The 116th Congress, January 3, 2019–January 3, 2021

United States House of Representatives

Democrats: 233 Republicans: 200 Undecided: 2 **2018 Election Results:** Democrats gained control of the House*

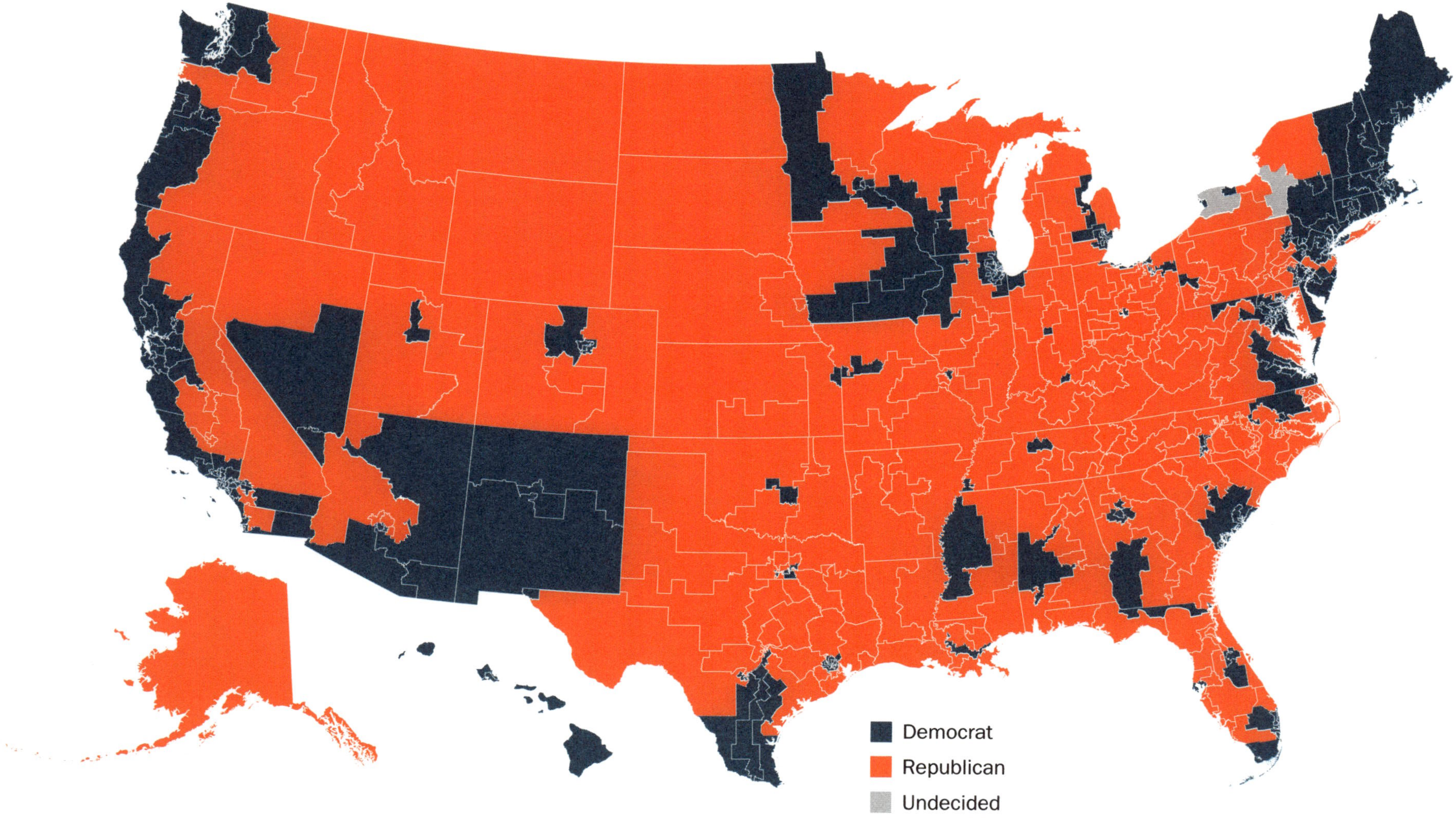

United States Senate

Democrats: 45 Republicans: 52 Independents: 2 **2018 Election Results:** Republicans retained control of the Senate*

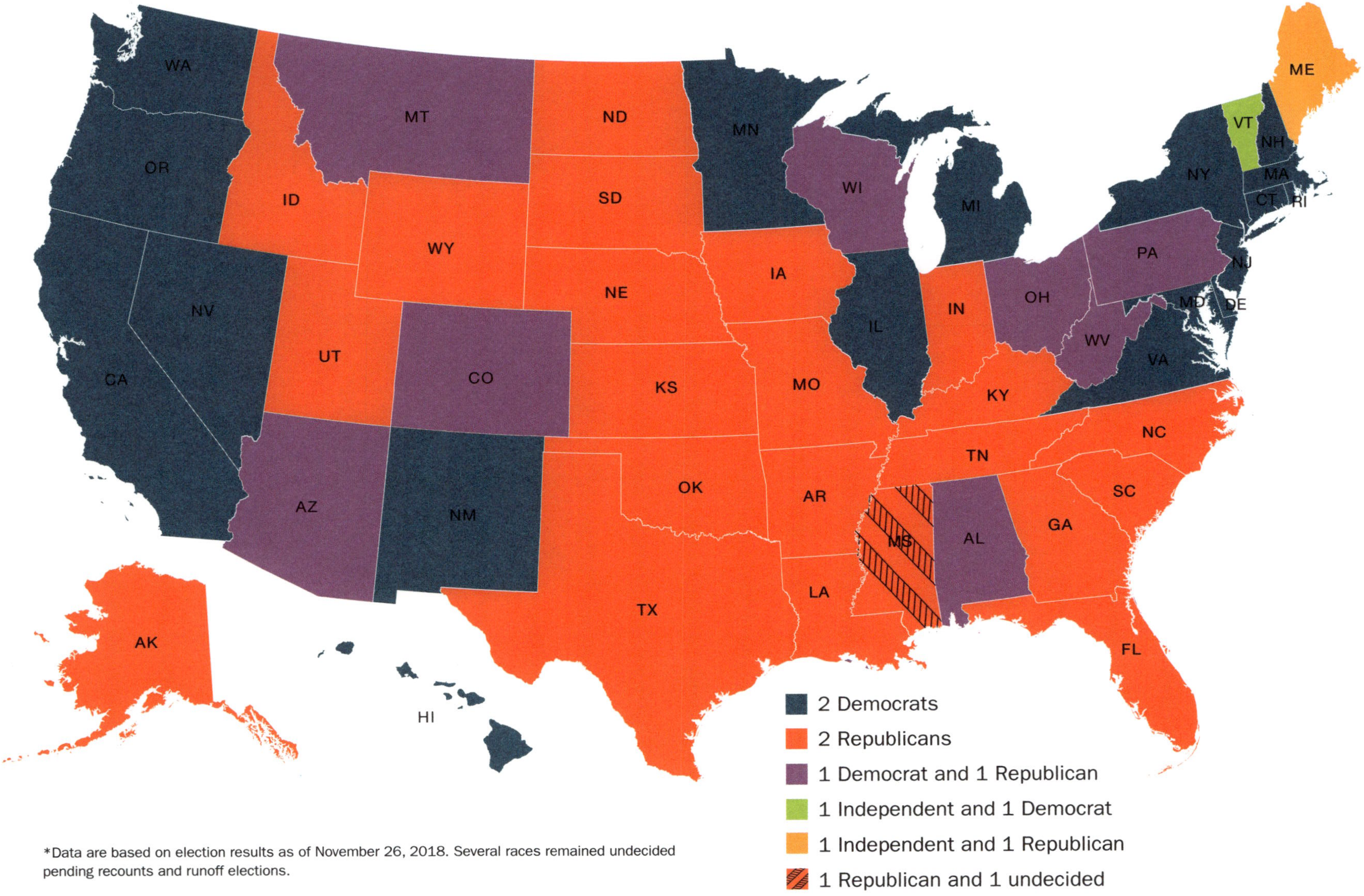

*Data are based on election results as of November 26, 2018. Several races remained undecided pending recounts and runoff elections.

CORE
edition
12

We the People

An Introduction to American Politics

CORE ★ edition ★ 12

We the People

An Introduction to American Politics

★ **BENJAMIN GINSBERG**
THE JOHNS HOPKINS UNIVERSITY

★ **THEODORE J. LOWI**
LATE OF CORNELL UNIVERSITY

★ **MARGARET WEIR**
BROWN UNIVERSITY

★ **CAROLINE J. TOLBERT**
UNIVERSITY OF IOWA

★ **ANDREA L. CAMPBELL**
MASSACHUSETTS INSTITUTE OF TECHNOLOGY

W. W. NORTON & COMPANY
NEW YORK LONDON

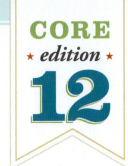

W. W. Norton & Company has been independent since its founding in 1923, when William Warder Norton and Mary D. Herter Norton first published lectures delivered at the People's Institute, the adult education division of New York City's Cooper Union. The firm soon expanded its program beyond the Institute, publishing books by celebrated academics from America and abroad. By mid-century, the two major pillars of Norton's publishing program—trade books and college texts—were firmly established. In the 1950s, the Norton family transferred control of the company to its employees, and today—with a staff of four hundred and a comparable number of trade, college, and professional titles published each year—W. W. Norton & Company stands as the largest and oldest publishing house owned wholly by its employees.

Printed in Canada

Editor: Peter Lesser
Project Editor: Christine D'Antonio
Assistant Editor: Anna Olcott
Manuscript Editor: Lynne Cannon
Managing Editor, College: Marian Johnson
Managing Editor, College Digital Media: Kim Yi
Production Manager, College: Ashley Horna
Media Editor: Spencer Richardson-Jones
Associate Media Editor: Michael Jaoui
Media Editorial Assistant: Tricia Vuong
Ebook Production Manager: Danielle Lehmann
Marketing Manager, Political Science: Erin Brown
Art Director: Rubina Yeh
Text Design: Jen Montgomery
Photo Editor: Stephanie Romeo
Photo Researcher: Elyse Rieder
Director of College Permissions: Megan Schindel
Permissions Associate: Elizabeth Trammell
Information Graphics: Kiss Me I'm Polish LLC, New York
Composition: Graphic World, Inc.
Manufacturing: TransContinental

Permission to use copyrighted material is included in the credits section of this book, which begins on page A75.

The Library of Congress has cataloged the full edition as follows:
Library of Congress Cataloging-in-Publication Data
Names: Ginsberg, Benjamin, author.
Title: We the people : an introduction to American politics / Benjamin Ginsberg, The Johns Hopkins University, Theodore J. Lowi, Cornell University, Margaret Weir, Brown University, Caroline J. Tolbert, University of Iowa, Andrea L. Campbell, Massachusetts Institute of Technology.
Description: Twelfth Edition. | New York : W.W. Norton & Company, [2018] | Includes bibliographical references and index.
Identifiers: LCCN 2018046033 | ISBN 9780393644326 (hardcover)
Subjects: LCSH: United States—Politics and government—Textbooks.
Classification: LCC JK276 .G55 2018 | DDC 320.473—dc23 LC record available at https://lccn.loc.gov/2018046033
ISBN: 978-0-393-66463-8 (pbk.)

W. W. Norton & Company, Inc., 500 Fifth Avenue, New York, NY 10110
wwnorton.com

W. W. Norton & Company Ltd., 15 Carlisle Street, London W1D 3BS

2 3 4 5 6 7 8 9 0

To:

Sandy, Cindy, and Alex Ginsberg

David, Jackie, Eveline, and Ed Dowling

Dave, Marcella, Logan, and Kennah Campbell

Contents

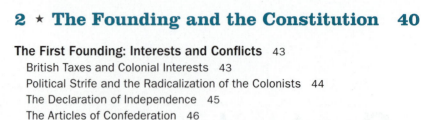

2 ★ The Founding and the Constitution 40

3 ★ Federalism 76

5 ★ Civil Rights 158

PART II POLITICS

WE ARE
A POWERFUL,
PISSED-OFF
MOVEMENT
OF YOUNG
PEOPLE
nextgen america

T TREAD
ME
EAD ON ME

10 ★ Campaigns and Elections 378

11 ★ Groups and Interests 428

PART III INSTITUTIONS

13 ★ The Presidency 512

14 ★ Bureaucracy in a Democracy 550

15 ★ The Federal Courts 590

Appendix

Preface

This book has been and continues to be dedicated to developing a satisfactory response to the question more and more Americans are asking: Why should we be engaged with government and politics? Through the first eleven editions, we sought to answer this question by making the text directly relevant to the lives of the students who would be reading it. As a result, we tried to make politics interesting by demonstrating that students' interests are at stake and that they therefore need to take a personal, even selfish, interest in the outcomes of government. At the same time, we realized that students needed guidance in how to become politically engaged. Beyond providing students with a core of political knowledge, we needed to show them how they could apply that knowledge as participants in the political process. The "Who Participates?" and "What You Can Do" sections in each chapter help achieve that goal.

As events from the last several years have reminded us, "what government does" inevitably raises questions about political participation and political equality. The size and composition of the electorate, for example, affect who is elected to public office and what policy directions the government will pursue. Hence, the issue of voter ID laws became important in the 2016 election, with some arguing that these laws reduce voter fraud and others contending that they decrease participation by poor and minority voters. Charges of Russian meddling in the 2016 election have raised questions about the integrity of the voting process. Fierce debates about the policies of the Trump administration have heightened students' interest in politics. Other recent events have underscored how Americans from different backgrounds experience politics. Arguments about immigration became contentious during the 2016 election as the nation once again debated the question of who is entitled to be an American and have a voice in determining what the government does. And charges that the police often use excessive violence against members of minority groups have raised questions about whether the government treats all Americans equally. Reflecting all of these trends, this new Twelfth Edition shows more than any other book on the market (1) how students are connected to government, (2) why students should think critically about government and politics, and (3) how Americans from different backgrounds experience and shape politics.

To help us explore these themes, Professor Andrea Campbell has joined us as the most recent in a group of distinguished coauthors. Professor Campbell's scholarly work focuses on the ways in which government and politics affect the lives of ordinary citizens. Among her contributions are new chapter introductions that focus on stories of individuals and how government has affected them. Many Americans, particularly the young, can have difficulty seeing the role of government in their everyday lives. Indeed, that's a chief explanation of low voter participation among younger citizens. The new chapter openers profile various individuals and illustrate their interactions with government, from a rock band that gets its controversial name approved by the Supreme

Court (Chapter 4), to a young mother who realizes the tap water in her Flint, Michigan, home is poisoning her children after local officials switched the source (Chapter 14), to teenagers protesting the end of net neutrality and the internet as they have known it (Chapter 7). The goal of these stories is to show students in a vivid way how government and politics mean something to their daily lives.

Several other elements of the book also help show students why politics and government should matter to them. These include:

- **A twenty-first-century perspective on demographic change** moves beyond the book's strong coverage of traditional civil rights content with expanded coverage of contemporary group politics.
- **"Who Are Americans?" infographics**—many new and updated for the twelfth edition—ask students to think critically about how Americans from different backgrounds experience politics. These sections use bold, engaging graphics to present a statistical snapshot of the nation related to each chapter's topic. Critical-thinking questions are included in each infographic.
- **"Who Participates?" infographics at the end of every chapter** show students how different groups of Americans participate in key aspects of politics and government. Each concludes with a "What You Can Do" section that provides students with specific, realistic steps they can take to act on what they've learned and get involved in politics. The InQuizitive course includes accompanying exercises that encourage students to engage with these features.
- **"America Side by Side" boxes** in every chapter use data figures and tables to provide a comparative perspective. By comparing political institutions and behavior across countries, students gain a better understanding of how specific features of the American system shape politics.
- **Up-to-date coverage**, with more than 20 pages and numerous graphics on the 2016 and 2018 elections, including a 12-page section devoted to analysis of these momentous elections in Chapter 10, as well as updated data, examples, and other information throughout the book.
- **"For Critical Analysis" questions** are incorporated throughout the text. "For Critical Analysis" questions in the margins of every chapter prompt students' own critical thinking about the material in the chapter, encouraging them to engage with the topic.
- **"What Do We Want" chapter conclusions** step back and provide perspective on how the chapter content connects to fundamental questions about the American political system. The conclusions also reprise the important point made in the personal profiles that begin each chapter that government matters to the lives of individuals.
- **This Twelfth Edition is accompanied by InQuizitive**, Norton's award-winning formative, adaptive online quizzing program. The InQuizitive course for *We the People* guides students through questions organized around the text's chapter learning objectives to ensure mastery of the core information and to help with assessment. More information and a demonstration are available at digital.wwnorton.com/wethepeople12core.

We note with regret the passing of Theodore Lowi as well as Margaret Weir's decision to step down from the book. We miss them but continue to hear their voices and to benefit from their wisdom in the pages of our book We also continue to hope that our book will itself be accepted as a form of enlightened political action. This Twelfth Edition is another chance. It is an advancement toward our goal. We promise to keep trying.

Acknowledgements

We are pleased to acknowledge the many colleagues who had an active role in criticism and preparation of the manuscript. Our thanks go to:

First Edition Reviewers

Sarah Binder, Brookings Institution
Kathleen Gille, Office of Representative David Bonior
Rodney Hero, University of Colorado at Boulder
Robert Katzmann, Brookings Institution
Kathleen Knight, University of Houston
Robin Kolodny, Temple University
Nancy Kral, Tomball College
Robert C. Lieberman, Columbia University
David A. Marcum, University of Wyoming
Laura R. Winsky Mattei, State University of New York at Buffalo
Marilyn S. Mertens, Midwestern State University
Barbara Suhay, Henry Ford Community College
Carolyn Wong, Stanford University
Julian Zelizer, State University of New York at Albany

Second Edition Reviewers

Lydia Andrade, University of North Texas
John Coleman, University of Wisconsin at Madison
Daphne Eastman, Odessa College
Otto Feinstein, Wayne State University
Elizabeth Flores, Delmar College
James Gimpel, University of Maryland at College Park
Jill Glaathar, Southwest Missouri State University
Shaun Herness, University of Florida
William Lyons, University of Tennessee at Knoxville
Andrew Polsky, Hunter College, CUNY
Grant Reeher, Syracuse University
Richard Rich, Virginia Polytechnic
Bartholomew Sparrow, University of Texas at Austin

Third Edition Reviewers

Bruce R. Drury, Lamar University
Andrew I. E. Ewoh, Prairie View A&M University
Amy Jasperson, University of Texas at San Antonio
Loch Johnson, University of Georgia
Mark Kann, University of Southern California
Robert L. Perry, University of Texas of the Permian Basin
Wayne Pryor, Brazosport College
Elizabeth A. Rexford, Wharton County Junior College
Andrea Simpson, University of Washington
Brian Smentkowski, Southeast Missouri State University
Nelson Wikstrom, Virginia Commonwealth University

Fourth Edition Reviewers

M. E. Banks, Virginia Commonwealth University
Lynn Brink, North Lake College
Mark Cichock, University of Texas at Arlington
Del Fields, St. Petersburg College
Nancy Kinney, Washtenaw Community College
William Klein, St. Petersburg College
Dana Morales, Montgomery College
Christopher Muste, Louisiana State University
Larry Norris, South Plains College
David Rankin, State University of New York at Fredonia
Paul Roesler, St. Charles Community College
J. Philip Rogers, San Antonio College
Greg Shaw, Illinois Wesleyan University
Tracy Skopek, Stephen F. Austin State University
Don Smith, University of North Texas
Terri Wright, Cal State, Fullerton

Fifth Edition Reviewers

Annie Benifield, Tomball College
Denise Dutton, Southwest Missouri State University
Rick Kurtz, Central Michigan University
Kelly McDaniel, Three Rivers Community College
Eric Plutzer, Pennsylvania State University
Daniel Smith, Northwest Missouri State University
Dara Strolovitch, University of Minnesota
Dennis Toombs, San Jacinto College–North
Stacy Ulbig, Southwest Missouri State University

Sixth Edition Reviewers

Janet Adamski, University of Mary Hardin–Baylor
Greg Andrews, St. Petersburg College
Louis Bolce, Baruch College
Darin Combs, Tulsa Community College
Sean Conroy, University of New Orleans
Paul Cooke, Cy Fair College
Vida Davoudi, Kingwood College
Robert DiClerico, West Virginia University
Corey Ditslear, University of North Texas
Kathy Dolan, University of Wisconsin, Milwaukee
Randy Glean, Midwestern State University
Nancy Kral, Tomball College
Mark Logas, Valencia Community College
Scott MacDougall, Diablo Valley College
David Mann, College of Charleston
Christopher Muste, University of Montana
Richard Pacelle, Georgia Southern University
Sarah Poggione, Florida International University
Richard Rich, Virginia Tech
Thomas Schmeling, Rhode Island College
Scott Spitzer, California State University–Fullerton
Robert Wood, University of North Dakota

Seventh Edition Reviewers

Molly Andolina, DePaul University
Nancy Bednar, Antelope Valley College
Paul Blakelock, Kingwood College
Amy Brandon, San Jacinto College
Jim Cauthen, John Jay College, CUNY
Kevin Davis, North Central Texas College
Louis DeSipio, University of California–Irvine
Brandon Franke, Blinn College
Steve Garrison, Midwestern State University
Joseph Howard, University of Central Arkansas
Aaron Knight, Houston Community College
Paul Labedz, Valencia Community College
Elise Langan, John Jay College, CUNY
Mark Logas, Valencia Community College
Eric Miller, Blinn College
Anthony O'Regan, Los Angeles Valley College
David Putz, Kingwood College
Chis Soper, Pepperdine University
Kevin Wagner, Florida Atlantic University
Laura Wood, Tarrant County College

Eighth Edition Reviewers

Brian Arbour, John Jay College, CUNY
Ellen Baik, University of Texas–Pan American
David Birch, Lone Star College–Tomball
Bill Carroll, Sam Houston State University
Ed Chervenak, University of New Orleans
Gary Church, Mountain View College
Adrian Stefan Clark, Del Mar College
Annie Cole, Los Angeles City College
Greg Combs, University of Texas at Dallas
Cassandra Cookson, Lee College
Brian Cravens, Blinn College
John Crosby, California State University–Chico
Scott Crosby, Valencia Community College
Courtenay Daum, Colorado State University, Fort Collins
Peter Doas, University of Texas–Pan American
John Domino, Sam Houston State University
Doug Dow, University of Texas–Dallas
Jeremy Duff, Midwestern State University
Heather Evans, Sam Houston State University
Hyacinth Ezeamii, Albany State University
Bob Fitrakis, Columbus State Community College
Brian Fletcher, Truckee Meadows Community College
Paul Foote, Eastern Kentucky University
Frank Garrahan, Austin Community College
Jimmy Gleason, Purdue University
Steven Greene, North Carolina State University
Jeannie Grussendorf, Georgia State University
M. Ahad Hayaud-Din, Brookhaven College
Alexander Hogan, Lone Star College–CyFair
Glen Hunt, Austin Community College
Mark Jendrysik, University of North Dakota
Krista Jenkins, Fairleigh Dickinson University
Carlos Juárez, Hawaii Pacific University
Melinda Kovas, Sam Houston State University
Boyd Lanier, Lamar University
Jeff Lazarus, Georgia State University
Jeffrey Lee, Blinn College
Alan Lehmann, Blinn College
Julie Lester, Macon State College
Steven Lichtman, Shippensburg University
Fred Lokken, Truckee Meadows Community College
Shari MacLachlan, Palm Beach Community College
Guy Martin, Winston-Salem State University
Fred Monardi, College of Southern Nevada
Vincent Moscardelli, University of Connecticut
Jason Mycoff, University of Delaware
Sugmaran Narayanan, Midwestern State University
Anthony Nownes, University of Tennessee, Knoxville
Elizabeth Oldmixon, University of North Texas
John Osterman, San Jacinto College–Central
Mark Peplowski, College of Southern Nevada
Maria Victoria Perez-Rios, John Jay College, CUNY
Sara Rinfret, University of Wisconsin, Green Bay
Andre Robinson, Pulaski Technical College
Susan Roomberg, University of Texas at San Antonio
Ryan Rynbrandt, Collin County Community College
Mario Salas, Northwest Vista College
Michael Sanchez, San Antonio College
Mary Schander, Pasadena City College
Laura Schneider, Grand Valley State University

Subash Shah, Winston-Salem State University
Mark Shomaker, Blinn College
Roy Slater, St. Petersburg College
Debra St. John, Collin College
Eric Whitaker, Western Washington University
Clay Wiegand, Cisco College
Walter Wilson, University of Texas at San Antonio
Kevan Yenerall, Clarion University
Rogerio Zapata, South Texas College

Ninth Edition Reviewers

Amy Acord, Lone Star College–CyFair
Milan Andrejevich, Ivy Tech Community College
Steve Anthony, Georgia State University
Phillip Ardoin, Appalachian State University
Gregory Arey, Cape Fear Community College
Joan Babcock, Northwest Vista College
Evelyn Ballard, Houston Community College
Robert Ballinger, South Texas College
Mary Barnes-Tilley, Blinn College
Robert Bartels, Evangel University
Nancy Bednar, Antelope Valley College
Annie Benifield, Lone Star College–Tomball
Donna Bennett, Trinity Valley Community College
Amy Brandon, El Paso Community College
Mark Brewer, The University of Maine
Gary Brown, Lone Star College–Montgomery
Joe Campbell, Johnson County Community College
Dewey Clayton, University of Louisville
Jeff Colbert, Elon University
Amanda Cook-Fesperman, Illinois Valley Community College
Kevin Corder, Western Michigan University
Kevin Davis, North Central Texas College
Paul Davis, Truckee Meadows Community College
Terri Davis, Lamar University
Jennifer De Maio, California State University, Northridge
Christopher Durso, Valencia College
Ryan Emenaker, College of the Redwoods
Leslie Feldman, Hofstra University
Glen Findley, Odessa College
Michael Gattis, Gulf Coast State College
Donna Godwin, Trinity Valley Community College
Precious Hall, Truckee Meadows Community College
Sally Hansen, Daytona State College
Tiffany Harper, Collin College
Todd Hartman, Appalachian State University
Virginia Haysley, Lone Star College–Tomball
David Head, John Tyler Community College
Rick Henderson, Texas State University–San Marcos
Richard Herrera, Arizona State University
Thaddaus Hill, Blinn College
Steven Holmes, Bakersfield College
Kevin Holton, South Texas College
Robin Jacobson, University of Puget Sound
Joseph Jozwiak, Texas A&M–Corpus Christi
Casey Klofstad, University of Miami
Samuel Lingrosso, Los Angeles Valley College
Mark Logas, Valencia College
Christopher Marshall, South Texas College
Larry McElvain, South Texas College
Elizabeth McLane, Wharton County Junior College
Eddie Meaders, University of North Texas
Rob Mellen, Mississippi State University
Jalal Nejad, Northwest Vista College
Adam Newmark, Appalachian State University
Stephen Nicholson, University of California, Merced
Cissie Owen, Lamar University
Suzanne Preston, St. Petersburg College
David Putz, Lone Star College–Kingwood
Auksuole Rubavichute, Mountain View College
Ronnee Schreiber, San Diego State University
Ronald Schurin, University of Connecticut
Jason Seitz, Georgia Perimeter College
Jennifer Seitz, Georgia Perimeter College
Shannon Sinegal, The University of New Orleans
John Sides, George Washington University
Thomas Sowers, Lamar University
Jim Startin, University of Texas at San Antonio
Robert Sterken, University of Texas at Tyler
Bobby Summers, Harper College
John Theis, Lone Star College–Kingwood
John Todd, University of North Texas
Delaina Toothman, The University of Maine
David Trussell, Cisco College
Ronald Vardy, University of Houston
Linda Veazey, Midwestern State University
John Vento, Antelope Valley Community College
Clif Wilkinson, Georgia College
John Wood, Rose State College
Michael Young, Trinity Valley Community College
Tyler Young, Collin College

Tenth Edition Reviewers

Stephen P. Amberg, University of Texas at San Antonio
Juan F. Arzola, College of the Sequoias
Thomas J. Baldino, Wilkes University
Christina Bejarano, University of Kansas
Paul T. Bellinger, Jr., University of Missouri
Melanie J. Blumberg, California University of Pennsylvania
Matthew T. Bradley, Indiana University Kokomo
Jeffrey W. Christiansen, Seminole State College
McKinzie Craig, Marietta College
Christopher Cronin, Methodist University
Jenna Duke, Lehigh Carbon Community College
Francisco Durand, University of Texas at San Antonio
Carrie Eaves, Elon University
Paul M. Flor, El Camino College Compton Center
Adam Fuller, Youngstown State University

Christi Gramling, Charleston Southern University
Sally Hansen, Daytona State College
Mary Jane Hatton, Hawaii Pacific University
David Helpap, University of Wisconsin–Green Bay
Theresa L. Hutchins, Georgia Highlands College
Cryshanna A. Jackson Leftwich, Youngstown State University
Ashlyn Kuersten, Western Michigan University
Kara Lindaman, Winona State University
Timothy Lynch, University of Wisconsin–Milwaukee
Larry McElvain, South Texas College
Corinna R. McKoy, Ventura College
Eddie L. Meaders, University of North Texas
Don D. Mirjanian, College of Southern Nevada
R. Shea Mize, Georgia Highlands College
Nicholas Morgan, Collin College
Matthew Murray, Dutchess Community College
Harold "Trey" Orndorff III, Daytona State College
Randall Parish, University of North Georgia
Michelle Pautz, University of Dayton
Michael Pickering, University of New Orleans
Donald Ranish, Antelope Valley College
Glenn W. Richardson, Jr., Kutztown University of Pennsylvania
Jason Robles, Colorado State University
Ionas Aurelian Rus, University of Cincinnati–Blue Ash
Robert Sahr, Oregon State University
Kelly B. Shaw, Iowa State University
Captain Michael Slattery, Campbell University
Michael Smith, Sam Houston State University
Maryam T. Stevenson, University of Indianapolis
Elizabeth Trentanelli, Gulf Coast State College
Ronald W. Vardy, University of Houston
Timothy Weaver, University of Louisville
Christina Wolbrecht, University of Notre Dame

Eleventh Edition Reviewers

Maria J. Albo, University of North Georgia
Andrea Aleman, University of Texas at San Antonio
Juan Arzola, College of the Sequoias
Ross K. Baker, Rutgers University
Daniel Birdsong, University of Dayton
Phil Branyon, University of North Georgia
Sheryl Edwards, University of Michigan–Dearborn
Lauren Elliott-Dorans, University of Toledo
Heather Evans, Sam Houston State University
William Feagin, Jr., Wharton County Junior College
Glen Findley, Odessa College
Heather Frederick, Slipper Rock University
Jason Ghibesi, Ocean County College
Patrick Gilbert, Lone Star–Tomball
Steven Horn, Everett Community College
Demetra Kasimis, California State University, Long Beach
Eric T. Kasper, University of Wisconsin–Eau Claire
Mary Linder, Grayson County College
Phil McCall, Portland State University
Carolyn Myers, Southwestern Illinois College–Belleville
Gerhard Peters, Citrus College
Michael A. Powell, Frederick Community College
Allen K. Settle, California Polytechnic State University
Laurie Sprankle, Community College of Allegheny County
Ryan Lee Teten, University of Louisiana at Lafayette
Justin Vaughn, Boise State University
John Vento, Antelope Valley College
Aaron Weinschenk, University of Wisconsin–Green Bay
Tyler Young, Collin College

Twelfth Edition Reviewers

Craig Albert, Augusta University
Alexa Bankert, University of Georgia
Nathan Barrick, University of South Florida
Jeff Birdsong, Northeastern Oklahoma A&M College
Sara Butler, College of the Desert
Cory Colby, Lone Star College
Anthony Daniels, University of Toledo
Dennis Falcon, Cerritos College
Kathleen Ferraiolo, James Madison University
Patrick Gilbert, Lone Star College, Tomball
Matthew Green, Catholic University of America
Matt Guardino, Providence College
Barbara Headrick, Minnesota State University, Moorhead
Justin Hoggard, Three Rivers Community College
John Patrick Ifedi, Howard University
Cryshanna Jackson Leftwich, Youngstown State University
Douglas Kriner, Boston University
Thom Kuehls, Weber State University
Jennifer Lawless, American University
LaDella Levy, College of Southern Nevada
Timothy Lim, California State University, Los Angeles
Sam Lingrosso, Los Angeles Valley College
Mandy May, College of Southern Maryland
Suzanne Mettler, Cornell University
Michael Miller, Barnard College
Joseph Njoroge, Abraham Baldwin Agricultural College
Michael Petri, Santa Ana College
Christopher Poulios, Nassau Community College
Andrew Rudalevige, Bowdoin College
Amanda Sanford, Louisiana Tech University
Elizabeth Saunders, George Washington University
Kathleen Searles, Louisiana State University
Matthew Snyder, Delgado Community College
Steven Sylvester, Utah Valley University
Linda Trautman, Ohio University Lancaster
Donald Williams, Western New England University
Peter Yacobucci, Buffalo State College

We are also grateful to Melissa Michelson, of Menlo College, who contributed to the "Who Are Americans?" and "Who Participates?" infographics for this edition; Holley Hansen, of Oklahoma State University, who contributed to the "America Side by Side" boxes.

Perhaps above all, we thank those at W. W. Norton. For its first five editions, editor Steve Dunn helped us shape the book in countless ways. Lisa McKay contributed smart ideas and a keen editorial eye to the Tenth Edition. Ann Shin carried on the Norton tradition of splendid editorial work on the Sixth through Ninth Editions and on the Eleventh Edition. Peter Lesser brought intelligence, dedication, and keen insight to the development of this Twelfth Edition. For our InQuizitive course, Coursepack, and other instructor resources, Spencer Richardson-Jones has been an energetic and visionary editor. Ashley Horna, Michael Jaoui, Tricia Vuong, and Anna Olcott also kept the production of the Twelfth Edition and its accompanying resources coherent and in focus. Lynne Cannon copyedited the manuscript, and our superb project editor Christine D'Antonio devoted countless hours to keeping on top of myriad details. We thank Elyse Rieder for finding new photos and our photo editor Stephanie Romeo for managing the image program. Finally, we thank Roby Harrington, the head of Norton's college department.

Benjamin Ginsberg
Caroline J. Tolbert
Andrea Campbell

October 2018

CORE ★ edition ★ 12

We the People

An Introduction to American Politics

★ chapter ★

01

American Political Culture

WHAT GOVERNMENT DOES AND WHY IT MATTERS Meet two of the nation's youngest elected officials. Saira Blair became the youngest member of West Virginia's House of Delegates when she won election as an 18-year-old college freshman. The day after her victory party in November 2014, she was back in class at West Virginia University. In May 2017, Prairie View A&M senior Kendric D. Jones similarly achieved electoral victory, becoming the youngest city council member in the state of Texas. What got Blair and Jones involved in politics? Both had sources of political inspiration. Blair followed in the footsteps of her father, a West Virginia state senator, who she had accompanied at political events since childhood. Jones was inspired by the long history of activism at Prairie View, which was founded in 1876 during Reconstruction by some of the first African American members of the Texas state legislature. A further spur to action was President Obama's call in his 2017 farewell address to "grab a clipboard, get some signatures, and run for office yourself." Both also had strong commitments to issues. Saira Blair believes in limited government, lower taxes, and Second Amendment gun rights. Kendric Jones has a long history of working in the community, serving in student government,

While Americans share a belief in the values of liberty, equality, and democracy, debates rage about how to live up to those values. To advocate for their beliefs, Republican Saira Blair (left) and Democrat Kendric Jones (right)—both college students—ran for office and won. What is the citizen's role in America's democratic system?

and founding a mentoring program for middle-school boys. Many Prairie View students also have concerns about police relations. Sandra Bland, the 28-year-old who hanged herself in jail after being arrested in a traffic stop, was an alumna of Prairie View.

Both Blair and Jones also believe deeply in political participation, especially that of young people. As Jones said, "The students of Prairie View A&M University's voices have not been heard. Since I have been here, the city has been stagnant and has not made any progression—outside of the university. I feel as though a young, innovative mind can push this city forward." After participating in a mock government program in high school, Blair saw that young people were just as capable as lawmakers decades older: "When I saw how capable the students were of creating . . . legislation and really getting work done, it really made me realize that we really didn't need to wait."[1]

Saira Blair's and Kendric Jones's experiences show that citizens are at the center of democratic government. They ran for office because they care about public issues and want to have a hand in shaping policy outcomes. What are you passionate about? How does government affect your everyday life and that of your family, friends, and community? And how are differences in political views adjudicated in the political realm? There are some core values that Americans hold dear, including liberty, equality, and democracy. But there are also disagreements about what those values mean and what the role of government should be. Not everyone has to run for political office as Blair and Jones did. But all of us are affected by government in ways small and large every day. The purpose of this book is to show what government does, how, and why—and what you can do about it.

CHAPTER GOALS

★ **Define government and forms of government (pp. 5–10)**

★ **Describe the role of the citizen in politics (pp. 10–13)**

★ **Show how the social composition of the American population has changed over time (pp. 13–22)**

★ **Analyze whether the U.S. system of government upholds American political values (pp. 22–29)**

★ **Explore Americans' attitudes toward government (pp. 29–33)**

Government

Define government and forms of government

Government is the term generally used to describe the formal institutions through which a land and its people are ruled. A government may be as simple as a town meeting in which community members make policy and determine budgets together or as complex as the vast establishments found in many large countries today, with their extensive procedures, laws, and bureaucracies. In the history of civilization, governments have not been difficult to establish. There have been thousands of them. The hard part is establishing a government that lasts. Even more difficult is developing a stable government that is true to the key American political values of liberty, equality, and democracy.

government institutions and procedures through which a territory and its people are ruled

Most Americans find it easy to affirm these three values in principle. In practice, however, these values mean different things to different people, and they often seem to conflict. This is where politics comes in. **Politics** refers to conflicts and struggles over the leadership, structure, and policies of governments. As we will see in this chapter and throughout this book, much political conflict concerns policies and practices that seem to affirm one of the key American political values but may contradict another.

politics conflict over the leadership, structure, and policies of governments

IS GOVERNMENT NEEDED?

Americans have always harbored some suspicion of government and have wondered how extensive a role it should play in their lives. Thomas Jefferson famously observed that the best government was one that "governed least." Indeed, a desire for limited government has also been a central feature of American political culture and history since the nation's founding. Generally speaking, a government is needed to provide those services, sometimes called "public goods," that all citizens need but are not likely to be able to provide adequately for themselves. These might include defense against foreign aggression, maintenance of public order, a stable currency, enforcement of contractual obligations and property rights, and a guarantee of some measure of social justice. These are goods that benefit everyone but that no individual or group on its own can afford to supply. Government, with its powers to tax and regulate, is typically viewed as the best way to provide public goods. However, there is often disagreement about which public goods are essential and how they should be provided. The precise extent to which government involvement in American society is needed has been debated throughout the nation's history and will continue to be a central focus of political contention.

Much of what citizens have come to depend on and take for granted as somehow part of the natural environment is in fact created by government. Take the example of a typical college student's day, throughout which that student relies on a host of services and activities organized by national, state, and local government agencies. The extent of this dependence on government is illustrated by Table 1.1 on page 6.

FORMS OF GOVERNMENT

Governments vary in their structure, their size, and the way they operate. Two questions are of special importance in determining how governments differ: Who governs? And how much government control is permitted?

TABLE 1.1

The Presence of Government in the Daily Life of a Student at "State University"

TIME OF DAY	SCHEDULE
7:00 A.M.	Wake up. Standard time set by the national government.
7:10 A.M.	Shower. Water courtesy of local government, either a public entity or a regulated private company. Brush your teeth with toothpaste whose cavity-fighting claims have been verified by a federal agency. Dry your hair with an electric dryer manufactured according to federal government agency guidelines.
7:30 A.M.	Have a bowl of cereal with milk for breakfast. "Nutrition Facts" on food labels are a federal requirement, pasteurization of milk required by state law, freshness dating on milk based on state and federal standards, recycling the empty cereal box and milk carton enabled by state or local laws.
8:30 A.M.	Drive or take public transportation to campus. Air bags and seat belts required by federal and state laws. Roads and bridges paid for by state and local governments, speed and traffic laws set by state and local governments, public transportation subsidized by all levels of government.
8:45 A.M.	Arrive on campus of large public university. Buildings are 70 percent financed by state taxpayers.
9:00 A.M.	First class: Chemistry 101. Tuition partially paid by a federal loan (more than half the cost of university instruction is paid for by taxpayers), chemistry lab paid for with grants from the National Science Foundation (a federal agency) and smaller grants from business corporations made possible by federal income tax deductions for charitable contributions.
Noon	Eat lunch. College cafeteria financed by state dormitory authority on land grant from federal Department of Agriculture.
12:47 P.M.	Felt an earthquake! Check the U.S. Geological Survey at www.usgs.gov to see that it was a 3.9 on the Richter scale.
2:00 P.M.	Second class: American Government 101 (your favorite class!). You may be taking this class because it is required by the state legislature or because it fulfills a university requirement.
4:00 P.M.	Third class: Computer Science 101. Free computers, software, and internet access courtesy of state subsidies plus grants and discounts from Apple and Microsoft, the costs of which are deducted from their corporate income taxes; internet built in part by federal government. Duplication of software prohibited by federal copyright laws.
6:00 P.M.	Eat dinner: hamburger and french fries. Meat inspected for bacteria by federal agencies.
7:00 P.M.	Work at part-time job at the campus library. Minimum wage set by federal, state, or local government; books and journals in library paid for by state taxpayers.
8:15 P.M.	Go online to check the status of your application for a federal student loan (FAFSA) on the Department of Education's website at studentaid.ed.gov.
10:00 P.M.	Go home. Street lighting paid for by county and city governments, police patrols by city government.
10:15 P.M.	Watch TV. Networks regulated by federal government, cable public-access channels required by city law. Weather forecast provided to broadcasters by a federal agency.
10:45 P.M.	To complete your economics homework, visit the Bureau of Labor Statistics at www.bls.gov to look up unemployment levels since 1972.
Midnight	Put out the trash before going to bed. Trash collected by city sanitation department, financed by user charges.

Some nations are governed by a single individual—a king or dictator, for example. This state of affairs is called **autocracy**. Where a small group—perhaps landowners, military officers, or the wealthy—controls most of the governing decisions, that government is said to be an **oligarchy**. If citizens are vested with the power to rule themselves, that government is a **democracy**.

Governments also vary considerably in terms of how they govern. In the United States and a small number of other nations, governments are limited as to what they are permitted to control (substantive limits) and how they go about it (procedural limits). Governments that are limited in this way are called **constitutional governments**, or liberal governments. In other nations, including some in Latin America, Asia, and Africa, the law imposes few real limits. The government, however, is nevertheless kept in check by other political and social institutions that it is unable to control and must come to terms with—such as autonomous territories, an organized religion, organized business groups, or organized labor unions. Such governments are generally called **authoritarian**. In a third group of nations, including the Soviet Union under Joseph Stalin, Nazi Germany, perhaps prewar Japan and Italy, and North Korea today, governments not only are free of legal limits but also seek to eliminate those organized social groups that might challenge or limit their authority. These governments typically attempt to dominate or control every sphere of political, economic, and social life and, as a result, are called **totalitarian** (see Figure 1.1).

Americans have the good fortune to live in a nation in which limits are placed on what governments can do and how they can do it. Many of the world's people do not. By one measure, just 40 percent of the global population (those living in 86 countries) enjoy sufficient levels of political and personal freedom to be classified as living in a constitutional democracy.[2] And constitutional democracies were unheard of before the modern era. Prior to the eighteenth and nineteenth centuries, governments seldom sought—and rarely received—the support of their subjects. The available evidence strongly suggests that ordinary people often had little love for the government or for the social order. After all, they had no stake in it.[3]

Beginning in the seventeenth century, in a handful of Western nations, two important changes began to take place in the character and conduct of government. First, governments began to acknowledge formal limits on their power. Second, a small number of governments began to provide ordinary citizens with a formal

autocracy a form of government in which a single individual—a king, queen, or dictator—rules

oligarchy a form of government in which a small group—landowners, military officers, or wealthy merchants—controls most of the governing decisions

democracy a system of rule that permits citizens to play a significant part in the governmental process, usually through the election of key public officials

constitutional government a system of rule in which formal and effective limits are placed on the powers of the government

authoritarian government a system of rule in which the government recognizes no formal limits but may nevertheless be restrained by the power of other social institutions

totalitarian government a system of rule in which the government recognizes no formal limits on its power and seeks to absorb or eliminate other social institutions that might challenge it

FIGURE 1.1

Forms of Government

Who governs	Type of government
One person	Autocracy
Small group (e.g., landowners, military officers, or wealthy merchants)	Oligarchy
Many people	Democracy

Limits on government	Type of government
Codified, legal substantive and procedural limits on what government can or cannot do	Constitutional
Few legal limits; some limits imposed by social groups	Authoritarian
No limits	Totalitarian

America's Founders were influenced by the English thinker John Locke (1632–1704). Locke argued that governments need the consent of the people.

voice in public affairs—through the vote. Obviously, the desirability of limits on government and the expansion of popular influence were at the heart of the American Revolution in 1776. "No taxation without representation," as we shall see in Chapter 2, was fiercely asserted from the beginning of the Revolution through the Founding in 1789. But even before the Revolution, a tradition of limiting government and expanding participation in the political process had developed throughout western Europe.

LIMITING GOVERNMENT

The key force behind the imposition of limits on government power was a new social class, the bourgeoisie, which became an important political force in the sixteenth and seventeenth centuries. *Bourgeois* is a French word for "freeman of the city," or *bourg*. Being part of the bourgeoisie later became associated with being "middle class" and with involvement in commerce or industry. In order to gain a share of control of government, joining or even displacing the kings, aristocrats, and gentry who had dominated government for centuries, the bourgeoisie sought to change existing institutions—especially parliaments—into instruments of real political participation. Parliaments had existed for centuries but were generally aristocratic institutions. The bourgeoisie embraced parliaments as means by which they could exert the weight of their superior numbers and growing economic advantage over their aristocratic rivals. At the same time, the bourgeoisie sought to place restraints on the capacity of governments to threaten these economic and political interests by placing formal or constitutional limits on governmental power.

Although motivated primarily by the need to protect and defend their own interests, the bourgeoisie advanced many of the principles that would define the central underpinnings of individual liberty for all citizens—freedom of speech, freedom of assembly, freedom of conscience, and freedom from arbitrary search and seizure. The work of political theorists such as John Locke (1632–1704) and, later, John Stuart Mill (1806–73) helped shape these evolving ideas about liberty and political rights. However, it is important to note that the bourgeoisie generally did not favor democracy as we know it. They were advocates of electoral and representative institutions, but they favored property requirements and other restrictions so as to limit participation to the middle and upper classes. Yet once these institutions of politics and the protection of the right to engage in politics were established, it was difficult to limit them to the bourgeoisie.

John Stuart Mill (1806–73) presented a ringing defense of individual freedom in his famous treatise *On Liberty*. Mill's work influenced Americans' evolving ideas about the relationship between government and the individual.

ACCESS TO GOVERNMENT: THE EXPANSION OF PARTICIPATION

The expansion of participation from the bourgeoisie to ever-larger segments of society took two paths. In some nations, popular participation was expanded by the Crown or the aristocracy, which ironically saw common people as potential political allies against the bourgeoisie. Thus, in nineteenth-century Prussia, for example, it was the emperor and his great minister Otto von Bismarck who expanded popular participation in order to build political support among the lower orders.

In other nations, participation expanded because competing segments of the bourgeoisie sought to gain political advantage by reaching out to and mobilizing the support of working- and lower-class groups that craved the opportunity to take part in politics—"lining up the unwashed," as one American historian put it.[4] To be sure, excluded groups often agitated for greater participation. But seldom was such agitation by itself enough to secure the right to participate. Usually, expansion of voting rights resulted from a combination of pressure from below and help from above.

The gradual expansion of voting rights by groups hoping to derive some political advantage has been typical of American history. After the Civil War, one of the chief reasons that Republicans moved to enfranchise newly freed slaves was to use the support of the former slaves to maintain Republican control over the defeated southern states. Similarly, in the early twentieth century, upper-middle-class Progressives advocated women's suffrage because they believed that women were likely to support the reforms espoused by the Progressive movement.

INFLUENCING THE GOVERNMENT THROUGH PARTICIPATION: POLITICS

Expansion of participation means that more and more people have a legal right to take part in politics. *Politics* is an important term. In its broadest sense, it refers to conflicts over the character, membership, and policies of any organization to which people belong. As Harold Lasswell, a famous political scientist, once put it, politics is the struggle over "who gets what, when, how."[5] Although politics is a phenomenon that can be found in any organization, our concern in this book is narrower. Here, politics will be used to refer only to conflicts and struggles over the leadership, structure, and policies of governments. The goal of politics, as we define it, is to have a share or a say in the composition of the government's leadership, how the government is organized, or what its policies are going to be. Having a share is called having **power** or influence.

power influence over a government's leadership, organization, or policies

Participation in politics can take many forms, including blogging and posting opinion pieces online, sending emails to government officials, voting, lobbying legislators on behalf of particular programs, and participating in protest marches and even violent demonstrations. A system of government that gives citizens a regular opportunity to elect the top government officials is usually called a **representative democracy**, or **republic**. A system that permits citizens to vote directly on laws and policies is often called a **direct democracy**. At the national level, the United States is a representative democracy in which citizens select government officials but do not vote on legislation. Some states and cities, however, have provisions for direct legislation through popular initiatives and ballot referenda. These procedures allow citizens to collect petitions requiring an issue to be brought directly to the voters for a decision. In 2018, 169 initiatives appeared on state ballots, often dealing with hot-button issues. Five states considered measures legalizing medical or recreational marijuana. Eight states considered restrictions on taxes, 3 considered initiatives on abortion access and funding, and 21 voted on elections policies such as redistricting, voting requirements, and campaign finance. In 2017 voters in Maine decided to expand Medicaid under the Affordable Care Act after the governor had vetoed expansion multiple times, becoming the first state to decide the issue by direct democracy.[6]

representative democracy (republic) a system of government in which the populace selects representatives, who play a significant role in governmental decision-making

direct democracy a system of rule that permits citizens to vote directly on laws and policies

Groups and organized interests also participate in politics. Their political activities include providing funds for candidates, lobbying, and trying to influence public opinion. The pattern of struggles among interests is called group politics, or **pluralism**. Americans have always been ambivalent about pluralist politics. On the one hand, the right of groups to press their views and compete for influence in the government is the essence of liberty. On the other hand, Americans often fear that

pluralism the theory that all interests are and should be free to compete for influence in the government; the outcome of this competition is compromise and moderation

Politics sometimes involves direct action. People often hold public rallies or protests to draw attention to issues. These concerns can range from inequality in police practices (left), animal rights (center), taxes and government spending (right).

organized groups may sometimes exert too much influence, advancing special interests at the expense of larger public interests. (We return to this problem in Chapter 11.)

Sometimes, of course, politics does not take place through formal channels at all but instead involves direct action. Direct action politics can include either violent politics or civil disobedience, both of which attempt to shock rulers into behaving more responsibly. Direct action can also be a form of revolutionary politics, which rejects the system entirely and attempts to replace it with a new ruling group and a new set of rules. In recent years in the United States, groups ranging from animal rights activists to right-to-life advocates to the Tea Party to Black Lives Matter protesters have used direct action to underline their demands. Many forms of peaceful direct political action are protected by the U.S. Constitution. The country's Founders knew that the right to protest is essential to the maintenance of political freedom, even where the ballot box is available.

Citizenship: Participation, Knowledge, and Efficacy

Describe the role of the citizen in politics

Citizen participation is the hallmark of the democratic form of government. "Government by the people" depends on lively citizen involvement in public discussion, debate, and activity designed to improve the welfare of one's community. The very legitimacy of democratic government depends on political participation, which takes a variety of forms, from the conventional—voting, contacting elected officials, working on a campaign, making political donations, attending political meetings—to the unconventional—protesting, boycotting, and signing petitions.

political knowledge possessing information about the formal institutions of government, political actors, and political issues

One key ingredient for political participation is **political knowledge** and information. Democracy functions best when citizens are informed and have the knowledge

needed to participate in political debate. Indeed, our definition of **citizenship** derives from the ideal put forth by the ancient Greeks: *enlightened* political engagement.[7] Political knowledge means more than having a few opinions to offer a pollster or to guide your decisions in a voting booth. It is important to know the rules and strategies that govern political institutions and the principles on which they are based, *and* to know them in ways that relate to your own interests. If your street is rendered impassable by snow, what can you do? Is snow removal the responsibility of the federal government? Is it a state or municipal responsibility? Knowing that you have a stake in a clear road does not help much if you do not know that snow removal is a city or a county responsibility and if you cannot identify the municipal agency that deals with the problem. Americans are fond of complaining that government is not responsive to their needs, but in some cases, it is possible that citizens simply lack the information they need to present their problems to the appropriate government officials.

citizenship informed and active membership in a political community

Without political knowledge, citizens cannot be aware of their stakes in political disputes. For example, during the debate in 2017 about whether to repeal the Obama health care reform, one-third of Americans did not know that "Obamacare" and the "Affordable Care Act" are the same thing.[8] That meant that some Americans who had enrolled in "Obamacare" did not realize their access to health insurance would be affected if the ACA were repealed. Citizens need knowledge in order to assess their interests and to know when to act on them.

The internet can greatly facilitate acquisition of knowledge about politics. A 2015 Pew survey found that over the previous year, 65 percent of Americans had used the internet to find data or information about government, including visiting a local, state, or federal government website.[9] Such **digital citizenship**—the ability to participate in society online—benefits individuals and provides advantages to society as a whole. Digital citizens are more likely to be interested in politics and to discuss politics with friends, family, and coworkers than individuals who do not use online political information. They are also more likely to vote and participate in other ways in elections. A lingering concern is that lower-income and less-educated Americans,

digital citizenship using the internet, social media, and other information technology to engage in society and government rural residents, racial and ethnic minorities, and the elderly are all less likely to have internet access. This digital divide (which we discuss further in Chapters 7 and 8) exacerbates inequalities in political participation.

FOR CRITICAL ANALYSIS

Many studies seem to show that most Americans know very little about government and politics. Can we have democratic government without knowledgeable and aware citizens?

Even though the internet has made it easier than ever to learn about politics, the state of political knowledge in the United States today is spotty. Most Americans know little about current issues or debates, or even the basics of how government works. For example, in 2017 only 26 percent of those surveyed could identify all three branches of the federal government and only 54 percent knew that Congress has the power to declare war. During the summer before the 2016 presidential election, just 22 percent of the public could identify the Democratic vice-presidential candidate and 37 percent could identify the Republican vice-presidential candidate. On the other hand, more than three-quarters of those surveyed knew that Congress has the power to raise taxes and cannot establish an official religion for the nation (see Table 1.2). Those of you who make the effort to become more knowledgeable will be much better prepared to influence the political system regarding the issues and concerns that you care most about.

political efficacy the ability to influence government and politics

Another ingredient in political participation is **political efficacy**, the belief that ordinary citizens can affect what government does. The feeling that you can't affect government decisions can lead to apathy, declining political participation, and withdrawal from political life. Why bother to participate if you believe it makes no difference? Americans' sense of political efficacy has declined over time. In 1960, only 25 percent felt shut out of government. In 2015, 74 percent of Americans said that elected officials don't care what people like them think.[10]

TABLE 1.2

What Americans Know about Government

RESPONDENTS WHO	PERCENTAGE
Could identify all three branches of government	26
Knew Congress has the power to declare war	54
Knew Congress has the power to raise taxes	83
Knew Congress cannot establish an official religion of the United States	77
Could not name any of the rights guaranteed by the First Amendment	37
In 2016, could name the Republican vice-presidential candidate (Mike Pence).	37
In 2016, could name the Democratic vice-presidential candidate (Tim Kaine)	22

SOURCES: Annenberg Constitution Day Civics Survey, July 14–18, 2016, cdn.annenbergpublicpolicycenter.org/wp-content/uploads/Constitution_Day_2016_Civics_Appendix.pdf; and Annenberg Constitution Day Civics Survey, August 9–13, 2017, www.annenbergpublicpolicycenter.org/americans-are-poorly-informed-about-basic-constitutional-provisions/ (accessed 2/17/18).

Accompanying this sense that ordinary people are not heard is a growing belief that government is not run for the benefit of all. In 2015, 76 percent of the public disagreed with the idea that the "government is really run for the benefit of all the people."[11]

This widely felt loss of political efficacy is bad news for American democracy: the belief that you can be effective is the first step needed to influence government. Not every effort of ordinary citizens to influence government will succeed, but without any such efforts, government decisions will be made by a smaller and smaller circle of powerful people. Such loss of broad popular influence over government actions undermines the key feature of American democracy—government by the people.

There are ways that individuals can build their sense of political efficacy. Research shows that the relationship between efficacy and participation is two-way: a feeling that one can make a difference leads to participation, but in addition, joining in can increase one's efficacy. Most people do not want to be politically active every day of their lives, but it is essential to American political ideals that all citizens be informed and able to act.

Who Are Americans?

Show how the social composition of the American population has changed over time

While American democracy aims to give the people a voice in government, the meaning of "we the people" has changed over time. Who are Americans? Through the course of American history, politicians, religious leaders, prominent scholars, and ordinary Americans have puzzled over and fought about the answer to this fundamental question. Since the Founding, the American population has grown from 3.9 million in 1790, the year of the first official census, to 327 million in 2018.[12] As the American population has grown, it has become more diverse on nearly every dimension imaginable.[13] (See the "Who Are Americans?" feature on p. 15.)

At the time of the Founding, when the United States consisted of 13 states along the Eastern Seaboard, 81 percent of Americans counted by the census traced their roots to Europe, mostly England and northern Europe; and nearly 20 percent were of African origin, the vast majority of whom were slaves.[14] Only 1.5 percent of the black population was free. There was also an unknown number of Native Americans, the original inhabitants of the land, not counted by the census because the government did not consider them Americans. The first estimates of Native Americans and Hispanics in the mid-1800s showed that each group made up less than 1 percent of the total population.[15]

Fast-forward to 1900. The country now stretched across the continent, and waves of immigrants, mainly from Europe, boosted the population to 76 million. In 1900 the United States was predominantly composed of whites of European ancestry, but this number now included many from southern and eastern as well as northern Europe; the black population stood at 12 percent. Residents who traced their origin to Latin America or Asia each accounted for less than 1 percent of the entire population.[16] The large number of new immigrants was reflected in the high proportion of foreign-born people in the United States: the foreign-born population reached its height at 14.7 percent in 1910.[17]

Native American societies, with their own forms of government, existed for thousands of years before the first European settlers arrived. By the time this photo of Red Cloud and other Sioux warriors was taken, around 1870, Native Americans made up about 1 percent of the American population.

IMMIGRATION AND ETHNIC DIVERSITY

As the European-origin population grew more diverse, anxiety about Americans' ethnic identity mounted. The growing numbers of immigrants from southern and eastern Europe who were crowding into American cities spurred heated debates about how long those with United Kingdom and northern European ancestry could dominate. Much as today, politicians and scholars argued about whether the country could absorb such large numbers of immigrants. Concerns ranged from whether their political and social values were compatible with American democracy to whether they would learn English to alarm about the diseases they might bring into the United States.

Those worried about new immigrants noted their different religious affiliations as well. The first immigrants to the United States were overwhelmingly Protestant, many of them fleeing religious persecution. The arrival of Germans and Irish in the mid-1800s began to shift that balance with increasing numbers of Catholics. Even so, in 1900 four out of five Americans were still Protestants. The large-scale immigration of the early twentieth century threatened to reduce the proportion of Protestants significantly. Many of the eastern European immigrants pouring into the country, especially those from Russia, were Jewish; the southern Europeans, especially the Italians, were Catholic. A more religiously diverse country challenged the implicit Protestantism embedded in many aspects of American public life. For example, religious diversity introduced new conflicts into public schooling as Catholics sought public funding for parochial schools and dissident Protestant sects lobbied to eliminate Bible reading and prayer in the schools.

Anxieties about immigration sparked intense debate. Should the numbers of immigrants entering the country be limited? Should restrictions be placed on the types of immigrants to be granted entry? After World War I, Congress responded to the fears swirling around immigration with new laws that sharply limited the number who could enter the country each year. It also established a new National Origins quota system, based on the nation's population in 1890, before the wave of immigrants from eastern and southern Europe arrived.[18] Supporters of ethnic quotas

WHO ARE AMERICANS?

An Increasingly Diverse Nation

Since the Founding, the American people have become increasingly diverse. This diversity and the changes in the population have frequently raised challenging questions in American politics.

Race

1790*

1900*

2015

= 1 million people

White 81%
Black 19%

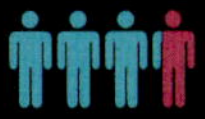

White 88%
Black 12%
Other 1%

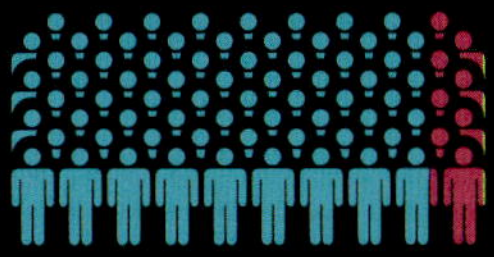

White 62%
Black 12%
Hispanic 17%
Asian 5%
Native American 1%
Other 0.4%
2 or more races 2%

TOTAL POPULATION =	1790	1900	2015
	3,929,214	75,994,575	323,127,513

Geography

1790

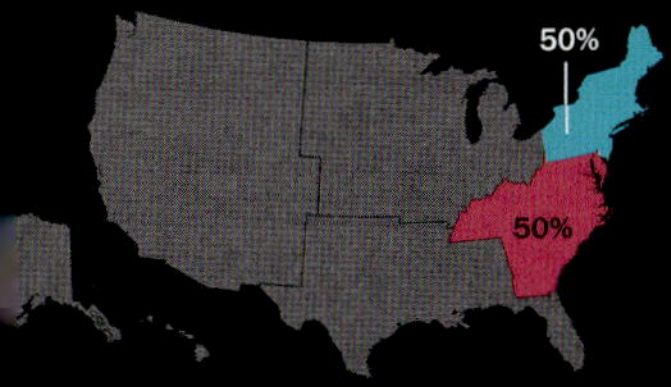

Northeast 50% South 50%

1900

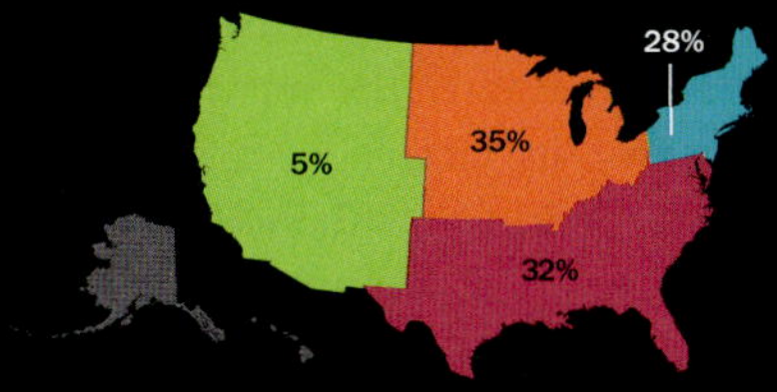

Northeast 28% Midwest 35%
South 32% West 5%

2015

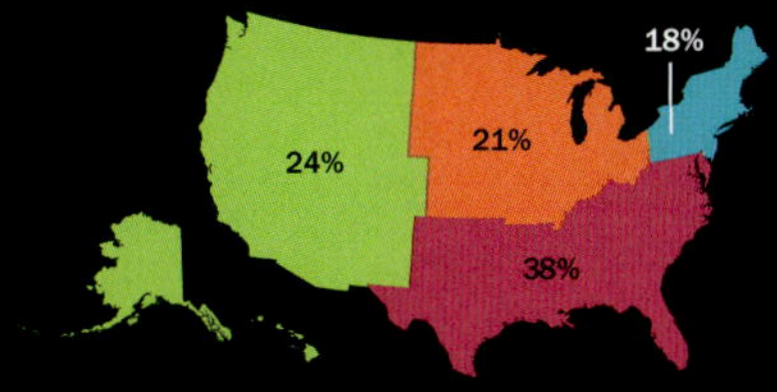

Northeast 18% Midwest 21%
South 38% West 24%

Age

1900

0–19 44%
20–44 38%
45–64 14%
65 + 4%

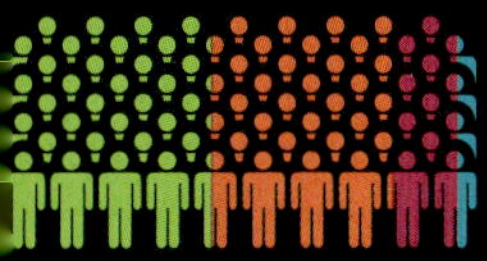

2015

0–19 26%
20–44 34%
45–64 26%
65 + 14%

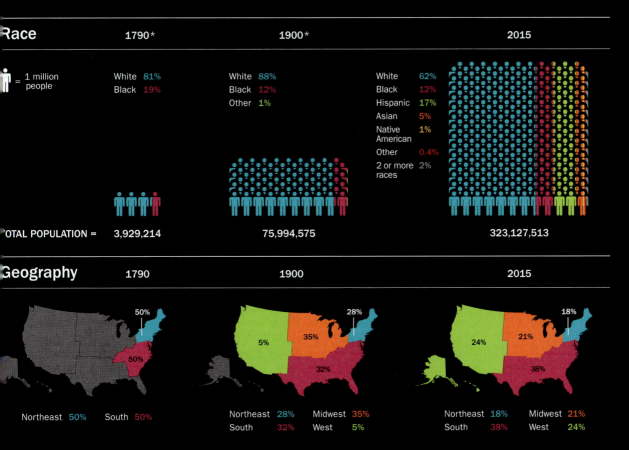

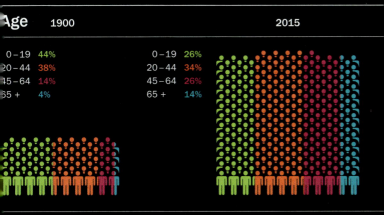

*The 1790 census does not accurately reflect the population because it only counted blacks and whites. It did not include Native Americans or other groups. The 1900 census did not count Hispanic Americans.

SOURCE: U.S. Census Bureau, 2011–2015 American Community Survey 5-Year Estimates, https://factfinder.census.gov (accessed 8/27/16).

FOR CRITICAL ANALYSIS

1. In 2015, the U.S. Census Bureau estimated that the population of the South and the West continued to grow more rapidly than the Northeast and Midwest. What are some of the political implications of this trend?
2. Today, Americans over age 37 outnumber Americans under 37—and older adults are more likely to participate in the political process. What do you think this means for the kinds of issues and policies taken up by the government?

In the 1900s many immigrants entered the United States through New York's Ellis Island, where they were checked for disease before being admitted. Today, individuals hoping to immigrate to the United States often apply for a visa at the U.S. consulate in their home country before traveling to the United States, where the U.S. Customs and Border Protection checks their identity and legal status.

hoped to turn back the clock and revert to an earlier America in which northern Europeans dominated. The new system set up a hierarchy of admissions: northern European countries received generous quotas for new immigrants, whereas eastern and southern European countries were granted very small quotas. These restrictions ratcheted down the numbers of immigrants so that by 1970 the foreign-born population in the United States reached an all-time low of 5 percent.

IMMIGRATION AND RACE

Official efforts to use racial and ethnic criteria to restrict the American population were not new but had been used to draw boundaries around the American community from the start. The very first census, as just mentioned, did not count Native Americans; in fact, no Native Americans became citizens until 1924. Although the Constitution infamously declared that each slave would count as three-fifths of a person for purposes of apportioning representation among the states, most people of African descent were not officially citizens until 1868, when the Fourteenth Amendment to the Constitution conferred citizenship on the freed slaves (see Chapter 2).

Over half a century earlier, the federal government had sought to limit the nonwhite population with a 1790 law stipulating that only free whites could become naturalized citizens. Not until 1870 did Congress lift the ban on the naturalization of nonwhites. In addition to the restrictions on blacks and Native Americans, restrictions applied to Asians. The Chinese Exclusion Act of 1882 outlawed the entry of Chinese laborers to the United States. These provisions were not lifted until 1943, when China became America's ally during World War II. Additional barriers enacted after World War I meant that virtually no Asians entered the country as immigrants until the 1940s. People of Hispanic origin do not fit simply into the American system of racial classification. In 1930, for example, the census counted people of Mexican origin as nonwhite but reversed this decision a decade later—after protests by the Mexican-origin population and the Mexican government. Only in 1970 did the census officially begin counting persons of Hispanic origin, noting that they could be any race.[19] As this history suggests, American citizenship has always been tied to "whiteness" even as the meaning of "white" shifted over time.

TWENTY-FIRST-CENTURY AMERICANS

Race and Ethnicity By the year 2000 immigration had profoundly transformed the nation's racial and ethnic profile once again. The primary cause was Congress's decision in 1965 to lift the tight restrictions of the 1920s, allowing for much-expanded immigration from Asia and Latin America (see Figure 1.2). One consequence of the shift has been the growth in the Hispanic, or Latino, population. Census figures for 2016 show that Hispanics, who can be of any race, constitute 17.8 percent of the population. The black, or African American, population is 12.7 percent of the total population, while Asians make up 5.4 percent. Non-Hispanic white Americans account for 61 percent of the population—their lowest share ever. Moreover, 3.2 percent of the population now identifies itself as of "two or more races," a new

FIGURE 1.2

Immigration by Continent of Origin

Where did most immigrants come from at the start of the twentieth century? How does that compare with immigration in the twenty-first century?

*Less than 1 percent not shown.

SOURCE: Department of Homeland Security 2016 Yearbook of Immigration Statistics Table 2, November 2017, www.dhs.gov/immigration-statistics/yearbook/2016 (accessed 2/16/18). Figure shows those who have obtained "lawful permanent resident status" by continent of origin.

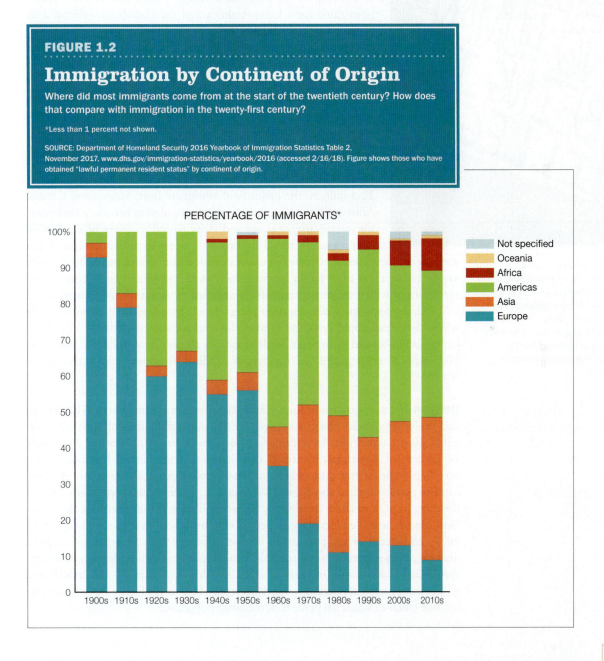

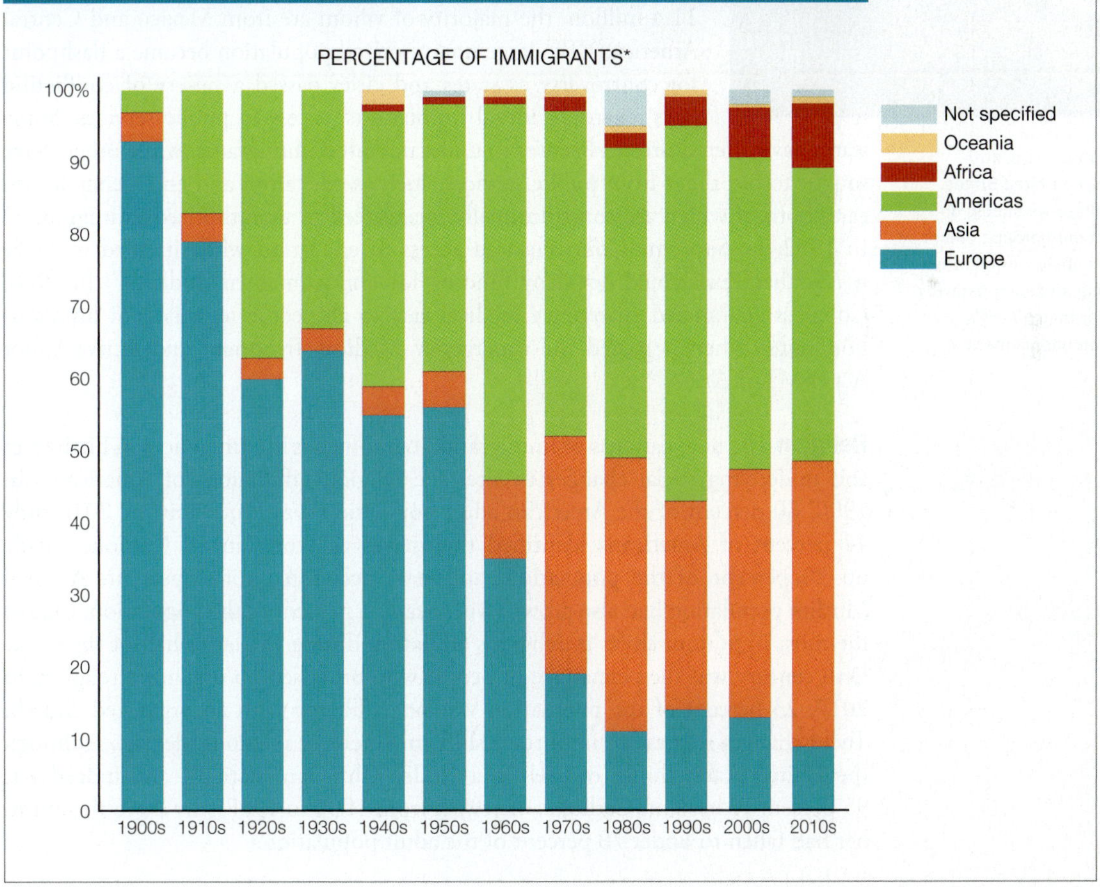

Immigration remains a controversial issue in the United States. While many believe we should do more to protect our borders, others call for comprehensive immigration reform, including an easier pathway to citizenship for the country's nearly 12 million undocumented immigrants.

category that the census added in 2000.[20] Although it is only a small percentage of the population, the multiracial category points toward a future in which the traditional labels of racial identification may be blurring, marking a major shift in the long-standing American tradition of strict racial categorization. The blurring of racial categories poses challenges to a host of policies—many of them put in place to remedy past discrimination—that rely on racial counts of the population.

Large-scale immigration means that many more residents are foreign-born. In 2016, 13.5 percent of the population was born outside the United States, a figure comparable to foreign-born rates at the turn of the previous century.[21] About half of the foreign-born came from Latin America and the Caribbean—almost 1 in 10 from the Caribbean, just over one-third from Central America (including Mexico), and 1 in 15 from South America.[22] Those born in Asia constituted the next-largest group, making up 31 percent of foreign-born residents.[23] In sharp contrast to the immigration patterns of a century earlier, fewer immigrants came from Europe. By 2016 just 10.9 percent of those born outside the United States came from Europe.[24]

One contemporary feature of American society is the large number of immigrants who live in the country without legal authorization. Estimates put the number of undocumented immigrants at 11.4 million, the majority of whom are from Mexico and Central America.[25] The large unauthorized population became a flashpoint for controversy as states and cities passed a variety of conflicting laws regarding illegal immigrants' access to public services. Some states have offered driver's licenses to undocumented immigrants, while others have sought to bar them from public services, such as education and emergency health care, both of which are constitutionally guaranteed to unauthorized immigrants.[26] In 1982 the Supreme Court ensured access to education when it ruled in *Plyler v. Doe* that Texas could not deny funding for undocumented students.[27] In 1986, Congress guaranteed emergency medical care to all people regardless of immigration status when it passed the Emergency Medical Treatment and Active Labor Act (EMTALA).

Religion The new patterns of immigration combined with differences in birth rates and underlying social changes to alter the religious affiliations of Americans. In 1900, 80 percent of the American adult population was Protestant; by 2016 only 44 percent of Americans identified themselves as Protestants.[28] Catholics made up 20 percent of the population, and Jews accounted for 2 percent. A small Muslim population had also grown, with nearly 1 percent of the population. One of the most important shifts in religious affiliation during the latter half of the twentieth century was the percentage of people who professed no organized religion: in 2017, 23 percent of the population was not affiliated with an organized church. These changes suggest an important shift in American religious identity. Although the United States thinks of itself as a "Judeo-Christian" nation—and indeed was 95 percent Protestant, Catholic, or Jewish from 1900 to 1968—by 2016 this number had fallen to under 70 percent of the adult population.[29]

AMERICA SIDE by SIDE

Global Diversity

The United States has become an increasingly diverse country over time particularly in regard to its racial and ethnic makeup. How does the racial and ethnic diversity of the United States compare to that of other countries around the world?

As a "nation of immigrants," the United States is more diverse than many Western countries, but some former colonies are even more diverse than the United States. Racial and ethnic diversity stem not only from immigration but also geography, historical legacies, and whether the government has favored certain groups over others. Many countries in sub-Saharan Africa were colonized by multiple empires, whose governments often drew borders that encompassed multiple ethnic groups in the region. State-building and nationalism are also very new to these regions, meaning that local identities remain stronger than national ones.

In contrast many western European and Asian countries have histories of past conflict and strong state-building efforts, resulting in less diversity either by eliminating rival groups or forcibly assimilating them. For example, Japan's geographic isolation has created a racially homogeneous society, which was reinforced by the government's use of isolationism as a means to consolidate power.[a] Modern policies limiting immigration continue these historic trends. To take another example, France has historically pursued both political and cultural assimilation, using its schools as tools to socialize its citizens into a common "republican" identity. More recent waves of immigrants, however, have highlighted potential problems with this policy.[b]

How might the degree of diversity shape political values in specific countries? What types of values and policies would we expect to see in countries with a high degree of diversity versus those with less diversity?

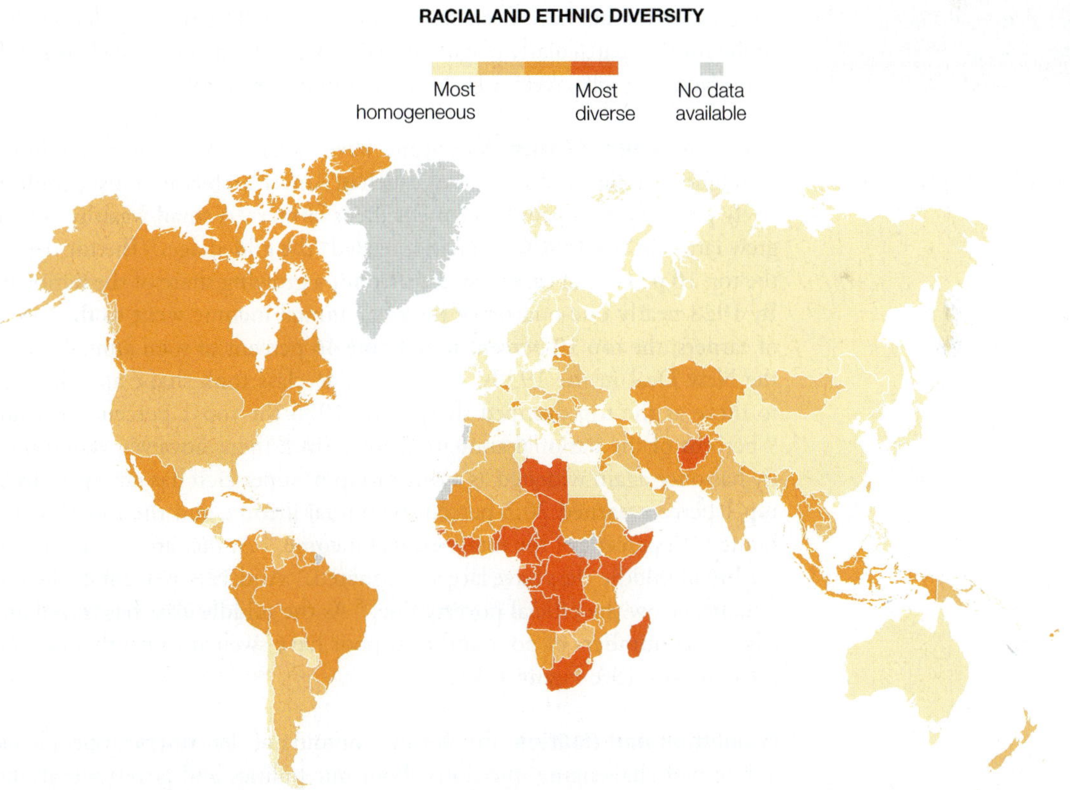

SOURCE: Alberto Alesina, Arnaud Devleeschauwer, William Easterly, Sergio Kurlat, and Romain Wacziarg, "Fractionalization," *Journal of Economic Growth*, 8 (2003): 155–94.

[a] Benedict Anderson, *Imagined Communities: Reflections on the Origin and Spread of Nationalism* (London: Verso, 2006), 94–99.

[b] John R. Bowen, *Why the French Don't Like Headscarves: Islam, the State, and Public Space* (Princeton, NJ: Princeton University Press, 2007).

Age As America grew and its population expanded and diversified, the country's age profile shifted with it. In 1900 only 4 percent of the population was over age 65. As life expectancy increased, the number of older Americans grew with it: by 2016, 15.2 percent of the population was over 65. Over the same period, the percentage of children under the age of 18 fell, from 40.5 percent of the American population in 1900 to 22.8 percent in 2016.[30] Even though the population is aging, Americans tend to be younger than citizens of many industrialized countries, mainly because of the large immigrant population in the United States. The share of the population aged 65 and over is 20 percent in the European Union and 27 percent in Japan.[31] But an aging population poses challenges to the United States as well. As the elderly population grows and the working-age population shrinks, questions arise about how we will fund programs for the elderly such as Social Security.

Geography Over the nation's history, Americans have changed in other ways, moving from mostly rural settings and small towns to large urban areas. Before 1920 less than half the population lived in urban areas; today 82 percent of Americans do.[32] Critics charge that the American political system—created when America was a largely rural society—underrepresents urban areas. The constitutional provision allocating each state two senators, for example, overrepresents sparsely populated rural states and underrepresents urban states, where the population is far more concentrated. In addition to becoming more urban over time, the American population has shifted regionally. During the past 50 years especially, many Americans left the Northeast and Midwest and moved to the South and Southwest. As congressional seats have been reapportioned to reflect the population shift, many problems that particularly plague the Midwest and Northeast, such as the decline in manufacturing jobs, receive less attention in national politics.

FOR CRITICAL ANALYSIS

What trend in America's changing population has had the biggest influence on politics? Increasing racial and ethnic diversity? Aging? Increasing urbanization? Increased economic inequality? Why?

Socioeconomic Status Americans have fallen into diverse economic groups throughout American history. For much of American history most people were relatively poor working people, many of them farmers. A small wealthy elite, however, grew larger in the 1890s, in a period called "the gilded age." The top 1 percent and the top 10 percent of earners accounted for a growing share of the national income. By 1928 nearly one-quarter of the total annual income went to the top 1 percent of earners; the top 10 percent took home 46 percent of total annual income. After the New Deal in the 1930s, a large middle class took shape and the share going to those at the top dropped sharply. By 1976 the top 1 percent took home only 9 percent of the national annual income. Since then, however, economic inequality has once again widened as a tiny group of super-rich has emerged. By 2015 the top 1 percent earned 20.3 percent of annual income and the top 10 percent took home 48.8 percent of the total national income.[33] At the same time, the incomes of the broad middle class have largely stagnated.[34] And 12.7 percent of the population remains below the official poverty line.[35] As the middle class has frayed around the edges, the numbers of poor and near poor have swelled to nearly one-third of the population.[36] (See Figure 1.3.)

Population and Politics The shifting contours of the American people have regularly raised challenging questions about our politics and governing arrangements. Population growth and shifts have spurred politically charged debates about how the population should be apportioned among congressional districts and how those

FIGURE 1.3

Income in the United States

The top graph shows that while the income of most Americans has risen only slightly since 1975, the income of the richest Americans (the top 5 percent) has increased dramatically. The lower graph shows the portion of all income in the United States that goes to each group, with an increasing share going to the richest Americans in recent years. What are some of the ways that this shift might matter for American politics? Does the growing economic gap between the richest groups and most other Americans conflict with the political value of equality?

*Dollar values are given in constant 2016 dollars, which are adjusted for inflation so that we can compare a person's income in 1975 with a person's income today.

SOURCE: U.S. Census Bureau, "Income and Poverty in the United States: 2016" Table A-2, www.census.gov/content/dam/Census/library/publications/2017/demo/P60-259.pdf (accessed 4/16/18).

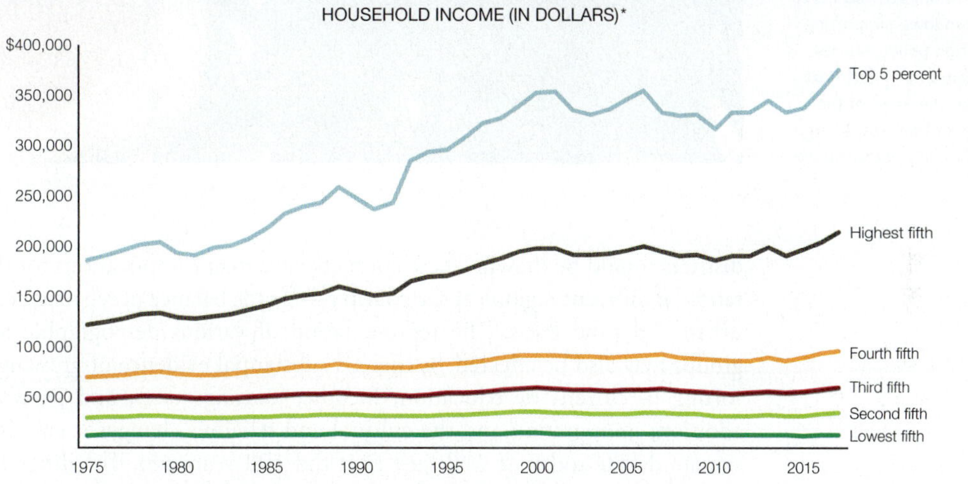

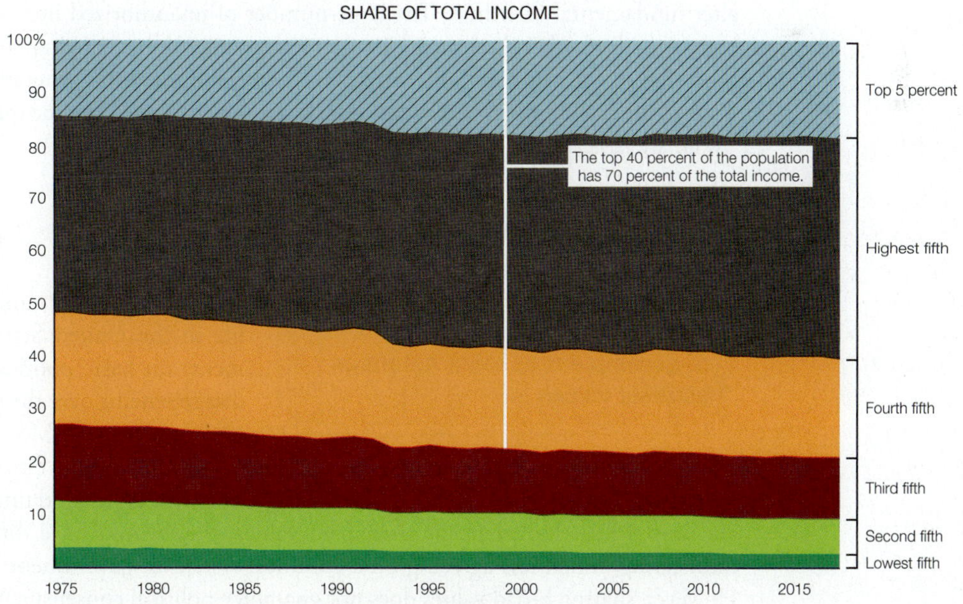

America continues to become more racially and ethnically diverse. These changes have sparked controversy over political issues. Here, Gregg Cummings, a Tea Party conservative from Iowa supporting strong immigration policy, stands outside of the Supreme Court next to Janet Murgu'a, the head of the National Council of La Raza, a large Latino rights advocacy organization.

districts should be drawn. These conflicts have major implications for the representation of different regions of the country—for the balance of representation between urban and rural areas. The representation of various demographic and political groups may also be affected, as there is substantial evidence of growing geographic sorting of citizens by education, income, marriage rates, and party voting.[37] In addition, immigration and the cultural and religious changes it entails sparks passionate debate today as well, just as it did 100 years ago. The different languages and customs that immigrants bring to the United States trigger fears among some that the country is changing in ways that may undermine American values and alter fundamental identities. The large number of unauthorized immigrants in the country today makes these anxieties even more acute. Yet a changing population has been one of the constants of American history. Indeed, each generation has confronted the myriad political challenges associated with answering the question anew, "Who are Americans?"

American Political Culture

Analyze whether the U.S. system of government upholds American political values

Underlying and framing political life in the United States are agreements on basic political values but disagreements over the ends or goals of government. Most Americans affirm the values of liberty, equality, and democracy. Values shape citizens' views of the world and define their sense of what is right and wrong, just and unjust, possible and impossible. If Americans shared no values, they would have difficulty communicating, much less agreeing on a common system of government and politics. However, sharing broad values does not guarantee political consensus. We can agree on principles but disagree over their application or how they are to be balanced.

Much of the debate over the role of government has been over what government should do and how far it should go to reduce the inequalities within our society and political system while still preserving essential liberties.

Even though Americans have disagreed over the meaning of such political ideals as equality, they still agree on the importance of those ideals. The values, beliefs, and attitudes that form our **political culture** and hold together the United States and its people date back to the time of the founding of the Union.

political culture broadly shared values, beliefs, and attitudes about how the government should function; American political culture emphasizes the values of liberty, equality, and democracy

The essential documents of the American Founding—the Declaration of Independence and the Constitution—enunciated a set of political principles about the purposes of the new republic. In contrast with many other democracies, in the United States these political ideals did not just remain words on dusty documents. Americans actively embraced the principles of the Founders and made them central to the national identity. Let us look more closely at three of these ideals: liberty, equality, and democracy.

LIBERTY

No ideal is more central to American values than liberty. The Declaration of Independence defined three inalienable rights: "Life, Liberty and the pursuit of Happiness." The preamble to the Constitution likewise identified the need to secure "the Blessings of Liberty" as one of the key reasons for drawing up the Constitution. For Americans, **liberty** means both personal freedom and economic freedom. Both are closely linked to the idea of **limited government**.

liberty freedom from governmental control

limited government a principle of constitutional government; a government whose powers are defined and limited by a constitution

The Constitution's first 10 amendments, known collectively as the Bill of Rights, above all preserve individual personal liberties and rights. In fact, the word *liberty* has come to mean many of the freedoms guaranteed in the Bill of Rights: freedom of speech and writing, the right to assemble freely, and the right to practice religious beliefs without interference from the government. Over the course of American history, the scope of personal liberties has expanded as laws have become more tolerant and as individuals have successfully used the courts to challenge restrictions on their individual freedoms. Far fewer restrictions exist today on the press, political speech, and individual moral behavior than in the early years of the nation. Even so, conflicts persist over how personal liberties should be extended and when personal liberties violate community norms. For example, a number of cities have recently passed "sit-lie" ordinances, which limit the freedom of individuals to sit or lie down on sidewalks. Designed to limit the presence of the homeless and make city streets more attractive to pedestrians, the ordinances have also been denounced as infringements on individual liberties.

Patrick Henry's famous "Give Me Liberty or Give Me Death" speech demanded freedom at any cost and has resonated with Americans throughout the nation's history.

The central historical conflict regarding liberty in the United States was about the enslavement of blacks. The facts of slavery and the differential treatment of the races have cast a long shadow over all of American history. In fact, scholars today note that the American definition of freedom has been formed in relation to the concept of slavery. The right to control one's labor and the right to receive rewards for that labor have been central elements of our definition of freedom precisely because these freedoms were denied to slaves.[38]

In addition to personal freedom, the American concept of liberty means economic freedom. Since the Founding, economic freedom has been linked to capitalism, free markets, and the protection of private property. Free competition, unfettered movement of goods, and the right to enjoy the fruits of one's labor are all essential aspects of economic freedom and American capitalism.[39] In the first century of the

laissez-faire capitalism an economic system in which the means of production and distribution are privately owned and operated for profit with minimal or no government interference

Republic, support for capitalism often meant support for the doctrine of *laissez-faire* (literally, "leave alone" in French). **Laissez-faire capitalism** allowed very little room for the national government to regulate trade or restrict the use of private property, even in the public interest. Americans still strongly support capitalism and economic liberty, but they now also endorse some restrictions on economic freedoms to protect the public. Today, federal and state governments deploy a wide array of regulations in the name of public protection. These include health and safety laws, environmental rules, and workplace regulations.

Not surprisingly, fierce disagreements often erupt over what the proper scope of government regulation should be. What some people regard as protecting the public, others see as an infringement on their own freedom to run their businesses and use their property as they see fit. For example, many business leaders opposed the Affordable Care Act, the health care reform legislation informally known as Obamacare, because it required businesses with over 50 employees to provide health coverage for their employees and establishes standards about which health services should be covered by the insurance. In addition, the law required that insurers pay for access to contraceptive care. From the perspective of the law's supporters, this provision simply ensured that women have access to basic health care. Many businesses, however, opposed the law as unwanted government intrusion. And some businesses strongly denounced the requirement to cover contraception, in particular, as a violation of their fundamental liberties to run their businesses as they see fit. In fact, in 2014 a company called Hobby Lobby successfully challenged this provision of the act when the Supreme Court ruled that family firms could be exempted on the basis of religious objections.[40]

Concerns about liberty have also arisen in relation to the government's efforts to combat terrorism and protect the nation's security. These concerns escalated in 2013 when Edward Snowden, a former National Security Agency (NSA) contractor, leaked top-secret documents from the NSA to the press. The NSA is the agency charged with protecting the United States by monitoring electronic data flows—including radio, email, and cellular telephone calls—for foreign threats. The leaked documents revealed that the American government was listening in on the private communications of foreign governments, including many American allies, such as Germany and Brazil. The leaks also revealed information about domestic surveillance: the NSA had access to Americans' Facebook, Google, Apple, and Yahoo! accounts, among many other electronic data sources. It was using these "metadata" to track the connections among people, searching for suspicious ties. The revelation that the NSA had been collecting this information for three years without public knowledge set off a storm of controversy since the NSA is supposed to monitor foreign communications, not track Americans. The controversy reinforced the tech companies' commitment to privacy. In 2016, Apple refused an FBI order to unlock the iPhone used by a terrorist who killed 14 people in San Bernardino, California. The FBI dropped the case after it was able to open the phone without Apple's help. However, a new court order to Apple related to an iPhone used in a drug conspiracy case made it clear that the tension between privacy and security will continue.[41]

Concerns about terrorism leave us with an extraordinary dilemma. On the one hand, we treasure liberty; but on the other hand, we recognize that the lives of thousands of Americans have already been lost and countless others are threatened by terrorism. Can we reconcile liberty and security? Liberty and order? In previous national emergencies, Americans accepted restrictions on liberty with the understanding that these would be temporary. But because the threat of terrorism has no clear end point, doubts have grown about whether special government powers that infringe on liberties should be continued.

EQUALITY

The Declaration of Independence declares as its first "self-evident" truth that "all men are created equal." As central as it is to the American political creed, however, equality has been an even less well-defined ideal than liberty because people interpret "equality" in different ways. Few Americans have wholeheartedly embraced the ideal of full equality of results, but most Americans share the ideal of **equality of opportunity**—that is, the notion that each person should be given a fair chance to go as far as his or her talents will allow. Yet it is hard for Americans to reach agreement on what constitutes equality of opportunity. Must a group's *past* inequalities be remedied in order to ensure equal opportunity in the *present*? Should inequalities in the legal, political, and economic spheres be given the same weight? In contrast to liberty, which requires limits on the role of government, equality implies an *obligation* of the government to the people.[42]

equality of opportunity a widely shared American ideal that all people should have the freedom to use whatever talents and wealth they have to reach their fullest potential

Americans do make clear distinctions between political equality and social or economic equality. **Political equality** means that members of the American political community have the right to participate in politics on equal terms. Beginning from a very restricted definition of political community, which originally included only propertied white men, the United States has moved much closer to an ideal of political equality that can be summed up as "one person, one vote." Broad support for the ideal of political equality has helped expand the American political community and extend to all the right to participate. Although considerable conflict remains over whether the political system makes participation in it harder for some people and easier for others and whether the role of money in politics has drowned out the public voice, Americans agree that all citizens should have an equal right to participate and that government should enforce that right.

political equality the right to participate in politics equally, based on the principle of "one person, one vote"

In part because Americans believe that individuals are free to work as hard as they choose, they have always been less concerned about social or economic inequality. Many Americans regard economic differences as the consequence of individual choices, virtues, or failures. Because of this, Americans tend to be less supportive than most Europeans of government action to ensure economic equality. Yet when

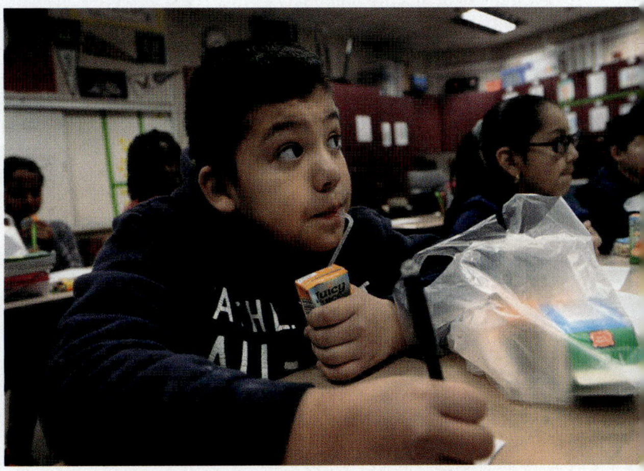

Americans struggle to define how equality of opportunity can be provided at the same time as individual liberty. One area of debate is in education. Does the fact that New York (left) spends on average $21,206 per student each year while Utah (right) spends on average $6,575 per student, mean that there is not an equality of opportunity for schoolchildren? *(Data from www.census.gov.)*

major economic forces, such as the Great Depression of the 1930s, affect many people or when systematic barriers appear to block equality of opportunity, Americans support government action to promote equality. Even then, however, they have endorsed only a limited government role designed to help people get back on their feet or to open up opportunity.

Because equality is such an elusive concept, many conflicts have arisen over what it should mean in practice. Americans have engaged in three kinds of controversies about the public role in addressing inequality. The first is determining what constitutes equality of access to public institutions. In 1896 the Supreme Court ruled in *Plessy v. Ferguson* that "separate but equal" accommodation for blacks and whites was constitutional.[43] In 1954, in a major legal victory for the civil rights movement, the Supreme Court's decision in *Brown v. Board of Education* overturned the "separate but equal" doctrine (see Chapter 5).[44] Today, new questions have been raised about what constitutes equal access to public institutions. Some argue that the unequal financing of public schools in cities, suburbs, and rural districts is a violation of the right to equal education. To date, these claims have not been supported by the federal courts, which have rejected the notion that the unequal economic impacts of public policy outcomes are a constitutional matter, leaving the issue to the states.[45] Lawsuits arguing a right to "economic equal protection" stalled in 1973 when the Supreme Court ruled that a Texas school-financing law did not violate the Constitution even though the law affected rich and poor students differently.[46]

A second debate concerns the public role in ensuring equality of opportunity in private life. Although Americans generally agree that discrimination should not be tolerated, people disagree over what should be done to ensure equality of opportunity (see Table 1.3).[47] Controversies about affirmative action programs reflect these disputes. Supporters of affirmative action claim that such programs are necessary to compensate for past discrimination in order to establish true equality of opportunity today. Opponents maintain that affirmative action amounts to reverse discrimination and that a society that espouses true equality should not acknowledge gender or racial differences. The question of the public responsibility for private inequalities is central to gender issues. The traditional view, still held by many today, takes for

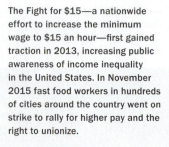

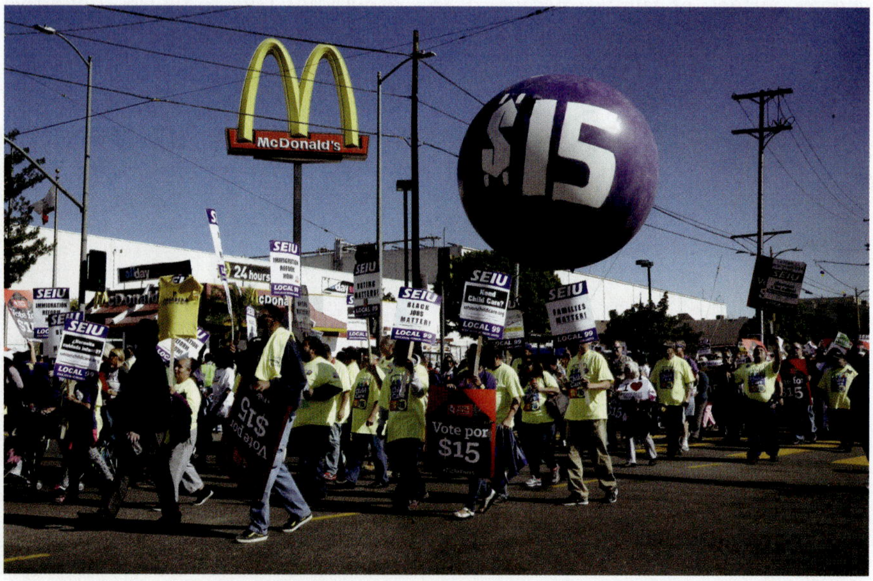

The Fight for $15—a nationwide effort to increase the minimum wage to $15 an hour—first gained traction in 2013, increasing public awareness of income inequality in the United States. In November 2015 fast food workers in hundreds of cities around the country went on strike to rally for higher pay and the right to unionize.

TABLE 1.3

Equality and Public Opinion

Americans believe in some forms of equality more than others. How do these survey results reflect disagreement about what equality means in practice?

STATEMENT	PERCENTAGE WHO AGREE
It is very important that women have the same rights as men in our country.	91
Our society should do what is necessary to make sure that everyone has an equal opportunity to succeed.	86
Our country should have laws that protect gay, lesbian, bisexual, and transgender people against discrimination in jobs, public accommodations, and housing.	69
It should be legal for gay and lesbian couples to get married.	62
The fact that some are rich and some are poor is an acceptable part of the economic system.	52
Our country needs to continue making changes to give blacks equal rights with whites (according to whites).	54
Our country needs to continue making changes to give blacks equal rights with whites (according to blacks).	88
The country hasn't gone far enough when it comes to gender equality (according to women).	57
The country hasn't gone far enough when it comes to gender equality (according to men).	42

SOURCE: Pew Research Center, www.pewresearch.org/. See endnote 47 for specific reports.

granted that women should bear special responsibilities in the family. In this perspective, the challenges women face in the labor force due to family responsibilities fall outside the range of public concern. In the past 30 years especially, these traditional views have come under fire as advocates for women have argued that private inequalities *are* a topic of public concern.[48]

A third debate about equality concerns differences in income and wealth. Unlike in other countries, income inequality has not been an enduring topic of political controversy in the United States, which currently has the largest gap in income and wealth between rich and poor citizens of any developed nation. Americans have generally tolerated great differences among rich and poor citizens, in part because of a pervasive belief that mobility is possible and that economic success is the product of individual effort.[49] This tolerance for inequality is reflected in America's tax code, which is more advantageous to wealthy taxpayers than that of almost any other Western nation.

FOR CRITICAL ANALYSIS

Economic inequality among Americans has been widening since at least the 1970s. Many politicians and news commentators say that inequality is threatening the middle class. Is there any evidence that the American public is worried about the growth in inequality?

Since the Great Recession, however, income inequality has risen on the political agenda. During the 2016 presidential race, Democratic candidates Hillary Clinton and Bernie Sanders discussed economic inequality, as did Republican candidates such as Donald Trump and Marco Rubio, although their proposed solutions differed. Public opinion polls revealed concerns about inequality as well. In 2015 two-thirds of Americans said the distribution of wealth and money is not fair and should be more evenly distributed; in 2017, 63 percent of Americans said upper-income people pay too little in taxes, and 67 percent said corporations pay too little.[50] Nonetheless, the tax bill passed by the Republican-led Congress and signed by President Trump at the end of 2017 lowered taxes on corporations and wealthy households, raising concerns among some critics about lack of responsiveness to public opinion.

DEMOCRACY

The essence of democracy is the participation of the people in choosing their rulers and the people's ability to influence what those rulers do. In a democracy, political power ultimately comes from the people. The idea of placing power in the hands of the people is known as popular sovereignty. In the United States, **popular sovereignty** and political equality make politicians accountable to the people. Ideally, democracy envisions an engaged citizenry prepared to exercise its power over rulers. As we noted earlier, the United States is a representative democracy, meaning that the people do not rule directly but instead exercise power through elected representatives. Forms of participation in a democracy vary greatly, but voting is a key element of the representative democracy that the American Founders established.

popular sovereignty a principle of democracy in which political authority rests ultimately in the hands of the people

American democracy rests on the principle of **majority rule** with **minority rights**. Majority rule means that the wishes of the majority determine what government does. The House of Representatives—a large body elected directly by the people—was designed in particular to ensure majority rule. But the Founders feared that popular majorities could turn government into a "tyranny of the majority" in which individual liberties would be violated. Concern for individual rights has thus been a part of American democracy from the beginning. The rights enumerated in the Bill of Rights and enforced through the courts provide an important check on the power of the majority.

majority rule, minority rights the democratic principle that a government follows the preferences of the majority of voters but protects the interests of the minority

Despite Americans' deep attachment to the *ideal* of democracy, many questions can be raised about our *practice* of democracy. The first is the restricted definition of the political community during much of American history. Property restrictions on the right to vote were eliminated by 1828; in 1870 the Fifteenth Amendment to the Constitution granted African Americans the vote, although later exclusionary practices denied them that right; in 1920 the Nineteenth Amendment guaranteed women the right to vote; and in 1965 the Voting Rights Act finally secured the right of African Americans to vote. The Twenty-Sixth Amendment, ratified in 1971 during the Vietnam War, gave 18- to 20-year-olds the right to vote.

FOR CRITICAL ANALYSIS

In the United States, do citizens make the decisions of government, or do they merely influence them?

Just securing the right to vote does not end concerns about democracy, however. The organization of electoral institutions can have a significant impact on access to elections and on who can get elected. During the first two decades of the twentieth century, states and cities enacted many reforms, including strict registration requirements and scheduling of elections, that made it harder to vote. The aim was to rid politics of corruption, but the consequence was to reduce participation. More recently, voter ID laws requiring government identification to register or to vote have been enacted for similar reasons and with similar consequences. Other

While levels of participation in politics are relatively low for young Americans, the presidential primary campaigns of 2008 and 2016 saw the highest levels of youth turnout—to volunteer and to vote—in decades. What factors might have energized young people to become involved in these particular campaigns?

institutional decisions affect which candidates stand the best chance of getting elected (see Chapter 10).

A further consideration about democracy concerns the relationship between economic power and political power. Money has always played an important role in elections and governing in the United States. Many argue that the pervasive influence of money in American electoral campaigns and lobbying activities today undermines democracy. With the decline of locally based political parties that depend on party loyalists to turn out the vote and the rise of political action committees, political consultants, and expensive media campaigns, money has become the central fact of life in American politics. Money often determines who runs for office; it can exert a heavy influence on who wins; and some argue that it affects what politicians do once they are in office.[51]

Low turnout for elections and a pervasive sense of apathy and cynicism characterized American politics for much of the past half-century. The widespread interest in the 2008 election and the near-record levels of voter turnout, which, at 61.6 percent, was the highest turnout since 1968, reversed this trend.[52] Nine million voters registered and voted for the first time in 2008, including near-record numbers of voters under the age of 24.[53] Despite strong engagement in the presidential primaries and in the general election campaigns, lower turnout in the 2012 and 2016 elections suggested that public disengagement remains a challenge for American democracy.

What Americans Think about Government

Explore Americans' attitudes toward government

Since the United States was established as a nation, Americans have been reluctant to grant government too much power, and they have often been suspicious of politicians. But over the course of the nation's history, Americans have also turned to government for assistance in times of need and have strongly supported the government in periods of war. In 1933 the power of the

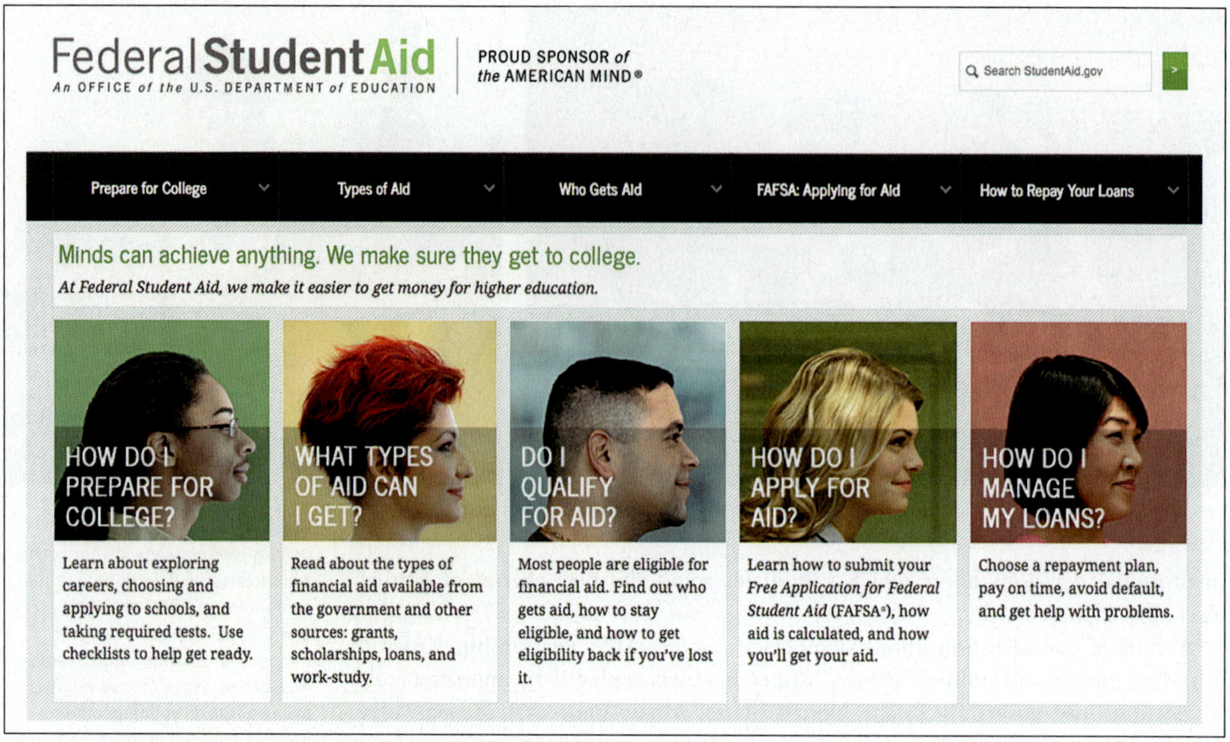

The federal government maintains a large number of websites that provide useful information to citizens on such topics as loans for education, civil service job applications, the inflation rate, and how the weather will affect farming. These sites are just one way in which the government serves its citizens.

government began to expand to meet the crises created by the stock market crash of 1929, the Great Depression, and the run on banks of 1933. Congress passed legislation that brought the government into the businesses of home mortgages, farm mortgages, credit, and relief of personal distress. More recently, when the economy threatened to fall into a deep recession in 2008 and 2009, the federal government took action to shore up the financial system, oversee the restructuring of the ailing auto companies, and inject hundreds of billions of dollars into the faltering economy. In 2017 federal government funds helped fight wildfires in the American West and provide hurricane relief in Texas and Florida. Today the national government is enormous, with programs and policies reaching into every corner of American life. It oversees the nation's economy, it is the nation's largest employer, it provides citizens with a host of services, it controls the world's most formidable military, and it regulates a wide range of social and commercial activities. Americans use government services, benefits, and infrastructure every day and are simultaneously skeptical about the role of government in society. We might consider these contradictory feelings and low government trust additional aspects of contemporary American political culture.

CONSERVATIVE IN THEORY, LIBERAL IN PRACTICE

The Constitution lays out a system of limited government, which largely reflects the preferences of the majority of Americans. When asked questions about the role of government in general, the majority of Americans give answers on the conservative side of the political spectrum. More Americans consider themselves politically conservative than liberal (36 versus 26 percent in 2017; 40–21 in 2009).[54] In 2017, 55 percent of Americans said "the federal government has too much power," and 56 percent said that the "government is almost always wasteful and inefficient."[55]

At the same time, however, when asked about specific government programs, majorities offer strong support. In 2017, 86 percent of Republicans and 95 percent of Democrats wanted federal spending on Social Security to be kept the same or increased; 91 percent of Republicans and 92 percent of Democrats wanted spending on highways, bridges, and roads to be the same or higher; and 61 percent of Republicans and 93 percent of Democrats wanted spending on economic assistance to needy people kept the same or increased.[56] Thus many Americans prefer small government in the abstract, but very much like what government does in some specific issue areas. They are simultaneously "abstract conservatives" and "operational liberals."[57] That both sentiments are prevalent in American public opinion helps explain why there can be calls both for more government action and for less, depending on the situation.

TRUST IN GOVERNMENT

Another characteristic of contemporary political culture is low trust in government. Ironically, even as popular dependence on the government has grown, the American public's view of government has turned sour. In the early 1960s three-quarters of Americans said they trusted government most of the time or always. By 2017 only 18 percent of Americans expressed such trust in government[58] (see Figure 1.4). Different groups vary somewhat in their levels of trust: African Americans and Latinos express slightly more confidence in the federal government than do whites. But even among the most supportive groups, considerably more than half only trust the government some of the time.[59] These developments are important because politically engaged citizens and public confidence in government are vital for the health of a democracy.

Trust spiked higher after the September 11 terrorist attacks, but fell to pre-attack levels within three years, and the trend has continued its downward path. Distrust of government greatly influenced the primary elections in 2015 and 2016, when a

With a few upticks, trust in government has been on the decline since the 1960s. What factors might reverse the trend? Have high-profile populist presidential candidates like Donald Trump and Bernie Sanders helped to raise or lower trust in government?

FIGURE 1.4

Public Trust in Government, 1958–2017

Since the 1960s, general levels of public trust in government have declined. What factors might help to account for changes in the public's trust in government? Why has confidence in government dropped again since September 11, 2001?

SOURCE: The American National Election Studies, 1958–2004; Pew Research Center, www.people-press.org/2017/05/03/public-trust-in-government-1958-2017/ (accessed 12/27/17). The Pew data after 2004 represent a "three survey moving average."

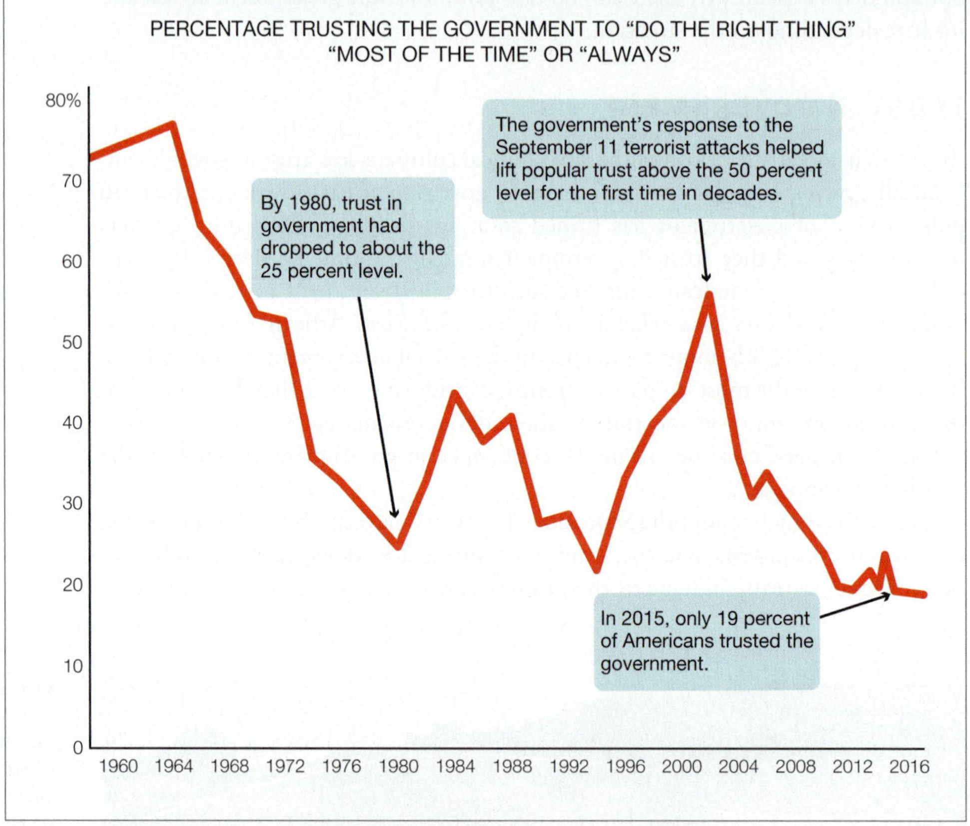
PERCENTAGE TRUSTING THE GOVERNMENT TO "DO THE RIGHT THING" "MOST OF THE TIME" OR "ALWAYS"
80%
70
60
50
40
30
20
10
0
1960 1964 1968 1972 1976 1980 1984 1988 1992 1996 2000 2004 2008 2012 2016
By 1980, trust in government had dropped to about the 25 percent level.
The government's response to the September 11 terrorist attacks helped lift popular trust above the 50 percent level for the first time in decades.
In 2015, only 19 percent of Americans trusted the government.

number of "outsider" candidates, critical of government, attracted wide support. This trend was especially pronounced in the Republican primaries, in which candidates known for their strong anti-government rhetoric, such as Ted Cruz, and candidates with no government experience, notably Donald Trump, unexpectedly attracted wide support. Among Democratic primary voters, strong support for Bernie Sanders, a democratic socialist, also indicated a desire to depart from business as usual in Washington. Sanders vigorously faulted the government for failing to take more forceful action against corporate misconduct and growing inequality.

Does it matter if Americans trust their government? For the most part, the answer is yes. As we have seen, most Americans rely on government for a wide range of services and laws that they simply take for granted. But long-term distrust in government can result in public refusal to pay the taxes necessary to support such widely approved public activities. Low levels of confidence may also make it difficult for government to attract talented and effective workers to public service.[60] The weakening of government as a result of prolonged levels of distrust may ultimately harm the United States' capacity to defend its national interest in the world economy and may jeopardize its national security. Likewise, a weak government can do little to assist citizens who need help in weathering periods of sharp economic or technological change.

FOR CRITICAL ANALYSIS

What recent events have affected Americans' trust in government? What might it take to restore Americans' trust in the federal government?

American Political Culture
WHAT DO WE WANT?

Americans express mixed views about government. Almost everyone complains about government at one time or another, but in the past three decades, general trust in government has declined significantly. Despite mounting distrust, when asked about particular government activities or programs, a majority of Americans are more than likely to support the activities that government undertakes. These conflicting views reflect the tensions in American political culture: there is no perfect balance between liberty, equality, and democracy. In recent years, finding the right mix of government actions to achieve these different goals has become especially troublesome. Some charge that government initiatives designed to promote equality infringe on individual liberty, while others point to the need for government to take action in the face of growing inequality. Sharp political debate over competing goals alienates many citizens, who react by withdrawing from politics. Yet, in contrast to totalitarian and authoritarian forms of government, democracy rests on the principle of popular sovereignty. No true democracy can function properly without knowledgeable and engaged citizens. The "**Who Participates?**" feature on page 35 shows which Americans voted in the 2016 presidential election.

The remarkable diversity of the American people represents a great strength for American democracy as well as a formidable challenge. The shifting religious, racial and ethnic, and immigration status of Americans throughout history has always provoked fears about whether American values could withstand such dramatic shifts.

Demographic changes will continue to raise thorny new questions in the coming decades. For example, as the American population grows older, programs for the elderly are expected to take up an increasing share of the federal budget. Yet to be successful, a nation must invest in its young people. And, as any college student knows, the cost of college has risen in recent years. Many students drop out as they discover that the cost of college is too high. Or they graduate and find themselves saddled with loans that will take decades to pay back. Yet, in a world of ever-sharper economic competition, higher education has become increasingly important for individuals seeking economic security. Moreover, an educated population is critical to the future prosperity of the country as a whole. Are there ways to support the elderly and the young at the same time? Is it fair to cut back assistance to the elderly, who have worked a lifetime for their benefits? If we decrease assistance to the elderly, will they stay in the labor market and make the job hunt for young people even more difficult?

As these trade-offs suggest, there are no easy answers to the demographic changes that will unfold in the coming years. Undoubtedly, these questions will provoke heated political conflict as politicians and interest groups propose different strategies for supporting the young in an aging country. Informed participation of the American public, especially the participation of young people, is the only way to ensure that the steps taken to address these challenges best reflect the will of the people. The young politicians mentioned at the beginning of the chapter, Saira Blair and Kendric Jones, have become engaged in a particularly deep way, by running for office. But there are many ways to become informed and involved, and the goal of this book is to show you how and why it matters.

WHO PARTICIPATES?

Who Voted in 2016?

Age

46%	59%	67%	71%
18–29	30–44	45–64	65+

Income

55%	69%	78%
<$50,000	$50,000–$99,999	$100,000+

Race / Ethnicity

65%	48%	59%	49%
White	Hispanic	Black	Asian

Sex

59%	63%
Male	Female

Education*

35%	52%	63%	74%	80%
Some high school	High school graduate	Some college	College graduate	Postgraduate study

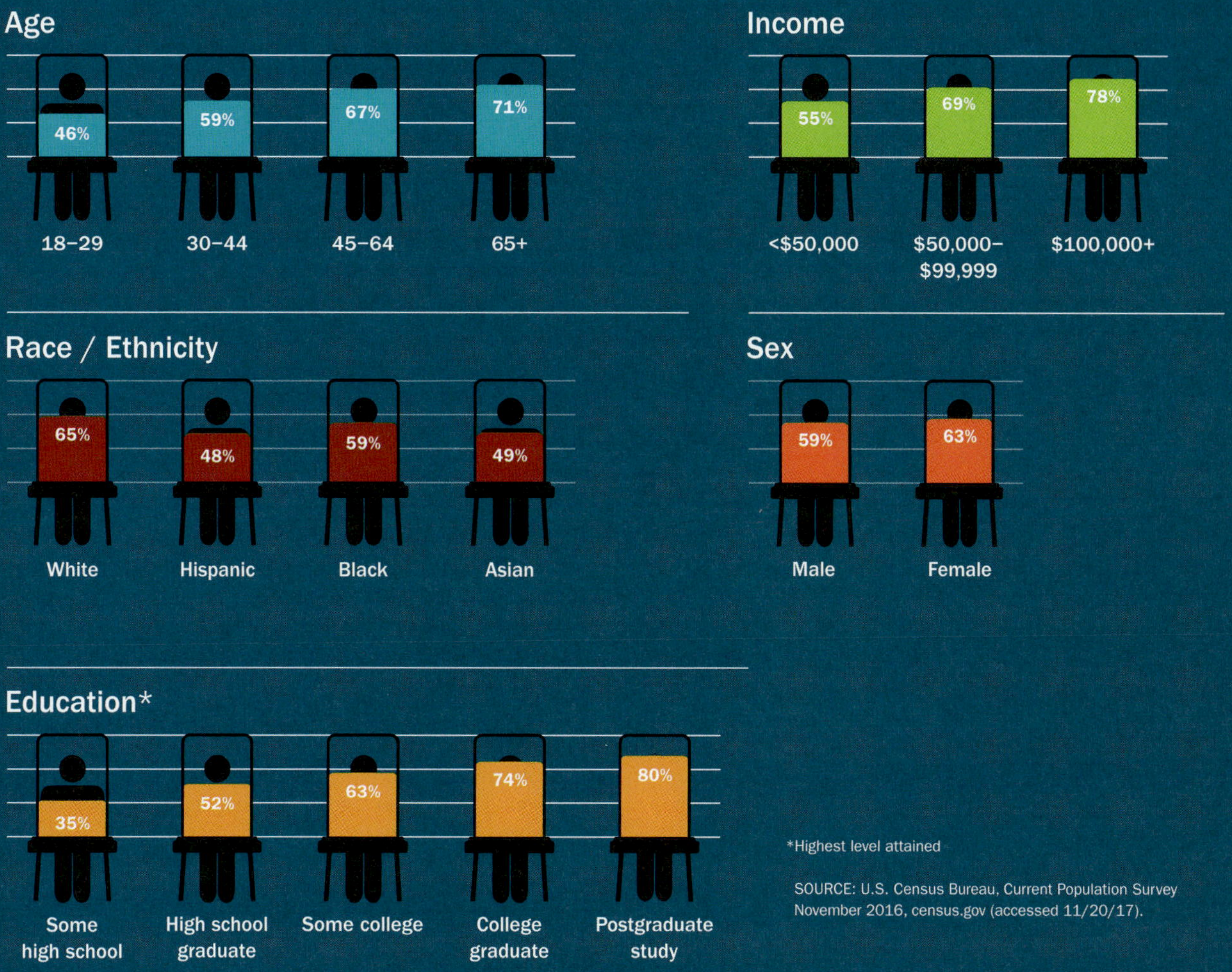

*Highest level attained

SOURCE: U.S. Census Bureau, Current Population Survey November 2016, census.gov (accessed 11/20/17).

★ WHAT YOU CAN DO ★

Vote

 ☑ Register to vote. See page 329.

 ☑ Find out what's on the ballot in upcoming elections in your state and district by entering your address at **www.vote411.org** (a website from the League of Women Voters).

 ☑ Cast your vote on Election Day. Consider encouraging others to vote too. Research shows that people are more likely to turn out to vote if a friend or family member asks them to.

STUDY GUIDE

Government

Define government and forms of government (pp. 5–10)

Government is needed to provide those services, sometimes called "public goods," that citizens need but are not likely to be able to provide adequately for themselves. There are many different kinds of government. Prior to the modern era, governments accepted almost no limits on their behavior and provided citizens with few opportunities to participate in public affairs. Today, numerous countries, including the United States, are constitutional democracies. America's democracy provides citizens with the chance to elect top officials at all levels of government and even allows them to vote directly on laws in many states and localities.

Key Terms

government (p. 5)
politics (p. 5)
autocracy (p. 7)
oligarchy (p. 7)
democracy (p. 7)
constitutional government (p. 7)
authoritarian government (p. 7)
totalitarian government (p. 7)
power (p. 9)
representative democracy (republic) (p. 9)
direct democracy (p. 9)
pluralism (p. 9)

Practice Quiz

1. Services that citizens need but are unlikely to provide for themselves, such as national defense, maintenance of public order, and a stable currency, are called
   a) laissez-faire goods.
   b) pluralist goods.
   c) provisional goods.
   d) public goods.
   e) private goods.
2. What is the basic difference between an autocracy and an oligarchy?
   a) the extent to which average citizens have a say in government affairs
   b) the means of collecting taxes and conscripting soldiers
   c) the number of people who control governing decisions
   d) the size and political influence of the military
   e) there are no differences between autocracies and oligarchies
3. A government that is formally limited in what it can control and how it controls it is known as
   a) a totalitarian government.
   b) a authoritarian government.
   c) a constitutional government.
   d) a autocracy.
   e) a oligarchy.
4. A system of government that allows citizens to vote directly on the law through popular initiatives and ballot referendums is called a
   a) republic
   b) representative democracy
   c) direct democracy
   d) pluralism
   e) laissez-faire capitalism

Citizenship: Participation, Knowledge, and Efficacy

Describe the role of the citizen in politics (pp. 10–13)

Citizenship requires political knowledge. When citizens know about politics, they are better able to understand their interests and to identify the best way to act on those interests. Most Americans, however, do not know much about politics. While the internet has made it easier to learn about and participate in politics, many Americans still do not go online to find information about government. Internet access and digital literacy are increasingly important for full participation in American politics.

Key Terms

political knowledge (p. 10)
citizenship (p. 11)
digital citizenship (p. 11)
political efficacy (p. 12)

Practice Quiz

5. What is *digital citizenship*?
   a) a new government initiative to expand online voter registration
   b) the ability to vote online
   c) an online certification program that allows immigrants to become American citizens
   d) the ability to participate in society online
   e) a new government initiative to provide daily legislative updates online

6. *Political efficacy* is the belief that
   a) government is wasteful and corrupt.
   b) government operates efficiently.
   c) government has grown too large.
   d) government cannot be trusted.
   e) ordinary citizens can influence what government does.

Who Are Americans?

Show how the social composition of the American population has changed over time (pp. 13–22)

The United States is defined, in part, by its ever-growing and changing population. During the last 200 years, America has become more racially, ethnically, geographically, and religiously diverse. Immigration has been an important reason for the country's shifting demographics, and it has frequently sparked intense debate about the nature of American identity and American democracy.

Practice Quiz

7. In 1910 residents who traced their origin to Latin America or Asia each accounted for
   a) less than 1 percent of the U.S. population.
   b) approximately 5 percent of the U.S. population.
   c) approximately 10 percent of the U.S. population.
   d) approximately 15 percent of the U.S. population.
   e) more than 20 percent of the U.S. population.

8. Which of the following statements best describes the history of income inequality in the United States?
   a) The top 1 percent has never earned more than 10 percent of the nation's annual income.
   b) The top 1 percent has never earned less than 10 percent of the nation's annual income.
   c) Income inequality has remained fairly constant since the late 1970s.
   d) Income inequality has increased considerably since the late 1970s.
   e) Income inequality has decreased considerably since the late 1970s.

American Political Culture

Analyze whether the U.S. system of government upholds American political values (pp. 22–29)

Most Americans express strong support for liberty, equality, and democracy. Agreement on these basic values does not mean, however, that political debate in the United States is without conflict. Questions about how to apply and balance the different elements of American political culture have motivated disagreements throughout the country's history.

Key Terms

political culture (p. 23)
liberty (p. 23)
limited government (p. 23)
laissez-faire capitalism (p. 24)
equality of opportunity (p. 25)
political equality (p. 25)
popular sovereignty (p. 28)
majority rule, minority rights (p. 28)

Practice Quiz

9. "Life, Liberty and the pursuit of Happiness" are the three inalienable rights mentioned in
   a) the Constitution.
   b) the Declaration of Independence.
   c) the Bill of Rights.
   d) the Articles of Confederation.
   e) the Pledge of Allegiance.

10. Which of the following is *not* related to the American conception of liberty?
    a) freedom of speech
    b) economic freedom
    c) freedom of religion
    d) freedom of assembly
    e) All of the above are related to the American conception of liberty.

11. The principle of political equality can be best summed up as
    a) "equality of results."
    b) "equality of opportunity."
    c) "one person, one vote."
    d) "equality between the sexes."
    e) "leave everyone alone."

12. Which of the following is *not* part of American political culture?
    a) belief in equality of results
    b) belief in democracy
    c) belief in personal freedom
    d) belief in economic freedom
    e) belief in equality of opportunity

13. Which of the following restrictions on voting have been repealed over the last 200 years in the United States?
    a) property, gender, and race
    b) gender only
    c) race only
    d) property only
    e) race and gender only

What Americans Think about Government

Explore Americans' attitudes toward government (pp. 29–33)

While Americans have always been hesitant about granting government too much power, they have frequently relied on it during times of national crisis and have become increasingly dependent on it to provide important services. Over the last few decades, Americans' trust in government has declined significantly. Low levels of trust and efficacy may threaten American democracy by weakening the government and reducing the public's willingness to participate in political life.

Practice Quiz

14. What does it mean to say that Americans are "abstract conservatives" and "operational liberals"?
    a) The majority of Americans have no opinions about government in general or about the specific programs government implements.
    b) The majority of Americans prefer large government in the abstract and are very supportive of most specific government programs.
    c) The majority of Americans prefer large government in the abstract but are very opposed to most specific government programs.
    d) The majority of Americans prefer small government in the abstract but are very supportive most specific government programs.
    e) The majority of Americans prefer small government in the abstract and are very opposed to most specific government programs.

15. Americans' trust in their government
    a) rose significantly between 1964 and 1980.
    b) increased immediately following September 11, 2001, but declined shortly thereafter.
    c) declined immediately after the September 11 attacks but has risen dramatically since 2004.
    d) reached its highest point ever in the fall of 2011.
    e) has remained the same over the last 50 years.

For Further Reading

Dahl, Robert. *How Democratic Is the American Constitution?* New Haven, CT: Yale University Press, 2002.

Dalton, Russell. *The Good Citizen: How a Younger Generation Is Reshaping American Politics*, 2nd ed. Washington, DC: CQ Press, 2015.

Delli Carpini, Michael X., and Scott Keeter. *What Americans Know about Politics and Why It Matters*. New Haven, CT: Yale University Press, 1996.

Fischer, Claude S., and Michael Hout. *A Century of Difference: How America Changed in the Last One Hundred Years*. New York: Russell Sage Foundation, 2006.

Hetherington, Marc J., and Thomas J. Rudolph. *Why Washington Won't Work: Polarization, Political Trust, and the Governing Crisis*. Chicago: University of Chicago Press, 2015.

Hibbing, John R., and Elizabeth Theiss-Morse. *Stealth Democracy: Americans' Belief about How Government Should Work*. New York: Cambridge University Press, 2002.

Hochschild, Jennifer L. *Facing Up to the American Dream: Race, Class, and the Soul of the Nation*. Princeton, NJ: Princeton University Press, 1995.

Huntington, Samuel. *Who Are We? The Challenges to America's National Identity*. New York: Simon & Schuster, 2004.

Lasswell, Harold. *Politics: Who Gets What, When, How*. New York: Meridian Books, 1958.

McCarty, Nolan, Keith T. Poole, and Howard Rosenthal. *Polarized America: The Dance of Ideology and Unequal Riches*. Cambridge, MA: MIT Press, 2008.

Mettler, Suzanne. *The Submerged State: How Invisible Government Policies Undermine American Democracy*. Chicago: University of Chicago Press, 2011.

Page, Benjamin I., and Lawrence R. Jacobs. *Class War? What Americans Really Think about Economic Inequality*. Chicago: University of Chicago Press, 2009.

Putnam, Robert. *Making Democracy Work: Civic Traditions in Modern Italy*. Princeton, NJ: Princeton University Press, 1993.

Tocqueville, Alexis de. *Democracy in America*. Translated by Phillips Bradley. New York: Knopf, Vintage Books, 1945. First published 1835.

Winters, Jeffrey A. *Oligarchy*. New York: Cambridge University Press, 2011.

Recommended Websites

American Democracy Project
www.aascu.org/programs/adp
This is an effort by the American Association of State Colleges and Universities to increase political engagement among college students. See what opportunities are available for you to become politically active.

Americans for Informed Democracy
www.aidemocracy.org
A nonpartisan organization that promotes democracy and seeks to build a new generation of globally conscious leaders. Find out how you can be politically active and coordinate a town hall meeting on campus, attend a leadership retreat, or publish your opinions on democracy.

DiversityInc
http://diversityinc.com
This site is dedicated to the promotion of American diversity and education. Here you can read about the issues that directly affect American minorities.

Future of Freedom Foundation
www.fff.org
This organization promotes individual liberty, free markets, private property, and limited government. Find out how some people are trying to protect freedom in the United States.

Mobilize.org
http://mobilize.org
This all-partisan network is dedicated to educating, empowering, and energizing young people. Find out how politics affects America's youth and what they are doing about it by being engaged and active.

Pew Research Center, U.S. Politics and Policy
www.people-press.org
A nonpartisan "fact tank" that provides public opinion data about a wide range of topics related to American government and society. This site covers current issues as well as provides analyses of change over time in American politics and demographics.

The Youth Participatory Politics Research Network
http://ypp.dmlcentral.net
A network of researchers and writers supported by the MacArthur Foundation. The network conducts studies of youth participation and contains short videos, blogs, and links to other resources about youth participation. The website provides many resources for understanding the impact of digital media on youth engagement in politics.

U.S. Census Bureau
www.census.gov
The website for the Census Bureau offers a statistical look at our country's population and economy. Check out some of the statistics to get a better idea of American diversity.

★ chapter ★

02

The Founding and the Constitution

WHAT GOVERNMENT DOES AND WHY IT MATTERS Often we are barely aware of the many ways the U.S. Constitution shapes Americans' lives every day, but at some moments, its features leap dramatically into view, highlighting the framers' views about the nature of government. One of their worries was the concentration of government powers and the possible infringement of individual liberties. One solution was to divide the executive, legislative, and judicial powers of government across different institutions with separate powers, each checking the other. Governmental power was further divided across the levels of government in the federal system, between the national and state governments. Sometimes, this constitutional system and its effect on average Americans come vividly to life.

Jim Obergefell was a real estate agent and IT consultant in Cincinnati, Ohio, in 1992 when he met and fell in love with John Arthur.[1] Although their relationship would last for decades, they were unable to marry. In 1996, Congress passed and President Bill Clinton signed the Defense of Marriage Act (DOMA), a federal law defining marriage as between one man and one woman. States could still permit same-sex marriage, but the marriages would not be recognized for federal purposes such as filing taxes or earning Social Security survivor benefits. The law also permitted states to refuse to recognize same-sex marriages

From America's founding to today, debates over the role of the government in citizens' lives have persisted. After the historic decision to rule same-sex marriage a right guaranteed by the Constitution, Jim Obergefell holds a photo of his late husband on the steps of the Supreme Court to celebrate his bittersweet victory.

performed in other states. Then the state of Ohio enacted its own DOMA in 2004, which prohibited same-sex marriage and refused to recognize those performed elsewhere.

Thus Obergefell and Arthur were unable to marry due to the actions of two branches of the federal government—the executive and legislative—and their state. The issue became more acute when Arthur was diagnosed with ALS, or Lou Gehrig's disease—a progressive debilitating disease. Obergefell served as Arthur's primary caregiver, and the couple traveled to Maryland in 2013 and wed on the airport tarmac. Then they filed a lawsuit with the state of Ohio for Obergefell to be recognized as the surviving spouse on Arthur's imminent death certificate. "We decided to stand up for our marriage and to no longer accept being treated as second-class citizens."[2] Arthur passed away three months later.

The case made it to the Supreme Court, the top of the judicial branch of government. In 2015 the high court ruled in *Obergefell v. Hodges* that the fundamental right to marry is guaranteed to same-sex couples by the due process and equal protection clauses of the Fourteenth Amendment to the U.S. Constitution. The ruling secured a right to marry on the same terms and conditions as opposite-sex couples nationwide.[3] Thus the Court secured a civil right that the executive and legislative branches and a number of states had denied. Obergefell said, "Some have called me a hero; I'm not comfortable with that term, and I doubt I ever will be. But I can now accept it from others because I see what this fight means to them."[4]

The U.S. Constitution lays out the purpose of government: to promote justice, to maintain peace at home, to defend the nation from foreign foes, to provide for the welfare of the citizenry, and, above all, to secure the "blessings of liberty" for Americans. It also spells out a plan for achieving these objectives, including provisions for the exercise of legislative, executive, and judicial powers and a recipe for the division of powers among the federal government's branches and between the national and state governments. Jim Obergefell's quest to marry the love of his life intersected with all three branches and both levels of government.

His story also shows that although many Americans believe strongly in the long-standing values of liberty, equality, and democracy, how those values are defined and implemented by the political institutions that the Constitution created are a source of considerable controversy. The framers believed that a good constitution created a government with the capacity to act forcefully. But they also believed that government should be compelled to take a variety of interests and viewpoints into account when it formulates policies. Sometimes the deliberation and compromise encouraged by the constitutional arrangements of "separated institutions sharing powers" can result in policymaking that is slow or even gridlocked.[5] Public policy is always a product of political bargaining. But so was the Constitution itself. As this chapter will show, the Constitution reflects high principle as well as political self-interest and defines the relationship between American citizens and their government.

CHAPTER GOALS

- ★ **Describe the events that led to the Declaration of Independence and the Articles of Confederation (pp. 43–46)**
- ★ **Analyze the reasons many Americans thought a new Constitution was needed, and assess the obstacles to a new Constitution (pp. 47–53)**
- ★ **Explain how the Constitution attempted to improve America's governance, and outline the major institutions established by the Constitution (pp. 53–60)**
- ★ **Present the controversies involved in the struggle for ratification (pp. 60–65)**
- ★ **Trace how the Constitution has changed over time through the amendment process (pp. 65–69)**

The First Founding: Interests and Conflicts

Describe the events that led to the Declaration of Independence and the Articles of Confederation

Competing ideals and principles often reflect competing interests, and so it was in Revolutionary America. The American Revolution and the American Constitution were outgrowths and expressions of a struggle among economic and political forces within the colonies. Five sectors of society had interests that were important in colonial politics: (1) New England merchants; (2) southern planters; (3) "royalists"—holders of royal lands, offices, and patents (licenses to engage in a profession or business activity); (4) shopkeepers, artisans, and laborers; and (5) small farmers. Throughout the eighteenth century, these groups were in conflict over issues of taxation, trade, and commerce. For the most part, however, the southern planters, the New England merchants, and the royal office and patent holders—groups that together made up the colonial elite—were able to maintain a political alliance that held in check the more radical forces representing shopkeepers, laborers, and small farmers. After 1760, however, by seriously threatening the interests of New England merchants and southern planters, British tax and trade policies split the colonial elite, permitting radical forces to expand their political influence and seting in motion a chain of events that culminated in the American Revolution.[6]

BRITISH TAXES AND COLONIAL INTERESTS

During the first half of the eighteenth century, Britain ruled its American colonies with a light hand. Evidence of British rule was hardly to be found outside the largest towns, and the enterprising colonists had found ways of evading most of the taxes levied by the distant British regime. Beginning in the 1760s, however, the debts and other financial problems confronting the British government forced it to search for new revenue sources. This search rather quickly led to the Crown's North American colonies, which, on the whole, paid remarkably little in taxes to their parent country. The British government reasoned that a sizable fraction of its debt was, in fact, attributable to the expenses it had incurred in defense of the colonies during the French and Indian War, which ended in 1763, driving France from North America. The British also considered the cost of the continuing protection that British forces were giving the colonists from Indian attacks and that the British navy was providing for colonial shipping. Thus, during the 1760s, Britain sought to impose new, though relatively modest, taxes on the colonists.

British colonists in America shipped many goods back to England, such as furs obtained by trading with Native Americans. The British government claimed that the colonists should pay more in taxes in light of the protection their shipments received from the British navy and the expenses Britain incurred defending the colonies.

Like most governments of the period, the British regime had limited ways in which to collect revenues. The income tax, which in the twentieth century became the single most important source of governmental revenues, had not yet been developed. In the mid-eighteenth century, governments relied mainly on tariffs, duties, and other taxes on commerce; and it was to such taxes, and to the Stamp Act, that the British turned during the 1760s.

The Stamp Act, and other taxes on commerce such as the Sugar Act of 1764, which taxed sugar, molasses, and other commodities, most heavily affected the two groups in colonial society whose commercial interests and activities were most extensive—the New England merchants and the southern planters. United under the famous slogan "No taxation without representation," the merchants and planters sought to organize opposition to these new taxes. In the course of the struggle against British tax measures, the planters and merchants broke with their royalist allies and turned to their former adversaries—the shopkeepers, small farmers, laborers, and artisans—for help. With the assistance of these groups, the merchants and planters organized demonstrations and a boycott of British goods that ultimately forced the Crown to rescind most of its hated new taxes.

From the perspective of the merchants and planters, this was a victorious conclusion to their struggle with the mother country. In contrast to the shopkeepers, small farmers, laborers, and artisans whom they had helped mobilize initially, merchants and planters were now anxious to end the unrest they had helped arouse; and they supported the British government's efforts to restore order. Indeed, most respectable Bostonians supported the actions of the British soldiers involved in the Boston Massacre—the 1770 killing of five colonists by British soldiers who were attempting to repel an angry mob gathered outside the Town House, the seat of the colonial government. In their subsequent trial, the soldiers were defended by John Adams, a pillar of Boston society and a future president of the United States. Adams asserted that the soldiers' actions were entirely justified, provoked by "a motley rabble of saucy boys, negroes and mulattoes, Irish teagues and outlandish Jack tars." All but two of the soldiers were acquitted.[7]

Despite the efforts of the British government and the elite members of colonial society, it proved difficult to bring an end to the political strife. The more radical forces continued to agitate for political and social change. These radicals, whose leaders included Samuel Adams, a cousin of John Adams, asserted that British power supported an unjust political and social structure within the colonies and began to advocate an end to British rule.[8]

POLITICAL STRIFE AND THE RADICALIZATION OF THE COLONISTS

The political strife within the colonies was the background for the events of 1773–74. In 1773 the British government granted the politically powerful East India Company a monopoly on the export of tea from Britain, eliminating a lucrative form of trade for colonial merchants. To add to the injury, the East India Company sought to sell the tea directly in the colonies instead of working through the colonial merchants. Tea was an extremely important commodity during the 1770s, and these British actions posed a serious threat to the New England merchants. Together with their southern allies, the merchants once again called on their radical adversaries for support. The most dramatic result was the Boston Tea Party. In three other colonies, antitax Americans succeeded in blocking the unloading of taxed tea, which then had to be returned to Britain. The royal governor of Massachusetts, however, refused to allow three shiploads of unsold tea to leave Boston Harbor. Anti-British radicals seized this opportunity: on the night of December 16, 1773, a group led by Samuel Adams, some of them hastily "disguised" as Mohawk Indians, boarded the three vessels and threw the entire cargo of 342 chests of tea into the harbor.

The British helped radicalize colonists through bad policy decisions in the years before the Revolution. For example, Britain gave the ailing East India Company a monopoly on the tea trade in the American colonies. Colonists feared that the monopoly would hurt colonial merchants' business and protested by throwing East India Company tea into Boston Harbor in 1773.

This event was of decisive importance in American history. The merchants had hoped to force the British government to rescind the Tea Act, but they did not support any further demands and did not seek independence from Britain. Samuel Adams and the other radicals, however, did hope to provoke the British government to take actions that would alienate its colonial supporters and pave the way for a rebellion. This was precisely the purpose of the Boston Tea Party, and it succeeded. By dumping the East India Company's tea into Boston Harbor, Adams and his followers goaded the British into enacting a number of harsh reprisals, including closing the port of Boston to commerce, changing the provincial government of Massachusetts, providing for the removal of accused persons to Britain for trial, and, most important, restricting movement to the West—further alienating the southern planters, who depended on access to new western lands. These acts of retaliation confirmed the worst criticisms of British rule and helped radicalize Americans. Radicals such as Samuel Adams had been agitating for more violent measures against the British for some time, but ultimately they needed Britain's political repression to create widespread support for independence.

Thus, the Boston Tea Party set in motion a cycle of provocation and retaliation that in 1774 resulted in the convening of the First Continental Congress—an assembly of delegates from all parts of the country—that called for a total boycott of British goods and, under the prodding of the radicals, began to consider the possibility of independence from British rule. The eventual result was the Declaration of Independence.

FOR CRITICAL ANALYSIS

Conflicts over taxes did not end with the American Revolution. Why is tax policy almost always controversial? What differences and similarities are there between the debates over taxes in the 1760s and today?

THE DECLARATION OF INDEPENDENCE

In 1776, more than a year after open warfare had commenced in Massachusetts, the Second Continental Congress appointed a committee consisting of Thomas Jefferson of Virginia, Benjamin Franklin of Pennsylvania, Roger Sherman of Connecticut, John Adams of Massachusetts, and Robert Livingston of New York to draft a statement of American independence from British rule. The Declaration of Independence, written by Jefferson and adopted by the Second Continental Congress, was an extraordinary document both philosophically and politically. Philosophically, the Declaration was remarkable for its assertion that certain rights—the "unalienable rights" that include life, liberty, and the pursuit of happiness—could not be abridged by governments. In the world of 1776, in which some kings still claimed to rule by divine right, this was a dramatic statement. This philosophical view was heavily influenced by the works of the philosopher John Locke, one of England's foremost liberal theorists of the seventeenth century. In his treatises on government, widely read by educated colonists, Locke asserted that all individuals were equal and possessed a natural right to defend their own lives, liberties, and possessions. Individuals created governments to help them protect these rights, and if a government failed in its duties, the citizenry had the right to alter or abolish it. Politically, the Declaration was remarkable because, despite the differences of interest that divided the colonists along economic, regional, and philosophical lines, it focused on grievances, aspirations, and principles that might unify the various colonial groups. The Declaration was an attempt to identify and articulate a history and set of principles that might help forge national unity.[9]

The Declaration of Independence held that government could not curtail certain rights and helped to inspire national unity. Every year, Americans celebrate the signing of the Declaration on the Fourth of July.

THE ARTICLES OF CONFEDERATION

Having declared their independence, the colonies needed to establish a governmental structure. In November 1777 the Continental Congress adopted the **Articles of Confederation**—the United States' first written constitution. Although it was not ratified by all the states until 1781, it was the country's operative constitution until the final months of 1788.

The first goal of the Articles was to limit the powers of the central government. The relationship between the national government and the states was called a **confederation**; as provided under Article II, "each state retains its sovereignty, freedom, and independence." The central government was given no president or any other presiding officer. The entire national government was vested in a Congress, with execution of its few laws to be left to the individual states. And the Articles gave Congress very little power. Its members were not much more than delegates or messengers from the state legislatures: their salaries were paid out of the state treasuries; they were subject to immediate recall by state authorities; and each state, regardless of its size, had only one vote. All 13 states had to agree to any amendments to the Articles of Confederation after it was ratified.

Articles of Confederation America's first written constitution; served as the basis for America's national government until 1789

confederation a system of government in which states retain sovereign authority except for the powers expressly delegated to the national government

Under the Articles of Confederation, Congress was given the power to declare war and make peace, to make treaties and alliances, to coin or borrow money, and to regulate trade with the Native Americans. It could also appoint the senior officers of the U.S. Army, but the national government had no army for those officers to command because the nation's armed forces were composed of the state militias. Moreover, the central government could not prevent one state from discriminating against other states in the competition for foreign commerce. These extreme limits on the power of the national government made the Articles of Confederation hopelessly impractical.[10]

The Second Founding: From Compromise to Constitution

Analyze the reasons many Americans thought a new Constitution was needed, and assess the obstacles to a new Constitution

The Declaration of Independence and the Articles of Confederation were not sufficient to hold the new nation together as an independent and effective nation-state. A series of developments following the armistice with the British in 1783 highlighted the shortcomings of the Articles of Confederation.

First, many of the new country's leaders worried that the Articles of Confederation would not allow the United States to conduct its foreign affairs successfully, as the federal government was unable to enforce existing treaties and there was no national military. Furthermore, competition among the states for foreign commerce allowed the European powers to play the states off one another, which created confusion on both sides of the Atlantic. At one point during the winter of 1786–87, John Adams of Massachusetts, a leader in the independence struggle, was sent to negotiate a new treaty with the British, one that would cover disputes left over from the war. The British government responded that since the United States under the Articles of Confederation was unable to enforce existing treaties, it would negotiate with each of the 13 states separately. At the same time, the United States faced a threat from Spain, which still held vast territories in North and South America. Without a national military, the nation's borders were difficult to protect against this potentially hostile foreign power.

Second, the Articles of Confederation allowed for only a weak federal government, with state governments retaining most of the powers of government. This situation became alarming to well-to-do Americans, in particular New England merchants and southern planters, when "radical" forces began to exert considerable influence in a number of state governments. As a result of the Revolution, one key segment of the colonial elite—the royal land, office, and patent holders—was stripped of its economic and political privileges. And although the prerevolutionary elite was weakened, the prerevolutionary radicals were better organized than ever and now controlled such states as Pennsylvania and Rhode Island, where they pursued economic and political policies that struck terror in the hearts of the prerevolutionary political establishment. In Rhode Island, for example, between 1783 and 1785, a legislature dominated by representatives of small farmers, artisans, and shopkeepers had instituted economic policies, including drastic currency inflation, that frightened business and property owners throughout the country. Of course, the central government under the Articles of Confederation was powerless to intervene. Similarly, the Pennsylvania government engaged in land redistribution, to the chagrin of property owners.

However, the Articles of Confederation were by no means a complete failure. The Congress of the Confederation agreed upon two laws that helped to shape American history. These were the Land Ordinance of 1785 and the Northwest Ordinance of 1787. The Land Ordinance established the principles of land surveying and landownership that governed America's westward expansion. Under the Northwest Ordinance, the individual states agreed to surrender their western land claims, which opened the way for the admission of new states to the Union.

These legislative successes were not adequate to sustain the fledgling federal government, however. During the 1780s, the political and economic position of the new American states deteriorated. Europe's great powers—Britain, France, and Spain—hurt colonial commerce by adopting policies that excluded American trade. At the same time, political unrest within the 13 new states further undermined trade and investment. Something had to be done.

THE ANNAPOLIS CONVENTION

The continuation of international weakness and domestic economic turmoil led many Americans to consider whether their newly adopted form of government might not already require revision. In the fall of 1786, many state leaders accepted an invitation from the Virginia legislature for a conference of representatives of all the states, to be held in Annapolis, Maryland. Delegates from only five states actually attended, so nothing substantive could be accomplished. Still, this conference was the first step toward what is now known as the second founding. The one positive result that came out of the Annapolis Convention was a carefully worded resolution calling on the Congress to send commissioners to Philadelphia at a later time "to devise such further provisions as shall appear to them necessary to render the Constitution of the Federal Government adequate to the exigencies of the Union."[11] But the resolution did not necessarily imply any desire to do more than improve and reform the Articles of Confederation.

SHAYS'S REBELLION

It is quite possible that the Constitutional Convention of 1787 in Philadelphia would never have taken place at all except for a single event that occurred during the winter following the Annapolis Convention: Shays's Rebellion.

Daniel Shays, a former army captain, led a mob of farmers in a rebellion against the government of Massachusetts. The purpose of the rebellion was to prevent foreclosures on their debt-ridden land by keeping the county courts of western Massachusetts from sitting until after the next election. A militia force organized by the Governor of Massachusetts and privately funded by a group of prominent merchants dispersed the mob, but for several days in February 1787, Shays and his followers terrified the state government by attempting to capture the federal arsenal at Springfield, provoking an appeal to the Congress to help restore order. Within a few days, the state government regained control and captured 14 of the rebels. Later that year, a newly elected Massachusetts legislature granted some of the farmers' demands.

Daniel Shays's rebellion proved the Articles of Confederation were too weak to protect the fledgling nation.

The effects of the incident lingered and spread. George Washington summed it up: "I am mortified beyond expression that in the moment of our acknowledged independence we should by our conduct verify the predictions of our transatlantic foe, and render ourselves ridiculous and contemptible in the eyes of all Europe."[12]

The Congress under the Confederation had been unable to act decisively in a time of crisis. This provided critics of the Articles of Confederation with precisely the evidence they needed to push the Annapolis resolution through the Congress. Thus, the states were asked to send representatives to Philadelphia to discuss constitutional revision. Seventy-four delegates were chosen. Of these, 55 would actually attend the convention, representing every state except Rhode Island, and 39 would eventually sign the newly drafted Constitution.

THE CONSTITUTIONAL CONVENTION

The delegates who convened in Philadelphia in May 1787 had political strife, international embarrassment, national weakness, and local rebellion fixed in their minds. Recognizing that these issues were symptoms of fundamental flaws in the Articles of Confederation, the delegates soon abandoned the plan to revise the Articles and committed themselves to a second founding—a second, and ultimately successful, attempt to create a legitimate and effective national system of government. This effort would occupy the convention for the next five months.

A Marriage of Interest and Principle For years, scholars have disagreed about the motives of the Founders in Philadelphia. Among the most controversial views of the framers' motives is the "economic interpretation" put forward by the historian Charles Beard and his disciples.[13] According to Beard's account, America's Founders were a collection of securities speculators and property owners whose only aim was personal enrichment. From this perspective, the Constitution's lofty principles were little more than sophisticated masks behind which the most venal interests sought to enrich themselves.

Of course, the opposite view is that the framers of the Constitution *were* concerned with philosophical and ethical principles—that, indeed, they sought to devise a system of government consistent with the dominant philosophical and moral principles of the day. But in fact these two views belong together: the Founders' interests were reinforced by their principles. The convention that drafted the American Constitution was chiefly organized by the New England merchants and southern planters. Although the delegates representing these groups did not all hope to profit personally from an increase in the value of their securities, as Beard would

The Constitutional Convention took place from May to September 1787 at Independence Hall in Philadelphia, where the Declaration of Independence had been signed 11 years prior. In order to keep their deliberations secret, the delegates voted to keep the hall's windows shut throughout the hot summer.

have it, they did hope to benefit in the broadest political and economic sense by breaking the power of their radical foes and establishing a system of government more compatible with their long-term economic and political interests. Thus, the framers sought to create a new government capable of promoting commerce and protecting property from radical state legislatures and populist forces hostile to the interests of the commercial and propertied classes.

The Great Compromise The proponents of a new government fired their opening shot on May 29, 1787, when Edmund Randolph of Virginia offered a resolution that proposed corrections and enlargements in the Articles of Confederation. The proposal, which showed the strong influence of James Madison, was not a simple motion. Rather, it provided for virtually every aspect of a new government.

Virginia Plan a framework for the Constitution, introduced by Edmund Randolph, that called for representation in the national legislature based on the population of each state

The portion of Randolph's motion that became most controversial was called the **Virginia Plan.** This plan provided for a system of representation in the national legislature based on the population of each state or the proportion of each state's revenue contribution to the national government, or both. (Randolph also proposed a second chamber of the legislature, to be elected by the members of the first chamber.) Since the states varied enormously in size and wealth, the Virginia Plan was thought to be heavily biased in favor of the large states.

New Jersey Plan a framework for the Constitution, introduced by William Paterson, that called for equal state representation in the national legislature regardless of population

While the convention was debating the Virginia Plan, opposition to it began to mount as more delegates arrived in Philadelphia. William Paterson of New Jersey introduced a resolution known as the **New Jersey Plan.** Its main proponents were delegates from the less populous states, including Delaware, New Jersey, Connecticut, and New York, who asserted that the more populous states—Virginia, Pennsylvania, North Carolina, Massachusetts, and Georgia—would dominate the new government if representation were to be determined by population. The smaller states argued that each state should be equally represented in the new regime regardless of the state's population.

The issue of representation threatened to wreck the entire constitutional enterprise. Delegates conferred, factions maneuvered, and tempers flared. James Wilson of Pennsylvania told the small-state delegates that if they wanted to disrupt the union, they should go ahead. The separation, he said, could "never happen on better grounds." Small-state delegates were equally blunt. Gunning Bedford of Delaware declared that the small states might, if forced, look elsewhere for friends. "The large states," he said, "dare not dissolve the confederation. If they do the small ones will find some foreign ally of more honor and good faith, who will take them by the hand and do them justice." These sentiments were widely shared. The union, as Luther Martin of Maryland put it, was "on the verge of dissolution, scarcely held together by the strength of a hair."[14]

Great Compromise the agreement reached at the Constitutional Convention of 1787 that gave each state an equal number of senators regardless of its population but linked representation in the House of Representatives to population

The outcome of this debate was the Connecticut Compromise, also known as the **Great Compromise.** Under the terms of this compromise, in the first chamber of Congress—the House of Representatives—the representatives would be apportioned according to the population in each state. This, of course, was what delegates from the large states had sought. But in the second branch—the Senate—each state would have equal representation regardless of its size; this provision addressed the concerns of small states. This compromise was not immediately satisfactory to all the delegates. Indeed, two of the most vocal members of the small-state faction, John Lansing and Robert Yates of New York, were so angered by the concession that their colleagues had made to the large-state forces that they stormed out of the

Who Benefits from the Great Compromise?

The Great Compromise attempted to balance power between large and small states in the new Congress. The figure shows the difference in representation for states in the House and Senate in the first Congress (1789–91). In the Senate each state has equal representation, which in the first Congress meant each had 1/13 of all seats. In the House the number of seats apportioned to each state is based on population; thus, the larger states have more representation.

Representation in the First Congress

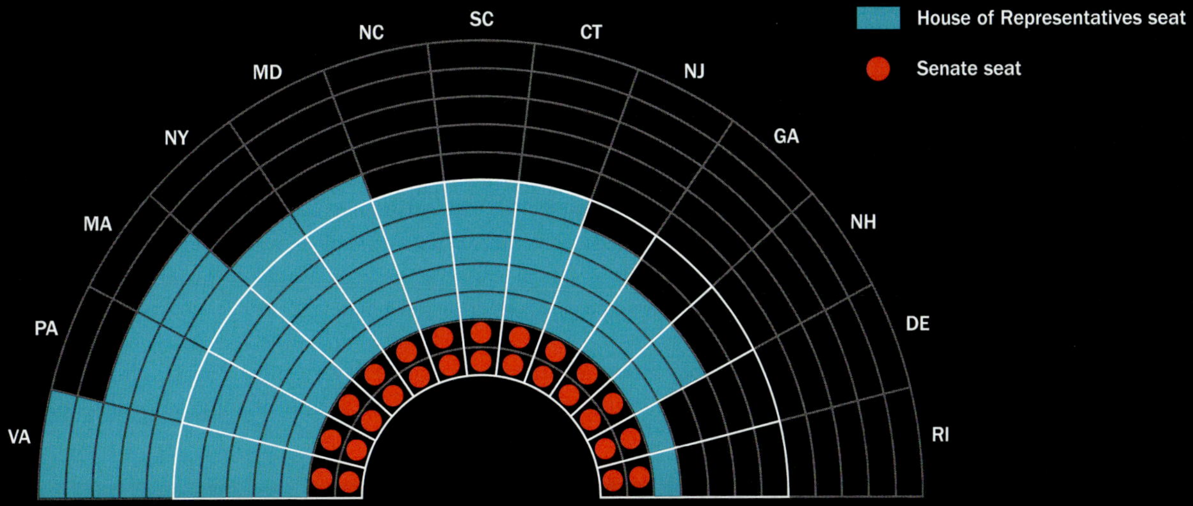

State Populations, 1790*

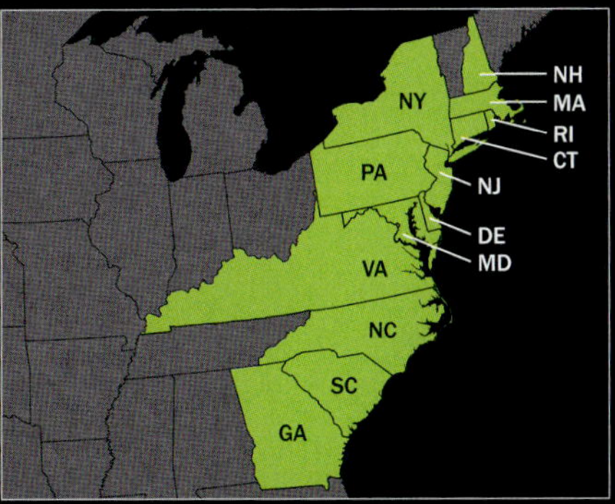

1.	Virginia	747,610
2.	Pennsylvania	433,373
3.	North Carolina	393,751
4.	Massachusetts	378,787
5.	New York	340,120
6.	Maryland	319,728
7.	South Carolina	249,073
8.	Connecticut	237,946
9.	New Jersey	184,139
10.	New Hampshire	141,885
11.	Georgia	82,548
12.	Rhode Island	68,825
13.	Delaware	59,096

These numbers represent the total number of persons in each state according to the 1790 census (including free white males, free white females, "all other free persons," and slaves). For the purpose of representation in the first Congress, the framers calculated the number of representatives per state in 1787 based on population estimates, which counted each slave as three-fifths of a person. This calculation is why the representation in the first Congress does not match perfectly with the total population counts reported here.

SOURCE: U.S. Census Bureau, www.census.gov (accessed 8/16/12); U.S. House of Representatives, www.history.house.gov/Institution/Apportionment/Apportionment (accessed 4/11/14).

FOR CRITICAL ANALYSIS

1. At the Constitutional Convention, large states supported the Virginia Plan, which would have made the whole Congress look like the House. Small states supported the New Jersey Plan, which would have made the whole Congress look like the Senate. How would each group have benefited from its favored plans?
2. What are the advantages of equal representation by states? What are the drawbacks? In your opinion, do the advantages outweigh the disadvantages?

convention. In the end, however, most of the delegates preferred compromise to the breakup of the Union, and the plan was accepted.

The Question of Slavery: The Three-Fifths Compromise Many of the conflicts that emerged during the Constitutional Convention were reflections of the fundamental differences between the slave and the nonslave states—differences that pitted the southern planters against the New England merchants and would almost destroy the Republic in later years. Even in the midst of debate over large versus small states, James Madison observed that "the great danger" lay in the opposition of "southern and northern interests."[15] More than 90 percent of the country's slaves resided in five states—Georgia, Maryland, North Carolina, South Carolina, and Virginia—where they accounted for 30 percent of the total population. In some places, slaves outnumbered nonslaves by as many as 10 to 1. Were they to be counted in as part of a state's population even though they had no rights, thereby giving slave states increased representation in the House? If the Constitution were to embody any principle of national supremacy, some basic decisions would have to be made about the place of slavery in the general scheme. Madison hit on this point on several occasions as different aspects of the Constitution were being discussed. For example, he observed,

> It seemed now to be pretty well understood that the real difference of interests lay, not between the large and small but between the northern and southern states. The institution of slavery and its consequences formed the line of discrimination. There were five states on the South, eight on the northern side of this line. Should a proportional representation take place it was true, the northern side would still outnumber the other: but not in the same degree, at this time; and every day would tend towards an equilibrium.[16]

Whatever they thought of the institution of slavery, most delegates from the northern states opposed counting slaves in the distribution of congressional seats. James

Despite the Founders' emphasis on liberty, the new Constitution allowed slavery, counting three-fifths of all slaves in apportioning seats in the House of Representatives. In this 1792 painting, *Liberty Displaying the Arts and Sciences*, the books, instruments, and classical columns at the left contrast with the kneeling slaves at the right—illustrating the divide between America's rhetoric of liberty and equality and the reality of slavery.

Wilson of Pennsylvania, for example, argued that if slaves were citizens, they should be treated and counted like other citizens. If, on the other hand, they were property, then why should not other forms of property be counted toward the apportionment of representatives? But southern delegates made it clear that they would never agree to the new government if the northerners refused to give in; William R. Davie of North Carolina, for example, heatedly asserted that the people of North Carolina would never enter the Union if slaves were not counted as part of the basis for representation. Without such agreement, he asserted ominously, "the business was at an end."

Northerners and southerners eventually reached agreement through the **Three-Fifths Compromise**. The seats in the House of Representatives would be apportioned according to a "population" in which only three-fifths of slaves would be counted. The slaves would not be allowed to vote, of course, but the number of representatives would be apportioned accordingly.

Three-Fifths Compromise the agreement reached at the Constitutional Convention of 1787 that stipulated that for purposes of the apportionment of congressional seats only three-fifths of slaves would be counted

The issue of slavery was the most difficult one faced by the framers, and it nearly destroyed the Union. Although some delegates believed slavery to be morally wrong, an evil and oppressive institution that made a mockery of the ideals and values espoused in the Constitution, morality was not the issue that caused the framers to support or oppose the Three-Fifths Compromise. Indeed, northerners even agreed to permit a continuation of the odious slave trade in order to keep the South in the Union. But in due course, the disparate interests of the North and the South could no longer be reconciled, and a bloody civil war was the result.

The Constitution

Explain how the Constitution attempted to improve America's governance, and outline the major institutions established by the Constitution

The political significance of the Great Compromise and the Three-Fifths Compromise was to reinforce the unity of the mercantile and planter forces that sought to create a new government. The Great Compromise reassured those in both groups who feared that a new governmental framework would reduce the importance of their own local or regional influence. The Three-Fifths Compromise temporarily defused the rivalry between the merchants and planters. Their unity secured, members of the alliance supporting the establishment of a new government moved to fashion a constitutional framework consistent with their economic and political interests.

In particular, the framers sought a new government that, first, would be strong enough to promote commerce and protect property from radical state legislatures such as Rhode Island's. This became the constitutional basis for national control over commerce and finance and for the establishment of national judicial supremacy and the effort to construct a strong presidency. (See Table 2.1 for a comparison of the Articles of Confederation to the Constitution.)

Second, the framers sought to prevent what they saw as the threat posed by the "excessive democracy" of the state and national governments under the Articles of Confederation. This led to such constitutional principles as a **bicameral** legislature, **checks and balances**, staggered terms in office, and indirect election (selection of the president by an electoral college rather than directly by voters and election of senators by state legislatures).

bicameral having a legislative assembly composed of two chambers or houses; distinguished from *unicameral*

checks and balances mechanisms through which each branch of government is able to participate in and influence the activities of the other branches; major examples include the presidential veto power over congressional legislation, the power of the Senate to approve presidential appointments, and judicial review of congressional enactments

Bill of Rights the first 10 amendments to the U.S. Constitution, ratified in 1791; they ensure certain rights and liberties to the people

separation of powers the division of governmental power among several institutions that must cooperate in decision making

federalism a system of government in which power is divided, by a constitution, between a central government and regional governments

Third, the framers, lacking the power to force the states or the public at large to accept the new form of government, sought to identify principles that would help secure support. This became the basis of the constitutional provision for direct popular election of representatives and, subsequently, for the addition of the **Bill of Rights** to the Constitution.

Finally, the framers wanted to be certain that the government they created did not pose an even greater threat to its citizens' liberties and property rights than did the radical state legislatures they feared and despised. To prevent the new government from abusing its power, the framers incorporated principles such as the **separation of powers** and **federalism** into the Constitution. In Table 2.1, we assess the major provisions of the Constitution's seven articles to see how each relates to these objectives.

If the Declaration of Independence drew its philosophical inspiration from John Locke, the Constitution drew upon the thought of the French political philosopher Baron de La Brède et de Montesquieu (1689–1755). In Montesquieu's view,

TABLE 2.1

Comparing the Articles of Confederation and the Constitution

MAJOR PROVISIONS	ARTICLES OF CONFEDERATION	CONSTITUTION
Executive branch	None	President of the United States
Judiciary	No federal court system. Judiciary exists only at state level.	Federal judiciary headed by Supreme Court
Legislature	Unicameral legislature with equal representation for each state. Delegates to the Congress of the Confederation were appointed by the states.	Bicameral legislature consisting of Senate and House of Representatives. Each state is represented by two senators, while apportionment in the House is based on each state's population. Senators are chosen by the state legislatures (changed to direct popular election in 1913) for six-year terms and members of the House by popular election for two-year terms.
Fiscal and economic powers	The national government is dependent upon the states to collect taxes. The states are free to coin their own money and print paper money. The states are free to sign commercial treaties with foreign governments.	Congress given the power to levy taxes, coin money, and regulate international and interstate commerce. States prohibited from coining money or entering into treaties with other nations.
Military	The national government is dependent upon state militias and cannot form an army during peacetime.	The national government is authorized to maintain an army and navy.
Legal supremacy	State constitutions and state law are supreme.	National Constitution and national law are supreme.
Constitutional amendment	Must be agreed upon by all states.	Must be agreed upon by three-fourths of the states.

the powers of government must be divided in order to prevent any one group or institution from exercising tyrannical control over the nation. Montesquieu recommended a tripartite division, placing the executive, legislative, and judicial powers in different governmental bodies. He claimed that such a tripartite division had worked very well in the Roman Republic and in Britain. The delegates to America's Constitutional Convention referred frequently to Montesquieu's writings in devising America's new governmental structure.

THE LEGISLATIVE BRANCH

In Article I, Sections 1–7, the Constitution provides for a Congress consisting of two chambers: a House of Representatives and a Senate. Members of the House of Representatives were given two-year terms in office and were to be elected directly by the people. Members of the Senate were to be appointed by the state legislatures (this was changed in 1913 by the Seventeenth Amendment, which instituted direct election of senators) for six-year terms. These terms were staggered so that the appointments of one-third of the senators would expire every two years. The Constitution assigned somewhat different tasks to the House and Senate. Though the approval of each body is required for the enactment of a law, the Senate alone is given the power to ratify treaties and approve presidential appointments. The House, on the other hand, is given the sole power to originate revenue bills.

The character of the legislative branch was related to the framers' major goals. The House of Representatives was designed to be directly responsible to the people in order to encourage popular consent for the new Constitution and to help enhance the power of the new government. At the same time, to guard against "excessive democracy," the power of the House of Representatives was checked by the Senate, whose members were to be appointed by the states for long terms rather than elected directly by the people. The purpose of this provision, according to Alexander Hamilton, was to avoid "an unqualified complaisance to every sudden breeze of passion, or to every transient impulse which the people may receive."[17] Staggered terms of service in the Senate, moreover, were intended to make that body even more resistant to popular pressure. Since only one-third of the senators would be selected at any given time, the composition of the institution would be protected from changes in popular preferences transmitted by the state legislatures. Thus, the structure of the legislative branch was designed to contribute to governmental power, to promote popular consent for the new government, and at the same time to place limits on the popular political currents that many of the framers saw as a radical threat to the economic and social order.

The issues of power and consent are important throughout the Constitution. Section 8 of Article I specifically lists the powers of Congress, which include the authority to collect taxes, borrow money, regulate commerce, declare war, and maintain an army and navy. By granting Congress these powers, the framers indicated very clearly that they intended the new government to be far more influential than its predecessor. At the same time, by defining the new government's most important powers as belonging to Congress, the framers sought to promote popular acceptance of this critical change by reassuring citizens that their views would be fully represented whenever the government exercised its new powers.

As a further guarantee to the people that the new government would pose no threat to them, the Constitution implies that any powers not listed were not

expressed powers specific powers granted by the Constitution to Congress (Article I, Section 8) and to the president (Article II)

elastic clause The concluding paragraph of Article I, Section 8, of the Constitution (also known as the "necessary and proper clause"), which provides Congress with the authority to make all laws "necessary and proper" to carry out its enumerated powers

granted at all. This is what Chief Justice John Marshall named the doctrine of **expressed powers:** the Constitution grants only those powers specifically expressed in its text. But the framers intended to create an active and powerful government, so they also included the necessary and proper clause, sometimes known as the **elastic clause**, which declares that Congress could write laws needed to carry out its expressed powers. This clause indicates that the expressed powers could be broadly interpreted and were meant to be a source of strength to the national government, not a limitation on it. In response to the charge that they intended to give the national government too much power, the framers included language in the Tenth Amendment stipulating that powers not specifically granted by the Constitution to the federal government were reserved to the states or to the people. As we will see in Chapter 3, the resulting tension between the elastic clause and the Tenth Amendment has been at the heart of constitutional struggles between federal and state powers.

THE EXECUTIVE BRANCH

The Articles of Confederation had not provided for an executive branch, and the framers viewed this omission as a source of weakness. Accordingly, the Constitution provides for the establishment of the presidency in Article II. As Alexander Hamilton commented, the presidential article aims toward "energy in the Executive."[18] It does so in an effort to overcome the natural tendency toward stalemate that was built into the bicameral legislature and into the separation of powers among the three branches. The Constitution affords the president a measure of independence from the people and from the other branches of government—particularly the Congress.

In line with the framers' goal of increased power to the national government, the president is granted the unconditional power to accept ambassadors from other countries—this amounts to the power to "recognize" other countries—as well as the power to negotiate treaties, although their acceptance requires the approval of the Senate by a two-thirds vote. The president is also given the unconditional right to grant reprieves and pardons, except in cases of impeachment, and the powers to appoint major departmental personnel, to convene Congress in special session, and to veto congressional enactments. The veto power is formidable, but it is not absolute since Congress can override it by a two-thirds vote, reflecting the framers' concern with checks and balances.

The framers hoped to create a presidency that would make the federal government rather than the states the agency capable of timely and decisive action to deal with public issues and problems—hence the "energy" that Hamilton hoped to impart to the executive branch. At the same time, however, the framers sought to help the presidency withstand excessively democratic pressures by creating a system of indirect rather than direct election through a separate electoral college.

THE JUDICIAL BRANCH

In establishing the judicial branch in Article III, the Constitution reflects the framers' preoccupations with nationalizing governmental power and checking radical democratic impulses while preventing the new national government itself from interfering with liberty and property.

Under the provisions of Article III, the framers created a court that was literally a supreme court of the United States and not merely the highest court of the national government alone. The most important expression of this intention is granting the Supreme Court the power to resolve any conflicts that might emerge between federal and state laws. In particular, the Supreme Court is given the right to determine whether a power is exclusive to the national government, concurrent with the states, or exclusive to the states. In addition, the Supreme Court is assigned jurisdiction over controversies between citizens of different states. The long-term significance of this provision was that as the country developed a national economy, it came to rely increasingly on the federal judiciary, rather than on the state courts, for the resolution of disputes.

Article I of the Constitution establishes the structure of Congress and lists certain specific powers of Congress. The language of the Constitution reflects the framers' desire to create government that was powerful enough to be effective but not so powerful that it would threaten individual liberty.

Federal judges are given lifetime appointments to protect them from popular politics and from interference by the other branches. This, however, does not mean that the judiciary remains totally impartial to political considerations or to the other branches, for the president is to appoint the judges and the Senate to approve the appointments. Congress also has the power to create inferior (lower) courts, change the jurisdiction of the federal courts, add or subtract federal judges, and even change the size of the Supreme Court.

No explicit mention is made in the Constitution of **judicial review**—the power of the courts to render the final decision when there is a conflict of interpretation of the Constitution or of laws between the courts and Congress, the courts and the executive branch, or the courts and the states. The Supreme Court eventually assumed the power of judicial review. Its assumption of this power, as we shall see in Chapter 15, was based not on the Constitution itself but on the politics of later decades and the membership of the Court.

judicial review the power of the courts to review and, if necessary, declare actions of the legislative and executive branches invalid or unconstitutional; the Supreme Court asserted this power in *Marbury v. Madison* (1803)

NATIONAL UNITY AND POWER

Various provisions in the Constitution addressed the framers' concern with national unity and power, including Article IV's provisions for comity (reciprocity) among states and among citizens of all states. Each state is prohibited from discriminating against the citizens of other states in favor of its own citizens. The Supreme Court is charged with deciding in each case whether a state had discriminated against goods or people from another state. The Constitution restricts the power of the states in favor of ensuring enough power to the national government to give the country a free-flowing national economy.

The framers' concern with national supremacy was also expressed in Article VI, in the **supremacy clause**, which provides that national laws and treaties "shall be the supreme Law of the Land." This means that all laws made under the "Authority of the United States" would be superior to all laws adopted by any state or any other subdivision and that the states would be expected to respect all treaties made under that authority. The supremacy clause also binds the officials of all governments—state and local as well as federal—to take an oath of office to support the national

supremacy clause Article VI of the Constitution, which states that laws passed by the national government and all treaties are the supreme law of the land and superior to all laws adopted by any state or any subdivision

Constitution. This means that every action taken by the U.S. Congress has to be applied within each state as though the action were in fact state law.

AMENDING AND RATIFYING THE CONSTITUTION

The Constitution establishes procedures for its own revision in Article V. Its provisions are so difficult that, as we shall see below, Americans have successfully availed themselves of the amending process only 17 times since 1791, when the first 10 amendments were adopted. The rules for the ratification of the Constitution are set forth in Article VII. Nine of the 13 states would have to ratify, or agree to, the terms in order for the Constitution to be formally adopted. Even if all the states did not ratify the Constitution it would take effect for those that did once the threshold of nine had been crossed.

CONSTITUTIONAL LIMITS ON THE NATIONAL GOVERNMENT'S POWER

Although the framers sought to create a powerful national government, they also wanted to guard against possible misuse of that power. To that end, the framers incorporated two key principles into the Constitution—federalism and the separation of powers. A third set of limitations, in the form of the Bill of Rights, was added to the Constitution in the form of 10 amendments proposed by the first Congress and ratified by the states. Most of the framers had thought a Bill of Rights to be unnecessary but accepted the idea during the ratification debates that took place when the new constitution was submitted to the states for approval.

FOR CRITICAL ANALYSIS

How does the separation of powers limit the national government's power? What are the consequences for the ability of the federal government to govern?

The Separation of Powers No principle of politics was more widely shared at the time of the 1787 Founding than the principle that power must be used to balance power. As noted earlier, the French political theorist Montesquieu believed that this balance was an indispensable defense against tyranny. His writings, especially his major work, *The Spirit of the Laws*, "were taken as political gospel" at the Philadelphia Convention.[19] Although the principle of the separation of powers is not explicitly stated in the Constitution, the entire structure of the national government was built precisely on Article I, the legislature; Article II, the executive; and Article III, the judiciary (see Figure 2.1).

However, separation of powers is nothing but mere words on parchment without a method to maintain that separation. The method became known by the popular label "checks and balances" (see Figure 2.2). Each branch is given not only its own powers but also some power over the other two branches. Among the most familiar checks and balances are the president's veto power over Congress and Congress's power over the president through its control of appointments to high executive posts and to the judiciary. Congress also has power over the president with its control of appropriations (the spending of government money) and (by the Senate) the right of approval of treaties. The judiciary has the power of judicial review over the other two branches.

Another important feature of the separation of powers is the principle of giving each of the branches a distinctly different constituency. Theorists such as Montesquieu called this a "mixed regime," with the president chosen, indirectly, by electors; the House, by popular vote; the Senate (originally), by state

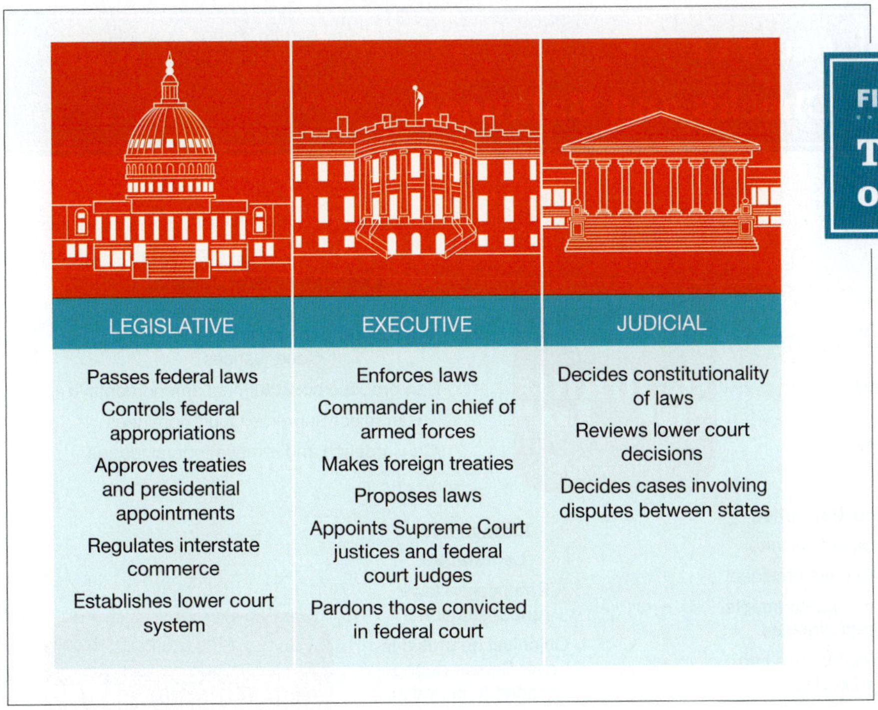
LEGISLATIVE
Passes federal laws
Controls federal appropriations
Approves treaties and presidential appointments
Regulates interstate commerce
Establishes lower court system
EXECUTIVE
Enforces laws
Commander in chief of armed forces
Makes foreign treaties
Proposes laws
Appoints Supreme Court justices and federal court judges
Pardons those convicted in federal court
JUDICIAL
Decides constitutionality of laws
Reviews lower court decisions
Decides cases involving disputes between states

FIGURE 2.1

The Separation of Powers

legislatures; and the judiciary, by presidential appointment. By these means, the occupants of each branch would tend to develop very different outlooks on how to govern, different definitions of the public interest, and different alliances with private interests.

Federalism Compared with the confederation principle of the Articles of Confederation, federalism was a step toward greater centralization of power. The delegates agreed that they needed to place more power at the national level, without completely undermining the power of the state governments. Thus, they devised a system of two sovereigns—the states and the nation—with the hope that competition between the two would be an effective limitation on the power of both.

The Bill of Rights Late in the Philadelphia Convention, a motion was made to include a list of citizens' rights in the Constitution. After a brief debate in which hardly a word was said in its favor and only one speech was made against it, the motion was almost unanimously turned down. Most delegates sincerely believed that since the federal government was already limited to its expressed powers, further protection of citizens was not needed. The delegates argued that the states should adopt bills of rights because their greater powers needed greater limitations. But almost immediately after the Constitution was ratified, a movement arose to adopt a national bill of rights. This is why the Bill of Rights, adopted in 1791, comprises the first 10 amendments to the Constitution rather than being part of the body of it. (We will have a good deal more to say about the Bill of Rights in Chapter 4.)

FIGURE 2.2

Checks and Balances

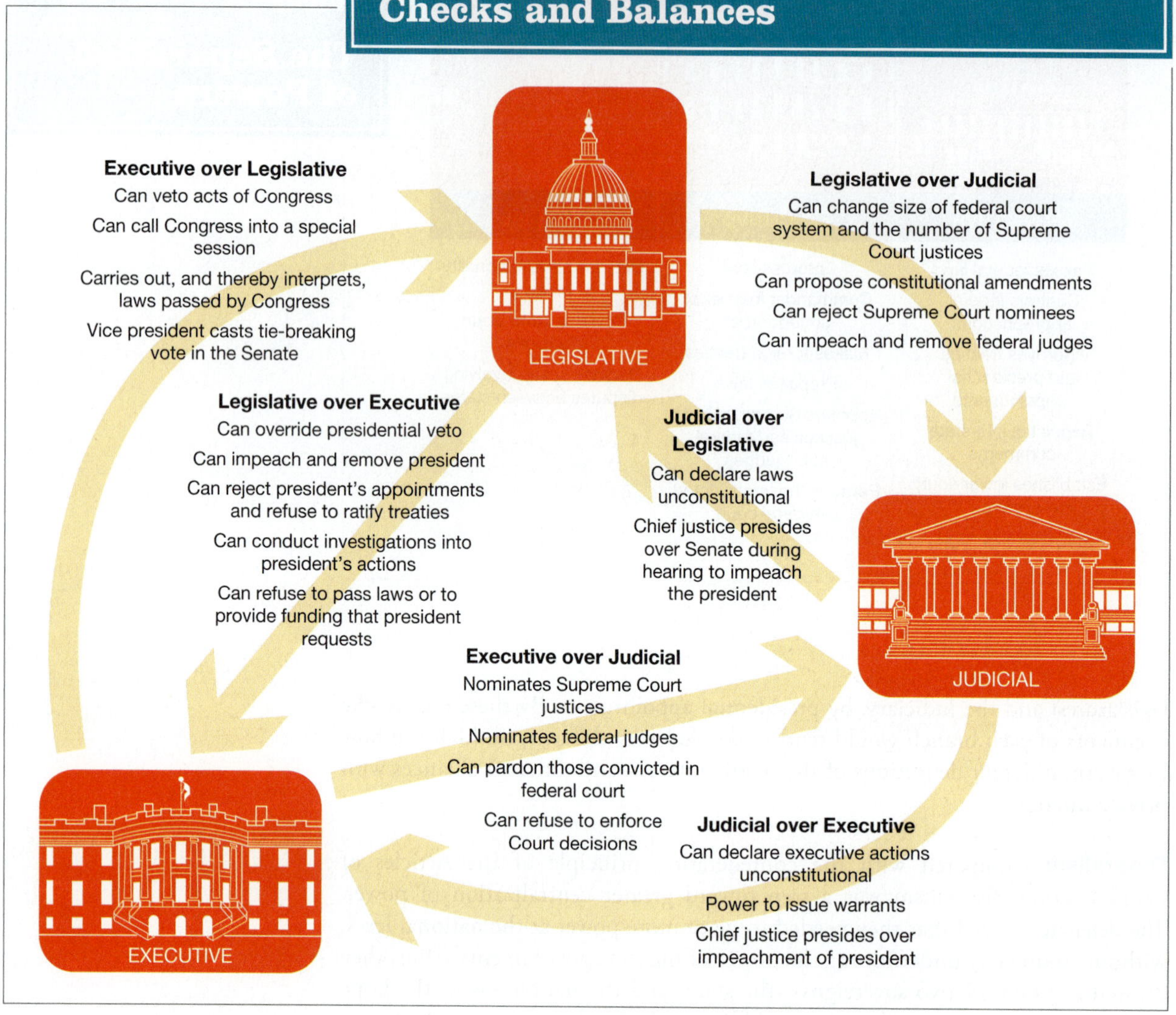

LEGISLATIVE
JUDICIAL
EXECUTIVE
Executive over Legislative
Can veto acts of Congress
Can call Congress into a special session
Carries out, and thereby interprets, laws passed by Congress
Vice president casts tie-breaking vote in the Senate
Legislative over Judicial
Can change size of federal court system and the number of Supreme Court justices
Can propose constitutional amendments
Can reject Supreme Court nominees
Can impeach and remove federal judges
Legislative over Executive
Can override presidential veto
Can impeach and remove president
Can reject president's appointments and refuse to ratify treaties
Can conduct investigations into president's actions
Can refuse to pass laws or to provide funding that president requests
Judicial over Legislative
Can declare laws unconstitutional
Chief justice presides over Senate during hearing to impeach the president
Executive over Judicial
Nominates Supreme Court justices
Nominates federal judges
Can pardon those convicted in federal court
Can refuse to enforce Court decisions
Judicial over Executive
Can declare executive actions unconstitutional
Power to issue warrants
Chief justice presides over impeachment of president

Federalists those who favored a strong national government and supported the Constitution proposed at the American Constitutional Convention of 1787

Antifederalists those who favored strong state governments and a weak national government and who were opponents of the Constitution proposed at the American Constitutional Convention of 1787

The Fight for Ratification

Present the controversies involved in the struggle for ratification

The first hurdle faced by the proposed Constitution was ratification by state conventions of delegates elected by the people of each state. This struggle for ratification was carried out in 13 separate campaigns. Each involved different people, moved at a different pace, and was influenced by local and national considerations. Two sides faced off throughout the states, however, calling themselves **Federalists** and **Antifederalists** (see Table 2.2). The Federalists (who more accurately should have called themselves "Nationalists," but who

AMERICA SIDE by SIDE

Comparing Systems of Government

All democracies possess some form of an executive, a legislature, and a judiciary; however, the amount of power that each branch has varies. In the United States, the Founding Fathers sought to prevent any one branch from becoming too powerful by creating the system of checks and balances, as described in this chapter and outlined in Figure 2.2. Fearing monarchic dominance, the writers of the U.S. Constitution preferred limited government power in all branches rather than risk an overly powerful central government. In contrast, France's Fifth Republic has an extremely powerful president, so much so that the office has sometimes been referred to as the "republican monarchy."[a] Written during a period of intense upheaval and political violence, France's 1958 constitution created a strong executive who could act decisively (if not always democratically) in the midst of crisis.

However, what is "on paper" in a constitution does not always define the true balance of power in daily political life. Through usage and reinterpretation, constitutional provisions may take new shape over time. For example, as written in the U.S. Constitution (and shown below), the presidency is less powerful than Congress. Over time, however, presidential power has grown as Congress has delegated significant powers, such as the war power, to the president, Even constitutions that are less open to interpretation, such as India's 146,385-word constitution, have seen significant shifts in power over time. India's past prime ministers, especially when faced with a crisis, have sometimes reinterpreted their constitutional powers in ways that have benefited the power of their office.

COUNTRY	WRITTEN CONSTITUTION?	FEDERAL OR UNITARY SYSTEM	STRENGTH OF EXECUTIVE	STRENGTH OF LEGISLATURE	JUDICIAL INDEPENDENCE
BRAZIL	Yes	Federal	High	Medium	High
FRANCE	Yes	Unitary	High	Low	Low
INDIA	Yes	Federal	Medium	Low	Medium
ISRAEL	No	Unitary	Low	Low	Medium
SOUTH AFRICA	Yes	Unitary	Medium	Low	High
TUNISIA	Yes	Unitary	High	Medium	Low
UNITED STATES	Yes	Federal	High*	Medium	High*
UNITED KINGDOM	No	Unitary	Low	Low	Medium

*Although the Comparative Constitutions Project classifies the formal powers of both the American presidency and the judicial branch, as originally provided for in the Constitution, as relatively *weak*, we have classified both here as strong, based on the greater powers that have developed over time.

SOURCE: Comparative Constitutions Project, "CCP Rankings," http://comparativeconstitutionsproject.org/ccp-rankings/ (accessed 4/6/18).

[a]Catherine Field, "France's 'Republican Monarchy': When the President Is Treated Like a King," *New York Times*, September 1, 2004, www.nytimes.com/2004/09/01/opinion/frances-republican-monarchy-when-the-president-is-treated-like-a.html (accessed 4/6/18).

TABLE 2.2

Federalists versus Antifederalists

	FEDERALISTS	ANTIFEDERALISTS
Who were they?	Property owners, creditors, merchants	Small farmers, frontiersmen, debtors, shopkeepers, some state government officials
What did they believe?	Believed that elites were most fit to govern; feared "excessive democracy"	Believed that government should be closer to the people; feared concentration of power in hands of the elites
What system of government did they favor?	Favored strong national government; believed in "filtration" so that only elites would obtain governmental power	Favored retention of power by state governments and protection of individual rights
Who were their leaders?	Alexander Hamilton, James Madison, George Washington	Patrick Henry, George Mason, Elbridge Gerry, George Clinton

took their name to appear to follow in the revolutionary tradition) supported the Constitution and preferred a strong national government. The Antifederalists opposed the Constitution and preferred a federal system of government that was decentralized; they took their name by default, in reaction to their better-organized opponents. The Federalists were united in their support of the Constitution, whereas the Antifederalists were divided over possible alternatives to the Constitution.

During the struggle over ratification of the Constitution, Americans argued about great political issues and principles. How much power should the national government be given? What safeguards would most likely prevent the abuse of power? What institutional arrangements could best ensure adequate representation for all Americans? Was tyranny of the many to be feared more than tyranny of the few?

FEDERALISTS VERSUS ANTIFEDERALISTS

Federalist Papers a series of essays written by Alexander Hamilton, James Madison, and John Jay supporting ratification of the Constitution

During the ratification struggle, thousands of essays, speeches, pamphlets, and letters were presented in support of and in opposition to the proposed Constitution. The best-known pieces supporting ratification were the 85 essays written between the fall of 1787 and the spring of 1788 under the name of "Publius," by Alexander Hamilton, James Madison, and John Jay. These ***Federalist Papers***, as they are collectively known today, defended the principles of the Constitution and sought to dispel fears of a national authority. The Antifederalists published essays of their own, arguing that the new Constitution betrayed the Revolution and was a step toward monarchy. Among the best of the Antifederalist works were the essays, usually attributed to the New York State Supreme Court justice Robert Yates, that were written under the name of "Brutus" and published in the *New York Journal* at the same time the *Federalist Papers* appeared. The Antifederalist view was also ably presented in the pamphlets and letters written by a former delegate to the Continental Congress and future U.S. senator, Richard Henry Lee of Virginia, using the pen name "The Federal Farmer." These essays highlight the major differences of opinion between

Federalists and Antifederalists. Federalists appealed to basic principles of government in support of their nationalist vision. Antifederalists cited equally fundamental precepts to support their vision of a looser confederacy of small republics.

Representation One major area of contention between the two sides was the question of representation. The Antifederalists asserted that representatives must be "a true picture of the people... [possessing] the knowledge of their circumstances and their wants."[20] This could be achieved, argued the Antifederalists, only in small, relatively homogeneous republics such as the existing states. In their view, the size and extent of the entire nation precluded the construction of a truly representative form of government. As Brutus put it, "Is it practicable for a country so large and so numerous... to elect a representation that will speak their sentiments?... It certainly is not."[21]

Federalists, for their part, saw no reason that representatives should be precisely like those they represented. In the Federalist view, one of the great advantages of representative government over direct democracy was precisely the possibility that the people would choose as their representatives individuals possessing ability, experience, and talent superior to their own. In Madison's words, rather than serving as a mirror or reflection of society, representatives must be "[those] who possess [the] most wisdom to discern, and [the] most virtue to pursue, the common good of the society."[22]

FOR CRITICAL ANALYSIS

The Antifederalists worried that the size and diversity of the United States made democratic government impossible. In what ways might a large heterogeneous population limit democracy and enhance democracy?

Tyranny A second important issue dividing Federalists and Antifederalists was the threat of **tyranny**—unjust rule by the group in power. Both opponents and defenders of the Constitution frequently affirmed their fear of tyrannical rule. Each side, however, had a different view of the most likely source of tyranny and, hence, of the way in which to forestall the threat.

tyranny oppressive government that employs cruel and unjust use of power and authority

From the Antifederalist perspective, the great danger was the tendency of all governments—including republican governments—to become gradually more and more "aristocratic" in character, wherein the small number of individuals in positions of authority would use their stations to gain more and more power over the general citizenry. In essence, the few would use their power to tyrannize the many. For this reason, Antifederalists were sharply critical of those features of the Constitution that divorced governmental institutions from direct responsibility to the people—institutions such as the Senate, the executive, and the federal judiciary. The last, appointed for life, presented a particular threat: "I wonder if the world ever saw... a court of justice invested with such immense powers, and yet placed in a situation so little responsible," protested Brutus.[23]

The Federalists, too, recognized the threat of tyranny, but they believed that the danger particularly associated with republican governments was not aristocracy but majority tyranny. The Federalists were concerned that a popular majority, "united and actuated by some common impulse of passion, or of interest, adverse to the rights of other citizens," would endeavor to "trample on the rules of justice."[24] From the Federalist perspective, it was precisely those features of the Constitution that the Antifederalists attacked as potential sources of tyranny that actually offered the best hope of averting the threat of oppression. The size and extent of the nation, for instance,

Article VII of the Constitution required 9 of the 13 states to ratify the Constitution in order for it to be adopted. In this image from January 1788, the pillars represent the first five states that ratified the Constitution, with Massachusetts as the likely sixth.

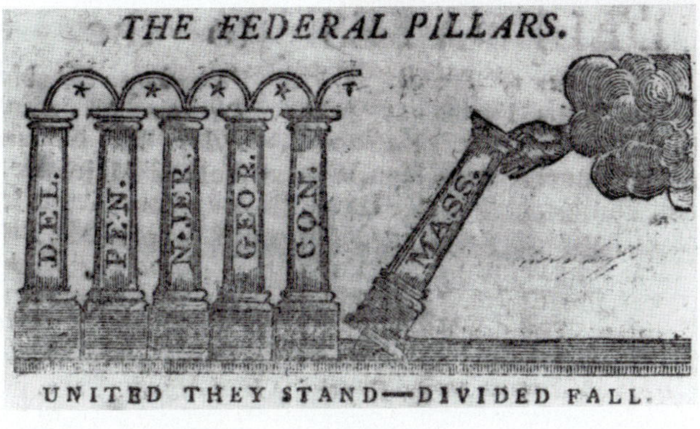

Debates over how much power the national government should have continue today. After the San Bernardino shooting in 2015, the FBI demanded Apple unlock the perpetrator's iPhone for details into his criminal activity. Here, a group protests the FBI's infringement on the right to privacy.

was for the Federalists a bulwark against tyranny because a majority would have difficulty uniting in a large and populous nation.

Governmental Power A third major difference between Federalists and Antifederalists was the issue of governmental power. Both opponents and proponents of the Constitution agreed on the principle of **limited government**. They differed, however, on the fundamentally important question of how to place limits on governmental action. Antifederalists favored limiting and enumerating the powers granted to the national government in relation both to the states and to the people at large. To them, the powers given the national government ought to be "confined to certain defined national objects."[25] Otherwise, the national government would "swallow up all the power of the state governments."[26] Antifederalists bitterly attacked the supremacy clause and the elastic clause of the Constitution as unlimited and dangerous grants of power to the national government.[27] Antifederalists also demanded that a bill of rights be added to the Constitution to place limits on the government's exercise of power over the citizenry.

limited government a principle of constitutional government; a government whose powers are defined and limited by a constitution

Federalists favored the construction of a government with broad powers to defend the nation against foreign foes, guard against domestic strife and insurrection, promote commerce, and expand the nation's economy. Antifederalists shared some of these goals but still feared governmental power. In reply, Federalists such as Hamilton acknowledged that every power could be abused but argued that the way to prevent misuse of power was not by depriving the government of the powers needed to achieve national goals but by adopting the Constitution's internal checks and controls. As Madison put it, "the power surrendered by the people is first divided between two distinct governments (state and national), and then the portion allotted to each subdivided among distinct and separate departments. Hence, a double security arises to the rights of the people. The different governments will control each other, at the same time that each will be controlled by itself."[28] The Federalists' concern with avoiding unwarranted limits on governmental power led them to oppose a bill of rights, which they saw as nothing more than a set of unnecessary restrictions on the government.

Federalists acknowledged that abuse of power remained a possibility but felt that the risk had to be taken in order to achieve essential goals. "The very idea of power included a possibility of doing harm," said the Federalist John Rutledge during the South Carolina ratification debates. "If the gentleman would show the power that could do no harm," Rutledge continued, "he would at once discover it to be a power that could do no good."[29] This aspect of the debate between Federalists and Antifederalists, perhaps more than any other, continues to reverberate through American politics. Should the nation limit the federal government's power to tax and spend? Should Congress limit the capacity of federal agencies to issue new regulations? Should the government endeavor to create new rights for minorities, the disabled, and others? Though the details have changed, these are the same great questions that have been debated since the Founding.

FOR CRITICAL ANALYSIS

Do you agree with Rutledge that a power that can do no harm can also do no good? How can a system of government maximize the ability of government to do good while minimizing the possibility of harm?

REFLECTIONS ON THE FOUNDING

The final product of the Constitutional Convention was an extraordinary victory for the groups that had most forcefully called for the creation of a new system of government to replace the Articles of Confederation. While Antifederalist criticisms did force the Constitution's proponents to accept the addition of a bill of rights designed to limit the powers of the national government, overall it was the Federalist vision of America that triumphed. The Constitution adopted in 1789 created the framework for a powerful national government that for more than 200 years has defended the nation's interests, promoted its commerce, and maintained national unity. In one notable instance, the national government fought and won a bloody war to prevent the nation from breaking apart. And despite this powerful national government, the system of internal checks and balances has functioned reasonably well, as the Federalists predicted, to prevent the government from tyrannizing its citizens. The national unity created under the Constitution also gradually helped America become a great world power—as many of the framers had hoped.

Although they were defeated in 1788, the Antifederalists present us with an important picture of an America that might have been. Would Americans in the eighteenth century have been worse off if they had been governed by a confederacy of small republics linked by a national administration with severely limited powers? Were the Antifederalists correct in predicting that a government given great power in the hope that it might do good would, through "insensible progress," inevitably turn to evil purposes?

The Citizen's Role and the Changing Constitution

Trace how the Constitution has changed over time through the amendment process

The Constitution has endured for more than two centuries as the framework of government. But it has not gone unchanged. The Constitution assigns citizens an indirect but important role in this process of change. Figure 2.3 outlines the ways in which the Constitution might be amended, all of which involve citizens through the election of members of Congress and state legislatures or, hypothetically, through the election of delegates to national and state constitutional conventions. Amending the Constitution may be difficult, but it is ultimately controlled by institutions elected by the people. Of course, the federal courts, whose judges are not elected by the people but appointed by the president with the consent of the Senate, also interpret the Constitution and adapt it to changing circumstances. Many voters are aware that their presidential ballots may also help to shape the character of the Supreme Court and other federal courts.

AMENDMENTS: MANY ARE CALLED; FEW ARE CHOSEN

The inevitable need for change was recognized by the framers of the Constitution, and provisions for **amendment** were incorporated into Article V. Four methods of amendment are described:

amendment a change added to a bill, law, or constitution

1. Passage in House and Senate by two-thirds vote, then ratification by majority vote of the legislatures of three-fourths (now 38) of the states
2. Passage in House and Senate by two-thirds vote, then ratification by conventions called for the purpose in three-fourths of the states

FIGURE 2.3

Four Ways the Constitution Can Be Amended

*This method of proposal has never been employed. Thus, amendment routes 3 and 4 have never been attempted.
**For each amendment proposal, Congress has the power to choose the method of ratification, the time limit for consideration by the states, and other conditions of ratification. The movement to repeal Prohibition in the Twenty-First Amendment was the only occasion in which route 2 was used successfully.

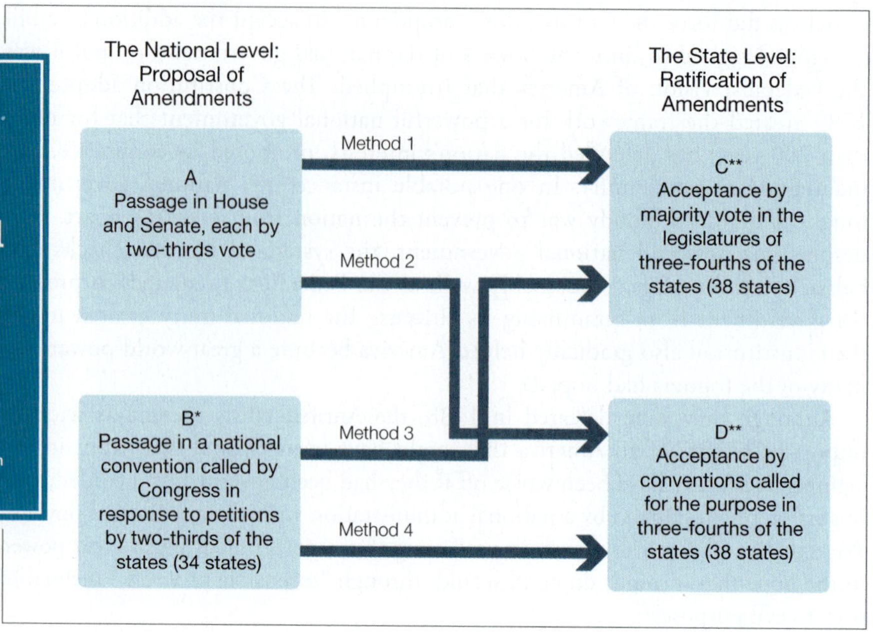

The National Level: Proposal of Amendments
The State Level: Ratification of Amendments
A
Passage in House and Senate, each by two-thirds vote
B*
Passage in a national convention called by Congress in response to petitions by two-thirds of the states (34 states)
Method 1
Method 2
Method 3
Method 4
C**
Acceptance by majority vote in the legislatures of three-fourths of the states (38 states)
D**
Acceptance by conventions called for the purpose in three-fourths of the states (38 states)

3. Passage in a national convention called for by Congress in response to petitions by two-thirds of the states, then ratification by majority vote of the legislatures of three-fourths of the states
4. Passage in a national convention (as in method 3), then ratification by conventions called for the purpose in three-fourths of the states

Figure 2.3 illustrates each of these possible methods. Since no amendment has ever been proposed by national convention, however, methods 3 and 4 have never been employed. And method 2 has been employed only once (the Twenty-First Amendment, which repealed the Eighteenth Amendment, or Prohibition). Thus, method 1 has been used for all the others.

The Constitution has proved to be extremely difficult to amend. Since 1789, more than 11,000 amendments have been formally offered in Congress. Of these, Congress officially proposed only 29, and 27 of these were eventually ratified by the states. Two of these—Prohibition and its repeal—cancel each other out, so for all practical purposes, only 25 amendments have been added to the Constitution since 1791.

FOR CRITICAL ANALYSIS

It is very difficult to amend the Constitution. Should the amendment process be made easier? Would the American system of government be more democratic if the Constitution could be revised more easily?

WHICH WERE CHOSEN? AN ANALYSIS OF THE 27

There is more to the amending difficulties than the politics of campaigning and voting. It would appear that only a limited number of changes can actually be made to the Constitution. Most efforts to amend the Constitution have failed because they were simply attempts to use the Constitution as an alternative to legislation for dealing directly with a specific public problem.

The 25 successful amendments, on the other hand, are concerned with the structure or composition of government (see Table 2.3). This is consistent with the

TABLE 2.3

Amendments to the Constitution

AMENDMENT	PURPOSE	YEAR PROPOSED	YEAR ADOPTED
I	Congress is not to make any law establishing a religion or abridging free exercise of religion, speech, press, assembly, or petitioning the government for redress of grievances.	1789	1791
II, III, IV	No branch of government may infringe on the right of people to keep arms (II), is not arbitrarily to occupy homes for a militia (III), and is not to engage in the search or seizure of evidence without a court warrant swearing to belief in the probable existence of a crime (IV).	1789	1791
V, VI, VII, VIII	The courts* are not to hold trials for serious offenses without provision for a grand jury (V), a petit (trial) jury (VII), a speedy trial (VI), presentation of charges (VI), confrontation of hostile witnesses (VI), immunity from testimony against oneself (V), and immunity from more than one trial for the same offense (V). Neither bail nor punishment can be excessive (VIII), and no property can be taken without just compensation (V).	1789	1791
IX, X	All rights and powers not enumerated are reserved to the states or the people.	1789	1791
XI	Limited jurisdiction of federal courts over suits involving the states.	1794	1795
XII	Provided separate ballot for vice president in the electoral college.	1803	1804
XIII	Eliminated slavery and eliminated the right of states to treat persons as property.	1865	1865
XIV	Asserted the principle of national citizenship and prohibited the states from infringing upon the rights of citizens of the nation, no matter that they happened to live in that state. Also prohibited states from denying voting rights to male citizens over the age of 21.**	1866	1868
XV	Extended voting rights to all races.	1869	1870
XVI	Established national power to tax incomes.	1909	1913
XVII†	Provided for direct election of senators. This diminished the power of the state legislatures and underscored the idea of a direct connection between Americans and the government of the United States.	1912	1913
XIX	Extended voting rights to women.	1919	1920
XX	Eliminated "lame-duck" session of Congress.	1932	1933
XXII	Limited presidential term.	1947	1951
XXIII	Extended voting rights to residents of the District of Columbia.	1960	1961
XXIV	Extended voting rights to all classes by abolition of poll taxes.	1962	1964
XXV	Provided presidential succession in case of disability.	1965	1967
XXVI	Extended voting rights to citizens aged 18 and over.	1971	1971††
XXVII	Limited Congress's power to raise its own salary.	1789	1992

*These amendments also impose limits on the law-enforcement powers of federal, state, and local executive branches.

**In defining *citizenship*, the Fourteenth Amendment actually provided the constitutional basis for expanding the electorate to include all races, women, and residents of the District of Columbia. Only the "18-year-olds' amendment" should have been necessary since it changed the definition of citizenship. The fact that additional amendments were required following the Fourteenth suggests that voting is not considered an inherent right of U.S. citizenship. Instead, it is viewed as a privilege.

†The Eighteenth Amendment, ratified in 1919, outlawed the sale and transportation of liquor. It was repealed by the Twenty-First Amendment, ratified in 1933.

††The Twenty-Sixth Amendment holds the record for speed of adoption. It was proposed on March 23, 1971, and adopted on July 5, 1971.

dictionary, which defines *constitution* as the makeup or composition of something. And it is consistent with the concept of a constitution as "higher law" because the whole point and purpose of a higher law is to establish a framework within which government and the process of making ordinary law can take place. Even those who would have preferred more changes to the Constitution have to agree that there is great wisdom in this principle. A constitution ought to enable legislation and public policies to be enacted, but it should not determine what that legislation or those public policies ought to be.

Private property is an excellent example. Property is one of the most fundamental and well-established rights in the United States; but it is well established not because it is recognized in so many words in the Constitution but because legislatures and courts, working within an agreed-upon constitutional framework, have made it a crime for anyone, including the government, to trespass or to take away property without compensation. A constitution is good if it produces the cause of action that leads to good legislation, good case law, and appropriate police behavior. Its principles can be a citizen's dependable defense against the abuse of power.

And ordinary citizens, including students, can influence America's constitution. Take the case of the Twenty-Seventh Amendment, which declares that no congressional pay increase can take effect until the next Congress is elected. This idea was proposed in 1789 along with the 10 amendments that became the Bill of Rights. This proposed amendment was ratified by several states but never achieved the three-fourths needed to be added to the Constitution. The idea was forgotten until a University of Texas undergraduate, Gregory Watson, wrote his class term paper on the subject in 1982. Watson proposed a campaign to complete the ratification process. His professor awarded Watson a C grade, asserting that the proposal was unrealistic. Watson, however, was undeterred and launched a student-led campaign to complete the ratification process. In 1992 the Twenty-Seventh Amendment was added to the Constitution, more than two centuries after it was proposed.

The Twenty-Sixth Amendment addressed an issue of representation that came to the fore when 18-, 19-, and 20-year-olds were drafted to serve in the Vietnam War but could not vote for Congress or the president who enacted the policies that affected their lives and deaths.

THE SUPREME COURT AND CONSTITUTIONAL CHANGE

Although the process of constitutional amendment outlined in Article V has seldom been used successfully, another form of constitutional revision is constantly at work in the United States: judicial interpretation of the Constitution and its amendments by the Supreme Court as it reviews cases. In some instances, the Court may give concrete definition to abstract constitutional principles. For example, the Constitution's Fifth Amendment asserts in general terms that individuals accused of crimes are entitled to procedural rights. The Supreme Court, in a series of decisions, established principles giving effect to those rights. Every viewer of television crime programs knows that, upon being arrested, individuals must receive Miranda warnings informing them of their right to refuse to speak and their right to counsel. These required warnings are the result of a 1966 Supreme Court decision interpreting the meaning and implications of the Fifth Amendment.

In some instances, the Supreme Court does more than interpret or flesh out constitutional provisions: it seems to modify or augment the text itself. For example, in decisions in 1965 and 1973 on birth control and abortion, respectively, the Court said that Americans were constitutionally entitled to a right of privacy. The Constitution does not explicitly mention the right to privacy; it is derived from the Fourteenth Amendment and several provisions in the Bill of Rights.

As we examine in more depth later in the book, much of the Supreme Court's power is itself based on constitutional interpretation rather than on the text of the document. The Supreme Court claims the power of judicial review—the power to render the final decision when there is a conflict of interpretations of the Constitution or federal law among the courts, Congress, the executive branch, or the states. Nowhere does the Constitution mention this power. In a number of early cases, however, the Supreme Court asserted that the Constitution gave it the power of judicial review; and this interpretation has prevailed, enhancing the Court's power. Some commentators denounce this as constitutional amendment by the judiciary and demand that judges limit themselves to "strict construction" of the Constitution, adhering closely to the words of the document's text. Proponents of the idea of the *living Constitution*, on the other hand, assert that the Constitution is subject to change as conditions warrant; and they argue that the judiciary is the institution best qualified to adjust the Constitution's principles to new problems and times.

The Equal Rights Amendment (ERA) is an example of an amendment that almost succeeded. The proposed amendment guaranteed equality under the law for women and made gender discrimination illegal. The ERA was ratified by 35 state legislatures but failed to get the 38 necessary to equal three-fourths of the states.

The Constitution
WHAT DO WE WANT?

The Constitution's framers placed individual liberty ahead of all other political values, a concern that led many of the framers to distrust both democracy and equality. They feared that democracy could degenerate into a majority tyranny in which the populace, perhaps led by rabble-rousing demagogues, trampled on liberty. As for equality, the framers were products of their time and place; our contemporary ideas of racial and gender equality would have been foreign to them. The framers were concerned primarily with another manifestation of equality: they feared that those without property or position might be driven by what some called a "leveling spirit" to infringe on liberty in the name of greater economic or social equality. Indeed, the framers believed that this leveling spirit was most likely to produce demagoguery and majority tyranny. As a result, the basic structure of the Constitution—separated powers, internal checks and balances, and federalism—was designed to safeguard liberty, and the Bill of Rights created further safeguards for liberty. At the same time, however, many of the Constitution's other key provisions, such as indirect election of senators and the president and the appointment of judges for life, were designed to limit democracy and, hence, the threat of majority tyranny.

FOR CRITICAL ANALYSIS

What are the U.S. Constitution's greatest strengths? What are its most pronounced weaknesses? If you were revising the Constitution today, what would you change? Why?

By championing liberty, however, the framers virtually guaranteed that democracy and even a measure of equality would sooner or later evolve in the United States. Liberty promotes the growth of political activity and the expansion of political participation, as in James Madison's famous phrase "Liberty is to faction as air is to fire."[30] The "**Who Participates?**" feature on the facing page traces the expansion of the right to vote in the United States from the Founding to today. Where they have liberty, more and more people, groups, and interests will engage in politics and gradually overcome whatever restrictions might have been placed on participation. They will fight for their rights and interests, and in doing so, may achieve greater equality, as Jim Obergefell did in securing marriage equality for same-sex couples. By granting citizens the freedom to exercise voice, liberty over time is conducive to democracy.

Who Gained the Right to Vote through Amendments?

Adult Citizens Eligible to Vote in National Elections*

27.9%	31.7%	92.6%	99.9%

1789	**1869**	**1920**	**1971**
The Founding: White men of property, age 21+	15th Amendment: All men, age 21+	19th Amendment: All men and women, age 21+	26th Amendment: All men and women, age 18+

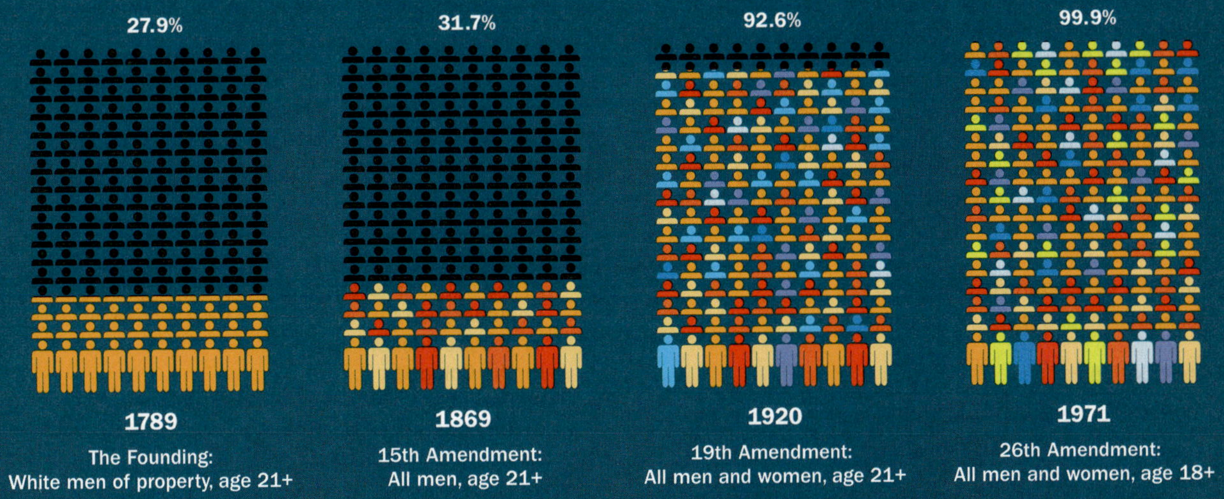

*Percentages are of the adult (18+) population. These figures are approximate for 1789 and 1869. The voting rights of convicted felons are restricted in some states, and of noncitizens in all states.

SOURCES: U.S. Census of Population and Housing, 1790–2010, www.census.gov/prod/www/decennial.html (accessed 9/28/15); United States Elections Project, www.electproject.org/national-1789–present (accessed 9/27/15).

★ WHAT YOU CAN DO ★

Know Your Constitutional Rights

- ☑ Review your rights as outlined in the Constitution, a copy of which is reproduced in the appendix of this book.

- ☑ Find out what voting rights are retained by individuals who have been convicted of a felony. Go to **www.ncsl.org** and search "felon voting rights" for more information.

- ☑ Find out what voting rights are retained by individuals with mental illness. Go to **www.bazelon.org** and search "voting" for more information.

- ☑ Should noncitizens (such as longtime permanent legal residents) have the right to vote? Go to **www.latimes.com/citizenship** to read more and to join the conversation online.

in fighting illegal drugs and criminal activity."[4] It remains to be seen whether marijuana will be a focus of a possibly renewed War on Drugs in the Trump administration.[5]

Larry Harvey's situation and the debates about marijuana policy engage some of the oldest questions in American government: What is the responsibility of the federal government, and what is the responsibility of the states? When should there be uniformity across the states, and when is it better to let states adopt their own laws based on the needs and desires of their population, which may result in a diverse set of laws across the country? Which approach serves the common good?

The United States is a federal system, in which the national government shares power with lower levels of government. Throughout American history, lawmakers, politicians, and citizens have wrestled with questions about how responsibilities should be allocated across the different levels of government. Some responsibilities, such as international relations, clearly lie with the federal government. Others, such as divorce laws, are controlled by state governments. In fact, most of the rules and regulations that Americans face in their daily lives are set by state and local governments. However, many government responsibilities are shared in American federalism and require cooperation among local, state, and federal governments. The debate about "who should do what" remains one of the most important discussions in American politics.

CHAPTER GOALS

- ★ **Describe what the Constitution says about the powers of the national government and of the states (pp. 79–84)**
- ★ **Consider how the relationship between the federal and state governments evolved during the nation's first 140 years (pp. 84–88)**
- ★ **Trace developments in the federal framework leading to a stronger national government (pp. 89–94)**
- ★ **Analyze the changing role of the states in the federal framework (pp. 94–102)**
- ★ **Analyze contemporary relationships among national, state, and local governments (pp. 102–7)**

Federalism in the Constitution

Describe what the Constitution says about the powers of the national government and of the states

The Constitution has had a profound influence on American life through **federalism**, the division of powers and functions between the national government and the state governments. Governments can organize power in a variety of ways. One of the most important distinctions is between unitary and federal governments. In a **unitary system**, the central government makes the important decisions and lower levels of government have little independent power. In such systems, lower levels of government primarily implement decisions made by the central government. In France, for example, the central government was once so involved in the smallest details of local activity that the minister of education boasted that by looking at his watch he could tell what all French schoolchildren were learning at that moment because the central government set the school curriculum. In a federal system, by contrast, the central government shares power or functions with lower levels of government, such as regions or states. Nations with diverse ethnic or language groupings, such as Switzerland and Canada, are most likely to have federal arrangements. In federal systems, lower levels of government often have significant independent power to set policy in some areas, such as education and social programs, and to impose taxes. Yet the specific ways in which power is shared vary greatly: no two federal systems are exactly the same.

federalism a system of government in which power is divided, by a constitution, between a central government and regional governments

unitary system a centralized government system in which lower levels of government have little power independent of the national government

The United States was the first nation to adopt federalism as its governing framework. With federalism, the framers sought to limit the national government by creating a second layer of state governments. By granting a few "expressed powers" to the national government and reserving all the rest to the states, the original Constitution recognized two sovereigns: state governments and the federal government. Table 3.1 indicates which level of government has responsibility for some of the actions that affect our everyday lives.

THE POWERS OF THE NATIONAL GOVERNMENT

As we saw in Chapter 2, the **expressed powers** granted to the national government are found in Article I, Section 8 of the Constitution. These 17 powers include the power to collect taxes, coin money, declare war, and regulate commerce. Article I, Section 8 also contains another important source of power for the national government: the **implied powers** that enable Congress "to make all Laws which shall be necessary and proper for carrying into Execution the foregoing Powers." Not until several decades after the Founding did the Supreme Court allow Congress to exercise the power granted in this **necessary and proper clause**, but as we shall see later in this chapter, this doctrine allowed the national government to expand considerably the scope of its authority, although the process was a slow one. In addition to these expressed and implied powers, the Constitution affirmed the power of the national government in the supremacy clause (Article VI), which made all national laws and treaties "the supreme Law of the Land."

expressed powers specific powers granted by the Constitution to Congress (Article I, Section 8) and to the president (Article II)

implied powers powers derived from the necessary and proper clause of Article I, Section 8 of the Constitution; such powers are not specifically expressed but are implied through the expansive interpretation of delegated powers

necessary and proper clause Article I, Section 8 of the Constitution, which provides Congress with the authority to make all laws "necessary and proper" to carry out its expressed powers

TABLE 3.1

The Presence of Federal, State, and Local Government in the Daily Life of a Student at "State University"

TIME	SCHEDULE	LEVEL OF GOVERNMENT
7:00 A.M.	Wake up. Standard time set by the national government.	Federal and state
7:10 A.M.	Shower. Water courtesy of local government, either a public entity or a regulated private company.	Local
7:18 A.M.	Brush your teeth with toothpaste whose cavity-fighting claims have been verified by a federal agency.	Federal
7:30 A.M.	Have a bowl of cereal with milk for breakfast. "Nutrition Facts" on food labels are a federal requirement, pasteurization of milk required by state law, freshness dating on milk based on state and federal standards.	Federal and state
7:57 A.M.	Recycle the empty cereal box and milk carton.	State or local
8:30 A.M.	Drive or take public transportation to campus. Airbags and seat belts required by federal and state laws. Roads and bridges paid for by state and local governments, speed and traffic laws set by state and local governments, public transportation subsidized by all levels of government.	Federal, state, and local
8:45 A.M.	Arrive on campus of large public university. Buildings are 70 percent financed by state taxpayers.	State
9:00 A.M.	First class: Chemistry 101. Tuition partially paid by a federal loan (more than half the cost of university instruction is paid for by taxpayers), chemistry lab paid for with grants from the National Science Foundation (a federal agency) and smaller grants from business corporations made possible by federal income tax deductions for charitable contributions.	Federal
2:00 P.M.	Second class: American Government 101 (your favorite class!). You may be taking this class because it is required by the state legislature or because it fulfills a university requirement.	State
4:00 P.M.	Third class: Computer Science 101. Free computers, software, and internet access courtesy of state subsidies plus grants and discounts from Apple and Microsoft, the costs of which are deducted from their corporate income taxes; internet built in part by federal government. Duplication of software prohibited by federal copyright laws.	Federal and state
6:00 P.M.	Eat dinner: hamburger and french fries. Meat inspected for bacteria by federal agencies.	Federal
7:00 P.M.	Work at part-time job at the campus library. Minimum wage set by federal government; some states and cities set a higher minimum. Books and journals in library paid for by state taxpayers.	Federal, state, local
8:15 P.M.	Go online to check the status of your application for a federal student loan (FAFSA) on the Department of Education's website at studentaid.ed.gov.	Federal
10:00 P.M.	Go home. Street lighting paid for by county and city governments, police patrols by city government.	Local
10:15 P.M.	Watch Netflix. Broadband internet service regulated by federal government. Check app for tomorrow's weather. Weather forecast provided by a federal agency.	Federal
10:45 P.M.	To complete your economics homework, visit the Bureau of Labor Statistics at www.bls.gov to look up unemployment levels since 1972.	Federal
Midnight	Put out the trash before going to bed. Trash collected by city sanitation department, financed by "user charges."	Local

THE POWERS OF STATE GOVERNMENT

One way in which the framers sought to preserve a strong role for the states was through the Tenth Amendment to the Constitution. The Tenth Amendment states that the powers the Constitution does not delegate to the national government or prohibit to the states are "reserved to the States respectively, or to the people." The Antifederalists, who feared that a strong central government would encroach on individual liberty, repeatedly pressed for such an amendment as a way of limiting national power. Federalists agreed to the amendment because they did not think it would do much harm, given the powers of the Constitution already granted to the national government. The Tenth Amendment is also called the "**reserved powers** amendment" because it aims to reserve powers to the states.

reserved powers powers, derived from the Tenth Amendment to the Constitution, that are not specifically delegated to the national government or denied to the states

The most fundamental power that the states retain is that of coercion—the power to develop and enforce criminal codes, to administer health and safety rules, and to regulate the family via marriage and divorce laws. These issues touch closely on state and local values, which the Founders saw as appropriately differing from state to state (see Figure 3.1). States also have the power to

FIGURE 3.1

The Size of State Governments

The Founders believed that local needs and values varied from state to state and thus left many powers and responsibilities to state governments rather than the national government. State governments vary substantially in their relative size (how many state employees per 100 residents). How might these differences reflect differing needs and values?

SOURCES: U.S. Census Bureau, "2016 Annual Survey of Public Employment and Payroll," October 19, 2017, factfinder.census.gov/faces/tableservices/jsf/pages/productview.xhtml?src=bkmk/ (accessed 6/8/18); U.S. Census Bureau, "Annual Estimates of the Resident Population for the United States, Regions, States, and Puerto Rico: April 1, 2010 to July 1, 2017," May 8, 2018, www.census.gov/data/tables/2017/demo/popest/state-total.html (accessed 6/8/18).

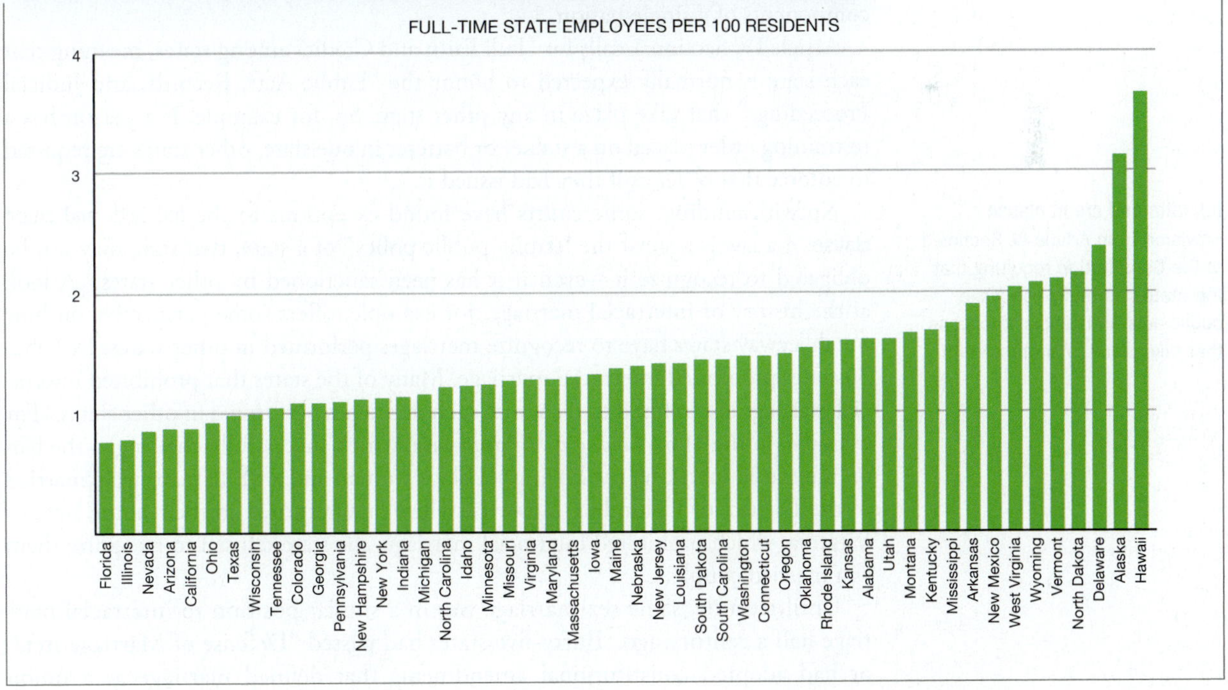

regulate individuals' livelihoods; if you're a doctor or a lawyer or a plumber or a barber, you must be licensed by the state. Even more fundamentally, the states have the power to define private property—private property exists because state laws against trespass define who is and is not entitled to use a piece of property. If you own a car, your ownership isn't worth much unless the state is willing to enforce your right to possession by making it a crime for anyone else to drive your car without your consent. These are fundamental matters, and the powers of the states regarding these domestic issues are much greater than the powers of the national government.

police power power reserved to the state government to regulate the health, safety, and morals of its citizens

A state's authority to regulate these fundamental matters is commonly referred to as the **police power** of the state and encompasses the state's power to regulate the health, safety, welfare, and morals of its citizens. Policing is what states do—they coerce you in the name of the community in order to maintain public order. And this was exactly the type of power that the Founders intended the states, not the federal government, to exercise.

concurrent powers authority possessed by *both* state and national governments, such as the power to levy taxes

In some areas, the states share **concurrent powers** with the national government, whereby they retain and share some power to regulate commerce and affect the currency—for example, by being able to charter banks, grant or deny corporate charters, grant or deny licenses to engage in a business or practice a trade, regulate the quality of products or the conditions of labor, and levy taxes. Wherever there is a direct conflict of laws between the federal and the state levels, the issue will most likely be resolved in favor of national supremacy.

STATES' OBLIGATIONS TO ONE ANOTHER

The Constitution also creates obligations among the states. These obligations, spelled out in Article IV, were intended to promote national unity. By requiring the states to recognize actions and decisions taken in other states as legal and proper, the framers aimed to make the states less like independent countries and more like components of a single nation.

Article IV, Section 1 calls for "Full Faith and Credit" among states, meaning that each state is normally expected to honor the "Public Acts, Records, and Judicial Proceedings" that take place in any other state. So, for example, if a person has a restraining order placed on a stalker or batterer in one state, other states are required to enforce that order as if they had issued it.

full faith and credit clause provision from Article IV, Section 1 of the Constitution requiring that the states normally honor the public acts and judicial decisions that take place in another state

Notwithstanding, some courts have found exceptions to the **full faith and credit clause**: if a law is against the "strong public policy" of a state, that state may not be obligated to recognize it—even if it has been sanctioned by other states.[6] A look at the history of interracial marriage, for example, offers some perspective on how much leeway states have to recognize marriages performed in other states. In 1952, 30 states prohibited interracial marriage. Many of the states that prohibited interracial marriage also refused to recognize such marriages performed in other states.[7] For example, in the 1967 *Loving v. Virginia* case, which successfully challenged the ban on interracial marriage, the Lovings (a black woman and a white man) were married in the District of Columbia. However, when they returned to their home state of Virginia, which prohibited interracial marriage, the state refused to recognize them as a married couple.[8]

Until recently, same-sex marriage was in a similar position to interracial marriage half a century ago. Thirty-five states had passed "Defense of Marriage Acts" or had adopted constitutional amendments that defined marriage as a union between one man and one woman. Anxious to show its disapproval of gay marriage, Congress passed the Defense of Marriage Act in 1996, which declared that states would not have to recognize a same-sex marriage from another state. The act also said that the federal government would not recognize same-sex marriage—even if it were legal under state law—and that same-sex marriage partners would not be eligible for the federal benefits, such as Medicare and Social Security, normally available to spouses.[9] In 2013, however, the Supreme Court in *United States v. Windsor* struck down the Defense of Marriage Act in part, requiring that same-sex married couples receive equal treatment on issues relating to taxes, inheritance, and other federal laws.[10] After *Windsor*, many state courts struck down the state bans on same-sex marriage.

Previously a state-level policy, same-sex marriage was declared a fundamental right nationwide by the Supreme Court in 2015. The decision prompted a brief backlash when clerks in some states, such as Kim Davis from Kentucky, pictured here, refused to issue marriage licenses to same-sex couples.

On the second anniversary of the *Windsor* ruling, the Supreme Court, in a historic and long-awaited decision, ruled that the Fourteenth Amendment guaranteed a fundamental right to same-sex marriage. The case, *Obergefell v. Hodges*, combined four lawsuits by same-sex couples challenging their home states' refusals to grant same-sex marriage licenses or recognize same-sex marriages performed out of state.[11] While 37 states recognized same-sex marriage on the eve of the *Obergefell* announcement, the Court's 5–4 decision immediately required that number to jump to 50: all states must offer marriage licenses to two people of the same sex and recognize same-sex marriages licensed out of state. In one stroke, same-sex marriage turned from a state-level policy choice to a nationally recognized right. In the aftermath of the *Obergefell* decision, several of the 13 states that were mandated to lift their bans on same-sex marriage protested the ruling. Ken Paxton, the attorney general of Texas, for example, called the decision "unlawful" and pledged to provide legal assistance to local officials who refused to carry out the new law.[12] However, such resistance ebbed as it became clear that the courts would enforce the constitutional right to same-sex marriage.

Article IV, Section 2, known as the "comity clause," also seeks to promote national unity. It provides that citizens enjoying the **privileges and immunities** of one state should be entitled to similar treatment in other states. What this has come to mean is that a state cannot discriminate against someone from another state or give special privileges to its own residents. For example, in the 1970s, when Alaska passed a law that gave residents preference over nonresidents in obtaining work on the state's oil and gas pipelines, the Supreme Court ruled the law illegal because it discriminated against citizens of other states.[13] The comity clause also regulates criminal justice among the states by requiring states to return fugitives to the states from which they have fled. Thus, in 1952, when an inmate escaped from an Alabama prison and sought to avoid being returned to Alabama on the grounds that he was being subjected to "cruel and unusual punishment" there, the Supreme Court ruled that he must be returned according to Article IV, Section 2.[14]

privileges and immunities clause provision, from Article IV, Section 2 of the Constitution, that a state cannot discriminate against someone from another state or give its own residents special privileges

States' relationships with one another are also governed by the interstate compact clause (Article I, Section 10), which states that "No State shall, without the Consent of Congress . . . enter into any Agreement or Compact with another State." The Court has interpreted the clause to mean that states may enter into agreements with one another, subject to congressional approval. Today compacts are used for a wide range of issues from adult offender supervision to pest control, but are especially important in regulating the distribution of river water, addressing

TABLE 3.2

90,107 Governments in the United States

TYPE	NUMBER
National	1
State	50
County	3,031
Municipal	19,519
Townships	16,360
School districts	12,880
Other special districts	38,266

SOURCE: U.S. Census Bureau, www2.census.gov/govs/cog/g12_org.pdf (accessed 11/2/13).

environmental concerns, and operating transportation systems that cross state lines.[15]

LOCAL GOVERNMENT AND THE CONSTITUTION

Local government occupies a peculiar but very important place in the American system (see Table 3.2). In fact, the status of American local government is probably unique in world experience. First, it must be pointed out that local government has no status in the U.S. Constitution. *State* legislatures created local governments, and *state* constitutions and laws permit local governments to take on some of the responsibilities of the state governments. Thus local governments are subject to ultimate control by the states. This imbalance of power means that state governments could legally dissolve local governments or force multiple local governments to consolidate into one large locality. Most states amended their own constitutions to give their larger cities **home rule**—a guarantee of noninterference in various areas of local affairs.[16] In recent years, as discussed below, some local governments have passed laws making policy on matters from minimum wage to public broadband, only to have state legislatures preempt, or remove, that authority, illustrating the degree to which local governments are creations of the state.

home rule power delegated by the state to a local unit of government to manage its own affairs

FEDERALISM IN PRACTICE

The formally enumerated powers of the national and state governments in the Constitution represent only part of the story. What makes the federal form of government relevant for the nature of American democracy is its shifting practice over time. As we'll see, the states dominated for the nation's first 140 years or so, with the federal government becoming much more important after the New Deal in the 1930s. Over the last 80 years, even as the trend has been toward centralization of government power, the states have asserted themselves at certain times and in certain policy areas, sometimes aided by the courts. But then at other moments a crisis shifts power toward the national government again, as during the Great Depression, the September 11, 2001, terror attacks, and the fiscal crisis that began in 2008. Federalism creates a complex, flexible form of government whose workings shift over time.

The Traditional System of Federalism

Consider how the relationship between the federal and state governments evolved during the nation's first 140 years

At the time of the Founding, the states far surpassed the federal government in their power to influence the lives of ordinary Americans. In the system of shared powers between the states and the federal government, the states were most active in economic and social regulation, while the federal government took a much more hands-off approach. Even so, the federal government gradually expanded its powers in the wake of important Supreme Court decisions. However, it was not until the New Deal in the 1930s that the federal government gained vast new powers.

RESTRAINING NATIONAL POWER WITH DUAL FEDERALISM

As we have noted, the Constitution created two layers of government: the national government and the state governments. The consequences of this **dual federalism** are fundamental to the American system of government; they have meant that states have done most of the fundamental governing. For evidence, look at Table 3.3, which lists the major types of public policies by which Americans were governed for the first century and a half under the Constitution. We call it the "traditional system" because it prevailed for much of American history.

dual federalism the system of government that prevailed in the United States from 1789 to 1937 in which most fundamental governmental powers were shared between the federal and state governments

Under the traditional system, the national government was quite small compared with both the state governments and the governments of other Western nations. It was also very narrowly specialized in the functions it performed. The national government built or sponsored the construction of roads, canals, and bridges (internal improvements). It provided cash subsidies to shippers and shipbuilders and distributed free or low-priced public land to encourage western settlement and business ventures. It placed relatively heavy taxes on imported goods (tariffs), not only to raise revenues but also to protect "infant industries" from competition from the more advanced European enterprises. It protected patents and provided for a common currency, which encouraged and facilitated enterprises and expanded markets.

What do these functions of the national government reveal? First, virtually all the functions were aimed at assisting commerce. Second, virtually none of the national

TABLE 3.3

The Federal System: Specialization of Governmental Functions in the Traditional System, 1789–1937

NATIONAL GOVERNMENT POLICIES (DOMESTIC)	STATE GOVERNMENT POLICIES	LOCAL GOVERNMENT POLICIES
Internal improvements	Property laws (including slavery)	Adaptation of state laws to local conditions
Subsidies	Estate and inheritance laws	Public works
Tariffs	Commerce laws	Contracts for public works
Public land disposal	Banking and credit laws	Licensing of public accommodation
Patents	Corporate laws	Zoning and other land-use regulation
Currency	Insurance laws	Basic public services
	Family laws	
	Morality laws	
	Public health laws	
	Education laws	
	General penal laws	
	Eminent domain laws	
	Construction codes	
	Land-use laws	
	Water and mineral laws	
	Criminal procedure laws	
	Electoral and political party laws	
	Local government laws	
	Civil service laws	
	Occupations and professions laws	

In 1815, President James Madison called for a federally funded program of "internal improvements," which was one of the few policy roles for the national government during the first half of the nineteenth century. By improving transportation through the construction of roads and canals, the government fostered the growth of the market economy and boosted federal power.

government's policies directly coerced citizens. The emphasis of governmental programs was on assistance, promotion, and encouragement—the allocation of land or capital to meet the needs of economic development.

Meanwhile, state legislatures were also actively involved in economic regulation during the nineteenth century. In the United States, then and now, private property exists only in state laws and in state court decisions regarding property, trespass, and real estate. American capitalism took its form from state property and trespass laws and from state laws and court decisions regarding contracts, markets, credit, banking, incorporation, and insurance. Laws concerning slavery were a subdivision of property law in states where slavery existed, though Article I, Section 2 of the Constitution (known as the fugitive slave clause) ensured that slavery would be protected even in free states. This clause obliged free states to return runaway slaves to the state from which they escaped (although it was rendered moot by the Thirteenth Amendment abolishing slavery). Even today, states control many policy areas, including the licensing of professions such as law and medicine, requirements for children's education, and, until recent decades, virtually all criminal laws—regarding everything from trespass to murder.

All this (and more, as shown in the middle column of Table 3.3) demonstrates that in the United States' first 150 years, most of the fundamental governing was done by the states. The contrast between national and state policies, as shown by Table 3.3, demonstrates the difference in the power vested in each. The list of items in the middle column could actually have been made longer. Moreover, each item on the list is a category of law that fills many volumes of statutes and court decisions.

By allowing state governments to do most of the fundamental governing, the Constitution saved the national government from many policy decisions that might have proven too divisive for a large and very young country. And the state and regional variation in policy the federal framework allows continues to facilitate governance in this large and diverse nation. The most fundamental impact of federalism on the way the United States is governed comes not from any particular provision of the Constitution but from the framework itself, which has determined which level of government does what and, through that, the political development of the country. As we shall see, some important aspects of federalism have changed, but the federal framework has survived two centuries and a devastating civil war.

FOR CRITICAL ANALYSIS

Which level of government had the most influence over citizens' lives when the country was founded? Why did this allocation of responsibilities make sense at the time?

FEDERALISM AND THE SLOW GROWTH OF THE NATIONAL GOVERNMENT'S POWER

As the nation grew, disputes arose about the powers of the federal government versus the powers of the states. In the first several decades after the Founding, the Supreme Court decided several critical cases that expanded federal powers and facilitated trade across the states. These decisions removed barriers to trade in the new nation and laid the groundwork for a national economy. However, by the end of the nineteenth century, as reformers began to enact laws regulating businesses through such measures as child labor restrictions, the Court took a much more restrictive view of federal power. Not until well into the New Deal in 1937 did the federal government gain the expansive powers it exercises today.

The Supreme Court's early decisions to expand federal power rested on its pro-national interpretation of Article I, Section 8 of the Constitution. That article enumerates the powers of Congress, including the power to tax, raise an army, declare war, establish post offices, and "regulate commerce with foreign nations, and among the several States and with the Indian tribes." This **commerce clause** would later form the basis for expansive federal government control over the economy, but its scope initially remained unclear.

commerce clause Article I, Section 8 of the Constitution, which delegates to Congress the power "to regulate commerce with foreign nations, and among the several States and with the Indian tribes"; this clause was interpreted by the Supreme Court in favor of national power over the economy

The Court's early decisions began to define national power by favoring federal control over the economy when there was a conflict between the states and the federal government. The first and most important such case was *McCulloch v. Maryland* (1819), which involved the question of whether Congress had the power to charter a national bank—an explicit grant of power nowhere to be found in Article I, Section 8.[17] Chief Justice John Marshall answered that this power could be "implied" from other powers that were expressly delegated to Congress, such as the "powers to lay and collect taxes; to borrow money; to regulate commerce; and to declare and conduct a war." Marshall's decision rested on the necessary and proper clause of Article I, Section 8, which gave Congress the power to enact laws "necessary and proper" for executing its substantive powers.

By allowing Congress to use the necessary and proper clause to interpret its delegated powers expansively, the Supreme Court created the potential for an unprecedented increase in national government power. Marshall also concluded that whenever a state law conflicted with a federal law (as in *McCulloch*), the state law would be deemed invalid since the Constitution states that "the Laws of the United States . . . shall be the supreme Law of the Land." Both parts of this great case are pro-national, yet Congress did not immediately seek to expand the policies of the national government.

Another major case, *Gibbons v. Ogden* (1824), reinforced this nationalistic interpretation of the Constitution. The important but relatively narrow issue was whether the state of New York could grant a monopoly to Robert Fulton's steamboat company to operate an exclusive service between New York and New Jersey. Chief Justice Marshall argued that New York State did not have the power to grant this particular monopoly, so Marshall had to define what Article I, Section 8 meant by "commerce among the several states." He insisted that the definition was "comprehensive," extending to "every species of commercial intercourse." However, this comprehensiveness was limited "to that commerce which concerns more states than one." *Gibbons* is important because it established the supremacy of the national government in all matters affecting what later came to be called "interstate commerce."[18] But the precise meaning of interstate commerce would remain uncertain during

In 1916 the national government passed the Keating-Owen Child Labor Act, which excluded from interstate commerce all goods manufactured by children under age 14. The act was ruled unconstitutional by the Supreme Court, and the regulation of child labor remained in the hands of state governments until the 1930s.

several decades of constitutional discourse. Backed by the implied-powers decision in *McCulloch* and by the broad definition of "interstate commerce" in *Gibbons*, Article I, Section 8 was a source of power for the national government as long as Congress sought to facilitate commerce through subsidies, services, and land grants.

Later in the nineteenth century, though, any effort of the national government to *regulate* commerce in such areas as fraud, the production of substandard goods, the use of child labor, or the existence of dangerous working conditions or long hours was declared unconstitutional by the Supreme Court as a violation of the concept of interstate commerce. Such legislation meant that the federal government was entering the factory and the workplace—local areas—and was attempting to regulate goods that had not yet passed into interstate commerce. To enter these local workplaces was to exercise police power—a power reserved to the states. No one questioned the power of the national government to regulate businesses that intrinsically involved interstate commerce, such as railroads, gas pipelines, and waterway transportation. But well into the twentieth century the Supreme Court used the concept of interstate commerce as a barrier against most efforts by Congress to regulate local conditions.

Thus, federalism, as interpreted by the Supreme Court for 70 years after the Civil War, made it possible for business to have its cake and eat it, too: entrepreneurs enjoyed the benefits of national policies facilitating commerce and were protected by the courts from policies regulating commerce by protecting the rights of consumers and workers.[19]

All this changed after 1937, when the Supreme Court issued a series of decisions that laid the groundwork for a much stronger federal government. Most significant was the Court's dramatic expansion of the commerce clause. By throwing out the old distinction between interstate and intrastate commerce, the Court converted the commerce clause from a source of limitations to a source of power for the national government. The Court upheld acts of Congress protecting the rights of employees to organize and engage in collective bargaining, regulating the amount of farmland in cultivation, extending low-interest credit to small businesses and farmers, and restricting the activities of corporations dealing in the stock market.[20] The Court also upheld many other laws that contributed to the construction of the "welfare state." With these rulings, the Court decisively signaled that the era of dual federalism was over. In the future, Congress would have very broad powers to regulate activity in the states.

Federalism in the Modern Era

Trace developments in the federal framework leading to a stronger national government

The economic crisis of the Great Depression and the nature of the government response signaled a new era in the age-old question of the meaning and operation of federalism in the United States. In this section we will look at how the balance of state and federal power has shifted since the 1930s, with growth in the size and scope of the federal government. We will examine the changing nature of federalism and the tools the federal government has used both to elicit state effort and to shape resultant state policy.

THE NEW DEAL AND WORLD WAR II: NEW ROLES FOR GOVERNMENT

The door to increased federal action opened when states proved unable to cope with the demands brought on by the Great Depression of the 1930s. Before this national economic catastrophe, states and localities took responsibility for addressing the needs of the poor, usually through private charity. But the extent of the depression quickly exhausted local and state capacities. By 1932, 25 percent of the workforce was unemployed. The jobless lost their homes and settled into camps all over the country, called "Hoovervilles," after President Herbert Hoover. Elected in 1928, the year before the depression hit, Hoover steadfastly maintained that the federal government could do little to alleviate the misery caused by the depression. It was a matter for state and local governments, he said.

Yet demands mounted for the federal government to take action. In Congress, some Democrats proposed that the federal government finance public works to aid the economy and put people back to work. Other members of Congress introduced legislation to provide federal grants to the states to assist them in their relief efforts. Most of these measures failed to win congressional approval or were vetoed by President Hoover.

When Franklin Delano Roosevelt took office in 1933, he energetically threw the federal government into the business of fighting the depression through a number of proposals known collectively as the New Deal. He proposed a variety of temporary measures to provide federal relief and work programs. Most of the programs he proposed were to be financed by the federal government but administered by the states. In addition to these temporary measures, Roosevelt presided over the creation of several important federal programs designed to provide future economic security for Americans. The New Deal signaled the rise of a more active national government.

The New Deal expanded the scope of the federal government. One of the largest and most effective New Deal programs, the Works Progress Administration (WPA) employed millions of Americans in projects such as constructing highways, bridges, and public parks.

FROM LAYER CAKE TO MARBLE CAKE: COOPERATIVE FEDERALISM AND THE USE OF CATEGORICAL GRANTS

For the most part, the new national programs that the Roosevelt administration developed did not directly take power away from the states. Instead, the national government

grants-in-aid programs through which Congress provides money to state and local governments on the condition that the funds be employed for purposes defined by the federal government

typically redirected states by offering them **grants-in-aid**, whereby Congress appropriates money to state and local governments on the condition that the money be spent for a particular purpose defined by Congress (see Figure 3.2). Franklin Roosevelt's New Deal expanded the range of grants-in-aid into social programs, providing grants to the states for financial assistance to poor children. Congress added more grants after World War II, creating new programs to help states fund activities such as providing school lunches and building highways. Sometimes the national government required state or local governments to match the national contribution dollar for dollar, but in some programs, such as the development of the interstate highway system, the congressional grants provided 90 percent of the cost of the program.

FIGURE 3.2

Historical Trend of Federal Grants-in-Aid,* 1950–2019 (in billions of dollars)

Spending on federal grants-in-aid to the states and local governments has grown dramatically since 1990. These increases reflect the growing public expectations about what government should do. What has been the most important cause of the steady increase in these grants?

*Excludes outlays for national defense, international affairs, and net interest.
**Estimate.
†Data in constant (fiscal year 2009) dollars.

SOURCE: Office of Management and Budget, U.S. Budget for Fiscal Year 2019, "Historical Tables: Table 12.1, Summary Comparison of Total Outlays for Grants to State and Local Governments: 1940–2023," www.whitehouse.gov/omb/historical-tables/ (accessed 6/8/18).

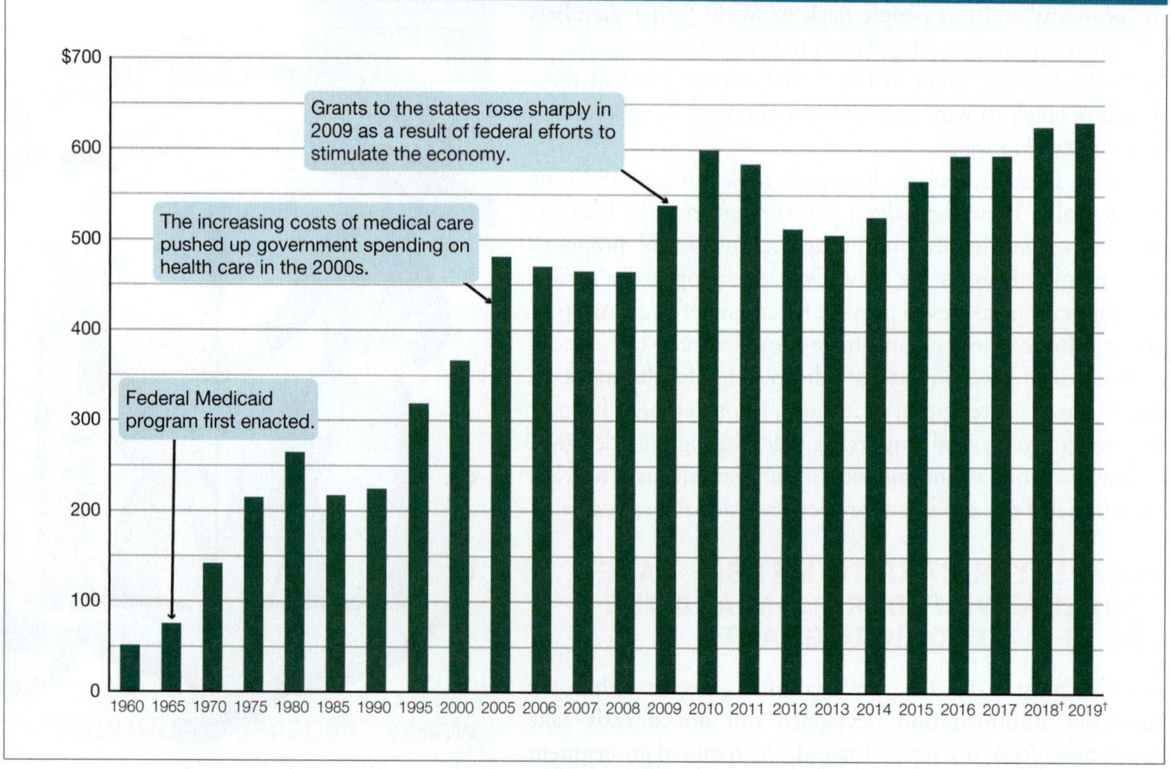

These types of federal grants-in-aid are called **categorical grants** because the national government determines the purposes, or categories, for which the money can be used. For the most part, the categorical grants created before the 1960s simply helped the states perform their traditional functions.[21] During the 1960s, however, the national role expanded and the number of categorical grants increased dramatically.[22] The grants authorized during the 1960s announced national purposes much more strongly than did earlier grants. One of the most important—and expensive—was the federal Medicaid program, which provides states with grants to pay for medical care for the poor, the disabled, and many nursing home residents. Over time the *value* of categorical grants has risen dramatically, increasing from $2.3 billion in 1950 to an estimated $675 billion in 2017.

categorical grants congressional grants given to states and localities on the condition that expenditures be limited to a problem or group specified by law

The growth of categorical grants created a new kind of federalism. If the traditional system of two sovereigns performing highly different functions could be called dual federalism, historians of federalism suggest that the system since the New Deal could be called **cooperative federalism**. The political scientist Morton Grodzins characterized this as a move from "layer cake federalism" to "marble cake federalism,"[23] in which intergovernmental cooperation and sharing have blurred a once-clear distinguishing line, making it difficult to say where the national government ends and the state and local governments begin (see Figure 3.3). Figure 3.4 demonstrates the financial basis of the "marble-cake" idea.

cooperative federalism a type of federalism existing since the New Deal era in which grants-in-aid have been used strategically to encourage states and localities (without commanding them) to pursue nationally defined goals; also known as *intergovernmental cooperation*

As important as the states were in this new system of grants, some new federal grants, particularly during the War on Poverty of the 1960s, bypassed the states and instead sent money directly to local governments and even to local nonprofit organizations. The theme heard repeatedly in Washington was that the states simply could not be trusted to carry out national purposes.[24]

One of the reasons that Washington distrusted the states was the way African American citizens were treated in the South. The southern states' forthright defense of segregation, justified on the grounds of states' rights, helped tarnish the image of the states as the civil rights movement gained momentum. The national officials who planned the War on Poverty pointed to the racially exclusionary practices of the southern states as a reason for bypassing state governments. The political scientist James Sundquist described their thinking: "In the drafting of the Economic

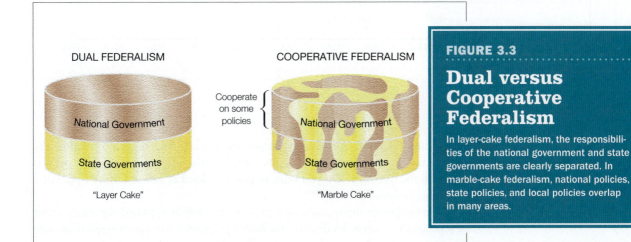

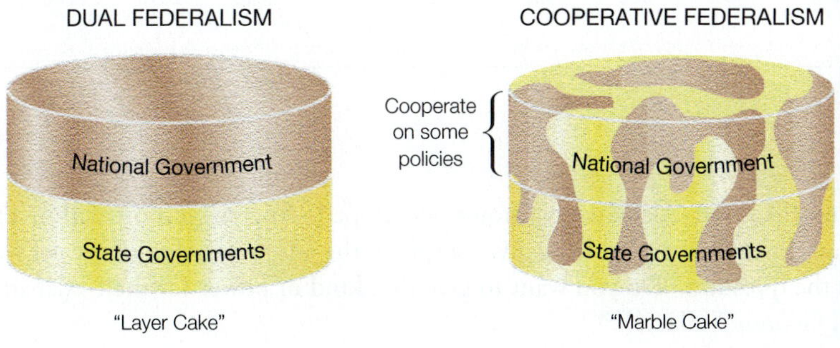

FIGURE 3.3

Dual versus Cooperative Federalism

In layer-cake federalism, the responsibilities of the national government and state governments are clearly separated. In marble-cake federalism, national policies, state policies, and local policies overlap in many areas.

FIGURE 3.4

The Rise, Decline, and Recovery of Federal Aid, 1960–2019*

The level of federal aid has varied over the past several decades as program costs and politics have affected the role the national government plays in funding state and local services. The data in this figure show the rise, decline, and recovery of federal aid. What factors contributed to each of these trends?

*Excludes national defense, international affairs, net interest, and undistributed offsetting receipts. Data for 2018 and 2019 are estimated.
**Estimates for state and local expenditures in 2018 and 2019 are not available.

SOURCES: Office of Management and Budget, U.S. Budget for Fiscal Year 2019, Analytical Perspectives, Table 14-2, "Trends in Federal Grants to State and Local Governments," www.whitehouse.gov/wp-content/uploads/2018/02/spec-fy2019.pdf (accessed 6/8/18). Government Publishing Office, Budget of the United States Government, www.gpo.gov/fdsys/browse/collectionGPO.action?collectionCode=BUDGET (accessed 4/13/16).

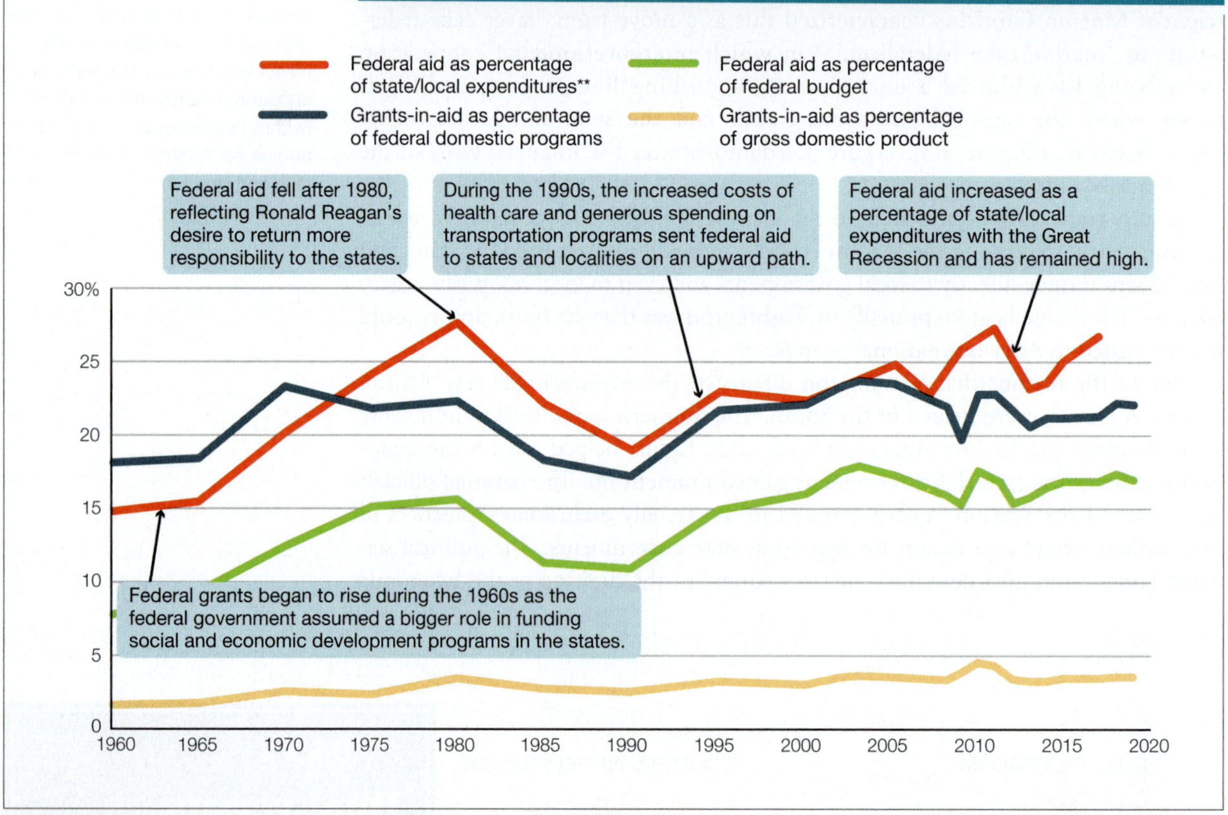

Federal aid as percentage of state/local expenditures**
Federal aid as percentage of federal budget
Grants-in-aid as percentage of federal domestic programs
Grants-in-aid as percentage of gross domestic product
Federal aid fell after 1980, reflecting Ronald Reagan's desire to return more responsibility to the states.
During the 1990s, the increased costs of health care and generous spending on transportation programs sent federal aid to states and localities on an upward path.
Federal aid increased as a percentage of state/local expenditures with the Great Recession and has remained high.
Federal grants began to rise during the 1960s as the federal government assumed a bigger role in funding social and economic development programs in the states.
30%
25
20
15
10
5
0
1960
1965
1970
1975
1980
1985
1990
1995
2000
2005
2010
2015
2020

Opportunity Act, an 'Alabama syndrome' developed. Any suggestion within the poverty task force that the states be given a role in the administration of the act was met with the question, 'Do you want to give that kind of power to [then–Alabama governor] George Wallace?'"[25]

Yet even though many national policies of the 1960s bypassed the states, other new programs, such as Medicaid—the health program for the poor—relied on state governments for their implementation. In addition, as the national government expanded existing programs run by the states, states had to take on more responsibilities. These new responsibilities meant that the states were playing a critical role in the federal system.

NATIONAL STANDARDS, REGULATION, AND PREEMPTION

Giving policy responsibilities to states introduces the possibility of variation and raises questions about how different things should be when one crosses a state line, or in what policy areas it is acceptable for states to differ. Supreme Court decisions about the fundamental rights of American citizens have provided important answers to these questions, typically pushing for greater uniformity across the states. But in other policy areas, national government has at times provided incentives or imposed rules in order to create greater uniformity.

Federal grants, as we have seen, are one such tool: Congress provides an incentive by giving money to state and local governments if they agree to spend it for the purposes Congress specifies. But as Congress in the 1970s began to enact legislation in new areas, such as environmental policy, it resorted to another tool: regulations on states and localities. Some political scientists call this a move toward **regulated federalism**.[26] The national government began to set standards of conduct or to require the states to set standards that met national guidelines. The effect of these national standards is that state and local policies in the areas of environmental protection, social services, and education are more uniform from coast to coast than are other nationally funded policies.

regulated federalism a form of federalism in which Congress imposes legislation on states and localities, requiring them to meet national standards

Some national standards require the federal government to take over areas of regulation formerly overseen by state or local governments. Such **preemption** occurs when state and local actions are found to be inconsistent with federal requirements. In some cases, federal laws and regulations are more stringent than state laws. In the 1970s, preemptions required the states to abide by tougher federal rules in policies as diverse as air and water pollution, occupational health and safety, and access for the disabled. The regulated industries often oppose such laws because they increase the cost of doing business. After 1994, when Republicans retook control of Congress, the federal government used its preemption power in business's favor, limiting the ability of states to tax and regulate industry. For example, the Internet Tax Freedom Act, first enacted by Congress in 1998 and subsequently renewed, prohibits states and localities from taxing internet access services.

preemption the principle that allows the national government to override state or local actions in certain policy areas; in foreign policy, the willingness to strike first in order to prevent an enemy attack

Congress is not the only federal body that can preempt the states; federal regulatory agencies can also issue rules that override state law. One controversial case involved a 2006 Food and Drug Administration drug-labeling rule preempting state laws that allow individuals to sue drug companies in state courts. Opponents—many of them trial lawyers—charged that such rules amounted to "stealth preemption" that "will deprive consumers of their right to hold negligent corporations accountable for injuries caused by defective products."[27] Supporters claimed that the rules were a proper use of federal authority.

State and local governments often contest federal preemptions. For example, in 2001, Attorney General John Ashcroft declared that Oregon's law permitting doctor-assisted suicide was illegal under federal drug regulations. The state, a physician, a pharmacist, and several terminally ill state residents challenged Ashcroft's rule, and in January 2006 the Supreme Court ruled in a 6–3 vote that the attorney general did not have the authority to outlaw the Oregon law.[28] Individuals have also challenged federal preemption. In 2009 the Supreme Court ruled against a drug manufacturer and in favor of a woman whose arm had to be amputated after she was improperly

FOR CRITICAL ANALYSIS

When is federal preemption of local laws desirable? Is preemption justified for some issues more than for others?

injected with a drug designed to counter nausea.[29] Although the drug company knew that such complications could arise, it argued that it was not responsible for the amputation because federal regulations did not require it to warn against this danger in labeling the drug. The Court, however, found the company liable for the damage. In its decision, the Court made it clear that federal regulations could not preempt state consumer protections and that states had the power to adopt stricter protections than those of the federal government.

In 2009, after only a few months in office, President Obama reversed the George W. Bush administration's use of federal regulations to limit state laws. Under the new policy, federal regulations should preempt state laws only in extraordinary cases. The president directed agency leaders to review the regulations that had been put in place over the previous 10 years and consider amending them if they interfered with the "legitimate prerogatives of the states."[30] But as we will see, the Obama administration did use its power of preemption to challenge state immigration laws, charging that states were making laws in a domain reserved for federal authority. The Trump administration has moved in the opposite direction. California has long had more stringent vehicle emissions and mileage targets than the federal government, but a Trump administration proposal would revoke the ability of any state to set rules different from federal levels.[31] In May 2018, California and 16 other states sued the Trump administration to keep the stricter regulations in place.

Evolving Role of the States

Analyze the changing role of the states in the federal framework

The federal government's fluid strategies vis-à-vis the states—from cooperating with them to regulating them—raise the question of the appropriate role for the states in the federal system. Do some divisions of responsibility between states and the federal government work better than others? Might states be sources of experimentation and innovation, the "laboratories of democracy" that Supreme Court Justice Louis Brandeis suggested?[32] Which responsibilities are states administratively and fiscally capable of carrying out? And what are the implications of the variation across the nation that might result from having states determine policy? States are sovereign actors in the federal system. In addition to receiving funding from the national government, they raise their own revenues. They make policy in a number of areas and decide which policy areas lower levels of government such as cities and counties can control. Forty-nine states have to balance their budgets, unlike the federal government, which can run budget deficits. Hence states embody both the promise and the constraints of a federal form of government.

FOR CRITICAL ANALYSIS

How have Supreme Court decisions affected the balance of power between the federal government and the states? Has the Supreme Court favored the federal government or the states?

STATES' RIGHTS

The Tenth Amendment, which reserves to the states the powers the Constitution does not specifically delegate to the national government, has been used over the decades by different groups, for different purposes, to bolster the role of the states in the federal system. For much of the nineteenth century, when federal power remained limited, the Tenth Amendment was used to argue in favor of **states' rights**, which in their extreme version claimed that the states did not have to submit to national laws whenever they believed the national government had exceeded its authority. Prior to

states' rights the principle that the states should oppose the increasing authority of the national government; this principle was most popular in the period before the Civil War the Civil War, sharp differences between the North and the South over tariffs and slavery gave rise to arguments supporting nullification. Most fully articulated by John C. Calhoun, vice president under Andrew Jackson and later a senator from South Carolina, the doctrine of nullification proposed that states were not bound by federal laws that they considered unconstitutional. Such arguments were voiced less often after the Civil War, but the Supreme Court continued to use the Tenth Amendment to strike down laws that it thought exceeded national power, including the Civil Rights Act passed in 1875, which would have eliminated discrimination against African Americans in public accommodations and transportation.

In 1995 the Supreme Court ruled that the Gun-Free School Zones Act was an unconstitutional application of the commerce clause, leaving this area of regulation to the states. In striking down a federal law, the Supreme Court ruled that regulating guns near schools is a state prerogative.

By the late 1930s, although the Supreme Court had struck down some national regulations limiting the power of large corporations and preserving the health and welfare of citizens, the overall direction of the Court's decisions expanded federal power. Indeed, so much so that the Tenth Amendment appeared irrelevant. In 1941, Justice Harlan Fiske Stone declared that the Tenth Amendment was simply a "truism," that it had no real meaning.[33]

Yet the idea that some powers should be reserved to the states did not go away. One reason is that groups with substantive policy interests often support states' rights as a means for achieving their policy goals. For example, in the 1950s, southern opponents of the civil rights movement revived the idea of states' rights to support racial segregation. In 1956, 96 southern members of Congress issued a "Southern manifesto" in which they declared that southern states were not constitutionally bound by Supreme Court decisions outlawing racial segregation. They believed that states' rights should override individual rights to liberty and formal equality. With the eventual triumph of the civil rights movement, the slogan of "states' rights" became tarnished by its association with racial inequality.

The 1990s saw a revival of interest in the Tenth Amendment and important Supreme Court decisions limiting federal power. Much of the interest in the Tenth Amendment stemmed from conservatives who believed that a strong federal government encroached on individual liberties. They believed such freedoms were better protected by returning more power to the states through the process of devolution, as we'll see later.[34] The Supreme Court's 1995 ruling in *United States v. Lopez* fueled further interest in the Tenth Amendment.[35] In that case, the Court, stating that Congress had exceeded its authority under the commerce clause, struck down a federal law that barred handguns near schools. This was the first time since the New Deal that the Court had limited congressional powers in this way. In 1997 the Court again relied on the Tenth Amendment to limit federal power in *Printz v. United States*.[36] The decision declared unconstitutional a provision of the Brady Handgun Violence Prevention Act that required state and local law-enforcement officials to conduct background checks on handgun purchasers. The Court declared that this provision violated state sovereignty guaranteed by the Tenth Amendment because it required state and local officials to administer a federal regulatory program.

Thus, the expansion of the power of the national government since the 1930s has not left the states powerless. State governments continue to make important laws. No better demonstration of the continuing influence of the federal framework can be offered than that in the middle column of Table 3.3, which is still a fairly accurate characterization of state government today. In each of these domains, however, states must now share power with the federal government.

John C. Calhoun, one of the most prominent advocates of states' rights, argued that states should have the right to veto any federal law they found to be unconstitutional.

DEVOLUTION

devolution a policy to remove a program from one level of government by delegating it or passing it down to a lower level of government, such as from the national government to the state and local governments

diffusion policy decisions in one political jurisdiction are influenced by choices made in another jurisdiction

block grants federal grants-in-aid that allow states considerable discretion in how the funds are spent

New Federalism attempts by presidents Nixon and Reagan to return power to the states through block grants

general revenue sharing the process by which one unit of government yields a portion of its tax income to another unit of government, according to an established formula; revenue sharing typically involves the national government providing money to state governments

Since the 1970s, as states became more capable of administering large-scale programs, the idea of **devolution**—transferring responsibility for policy from the federal government to the states and localities—has become popular. Proponents of devolution champion states' potential as innovators and experimenters, whose good ideas might spread horizontally to other states and even vertically to the federal government through policy **diffusion**. Devolution's supporters also assert that government closer to the people can better tailor policies to local needs than can the federal government in far-off Washington, D.C. Political conservatives have been the chief proponents of such views, but as we will see later, there is some expedience to views about federalism that depend on which party controls which levels of government.

Block Grants as a Tool of Devolution Proponents of more state authority have looked to **block grants** as a way of reducing federal control. Block grants are federal grants that allow the states considerable leeway in spending federal money. President Nixon led the first push for block grants in the early 1970s, as part of his **New Federalism**. Nixon's approach consolidated programs in the areas of job training, community development, and social services into three large block grants. These grants imposed some conditions on states and localities as to how the money should be spent, but not the narrow regulations contained in categorical grants. In addition, Congress provided an important new form of federal assistance to state and local governments, called **general revenue sharing**. Revenue sharing provided money to local governments and counties with no strings attached; localities could spend the money as they wished. (see Figure 3.5)

In his version of the New Federalism in the 1980s, President Reagan also looked to block grants to reduce the national government's control and return power to the states. But unlike Nixon, he used them to cut federal spending as well. General revenue sharing ended—members of Congress never liked it because they couldn't claim credit for projects implemented by state and local officials—and the 12 new

FIGURE 3.5

Regulated versus New Federalism

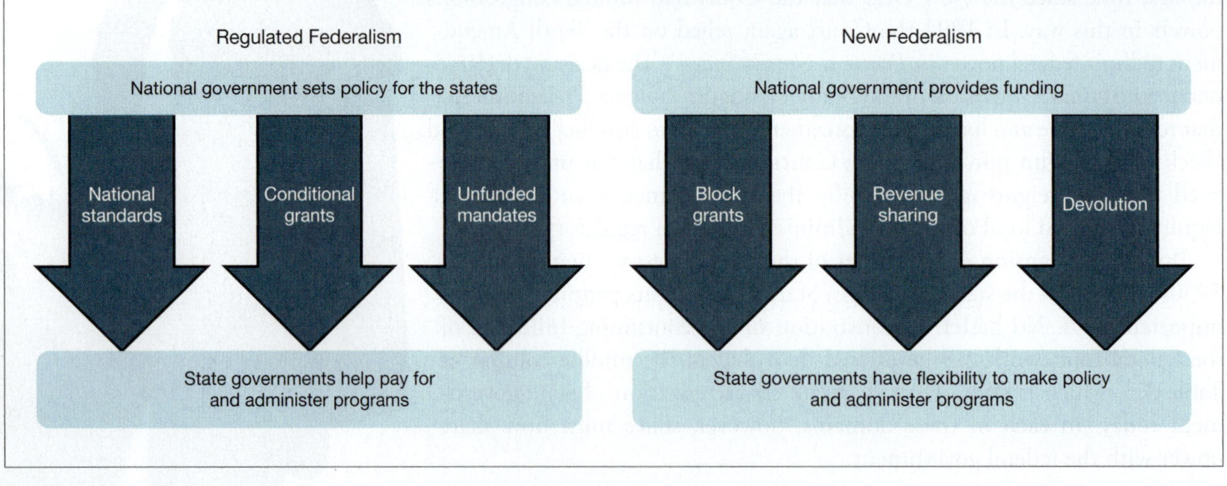
Regulated Federalism
National government sets policy for the states
National standards
Conditional grants
Unfunded mandates
State governments help pay for and administer programs
New Federalism
National government provides funding
Block grants
Revenue sharing
Devolution
State governments have flexibility to make policy and administer programs

AMERICA SIDE by SIDE

Cooperative Federalism: Competition or a Check on Power?

While the United States has evolved into a system of cooperative federalism, some democracies began that way. Germany's constitution, adopted in 1949, was designed to use a cooperative federal system to help prevent the abuses of central government power seen in Hitler's Germany. For example, the upper house of the German parliament comprises delegates from the *Länder* ("states") governments, giving the states an official check on all national policy.

The most interesting blending of power, however, is in taxation and spending. Unlike U.S. states, German states and local governments have no taxation powers, making them fully dependent on federal funding. However, German states are responsible for implementing most government policy. As a result, almost two-thirds of German government spending is carried out by states and local governments, compared to less than half of U.S. spending. This emphasis on local spending includes the running of Germany's extensive social security program, a complex system carried out at the national, state, and local levels. In the United States, comparable social spending is both carried out and financed by national, state, and local government or is left to Americans to pay out of pocket.

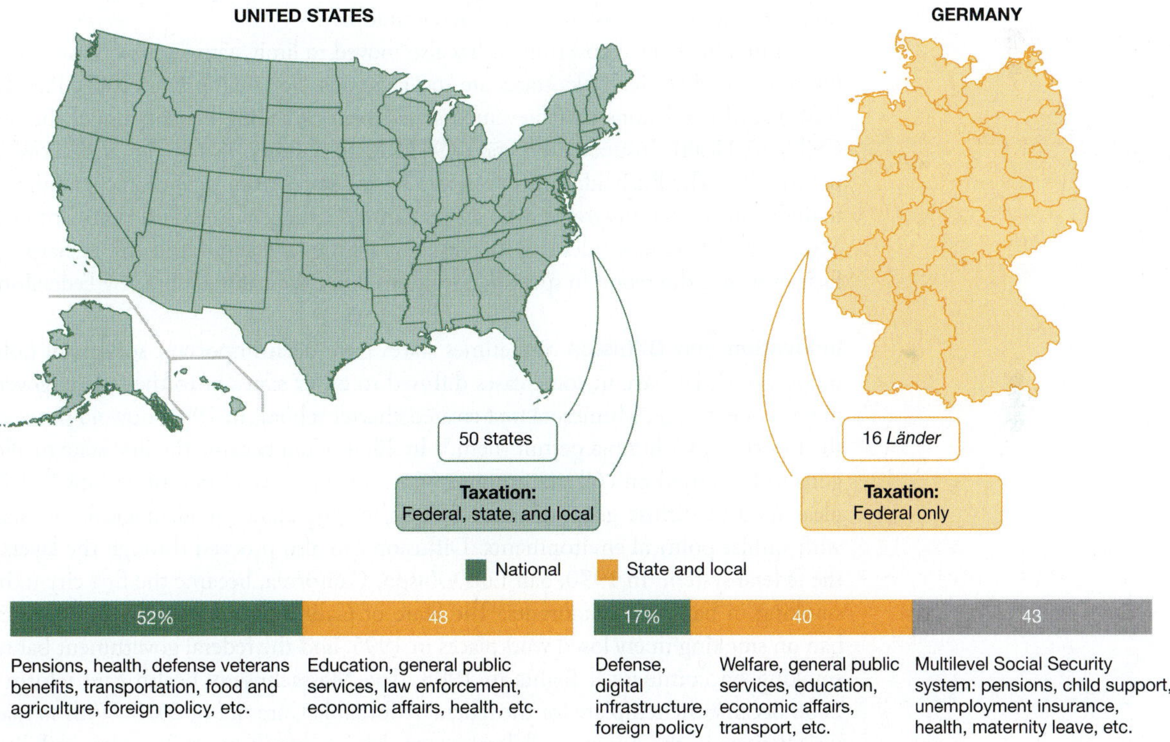

SOURCE: OECD, "Figure 2.42. Distribution of general government expenditures across levels of government, 2015 and 2016," Government at a Glance 2017, www .oecd-ilibrary.org/governance/government-at-a-glance-2017_gov_glance-2017-en; "Regional Policy Profile: United States," www.oecd.org/regional/regional-policy/ profile-United-States.pdf and "Regional Policy Profile: Germany," www.oecd.org/regional/regional-policy/profile-Germnay.pdf (acessed 6/7/18).

block grants enacted between 1981 and 1990 cut federal spending in those areas by 12 percent.[37] Reagan's view was that states could spend their own funds to make up the difference if they chose to do so.

The Republican Congress elected in 1994 attempted to take the devolution strategy even further, continuing to support block grants and proposing substantial cuts in federal programs. Their biggest success was the 1996 welfare reform law, which delegated to states important new responsibilities. Most of the other major proposed block grants or spending reductions, however, failed to pass Congress or were vetoed by President Clinton.[38]

Trade-Offs of State Control Neither block grants nor reduced federal funding have proven to be magic solutions to the problems of federalism. For one thing, there is always a trade-off between accountability—that is, whether the states are using funds for the purposes intended—and flexibility. If the objective is to have accountable and efficient government, it is not clear that state bureaucracies are any more efficient or more capable than national agencies. In Mississippi, for example, the state Department of Human Services spent money from the child care block grant for office furniture and designer salt and pepper shakers that cost $37.50 a pair. As one Mississippi state legislator said, "I've seen too many years of good ol' boy politics to know they shouldn't [transfer money to the states] without stricter controls and requirements."[39] Even after block grants were created, Congress reimposed regulations in order to increase the states' accountability.

At times the federal government has also moved to limit state discretion over spending in cases where it thinks states are too generous. For example, in 2007, President Bush issued regulations that prevented states from providing benefits under the State Children's Health Insurance Program (SCHIP) to children in families well above the poverty line. The Bush administration also barred states from providing chemotherapy to undocumented immigrants, who are guaranteed emergency medical treatment under Medicaid.[40] These new rules embroiled states and the federal government in sharp conflicts over state discretion in spending decisions, once the hallmark of New Federalism.

Innovation and Diffusion Sometimes states have been important sources of policy innovations that have in some cases diffused to other states or to the federal government. For example, Minnesota first created charter schools in 1991; now 44 states and the District of Columbia permit them.[41] In 2004, Utah became the first state to allow guns to be carried on college campuses; now 12 states have such provisions.[42] Policy ideas tend to diffuse geographically to neighboring states or ideologically to states with similar political environments. Diffusion can also proceed through the layers of the federal system. In 1990, San Luis Obispo, California, became the first city to ban smoking in bars and restaurants. The State of California followed with a statewide ban on smoking in enclosed workplaces in 1995, and the federal government banned smoking on commercial flights in 1998. The Massachusetts health care reform of 2006 became the template for the federal Affordable Care Act of 2010. With so many jurisdictions in the American federal system having significant policy responsibilities, the possibilities for generating and disseminating new ideas are endless.

States and Fiscal Constraint One reason states have been such important sources of innovation is the creativity spurred by fiscal constraint. The states raise their own revenue, in addition to receiving federal funds, and operate under stringent fiscal constraints. Forty-nine states have legal or constitutional provisions requiring their proposed budgets to balance; most are also prohibited from carrying deficits into the next fiscal year.[43] Both the growth of national standards and devolution have created fiscal challenges for states and heightened questions about which level of government should pay for various public priorities.

One problem that emerged in the 1970s and especially in the 1980s was the increase in **unfunded mandates**—the product of a Democratic Congress that wanted to achieve liberal social objectives and Republican presidents who opposed increased social spending. For example, the 1973 Rehabilitation Act prohibited discrimination against the disabled in programs that were partly funded by the federal government. The new law required state and local governments to make public transit accessible to disabled people with wheelchair lifts in buses, elevators in train stations, and special transportation systems where needed. These requirements were estimated to cost state and local governments $6.8 billion over 30 years.[44] But Congress did not supply additional funding to help states meet these new requirements; the states had to shoulder the increased financial burden themselves. Between 1983 and 1991, Congress mandated standards in many policy areas, including social services and environmental regulations, without providing additional funds to help the states meet those standards. Altogether, Congress enacted 27 laws that imposed new regulations or required states to expand existing programs.[45]

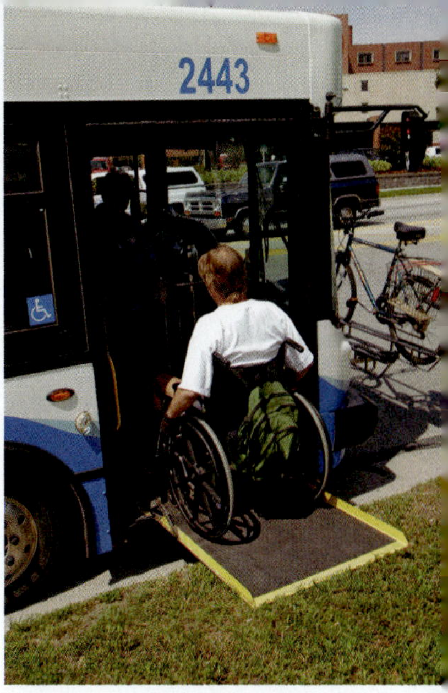

The federal government frequently passes laws that impose mandates on the states, such as the 1990 Americans with Disabilities Act, which protects against discrimination based on disability. States were required to pay for changes to meet federal standards for accessibility in public transportation and public facilities.

unfunded mandate a law or regulation requiring a state or local government to perform certain actions without providing funding for fulfilling the requirement

States and localities quickly began to protest the cost of unfunded mandates, complaining that they were unable to set their own priorities due to the unreimbursed costs. These burdens became part of a rallying cry to reduce the power of the federal government—a cry that took center stage in 1994 when a Republican Congress was elected. One of the first measures the new Congress passed was an act to limit the cost of unfunded mandates, the Unfunded Mandates Reform Act (UMRA). Under this law, the Congressional Budget Office must assess the cost of any mandate that it believes would exceed the threshold established in UMRA ($76 million in 2014 adjusted for inflation). Bills that would impose sizable costs on the private sector must also be assessed. The goal is to ensure that Congress knows how much it is expecting of state and local governments and the private sector. Congress must identify funding sources for bills that exceed the threshold established in UMRA. Of all public laws enacted since 1996, fewer than 5 percent have included private-sector mandates with costs estimated to exceed the threshold, while fewer than 1 percent have contained intergovernmental mandates (mandates on state or local governments) with such costs.[46]

Recently, concern about unfunded mandates has arisen around health care reform. The major health care reform enacted under President Obama, the Affordable Care Act of 2010, called for a major expansion of Medicaid. Because Medicaid is partly funded by the states, any major increase in the number of Medicaid recipients could impose a significant fiscal burden on the states. Although the ACA provided additional federal aid to support the new requirements, the Medicaid provisions became a target for state challenges to the health care law. One of the central claims in the 26 states' lawsuits charged that the federal government did not have the power to withhold Medicaid funds from states that did not implement the new expansions.[47] The Supreme Court ultimately ruled that states could decline to expand Medicaid coverage without losing their existing Medicaid funds. After the Court's decision, 25 states, all led by Republican governors, announced that they would not implement the expanded coverage. Some began to reconsider this decision. By late 2018, 36 states plus the District of Columbia had decided to expand Medicaid, and 14 had decided to not expand.[48] It is clear that in programs where the national and state governments share responsibility, the question of who pays remains acute.

FOR CRITICAL ANALYSIS

Should states be required to implement unfunded mandates? How much of the funding should the federal government provide for policies or standards that it sets?

DEVOLUTION: FOR WHOSE BENEFIT?

As Figure 3.6 indicates, federalism has changed dramatically over the course of American history. Finding the right balance among states and the federal government is an evolving challenge for American democracy, and since the expansion of the national government in the 1930s, questions about "who does what" have frequently provoked conflict. Why does such an apparently simple choice set off such highly charged political debate? One reason is that many decisions about federal-versus-state responsibility have implications for who benefits from government action.

redistributive programs economic policies designed to transfer income through taxing and spending, with the goal of benefiting the poor

Let's consider the benefits of federal control versus devolution in the realm of **redistributive programs**—programs designed primarily for the benefit of the poor. Many political scientists and economists maintain that states and localities should not be in charge of redistributive programs. They argue that since states and local governments have to compete with one another, they do not have the incentive to spend their money on the needy people in their areas. Instead, they want to keep taxes low and spend money on things that promote economic development.[49] In this situation, states might engage in a "race to the bottom": if one state cuts assistance to the poor, neighboring states will institute similar or deeper cuts both to reduce expenditures and to discourage poorer people from moving to their states. As one New York legislator put it, "The concern we have is that unless we make our welfare system and our tax and regulatory system competitive with the states around us, we will have too many disincentives for business to move here. Welfare is a big part of that."[50]

In 1996, when Congress enacted major welfare reform, it followed a different logic. By changing welfare from a combined federal–state program into a block grant to the states, Congress gave the states more responsibility for programs that serve the poor. Supporters of the change hoped to reduce welfare spending and argued that states could act as laboratories of democracy by experimenting with many different approaches in order to find those that best met the needs of their citizens. As states altered their welfare programs in the wake of the new law, they did indeed design diverse approaches. For example, Minnesota adopted an incentive-based approach that offers extra assistance to families that take low-wage jobs, while six other states imposed very strict time limits on receiving benefits, allowing welfare recipients less than the five-year limit in the federal legislation. After the passage of the law, welfare rolls declined dramatically. On average, they declined by more than half from their peak in 1994. In 12 states the decline was 70 percent or higher. Politicians have cited these statistics to claim that the poor have benefited from greater state control of welfare, yet most studies have found that the majority of those leaving welfare remain in poverty.

More broadly, devolution and state control in areas such as redistributive policy has resulted in substantial interstate variation in program rules. As of 2018

FIGURE 3.6

The Changing Federal Framework

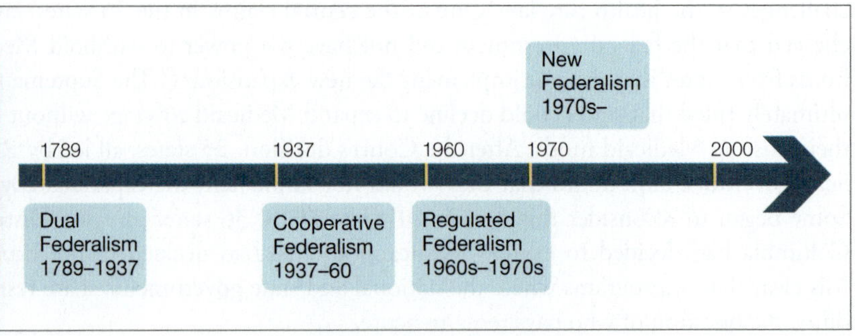

cash welfare benefits for a family of three are $714 in California, $462 in Colorado, and $290 in Texas.[51] The lifetime limit for receiving welfare benefits is 60 months in most states, but 48 months in Michigan, 21 months in Connecticut, and 12 months in Arizona.[52] Under federal Medicaid rules, dental and vision services are required for children but optional for adults. In most states Medicaid does not cover eyeglasses for adults, but in Texas it does. Utah provides eyeglasses only to pregnant Medicaid recipients, while Tennessee provides them only after cataract surgery. Most Medicaid adults do not have dental care coverage; they can get cavities filled in Massachusetts, but only in the front twelve teeth, not in the molars.[53] Whether one is eligible, under what criteria, and for which benefits vary widely across states; the same person could be eligible in one state but not another, or could receive a differing level of assistance depending on where they live. These differences in policy parameters arise from differences in state wealth and political environment.[54]

In some decisions about federalism, local concerns are overridden in the name of the national interest. The question of speed limits, traditionally a state and local responsibility, provides an example. In 1973, at the height of the oil shortage, Congress passed legislation to withhold federal highway funds from states that did not adopt a maximum speed limit of 55 miles per hour in order to reduce fuel consumption. Although Congress had not formally taken over the authority to set speed limits, the power of its purse was so important that every state adopted the new speed limit. As the crisis faded, concern about energy conservation diminished. The national speed limit lost much of its support, even though it was found to have reduced the number of traffic deaths. In 1995, Congress repealed the penalties for higher speed limits, and states once again became free to set their own speed limits. Many states with large rural areas raised their maximum to 75 miles per hour; Montana initially set unlimited speeds in its rural areas during daylight hours. Research indicates that the number of highway deaths has indeed risen in the states that increased the limits.[55]

Because the division of responsibility in the federal system has important implications for who benefits, few conflicts over state-versus-national control will ever be settled once and for all. New evidence about the costs and benefits of different arrangements provides fuel for ongoing debates about what are properly the states' responsibilities

The debate over national-versus-state control of speed limits arose in 1973, when gas prices skyrocketed and supplies became scarce. Drivers nationwide were forced to wait in long lines at gas stations. The federal government responded to the gas crisis by instituting a national 55-mile-per-hour speed limit. In 1995, Congress removed its speed limit restrictions and allowed states to raise the limit above 55 miles per hour without losing federal highway funds.

and what the federal government should do. Likewise, changes in the political control of the national government usually provoke a rethinking of responsibilities as new leaders seek to alter federal arrangements for the benefit of the groups they represent.

The Politics of Federalism Today

Analyze contemporary relationships among national, state, and local governments

Since the year 2000, the political polarization between Republicans and Democrats that has characterized national politics and divided states has been played out through the federal system as well. Not all decisions about federalism have divided along political lines. But many of the most controversial issues in American politics—including the appropriate amount of public social spending, the rights and benefits of immigrants (legal and undocumented), government response to global climate change, and questions about whether and how government should regulate business and moral behavior—have been fought through the federal system. Politicians of all stripes have regularly turned to the federal government to override policies they don't like that were made at the state level. The reverse is also true: when the federal government proves unable or unwilling to act, activists and politicians instead try to achieve their goals in states and localities. Sometimes, states seek to go their own way regardless of federal law. It is often then up to the courts to decide which level of government should have the final say. In many cases, the federal government has succeeded in advancing its policy agenda through the states. However, the era since 2000 has been marked by a considerable amount of back-and-forth between the states, the federal government, and even localities as debates over federalism have become politically prominent.

EXPEDIENCY VERSUS IDEOLOGY IN FEDERALISM

FOR CRITICAL ANALYSIS

The role of the national government has changed significantly from the Founding era to the present. Do you think the framers of the Constitution would be pleased with the current balance of power between the national government and the state governments?

Although conservatives proclaim their preference for a small federal government and their support for more state autonomy, in fact they often expand the federal government and limit state autonomy. During the presidency of George W. Bush, the growth of government; the activist, free-spending Republican Congress; and a series of Supreme Court rulings supporting federal power over the states made it clear that conservatives do not always support small government, nor do they always favor returning power to the states. Once in power, many conservatives discovered not only that they needed a strong federal government to respond to public demands but also that they could use federal power to advance conservative policy goals.

For President Bush, the importance of a strong federal government dawned with force after the terrorist attacks in 2001. Aware that the American public was looking to Washington for protection, Bush worked with Congress to pass the USA PATRIOT Act, which greatly increased the surveillance powers of the federal government. A year later he created the enormous new federal Department of Homeland Security. Democrats supported the president in both initiatives. President Bush, with the support of Democrats, also expanded federal control and increased spending in policy areas far removed from concerns about security. The 2001 No Child Left Behind Act introduced unprecedented federal intervention in public education, traditionally a state and local responsibility. New, detailed federal testing requirements and provisions stipulating how states should treat failing schools were major expansions of federal authority in education. When a number of states

Who Benefits from Federal Spending?

Federal Grants to State and Local Governments, 2016

Although Americans often think they pay a lot in federal taxes, they receive much in return in the form of federal money for state and local programs. Federal outlays for grants to state and local governments have grown from $51.5 billion in 1960 to $593.5 billion in 2016 (in constant dollars).

Fiscal Transfers between the States and the Federal Government, 2015

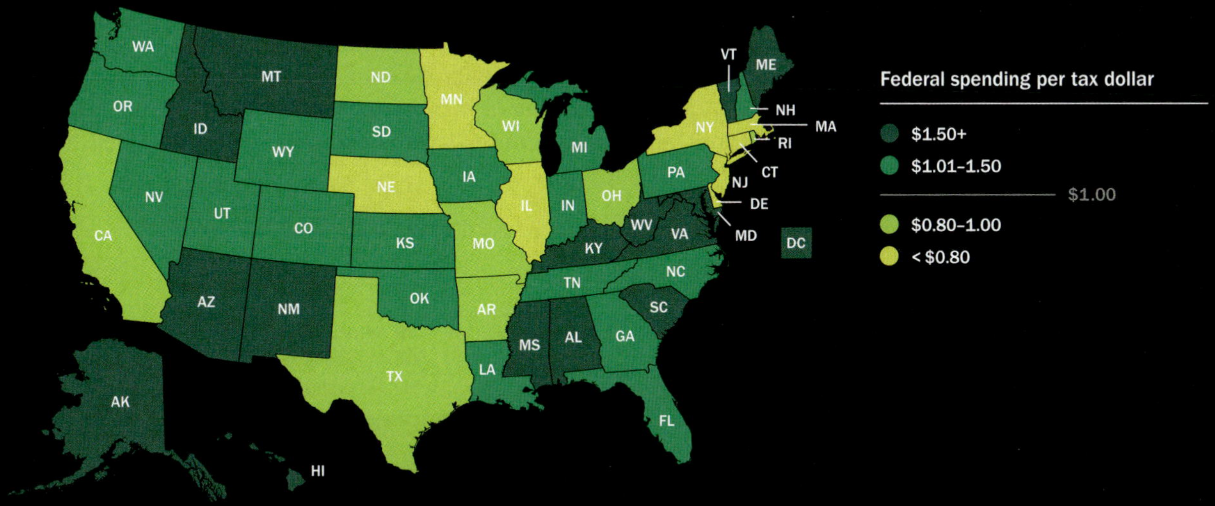

Every U.S. state contributes to the federal government through the federal taxes paid by the state's citizens, and every state receives money from federal spending. Federal spending is a broad category that includes the federal grants described above as well as spending on military bases and federal procurement. Not every state receives the same amount from the federal government, however. The map above shows how much federal spending each state received for each dollar paid in federal taxes in 2015.

SOURCES: Federal Grants to State and Local Governments: A Historical Perspective on Contemporary Issues, https://fas.org; Federal Spending in the States, 2015, http://knowledgecenter.csg.org; IRS 2015 Data Book, https://www.irs.gov, (accessed 3/16/18).

FOR CRITICAL ANALYSIS

1. What are some of the benefits of federal grants to state and local governments?
2. What is the rationale behind transfers from one state to another? Is it fair that some states pay more in federal taxes than they receive? What might explain why some states are net recipients and some net contributors?

threatened to defy some of the new federal requirements, Bush's Department of Education relaxed its tough stance and became more flexible in enforcing the act. President Obama later released the states from the federal NCLB mandates and in 2015 enacted a new education law called Every Student Succeeds, returning power to the states to evaluate schools, a move that might be expected more from a conservative president.

In the Supreme Court, too, many decisions began to support a stronger federal role over the states. This was surprising to many observers because in the 1990s it had appeared that the Court then was embarked on a "federalism revolution" designed to return more power to the states. Instead, in several key decisions, the Court reaffirmed the power of the federal government. Decisions to uphold the federal Family and Medical Leave Act and the Americans with Disabilities Act asserted federal authority against state claims of immunity from the acts. In one important 2005 case, the Court upheld the right of Congress to ban medical marijuana, even though 11 states had legalized its use. Overturning a lower-court ruling that said Congress did not have authority to regulate marijuana when it had been grown for noncommercial purposes in a single state, the Supreme Court ruled that the federal government did have the power to regulate use of all marijuana under the commerce clause precipitating the type of raid that Larry Harvey of the chapter opener experienced.[56] Even so, by 2018, 33 states and the District of Columbia had legalized medical marijuana (see Figure 3.7). Amid this legal confusion, a medical marijuana industry began to flourish. In 2012, Colorado and Washington went further by legalizing recreational marijuana soon followed by eight more states even though it is a prohibited substance by federal law. The federal government has not endorsed these laws, and while it made prosecution of marijuana in these states a low priority during the Obama administration, the Trump administration's first attorney general, Jeff Sessions, vowed to increase such prosecutions.

FIGURE 3.7

Marijuana Laws across the States

SOURCE: The National Organization for the Reform of Marijuana Laws, State Laws, norml.org/laws; "33 Legal Medical Marijuana States and DC," November 7, 2018, https://medicalmarijuana.procon.org/view.resource.php?resourceID=000881 (accessed 11/7/18).

CREDIT: State Marijuana Laws in 2018 Map, originally published by Governing.com, March 30, 2018. Reprinted by permission of Governing.

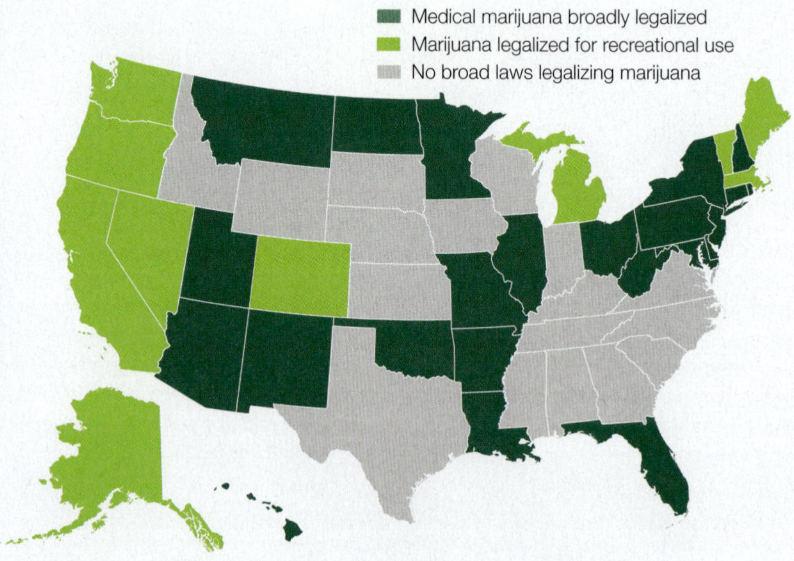

POLARIZATION AND NATIONAL GRIDLOCK: STATES STEP IN

The move to a stronger federal role has not been uniform. In some cases the Supreme Court has granted more authority to the states. One closely watched federalism case in 2006 was the challenge to Oregon's "right to die" law, discussed earlier, which allows doctors to prescribe lethal doses of medicine for terminally ill patients who request it. Challengers claimed the law was illegal because Congress has the right to outlaw such use of drugs under the Controlled Substances Act, which regulates prescription drugs. In a 6–3 decision, the Court ruled in Oregon's favor.[57] Washington State, Vermont, Montana, California, and Colorado followed in Oregon's footsteps to make physician-assisted suicide legal.[58]

States have also responded to gridlock at the national level by taking action themselves. On some issues, the majority of the states have pressed the federal government to act, but it has not responded. One issue on which most states would like the federal government to establish uniform law is internet sales. Current law requires internet retailers to collect sales tax on online purchases only when the business has a physical presence in the buyer's state. This has become a major issue for states, most of which rely on sales taxes for a significant part of their revenue. One study estimated that states lost $23 billion in 2012 from internet sales on which no taxes were collected.[59] In 2013 the Senate—with support from both Democrats and Republicans—passed the Marketplace Fairness Act, which would require online retailers to collect state sales taxes. However, in the House, some Republicans opposed the measure as a tax increase. By 2016, with the issue still unresolved in Congress, officials in 13 states had begun to impose taxes on out-of-state internet sales. Frustrated by congressional inaction, the states aimed to push Congress to act or to throw the matter into the courts, where they hoped for a decision that would support them.[60]

STATE-FEDERAL TUG OF WAR

The long-standing tug-of-war between the federal and state governments has continued in recent years. Indeed, immigration policy has been a center of federal-state conflict. Frustrated by congressional inaction on immigration reform, President Obama issued executive memoranda in 2012 that would provide temporary legal status and work permits to those who had been brought to the United States as children, termed the "Dreamers." However, when Obama moved to expand this Deferred Action for Childhood Arrivals program (DACA) in 2014 and extend legal status to some parents of U.S. citizens and legal residents (called Deferred Action for Parents of Americans, or DAPA), 26 states led by Texas challenged the executive order in court. They charged the expansion exceeded executive authority and would impose unreasonable costs on states, which would bear additional costs such as issuing driver's licenses. The expansion was never implemented because the Supreme Court, in the wake of the death of Justice Antonin Scalia, deadlocked in a 4–4 decision, leaving in place lower-court decisions that sided with the states.[61] The Trump administration began a six-month phaseout of the DACA program in September 2017, giving Congress until March 2018 to devise a legislative solution.[62] Congressional action failed, but as of late 2018 DACA remained in place due to two federal judges' rulings.

Whether states and localities have to enforce federal immigration laws has been a particular center of controversy. For example, the Secure Communities program, launched in 2008, required state and local authorities to check the fingerprints of people being booked into jail against a Homeland Security database. The policy led to a record number of deportations in 2009 and 2010, leading several states and

Since the Trump administration's announcement of the six-month phaseout of the DACA program put in place by the Obama administration, the legislative branch on the federal level has failed to implement a solution. State-level challenges to the termination of the policy, however, have been successful in protecting those covered by the program.

localities to pull out of the agreement with the federal government on the grounds that the law was detaining too many undocumented immigrants who had never committed a crime. The Obama administration softened its deportation policy in 2011 but sustained opposition, as well as federal court decisions that challenged the constitutionality of elements of the policy, ultimately led the government to end the program in late 2014. In its place, the Obama administration launched the Priority Enforcement Program in July 2015, which adopts a more limited deportation policy than the one formerly mandated by Secure Communities.[63]

President Donald Trump campaigned on promises for more rigorous immigration enforcement. In January 2017 he signed an executive order increasing the number of immigrants considered a priority for deportation, from those convicted of serious crimes such as felonies or multiple misdemeanors (as under Obama) to those accused or convicted of minor crimes as well.[64] In response, a growing number of cities, counties, and states declared themselves "sanctuaries" that limit cooperation with national government enforcement of immigration law. President Trump pledged to cancel funding for sanctuary cities and states, but in 2017 a federal judge blocked the Trump administration from withholding federal grants from these jurisdictions because of sanctuary policies.[65] In January 2018, the Justice Department began considering whether state and local officials could be subject to criminal charges if they implement sanctuary status, which opponents say would be illegal.[66]

The 2010 Affordable Care Act has also been the object of contestation between the federal and state governments. As we have seen, one controversial part of that legislation required states to expand their Medicaid programs to cover more low-income residents. The Court's 2012 ruling in *National Federation of Independent Business v. Sebelius* that the federal government could not impose all-or-nothing conditions on the states—implement the expansion or lose all Medicaid funding—represented a sharp departure from the past.[67] The ruling has far-reaching potential to change the federal government's power to impose conditions on the states when it supplies the funds. The other controversial provision of the Affordable Care Act was the "individual mandate," the requirement that individuals without health care insurance be required to purchase such insurance. The 26 states suing the federal government charged that Congress had no power to force individuals to purchase a product and that it had exceeded its power under the commerce clause. In defending the law, the federal government argued the opposite: that the complex interactions of the health care market made the individual mandate constitutional under the commerce clause.[68] Everyone is part of the health care economy. Even if a person does not have health insurance, federal law requires that hospitals provide treatment in an emergency, costs which are borne by all of the people who do pay for health insurance. The Court rejected this argument on the grounds that the federal government cannot regulate economic inactivity, that is, the failure to purchase health insurance. Instead, it found that the Affordable Care Act could be justified by Congress's power to tax. The law required individuals who do not receive insurance from their employers or their parents and who are not eligible for Medicaid to purchase insurance or pay a penalty. The Court reasoned that the penalty could be considered a tax and, in that sense, passed constitutional muster. The complex and surprising decision marked a new era in American federalism. The Court placed limits on two of the key powers that have expanded the reach of the federal government since the New Deal—the power to regulate commerce and the power to spend for the general welfare. The decision will surely invite challenges to federal power in diverse areas, possibly including education programs, the drinking age, and environmental regulations.

The Affordable Care Act law survived another challenge in 2015 when the Supreme Court ruled that federal subsidies to help pay for insurance should be available to residents in states that offered insurance through the federal exchange as well as in states that had formed their own state insurance marketplaces. The outcome of *King v. Burwell* ensured that subsidies would be available in all states.[69] The ACA also survived a repeal attempt after the 2016 election, when Republicans took control of Congress and the Presidency. However, the Tax Cuts and Jobs Act passed in late 2017 did repeal the individual mandate requiring Americans to have health insurance.

FOR CRITICAL ANALYSIS

Why was the 2010 Affordable Care Act controversial? How did the Supreme Court's decisions about the law reflect the principles of federalism?

STATE PREEMPTION OF LOCAL GOVERNMENT POLICY

Another notable development in the recent politics of federalism has been the willingness of state governments to preempt local policy. Just as states sometimes seize the initiative and make policy in areas where the federal government has failed to do so, so too have cities made policy in areas of state inaction or where policy preferences differ in the city compared to the state at large. In recent years some cities have set higher minimum wages than their surrounding state; implemented paid sick leave regulations on employers; regulated the "sharing economy" of car- and home-sharing; passed laws prohibiting discrimination in public facilities such as bathrooms; and attempted to establish public broadband services. In each of these cases, some state legislatures that disagreed with the direction of municipal policy have responded with preemption, passing laws nullifying municipal law or authority. As of 2017, 25 states preempt local minimum wage ordinances, 17 preempt local paid leave ordinances, 37 limit local authority to regulate ride sharing, and 3 limit local authority on home sharing. Michigan banned cities from banning plastic bags; Texas banned cities from banning fracking. Seventeen states prohibit localities from establishing municipal broadband service, and three—most famously North Carolina—preempt local anti-discrimination ordinances.[70]

In February 2016, the Charlotte City Council passed an ordinance prohibiting sex discrimination in public facilities. The following month the North Carolina legislature passed HB2, the Public Facilities Privacy and Security Act. The "Charlotte bathroom bill," as it came to be known, eliminated local authority to regulate access to public facilities and required people to use the bathroom of their designated gender at birth. The state faced strong objections to the law, which was viewed by opponents as a violation of transgender rights, and the state lost nearly $400 million in investment as plans for new jobs and events such as the NBA all-star game, NCAA championship, and business conferences were canceled.[71] Other preemption laws similarly unmake local provisions. In St. Louis, the minimum wage rose to $10 an hour in May 2017. Two months later, the Missouri legislature nullified the law. Some business owners pledged to keep the new higher wage, but other owners of fast food restaurants and grocery stores reset wages to the state's minimum of $7.70 an hour ($7.85 as of January 1, 2018).[72]

Like struggles between the federal and state governments since 2000, the more recent episodes of municipal preemption reflect the era's political polarization, with conservative state legislatures preempting the authority of more liberal municipal governments. Although conservatives have historically extolled the virtues of local control, views on federalism can depend more on party control of government than traditional ideological stances.

Despite the Charlotte City Council's ordinance prohibiting sex discrimination in public facilities, state preemption allowed for the North Carolina legislature to pass the "Charlotte bathroom bill," which undid the provisions originally set out by the city council. Opponents to this legislation saw the bill as a clear violation of transgender rights, and protested its passage.

Federalism
WHAT DO WE WANT?

FOR CRITICAL ANALYSIS

What would be the advantages and disadvantages of a unitary system in which the federal government had all the power? What would be the advantages and disadvantages of a fully decentralized system in which the states had all the power?

In recent years, sharp differences in Americans' views on many economic and social issues have been reflected in the federal system. Until 2015, when the Supreme Court ruled that state-level bans on same-sex marriage were unconstitutional, 37 states allowed same-sex marriage and 13 did not. Today, over half of the 50 states have legalized medical marijuana, while 10 and Washington, D.C., have gone further and legalized recreational marijuana.[73] More states are likely to change their laws on marijuana, but differences across the states are likely to persist for many years. Half of the states welcomed the expansion of Medicaid, the program that provides medical assistance to the poor. The other half, concerned about costs and the growing role of government in the economy, initially declined to implement the expansion. Some states actively welcome immigrants and seek to opt out of restrictive federal laws; other states go beyond the federal government in enacting restrictive immigration laws. Yet while states have the authority to devise their own laws on a variety of important issues, Americans' participation in state and local politics remains low (see the "**Who Participates?**" feature on the facing page).

As described in the opening of this chapter, Larry Harvey's arrest for using medical marijuana, legal in his state but illegal under federal law, raises questions about the promise, conflict, and ambiguity inherent in a federal system of government. Our history of federalism means that we are comfortable with the idea that states should have the freedom to enact laws that best serve their residents, within the bounds set by Congress and the courts. We expect states to act as "laboratories of democracy" that try out new policies. But the great variation across the states today poses questions that will have to be answered in the coming decades. Is the federal government endangering people by allowing states to legalize marijuana? Or is the federal government endangering critically ill people by prosecuting medical marijuana use even in states with legalization? Is it fair that a transgender person in California can legally change the sex on her birth certificate, but a transgender person in Tennessee would be denied the same? Is it reasonable that a gun owner can openly carry a handgun in Georgia but not in Florida? Each generation confronts a different set of questions about how much variation across the states is appropriate. Are some of the issues on which the states differ fundamental rights that should be uniform across the country? Is it important to preserve state choice on most matters? As today's youth help to answer these questions in the coming decades, they will be remaking American federalism.

Thus, American federalism remains a work in progress. As public problems shift and as local, state, and federal governments change, questions about the relationship between American values and federalism naturally emerge. The different views that people bring to this discussion suggest that federalism will remain a central issue in American democracy.

WHO PARTICIPATES?

Who Participates in State and Local Politics?

Turnout in Recent Gubernatorial Elections

Percentage of voting-eligible population*

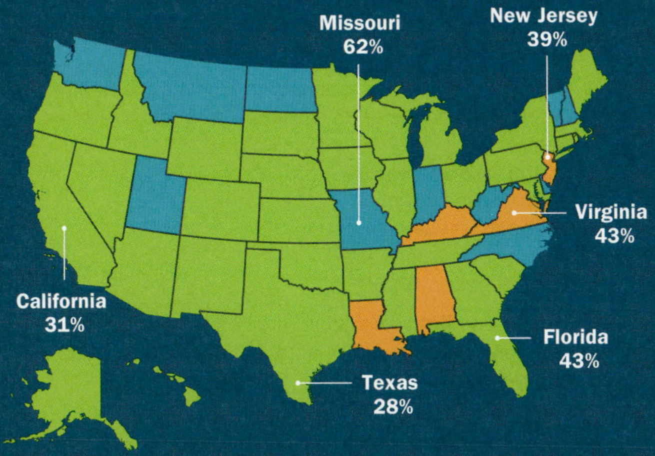

Median % of voters to turn out in the following years:

Non-presidential, non-congressional	Non-presidential congressional	Presidential
2015, 2017	2014	2016
39%	40%	65%

Turnout in Most Recent Municipal Election

Percentage of voting-age population in selected cities*

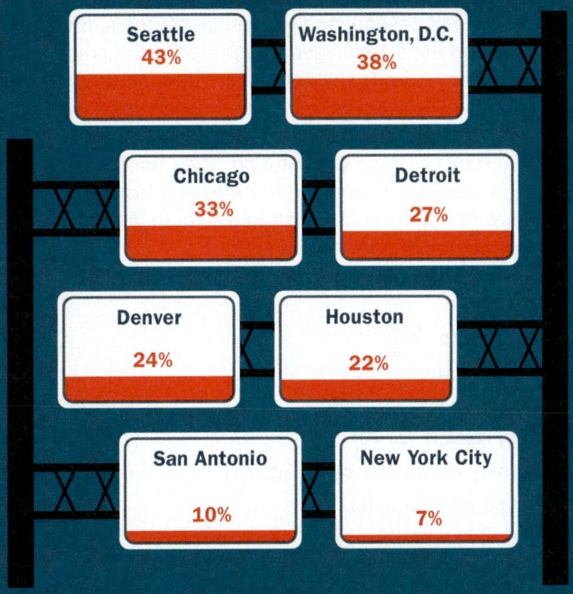

*The voting-eligible population excludes noncitizens and people who are institutionalized or not allowed to vote in some states because they are ex-felons. The voting-age population includes everyone over 18.

NOTE: Oregon had an additional election in 2016 to fill a vacancy.

SOURCES: Elect Project, electproject.org; Voter Turnout, elect.ky.gov; Post Election Statistics, electionstatistics.sos.la.gov; 2017 Results, state.nj.us; 2017 Results Report, elections.virginia.gov (accessed 3/10/18).

WHAT YOU CAN DO

Get Involved in State and Local Politics

- Attend a board of supervisors, city council, planning commission, or other local government meeting. Agendas and minutes will usually be available on county and city websites.
- Visit the state capitol. If you make an appointment, you might be able to meet with your local representative. Committee meetings and hearings are generally open to the public, as are meetings of the legislature.
- Attend a session of your local or state judiciary. Cases on the docket are available online, as are rules for attendance and behavior when the court is in session.

STUDY GUIDE

Federalism in the Constitution

Describe what the Constitution says about the powers of the national government and of the states (pp. 79–84)

While the Founders wanted a national government that was stronger than it had been under the Articles of Confederation, they also wanted to preserve the autonomy of the states. The necessary and proper clause, the supremacy clause, and the specific powers granted to Congress in Article I demonstrate the nation-centered focus of the Constitution. The Tenth Amendment, which grants all undelegated powers to the states, shows the state-centered focus of the Constitution. The Constitution also creates obligations among the states and includes some concurrent powers that are shared by both the federal government and state governments.

Key Terms

federalism (p. 79)
unitary system (p. 79)
expressed powers (p. 79)
implied powers (p. 79)
necessary and proper clause (p. 79)
reserved powers (p. 81)
police power (p. 82)
concurrent powers (p. 82)
full faith and credit clause (p. 82)
privileges and immunities clause (p. 83)
home rule (p. 84)

Practice Quiz

1. Which term describes the division of powers between the national government and the state governments?
   a) home rule
   b) separation of powers
   c) federalism
   d) checks and balances
   e) unitary system

2. Which amendment to the Constitution stated that the powers not delegated to the national government or prohibited to the states were "reserved to the states"?
   a) First Amendment
   b) Fifth Amendment
   c) Tenth Amendment
   d) Fourteenth Amendment
   e) Twenty-Sixth Amendment

3. A state government's authority to regulate the health, safety, and morals of its citizens is frequently referred to as
   a) the reserved power.
   b) the police power.
   c) the expressed power.
   d) the concurrent power.
   e) the implied power.

4. Which constitutional clause requires that states normally honor the public acts and judicial decisions of other states?
   a) privileges and immunities clause
   b) necessary and proper clause
   c) interstate commerce clause
   d) preemption clause
   e) full faith and credit clause

5. Many states have amended their constitutions to guarantee that large cities will have the authority to manage local affairs without interference from state government. This power is called
   a) home rule.
   b) devolution.
   c) preemption.
   d) states' rights.
   e) New Federalism.

The Traditional System of Federalism

Consider how the relationship between the federal and state governments evolved during the nation's first 140 years (pp. 84–88)

The relative importance of states and the federal government has changed significantly over time. For the first 140 years of American history, the national government was small, reluctant to directly coerce citizens, and focused primarily on assisting commerce. Most of the fundamental governing in the United States during this period was done by the states. Beginning in the 1930s, the Supreme Court dramatically expanded the power of the federal government through its expansive interpretation of the commerce clause.

Key Terms

dual federalism (p. 85)
commerce clause (p. 87)

Practice Quiz

6. The relationship between the states and the national government from 1789 to 1937 is known as
   a) unitary government.
   b) New Federalism.
   c) dual federalism.
   d) cooperative federalism.
   e) regulated federalism.
7. In which case did the Supreme Court create the potential for increased national power by ruling that Congress could use the necessary and proper clause to interpret its delegated powers broadly?
   a) *United States v. Lopez*
   b) *Printz v. United States*
   c) *Loving v. Virginia*
   d) *McCulloch v. Maryland*
   e) *Gibbons v. Ogden*
8. In 1937 the Supreme Court laid the groundwork for a stronger federal government by issuing a number of decisions that
   a) dramatically narrowed the definition of the commerce clause.
   b) dramatically expanded the definition of the commerce clause.
   c) struck down the supremacy clause.
   d) struck down the privileges and immunities clause.
   e) struck down the full faith and credit clause.

Federalism in the Modern Era

Trace developments in the federal framework leading to a stronger national government (pp. 89–94)

The Great Depression effectively ended the traditional system of dual federalism in which the states and the federal government performed very different functions and instituted a new system of cooperative federalism. Under this new system, the size and scope of the national government grew dramatically. As Congress began to enact legislation in previously unregulated areas during the 1970s, the national government began to set an increasingly large number of standards that required states to meet national guidelines. This more recent trend is often referred to as regulated federalism.

Key Terms

grants-in-aid (p. 90)
categorical grants (p. 91)
cooperative federalism (p. 91)
regulated federalism (p. 93)
preemption (p. 93)

Practice Quiz

9. The value of categorical grants
   a) increased from \$2.3 billion in 1950 to approximately \$31 billion in 2016.
   b) increased from \$2.3 billion in 1950 to approximately \$675 billion in 2016.
   c) decreased from \$31 billion in 1950 to approximately \$2 billion in 2016.
   d) decreased from \$667 billion to approximately \$2 billion in 2016.
   e) remained the same between 1950 and 2016.
10. The principle that allows the federal government to take over areas of regulation formerly overseen by states or local governments is called
    a) regulated federalism.
    b) preemption.
    c) devolution.
    d) "layer cake" federalism.
    e) exemption.

Evolving Role of the States

Analyze the changing role of the states in the federal framework (pp. 94–102)

Throughout the history of American federalism, questions about "who does what" have provoked intense political conflict. Despite the national government's expansion since the 1930s and more recent attempts to enhance state authority through block grants and revenue sharing, both the federal and state governments remain important players in American democracy. Most of the important public policy issues in recent years, including controversies about government spending, immigration, climate change, health care, and economic regulation, are debated and addressed through the United States' unique system of federalism.

Key Terms

states' rights (p. 94)
devolution (p. 96)
diffusion (p. 96)
block grants (p. 96)
New Federalism (p. 96)
general revenue sharing (p. 96)
unfunded mandates (p. 99)
redistributive programs (p. 100)

Practice Quiz

11. The process of returning more of the responsibilities of governing from the national level to the state level is known as
a) devolution.
b) diffusion
c) incorporation.
d) home rule.
e) preemption.

12. To what does the term *New Federalism* refer?
a) the era of federalism initiated by President Roosevelt during the late 1930s
b) the national government's regulation of state action through grants-in-aid
c) the type of federalism that uses categorical grants to influence state action
d) efforts to return more policy-making discretion to the states through the use of block grants
e) the recent emergence of local governments as important political actors

13. When state and local governments must conform to costly federal regulations or conditions in order to receive grants but do not receive reimbursements for their expenditures it is called
a) states' rights.
b) block grants.
c) general revenue sharing.
d) unfunded mandate.
e) redistributive programs.

The Politics of Federalism Today

Analyze contemporary relationships among national, state, and local governments (pp. 102–7)

Since the year 2000, the political polarization between Republicans and Democrats has been played out through the federal system as well as in national politics. Sometimes, states seek to go their own way regardless of federal law, and the federal government has succeeded in advancing its policy agenda through the states. It is often up to the courts to decide who gets the final say. However, the era since 2000 has been marked by a considerable amount of back-and-forth between the states, the federal government, and even localities as debates over federalism have become politically prominent.

14. The Supreme Court's decision in *National Federation of Independent Business v. Sebelius* was significant because
a) it affirmed the federal government's absolute power to impose all-or-nothing conditions on state governments attempting to receive federal funding.
b) it limited the federal government's power to impose all-or-nothing conditions on state governments attempting to receive federal funding.
c) it struck down the individual mandate of the Affordable Care Act as a violation of the interstate commerce clause.
d) it eliminated the federal government's ability to provide subsidies for health insurance coverage.
e) it invalidated the educational standards and testing requirements imposed by the 2001 No Child Left Behind Act.

For Further Reading

Derthick, Martha. *Keeping the Compound Republic: Essays on American Federalism*. Washington, DC: Brookings Institution Press, 2001.

Elazar, Daniel. *American Federalism: A View from the States*. 3rd ed. New York: Harper & Row, 1984.

Feiock, Richard C., and John T. Scholz. *Self-Organizing Federalism: Collaborative Mechanisms to Mitigate Institutional Collective Action Dilemmas*. New York: Cambridge University Press, 2009.

Gerston, Larry N. *American Federalism: A Concise Introduction*. Armonk, NY: M. E. Sharpe, 2007.

Grodzins, Morton. *The American System*. Chicago: Rand McNally, 1974.

Johnson, Kimberly S. *Governing the American State: Congress and the New Federalism, 1877–1929*. Princeton, NJ: Princeton University Press, 2007.

Karch, Andrew. *Democratic Laboratories: Policy Diffusion among the American States*. Ann Arbor: University of Michigan Press, 2007.

Kettl, Donald. *The Regulation of American Federalism*. Baltimore: Johns Hopkins University Press, 1987.

Mettler, Suzanne. *Dividing Citizens: Gender and Federalism in New Deal Public Policy*. Ithaca, NY: Cornell University Press, 1998.

Michener, Jamila. *Fragmented Democracy: Medicaid, Federalism, and Unequal Politics*. New York: Cambridge University Press, 2018.

Pierceson, Jason. *Same-Sex Marriage in the United States: The Road to the Supreme Court*. Lanham, MD: Rowman and Littlefield, 2013.

Robertson, David Brian. *Federalism and the Making of America*. New York: Routledge, 2011.

Van Horn, Carl E. *The State of the States*. 4th ed. Washington, DC: CQ Press, 2005.

Recommended Websites

Constitution Finder
http://confinder.richmond.edu
Governments can organize power in either a unitary or a federal system. Examine the constitutions of different countries throughout the world, and try to identify how those governments organize power.

Council of State Governments
www.csg.org
This organization provides information on a variety of state–federal policy areas. See what current issues concerning federalism are of prime importance to the state governments on this site.

Governing.com
www.governing.com
See what state–federal issues are important to your local government officials on the website for *Governing* magazine.

National Conference of State Legislatures
www.ncsl.org

National Governors Association
www.nga.org
These are two of the largest organizations dedicated to representing state and local government interests at the federal level.

Oyez: U.S. Supreme Court Media
www.oyez.org
Read here about one of the most important U.S. Supreme Court decisions regarding the division of federal and state power in the case of *McCulloch v. Maryland*.

Pew Charitable Trusts Stateline
www.pewtrusts.org/en/research-and-analysis/blogs/stateline/about
This nonprofit site provides news coverage in the states, focusing on four issues: fiscal and economic issues, health care, demographics, and the business of government. It also offers a weekly newsletter that includes the highlights of its reporting.

Supreme Court of the United States Blog
www.scotusblog.com
Supreme Court of the United States blog provides independent scholarly analysis of court rulings. The site provides timely discussion of pending and recent court decisions including *Obergefell v. Hodges*, the decision that made same-sex marriage legal in all states.

U.S. Census Bureau
www.census.gov
The Census Bureau maintains one of the largest collections of data about social and economic conditions of the nation's 50 states.

World Federalist Movement
www.wfm.org
This international organization is dedicated to the division of power and authority among all local, state, and international governmental agencies. Generally, it promotes federalism and constitutional democracy throughout the world.

★ chapter ★

04

Civil Liberties

WHAT GOVERNMENT DOES AND WHY IT MATTERS In Portland in 2006, Simon Tam founded what *Oregon Music News* called the first and only all Asian American dance-rock band, or "Chinatown Dance Rock," as the band prefers. The various members of the band are of Chinese, Taiwanese, Vietnamese, and Filipino descent. In addition to playing at anime conventions and cultural festivals, they are known for their community involvement battling Asian stereotypes and supporting young Asian people.[1]

They are also known for a First Amendment case over the band's name, the Slants. The name has three sources. The first two reference the members' "slant" on life and the guitar chords they use: "It actually sounds like a fun, 80s, New Wave kind of band. And it's a play on words. We can share our personal experiences about what it's like being people of color—our own slant on life, if you will. It's also a musical reference. There are slant guitar chords that we use in our music," Tam said. The third source was a reclaiming and repurposing of the old ethnic slur about Asian people. "We grew up and the notion of having slanted eyes was always considered a negative thing," Tam said. "Kids would pull their eyes back in a slant-eyed gesture to make fun of

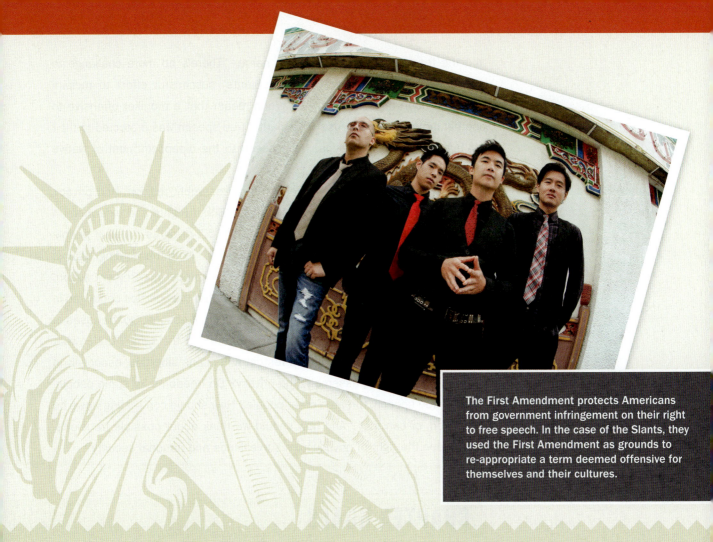

The First Amendment protects Americans from government infringement on their right to free speech. In the case of the Slants, they used the First Amendment as grounds to re-appropriate a term deemed offensive for themselves and their cultures.

us.... I wanted to change it to something that was powerful, something that was considered beautiful or a point of pride instead."

The U.S. Patent and Trademark Office had a different view. Tam's application for a trademark on the band's name was rejected as a violation of the Disparagement Clause of the Lanham Act of 1946, which prohibits trademarks that disparage a racial or ethnic group. The denial stated that although the "applicant, or even the entire band, may be willing to take on the disparaging term as a band name, in what may be considered an attempt ... to wrest 'ownership' of the term," that "does not mean that all [Asian Americans] share the applicant's view." The case ultimately went to the Supreme Court, which in 2017 ruled unanimously that the disparagement clause violated the First Amendment's free speech clause. The band could keep the name.

But in a further twist, the band's victory inadvertently undermined legal challenges to the name of the Washington Redskins football team. A group of Native Americans who found the "Redskins" name offensive had filed a petition to revoke the team's trademark, using the Lanham Act's disparagement clause. Once the Court declared the clause unconstitutional, they lost the legal basis for their argument, and the team was able to keep the name. "There's no more challenge to make," said their attorney. Thus the Slants' successful effort to reclaim what had been an epithet to their group meant that a moniker offensive to another group remains in use. The Slants' free speech was protected to their joy, but so was the Redskins' free speech to the disappointment of Native American groups.

Free speech, along with the freedoms of assembly, religion, and privacy, are among the civil liberties contained in the Bill of Rights and elsewhere in the Constitution. Thomas Jefferson said that a bill of rights "is what people are entitled to against every government on earth." Note the wording: *against government*. Civil liberties are *protections from* improper government action. Today in the United States, we often take for granted the liberties contained in the Constitution. But these freedoms raise difficult questions. Do the cases of the Slants and the Redskins strike you as different or the same? Under what circumstances can the government restrict Americans' liberties, especially in the realms of speech, assembly, and privacy? Do freedoms for some people, such as free speech, threaten other people? How should contrasting views be reconciled, or can they? And how should we think about possible trade-offs, as between the right of privacy from surveillance and national security?

CHAPTER GOALS

- **Explain the origins and evolution of the civil liberties in the Bill of Rights as they apply to the federal government and the states (pp. 117–22)**
- **Describe how the First Amendment protects freedom of religion (pp. 123–27)**
- **Describe how the First Amendment protects free speech and freedom of the press (pp. 127–36)**
- **Explore whether the Second Amendment means people have a right to own guns (pp. 136–38)**
- **Explain the major rights that people have if they are accused of a crime (pp. 138–46)**
- **Assess whether people have a right to privacy under the Constitution (pp. 146–51)**

Civil Liberties and the Constitution

Explain the origins and evolution of the civil liberties in the Bill of Rights as they apply to federal government and the states

Civil liberties are related to but different from civil rights. Civil rights, which we will discuss in Chapter 5, are obligations (what the government must do) to guarantee equal citizenship and to define how people will be treated by the government. The foundations of civil liberties as well as civil rights are to be found in the state and federal constitutions which guarantee free speech, freedom of the press, freedom of assembly and so forth. The federal Constitution's Bill of Rights includes both liberties and rights. However, because civil liberties are limits on government power, the evolution and expansion of civil liberties in the United States is mainly a story of judicial action to overturn state and federal government policies that placed limits on liberty. Civil rights, on the other hand, were shaped as much or more by the actions of the Congress and state legislatures as by the decisions of the courts. Thus, in Chapter 5 we will consider such pieces of federal legislation as the Voting Rights Act and the 1964 Civil Rights Act.

Why might the actions of the federal and state governments threaten civil liberties? There may be a variety of reasons, but the fundamental problem is the clash between the basic duty of governments to protect the public's health, safety, and general welfare from such dangers as crime, environmental hazards, and terrorism, and the freedom of citizens to go about their own business without governmental interference. Most Americans wish to be protected against violent criminals, but few would say there should be no restraint on police conduct in conducting investigations and interrogations. Most Americans want to be protected against terrorist plots, but few approve of unrestricted government surveillance and intrusions into their own communications. How do we balance safety and freedom? Where do we draw the line between anarchy and a police state?

In the United States, the federal and state constitutions establish the basic limits on government action and the decisions of the courts, interpreting constitutional principles, attempt to balance public safety and individual freedom. This balance is never carved in stone but needs to constantly be reexamined and revisited in light of changing circumstances.

A BRIEF HISTORY OF THE BILL OF RIGHTS

When the first Congress under the newly ratified Constitution met in late April of 1789, the most important item of business was the consideration of a proposal to add a bill of rights to the Constitution. Such a proposal had been turned down with little debate in the waning days of the Philadelphia Constitutional Convention in 1787, not because the delegates were against rights but because, as the Federalists, led by Alexander Hamilton, later argued, it was "not only unnecessary in the proposed Constitution but would even be dangerous."[2] First, according to Hamilton, a bill of rights would be irrelevant to a national government that was given only delegated powers in the first place. To put restraints on "powers which are not granted" could provide a pretext for governments to claim more powers than were in fact granted: "For why declare that things shall not be done which there is no power to do?"[3] Second, the Constitution was to Hamilton and the Federalists a bill of rights in itself, containing provisions that amounted to a bill of rights without requiring

TABLE 4.1

Rights in the Original Constitution (Not in the Bill of Rights)

CLAUSE	RIGHT ESTABLISHED
Article I, Section 9	Guarantee of habeas corpus
Article I, Section 9	Prohibition of bills of attainder
Article I, Section 9	Prohibition of ex post facto laws
Article I, Section 9	Prohibition against acceptance of titles of nobility, etc., from any foreign state
Article III	Guarantee of trial by jury in state where crime was committed
Article III	Treason defined and limited to the life of the person convicted, not to the person's heirs

habeas corpus a court order demanding that an individual in custody be brought into court and shown the cause for detention

additional amendments (see Table 4.1). For example, Article I, Section 9 included the right of **habeas corpus**, which prohibits the government from depriving a person of liberty without an open trial before a judge. Many of the framers, moreover, saw the very structure of the Constitution, including checks and balances, as protective of citizens' liberties.

Despite the power of Hamilton's arguments, when the Constitution was submitted to the states for ratification, Antifederalists, most of whom had not been delegates in Philadelphia, picked up on the argument of Thomas Jefferson (who also had not been a delegate) that the omission of a bill of rights was a major imperfection of the new Constitution. The Federalists conceded that to gain ratification they would have to make an "unwritten but unequivocal pledge" to add a bill of rights that would include a confirmation (in what would become the Tenth Amendment) of the understanding that all powers not expressly delegated to the national government or explicitly prohibited to the states were reserved to the states.[4]

"After much discussion and manipulation...at the delicate prompting of Washington and under the masterful prodding of Madison," the House of Representatives approved 17 amendments; of these, the Senate accepted 12. Ten of the amendments were ratified by the necessary three-fourths of the states on December 15, 1791; from the start, these 10 were called the **Bill of Rights** (see Table 4.2).[5] The protections against improper government action contained in the Constitution and the Bill of Rights represent important **civil liberties**.

Bill of Rights the first 10 amendments to the U.S. Constitution, ratified in 1791; they ensure certain rights and liberties to the people

civil liberties areas of personal freedom constitutionally protected from government interference

NATIONALIZING THE BILL OF RIGHTS

The First Amendment provides that "Congress shall make no law. . . ." But this is the only amendment in the Bill of Rights that addresses itself exclusively to the national government. For example, the Second Amendment provides that "the right of the people to keep and bear Arms, shall not be infringed." And the Fifth Amendment

TABLE 4.2

The Bill of Rights

Amendment I	Congress cannot make any law establishing a religion or abridging freedoms of religious exercise, speech, assembly, or petition.
Amendments II, III, IV	No branch of government may infringe upon the right of the people to keep arms (II), cannot arbitrarily take houses for militia (III), and cannot search for or seize evidence without a court warrant swearing to the probable existence of a crime (IV).
Amendments V, VI, VII, VIII	The courts cannot hold trials for serious offenses without provision for a grand jury (V), a trial jury (VII), a speedy trial (VI), presentation of charges and confrontation by the accused of hostile witnesses (VI), and immunity from testimony against oneself and immunity from trial more than once for the same offense (V). Furthermore, neither bail nor punishment can be excessive (VIII), and no property can be taken without "just compensation" (V).
Amendments IX, X: Limits on the national government	Any rights not enumerated are reserved to the state or the people (X), and the enumeration of certain rights in the Constitution should not be interpreted to mean that those are the only rights the people have (IX).

says, among other things, that "no person shall . . . be twice put in jeopardy of life or limb" for the same crime. Since the First Amendment is the only part of the Bill of Rights that is explicit in its intention to put limits on Congress and therefore on the national government, a fundamental question inevitably arises: Do the remaining provisions of the Bill of Rights put limits only on the national government, or do they limit the state governments as well?

The Supreme Court first answered this question in 1833 by ruling that the Bill of Rights limited only the national government and not the state governments.[6] This meant that the actions of state governments were restricted only by their own constitutions as interpreted by their own courts. But in 1868, when the Fourteenth Amendment was added to the Constitution, the question arose once again. The Fourteenth Amendment reads as if it were meant to impose the Bill of Rights on the states:

> No State shall make or enforce any law which shall abridge the privileges or immunities of citizens of the United States; nor shall any State deprive any person of life, liberty, or property, without due process of law; nor deny to any person within its jurisdiction the equal protection of the laws.

This language sounds like an effort to extend the Bill of Rights in its entirety to all citizens, wherever they might reside.[7] Yet this was not the Supreme Court's interpretation of the amendment for nearly 100 years. Within five years of ratification of the Fourteenth Amendment, the Court was making decisions as though the amendment had never been adopted.[8]

The only change in civil liberties during the first 50-odd years following the adoption of the Fourteenth Amendment came in 1897, when the Supreme Court held that the due process clause of the Fourteenth Amendment did in fact prohibit states from taking property for a public use without just compensation.[9] However, the Supreme Court had selectively "incorporated" into the Fourteenth Amendment only the property protection provision of the Fifth Amendment and no other clause of the Fifth or any other amendment of the Bill of Rights. In other words, although according to the Fifth Amendment "due process" applied to the taking of life and liberty as well as property, only property was incorporated into the Fourteenth Amendment as a limitation on state power.

No further expansion of civil liberties via the Fourteenth Amendment occurred until 1925, when the Supreme Court held that freedom of speech is "among the fundamental personal rights and 'liberties' protected by the due process clause of the Fourteenth Amendment from impairment by the states."[10] In 1931 the Court added freedom of the press to that short list of freedoms protected by the Bill of Rights from state action; in 1939 it added freedom of assembly.[11]

But that was as far as the Court was willing to go. In the 1937 case of *Palko v. Connecticut*, the Court gave its blessing to the preservation of a legal framework in which the states had the power to determine their own laws on a number of fundamental issues. In that case, a Connecticut court had found Frank Palko guilty of second-degree murder and sentenced him to life in prison. Unhappy with the verdict, the state of Connecticut appealed the conviction to its highest court, won the appeal, got a new trial, and then succeeded in getting Palko convicted of first-degree murder. Palko appealed to the Supreme Court on what seemed an open-and-shut case of double jeopardy, which is prohibited by the Fifth Amendment. Yet, although the majority of the Court agreed that this could indeed be considered a case of double jeopardy, they decided that double jeopardy was *not* one of the provisions of the Bill of Rights incorporated into the Fourteenth Amendment as a restriction on the powers of the states. It took more than 30 years for the Court to nationalize the constitutional protection against double jeopardy. Because Frank Palko lived in the state of Connecticut rather than in a state whose constitution included a guarantee against double jeopardy, he was eventually executed for the crime.

selective incorporation the process by which different protections in the Bill of Rights were incorporated into the Fourteenth Amendment, thus guaranteeing citizens protection from state as well as national governments

The *Palko* case established the principle of **selective incorporation**, by which the provisions of the Bill of Rights were to be considered one by one and selectively applied as limits on the states through the Fourteenth Amendment. In order to make clear that "selective incorporation" should be narrowly interpreted, Justice Benjamin Cardozo, writing for an 8–1 majority, asserted that although many rights have value and importance, some rights do not represent a "principle of justice so rooted in the traditions and conscience of our people as to be ranked as fundamental."[12] *Palko* left states with most of the powers they had possessed even before the adoption of the Fourteenth Amendment, such as the power to engage in searches and seizures without a warrant, to deprive accused persons of trial by jury, and to prosecute accused persons more than once for the same crime.[13] Few states chose to use these kinds of powers, but some did.

So, until 1961 (see Table 4.3), only the First Amendment and one clause of the Fifth Amendment had been clearly incorporated into the Fourteenth Amendment as binding on the states as well as on the national government.[14] After that, one by one, almost all the provisions of the Bill of Rights were incorporated into the Fourteenth Amendment and applied to the states. Table 4.3 shows the progress of this revolution in the interpretation of the Constitution. Before we leave the topic, it is worth mentioning that one element of the Fourteenth Amendment is being called into question today. This is the idea that all persons "born or naturalized" in the United States are citizens. Some politicians and public figures, most notably Donald Trump, have argued that the children of undocumented immigrants should not be considered U.S. citizens and might be subject to deportation. Though we are

TABLE 4.3

Incorporation of the Bill of Rights into the Fourteenth Amendment

These cases are significant because they represent the first instance that the Supreme Court acknowledged that the selected provision or amendment was binding on the states. In some cases this meant the Supreme Court overturned the state or local law under contention. In other cases the Court held that the law did not violate the Constitution, so the law was upheld.

SELECTED PROVISIONS AND AMENDMENTS	INCORPORATED	KEY CASE
Eminent domain (V)	1897	*Chicago, Burlington, and Quincy R.R. v. Chicago* The city of Chicago was required to compensate a railroad company for seizing its property for the purpose of widening a city road.
Freedom of speech (I)	1925	*Gitlow v. New York* Upheld Gitlow's conviction for "criminal anarchy" for publishing a left-wing manifesto. The Court held the First Amendment allowed the states to suppress speech directly advocating the overthrow of the government.
Freedom of press (I)	1931	*Near v. Minnesota* Overturned Minnesota's permanent injunction against those who created a "public nuisance" by publishing, selling, or distributing a "malicious, scandalous and defamatory newspaper, magazine or other periodical" as an infringement on freedom of the press.
Free exercise of religion (I)	1934	*Hamilton v. Regents of the University of California* Students filed suit to protest mandatory military training at the University of California on religious grounds. The Court upheld the right of California to mandate that its students receive military training as permissible under the First Amendment's free exercise of religion clause.
Freedom of assembly (I) and freedom to petition the government for redress of grievances (I)	1937	*DeJonge v. Oregon* DeJonge's conviction for addressing a meeting of the Communist Party was overturned as an infringement on freedom of assembly.
Free exercise of religion (I)	1940	*Cantwell v. Connecticut* State governments may not prohibit the dissemination or expression of religious views.
Nonestablishment of state religion (I)	1947	*Everson v. Board of Education* Applying the establishment clause, the Court found that using taxpayer money to bus students to private religious schools did not constitute establishing a religion because busing was a "separate" function from the school's religious purpose.
Freedom from warrantless search and seizure (IV) ("exclusionary rule")	1961	*Mapp v. Ohio* The Court overturned the conviction of Dollree Mapp for possession of obscene materials because the evidence was obtained in violation of the Fourth Amendment's requirement of a warrant for conducting a search.

Continued

TABLE 4.3

Incorporation of the Bill of Rights into the Fourteenth Amendment—cont'd

SELECTED PROVISIONS AND AMENDMENTS	INCORPORATED	KEY CASE
Freedom from cruel and unusual punishment (VIII)	1962	*Robinson v. California* The Court overturned a California law imposing a 90-day jail sentence on persons found guilty of "addiction to the use of narcotics" as cruel and unusual punishment for what amounted to illness.
Right to counsel in any criminal trial (VI)	1963	*Gideon v. Wainwright* Gideon requested a lawyer at his trial for a felony crime but was denied under Florida law. The Supreme Court held the right to counsel in the Sixth Amendment applied to the states, so Gideon got a new trial with counsel.
Right against self-incrimination and forced confessions (V)	1964	*Malloy v. Hogan* Malloy was imprisoned for contempt after refusing to answer questions about gambling activities on grounds it might implicate him. The Supreme Court held the Fifth Amendment secures defendants against self-incrimination, so Malloy could not be forced to testify.
Right to remain silent (V)	1964	*Escobedo v. Illinois* Police denied repeated requests by Escobedo to see his lawyer during interrogation; Escobedo eventually incriminated himself in a murder. The Court held Escobedo's Sixth Amendment rights to counsel and to the right to remain silent were violated.
Right to counsel and to remain silent (V)	1966	*Miranda v. Arizona* Miranda was questioned by police and signed a statement of confession without being informed of his right to counsel and protection from self-incrimination. The Court held defendants in police custody must be informed of their rights.
Right against double jeopardy (V)	1969	*Benton v. Maryland* Benton was tried twice for the same crime of larceny. The Supreme Court held "double jeopardy" as impermissible under the Fifth Amendment.
Right to bear arms (II)	2010	*McDonald v. Chicago* The Supreme Court struck down a Chicago firearms ordinance making it extremely difficult to own a gun within city limits as violating the Second Amendment.

a nation of immigrants, struggles over who may lawfully engage in the opportunities provided by American democracy can become bitter.

The best way to examine the Bill of Rights today is the simplest way: to take the major provisions one at a time. Some of these provisions are settled areas of law; others are not. The Court can reinterpret any one of them at any time.

The First Amendment and Freedom of Religion

Describe how the First Amendment protects freedom of religion

Congress shall make no law respecting an establishment of religion, or prohibiting the free exercise thereof; or abridging the freedom of speech, or of the press; or the right of the people peaceably to assemble, and to petition the Government for a redress of grievances.

The Bill of Rights begins by guaranteeing freedom of religion, and the First Amendment provides for that freedom in two distinct clauses: "Congress shall make no law [1] respecting an establishment of religion, or [2] prohibiting the free exercise thereof." The first clause is called the "establishment clause," and the second is called the "free exercise clause."

SEPARATION BETWEEN CHURCH AND STATE

The **establishment clause** and the idea of "no law" regarding the establishment of religion could be interpreted in several possible ways. One interpretation, which probably reflects the views of many of the First Amendment's authors, is that the government is prohibited from establishing an official church. Official state churches, such as the Church of England, were common in the eighteenth century and were viewed by many Americans as inconsistent with a republican form of government. Indeed, many American colonists had fled Europe to escape persecution for having rejected state-sponsored churches. A second possible interpretation is the view that the government may not take sides among competing religions but is not prohibited from providing assistance to religious institutions or ideas as long as it shows no favoritism. The United States accommodates religious beliefs in a variety of ways, from the reference to God on U.S. currency to the prayer that begins every session of Congress. These forms of religious establishment have never been struck down by the courts. The third view regarding religious establishment, the most commonly held today, is the idea of a "wall of separation" between church and state—Jefferson's formulation—that cannot be breached by the government. For two centuries, Jefferson's words have had a powerful impact on our understanding of the proper relationship between church and state in America.

establishment clause the First Amendment clause that says that "Congress shall make no law respecting an establishment of religion"; this law means that a "wall of separation" exists between church and state

FOR CRITICAL ANALYSIS

Despite the establishment clause, the United States still uses the motto "In God We Trust" and calls itself "one nation, under God." Do you think its reference to God is a violation of the separation of church and state?

Despite the seeming absoluteness of the phrase "wall of separation," there is ample room to disagree on how high the wall is. One area of contestation over the appropriate boundary between church and state is in public education. For example, the Court has been consistently strict in cases of school prayer, striking down such practices as Bible reading,[15] nondenominational prayer,[16] a moment of silence for meditation, and pregame prayer at public sporting events.[17] In each of these cases, the Court reasoned that school-sponsored religious observations, even of an apparently nondenominational character, are highly suggestive of school sponsorship and therefore violate the prohibition against establishment of religion.

For decades, the Court has faced cases involving government financial support for religious schools. In 1971 the Court attempted to specify some criteria to guide its decisions and those of lower courts, indicating the circumstances under which

Lemon test a rule articulated in *Lemon v. Kurtzman* that government action toward religion is permissible if it is secular in purpose, neither promotes nor inhibits the practice of religion, and does not lead to "excessive entanglement" with religion

state financial assistance to religious schools was constitutionally permissible. In its decision in *Lemon v. Kurtzman*, the Supreme Court established three criteria to guide future cases. Collectively, these came to be called the **Lemon test**. The Court held that government aid to religious schools would be accepted as constitutional if (1) it had a secular purpose, (2) its effect was neither to advance nor to inhibit religion, and (3) it did not entangle government and religious institutions in each other's affairs.[18]

Although these restrictions make the *Lemon* test hard to pass, imaginative authorities are finding ways to do so, and the Supreme Court has demonstrated a willingness to let them. For example, in 1995 the Court narrowly ruled that a student religious group at the University of Virginia could not be denied student activities funds merely because it was a religious group espousing a particular viewpoint about a deity. The Court called the denial "viewpoint discrimination" that violated the free speech rights of the group.[19]

In 2004 the question of whether the phrase "under God" in the Pledge of Allegiance violated the establishment clause was brought before the Court. Written without any religious references in 1892, the pledge had long been used in schools. But in 1954, in the midst of the Cold War, Congress voted to change the pledge in response to the "godless Communism" of the Soviet Union.

Ever since the change was made, there has been a steady murmuring of discontent from those who object to an officially sanctioned profession of belief in a deity as a violation of the establishment clause of the First Amendment. In 2003, Michael A. Newdow, the atheist father of a kindergarten student, brought suit against the local California school district, arguing that the reference to God turned the daily recitation of the pledge into a religious exercise. The case was appealed to the Supreme Court,

The First Amendment affects everyday life in a multitude of ways. Because of the amendment's ban on state-sanctioned religion, the Supreme Court ruled in 2000 that school-sponsored prayer in public schools is illegal. Requiring pregame prayer at public schools violates the establishment clause of the First Amendment.

In 2001, Alabama Supreme Court chief justice Roy Moore had a large granite statue of the Ten Commandments installed in the Alabama Supreme Court building. Despite a court injunction requiring Justice Moore to remove the statue, citing a violation of the Establishment Clause, the statue remained until the building manager was compelled to remove it.

which ruled that Newdow lacked a sufficient personal stake in the case to bring the complaint. This inconclusive decision by the Supreme Court left "under God" in the pledge while keeping the issue alive for possible resolution in a future case.[20]

Another realm of contestation over the meaning of the establishment clause is in public displays of religious symbols, such as city-sponsored nativity scenes in commercial or municipal areas. This realm remains contested, in part because the Supreme Court's rulings on such cases have been inconclusive, as demonstrated by two 2005 cases involving displays of the Ten Commandments. In *Van Orden v. Perry*, the Court decided that a display of the Ten Commandments outside the Texas state capitol did not violate the Constitution.[21] However, in *McCreary County v. American Civil Liberties Union of Kentucky*, the Court determined that a display of the Ten Commandments inside two Kentucky courthouses was unconstitutional.[22] Justice Stephen Breyer, the deciding vote in the two cases, said that the display in *Van Orden* had a secular purpose, whereas the displays in *McCreary* had a purely religious purpose. The key difference between the two cases is that the Texas display had been exhibited in a large park for 40 years with other monuments related to the development of American law, whereas the Kentucky display was erected much more recently and initially by itself, suggesting to some justices that its posting had a religious purpose. But most observers saw little difference between the two cases. Clearly, the issue of government-sponsored displays of religious symbols has not been settled.

FREE EXERCISE OF RELIGION

free exercise clause the First Amendment clause that protects a citizen's right to believe and practice whatever religion he or she chooses

The **free exercise clause** protects the right to believe and to practice whatever religion one chooses; it also protects the right to be a nonbeliever. The precedent-setting case involving free exercise is *West Virginia State Board of Education v. Barnette* (1943), which involved the children of a family of Jehovah's Witnesses who refused to salute and pledge allegiance to the American flag on the grounds that their religious faith did not permit it. Three years earlier, the Court had upheld such a requirement and had permitted schools to expel students for refusing to salute the flag. But the entry of the United States into a war to defend democracy, coupled with the ugly treatment to which the Jehovah's Witnesses' children had been subjected, induced the Court to reverse itself and to endorse the free exercise of religion even when it may be offensive to the beliefs of the majority.[23]

Although the Supreme Court has been fairly consistent and strict in protecting the free exercise of religious belief, it has taken pains to distinguish between religious beliefs and *actions* based on those beliefs. The 1940 case of *Cantwell v. Connecticut* established the "time, place and manner" rule. The case arose from the efforts of two Jehovah's Witnesses to engage in door-to-door fund-raising. Americans are free to adhere to any religious beliefs, but the time, place, and manner of their exercise are subject to regulation in the public interest.[24]

In recent years, the principle of free exercise has been bolstered by statutes prohibiting religious discrimination by public and private entities in a variety of realms including hiring, land use, and the treatment of prison inmates. Three recent cases illustrating this point are *Holt v. Hobbs*,[25] *Equal Employment Opportunity Commission v. Abercrombie & Fitch Stores, Inc.*,[26] and *Burwell v. Hobby Lobby Stores*.[27] The *Holt* case involved a Muslim prisoner in an Arkansas jail. The prisoner, Gregory Holt, asserted that his religious beliefs required him to grow a beard. Thus, according to Holt, an Arkansas prison policy prohibiting beards was a violation of his ability to exercise his religion. The Court held that the prison policy was a violation of the free exercise clause and violated a federal statute designed to protect the ability of prisoners to worship as they pleased. In the second case, the Equal Employment Opportunity Commission brought suit against Abercrombie & Fitch for refusing to hire a Muslim woman who wore a head scarf in violation of the company's dress code. The Court held that the store's actions amounted to religious discrimination in hiring, a violation of Title VII of the U.S. Code, which prohibits employers from hiring discrimination based upon race, color, religion, gender, and national origin.

The Hobby Lobby case involved the owners of a chain of craft stores who claimed that a section of the Affordable Care Act (ACA or Obamacare) requiring employers to provide their female employees with free contraceptive coverage violated their religious beliefs as protected by the Religious Freedom Restoration Act (RFRA). This law, enacted in 1993, requires the government to prove a "compelling interest" for requiring individuals to obey a law that violates their religious beliefs.

Does religious freedom lead to discrimination on the basis of religion? Here, senior counsel for Hobby Lobby stores speaks to supporters after the Supreme Court ruled that businesses were not required to provide free contraceptive coverage if they find it in violation of their religious beliefs.

The Supreme Court ruled in favor of Hobby Lobby. Currently, members of the LGBTQ community are concerned that RFRA will be used as the basis for discrimination in hiring or other realms against gay or transgender individuals by individuals claiming that such practices violate their own religious beliefs. In 2017 the Trump administration affirmed the Court's decision by declaring that under ACA employers who had religious or moral objections would no longer be required to provide birth control benefits.

The First Amendment and Freedom of Speech and of the Press

Describe how the First Amendment protects free speech and freedom of the press

Congress shall make no law... abridging the freedom of speech, or of the press.

Freedom of speech and freedom of the press have a special place in American political thought. To begin with, democracy depends on the ability of individuals to talk to one another and to disseminate information. It is difficult to conceive how democratic politics could function without free and open debate. Such debate, moreover, is seen as an essential mechanism for determining the quality or validity of competing ideas. As Justice Oliver Wendell Holmes said in 1919, "The best test of truth is the power of the thought to get itself accepted in the competition of the market... That at any rate is the theory of our Constitution."[28] What is sometimes called the "marketplace of ideas" receives a good deal of protection from the courts. In 1938 the Supreme Court held that any legislation that attempts to restrict speech "is to be subjected to a more exacting judicial scrutiny... than are most other types of legislation."[29] This higher standard of judicial review came to be called "strict scrutiny."

The doctrine of strict scrutiny places a heavy burden of proof on the government if it seeks to regulate or restrict speech. Americans are assumed to have the right to speak and to broadcast their ideas unless some compelling reason can be identified to stop them. But strict scrutiny does not mean that speech can never be regulated. Over the past 200 years, the courts have scrutinized many different forms of speech and constructed different principles and guidelines for each. According to the courts, although virtually all speech is protected by the Constitution, some forms of speech are entitled to a greater degree of protection than others.

POLITICAL SPEECH

Political speech was the activity of greatest concern to the framers of the Constitution, even though some found it the most difficult form of speech to tolerate. Within seven years of the ratification of the Bill of Rights in 1791, Congress adopted the infamous Alien and Sedition Acts (long since repealed), which, among other things, made it a crime to say or publish anything that might tend to defame or bring into disrepute the government of the United States.

The first modern free speech case arose immediately after World War I. It involved persons who had been convicted under the federal Espionage Act of 1917 for opposing U.S. involvement in the war. The Supreme Court upheld the

"clear and present danger" test test used to determine whether speech is protected or unprotected, based on its capacity to present a "clear and present danger" to society

Espionage Act and refused to protect the speech rights of the defendants on the grounds that their activities—appeals to draftees to resist the draft—constituted a **"clear and present danger"** to national security.[30] This is the first and most famous, though since discarded, "test" for when government intervention or censorship can be permitted.

It was only after the 1920s that real progress toward a genuinely effective First Amendment was made. Since then, political speech has been consistently protected by the courts even when it has been deemed "insulting" or "outrageous." In the 1969 case *Brandenburg v. Ohio*, the court ruled that as long as speech falls short of actually inciting action, it cannot be prohibited, even if it is hostile to or subversive of the government and its policies. This decision came in the case of a Ku Klux Klan leader, Charles Brandenburg, who had been arrested and convicted of advocating "revengent" action against the president, Congress, and the Supreme Court, among others, if they continued "to suppress the white, Caucasian race." Although Brandenburg was not carrying a weapon; some of the members of his audience were. Nevertheless, the Supreme Court reversed the state courts and freed Brandenburg while also declaring Ohio's Criminal Syndicalism Act unconstitutional because it punished persons who "advocate, or teach the duty, necessity, or propriety [of violence] as a means of accomplishing industrial or political reform" or who publish materials or "voluntarily assemble . . . to teach or advocate the doctrines of criminal syndicalism." The Supreme Court argued that the statute did not distinguish "mere advocacy" from "incitement to imminent lawless action."[31] It would be difficult to go much further in protecting freedom of speech.

Another area of political speech that has recently received much attention is the First Amendment status of monetary contributions to political campaigns. Campaign finance reform laws of the early 1970s, arising out of the Watergate scandal, sought to put severe limits on campaign spending. In the 1976 case *Buckley v. Valeo*, a number of important provisions were declared unconstitutional on the basis of a new principle that spending money by or on behalf of candidates is a form of speech protected by the First Amendment.[32] (For more details, see Chapter 10.)

The issue came up again in 2003 with passage of a new and still more severe campaign finance law, the Bipartisan Campaign Reform Act (BCRA). In *McConnell v. Federal Election Commission*, the 5–4 majority seriously reduced the area of speech protected by the *Buckley v. Valeo* decision by holding that Congress was well within its power to put limits on campaign spending. The Court argued that "the selling of access . . . has given rise to the appearance of undue influence [that justifies] regulations impinging on First Amendment rights . . . in order to curb corruption or the appearance of corruption."[33] In the *McConnell* case, the Court also upheld BCRA's limitations on "issue advertising." The act prohibited political advocacy groups from running ads that mentioned a candidate within 30 days of a primary election and 60 days of a general election. This ban was justified with the argument that wealthy special interests could affect election outcomes with last-minute ad campaigns. However, in its 2007 decision in the case of *Federal Election Commission v. Wisconsin Right to Life*, the Court reversed itself, declaring that such ads were protected speech and could not be prohibited so long as they focused mainly on issues and were not simply appeals to vote for or against a specific candidate.[34]

Even more recently, in the 2010 case of *Citizens United v. Federal Election Commission*, the Supreme Court declared that the First Amendment prohibited BCRA's

During the 2008 presidential primaries, the conservative organization Citizens United released a documentary criticizing Hillary Clinton. A lower court found that ads for the film violated the BCRA's ban on corporate funding of ads for or against a particular candidate. In 2010 the Court declared the BCRA ban unconstitutional under the First Amendment.

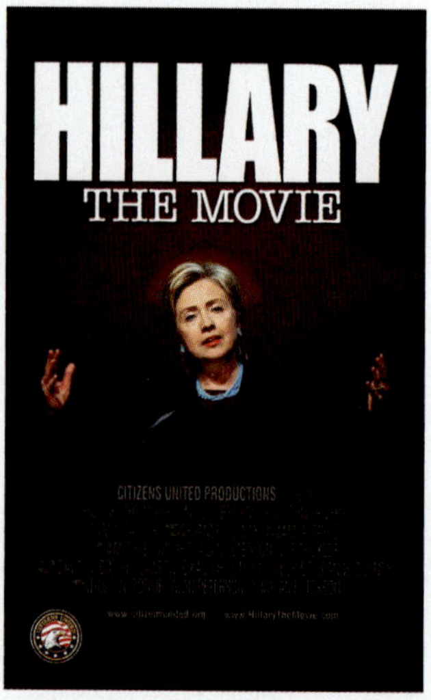

ban on corporate funding of independent political broadcasts aimed at electing or defeating particular candidates.[35] In its 5–4 decision, the Supreme Court ruled that the Constitution prohibits the government from regulating political speech and that therefore the government could not ban this type of political spending by corporations. In 2014 the Court again expanded its protection of campaign expenditures under the First Amendment by overturning aggregate limits restricting how much money a donor may contribute.[36] As a result of this decision several wealthy donors contributed more than $10 million to presidential candidates in 2016. The Court's decisions in both cases have been controversial. Republicans hailed the decisions as a victory for free speech, while Democrats denounced the decisions. President Obama called *Citizens United* "a major victory for big oil, Wall Street banks, health insurance companies, and the other powerful interests that marshal their power every day in Washington to drown out the voices of everyday Americans."[37]

FIGHTING WORDS AND HATE SPEECH

Freedom of speech does have limits, however. Speech can also lose its protected position when it moves toward the sphere of action. "Expressive speech," for example, is protected until it moves from the symbolic realm to the realm of actual conduct—to direct incitement of damaging conduct with the use of so-called **fighting words.** In 1942 a man called a police officer a "goddamned racketeer" and "a damn Fascist" and was arrested and convicted of violating a state law forbidding the use of offensive language in public. When his case reached the Supreme Court, the arrest was upheld on the grounds that the First Amendment provides no protection for such offensive language because such words "are no essential part of any exposition of ideas."[38] This decision was reaffirmed in the important 1951 case of *Dennis v. United States* when the Supreme Court held that there is no substantial public interest in permitting certain kinds of utterances: the lewd and obscene, the profane, the libelous, and the insulting or "fighting" words—those which by their very utterance inflict injury or tend to incite an immediate breach of the peace.[39] Since that time, however, the Supreme Court has reversed almost every conviction based on arguments that the speaker had used "fighting words."

fighting words speech that directly incites damaging conduct

In recent years, the increased activism of minority and women's groups has prompted a movement against words that might be construed as offensive to members of a particular group. Scores of universities have attempted to develop speech codes to suppress utterances deemed to be racial or ethnic or gender slurs. The drafting of such codes has been encouraged by the Department of Education's Office of Civil Rights (OCR) which has also interpreted Title IX of the Higher Education Act to require colleges to vigorously prosecute charges involving racial or sexual harassment. Critics have charged that the procedures encouraged by OCR ignore the rights of the accused and have led, on some campuses, to the creation of tribunals that assume the guilt of anyone charged with an offense. This issue is currently being fought out on college campuses across the country.[40] In 2017, Education Secretary Betsy Devos rescinded the department's previous guidelines, declaring they were unfair to those accused of sexual misconduct, and said new rules would soon be promulgated that would provide justice to all parties involved in a sexual misconduct case.

Similar issues have arisen in large corporations, both public and private, with many successful complaints and lawsuits alleging that the words of employers or their supervisors created a "hostile or abusive working environment." The Supreme Court has held that a "hostile working environment" results from "sexual harassment," including "unwelcome sexual advances, requests for sexual favors, and other *verbal* or physical conduct of a sexual nature [emphasis added]."[41] A fundamental free speech issue is involved in these regulations of hostile speech.

Many jurisdictions have drafted ordinances banning hate speech—forms of expression designed to assert hatred toward one or another group, be they African Americans, Jews, Muslims, or others. Such ordinances seldom pass constitutional muster. The leading Supreme Court case in this realm is the 1992 decision in *R.A.V. v. City of St. Paul.*[42] Here, a white teenager was arrested for burning a cross on the lawn of a black family in violation of a municipal ordinance that banned cross burning. The Court ruled that such an ordinance must be *content neutral*—that is, it must not prohibit actions directed at some groups but not others. The statute in question prohibited only cross burning, which is typically directed at African Americans. Since a statute banning all forms of hateful expression would be deemed overly broad, the *R.A.V.* standard suggests that virtually all hate speech is constitutionally protected.

The issue of hate speech has arisen on a number of college campuses. Some students and faculty at several colleges have demanded that (usually) conservative and far-right speakers be banned from campus on the grounds that they promote hatred. Student protesters have forced the cancellation of speeches by conservatives like Ann Coulter and Milo Yiannopoulos, disrupted talks by such prominent conservative scholars as Charles Murray, and have unsuccessfully sought to prevent "white nationalist" Richard Spencer from speaking. There seems little doubt that the right of all these individuals to speak is protected by the Constitution. The conflict arises when that Constitutional right comes up against university policies to emphasize safety. It is important to remember that not so long ago speakers on the political left were banned from campuses in the name of safety. Perhaps people of all political persuasions should think about the words of Supreme Court Justice Oliver Wendell Holmes, who said, "if there is any principle of the Constitution that more imperatively calls for attachment than any other, it is the principle of free thought—not free thought for those who agree with us but freedom for the thought that we hate."[43]

FOR CRITICAL ANALYSIS

Is there speech that should be banned because it does not contribute to the exchange of ideas? How do we determine what speech should be protected because it contributes to this exchange and what speech does not?

STUDENT SPEECH

One category of conditionally protected speech is the speech of high school students in public schools. In 1986 the Supreme Court backed away from a broad protection of student free speech rights by upholding the punishment of a high school student for making a sexually suggestive speech. The Court opinion held that such speech interfered with the school's goal of teaching students the limits of socially acceptable behavior.[44] Two years later the Supreme Court took another conservative step by restricting students' speech and press rights even further, defining them as part of the educational process and not to be treated with the same standard as adult speech in a regular public forum.[45] A later case involving high school students is the 2007 case of *Morse v. Frederick.*[46] This case dealt with the policies of Juneau-Douglas High School in Juneau, Alaska. In 2002 the Olympic torch relay had passed through Juneau on its way to Salt Lake City for the opening of the Winter Olympics. As the torch passed Juneau-Douglas High, a senior, Joseph Frederick, unfurled a banner reading "BONG HITS 4 JESUS." The school's principal promptly suspended Frederick, who then brought suit for reinstatement, alleging that his free speech rights had been violated. Like most of America's public schools, Juneau-Douglas

The Supreme Court has ruled that high school students' speech can be restricted. In a 2007 case involving a student who displayed the banner above, the Court found that the school principal had not violated the student's right to free speech by suspending him.

High prohibits assemblies or expressions on school grounds that advocate illegal drug use, saying that some federal aid is contingent on this policy. Civil libertarians, of course, see such policies as restricting students' right to free speech. Speaking for the Court's majority, Chief Justice Roberts said that the First Amendment did not require schools to permit students to advocate illegal drug use.

COMMERCIAL SPEECH

Commercial speech, such as newspaper or television advertisements, does not have full First Amendment protection because it cannot be considered political speech. Initially considered to be entirely outside the protection of the First Amendment, commercial speech today is subject to limited regulation. For example, the prohibition of false and misleading advertising by the Federal Trade Commission is an old and well-established power of the federal government. The Supreme Court has upheld city ordinances prohibiting the posting of all commercial signs on public property (as long as the ban is total so that there is no hint of selective censorship).[47]

However, the gains far outweigh the losses in the effort to expand the protection of commercial speech under the First Amendment. "In part, this reflects the growing appreciation that commercial speech is part of the free flow of information necessary for informed choice and democratic participation."[48] For example, in 1975 the Supreme Court struck down a state statute making it a misdemeanor to sell or circulate newspapers encouraging abortions; the Court ruled that the statute infringed on constitutionally protected speech and on the right of the reader to make informed choices.[49] On a similar basis, the Court reversed its own earlier decisions upholding laws that prohibited lawyers, dentists, and other professionals from advertising their services. For the Court, medical service advertising was a matter of health that could be advanced by the free flow of information.[50] And in a 2001 case, the Court ruled that a Massachusetts ban on all cigarette advertising violated the First Amendment right of the tobacco industry to advertise its products to adult consumers.[51] These instances of commercial speech, significant in themselves, are all the more significant because they indicate the breadth and depth of the freedom existing today to direct appeals to a large public, not only to sell goods and services but also to mobilize people for political purposes.

SYMBOLIC SPEECH, SPEECH PLUS, AND THE RIGHTS OF ASSEMBLY AND PETITION

The First Amendment treats the freedoms of religion and political speech as equal to the freedoms of assembly and petition—speech associated with action. For this reason, the long record of Supreme Court cases largely protects an individual's right to symbolic speech, assembly, and petition. Freedom of speech and freedom of assembly are closely related by the "public forum doctrine." In the 1939 case of *Hague v. Committee for Industrial Organization*, the Court declared that the government may not prohibit speech-related activities such as demonstrations or leafleting in public areas traditionally used for that purpose, though, of course, the government may impose rules designed to protect the public safety so long as these rules do not discriminate against particular viewpoints.[52]

Generally, the Supreme Court has sought to protect actions that are designed to send a political message. One example is the burning of the American flag as a protest. In 1984, at a political rally held during the Republican National Convention in Dallas, Texas, a political protester burned an American flag, thereby violating a Texas statute that prohibited desecration of a venerated object. In a 5–4 decision, the Supreme Court declared the Texas law unconstitutional on the grounds that flag burning was expressive conduct protected by the First Amendment.[53] Since 1995 the House of Representatives has seven times passed a resolution for a constitutional amendment to ban this form of expressive conduct, but each time the Senate has failed to go along.[54]

In the 2011 case of *Snyder v. Phelps*, the Court sought to protect another form of symbolic speech. Members of the Westboro Baptist Church had frequently demonstrated at military funerals, claiming that the deaths of the soldiers were a sign that

Should the First Amendment's protection of free speech apply even when that speech is seen as offensive? In 2011 the Supreme Court ruled 8–1 that members of the Westboro Baptist Church had a right to picket soldiers' funerals to demonstrate what they take as a sign of God's disapproval of homosexuality.

God disapproved of the acceptance of homosexuality in the United States. The father of a soldier killed in Iraq brought suit against the church and its pastor, claiming that the demonstrators had caused him and his family severe emotional distress. The Supreme Court ruled, however, that the First Amendment protected free speech in a public place against such suits.[55]

Closer to the original intent of the assembly and petition clause is the category of "**speech plus**"—following speech with physical activity such as picketing, distributing leaflets, and other forms of peaceful demonstration or assembly. Such assemblies are consistently protected by courts under the First Amendment; state and local laws regulating such activities are closely scrutinized and frequently overturned. But the same assembly on private property is quite another matter and can in many circumstances be regulated. For example, the directors of a shopping center can lawfully prohibit an assembly protesting a war or supporting a ban on abortion. Assemblies in public areas can also be restricted under some circumstances, especially when the assembly or demonstration jeopardizes the health, safety, or rights of others. This condition was the basis of the Supreme Court's decision to uphold a lower-court order that restricted the access that abortion protesters had to the entrances of abortion clinics.[56]

"speech plus" speech accompanied by conduct such as sit-ins, picketing, and demonstrations; protection of this form of speech under the First Amendment is conditional, and restrictions imposed by state or local authorities are acceptable if properly balanced by considerations of public order

FREEDOM OF THE PRESS

For all practical purposes, freedom of speech implies and includes freedom of the press. With the exception of the broadcast media, which are subject to federal regulation, the press is protected under the doctrine against **prior restraint**. Beginning with the landmark 1931 case of *Near v. Minnesota*, the U.S. Supreme Court has held that, except under the most extraordinary circumstances, the First Amendment of the Constitution prohibits government agencies from seeking to prevent newspapers or magazines from publishing whatever they wish.[57] Indeed, in the 1971 case *New York Times Co. v. United States* (the so-called Pentagon Papers case), the Supreme Court ruled that the government could not block publication of secret Defense Department documents furnished to the *New York Times* by an opponent of the Vietnam War who had obtained the documents illegally.[58]

prior restraint an effort by a governmental agency to block the publication of material it deems libelous or harmful in some other way; censorship; in the United States, the courts forbid prior restraint except under the most extraordinary circumstances

Should individuals be prosecuted for leaking classified information to the press? Then-Pfc. Bradley Manning and Edward Snowden were charged for the crime of leaking classified information related to government surveillance.

Another press freedom issue that the courts have often been asked to decide is the question of whether journalists can be compelled to reveal their sources of information. Journalists assert that if they cannot ensure their sources' confidentiality, the flow of information will be reduced and press freedom effectively curtailed. Government agencies, however, aver that names of news sources may be relevant to criminal or even national security investigations. More than 30 states have "shield laws," which, to varying degrees, protect journalistic sources. There is, however, no federal shield law and no special constitutional protection for journalists. The Supreme Court has held that the press has no constitutional right to withhold information in court.[59]

In addition to prosecuting journalists for refusing to reveal their sources, the government may seek to prosecute individuals who leak information to the press. During the Obama presidency, seven individuals were charged or prosecuted for disclosing classified information. These cases included Pfc. Bradley Manning, an army intelligence analyst sent to prison for providing classified documents to WikiLeaks, which published many of the documents, and Edward Snowden, an employee of the National Security Agency (NSA) who fled the country to escape arrest after revealing the details of NSA domestic spying operations. Manning, who took the name Chelsea after undergoing gender reassignment surgery, was released from prison in 2017.

Libel and Slander Some speech is not protected at all. If a written statement is made in "reckless disregard of the truth" and is considered damaging to the victim because it is "malicious, scandalous, and defamatory," it can be punished as **libel**. If such a statement is made orally, it can be punished as **slander**.

libel a written statement made in "reckless disregard of the truth" that is considered damaging to a victim because it is "malicious, scandalous, and defamatory"

slander an oral statement made in "reckless disregard of the truth" that is considered damaging to the victim because it is "malicious, scandalous, and defamatory"

Most libel suits today involve freedom of the press, and the realm of free press is enormous. Historically, newspapers were subject to the law of libel, which provided that newspapers that printed false and malicious stories could be compelled to pay damages to those they defamed. In recent years, however, American courts have greatly narrowed the meaning of libel and made it extremely difficult, particularly for politicians or other public figures, to win a libel case against a newspaper. In the important 1964 case of *New York Times Co. v. Sullivan*, the Court held that to be deemed libelous, a story about a public official not only had to be untrue but also had to result from "actual malice" or "reckless disregard" for the truth.[60] In other words, the newspaper had to print false and malicious material deliberately. In practice, it is nearly impossible to prove that a paper *deliberately* printed maliciously false information, and it is thus especially difficult for a politician or other public figure to win a libel case. Essentially, the print media have been able to publish anything they want about a public figure.

However, the Court has opened up the possibility for public officials to file libel suits against the press. The Court has held since the 1970s that the press was immune to libel suits only when the printed material was "a matter of public concern."[61] In other words, a newspaper would have to show that the public official was engaged in activities that were indeed *public*. This principle has made the press more vulnerable to libel suits, but it still leaves an enormous realm of freedom for the press. President Trump has said that stricter libel laws are needed to prevent what he likes to call "fake news," though no action or policies have changed.

With the emergence of the internet as an important communications medium, the courts have had to decide how traditional libel law applies to internet content. In 1995 the New York courts held that an online bulletin board could be held responsible for the libelous content of material posted by a third party. To protect internet service providers, Congress subsequently enacted legislation absolving them of responsibility for third-party posts. The federal courts have generally upheld this law and declared that service providers are immune from suits regarding the content of material posted by others.[62]

Obscenity and Pornography If libel and slander cases can be difficult because of the problem of determining the truth of statements and whether those statements are malicious and damaging, cases involving pornography and obscenity can be even trickier. Not until 1957 did the Supreme Court confront this problem, and it did so with a definition of obscenity that may have caused more confusion than it cleared up. In writing the Court's opinion, Justice William Brennan defined obscenity as speech or writing that appeals to the "prurient interest"—that is, whose purpose is to excite lust, as this appears "to the average person, applying contemporary community standards." Even so, Brennan added, the work should be judged obscene only when it is "utterly without redeeming social importance."[63] In 1964, Justice Potter Stewart confessed that, although he found pornography impossible to define, "I know it when I see it."[64]

The vague and impractical standards that had been developed meant ultimately that almost nothing could be banned on the grounds that it was pornographic and obscene. An effort was made to strengthen the restrictions in 1973, when the Supreme Court expressed its willingness to define pornography as a work that (1) as a whole, is deemed prurient by the "average person" according to "community standards"; (2) depicts sexual conduct "in a patently offensive way"; and (3) lacks "serious literary, artistic, political, or scientific value." This definition meant that pornography would be determined by local rather than national standards. Thus, a local bookseller might be prosecuted for selling a volume that was a best-seller nationally but that was deemed pornographic locally.[65] This new definition of standards did not help much either, and not long after 1973, the Court began again to review all such community antipornography laws, reversing most of them.

In recent years, the battle against obscene speech has targeted pornography on the internet. Opponents of this form of expression argue that it should be banned because of the easy access children have to the internet. The first major effort to regulate the content of the internet occurred in 1996, when Congress passed the Telecommunications Act. Attached to it was an amendment, called the Communications Decency Act (CDA), designed to regulate the online transmission of obscene material. The constitutionality of the CDA was immediately challenged in court by a coalition of interests led by the American Civil Liberties Union. In the 1997 case of *Reno v. American Civil Liberties Union*, the Supreme Court struck down the CDA, ruling that it suppressed speech that "adults have a constitutional right to receive" and that governments may not limit the adult population to messages that are fit for children. Supreme Court justice John Paul Stevens described the internet as the "town crier" of the modern age and said that the internet was entitled to the greatest degree of First Amendment protection possible.[66] In 2003, Congress enacted the PROTECT Act, which outlawed efforts to sell child pornography via the internet. The Supreme Court upheld this act in the 2008 case of *United States v. Williams*, in which the majority said that criminalizing efforts to purvey child pornography did not violate free speech guarantees.[67]

In 2000 the Supreme Court extended the highest degree of First Amendment protection to cable (not broadcast) television. In *United States v. Playboy Entertainment Group*, the Court struck down a portion of the 1996 Telecommunications

Act that required cable TV companies to limit the broadcast of sexually explicit programming to late-night hours. In its decision, the Court noted that the law already provided parents with the means to restrict access to sexually explicit cable channels through various blocking devices. Moreover, such programming could come into the home only if parents decided to purchase such channels in the first place.[68]

Closely related to the issue of obscenity is the matter of violent broadcast content. Can a state or the federal government prohibit broadcasts or publications deemed to be excessively violent? Here, too, the Court has generally upheld freedom of speech. For example, in the 2011 case of *Brown v. Entertainment Merchants Association*, the Court struck down a California law banning the sale of violent video games to children, saying that the law violated the First Amendment.[69]

The Second Amendment and the Right to Bear Arms

Explore whether the Second Amendment means people have a right to own guns

A well regulated Militia, being necessary to the security of a free State, the right of the people to keep and bear Arms, shall not be infringed.

The point and purpose of the Second Amendment is the provision for militias; they were to be the backing of the government for the maintenance of local public order. "Militia" was understood at the time of the Founding to be a military or police resource for state governments, and militias were specifically distinguished from armies and troops, which came within the sole constitutional jurisdiction of Congress. Many individuals, though, have argued that the Second Amendment also establishes an individual right to bear arms.

The judicial record of Second Amendment cases is far sparser than that of First Amendment cases, and for almost 60 years the Court made no Second Amendment decisions. In the absence of a ruling that would apply to the entire country, localities across the country have very different gun ownership standards, the result of a patchwork of state and local laws. For instance, in Wyoming, there is no ban on owning any type of gun, there is no waiting period to purchase a firearm, and individuals are not required to obtain a permit for carrying a concealed weapon. In California, in contrast, the possession of assault weapons is banned, there is a 10-day waiting period to purchase a firearm, and a permit is required to carry a concealed weapon. Figure 4.1 shows the background check requirements to purchase a firearm across the country.

The Court's silence on the application of the Second Amendment ended in 2008, when the Supreme Court made the first of two rulings in favor of expansive rights of gun ownership by individuals. In the case *District of Columbia v. Heller*, at issue was a strict Washington, D.C., law that banned handguns. In a 5–4 decision, the Court ruled that the Second Amendment provides a constitutional right to keep a loaded handgun at home for self-defense, a view that had long been subject to debate. In the majority opinion, Justice Antonin Scalia stated that the decision was not intended to cast doubt on all laws limiting firearm possession, such as the prohibition on gun ownership by felons or the mentally ill.[70] In his dissenting opinion, Justice Stevens asserted that the Second Amendment only protects the rights of individuals to bear arms as part of a militia force, not in an individual capacity. The District of Columbia

FIGURE 4.1

Gun Rights by State

Although state gun laws must conform to the Second Amendment as interpreted by the U.S. Supreme Court, laws concerning gun sales and ownership vary widely from state to state. It is much more difficult to buy a gun in, say, New York or California than in Texas or Kentucky. This map shows states that require criminal background checks for the sale of all firearms, only handguns, or none when purchasing firearms. While federal law requires background checks when purchasing a firearm from a licensed seller, only 21 states require them from unlicensed sellers as well.

*An answer of N/A indicates the state does not require criminal background checks for gun sales by unlicensed sellers.

SOURCE: Background Checks, Gun Law Navigator, www.everytownresearch.org/ (accessed 6/12/18).

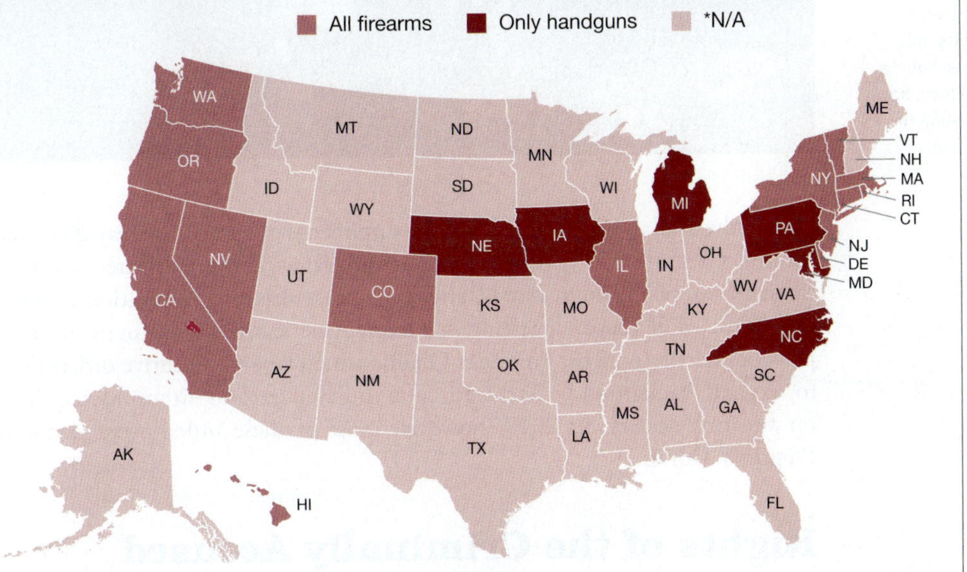

is an entity of the federal government, and the Court did not indicate that its ruling applied to state firearms laws. However, in the 2010 case of *McDonald v. Chicago*, the Supreme Court applied the Second Amendment to the states, making this decision the first new incorporation decision by the Court in 40 years. The case concerned a Chicago ordinance that made it extremely difficult to own a gun within city limits, and the Court's ruling had the effect of overturning the law.[71]

Despite these rulings, the debate over gun control continues to loom large in American politics today. A recent series of tragic shootings (including the killing of 20 elementary school students in Newtown, Connecticut; 9 parishioners at a Charleston, South Carolina, church; 50 people at a nightclub in Orlando, Florida; 59 individuals at a concert in Las Vegas, Nevada; 27 worshipers at a church in Sutherland Springs, Texas; and 17 students and staff members at a high school in Parkland, Florida) has kept the issue of gun laws firmly on the national agenda. Proponents of gun control point to these shootings as evidence of the need to

A string of mass shootings in the United States, including ones in which 59 people at a concert in Las Vegas and 17 students and staff members at a high school in Parkland, Florida, were killed, have prompted calls for legislation to limit the availability of guns.

restrict the availability of firearms while opponents of gun control say that shooting incidents demonstrate that Americans are not safe and should be free to carry arms for self protection. Interestingly, after each mass shooting opposition to gun control increased, perhaps suggesting that many Americans equate gun ownership with personal safety. In 2016, President Obama issued several executive orders designed to expand background checks for gun purchasers and licensure requirements for firearms dealers. In 2017, however, most of these orders were rescinded by President Trump.

Rights of the Criminally Accused

Explain the major rights that people have if they are accused of a crime

Except for the First Amendment, most of the battle to apply the Bill of Rights to the states has been fought over the various protections granted to individuals who are accused of a crime, who are suspects in the commission of a crime, or who are brought before the court as a witness to a crime (Table 4.4). The Fourth, Fifth, Sixth, and Eighth amendments, taken together, are the essence of the **due process of law**, even though these precise words for this fundamental concept do not appear until the end of the Fifth Amendment. In the next sections, we will look at specific cases that illuminate the dynamics of this important constitutional issue. The procedural safeguards that we will discuss may seem remote to most law-abiding citizens, but they help define the limits of government action against the personal liberty of every citizen. Many Americans believe that "legal technicalities" are responsible for setting many actual criminals free. In some cases, this is true. In fact, few convictions are actually lost because of excluded evidence. But one of America's traditional and most strongly held juridical values is that "it is far worse to convict an innocent man than to let a guilty man go free."[72] In civil suits, verdicts rest on "the preponderance of the evidence"; but in criminal cases, guilt has to be proven

due process of law the right of every individual against arbitrary action by national or state governments "beyond a reasonable doubt"—a far higher standard. The provisions for due process in the Bill of Rights were added in order to improve the probability that the standard of "reasonable doubt" would be respected.

TABLE 4.4

The Rights of the Accused from Arrest to Trial

No improper searches and seizures (Fourth Amendment)
No arrest without probable cause (Fourth Amendment)
Right to remain silent (Fifth Amendment)
No self-incrimination during arrest or trial (Fifth Amendment)
Right to be informed of charges (Sixth Amendment)
Right to counsel (Sixth Amendment)
No excessive bail (Eighth Amendment)
Right to grand jury (Fifth Amendment)
Right to open trial before a judge (Article I, Section 9)
Right to speedy and public trial before an impartial jury (Sixth Amendment)
Evidence obtained by illegal search not admissible during trial (Fourth Amendment)
Right to confront witnesses (Sixth Amendment)
No double jeopardy (Fifth Amendment)
No cruel and unusual punishment (Eighth Amendment)

THE FOURTH AMENDMENT AND SEARCHES AND SEIZURES

> The right of the people to be secure in their persons, houses, papers, and effects, against unreasonable searches and seizures, shall not be violated, and no Warrants shall issue, but upon probable cause, supported by Oath or affirmation, and particularly describing the place to be searched, and the persons or things to be seized.

The purpose of the Fourth Amendment is to guarantee the security of citizens against unreasonable (i.e., improper) searches and seizures. In 1990 the Supreme Court summarized its understanding of the Fourth Amendment brilliantly and succinctly: "A search compromises the individual interest in privacy; a seizure deprives the individual of dominion over his or her person or property."[73] But how are we to define what is reasonable and what is unreasonable?

The 1961 case of *Mapp v. Ohio* illustrates one of the most important of the principles that have grown out of the Fourth Amendment—the **exclusionary rule**, which prohibits evidence obtained during an illegal search from being introduced in a trial. Acting on a tip that Dollree (Dolly) Mapp was harboring a suspect in a bombing incident, several policemen forcibly entered Mapp's house, claiming they had a warrant to look for the bombing suspect. The police did not find the bombing suspect but, in an old trunk in the basement, did find some materials they declared to be obscene. Although no warrant was ever produced, the evidence that had been seized was admitted by a court, and Mapp was charged and convicted of illegal possession of obscene materials.

exclusionary rule the ability of courts to exclude evidence obtained in violation of the Fourth Amendment

The question before the Court was whether any evidence produced under the circumstances of the search of her home was admissible. The Court's opinion affirmed the exclusionary rule: under the Fourth Amendment (applied to the states through the Fourteenth Amendment), "all evidence obtained by searches and seizures in violation of the Constitution . . . is inadmissible."[74] This means that even people who are clearly guilty of the crime of which they are accused must not be convicted if the only evidence for their conviction was obtained illegally.

The exclusionary rule is the most dramatic restraint imposed by the courts on police behavior because it rules out precisely the evidence that produces a conviction; it frees those people who are *known* to have committed the crime of which they have been accused. Thus, in recent years the Court has softened the application of the exclusionary rule, and federal courts have relied on its discretionary use,

Under what circumstances can the police search an individual's car? The Fourth Amendment protects against "unreasonable searches and seizures," but the Supreme Court has had to interpret what is unreasonable.

whereby they make a judgment as to the "nature and quality of the intrusion."[75] In 2006, in the case of *United States v. Grubbs*, the Supreme Court ruled that the police could conduct searches using such "anticipatory warrants"—warrants issued when the police know that incriminating material is not yet present but have reason to believe that it will eventually arrive at a particular premises.[76] The warrants are held until the police are ready to conduct their search. In some instances, such as during an arrest, the authorities can conduct searches without obtaining any warrants at all.

The Fourth Amendment is also at issue in the controversy over mandatory drug testing. Such tests are most widely applied to public employees. In 1989 the Supreme Court upheld the U.S. Customs Service's drug-testing program for its employees[77] and drug and alcohol tests for railroad workers if they were involved in serious accidents.[78] Since then, more than 40 federal agencies have initiated mandatory employee drug tests, giving rise to public appeals against the general practice of "suspicionless testing" of employees, in violation of the Fourth Amendment. A 1995 case, in which the Court upheld a public school district's policy requiring all students participating in interscholastic sports to submit to random drug tests, surely contributed to the efforts of federal, state, and local agencies to initiate random and suspicionless drug and alcohol testing.[79]

The most recent cases suggest, however, that the Court is beginning to consider limits on the war against drugs. In a decisive 8–1 decision in 1997, the Court applied the Fourth Amendment as a shield against "state action that diminishes personal privacy" in cases that do not involve high-risk or safety-sensitive tasks.[80] And in 2013, the Court held that the use of a drug-sniffing dog on the front porch of a home constituted a search that violates the Fourth Amendment in the absence of consent of a warrant.[81]

Changes in technology have also had an impact on Fourth Amendment jurisprudence. In the 2012 case of *United States v. Jones*, the Court held that prosecutors violated Jones's rights when they attached a Global Positioning System (GPS) device to his Jeep and monitored his movements for 28 days.[82] On the other hand, in *Maryland v. King*, the Court upheld DNA testing of arrestees without the need for individualized suspicion. Writing for the majority, Justice Anthony Kennedy characterized DNA testing as an administrative tool for identifying the arrestee and thus legally indistinguishable from photographing and fingerprinting.[83] In the 2014 case of *Riley v. California*, the Court held that the police were constitutionally prohibited from seizing and searching the digital contents of a cell phone during an arrest. As new technologies develop, the Court will continue to face the question of what constitutes a reasonable search.[84] In 2016 the FBI sought to compel the Apple Corporation to unlock the cell phone used by Syed Farook, an alleged terrorist who, along with his wife Tashfeen Malik, had killed 14 people in San Bernardino, California. Apple asserted that creating new software to enable the FBI to unlock the phone would allow the agency to invade the privacy of millions of iPhone users. The case became moot when the FBI was able to unlock the phone without Apple's help.

Supporters of stop-and-frisk tactics argue that the practice reduces crime rates. However, since Mayor Bill de Blasio ended stop and frisk in New York City in 2014, crime rates have not increased or changed significantly. Here, plain clothes police officers stop and frisk Harlem residents.

Fourth Amendment issues have also been raised by aggressive police tactics, particularly the tactic known as "stop and frisk." This is a tactic in which the police confront an individual whom they believe to be acting "suspiciously," question the individual, and conduct a search for weapons. The practice was reviewed by the Supreme Court in the 1968 case of *Terry v. Ohio*, and the Court then held that if an officer had "probable cause" to believe the individual was armed, such a search was permitted.[85] In recent years, some police departments, most notably the New York City police, have made stop and frisk a routine practice, searching thousands and thousands of individuals whom they deemed to look suspicious. The police aver that this aggressive tactic has reduced crime rates. In August 2013 a federal judge, Shira Scheindlin, noted that most police stops occurred in minority communities and amounted to a form of racial profiling. The judge's order ending the practice, however, was stayed by a federal appeals court that removed Judge Scheindlin from the case and accused her of improper bias. In 2014 the City of New York dropped its appeal and agreed to engage in a process of mediation with community groups to curtail the practice. After his election in 2014, Mayor Bill de Blasio announced an end to aggressive stop-and-frisk tactics. Critics charged that the mayor's orders would lead to an increase in New York crime rates, though this has not occurred.

Finally, the Fourth Amendment places limits on government surveillance of individuals, an ongoing and controversial issue in the United States today. For example, a federal judge in Washington, D.C., recently ruled that an NSA program that collected millions of records of telephone calls was impermissible under the Fourth Amendment.[86]

THE FIFTH AMENDMENT

> No person shall be held to answer for a capital, or otherwise infamous crime, unless on a presentment or indictment of a Grand Jury, except in cases arising in the land or naval forces, or in the Militia, when in actual service in time of War or public danger; nor shall any person be subject for the same offence to be twice put in jeopardy of life or limb; nor shall be compelled in any criminal case to be a witness against himself, nor be deprived of life, liberty, or property, without due process of law; nor shall private property be taken for public use, without just compensation.

Grand Juries The first clause of the Fifth Amendment, the right to a **grand jury** to determine whether a trial is warranted, is considered "the oldest institution known to the Constitution."[87] A grand jury is a body of citizens that must agree that the

grand jury jury that determines whether sufficient evidence is available to justify a trial; grand juries do not rule on the accused's guilt or innocence prosecutor has sufficient evidence to bring criminal charges against a suspect. Grand juries play an important role in federal criminal cases. However, the provision for a grand jury is the one important civil liberties provision of the Bill of Rights that was not incorporated into the Fourteenth Amendment to apply to state criminal prosecutions. Thus, some states operate without grand juries. In such states, the prosecuting attorney simply files a "bill of information" affirming that there is sufficient evidence available to justify a trial. If the accused person is to be held in custody, the prosecutor must take the available information before a judge to determine that the evidence shows probable cause.

double jeopardy the Fifth Amendment right providing that a person cannot be tried twice for the same crime

Double Jeopardy "Nor shall any person be subject for the same offence to be twice put in jeopardy of life or limb" is the constitutional protection from **double jeopardy**, or being tried more than once for the same crime. The protection from double jeopardy was at the heart of the *Palko* case in 1937, which, as we saw earlier in this chapter, also established the principle of selective incorporation of the Bill of Rights. In the *Palko* case, the Supreme Court ruled that the Fifth Amendment's prohibition of double jeopardy did not apply to the states. However, in the 1969 case of *Benton v. Maryland*, the Court expressly overruled *Palko* and declared that the double jeopardy clause did, in fact, apply to the states.[88] In this case, the state of Maryland sought to try a defendant, John Benton, for larceny, even though he had previously been acquitted by a jury. Maryland's constitution did not prohibit such a proceeding, and at the second trial Benton was convicted. The Supreme Court, however, ruled that the second trial violated Benton's rights under the U.S. Constitution. Double jeopardy now joined those rights "incorporated" via the Fourteenth Amendment.

Self-Incrimination Perhaps the most significant liberty found in the Fifth Amendment, and the one most familiar to the many Americans who watch television crime shows, is the guarantee that no citizen "shall be compelled in any criminal case to be a witness against himself." The most famous case concerning self-incrimination is one of such importance that Chief Justice Earl Warren assessed its results as going "to the very root of our concepts of American criminal jurisprudence."[89] Twenty-three-year-old Ernesto Miranda was sentenced to between 20 and 30 years in prison for the kidnapping and rape of an 18-year-old woman. The woman had identified him in a police lineup, and after two hours of questioning, Miranda confessed, subsequently signing a statement that his confession had been made voluntarily, without threats or promises of immunity. These confessions were admitted into evidence and served as the basis for Miranda's conviction. After his conviction, Miranda argued that his confession had not been truly voluntary and that he had not been informed of his right to remain silent or his right to consult an attorney. The Supreme Court agreed and overturned the conviction. Following one of the most intensely and widely criticized decisions ever handed down by the Supreme Court, Ernesto Miranda's case produced the rules the police must follow before questioning an arrested criminal suspect. The reading of a person's "Miranda rights" became a standard scene in every police station and on virtually every dramatization of police action on television and in the movies. *Miranda* advanced the civil liberties of accused persons not only by expanding the scope of the Fifth Amendment clause covering coerced confessions and self-incrimination but also by confirming the right to counsel (discussed later). The Supreme Court under Burger and Rehnquist considerably softened the *Miranda*

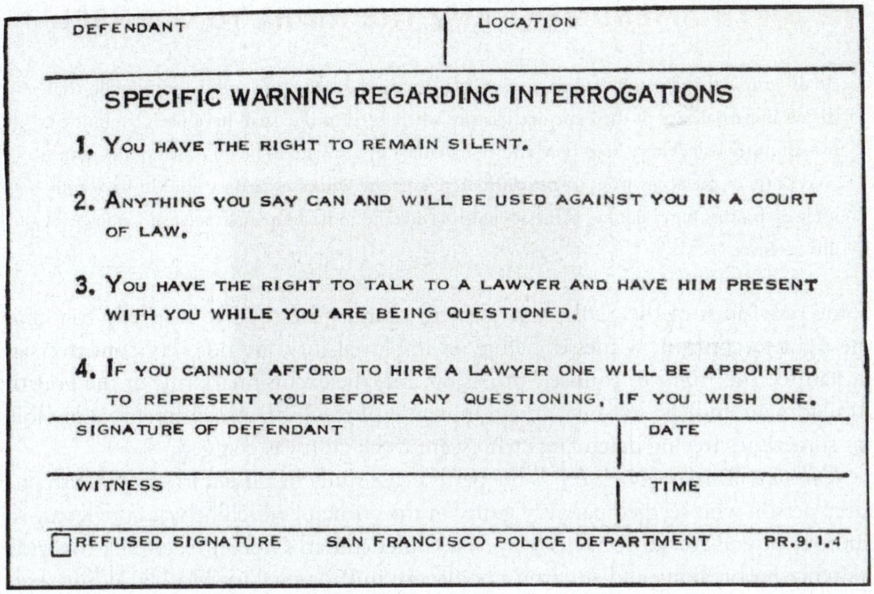

DEFENDANT | LOCATION

SPECIFIC WARNING REGARDING INTERROGATIONS

1. YOU HAVE THE RIGHT TO REMAIN SILENT.

2. ANYTHING YOU SAY CAN AND WILL BE USED AGAINST YOU IN A COURT OF LAW.

3. YOU HAVE THE RIGHT TO TALK TO A LAWYER AND HAVE HIM PRESENT WITH YOU WHILE YOU ARE BEING QUESTIONED.

4. IF YOU CANNOT AFFORD TO HIRE A LAWYER ONE WILL BE APPOINTED TO REPRESENT YOU BEFORE ANY QUESTIONING, IF YOU WISH ONE.

SIGNATURE OF DEFENDANT | DATE

WITNESS | TIME

☐ REFUSED SIGNATURE   SAN FRANCISCO POLICE DEPARTMENT   PR.9.1.4

The case of Ernesto Miranda resulted in the creation of Miranda rights, which must be read to those arrested to make them aware of their constitutional rights.

restrictions, but the **Miranda rule** still stands as a protection against egregious police abuses of arrested persons.

Miranda rule the requirement, articulated by the Supreme Court in *Miranda v. Arizona*, that persons under arrest must be informed prior to police interrogation of their rights to remain silent and to have the benefit of legal counsel

Eminent Domain The other fundamental clause of the Fifth Amendment is the "takings clause," which extends to each citizen a protection against the "taking" of private property "without just compensation." Although this part of the Fifth Amendment is not specifically concerned with protecting persons accused of crimes, it is nevertheless a fundamentally important instance where the government and the citizen are adversaries. The power of any government to take private property for public use—a power essential to the very concept of sovereignty—is called **eminent domain**. The Fifth Amendment puts limits on that inherent power through procedures that require a showing of a public purpose and the provision of fair payment for the taking of someone's property. This provision is now universally observed in all U.S. principalities, but it has not always been meticulously observed.

eminent domain the right of government to take private property for public use

The first modern case confronting the issue of public use involved a mom-and-pop grocery store in a run-down neighborhood of the District of Columbia. In carrying out a vast urban redevelopment program, the city government took the property as one of a large number of privately owned lots to be cleared for new housing and business construction. The owner of the grocery store took the government to court on the grounds that it was an unconstitutional use of eminent domain to take property from one private owner and eventually to turn that property back, in altered form, to another private owner. In 1945 the store owner lost the case. The Supreme Court's argument was a curious but very important one: the "public interest" can mean virtually anything a legislature says it means. In other words, since the overall slum clearance and redevelopment project was in the public interest, according to the legislature, the eventual transfers of property were justified.[90] This principle was reaffirmed in the 2005 case of *Kelo v. City of New London*, where the Court held that the city could seize land from one private owner and transfer it to another as part of a redevelopment plan.[91]

THE SIXTH AMENDMENT AND THE RIGHT TO COUNSEL

> In all criminal prosecutions, the accused shall enjoy the right to a speedy and public trial, by an impartial jury of the State and district wherein the crime shall have been committed, which district shall have been previously ascertained by law, and to be informed of the nature and cause of the accusation; to be confronted with the witnesses against him; to have compulsory process for obtaining witnesses in his favor, and to have the Assistance of Counsel for his defence.

Some provisions of the Sixth Amendment, such as the right to a speedy trial and the right to confront witnesses before an impartial jury, are not very controversial in nature. The "right to counsel" provision, like the exclusionary rule of the Fourth Amendment and the self-incrimination clause of the Fifth Amendment, is notable for sometimes freeing defendants who seem to be guilty as charged.

Gideon v. Wainwright (1963) is the perfect case study because it involved a disreputable person who seemed patently guilty of the crime of which he was convicted. In and out of jails for most of his 51 years, Clarence Earl Gideon received a five-year sentence for breaking and entering a poolroom in Panama City, Florida. While serving time in jail, Gideon became a fairly well-qualified "jailhouse lawyer," made his own appeal on a handwritten petition, and eventually won the landmark ruling on the right to counsel in all felony cases.[92]

The right to counsel has been expanded during the past few decades, even as the courts have become more conservative. For example, although at first the right to counsel was met by judges assigning lawyers from the community as a formal public obligation, now most states and cities have created an office of public defender; these state-employed professional defense lawyers typically provide poor defendants with much better legal representation. In addition, defendants have the right to appeal a conviction on the grounds that the counsel provided by the state was deficient. For example, in 2003 the Supreme Court overturned the death sentence of a Maryland death-row inmate, holding that the defense lawyer had failed to inform the jury fully of the defendant's history of "horrendous childhood abuse."[93] Moreover, the right to counsel extends beyond serious crimes to any trial, with or without a jury, that holds the possibility of imprisonment.[94]

THE EIGHTH AMENDMENT AND CRUEL AND UNUSUAL PUNISHMENT

> Excessive bail shall not be required, nor excessive fines imposed, nor cruel and unusual punishment inflicted.

Virtually all the debate over Eighth Amendment issues focuses on the last clause of the amendment: one of the greatest challenges in interpreting this provision consistently is that what is considered "cruel and unusual" varies from culture to culture and from generation to generation.

In 1972 the Supreme Court overturned several state death penalty laws, not because they were cruel and unusual but because they were being applied unevenly—that is, African Americans were much more likely than whites to be sentenced to death, the poor more likely than the rich, and men more likely than women.[95] Very soon after that decision, a majority of states revised their capital punishment provisions to meet the Court's standards, and the Court reaffirmed that the death penalty could be used if certain standards were met.[96] Since 1976, the Court has consistently upheld state laws providing for capital punishment, although the Court also continues to review death penalty appeals each year.

Between 1976 and April 2017, states executed 1,448 people. Most of those executions occurred in southern states, with Texas leading the way at 542. As of October 2018, 30 states had statutes providing for capital punishment for specified offenses, a policy supported by a majority of Americans, according to polls. On the other hand, 19 states bar the death penalty, and since the end of the 1990s, both the number of death sentences and the number of executions have declined annually.[97] In 2017, 23 people were executed in the United States, a slight increase over the 20 executed in 2016.

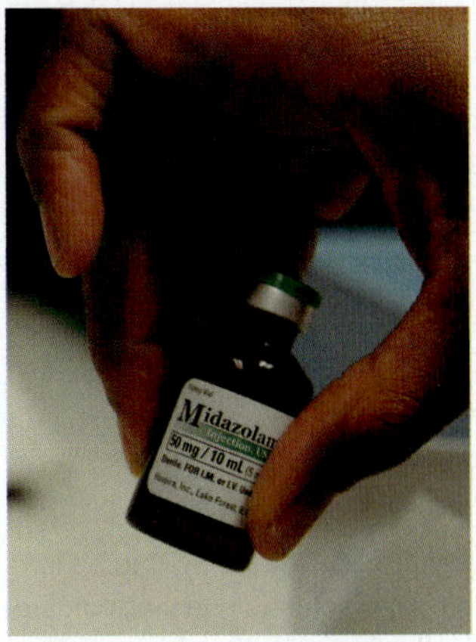

Opponents argue that the death penalty constitutes cruel and unusual punishment. In recent years the use of lethal injection drugs including Midazolam has come under scrutiny after some troubling executions where the process was drawn out and painful. In 2015 the Supreme Court upheld the use of lethal injection.

Despite the seeming popularity of the death penalty, the debate has become, if anything, more intense. Many death penalty supporters assert its deterrent effects on other would-be criminals. Although studies of capital crimes usually fail to demonstrate any direct deterrent effect, this failure may be due to the lengthy delays—typically years and even decades—between convictions and executions. A system that eliminates undue delays might enhance deterrence. And deterring even one murder or other heinous crime, proponents argue, is ample justification for such laws.

Death penalty opponents are quick to counter that the death penalty has not been proven to deter crime, either in the United States or abroad. In fact, America is the only Western nation that still executes criminals. If the government is to serve as an example of proper behavior, say foes of capital punishment, it has no business sanctioning killing when incarceration will similarly protect society. Furthermore, execution is time-consuming and expensive—more expensive than life imprisonment—precisely because the government must make every effort to ensure that it is not executing an innocent person. Curtailing legal appeals would make the possibility of a mistake too great. And although most Americans do support the death penalty, people also support life imprisonment without the possibility of parole as an alternative. Race also intrudes in death penalty cases: people of color are disproportionately more likely than whites charged with identical crimes to be given the ultimate punishment.

The Supreme Court has long struggled to establish principles to govern executions under the Eighth Amendment. In recent years, the Court has issued a number of death penalty opinions, declaring that death was too harsh a penalty for the crime of rape of a child,[98] prohibiting the execution of a defendant with an IQ under 70 and of a youthful defendant, and invalidating a death sentence for an African Americans defendant after the prosecutor improperly excluded African Americans from the jury.[99] In 2015 the Court upheld lethal injection as a mode of execution despite arguments that this form of execution was likely to cause considerable pain.[100]

The question of cruel and unusual punishment goes beyond the death penalty. Federal courts have on occasion held that overcrowding and other dangerous conditions within prisons, such as inadequate food, medical care, and sanitation, may constitute cruel and unusual punishment. Also, prison officials employing threats and beatings against inmates may be guilty of violating this Eighth Amendment right.[101] The Court has also been concerned with punishments meted out to the mentally disabled and to juveniles. In a recent case, the Court held that life imprisonment without parole for a juvenile, even one convicted of murder, constituted cruel and unusual punishment.[102] The "Who Are Americans?" feature takes a look at the U.S. prison population.

The Right to Privacy

Assess whether people have a right to privacy under the Constitution

A **right to privacy** was not granted in the Bill of Rights, but a clause in the Fourth Amendment provides for "the right of the people to be secure in their persons, houses, papers, and effects, against unreasonable searches and seizures." In a 1928 case, Justice Louis Brandeis argued in a dissent that the Fourth Amendment should be extended to a more general principle of "privacy in the home."[103] Another step in this direction was taken when several Jehovah's Witnesses directed their children not to salute the flag or say the Pledge of Allegiance in school because the first of the Ten Commandments prohibits the worship of "graven images." They lost their case in 1940, but the Supreme Court, reversing itself in 1943, held that the 1940 case had been "wrongly decided" and recognized "a right to be left alone" as part of the free speech clause of the First Amendment.[104] Another small step was taken in 1958, when the Supreme Court recognized "privacy in one's association" in its decision that the state of Alabama could not use the membership list of the National Association for the Advancement of Colored People (NAACP) in state investigations.[105]

right to privacy the right to be left alone, which has been interpreted by the Supreme Court to entail individual access to birth control and abortions

BIRTH CONTROL

The sphere of privacy was formally recognized in 1965, when the Court ruled that a Connecticut statute forbidding the use of contraceptives violated the right of marital privacy. Estelle Griswold, the executive director of the Planned Parenthood League of Connecticut, was arrested by the state of Connecticut for providing information, instruction, and medical advice about contraception to married couples. She and her associates were found guilty as accessories to the crime and fined $100 each. The Supreme Court reversed the lower-court decisions and declared the Connecticut law unconstitutional because it violated "a right of privacy older than the Bill of Rights—older than our political parties, older than our school system."[106] Justice William O. Douglas, author of the majority decision in the *Griswold* case, argued that this right of privacy is also grounded in the Constitution because it fits into a "zone of privacy" created by a combination of the Third, Fourth, and Fifth amendments. A concurring opinion, written by Justice Arthur Goldberg, attempted to strengthen Douglas's argument by adding that "the concept of liberty...embraces the right of marital privacy though that right is not mentioned explicitly in the Constitution [and] is supported by numerous decisions of this Court...and *by the language and history of the Ninth Amendment* [emphasis added]."[107] The Ninth Amendment provides that "the enumeration in the Constitution, of certain rights, shall not be construed to deny or disparage others retained by the people." According to Justice Goldberg, this language means, in effect, that just because the Constitution does not specifically mention a particular right to privacy does not mean that the people do not retain that right. The language of the Ninth Amendment, when taken with the evidence provided by the First, Third, Fourth, and Fifth amendments, was sufficient for the Court to find that the Bill of Rights implies a constitutional right to privacy.

FOR CRITICAL ANALYSIS

Read the Third, Fourth, Fifth, and Ninth amendments in the appendix at the end of this book. In your opinion, do American citizens have a constitutional right to privacy?

Vho Is in Prison?

espite the many freedoms protected by the Bill of Rights, the United States imprisons more of its people than ıy other country. Although African Americans make up only about 13 percent of the total U.S. population, they ake up 35.7 percent of the prison population. Incarceration rates by state range from a low of 189 per)0,000 residents in Maine to a high of 1,072 per 100,000 residents in Louisiana.*

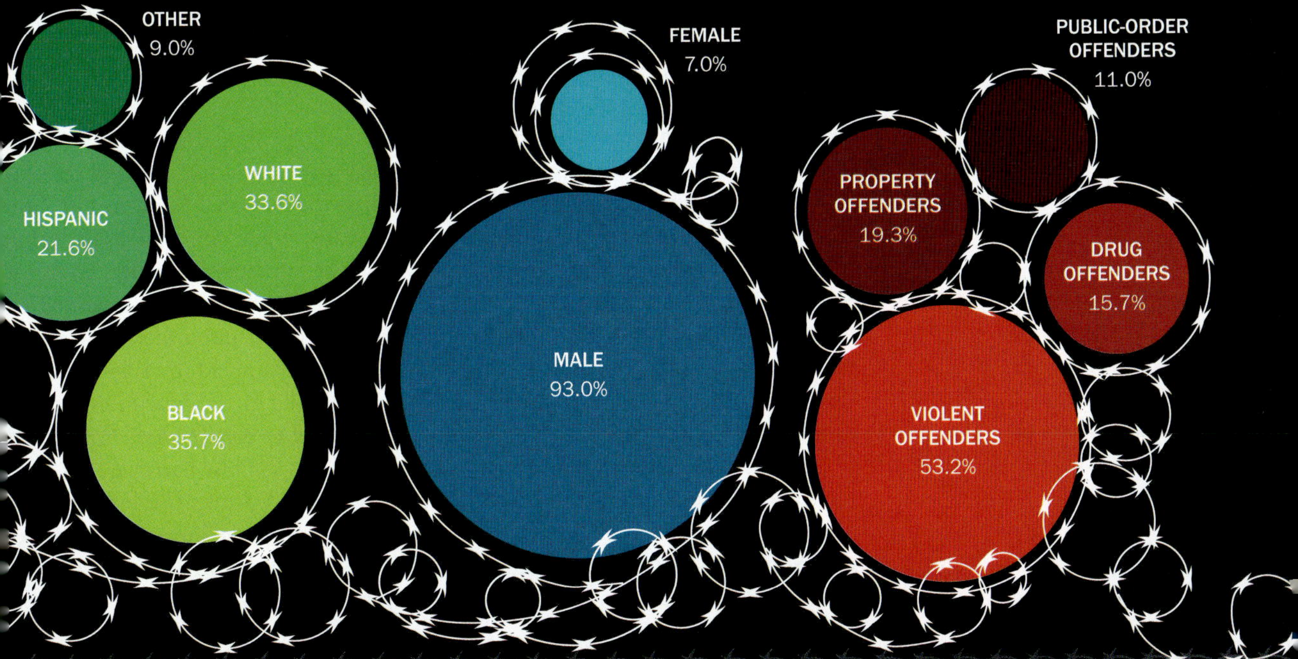

ılent offenses include murder, manslaughter, rape/sexual assault, robbery, and aggravated or simple assault. Property offenses include burglary, motor vehicle theft, ıd fraud. Drug offenses include trafficking and possession. Public order offenses include weapons, drunk driving, and indecency.

Incarceration Rates by State

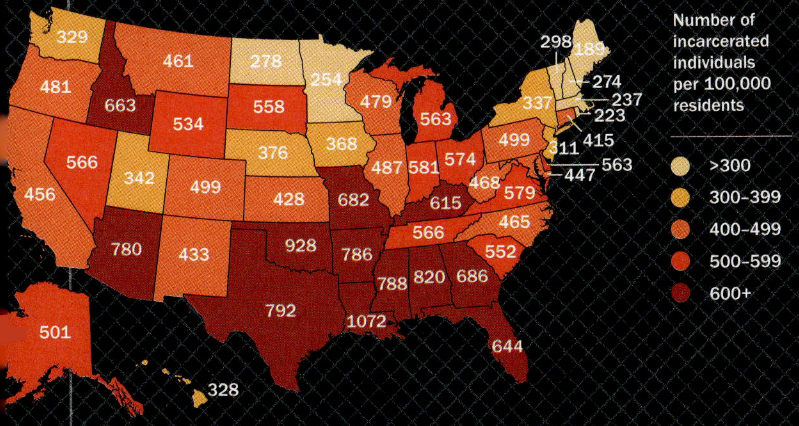

)URCE: U.S. Department of Justice, "Prisoners in 2014," September 2015, ıw.bjs.gov/index.cfm?ty=pbdetail&iid=5387 (accessed 2/18/16).

FOR CRITICAL ANALYSIS

1. Due process guarantees the same legal protections to anyone accused of a crime. However, studies have shown that African Americans and Hispanics are more likely to be jailed—and jailed for longer—than whites convicted of similar crimes. Is this a violation of civil liberties?
2. Some people have argued that prison terms for relatively minor drug offenses violate the Eighth Amendment's ban on cruel and unusual punishment. What do you think?

ABORTION

The right to privacy was confirmed and extended in 1973 in an important Supreme Court decision: *Roe v. Wade*. This decision established a woman's right to seek an abortion and prohibited states from making abortion a criminal act prior to the point at which the fetus becomes viable, which in 1973 was the twenty-seventh week.[108] The Burger Court's decision in *Roe* took a revolutionary step toward establishing the right to privacy. It is important to emphasize that the preference for privacy rights and for their extension to include the rights of women to control their own bodies was not something the Supreme Court invented in a vacuum. Most states did not regulate abortions in any fashion until the 1840s, at which time only six of the 26 existing states had any regulations governing abortion. In addition, many states had begun to ease their abortion restrictions well before the 1973 *Roe* decision, although in recent years a number of states have reinstated some restrictions on abortion including lowering the viability standard: 20 weeks (Texas), 12 weeks (Arkansas), and 6 weeks (North Dakota).

By extending the umbrella of privacy, this sweeping ruling dramatically changed abortion practices in America. In addition, it galvanized and nationalized the abortion debate. Groups opposed to abortion, such as the National Right to Life Committee, organized to fight the liberal new standard, while abortion rights groups have sought to maintain that protection. While the Supreme Court has continued to affirm a woman's right to seek an abortion, the Court has since qualified that right as the legal standard shifted against abortion rights supporters. In *Webster v. Reproductive Health Services* (1989), the Court narrowly upheld (by a 5–4 majority) the constitutionality of restrictions on the use of public medical facilities for abortion.[109] And in the 1992 case of *Planned Parenthood of Southeastern Pennsylvania v. Casey*, another 5–4 majority of the Court upheld *Roe* but narrowed its scope, refusing to invalidate a Pennsylvania law that significantly limits freedom of choice. The Court's decision defined the right to an abortion as a "limited or qualified" right subject to regulation by the states as long as the regulation does not constitute an "undue burden."[110] In the 2006 case of *Ayotte v. Planned Parenthood of Northern*

One of the most important cases related to the right to privacy was *Roe v. Wade*, which established a woman's right to seek an abortion. However, the decision has remained highly controversial, with opponents arguing that the Constitution does not guarantee this right.

New England, the Court held that a law requiring parental notification before a minor could obtain an abortion was not an undue burden.[111] And in the 2007 *Gonzales v. Carhart* decision, the Court effectively upheld the federal partial-birth abortion ban, which outlaws a particular type of abortion procedure.[112]

SEXUAL ORIENTATION

In the last three decades, the right to be left alone began to include the privacy rights of gay people. One morning in Atlanta, Georgia, in the mid-1980s, a police officer came to the home of Michael Hardwick to serve a warrant for Hardwick's arrest for failure to appear in court to answer charges of drinking in public. One of Hardwick's unknowing housemates invited the officer to look in Hardwick's room, where he found Hardwick and another man engaging in "consensual sexual behavior" and then proceeded to arrest him under Georgia's laws against heterosexual and homosexual sodomy. Hardwick filed a lawsuit against the state, challenging the constitutionality of the Georgia law, and won his case in the federal court of appeals. The state of Georgia, in an unusual move, appealed the court's decision to the Supreme Court. In 1986 the majority of the Court reversed the lower-court decision, holding against Hardwick on the grounds that "the federal Constitution confers [no] fundamental right upon homosexuals to engage in sodomy" and that therefore there was no basis to invalidate "the laws of the many states that still make such conduct illegal and have done so for a very long time."[113]

Seventeen years later, and to almost everyone's surprise, in *Lawrence v. Texas* (2003) the Court overturned *Bowers v. Hardwick* with a dramatic pronouncement that gays are "entitled to respect for their private lives"[114] as a matter of constitutional due process. Drawing from the tradition of negative liberty, the Court maintained, "In our tradition the State is not omnipresent in the home. And there are other spheres of our lives and existence outside the home, where the State should not be a dominant presence." Explicitly encompassing lesbians and gay men within the umbrella of privacy, the Court concluded that the "petitioners are entitled to respect for their private lives. The State cannot demean their existence or control their destiny by making their private sexual conduct a crime."[115] This decision added substance to the "right of privacy."[116] In 2015 the Court took another important step in the protection of gay rights by declaring that state bans on same-sex marriage were unconstitutional.[117] The Court said that the refusal to issue marriage licenses to same-sex couples constituted a violation of the Fourteenth Amendment's equal protection and due process clauses. See Chapter 5 for more on same-sex marriage.

THE RIGHT TO DIE

Another area ripe for litigation and public discourse is the so-called right to die. A number of highly publicized physician-assisted suicides in the 1990s focused attention on whether people have a right to choose their own death and to receive assistance in carrying it out. Can this become part of the privacy right? Or is it a new substantive right? The Supreme Court has not definitively answered this question. However, the Court refused to intervene in the well-publicized case of Terri Schiavo, a woman who suffered irreversible brain damage and was kept alive in a vegetative state via a feeding tube for 15 years. During this period, Schiavo's husband wanted to withdraw life support, citing his wife's wishes, while her

AMERICA SIDE by SIDE

Civil Liberties around the World

Elections are only a small part of what makes a democracy a democracy. *Liberal democracies*—a term political scientists use to refer to countries they consider fully democratic—also have extensive civil rights and civil liberties.

Freedom House, an independent watchdog organization focusing on freedom and democracy around the world, collects data on political rights and civil liberties from each country. They measure freedom of expression and belief, respect for the "rule of law,"[a] the right to organize and form associations, and personal autonomy and individual rights to rank countries as free, partly free, and not free (shown below).

All countries vary in how they prioritize specific liberties. The United States is generally comparable to other democracies when it comes to the freedom of expression and belief and the right to organize and form associations, but the United States places exceptionally high emphasis on personal autonomy and individual rights. In comparison, Latvia is ranked slightly higher on the right to organize and form associations, but concerns regarding the treatment of women and minorities mean its individual rights score is lower.

CIVIL LIBERTIES AND POLITICAL RIGHTS, 2018

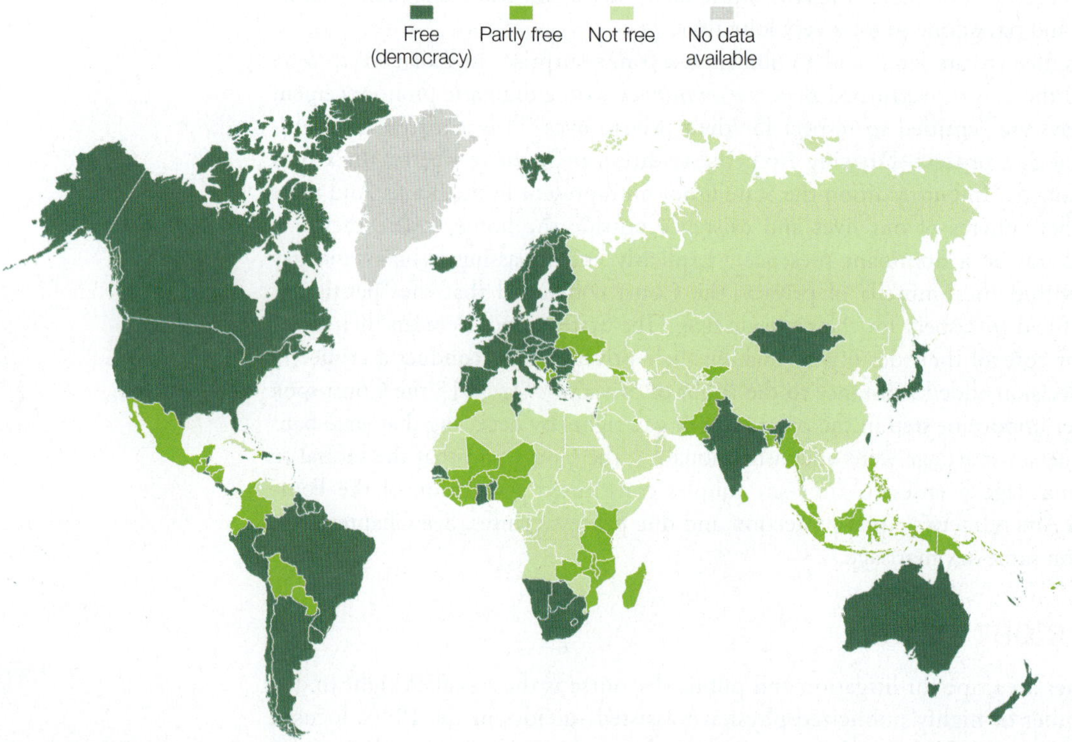

SOURCE: Freedom House, "Freedom in the World 2018 Democracy in Crisis," https://freedomhouse.org/report/freedom-world-aggregate-and-subcategory-scores (accessed 4/27/18).

[a] A legal principle that laws should govern a country—including its leaders—rather than having decisions made arbitrarily by individuals in the government.

parents wanted support continued indefinitely. The case was heard multiple times in the Florida state courts and the federal courts. In 2005, Schiavo's husband finally prevailed, and she was removed from life support and subsequently died.[118] In the 2006 case of *Gonzales v. Oregon*, the Supreme Court did intervene to uphold a law allowing doctors to use drugs to facilitate the deaths of terminally ill patients who requested such assistance.[119] Thus, although the Court has not ruled definitively on the right-to-die question, it does not seem hostile to the idea.

Civil Liberties
WHAT DO WE WANT?

The prominent place of civil liberties is one of the hallmarks of American government. The freedoms enshrined in the Constitution and its amendments help define the relationship between government and citizens by limiting what government can do to individuals.

But these freedoms also come with trade-offs. We saw in the chapter opener that the freedom afforded to the Slants rock band to reimagine an ethnic slur as a term of empowerment undermined Native Americans' efforts to end the use of an ethnic term they found offensive. Trade-offs are prominent in many areas of government. Surveillance is one where difficult trade-offs are particularly acute. Government eavesdropping on communications, travel, and personal conduct has become a fact of American life. Revelations in the summer of 2013 of extensive electronic surveillance by the NSA of Americans' phone and internet communications caused considerable consternation in Congress and in the news media. However, many Americans believe that they are the beneficiaries rather than the potential victims of government surveillance. Those who have nothing to hide, goes the saying, have nothing to fear. But as law professor Daniel Solove shows, surveillance can entrap even the most innocent individuals in a web of suspicions and allegations from which they may find it extremely difficult to extricate themselves.[120]

National Intelligence director James Clapper and other defense officials testified before Congress following revelations in 2013 of extensive government surveillance programs. Electronic monitoring allows the government to gather vast quantities of data from private communications.

The trade-off between individual privacy and government surveillance raises questions not just about security but also about political power. Popular government requires that citizens possess a good deal of knowledge about the actions of the state. In essence, citizens must undertake their own surveillance of the government and its officials as a precondition for exerting influence over them. At the same time, citizens' ability to exercise power also requires that they have considerable protection from the state's scrutiny. Those who disagree with government must be both free to organize and voice their opinions and free from government retaliation.

Thus, popular government requires a combination of government transparency and citizen privacy. Questions about privacy will continue to grow as surveillance technologies become more sophisticated and we, as citizens, will be challenged to adapt eighteenth-century constitutional protections to twenty-first-century issues. How have new technologies affected the government's ability to monitor its citizens? What are your expectations of privacy in your email conversations, your plane tickets, your reading habits?

These issues, along with questions about the right to bear arms, the use of the death penalty, and religious freedom (see the "**Who Participates?**" feature on the facing page) are unlikely to go away any time soon and will continue to challenge Americans in the years to come.

WHO PARTICIPATES?

Religious Affiliation and Freedom of Religion

Percentage of American Adults in Each Religious Tradition

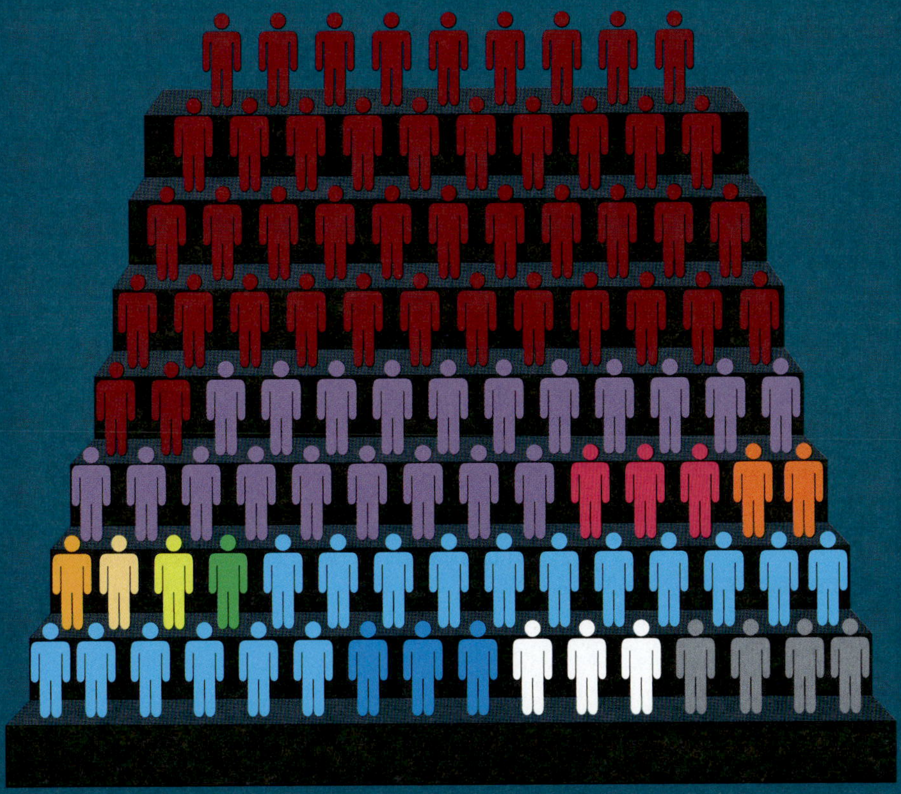

Under the First Amendment, Americans enjoy the freedom to practice (or not practice) the religion of their choice. Most Americans identify with and participate in some form of religion.

- Protestant **44%**
- Catholic **20%**
- Other Christian **3%**
- Jewish **2%**
- Muslim **1%**
- Buddhist **1%**
- Hindu **1%**
- Other faiths **1%**
- Nothing in particular **17%**
- Agnostic **3%**
- Atheist **3%**
- Don't know **4%**

SOURCE: Robert P. Jones and Daniel Cox, *America's Changing Religious Identity*, 2016, www.prri.org/ (accessed 11/4/17).

WHAT YOU CAN DO

Know Your First Amendment Rights

- ✓ Learn more about freedom of religion from a variety of legal scholars at **www.constitutioncenter.org**.
- ✓ Share your opinion about the First Amendment and religion on campus with your school newspaper. Find information about students' religious rights at **www.thefire.org**.
- ✓ Learn more about your other First Amendment rights, such as free speech on the internet, at **www.eff.org**.

STUDY GUIDE

Civil Liberties and the Constitution

Explain the origins and evolution of the civil liberties in the Bill of Rights as they apply to federal government and the states (pp. 117–22)

Although some of the framers believed that a bill of rights was unnecessary and potentially dangerous, the Federalists made a pledge to add one in order to secure support for the Constitution during the ratification process. Over the course of the first 100 years of American history, the Bill of Rights was interpreted to limit only the actions of the federal government. One by one, most of the important provisions of the first 10 amendments have been incorporated into the Fourteenth Amendment and applied to the states.

Key Terms

habeas corpus (p. 118)
Bill of Rights (p. 118)
civil liberties (p. 118)
selective incorporation (p. 120)

Practice Quiz

1. From 1791 until the end of the nineteenth century, the Bill of Rights was interpreted to put limits on
   a) the national government only.
   b) the state government only.
   c) both the national and state governments.
   d) neither the national nor the state government.
   e) political parties and interest groups.
2. Which of the following rights was *not* included in the original Constitution?
   a) prohibition of bills of attainder
   b) prohibition of ex post facto laws
   c) guarantee of habeas corpus
   d) guarantee of trial by jury in the state where the crime was committed
   e) None. They were all included in the original Constitution.
3. The process by which some of the liberties in the Bill of Rights were applied to the states is known as
   a) preemption.
   b) selective incorporation.
   c) judicial activism.
   d) civil liberties.
   e) establishment.
4. Which of the following provisions of the Bill of Rights was incorporated in the 1897 Supreme Court case *Chicago, Burlington, and Quincy R.R. v. Chicago*?
   a) the right to counsel in any criminal trial
   b) the right against self-incrimination
   c) freedom from unnecessary searches and seizures
   d) freedom to petition the government for redress of grievances
   e) protection against the "taking" of private property by state governments "without just compensation"

The First Amendment and Freedom of Religion

Describe how the First Amendment protects freedom of religion (pp. 123–27)

Two parts of the First Amendment touch on religious freedom: the establishment clause and the free exercise clause. The courts have been somewhat inconsistent in determining how solid the establishment clause's "wall of separation" between church and state actually is in practice. While the courts have been more consistent in protecting the free exercise of religious beliefs, they have taken pains to distinguish between religious beliefs and actions based on those beliefs.

Key Terms

establishment clause (p. 123)
***Lemon* test (p. 124)**
free exercise clause (p. 125)

Practice Quiz

5. The Supreme Court's ruling in *Lemon v. Kurtzman*, which led to the *Lemon* test, concerned the issue of
   a) school desegregation.
   b) financial assistance to religious schools.
   c) cruel and unusual punishment.
   d) obscenity.
   e) prayer in school.

The First Amendment and Freedom of Speech and of the Press

Describe how the First Amendment protects free speech and freedom of the press (pp. 127–36)

Given the importance of freedom of speech and of the press to the functioning of democratic government, Americans are assumed to have the right to speak and broadcast their ideas unless there is some compelling reason to stop them. According to the courts, although virtually all speech is protected by the Constitution, some forms of speech are entitled to a greater degree of protection than others. Libel, slander, and speech that incites lawless action are examples of speech that can be limited by the government.

Key Terms

"clear and present danger" test (p. 128)
fighting words (p. 129)
"speech plus" (p. 133)
prior restraint (p. 133)
libel (p. 134)
slander (p. 134)

Practice Quiz

6. The judicial doctrine that places a heavy burden of proof on the government when it seeks to regulate or restrict speech is called
   a) judicial restraint.
   b) judicial activism.
   c) habeas corpus.
   d) prior restraint.
   e) strict scrutiny.

7. The standard articulated by the Supreme Court in *R.A.V. v. City of St. Paul* suggests that
   a) virtually all "hate speech" is not constitutionally protected by the First Amendment.
   b) virtually all "hate speech" is constitutionally protected by the First Amendment.
   c) "hate speech" is not constitutionally protected by the First Amendment when it is directed at religious groups.
   d) "hate speech" is not constitutionally protected by the First Amendment when it is directed at racial or ethnic minority groups.
   e) "hate speech" is not constitutionally protected by the First Amendment when it is expressed on college campuses.

8. Which of the following describes a written statement made in "reckless disregard of the truth" that is considered damaging to a victim because it is "malicious, scandalous, and defamatory"?
   a) slander
   b) libel
   c) speech plus
   d) fighting words
   e) expressive speech

The Second Amendment and the Right to Bear Arms

Explore whether the Second Amendment means people have a right to own guns (pp. 136–38)

The Second Amendment granted Americans the right "to keep and bear Arms" in order to provide for state militias. Prior to 2010, the Second Amendment was not incorporated. In *McDonald v. Chicago*, the Supreme Court asserted that the right to bear arms applies to both state governments and the federal government.

Practice Quiz

9. In *District of Columbia v. Heller*, the Supreme Court ruled that
   a) states can require citizens to own firearms.
   b) federal grants can be used to support the formation of state militias.
   c) felons cannot be prevented from purchasing assault rifles.
   d) the Second Amendment provides a constitutional right to keep a loaded handgun at home for self-defense.
   e) the Second Amendment applies only to the federal government and not to states.

Rights of the Criminally Accused

Explain the major rights that people have if they are accused of a crime (pp. 138–46)

The essence of the Constitution's due process of the law is found in the Fourth, Fifth, Sixth, and Eighth amendments. The Fourth Amendment protects individuals from unreasonable searches and seizures. The Fifth Amendment provides individuals with the right to a grand jury, protection from double jeopardy, and a guarantee against self-incrimination. The Sixth Amendment provides the right to legal counsel, the right to a speedy trial, and the right to confront witnesses before an impartial jury. The Eighth Amendment protects individuals against "cruel and unusual" punishment.

Key Terms

due process of law (p. 138)
exclusionary rule (p. 139)
grand jury (p. 141)
double jeopardy (p. 142)
Miranda rule (p. 143)
eminent domain (p. 143)

Practice Quiz

10. In *Mapp v. Ohio*, the Supreme Court ruled that
a) evidence obtained from an illegal search could not be introduced in a trial.
b) the government must provide legal counsel for defendants who are too poor to provide it for themselves.
c) persons under arrest must be informed prior to police interrogation of their rights to remain silent and to have the benefits of legal counsel.
d) the government has the right to take private property for public use if just compensation is provided.
e) a person cannot be tried twice for the same crime.

11. Which of the following is called "the oldest institution known to the Constitution"?
a) The Third Amendment's freedom from forced quartering of soldiers during peacetime.
b) The Fourth Amendment's freedom from warrantless search and seizure.
c) The Fifth Amendment's right to remain silent.
d) The Fifth Amendment's right against self-incrimination and forced confessions.
e) The Fifth Amendment's right to a grand jury in order to determine whether a trial is warranted.

12. Which famous case deals with the Sixth Amendment's guarantee of the right to counsel?
a) *Roe v. Wade*
b) *Mapp v. Ohio*
c) *Gideon v. Wainwright*
d) *Terry v. Ohio*
e) *Miranda v. Arizona*

The Right to Privacy

Assess whether people have a right to privacy under the Constitution (pp. 146–51)

A right to privacy is never explicitly mentioned in the Constitution. In fact, it was not until 1965 that the Supreme Court interpreted the Third, Fourth, Fifth, and Ninth amendments to create a constitutional "zone of privacy." The right to privacy has since been used to strike down laws limiting access to birth control, outlawing abortion, and criminalizing gay and lesbian sexual activity. The Supreme Court has not yet definitively answered the question of whether the right to privacy also gives individuals a right to choose their own death and to receive assistance in carrying it out.

Key Term

right to privacy (p. 146)

Practice Quiz

13. In which case was a right to privacy related to the use of birth control first formally recognized by the Court?
a) *Griswold v. Connecticut*
b) *Roe v. Wade*
c) *Lemon v. Kurtzman*
d) *Planned Parenthood v. Casey*
e) *Baker v. Carr*

14. In which case did the Supreme Court rule that state governments no longer had the authority to make private sexual behavior a crime?
a) *Texas v. Johnson*
b) *Webster v. Reproductive Health Services*
c) *Gonzales v. Oregon*
d) *Lawrence v. Texas*
e) *Bowers v. Hardwick*

For Further Reading

Amar, Akhil Reed. *The Law of the Land: A Grand Tour of Our Constitutional Republic*. New York: Basic Books, 2015.

Ash, Timothy Garton. Free Speech. New Haven, CT: Yale University Press, 2017.

Barbas, Samantha. *Newsworthy: The Supreme Court Battle over Privacy and Press Freedom*. Stanford, CA: Stanford University Press, 2017.

Brandon, Mark. *The Constitution in Wartime*. Durham, NC: Duke University Press, 2005.

Friendly, Fred W. *Minnesota Rag: The Dramatic Story of the Landmark Supreme Court Case That Gave New Meaning to Freedom of the Press*. New York: Vintage, 1982.

Gray, David. *The Fourth Amendment in an Age of Surveillance*. New York: Cambridge University Press, 2017.

Lewis, Anthony. *Freedom for the Thought That We Hate: A Biography of the First Amendment*. New York: Basic Books, 2010.

Lewis, Anthony. *Gideon's Trumpet*. New York: Random House, 1964.

O'Brien, David M. *Constitutional Law and Politics: Civil Rights and Civil Liberties*. 10th ed. Vol. 2. New York: W. W. Norton, 2017.

Richards, Neil. *Intellectual Privacy: Rethinking Civil Liberties in the Digital Age*. New York: Oxford University Press, 2015.

Smith, Steven D. *The Rise and Decline of American Religious Freedom*. Cambridge, MA: Harvard University Press, 2014.

Solove, Daniel. *Nothing to Hide: The False Tradeoff between Privacy and Security*. New Haven, CT: Yale University Press, 2011.

Tebbe, Nelson. *Religious Freedom in an Egalitarian Age*. Cambridge, MA: Harvard University Press, 2017.

Waldron, Jeremy. *The Harm in Hate Speech*. Cambridge, MA: Harvard University Press, 2012.

Weinrib, Laura. *The Taming of Free Speech: America's Civil Liberties Compromise*. Cambridge, MA: Harvard University Press, 2016.

Winkler, Adam. *Gunfight: The Battle over the Right to Bear Arms in America*. New York: W. W. Norton, 2013.

Recommended Websites

The American Civil Liberties Union (ACLU)
www.aclu.org

The ACLU is committed to protecting for all individuals the freedoms found in the Bill of Rights. This sometimes controversial organization constantly monitors the government for violations of liberty and encourages its members to take political action.

Electronic Privacy Information Center
http://epic.org/privacy

For an extensive list of privacy issues, go to the web page for the Electronic Privacy Information Center. Here you will find civil liberties concerns as they relate to all forms of information technology, including the internet.

The Free Expression Network
www.freeexpression.org

The Free Expression Network is an organization "dedicated to preserving the right to free expression." On its website you can find links to important First Amendment issues and organizations.

Freedom Forum
www.freedomforum.org

Freedom of speech and freedom of the press are considered critical in any democracy; however, only some kinds of speech are fully protected against restrictions. Freedom Forum is a nonpartisan agency that investigates and analyzes such First Amendment restrictions.

National Abortion and Reproductive Rights Action League
www.naral.org

National Right to Life Committee
www.NRLC.org

The National Abortion and Reproductive Rights Action League and the National Right to Life Committee are two of the nation's largest interest groups weighing in on the abortion issue. See what these opposing groups have to say about privacy rights.

Religious Freedom
http://guides.lib.virginia.edu/content.php?pid5147534&sid51255449

The establishment clause of the U.S. Constitution has been interpreted to mean a "wall of separation" between government and religion. On the Religious Freedom Page you can find information on a variety of issues pertaining to religious freedom in the United States and around the world.

U.S. Supreme Court Media
www.oyez.org

This website for U.S. Supreme Court media has a great search engine for finding information on cases affecting civil liberties, such as *Lemon v. Kurtzman*, *Miranda v. Arizona*, *Mapp v. Ohio*, and *New York Times v. Sullivan*, to name a few.

transgender Americans were allowed to enlist beginning January 1, 2018.[3] Kibby's career was saved.

As we saw in the previous chapter, in the Bill of Rights, civil liberties are phrased as negatives—what government must *not* do. Civil rights, on the other hand, are positives—what the government *must* do to guarantee equal citizenship and protect citizens from discrimination. Civil liberties protect Americans from various forms of governmental abuse. Civil rights regulate *who* can participate in the political process and civil society and *how* they can participate: for example, who can vote, who can hold office, who can have a trial or serve on juries, and when and how citizens can petition the government to take action. Civil rights also define how people are treated in employment, education, and other aspects of American society.

As in the case of civil liberties, Americans agree with the basic principle of civil rights but quarrel frequently over their application. The question of who has the constitutional right to do what underlies some of the major controversies of American history. Fifty years ago, the African American struggle for equal rights took center stage. Many goals of the civil rights movement that once aroused bitter controversy are now widely accepted as part of the American commitment to equal rights. But even today the question of what is meant by "equal rights" is hardly settled. To what extent can states mandate racial preferences in college admissions? What rights do undocumented immigrants possess? Do transgender individuals have the right to use a public restroom based upon their gender identification rather than their physical characteristics, and can they serve in the military?

As we saw in Chapter 4, the evolution of civil liberties in the United States mainly, though not exclusively, involved the actions of the federal courts. Liberties are limits on government action, and the courts are the institution best situated to tell Congress, the president, and state governments what they may not do. Civil rights, though, involve the government's obligation to act, and the evolution of civil rights required much more action on the part of Congress and the president.

CHAPTER GOALS

- ★ **Trace the legal developments and social movements that expanded civil rights (pp. 161–79)**
- ★ **Describe how different groups have fought for and won protection of their civil rights (pp. 179–94)**
- ★ **Contrast arguments for and against affirmative action (pp. 195–97)**

The Struggle for Civil Rights

Trace the legal developments and social movements that expanded civil rights

In the United States the history of slavery and legalized racial **discrimination** against African Americans coexists uneasily with a strong tradition of individual liberty. Indeed, for much of our history Americans have struggled to reconcile such exclusionary racial practices with our notions of individual rights. With the adoption of the Fourteenth Amendment in 1868 **civil rights** became part of the Constitution, guaranteed to each citizen through "equal protection of the laws." This **equal protection clause** launched a century of political movements and legal efforts to press for racial equality.

discrimination the use of any unreasonable and unjust criterion of exclusion

civil rights obligation imposed on government to take positive action to protect citizens from any illegal action of government agencies and of other private citizens

equal protection clause provision of the Fourteenth Amendment guaranteeing citizens "the equal protection of the laws." This clause has been the basis for the civil rights of African Americans, women, and other groups

For African Americans, the central fact of political life for most of American history has been a denial of full citizenship rights. By accepting the institution of slavery, the Founders embraced a system fundamentally at odds with the "Blessings of Liberty" promised in the Constitution. Their decision set the stage for two centuries of African American struggles to achieve full citizenship.

For women, electoral politics was a decidedly masculine world. Until 1920, not only were women barred from voting in national politics but electoral politics was closely tied to such male social institutions as lodges, bars, and clubs. Yet the exclusion of women from this political world did not prevent them from engaging in public life. Instead, women carved out a "separate sphere" for their public activities. Emphasizing female stewardship of the moral realm, women became important voices in social reform well before they won the right to vote.[4] Prior to the Civil War, women played leading roles in the abolitionist movement.

SLAVERY AND THE ABOLITIONIST MOVEMENT

No issue in the nation's history so deeply divided Americans as that of slavery. The importation and subjugation of Africans kidnapped from their native lands was a practice virtually as old as the country itself: the first slaves brought to what became

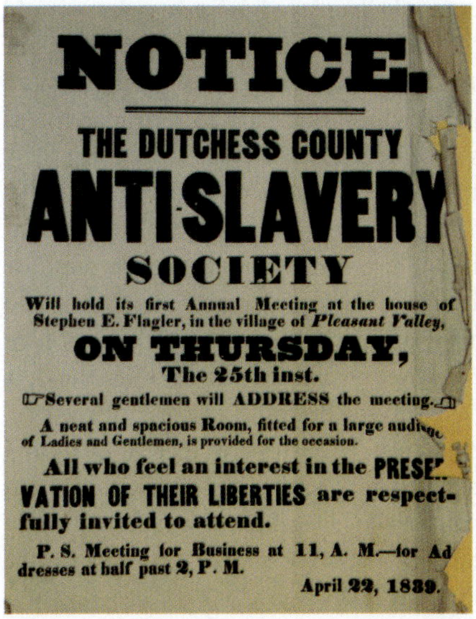

Slavery tore the nation apart and ultimately led to the Civil War. The abolition movement organized in the North and pushed to end slavery. Harriet Tubman (far left in photograph) was an abolitionist and ex-slave who helped many slaves escape bondage through a system of safe houses called the "underground railroad."

the United States arrived in 1619, a year before the Plymouth colony was established in Massachusetts. White southerners built their agricultural economy (especially cotton production) on a large slave labor force. By 1840 nearly half of the populations of Alabama and Louisiana consisted of black slaves. Even so, only about one-quarter of southern white families owned slaves.

Slavery was so much a part of southern culture that efforts to restrict or abolish the institution were met with fierce resistance. Despite the manifest cruelties of the slave system, southerners referred to it merely as their "peculiar institution." This quaint label meant little to slavery's opponents, however; and an abolitionist movement grew and spread among northerners in the 1830s (although abolitionist sentiment could be traced back to the prerevolutionary era). The abolitionist movement spread primarily through local organizations in the North. Soon two political parties emerged: the staunchly antislavery Liberty Party and the more moderate Free Soil Party, which sought primarily to restrict slavery from spreading into new western territories. Some opponents of slavery took matters into their own hands, aiding in the escape of runaway slaves along the Underground Railroad. In the South, a similar, if contrary, fervor prompted mobs to break into post offices in order to seize and destroy antislavery literature.

In 1857 the Supreme Court inflamed this tense atmosphere with its infamous decision in *Dred Scott v. Sanford*. Dred Scott was a slave who had been taken by his owner to the free state of Illinois and the territory of Wisconsin, where slavery was forbidden. Scott sued for his freedom, arguing that his residence in a free territory meant he was a free man. The Court, however, disagreed, holding that slaves—indeed, all blacks—were not citizens of the United States. Scott had no due process rights because, as a slave, he was his master's permanent property, regardless of his master's having taken him to a free state or territory.[5] This decision split the country deeply over the issue of slavery; the emotional power of the slavery issue was such that it precipitated the nation's bloodiest conflict, the Civil War. From the ashes of the Civil War came the Thirteenth, Fourteenth, and Fifteenth amendments, which would redefine civil rights from that time on.

THE WOMEN'S RIGHTS MOVEMENT

The quiet upstate New York town of Seneca Falls played host to what would later come to be known as the starting point of the modern women's movement. Convened in July 1848 and organized by the activists Elizabeth Cady Stanton and Lucretia Mott, the Seneca Falls Convention drew 300 delegates to formulate plans for advancing the political and social rights of women.

The centerpiece of the convention was its Declaration of Sentiments and Resolutions. Patterned after the Declaration of Independence, the Seneca Falls document declared, "We hold these truths to be self-evident: that all men and women are created equal" and "The history of mankind is a history of repeated injuries and usurpations on the part of man toward woman, having in direct object the establishment of an absolute tyranny over her." The most controversial provision of the declaration, nearly rejected as too radical, was the call for the right to vote for women. Although most of the delegates were women, about 40 men participated, including the renowned abolitionist Frederick Douglass. The link to the antislavery movement was not new. Stanton and Mott had attended the World Anti-Slavery Convention in London in 1840 but had been denied delegate seats because of their sex. This rebuke helped precipitate the 1848 convention in Seneca Falls.

The convention and its participants were subjected to widespread ridicule, but similar conventions were organized in other states. And in the same year as the Seneca Falls Convention, New York State passed the Married Women's Property Act in order to restore the right of married women to own property.

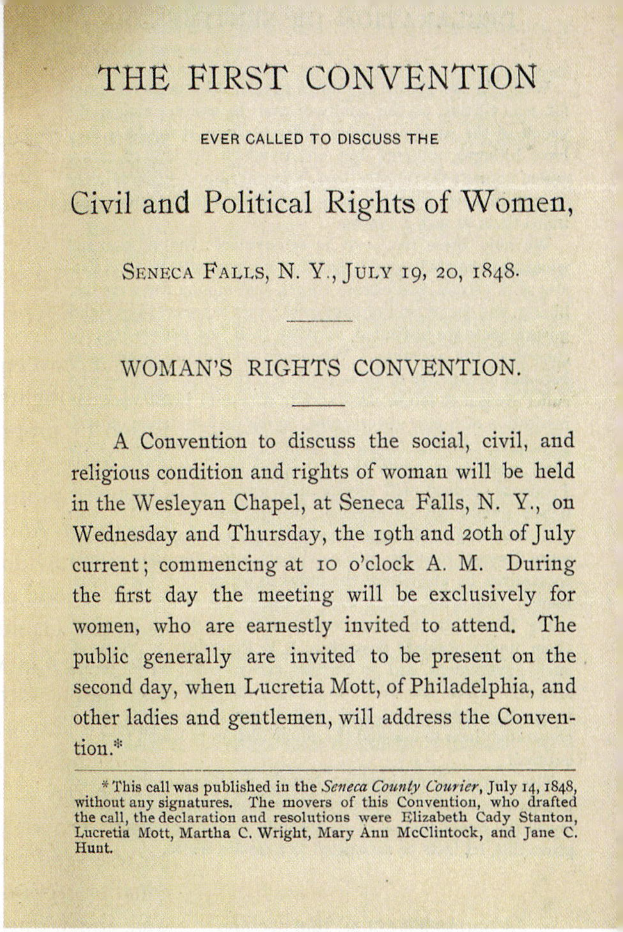

THE FIRST CONVENTION

EVER CALLED TO DISCUSS THE

Civil and Political Rights of Women,

SENECA FALLS, N. Y., JULY 19, 20, 1848.

WOMAN'S RIGHTS CONVENTION.

A Convention to discuss the social, civil, and religious condition and rights of woman will be held in the Wesleyan Chapel, at Seneca Falls, N. Y., on Wednesday and Thursday, the 19th and 20th of July current; commencing at 10 o'clock A. M. During the first day the meeting will be exclusively for women, who are earnestly invited to attend. The public generally are invited to be present on the second day, when Lucretia Mott, of Philadelphia, and other ladies and gentlemen, will address the Convention.*

* This call was published in the *Seneca County Courier*, July 14, 1848, without any signatures. The movers of this Convention, who drafted the call, the declaration and resolutions were Elizabeth Cady Stanton, Lucretia Mott, Martha C. Wright, Mary Ann McClintock, and Jane C. Hunt.

Many see the Seneca Falls Convention of 1848 as the starting point of the modern women's rights movement. Its Declaration of Sentiments proclaiming equality for women is one of the movement's most important documents.

THE CIVIL WAR AMENDMENTS TO THE CONSTITUTION

The hopes of African Americans for achieving full citizenship rights initially seemed fulfilled when three constitutional amendments were adopted after the Civil War: the **Thirteenth Amendment** abolished slavery, the **Fourteenth Amendment** guaranteed equal protection and due process under the law, and the **Fifteenth Amendment** guaranteed voting rights for blacks. Protected by the presence of federal troops, African American men were able to exercise their political rights immediately after the war. Between 1869 and 1877 blacks were elected to many political offices: two black senators were elected from Mississippi, and a total of 14 African Americans were elected to the House of Representatives. African Americans also held many state-level political offices. As voters and public officials, black citizens found a home in the Republican Party, which had secured the ratification of the three constitutional amendments guaranteeing black rights. After the war, the Republican Party continued to reach out to black voters as a means to build party strength in the South.[6]

This political equality was short-lived, however. The national government withdrew its troops from the South and turned its back on African Americans in 1877, when Reconstruction ended. In the Compromise of 1877, southern Democrats agreed to allow the Republican candidate, Rutherford B. Hayes, to become president after a disputed election. In exchange, northern Republicans dropped their support for the civil liberties and political participation of African Americans. After that, southern states erected a "Jim Crow" system of social, political, and economic inequality that made a mockery of the promises in the Constitution. The first **Jim Crow laws** were adopted in the 1870s, in each southern state, to criminalize intermarriage of the races and to segregate trains and depots. These were promptly followed by laws segregating all public accommodations, and within 10 years all southern states had adopted laws segregating the schools.

Immediately after the Civil War, when male ex-slaves won the franchise, some women pressed for the right to vote at the national level; but politicians in both parties rejected women's suffrage as disruptive and unrealistic. Women also started to press for the vote at the state level in 1867, when a referendum to give women the vote in Kansas failed. Frustration with the general failure to win reforms accelerated suffrage activism. In 1872, Susan B. Anthony and several other women were arrested in Rochester, New York, for illegally registering and voting in that year's national election. (The men who allowed the women to register and vote were also indicted. Anthony paid their expenses and eventually won presidential pardons for them.) At Anthony's trial, Judge Ward Hunt ordered the jury to find her guilty without deliberation. Yet Anthony was allowed to address the court, saying, "Your denial of my citizen's right to vote is the denial of my right of consent as one of the

Thirteenth Amendment one of three Civil War amendments; it abolished slavery

Fourteenth Amendment one of three Civil War amendments; it guaranteed equal protection and due process

Fifteenth Amendment one of three Civil War amendments; it guaranteed voting rights for African American men

Jim Crow laws laws enacted by southern states following Reconstruction that discriminated against African Americans governed, the denial of my right of representation as one of the taxed, the denial of my right to a trial of my peers as an offender against the law."[7] Hunt assessed Anthony a fine of $100 but did not sentence her to jail. She refused to pay the fine.

CIVIL RIGHTS AND THE SUPREME COURT: "SEPARATE BUT EQUAL"

Resistance to equality for African Americans in the South led Congress to adopt the Civil Rights Act of 1875, which attempted to protect blacks from discrimination by proprietors of hotels, theaters, and other public accommodations. But the Court declared the legislation unconstitutional on the grounds that the act sought to protect blacks against discrimination by *private* businesses, whereas the Fourteenth Amendment, according to the Court's interpretation, was intended to protect individuals from discrimination only against actions by *public* officials of state and local governments.

In the infamous case of *Plessy v. Ferguson* (1896), the Court went still further by upholding a Louisiana statute that *required* segregation of the races on trolleys and other public carriers (and, by implication, in all public facilities, including schools). Homer Plessy, a man defined as "one-eighth black," sat in a trolley car reserved for whites and was found guilty of violating a Louisiana law that provided for "equal but separate accommodations" on trains and levied a $25 fine on any white passenger who sat in a car reserved for blacks or on any black passenger who sat in a car reserved for whites. The Supreme Court held that the Fourteenth Amendment's equal protection clause was not violated by racial distinction as long as the facilities were equal, thus establishing the **"separate but equal" rule** that prevailed through the mid-twentieth century. White people generally pretended that segregated accommodations were equal as long as some accommodation for blacks existed. The Court said that although "the object of the [Fourteenth] Amendment was undoubtedly to enforce the absolute equality of the two races before the law... it could not have

"separate but equal" rule doctrine that public accommodations could be segregated by race but still be considered equal

The 1896 Supreme Court case of *Plessy v. Ferguson* upheld legal segregation and created the "separate but equal" rule, which fostered national segregation. Overt discrimination in public accommodations was common.

intended to abolish distinctions based on color, or to enforce social, as distinguished from political, equality, or a commingling of the two races upon terms unsatisfactory to either."[8] What the Court was saying in effect was that the use of race as a criterion of exclusion in public matters was reasonable.

> **FOR CRITICAL ANALYSIS**
>
> **What were the consequences of the "separate but equal" policy for southern society and for blacks' civil rights?**

ORGANIZING FOR EQUALITY

The creation of a Jim Crow system in the southern states and the lack of a legal basis for "equal protection of the laws" prompted the beginning of a long process in which African Americans built organizations and devised strategies for asserting their constitutional rights.

The National Association for the Advancement of Colored People One such strategy sought to win political rights through political pressure and litigation. This approach was championed by the National Association for the Advancement of Colored People (NAACP), established in 1909 by a group of black and white reformers that included W. E. B. Du Bois, one of the twentieth century's most influential and creative thinkers on racial issues. Because the northern black vote was so small in the early 1900s, the NAACP relied primarily on the courts to press for black political rights. After the 1920s it built a strong membership base, with some strength in the South, which would be critical when the civil rights movement gained momentum in the 1950s.

Women's Organizations and the Right to Suffrage The 1886 unveiling in New York Harbor of the Statue of Liberty, depicting liberty as a woman, prompted women's rights advocates to call it "the greatest hypocrisy of the nineteenth century," in that "not one single woman throughout the length and breadth of the Land is as yet in possession of political Liberty."[9]

The climactic movement toward women's suffrage had been formally launched in 1878 with the introduction of a proposed constitutional amendment in Congress. Parallel efforts were made in the states. Many states granted women the right to vote before the national government did. Western states with less entrenched political systems opened politics to women earliest. When Wyoming became a state in 1890, it was the first state to grant full suffrage to women. Colorado, Utah, and Idaho all

Women fought for decades for the right to vote. The Nineteenth Amendment, ratified in 1920 over the opposition of President Wilson, guaranteed that right. Pictured here on the right are women voting for the first time after the passage of the amendment.

followed suit in the next several years. Suffrage organizations grew—the National American Woman Suffrage Association (NAWSA), formed in 1890, claimed 2 million members by 1917 and staged mass meetings, parades, petitions, and protests. NAWSA organized state-by-state efforts to win the right for women to vote. Members of a more militant group, the National Woman's Party, staged pickets and got arrested in front of the White House to protest President Wilson's opposition to a constitutional amendment granting women this right. When the Nineteenth Amendment was ratified in 1920, women were finally guaranteed the right to vote.

LITIGATING FOR EQUALITY AFTER WORLD WAR II

The shame of discrimination against black military personnel during World War II, plus revelations of Nazi racial atrocities, moved President Harry S. Truman finally to bring the problem of racial discrimination to the White House and national attention, with the appointment in 1946 of the President's Commission on Civil Rights. In 1948 the commission submitted its report, *To Secure These Rights*, which laid bare the extent of the problem and its consequences and revealed the success of experiments with racial integration in the armed forces during World War II. This was intended to demonstrate to southern society that it had nothing to fear. But the commission recognized that the national government had no clear constitutional authority to pass and implement civil rights legislation. It proposed tying such legislation to the commerce power described in Article I of the Constitution, which allows Congress to regulate interstate commerce, although it was clear that discrimination was not itself related to the flow of interstate commerce.[10] The committee even suggested using the treaty power as a source of constitutional authority for civil rights legislation.[11]

The Supreme Court had begun to change its position on racial discrimination before World War II by being stricter about the criterion of equal facilities in the "separate but equal" rule. In 1938, for example, the Court rejected Missouri's policy of paying the tuition of qualified blacks to out-of-state law schools rather than admitting them to the University of Missouri Law School.[12]

After the war, modest progress resumed. In 1950 the Court rejected Texas's claim that its new "law school for Negroes" afforded education equal to that of the all-white University of Texas Law School, anticipating its future civil rights rulings by opening the question of whether *any* segregated facilities could be truly equal.[13] But in ordering the admission of blacks to all-white state law schools, the Supreme Court did not directly confront the "separate but equal" rule. The most important pre-1954 decision was probably *Shelley v. Kraemer*, in which the Court ruled against the widespread practice of "restrictive covenants" whereby the seller of a home added a clause to the sales contract requiring the buyer to agree never to sell the home to any non-Caucasian, non-Christian, and so on. The Court ruled that such covenants could not be judicially enforced since the Fourteenth Amendment prohibits any organ of the state, including the courts, from denying equal protection of its laws.[14]

Although none of those pre-1954 cases confronted "separate but equal" and the principle of racial discrimination as such, they were extremely significant to black leaders in the 1940s and gave them encouragement to believe that at last they had an opportunity and enough legal precedent to change the constitutional framework itself. Much of this legal work was done by the Legal Defense and Educational Fund of the NAACP, which until the late 1940s had concentrated on winning small victories within the existing framework. In 1948 the Legal Defense Fund upgraded its approach by simultaneously filing suits in different federal districts and through each level of schooling. After nearly two years of these mostly successful equalization suits, the lawyers decided the time was ripe to confront the "separate but equal" rule head-on, but they felt they needed some heavier artillery to lead the attack. Their choice was the African American lawyer Thurgood Marshall, who had been fighting, and often winning, equalization suits since the early 1930s. Marshall was pessimistic about the readiness of the Supreme Court for a full confrontation with segregation itself and the constitutional principle sustaining it. But the unwillingness of Congress after the 1948 election to consider fair-employment legislation seems to have convinced Marshall that the courts were the only hope.

In the fall of 1952 the Court had on its docket cases from Delaware, Kansas, South Carolina, Virginia, and the District of Columbia challenging the constitutionality of school segregation. Of these, the case filed in Kansas became the one chosen by the NAACP. This case was further along in the process of adjudication in its district court, and it had the advantage of being located in a state outside the Deep South, a fact that would minimize any local opposition to a favorable decision.[15]

Oliver Brown, the father of three girls, lived "across the tracks" in a low-income, racially mixed Topeka neighborhood. Every school day, Linda Brown took the school bus to the Monroe Elementary School, for black children, about a mile away. In September 1950, Oliver Brown took Linda to the all-white Sumner School, which was closer to home, to enter her into the third grade, in defiance of state law and local segregation rules. When they were refused, Brown took his case to the NAACP, and soon thereafter, the case **Brown v. Board of Education** was born. In mid-1953 the Court announced that the several cases on their way up would be reargued within a set of questions having to do with the intent of the Fourteenth Amendment. Almost exactly a year later, the Court responded to those questions in one of the most important decisions in its history:

> Does segregation of children in public schools solely on the basis of race, even though the physical facilities and other "tangible" factors may be equal, deprive the children of the minority group of equal educational opportunities? We believe that it does. . . . We conclude that in the field of public education the doctrine of "separate but equal" has no place. Separate educational facilities are inherently unequal.[16]

Brown v. Board of Education the 1954 Supreme Court decision that struck down the "separate but equal" doctrine as fundamentally unequal; this case eliminated state power to use race as a criterion of discrimination in law and provided the national government with the power to intervene by exercising strict regulatory policies against discriminatory actions

The *Brown* decision altered the constitutional framework by indicating that racial discrimination violated the Constitution.

CIVIL RIGHTS AFTER *BROWN V. BOARD OF EDUCATION*

Brown v. Board of Education withdrew all constitutional authority to use race as a criterion of exclusion, and it signaled more clearly the Court's determination to use the **strict scrutiny** test in cases related to racial discrimination. This meant that the burden of proof would fall on the government to show that the law in question *was* constitutional—not on the challengers to show the law's *un*constitutionality.[17] Although the use of strict scrutiny would give an advantage to those attacking racial discrimination, the historic decision in *Brown v. Board of Education* was merely a small opening move. First, most states refused to cooperate until sued, and many ingenious schemes were employed to delay obedience (such as paying the tuition for white students to attend newly created "private" academies). Second, even as southern school boards began to cooperate by eliminating their legally enforced

strict scrutiny a test used by the Supreme Court in racial discrimination cases and other cases involving civil liberties and civil rights that places the burden of proof on the government rather than on the challengers to show that the law in question is constitutional

"Massive resistance" among white southerners attempted to block the desegregation efforts of the national government. For example, at Little Rock Central High School in 1957, an angry mob of white students prevented black students from entering the school.

de jure literally, "by law"; refers to legally enforced practices, such as school segregation in the South before the 1960s

de facto literally, "by fact"; refers to practices that occur even when there is no legal enforcement, such as school segregation in much of the United States today

FOR CRITICAL ANALYSIS

Describe the changes in American society between the *Plessy v. Ferguson* and the *Brown v. Board of Education* decisions. How have changes in civil rights policy since the *Brown* case impacted society?

(**de jure**) school segregation, extensive actual (**de facto**) school segregation remained, in the North as well as in the South, as a consequence of racially segregated housing that could not be addressed by the 1954–55 *Brown* principles. Third, discrimination in employment, public accommodations, juries, voting, and other areas of social and economic activity was not directly touched by *Brown*.

School Desegregation, Phase One Although the District of Columbia and some of the school districts in the border states began to respond almost immediately to court-ordered desegregation, the states of the Deep South responded with a carefully planned delaying tactic commonly called "massive resistance." Southern politicians stood shoulder to shoulder to declare that the Supreme Court's decisions and orders were without effect. The legislatures in these states enacted statutes ordering school districts to maintain segregated schools and state superintendents to terminate state funding wherever there was racial mixing in the classroom. Some southern states violated their own long traditions of local school autonomy by centralizing public school authority under the governor or the state board of education, and they gave themselves the power to close the schools and to provide alternative private schooling wherever local school boards might be inclined to obey the Supreme Court.

Most of these plans of "massive resistance" were tested in the federal courts and struck down as unconstitutional.[18] But southern resistance was not confined to legislation. Perhaps the most serious incident occurred in Arkansas in 1957, when Governor Orval Faubus mobilized the Arkansas National Guard to intercede against enforcement of a federal court order to integrate Little Rock Central High School. President Eisenhower was compelled to deploy U.S. troops and place the city under martial law. This action by the federal government underlined that a right was at issue. The Supreme Court considered the Little Rock confrontation so historically important that the opinion it rendered in that case was not only agreed to unanimously but, unprecedentedly, signed personally by every one of the justices.[19]

The end of massive resistance, however, became simply the beginning of still another southern strategy. "Pupil placement" laws authorized school districts to place each pupil in a school according to a variety of academic, personal, and psychological considerations, never mentioning race at all. This put the burden of transferring to an all-white school on the nonwhite children and their parents, making it almost impossible for a single court order to cover a whole district, let alone a whole state, thereby delaying desegregation awhile longer.[20]

Social Protest after *Brown* Ten years after *Brown*, fewer than 1 percent of black school-age children in the Deep South were attending schools with whites.[21] A decade of frustration made it fairly obvious to all observers that adjudication alone would not succeed. The goal of "equal protection" required positive, or affirmative, action by Congress and by administrative agencies. And given massive southern resistance and a generally negative national public opinion toward racial integration, progress would not be made through courts, Congress, or federal agencies without intense, well-organized support. Figure 5.1 shows the increase in the number of civil rights demonstrations for voting rights and public accommodations during the years following *Brown*.

The number of organized demonstrations began to mount slowly but surely after *Brown v. Board of Education*. Only a year after *Brown*, black citizens in Montgomery, Alabama, challenged the city's segregated bus system with a yearlong boycott. The boycott began with the arrest of Rosa Parks, who refused to give up her seat for a white man. A seamstress who worked with civil rights groups, Parks eventually became a civil rights icon, as did one of the ministers leading the boycott, Martin Luther King, Jr. After a year of private carpools and walking, Montgomery's bus system desegregated, but only after the Supreme Court ruled the system unconstitutional.

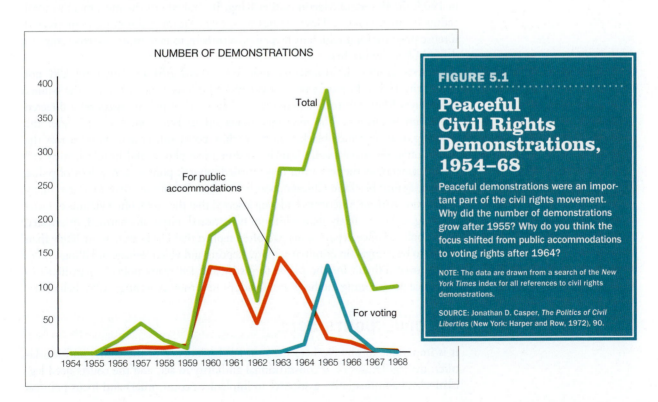

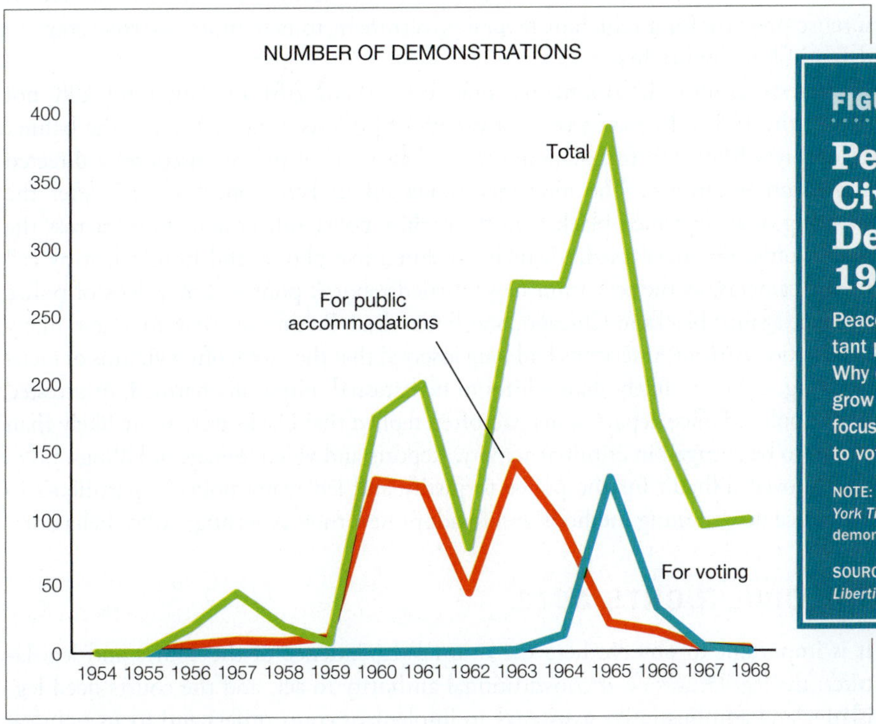

FIGURE 5.1

Peaceful Civil Rights Demonstrations, 1954–68

Peaceful demonstrations were an important part of the civil rights movement. Why did the number of demonstrations grow after 1955? Why do you think the focus shifted from public accommodations to voting rights after 1964?

NOTE: The data are drawn from a search of the *New York Times* index for all references to civil rights demonstrations.

SOURCE: Jonathan D. Casper, *The Politics of Civil Liberties* (New York: Harper and Row, 1972), 90.

The struggle for African American civil rights has spanned decades. Among the key moments are Rosa Parks and the Montgomery Bus Boycott (1955–56), sit-ins at segregated lunch counters throughout the South, the March on Washington and Martin Luther King, Jr.'s famous "I Have a Dream" speech (1963), and the Black Lives Matter movement that persists today.

By the 1960s the many organizations that made up the civil rights movement had accumulated experience and built networks capable of launching large-scale direct action campaigns against southern segregationists. The Southern Christian Leadership Conference, the Student Nonviolent Coordinating Committee, and many other organizations had built a movement that stretched across the South, using the media to attract nationwide attention and support. The image of protesters being beaten, attacked by police dogs, and set upon with fire hoses did much to win broad sympathy for the cause of black civil rights and to discredit state and local governments in the South. In the massive March on Washington in 1963, the Reverend Martin Luther King, Jr., staked out the movement's moral claims in his famous "I Have a Dream" speech. Steadily, the movement created intense pressure for a reluctant federal government to take more assertive steps to defend black civil rights.

Protests against discriminatory practices toward African Americans did not end in the 1960s. In recent years, a variety of protests coalesced under the banner Black Lives Matter to focus attention on allegations of police misconduct directed at African Americans. The movement took off in Ferguson, Missouri, after the shooting of an unarmed black man by a white police officer and spread across the nation often via social media, which presented live photos and films taken by cell phone cameras, as the television news carried reports, photos, and videos of police violence against blacks in Chicago, South Carolina, Baltimore, New York, and many other cities. African Americans had long asserted that they were often victims of racial profiling and more likely than whites to be harassed, physically harmed, or arrested by the police. Police departments had often replied that blacks were more likely than whites to be engaged in criminal activity. Reports and video footage of killings, however, proved difficult for the police to justify and led many police departments to introduce new training methods and to adopt new rules governing police behavior.

THE CIVIL RIGHTS ACTS

It is important to observe here the mutual dependence of the courts and legislatures: the legislatures need constitutional authority to act, and the courts need legislative and administrative assistance to implement court orders and focus political

support. Consequently, even as the U.S. Congress finally moved into the field of school desegregation (and other areas of "equal protection"), the courts continued to exercise their powers, not only by placing court orders against recalcitrant school districts but also by extending and reinterpreting aspects of the equal protection clause to support legislative and administrative actions (see Table 5.1).

Three civil rights acts were passed during the first decade after the 1954 Supreme Court decision in *Brown v. Board of Education*. But these acts were of only marginal importance.

By far the most important piece of legislation passed by Congress concerning equal opportunity was the Civil Rights Act of 1964. It not only put some teeth in the voting rights provisions of the 1957 and 1960 acts but also went far beyond voting to attack discrimination in public accommodations, segregation in the schools, and, at long last, the discriminatory conduct of employers in hiring, promoting, and laying off their employees. Discrimination against women was also included, extending the important 1963 provisions. The 1964 act seemed bold at the time, but it was enacted fully 10 years after the Supreme Court had declared racial discrimination "inherently unequal" and long after blacks had demonstrated that discrimination was no longer acceptable. With the Civil Rights Act of 1964, Congress pointed to a different part of the Constitution as the primary source of its authority to ban racial discrimination in some businesses: the "commerce clause," which empowers Congress to "regulate commerce . . . among the several states." Over the previous twenty years, Congress and the courts had come to agree that this clause empowered Congress to regulate commercial activity broadly defined. And this time, when southern business owners challenged the law, the Supreme Court upheld it.

Public Accommodations After the passage of the 1964 Civil Rights Act, public accommodations quickly removed some of the most blatant forms of racial discrimination. Signs defining "colored" and "white" restrooms, water fountains, waiting rooms, and seating arrangements were removed; and a host of other practices that relegated black people to separate and inferior arrangements were ended. In addition, the federal government filed more than 400 antidiscrimination suits in federal courts against hotels, restaurants, taverns, gas stations, and other "public accommodations."

TABLE 5.1

Cause and Effect in the Civil Rights Movement

Political action and government action worked in tandem to produce dramatic changes in American civil rights policies.

JUDICIAL AND LEGAL ACTION	POLITICAL ACTION
1954 *Brown v. Board of Education*	**1955** Montgomery, Alabama, bus boycott
1956 Federal courts order school integration; of special note is one ordering Autherine Lucy admitted to the University of Alabama, with Governor Wallace officially protesting	
1957 Civil Rights Act creating Civil Rights Commission; President Eisenhower sends 101st Airborne Division paratroops to Little Rock, Arkansas, to enforce integration of Central High School	**1957** Southern Christian Leadership Conference formed, with Martin Luther King, Jr., as president
1960 First substantive Civil Rights Act, primarily voting rights	**1960** Student Nonviolent Coordinating Committee formed to organize protests, sit-ins, freedom rides
1961 Interstate Commerce Commission orders desegregation on all buses and trains and in terminals; President Kennedy (JFK) favors executive action over civil rights legislation	
1963 JFK shifts, supports strong civil rights law; JFK's assassination; President Johnson asserts strong support for civil rights	**1963** Nonviolent demonstrations in Birmingham, Alabama, lead to King's arrest and his "Letter from Birmingham Jail"; March on Washington
1964 Congress passes historic Civil Rights Act covering voting, employment, public accommodations, education	
1965 Voting Rights Act	**1965** King announces drive to register 3 million blacks in the South
1966 War on Poverty in full swing	**Late 1960s** Movement diverges: part toward litigation, part toward community action programs, part toward war protest, part toward more militant "Black Power" actions

Many aspects of legalized racial segregation—such as separate Bibles to swear in black and white witnesses in the courtroom—seem like ancient history today. But the issue of racial discrimination in public settings is by no means over. In 2014, for example, an African American customer at a Vancouver, Washington "Elmer's" restaurant noticed that he was being asked to prepay for his food while white customers were presented with their bills after they had finished their meals. The case was settled out of court for an undisclosed amount.[22] Other forms of racial discrimination in public accommodations are harder to challenge, however. For example, there is considerable evidence that taxicabs often refuse to pick up black passengers.[23] Such practices may be common, but they are difficult to prove and remedy through the law.

School Desegregation, Phase Two The 1964 Civil Rights Act also declared discrimination by private employers and state governments (school boards, etc.) illegal and then went further to provide for administrative agencies to help the courts implement these laws. Title IV of the act, for example, authorized the executive branch, through the Justice Department, to implement federal court orders to desegregate schools and to do so without having to wait for individual parents to bring complaints. Title VI of the act vastly strengthened the role of the executive branch and the credibility of court orders by providing that federal grants-in-aid to state and local governments for education must be withheld from any school system practicing racial segregation. Title VI became the most effective weapon for desegregating schools outside the South because the situation in northern communities was subtler and more difficult to address. In the South, the problem was segregation by law coupled with overt resistance to the national government's efforts to change the situation. In contrast, outside the South, segregated facilities were the outcome of hundreds of thousands of housing choices made by individuals and families. Once racial residential patterns emerged, racial homogeneity, property values, and neighborhood schools and churches were defended by real estate agents, neighborhood organizations, and the like. Thus, in order to eliminate discrimination nationwide, the 1964 Civil Rights Act gave (1) the president, through the Justice Department's Office for Civil Rights, the power to withhold federal education grants[24] and (2) the attorney general of the United States the power to initiate suits (rather than having to await complaints) wherever there was a "pattern or practice" of discrimination.[25]

In the decade following the 1964 Civil Rights Act, the Justice Department brought legal action against more than 500 school districts. During the same period, administrative agencies filed lawsuits against 600 school districts, threatening to suspend federal aid to education unless real desegregation steps were taken.

Busing One step taken toward desegregation was busing children from poor urban school districts to wealthier suburban ones. In 1971 the Supreme Court held that state-imposed desegregation could be brought about by busing children across

The 1964 Civil Rights Act made desegregation a legal requirement. The policy of busing from black neighborhoods to white schools bitterly divided the black and white communities in Boston. In 1976 a protester waved an American Flag threateningly at an innocent black bystander—a lawyer on his way to his office—as another white man sought to help him get out of the way.

school districts.[26] But the decision went beyond that, adding that under certain limited circumstances even racial quotas could be used as the "starting point in shaping a remedy to correct past constitutional violations" and that pairing or grouping schools and reorganizing school attendance zones would also be acceptable.

Three years later, however, this principle was severely restricted when the Supreme Court determined that only cities found guilty of deliberate and de jure racial segregation would have to desegregate their schools,[27] effectively exempting most northern states and cities from busing because school segregation in northern cities is generally the de facto result of segregated housing and thousands of acts of private discrimination against blacks and other minorities.

Boston provides a good illustration of the agonizing problem of making further progress in civil rights in the schools under the constitutional framework established by these decisions. Boston school authorities were found guilty of deliberately building school facilities and drawing school district boundaries "to increase racial segregation." After vain efforts by Boston school authorities to draw up an acceptable plan to remedy the segregation, in 1974 federal judge W. Arthur Garrity ordered an elaborate desegregation plan of his own, involving busing between the all-black neighborhood of Roxbury and the nearby white, working-class community of South Boston. The city's schools were so segregated and uncooperative that even the conservative administration of President Richard Nixon had already initiated a punitive cutoff of funds. But even many liberals criticized Judge Garrity's plan as being badly conceived for involving two neighboring communities with a history of tension and mutual resentment. The plan did work well at the elementary school level, but proved explosive at the high school level, generating a continuing crisis for the city of Boston and for the whole nation.[28]

The prospects for further school integration diminished with a 1991 Supreme Court decision holding that lower federal courts could end supervision of local school boards if they could show "good faith" compliance with court orders to desegregate and that "vestiges of past discrimination" had been eliminated "to the extent practicable."[29] It is not necessarily easy for a school board to prove that the new standard has been met, but this was the first time since *Brown* and the 1964 Civil Rights Act that the Court had opened the door at all to retreat.

In 2007 the Court's ruling in *Parents Involved in Community Schools v. Seattle School District No. 1* limited school integration measures still further.[30] By making race one factor in assigning students to schools, the cities of Seattle, Washington, and Louisville, Kentucky, had hoped to achieve greater racial balance across the public schools. The Court ruled that these plans were unconstitutional because there was no compelling government interest in using race as a criterion in assigning students to schools. Many observers described the decision as the end of the *Brown* era because it attacked one of the few public strategies left to promote racial integration.

FOR CRITICAL ANALYSIS

Brown v. Board of Education **led to the end of de jure segregation. However, de facto segregation remains in many areas, including housing and schooling. Should there be legal or social efforts to address de facto segregation?**

Outlawing Discrimination in Employment Despite the agonizingly slow progress of school desegregation, some progress was made in other areas of civil rights during the 1960s and '70s. Voting rights were established and fairly quickly began to revolutionize southern politics. Service on juries was no longer denied to minorities. But progress in the right to participate in politics and government dramatized the relative lack of progress in the economic domain, where battles over civil rights were increasingly being fought.

The federal courts and the Justice Department entered this area through Title VII of the Civil Rights Act of 1964, which outlawed job discrimination by all private and public employers, including governmental agencies (such as fire and police departments) that employed more than 15 workers. Title VII makes it unlawful to discriminate in employment on the basis of color, religion, sex, or national origin, as well as race.

Title VII delegated some of the powers to enforce fair-employment practices to the Justice Department's Civil Rights Division and others to a new agency created in the 1964 act, the Equal Employment Opportunity Commission (EEOC). By executive order, these agencies had the power of the national government to revoke public contracts for goods and services and to refuse to engage in contracts with any private company that could not guarantee that its rules for hiring, promotion, and firing were nondiscriminatory. And in 1972, President Nixon and a Democratic Congress cooperated to strengthen the EEOC by giving it authority to initiate suits rather than wait for grievances.

But one problem with Title VII was that the accusing party had to show that deliberate discrimination was the cause of the failure to get a job or a training opportunity. The courts have since allowed aggrieved parties (the plaintiffs) to make their case if they can show that an employer's hiring practices had the *effect* of exclusion. A leading case in 1971 involved a "class action" by several black employees in North Carolina attempting to show with statistical evidence that blacks had been relegated to only one department in the Duke Power Company, which involved the least desirable manual-labor jobs, and that they had been kept out of contention for better jobs because the employer had added attainment of a high school education and the passing of specially prepared aptitude tests as qualifications for higher jobs. The Supreme Court held that although the statistical evidence did not prove intentional discrimination and although the requirements were race-neutral in appearance, their effects were sufficient to shift the burden of justification to the employer to show that the requirements were a "business necessity" that bore "a demonstrable relationship to successful performance."[31] The ruling in this case was subsequently applied to other hiring, promotion, and training programs.[32]

Voting Rights In the 1965 Voting Rights Act, Congress significantly strengthened legislation protecting voting rights by barring literacy and other tests as a condition for voting in six southern states,[33] by setting criminal penalties for interference with efforts to vote, and by providing for the replacement of local registrars with federally appointed registrars in counties designated by the attorney general as significantly resistant to registering eligible blacks to vote. The right to vote was further strengthened with ratification in 1964 of the Twenty-Fourth Amendment, which abolished the poll tax, and in 1975 with legislation permanently outlawing literacy tests in all 50 states and mandating bilingual ballots or oral assistance for Spanish, Chinese, Japanese, and Korean speakers; and Native Americans and Alaska natives.

In the long run, the laws extending and protecting voting rights could prove to be the most effective of all the great civil rights legislation because the progress in black political participation produced by these acts has altered the shape of American politics. In 1965, in the seven states of the Old Confederacy covered by the Voting Rights Act, 29.3 percent of the eligible black residents were registered to vote, compared with 73.4 percent of the white residents (see Table 5.2). By 1972 the gap between black and white registration in the seven states was only 11.2 points. At one time, white leaders in Mississippi had attempted to dilute the influence of this growing black vote by **gerrymandering** districts to ensure that no blacks would

gerrymandering the apportionment of voters in districts in such a way as to give unfair advantage to one racial or ethnic group or political party

TABLE 5.2

Registration by Race and State in Southern States Covered by the Voting Rights Act (VRA)

The VRA had a direct impact on the rate of black voter registration in the southern states, as measured by the gap between white and black voters in each state. Further insights can be gained by examining changes in white registration rates before and after passage of the VRA and by comparing the gaps between white and black registration. Why do you think registration rates for whites increased significantly in some states and dropped in others? What impact could the increase in black registration have had on public policy?

	BEFORE THE ACT*			AFTER THE ACT* 1971–72		
	WHITE %	BLACK %	GAP** %	WHITE %	BLACK %	GAP %
Alabama	69.2	19.3	49.9	80.7	57.1	23.6
Georgia	62.6	27.4	35.2	70.6	67.8	2.8
Louisiana	80.5	31.6	48.9	80.0	59.1	20.9
Mississippi	69.9	6.7	63.2	71.6	62.2	9.4
North Carolina	96.8	46.8	50.0	62.2	46.3	15.9
South Carolina	75.7	37.3	38.4	51.2	48.0	3.2
Virginia	61.1	38.3	22.8	61.2	54.0	7.2
TOTAL	73.4	29.3	44.1	67.8	56.6	11.2

*Available registration data as of March 1965 and 1971–72.

**The gap is the percentage-point difference between white and black registration rates.

SOURCE: U.S. Commission on Civil Rights, *Political Participation* (1968), Appendix VII: Voter Education Project, attachment to press release, October 3, 1972.

be elected to Congress. But the black voters changed Mississippi before Mississippi could change them. In 1988, 11 percent of all elected officials in Mississippi were black—still well below the percentage of blacks in the state's voting-age population, which was 32 percent in 1990, but progress nonetheless.[34]

Several provisions of the 1965 act were scheduled to expire in 2007. However, in 2006, responding to charges that black voters still faced discrimination at the polls, Congress renewed the act for another 25 years. Pressure for renewal of the act had been intense since the disputed 2000 presidential election. The U.S. Commission on Civil Rights conducted hearings on the election in Florida, at which black voters testified about being turned away from the polls and wrongly purged from the voting rolls and about the unreliable voting technology in their neighborhoods. On the basis of this testimony and after an analysis of the vote, the commission charged that there had been extensive racial discrimination.[35] Recently, Texas has come under fire for gerrymandering congressional districts that discriminate against Latino voters. Due to population growth, most of it among Latinos, Texas gained four new congressional seats after the 2010 census. The heavily Republican state legislature drew a map designed to ensure that three of the new seats would go to Republican candidates. However, a coalition of minority groups and the Justice Department contested the map in court, charging that it failed to create a sufficient number of majority-minority districts. After extensive legal wrangling, the new redistricting plan included three majority-minority districts.[36]

The 1965 Voting Rights Act had also required some state and local governments to obtain federal preclearance before making any changes to their voting laws or practices. The designation of which jurisdictions needed preclearance was based upon a formula that calculated each jurisdiction's history of past voting discrimination. In the 2013 case *Shelby County v. Holder*, the Supreme Court overturned the formula, saying it was based on data more than 40 years old.[37] The Obama administration was critical of the decision, but there seemed little possibility that Congress would take action to devise a new preclearance formula.

A new area of controversy in the realm of voting rights concerns is so-called voter ID laws. Some 34 states have enacted legislation requiring voters to show positive identification at the polls. As of 2018, 18 of these states required prospective voters to show an official photo ID before they would be allowed to cast ballots. Republicans generally support such laws, arguing that they deter voter fraud. Democrats generally oppose such laws, countering that they are particularly burdensome to poor and minority voters, who they say are less likely than others to possess such IDs. Cases challenging the laws on equal protection grounds have met mixed success. In 2008 the Supreme Court upheld the constitutionality of Indiana's voter ID law, affirming the states' "valid interest" in improving election procedures and deterring fraud.[38] On the other hand, in 2013 the Supreme Court struck down an Arizona law requiring that individuals produce proof of U.S. citizenship in order to register to vote. In 2016 voter ID laws were struck down or modified by courts in Kansas, North Carolina, North Dakota, Texas, and Wisconsin, indicating increased judicial suspicion of these statutes. Given the political controversy over voter ID laws, it seems likely that the Court will be asked to rule yet again on the question.

Housing The Civil Rights Act of 1964 did not address housing, but in 1968 Congress passed another civil rights act specifically to outlaw housing discrimination. Called the Fair Housing Act, the law prohibited discrimination in the sale or rental of most housing—eventually covering nearly all the nation's housing. Housing was among the most controversial of discrimination issues because of deeply entrenched patterns of residential segregation across the United States. Such segregation was not simply a product of individual choice. Local housing authorities deliberately segregated public housing, and federal guidelines had sanctioned discrimination in Federal Housing Administration mortgage lending, effectively preventing blacks from joining the exodus to the suburbs in the 1950s and '60s. Nonetheless, Congress had been reluctant to tackle housing discrimination, fearing the tremendous controversy it could arouse. But just as the housing legislation was being considered in April 1968, the civil rights leader Martin Luther King, Jr., was assassinated; this tragedy brought the measure unexpected support in Congress.

Although it pronounced sweeping goals, the Fair Housing Act had little effect on housing segregation because its enforcement mechanisms were so weak. Individuals who believed they had been discriminated against had to file suit themselves. The burden was on the individual to prove that housing discrimination had occurred, even though such discrimination is often subtle and difficult to document. Although local fair housing groups emerged to assist

The mortgage crisis that led to foreclosures on many homes in 2008 and 2009 hit minority communities especially hard. Civil rights organizations argued that some lenders discriminated against African Americans and Latino home buyers, making it harder for them to get a fair deal on a mortgage.

individuals in their court claims, the procedures for proving discrimination constituted a formidable barrier to effective change. These procedures were not altered until 1988, when Congress passed the Fair Housing Amendments Act. This new law put more teeth in the enforcement procedures and allowed the Department of Housing and Urban Development (HUD) to initiate legal action in cases of discrimination.[39]

redlining a practice in which banks refuse to make loans to people living in certain geographic locations

Efforts to prohibit discrimination in lending have met some success. Several laws passed in the 1970s required banks to report information about their mortgage lending patterns, making it more difficult for them to engage in **redlining**, the practice of refusing to lend to entire neighborhoods. The 1977 Community Reinvestment Act required banks to lend in neighborhoods in which they do business. Through vigorous use of this act, many neighborhood organizations have reached agreements with banks that, as a result, have significantly increased investment in some poor neighborhoods.

Even so, racial discrimination in home mortgage lending remains a significant issue. In 2007 the issue of predatory lending—offering loans well above market rates, often with complex provisions that borrowers do not understand—attracted nationwide attention as the number of home foreclosures skyrocketed. In 2009 civil rights organizations, several states, and some cities filed charges against banks and other lenders claiming they had illegally discriminated against African American and Latino home buyers. Minority home buyers, the suits charged, had been offered subprime mortgage products with higher interest rates, in contrast to whites with similar income levels, who were offered loans at lower interest rates. By 2012 some of these lawsuits had resulted in the largest financial settlements ever issued for lending discrimination. In announcing one settlement, the Justice Department vowed to "vigorously pursue those who would take advantage of certain Americans because of their race, national origin, gender or disability," noting that such discrimination "betrays the promise of equal opportunity that is enshrined in our Constitution and our legal framework."[40]

Marriage The Civil Rights Act of 1964 was also silent on the question of interracial marriage, which 16 states continued to outlaw in 1967. In that year, the Supreme Court ruled in *Loving v. Virginia* that such state laws were unconstitutional. The case concerned a Virginia couple, a white man and a black woman, who married in Washington, D.C., where such unions were legal. When they moved back to Virginia, which outlawed interracial marriage, authorities charged the couple with violating Virginia law. The Lovings moved back to Washington, D.C., and challenged the Virginia law. Nine years later the Supreme Court struck down state laws banning marriage on the basis of racial classifications. In so doing, the Court declared marriage "one of the 'basic civil rights of man,' fundamental to our very existence and survival."[41]

The Supreme Court ruled in 1967 that state laws banning interracial marriage were unconstitutional. The case *Loving v. Virginia* was invoked numerous times in the Court's decision almost 50 years later, declaring marriage a fundamental right for same-sex couples.

Extending Civil Rights

Describe how different groups have fought for and won protection of their civil rights

Even before equal employment laws began to have a positive effect on the economic situation of blacks, something equally dramatic began happening: the extension of civil rights to other groups. The right not to be discriminated against was being successfully claimed by the other groups listed in Title VII of the 1964 Civil Rights Act, those defined by sex, religion, or national origin, and eventually by still other groups defined by age or sexual orientation. This extension of civil rights has become the new frontier of the civil rights struggle.

Once racial discrimination began to be seen as an important civil rights issue, other groups rose to demand recognition and active protection of their civil rights. Under Title VII, any group or individual can try, and in fact is encouraged to try, to convert goals and grievances into questions of rights and of the deprivation of those rights. A plaintiff must establish only that his or her membership in a group is an unreasonable basis for discrimination. In the United States today, a large number of individuals and groups have and are claiming illegal discrimination.

LEVELS OF SCRUTINY UNDER THE EQUAL PROTECTION CLAUSE

Before we examine the civil rights movements of the past 60 years, it is useful to take a moment to describe how the courts have analyzed laws in cases where an individual or group has claimed discrimination. As has already been made clear, the courts have been a very important actor in the contest for rights protections. Recall that civil rights are the rules governing who may participate in the political process and regulating the ways in which the government may or may not treat its citizens. The equal protection clause of the Fourteenth Amendment does not require that everyone be treated equally. State and federal laws often create classifications allowing some, but not other, individuals to engage in activities or receive benefits. States, for example, allow only those with certain qualifications to engage in various occupations (such as medical professions) and set a minimum age for driving automobiles, voting, and consuming alcohol. Courts generally recognize the need for such systems of classification. Some systems of classification, on the other hand, such as those based on race, gender, or religion, raise serious constitutional questions. When dealing with challenges to state-imposed systems of classification, the courts employ a three-tiered approach, placing a greater burden of proof on the government to defend some types of classificatory schemes than others. The three tiers are often called "levels of scrutiny."

First Level The first and lowest level of scrutiny is applied by the courts to most state and federal regulatory schemes, such as motor vehicle and occupational licensing, as well as laws setting a minimum age for the purchase of alcohol and cigarettes. Here, the courts will generally apply the "rational basis test." Under this level of scrutiny, the burden of proof is on the plaintiff to show that there is no rational basis whatsoever for the government's rules. Such a showing is extremely difficult, and few plaintiffs succeed.

intermediate scrutiny a test used by the Supreme Court in gender discrimination cases that places the burden of proof partially on the government and partially on the challengers to show that the law in question is unconstitutional

Second Level The next level of judicial review of state action under the equal protection clause is **intermediate scrutiny** (or exacting scrutiny). Here, there is a greater burden on the government to show that its classification scheme not only is rational but also serves an important interest. Courts generally apply intermediate scrutiny to laws that afford differential treatment to men and women or that discriminate against the inheritance and property rights of illegitimate children. In recent years, federal courts have generally applied intermediate scrutiny in cases involving gender orientation. For example, in the 2013 case of *Windsor v. United States* the Second Circuit Courts of Appeals employed intermediate scrutiny in holding that the federal Defense of Marriage Act, which applied the terms *marriage* and *spouse* only to heterosexual unions, served no legitimate state interest.[42] The U.S. Supreme Court affirmed the decision but did not indicate which level of scrutiny it had applied.

Third Level The highest level of scrutiny employed by the courts, "strict scrutiny," places the burden of proof on the government to show that discrimination serves a "compelling interest," that the law is "narrowly tailored to achieve that goal," and that the government has used the "least restrictive means" for achieving its compelling interest. Strict scrutiny generally applies to laws that discriminate on the basis of race, religion, or national origin. These are termed *suspect classifications*. Strict scrutiny also applies to laws that hinder the exercise of fundamental rights, such as access to the courts or the right to vote. When a federal court employs strict scrutiny, the government is seldom able to meet its burden of proof. All race-based classifications are automatically subject to strict scrutiny.[43] In 2013 the Supreme Court also applied strict scrutiny to a case involving a claim of reverse discrimination. In the case of *Fisher v. University of Texas*, a white plaintiff charged that she had been rejected in favor of less qualified minority applicants.[44] The Supreme Court remanded the case for reconsideration by a lower federal court, which was instructed to apply strict scrutiny to the school's admissions process. The court of appeals still rejected Fisher's claim, and in 2016 the Supreme Court upheld the university's procedures.[45]

WOMEN AND GENDER DISCRIMINATION

Title VII provided a valuable tool for the growing women's movement in the 1960s and '70s. In fact, in many ways the law fostered the growth of the women's movement. The first major campaign of the National Organization for Women (NOW)

involved picketing the EEOC for its refusal to ban sex-segregated employment advertisements. NOW also sued the *New York Times* for continuing to publish such ads after the passage of Title VII. Another organization, the Women's Equity Action League (WEAL), pursued legal action on a wide range of gender-discrimination issues, filing lawsuits against law schools and medical schools for discriminatory admission policies, for example.

Building on these victories and the growth of the women's movement, feminist activists sought an "Equal Rights Amendment" (ERA) to the Constitution. The proposed amendment was short: its substantive passage stated that "equality of rights under the law shall not be denied or abridged by the United States or by any State on account of sex." The amendment's supporters believed that such a sweeping guarantee of equal rights was a necessary tool for ending all discrimination against women and for making gender roles more equal. Opponents charged that the amendment would be socially disruptive and would introduce changes (such as unisex restrooms) that most Americans did not want. The amendment easily passed Congress in 1972 and won quick approval in many state legislatures, but it fell three states short of the 38 needed to ratify it by the 1982 deadline.[46]

Despite the failure of the ERA, efforts to stop gender discrimination expanded dramatically as an area of civil rights law. In the 1970s the conservative Burger Court (under Chief Justice Warren Burger) helped establish gender discrimination as a major and highly visible civil rights issue. Although the Supreme Court refused to treat gender discrimination as the equivalent of racial discrimination,[47] it did make it easier for plaintiffs to file and win suits on the basis of gender discrimination by applying an "intermediate" level of review to these cases, as described earlier.[48]

In recent years, laws and court decisions designed to deal with discrimination against women have been used by groups representing transgender individuals to press for equal rights, especially in the realm of employment. For example, Title VII of the 1964 Civil Rights Act makes it unlawful to discriminate in employment on the basis of color, religion, sex, national origin, or race. The act is enforced by the EEOC. Pressed by groups representing transgender workers, in July 2015 President Obama issued an executive order prohibiting federal contractors from discriminating against workers based on their sexual orientation or gender identity. Two months later, the EEOC filed its first-ever lawsuits to protect transgender workers under Title VII. In late December, then–attorney general Eric Holder announced that, going forward, the Justice Department would consider discrimination against transgender people as covered by the Civil Rights Act's prohibition of sex discrimination.[49] Nonetheless, attempts have been made to pass legislation requiring transgender individuals to use public bathrooms that correspond to the gender designated on their birth certificates. In 2016, North Carolina enacted such a law, leading to boycotts and protests, with several corporations announcing plans to reduce their operations in the state. When the Department of Justice warned North Carolina that the law violated the Civil Rights Act, the state sued the federal government in order to defend its new law. In 2017, under pressure from the business community, North Carolina repealed its ordinance.

As discussed in this chapter's introduction, more recently, President Trump tweeted that transgender individuals would be barred from the armed forces, though there has been no plan to implement the president's tweet pending further clarification.

Gains for women in the area of civil rights have come, but slowly. Title IX of the 1972 Education Act has helped promote gender equality in education and helped increase women's participation in college sports, though women continue to be underrepresented in science, technology, engineering, and math. In 2009, President Obama signed the Lily Ledbetter Fair Pay Act to help combat pay discrimination. After serving in the military for decades, women were finally allowed to serve in combat in 2013. Despite these steps forward, gender inequity persists in American life.

Equality in Education Title IX of the 1972 Education Act forbade gender discrimination in education, but it initially sparked little litigation because of its weak enforcement provisions. In 1992 the Supreme Court ruled in *Franklin v. Gwinnett County Public Schools* that monetary damages could be awarded for gender discrimination, opening the door for more legal action in the area of education.[50] The greatest impact has been in the areas of sexual harassment (the subject of the *Franklin* case) and in equal treatment of women's athletic programs. The potential for monetary damages has made universities and public schools take the problem of sexual harassment more seriously. And in the two years after the *Franklin* case, complaints to the Education Department's Office for Civil Rights about unequal treatment of women's athletic programs nearly tripled. In several high-profile legal cases, some prominent universities were ordered to create more women's sports programs, prompting many other colleges and universities to follow suit in order to avoid potential litigation.[51] In 1997 the Supreme Court refused to hear a petition by Brown University challenging a lower-court order that the university establish strict sex equity in its athletic programs. The Court's decision meant that in colleges and universities across the country, varsity athletic positions for men and women must reflect the schools' overall enrollment numbers.[52] Though the ruling has a major impact on college athletic programs, advocates for gender equality note that many differences between male and female students continue to exist. They point to gender barriers in important fields such as science, technology, engineering, and math, which female students are much less likely to enter.[53]

FOR CRITICAL ANALYSIS

Has Title IX created equality in men's and women's college athletic programs? Should there be public efforts to encourage more female students to enter well-paid fields such as science and technology, or is that mainly a matter of individual choice?

In 1996 the Supreme Court made another important decision about gender and education by putting an end to all-male schools supported by public funds. It ruled that the Virginia Military Institute's (VMI) policy of not admitting women was unconstitutional.[54] Along with the Citadel, an all-male military college in South Carolina, VMI had never admitted women in its 157-year history. VMI argued that the unique educational experience it offered (including intense physical training and the harsh treatment of freshmen) would be destroyed if women were admitted. The Court, however, ruled that the male-only policy denied "substantial equality" to women. Two days after the ruling, the Citadel announced that it would accept women. Even without formal barriers to entry, the experience of the new female cadets at these schools was not easy. Of the four women admitted to the Citadel

immediately after the Supreme Court decision, two quit within months. They charged harassment from male students, including attempts to set the female cadets on fire.[55] Women persevered, and today women constitute nearly 10 percent of the Citadel's corps of cadets.[56]

Sexual Harassment Courts began to find sexual harassment to be a form of sex discrimination during the late 1970s. Most such law has been developed by courts through interpretation of Title VII of the 1964 Civil Rights Act. In 1986 the Supreme Court recognized two forms of sexual harassment. One type is "quid pro quo" harassment, which involves an explicit or strongly implied threat that submission is a condition of continued employment. The second is harassment that creates offensive or intimidating employment conditions amounting to a "hostile environment."[57] Employers and many employees have complained that "hostile environment" sexual harassment is too ambiguous. When can an employee bring charges? When is the employer liable? In 1986 the Court said that sexual harassment may be legally actionable even if the employee did not suffer tangible economic or job-related losses in relation to it and in 1993 added that tangible psychological costs did not have to be a result either to warrant legal action.[58] In two 1998 cases, the Court further strengthened the law when it said that whether or not sexual harassment results in economic harm to the employee, an employer is liable for the harassment if it was committed by someone with authority over the employee—by a supervisor, for example. But the Court also said that an employer may defend itself by showing that it had a sexual harassment prevention and grievance policy in effect.[59]

In 2011 the Department of Education's Office of Civil Rights (OCR) issued a "Dear Colleague" letter to the more than 7,000 colleges and universities receiving federal money, advising them, under the authority of Title IX, to adopt stringent procedures to adjudicate charges of sexual assault and harassment on campus. OCR told colleges to shift the burden of proof from the accuser toward the accused in such cases, to allow accusers to appeal not-guilty findings (double jeopardy contrary to the language of the Fifth Amendment) and to refrain from allowing accused persons from cross-examining their accusers (contrary to the Sixth Amendment). These procedures have led to a furor on many campuses and a flurry of charges of false accusations and unfair proceedings.[60]

Sexual harassment remains an issue today. Recently, a number of cases of sexual harassment of female members of the U.S. military have come to light. These cases have led to several courts-martial of both officers and noncommissioned officers. Some observers argue that the problem is systemic, however, and have urged the military to enact reforms that would hopefully have the effect of stemming the abuse of women in the military.

Equality in Employment Women have also pressed for civil rights in employment. In particular, women have fought against pay discrimination—when a male employee is paid more than a female employee of equal qualifications in the same job. After the Equal Pay Act of 1963 made such discrimination illegal, women's pay slowly moved toward the level of men's pay. In 2007 this movement received a setback when the Supreme Court ruled against a claim of pay discrimination. The case, *Ledbetter v. Goodyear Tire and Rubber Co.*, involved a female supervisor named Lily Ledbetter, who learned late in her career that she was being paid up to 40 percent less than male supervisors, including those with less seniority. Ledbetter filed a grievance with the EEOC, charging sex discrimination.[61] The Supreme Court denied her claim, ruling that, according to the law, workers must file their grievance 180 days after the discrimination occurs. Many observers found the ruling unfair because workers often do not know about pay differentials until well after the initial decision to discriminate has been made. Justice Ruth Bader Ginsburg, the only female member of the Court at the time, marked her disagreement by reading her dissent aloud, a rare occurrence. In January 2009 the Lily Ledbetter Fair Pay Act became the first bill that President Obama signed into law. The new law gave workers expanded rights to sue in cases, such as Ledbetter's, when an employee learns of discriminatory treatment well after it has started. Despite such cases, women continue to earn about 20 percent less than men in the U.S. workforce.[62]

The fight against gender discrimination as an important part of the civil rights struggle has coincided with the rise of women's politics as a discrete movement in American politics. As with the struggle for racial equality, the relationship between changes in government policies and political action suggests that, to a great degree, changes in government policies produce political action. The inclusion of gender as a protected class in the 1964 Civil Rights Act prompted women to take steps to press for their rights where they were denied in education and employment. The "Who Are Americans?" feature on page 185 considers the progress on women's rights.

LATINOS

The labels *Latino* and *Hispanic* encompass a wide range of groups with diverse national origins, distinctive cultural identities, and particular experiences. As a result, civil rights issues for them have varied considerably by group and by place. For example, the early political experiences of Mexican Americans were shaped by race and by region. In 1848, under the Treaty of Guadalupe Hidalgo, Mexico ceded to the United States territory that now comprises Arizona, California, New Mexico, and parts of Colorado, Nevada, and Utah, as well as extended the Texas border to the Rio Grande. Although the treaty guaranteed full civil rights to the residents of these territories, Mexican Americans in fact experienced ongoing discrimination, which they sought to remedy through the courts. In 1898 the courts reconfirmed Mexican Americans' formal political rights, including the right to vote. In many places, however, and especially in Texas, Mexican Americans were segregated and

Have Women Achieved Equal Rights?

Title VII of the 1964 Civil Rights Act prohibits gender discrimination, and the Supreme Court has consistently upheld the principle that women should have the same rights as men. Since 1960 the United States has made great strides toward gender equality in some areas but, as the data show, still has a long way to go in other areas.

Education

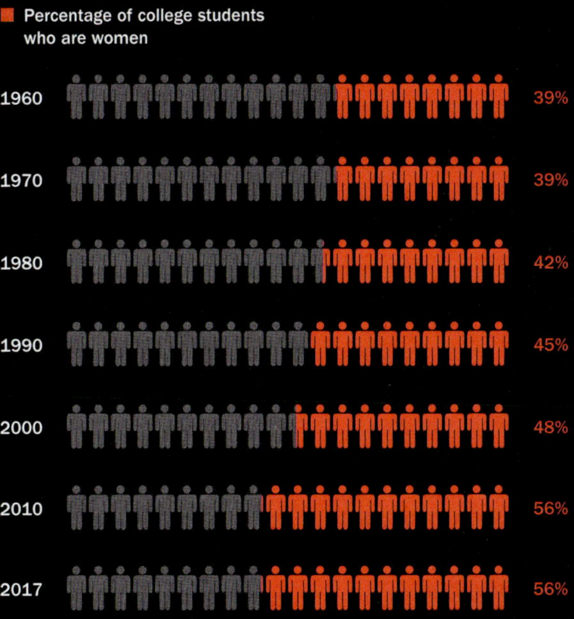

Politics

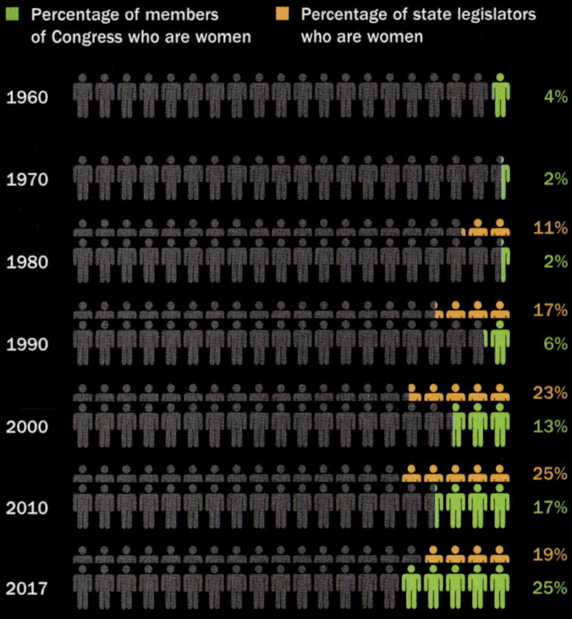

Median Weekly Earnings by Race and Gender

In 2016 women who were full-time wage and salary workers had median usual weekly earnings that were 82 percent of those of male full-time wage and salary workers.

SOURCES: National Center for Education Statistics, www.nces.ed.gov (accessed 11/4/17); Congressional Research Service, www.fas.org; National Conference of State Legislators, www.ncsl.org; Bureau of Labor Statistics, www.bls.gov (accessed 11/4/17).

FOR CRITICAL ANALYSIS

1. How much does each of these factors—education, political office, and income—say about gender equality in the United States?
2. While most Americans support the principle of equal opportunity for all groups, there is disagreement over how much the government should do to ensure equal outcomes. Discuss the difference between equal opportunity and equal outcomes in the context of women's rights.

Immigration is one of today's most controversial issues. President Trump campaigned on a promise to build a protective wall on the U.S.-Mexico border. Supporters of stricter immigration policies believe they will help protect jobs for American citizens. Others support the rights of undocumented people—especially young people brought to the United States by their parents—and believe that they should have a path to American citizenship.

prevented from voting through such means as the white primary and the poll tax.[63] Texas established separate schools for Mexicans, a practice also common in southern California. In the housing markets, Mexicans were often banned by restrictive covenants from buying or renting houses in many neighborhoods.

The earliest Mexican American independent political organizations included the League of United Latin American Citizens (LULAC), founded in 1929, and the GI Forum, created in 1948. Both groups worked to stem discrimination against Mexican Americans. LULAC pursued a legal strategy like the NAACP's to eliminate the segregation of Mexican American students. One of its earliest victories came in 1930, when it successfully challenged a Texas school district's decision to establish separate schools for Anglos and Mexicans.[64] LULAC also litigated the 1946–47 *Mendez v. Westminster* case, which overturned school segregation in Orange County, California.[65] This case was an important precursor to *Brown v. Board of Education*, and many of the same actors were involved.

In the 1960s a new kind of Mexican American political movement was born. By the late 1950s the first Mexican American was elected to Congress, and four others followed in the 1960s. A central inspiration for political mobilization emerged from the United Farm Workers union and its charismatic leader, César Chávez. In an era of unprecedented economic prosperity, California's farmworkers, mainly Mexican migrants, remained poorly paid and lacked basic rights for fair treatment on the job. Employing novel tactics such as the national grape boycott, the union drew Americans' attention to the plight of farmworkers and the injustices that confronted Mexican migrants and Mexican Americans in the fields. Chávez, whose hunger strikes and inspirational speeches kept the movement in the public eye, came to symbolize the quest for Mexican American civil rights more broadly.[66] The fields were not the only focus of conflict. In the late 1960s, Mexican American students, inspired by the black civil rights movement, launched boycotts of high school classes in East Los Angeles, Denver, and San Antonio, demanding bilingual education, an end to discrimination, and more cultural recognition. They were soon joined by students in colleges and universities across California.

Since that time, Latino political strategy has developed along two tracks. One is a traditional ethnic group path of voter registration and voting along ethnic lines. The other is a legal strategy using the various civil rights laws designed to ensure fair

access to the political system. The Mexican American Legal Defense and Education Fund (MALDEF), founded in 1968, has played a key role in designing and pursuing the latter strategy.

Immigrants and Civil Rights Since the 1960s, rights for Latinos have been intertwined with immigrant rights. For much of American history, legal immigrants were treated much the same as citizens. But continuing immigration and mounting economic insecurity have undermined this sense of equality. Groups of voters across the country now strongly support drawing a sharper line between immigrants and citizens. The Supreme Court has ruled that unauthorized immigrants are eligible for education and emergency medical care but can be denied other social benefits. The movement to deny benefits to noncitizens gathered steam in California, which experienced sharp economic distress in the early 1990s and has the highest levels of immigration of any state. In 1994 an ultimately unsuccessful movement in California sought to deny unauthorized immigrants all services except emergency medical care in an attempt to discourage unauthorized immigration and to pressure those already in the country to leave.

Unauthorized immigration has continued to be a hot-button political issue. One priority for advocacy groups has been the issue of undocumented immigrants who came to the United States as young children, were raised in the United States, and have no real ties to the nation in which they were born. One proposed piece of legislation to benefit such individuals is the Development, Relief, and Education Act for Alien Minors, known as the DREAM Act. This proposal would provide a route to permanent residency for such individuals via military service or college attendance. The DREAM Act was introduced in Congress in 2001 but has been defeated every year on the grounds that it would encourage illegal immigration. Absent legislation, the Department of Homeland Security has instituted its own policy, Deferred Action for Childhood Arrivals (DACA), instructing immigration officials to take no action to deport law-abiding individuals who entered the United States illegally as children. In 2014, President Obama issued executive memoranda granting quasi-legal status and work permits to some 5 million individuals who entered the United States illegally as children or who have children who are American citizens. The president's orders were challenged in the federal courts, and in 2016 a 4–4 tie in the Supreme Court left in place a lower-court decision disallowing the president's plan.[67] In 2018 the Supreme Court declined to hear the Trump administration's appeal from a lower-court ruling requiring continuation of the DACA program. However, DACA cases before several U.S. district courts at the end of 2018 may result in competing rulings that could force the Supreme Court to address the question.

Efforts to curb illegal immigration have led to civil rights violations of legal immigrants. Latino organizations opposed the Immigration Reform and Control Act of 1986 because it imposed sanctions on employers who hire undocumented workers. Such sanctions, they feared, would lead employers to discriminate against Latinos. These suspicions were confirmed in a 1990 report by the General Accounting Office, which found employer sanctions had created a "widespread pattern of discrimination" against Latinos and others who appear foreign.[68]

Another ongoing issue is federal cooperation with local and state law-enforcement agencies to enforce federal immigration laws. Programs initiated by the Department of Homeland Security in the final years of the George W. Bush administration led to immigrant "sweeps," which rounded up Latinos, many of whom were legal immigrants or even American citizens. A broad coalition of civil rights organizations opposed the program for engaging in racial profiling and violating civil rights, and the congressional Hispanic Caucus called on the next president to end it. Yet, the Obama administration's Secure Communities program, which initially sought to focus on major drug offenders, violent criminals, and those already in prison, came under fire for illegally detaining citizens and legal immigrants. The Secure Communities Program was terminated in 2014 in favor of an effort to refocus law enforcement attention on serious criminals.

In 2017, however, President Trump ordered stricter immigration enforcement and began to expand the ranks of Immigration and Customs Enforcement (ICE) agents. Many thousands of immigrants who had not committed serious crimes were slated for deportation, and immigration enforcement at the border was stepped up as well. Several cities and a handful of states declared themselves "sanctuaries" and declined to cooperate with ICE agents. The administration responded by threatening to cut off federal funding from local governments that failed to help federal authorities.

Finally, as we saw in Chapter 3, while some local governments declared themselves to be sanctuaries, a number of states, including Arizona, Utah, South Carolina, Indiana, Georgia, and Alabama, passed very strict immigration laws within the past few years. Civil rights groups have contested the laws in court, and the federal Justice Department has instituted its own legal challenges. Arizona's 2010 law provided the inspiration for these far-reaching state measures. Arizona's law required immigrants to carry identity documents with them at all times, made it a crime for an undocumented immigrant to apply for a job, gave the police greater powers to stop anyone they suspected of being an unauthorized immigrant, and required them to check the immigration status of a person they detain if they suspect that person is an unauthorized immigrant. The Justice Department challenged the law on the grounds that the federal government was responsible for making immigration law, not the states. The Supreme Court's 2012 decision was a partial victory for the federal government. The Court struck down three parts of the Arizona law on the grounds that they intruded upon federal responsibility. These included the provision that immigrants carry identity papers, that undocumented immigrants cannot apply for jobs, and that police can stop persons they suspect of being undocumented immigrants. The Court let stand the provision that required local police to check the immigration status of an individual detained for other reasons if they had grounds

FOR CRITICAL ANALYSIS

Why are immigration and the rights of immigrants so controversial?

Soon after taking office, President Trump instituted a "travel ban" on people from some predominantly Muslim countries. He claimed that the move would cut down on foreign terrorism in the United States. Opponents protested this ban on the grounds that it was singling out certain religious groups and not others. The matter moved quickly to the U.S. Supreme Court, which ruled that a modified version of the ban could remain in place.

to suspect that the person was in the country illegally. Opponents of the police checks vowed to challenge that part of the law on the grounds that it led to illegal racial profiling.[69]

Immigration was, of course, a very divisive topic during the 2016 presidential election. During the campaign for the Republican nomination, Donald Trump asserted that he would build a wall along the U.S. border with Mexico, institute a temporary ban on Muslims seeking to travel to the United States, and end the Obama administration's program to accept several thousand Syrian refugees every year. When Trump took office, he lost little time in seeking to implement these campaign promises pertaining to immigration, though not all have come to fruition. As of 2018, while the fence on the U.S.-Mexico border had been extended in some places, no wall had been built.

However, in January 2017, Trump issued executive orders barring entry into the United States for travelers from six predominantly Muslim countries and blocking the admission of all refugees seeking admission to the United States for 120 days. Critics charged Trump, who had frequently stated his concerns that Muslim immigrants might include terrorists, with religious discrimination, and in particular with violating the 1965 Immigration Act, which states that people should not experience preferences or discrimination on account of their "race, sex, nationality, place of birth or place of residence." At least one federal appeals court agreed with this argument, though other immigration laws seem to give the president broad discretion in the matter. In a 5–4 decision, the U.S. Supreme Court upheld the ban, though the dissenting opinion argued the ban infringed on the right to religious liberty.

ASIAN AMERICANS

Like the term *Latino*, the label *Asian American* encompasses a wide range of people from very different national backgrounds who came to the United States at different moments in history. As a consequence, Asian Americans have had very diverse experiences.

The early Asian experience in the United States was shaped by a series of naturalization laws dating back to 1790, the first of which declared that only white aliens were eligible for citizenship. Chinese immigrants began arriving in California in the 1850s, drawn by the boom of the gold rush, but they were immediately met with virulent antagonism. In 1870, Congress declared Chinese immigrants ineligible for citizenship; in 1882 the first Chinese Exclusion Act suspended the entry of Chinese laborers.

At the time of the Exclusion Act, the Chinese community was composed predominantly of single male laborers, with few women and children. The few Chinese children in San Francisco were initially denied entry to the public schools; only after parents of American-born Chinese children pressed legal action were the children allowed to attend public school. Even then, however, they were segregated into a separate Chinese school. American-born Chinese children could not be denied citizenship, however; this right was confirmed by the Supreme Court in 1898, when it ruled in *United States v. Wong Kim Ark* that anyone born in the United States was entitled to full citizenship.[70] Still, new Chinese immigrants were barred from the United States until 1943, after China had become a key wartime ally and Congress repealed the Chinese Exclusion Act and permitted Chinese residents to become citizens.

The earliest Japanese immigrants, who came to California in the 1880s, at the height of the anti-Chinese movement, faced similar discrimination. Like Chinese immigrants, Japanese immigrants were ineligible to become citizens because of their race. During the first part of the twentieth century, California and several other western states enacted laws that denied Japanese immigrants the right to own property. The denial of basic civil rights to Japanese Americans culminated in the decision to forcibly remove Americans of Japanese descent as well as Japanese noncitizen residents from their homes and confine them in internment camps during World War II. After the Japanese government launched its attack on Pearl Harbor, America's Japanese residents and citizens were suspected of disloyalty. Some 120,000 individuals of Japanese descent or heritage, including 90,000 American citizens, were forcibly relocated from their homes to 10 internment camps located in California, Idaho, Utah, Arizona, Wyoming, Colorado, and Arkansas. Conditions in the camps were poor and characterized by overcrowding, food rationing, and primitive sanitary facilities. Despite a vigorous legal challenge, the Supreme Court ruled that the internment was constitutional on the grounds of military necessity.[71] In 1944, President Roosevelt rescinded the order that began the internment process and closed the camps. Many of the internees, however, had suffered property losses and health problems during the period of internment and would never recover from its effects. Not until the Civil Liberties Act of 1988 did the federal government formally acknowledge this denial of civil rights as a "grave injustice" that had been "motivated largely by racial prejudice, wartime hysteria, and a failure of political leadership."[72]

Asian immigration increased rapidly after the 1965 Immigration Act, which lifted discriminatory quotas. In spite of this and other developments, societal discrimination coupled with limited English proficiency barred many new Asian American (in addition to Latino) immigrants from full participation in American life. Two developments in the 1970s, however, established rights for language minorities. In 1974 the Supreme Court ruled in *Lau v. Nichols*, a suit filed on behalf of Chinese students in San Francisco, that school districts have to provide education for students whose English is limited.[73] It did not mandate bilingual education, but it established a duty to provide instruction that the students could understand. As we saw earlier, the 1970 amendments to the Voting Rights Act permanently outlawed literacy tests in all 50 states and mandated bilingual ballots or oral assistance for those who speak Chinese, Japanese, Korean, Spanish, or Native American or Alaskan languages.

NATIVE AMERICANS

The political status of Native Americans was left unclear in the Constitution. But by the early 1800s the courts had defined each of the Indian tribes as a nation. As members of Indian nations, Native Americans were thus declared noncitizens of the United States. The political status of Native Americans changed in 1924, when congressional legislation granted citizenship to all persons born in the United States. A variety of changes in federal policy toward Native Americans during the 1930s paved the way for a later resurgence of their political power. Most important was the federal decision to encourage Native Americans on reservations to establish local self-government.[74] Since the 1920s and '30s, Native American tribes have sued the federal government for illegal land seizures; both monetary reparations and land have been awarded as damages but only in small amounts. Native American tribes have been more successful at winning federal recognition of their sovereignty.

The Native American political movement gathered force in the 1960s as Native Americans began to use protest, litigation, and assertion of tribal rights to improve their situation. The federal government responded to the rise in Native American activism with the Indian Self-Determination and Education Assistance Act, which began to give Native Americans more control over their own land.[75]

As a language minority, Native Americans also benefited from the 1975 amendments to the Voting Rights Act and the *Lau* decision, which established the right of Native Americans to be taught in their own languages. This marked quite a change from the boarding schools run by the Bureau of Indian Affairs, where members of Native American tribes were forbidden to speak their own languages until reforms began in the 1930s. In addition to these language-related issues, Native Americans have sought to expand their rights on the basis of their sovereign status. Most significant in economic terms was a 1987 Supreme Court decision that freed Native American tribes from most state regulations prohibiting gambling. The establishment of casino gambling on Native American lands has brought a substantial flow of new income to desperately poor reservations.

DISABLED AMERICANS

The concept of rights for the disabled began to emerge in the 1970s as the civil rights model spread to other groups. The seed was planted in a little-noticed provision of the 1973 Rehabilitation Act, which outlawed discrimination against individuals on the basis of disabilities. As in many other cases, the law itself helped give rise to the movement demanding rights for the disabled.[76] Inspired by the NAACP's use of a legal defense fund, the disability movement founded the Disability Rights Education and Defense Fund to press its legal claims. The movement achieved its greatest success with the passage of the Americans with Disabilities Act (ADA) of 1990, which guarantees equal employment rights and access to public businesses for the disabled and prohibits discrimination in employment, housing, and health care. Claims of discrimination in violation of this act are considered by the EEOC.

The impact of the law has been far-reaching as businesses and public facilities have installed ramps, elevators, and other devices to meet the act's requirements.[77]

LGBTQ AMERICANS

In less than 50 years, the lesbian, gay, bisexual, transgender, and queer (LGBTQ) movement has become one of the largest civil rights movements in contemporary America. For much of the country's history, any sexual orientation other than heterosexuality was considered "deviant," and many states criminalized sexual acts considered to be "unnatural." Gay people were often afraid to reveal their sexual orientation for fear of reprisals, including being fired from their jobs; and the police in many cities raided bars and other establishments where it was believed that gay people gathered. While no formal restrictions existed on their political participation, gay people faced the possibility of ostracization, discrimination, and even prosecution.[78]

The contemporary gay rights movement began in earnest in the 1960s. In 1962, Illinois became the first state to repeal its sodomy laws. The movement drew national attention in 1969, when patrons at the Stonewall Inn, a popular gay bar in Greenwich Village, New York, rioted when police attempted to raid the establishment. The first gay pride parade was held in New York City the following year to commemorate the anniversary of the Stonewall riots, and gay pride parades now take place in dozens of cities across the country.

Gay rights drew national attention again in 1993, when President Bill Clinton confronted the question of whether gays should be allowed to serve in the military. As a candidate, Clinton had said he favored lifting the ban on gay people in the military. The issue set off a huge controversy in the first months of Clinton's presidency. After nearly a year of deliberation, the administration enunciated a compromise: its "Don't Ask, Don't Tell" policy allowed gay men and lesbians to serve in the military as long as they did not openly proclaim their sexual orientation or engage in homosexual activity. Many gay rights advocates expressed disappointment, charging the president with reneging on his campaign promise. After nearly 20 years of challenges, President Obama signed an executive order in 2010 repealing "Don't Ask, Don't Tell," allowing gay men and lesbians to serve openly in the military.

No Supreme Court ruling or national legislation explicitly protected gay men and lesbians from discrimination until 1996. In its first gay rights case, *Bowers v. Hardwick*, the Court ruled against a right to privacy that would protect consensual homosexual activity.[79] After the *Bowers* decision, the gay rights movement sought suitable legal cases to test the constitutionality of discrimination against gay men and lesbians, much as the African American civil rights movement had done in the late 1940s and '50s. Test cases stemmed from local ordinances restricting gay rights (including the right to marry), allowing job discrimination, and affecting family law issues such as adoption and parental rights. In 1996 the Supreme Court, in *Romer v. Evans*, explicitly extended fundamental civil rights protections to gay men and lesbians by declaring unconstitutional a 1992 amendment to the Colorado state constitution that prohibited local governments from passing ordinances to protect gay rights.[80] In its decision, the Court highlighted the connection between gay rights and civil rights.

It was not until 2003, in *Lawrence v. Texas*, that the Court overturned *Bowers* and struck down a Texas statute criminalizing certain intimate sexual conduct between consenting partners of the same sex.[81] This significant victory for gay men and lesbians extends the right to privacy to sexual minorities.

However, this decision did not undo the various exclusions that deprive gay men and lesbians of full civil rights, including the right to marry. In 1993, Hawaii's supreme court declared the state's ban on same-sex marriage discriminatory, raising the possibility that such marriages could become legal. In Washington, D.C., the Republican congressional majority responded with the Defense of Marriage Act, which defined marriage as the union of a man and a woman for purposes of federal law and benefits, such as Social Security.

In 2015 the Supreme Court legalized same-sex marriage nationwide with its decision in *Obergefell v. Hodges*. The Obama administration showed its support by illuminating the White House in rainbow light.

More than a decade later, in 2015, the Supreme Court clarified the law concerning same-sex marriage. In the case of *Obergefell v. Hodges*, the Court ruled that the Constitution's equal protection clause and the Fourteenth Amendment's due process clause guarantee same-sex couples the right to marry in all states and require states to recognize same-sex marriages performed in other jurisdictions (see Chapter 2).[82] Some local officials briefly refused to issue marriage licenses to same-sex couples, but opposition soon melted away. Though the Court was closely divided in the case, the Court's opinion appeared to reflect a shift in public opinion on same-sex unions, with a majority of Americans favoring the right of same-sex couples to wed.[83]

Gay rights advocates won a significant victory of a different kind in national politics in 2009 when new legislation extended the definition of hate crimes to include crimes against gay and transgender people. Such legislation had been sought since the 1998 murder of Matthew Shepard, a Wyoming college student who was brutally slain because of his sexual orientation. The new law allowed for tougher penalties when a crime is designated a hate crime. In another win in 2013, the Senate approved a law that bans discrimination in the workplace based on sexual orientation and gender identity (discussed earlier), with a vote of 64 to 32 in which 10 Republicans joined 54 Democrats. The House did not take up the bill, however, so it has not yet become law. Like other minorities fighting for civil rights, the LGBTQ community is organized politically to support such measures. The Human Rights Campaign is the primary national political action committee focused on gay rights; it provides campaign financing and volunteers to work for political candidates endorsed by the group. The movement has also formed legal rights organizations, including the Lambda Legal Defense and Education Fund.

FOR CRITICAL ANALYSIS

Political conflicts over gay rights have been carried out in the courts, in state legislatures, in Congress, and in elections. What are some of the decisions that have been reached in each of these different decision-making arenas? Where should decisions about gay rights be made?

DO THE POOR HAVE CIVIL RIGHTS?

One category often omitted from discussions of rights is the poor. Yet America's poor have also struggled for recognition as a group with rights that should be protected. From the colonial period until the early nineteenth century, state income and property restrictions excluded poor people from voting and officeholding. In modern times, advocates have argued that the poor have a right to education, health care, and other social benefits. Such rights are guaranteed in many European constitutions. And, in the United States, various social policies appear to recognize such rights.

AMERICA SIDE by SIDE

Women's Rights

Every year, the World Economic Forum (a nonprofit based in Switzerland) ranks countries based on how close they are to achieving gender equality. In 2017 the United States was ranked 49th out of 144 countries, comparable to countries such as Peru and Zimbabwe.[a] One of the interesting findings in this report is that the United States has reached full gender parity in regards to educational attainment, yet lags regarding women's economic participation and opportunity, health and survival, and political empowerment.

When we compare the United States to other democracies, we notice that the United States lacks key legislation that impacts how women interact in the workforce. While most wealthy democracies mandate employers provide *paid* maternity and paternity leave, the United States has no legislation that guarantees even *unpaid* leave. As a result, it is more difficult for women in the United States to balance motherhood and pursuing a career. Largely thanks to various court decisions, U.S. law protects women from gender-based discrimination in hiring and, increasingly, from sexual harassment in the workplace, yet lacks sufficient protections guaranteeing equal pay for equal work.

	CONSTITUTION CONTAINS A NON-DISCRIMINATION CLAUSE BASED ON GENDER	ABORTION PERMITTED UPON REQUEST	GENDER PARITY REACHED IN LITERACY AND IN PRIMARY, SECONDARY, AND TERTIARY EDUCATION	LAW MANDATES NON-DISCRIMINATION BASED ON GENDER IN HIRING	LAW MANDATES EQUAL PAY FOR EQUAL WORK	LAW MANDATES MATERNITY LEAVE (PAID OR UNPAID)
Australia		✓	✓	✓	✓	
Brazil	✓		✓			✓
Canada	✓	✓	✓		✓	✓
France		✓	✓	✓	✓	✓
Germany		✓		✓		✓
India	✓			✓		✓
Japan	✓			✓		✓
Mexico	✓	✓		✓		✓
South Africa	✓	✓		✓	✓	✓
United States		✓	✓	✓		

SOURCES: World Bank, "Gender Data Portal," 2018, www.datatopics.worldbank.org (accessed 7/2/18); Pew Research Center, "Worldwide Abortion Politics," October 5, 2015, www.pewresearch.org (accessed 7/2/18); World Economic Forum, "Global Gender Gap Report," 2017, www.reports.webforum.org (accessed 7/2/18).

[a] World Economic Forum, "Global Gender Gap Report," 2017, www.reports.weforum.org/global-gender-gap-report-2017/dataexplorer/ (accessed 5/28/18).

Affirmative Action

Contrast arguments for and against affirmative action

Over the past half-century or so, the relatively narrow goal of equalizing opportunity by eliminating discriminatory barriers evolved into the broader goal of **affirmative action**, compensatory action to overcome the consequences of past discrimination and encourage greater diversity. Affirmative action policies take race or some other status into account in order to provide greater opportunities to groups that have previously been at a disadvantage due to discrimination.

affirmative action government policies or programs that seek to redress past injustices against specified groups by making special efforts to provide members of those groups with access to educational and employment opportunities

In 1965, President Lyndon Johnson issued executive orders promoting minority employment in the federal civil service and in companies doing business with the government. But affirmative action did not become a prominent goal of the national government until the 1970s.

Affirmative action also took the form of efforts by the agencies in the Department of Health, Education, and Welfare to shift their focus from "desegregation" to "integration."[84] Federal agencies, sometimes with court orders and sometimes without them, required school districts to present plans for busing children across district lines, for closing certain schools, and for redistributing faculties as well as students or face the loss of grants-in-aid from the federal government. These efforts dramatically increased the number of black children attending integrated classes.

THE SUPREME COURT AND THE BURDEN OF PROOF

Efforts by the executive, legislative, and judicial branches to shape the meaning of affirmative action today tend to center on one key issue: What is the appropriate level of review in affirmative action cases—that is, on whom should the burden of proof be placed: the plaintiff, to show that discrimination has not occurred, or the defendant, to show that discrimination has occurred? The reason this question is difficult is because the cases in which the Court critically scrutinized and struck down racially discriminatory laws—cases like *Brown* and *Loving*—all involved historically disadvantaged racial minority groups. The Court struck down those laws partly because it concluded they were motivated by racial hostility—which is not a valid government purpose—and partly because the Court concluded that disadvantaged minority groups were effectively unable to use the political process to challenge laws that harmed them. The new cases, however, did not fit this pattern. Instead of being motivated by racial hostility, they were enacted with the objective of assisting victims of past injustice. And instead of harming minority groups, they disadvantaged members of the dominant majority racial group. Yet critics argued that discriminating against *any* individual because of their race violated the Equal Protection clause.

This question was addressed directly by the Supreme Court in the case of Allan Bakke (see Table 5.3). Bakke, a white male, brought suit against the University of California at Davis Medical School on the grounds that, in denying him admission, the school had discriminated against him on the basis of his race. (That year, the school had reserved 16 of 100 available slots for minority applicants.) Bakke argued that his grades and test scores ranked him well above many students who were accepted and that he had been rejected because he was white, whereas those others accepted were black or Latino. In 1978, Bakke won his case before the Supreme Court and was admitted to the medical school, but the Court stopped short of

TABLE 5.3

Supreme Court Rulings on Affirmative Action

CASE	COURT RULING
Regents of the University of California v. Bakke, 438 U.S. 265 (1978)	Affirmative action upheld, but quotas and separate admission for minorities rejected; burden of proof on defendant
Wards Cove Packing Co., Inc. v. Atonio, 490 U.S. 642 (1989)	All affirmative action programs put in doubt: burden of proof shifted from defendant to plaintiff (victim), then burden of proof shifted back to employers (defendants)
St. Mary's Honor Center v. Hicks, 509 U.S. 502 (1993)	Required victim to prove discrimination was intentional
Adarand Constructors Inc. v. Peña, 515 U.S. 200 (1995)	All race-conscious policies must survive "strict scrutiny," with burden of proof on government to show the program serves "compelling interest" to redress past discrimination
Hopwood v. Texas, 78 F.3d 932 (5th Cir., 1996)	Race can *never* be used as a factor in admission, even to promote diversity (Supreme Court refusal to review limited application to the Fifth Circuit—Texas, Louisiana, Mississippi)
Gratz v. Bollinger, 539 U.S. 244 (2003)	Rejection of a "mechanical" point system favoring minority applicants to University of Michigan as tantamount to a quota; *Bakke* reaffirmed
Grutter v. Bollinger, 539 U.S. 306 (2003)	Upheld race-conscious admission to Michigan Law School, passing strict scrutiny with diversity as a "compelling" state interest, as long as admission was "highly individualized" and not "mechanical," as in *Gratz*
Fisher v. University of Texas, 570 U.S. __ (2013)	Held that strict scrutiny should be applied to college admissions policies that used race as a factor even if the intent was to favor black applicants

declaring affirmative action unconstitutional. The Court rejected the procedures at the University of California because its medical school had used both a quota *and* a separate admissions system for minorities. The Court accepted the argument that achieving "a diverse student body" was a "compelling public purpose" but found that the method of a rigid quota of student slots assigned on the basis of race was incompatible with the Fourteenth Amendment's equal protection clause. Thus, the Court permitted universities (and presumably other schools, training programs, and hiring authorities) to continue to consider minority status but limited the use of quotas to situations (1) in which previous discrimination had been shown and (2) where quotas served more as a guideline for social diversity than as a mathematically defined ratio.[85]

For nearly a decade after *Bakke*, the Court was tentative and permissive about efforts by universities, corporations, and governments to experiment with affirmative action programs.[86]

But in 1995 another Supreme Court ruling further weakened affirmative action. This decision stated that race-based policies, such as preferences given by the government to minority contractors, must survive strict scrutiny, placing the burden on the government to show that such affirmative action programs serve a compelling government interest and address identifiable past discrimination.[87]

This ambiguous status of affirmative action was how things stood in 2003, when the Supreme Court took two cases against the University of Michigan. The first suit alleged that by automatically awarding 20 points (out of 150) to African American, Latino, and Native American applicants, the university discriminated unconstitutionally against white students of otherwise equal or superior academic qualifications. The Supreme Court agreed, arguing that something tantamount to a quota was involved because undergraduate admissions lacked the necessary "individualized consideration" and had employed instead a "mechanical one," based too much on the favorable minority points.[88]

The second case, *Grutter v. Bollinger*, broke new ground. Barbara Grutter sued the law school on the grounds that it had discriminated in a race-conscious way against white applicants with equal or superior grades and law boards. A 5–4 decision for the first time aligned the majority of the Supreme Court with Justice Powell's lone plurality opinion in *Bakke*. Powell had argued that (1) diversity in education is a compelling state interest and (2) race could be constitutionally considered as a plus factor in admissions decisions. In *Grutter*, the Court reiterated Powell's holding and, applying strict scrutiny to the law school's policy, found that the law school's admissions process was tailored to the school's compelling state interest in diversity because it gave a "highly individualized, holistic review of each applicant's file" in which race counted but was not used in a "mechanical" way.[89] The Court's ruling that racial categories can be deployed to serve a compelling state interest put affirmative action on stronger ground. The Court reaffirmed the *Grutter* decision in 2013 when it decided *Fisher v. University of Texas*, in which a white student challenged the use of race as one factor among many in the admissions decision. In a 7–1 decision, the Court sent the case back to the district court with instructions to apply "strict scrutiny" to the school's policy, as articulated in *Grutter*.[90] As noted earlier, the Court eventually accepted the university's plan.

Civil Rights
WHAT DO WE WANT?

The debate about civil rights and affirmative action is ongoing because Americans hold fundamentally different views about whether and how the government should recognize racial distinctions. At the risk of gross oversimplification, we can divide those with differing views into two groups and label them *liberals* and *conservatives*.[91] Conservatives argue, first, that rights in the American tradition are *individual* rights and that affirmative action violates this concept by concerning itself with "group rights," an idea said to be alien to the American tradition. Second, conservatives argue that the Constitution is "color-blind" and that any discrimination, even if it is called positive or benign, must inevitably rely on quotas and thus ultimately violate the equal protection clause.

Liberals agree that rights ultimately come down to individuals but argue that since the essence of discrimination is the unreasonable and unjust exclusion of *an entire group* from something valuable the society has to offer, discrimination itself has to be attacked on a group basis. Despite progress toward racial equality, liberals argue that race still matters. They can also cite Supreme Court history because the first definitive interpretation of the Fourteenth Amendment by the Court, in 1873, stated that

> the existence of laws in the state where the newly emancipated Negroes resided, which discriminated with gross injustice and hardship against them *as a class*, was the evil to be remedied by this clause [emphasis added].[92]

As to the conservative argument concerning quotas, the liberal response is that the Supreme Court has already accepted ratios (a form of quota) that are admitted as evidence to prove a "pattern or practice of discrimination" sufficient to reverse the burden of proof—to obligate the employer to show that there was *not* an intent to discriminate. Further, benign quotas have often been used by Americans both to compensate for some bad action in the past and to provide some desired distribution of social characteristics—that is, diversity. For example, a long-respected policy in the United States is the "veterans' preference" by which the government automatically gives extra consideration in hiring to persons who have served in the country's armed forces. And the goal of social diversity has long justified "positive discrimination," especially in higher education. For example, many private colleges and universities regularly reserve admissions places for the children of loyal alumni and of their own faculty, even when, in a pure competition based solely on test scores and high school records, many of those same students would not have been admitted. These practices underscore the liberal argument that affirmative or compensatory action for minorities is not alien to American experience. Because our nation has a history of slavery and legalized racial discrimination and because discrimination continues to exist (although it has declined), the issue of racial justice, more than any other, highlights the difficulty of reconciling our values to our practice.

The civil rights revolution, a revolution that began with African Americans, has broadened to include women and Latinos and to address such matters as sexual orientation, sexual identification, and immigration status. The "**Who Participates?**" feature on the facing page shows a time line of groups that have fought for their rights throughout American history. As our nation becomes more and more diverse, equal protection of the laws will become more and more important. If we are to succeed and prosper as a nation, we must be inclusive. The tumultuous history of civil rights in America demonstrates that exclusion is a recipe for national calamity. It also demonstrates that struggles for civil rights often take a long time, beginning with political action by a small group of committed individuals and often ending with legislation and legal decisions from the highest court in the country. What civil rights battles now appear on the country's horizon? What can and should be done to remedy past wrongs that have current consequences, such as when past discrimination results in an economic underclass for a racial or ethnic minority? And, most fundamentally, how does a country based on the democratic principle of majority rule ensure that the civil rights of minorities are protected? In 2017 the Department of Justice declared that it was planning to investigate discrimination against whites. Some said it was high time for such an investigation, while others lamented what they saw as a step backward for the nation. Civil rights continue to be contested terrain in America.

Who Has Fought for Their Rights?

Time Line of Major Civil Rights Movements

LABOR MOVEMENT
Workers
1930s

NATIVE AMERICAN MOVEMENT
Native Americans
1968–present

GAY RIGHTS MOVEMENT
LGBTQ Americans
1969–present

WOMEN'S SUFFRAGE MOVEMENT
Women
1848–1920

BLACK CIVIL RIGHTS MOVEMENT
Black Americans
1955–1968

DISABILITY RIGHTS MOVEMENT
Disabled Americans
1960s–present

THE AMERICAN REVOLUTION
Colonists
1775–1783

THE ABOLITION MOVEMENT
Slaves
1830s–1865

FEMINIST MOVEMENT 2ND WAVE
Women
1963–1982

CHICANO MOVEMENT
Mexican Americans
1960s–1970s

1750 1800 1850 1900 1950 2000

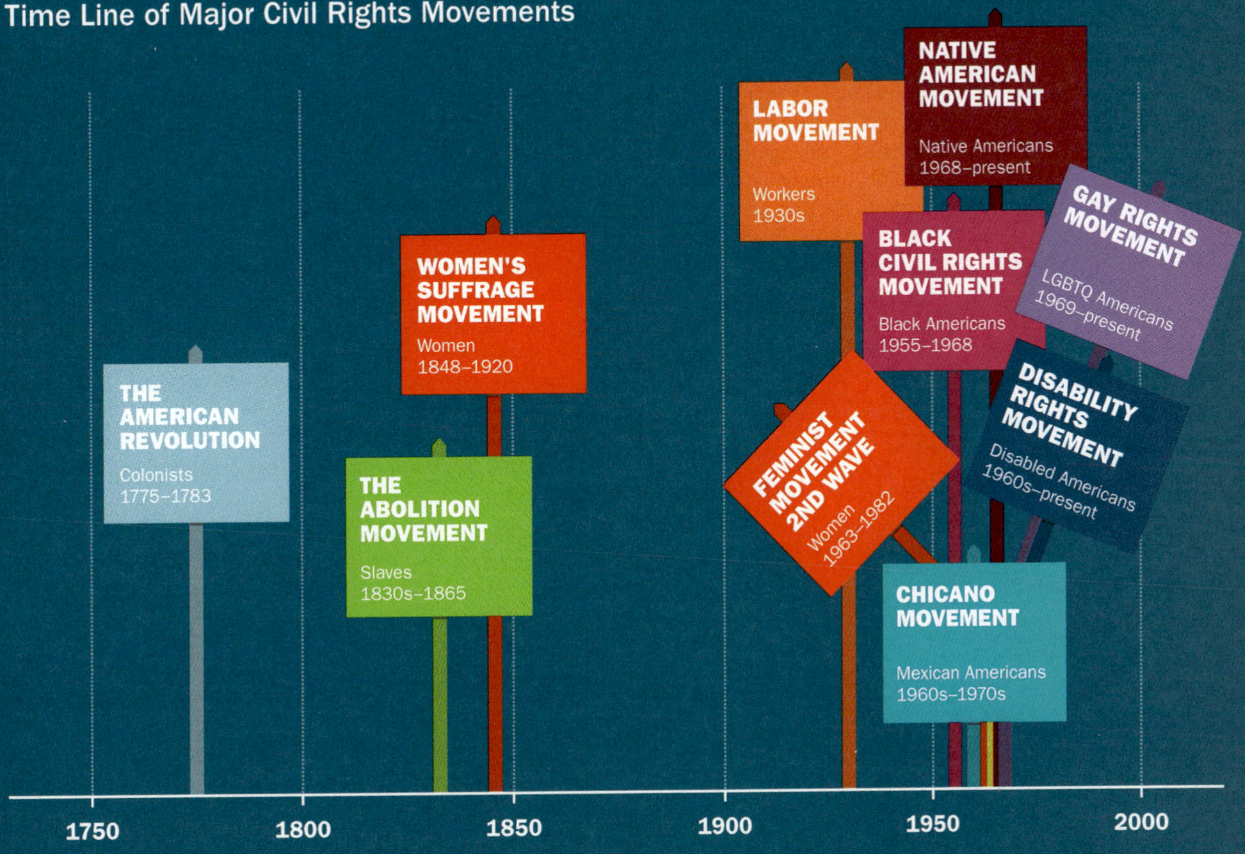

★ WHAT YOU CAN DO ★

Advocate Your Position on Civil Rights

✓ To learn more about your civil rights, explore the Civil Rights page of the U.S. Department of Health and Human Services at **www.hhs.gov/ocr**.

✓ Do you think the government should do more to protect civil rights in your community? Speak out about civil rights on social media. Post to your Facebook page or Tumblr, launch a hashtag campaign on Twitter, or start an online petition at **www.change.org**.

✓ Make a phone call to voice your opinion on civil rights. Call the White House (**202-456-1111**) or your members of Congress (**202-224-3121**). You can also contact the White House online (**www.whitehouse.gov/contact**) or email your members of Congress (**www.congress.gov/members**).

STUDY GUIDE

The Struggle for Civil Rights

Trace the legal developments and social movements that expanded civil rights (pp. 161–79)

Discrimination against individuals on the basis of their race and gender was tolerated and even enforced by government policy through much of American history. With the adoption of the Fourteenth Amendment in 1868, civil rights became a part of the Constitution. The political struggles of African Americans and women have narrowed the gap between Americans' belief in equality and the reality of life in the United States, but they have not eliminated it.

Key Terms

discrimination (p. 161)
civil rights (p. 161)
equal protection clause (p. 161)
Thirteenth Amendment (p. 163)
Fourteenth Amendment (p. 163)
Fifteenth Amendment (p. 163)
Jim Crow laws (p. 163)
"separate but equal" rule (p. 164)
***Brown v. Board of Education* (p. 167)**
strict scrutiny (p. 167)
de jure (p. 168)
de facto (p. 168)
gerrymandering (p. 175)
redlining (p. 178)

Practice Quiz

1. When did civil rights first become part of the Constitution?
   a) in 1789 at the Founding
   b) with the adoption of the Fourteenth Amendment in 1868
   c) in 2008 when Barack Obama was elected president
   d) with the adoption of the Nineteenth Amendment in 1920
   e) in the 1954 *Brown v. Board of Education* decision
2. Which of the following could be described as a Jim Crow law?
   a) a law forcing blacks and whites to ride on separate trains
   b) a law criminalizing interracial marriage
   c) a law requiring blacks and whites to attend different schools
   d) a law segregating all public accommodations, such as hotels, restaurants, and theaters
   e) All of the above are examples of Jim Crow laws.
3. Which civil rights case established the "separate but equal" rule?
   a) *Plessy v. Ferguson*
   b) *Grutter v. Bollinger*
   c) *Brown v. Board of Education*
   d) *Regents of the University of California v. Bakke*
   e) *Adarand Constructors Inc. v. Peña*
4. Which of the following organizations established a legal defense fund to challenge segregation?
   a) the Association of American Trial Lawyers
   b) the National Association of Evangelicals
   c) the National Association for the Advancement of Colored People
   d) the Student Nonviolent Coordinating Committee
   e) the Southern Christian Leadership Council
5. *Massive resistance* refers to efforts by southern states during the late 1950s and early 1960s to
   a) build public housing for poor blacks.
   b) defy federal mandates to desegregate public schools.
   c) give women the right to have an abortion.
   d) bus black students to white schools.
   e) stage large-scale protests against Jim Crow laws.
6. Which of the following outlawed discrimination by employers in hiring, promoting, and laying off their employees and state governments illegal?
   a) the Fourteenth Amendment
   b) the Fifteenth Amendment
   c) *Brown v. Board of Education*
   d) the 1964 Civil Rights Act
   e) *Regents of the University of California v. Bakke*
7. The Voting Rights Act of 1965 significantly extended and protected voting rights by doing which of the following?
   a) barring literacy tests as a condition for voting in six southern states
   b) requiring all voters to register two weeks before any federal election
   c) eliminating all federal-level registration requirements
   d) allowing voters to sue election officials for monetary damages in civil court
   e) requiring that all voters show a valid government-issued photo ID

Extending Civil Rights

Describe how different groups have fought for and won protection of their civil rights (pp. 179–94)

In the 1970s the civil rights model created by African Americans began to spread beyond racial and ethnic groups to include groups defined by sex, religion, national origin, age, disabilities, and sexual orientation. For many of these groups, government policies played an important role in giving rise to movements that demanded equal treatment.

Key Term

intermediate scrutiny (p. 180)

Practice Quiz

8. The judicial test that places the burden of proof on government to show that a race-based policy serves a "compelling interest," is "narrowly tailored," and uses the "least restrictive means" for achieving its compelling interest is called

a) strict scrutiny.
b) intermediate scrutiny.
c) limited scrutiny.
d) de facto segregation.
e) de jure segregation.

9. Which of the following declared that "equality of rights under the law shall not be denied or abridged by the United States or by any State on account of sex"?

a) the Lily Ledbetter Fair Pay Act
b) Title IV of the 1964 Civil Rights Act
c) the DREAM Act
d) the Equal Rights Amendment
e) *Obergefell v. Hodges*

10. The Supreme Court's decision in *Mendez v. Westminster* was significant because it

a) served as a precursor for *Brown v. Board of Education* by ruling that the segregation of Anglos and Mexican Americans into separate schools was unconstitutional.
b) determined that anyone born in the United States was entitled to full citizenship.
c) allowed school districts to achieve racial integration through busing.
d) held that public accommodations could be segregated by race but still be equal.
e) eliminated state power to use race as a criterion for discrimination in law.

11. In *United States v. Wong Kim Ark,* the Supreme Court ruled that

a) school districts must provide bilingual education for students whose English is limited.
b) the internment of Japanese Americans during World War II was constitutional on the grounds of military necessity.
c) the 1882 Chinese Exclusion Act was an unconstitutional form of racial discrimination.
d) anyone born in the United States was entitled to full citizenship.
e) Chinese immigrants were ineligible for citizenship in the United States.

12. Which two Supreme Court decisions reached opposite conclusions about the constitutionality of state laws criminalizing intimate sexual conduct between consenting partners of the same sex?

a) *Bowers v. Hardwick* and *Lawrence v. Texas*
b) *Lau v. Nichols* and *Korematsu v. United States*
c) *Romer v. Evans* and *Obergefell v. Hodges*
d) *Grutter v. Bollinger* and *Gratz v. Bollinger*
e) *Lawrence v. Texas* and *Texas v. Johnson*

Affirmative Action

Contrast arguments for and against affirmative action (pp. 195–97)

Affirmative action policies take race or some other status into account in order to provide greater educational and employment opportunities to groups that have been discriminated against. The Supreme Court has ruled that the government must show evidence that affirmative action programs serve a compelling government interest and are narrowly tailored to address identifiable past discrimination in order to be ruled constitutional. In recent years, challenges to affirmative action have also emerged at the state and local levels.

Key Term

affirmative action (p. 195)

Practice Quiz

13. In *Regents of the University of California v. Bakke,* the Supreme Court ruled that

a) race can never be used as a factor in university admissions, even to promote diversity.

b) achieving "a diverse student body" was a "compelling public purpose," and the method of a rigid quota of student slots assigned on the basis of race was consistent with the Fourteenth Amendment's equal protection clause.

c) achieving "a diverse student body" was a "compelling public purpose," but the method of a rigid quota of student slots assigned on the basis of race was incompatible with the Fourteenth Amendment's equal protection clause.

d) achieving "a diverse student body" was a "compelling public purpose," but affirmative action policies can only be used to give preferences to African Americans.

e) achieving "a diverse student body" was a "compelling public purpose," but affirmative action policies can only be used to give preferences to Asian Americans.

14. In which case did the Supreme Court rule that that the burden of proof is on the government to show that race-based policies, such as preferences given by the government to minority contractors, serve a compelling government interest and address identifiable past discrimination?

a) *Wards Cove Packing Co., Inc. v. Atonio*

b) *St. Mary's Honor Center v. Hicks*

c) *Adarand Constructors v. Peña*

d) *Gratz v. Bollinger*

e) *Fisher v. University of Texas*

For Further Reading

Ackerman, Bruce. *We the People*. Vol. 3, *The Civil Rights Revolution*. Cambridge, MA: Harvard University Press, 2014.

Ancheta, Angelo. *Race, Rights and the Asian American Experience*. New Brunswick, NJ: Rutgers University Press, 2006.

Chen, Anthony S. *The Fifth Freedom: Jobs, Politics, and Civil Rights in the United States, 1941–1972*. Princeton, NJ: Princeton University Press, 2009.

Chermerinsky, Erwin. *Closing the Courthouse Door: How Your Constitutional Rights Became Unenforceable*. New Haven, CT: Yale University Press, 2017.

Davis, Lennard J. *Enabling Acts: The Hidden Story of How the Americans with Disabilities Act Gave the Largest US Minority Its Rights*. Boston: Beacon Press, 2015.

Faderman, Lillian. *The Gay Revolution: The Story of the Struggle*. New York: Simon & Schuster, 2015.

Garrow, David J. *Bearing the Cross: Martin Luther King, Jr., and the Southern Christian Leadership Conference: A Personal Portrait*. New York: Morrow, 1986.

Gonzales, Roberto. *Lives in Limbo: Undocumented and Coming of Age in America*. Los Angeles: University of California Press, 2015.

Greenberg, Jack. *Crusaders in the Courts: How a Dedicated Band of Lawyers Fought for the Civil Rights Revolution*. New York: Basic Books, 1994.

Katznelson, Ira. *When Affirmative Action Was White: The Untold Story of Racial Inequality in Twentieth-Century America*. New York: W. W. Norton, 2006.

Lee, Sonia Song-Ha. *Building a Latino Civil Rights Movement*. Chapel Hill: University of North Carolina Press, 2014.

Nichols, Walter J. *The DREAMers: How the Undocumented Youth Movement Transformed the Immigrant Rights Debate*. Stanford, CA: Stanford University Press, 2013.

Rosenberg, Gerald N. *The Hollow Hope: Can Courts Bring about Social Change?* Chicago: University of Chicago Press, 2008.

Stone, Geoffrey. *Sex and the Constitution: Sex, Religion and Law From America's Origins to the Twenty-First Century*. New York: Liveright, 2017.

Taylor, Jami Kathleen, and Donald P. Halder-Markel, eds. *Transgender Rights and Politics*. Ann Arbor: University of Michigan Press, 2015.

Waldman, Michael. *The Fight to Vote*. New York: Simon & Schuster, 2016.

Recommended Websites

ADA Home Page
www.ada.gov
The Americans with Disabilities Act (ADA), enacted in 1990, guarantees equal employment rights and access to public businesses for the physically disabled. The U.S. Department of Justice maintains this website, which offers general information on ADA standards, changes in regulation, and policy enforcement.

Equal Employment Opportunity Commission
www.eeoc.gov
This website provides information on the federal agency and current employment laws. At this site you can even find out how someone might file a harassment or discrimination charge against an employer.

Equality Now
www.equalitynow.org
This is an organization dedicated to ending gender discrimination around the world. Read about how this group is fighting for the rights of women in Africa or campaigning against female genital mutilation and sex trafficking.

Federal Bureau of Investigation
www.fbi.gov/hq/cid/civilrights/hate.htm
Civil rights violations fall under the jurisdiction of the Federal Bureau of Investigation (FBI). Find out what steps the FBI is taking to combat the problem of hate crimes, and view some comprehensive statistical data.

Feminist Majority Foundation
www.feminist.org
This organization seeks to promote the legal, social, and political equality of women. They develop public policy, participate in grassroots organizing, and train leaders to promote their cause.

Gay and Lesbian Alliance against Defamation
www.glaad.org

Human Rights Campaign
www.hrc.org
These two prominent interest groups are dedicated to equal rights for lesbians and gay men and ending gender discrimination.

League of United Latin American Citizens
www.lulac.org
The League of United Latin American Citizens has worked to stem discrimination against Mexican Americans since World War II and is now the largest and oldest Latino organization in the United States. See what this group is doing to guarantee racial equality based on the Fourteenth Amendment's equal protection clause.

The Martin Luther King, Jr., Research and Education Institute
http://mlk-kpp01.stanford.edu
Dr. Martin Luther King, Jr., was a key leader in the fight for civil rights and desegregation. At this website you can find Dr. King's important speeches and papers, as well as other information about social injustice.

Mexican American Legal Defense and Education Fund
www.maldef.org
The Mexican American Legal Defense and Education Fund (MALDEF) is the leading nonprofit Latino litigation, advocacy, and educational outreach institution in the United States. At this site, you will learn about litigation and other activities that MALDEF has initiated related to the rights of Latinos and of immigrants more generally.

NAACP
www.naacp.org
The NAACP is one of the oldest and largest civil rights organizations that is dedicated to equal rights and putting an end to racial discrimination. This group was particularly influential in the landmark case *Brown v. Board of Education*, which led to the desegregation of public schools.

National Organization for Women
www.now.org
This leading women's rights group continues to fight for gender equality and equal rights.

U.S. Commission on Civil Rights
www.usccr.gov
The U.S. Commission on Civil Rights was created by Congress in the late 1950s and continues to investigate complaints of discrimination in American society.

U.S. Supreme Court Media
www.oyez.org
This website has a good search engine for finding information on such landmark civil rights cases as *Plessy v. Ferguson*, *Brown v. Board of Education*, *Lawrence v. Texas*, and *United States v. Wong Kim Ark*, to name only a few.

★ chapter ★

06

Public Opinion

WHAT GOVERNMENT DOES AND WHY IT MATTERS Americans can have quite different opinions on important issues, even citizens who have had similarly vivid, harrowing experiences. In 1991, Suzanna Hupp was eating lunch in a Texas restaurant when a man drove his truck through the window and began shooting people. Hupp had often carried a handgun in her purse, but had recently taken it out because Texas did not allow concealed carry at the time, and she was afraid she would lose her license as a chiropractor if caught. "Could I have hit the guy? He was fifteen feet from me. . . . Could I have missed? Yeah, it's possible. But the one thing nobody can argue with is that it would have changed the odds." The gunman killed 23 people, including her parents. She has become a strong proponent of gun rights since then. "One of my bugaboos is gun laws. Anytime we list a place where you can't carry guns, to me, that's like a shopping list for a madman. . . . If you think about nearly every one of these mass shootings, they have occurred at places where guns weren't allowed. That's frustrating to me, particularly when you talk about schools. Where do these madmen go? They go to schools and slaughter people."[1]

Fifteen-year-old Justin Gruber also survived a terrible shooting incident, in a school: the shooting

Suzanna Hupp (left) and Justin Gruber (right) were both present during episodes of gun violence. These events pushed Hupp to advocate for more gun rights, and Gruber to speak out for more restrictive gun laws. How do political opinions form? And how do government officials respond to shifts in public opinion?

at the Marjory Stoneman Douglas High School in Parkland, Florida, in February 2018. The incident left 17 students and teachers dead. But Gruber and many of his schoolmates reached the opposite view of Suzanna Hupp, arguing for greater gun control such as assault weapon bans and increased age limits for purchase. Objecting to one suggestion raised after the shooting, Gruber said that arming teachers is a "terrible idea." "Adding guns to solve a gun problem will increase the possible negative outcomes," he said. "Teachers shouldn't have to be trained to carry weapons. They are supposed to mold the minds of the next generation."[2] Some students formed a group, Never Again MSD, known by the hashtag #NeverAgain, to advocate for tighter gun control.

After mass shootings, support for stronger gun control measures tends to increase among the general public. The percentage of Americans telling the Gallup Organization that they wanted stricter laws covering the sale of firearms increased 5 points after the October 2017 mass shooting in Las Vegas and 7 more points after the Parkland shooting five months later, to 67 percent overall.[3] At the same time, gun sales typically increase after mass shootings as gun supporters fear tighter controls (although this pattern is more muted under Trump than it was under Obama).[4] Soon after, however, public outcry tends to fade—after the 2012 Sandy Hook Elementry School shooting in Connecticut, support for more gun control spiked then subsided—and elected politicians seem to take no action. In these cases, are politicians following public opinion or are they ignoring it?

The "consent of the governed," which is demanded in the Declaration of Independence, is critical for the functioning of a democracy. We expect government to pay attention to the people. But whose opinion gets represented in public policy, particularly on issues, such as gun rights and gun control, where there are strong divides among the public? What is the role of public opinion compared to that of other political actors, such as organized interests? How well informed are people, and by what channels can individuals have their voices heard? As we will see in this chapter, research shows that public opinion does indeed have a significant impact on public policy. But there are debates among scholars about whether the public is sufficiently informed about politics, as well as whether elected officials represent the interests of all Americans or only some Americans.

CHAPTER GOALS

★ **Define public opinion, and identify broad types of values and beliefs Americans have about politics (pp. 207–15)**

★ **Explain the major factors that shape specific individual opinions (pp. 216–25)**

★ **Explore when and why public opinion changes and what role political knowledge plays (pp. 225–32)**

★ **Describe the major forces that shape public opinion (pp. 232–34)**

★ **Analyze how public opinion shapes government policy and influences elected officials (pp. 234–37)**

★ **Describe basic survey methods and other techniques researchers use to measure public opinion (pp. 237–47)**

Defining Public Opinion

Define public opinion, and identify broad types of values and beliefs Americans have about politics

The term **public opinion** refers to the attitudes that people have about policy issues, events, elected officials, and politics. It is useful to distinguish between values and beliefs, on the one hand, and attitudes and opinions, on the other. **Values (or beliefs)** constitute a person's basic orientation to politics and include guiding principles. Values are not limited to the political arena, but they include deep-rooted morals, ethics, aspirations, and ideals that shape an individual's perceptions of society, government, and the economy. Liberty (i.e. freedom), democracy, and equality of opportunity, for example, are basic political values held by most Americans.

public opinion citizens' attitudes about political issues, leaders, institutions, and events

values (or beliefs) basic principles that shape a person's opinions about political issues and events

Another useful term for understanding public opinion is *ideology*. **Political ideology** refers to a set of beliefs and values that, as a whole, form a general philosophy about government. For example, many Americans believe that governmental solutions to problems are inherently inferior to solutions offered by the private sector and free markets. Such a philosophy about government may predispose individuals to form negative views of specific government programs, even before they know much about the policy.

political ideology a cohesive set of beliefs that forms a general philosophy about the role of government

An **attitude (or opinion)** is a view about a particular issue, person, or event. An individual may have an attitude toward American policy in the Middle East or an opinion about economic inequality in America. The attitude may have emerged from a broad belief about military intervention or about the role of government in the economy, but the opinion itself is very specific. Some attitudes may be short-lived and can change based on changing circumstances or new information; others may change over a few years and still others may not change over a lifetime.

attitude (or opinion) a specific preference on a particular issue

To measure public opinion on an issue, one must study the individual opinions of thousands or millions of people aggregated together; it is a way to gauge what Americans think about politics and policy. When we think of public opinion, we often think in terms of differences of opinion. The media are fond of reporting political differences between Republicans and Democrats, blacks and whites, women and men, the young and the old, and so on. Certainly, Americans differ on many issues, and often these differences are associated with partisanship, economic status, or social and demographic characteristics such as race and ethnicity, gender, income, education, age, religion, and region. For example, individuals whose incomes differ substantially have varying views on many important economic and social programs, including government health care. In general, the poor, who are the chief beneficiaries of these programs, support them more strongly than do those who are wealthier and pay more of the taxes that fund the programs.

Political attitudes are increasingly influenced by partisanship (Republicans versus Democrats) and ideology (conservatives versus liberals). For example, shortly after taking office in January 2017 President Trump signed a controversial executive order immediately halting the U.S. refugee program and banning immigration to the United States from a half dozen predominantly Muslim countries, including Syria. In 2018 the Supreme Court upheld the travel ban as constitutional, despite legal challenges. Opinion polls show that while 63 percent of Republicans say refugees from the Middle East are a threat, only 30 percent of Democrats say the same.[5]

Traditionally, there was an assumption that political attitudes were rooted in rational factors, such as self-interest. Now political scientists understand that opinions about issues and politics have emotional underpinnings as well.[6] Emotional responses to candidates, events, or policies run the gamut from strongly positive to strongly negative. These emotions are usually measured by survey questions asking if a candidate (or another individual, event, or issue) makes the respondent feel angry, fearful, anxious, or enthusiastic. Donald Trump's 2016 presidential campaign, for example, benefited from high enthusiasm from his supporters. Similarly high positive emotions may have given Barack Obama an advantage as the first African American president in 2008, overcoming racial resentment among some citizens.[7] Contrary to the idea that public opinion is purely rational, feelings are complicated and often irrational; once individuals become emotionally attached to particular beliefs, they tend to hold on to them even in the face of contradictory information. Using emotions as a guide, individuals form opinions quickly in response to current events. An important study called this "affective [meaning emotional] intelligence."[8]

Research has shown that individuals usually monitor political news by responding to familiar political figures or issues in a habitual and unthinking manner. However, when we encounter a new political actor, event, or issue, we tend to form a new evaluation. Anxiety triggered by a change in the political environment, such as a foreign enemy (e.g., Russia, North Korea, or ISIS) or an opposing party's candidate can trigger increased interest, attention, and information seeking, which in some cases prompts a change of opinion. These findings suggest that even individuals with strong opinions might abandon their political habits if they have feelings of anxiety and feel threatened.

For example, the mass shooting at Marjory Stoneman Douglas High School in Parkland, Florida, described in the beginning of this chapter, caused strong emotional responses, including fear and outrage among students and parents, and reopened a national debate about gun regulation. One month after the shooting, on March 14, 2018, thousands of students and teachers walked out of school to protest the government's lack of response to gun violence in the United States. In response

Dramatic events, and the emotions they stir, can alter public opinion. In the aftermath of the violence erupting at a 2017 white nationalist rally in Charlottesville, Virginia, seemingly everyone had an opinion on the state of race relations in America.

to the shooting and reactions to it, the Republican-controlled Florida state legislature passed a law raising the minimum age to purchase a gun from 18 to 21, despite opposition from the National Rifle Association. Alternatively, President Trump has suggested arming some teachers with handguns. Though most U.S. adults (55 percent) would oppose allowing teachers to carry guns in K–12 schools, a sizable minority (45 percent) said they favored such a measure. Among Republicans, the number was even larger, with about 7 in 10 Republicans and independents who lean Republican (69 percent) in support of this proposal.[9]

Emotions play a major role in public opinion about gun ownership and school violence; anxiety triggered by an event such as a mass shooting often leads to increased interest and attention around an issue, as well as motivation to fight for change in government policy.

POLITICAL VALUES

Despite their differences, most Americans share a common set of values, including a belief in the principles, if not always the actual practice, of liberty, equality, and democracy. The United States was founded on the principle of individual **liberty**, or freedom. Americans have always voiced strong support for the idea of liberty and typically support the notion that governmental interference with individuals' lives and property should be kept to a minimum. Liberty is, after all, tied inextricably to the birth of our nation—Puritans fled to America to escape persecution in England for their religious beliefs—and it remains as important in contemporary politics as it was during the Founding era when the colonists fought for their freedom from Britain during the Revolutionary War. Americans have stronger views about the importance of liberty and freedom of expression than do citizens in other democratic countries. One example is the growing concern with civil liberties related to privacy and security of personal information online. Three in four Americans don't see a need to sacrifice liberty (privacy and freedom) to be safe from terrorism.[10] Support for freedom of speech, a free internet, and a free press is higher in the United States than in most other countries in the world: 71 percent of Americans believe it is very important that "people can say what they want without state or government censorship," compared to a global average of 56 percent.[11] These data underscore the fact that government surveillance is of increasing concern to most Americans and that the value of liberty matters.

liberty freedom from governmental control

Similarly, **equality of opportunity** has always been an important theme in American society. Most Americans believe that all individuals should be allowed to seek personal and economic success. Moreover, most people generally believe that such success should be the result of individual effort and ability, rather than family connections or other forms of special privilege. Quality public education is one of the most important mechanisms for obtaining equality of opportunity in that it allows individuals, regardless of personal or family wealth, a chance to get ahead. Education is one of the most important pathways to a high paying job, but rising tuition limits access to a college degree for many people. Student loan debt has skyrocketed in the United States; Americans owed more than $1.3 trillion in loans in 2017.[12] Today 17 states offer free college for eligible students, reflecting the principle of equality of opportunity.

equality of opportunity a widely shared American ideal that all people should have the freedom to use whatever talents and wealth they have to reach their fullest potential

Most Americans also believe in democracy and the rule of law. They believe that every citizen should have the opportunity to take part in the nation's governmental and policy-making processes and to have some say in determining how they are

FIGURE 6.1

Americans Agree on Many Core Democratic Values

SOURCE: Pew Research Center, "Broad Public Agreement on Importance of Many Aspects of a Strong Democracy," March 2, 2017, www.people-press.org (accessed 1/23/18).

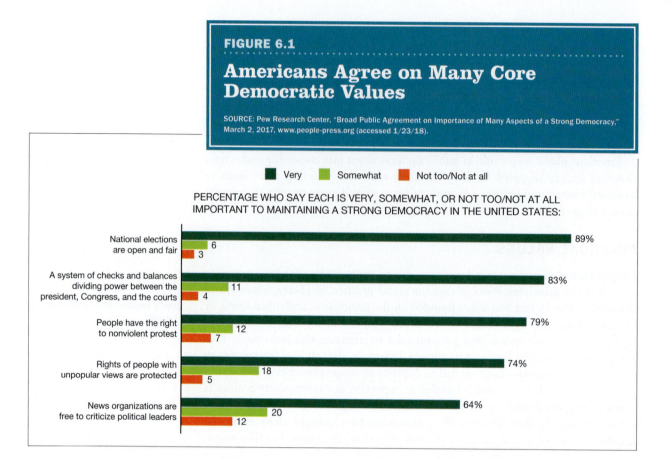

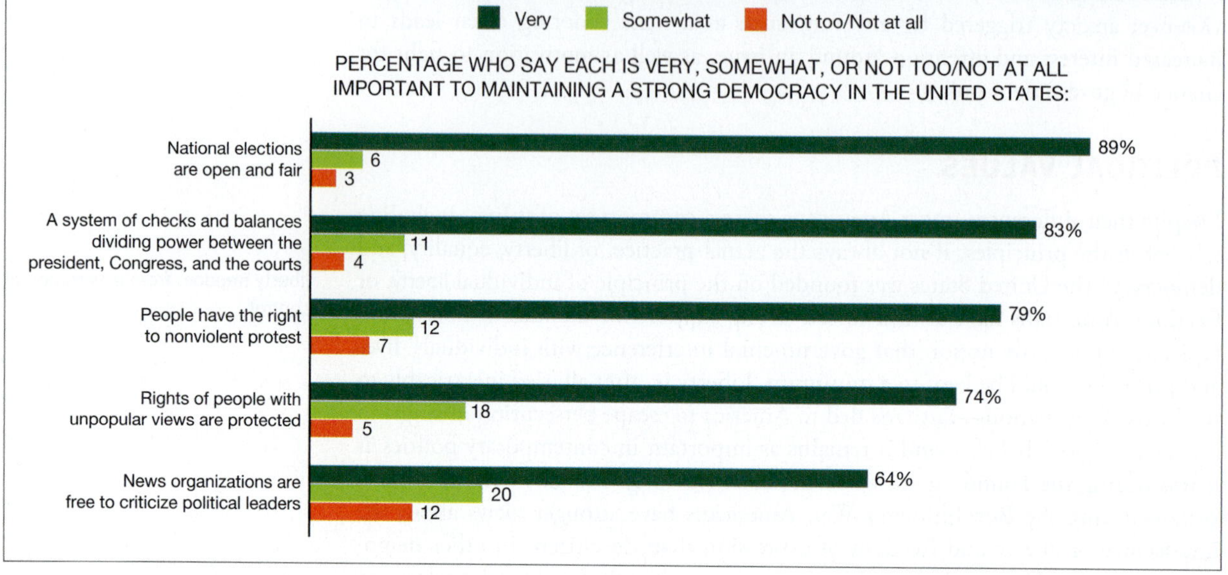

governed, including the right to vote in elections.[13] (See Chapter 8 for a discussion of rules affecting voting in elections.) Figure 6.1 shows there is consensus among Americans on fundamental values: for instance, nearly 90 percent of Americans believe free and fair elections are essential to U.S. democracy, while 83 percent say checks and balances with power divided between the president, Congress, and the courts is also very important for democracy. Eighty percent believe people should be able to make statements that criticize the government, including nonviolent protest, and 74 percent believe democracy requires protecting the rights of people with unpopular views. But there are emerging partisan divisions, even over core values. For example, Republicans and Democrats differ significantly on the importance of the freedom of the press. Roughly half (49 percent) of Republicans say a free press is very important to maintaining a strong democracy, compared to 76 percent of Democrats.[14]

Threats to Political Values and the Rule of Law Nearly 90 percent of Americans believe a strong democracy in America depends on open and fair elections. In 2016, America's free and fair elections were threatened by Russia's leader Vladimir Putin, who orchestrated cyberattacks intended to sway the 2016 presidential election to favor Donald Trump and undermine his opponent, Hillary Clinton. The Central Intelligence Agency and the FBI confirmed the Russians hacked the Democratic National Committee (DNC) and the campaign of Hillary Clinton, releasing large amounts of data in an effort to undermine her campaign. The hacks produced a stream of leaked emails resulting in negative news about Clinton's campaign in the run-up to the election. In June 2017 the Department of Homeland Security confirmed that the computerized election systems of 21 states had been hacked by the Russians, although they could not confirm vote tallies had been changed. The National Security Administration (NSA) found Russian intelligence agents tried to hack the U.S. company that maintains and verifies voter rolls in multiple states. In Illinois, for example, Russian actors stole driver's license and social security numbers from 90,000 voter records.

In response to these events, most Americans believe Russia interfered with the 2016 U.S. presidential election. Eighty-eight percent of U.S. adults had heard about allegations that Russia was involved in hacking the Democratic National Committee and Hillary Clinton's campaign, and roughly 3 in 4 Americans believe Russia was definitely or probably behind the cyberattacks, according to a Pew survey. Today 73 percent of Americans see Russia as a serious problem or an adversary, more than any other foreign nation.[15] Historically Republicans have been more concerned with Russia than Democrats. But 39 percent of Democrats name Russia as the country representing the greatest danger to the United States, ahead of North Korea, countries in the Middle East, or China. Pew reports this is the highest percentage naming Russia in nearly three decades. In contrast, only 21 percent of Republicans say Russia represents the greatest threat to the United States.[16]

Obviously, the political values that Americans espouse have not always been put into practice. For 200 years, Americans embraced the principles of equality of opportunity and individual liberty while denying them in practice to generations of African Americans. Ultimately, proponents of slavery and, later, of segregation were defeated in the arena of public opinion because their practices differed so sharply from the fundamental principles accepted by most Americans.

Yet even when there is broad agreement over principles, practical *interpretations* of principles can differ. For example, in contemporary politics Americans' fundamental commitment to equality of opportunity has led to divisions over affirmative action programs, with both proponents and opponents citing their belief in equality of opportunity as the justification for their position (see Figure 6.2). Proponents of these programs see them as necessary to ensure equality of opportunity, whereas opponents believe that affirmative action is a form of preferential treatment that violates basic American values (see Chapter 5).[17] We form our individual preferences and interpretation of values through interaction with family members, friends, teachers, coaches, mentors, and others in our social groups and networks in a process called *socialization*. This process of socialization is discussed in more detail later, under family and social networks.

FOR CRITICAL ANALYSIS

The news often focuses on issues on which public opinion is sharply divided, but in fact there are many issues on which Americans largely agree. What other issues do you think have strong consensus among Americans?

POLITICAL IDEOLOGY

Americans share many fundamental political values, but the application of these values to specific policies varies. The set of underlying ideas and beliefs through which we come to understand and interpret politics is called a *political ideology*.

In the United States the definitions of the two most common political ideologies—liberalism and conservatism—have changed over time. To some extent, contemporary

FIGURE 6.2

Americans' Support for Fundamental Values

Americans support equality of opportunity, liberty, and democracy in principle; but do they always support these values in practice? What limits, if any, do you think Americans favor when it comes to equality, liberty, and democracy?

SOURCES: Pew Research Center for the People and the Press Values Survey, www.pewresearch.com (accessed 2/5/14); Jacob Poushter and Dionna Givens, "Where the World Sees Limits to Free Speech," Pew Research Center, November 18, 2015, www.pewresearch.com (accessed 11/18/15); First Amendment Center, www.firstamendmentcenter.org (accessed 11/18/15).

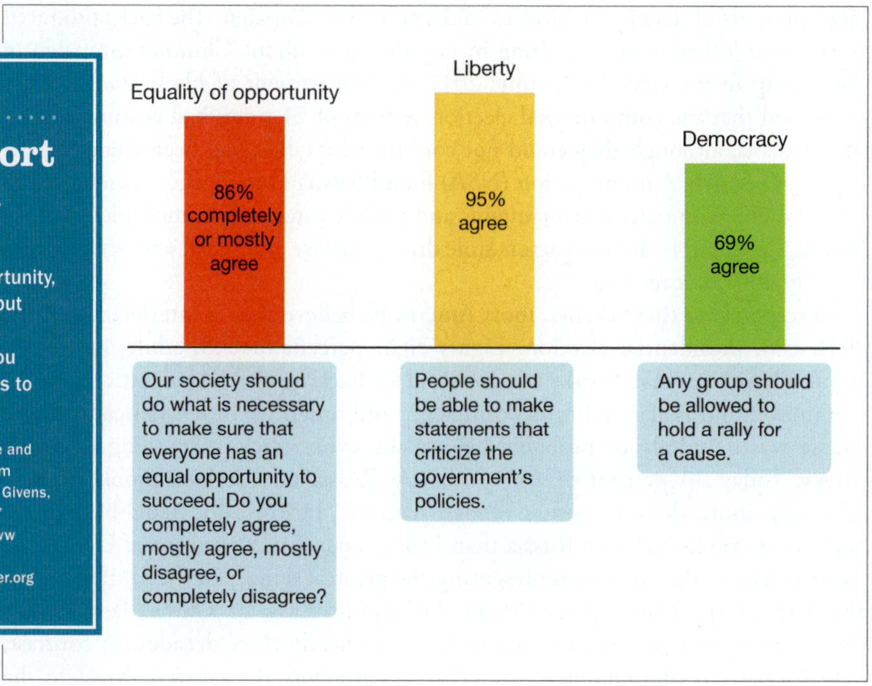

Equality of opportunity
86% completely or mostly agree
Our society should do what is necessary to make sure that everyone has an equal opportunity to succeed. Do you completely agree, mostly agree, mostly disagree, or completely disagree?
Liberty
95% agree
People should be able to make statements that criticize the government's policies.
Democracy
69% agree
Any group should be allowed to hold a rally for a cause.

liberalism and conservatism can be seen as differences in emphasis with regard to the fundamental American political values of liberty and equality. For liberals, equality is the most important of the core values. Liberals encourage government action in such areas as the economy and progressive taxation, health care and workers' rights, financial aid for college, environmental protection, and business practices to enhance race, class, and gender equality of opportunity. For conservatives, on the other hand, liberty is the core value. Conservatives oppose many efforts of the government, however well intentioned, to interfere in private life and free markets, including government regulations.

Liberalism In classical political theory, a liberal was someone who favored individual initiative and was suspicious of the motives of government and of its ability to manage economic and social affairs—a definition akin to that of today's libertarian. The proponents of a larger and more active government called themselves progressives. In the early twentieth century, many liberals and progressives coalesced around the doctrine of "social liberalism," which held that government action (laws and policy) might be needed to preserve individual liberty. Today's liberals are social liberals rather than classical liberals.

In contemporary politics being a **liberal** has come to mean supporting government policies to create a fairer economic system and opportunity for upward mobility, including raising taxes on the wealthy; the expansion of federal social services and health care; government spending on roads, infrastructure, science, technology, and alternative energy; more vigorous efforts on behalf of the poor and minorities; and greater concern for protecting the environment. For example, Senator Elizabeth Warren (D-Mass.) is a leading liberal politician. Warren is an

liberal today this term refers to those who generally support social and political reform, governmental intervention in the economy, more economic equality, expansion of federal social services, and greater concern for consumers and the environment

BOX 6.1

Profile of a Liberal: Senator Elizabeth Warren

- ★ Supports stricter environmental protections
- ★ Favors expanded health coverage for all Americans
- ★ Advocates increased funding for education
- ★ Supports same-sex marriage
- ★ Supports abortion rights and birth control
- ★ Supports an increase in the minimum wage
- ★ Supports more equitable tax policy that benefits middle-class Americans and imposes higher taxes on corporations

active consumer protection advocate whose work led to the establishment of the U.S. Consumer Financial Protection Bureau, which protects individuals from bankruptcy and banks selling high-interest loans. Liberals generally support reproductive rights for women, rights for gays and lesbians, and are concerned with protecting the rights of people accused of crimes, refugees, and immigrants. In international affairs, liberals often support foreign aid to poor nations, arms control, and international organizations that promote peace such as the United Nations and the European Union. Many liberals are opposed to military wars, but under President Obama some liberals tolerated military interventions in other countries. Liberals are also divided on issues of international trade, with some liberals seeking to support local businesses and locally sourced products.

Conservatism By contrast, **conservatives** believe strongly that a large government poses a threat to the freedom of individual citizens and to free markets and democracy. Ironically, today's conservatives support the views of classical liberalism. Today, conservatives generally oppose the expansion of governmental activity, asserting that solutions to many social and economic problems can and should be developed in the private sector, local communities, or by religious organizations. Conservatives support cutting taxes and reducing government spending. Conservatives generally oppose efforts to impose government regulation on business, maintaining that regulation frequently leads to economic inefficiency, is costly, and can lower the entire nation's standard of living by making U.S. manufactured products more expensive and less competitive. Former Speaker of the House Paul Ryan (R-Wisc.) is a leading conservative politician who is known to support cutting taxes and reducing regulations on businesses, among other conservative positions. In terms of social policy, many conservatives support traditional family values and generally oppose

conservative today this term refers to those who generally support the social and economic status quo and are suspicious of efforts to introduce new political formulas and economic arrangements; conservatives believe that a large and powerful government poses a threat to citizens' freedom

BOX 6.2

Profile of a Conservative: Former House Speaker Paul Ryan

- ★ Wants to trim the size of the federal government
- ★ Wants to reduce government regulation of business
- ★ Supports capital punishment for certain crimes
- ★ Opposes restrictions on the right to bear arms
- ★ Supports using traditional energy sources and opposes climate change action that reduces manufacturing jobs
- ★ Opposes many affirmative action programs
- ★ Favors tax cuts

abortion and same-sex marriage. They often oppose environmental protections that interfere with private business. Many conservatives prefer stricter criminal justice laws, oppose drug legalization, and seek to reduce immigration to the United States. Conservatives today are deeply divided on issues such as immigration, international trade, and the fairness of the U.S. economic system. In international affairs, conservatism has come to mean support for military intervention and the maintenance of American military power. There is a split among conservatives in terms of immigration, with pro-business conservatives often accepting immigration and social conservatives strongly opposing immigration to the United States.

libertarian someone who emphasizes freedom and believes in voluntary association with small government

Libertarianism Other political ideologies also influence American politics. **Libertarians**, for example, argue that government interferes with freedom of expression, free markets, and society, and thus should be limited to as few spheres of activity as possible (public education being a notable exception for many libertarians). In 2016, Republican Senator and libertarian Rand Paul ran for president based on his opposition to foreign wars and his commitment to civil liberties and smaller government.

socialist someone who generally believes in social ownership, strong government, free markets, and reducing economic inequality

Socialism and the Green Party While libertarians believe in less government intervention in economic and social realms, **socialists** argue that more government is necessary to promote justice and to reduce economic and social inequality. In 2016, Democratic presidential candidate Bernie Sanders called himself a "democratic socialist," gaining widespread support from Democrats, especially millennials. Like the Social Democratic parties in Europe, Sanders supports free markets and private enterprise but wants government to ensure more equality of opportunity for citizens such as free public college, single payer health care, and increased taxation on the very affluent. He also supports government policies to protect workers' rights and unions. Socialists are more to the ideological left than the mainstream Democratic Party although they share many policy issues. MoveOn.org, a massive online organization with millions of members, advocates a policy agenda consistent with social democrats, as does 2016 Green Party candidate Jill Stein and 2020 presidential candidate Tom Steyer.

Americans' Ideologies Today Although many Americans subscribe to libertarianism, socialism, or other ideologies in part, most describe themselves as either liberals, conservatives, or moderates. Figure 6.3 shows that the percentage of Americans who consider themselves moderates, liberals, or conservatives has remained relatively constant for the past 15 years. Gallup surveys indicate that as of 2017, 35 percent of Americans considered themselves conservatives, 35 percent moderates, and 26 percent liberals. But among young people aged 18-33, trends are different: just 15 percent identify as conservative, while 41 percent identify as liberals and 44 percent as moderates (and independent from the political parties).[18]

Within each ideological group, individual beliefs often vary. Many conservatives support at least some government social programs. Republican president George W. Bush called himself a "compassionate conservative," to indicate that he favored programs that assist the poor and needy. In contrast, staunch conservatives hold much more critical views of government's role in the economy and society. Many joined the rising Tea Party movement in 2009 to protest President Obama's efforts to expand the role of the federal government, especially in health care.

And while President Obama supported health care reform and other social programs, he was criticized by those on the left for extending the tax policies of his Republican predecessor, George W. Bush, which benefited the affluent; for expanding U.S. military involvement overseas; and for deportations of undocumented immigrants. In short, some of Obama's domestic, economic, and foreign policies are associated with conservatives and some with liberals. The real political world is far too complex to be seen simply in terms of a struggle between liberals and conservatives.

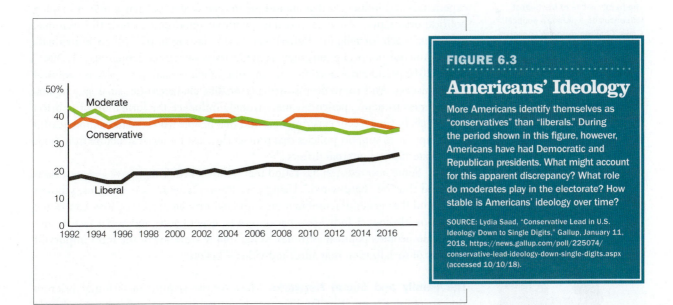

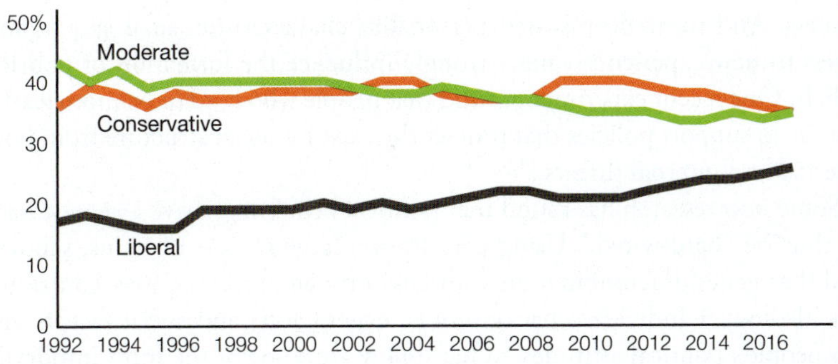

FIGURE 6.3

Americans' Ideology

More Americans identify themselves as "conservatives" than "liberals." During the period shown in this figure, however, Americans have had Democratic and Republican presidents. What might account for this apparent discrepancy? What role do moderates play in the electorate? How stable is Americans' ideology over time?

SOURCE: Lydia Saad, "Conservative Lead in U.S. Ideology Down to Single Digits," Gallup, January 11, 2018, https://news.gallup.com/poll/225074/conservative-lead-ideology-down-single-digits.aspx (accessed 10/10/18).

How We Form Political Opinions

Explain the major factors that shape specific individual opinions

As noted above, broad ideologies do not necessarily determine every political opinion a person holds. Though conservatives generally support small government, most also support some federal programs, such as the military, national parks, national security, and wish to see them—and hence the government—expanded. Some conservatives are not opposed to immigration and accept same-sex marriage. Though most liberals do not favor American military intervention abroad, many do favor military intervention for what they deem to be humanitarian purposes or to prevent terrorist attacks. How are political opinions like these formed?

POLITICAL SOCIALIZATION

People's attitudes about political issues and elected officials tend to be shaped by their underlying political beliefs and values. For example, an individual who has negative feelings about government regulation of the economy would probably be predisposed to oppose the development of new health care programs. Similarly, someone who distrusts the military tends to be suspicious of the use of U.S. force for most foreign conflicts. The processes through which these underlying political beliefs and values are formed are collectively called **political socialization**.

political socialization the induction of individuals into the political culture; learning the underlying beliefs and values on which the political system is based

Probably no nation, and certainly no democracy, could survive if its citizens did not share some fundamental beliefs. In contemporary America, the **agents of socialization** that foster differences in political opinions include the family and social networks, education, membership in social groups, religion, party affiliation, self-interest, and political environment. Other agents of socialization, such as public education, promote similarities.

agents of socialization social institutions, including families and schools, that help to shape individuals' basic political beliefs and values

Of course, no list of the agents of socialization can fully explain an individual's basic political beliefs. In addition to the factors that are important for everyone, experiences and influences that are unique to each individual play a role in shaping political orientation. An early encounter with an important mentor (for example, a teacher, coach, or religious leader), can have a lasting impact on an individual's views. A major political event, such as the terrorist attacks of September 11, 2001, or the 2016 presidential election, can leave an indelible mark on a person's political consciousness. And some deep-seated personality characteristic, such as paranoia or openness to new experiences, may strongly influence the formation of political beliefs. One recent experiment found that people who tend to be more fearful appear to support policies that protect the existing social structure from both external and internal threats.[19]

Some new research has found that political beliefs may have a genetic basis and thus be "hard-wired." Using data from a large sample of twins, scholars found that genes, in combination with environmental factors, may contribute to our ideology.[20] Individual backgrounds, experiences, and social factors also explain people's political attitudes. What follow are some of the most important agents of socialization that affect individuals' beliefs.

The family is one of the largest influences on a person's political views. Children raised in conservative or liberal families, usually, but not always, hold those same views later in life.

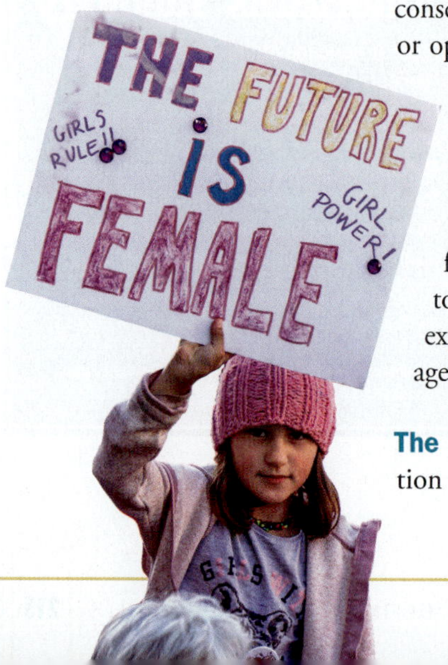

The Family and Social Networks Most people acquire their initial orientation to politics from their families. As might be expected, differences in family

background tend to produce divergent political perspectives. Although relatively few parents spend significant time directly teaching their children about politics, political conversations occur in many households, and children tend to absorb the political views of parents and other caregivers, often without realizing it. Studies find, for example, that party preferences are initially acquired at home, even in households that don't explicitly talk about politics. Children raised in households in which both primary caregivers are Democrats or Republicans tend to become Democrats or Republicans respectively.[21] Of course, not all children absorb their parents' political views. Two of the late Republican president Ronald Reagan's three children, for instance, rejected their parents' conservative values and became active on behalf of Democratic candidates.

By sharing their personal stories with the #MeToo hashtag, woman and men were able to network and organize (online and offline) to draw attention to what they saw as pervasive sexual harassment in American life.

Nevertheless, family, friends, coworkers, and neighbors are an important source of political orientation for nearly everyone. Political scientist Betsy Sinclair argues that individuals are "social citizens" whose political opinions and behavior are significantly shaped by peer influence, including friends and family.[22] Sinclair shows that social networks can and do have the power to change an individual's opinion. When members of a social network express a particular political opinion or belief, Sinclair finds, others notice and conform, particularly if their conformity is likely to be highly visible. The conclusion is that basic political acts are surprisingly subject to social pressures.

Online social networks such as Facebook and Twitter may increase the role of peers in shaping public opinion. For example, the widely shared Facebook meme of an equal sign against a red background in 2013 communicated support for gay rights at the same time that the U.S. Supreme Court was deciding two controversial court cases affecting gay and lesbian marriage rights. This social media discussion was associated with upticks in public support for gay marriage nationally. Public opinion on this issue changed rapidly over a decade. In 2017, 62 percent of Americans believed marriages between same-sex couples should be recognized by law, an increase of over 20 percent from 2005 when only 36 percent of Americans felt this way.[23] Similarly, the #MeToo movement that emerged in 2017 to highlight and combat sexual harassment, used social media to organize online and offline.

Education After family, formal education can be an important source of differences in political perspectives. Governments use public education to try to teach all children a common set of civic values; it is mainly in school that Americans acquire their basic beliefs in liberty, equality, and democracy. In history classes, students are taught that the Founders fought for the principle of liberty (freedom). In the course of studying such topics as the Constitution, the Civil War, and the civil rights movement, students are taught the importance of equality. Research finds formal education is a strong predictor of tolerance for racial, ethnic, and religious minorities.[24]

At the same time, differences in formal education are strongly associated with differences in political opinions. In particular, those who attend college are often exposed to modes of thought that will distinguish them from their friends and neighbors who do not pursue college diplomas. Education is one of the most important factors in predicting who engages in behaviors that increase political knowledge, such as regularly following the news, voting, and participating in politics as well as higher earnings over a lifetime.[25]

SOCIAL GROUPS AND PUBLIC OPINION

The social groups to which individuals belong comprise another important source of political values. Social groups include those that individuals haven't chosen (national, religious, gender, and racial groups, for example) and those they join willingly (political parties, labor unions, the military, and environmental, educational, and occupational groups). Membership in a particular group can give individuals experiences and perspectives that shape their view of political and social life.

Race Race plays an important role in shaping political attitudes and opinions, among both minorities and whites. The experiences of blacks, whites, and Asian Americans, for example, can differ significantly. By 2045 the U.S. population is predicted to become majority minority, as the size of minority populations will outnumber white non-Hispanics, in large part due to youthful minorities.[26] Blacks are a minority and have been victims of persecution and discrimination throughout American history, while many Asians are relatively recent immigrants to the United States. Blacks and whites also have different occupational opportunities, often live in separate communities, and frequently attend separate schools. Such differences tend to produce distinctive political views. Many black Americans perceive other blacks as members of a group with a common identity and a shared political interest in overcoming persistent racial and economic inequality. Political scientists refer to this phenomenon as "linked fate": African Americans see their fate as linked to other members of the black community.[27] This linked fate acts as a sort of filter through which black Americans evaluate information and determine their own opinions and policy preferences.

That black and white Americans have different views is reflected in public perception of fair treatment across racial groups in the United States. Figure 6.4 shows that 84 percent of African Americans believe that blacks are treated less fairly than whites in dealing with the police, compared to 50 percent of whites. In a striking difference, 66 percent of blacks believe blacks are treated unfairly in applying for a loan or home mortgage compared to 25 percent of whites who share this perspective of racial discrimination, while 64 percent of blacks believe they are treated less fairly in the workplace compared to just 25 percent of whites. Blacks are over twenty percentage points more likely to believe blacks face racial discrimination in voting in elections compared to whites.[28]

Events and circumstances can cause opinions to change. In 2009, 80 percent of African Americans said blacks and other minorities do not get equal treatment under the law; the number of whites giving this response was just 40 percent.[29] In the past few years, however, widely publicized incidents of excessive use of police force against African Americans have begun to cause a shift in public opinion on this issue. The activist movement Black Lives Matter gained momentum in 2014 after the killing of Michael Brown, an unarmed, 18-year-old African American, by a white police officer in Ferguson, Missouri. Protests erupted across the nation when the officer, Daren Wilson, was not indicted. One month after that verdict, a white police officer in New York was not indicted despite video evidence that he had used a chokehold and other means of force on Eric Garner, an African American man, heard repeatedly saying that he could not breathe. By 2015, 90 percent of African Americans agreed that blacks and whites are not treated equally by police, and 54 percent of whites felt the same way (see Figure 6.4), showing that while there is still a racial divide on this issue, opinions on it have changed

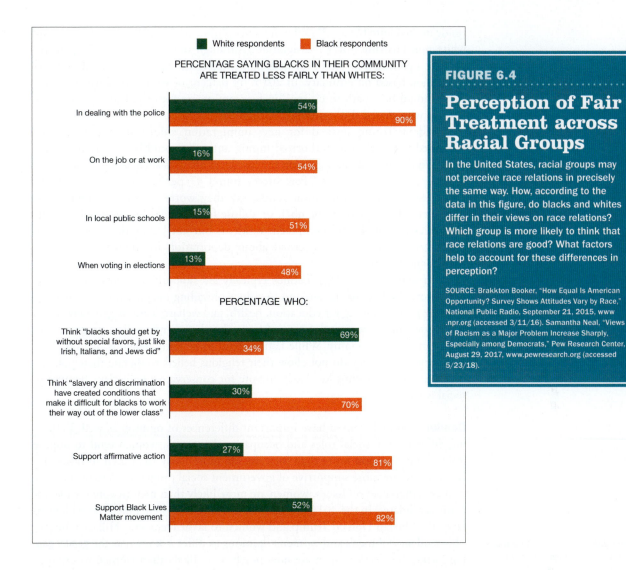

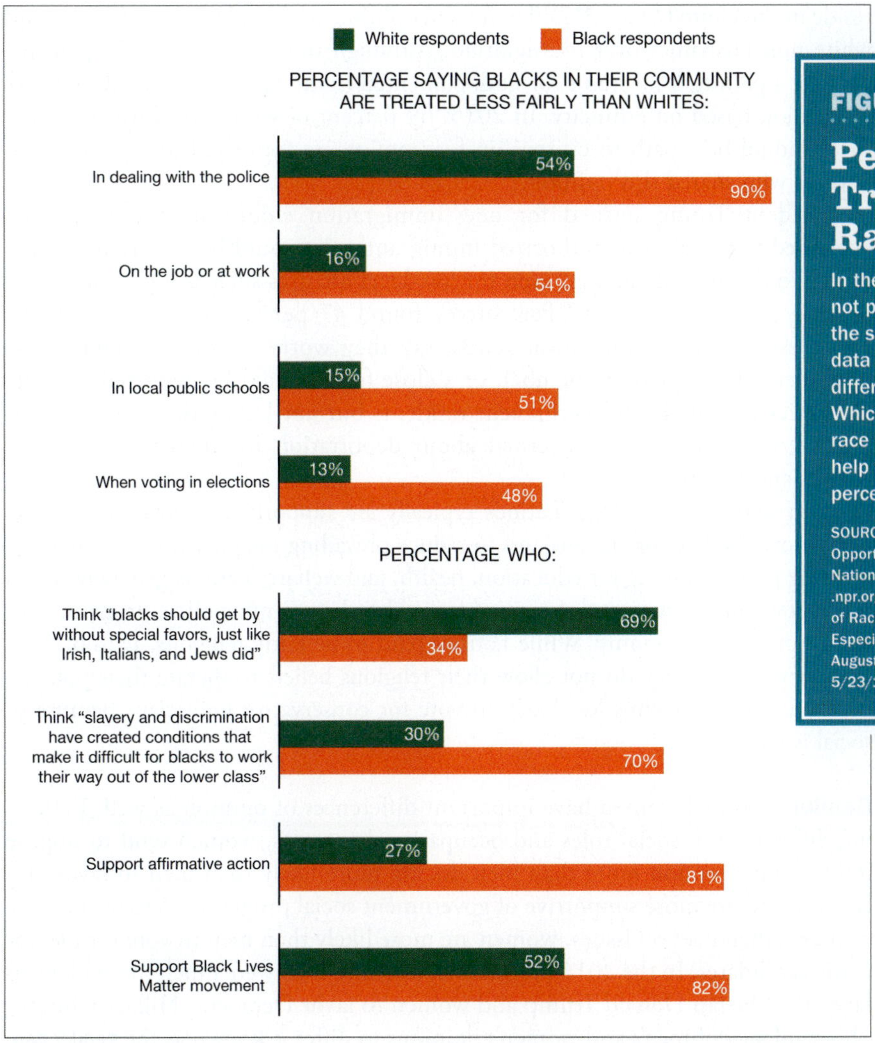

FIGURE 6.4

Perception of Fair Treatment across Racial Groups

In the United States, racial groups may not perceive race relations in precisely the same way. How, according to the data in this figure, do blacks and whites differ in their views on race relations? Which group is more likely to think that race relations are good? What factors help to account for these differences in perception?

SOURCE: Brakkton Booker, "How Equal Is American Opportunity? Survey Shows Attitudes Vary by Race," National Public Radio, September 21, 2015, www.npr.org (accessed 3/11/16). Samantha Neal, "Views of Racism as a Major Problem Increase Sharply, Especially among Democrats," Pew Research Center, August 29, 2017, www.pewresearch.org (accessed 5/23/18).

significantly over the past few years.[30] Strikingly, half of all Americans now agree that racism is a big problem, compared to only 26 percent in 2009.[31]

Ethnicity Ethnicity also affects policy attitudes. Latinos are the fastest-growing minority population in the United States. While most Latinos are white in race, their shared Hispanic ethnicity contributes to a group consciousness that shapes opinions. The U.S. Latino population, which makes up 17 percent of the total population and 12 percent of the electorate, is diverse, comprising individuals of Central American, South American, and Caribbean descent, and thus their backgrounds and circumstances can be quite different.[32] In spite of the differences, however, the Latino population has a growing sense of "linked fate."

Unsurprisingly, immigration is one of the most important policy issues among Latinos, with significant majorities of Latinos concerned about restrictive immigration policies and the threat of deportation. The number of first-generation immigrants—or foreign-born citizens—living in the United States quadrupled from almost 10 million in 1970 to over 40 million today. Most immigrants legally reside in the United States.[33] Differences in opinion are found between Latinos and white non-Hispanics over immigration. Although most Americans (72 percent) support a path to legal status for undocumented immigrants, there are differences in opinion based on ethnicity. In 2015, 69 percent of white non-Hispanics said there should be a path to citizenship for immigrants compared to 86 percent of Latinos who shared this opinion.[34]

President Trump pushed for new immigration enforcement policies that expanded the pool of unauthorized immigrants who could be deported because of previous criminal charges, even for low-level offenses such as a parking ticket or drug possession. A 2017 Pew survey found 47 percent of Hispanic adults, regardless of their immigration status, say they worry "a lot" or "some" that they themselves, a family member, or a close friend could be deported. Among Hispanics that are lawful permanent residents but not U.S. citizens, 66 percent were very or somewhat concerned about deportation for themselves or their friends and family.[35]

With respect to ideology, Latinos typically are supportive of government laws to improve the lives of citizens and to reduce prevailing inequality, which includes favoring public funding for education, health, and welfare; Latinos generally see an active government as a good thing and favor liberal economic policies to create jobs and improve the economy. While Latinos tend to be fairly religious, Latino Decision surveys find they do not allow their religious beliefs to dictate their political decisions—they are thus less likely to vote for conservative politicians because of social issues.[36]

Gender Men and women have important differences of opinion as well. Reflecting differences in social roles and occupational patterns, women tend to oppose military intervention more than men do, are more likely than men to favor gun control, and are more supportive of government social programs. Perhaps because of these differences on issues, women are more likely than men to vote for Democratic candidates. In the 2016 presidential election, men were much more likely to favor Republican Donald Trump and women to favor Democrat Hillary Clinton. This tendency of men's and women's opinions to differ is known as the **gender gap**. Following the election, men are now much more likely than women to say they have "quite a lot" of confidence in the future of the United States then women; this represents a significant change from 2015 when men and women had similar levels of confidence. As of 2018, only 30 percent of women approved of the job Trump was doing as president, compared to 46 percent of men. This 16 percent gender gap in presidential approval is wider than for any other modern president.[37] (See Figure 6.5.)

gender gap a distinctive pattern of voting behavior reflecting the differences in views between women and men

Religion Religion is an important predictor of opinion on a wide range of issues. Religious individuals are usually defined in surveys regarding religious affiliation, frequency of church attendance, and the belief that religion and prayer are important in their lives. One of the fastest-growing groups in America are those without religious affiliation, rising from 5-6 percent of the population in the 1990s to almost 25 percent today.[38] Among religious groups, white evangelical Protestants tend to be even more conservative than Catholics. Just over 30 percent of evangelical Protestants believe abortion rights for women should always be permitted, compared to 75 percent of those without religious affiliation.

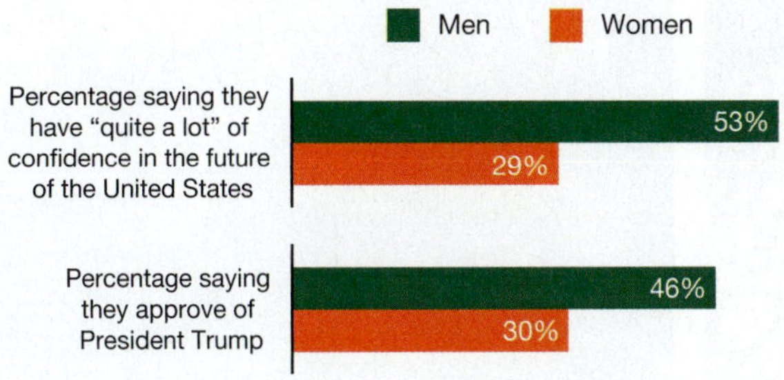

FIGURE 6.5

Differences in Public Opinion by Gender, 2018

Data reveal significant differences in men's and women's opinions about the political world. What might explain the differences we see in how optimistic men and women are about the future of the United States? What might explain the differences in how men and women view specific presidents?

SOURCE: Samantha Smith, "In Trump Era, Women's Views of Nation's Prospects Take a Negative Turn," Pew Research Center, May 15, 2017, www.pewresearch.org (accessed 5/23/18); "Trump Gets Negative Ratings for Many Personal Traits, but Most Say He Stands Up for His Beliefs," Pew Research Center, October 1, 2018, www.people-press.org/2018/10/01/trump-gets-negative-ratings-for-many-personal-traits-but-most-say-he-stands-up-for-his-beliefs/ (accessed 10/10/18).

Similarly sharp differences in opinion are also found in terms of attitudes about same-sex marriage: only 35 percent of evangelical Protestants support same-sex marriage compared to 76 percent of the nonreligious.[39] Religion also helps us understand opinions on teaching evolution in the public schools, environmental policy, immigration, partisanship, ideology, and other issues. White evangelicals and weekly churchgoers are much more likely to hold conservative views and be Republican, while the religiously unaffiliated are more likely to hold liberal views and favor the Democratic Party.

Party Affiliation Political party membership is one of the most important factors affecting political attitudes. We can think of partisanship as red- or blue-tinted glasses that color opinion on a vast array of issues. Self-identified partisans (individuals affiliating with the Republican or Democratic Party) tend to rely on party leaders and the media for cues on the appropriate positions to take on major political issues.[40]

In recent years, party polarization has become a defining feature of Congress and many state legislatures. As a result, the leadership of the Republican Party has become increasingly conservative, whereas that of the Democratic Party has become more liberal, a shift reflected in public opinion. Geographic sorting—where liberals choose to live in neighborhoods, cities, counties, and states that are more liberal, while conservatives move to areas with populations with more conservative views—also contributes to mass polarization. Large cities, such as New York City, Chicago, and Los Angeles, have predominantly Democratic populations, while Republicans are more numerous in rural and suburban areas.

According to recent studies, differences between Democratic and Republican partisans on a variety of political and policy questions are greater today than during any other period for which data are available. Across a wide range of issues, Democrats and Republicans strongly disagree. For example, 76 percent of Democrats strongly favor government policies to protect the environment compared to just

FOR CRITICAL ANALYSIS

Political scientists have observed "geographic sorting" in the United States, where liberals live in areas with other liberals and conservatives live in areas with other conservatives. Is the area where you live strongly liberal, conservative, or evenly mixed? What are the political consequences of geographic sorting?

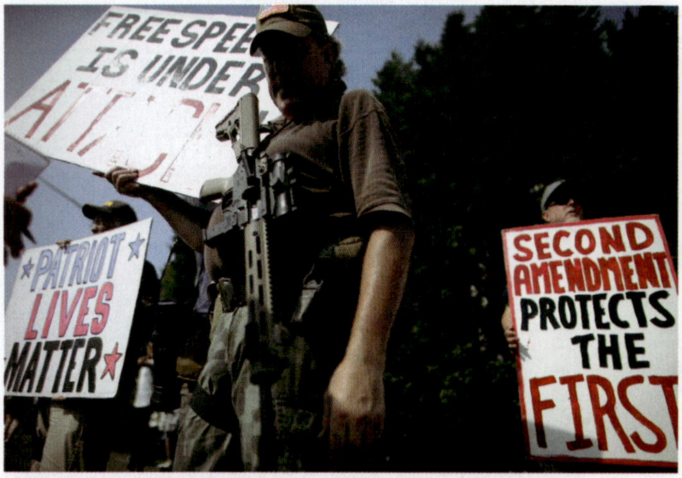

The opinions of women and men diverge greatly on some, but by no means all, political issues. One of the biggest gender gaps appears around gun control. Many more women than men favor more restrictions on gun ownership.

30 percent of Republicans, and while 72 percent of Republicans oppose granting legal citizenship for immigrants with jobs in the United States, only 34 percent of Democrats do.[41] Figure 6.6 offers a more detailed look at Americans' attitudes toward immigration, broken down by party affiliation and by education. Wide differences in public opinion exist based on partisanship involving immigration, energy, income inequality, infrastructure, job creation, climate change and energy, national defense, budget deficit, taxes, terrorism, trade, and much more.

Despite the fact that the rift between the "red" (Republican-leaning) and "blue" (Democrat-leaning) states seems deeper than ever, political scientist Morris Fiorina and colleagues argue that most Americans hold moderate opinions.[40] While political elites and members of Congress may be highly polarized, there is general agreement among most Americans even on those issues thought to be most divisive. Thus, evidence of partisan polarization in public opinion is mixed: some see deep divisions while others see evidence of popular consensus.

Economic Class and Group Self-Interest Another way that membership in groups can affect political beliefs is through what might be called rational political interest. On many economic issues, for example, the interests of the rich and the poor differ significantly. Inevitably, these differences in interests will produce differences in political outlook.

The framers of the Constitution thought that the inherent gulf between the rich and the poor would always be the most important source of conflict in political life. Today significant numbers of Republicans and Democrats bemoan the chasm between the 99 percent of income earners and the top 1 percent. Donald Trump (on the right) and Bernie Sanders and Hillary Clinton (on the left) made income inequality a major piece of their 2016 campaigns. But while there might be agreement on the problem, there are huge disagreements about the solution. Republicans favor cutting taxes on business and wealthier Americans. In addition, President Trump favors creating jobs by promoting an isolationist foreign policy with reduced reliance on free-trade, tariffs on steel and aluminum, and limiting foreign immigration. Liberals tend to favor government policies to promote equality, such as raising the minimum wage to $15 an hour, free college education, and raising taxes on the wealthy, as well as incentives to encourage employee-owned

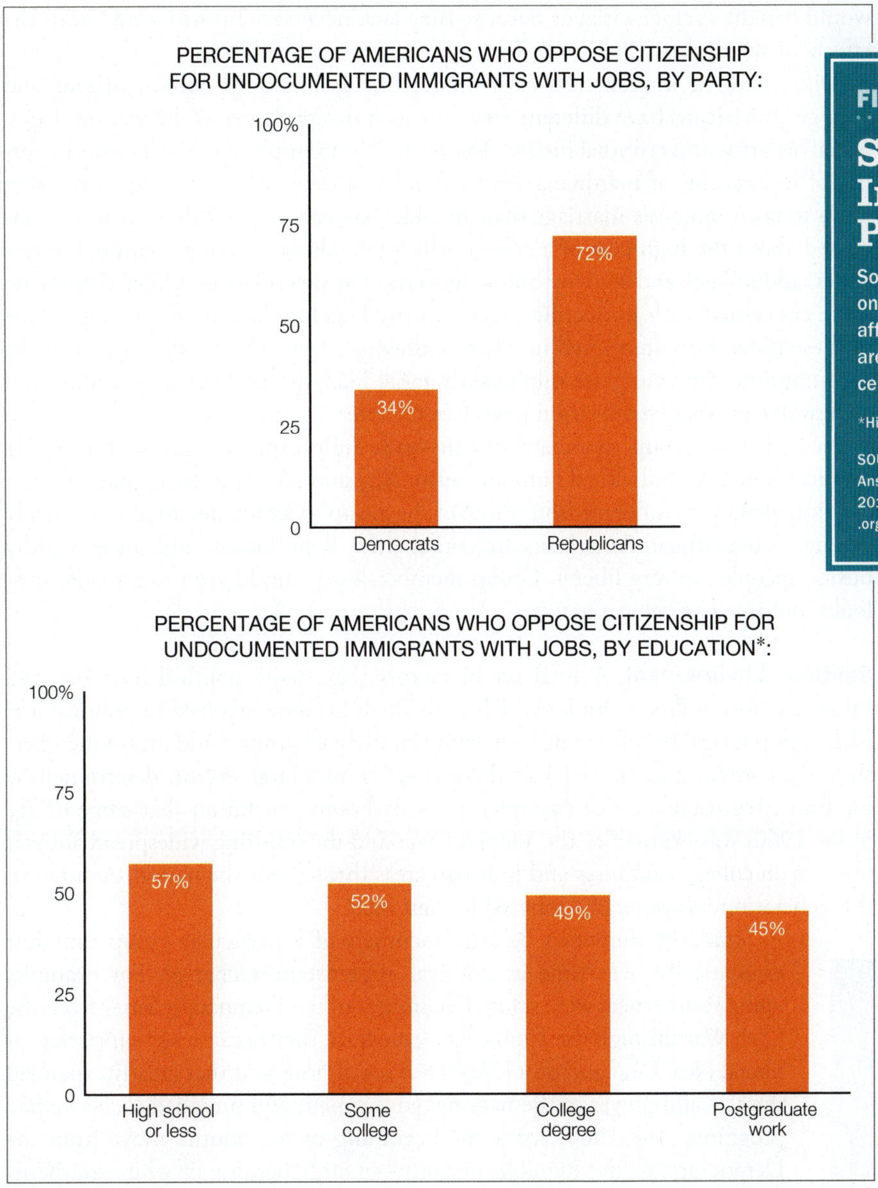

FIGURE 6.6

Social Group Influence on Public Opinion

Social groups have strong impacts on individuals' opinions. Party affiliation and level of education are two predictors of opinion on certain issues, like immigration.

*Highest level attained.

SOURCE: Brian Schaffner and Stephen Ansolabehere, "CCES Common Content, 2014," Harvard Dataverse, V2 http://dx.doi .org/10.7910/DVN/XFXJVY (accessed 5/4/16).

companies and strengthen employee unions. Wealthier individuals tend to favor the Republican solutions, including tax cuts, while the less wealthy tend to favor the liberal policies including government benefits.

However, some researchers have found that people don't necessarily translate broad concerns about inequality or their own economic self-interest into specific policy preferences.[43] For instance, two-thirds of Americans favored the 2001 and 2003 federal tax cuts supported by President George W. Bush, even though the tax reduction disproportionately benefited the very wealthy and therefore increased inequality. The poor, middle class, and affluent alike favored the tax cuts. Political scientist Larry Bartels concluded that the public is not always able to translate a concern for economic self-interest into policy preferences that would benefit average citizens because they lack necessary information about the effects of the tax cuts.[44]

FOR CRITICAL ANALYSIS

An individual's family, social networks, group membership, party affiliation, education, self-interest, and political environment can influence his or her political perspectives. What influences in your life have affected your political opinions and beliefs?

Differences in interest also exist among the generations. Senior citizens and younger Americans have different views on such diverse issues as the war on drugs, Social Security, and criminal justice. The young, for example, are much more accepting of legalization of marijuana than are older citizens. The young are also more likely to favor same-sex marriage than are older age cohorts, and they are more concerned about the high cost of a college education, climate change, criminal justice issues, and privacy and security online (government surveillance). Older citizens are more concerned with protecting social security benefits than are the young. Some of these differences are rooted in where individuals learn about politics and media consumption; the young are significantly more likely to get their news online and are less likely to watch television news (see Chapter 7).

Nevertheless, group membership can never fully explain a given individual's political views. An individual's unique personality and life experiences may produce political views very different from those of the group to which one might nominally belong. Some African Americans are conservative Republicans, and some wealthy businesspeople are very liberal. Group membership is conducive to particular outlooks, but it is not determinative.

Political Environment A final set of factors that shape political attitudes and values are the conditions under which individuals become involved in political life. Although political beliefs are influenced by family background and group membership, the content and character of these views is, to a large extent, determined by political circumstances. For example, the baby-boom generation that came of age in the 1960s was exposed to the Vietnam War and the resulting widespread antiwar protests on college campuses and in urban areas throughout the nation. As a result, this generation has generally opposed foreign wars.

The terrorist attacks of September 11, 2001, certainly influenced public opinion in the months immediately following the attacks and likely also had a long-term effect on many Americans' basic political beliefs.

Similarly, the views held by members of a particular group can shift dramatically over time as political circumstances change. For example, white southerners were staunch members of the Democratic Party from the Civil War through the 1960s. As Democrats, they became key supporters of liberal New Deal and post–New Deal social programs that greatly expanded the size and power of the national government and provided social welfare programs. The 1960s mark the beginning of the South's move from the Democratic to the Republican camp—mainly because of white southerners' opposition to racial integration of schools and public facilities.

Since the 1960s a majority of southern whites have shifted to the Republican Party and away from the Democrats. Today Southern whites provide a solid base of support for efforts to scale back social programs and sharply reduce the size and power of the national government—hence the popularity of the Tea Party movement.[45] This major shift in partisanship in the South was the result of changes in the political environment and the policies promoted by the parties.

Another example of public opinion change can be seen in the evolving political environment in the West. California's Republican governor in the 1970s, Ronald Reagan, went on in the 1980s to become one of the most admired Republican presidents, ushering in major tax reform and scaling back the size and reach of the federal government. But since the 1990s, California, once a Republican stronghold, has become solidly

Democratic. Some argue that the shift began with a series of Republican-endorsed ballot measures targeting racial and ethnic minorities—including immigration, affirmative action, and bilingual education—which triggered a backlash especially among Latinos, who had previously participated in politics in very low numbers. In the 1990s, the number of Latino voters who favored more liberal public policy increased dramatically. With Latinos and blacks combined making up more than 50 percent of California's population, this demographic environmental change moved California to a solid Democratic state.[46] In this case, immigration and demographic change, two environmental factors, caused public opinion in the nation's largest state to change over time.

In sum, public opinion and orientations are shaped by the political circumstances in which individuals and groups find themselves, and those outlooks can change as circumstances change.

Political Knowledge and Changes in Public Opinion

Explore when and why public opinion changes and what role political knowledge plays

The section above described what factors shape individuals' opinions, including political socialization, group identity, and political environment. These factors are relatively constant: one's level of education, for example, is generally set by early adulthood. However, these are not the only influences on public opinion. Individuals encounter new information from political leaders and the media throughout their lives. What role does political knowledge and information play in forming opinions? What causes people's opinions to change over time?

STABILITY AND CHANGE OF PUBLIC OPINION

One of the most important studies of how public opinion is formed is by political scientist John Zaller.[47] Zaller argues that individuals learn about politics by converting information from the news, elected officials, and other sources into opinions. His model of opinion formation works in three stages. In the "receive" stage, an individual receives information from a number of different sources. In the "accept" stage, the individual assesses this information through the lens of her own political views and accepts only those messages that are in line with previously held beliefs, meaning that some political information will be rejected. Finally, in the "sample" stage, the individual selects some of the accepted information—often the information that is most recent—and forms an opinion from it. So, according to this theory, if you receive information from various sources about a proposed tax cut, you will then assess the different messages based on your own previously held beliefs about tax cuts. If you believe tax cuts are generally good, you will likely reject information that suggests this particular cut is bad and accept only the messages suggesting that it is good.

The decision to accept or reject information is based on political knowledge. When asked about his opinion on a topic, the individual selects the most relevant or most recently acquired and accepted information from his "bucket" of information (the third stage above). Citizens with more political knowledge can differentiate between information that fits or does not fit with their beliefs—and then correctly accept or

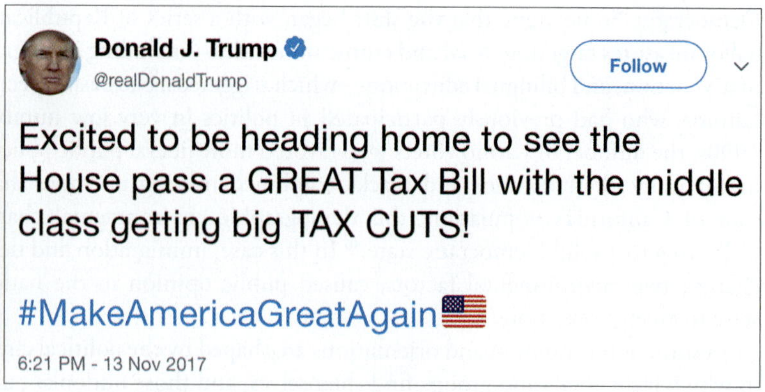

Donald J. Trump
@realDonaldTrump
Follow
Excited to be heading home to see the House pass a GREAT Tax Bill with the middle class getting big TAX CUTS!
#MakeAmericaGreatAgain
6:21 PM - 13 Nov 2017

After political opinions form, they remain relatively stable. The most knowledgeable people are generally able to discern whether new information fits or contradicts their previously held beliefs. Do you think the people in this protest (left) would change their opinions about tax cuts after seeing President Trump's tweet (right)?

reject it. For less-informed individuals, the media and political leaders may play a larger role in influencing public opinion. Low-informed individuals are more susceptible to fake news, partisan news, and political propaganda from elites than more-informed individuals. This reliance on politicians and the media, Zaller concludes, means that the public's opinions are often unstable and unreliable because these sources provide competing, changing information. As a result, public opinion is often a reflection of whatever recent campaign message (or media story) an individual has stored in her short-term memory. As we will see in Chapter 7, this effect is called *priming*.

Another way of understanding how individuals form political opinions is the online-processing model.[48] According to this model, an individual keeps a running tally of information and uses that tally to form an opinion on a policy issue or to decide which candidate to vote for. However, by the time an individual actually votes or voices an opinion on a specific issue, she may have forgotten some of the older information included in her decision-making process. This effect leads to the misconception that voters are uninformed, when in fact their opinion is informed but they have not retained all of the facts used to form that opinion. This model also implies a large role for political elites and the media but does not necessarily suggest that opinion is unstable. If public opinion is easily manipulated, the democratic process, which relies on citizens to play a significant part in the government, would be at risk. But other research has shown that individuals are quite stable in their policy attitudes.[49]

To take a closer look at whether and how public opinion changes, see Figure 6.7. The Pew Research Center tracks public opinion over time with annual surveys asking identical questions. Some opinions are relatively stable: support for abortion, for example, has remained virtually unchanged over the past decade, with over half of Americans saying abortion should be legal in all or most cases. Optimism about the economy and personal finances, however, experienced a gradual decline triggered by the financial crisis in 2008. In contrast, opinion on same-sex marriage has changed dramatically over the past two decades, with approval of marriage rights increasing by 25 percentage points. Notice that when public opinion has shifted, the shift has occurred fairly steadily in one direction; it doesn't simply jump around.[50]

The shift in public opinion on same-sex marriage has occurred partly in response to government policy. Political scientists call this "policy feedback." In 2009, Iowa was just the third U.S. state to allow same-sex marriages when the state Supreme Court issued a unanimous and at the time unpopular decision in the case *Varnum v. Brien*.[51] Changes in opinion immediately before and after the court decision were large. A survey of Iowans conducted immediately before and after the court legalized

FIGURE 6.7

Stability and Change in Public Opinion

Public opinion on some issues has stayed stable in the last two decades, while opinion on other issues has shifted. What might explain why opinion on personal finance and same-sex marriage has changed, while opinion on abortion and the environment has stayed relatively constant?

NOTE: Personal finance data are from 2015.

SOURCES: "Changing Attitudes on Gay Marriage," Pew Research Center, June 26, 2017 www.pewforum.org (accessed 5/23/18); "Views on Abortion, 1995–2017," Pew Research Center, July 7, 2017 www.pewforum.org (accessed 5/23/18); "Public Views about Guns," Pew Research Center, June 22, 2017, www.people-press.org (accessed 5/23/18); "Economics and Personal Finances," Pew Research Center, www.pewresearch.org (accessed 12/23/15).

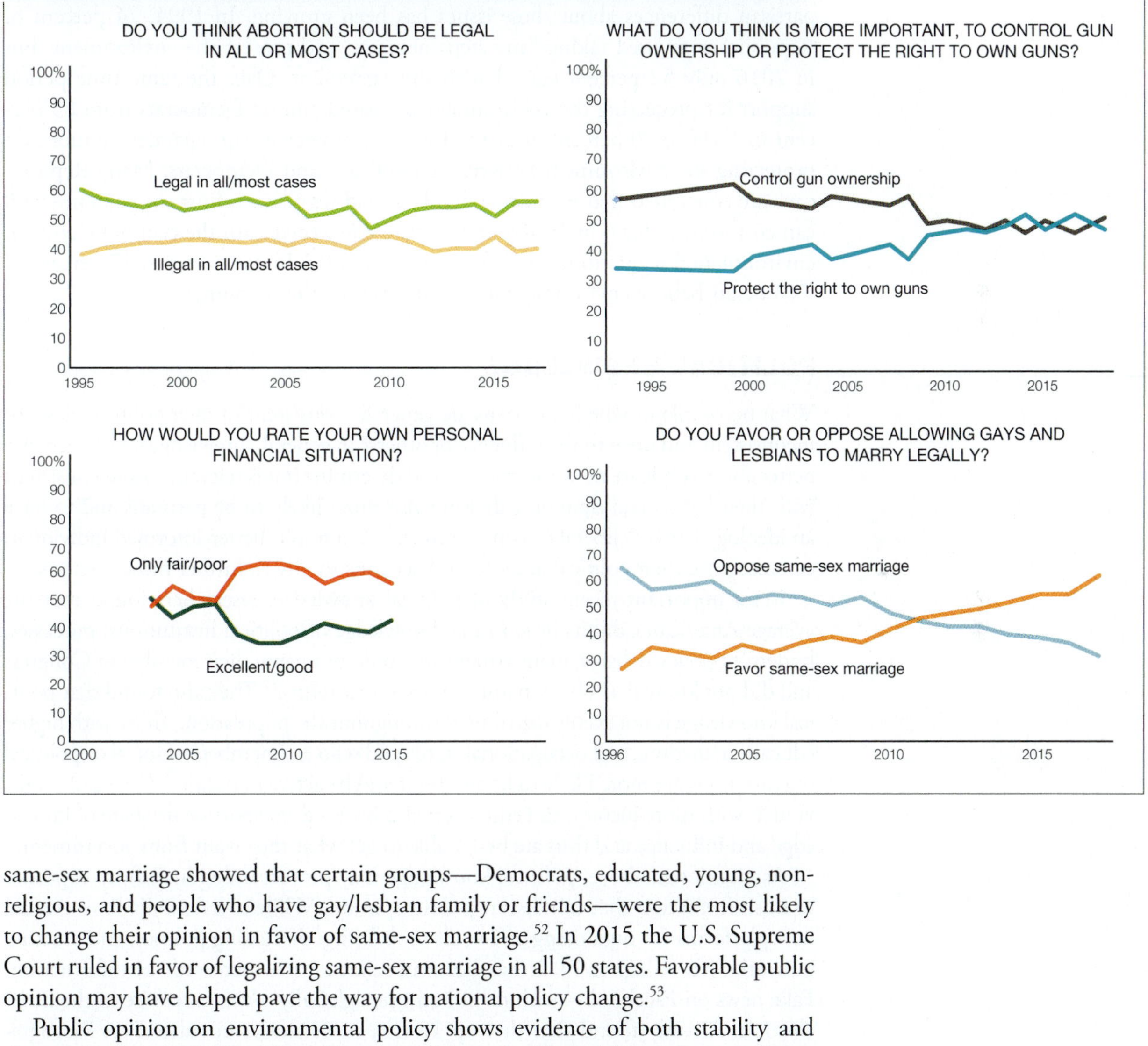

same-sex marriage showed that certain groups—Democrats, educated, young, nonreligious, and people who have gay/lesbian family or friends—were the most likely to change their opinion in favor of same-sex marriage.[52] In 2015 the U.S. Supreme Court ruled in favor of legalizing same-sex marriage in all 50 states. Favorable public opinion may have helped pave the way for national policy change.[53]

Public opinion on environmental policy shows evidence of both stability and change. In June 2017 President Trump withdrew the United States from an international treaty signed by nearly 200 nations to protect the earth's environment. The political decision was widely criticized by global political leaders. The Paris Agreement sought to prevent rising temperatures and climate change by reducing reliance on fossil fuels such as coal, oil, and gas and develop alternative energy sources. Surveys reveal most Americans favor protecting the environment consistent with the terms of the Paris Agreement. In 2016 roughly three quarters (74 percent) of Americans believed "the country should do whatever it takes to protect the environment." Less than a quarter say "the country has gone too far in its efforts to protect the environment." Opinions on environmental protection go hand in hand with energy policy, as scientists find burning fossil fuels is linked to rising global temperatures. While Trump favors increasing coal production, most Americans (65 percent) favor developing alternative energy sources, such as wind and solar. This is a five percent increase from 2014. In some states, such as Iowa, 37 percent of energy is produced from wind power. Public opinion favoring alternative energy development may drive policy change.[54]

Though there might seem to be broad agreement on protecting the environment, partisan differences about these issues has been growing. In 1994, 74 percent of Republicans favored taking "any steps necessary" to protect the environment, but in 2016 only 52 percent agreed with this statement. Over the same time period support for protecting the environment increased among Democrats from 85 percent in 1994 to 90 percent in 2016. Today a 38 percent gap separates opinions on protecting the environment between Republicans and Democrats. Many Republicans are concerned that environmental laws and regulations hurt the economy and can cost jobs; today 6 in 10 Republicans are concerned with the economic costs of environmental regulations, up from 3 in 10 in 2007. In contrast, just 17 percent of Democrats believe environmental regulations hurt the economy.

POLITICAL KNOWLEDGE

What best explains whether citizens are generally consistent in their political views or inconsistent and open to the influence of others? In general, knowledgeable citizens are better able to evaluate new information and determine if it is relevant to and consistent with their beliefs and opinions; they are also more likely to be partisans and to have an ideology (such as liberal or conservative).[55] As a result, better-informed individuals can recognize their political interests and act consistently to further those interests.[56]

In an important recent study of political knowledge, researchers found that the average American exhibits little formal knowledge of political institutions, processes, leaders, or policy debates; many Americans could not name their member of Congress and did not know that U.S. senators serve six-year terms.[57] They also found that political knowledge is not evenly distributed throughout the population. Those with higher education, income, and occupational status and who are members of social or political organizations are more likely to know about and be active in politics. As a result, individuals with more income and education also have a disproportionate share of knowledge and influence and thus are better able to get what they want from government.

As mentioned above, political knowledge may protect individuals from exposure to misinformation that can distort public opinion. While social media have created new platforms for organizing and voter mobilizing, discussing politics, and creating networks (see Chapter 7), it has been associated with increased misinformation. Fake news on Facebook—with its billion users globally—was extensive in the 2016 election. A study found that the top 10 fake news stories circulated on Facebook were shared more widely than the top 10 authentic news stories about the election. The most viral story on Facebook was that the Pope had endorsed Trump for president. Russian Twitter "bot" accounts have been linked to breaking many of the fake news stories. Since the election, both Google and Facebook have implemented new protocols to block content from deceptive outlets, and Twitter, Reddit, and Instagram deleted thousands of fake accounts. Misinformation from elected officials and online news has encouraged more Americans to seek websites such as PolitiFact, FactCheck.org, and Snopes.com to verify the content of political information. It has also encouraged more Americans to turn to established media outlets, such as the *Washington Post*, *Wall Street Journal*, or *New York Times*, for news. Political knowledge and accurate political news is more important now than ever.

Shortcuts and Cues Because being informed politically requires a substantial investment of time and energy, most Americans seek to acquire political information and to make political decisions "on the cheap" by making use of shortcuts for political evaluation and decision making rather than engaging in a lengthy process of information-gathering. As noted above, researchers have found that individuals rely on cues from trusted party elites, interest groups, and the media to aid in attitude formation.[58] Today, tweets from elected officials are an increasingly important source of news; Donald Trump relies on Twitter more extensively than any other president, often tweeting multiple times a day. Other "inexpensive" ways to become informed involve taking cues from trusted friends, social networks and social media, relatives, colleagues, and perhaps religious leaders. Political scientists Richard Lau and David Redlawsk contend that by using informational shortcuts, average citizens can form political opinions that are, in most instances, consistent with their underlying preferences. They call this "voting correctly."[59] Even individuals with low levels of political knowledge are able to make relatively informed political choices by relying on these voter cues. It is generally accepted by scholars that people rely on shortcuts in forming public opinion on politics and public policy.[60] From this perspective, lower levels of political knowledge about politics, or instability of opinions, may not be a serious problem.

The public's reliance on elite cues has taken on new significance in today's era of party polarization. As elected officials have become increasingly polarized, has this change affected the way that citizens arrive at their opinions? Political scientists have found stark evidence that polarized political environments change how citizens make

People use cues from political elites and other trusted sources as a shortcut to forming opinions. Someone might not know the details about immigration and the DREAM act, but if they were a liberal or democrat, they might hear Senator Kamala Harris (D-Calif.) speaking on behalf of the bill and then feel they too supported it.

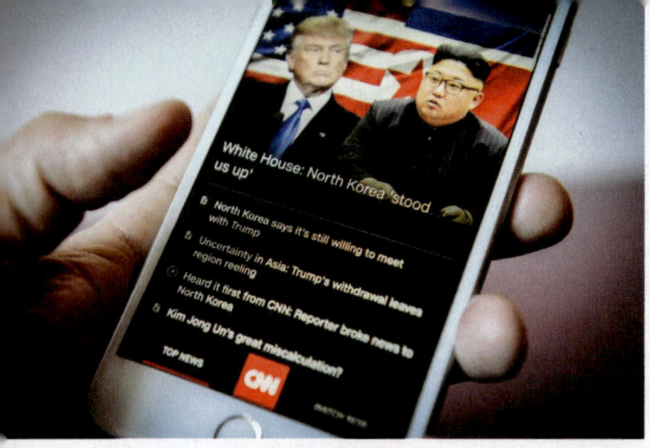

More and more people getting their news online, which seems to have altered reading habits. News articles have become shorter, and people are spending more time scanning headlines and less reading in-depth coverage.

decisions and form opinions. Notably, polarization between the parties means that party endorsements (of an issue or candidate) have a larger impact on public opinion formation than they used to. For example, if Republican leaders in Congress support a plan to impose higher taxes (tariffs) on foreign goods, citizens that identify as Republicans are more likely to support the plan as well. At the same time, polarization decreases the impact of other information on public opinion—that is, party polarization may actually reduce levels of political knowledge. Thus, elite polarization may have negative implications for public opinion formation.[61]

Skim and Scan Another factor affecting political knowledge is the *form* in which people consume information. The transformation of political information in the digital era has had a profound effect on the way the news is reported and how citizens learn about politics. Today more than three in four Americans read the news online or seek political information online.[62] Recent research also indicates a trend in journalism toward shorter articles and flashier headlines, and Twitter limits text to 280 characters. Americans today are likely to read the news by skimming and scanning multiple headlines online, in bits and bytes, rather than by reading long news articles.[63] There is a debate about whether the shift to digital media creates a more informed public, given the broader diversity of information sources and more personalized communication of the news via social media, or a public that is less informed because of a tendency to favor skimming and scanning over in-depth reading. However, as we've seen in this chapter, some research indicates that most individuals use simple cues and shortcuts to process political information. If this is correct, skimming and scanning headlines might provide a reasonable way to be informed about politics without extensive time or effort.

Costs to Democracy Political knowledge is necessary for effective citizenship. Those who lack political information cannot effectively defend their own political interests, rights, and freedoms and can easily become losers in political struggles and government policy. The presence of large numbers of politically ignorant individuals means that power can more easily be manipulated by political elites, the media, foreign governments and wealthy special interests that seek to shape public opinion. If knowledge is power, then a lack of knowledge can contribute to growing political and economic inequality. When individuals are unaware of their interests or how to pursue them, it is virtually certain that political outcomes will not favor them. The answer is to get informed and stay informed.

One of the most important areas of government policy is taxation. The United States has one of the largest gaps between the rich and the poor of any nation in the world. But rather than raise taxes, over the past several decades the United States has substantially reduced the rate of taxation levied on its wealthiest citizens. George W. Bush signed major tax cuts into law in 2001, providing a substantial tax break mainly for the top 1 percent of the nation's wage earners. Political scientist Larry Bartels has shown that, surprisingly, most Americans favored the 2001 tax cuts, including millions of middle- and lower-middle-class citizens who did not stand to benefit from the tax policy. Additionally, 40 percent of Americans had no opinion at all regarding the Bush tax cuts. The explanation for this odd state of affairs appears to be a lack of political knowledge. Millions of individuals who were unlikely to derive benefit from President Bush's tax policy thought they would. Since most Americans think they

Where Does Income Inequality Stem From?

In your opinion, which generally has more to do with . . .

Why a person is rich

Worked harder / Had advantages in life

	Worked harder	Had advantages in life
Overall	45%	43%
By gender: Men	49%	39%
By gender: Women	41%	47%
By party: Republican	66%	21%
By party: Democrats	29%	60%
By education: High school or less	47%	41%
By education: College grad	42%	47%
By income: Family income <$30K	39%	49%
By income: Family income $30K–$74,999	46%	44%
By income: Family income $75K+	51%	37%

Why a person is poor

Lack of effort / Circumstances beyond control

	Lack of effort	Circumstances beyond control
Overall	34%	53%
By gender: Men	42%	46%
By gender: Women	26%	60%
By party: Republican	56%	32%
By party: Democrats	19%	71%
By education: High school or less	38%	49%
By education: College grad	28%	59%
By income: Family income <$30K	31%	56%
By income: Family income $30K–$74,999	38%	51%
By income: Family income $75K+	33%	57%

An individual's party identification, gender, and income may influence his or her opinions on specific issues. A recent study showed there are significant differences of opinion about the government's role in reducing the income gap between men and women and across income groups, but the most pronounced differences were between Democrats and Republicans.

SOURCE: Pew Research Center, "Why People Are Rich and Poor: Republicans and Democrats Have Very Different Views," www.pewresearch.org (accessed 11/19/17).

FOR CRITICAL ANALYSIS

1. Do the findings in this study show that opinions are shaped by economic self-interest? Why or why not?
2. Which of these groups is most likely to support government action to address inequality? Are the other groups not concerned about inequality? Use the data to explain your answers.

pay too much in taxes, they favored the policy, even if the wealthy benefited much more than the middle class. (See the "Who Are Americans?" feature for public opinion on income inequality.) President Trump and the Republican-controlled Congress adopted even larger tax cuts for the affluent and corporations in 2017. Opinion polls showed a majority of Americans were opposed to the 2017 tax reform. Had political knowledge around taxes increased, or did the opposition reflect the low public opinion about President Trump and Congress at the time?

The Media, Government, and Public Opinion

Describe the major forces that shape public opinion

When individuals attempt to form opinions about particular political issues, events, and political leaders, they seldom do so in isolation. Typically, they are confronted with—sometimes bombarded by—the efforts of a host of individuals and groups seeking to persuade them to adopt a particular point of view. In the approach to the 2016 presidential election, someone trying to decide what to think about Hillary Clinton or Donald Trump could hardly avoid an avalanche of opinions expressed through the media, in meetings, or in conversations with friends. The **marketplace of ideas** is the interplay of opinions and views that takes place as competing forces attempt to persuade as many people as possible to accept a particular position on a particular issue. Given this constant exposure to the ideas of others, it is virtually impossible for most individuals to resist some modification of their own beliefs. Three forces that play important roles in shaping opinions in the marketplace are the government, private groups, and the news media.[64]

marketplace of ideas the public forum in which beliefs and ideas are exchanged and compete

POLITICAL LEADERS

All governments try to influence, manipulate, or manage their citizens' beliefs. But the extent to which public opinion is actually affected by governmental public relations can be limited. Often, governmental claims are disputed by the media, by interest groups, and increasingly by the opposing political party.

This hasn't stopped modern presidents from focusing a great deal of attention on shaping public opinion to boost support for their policy agendas. Franklin Delano Roosevelt promoted his policy agenda directly to the American people through his famous "fireside chat" radio broadcasts. A hallmark of the Clinton administration was the establishment of a political "war room" similar to the one that operated in his campaign headquarters, where staff met daily to discuss and coordinate the president's public-relations efforts.[65] The George W. Bush administration developed an extensive public-relations program to bolster popular support for the president's policies, including the war against terrorism.[66]

Like his predecessors, President Obama was effective in shaping public opinion. He built support for national health care reform by relying upon the power of his oratorical skills to build support for his administration's initiatives in domestic and foreign policy. Obama's White House was the first to use digital and social media to promote the president's policy agenda. Facebook posts promoted his policies and served to personalize the president. Obama was especially adept at using Twitter, with 70 million followers on that network. His use of multiple Twitter accounts to shape public opinion in favor of his policies allowed him to communicate directly with the people without having to be interviewed by the media.

Though Obama was the first president to use Twitter, Donald Trump is the nation's first Twitter president. Twitter was a key tool that helped Trump win the presidency; as president he uses it to promote his policy agenda and shape public opinion. Often tweeting in the early morning hours, Trump communicates his sentiments on politics like no other president in modern history. A website, the Trump Twitter Archives, lists thousands of Trump tweets searchable by topic. Former White House press secretary Sean Spicer said that although they often circumvent or contradict his own staff—and sometimes even himself—Trump's tweets will continue: "He has this direct pipeline to the American people, where he can talk back and forth." Trump uses Twitter for policy proposals, government announcements, attacking his enemies, defending himself and his campaign, building support for his party and his policies, and just plain venting. Laced with emotion and frequent typos, his tweets are authentic, if not always factually correct. He is known for Twitter rants, with multiple tweets on the same topic. For example, facing mounting criticism and a federal investigation into whether the Trump campaign coordinated with the Russians to sway the 2016 election, Trump tweeted in June 2017, "I am being investigated for firing the FBI Director by the man who told me to fire the FBI Director! Witch Hunt"[67] and "You are witnessing the single greatest WITCH HUNT in American political history - led by some very bad and conflicted people! #MAGA" ("Make America Great Again"—Trump's campaign slogan).[68] New scholarship argues political leaders like Trump prefer social media to traditional media since they can control the content unmitigated by the mainstream press.[69]

INTEREST GROUPS

The ideas that become prominent in political life are developed and spread not only by government officials and parties but also by important economic and political groups searching for issues that will advance their causes. One notable example is the abortion issue, which has inflamed American politics over the past 30 years. The notion of a fetal "right to life," whose proponents seek to outlaw abortion and overturn the Supreme Court's 1973 *Roe v. Wade* decision, was developed by conservative politicians who saw of abortion as a means of uniting Catholic and Protestant conservatives and linking both groups to the Republican Party.[70] To advance their cause, leaders of the right-to-life movement sponsored well-publicized

Interest groups focus much of their efforts on influencing public opinion. (Left) A member of the liberal group MoveOn.org hand delivers petitions in support of the Iran Nuclear agreement to New Jersey senators Cory Booker and Robert Menendez. (Right) Indivisible is another liberal group that formed after the 2016 elections to protest Donald Trump and Republican policies.

Senate hearings at which testimony, photographs, films (such as *The Silent Scream*), and other exhibits were presented to illustrate the movement's claim that abortion amounted to the murder of millions of unborn human beings. Finally, Catholic and Evangelical Protestant religious leaders were organized to denounce abortion from their church pulpits and, increasingly, from their electronic pulpits on the Christian Broadcasting Network and the various other television forums available for religious programming. Religious leaders have also organized demonstrations, pickets, and disruptions at abortion clinics throughout the nation.[71]

THE MASS MEDIA

FOR CRITICAL ANALYSIS

Does it matter what news sources an individual reads? How can the news influence public attitudes on issues of public policy?

The media are among the most powerful forces operating in the marketplace of ideas. As we shall see in Chapter 7, the mass media are not simply neutral messengers for ideas developed by others. Instead, the media are opinion makers and have an enormous impact on popular attitudes. For example, since the publication of the Pentagon Papers by the *New York Times* and the exposure of the Watergate scandal led by the *Washington Post* in the 1970s, the national news media have relentlessly investigated personal and official wrongdoing on the part of politicians and public officials. Today, the national media plays a similar role in exposing potential government corruption and Russian interference in the 2016 election, as discussed earlier. Media revelation of corruption in government has contributed to the cynicism and distrust of government that prevail in much of the general public.

At the same time, the ways in which media coverage interprets or "frames" specific events can have a major impact on popular responses and opinions about these events (see Chapter 7).[72] Given the critical importance of media framing to the way the public perceives the news, President George W. Bush went to great lengths to persuade broadcasters to follow his administration's lead in their coverage of both terrorism and America's response to terrorism in the months following the September 11, 2001, attacks. The media acquiesced, presenting the administration's military campaigns in Afghanistan and Iraq, as well as its domestic antiterrorist efforts, in a positive light. Even supposedly liberal newspapers such as the *New York Times* published articles supportive of the military invasion of Iraq in March 2003, when President Bush ordered the invasion. In 2002, Congress passed the Joint Resolution to Authorize the Use of United States Armed Forces Against Iraq. Public opinion in favor of invading Iraq remained above 50 percent between June and November of 2002, according to Gallup polls. By the time the invasion occurred, in March 2003, after months of presidential messages and media coverage focused on the threat of terrorism, public support had reached over 70 percent.[73]

Public Opinion and Government Policy

Analyze how public opinion shapes government policy and influences elected officials

In 1960 the authors of a book titled *The American Voter* argued that few Americans think about politics ideologically or consistently, so one would naturally expect public opinion to vary, as discussed earlier.[74] Given generally low levels of political knowledge among voters and the changing nature of public opinion, it's little wonder that politicians are sometimes unwilling to act solely on the basis of public opinion. But one could argue that consulting public opinion is a duty of elected officials in a democracy. Is government policy responsive to public opinion?

GOVERNMENT RESPONSIVENESS TO PUBLIC OPINION

Studies generally find that elected officials are influenced by the preferences of the public. Political scientists Benjamin Page and Robert Shapiro explored the relationship between broad changes in opinion toward various political issues and the policy outcomes that most closely correspond to the issues.[75] The results showed that shifts in public opinion on particular issues do in fact tend to lead to changes in public policy. This is especially true when there are wide swings in opinion regarding particularly high-profile issues that are relatively simple, such as legalization of same-sex marriage. Other studies have found similar evidence that government policy generally does track public opinion. Unsurprisingly, states where conservative opinions predominate tend to adopt more conservative laws and states with more liberal public opinion adopt more liberal policies.[76] Another example is in health care. A July 2009 Pew survey found that 65 percent of Americans favored a law "requiring all Americans to have health insurance, and government aid for those unable to afford it."[77] The federal government adopted the Affordable Health Care Act for America in 2010, which required health insurance for all citizens.

However, there is reason to question whether prevailing public opinion causes politicians to make policies that reflect the general will or whether government policy in fact causes changes in public opinion. The relationship between government policy and opinion may be dynamic, wherein policy responds to opinion but opinion also shifts based on new government policies.[78] Recent studies have found government policy to have an effect on opinion in various areas, such as the environment, health care, welfare reform, the death penalty, and smoking bans. For example, researchers found that in states that adopted smoking bans, public opinion then shifted to become more critical of cigarette smoking than in states without such bans.[79] Scholars have suggested a number of possible mechanisms to explain this process. New policy may expose the public to new ideas, causing opinion to change, or experience with a successful or unsuccessful policy may give the public new information. A policy might act as a "signal" of a moral or ethical view (such as a smoking ban acting as a "signal" that smoking should be stigmatized).

To what extent do political leaders listen to the opinions of their constituents? To what extent should they listen? Is Calvin's father right that leaders should do what they believe is right, not what the public wants?

Of course, sometimes public opinion and policy do not align, as the prior discussion of environmental policy and the Paris Agreement. Sometimes public officials act on their own preferences if they believe it will benefit government or society, and lawmakers typically do use their own judgment when making policy choices.[80] When elected officials pursue policies not aligned with public opinion, it is often because they view particular groups of the electorate as more important than others. Inevitably, loyal voting blocs or interest groups that regularly contribute to a candidate may have their interests more closely represented than the general public.[81]

DOES EVERYONE'S OPINION COUNT EQUALLY?

In a democracy, it is assumed that elected representatives will implement the policies favored by the majority of the people, and in a general sense this happens in the United States. But when policy issues are more complicated (such as taxation or foreign policy), the public is likely to have less of a voice. Further, citizens who are more affluent and more educated may have a disproportionate influence over politics and public policy decisions. This has been shown when comparing the responsiveness of elected officials to low- and high-income individuals, voters and nonvoters, and whites and minorities. The view that some groups in a society have more influence in politics is not new, but it is quite a departure from the traditional pluralist view of all citizens having equal access to the political sphere.

How do more affluent and educated citizens manage to wield outsize influence over policy makers? One way is obvious: they vote at higher rates, and they are more likely to contribute money to political campaigns. As we will discuss in Chapter 8, voters and individuals making political contributions tend to be more affluent and educated than nonvoters. Indeed, there is new evidence supporting the common, but generally untested, assumption that voters are better represented than nonvoters. In a comparative study of the roll-call votes of U.S. senators, political scientists John Griffin and Brian Newman demonstrated that elected officials are indeed responsive to the policy preferences of voters but not to those of nonvoters.[82]

In regard to income group, research has found that U.S. senators from both the Republican and Democratic parties are less likely to respond to the opinions of low-income constituents than to those of constituents with higher incomes.[83] Senate votes on such varied issues as the minimum wage, civil rights, and abortion are more likely to reflect the opinions of the rich. The influence of affluent Americans may explain government policies such as failure to increase the minimum wage and the 2017 tax reform that significantly reduced corporate taxes and reduced taxes paid by the wealthiest citizens, all of which contribute to growing income inequality.[84]

Charles Koch, one of the wealthiest people in the world, is a major donor to Republican candidates and causes. Some say that the opinions of wealthier individuals have more influence on politicians and government policy, though this has been difficult to prove unequivocally.

As an alternative to analyzing legislative votes, political scientist Martin Gilens has used survey results to confirm that those with higher incomes are more likely to have their policy preferences represented by actual policies.[85] He considered public opinion surveys on a wide variety of policy issues conducted over 20 years and compared the responses of upper- and lower-income groups with related federal policy outcomes. Gilens found a relationship between what the public wants and what the government actually does, albeit with a strong bias toward the status quo. But when Americans with different income levels differ in their policy preferences, policies strongly reflect the preferences of the most affluent and show little or no relationship to the preferences of poor or middle-income Americans.

Some argue that every American citizen has an equal right to voice opinions in the political arena, but others point out that some voices receive a very attentive listening, while others are hardly heard at all.[86]

Measuring Public Opinion

Describe basic survey methods and other techniques researchers use to measure public opinion

A century ago American political leaders gauged public opinion by the presence of crowds at meetings and their applause. This direct exposure to the people's views did not necessarily produce accurate knowledge of public opinion. It did, however, give political leaders confidence in their public support—and therefore confidence in their ability to govern by consent.

Today, public officials make extensive use of **public-opinion polls** to help them decide whether to run for office, what policies to support, how to vote on important legislation, and what types of appeals to make in their campaigns. All recent presidents and other major political figures have worked closely with polls and pollsters.

public-opinion polls scientific instruments for measuring public opinion

MEASURING PUBLIC OPINION FROM SURVEYS

It is not feasible to interview the more than 300 million Americans residing in the United States on their opinions of who should be the next president or what should be done about important policy issues such as how to improve the economy and create jobs. Instead, pollsters take a **sample** of the population and use it to make inferences (e.g., predictions and educated guesses) about the preferences of the population as a whole. For a political survey to be an accurate representation of the population, it must meet certain requirements, including an appropriate sampling method (i.e., randomization), a sufficient sample size, and the avoidance of selection bias.[87] While some are skeptical of sampling, random sample surveys, which are used extensively in business and marketing as well as politics, ensure that the samples are accurate and reliable predictions of the underlying population.

sample a small group selected by researchers to represent the most important characteristics of an entire population

Websites such as RealClearPolitics.com list the results of every political survey released each day; during elections, this can be dozens of different surveys daily. Every week, the opinions of Americans regarding candidates and public policies are measured, as well as opinions on a vast array of products (toothpaste), entertainment (movie star romances), and even college political science textbooks!

Representative Samples One way to obtain a representative sample is what statisticians call a **simple random sample (or probability sample)**. To take such a sample, one would need a complete list of all the people in the United States, and individuals would be randomly selected from that list. Imagine that everyone's name was entered into a lottery, with names then drawn blindly from an enormous box. If everyone had an equal chance of selection, the result is a random sample. Since we don't have a complete list of all Americans, pollsters use census data, lists of households (for in-person or telephone surveys), and telephone numbers to create lists, drawing samples from regions and then neighborhoods within regions. State voter registration files are often used in political surveys designed to predict the outcome of an election or public opinion. If respondents are chosen randomly and everyone has an equal chance of being selected, then their results can be used to predict

simple random sample (or probability sample) a method used by pollsters to select a representative sample in which every individual in the population has an equal probability of being selected as a respondent

Confidence in Democratic Institutions

AMERICA SIDE by SIDE

Parliaments, political parties, and the press are three institutions that play an important role in making democracy work. Parliament is the branch of government that most directly represents the voters; it serves as a major forum for policy debate and prevents abuse of executive power. Political parties offer different ideological goals, thereby helping to organize government, mobilize voters, and ensure political competition and accountability. Finally, the press plays an important "watchdog" role in politics, informing voters and helping them hold their leaders accountable for their actions.

While these institutions are important to all democracies, we do notice that Americans tend to be much less confident in these institutions than are citizens in other democracies. This raises two important questions: Why are the U.S. scores so low, and what does it mean for politics when a large percentage of a population loses confidence in the institutions that keep its democracy functioning?

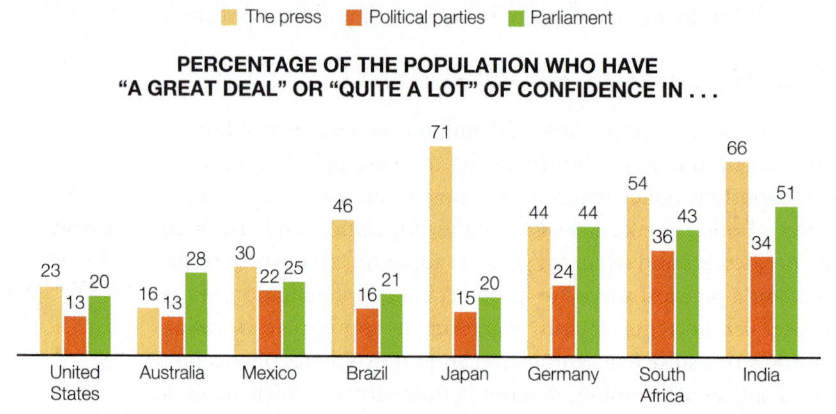

SOURCE: R. Inglehart et al., eds., "World Values Survey: Round Six—Country-Pooled Datafile Version," 2014, www.worldvaluessurvey.org (accessed 6/5/18).

behavior for the overall population. If randomization is not used or some people are excluded from the chance to be selected, then the sample will be biased and cannot be used to generalize to the population accurately.

Another method of drawing samples of the national population is a technique called **random digit dialing**. A computer random number generator is used to produce a list of 10-digit telephone numbers. Given that 95 percent of Americans have telephones (cell phones or landlines), this technique usually results in a random national sample because almost every citizen has a chance of being selected for the survey. Telephone surveys are fairly accurate, cost-effective, and flexible in the type of questions that can be asked; but many people refuse to answer political surveys, and response rates—the percent of those called who actually answer the survey—have been falling steadily, averaging less than 15 percent.[88]

random digit dialing a polling method in which respondents are selected at random from a list of 10-digit telephone numbers, with every effort made to avoid bias in the construction of the sample

Sample Size A sample must be large enough to provide an accurate representation of the population. Surprisingly, though, the size of the population being measured doesn't matter, only the size of the sample. A survey of 1,000 people is almost as effective for measuring the opinions of all Texans (28 million residents) as the opinions of all Americans (over 323 million residents).

Flipping a coin shows how this works. After tossing a coin 10 times, the number of heads and tails may not be close to 5 and 5. After 100 tosses of the coin, though, the percentage of heads should be close to 50 percent and after 1,000 tosses, very close to 50 percent. In fact, after 1,000 tosses, there is a 95 percent chance that the number of heads will be somewhere between 46.9 percent and 53.1 percent. This 3.1 percent variation from 50 percent is called the **sampling error (or margin of error)**: the chance that the sample used does not accurately represent the population from which it is drawn. In this case, 3.1 percent is the amount of uncertainty we can expect with a typical 1,000-person survey. If we conduct a national survey and find candidate A leads candidate B by 5 percent in the upcoming election and the uncertainty in the survey is 3 percent, it means candidate A leads candidate B by anywhere between 2 (5−3) and 8 (5 + 3) percentage points. Normally, samples of 1,000 people are considered sufficient for accurately measuring public opinion through the use of surveys.

sampling error (or margin of error) polling error that arises based on the small size of the sample

Larger sample sizes can yield more accurate predictions of the opinions of a population, but there is a trade-off in terms of cost since it is also more expensive to survey more people. Why is a sample size of only 1,000 generally accepted as adequately representative of much larger populations? Consider the "diminishing returns" of sampling more and more people. The sample error from a sample of 500 people is 4.4 percent. With 1,000 respondents, it drops to 3.1 percent and with 1,500 to 2.5 percent. That is, the smaller and smaller gains in accuracy have to be weighed against the increasing costs of polling more people. The consensus among statisticians and pollsters is that the optimal trade-off point is 1,000—hence 1,000 is the "gold standard." But today many surveys conducted online include thousands of respondents, making their predictions potentially even more accurate.

When an election poll of 1,000 people indicates that 51 percent of voters surveyed favor the Republican candidate and 49 percent support the Democratic candidate, the outcome is considered too close to call because the difference, 2 percent, is within the margin of error of 3.1 percent. That is, a figure of 51 percent really means that between 48 percent and 54 percent of voters in the population *probably* favor the Republican, while a figure of 49 percent indicates that between 46 percent and 52 percent of all voters *probably* support the Democrat. Thus, in this example, a 52-to-48 percent Democratic victory would still be consistent with polls predicting a 51-to-49 percent Republican triumph.

Survey Design and Question Wording Even with a good sample design, surveys may fail to reflect the true distribution of opinion within a target population. One frequent source of measurement error is the wording of survey questions. The words used in a question can have an enormous impact on the answers it elicits. The reliability of survey results can also be adversely affected by poor question format, the ordering of questions, poor vocabulary, ambiguity of questions, or questions with built-in biases.

Often, minor differences in the wording of a question can convey vastly different meanings to respondents and thus produce quite different response patterns (see Box 6.3). For example, for many years the University of Chicago's National Opinion Research Center has asked respondents whether they think the federal government is spending too much, too little, or about the right amount of money on "assistance for the poor." Answering the question posed this way, about two-thirds of all respondents seem to believe that the government is spending too little. However, the same survey also asks whether the government spends too much, too little, or about the right amount for welfare. When the word *welfare* is substituted for "assistance for the poor," about half of all respondents indicate that too much is being spent.[89]

Online Surveys Today, pollsters are increasingly turning to the use of online surveys, often using similar techniques to those of telephone surveys. Internet surveys can be more efficient, less costly, and more accurate than standard phone surveys; and they include much larger samples of young people and yield more accurate results within age cohorts. But many surveys you will find online do not use

BOX 6.3

It Depends on How You Ask

THE SITUATION

The public's desire for tax cuts can be hard to measure. In 2000, pollsters asked what should be done with the nation's budget surplus and got different results depending on the specifics of the question.

THE QUESTION

President [Bill] Clinton has proposed setting aside approximately two-thirds of an expected budget surplus to fix the Social Security system. What do you think the leaders in Washington should do with the remainder of the surplus?

VARIATION 1

Should the money be used for a tax cut, or should it be used to fund new government programs?

VARIATION 2

Should the money be used for a tax cut, or should it be spent on programs for education, the environment, health care, crime fighting, and military defense?

SOURCE: Pew Research Center, reported in the *New York Times*, January 30, 2000, WK 3.

probability sampling (random sampling) and thus are not representative of the American population. Instead, they reflect those willing to take a quiz online.

Knowledge Networks and YouGov are leaders in internet polling using sampling methods in which respondents complete surveys online instead of being interviewed on the phone. YouGov has a large population of respondents (hundreds of thousands of individuals) identified using probability sampling, so the sample is representative of the American population. Individuals without internet access are given free subscriptions or complete the surveys using the TV. If a client commissions a survey, YouGov randomly draws a sample of, say, 1,000 people from its population of online respondents. Because respondents have agreed to complete a number of surveys in exchange for free internet access, they are more likely to complete the surveys. YouGov has been more accurate in predicting the outcomes of recent presidential elections than other firms.[90]

Other polling companies use different methods for conducting internet surveys, often by using statistical weights to make the surveys generally representative of the American population.[91] Internet surveys such as the Cooperative Congressional Election Study can have very large samples, up to 50,000 people, and rolling panel survey designs, where the same respondents are interviewed repeatedly over months. In the future, internet surveys may be more representative of the American population than traditional telephone surveys and may replace telephone surveys entirely, especially given falling response rates and the growing number of households without landline phones but using cell phones exclusively.

Critics of internet surveys contend that the samples may still be biased by not including enough respondents from groups that are more likely to be offline, especially non-English speakers, Latinos, the elderly, and the poor. Online surveys may include more respondents who are interested in politics than the normal population. Proponents contend that minorities and the poor are increasingly online, even via mobile access, and that the samples are representative of the American population. Because online surveys from sites such as YouGov have proved to be more accurate in forecasting elections than many telephone surveys relying on cell phones and landlines, online surveys are likely here to stay.[92]

In contrast to online surveys, with more than 60 years' experience studying American public opinion, the American National Election Studies (ANES) is the premier broad general survey. The ANES traditionally has conducted surveys using face-to-face interviews, but because interviewing respondents in person is very costly, the ANES increasingly conducts online surveys as well. The ANES is considered the gold standard for political survey research because of its accuracy, design and question wording.

Telephone and online surveys increasingly embed experimental techniques within the design, in which one group of respondents is given a treatment, or unique question wording, and responses are compared with a control group of respondents that does not receive the treatment. The researcher is interested in the difference in responses between the treatment and control group. Experiments are one of the most rigorous methods for detecting causal relationships. During Obama's 2012 presidential campaign, for example, mobilizers found that if they asked individuals to list everything in their daily schedule, and state the time of day they planned to vote within that schedule, the individual was more likely to actually vote, compared to individuals who were simply asked to vote for the candidate. In another survey framing experiment, individuals in one group were exposed to a frame arguing that affirmative action is necessary to correct past discrimination, while those in a second group received a competing frame arguing that affirmative action gives African Americans special treatment. Not surprisingly, those in the first group showed greater support for affirmative action than did those in the second group for the same policies. By using a treatment and control group design, framing experiments provide more leverage in assessing cause and effect in measuring changes in public opinion. Framing experiments are an important way to understand how public opinion changes in response to political elites and the mass media.

WHEN POLLS ARE WRONG

The history of polling over the past century contains many instances of getting it wrong and learning valuable lessons in the process. As a result, polling techniques have grown more and more sophisticated, and pollsters have a more nuanced understanding of how public opinion is formed and how it is revealed. Polls are best understood as best guesses of a political outcome but not a prediction of fact. The 2016 election provides a recent example of inaccurate polling: the vast majority of opinion polls leading up to the election predicted that Hillary Clinton would win by a landslide.

social desirability effect the effect that results when respondents in a survey report what they expect the interviewer wishes to hear rather than what they believe

Social Desirability Effects Political scientists have found that survey results can be inaccurate when the surveys include questions about sensitive issues for which individuals do not wish to share their true preferences. For example, respondents tend to overreport voting in elections and the frequency of their church attendance because these activities are deemed socially appropriate. Political scientists call this the **social desirability effect**, whereby respondents report what they expect the interviewer wishes to hear or whatever they think is socially acceptable, rather than what they actually believe or know to be true.[93] On other topics, such as questions about income or alcohol and drug use, respondents may feel self-conscious and choose not to answer.

Given the failure of public opinion polls to predict the outcome of the 2016 election, many people question if polls systematically underreported support for Trump and his policies. Explanations for why Trump performed better at the ballot box than in the polls include that Trump did better in polls of voters (either registered or likely voters) than in polls of all adults, and he also performed better in polls conducted online or by automated script surveys with a live-telephone caller. This latter finding may be the result of the social desirability effect. Because Trump is a polarizing and controversial figure, some people may have been reluctant to tell an interviewer they support Trump or his policies; online surveys may allow respondents to reveal their true preferences without facing social pressure to conform.

Pew studied if telephone surveys were systematically underestimating public support for Trump. The researchers compared public support for the president's agenda using telephone surveys with live interviewers to online public support for his agenda using surveys. They expected the online surveys to show higher support for the president and his policies, because self-administered online surveys should reduce respondents' reluctance to reveal their true preferences. The study found little statistical difference in evaluations of Trump or his policies when varying the mode of the interview from online to telephone.[94] The fact that Clinton won 3 million more votes than Trump may be evidence that the 2016 election polls were partially right after all.

Questions that ask directly about race or gender are particularly problematic. Social desirability makes it difficult to learn voters' true opinions about touchy subjects such as racial attitudes because respondents hide their preferences from the interviewer for fear of social retribution (against what might be deemed "politically incorrect" opinions). For example, researchers have found respondents in surveys didn't want to admit that they opposed school integration and would not vote for the black candidate and, therefore, abstained from answering the question. Measuring public opinion can be a challenge; measuring opinions incorrectly can bias the findings. However, surveys using experiments can be designed to tap respondents' latent or hidden feelings about sensitive issues without directly asking them to express overt opinions.

Selection Bias The importance of accurate sampling was brought home early in the history of political polling. A 1936 *Literary Digest* poll predicted that the Republican candidate, Alf Landon, would defeat the Democratic incumbent, Franklin Roosevelt, in that year's presidential election. The actual election ended in a Roosevelt landslide. The main problem with the survey was what is called **selection bias** in drawing the sample. The pollsters had relied on telephone directories and automobile registration rosters to produce the survey sample. During the Great Depression, though, only wealthier Americans owned telephones and automobiles. Thus, the millions of working-class Americans who constituted Roosevelt's base of support were excluded from the sample.

selection bias polling error that arises when the sample is not representative of the population being studied, which creates errors in overrepresenting or underrepresenting some opinions

Selection bias was also at play in preelection polls in the 2012 presidential election, when Gallup significantly overestimated Latino support for the Republican candidate, suggesting a close race between the Republican candidate, Mitt Romney, and the Democratic candidate, Barack Obama. The Gallup numbers were incorrect because of selection bias (that is, they had too few Latinos in their sample and therefore their predictions were inaccurate). Estimates based on aggregating information from many different statewide public opinion polls were more accurate.[95]

As discussed, in the 2016 presidential election, although most polls predicted the direction of the popular vote correctly in Hillary Clinton's favor, they failed

Though public opinion is important, it is not always easy to interpret, and polls often fail to predict how Americans will vote. In 1948 election-night polls showed Thomas Dewey defeating Harry S. Truman for the presidency, which caused the *Chicago Daily Tribune* to incorrectly print a banner announcing Dewey's win. In 2016 polls considerably favored Hillary Clinton over Donald Trump, causing many to doubt the possibility of Trump winning the election.

FIGURE 6.8

Accuracy of Final Preelection Polls, 2016

A large number of news organizations conducted polls to predict the outcome of the 2016 election. For how many of these polls was the actual result within their margin of error, assuming a sample size of 1,000 and a margin of error of plus or minus 3.1 percent? What might explain why some respected organizations, like Pew and Politico, were so far off the mark?

SOURCES: All poll data, except LA Times/USC, from HuffPost Pollster, www.elections.huffingtonpost.com/pollster (accessed 11/10/16). Poll results are from the most recent polls prior to election day in the database. USC/LATimes data from www.cesrusc.org/election/ (accessed 11/11/16). Popular vote margin data from "CNN 2016 Election Results," www.cnn.com/election/results (accessed 11/11/16).

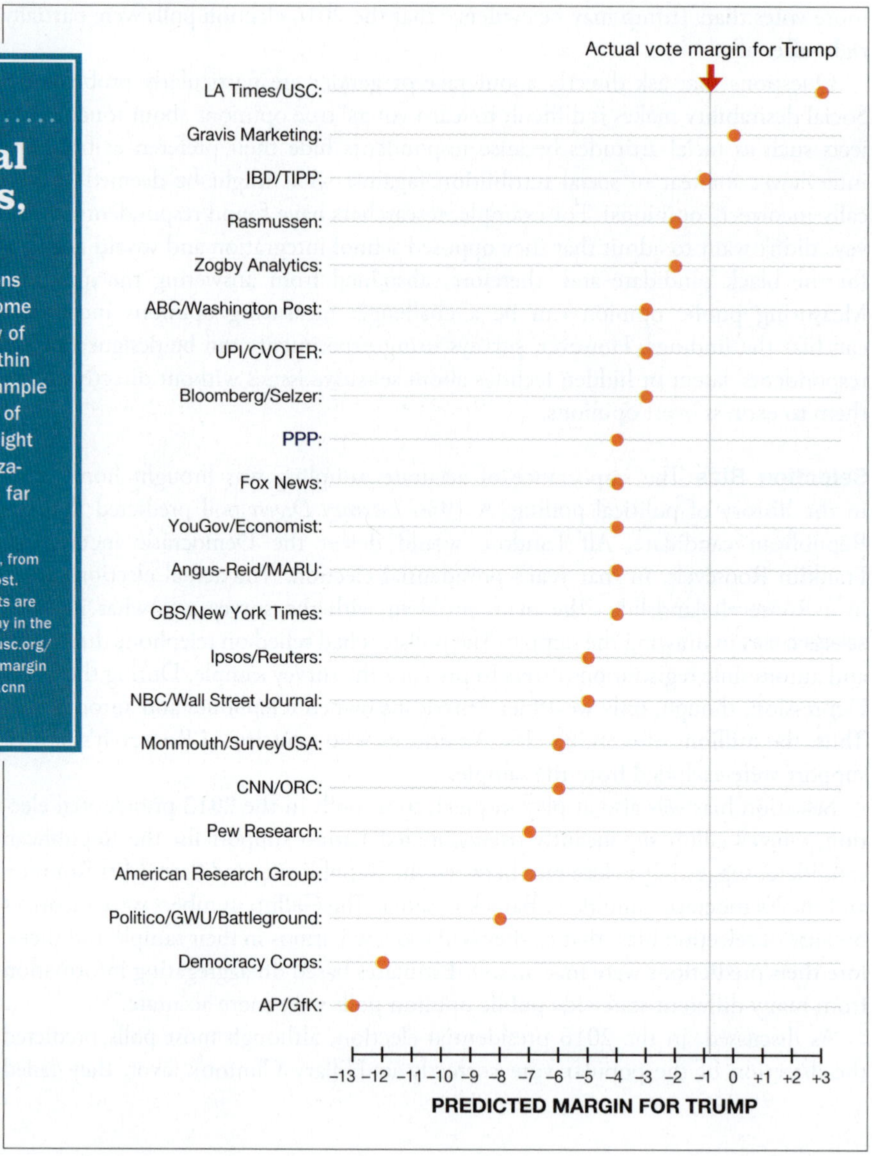

to predict the size of the vote margin and the election outcome (see Figure 6.8). Other possible explanations for the polling inaccuracies included the use of "likely voter models," which left out some groups that ended up voting at higher-than-usual rates, such as rural, non-college educated, blue-collar voters who supported Trump in large numbers. Trump called these voters the "silent majority." Selection bias may have been at play in why the polls failed to predict the 2016 election outcome. Nonresponse bias may have also occurred, where Trump supporters were less likely to respond to surveys.

The *LA Times*/USC survey accurately predicted a Trump win, relying on a different methodology than the others. It used rolling panel surveys, where the same individuals were interviewed repeatedly over time. Panel surveys have a stronger internal research design, where the researcher can measure opinion change for the same sample of individuals. Scholars increasingly recognize that measuring change over time is the key to accurately measuring public opinion.

In recent years, the issue of selection bias has been complicated by the fact that growing numbers of individuals refuse to answer pollsters' questions, or they use voice mail or caller ID to screen unwanted callers. If pollsters could be certain that those who responded to their surveys simply reflected the views of those who refused to respond, there would be no problem. Some studies, however, suggest that the views of respondents and nonrespondents can differ, especially along social class lines. This can lead to incorrect inferences of public opinion.

Push Polling **Push polls** are not scientific polls and are not intended to yield accurate information about a population. Instead, they involve asking a respondent a loaded question about a political candidate designed to elicit the response sought by the pollster and, simultaneously, to shape the respondent's perception of the candidate in question. One of the most notorious uses of push polling occurred in the 2000 South Carolina Republican presidential primary, in which George W. Bush defeated John McCain and went on to win the presidency. Callers working for Bush supporters asked conservative white voters if they would be more or less likely to vote for McCain if they knew he had fathered an illegitimate black child (a false statement).

push poll a polling technique in which the questions are designed to shape the respondent's opinion

The Bandwagon Effect Public-opinion polls can influence political realities and elections. In fact, sometimes polling can even create its own reality. The so-called **bandwagon effect** occurs when polling results convince people to support a candidate marked as the probable victor. This is especially true in the presidential nomination process, where there may be multiple candidates within one party vying to be the party's nominee. Researchers found that the change in national media coverage received by a candidate before and after the Iowa caucuses, the first nominating event, was a major predictor of how well the candidate would do in the New Hampshire primary (the second nominating event) and in presidential primaries nationwide, controlling for other factors including money and standing in the polls.[96] A candidate who has "momentum"—that is, one leading in the polls—usually finds it considerably easier to raise campaign funds than a candidate whose poll standing is poor. Wanting to highlight the momentum he felt he had, Trump frequently cited his lead in the polls during the 2016 presidential primaries and general election to mobilize his base.

bandwagon effect a shift in electoral support to the candidate whom public opinion polls report as the front-runner

BIG DATA, POLLING AGGREGATORS, AND MEASURING PUBLIC OPINION

Computational data analysis and social media have opened new ways to measure mass opinion. Some of the most fundamental questions about politics and public opinion are now being measured not with surveys but in terms of actual behavior online, including Google searches. Big data refers to data sets that are so large and complex that they require advanced analytics, rather than traditional methods, to reveal insights on a massive scale. Journalist Sasha Issenberg shows how big data played a critical role in Obama's presidential election campaigns. By analyzing Netflix movie queues, for example, campaign consultants were able to investigate concern for global warming based on the titles a person puts into her rental queue, even if she does not actually end up watching the film. Opinions about a wide range of

FOR CRITICAL ANALYSIS

Is it important that public-opinion polls be accurate? How might polls fail to be accurate? What are the consequences if polls are systematically inaccurate?

policy issues could be gleaned from the aggregate preferences of millions of movie viewers. This type of analysis is called *data mining*.[97]

Twitter, the preferred medium of candidates and political elites, introduces another way to measure public opinion and agenda setting using text analysis. One study analyzed the number of Twitter followers for the 2016 presidential candidates and tracked changes over time, as well as tracked mentions of any of the candidates based on millions of tweets.[98] A candidate's lead in positive Twitter coverage may be more important to winning the White House than a lead in traditional public-opinion polls. Coding large amounts of Twitter data can also be valuable for measuring phenomena that are difficult or impossible to measure with standard telephone surveys, such as the use of racial slurs.

Rather than rely on surveys to measure the opinions of U.S. citizens, researchers are now using Google search data. An example is public response in Flint, Michigan, and the surrounding communities when the city's water supply was found to be contaminated by lead. The Flint drinking water disaster exposed roughly 100,000 residents to harmful contaminants, requiring residents to drink filtered or bottled water. Local residents used online search engines as way to follow the news and understand the health problems from drinking contaminated water. Pew Research Center analyzed 18 months of Google search data to track public interest in the Flint water contamination crisis. The study covered events including boiling-water advisories from bacteria, reports of elevated lead levels in children's blood and tap water samples, bottled-water distribution, emergency warnings, and criminal charges. The data based on 2,700 different search terms reveals that residents of Flint were searching for information about their water long before the government recognized the contamination and before the media drew national attention to the problem. Similarly, Google search data has been able to predict local flu outbreaks based on search terms of symptoms (fever, etc.) considerably earlier than the Centers for Disease Control (CDC) declares a flu outbreak in a local area.[99]

Beyond Twitter, big data are playing a role in election forecasting, predictive analytics, and measuring public opinion. For example, polling aggregators can be used to track public opinion more accurately. Blogger Nate Silver became an overnight sensation in 2008 by aggregating thousands of public-opinion polls conducted in each of the 50 states to predict the winner of the presidential election state by state more accurately than any single polling house—a feat he repeated in 2012 (though he was often incorrect in predicting the winner in the tumultuous 2016 primaries).[100]

Silver and FiveThirtyEight.com also use statistics to average thousands of public opinion polls overtime to create a more accurate estimate of presidential approval than any one single poll. The thousands of polls they draw from are weighted based on their sample size, methodological rigor, and past accuracy—polls that historically have been more accurate count more.[101] Five months after his victory in the 2016 election, Trump had the lowest approval ratings of any president in modern history during the first 150 days in office.

The Democratic Party and the Republican Party now use a database of 240 million Americans, including a wide range of data from voting history and party registration, social media, consumer purchasing patterns, and so on. Using big data and data mining, researchers can predict factors that make a person more likely to vote in the first place and whether he will cast a vote for the Republican or Democratic candidate. Data mining has been used for years in business, marketing, and economics but is growing in importance in campaigns, elections, and policy. The study of politics has been on the forefront of this big data revolution with sophisticated analyses of massive amounts of data including text scraping and text analysis of social media. These are just a few examples of how very large sample data—millions and millions of data points—are changing how we measure public opinion in the digital age.

Public Opinion and Democracy
WHAT DO WE WANT?

This chapter has focused on the role of public opinion in American politics. A major purpose of democratic government, with its participatory procedures and representative institutions, is to ensure that political leaders will heed the public will. And, indeed, a good deal of evidence suggests that they do. There are many instances in which public policy and public opinion do not coincide, but often the government's actions are consistent with citizens' preferences, at least in the most general sense.[102]

However, it is not always clear what the public will is. Mass shootings heighten the preferences of supporters of both gun control and gun rights. *Whose* preferences prevail when attitudes differ among groups? Or when they differ between the public and elites? Or between the affluent and the poor? Some political scientists argue that government policy is much less responsive to public opinion on the issues that really count and that when the interests of elites are at stake, government officials are much more likely to represent the opinions of the affluent than the poor.[103] People in lower income groups, moreover, are less likely to actively seek out ways to express their political opinions than are wealthier people (see the "**Who Participates?**" feature on p. 249).

New technology may be able to help. The migration of politics online has greatly expanded the amount of information available and the ease of becoming informed. And as we will see in Chapter 7, online media are more diverse than traditional media. Given this new media environment, we might expect public opinion to be more accurate, even about the nuances of public policy. Digital citizenship offers the promise of a more informed electorate, with citizens having multiple venues in which to translate their opinions into political action and demand improved representation from political leaders. The use of social media by students from the Marjory Stoneman Douglas High School to argue for greater gun regulations shows digital citizenship in action.

At the same time, the internet raises new concerns about the accuracy and consistency of public opinion and whether people hold opinions that depart from facts and the truth. As Chapter 7 will show, Americans may become trapped in a "filter bubble" in which they are exposed only to news consistent with their political preferences. There are internet vandals, or "bomb throwers," who defame other people and their opinions in ways that may negatively color public opinion. Misinformation—rumor masked as legitimate news—may be more common, especially in blogs or social media sites. Some research finds that the gap between the haves and the have-nots in terms of political knowledge actually increases with the availability of more information. The implications are significant, given the explosion of political coverage online. The research suggests that with more information, public opinion may actually be less consistent.[104]

Social media may be reshaping what is public opinion. The effects of new media—vast and still unfolding—include the wide dissemination of public-opinion polls and the rise of internet polling. Do new media make public opinion more or less important? Do they make elected officials more or less responsive to the citizens? Time will tell.

Who Expresses Their Political Opinions?

By income group

● < $20,000 ● $20,000–$39,999 ● $40,000–$74,999 ● $75,000+

Attended a town or city council meeting

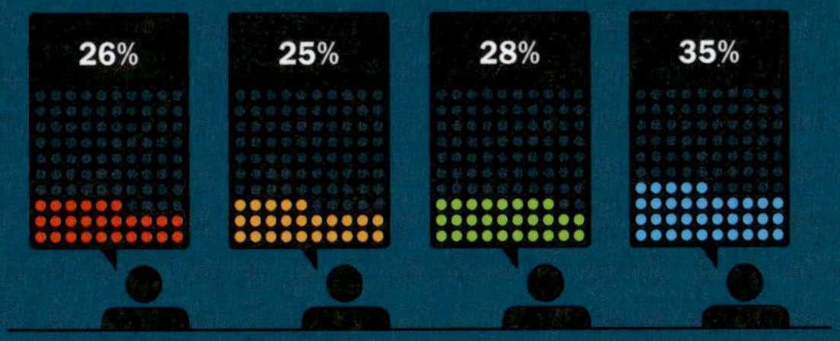

26% 25% 28% 35%

Signed a petition

19% 24% 24% 28%

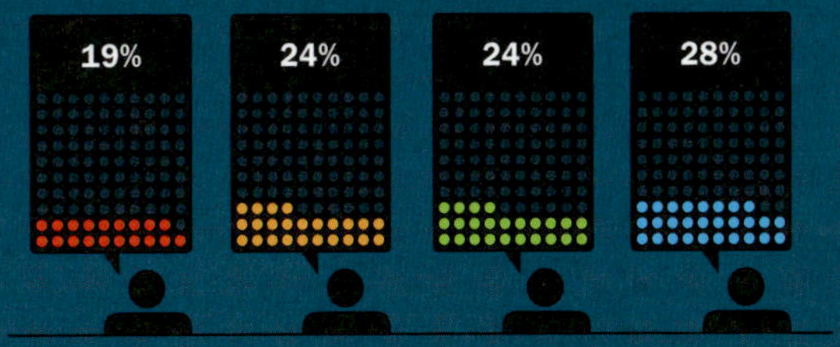

Attended a protest march

4% 4% 4% 3%

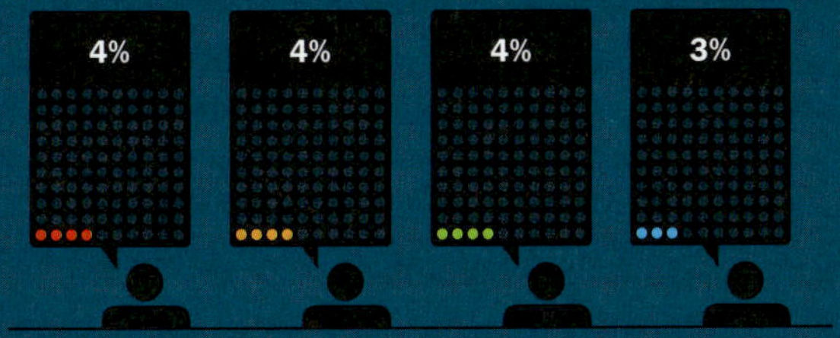

Tried to contact a member of Congress

7% 9% 10% 15%

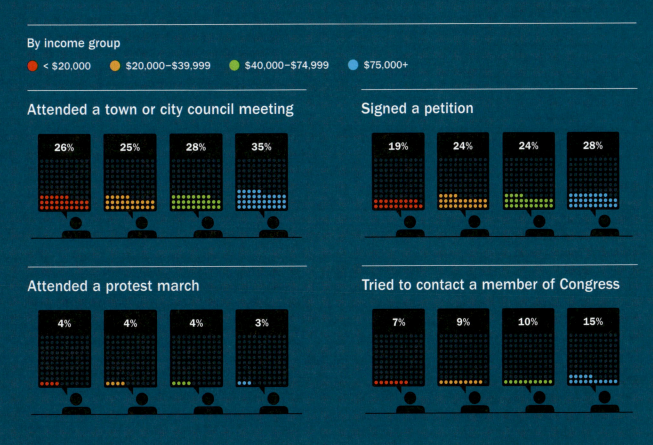

SOURCE: American National Election Study 2016 time series, www.electionstudies.org (accessed 11/4/17).

★ WHAT YOU CAN DO ★

Be an Informed Consumer of Opinion Polls

 When you encounter information from opinion polls, consider the source of the poll, the wording of the questions, and whether individuals were randomly selected to participate. Learn more at **www.umich.edu/~numbers/polls**.

 Go to **www.realclearpolitics.com** to see polls about the same issues from different sources. Note the margins of error, and notice how aggregating polls makes a difference.

 If asked, consider responding to an opinion poll—or take the initiative and express your views through one of the actions above.

condition for both liberty and democratic politics. Today, as the means of communication has expanded, the media continue to play a central role in American politics, not only in setting the agenda of topics that Americans think about and discuss but also in shaping public opinion on political issues and politicians. The political implications of this media system are significant. Politics is increasingly defined by the individuals and groups who are best able to blend older and newer media—using, for example, both television and digital media to promote their message.

Discussing the right of press freedom, Thomas Jefferson wrote, "The basis of our government being the opinion of the people, the very first object should be to keep that right; and were it left to me to decide whether we should have a government without newspapers or newspapers without a government, I should not hesitate a moment to prefer the latter."[4] As the nature of media has evolved, its centrality to government and politics has never waned. In fact, in an era when politicians accuse each other and media members of promoting "fake news," and people fight for or against control of internet communications, a full understanding of America's dynamic media landscape may be more important than ever.

CHAPTER GOALS

- ★ **Describe the key roles the media play in American political life (pp. 257–60)**
- ★ **Discuss how digital media have transformed how citizens learn about politics (pp. 261–77)**
- ★ **Analyze the ways the media can influence public opinion and politics (pp. 277–82)**
- ★ **Explain how politicians and others try to shape the news (pp. 283–85)**
- ★ **Trace the evolution of rules that govern broadcast media (pp. 285–87)**

The Media in American Democracy

Describe the key roles the media play in American political life

Freedom of the press is protected under the First Amendment to the U.S. Constitution, along with the most cherished individual rights in American democracy, including freedom of speech and religion. Freedom of the press is the right to circulate opinions in print and digital media without censorship by the government. In the United States, citizens and private companies have the right to publish newspapers, magazines, and other forms of digital media with few government restrictions. In many authoritarian countries there is no freedom of the press and the government controls the news and political information through state-sponsored media.

Why would the Founders care so much about the rights of the media to report the news without interference from government? In the 1700s, when they were still under British control, freedom of speech did not exist in the American colonies. Criticizing the King of England was a crime punishable, in some cases, by death. When the colonists won their freedom from England they wanted to be able to freely express their political opinions without fear of retaliation. The first of 10 amendments to the U.S. Constitution adopted during the Founding period states, "Congress shall make no law respecting an establishment of religion, or prohibiting the free exercise thereof; or abridging the freedom of speech, or of the press; or the right of the people peaceably to assemble, and to petition the Government for a redress of grievances." Despite attacks from both Republicans and Democrats that claim major media outlets are biased, most Americans believe freedom of the press is very important for maintaining a strong democracy, and that "news organizations are free to criticize political leaders" (see Figure 6.1 in Chapter 6).

The **media** serve three important roles in American democracy: helping to inform the public about current political issues and events; providing a forum through which candidates, politicians, and even the public can debate policies and issues; and acting as a watchdog on the actions of politicians and other political actors. Part of the media's role of informing the public involves providing a variety of perspectives on current events and fact-checking sources to provide unbiased coverage of current events. The media serve as a type of public square where citizens become informed about their government, political leaders, societal problems, and possible solutions—a forum where information necessary for democracy is exchanged.

media print and digital forms of communication, including television, newspapers, radio, and the internet, intended to convey information to large audiences

Without the work of journalists and the media, democracy and self-government would not be possible. The news media are how individuals learn about politics and current events, government policy, candidates, and political parties. The information presented by the media allows citizens to cast informed decisions in elections and to form opinions about policy issues. American philosopher John Dewey believed the media served to educate the public. A strong democracy, he said, was based not only on voting rights, but ensuring that public opinion on current issues is based on communication among citizens, experts, and elected officials. This communication ensures elected officials adopt policies consistent, for the most part, with the preferences of the citizens and serves as a counterweight to communication among elites, the wealthy, and corporations. In other words, the mass media help level the playing field between political elites and "the people," giving citizens a more potent voice in society. Without the media, citizens would not know the actions of political

One of the media's role in American democracy is that of a watchdog, investigating and highlighting alleged and actual wrongdoing by public officials. Recently, the media have exposed episodes of alleged sexual misconduct by several politicians including Senator Al Franken (D-Minn.), senatorial candidate Roy Moore (R-Ala.), and Donald Trump.

leaders, corporations, or foreign governments and would be powerless to change the system. Journalists (people trained to report the news) give ordinary citizens information and knowledge, and this information is ultimately power.

Finally, the media serve as a watchdog for the public, scrutinizing the actions of elected officials on behalf of citizens—most of whom do not have the opportunity to closely follow the actions of politicians and government. Like an alarm system for a home, the media notify the public of actions taken by government that may harm them.

The watchdog role of the media is the most important for the study of politics. Political news is reported on page 1 of print newspapers or in news alerts on your cell phone. The media inform the public about what policy issues are at stake in terms of changes in government laws and regulations. The media seek to expose which individuals and groups are exerting power in politics and what are their tactics and strategies, and sheds light on the different perspectives being used by political actors (e.g., the arguments for and against building a wall between the United States and Mexico, a major federal tax cut or raise, or adopting a law to create free college tuition). The media often expose how financial interests are tied to political leaders and policy making, or scandalous behavior of politicians and other public figures, like allegations of sexual assault against Republican senatorial candidate Roy Moore or Democratic senator Al Franken (Minn.). By reporting the news in the public interest the media continuously monitor the actions of public officials in its surveillance mode and strives to protect the public from government overreach and corruption by serving as a check on political power.

Informing the public, creating a forum for debate, and keeping a watchful eye on government action are critical components to democracy. And it seems like a lot to ask of the media. Do the media meet these goals?

JOURNALISM

Most practicing journalists receive training in schools of journalism and mass communication. Journalists are guided by standards in reporting the news in the public interest, known as the principles of journalism. Above all the news media seek to report the truth via fact-checking, verification of sources, and investigative journalism (defined in more detail later). This includes reporting factual claims by relying on legitimate sources and citing people with credible positions, eyewitnesses and participants in events, and documents associated with recognizable and credible institutions. The traditional news media aim to balance coverage of current events by providing objective treatment of opposing sides, and it avoids including personal views of reporters or editors. While reporting the news without any bias—objectivity—is ultimately unattainable because all individuals have biases that influence how they understand events, objectivity is a method used by journalists to report both sides of a story.

THE PROFIT MOTIVE

The media are sometimes referred to as the fourth branch of government, providing a check on the power of government and political leaders. But who checks or controls the media? In the United States the media are not part of government and not subject to checks and balances like Congress, the presidency, and the courts. Instead most media in the United States are privately owned companies. Media companies, like technology companies such as Verizon, Amazon, or Apple, are for-profit corporations.

Public broadcasting refers to television, radio, and digital media that receive funding from the public through license fees, subsidies, or tax dollars. In most other democratic countries public broadcasting plays a major role in informing the public about politics and current events. In contrast, public broadcasting in the United States—such as National Public Radio or PBS—plays a very small role in the media system, at just 2 percent of market share, compared to 35 percent in France, 40 percent in Germany, and 65 percent in Denmark. What is unique about the media in the United States is that most are entirely privately owned and operated. There is evidence from cross-national surveys that U.S. citizens have lower levels of political knowledge than those in European democracies who consume more public broadcasting.[5]

Because of the U.S. media's profit motive, they tend to focus on highly conflictual political events like presidential debates and less on the subtle details of changes in public policy.

Public media usually come with greater restrictions. Swiss law, for example, prohibits political campaign ads on radio and TV programs; they are only allowed in newspapers. In France, the media are prohibited from covering news about candidates running for public office the last few days before the election. American media face many fewer government regulations, as will be discussed later in this chapter.

U.S. media companies earn most of their revenue from advertising, rather than subscriptions, although revenue from subscriptions has been increasing. This means media actors—from journalists to editors to the owners of the media companies—are motivated by what audiences want, because higher ratings generate more advertising revenue. Because of the need to reach wide audiences to sell advertisements, the U.S. media are more focused on soft news, such as entertainment, sports, and celebrity news, than are European media, which provide more hard news coverage of politics and civic events. And when it comes to political news, American media tend to focus increasingly on more dramatic, highly conflictual events and issues. Sensational stories of scandals or candidate attacks often generate more interest—and thus revenue—than the stories of everyday governing and details of public policy. Nonetheless, objectivity is still the goal, and standard practice is that news, opinion, and ads should be separate and distinct; that is why the opinions of editors are reserved for the opinion pages.

The profit motive of the news industry may have contributed to Donald Trump's unexpected victory in the 2016 election. Due to the novelty of a television celebrity running for president, Trump's campaign was a financial boon for the media industry. His candidacy received double the media coverage of his Democratic opponent, Hillary Clinton, and his Republican challengers in the primaries. The head of CBS, Les Moonves, said the Trump phenomena "may not be good for America, but it's damn good for CBS..."[6] Throughout the election and Trump's first year in office, the cable news channels profited from higher ratings because of the public's fascination with Trump; CNN, for example, earned about $100 million in television and advertising revenue more than expected in 2016.[7] Newspapers and digital news outlets found that if the word *Trump* was mentioned in a title, it was more likely to be read and shared online.

MASS MEDIA OWNERSHIP

One noteworthy feature of the traditional media in the United States is the concentration of its ownership. A small number of giant corporations control a wide swath of media holdings, including television networks, movie studios, record companies, cable channels and local cable providers, book publishers, magazines, newspapers, and increasingly, online and digital media outlets. Large global corporations own much of the media offline and online.[8] **Media monopolies**, such as Disney, have prompted questions about whether enough competition exists among traditional media to produce a truly diverse set of views on political matters.[9] In 2019, for example, Disney purchased 21st Century Fox to become the third largest media company in the United States. As major newspapers, television stations, and radio networks fall into fewer hands, the risk increases that politicians and citizens who express less popular or minority viewpoints will have difficulty finding a public forum.

media monopoly the ownership and control of the media by a few large corporations

FOR CRITICAL ANALYSIS

In recent years, a number of major media corporations have acquired numerous newspapers, television stations, and radio properties. Is media concentration a serious problem? Why or why not?

Despite the appearance of substantial numbers overall, the number of traditional news-gathering sources operating nationally is actually quite small—several wire services, four broadcast networks, a few elite print newspapers, and a smattering of other sources, such as a few large local papers and several small, independent radio networks. More than three-fourths of the daily print newspapers in the United States are owned by large media conglomerates such as the Hearst, McClatchy, and Gannett corporations. Much of the national news that is published by local newspapers is provided by one wire service, the Associated Press. More than 500 of the nation's television stations are affiliated with one of just four networks and carry that network's evening news programs.

The trend in concentration of traditional media ownership occurred in large part due to the relaxation of government regulations in the 1980s and '90s. The enactment of the 1996 Telecommunications Act opened the way for additional consolidation in the media industry, and a wave of mergers and consolidations has further reduced the field of independent media across the country. But as more digital-only news sources come online, these trends toward concentration in media ownership may reverse.

The Media Today

Discuss how digital media have transformed how citizens learn about politics

The past three decades have resulted in a massive transformation of the U.S. news media. New competition from free digital sources has put pressure on traditional subscription-based news sources as Americans migrated to reading the news online. Today 93 percent of adults read the news online.[10] This picture is very different from the early 2000s, when most Americans said that after television, print newspapers were their main source for news and less than 20 percent read the news online (see Figure 7.1).[11] Though not replacing losses in subscription and traditional advertising revenue, digital advertising revenue continues to grow.[12]

Despite the digital transformation of the news media, much of what makes the media important in American politics remains the same. Major newspapers and TV networks—even if their content is increasingly delivered in digital form—remain popular and important sources of news. Political leaders are successful in making headline news and setting the news agenda. And journalists trained in professional schools create and develop much of what we consume as news, including original reporting.

But more and more, the media are online companies facing an environment where anyone with access to an internet connection can publish the news. It is still only a small number of organizations that have credibility and the largest audiences, however;[13] the leading newspapers in the United States, such as the *New York Times*, the *Wall Street Journal*, and the *Washington Post*, receive some of the highest traffic online. Nevertheless, the digital transformation of the media has created a reorganization of the media industry that impacts how the news is made and how consumers learn about politics.

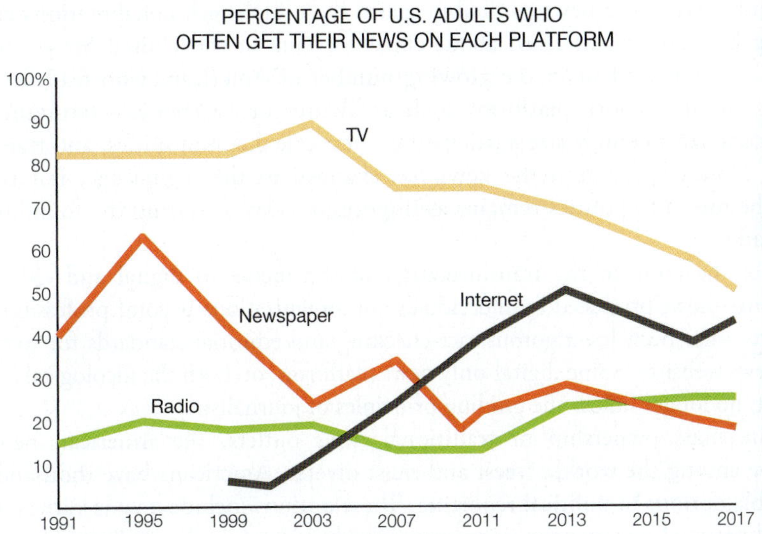

FIGURE 7.1

Use of Online News Continues to Grow

The media landscape for news has seen remarkable shifts in a short period of time. Twenty years ago, more than 80 percent of Americans watched news on television and more than half read news in a newspaper. Today, fewer Americans watch news on TV and just over one-quarter read the newspaper. What media source has gained rather than lost its audience?

SOURCE: "Americans' Online News Use Is Closing in on TV News Use," Pew Research Center, September 5, 2017, www.pewresearch.org (accessed 5/23/18).

Two trends in media have been the consolidation of media outlets into large conglomerates and the growing influence of technology on media. Founded by Rupert Murdoch (left), News Corp is a media conglomerate that has owned Fox News and the *Wall Street Journal*, among other news outlets. Since he acquired the *Washington Post*, Amazon's Jeff Bezos (right) has deepened the paper's focus on investigative journalism, which some say has made the *Post* profitable again.

Before the internet, journalism organizations largely controlled the news, including original reporting, writing and production, packaging and delivery, and selecting editors. Over time, technology companies like Facebook, Apple, Google, and Amazon have become major players in the content and delivery of the news. These companies are partners in the business of journalism from the financial side to how the news is produced and delivered to consumers. They report the news using advanced technology, engineering, and market research to push specific news alerts to specific people, based on their interests and preferences. And it seems to be working: Facebook and Google, for example, generate the most digital advertising revenue for newspapers.[14]

The interdependence between technology and media companies continues to grow. In one of the latest trends, technology companies and their CEOs have been purchasing or developing major news media companies, such as the creation of the *Intercept* by Ebay founder Pierre Omidyar, or the purchase of the *Washington Post* by Amazon CEO Jeff Bezos. Both the *Intercept* and *Washington Post* have a reputation for forceful investigative journalism and original reporting. And Facebook editors control trending topics in the news on the global platform, a key editorial role in what makes the headline news.

Beyond making the news profitable again, these high-tech collaborations are changing how Americans learn about current events in the United States and globally.[15] This is evident in the growing number of Americans who read news by using social network platforms such as Twitter or Facebook—community forums designed to emphasize participation, networked communities, and transparency. How citizens read the news has changed in the digital age, but the role of the media in politics remains as important today as during the founding of our nation.

One of the costs of the transformation of the media to digital and citizen journalism—news produced by individuals and organizations beyond professional journalists—has been less rigorous fact-checking and editorial standards for some online news websites. Some digital-only news platforms, on both the ideological left and right, no longer follow the guiding principles of journalism.

Despite mass ownership of traditional news outlets, the American news media are among the world's freest and most diverse. Americans have thousands of available options in political reporting. These options include a wide variety of local and national newspapers, newsmagazines, broadcast media, radio, podcasts, and digital sources. The freedom to speak one's mind is one of the most cherished of American political values. Without the news media's investigations, citizens would be forced to rely entirely on information provided by politicians and the government, and would be deprived of information necessary to evaluate issues carefully and form reasoned opinions. Americans get their news from (1) newspapers and magazines; (2) broadcast media (radio and television); and increasingly, (3) digital media. Each of these three sources—newspapers, broadcast, and digital—has distinctive characteristics.

NEWSPAPERS

Newspapers are the oldest medium for the dissemination of the news, though most Americans read digital versions of print media today. Newspapers have an especially influential audience because they help set the political agenda for the nation. Their audience of political elites relies on the detailed coverage provided by professional journalists to inform their views about public matters.

The emergence of newspapers (and later radio and television networks) as mass-production businesses driven primarily for profit had major implications for the role of the media in politics in the late nineteenth and early twentieth centuries. The development of standardized reporting and writing practices emphasizing objectivity in political news coverage was due in large part to generate revenue for media organizations. The owners of large newspaper companies determined that the best way to make a profit was to appeal to as broad an audience as possible, which meant not alienating potential readers who held liberal or conservative political views. This, in turn, required methods to train and "discipline" reporters to produce a standardized, seemingly neutral news product. In contrast, some native digital news is less likely than like journalism from legacy media outlets to be value neutral.

These journalistic practices were successful in attracting audiences, and for a long time most cities and towns in the country had their own newspaper. However, for most traditional newspapers, recent decades have been financially challenging. Competition from broadcast media and free content online, combined with simultaneous declines in advertising revenue and circulation levels, have undermined the traditional business model of newspapers.[16] In 2018 there were roughly 39,210 working journalists, down from a high of 60,000 a decade before.[17] Estimates indicate daily newspaper print circulation has declined by over 30 percent over the past 20 years.[18] And lower circulation leads to lower advertising revenue.

Following the 2016 election, however, some major U.S. newspapers reported a sharp increase in digital subscriptions.[19] The *New York Times* added more than 500,000 digital subscriptions in 2016—a 47 percent increase from the previous year, while the *Wall Street Journal* had a 23 percent increase over the previous year, and the *Chicago Tribune* a 76 percent increase. The newspaper industry as a whole, however, continues to face declines in circulation and ad revenue. The *New York Times* saw a 9 percent decline in advertising revenue but a 3 percent rise in circulation revenue, for an overall revenue decline of 2 percent in 2016.[20]

The *Washington Post*, in contrast, may be a model for making the news media profitable. The *Post* is a private company owned by Amazon CEO Jeff Bezos. While revenues for most newspapers continued to decline (see Figure 7.2), the *Post* experienced double-digit revenue growth for three straight years. Along with a viable financial model, the *Post* has emerged as a leader in investigative reporting, data analytics, and marketing. Bezos rebuilt the *Post* into a media technology company,

The circulation and newsstand sales of traditional newspapers and news magazines have fallen in the last decade. However, because the remaining audience includes political elites and politically engages citizens, they remain important forums in the marketplace of ideas.

FIGURE 7.2

Advertising Revenue

Media is a business, not a branch of government, so media rely on subscription and advertising money to fund their services. As print newspapers' readership declined, their advertising revenue fell sharply. Some of this money shifted to online advertising, including ads for mobile devices.

SOURCE: Newspaper Association of America (2003–2013), Pew Research analysis of BIA/Kelsey data (2014), www.journalism.org/media-indicators/newspaper-print-and-online-ad-revenue/ (accessed 2/3/17).

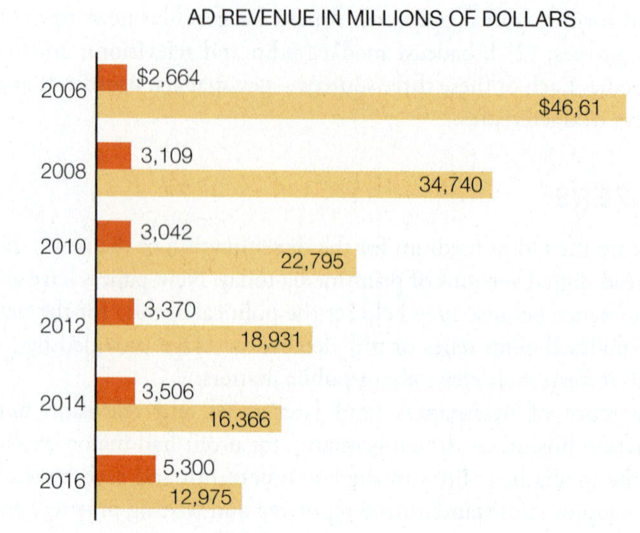

producing 1,200 articles per day, an exploding readership, and dynamic digital content. The paper's content-distribution uses social media like Facebook and Twitter, offers discounts to Amazon Prime members, and the *Post* app is preinstalled on Amazon's Fire tablets. The *Post* now tracks how different headlines and story framings affect readership of each story. One of the three major newspapers in the United States, the 140-year-old *Washington Post* is known for investigative reporting and for breaking the story that revealed the Watergate scandal in 1970 that led to the impeachment and removal from office of President Nixon. Today the *Post* focuses on adversarial journalism of the Trump Administration and extensive reporting of Russian interference in U.S. elections.[21]

News organizations such as the *Washington Post*, the *New York Times*, and the *Economist* were among the first to charge customers for reading the news online. For most newspapers today, non-ad revenue comes mainly from digital subscriptions rather than print circulation. This model allows a certain number of free visits before requiring users to pay and appears to be a viable business model for the digital press. Elite newspapers have been able to create a viable business model whereby people will pay digital subscriptions to access content, and paid digital news is increasing revenue and improving content. Digital subscription models have not been as viable for many smaller or mid-sized local, regional, and even big-city papers, however.

Legacy newspapers face the greatest competition from digital-only news outlets, such as Politico, Bloomberg News, the Drudge Report, the National Review, and a host of others. And the pace of technological change in the news media shows no signs of slowing down.[22]

While the media were widely criticized during the 2016 presidential campaign for a lack of scrutiny and uneven coverage of candidates, the media's investigative reporting on the Trump campaign is noteworthy. During the election investigative articles in the *Washington Post*, for example, revealed the history around candidate Donald Trump's casino bankruptcies, failure to release his taxes, and ties between Russia and the Trump campaign, while others focused on the defunct and fraudulent Trump University.[23] Russia's involvement in the election was especially troubling, and public knowledge of possible foul play in what are normally free and fair elections would not be possible without the deep investigative reporting by the media.[24]

BROADCAST MEDIA

Television news reaches more Americans than any other single news source. It is estimated that over 95 percent of Americans have a television, and tens of millions of people watch national and local news programs every day. Pew reports that combined average viewership for the ABC, CBS, and NBC evening newscasts remained stable in 2016 at about 24 million.[25] Despite the rise of digital media, television news (local, national network, and cable) still commands truly massive audiences, much larger than other sources. Television news, however, generally covers relatively few topics and provides little depth of coverage. It serves the important function of alerting viewers to issues and events—headline news—via brief quotes and short characterizations of the day's events. Furthermore, **broadcast media** do very little of their own reporting, instead relying on leading newspapers or digital media to set their news agenda. Print and digital media, as written text, also provide more detailed and complete information than radio or television media, offering a better context for analysis.

broadcast media television, radio, or other media that transmit audio and/or video content to the public

Because they are aware of the character of television news coverage, politicians and others often seek to manipulate the news by providing the media with sound bites that will dominate news coverage. Sound bites can work for or against politicians. During the 2016 presidential election, calls for deporting undocumented immigrants were a frequent sound bite topic from candidates such as Donald Trump.

Twenty-four-hour cable news stations such as MSNBC, CNN, and Fox News offer more detail and commentary than the half-hour evening news shows found on the three broadcast news stations—ABC, NBC, and CBS. But even these channels offer more headlines and sound bites than newspapers, especially during their prime-time broadcasts.

Politicians generally consider local broadcast news a friendlier venue than the national news. National reporters are often inclined to criticize and question, whereas local and state reporters are more likely to accept the pronouncements of national leaders at face value. Local TV continues to be a major source of news, especially for older Americans, though its importance as a news source is decreasing among the younger generation in favor of social media such as Facebook (see Figure 7.3). Generally, however, Americans' reliance on television does not appear to be going away.

RADIO

Radio is another broadcast news source that has evolved with the popularity of podcasting. In the 1990s, talk radio became an important source of commentary as well as entertainment. Conservative radio hosts, such as Rush Limbaugh and Sean Hannity, have huge audiences and have helped to mobilize support for conservative political causes and candidates. In the political center or center left, National Public Radio (NPR) is a coveted source for in-depth political reporting. In recent years radio news listening has experienced significant growth; in 1990 there were 400 radio stations, a number that has grown to over 2,000 today.

FIGURE 7.3

Where People Get the News, by Age

Younger people get their news from the internet more than older Americans. What does this trend mean for the future of other news media?

SOURCE: Amy Mitchell et al., "Pathways to News," Pew Research Center, July 7, 2016, www.journalism.org (accessed 5/23/18).

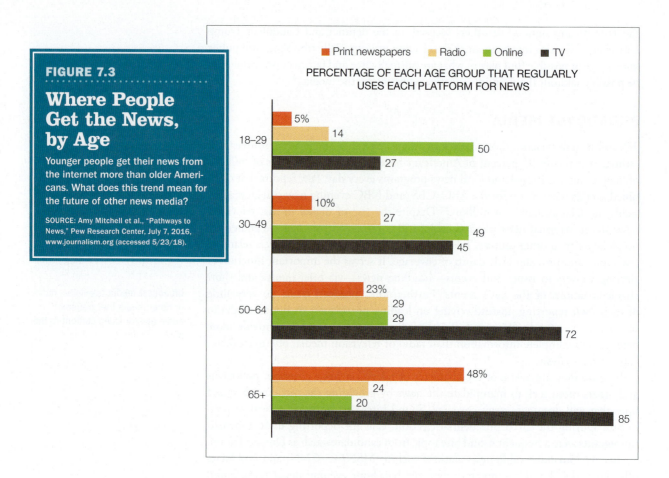

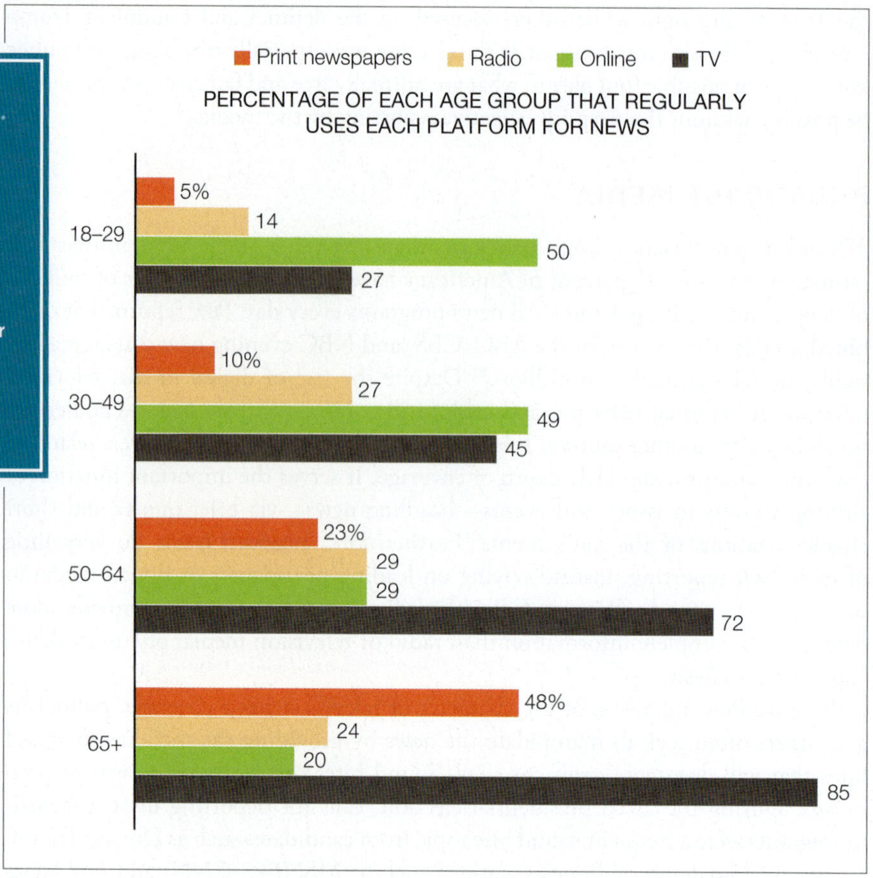

Broadcast radio includes traditional AM/FM radio and digital formats such as online radio and podcasting. While AM/FM radio reaches almost all Americans and remains steady in its revenue, online radio and podcasting has expanded rapidly in the past decade, steadily growing to 64 percent of Americans who reported tuning in during the last month in 2018, up from 12 percent in 2007. While public broadcasting has a much smaller share of the total media market in the United States than in other countries, NPR is still popular and an important way for people to learn about politics each day. In 2017 there were 5.4 million unique downloads of NPR podcasts every week, a number that continues to grow.[26] Mobile devices, including satellite radios and cell phones, have triggered a growth in radio use as online radio listening can occur nearly anywhere. Listening to radio news while commuting is a primary way many Americans become informed about politics.[27]

Comedy Comedy talk shows with political content, such as *The Daily Show*, *The Late Show*, and *Saturday Night Live* attract millions of television viewers. These shows use humor, sarcasm, and social criticism to discuss serious topics, generally covering almost every major political event. Pew surveys have shown that these talk shows are important sources of political news, especially for young people and liberals, and that followers of comedic talk shows are well informed about politics.[28] It is also likely that more-informed viewers are self-selecting into watching comedy news. These shows combine political news and entertainment and are an important source of news for young people.

DIGITAL MEDIA

The twenty-first century has experienced a profound transformation of the media, as discussed in the introduction. The impact of the internet in mass communication parallels that of the printing press in nineteenth-century America, which saw the rise of the **penny press** and widespread literacy.[29] Today, even as the print newspaper business has consolidated, readership of online news has soared. Digital has become the medium of choice to consume entertainment, news, and information about politics for all age groups below 50. In 2000 just 35 percent of adult internet users said they looked for news or information about politics or the upcoming campaigns online. Today 94 percent of young people get news online from mobile devices, and even 67 percent of Americans over age 65 go online for news.[30] In 2017 online news closed in on TV as the major source for news; 43 percent of Americans primarily get news online, compared to 50 percent who rely on TV.[31]

penny press cheap, tabloid-style newspaper produced in the nineteenth century, when mass production of inexpensive newspapers first became possible due to the steam-powered printing press; a penny press newspaper cost one cent compared with other papers, which cost more than five cents

Streaming videos is a growing substitute for television for some viewers, fundamentally altering broadcast news, as dedicated channels provide political analysis, commentary, full-length features, and comedy. Presidential addresses are now regularly streamed live, and millions of people tune in to hear the president in this format.[32] Similarly, podcasts are restructuring radio news by allowing listeners to tune in to the news at any time online.

While many traditional news sources, such as newspapers, now publish online, other digital-only outlets tend to be smaller and more specialized and have lower personnel and overhead costs than mainstream publishers. Besides digital-only news outlets, other digital news sources include news websites, citizen journalism such as blogs, social media such as Twitter and YouTube, podcasts, and nonprofit journalism. (See the "Who Are Americans?" feature on p. 279 for more information on where Americans get their news.) Do digital media ultimately help or hinder progress toward the ideal of a well-informed citizenry that can govern itself effectively? The following discussion helps to answer this question.

News aggregators such as Google News, Reddit, and RealClear Politics generally compile and repackage stories that were created by other sources, and then deliver them online to consumers in convenient formats. They serve as a platform that allows users to share and comment on the news. Some of this content is produced by digital-only news organizations, mainstream media, social movement organizations, ordinary users and other "amateurs," as well as powerful political groups, governments, candidates, nonprofits, corporations, and professional media organizations. News aggregators cover thousands of news stories each day, as well as the latest public-opinion polls and their own synthesis of the headline news. Mirroring the digital revolution, digital advertising has grown as a percentage of total media advertising across all platforms. The main benefactors of digital advertising continue to be social media and technology companies, such as Google and Facebook.[33]

news aggregator an application or feed that collects web content such as news headlines, blogs, podcasts, online videos, and more in one location for easy viewing

Social media sites are particularly convenient for obtaining breaking news 24 hours a day, and formats for doing so are becoming more diverse and interactive. Fully 73 percent of Americans use YouTube, the most commonly used social media platform, followed by Facebook (68 percent).[34] Rather than merely providing a forum to connect with friends and family, social media are spaces for learning about politics and now a primary source for news—a dramatic change from just a few years ago. A majority of American adults—67 percent—gets news on social media. The trend in using social media for political information continues to grow at a rapid rate across all demographic groups.

The rise of digital media has made it easier for Americans to get political news, but one in five Americans still lacks home internet access. People without high-speed internet access at home often get free access in public libraries, but access is restricted to certain times.

The rise of digital media has changed the way that people get information and share it, affecting everything from political activism, campaign advertising, and voter mobilization to public opinion. Online media are more diverse and have created a more participatory press, one in which citizens and nonprofit organizations now play a prominent role, and journalists regularly interact with readers via social media, especially Twitter. Readers can now post comments online, upload videos, and participate in a community, providing feedback on almost all online news articles. Digital media, by representing a wider range of political views than traditional media, have created more information and a more vibrant media environment.

The term *digital citizenship* refers to the ability to participate in culture and politics online. Today's internet has the potential to benefit society as a whole by facilitating political participation and social inclusion through greater access to political information and news.[35] The internet helps provide the information and skills needed for democratic engagement and economic opportunity. However, regular and effective use of the internet requires high-speed access and digital literacy to evaluate and use information online.[36] Individuals without the access or skills to use the internet may be increasingly uninformed and excluded from the world of politics online. In 2018, 73 percent of Americans were **digital citizens**, individuals with home high-speed access and the technology and literacy skills to use it.[37] Access to the internet is shaped by income and education. While only half of the working poor (those earning less than $20,000 a year) had home broadband, 85 percent of those earning more than $100,000 a year did. Sixty-three percent of high school graduates have home broadband compared with almost 90 percent of college graduates.[38] These data suggest that there are significant inequalities in access to digital media, what is called the **digital divide.**[39] Because digital media are essential to participation in society, some argue that government has a responsibility to provide affordable and universal access, as is provided by most other democratic countries.

digital citizen a daily internet user with broadband (high-speed) home internet access and the technology and literacy skills to go online for employment, news, politics, entertainment, commerce, and other activities

digital divide the gap in access to the internet among demographic groups based on education, income, age, geographic location, and race/ethnicity

Today, mobile internet on smartphones is increasingly important for news and participation in society, especially for the young, racial and ethnic minorities, and foreign-born populations. Similar inequalities based on demographic factors, such as income and education, are also found for mobile internet access. While many people see smartphone access as the bridge over the digital divide, others consider it an inferior form of access because many human capital–intensive activities—applying for a job, research for school, or work—require a computer and a broadband internet connection.[40] So while young people may think of smartphone access as a panacea, and the percentage of those reading the news on mobile phones has soared, it is definitely far from a perfect replacement for a computer and broadband.

social media web- and mobile-based technologies that are used to turn communication into interactive dialogue among organizations, communities, and individuals; social media technologies take on many different forms including text, blogs, podcasts, photographs, streaming video, Facebook, and Twitter

Social Media and Filtering **Social media**, such as Facebook and Twitter, tend to be a secondary source for news after television for many Americans but are a primary source for the young. While television remains the main source of news for one in two Americans, young people ages 18–33 increasingly learn about politics and news online and are significantly less likely than older Americans to turn to local TV. Seventy-eight percent of people under age 50 get their news from social media.[41]

The high rate of exposure to political news via social media is notable since young Americans overall are less engaged in politics—just 46 percent of people age 18–29

As the Hispanic population continues to grow, Latino-oriented news outlets are increasingly influential. Jorge Ramos is a popular news anchor on the Spanish-language network Univision, which in recent years has beat out major networks ABC, CBS, Fox, and NBC for the number 1 primetime spot.

voted in the 2016 election compared to 59 percent for the 30–44 age group.[42] As the web becomes an increasingly important source for political news, young people may become more engaged in politics.[43]

Because they are more personalized and interactive than anonymous news organizations, social media allow Americans to learn about politics and political news from each other. Growing use of social media for news is evident across *all* demographic groups, including older people, women and men, and groups defined by race, education, and income. Figure 7.4 shows the percentage of adults who use each social networking site as well as the percentage who get news from that site. Worldwide, Facebook had over 2.2 billion users in 2018, with 214 million users in the United States. Two-thirds of Americans use social media.[44] As of 2018, roughly 68 percent use Facebook and 24 percent use Twitter, both of which have high rates of exposure to political news.[45] With President Trump tweeting multiple times per day, as well as the use of Twitter and Facebook by congressional leaders and other politicians, social media sites have become a news source in their own right, as well as forums to share news published in the mainstream media.

Facebook provides a more interactive forum for learning about politics than does Twitter, with users more likely to post and respond to news about government and politics, while Twitter's strength is in providing news coverage as it happens, focusing on live events. More than two-thirds of users of both sites say they have posted about news at least at some point. Compared to passively watching television or reading the news, this is a high rate of engagement with political news.[46]

Before social media, most people read a daily newspaper or tuned into a television program to keep up with the daily news. Social media, now a key way to disseminate the news, have changed how people access news and have also increased filtering of the news. Both Facebook and Twitter have contributed to political mobilization and information sharing by creating virtual social networks where groups of like-minded individuals can quickly and easily share information. While many news stories posted on social media are still produced by major newspapers and digital media organizations, they are consumed differently. Political scientists Jason Gainous and Kevin Wagner use the metaphor of social media as the new dinner table, in that discussions of politics and current events occur within digital social networks of friends and family. Their research shows people prefer news that is consistent with their pre-existing beliefs; social networks tend to be more homogeneous

FIGURE 7.4

Social Media and the News

Many Americans who use social media use those sites as a way to obtain political news. This graph shows the percentage of American adults who use each social media site compared with the percentage who report getting news from that site. What are the advantages of getting news on social media, and what are some potential drawbacks?

SOURCE: Jeffrey Gottfried and Elisa Shearer, "News Use across Social Media Platforms 2017," Pew Research Center, September 7, 2017, www.journalism.org (accessed 5/23/18).

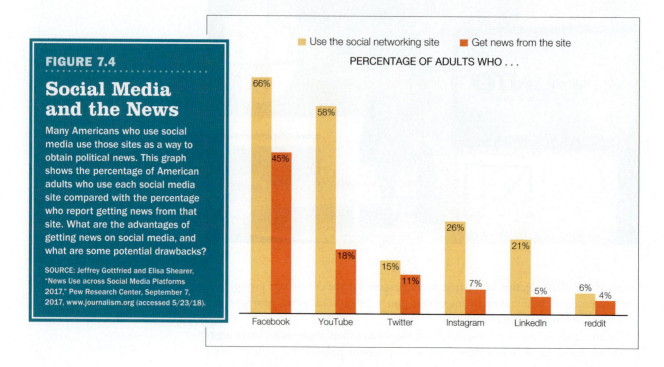

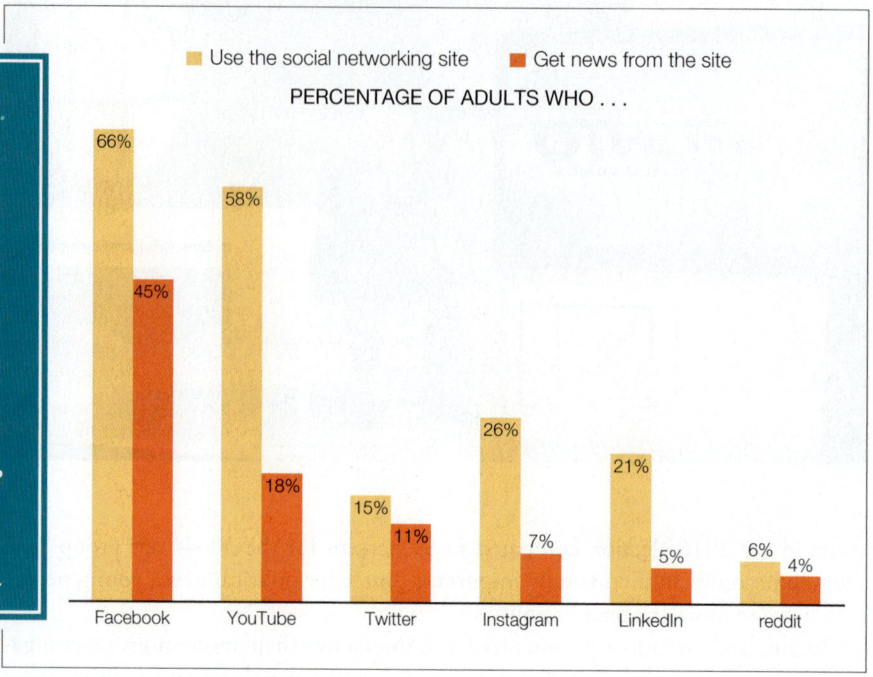

with people holding similar perspectives. This has contributed to growing party polarization in politics.[47]

Social media also provide a platform for citizens to be directly engaged with political candidates and elected officials, who have been quick to adopt Facebook and Twitter as means of communicating with their supporters and filtering the daily news for them. Gainous and Wagner, in their book *Tweeting to Power,* argue that social media is how citizens learn about politics: "Social media alters the political calculus in the United States by filtering who controls information, who consumes information, and how that information is distributed."[48] Because the networks operate outside of traditional media, and users pick their own friend networks and can avoid disagreeable ideas and information, parties, groups, and political candidates are able to directly dictate the content of these information networks. This study found individuals who are more active politically online and read the news using social media hold stronger partisan opinions. This means using social media for reading the news can exaggerate party polarization among the mass public.

Obama was the first American president to use social media extensively in his campaign and during his administration. Political candidates and organizations representing the ideological right, such as the Tea Party, and the left, such as MoveOn.org, have taken advantage of this power to filter the news for their audiences. But Donald Trump is the nation's first "Twitter President," directly communicating his opinions on issues and other politicians directly to the people, unmediated by the media or even his White House press staff. With more than 50 million Twitter followers, Trump has an enormous audience. His unconventional political strategy involves using social media and rallies to communicate directly with the American people and set the media agenda, while attacking the credibility of other sources that provide information countering his statements. On any given day, the president tweets multiple times, often calling out his opponents in his famous celebrity takedown mode he perfected from his experience as a reality TV host. Among his core supporters, the truth is what Trump says it is on Twitter or in emotional speeches before rally crowds. However, fact-checking websites such as PolitiFact have found 70 percent of Trump's statements are false or misleading and another 15 percent are only half true.[49]

While Trump effectively used Twitter to his advantage to filter the news for his supporters during the election and then set the media's agenda, his strategy of going public all the time may backfire. While most Americans believe Twitter does allow Trump to communicate directly to the people, few Americans think this is a good idea. A 2017 Gallup survey found a majority (52 percent) say his tweets are not an effective way for him to share his views on important issues, and 72 percent say the tweets do not send the right message to other world leaders. Seven in 10 Americans believe Trump's tweets are often in response to TV news the president has heard, and 71 percent say Twitter is a "risky way for a president to communicate," leading to misunderstandings.[50]

Social media used for news make citizens more informed and engaged in politics, and more likely to participate. On the down side, citizens may be more vulnerable to misinformation from political actors and candidates, especially if the candidate or organization is their only source of news. Are social media empowering or disempowering? The answer may lie somewhere in between.

CITIZEN JOURNALISM

Digital news is creating a new generation of whistle-blowers, enhancing the media's traditional role as a watchdog for the people against government corruption. A distinguishing feature of this phenomenon is the development of **citizen journalism**, which is interactive and participatory. Citizen journalism includes news reporting and political commentary by ordinary citizens and even crisis coverage from eyewitnesses on the scene, thus involving a wider range of voices in gathering news and interpreting political events. The near-universal availability of cameras on cell phones gives millions of Americans the capacity to photograph or record events, thus providing eye-witness accounts. At the same time, social media permit users to upload videos that can be viewed by hundreds of thousands of subscribers or relayed by the mainstream media for even wider dissemination.

citizen journalism news reported and distributed by citizens, rather than professional journalists and for-profit news organizations

In 2017 a global firestorm erupted over United Airlines' treatment of a passenger, an older Asian man, who was violently dragged off a boarded plane for refusing to voluntarily give up his seat. The video footage of the bloodied passenger was filmed by other passengers using smartphones and uploaded to social media. The video was viewed by millions of people globally, creating an outcry against mistreatment of airline passengers. In response the CEO of United Airlines apologized for the mistreatment of the passenger and the airline changed its policies; this event also led to a congressional investigation of regulations on U.S. airlines.[51] The United example illustrates how the mechanism of social media and grassroots politics can fuel policy change as well as candidate campaigns.

Citizen journalism is enhanced by the ease of starting a blog. There are millions of blogs, covering virtually every topic imaginable, and a large share of these include political news and commentary on local, national, and world events. Many blogs are citizen-run and more and more representative of the diversity of

As we have seen with recent dramatic events like the Charlottesville white nationalist rally (left) and Black Lives Matter protests (right), social media and citizen journalism are transforming the news. Groups can mobilize and push out their messages quickly using social media, and citizen journalists can use mobile technology to capture and disseminate news without the filter of mainstream media outlets.

American views than traditional news, which generally reflects the priorities of political elites.

Citizen journalism supplements the work of professional journalists in many important ways. The diversity of online media has created new opinion leaders and new voices and has even, at times, improved information. In recent years, for example, bloggers have uncovered major factual errors in media reports and forced the networks and newspapers to issue corrections. Furthermore, because bloggers and social media posts do not have strict editorial boards, they can post a story within minutes. This ability to scoop the mainstream media means bloggers can frame stories about political candidates before those stories break in the mainstream media.[52] By sharply lowering the technological and financial barriers that previously prevented all but a few individuals from reaching mass audiences, blogs increase the ability of ordinary people to engage in effective political action.

The freewheeling nature of blogging and social media often means that there is less traditional quality control employed by professional journalists and institutional old media. Because they do not face the burden of fact-checking required for the mainstream media or some digital-only news outlets, even well-meaning bloggers can post false information. This is one reason why misinformation about some political issues is higher among blog readers than those reading online news from the mainstream press.[53]

NONPROFIT JOURNALISM

As traditional news organizations have cut budgets and investigative journalism, political information is increasingly emanating from universities, think tanks, nonprofits, and private foundations. Think tanks such as the Brookings Institution, the Cato Institute, and the Pew Research Center provide news and analysis on current events to influence public debate. While some are ideologically driven, these institutions often provide critical analysis of policy issues. Universities have expanded their public outreach, encouraging faculty to explain their findings for a general audience. Community-based nonprofit newspapers are supported by local foundations seeking to fill the void in local news as local papers close their doors. For example, the Bill and Melinda Gates Foundation, established by Microsoft founder Bill Gates, provides extensive funding to National Public Radio. Nonprofits can provide rigorous original reporting and critical analysis of current events.

BENEFITS OF ONLINE NEWS

As digital news media has become mainstream, it is worthwhile to reexamine why Americans appear to prefer online news. The reasons include (1) the convenience of getting news online, (2) the up-to-the-minute currency of the information available online, (3) the depth of the information available online, (4) the diversity of viewpoints, and (5) the low cost.[54] At the same time, changes to the media have raised some concerns, as we will see in the following sections.

Convenience Information online is convenient and always available for those with access to the internet on a computer or through mobile devices. Pew surveys show that nearly half of those who use online news and political information cite its convenience.[55] Because political knowledge is central to the formation of political attitudes, the convenience of online news may lead to a more informed and engaged citizenry. Use of digital media is associated with more interest in politics, greater knowledge of politics, and a greater likelihood of discussing politics with friends and family, as well as voting.[56]

Currency One of the fundamental changes ushered in by an era of online news is the speed with which local, national, and international events are covered, as well as the scope of coverage. Major news stories regularly break first online. Social media have accelerated even further the speed with which news travels around the globe. For example, news of President Trump firing FBI director James Comey in 2016 spread rapidly through messaging and social media even before it could be verified by traditional media.

Depth Online news provides more information than the 60-second sound bites found in television and radio news. By blending more detailed treatment of topics with the visual and emotive appeal of streaming videos, digital media shares qualities both of print media (promoting knowledge) and of the visual aspects of television (promoting interest and engagement).[57] The multimedia and even immersive (virtual reality) capacity of the digital media notwithstanding, most websites still rely heavily upon written text, and most political "web surfing" consists mainly of reading, which facilitates greater recall of information and, in turn, encourages the acquisition of political knowledge.[58]

Diversity Online sources are much more diverse than those found in the traditional media, and this diversity may lead to an increase in political knowledge and interest.[59] While major players online often include mainstream outlets,[60] the web remains populated by a wide range of information sources. By making foreign media such as the British Broadcasting Company (BBC) and Al Jazeera television easily available, digital media have reduced the importance of physical proximity and created more global news. Such a vast array of voices, of course, means that online sources also can provide misinformation or outright lies—just as can happen in mainstream media, campaign events, and even presidential debates.

CONCERNS ABOUT ONLINE NEWS

While online news holds significant promise for improving access to the political information citizens need, the shift toward online media has also given rise to several major concerns. These potential disadvantages include a decline in investigative journalism, uneven quality in news content, fake news, and negative effects on knowledge and tolerance.

Loss of Investigative Power In a democracy, the press is expected to be a watchdog for the people and to inform citizens about government abuses of power. The greatest challenge for journalism organizations is to generate enough revenue to finance original reporting and investigative journalism.[61] When readers paid subscription fees to read the news, circulation was high and advertising provided sufficient revenue to allow newspapers and broadcasters to cover both basic news (weather, sports, business) and political events. Revenue from publishing basic news subsidized political analysis and investigative journalism. The internet has made it harder for news outlets to draw advertising dollars, since ad firms are migrating online to deliver targeted ads directly to consumers via social media and search engines. Firms can now reach consumers without paying news organizations. By breaking apart mainstream news organizations, digital news may actually reduce the media's ability to engage in the kind of sustained, in-depth reporting that is critical to the media's watchdog role.

More Variation in the Quality of News As already noted, the growing diversity of digital news has led to substantial variation in the quality of available information. Multiple perspectives create a stronger marketplace of ideas, but the freewheeling nature of the internet also means that hate speech, unsubstantiated rumors, and factual errors can overwhelm thoughtful, original, and civic-oriented voices. This is especially so in anonymous online forums.

Fake News Political candidates and political leaders are particularly susceptible to attack when negative stories go viral and spread quickly without fact-checking

Without traditional media's commitment to fact-checking, digital media sometimes spread inaccurate information and rumors. In 2008, the false claim that President Obama was not a natural-born citizen spread rapidly online and remained a top story even after Obama released his official long-form certificate.

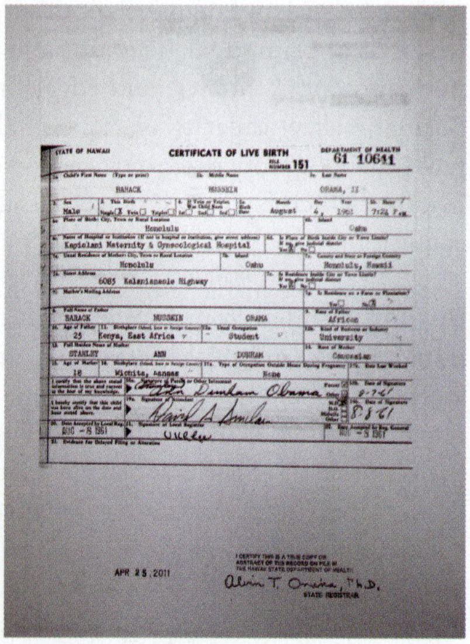
STATE OF HAWAII
CERTIFICATE OF LIVE BIRTH
DEPARTMENT OF HEALTH
151
61 10641
APR 25 2011

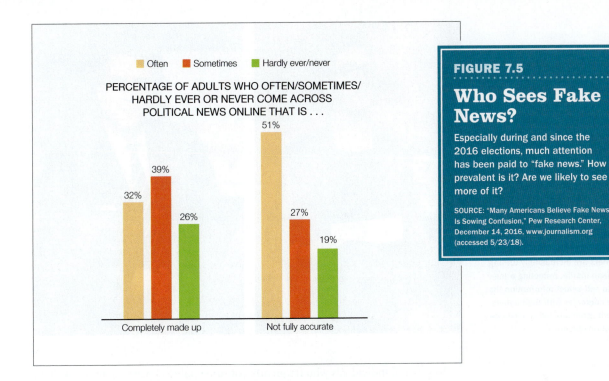

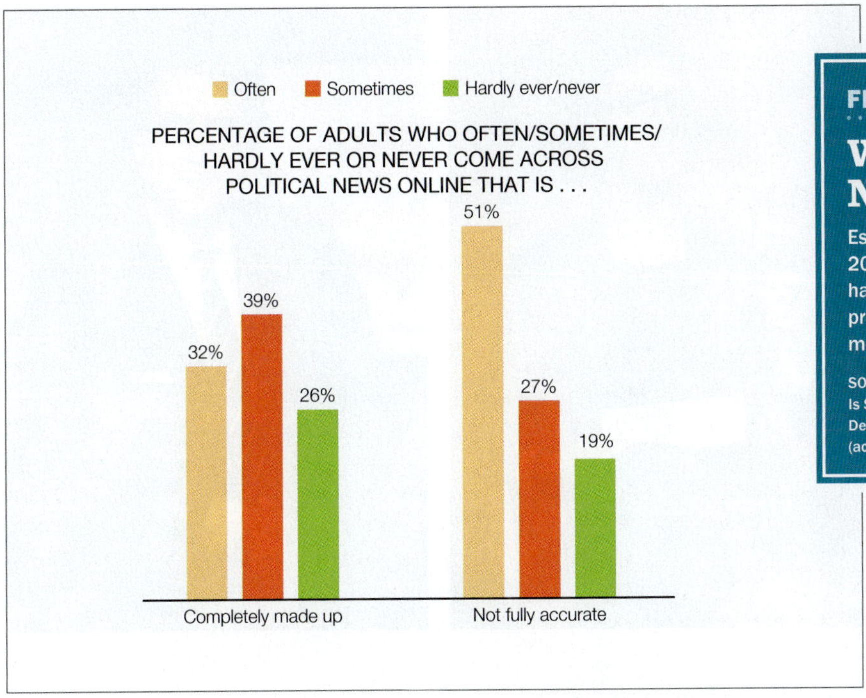

FIGURE 7.5

Who Sees Fake News?

Especially during and since the 2016 elections, much attention has been paid to "fake news." How prevalent is it? Are we likely to see more of it?

SOURCE: "Many Americans Believe Fake News Is Sowing Confusion," Pew Research Center, December 14, 2016, www.journalism.org (accessed 5/23/18).

or respect for the privacy of public figures. In contrast to legitimate new stories, *fake news* are false stories circulated to generate ad revenue or to benefit one political candidate or party over another. The most widely publicized fake news story in the 2016 election, for example, was that the Pope had endorsed Trump for president.[62] Circulation of the top 10 fake news stories on Facebook was more widespread than the top real news stories about the election (for more on who sees false news, see Figure 7.5). A study published by Stanford University found fake news stories on social media in the 2016 presidential election disproportionately favored Trump. The Russian government was involved in generating many of the fake news stories to discredit Clinton and her campaign.[63] To verify media reports found in both traditional and online media, there are websites such as FactCheck.org, Snopes.com, and PolitiFact.com devoted exclusively to checking the veracity of political claims.

Potential Effects on Knowledge and Tolerance Perhaps the greatest concern about politics in the digital age is that the very diversity of online news may actually *lower* tolerance for social, religious, and political diversity, leading to more partisan polarization and societal conflict. Digital media often do not abide by traditional media's principle of objective journalism. Instead, the specialization of information online and on cable television means that liberals and conservatives alike can self-select media that are consistent with their underlying assumptions and avoid exposure to information that might challenge their preconceived beliefs.[64] The natural tendency to select news that conforms with our own beliefs is exacerbated by the way search engines cater to our individual preferences—called the "filter bubble," or "self-selection bias"—which screens out exposure to information that might challenge or broaden our worldview.[65]

FOR CRITICAL ANALYSIS

Does digital news coverage differ from traditional print and television media? What impact does digital media have on American politics?

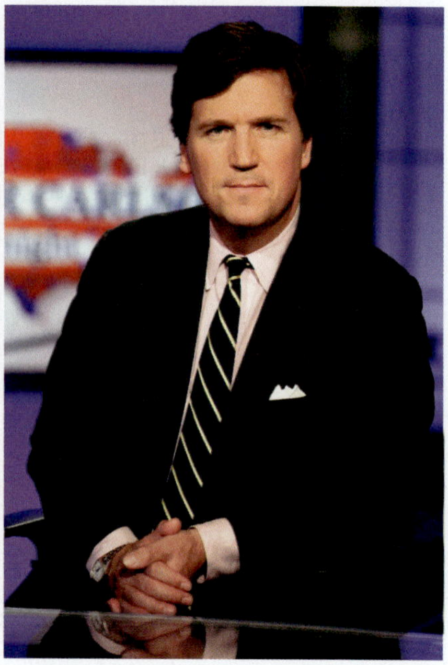

Though the media generally attempt to remain unbiased, a number of media figures and outlets are distinctly left- or right-leaning, such as Rachel Maddow of MSNBC and Tucker Carlson of Fox News. Consumers are increasingly turning to partisan media, reflecting a tendency to self-select information that already conforms with their beliefs, making it more difficult to evaluate information objectively.

In general, individuals who frequently consume political news are more likely to be interested in politics, to have political knowledge, and to vote in elections. But exposure to highly partisan news (Fox News for conservatives, MSNBC for liberals) or news on social media and blogs may lower political knowledge.

The media in all their varying forms—traditional and digital—lead to a more informed public, but also to growing gaps between the informed and uninformed.[66] And yet, despite the dramatic rise in political information and the diversity of the media, average levels of political knowledge in the population have remained constant for the last few decades, due to individuals "customizing" the political information they receive through their choice of news outlets, which, as discussed earlier, makes users less likely to encounter information that challenges their partisan viewpoints.[67]

If the new digital media are to create a more informed democratic process, citizens must have "information literacy" or the ability to find and evaluate information.[68] Greater access to information online makes education and critical thinking among citizens more important than ever before.

DO AMERICANS TRUST THE MEDIA TODAY?

One negative consequence of media concentration combined with party polarization may be a growing distrust of mainstream media. Political scientist Jonathan Ladd argues that fifty years ago the political parties were less polarized and were less likely to attack one another in the press, and newspaper editors also had less incentive to attack their competitors.[69] Ladd maintains that as competition increased in party politics and journalism, the public's distrust of the mass media grew, leading the public to reject the mainstream press's reporting and turn to alternative partisan media sources—those expressly favored by Republicans or Democrats. There are growing partisan divisions in confidence in the news media. Just 11 percent

FOR CRITICAL ANALYSIS

To what extent, do you think, are the media biased? As more news sources have become available, has this led to more or less bias in the media?

of Republicans have a lot of trust in national news media compared to 34 percent of Democrats, according to a 2017 Pew survey.[70]

Distrust in the mainstream media has increased with the Trump presidency. In response to the negative media coverage of his campaign and presidency, Trump has waged an unprecedented war on the American media, frequently referring to major newspapers and broadcast media as "fake news" to discredit them (though these mainstream sources are not producing fabricated news).

In February 2017, Trump upped the ante in a tweet where he called the press "the enemy of the American people." Conservative Republican senator John McCain publicly criticized Trump, warning that without a free and adversarial press, "That's how dictators get started . . . by suppressing free press. In other words, a consolidation of power when you look at history, the first thing that dictators do is shut down the press. And I'm not saying that President Trump is trying to be a dictator. I'm just saying we need to learn the lessons of history."[71]

In an age of digital media, it is more important than ever for citizens to find and evaluate information (see the "What You Can Do" section at the end of the chapter). Political fact-checking websites such as PolitiFact.com, Snopes.com, and FactCheck.org have grown in importance and popularity.

The internet has facilitated both diversity and specialization in the news media. Websites such as FactCheck.org exist solely for the purpose of evaluating statements made by U.S. politicians. The site corrects misinformation every day, such as the false story that CNN was shutting down because of poor ratings.

Media Influence

Analyze the ways the media can influence public opinion and politics

The content and character of news and public affairs programming—what the media choose to present and how they present it—can have far-reaching political consequences. The media can shape and modify, if not fully form, the public's perception of events, issues, and institutions. Media coverage can rally support for, or intensify opposition to, national policies on important matters such as health care, the economy, or international wars. Media disclosures can greatly enhance or fatally damage the careers of public figures, as discussed earlier. At the same time, the media are influenced by the individuals or groups who are subjects of the news. The president in particular has the power to set the news agenda through speeches and actions. All politicians, for that matter, seek to shape or manipulate their media images by cultivating good relations with reporters and through news leaks and staged news events.

In recent American political history, the media have played a central role in many major events. For example, the media were a critically important factor in the civil rights movement of the 1950s and '60s. Television images showing peaceful civil rights marchers attacked by club-swinging police helped to generate sympathy among northern whites for the civil rights struggle and greatly increased the pressure on Congress to bring an end to segregation.[72] To take another example, the media were also instrumental in compelling the Nixon administration to negotiate an end to American involvement in the Vietnam War by portraying the war as misguided and unwinnable.[73]

Conservatives have long charged that the liberal biases of reporters and journalists result in distorted news coverage.[74] Though some professional journalists

TABLE 7.1

Media and Viewers' Ideology

Percentage of each ideological group who report getting news about politics in the previous week from each source

SOURCE	CONSISTENTLY LIBERAL	MOSTLY LIBERAL	MIXED	MOSTLY CONSERVATIVE	CONSISTENTLY CONSERVATIVE
CNN	52	48	49	32	20
Fox News	10	24	39	61	84
ABC News	33	38	42	32	26
NBC News	37	44	40	29	21
CBS News	30	32	32	24	22
MSNBC	38	32	25	23	13
NPR	53	23	12	10	8

SOURCE: Pew Research Center, "Where News Audiences Fit on the Political Spectrum," www.journalism.org/interactives/media-polarization/table/consume/ (accessed 3/7/16).

do lean Democratic, they generally defend their professionalism, insisting that their personal political leanings do not affect the way they perform their jobs.[75] Today journalists represent liberals, conservatives, and moderates. Those who decry "the liberal media" seldom acknowledge the partisan or ideological leanings of media owners. Rupert Murdoch, for example, the chief executive officer of News Corporation and 21st Century Fox, is a politically active conservative. Sheldon Adelson is another wealthy media mogul with a clear conservative partisan and ideological agenda.

Many news sources are perceived as distinctly left- or right-leaning, and, as discussed earlier, people have a tendency to select news that conforms with their own ideology. Table 7.1 shows where different ideological groups get political news. With the exception of Fox News and, perhaps, MSNBC, there is not much credible empirical evidence for the idea that any particular mainstream news source is, as a whole, explicitly ideologically biased in one direction or another, at least in terms of the news coverage. Most have been found to be centrist.[76] Of course, many people perceive particular news stories to be biased. This perception may be what drives ideological self-selection of news sources.

HOW THE MEDIA INFLUENCE POLITICS

Traditional and digital media influence American politics in a number of important ways.[77] The power of all media collectively, both traditional and online, lies in their ability to shape what issues Americans think about (agenda setting) and what opinions Americans hold about those issues (framing and priming).

WHO ARE AMERICANS?

Where Do Americans Get Their News?

Percentage of each voter group who got news about politics and government in the previous week from ...

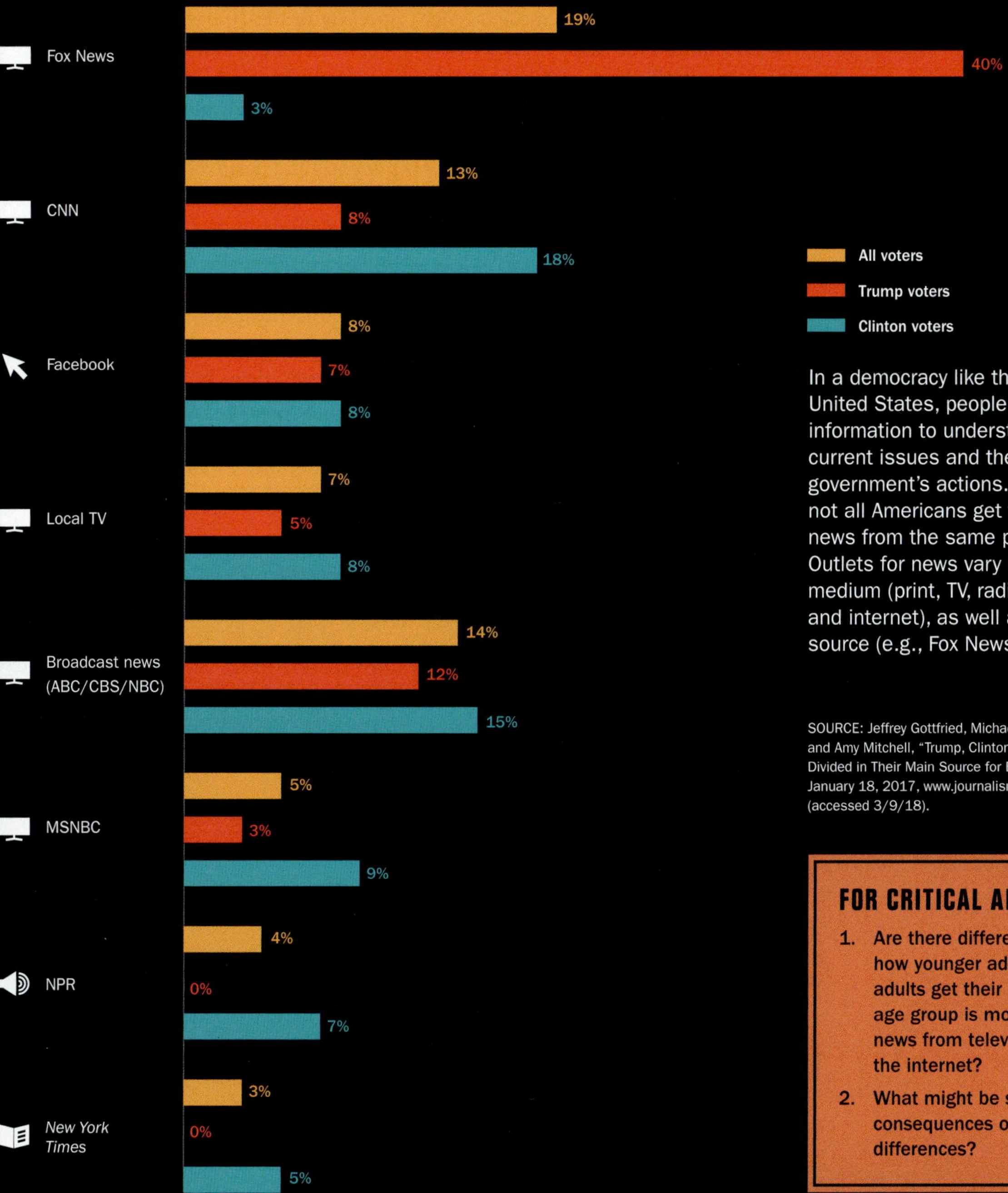

In a democracy like the United States, people need information to understand current issues and the government's actions. But not all Americans get their news from the same place. Outlets for news vary by medium (print, TV, radio, and internet), as well as source (e.g., Fox News).

SOURCE: Jeffrey Gottfried, Michael Barthel, and Amy Mitchell, "Trump, Clinton Voters Divided in Their Main Source for Election News," January 18, 2017, www.journalism.com (accessed 3/9/18).

FOR CRITICAL ANALYSIS

1. Are there differences between how younger adults and older adults get their news? Which age group is more likely to get news from television versus the internet?
2. What might be some consequences of such differences?

agenda setting the power of the media to bring public attention to particular issues and problems

Agenda Setting and Selection Bias The first source of media power is **agenda setting**; that is, the media help to set the agenda for political discussion. Agenda setting involves identifying the issues that politicians will pay attention to: some things are deemed important while others are not. Groups and forces that wish to bring their ideas before the public in order to generate support for policy proposals or political candidacies must secure media coverage. If the media are persuaded that an idea is newsworthy, then they may declare it an "issue" that must be confronted or a "problem" to be solved, thus clearing the first hurdle in the policy-making process. If, on the other hand, an idea lacks or loses media appeal, its chance of resulting in new programs or policies is diminished.

In the lead-up to the 2016 election, for example, the mainstream media and Donald Trump focused extensively on Hillary Clinton's use of a private email server during her tenure as Secretary of State, and the risk of jeopardizing government secrets. Clinton's email use dominated the media agenda, especially in the 10 days before the election when FBI director James Comey reopened the investigation into her email server.

Some stories have such overwhelming significance—such as wars, natural disasters, and domestic and international acts of terrorism—that in these cases the main concern of political leaders is not whether a story will receive attention but whether political leaders themselves will figure prominently and positively in media accounts. At the same time, many important issues are *not* on the media's agenda, such as alternative energy sources to fossil fuels like solar and wind power. Likewise, these issues are often absent from major policy discussions.

Media attention plays a central role in whether or not officials act on a policy issue, but how policy issues make the news in the first place has remained a puzzle. Political scientist Amber Boydstun has shown that the media have two modes: an "alarm mode" for breaking stories and a "patrol mode" for covering them in greater depth.[78] The incentive to reach a wider audience (and generate ad revenue) often initiates "alarm mode" around a story, after which news outlets go into watchdog "patrol mode" to monitor policy implications until the next big media storm hits. This pattern results in skewed coverage of political issues, with a few issues receiving the majority of media

Through agenda setting, the media have the power to influence which issues the public pays attention to. After FBI director James Comey released a letter indicating the reopening of the investigation into Hillary Clinton's use of a private email server days before the 2016 election, the media's intense coverage of the investigation caused the Clinton campaign to respond to the letter publicly.

During the 1960s, civil rights protesters learned a variety of techniques designed to elicit sympathetic media coverage. Television images of police brutality in Alabama led directly to the enactment of the 1965 Civil Rights Act.

attention while others receive none at all. Today, Twitter often sets off "alarm mode" by breaking news and causing it to go viral, setting the agenda for mainstream news.

Political candidates need the media's agenda-setting role to win elections. Candidates who receive positive news coverage gain momentum, pick up political endorsements, attract campaign contributions, and win support from voters.[79] In the 2008 Democratic primaries for president, Barack Obama exceeded the media's expectations with his early win in the Iowa caucuses. Obama's unexpected victory earned him increased press attention and eventually led the first African American president to the White House.[80] In 2016, Donald Trump exceeded media expectations by coming in second in Iowa and winning New Hampshire. But candidates who disappoint media expectations, such as 2016 Republican candidate Jeb Bush, see their political endorsements, campaign contributions, and polling numbers dwindle. The influence of the media on political candidates is just one example of the media's vitally important role in American democracy.

Because the media are businesses and seek to attract the largest possible audiences, they naturally tend to cover stories with dramatic or entertainment value, giving less attention to important stories that they deem less compelling. News coverage often focuses on crimes and scandals, especially those involving prominent individuals. **Selection bias** means that the news media may provide less information about important political issues that the public depends upon. For example, there was a media frenzy in January 1998 when reports surfaced that Democratic president Clinton might have had an affair with a White House intern. In 2016, Donald Trump's sensationalist statements during the course of his campaign dominated headline news for months. Partisanship and ideology notwithstanding, the age-old journalistic instinct for sensational stories often trumps both the media's responsibility to inform the public about what really matters and the public's responsibility to demand that from the media.

selection bias (news) the tendency to focus news coverage on only one aspect of an event or issue, avoiding coverage of other aspects

What the mainstream media decide to report on and what they ignore has important implications. For example, the Bush tax cuts of 2001 and 2003, extended under Obama in 2010, had widespread effects, dramatically increasing the federal budget deficit and widening the income gap between the super-rich and most other Americans. But the media provided little coverage of these measures, the result being that 40 percent of Americans had no opinion on whether they favored the massive tax cuts in 2001.[81] In contrast, the media paid more attention to the Trump administration's 2017 tax reform plan, and most Americans had definitive opinions about it. While the bill only had a 36 percent approval rating according to a Pew Research survey, it was adopted by Congress anyway.[82]

Access to the print and broadcast media is such an important political resource that political forces that have less media access, such as Black Lives Matter, have only a very limited opportunity to influence the political process. The skewed coverage of traditional media, however, may be partially balanced out by the diversity of media sources online, especially the growing influence of social media.

framing the power of the media to influence how events and issues are interpreted

Framing The language and context in which the media present the news, known as **framing**, can determine how the American people interpret political events. Robert Entman defines *framing* as the social construction of phenomena by the mass media, political or social movements, political leaders, or other political actors and organizations. Frames shape how individuals perceive meaning from words or phrases, photographs, or video.[83] Knowing this, politicians take care to choose language that presents their ideas in the most favorable light possible. For example, during the 2016 presidential campaign, Donald Trump framed Hillary Clinton as a criminal for her use of a private email server.

Because few citizens read legislation, when forming opinions about policy and politics, the public relies on media coverage. This means that arguments made by elected officials and other political actors—or frames—are critical in how the public interprets events and policy.

For example, Obama's health care initiative was framed differently by Democrats and Republicans. The Obama administration labeled the initiative the Patient Protection and Affordable Care Act, thus framing the proposal as a matter of compassionate responsibility and good economic sense. Early press coverage framed the bill as "health care reform." Sensing that Americans generally approve of the idea of "reform," Republican opponents of the legislation chose different language: the law's provisions for limiting excessive medical testing were labeled as "health care rationing," for example, and proposals to create committees to advise patients about end-of-life care were called "death panels."

priming process of preparing the public to bring specific criteria to mind when evaluating a politician or issue

Priming A third important way the media can shape political events is known as **priming**. Priming involves "calling attention to some matters while ignoring others" when evaluating political officials.[84] As a result, the public will be *primed* to use certain criteria when evaluating a politician or an issue and ignore other criteria. In the lead-up to the 2008 presidential election, for example, the serious economic recession took the media spotlight. As a result the economy—far more than other issues—became one of the most important lenses through which the public evaluated the 2008 presidential candidates.

In the case of political candidates, the media's focus on which candidate "has momentum" and "is winning the horse race" can prime the public to evaluate the candidates based on their likelihood to win the election rather than on their positions on policy issues. For example, when the media declared that Donald Trump had momentum after his unexpected victories and polling numbers exceeded expectations early in the primary season, he went on to win the Republican nomination. News media are not alone in agenda setting, framing, and priming; elected officials, interest groups, and other political players compete over all three in hopes of influencing public opinion.

FOR CRITICAL ANALYSIS

How do the media distort political reality? How do politicians use the media for their own purposes? What are the consequences for American democracy when the electorate is informed through such a filter? How might the quality of political information in America be improved?

News Coverage

Explain how politicians and others try to shape the news

News coverage, or the content of the news, comes from numerous sources. Governments, politicians, corporations, interest groups, nonprofit organizations, and others issue press releases to draw attention to an issue and tell their side of the story. The news media continues to be dominated by official government sources. Journalists also gain information through investigative journalism and media leaks.

The United States charged Julian Assange, founder of WikiLeaks, for breaching national security by publishing classified documents. Since 2012, Assange has been living in exile.

MEDIA LEAKS

The media may report information that is leaked by government officials. A leak is the disclosure of confidential information to the news media. Leaks may emanate from a variety of sources, including "whistle-blowers," lower-level officials who hope to publicize what they view as their bosses' or the government's improper activities. In 1971, for example, Daniel Ellsberg, a minor Defense Department staffer, sought to discredit official justifications for America's military involvement in Vietnam by leaking top-secret documents to the press. The Pentagon Papers—the Defense Department's own secret history of the war—were published by the *New York Times* and the *Washington Post* after the U.S. Supreme Court ruled that the government could not block their release.[85] The Pentagon's credibility was severely damaged, hastening the erosion of public support for the war. Most leaks, though, originate not with low-level whistle-blowers but rather with senior government officials, prominent politicians, and political activists. Journalists are likely to regard high-level sources of confidential information as valuable assets whose favor must be retained.

Digital technology has taken the cat-and-mouse game of leaks to a new level. WikiLeaks, an international organization dedicated to publishing classified information, posts leaked government documents to its website and uses an anonymous system so that leakers cannot be identified. In recent years, WikiLeaks has released thousands of secret government documents involving instances of government corruption, war crimes in Afghanistan and Iraq, torture at U.S. military detention camps, and stolen emails from the Democratic National Committee in the 2016 election.

In 2013, Edward Snowden, a former employee of the Central Intelligence Agency (CIA) and contractor for the National Security Agency (NSA), disclosed thousands of classified digital documents to journalists and international media. The leaks revealed widespread global surveillance programs by the U.S. government working with telecommunication companies. The world learned the NSA was searching millions of emails and tapping cell phones, even of foreign political leaders. For revealing the mass surveillance programs, Snowden has been called a hero, a whistleblower, a dissident, and a traitor. The leaks garnered intense media attention and sparked heated public debate over government surveillance and privacy of information for individuals. Critics of WikiLeaks and Snowden argue that governments must have some secrets and that the release of some government documents may jeopardize national security as well as American soldiers and their local allies by revealing their identities. Media leaks play a pivotal role in informing the public of government wrongdoings in terms of foreign policy and infringement of privacy and security in a digital age.

The famous photograph of the aftermath of a napalm attack was one of many media images that shaped the American public's views on the Vietnam War. Media accounts critical of the war helped to turn public opinion against it and hastened the withdrawal of American troops.

ADVERSARIAL JOURNALISM

The political power of the news media vis-à-vis the government has greatly increased in recent years through the growing prominence of *adversarial journalism*, a form of reporting in which the media adopt a skeptical or even hostile posture toward the government and public officials.

Presidents were the first national officials to make use of the opportunities presented by this development. By communicating directly to the electorate through newspapers and magazines, Theodore Roosevelt and Woodrow Wilson established political constituencies for themselves, independent of party organizations, and thereby strengthened their own power relative to that of Congress. President Franklin Delano Roosevelt used the radio, most notably in his famous fireside chats, to reach out to voters throughout the nation and to make himself the center of American political life. Subsequent presidents all sought to use the media to enhance their popularity and power, and the media became a cornerstone of presidential power.

The Vietnam War shattered this amicable relationship between the press and the presidency. During the early stages of U.S. involvement, American officials in Vietnam who disapproved of the way the war was being conducted leaked to reporters information critical of administrative policy. Publication of this material infuriated the White House, which pressured publishers to block its release, but the national broadcast media and especially the two leading national newspapers, the *Washington Post* and the *New York Times*, refused to do so. As the Vietnam War dragged on, adverse media coverage fanned antiwar sentiment. In turn, these shifts in popular and congressional sentiment emboldened journalists and publishers to continue to present news reports critical of the war. The media were also central actors in the Watergate affair, the cluster of scandals that ultimately forced President Nixon to resign from office in disgrace just two years later. A relentless series of investigations launched by the *Washington Post*, the *New York Times*, and the television networks led to disclosures of the various crimes of which Nixon was guilty, leading to threats of impeachment and his subsequent resignation. Gradually, a generation of journalists developed a commitment to adversarial journalism.

Adversarial journalism intensified during Trump's first year in office as the president became embroiled by a federal investigation into possible collusion between his campaign for president and Russia. The national news media, led by the *New York Times* and *Washington Post*, reported almost daily on breaking news revealing how Russia used a sophisticated cyber campaign to interfere in the 2016 election. The media's reporting has revealed that Russian president Vladimir Putin tried to discredit Hillary Clinton and tip the outcome of the 2016 election in favor of Donald Trump. The media first reported that Russian operatives hacked the accounts of the Democratic Party and publically released 30,000 embarrassing emails related to Clinton's presidential campaign. They have also reported frequently on the federal investigation by Robert Mueller and his team regarding whether anyone close to Trump participated in the Russian interference in the election. Trump's former campaign chairman, Paul Manafort, surrendered to the FBI and pleaded guilty to charges that he laundered millions of dollars through overseas shell companies after reaching a deal with the Justice Department. Rick Gates, Manafort's longtime associate as well as a campaign adviser, also pleaded guilty to federal crimes.

FOR CRITICAL ANALYSIS

Richard Nixon, Bill Clinton, Donald Trump, and many other presidents have criticized the media. Why are many politicians hostile to media? Do you share their views?

Without the rigorous investigative and adversarial journalism of the news media on behalf of political leaders, the people would not have the means (and information) necessary to hold their elected representatives accountable to the people. Throughout this chapter we have discussed the watchdog role of the media. Adversarial journalism, where the news media seeks to expose political corruption through reporting that is skeptical of government and public officials, is a critical part of what makes democratic governments work.

Aggressive use of the techniques of investigation, publicity, and exposure has allowed the national media to enhance their autonomy and carve out a prominent place for themselves in American government and politics. Without aggressive media coverage, important questions about the conduct of American foreign and domestic policy, police violence, drone attacks, election interference by foreign governments, political corruption, and civil liberty violations may not ever be raised. It is easy to criticize the media for their aggressive tactics, but our democracy may not function effectively without the critical role of the press. Independent media are needed as the watchdogs of American politics.

Regulation of the Media

Trace the evolution of rules that govern broadcast media

In many countries, such as China, the government exercises strict control over traditional media content. In others, the government owns the broadcast media (for example, the BBC in Britain) but does not tell the media what to say.

In the United States, the print and online media are essentially free from government interference. The broadcast media, on the other hand, are subject to federal regulation. American radio and television are regulated by the Federal Communications Commission (FCC), an independent agency established in 1934. Radio and TV stations must have FCC licenses, which must be renewed every five years. Through regulations prohibiting obscenity, indecency, and profanity, the FCC has sought to prohibit radio and television stations from airing explicit sexual and excretory references between 6 A.M. and 10 P.M., the hours when the audience is most likely to include children. Generally speaking, FCC regulation applies only to the over-the-air broadcast media. It does not apply to cable television, the internet, or satellite radio.

In 1996, Congress passed the Telecommunications Act, a broad effort to end most regulations. The legislation loosened restrictions on media ownership and allowed telephone companies, cable television providers, and broadcasters to compete with one another to provide telecommunication services. Following the passage of this act, mergers between telephone and cable companies and different entertainment media produced a greater concentration of media ownership than had been possible since regulation of the industry began in 1934.

Though the act loosened many regulations, it did include an attempt to regulate the content of material transmitted over the internet. This law, known as the Communications Decency Act, made it illegal to make "indecent" sexual material on the internet accessible to those under age 18. The act was immediately denounced by civil libertarians, and in 1997 the Supreme Court ruled that the Communications Decency Act was an unconstitutional infringement of the right to freedom of speech guaranteed by the First Amendment (see Chapter 4).

FOR CRITICAL ANALYSIS

In wartime, can media criticism of government action aid the nation's enemies? Should there be limits on media criticism of the government during times of war? Or does criticism actually enhance the nation's strength?

Although the government's ability to regulate the content of the internet is limited, the FCC has used its licensing power to impose several regulations that can affect the political content of radio and TV broadcasts. The first of these is the **equal time rule**, under which broadcasters must provide to candidates for the same political office equal opportunities to communicate their messages to the public. Under the terms of the Telecommunications Act, during the 45 days before an election, broadcasters are required to make time available to candidates at the lowest rate charged for that time slot.

equal time rule the requirement that broadcasters provide candidates for the same political office equal opportunities to communicate their messages to the public

right of rebuttal a Federal Communications Commission regulation giving individuals the right to have the opportunity to respond to personal attacks made on a radio or television broadcast

The second regulation affecting the content of broadcasts is the **right of rebuttal**, which requires that individuals be given the opportunity to respond to personal attacks. For many years, a third important federal regulation was the *fairness doctrine*. Under this rule, broadcasters that aired programs on controversial issues were required to provide time for opposing views. In addition, the fairness doctrine included a requirement that TV and radio stations cover controversial issues of public and social importance in their communities. In 1985, however, the FCC stopped enforcing the fairness doctrine on the grounds that there were so many radio and television stations—to say nothing of newspapers and newsmagazines—that in all likelihood many different viewpoints were already being presented without each station being required to try to present all sides of every argument. In 1987 the FCC officially revoked the fairness doctrine. Critics of this FCC decision charge that in many media markets the number of competing viewpoints is actually quite small.

The rise of online media challenges our thinking about regulation of the media as it is more difficult—some say impossible—to regulate political content online. In 2011 the United Nations declared that access to the internet is a human right.[86] While this declaration came in response to threats by authoritarian governments against internet access, it demonstrates the significance of information technology in modern life.[87]

The debate over net neutrality highlights fundamental questions about democracy. If the media are intended to be a marketplace of ideas, what should the government do to regulate that marketplace? Should any single entity be allowed to exert more influence or control, or should everyone be allowed to participate equally?

The Internet and Global Democracy

The internet and social media play an increasing role in elections, as demonstrated in this chapter. Critics of this trend have raised concerns that a lack of "quality control" allows the spreading of fake news by unscrupulous groups.[a] A number of foreign and domestic actors have used the open nature of this media to manipulate campaign rhetoric for political gain. The British government opened investigations into the spread of false news during the "Brexit" vote on leaving the European Union,[b] and Russia used internal techniques to manipulate elections in the United States and Europe.[c]

Supporters, however, point out that the internet and social media have allowed voters to connect better with their political systems. Nonprofit groups like GotToVote.cc run social media campaigns to help African citizens register to vote and identify their polling stations. In Kenya, biometric voter registration has made it more difficult for people to cast multiple ballots, and real-time texting has improved oversight on election counts, helping to combat voter fraud.[d]

While internet and social media are certainly transforming politics, it is important to remember that not all global citizens are part of this trend. Internet access may be near-universal in wealthy countries, but there are still many countries where less than a third of the population ever go online. If the future of politics is online, then many poor and older people around the world may be increasingly left behind.

INTERNET USAGE THROUGHOUT THE WORLD

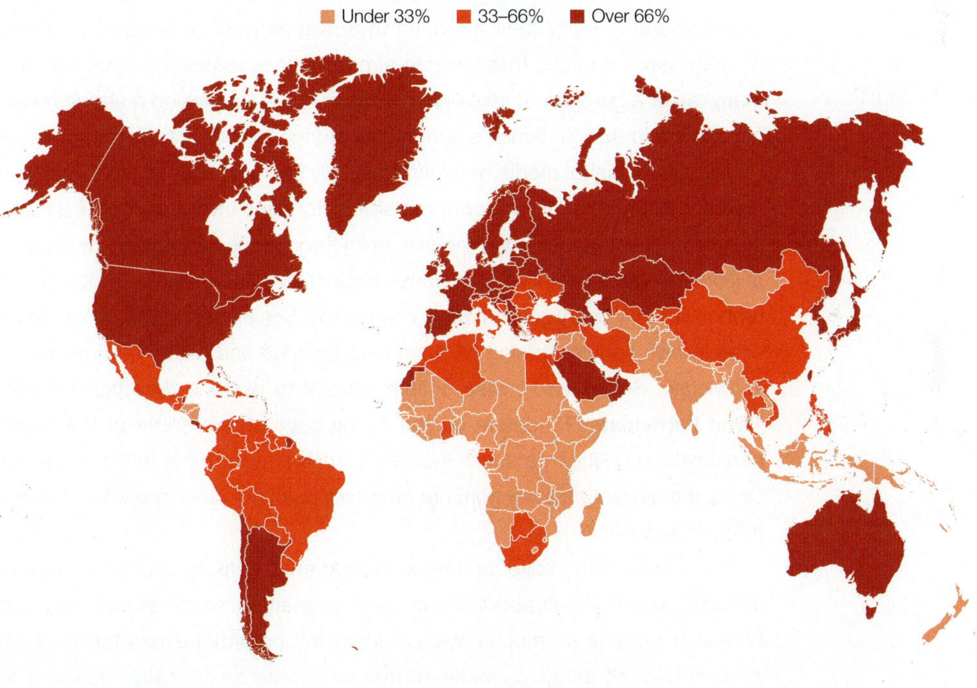

SOURCE: World Bank, "Individuals Using the Internet (% of Population)," 2016, data.worldbank.org (accessed 5/21/18).

[a] Thomas B. Edsall, "Opinion: Democracy, Disrupted," March 2, 2017, *New York Times*, www.nytimes.com/2017/03/02/opinion/how-the-internet-threatens-democracy.html (accessed 5/21/18).

[b] "What Are the Links between Cambridge Analytica and a Brexit Campaign Group?" Reuters, March 21, 2018, www.reuters.com/article/us-facebook-cambridge-analytica-leave-eu/what-are-the-links-between-cambridge-analytica-and-a-brexit-campaign-group-idUSKBN1GX2IO (accessed 5/21/18).

[c] Constanze Stelzenmüller, "Testimony: The Impact of Russian Interference on Germany's 2017 Election," June 28, 2017, www.brookings.edu/testimonies/the-impact-of-russian-interference-on-germanys-2017-elections/ (accessed 5/21/18).

[d] Loren Treisman, "How Kenyans Are Using Tech to Stop Election Fraud," August 3, 2017, *CNN*, www.cnn.com/2017/07/27/africa/kenya-elections-technology/index.html (accessed 5/21/18).

The Media and Democracy
WHAT DO WE WANT?

The freedom of the press is essential to democratic government. Ordinary citizens depend on the media to investigate wrongdoing, publicize and explain governmental policy, evaluate politicians, and bring to light matters that might otherwise be known to only a handful of governmental insiders. In short, without free and active media, democratic government would be virtually impossible. Citizens would have few means through which to know or assess the government's actions—other than the claims or pronouncements of the government itself. Moreover, without active (indeed, aggressive) media, citizens would be hard-pressed to make informed choices among competing candidates at the polls—one reason that the teenage defenders of net neutrality discussed at the beginning of the chapter hoped to keep the internet open as a source of information on public affairs.

Today's media are not only adversarial but also increasingly partisan. Blogs, digital-only news websites, social media, and others can be unabashedly partisan. To some extent, increasing ideological and partisan stridency is an inevitable result of the expansion and proliferation of news sources. When the news was dominated by three networks and a handful of national papers, each sought to appeal to the entire national audience. This required a moderate and balanced tone so that consumers would not be offended and transfer their attention to a rival network or newspaper. Today, there are so many news sources that few can aim for a broad-based national audience. Instead, many target a partisan or ideological niche and aim to develop a strong relationship with consumers in that audience segment by catering to their biases and predispositions.

The rise of digital media has fundamentally changed how political information is gathered and distributed. News today is participatory and involves citizens as well as professional journalists. Wikipedia, the free online encyclopedia founded by Jimmy Wales, has millions of pages compiled by legions of volunteers and provides relatively unbiased content on virtually every political topic imaginable. Social media, Wikipedia, and all Wiki-type sites involve people working collaboratively to write and create information and transmit knowledge. Social media also enable citizens to express their political opinions. (The "**Who Participates?**" feature on the facing page shows some of the ways Americans participate in politics via social media.) Is such a system the future of the news media? Or will the movement away from net neutrality push out smaller voices in favor of powerful media companies?

The media can make or break reputations, help to launch or destroy political careers, and build support for or rally opposition to programs and institutions.[88] Wherever there is so much power, at least the potential exists for its abuse or overly zealous use. All things considered, free media are so critically important to the maintenance of a democratic society that Americans must be prepared to take the risk that the media will occasionally abuse their power. Governmental controls that would prevent the media from misusing their power would also limit freedom. The ultimate beneficiaries of free and active media are the American people.

Civic Engagement in the Digital Age

In the last 12 months, did you send a message on Facebook or Twitter about political issues?

Percentage who said "yes" to this question

Age

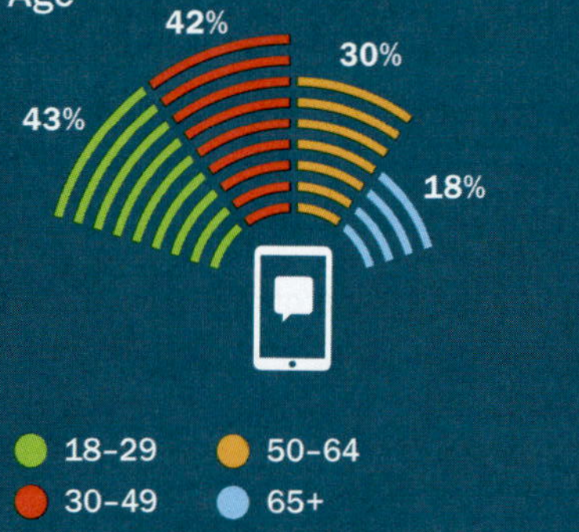

Income group

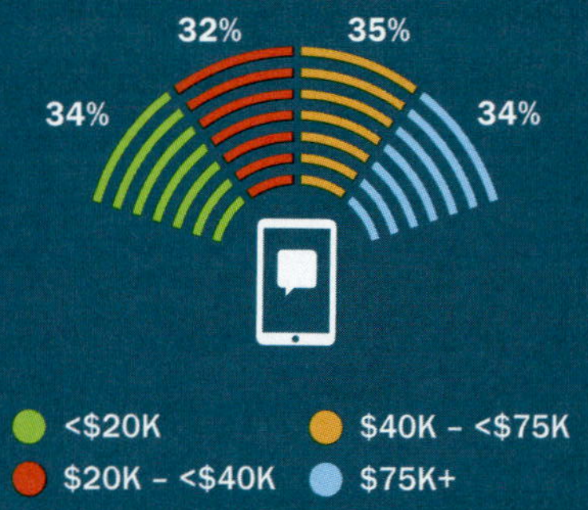

Partisanship

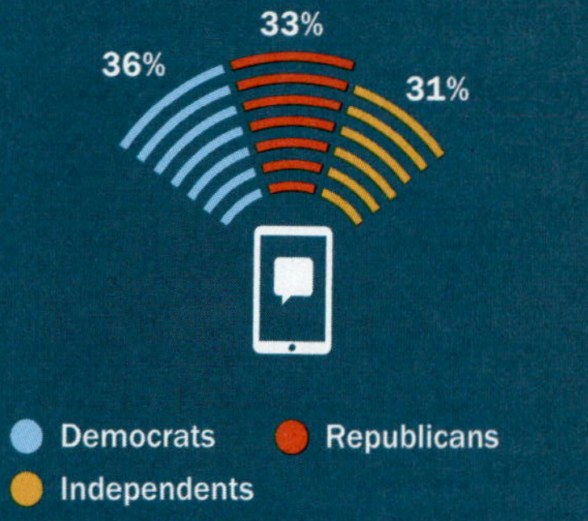

Education

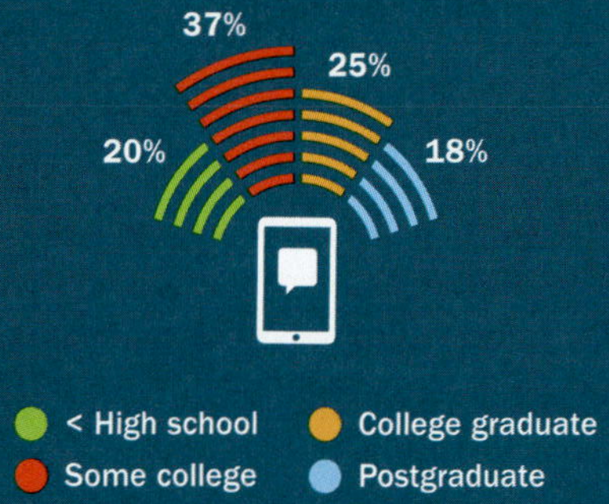

Sex

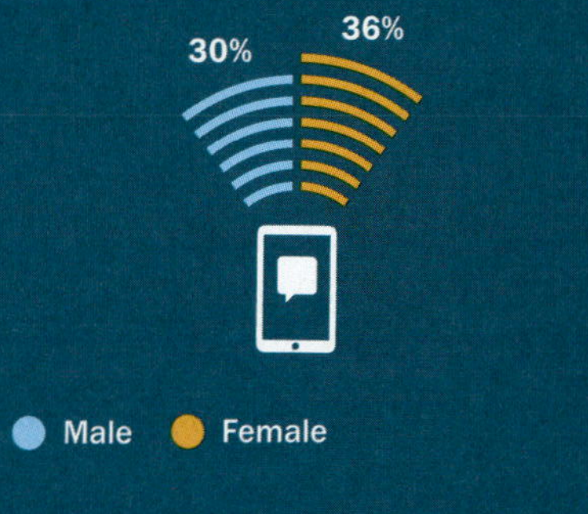

Race / ethnicity

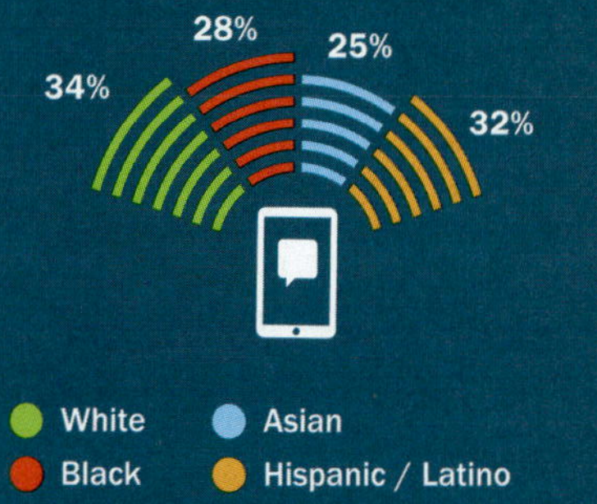

SOURCE: American National Election Study 2016 time series, www.electionstudies.org (accessed 11/4/17).

WHAT YOU CAN DO

Be an Informed Consumer of Media

- Gather information from a variety of news sources rather than relying on just one. You can set up a news aggregator with a variety of free downloadable apps, including Flipboard (**www.flipboard.com**) and Feedly (**www.feedly.com**).
- Check media watchdog organizations such as the Columbia Journalism Review (**www.cjr.org**), Fairness & Accuracy in Reporting (**www.fair.org**), and Accuracy in Media (**www.aim.org**) for reports of media bias and censorship.
- For information on the factual accuracy of what is said by political players, go to **www.factcheck.org**. For investigative journalism in the public interest, go to **www.propublica.org**. For reporting on the accuracy of news rumors, go to **www.snopes.com**.

STUDY GUIDE

The Media in American Democracy

Describe the key roles the media play in American political life (pp. 257–60)

The First Amendment to the U.S. Constitution guarantees the right to publish newspapers, magazines, and other forms of digital media without censorship by the government. The media serve three central roles in American democracy: informing the public about current political developments; providing a forum for debating political issues; and acting as a watchdog on the actions of political leaders. Unlike many other democracies, public broadcasting is a relatively small part of the American media landscape and a few giant corporations control a wide swath of media holdings in the United States.

Key Terms

media (p. 257)
media monopoly (p. 260)

Practice Quiz

1. Public broadcasting outlets that receive government funding through license fees, subsidies, or tax dollars
   a) are prohibited by the Constitution from operating in the United States.
   b) account for less than 5 percent of media market share in the United States.
   c) account for nearly one-third of media market share in the United States.
   d) account for approximately half of media market share in the United States.
   e) account for more than two-thirds of media market share in the United States.
2. More than three-fourths of the daily print newspapers in the United States are owned by
   a) large media conglomerates.
   b) the national government.
   c) small local companies.
   d) private individuals.
   e) the employees who run them.

The Media Today

Discuss how digital media have transformed how citizens learn about politics (pp. 261–77)

The rise of the internet over the last three decades has produced a massive transformation in the U.S. news media. While newspapers, magazines, television programs, and radio broadcasts are still important sources of news, many Americans now rely on digital media to learn about politics. The convenience, currency, depth, and diversity of online news has led many Americans to prefer it to more traditional sources. Changes arising from the emergence of the internet have, however, also raised concerns that online news may produce a decline in investigative journalism, a decrease in the quality of news content, and a reduction in political knowledge and tolerance.

Key Terms

broadcast media (p. 265)
penny press (p. 267)
news aggregator (p. 267)
digital citizen (p. 268)
digital divide (p. 268)
social media (p. 268)
citizen journalism (p. 271)

Practice Quiz

3. Digital citizenship requires
   a) an online subscription to one or more online newspapers.
   b) high-speed internet access and the skills to use and evaluate online information.
   c) a social media account.
   d) maintaining a political blog.
   e) registering one's computer with the government.
4. News reporting devoted to a targeted portion of readers based on content or ideological presentation is called
   a) nonprofit journalism.
   b) for-profit journalism.
   c) niche journalism.
   d) citizen journalism.
   e) adversarial journalism.
5. Which of the following is *not* a reason that many Americans appear to prefer online news?
   a) the convenience of getting news online
   b) the up-to-the-minute currency of the information available online
   c) the depth of the information available online
   d) the diversity of online viewpoints
   e) the accuracy and objectivity compared to traditional media outlets

Media Influence

Analyze the ways the media can influence public opinion and politics (pp. 277–82)

The content and character of news programming can have far-reaching political consequences. In recent American political history, the media have played a central role in numerous major events, such as the civil rights movement of the 1950s and '60s, the Vietnam War, and the Watergate affair. The power of the media lies in their ability to shape what issues Americans think about (agenda setting) and what opinions Americans hold about those issues (framing and priming).

Key Terms

agenda setting (p. 280)
selection bias (news) (p. 281)
framing (p. 282)
priming (p. 282)

Practice Quiz

6. The media's powers to determine what becomes a part of political discussion is known as
   a) framing.
   b) priming.
   c) agenda setting.
   d) selection bias.
   e) niche journalism.
7. The fact that Democrats discussed the Patient Protection and Affordable Care Act as a matter of compassionate responsibility and good economic sense while Republicans discussed it as a matter of "health care rationing" is an example of
   a) framing.
   b) priming.
   c) agenda setting.
   d) selection bias.
   e) niche journalism.

News Coverage

Explain how politicians and others try to shape the news (pp. 283–85)

While many politicians, corporations, interest groups, and nonprofit organizations attempt to shape media coverage, the content of news is typically dominated by official government sources. In addition to government sources, however, reporters frequently gain information through leaks and practicing adversarial journalism. Leaks, which are confidential pieces of information disclosed to members of the media, have driven press coverage on issues ranging from foreign policy to government corruption. Also incorporated into daily news coverage are thousands of press releases authored by advocates of influential political interests. Adversarial journalism, a form of reporting in which the media adopt a skeptical or even hostile posture toward public officials, has increased the political power of the press in recent years.

Practice Quiz

8. Most leaks originate with
   a) low-level government whistle-blowers.
   b) senior government officials, prominent politicians, and political activists.
   c) members of the public who witness misbehavior.
   d) ambassadors from foreign countries.
   e) members of the media.
9. Which organization has used the internet to anonymously release thousands of secret U.S. government documents relating to corruption, war crimes, and torture in recent years?
   a) the Federal Communications Commission
   b) WikiLeaks
   c) the National Security Agency
   d) the Project for Excellence in Journalism
   e) the Freedom of Information Agency
10. *Adversarial journalism* refers to
    a) the recent shift in American society away from general-purpose sources of information and toward narrowly focused niche sources.
    b) an era in American history when political parties provided all of the financing for newspapers.
    c) a form of reporting in which the media adopt a skeptical or even hostile posture toward the opinions and behaviors of their audience.
    d) a form of reporting in which the media adopt an accepting and friendly posture toward the government and public officials.
    e) a form of reporting in which the media adopt a skeptical or even hostile posture toward the government and public officials.
11. Which event shattered the amicable relationship between the press and the presidency?
    a) September 11, 2001
    b) the Vietnam War
    c) Watergate
    d) World War II
    e) the Monica Lewinsky affair

Regulation of the Media

Trace the evolution of rules that govern broadcast media (pp. 285–87)

Although American print and online media are free from government interference, broadcast media are subject to significant federal regulation. Radio and television stations in the United States are licensed by the Federal Communications Commission (FCC). The FCC has used its licensing power to impose several regulations, such as the equal time rule, the right of rebuttal, and the fairness doctrine, that affect the political content of radio and television broadcasts.

Key Terms

equal time rule (p. 286)
right of rebuttal (p. 286)

Practice Quiz

12. In general, FCC regulations apply only to
- a) cable television.
- b) internet websites.
- c) over-the-air broadcast media.
- d) satellite radio.
- e) newspapers and magazines.

13. The now defunct requirement that broadcasters provide time for opposing views when they air programs on controversial issues was called
- a) the equal time rule.
- b) the free speech doctrine.
- c) the fairness doctrine.
- d) the right of rebuttal.
- e) the response rule.

For Further Reading

Boydstun, Amber E. *Making the News: Politics, the Media, and Agenda Setting*. Chicago: University of Chicago Press, 2013.

Carr, Nicholas. *The Shallows: What the Internet Is Doing to Our Brains*. New York: W. W. Norton, 2011.

Chadwick, Andrew. *The Hybrid Media System: Politics and Power*. New York: Oxford University Press, 2013.

Timothy E. Cook, "The News Media as a Political Institution: Looking Backward and Looking Forward," *Political Communication* 23, no. 2 (September 2006).

Fenton, Tom. *Bad News: The Decline of Reporting, the Business of News, and the Danger to Us All*. New York: Harper Collins, 2005.

Hamilton, James T. *All the News That's Fit to Sell*. Princeton, NJ: Princeton University Press, 2004.

Iyengar, Shanto. *Media Politics: A Citizen's Guide*. New York: W. W. Norton, 2015.

Iyengar, Shanto, and Donald Kinder. *News That Matters: Television and American Public Opinion*. Chicago: University of Chicago Press, 2010.

Jamieson, Kathleen, and Paul Waldman. *The Press Effect*. New York: Oxford University Press, 2004.

Jenkins, Henry. *Convergence Culture: Where Old and New Media Collide*. New York: New York University Press, 2008.

Jenkins, Henry, Sam Ford, and Joshua Green. *Spreadable Media: Creating Value and Meaning in a Networked Culture*. New York: New York University Press, 2013.

Mossberger, Karen, Caroline Tolbert, and Ramona McNeal. *Digital Citizenship: The Internet, Society, and Participation*. Cambridge, MA: MIT Press, 2008.

Pariser, Eli. *The Filter Bubble: What the Internet Is Hiding from You*. New York: Penguin, 2011.

Shirky, Clay. *Here Comes Everybody: The Power of Organizing without Organizations*. New York: Penguin, 2009.

West, Darrell. *The Next Wave: Using Digital Technology to Further Social and Political Innovation*. Washington, DC: Brookings Institution Press, 2011.

Recommended Websites

Accuracy in Media
www.aim.org
This nonprofit watchdog group attempts to ensure accuracy in media reporting by identifying botched or slanted stories and then "setting the record straight."

Columbia Journalism Review
www.cjr.org
The Columbia Journalism Review is an organization committed to analyzing and critiquing trends in the media and journalism industries.

G. R. Boynton's New Media and Politics
ir.uiowa.edu/polisci_nmp/
This website contains a collection of research on new media trends such as microblogging, streaming video, and Twitter, with a focus on how these developments have shaped the way people share political information.

Journalism.org
www.journalism.org
This nonprofit, nonpolitical site, sponsored by the Project for Excellence in Journalism, examines the overall performance of the press as providers of information. Its aim is to help both consumers and producers of the news.

National Telecommunication and Information Administration
www.ntia.doc.gov
The National Telecommunication and Information Administration advises the president on telecommunications policies for the technological advancement of the nation. The "Broadband" section of the website includes "Digital Nation Reports" on internet usage in the United States.

Pew Internet, Science, and Tech
www.pewinternet.org
Pew Internet, Science, and Tech conducts public opinion polling, demographic research, and content analyses of trends around internet, science, and technology. Pew Research Center is an independent, nonpartisan think tank that also explores attitudes toward numerous other political issues.

Shorenstein Center on Media, Politics, and Public Policy
www.shorensteincenter.org
This research center based out of Harvard University explores the intersection of the press, politics, and public policy. The "News and Events" section includes a weekly roundup of "Must-Reads" on the media and politics.

★ chapter ★

08

Political Participation and Voting

WHAT GOVERNMENT DOES AND WHY IT MATTERS Who votes affects who is elected and what issues politicians put at the top of their agenda. Historically there's been a great deal of concern that young people turn out at lower rates than older Americans. But these days, although their turnout can still be low, the sheer number of Americans under age 35 means that they constitute a larger share of the electorate than baby boomers and older Americans.[1] And they are beginning to flex their electoral muscles, shaping election outcomes.

The 2017 Virginia race for governor is a case in point. Early polls showed Republican Ed Gillespie ahead of Democrat Ralph Northam. But in the end Northam won by nine percentage points. Much of Northam's margin came from Virginians under 30, whose turnout increased from just 18 percent in 2009 to 34 percent in 2017 and who supported Northam over Gillespie 69 to 30 percent.[2]

Groups on both the political right and left mobilized Virginia voters at double or triple the rates of the previous gubernatorial election. The National Rifle Association and Americans for Prosperity

For much of the country's history, large groups of Americans were denied the right to vote. Most restrictions on voting have been eliminated for Americans age 18 and older, but turnout remains relatively low, especially among young voters. Will changes in voting laws increase participation?

reached out to conservative voters. The Virginia League of Conservation Voters and BlackPAC knocked on Democrats' doors. NextGen America, a group founded by billionaire Tom Steyer to mobilize young voters, sponsored a petting zoo at Virginia Tech to pull students in with baby animals and tell them where to vote.[3]

As important as the youth vote was, 34 percent is a pretty low turnout rate. Turnout is generally higher in presidential elections, but even at the modern peak, the election of 2008, only 62 percent of Americans voted;[4] in 2016, the turnout rate was 59 percent.[5] In most democratic countries, residents are automatically registered to vote in elections at adult age. In the United States, citizens must actively register to vote and, in most states, must do so in advance of the election—sometimes 30 days beforehand. Young people especially are less likely to register to vote than are older Americans.[6] In an effort to boost voter turnout, a number of states have begun to offer same-day registration, which means that people can both register and vote when they go to the polls on Election Day. As of 2018, 18 states plus Washington, D.C., had enacted same-day registration laws.

Of the 10 states with the highest average voting rates, 7 offer same-day registration.[7]

Voting is just one form of political participation, and voter-registration requirements are just one factor that affects who participates in American politics. As we will see in this chapter, who participates and how they participate matter a great deal—in elections and in influencing government policy.

CHAPTER GOALS

- ★ **Describe the major forms of traditional and digital participation in politics (pp. 297–310)**
- ★ **Describe the patterns of participation among major demographic groups (pp. 310–19)**
- ★ **Explain the factors in the political environment that influence whether individuals vote or not (pp. 319–23)**
- ★ **Explain the effect of electoral laws on voting (pp. 323–27)**

Forms of Political Participation

Describe the major forms of traditional and digital participation in politics

We can think of political participation as falling into two major categories. Traditional participation in politics includes not only voting but also attending campaign events, rallies, and fund-raisers, volunteering on behalf of candidates and political organizations, canvassing, displaying campaign signs, contacting elected officials, contributing money to candidates and parties, or even challenging a law in court. Protests, demonstrations, and strikes, too, are age-old forms of participatory politics.

In addition to traditional participation, the growing world of digital politics includes not only the exchange of information but also fund-raising and voter mobilization. Though most experts now agree that digital politics is just a new way of engaging in traditional politics, as digital politics becomes more common, it continues to change participation in important ways that may increase engagement in politics overall.

TRADITIONAL POLITICAL PARTICIPATION

Traditional political participation refers to a wide range of activities designed to influence government, politics, and policy. For most citizens today, voting in elections is the most common form of participation in politics. Yet ordinary people took part in politics long before the advent of the election or any other formal mechanism of popular involvement in political life. If there is any natural or spontaneous form of popular political participation, it is not the election but the protest or riot. In fact, for much of American history, fewer Americans exercised their right to vote than participated in urban riots and rural uprisings, as voting for a long time was limited to white, male, landowning citizens.

traditional political participation activities designed to influence government, including voting, campaign contributions and face-to-face activities such as volunteering for a campaign or working on behalf of a candidate or political organization

The vast majority of Americans reject rioting or violence for political ends, but peaceful **protest** is protected by the First Amendment and generally recognized as a legitimate and important form of political activity. During the height of the civil rights movement in the 1960s, hundreds of thousands of Americans took part in peaceful protests to demand social and political rights for African Americans. Peaceful marches and demonstrations have been employed by a host of groups across the ideological spectrum, such as the conservative Tea Party Movement against big government and 2011 Occupy Wall Street protests against growing income inequality. To take a more recent example, in March 2018 thousands of people participated nationwide in March for Our Lives protests against gun violence and lack of gun regulations in the wake of a string of school shootings.

protest participation that involves assembling crowds to confront a government or other official organization

Protests have erupted particularly in response to the Trump presidency and some of his controversial measures. The nationwide Women's March the day after Trump's inauguration day was the largest single-day protest in U.S. history, with half a million protesters. The Women's March advocated policies to protect human rights, women's rights, LGBTQ rights, reproductive rights, racial equality, freedom of religion, workers' rights, immigration reform, universal health care, and protecting the environment. That same month there were massive protests against Trump's controversial travel restrictions on immigrants from seven predominantly

One advantage of protest is visibility: through media attention, protesters can raise awareness, attract like-minded individuals, and put pressure on politicians. That was the goal of (left to right) the Women's March, NFL players kneeling during the national anthem to protest police brutality, and white nationalists in Charlottesville, Virginia, protesting the removal of a Confederate statue.

Muslim countries. In August 2017 violent clashes erupted in Charlottesville, Virginia, between white nationalists, rallying against the city's decision to remove a statue of Confederate general Robert E. Lee, and counterprotesters. President Trump further inflamed emotions when he refused to denounce the white supremacists. The fallout from the controversial Charlottesville marches, and Trump's comments, led the CEOs of leading U.S. corporations to resign in protest from two White House advisory councils of American business leaders. Protests often lead to action and remain a common form of political participation across the ideological spectrum.

Growing concern over police discrimination and excessive use of force against African Americans has led to hundreds of protests across the nation in the past five years, including NFL players, coaches, and owners kneeling in locked arms during the playing of the national anthem in silent protest of racial inequality.

People participate in public protests to attract media attention, raise public awareness, and send a message to politicians about the policies they enact. The Black Lives Matter movement and protests by NFL players, for example, have prompted a national discussion and political action around police violence and reform, including revamped training programs and calls to equip police officers with body cameras. Opinion polls suggest that both white and black Americans increasingly feel that racism is a problem in American society.[8]

Elections, of course, are the hallmark of political participation in a democracy. In addition to voting (discussed below), citizens can give money to candidates or political organizations, volunteer to work on campaigns, contact political officials, sign petitions, attend public meetings, join organizations, display campaign signs and pins, write letters to the editor, and attend rallies. They can also lobby their representatives in Congress, and they can even sue the government or run for elected office. Such activities can communicate much more detailed information to public officials than voting can. By volunteering for a political campaign, writing or emailing their member of Congress, or contributing money to a political organization, people can convey their specific opinions, making these other political

activities often more satisfying than voting.[9] However, these other forms of political action generally require more time, effort, and/or money than voting. As a result, as Figure 8.1 shows, the percentage of the population that participates in ways other than voting is relatively low.

Participation through Voting For most Americans, voting is the single most important political act. Voting is the most common way that individuals interact with politics. The right to vote gives ordinary Americans an equal voice in politics as each vote has the same value. Voting is especially important because it selects the officials who make the laws that the American people must follow.

The right to vote, or **suffrage**, is a legal right. During early periods of American history, suffrage was restricted to white males over the age of 21. Many states further limited voting to those who owned property or paid more than a specified amount of annual tax. Until the early 1900s, state legislatures elected U.S. senators, and there were no direct elections for members of the Electoral College (who in turn elect the president). As a result, elections for the U.S. House as well as state and local offices were the primary venue for citizen participation in government.

suffrage the right to vote; also called *franchise*

During the nineteenth and early twentieth centuries, states often acted to restrict suffrage, initially through poll taxes (fees to vote) and literacy tests (reading tests) designed to curtail immigrant voting in northern cities. These laws were later imported to the southern states to prevent African Americans and poor whites from voting during the Jim Crow era, the period between the Civil War and the 1960s (see Chapter 5). Voter eligibility requirements often varied greatly from state to state. Some states openly prevented the right to vote on the basis of race; others did not. Some states required property ownership for voting; others had no such restrictions.[10]

Over the past two centuries of American history, a dominant trend has been federal statutes, court decisions, and constitutional amendments designed to override state voting laws and expand suffrage.[11] In the South, voting rights for

FIGURE 8.1

Political Participation

Political activities such as volunteering generally take more time and effort than voting. When asked about various forms of political participation, over 40 percent of respondents said they expressed support for a campaign on social media.

SOURCE: The ANES 2012 Time Series Study, www.electionstudies.org/studypages/anes_timesseries_2012/anes_timeseries_2012.htm (accessed 10/30/14). Based on a sample made up primarily of registered voters; "Political Engagement, Knowledge, and the Midterms," Pew Research Center, April 26, 2018, www.people-press.org/2018/04/26/10-political-engagement-knowledge-and-the-midterms/ (accessed 10/12/18).

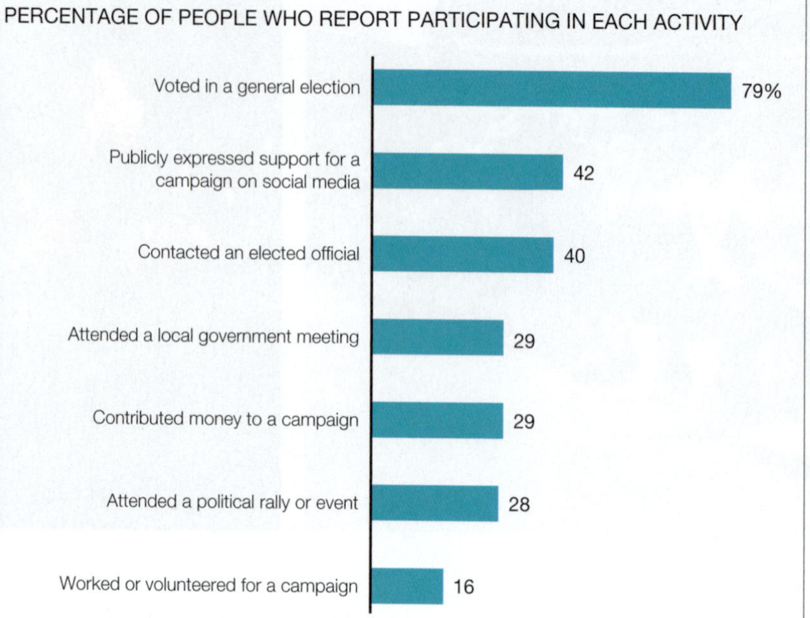

African American men were established by the Fifteenth Amendment in 1870, which prohibited denying the right to vote on the basis of race. Despite the Fifteenth Amendment, the voting rights of African American men were effectively rescinded during the 1880s by the states of the former Confederacy with voting laws such as poll taxes and literacy tests, as discussed above. A goal of the civil rights movement in the 1950s and '60s was voting rights for African Americans. This goal was partially achieved with the enactment of the 1965 Voting Rights Act, which authorized the federal government to register voters in states that discriminated against minority citizens and allowed the government to challenge voting rules and practices that systematically disenfranchise minority voters. The result was the re-enfranchisement of southern blacks for the first time since the 1860s.

Women won the right to vote in 1920 through the adoption of the Nineteenth Amendment to the Constitution. This amendment resulted primarily from the activism of the women's suffrage movement, led by Elizabeth Cady Stanton, Susan B. Anthony, and Carrie Chapman Catt, among others, during the late nineteenth and early twentieth centuries. The suffragists held rallies, demonstrations, and protest marches for more than half a century before achieving their goal. Before the federal government granted women the right to vote, numerous states and territories adopted women's suffrage, paving the way for women to earn the right to vote nationally.

The most recent expansion of the right to vote in the United States, the Twenty-Sixth Amendment, lowered the voting age from 21 to 18. Ratified during the Vietnam War, in 1971, it was intended to channel the disruptive protest activities of students involved in the anti–Vietnam War movement into peaceful participation at the ballot box.

FOR CRITICAL ANALYSIS

Describe the expansion of suffrage in the United States since the Founding. Why might the government have denied participation to so many for so long? What forces influenced the expansion of voting rights?

The campaign for women's suffrage gathered strength in the United States in the mid-eighteenth century. Activists fought for decades—with tactics ranging from protests to pickets to hunger strikes—before the Nineteenth Amendment to the Constitution granted all adult women the right to vote in 1920.

Current Trends in Voter Turnout Today, voting rights are granted to all American citizens aged 18 and above, although some states revoke this right from those who have committed a felony or are mentally impaired. Although eligibility to vote is now almost universal, America's overall rate of voting participation, or **turnout**, remains relatively low. The United States ranked 32nd in terms of voter turnout compared to other developed countries in 2016. Just over 58 percent voted in the 2012 and 2016 presidential elections. This pales in comparison to voting rates in the most recent national elections in other democracies: 87 percent in Belgium, 86 percent in Sweden, 71 percent in France, and 61 percent in the United Kingdom. Turnout in state and local elections, especially those that do not coincide with national contests or primaries, is typically much lower.[12]

turnout the percentage of eligible individuals who actually vote

Not only does the United States have relatively low rates of participation in elections, but those who do not vote are more likely to lack a college education and have lower incomes. That education and income tracks so closely with voter turnout is unique to the United States among other Western democracies. Low voter turnout coupled with unequal participation rates can have negative outcomes, including the election of candidates who do not reflect the interests of most voters, government policies that benefit wealthy voters over the middle and lower classes, and lower trust in government and perceptions of government legitimacy.

Participation in U.S. presidential elections has declined over the past four decades from a high of 64 percent in 1960. In 1996 participation reached a modern low when only 52 percent of eligible voters went to the polls. Since then, however, overall trends have improved in presidential elections due to highly contested elections and major efforts to get out the vote. Turnout reached a modern high of 62 percent in 2008 when Barack Obama's campaign mobilized many new voters. Turnout in 2016 was the third highest in the modern period and broke a record in terms of votes cast at 137.5 million ballots or 59 percent of eligible

FIGURE 8.2

Voter Turnout* in Presidential and Midterm Elections, 1892–2018

Since the 1890s, participation in elections has declined substantially. One pattern is consistent across time: more Americans tend to vote in presidential election years than in years when only congressional and local elections are held. What are some of the reasons that participation rose and fell during the last century?

*Percentage of voting-eligible population

SOURCES: Erik Austin and Jerome Clubb, *Political Facts of the United States since 1789* (New York: Columbia University Press, 1986); United States Election Project, www.electproject.org (accessed 11/14/16); "2018 November General Election Turnout Rates," United States Election Project, November 7, 2018, www.electproject.org/2018g (accessed 11/9/18).

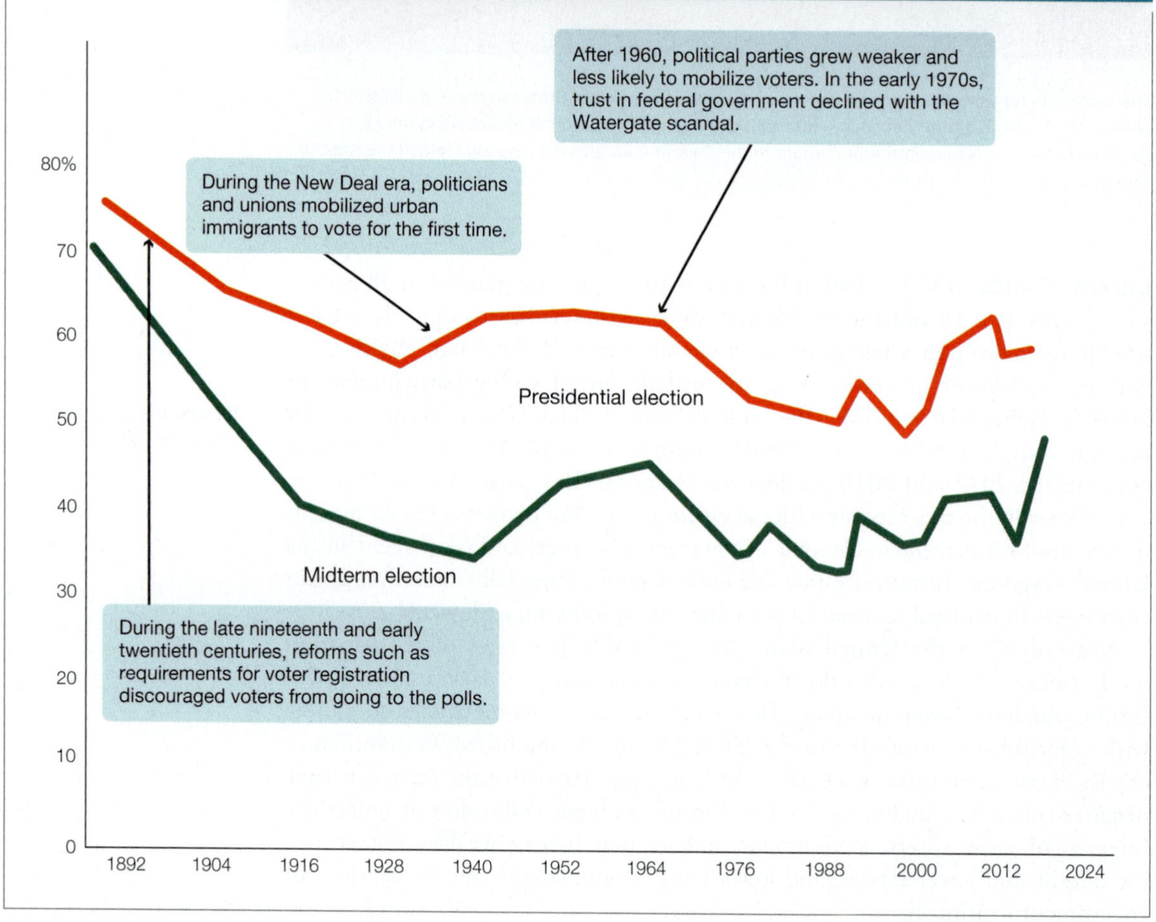

After 1960, political parties grew weaker and less likely to mobilize voters. In the early 1970s, trust in federal government declined with the Watergate scandal.
80%
70
60
50
40
30
20
10
0
During the New Deal era, politicians and unions mobilized urban immigrants to vote for the first time.
Presidential election
Midterm election
During the late nineteenth and early twentieth centuries, reforms such as requirements for voter registration discouraged voters from going to the polls.
1892
1904
1916
1928
1940
1952
1964
1976
1988
2000
2012
2024

voters.[13] Midterm elections with only congressional elections at the national level tend to have much lower voter turnout. In 2014, 36 percent voted though in 2018 turnout rose to 49 percent, a record high seen in non-presidential elections since 1966 (see Figure 8.2). Despite these overall trends, there are significant differences in voter turnout rates across the states. We'll learn about why later in this chapter.

DIGITAL POLITICAL PARTICIPATION

digital political participation
activities designed to influence politics using the internet, including visiting a candidate's website, organizing events online, and signing an online petition

Digital political participation is rapidly changing the way Americans experience politics. The internet and social media give citizens greater access to information about candidates and campaigns and a greater role in politics than ever before; digital politics is the new pulse of American democracy where political news frequently goes viral. Digital politics builds on traditional forms of participation but makes many of those activities easier and more immediate, giving citizens greater potential for community building and networked participation. The internet, and social media in particular, offers an active, two-way form of communication with feedback, rather than the more passive, one-way communication involved in reading printed newspapers, watching television, or listening to the radio. It allows for person-to-person communication as well as broadcast capability, especially through social media, where information can be widely shared.

Digital participation includes discussing issues or mobilizing supporters through social media, emailing and text messaging, reading blogs and online news stories, viewing YouTube videos and campaign ads, and sharing opinions on the internet, contributing money to candidates and political organizations, contacting political leaders and following them on Twitter, campaigning on social networking sites, working on behalf of candidates, and organizing face-to-face neighborhood meetings online. With 67 percent of Americans reading the news using social media, digital participation is the most common way average Americans participate in politics outside of voting.[14]

Why are digital media so effective for mobilization and political participation? Online mobilization works through emotional appeals, immediacy, personal networks, and social pressure. Political scientist Meredith Rolf argues that social connections are an essential component of political participation. Her work reveals that individual factors such as income and education are imperfect predictors of turnout, but one's social network *is* strongly predictive of political participation. When members of a social network indicate they have voted in an election or contributed to a candidate, for example, that can motivate others to do the same. Peer social pressure allows members of a social network to model and mimic actions of other members of their group.[15]

Social media in particular can efficiently coordinate the actions of millions of people required for political campaigns and winning elections. One in three social media users have encouraged others to vote, and roughly the same percentage have shared their own thoughts or comments on politics or government online.[16] Social media are characterized by tiny acts of political participation—sharing, following a candidate or organization, liking a post, commenting—that can scale up to dramatic changes, leading to real world political protests, voter mobilization drives, and the election of candidates and parties to government.[17] Small acts of political participation made possible by social media may give those uninterested in politics or who are rarely engaged a way of getting involved easily, which can than encourage them to do more.

Politicians, too, make much use of social media. In 2016 every serious presidential candidate had a Facebook page and Twitter account, with thousands or in some cases millions of fans who received daily updates from the candidates, political parties, and campaigns. These fans, in turn, signaled to their friends which candidates they supported for elected office, making politics a seamless part of everyday discussion. Donald Trump's supporters receive emails from his organization, follow him on Twitter and Facebook, and turn out for rallies and events. Based on a survey analysis of 65,000 registered voters and holding all other demographic factors constant, frequent social media users were more likely to vote for Trump than any other candidate in 2016.[18]

Unlike traditional social movements that gain momentum slowly over time, digital politics, and the use of social media especially, can create punctuated explosive bursts of collective action. For example, Bernie Sanders's supporters relied heavily on Reddit to organize rallies and rock concerts during the 2016 presidential primaries on behalf of the Vermont senator. Protests erupted after Trump won the 2016 election despite losing the popular vote by nearly 3 million votes. Over 700,000 people signed an online petition in a matter of days to eliminate the electoral college and elect the president based on actual votes cast.

Some have dismissed social media as *clicktivism*—forms of participation that require little effort and may or may not convert to offline acts of participation in politics. Others argue so-called clicktivism is the building block for sustained participation in politics. President Trump's extensive use of Twitter is evidence that audience-building on social media matters for political leadership and winning votes. The clicks of millions of Americans can and do add up.

Digital Politics Leads to Offline Participation An important question is whether online engagement in politics influences offline participation, especially voting. The discussion above suggests a number of mechanisms by which social networks and small acts of political participation lead to voting and offline engagement in politics. Many people use social media to facilitate organizing face-to-face neighborhood meetings or to get information about a local campaign event or where to vote. Digital politics encourages information-gathering and interaction among users and elected officials by combining the content of traditional media with interpersonal communication. The combination of information and interaction gives the internet the potential to promote interest in politics and increase participation. A growing body of research finds that online activities such as reading digital news, commenting on blogs, and using email or social media for politics increases the likelihood of voting and is associated with contributing to political campaigns, volunteering on behalf of candidates, and even contacting elected officials. Online participation is also linked with discussing politics with friends or family, developing an interest in politics in general, and being informed about politics.[19]

Additionally, the ease of making monetary contributions online has led to a dramatic increase in this form of political participation. The percentage of people who donated directly to candidates has doubled since 1992. Barack Obama was the first candidate to capitalize on online fundraising, raising much of the money needed to win the 2008 presidential election from small (less than $100) individual online donations. In fact, the 2008 presidential election and Obama's campaign ushered in the modern era of digital politics, building comprehensive online strategies to mobilize supporters, and citizens made unprecedented use of digital media to learn about candidates and to participate in campaigns.[20] In 2016, 12 percent of Americans said they contributed money to a candidate running for public office, up from 6 percent four years earlier. In large part because of online donations, 71 percent of Hillary Clinton's fundraising total[21] and 40 percent of Donald Trump's[22] in 2016 came from individual contributions.

AMERICA SIDE by SIDE

Voter Turnout in Comparison

Over the past 20 years, voter turnout in U.S. national elections has hovered around 45 percent of the voting-age population. While the number is significantly higher in presidential elections than in midterm elections (though in the 2018 midterm election turnout was roughly 49 percent),[a] voting rates in the United States still lag behind those in many other democratic countries. Australia, despite seeing their lowest turnout since 1925, had 78.9 percent of their voting-age population participate in the 2016 parliamentary election.[b]

So why does voter turnout vary so much from country to country? Part of the explanation rests in how we calculate who is eligible to vote. In the United States, noncitizens and ex-felons are denied voting rights. If we exclude those populations when calculating voter percentages, U.S. turnout would be at least two percentage points higher in each election.[c]

Another explanation relates to the rules governing elections. Some countries have rules that make it easier or harder for citizens to vote, while others penalize those who do not vote. In many democracies, citizens are automatically registered to vote when they reach a certain age; in contrast, U.S. citizens generally must register themselves, reregister if they move, and, in many states, register a certain number of days before the election. Many countries hold their elections on a Sunday, send their ballots through the mail, or declare their election day a national holiday, meaning that fewer voters must choose between going to work or going to the polls. Voting is also compulsory in many countries. Australia, for instance, charges a $20 fine (about US$16) unless a citizen can provide a good excuse for why she did not vote.[d] Countries with frequent elections like the United States and Switzerland often see depressed turnout as well, despite laws that ease or hinder access to the polls.

TURNOUT IN NATIONAL ELECTIONS*

	Turnout	Compulsory voting	Weekend or holiday voting	Automatic or compulsory registration
Australia	81%	✓	✓	✓
Brazil	76	✓	✓	✓
Germany	69		✓	✓
India	65		✓	✓
Japan	60		✓	✓
United Kingdom	60			✓
Canada	57			
Mexico	55	✓	✓	✓
South Africa	54		✓	✓
Tunisia	54			
United States	45			
Switzerland	39		✓	✓

*Average 1990–2018.

SOURCES: International Institute for Democracy and Electoral Assistance (IDEA) voter turnout database, www.idea.int/vt/viewdata.cfm, and the ACE Electoral Knowledge Network, www.aceproject.org/epic-en/CDMap?question=VR008&f= (accessed 3/27/18).

[a] International Institute for Democracy and Electoral Assistance (IDEA), Voter Turnout Database, www.idea.int/vt/viewdata.cfm (accessed 4/12/18).

[b] Nicole Hasham, "Election 2016: Voter Turnout Lowest since Compulsory Voting Began in 1925," *Sydney Morning Herald*, August 8, 2016, www.smh.com.au/politics/federal/election-2016-voter-turnout-lowest-since-compulsory-voting-began-in-1925-20160808-gqnij2.html (accessed 4/12/18).

[c] Michael P. McDonald, "National General Election VEP Turnout Rates, 1789–Present," United States Election Project, June 11, 2014, www.electproject.org/national-1789-present (accessed 4/12/18).

[d] Hasham, "Election 2016."

Twitter has become an especially important tool for voter mobilization. The percentage of Americans following elected officials on Twitter continues to soar. Citizens like following political figures on social media because they feel more emotionally connected to the candidates.[23] Social media also allow users to avoid exposure to information that challenges their preexisting views—it's easier to follow people online whom you agree with. Elected officials and organizations on the ideological left and right have taken advantage of this dynamic to filter the news and current events. Recent research finds people who use social media for politics frequently hold stronger opinions and are more polarized by party. A benefit of Twitter for politics, however, is that it leads to more interest in politics and higher rates of participation and voter turnout.[24]

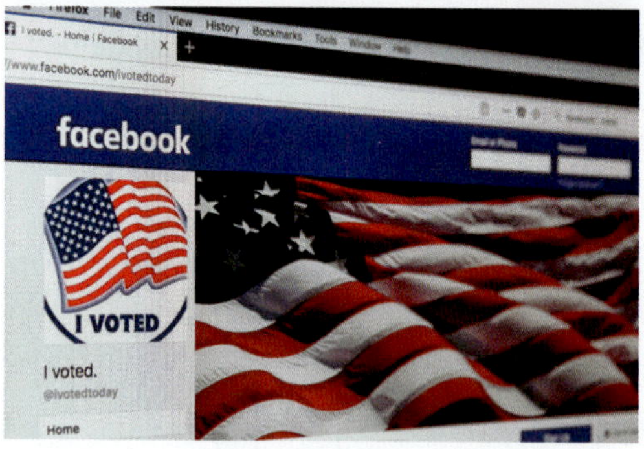

Like the traditional "I Voted" stickers, political messages shared on social media may remind and encourage others to participate too. In recent elections, Facebook users could click an "I Voted" button to announce that they had cast a ballot.

Researchers have suggested a number of possible reasons that digital politics may foster participation. First, information and political news are available 24 hours a day for those with internet access. Online news is often breaking news that can spread rapidly, and it is generally free. Digital politics may also engage individuals who otherwise would not be involved in politics. The internet creates a form of "accidental mobilization" for those who are greeted by political news on social media—sometimes politics finds the individual, rather than the other way around.[25] It is common for candidates to place political ads on social media sites and in Google searches, prompting the individuals exposed to these ads, who may be online for entirely separate reasons, to learn about politics. Donald Trump took advantage of online political ads in the 2016 campaign unlike any other modern candidate, spending millions of dollars on online ads. With two-thirds of Americans using social media, "Facebook was the 500-pound gorilla" that mobilized voters to support Trump. Facebook ads were more important than television ads in 2016.[26]

Further, digital media have unique characteristics that enhance participation. Streaming video online combines the qualities of print media that promote knowledge and in-depth reporting with the immediate and visual aspects of television that generate interest, engagement, and emotion.[27] Emotional responses to political candidates or issues learned from online media have been shown to trigger interest in politics and engagement.[28]And research has found that emotions are important in candidate evaluations and ultimately political behavior and participation. A recent study found Obama in 2008 and Trump in 2016 generated higher positive emotions from their supporters compared to other candidates. High emotional enthusiasm for these candidates was associated with their popularity, and ultimately their election victories.[29]

Finally, as we have discussed, online politics makes it easier for people to participate in politics because it requires less effort. By its very nature, digital politics occurs in ways that are less location-dependent than traditional politics: *community* takes on a very different meaning in an online social network compared with, say, a voter's actual neighborhood precinct. The internet facilitates participation that is potentially broad but with loose connections.[30] A large but more loosely knit online community may promote extensive organizing efforts and improve political knowledge, interest, and participation, but it also encourages forms of participation that can be low in intensity and sporadic—"clicktivism," as discussed above—possibly attracting individuals with only moderate political interest. Political scientist Bruce Bimber has shown that some interest groups are responding to this new political climate of sporadic participation by making it possible for individuals to support a specific issue or campaign without making a commitment to membership in the organization as a whole.[31] In this way, online politics widens the pool of political participation.

For all these reasons, digital media may foster a new kind of community building that has the potential to reverse the trends in declining political participation since the 1960s. Some analysts have cited reduced trust in government, unresponsive elected officials, and a diminishing stock of what Robert Putnam, author of *Bowling Alone*, calls social capital—community networks that motivate political participation—to explain low voter turnout in the United States.[32] By making political information, discussion, communication, and mobilization easier, the internet, and especially social media, may help Americans grow a new kind of digital social capital, one based on shared political experiences online.[33]

News about the Supreme Court's 2015 decision to legalize same-sex marriage spread rapidly, in part through viral activity on social media. Sites such as Twitter provided users with a highly visible platform to show support.

Expressive Politics Political scientist Russell Dalton has argued that participation in politics is becoming more expressive than ever before, largely aided by social media.[34] Today, individuals turn to social media to express their opinions on issues or candidates in many ways. This trend was exemplified by the response to the 2015 Supreme Court ruling that made same-sex marriage legal in all 50 states.

In the wake of the decision, digital politics created a media firestorm as responses to the decision took over the internet. The immediacy with which the news spread was remarkable. Traditional media and social media converged to celebrate or denounce the news that marriage for same-sex couples was the new law of the land. Social media enabled citizens to share their opinions in uniquely expressive ways. For example, the #LoveWins hashtag was used almost 5.5 million times in 24 hours, even by celebrities and President Obama, to recognize the Court's decision. Overall there were 10 million tweets about the Supreme Court decision in less than 12 hours.[35] And millions of people, too, used Facebook's tool to add a rainbow-colored background to their profile pictures or shared news stories and memes using rainbow images to show their support for marriage rights. Increased participation in digital politics, especially through social media, may force elected officials to better represent the people.[36]

Are There Drawbacks to Digital Participation? While social media can be effective in online political mobilization and activation, at the same time digital media create silos, echo chambers, and filter bubbles where individuals with shared views communicate to the exclusion of others, leading to increased ideological party polarization—and eventually hyper-partisanship. As mentioned earlier, people tend to surround themselves with news from like-minded sources. In such environments, people may uncritically believe news from outlets they trust while dismissing or ignoring information from sources they dislike. Social media algorithms can also create echo chambers that lead to extreme or biased views that get worse over time, creating a world of "alternative facts" where individuals cannot agree on basic principles.

There is evidence that social media—because of filter bubbles and polarized information environments—has exacerbated partisan conflict, social divisions, the culture wars, and intolerance based on race, ethnicity, gender, or religion. Anonymous social media discussion boards can have unintended consequences by allowing a forum for racism and hate speech, terrorist appeals, and sexual harassment—forums that have mobilized far right groups, including white nationalists. Some observers see a lack of civility in public discourse, or what is called a "coarsening of public discourse." Members of targeted groups—such as women and minorities—may opt out of participating in discussion of politics in what has been called the "disruption of the public square."[37]

THE DARK SIDE OF DIGITAL POLITICS: RUSSIAN VOTER SUPPRESSION AND MOBILIZATION

Free and fair elections are the foundation for democracies. But democratic elections may be increasingly vulnerable to manipulation by foreign governments and other extremists because of open networks and unregulated political advertising on social media. Donald Trump's campaign not only capitalized on social media and high enthusiasm from his supporters but also benefited from a Russian cyber campaign that used social media to discredit his opponent. Intelligence agencies have confirmed Russian interference in the election. Russian propaganda to disrupt the election was intended to mobilize Trump supporters to vote, demobilize Clinton supporters, promote third-party candidates to Bernie Sanders's supporters, and sow seeds of discord in the American public.

The first strategy focused on mobilizing voters to cast a ballot for Donald Trump. One notable ad featured a kneeling soldier and stated that the Constitution should be amended to take control of the army from Clinton should she be elected president. A similar ad had the false caption, "69 percent of veterans favor Trump" (in reality roughly 52 percent of veterans voted for Trump compared to 48 percent for Clinton—nearly a toss-up). As Senator Chris Coons (D-Del.) said, "This ad is nothing short of the Russian government directly interfering in our elections, lying to American citizens, duping folks who believe they are joining and supporting a group that is about veterans and based in Texas, when in fact it is paid for in rubles [Russian currency] by Russians."[38]

A second category of Russian propaganda worked to suppress votes for Clinton. These ads were targeted in sophisticated ways toward demographic and partisan groups in swing states such as Wisconsin, Michigan, and central Pennsylvania (three states Trump narrowly won over Clinton), but also nationwide. Fake news stories focused on Clinton's health and mental stability in the two weeks leading up to the election. The most troubling Russian propaganda ads encouraged people to cast a vote for Clinton by texting or tweeting their ballot, both of which are invalid forms of voting in the United States. Finally, to dissuade Bernie Sanders's supporters from turning out to vote for Clinton, the websites of Sanders supporters were found have extensive postings by fake eastern Europeans bot accounts.

The scope of Russian interference in the 2016 election and the foreign propaganda campaign was far greater than initially expected. Facebook and other social media platforms revealed thousands of false political ads appeared on their networks that were paid for by Russian operatives, with many of the ads focused on voter suppression. These ads are estimated to have reached 126 million people on Facebook alone, or 40 percent of the U.S. population. (To put this number in perspective, there were only 135 million votes cast in the 2016 election.) The information was shared hundreds of millions of times. Russian propaganda on Instagram during the election reached another 20 million people. Twitter found nearly 3,000 accounts controlled by Russian operatives and 36,000 more bot accounts that tweeted 1.4 million times during the election. A recent study from USC found that 1 in 5 tweets about the election were from bot accounts; the majority promoted stories damaging to Clinton.[39]

In addition to the aims described above, Russia's campaign on social media also sought more generally to divide the public over controversial issues such as race, immigration, abortion, gay rights, and gun ownership. Fake Facebook accounts linked to Russia included, for example, Infidels against Islam, Fed-up with Illegals, and Stop Killing White People.

Russian interference has exposed the outsized role played by platforms such as Facebook, Twitter, and Google in American politics and discourse—and that these companies don't always follow the same rules as government institutions. Russia's actions exposed the dark side of technology for democratic governance. Unlike traditional media (radio, television, print media) online political ads on Google and social media sites are not regulated. A foreign government was able to take advantage of the United States' open digital communication and media system to interfere in the election. In response Congress has enacted economic sanctions on Russia and is considering new regulations of online political advertising. The Honest Ads Act is aimed at preventing foreign influence on elections by subjecting political ads sold online to the same rules and transparency that apply to TV and radio.[40] The technology companies have also taken steps to crack down on fake accounts.

SUMMING UP DIGITAL PARTICIPATION

As we have seen, digital participation in politics has benefits and costs. It has the potential to foster innovation, free expression, social connections, information seeking, and political participation. But it may also foster misinformation, intolerance, a lack of civility, and breaches of privacy and even demobilization. A barrier to digital participation is the digital divide—defined as the gap between those with and those without home internet or mobile access. Growing inequalities online replicate existing societal inequalities based on race and economic class that threaten to widen gaps in who is informed about politics and who participates. Today, over 35 percent of Americans don't have home broadband, and those without access tend to be poorer, less educated, and older. The digital divide creates new inequalities as the world of politics moves online.

Perhaps the most transformative aspect of digital media is how they affect candidates and parties. Political candidates find campaigning online particularly attractive because it is cost-efficient and can reach a wide audience of prospective voters. Running for office can be enormously expensive, but social media may help level the playing field by reducing candidate reliance on money from corporations, special interests, and wealthy donors. Digital politics holds the promise of reinvigorating a more grassroots and participatory democracy. In 2016, Bernie Sanders largely rejected Super PAC funding for his campaign and relied heavily on digital media; Donald Trump did the same during the primaries. Grassroots funding in turn may allow political leaders to better connect to, and ultimately represent, the people.

Who Participates?

Describe the patterns of participation among major demographic groups

Individuals face a number of costs and benefits related to their decision to become involved in politics. Just as in any other activity in life, an individual is likely to vote in an election only if the benefits outweigh the costs.[41] One benefit associated with voting is the favorable policies that might result from having one's preferred candidate or party in office, which the potential voter weighs against the slim likelihood of her vote actually influencing the outcome of the election. Another benefit of voting is the sense of pride gained from fulfilling one's civic duty. The costs related to voting can include the time and resources needed to become informed and to cast a ballot, which may help explain why the poor and the less educated are less likely to vote and participate in politics in other ways.

To understand who votes, it helps to understand why some Americans don't vote. The U.S. Census indicates the top reason for not voting in the 2016 presidential election was "did not like the candidates or campaign issues." This reason was cited by almost 25 percent of nonvoters in 2016, compared to just 13 percent who gave this response in 2012. Fifteen percent of nonvoters said they were "not interested in politics"; 4 percent said they were "too busy or [had] conflicting schedules"; and almost 12 percent said they had an illness or disability that prevented them from voting. As we can see, even personal health can be a predictor of voting, with the healthier more likely to participate in politics.[42]

The factors that help us explain voting in elections can be grouped into three general categories: (1) a person's social and demographic characteristics and attitudes about politics; (2) the political environment in which elections take place, such as campaigns that seek to mobilize voters and whether an election is contested among two political candidates; and (3) the state electoral laws that shape the electoral process. We examine each in turn.

SOCIOECONOMIC STATUS

socioeconomic status status in society based on level of education, income, and occupational prestige

One of the most important and consistent findings from surveys about participation is that Americans with higher levels of education, more income, and higher-level occupations—collectively, what social scientists call higher **socioeconomic status**—participate much more in politics than do those with less education and less income.[43] Education is the single most important factor in predicting not only whether an individual will vote but also most kinds of participation. Unsurprisingly, income is another important factor when it comes to making contributions, as well as voting. People who are more affluent have the money, time, and capacity to participate effectively in the political system. Among people aged 45–64, for example, the 2016 Census found that 83 percent of individuals earning over $150,000 a year voted compared to 43 percent of those earning less than $20,000 per year.[44] These characteristics are also related to attitudes toward politics. Higher levels of political interest are associated with individuals higher on the socioeconomic scale.[45]

Figure 8.3 shows the differences in voter turnout linked to ethnic and racial groups, education level, employment status, and age. Just 52 percent of those with only a high school diploma voted in the recent presidential election, compared with 74 percent of college graduates.[46]

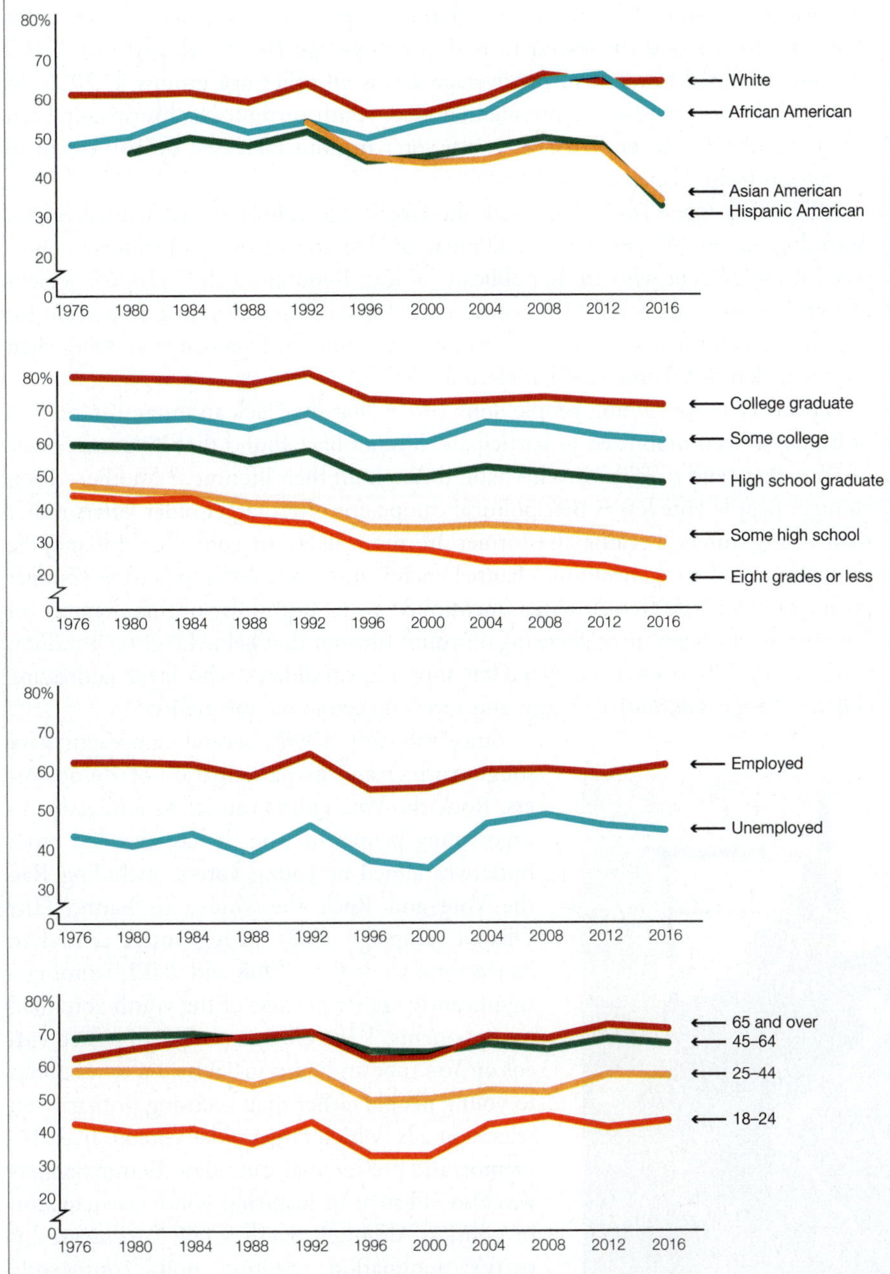

FIGURE 8.3

The Percentage of Americans Who Voted, 1976–2016

Voting rates vary substantially by race and ethnicity, education, employment status, and age. Which groups have the highest rates of voter turnout? Among which groups has participation increased the most since 1992?

SOURCES: U.S. Census Bureau, "Reported Voting and Registration by Race, Hispanic Origin, Sex, and Age Groups: November 1964 to 2016"; "Reported Voting and Registration by Region, Educational Attainment, and Labor Force: November 1964 to 2016," www.census.gov (accessed 3/24/18).

FOR CRITICAL ANALYSIS

As voter turnout has declined since its peak in the late 1800s, inequality in political participation has become more severe. Why are upper-income Americans more likely to be voters than lower-income Americans?

Education is one of the most important predictors of voting, and it is also associated with encouraging other people to vote or support an issue, as well making a donation to a candidate or cause.[47]

AGE AND PARTICIPATION

Older people have much higher rates of participation than do young people, in part because homeownership and property taxes, more common among older individuals, lead to a greater awareness of the importance of government. This pattern was evident in 2016 with citizens 65 years and older reporting the highest turnout (71 percent), followed by those age 45–66 (67 percent), 58 percent turnout for those age 30–44, and the lowest turnout for those age 18–29 (46 percent). Youth turnout remained lower than the average across all other age groups in 2016. In midterm elections without a presidential race, youth turnout has historically been extremely low. However, in 2018, youth voter turnout increased by 10 percent to 31 percent from 21 percent in 2014.[48]

Millennials (ages 18–35) are now the largest age cohort in the United States. According to Pew, 47 percent of millennials are Democrats or lean Democrat, compared to 34 percent who are Republicans or lean Republican. In 2018, 67 percent of young people supported Democratic candidates, compared to just 32 percent for Republican candidates, a larger gap than youth voting for Democrats in 2008 when President Barack Obama was first elected.[49]

A primary reason young people don't vote is that they lack an interest in politics or have not been mobilized to participate. Studies have found that if young people do vote, they tend to maintain this habit throughout their lifetime.[50] Another reason younger people vote less is that political campaigns often target older voters rather than young voters, because the former are more likely to vote. But this may be changing as more organizations channel energy and resources into getting younger people to vote. NextGen America (mentioned at the beginning of this chapter) for example, is an organization focusing on youth turnout that helped register 1 million voters in the 2016 election. NextGen supports candidates who favor addressing climate change, alternative energy, and reversing economic inequality.

Even though much time and effort is spent mobilizing young voters, people who actually vote tend to be older than the average American.

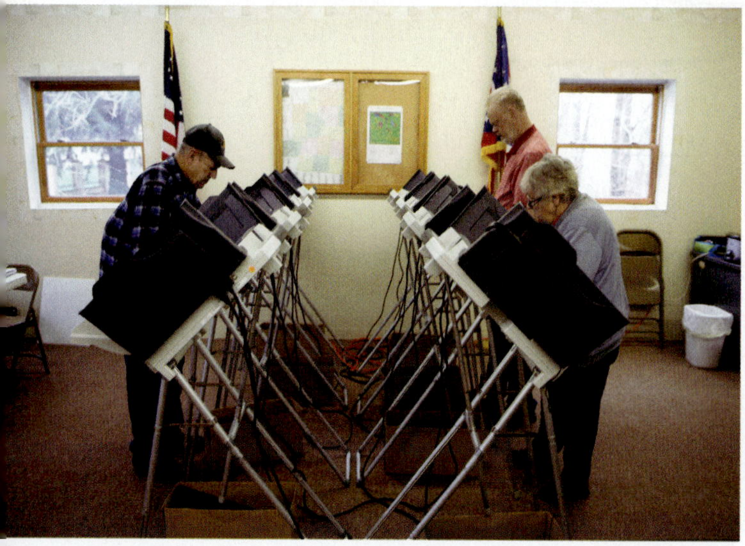

Since the early 1990s, several campaigns have sought to increase the participation of young voters. Rock the Vote enlists musicians and actors to urge young people to vote. It has spawned other initiatives aimed at young voters, including Rap the Vote and Rock the Vote a lo Latino. The Obama campaign made young voters central to its electoral strategy in 2008 and 2012, winning a significantly higher percent of the youth vote than his opponents.[51] The Obama campaign posted videos on YouTube and used social media to reach out to young people rather than focusing primarily on television ads (which target older voters). In 2016, Democratic presidential candidate Bernie Sanders was also effective in inspiring youth participation in politics. Although Sanders failed to secure his party's nomination, election polls consistently showed over 80 percent of people aged 18 to

In the 2016 presidential primaries, Democratic candidate Bernie Sanders energized young people and swept the youth vote, despite trailing Hillary Clinton overall. Still, 18- to 24-year-olds turned out at lower rates than all other age groups.

29 preferred him to his opponent, Hillary Clinton. Sanders called for a political revolution and focused on ending a corrupt campaign finance system, combating economic inequality, and providing free college tuition. Young people were drawn to the candidate's reputation of honesty and authenticity.

Relatively low voter turnout by the young has implications for the policies addressed by government at the local, state, and federal levels. For example, young people share older Americans' concerns about the economy and national security, but they tend to be more concerned about economic inequality and student debt, and express support for stronger environmental laws, funding for public education and colleges, and more tolerance for personal freedoms than older people do. A recent survey of 13- to 25-year-olds showed the consequences of coming of age in an era of hyper-partisanship and scandal; most saw the political system as ineffective and broken, and 9 out of 10 would not consider running for office.[52] At the same time young people have a strong interest in community service, and nearly 20 percent are involved in community service projects, with numbers higher among those with college experience.[53] The distinctive attitudes of today's young people suggest that higher levels of political participation by this group could significantly alter government policy and politics.

FOR CRITICAL ANALYSIS

When the Twenty-Sixth Amendment changed the voting age from 21 to 18 in 1971, observers expected that the youth vote would add a significant new voice to American politics. Why has the youth vote turned out to be less important than was hoped? What changes would engage more young people in the political system?

AFRICAN AMERICANS

As we saw in Chapter 5, during much of the twentieth century in the South, the widespread use of the poll tax, literacy tests, and other measures such as the white primary deprived African Americans of the right to vote. This system of legal segregation meant that African Americans in the South had few avenues for participating in politics. Through a combination of protest, legal action, and political pressure, the civil rights movement compelled a reluctant federal government to enforce black civil and political rights.

The victories of the civil rights movement made blacks full citizens and stimulated a tremendous growth in voter turnout. The movement drew on an organizational base and network of communication rooted in black churches, the National Association for the Advancement of Colored People (NAACP), and historically black colleges and universities. Because they tended to vote as a cohesive bloc, African American voters began to wield considerable political power, and the number of African American elected officials grew significantly as blacks exercised their newfound political rights. Despite this progress, today, state laws requiring government voter identification have created a new impediment for black and other minority voters in some states.

Being represented by a member of one's group appears to have positive effects on participation levels. African Americans are more likely to vote when residing in states with increased representation in the state legislature, as measured by the percentage of black lawmakers.[54] African Americans represented by a black member of Congress are more likely to vote in elections, have a sense of efficacy—the belief that the government is responsive to them—and higher levels of political knowledge.[55]

With Barack Obama running in 2008 as the first black major-party candidate for president, African American interest in the election surged. The black–white voting gap went from 7 percent in 2004 to 1 percent in 2008 as many African Americans voted for the first time (see Figure 8.3).[56] In 2012, blacks were more likely to vote than whites.[57] Exit polls indicated that 95 percent of African Americans who voted cast ballots for Obama.

In the 2016 election, black turnout in the presidential election declined 7 percentage points compared to 2012. Possible explanations for this decrease include strict voter ID laws and a reduction in the days allowed for early voting in some states, the lack of an African American presidential candidate on the ballot, and a divisive presidential campaign including anti-minority rhetoric.[58]

Racial segregation remains a fact of life in the United States along with the persistence of black urban poverty.[59] These conditions, often called *concentrated poverty*, post barriers to African American political participation. As the previous section on socioeconomic status described, participation (for blacks as well as whites) is highly correlated with more income, higher education, and higher-level occupations. Nevertheless, comparing citizens of similar socioeconomic status, African Americans are somewhat more likely to vote than whites.[60]

This may be because African Americans are a minority group. African Americans who feel a shared sense of collective identity, a concept called *linked fate*, are more likely to vote and participate politically. Political scientist Michael Dawson argues that black linked fate is a major predictor of political behavior. Dawson uses the construct of *linked fate* to measure the degree to which African Americans believe that their own self-interests are linked to the interests of the race.[61] That is, the experiences of African Americans with race and racial discrimination in the United States, including a history of slavery, unify their personal interests in seeking a candidate and policies that benefit their racial group. Black civic, community, religious, and political organizations are also important in increasing political participation for this group.

LATINOS

For many years, analysts called the Latino vote "the sleeping giant" because Latinos, while accounting for a large portion of the population, as a group had relatively low levels of political participation. For instance, 48 percent of Latinos voted in the

Though their turnout was lower than in 2012, Latinos and African Americans strongly favored Clinton over Trump in 2016.

2016 presidential election compared to 65 percent of non-Hispanic whites and just under 60 percent of African Americans. Despite continuing growth of the Latino population in the United States, just 12.7 million Latinos cast a ballot in the presidential election out of roughly 26 million eligible.[62]

Political scientists Matt Barreto and Gary Segura explain why voting rates are lower for Latinos compared to whites and African Americans. As a group, more Latinos are recent immigrants to this country and thus have fewer opportunities, such as access to a quality education, than do other ethnic and racial groups; therefore, they are more likely to lack resources for participation in politics such as money, time, and language skills.[63]

Today, politicians, political parties, and scholars view Latinos, the largest and fastest-growing minority in the United States, as a political group of critical importance. Latinos make up 17 percent of the population and represent 1 in 10 voters. In large states such as California and Texas, Latinos are approaching 50 percent of the population.[64] Although Latino registration and turnout are lower than those of other racial groups, these numbers have been increasing. Rapid population growth, increased registration rates, and uncertain party attachment all magnify the importance of the Latino vote.

FOR CRITICAL ANALYSIS

How significant a factor was the Latino vote in the 2016 election? Why does the percentage of eligible Latinos who vote still lag behind that of other groups?

While Latinos have tended to favor the Democrats in national elections, particularly due to staunch Republican opposition to immigration, Latinos tend to be religious, which may be expected to make them more socially conservative. But national surveys of Latinos find that they often do not allow their religious beliefs to dictate their political decisions. In addition to favoring an easier path to citizenship for immigrants, Latinos also favor more liberal economic policies. In 2016, Latinos strongly favored Clinton over Trump. Trump made ending illegal immigration a major theme of his campaign, proposing to build a wall between the United States and Mexico. The issue of immigration has continued to widen the partisan divide between minorities and white non-Hispanics. While 55 percent of white non-Hispanics voted for Republicans in 2018, 76 percent of nonwhites voted for Democrats. In 2018, 69 percent of Latinos voted Democratic.[65]

Similar to African Americans, Latinos are also more likely to vote when residing in states with increased representation in the state legislature, as measured by the percentage of Latino lawmakers, or in a district with a Latino member of Congress.[66] This phenomenon is commonly referred to as *descriptive representation*—when individuals are represented in government by officials of their same race, ethnicity, or gender, allowing minority groups to have a greater ability to affect policy outcomes. Descriptive representation may also confer symbolic benefits, such as reducing levels of political alienation among racial and ethnic minorities.[67] As the Latino population continues to grow, this group may influence more strongly who wins and who loses in U.S. elections.

ASIAN AMERICANS

Asian Americans are a smaller group than whites, Latinos, or African Americans, comprising roughly 6 percent of the population or 21 million citizens. In particular states, such as California, home to 33 percent of the nation's Asian American population, the group has become an important political presence. Asian Americans have education and income levels closer to those of whites than of Latinos or African Americans; but they are less likely to participate in politics than whites or African Americans.[68] Asian Americans have voter turnout rates similar to Latinos.[69]

No one national group dominates among the Asian American population, and this diversity has impeded the development of group-based political power. Asian Americans often have different political concerns from one another, stemming from their different national backgrounds and experiences in the United States. Historically, these groups have united most effectively around common issues of ethnic discrimination or anti-Asian violence, federal immigration policies, and discriminatory mortgage loan practices.

Asian American voter turnout rate increased to 49.3 percent in 2016, up from just under 47 percent in 2012 and surpassing Hispanics for the first time since 1996. But Asians constitute a much smaller share of the electorate than Latinos. In 2016, roughly 5 million Asians voted. Asian Americans have been moving, along with other minority groups, toward the Democratic Party in recent elections. Although a majority of Asian Americans voted Republican in the early 1990s, in the 2000s they have been voting increasingly Democratic; and 65 percent of Asian Americans voted for Hillary Clinton in 2016.[70]

The U.S. electorate in 2016 was the country's most racially and ethnically diverse ever; combined, African Americans, Latinos and Asians, and other racial or ethnic minorities accounted for nearly 27 percent of all voters almost an identical percentage as in 2012. However, since minority groups made up a larger share of the overall population in 2016 than 2012, this means many minorities chose not to vote in 2016. At the same time, turnout for non-Hispanic whites increased in 2016, in large part mobilized by Trump's campaign.

GENDER AND PARTICIPATION

gender gap a distinctive pattern of voting behavior reflecting the differences in views between women and men

Today, women register and vote at rates similar to or higher than those of men. The ongoing significance of gender issues in American politics is best exemplified by the **gender gap**—a distinctive pattern of male and female voting decisions—in electoral politics. Women tend to vote in higher numbers for Democratic candidates, whereas Republicans win more male votes. Behind these voting patterns are differing assessments of key policy issues. Women are more likely than men to oppose military activities, especially war, and to support gun control as well as social spending for health care, public education, and welfare. Though the gender gap generally runs around 10 points in presidential elections, the 2016 presidential election saw the first female major party candidate, Democrat Hillary Clinton, and the largest gender gap in history: surveys showed that 54 percent of women supported Clinton compared to 41 percent among men, a 13-point advantage.[71]

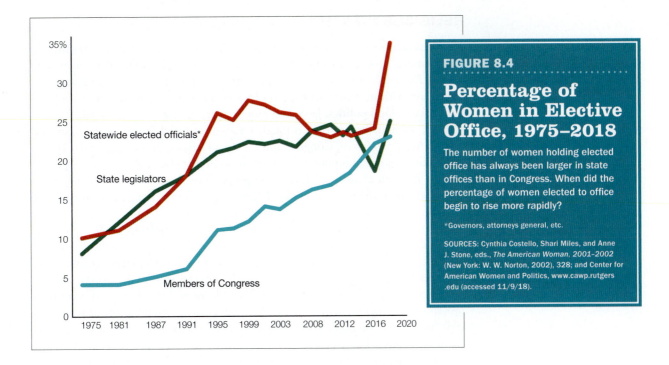

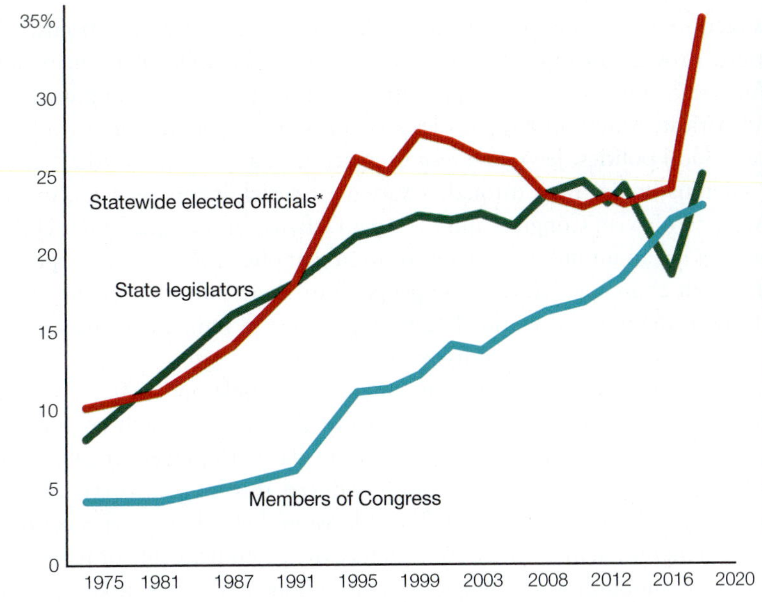

FIGURE 8.4

Percentage of Women in Elective Office, 1975–2018

The number of women holding elected office has always been larger in state offices than in Congress. When did the percentage of women elected to office begin to rise more rapidly?

*Governors, attorneys general, etc.

SOURCES: Cynthia Costello, Shari Miles, and Anne J. Stone, eds., *The American Woman, 2001-2002* (New York: W. W. Norton, 2002), 328; and Center for American Women and Politics, www.cawp.rutgers.edu (accessed 11/9/18).

One key development in gender politics in recent decades is the growing number of women in elective office (see Figure 8.4), an increasingly significant form of descriptive representation. A record number of women ran for office in 2018, and at least 125 women will serve in the 116th Congress, up from 107 in 2016. The numbers mark a new all-time high for the number of women in Congress. Over 100 women won House seats and at least 13 women won Senate seats, in addition to the 10 female senators who were not up for re-election this year.

Recent research has shown that one key to increasing the number of women in political office is to encourage more women to run for political office. Although women are just as likely as men to win an election, women are less likely to run for office, even if they are equally qualified. Because women are less likely than men to hold office, they also are less likely to benefit from the advantage of incumbency.[72] Organizations supporting female candidates have worked to encourage more women to run for office and have supported them financially. In addition to the bipartisan National Women's Political Caucus, the Women's Campaign Fund and EMILY's List provide prochoice Democratic women with early campaign financing, which is critical to establishing electoral momentum.

Why does the gender gap matter? Although women in public office by no means take uniform positions on policy issues, surveys show that, on the whole, female legislators are more supportive of women's rights, education, and health care spending and are also more attentive to children's and family issues. Nevertheless, partisanship matters more than gender in terms of representation of women's issues, especially in the current highly partisan political environment in Congress.[73] More women in Congress are Democrats, and Democratic lawmakers are much more likely to support these issues than Republican lawmakers regardless of gender.

RELIGIOUS IDENTITY

Religious identity plays an important role in American life. For many citizens, religious groups provide an organizational infrastructure for political participation. African American churches, for example, were instrumental in the civil rights movement, and African American religious leaders continue to play important roles in national and local politics. Jews have also been active as a group in politics but less through religious bodies than through a variety of social action agencies, including the American Jewish Congress and the Anti-Defamation League. In the United States churches are an important social institution that often fosters political participation. Through church activities many people learn civic skills that prepare them to participate in the political world. Today roughly one in four Americans are religiously unaffiliated and do not identify with any religion.

For most of American history, religious language, symbols, and values have been woven deeply into the fabric of public life. Until the mid-twentieth century, for example, public school students generally began the day with prayers or Bible readings. But a variety of court decisions greatly reduced this kind of overt religious influence on public life (see Chapter 4). These decisions helped to spawn a countermovement of religious activists seeking to restore the prominent role of religion in civic life and the mobilization of religious organizations has been one of the most significant political developments of the past half century. Some of the most divisive conflicts in politics today, such as those over abortion, birth control, and contraceptives, hinge on differences over religious beliefs. These divisions have become so salient that they now constitute what is called a "culture war," with repercussions throughout the political system and many policy areas.

One of the most significant drivers of this new politics was the mobilization of white evangelical Protestants into a cohesive political force. The Moral Majority, the first broad-based political organization of evangelical Christians, quickly rose to prominence in the 1980 election when it aligned with the Republican Party, eventually backing Ronald Reagan for president. Over the next few years, evangelicals strengthened their movement by registering voters and mobilizing them. Their success was evident in the 1984 election, when 8 in 10 evangelical Christian voters cast their ballots for Reagan. In 1988 the televangelist Pat Robertson ran for president. Although his candidacy was unsuccessful, his supporters gained control of some state Republican parties and won positions of power in others. President

Religious identity remains a significant factor in voting patterns. White evangelical Christians strongly support Republicans. Religious people of color tend to vote for Democrats, suggesting race may be a stronger predictor of voting behavior than religion.

George W. Bush was closely aligned with religious conservatives, and the religious right played an important role in electing him. In 2016 most evangelical Christians supported Trump in the general election.

Despite the influences of race and ethnicity, gender, age, religion, and socioeconomic status, these factors are not the only explanations for voter turnout or other forms of political participation. Our incomplete understanding of what motivates political participation is evident when we compare voting across countries. If more political resources lead to a greater likelihood of voting, why does the United States, one of the most prosperous countries in the world, have only moderate voting rates? And Americans have become more educated over the past century, with more people finishing high school and attending college. Given the well-documented links between educational attainment and voting, why has participation declined during this period?[74] These puzzles mean that we need to look beyond the socioeconomic characteristics of individuals and to the larger political environment in which participation occurs.

Political Environment and Voter Mobilization

Explain the factors in the political environment that influence whether individuals vote or not

Whether or not people feel engaged or are recruited to participate in politics depends on their political environment—that is, social setting, their friends and family, where they live, what associations they belong to. For example, citizens living in presidential battleground states (states with roughly equal numbers of Democrats and Republicans in the population) are exposed to a torrent of campaign ads, candidate visits, and grassroots mobilization efforts. These individuals are more knowledgeable about presidential elections, are more interested in the campaign, and have a higher probability of voting than residents of states that are "safe" for either the Republican Party, such as Texas, or the Democratic Party, such as New York or California.

MOBILIZATION

A critical aspect of political environments is whether people are mobilized—by parties, candidates, campaigns, interest groups, and social movements. A recent comprehensive study of the decline in political participation in the United States found that half of the drop-off could be accounted for by reduced **mobilization** efforts.[75] People become much more likely to participate when someone—especially someone they know—asks them to get involved.

mobilization the process by which large numbers of people are organized for a political activity

A series of experiments conducted by the political scientists Donald Green and Alan Gerber demonstrate the importance of personal contact for mobilizing voters. Evaluating the results of several get-out-the-vote drives, the researchers showed that face-to-face interaction with a canvasser greatly increased the chances that the person contacted would go to the polls, boosting overall voter turnout by almost 10 percent. The impact of direct mail was much smaller, increasing turnout by just 0.5 percent.[76] "Robocalls" (prerecorded phone calls) from a phone bank had no measurable effect on voter turnout. Social media networks can mimic face-to-face communication. In a large study involving 61 million users on Facebook, political scientists found voter turnout in the 2010 midterm election increased by 340,000 additional people (who otherwise would not have voted). Users' closest friends on the network had the most influence in getting them to vote.[77] Thus, online and offline networks both played a role in mobilizing voters.[78]

FOR CRITICAL ANALYSIS

Why do efforts toward direct mobilization seem to be more successful than television advertising in promoting voter turnout? How is the internet becoming an important tool for increasing political participation?

In previous decades, political parties and social movements relied on personal contact to mobilize voters. As we will see in Chapter 9, during the nineteenth century, American political party machines employed hundreds of thousands of workers to bring voters to the polls. The result was a very high turnout rate, typically more than 90 percent of eligible voters.[79] But political party machines began to decline in strength at the beginning of the twentieth century. By the late twentieth century, political parties had become essentially fund-raising and advertising organizations rather than mobilizers of people. Without party workers to encourage them to go to the polls, many eligible voters will not participate.

Nevertheless, competitive presidential elections since 2000 have once again motivated both parties to build strong grassroots organizations to reach voters and turn them out on Election Day. In the 2004 elections, Republicans were more successful in their organizational efforts than Democrats, building an organization with more than 1.4 million volunteers who were trained to make calls, go door to door to register voters, write letters in favor of President Bush, post blogs online, and phone local radio call-in shows. In 2008, Barack Obama's campaign made mobilization a centerpiece of its strategy, organizing a base of volunteers to go door to door seeking support for their candidate. Many of Obama's crucial primary victories relied on direct voter mobilization. The campaign then created a nationwide organization, opening more than 700 field offices. Obama campaigned in all 50 states, rather than focusing on battleground states as his predecessors had done. By mobilizing support in places where Democrats had not seriously contended in the past, the Obama campaign expanded the electoral map. For the first time in decades, turnout rates were comparable to those in 1960.

People are more likely to turn out to vote if someone asks them face to face. Direct mail and impersonal phone calls are less likely to have an effect on turnout.

In 2016 political campaigns shifted to social media as a primary way to mobilize voters and directly provide their supporters with election updates. Three in 10 Americans received digital messages about news and the elections, with far more Americans turning to the candidates' social media posts rather than to their websites or emails.[80] The Trump campaign was especially effective in mobilizing voters via social media networks.

DATA ANALYTICS AND VOTER MOBILIZATION

Today's modern campaigns use massive computer databases and sophisticated data analytics to identify individuals and members of the electorate to mobilize turnout in elections. Digital politics creates digital footprints that can be used by candidate and issue campaigns for micro-targeting to mobilize voters in elections or shape their opinions about politics. In *Hacking the Electorate*, political scientist Eitan Hersh argues that most of what campaigns know about voters comes from a core set of public records based on the voter rolls from all fifty states with data on 240 million Americans. States vary in the kinds of records they collect from voters, however, and these variations in data by state make campaigns more or less effective at micro-targeting voters in different states. States with better record keeping and computerized public records allow better mobilization of voters in campaigns.[81]

In the past, social movements, such as the labor movement in the 1930s and the civil rights movement in the 1960s, played an important role in mobilizing people into politics. Though interest groups and political parties have generally reduced their efforts at direct mobilization since then, some have revived direct mobilization in recent years. The Tea Party movement in particular has engaged in widespread grassroots mobilization, as have organizations on the left such as MoveOn.org.[82]

ELECTORAL COMPETITION

To be motivated to vote, individuals must be interested in the election and knowledgeable about the candidates. An important factor, often overlooked in analyzing political participation, is whether elections are competitive; that is, whether there are at least two parties (and their candidates) actively contesting a position in government.[83] Competitive elections, and the campaign spending and mobilization efforts that go along with them, play a key role in turnout in the United States and cross-nationally.[84] Conversely, limited exposure to competitive elections may be one reason for the lower levels of turnout since the 1960s. In many congressional, statewide, and local races, a candidate (often the incumbent) runs unopposed or is expected to win by such a large margin that the challenger's chances are virtually nil. When congressional districts are drawn to favor one political party over another—what is termed *gerrymandering* (see Chapter 10)—election outcomes are thus often highly lopsided in favor of one candidate over another. Relatively uncompetitive elections are a primary reason why most members of Congress win by landslides.

Political scientist Todd Donovan uses a sports analogy to explain the importance of competitive elections in mobilizing turnout: "People watch a game to see their team win, or because of interest in an important game. Uncontroversial calls by the umpire and high scoring is meaningless if only one team takes the field, and attendance will suffer if two teams are playing that no one can cheer for."[85] When candidates and political parties spend more effort and money to compete for an elected office, more information becomes available to voters in the form of media ads, news coverage, door-to-door campaigns, online campaigns, and more. Electoral competition reduces the cost to individuals of becoming informed, leading to higher turnout. Conversely, if elections are uncompetitive (where the winner beats the loser by more than 5 percent) or uncontested (where only one name appears on the ballot), they generate little political information. Without active campaigns, individuals have few opportunities to be interested in an election and may not vote.[86]

Unique rules for presidential elections in the United States create variation in electoral competition across the 50 states. No other country uses an electoral college to mediate between a national or direct vote for presidential candidates and the actual winner. To win, a U.S. presidential candidate must receive a majority of the votes in the electoral college. Each state is given a set number of votes in the electoral college based on the size of its congressional delegation. (The electoral college is covered in more detail in Chapter 10.) Some citizens reside in competitive battleground states, such as Florida, Ohio, and Pennsylvania. These states are defined by high levels of competition between the parties. Most Americans, however, live in nonbattleground states (also called "safe" states) such as California, New York, and Texas, where one of the major parties is generally assured of victory in presidential elections. Hence, presidential elections are often decided by a relatively small number of voters in the United States' dozen or so battleground states. (For example, if Hillary Clinton had won just 110,000 more votes across Michigan, Pennsylvania, and Wisconsin, she would have won the 2016 election.) Every four years, residents of battleground states get smothered with attention from candidates and media, while citizens in states with few electoral votes or where one political party has a solid majority barely get noticed. One study found that voter turnout is higher in battleground states than in nonbattleground states and less skewed in terms of lower participation by the poor and young.[87]

Even the rules for nominating presidential candidates create variation across the states in electoral competition that effects voter turnout. Selecting presidential candidates involves a sequence of statewide primary elections and caucuses. The early phase of this process is dominated by a handful of small-population states. The privileged position of Iowa and New Hampshire, sites of the nation's first caucus and first primary respectively, can boost political participation in those states. Similarly, studies have shown that citizens residing in "Super Tuesday" states (the 12 states that hold primaries or caucuses on a single day about six weeks after the New Hampshire primary) are more likely to vote in presidential primaries and be interested in the election.[88] Usually the nomination contest is essentially over quickly, as one candidate secures a significant lead in early primaries, leaving many citizens with no role in selecting their party's nominee. Turnout in states with later primaries, include large states like California and Texas, naturally plummets.

BALLOT MEASURES

Beyond candidate races, ballot measures (initiatives and referenda) have been found to increase voter turnout, especially in lower-profile, midterm elections but also in presidential elections.[89] Elections that include controversial initiatives on the state ballot—in which citizens vote directly on policy questions such as the minimum wage, immigration, or taxation—have also been found to increase voter turnout, political interest, and contributions to interest groups.[90] In many states, ballot-measure campaigns are important for mobilizing voters and can have spillover effects on candidate races.[91] When citizens are asked to vote directly on controversial policy issues,

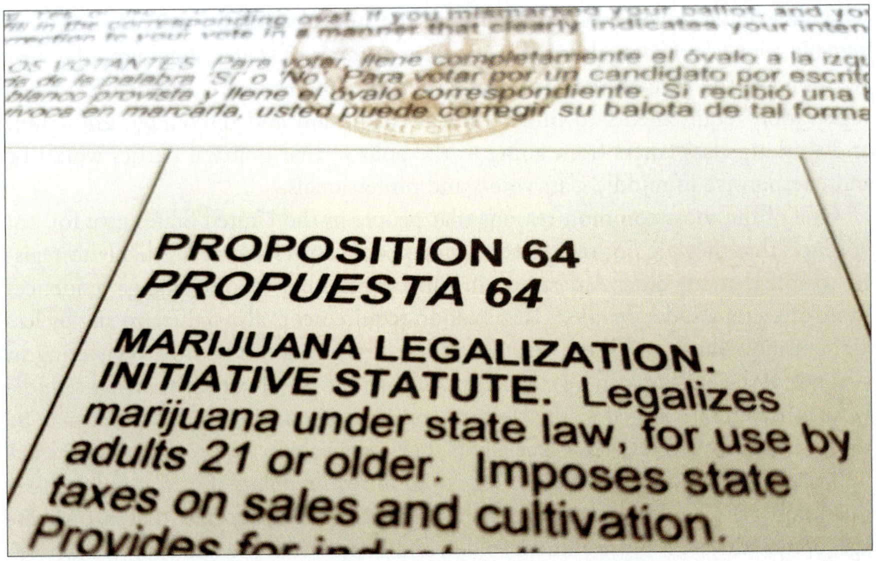
PROPOSITION 64
PROPUESTA 64
MARIJUANA LEGALIZATION.
INITIATIVE STATUTE. Legalizes
marijuana under state law, for use by
adults 21 or older. Imposes state
taxes on sales and cultivation.

Voters often turn out in higher numbers when there are controversial initiatives on the ballot. In 2016 groups for and against Proposition 64 in California, which would legalize recreational marijuana, spent millions of dollars on media and mobilization campaigns.

public awareness of politics and policy debates increases. Initiatives often involve high campaign spending by proponents and opponents of the proposed laws, which generates mass media coverage. The *Los Angeles Times* estimated that $452 million was spent in California alone in 2016 on controversial ballot measures including legalizing the recreational use of marijuana and repealing the death penalty.[92] Additionally, simply being asked to vote on issues—salient or otherwise—can increase participation. This has been called the "educative effects" of direct democracy as voters are forced to make a yes-or-no choice on the policy issue.[93]

Only 24 of the 50 states have the initiative process that lets citizens draft legislation, circulate petitions, and place the issue on the ballot for a popular vote. This is another reason that what state one lives in can matter for how likely they are to participate in politics.

State Electoral Laws and Participation

Explain the effect of electoral laws on voting

As stipulated by the Constitution, the states, not the federal government, control voter registration and voting itself. This decentralized system continues to create wide variation in the laws governing elections and voting, which affect participation in politics.[94] Voter turnout in presidential elections in the last decade ranges from a high of over 70 percent of eligible voters in Maine to 42 percent in Hawaii. State electoral laws can facilitate or create barriers to voting that can reduce participation and help explain the differences in turnout across states.

REGISTRATION REQUIREMENTS

In most democratic countries, residents are automatically registered to vote in elections at adult age. In the United States, citizens must actively register to vote and, in most states, must do so in advance of the election—sometimes 30 days beforehand. An important factor reducing voter turnout is our nation's unique state-by-state patchwork of registration rules. In every American state but North Dakota, individuals who are eligible to vote must register with the state election board before they are actually allowed to vote, although a growing number of states allow same-day registration. At the turn of the nineteenth century, progressive reformers introduced registration requirements to limit political corruption and discourage immigrant and working-class voters from going to the polls so that political parties would be more responsive to middle-class voters and professionals.

One of the most common reasons that people in the United States give for not voting is that they are not registered. Young people especially are less likely to register to vote than are older Americans, in part because they tend to change residences more often than older people.[95] Registration requirements also reduce voting by less affluent individuals and those with lower levels of education because registering in advance of the election can be more difficult than the act of voting itself. Once individuals become interested in the election and learn about the candidates, it may be too late for them to register, especially if they live in states that require registration up to a month before the election. Registration requirements thus not only reduce the number of people who vote but also tend to create an electorate that is, on average, better educated, more affluent, older, and whiter than the citizenry as a whole.

In an effort to boost voter turnout, a number of states have begun to offer same-day registration, which means that people can both register and vote when they go to the polls on Election Day. As of 2018, 18 states plus Washington, D.C., had enacted same-day registration laws. Thirteen states and the District of Columbia have recently gone even further, adopting laws to automatically register their residents to vote in elections by information sharing between government agencies collecting similar information: the Department of Motor Vehicles and the secretary of state's office.[96] Though these states have adopted these laws, automatic voter registration was only in effect in Oregon for the 2016 election. Though turnout in Oregon did not increase in 2016 from 2012, some scholars believe automatic voter registration is more likely to have an impact on turnout in state and local elections, rather than in presidential elections when voters are better informed and don't need a reminder to vote.[97]

Although many U.S. citizens are strong advocates of universal suffrage and voter turnout, this reform triggers controversial debate and deep partisan conflict. Opponents contend that these laws make the states' voter rolls more vulnerable to fraud. Supporters say the new system may be more secure than traditional paper registration because rather than simply attesting to their eligibility with a signature, individuals have to submit proof of citizenship. Automatic voter registration is generally favored by Democrats, who want expanded access to the ballot box. Republicans, on the other hand, often don't want to add new voters who may be more likely to support the Democratic Party. It is important to note, however, that lawmakers are not always correct about which party will benefit from increased voter registration.

Voter Identification Requirements Another barrier to voting is the requirement that voters provide proof of identity. Despite near universal adult suffrage in the United States, recent adoption of voter ID laws in many states has reduced turnout rates, especially for the low-income, racial minorities, the elderly, and people with disabilities—all of whom disproportionately lack government ID. Thirty-four states have some identification requirements to cast a ballot at the polls, but 10 states had strict ID laws in 2018 that required voters to present a government-issued photo ID or nonphoto ID in order to cast a ballot.[98] Estimates indicate that 11 percent

Which States Make Voting Easier?

Convenience Voting, 2018

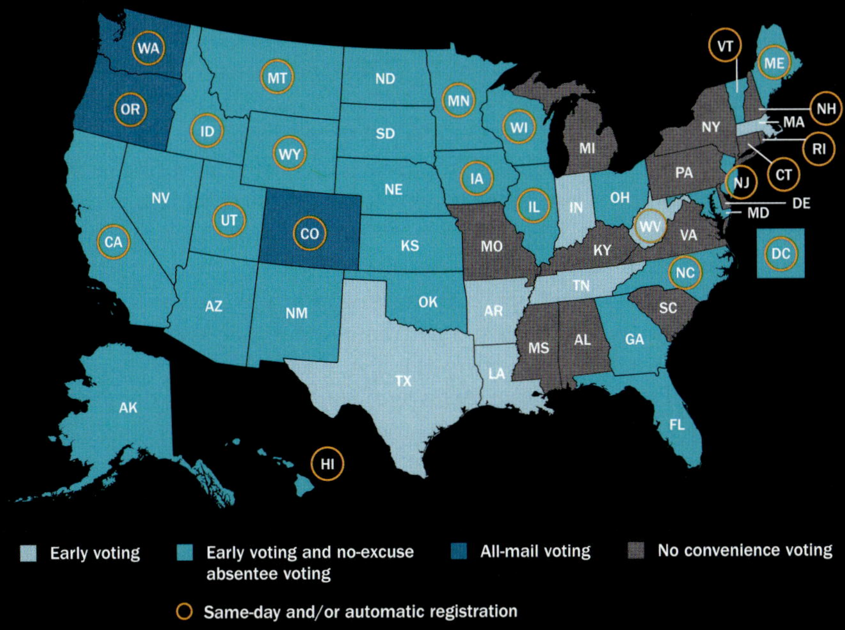

States have increasingly passed laws to make voting easier, such as early voting, which allows voters to cast a ballot before Election Day; "no-excuse" absentee voting, which permits voters to request an absentee ballot without providing justification; all-mail voting, whereby voters fill in their ballot at home and mail it, eliminating polling places altogether; and same-day and automatic voter registration. At the same time, many states have passed voter identification requirements, which make voting harder for some people. The maps show these laws by state as of the 2018 election.

* Two additional states have adopted same-day registration to take effect in 2019.

Voter ID Requirements, 2018

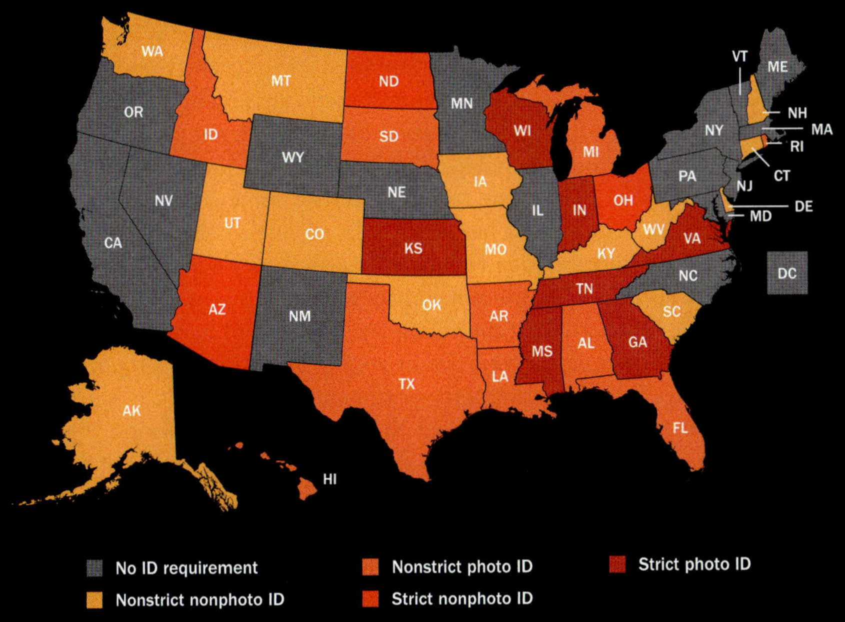

SOURCES: National Conference of State Legislatures, www.ncsl.org/research/elections-and-campaigns/absentee-and-early-voting.aspx (accessed 11/4/17); National Conference of State Legislatures, www.ncsl.org/research/elections-and-campaigns/voter-id.aspx#Table1 (accessed 11/4/17).

FOR CRITICAL ANALYSIS

1. Find your state on the maps. Do you think your state's voting laws affected turnout in the 2018 election?
2. In which regions of the country do we find the most states with convenience voting? Why might this be the case?

of U.S. citizens, or 21 million Americans, do not have government-issued photo identification, including one in five African Americans. Government identification can be difficult to obtain even if an ID is available for free, because citizens must pay for a birth certificate to apply for a government-issued identification. Travel to the Department of Motor Vehicles can be difficult for the elderly, disabled, and those living in rural areas. While the true effect of these laws is still not known, some government reports estimate that strict voter ID laws reduce turnout by 2–3 percentage points, which can amount to millions of people who are prevented from voting nationwide. Voter ID laws may change election outcomes in swing states.[99]

For example, out of 2.8 million votes cast in Wisconsin, just 22,748 votes separated Trump's victory over Clinton in the 2016 presidential election, one of the closest competitions of any state. Wisconsin's new voter ID law requires a citizen to show government identification in order to cast a ballot. One study found that nearly 17,000 registered Wisconsin voters were prevented from voting in the 2016 presidential election by the state's new strict voter identification law.[100] The results suggest that enough voters could have been deterred from participating that it flipped the outcome of the presidential election in the state.

Photo identification is a partisan issue. In Wisconsin and elsewhere, Republicans argue that such laws protect against voter fraud and ensure that the vote is fair, regardless of party. Opponents of voter ID laws, mainly Democrats, counter that there have been almost no significant instances of voter fraud in the modern era and that these laws suppress the vote of segments of the population most likely to vote for Democrats but also least likely to have photo ID—racial minorities and the poor.[101] Studies have shown that illegal voting via impersonating someone else is very rare in the United States.

There is also wide variation in implementation of voter ID laws. In Texas a student identification card does not count to vote, but a gun owner's license does. A study by Caltech/MIT scholars found that minority voters are more frequently questioned to provide ID than white voters. The adoption of strict voter ID laws in 14 states appears to coincide with a decline in African American turnout in the 2016 election.

VOTING RIGHTS OF FELONS

A barrier to voting that has grown more important in recent years is the restriction on the voting rights of people who have committed a felony. Forty-eight states and the District of Columbia prohibit prison inmates who are serving a felony sentence from voting. In 21 states, felons on probation or parole are not permitted to vote, but voting rights are restored automatically after parole or probation is complete. In 13 states, felons lose their voting rights forever for some crimes. On the other end of the spectrum, felons never lose their right to vote in Maine and Vermont. With the sharp rise in incarceration rates over the past three decades, restrictions on voting for felons have had a significant impact on voting rights. By one estimate, 5.3 million people (2.4 percent of the voting-age population) have lost their voting rights as a result of these restrictions. Felon voting restrictions disproportionately affect minorities because 59 percent of the prison population is African American or Latino, though these groups make up only 30 percent of the population.[102] One in eight black men cannot vote because of a criminal record.[103] The impact of felon disenfranchisement has been especially strong in the South. Concern over the impact of these voting restrictions has led to campaigns to restore voting rights to people who have committed a felony.[104]

VOTING AND REGISTRATION REFORMS

Election reform efforts over the past century have focused on making voter registration and voting more accessible and convenient. As mentioned above, **same-day registration** (SDR) allows citizens to both register to vote and cast a ballot on the same day. Seventeen states plus the District of Columbia have SDR laws.[105] Concern over SDR focuses on fraud and noncitizens voting. As might be expected, in states that allow registration on the day of the election, not only is voter turnout higher than the national average but younger and less educated voters are also more likely to participate.[106] On average, SDR increases overall turnout by 5 percent.[107]

In 1998, Oregon was also the first state to create a system for voting exclusively by mail, thus eliminating polling places altogether. Individual voters fill in their ballot at home and place it in the mail or in drop boxes throughout the state. In Washington State, Colorado, California, and many other states, many citizens now cast votes using **permanent absentee ballots**, which are mailed. Twenty-seven states and the District of Columbia allow "no-excuse" absentee voting, which means any voter can request an absentee ballot without providing a justification. Not only does mail voting increase turnout, it also saves the government money by not having to staff polling stations throughout the state. But because the western states tend to have higher voter turnout than most other parts of the country, it's difficult to disentangle whether mail voting or regional political culture drives higher turnout.

Another reform that has been adopted by many states is **early voting**, which allows registered voters to cast a ballot at their regular polling place up to 40 days before the election. Thirty-three percent of votes cast in the 2016 election were cast early, either in person or via mail. As of 2018, 37 states allow early voting in which any qualified voter may cast a ballot in person during a designated period prior to Election Day.[108] Three of these states go so far as to mail a ballot to all registered voters. Some studies find that the effects of early voting laws on turnout and the demographic composition of who votes are not yet clear.[109] One study from Oregon found that voting by mail tends to advantage upper-class and older citizens, who are more likely to vote anyway.[110] But others contend that early voting increases turnout among groups that are traditionally less likely to vote, including minorities. For a political campaign, a vote cast early is like securing another dollar in the bank. (See inside the back cover of your textbook to find voter-registration requirements in your state.)

Overall, SDR has been found to have the greatest effect in boosting voting rates and making participation by different demographic groups more equal. Having the ability to vote at the last minute helps many people who otherwise may not vote, particularly young adults and individuals with a high school–level education or less.[111] An individual need not become aware of the registration process in order to register to vote; he merely needs to know the date of the election and the location of the polling place, where registering to vote and voting can happen at the same time.

FOR CRITICAL ANALYSIS

Why is voter turnout so low in the United States? What are the consequences of low voter turnout?

same-day registration the option in some states to register on the day of the election, at the polling place, rather than in advance of the election

permanent absentee ballots the option in some states to have a ballot sent automatically to your home for each election, rather than having to request an absentee ballot each time

early voting the option in some states to cast a vote at a polling place or by mail before the election

Convenience voting, such as early voting and voting by mail, removes the need to stand in a potentially long line to cast a vote and may result in increased voter turnout.

Political Participation
WHAT DO WE WANT

The American political community has expanded over the course of history, with new groups winning and asserting political rights. This expansion has brought American politics more closely into line with the fundamental values of liberty, equality, and democracy. But for much of the twentieth century, the electoral system in the United States failed to mobilize an active citizenry, giving rise to an uneven pattern of political participation that gives some people more of a voice in politics than others. Since 2000 a series of highly competitive presidential elections has spurred political campaigns to pay more attention to drawing greater numbers of voters into the political process; even so, many Americans still do not participate in politics. The "**Who Participates?**" feature on the facing page shows who participated in the 2016 presidential election.

Naturally enough, one of the most important factors in sustaining participation is a sense of political efficacy, the feeling that average citizens can help shape what government actually does. One important study found that elected officials respond more to the preferences of voters than nonvoters, confirming long-held assumptions that affluent, more educated, and older citizens have more voice in politics and public policy.[112] A study by the political scientist Larry Bartels showed that senators (both Republicans and Democrats) are much less responsive to the policy preferences of low-income citizens—who are also less likely to be active voters.[113] If the voices of only the more affluent are heard during election time, the issues that concern lower-income Americans may not find a place at the top of the political agenda.

What would it take to increase political engagement among citizens of all backgrounds? Several recent developments promise to give a greater number of people more of a voice in American government. Over the past few decades, innovative states have led the way by reforming and modernizing America's patchwork election system, with reforms ranging from automatic and same-day voter registration to early and mail voting. Some states, such as Iowa and California, use nonpartisan boards to draw legislative districts, which tends to boost competition in congressional and state legislative races. Increased competition, in turn, often results in a more informed and energized electorate, thus increasing turnout. What if every state adopted automatic voter registration? Would this increase turnout for young voters who are the most mobile and are now the largest age cohort? Would reforming America's elections allow most citizens to vote and elected representatives that adopt policies in the interests of the greatest number of people, not just wealthy elites? Would true universal suffrage make American great again?

For much of American history, formal barriers restricted the right to vote and created a pattern of unequal participation in politics. Today, most of those barriers have been eliminated, but voter turnout remains relatively low, especially among young voters.

WHO PARTICIPATES?

Who Participated in the 2016 Presidential Election?

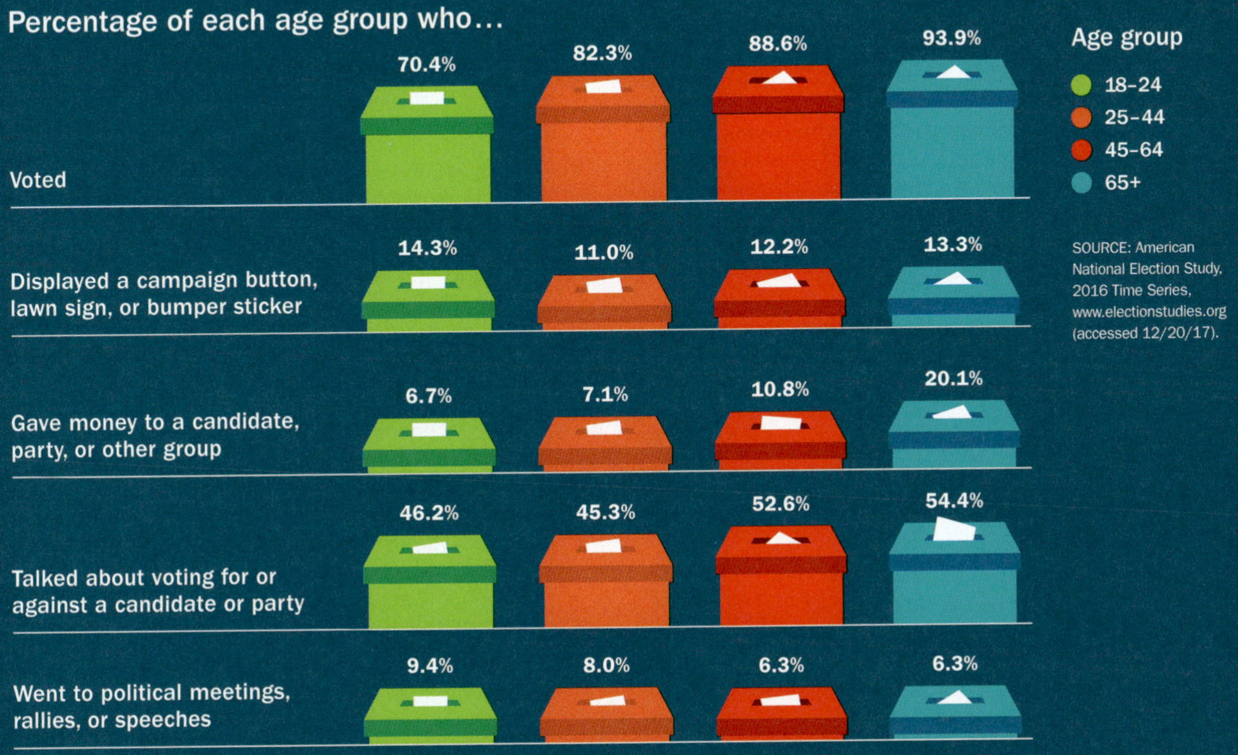

WHAT YOU CAN DO

Register to Vote

- In most states you can register to vote using the National Mail Voter Registration Form found at **www.eac.gov**. The Election Assistance Commission website also includes various tips about registering and voting.
- Find out when you need to register in order to vote in the next election. Visit **www.usa.gov/register-to-vote** for a list of registration deadlines.
- Many states allow online registration. Go to **www.ncsl.org** and search "online voter registration" to find a list of these states with links to their websites.
- If you've moved to attend college or for another reason, you can register with your new address.

STUDY GUIDE

Forms of Political Participation

Describe the major forms of traditional and digital participation in politics (pp. 297–310)

Political participation refers to a wide range of activities designed to influence government, politics, and policy. These activities fall into two major categories: traditional political participation, which includes voting, engaging in protest, volunteering, and contributing to a candidate; and digital political participation, which refers to a newer set of activities carried out through the internet, such as reading online news stories, posting comments on social media, and visiting a political party's website. Voting is the most common form of traditional political participation, but voter turnout is relatively low overall in the United States. While digital political participation has the potential to encourage innovation, free expression, and higher levels of traditional political participation, it may also produce misinformation, intolerance, and a lack of civility in public discourse.

Key Terms

traditional political participation (p. 297)
protest (p. 297)
suffrage (p. 299)
turnout (p. 301)
digital political participation (p. 303)

Practice Quiz

1. Which of the following is *not* a form of traditional political participation?
   a) volunteering for a campaign
   b) attending an abortion rights rally
   c) displaying a yard sign for a Republican congressional candidate
   d) voting in an election
   e) signing an online petition
2. Which group won voting rights most recently?
   a) 18- to 20-year-olds
   b) Asian Americans
   c) white property owners
   d) women
   e) African Americans
3. The *digital divide* means
   a) some citizens watch television news and some do not.
   b) newspapers rarely publish the same stories on their websites that they do in their print editions.
   c) few politicians maintain websites once they are elected to office.
   d) not all citizens have equal access to the internet.
   e) people who learn about politics online are less informed than those who learn about politics through traditional media.

Who Participates?

Describe the patterns of participation among major demographic groups (pp. 310–19)

Socioeconomic status, race, gender, age, and religious affiliation are associated with different levels and types of political participation. Generally speaking, whites, older people, women, and those with higher levels of education and income vote most frequently. In recent elections, African Americans, Latinos, women, and young people have been more likely to support Democratic candidates than whites, males, and older people.

Key Terms

socioeconomic status (p. 310)
gender gap (p. 316)

Practice Quiz

4. Which of the following statements about young people's political attitudes is most accurate?
   a) Younger people are less supportive of strong environmental laws than older people.
   b) Younger people are less concerned about economic inequality than older people.
   c) Younger people express less tolerance for personal freedoms than older people.
   d) Younger people are less concerned about national security than older people.
   e) Younger people are more supportive of funding for public education and colleges than older people.

5. African Americans
   a) almost never participate in politics.
   b) consistently support the Republican Party in elections.
   c) vote at much higher rates than whites.
   d) have never voted as a cohesive bloc.
   e) are more likely to participate when they feel a shared sense of collective identity.
6. Which of the following statements about Latinos is *not* accurate?
   a) Latinos have tended to favor Democratic candidates in recent national elections.
   b) In some large states, such as California and Texas, Latinos are approaching 50 percent of the population.
   c) Latinos have tended to favor Republican candidates in recent national elections.
   d) Latinos make up approximately 17 percent of the population.
   e) Latino registration and turnout rates have been lower than those of whites and African Americans in recent elections.
7. One reason that there are fewer women than men in elected office is that
   a) there is a limit set by the Constitution on the number of women who can serve in the House of Representatives.
   b) fewer women are eligible to run for office under the rules created by state and local governments.
   c) women are less likely to vote in elections than men.
   d) women are less likely to run for office than men.
   e) women are less likely to win elections than men.

Political Environment and Voter Mobilization

Explain the factors in the political environment that influence whether individuals vote or not (pp. 319–23)

Three general factors in the political environment influence whether individuals vote or not: mobilization efforts, electoral competitiveness, and the presence or absence of state-level ballot initiatives. People who are mobilized by political parties, candidates, campaigns, interest groups, and social movements are more likely to participate than those who are not. In competitive elections, turnout is higher because there are more opportunities for individuals to become interested in and informed about the race as each side campaigns to get its message out. People also make the effort to vote when ballot measures address issues that are important to them.

Key Term

mobilization (p. 319)

Practice Quiz

8. Which of the following techniques is considered most effective in mobilizing voters?
   a) direct mailings
   b) "robocalls"
   c) phone calls made by volunteers
   d) face-to-face contact
   e) television advertisements
9. How many states currently have an initiative process that lets citizens draft legislation, circulate petitions, and place measures on the ballot for a popular vote?
   a) 0
   b) 12
   c) 24
   d) 36
   e) 50

State Electoral Laws and Participation

Explain the effect of electoral laws on voting (pp. 323–27)

As stated in the Constitution, states retain control of voter registration and voting. In practice, there is wide variation in the laws governing elections and voting from state to state. Voter-registration requirements and other barriers, such as felony disenfranchisement and ID requirements, may reduce participation. States have experimented with reforms, such as same-day registration, permanent absentee ballots, automatic registration, and early voting, to make it easier to vote.

Key Terms

same-day registration (p. 327)
permanent absentee ballots (p. 327)
early voting (p. 327)

Practice Quiz

10. Voter-registration requirements and processes are determined and controlled by
    a) local governments.
    b) the federal government.
    c) the U.S. Constitution.
    d) the states.
    e) an independent organization.

11. Which of the following factors is *not* currently an obstacle to voting in the United States?
    a) registration requirements
    b) that elections occur on Tuesdays
    c) the restriction of voting rights for people who have committed a felony
    d) literacy tests
    e) voter identification laws

12. States that allow for same-day registration
    a) have lower overall voter turnout rates than states that do not allow for same-day registration.
    b) have the same overall voter turnout rates as states that do not allow for same-day registration.
    c) have higher rates of voter turnout among younger and less educated voters than states that do not allow for same-day registration.
    d) have overall turnout rates that are very close to 100 percent.
    e) have lower rates of voter turnout among younger and less educated voters than states that do not allow for same-day registration.

For Further Reading

Barreto, Matt, and Gary Segura. *Latino America: How America's Most Dynamic Population Is Poised to Transform the Politics of the Nation*. New York: Public Affairs, 2014.

Bowler, Shaun, and Todd Donovan. *The Limits of Electoral Reform*. Oxford: Oxford University Press, 2013.

Cain, Bruce E., Todd Donovan, and Caroline J. Tolbert, eds. *Democracy in the States: Experiments in Election Reform*. Washington, DC: Brookings Institution Press, 2008.

Crenson, Matthew A., and Benjamin Ginsberg. *Downsizing Democracy: How America Sidelined Its Citizens and Privatized Its Public*. Baltimore: Johns Hopkins University Press, 2004.

Dalton, Russell J. *The Good Citizen: How a Younger Generation Is Reshaping American Politics*. Washington, DC: CQ Press, 2008.

Donovan, Todd, and Shawn Bowler. *Reforming the Republic: Democratic Institutions for the New America*. Upper Saddle River, NJ: Pearson/Prentice Hall, 2004.

Green, Donald P., and Alan S. Gerber. *Get Out the Vote! How to Increase Voter Turnout*. Washington, DC: Brookings Institution Press, 2004.

Griffin, John D., and Brian Newman. *Minority Report: Evaluating Political Equality in America*. Chicago: University of Chicago Press, 2008.

Hanmer, Michael J. *Discount Voting: Voter Registration Reforms and Their Effects*. New York: Cambridge University Press, 2009.

Karpf, David. *The MoveOn Effect: The Unexpected Transformation of American Political Advocacy*. New York: Oxford University Press, 2012.

Lewis-Beck, Michael S., William G. Jacoby, Helmut Norpoth, and Herbert F. Weisberg. *The American Voter Revisited*. Ann Arbor: University of Michigan Press, 2008.

Manza, Jeff, and Christopher Uggen. *Locked Out: Felon Disenfranchisement and American Democracy*. New York: Oxford University Press, 2006.

McDonald, Michael P., and John Samples, eds. *The Marketplace of Democracy: Electoral Competition and American Politics*. Washington, DC: Brookings Institution Press, 2006.

Mossberger, Karen, Caroline Tolbert, and Ramona McNeal. *Digital Citizenship: The Internet, Society and Participation*. Cambridge, MA: MIT Press, 2008.

Nicholson, Steven P. *Voting the Agenda: Candidates, Elections, and Ballot Propositions*. Princeton, NJ: Princeton University Press, 2005.

Piven, Frances Fox, and Richard Cloward. *Why Americans Don't Vote*. New York: Pantheon, 1988.

Putnam, Robert. *Bowling Alone: The Collapse and Revival of American Community*. New York: Simon & Schuster, 2000.

Rosenstone, Steven J., and John Mark Hansen. *Mobilization, Participation, and Democracy in America*. New York: Macmillan, 1993.

Schattschneider, E. E. *The Semisovereign People: A Realist's View of Democracy in America*. Boston: Wadsworth-Cengage Learning, 1975.

Sinclair, Betsy. *The Social Citizen: Peer Networks and Political Behavior*. Chicago: University of Chicago Press, 2010.

Smith, Daniel, and Caroline Tolbert. *Educated by Initiative: The Effects of Direct Democracy on Citizens and Political Organizations in the American States*. Ann Arbor: University of Michigan Press, 2004.

Springer, Melanie. *American Electoral Institutions and Voter Turnout, 1920–2000*. Chicago: University of Chicago Press, 2014.

Verba, Sidney, Kay Lehman Schlozman, and Henry Brady. *Voice and Equality: Civic Voluntarism in American Politics*. Cambridge, MA: Harvard University Press, 1995.

Recommended Websites

League of Women Voters
www.lwv.org
Established in 1920 as part of the women's suffrage movement, the League of Women Voters encourages informed and active participation in government.

Open Secrets
www.opensecrets.org/elections/
Campaign contributions are a form of political participation that is both necessary and controversial. This website uses data from the Federal Election Commission to publish the names of those who give elected officials campaign money and those who may be receiving preferential treatment.

Project Vote
www.projectvote.org
Since 1982, Project Vote has worked to increase the participation of low-income, minority, youth, and other marginalized and underrepresented voters. The organization sponsors voter registration drives and get-out-the-vote programs and monitors election laws across the states. As a community organizer, Barack Obama worked for Project Vote, registering voters in Chicago.

Project Vote Smart
www.votesmart.org
This nonpartisan site is dedicated to providing citizens with information on political candidates and elected officials. Here you can easily view candidates' biographical information, positions on issues, and voting records so that you can make an informed choice on Election Day.

United States Election Project
www.electproject.org
Click on "Voter turnout data" for the best and most reliable source for voter turnout rates nationally and by state in presidential and midterm elections from 1980–2016.

U.S. Census Bureau: Voting and Registration
www.census.gov/population/www/socdemo/voting.html
The U.S. Census Bureau collects statistics on voting and registration by various demographic and socioeconomic characteristics. See if you can find differences in voter turnout by race, age, gender, or socioeconomic status.

Obama administration's plans for addressing the Great Recession. This conservative populist movement not only challenged Democratic policies but also the Republican party establishment. As political candidates associated with the Tea Party ran for office starting in the 2010 midterm elections, they sometimes won Republican Party endorsement but often ran against the mainstream party. Indeed, as a nontraditional Republican candidate, Donald Trump courted Tea Party supporters during his presidential campaign in 2016. As we will see in this chapter, parties play an important role in American democracy, mobilizing voters and organizing their choices. Revolts against the political parties by rank-and-file members occur very rarely in American history. But sometimes, parties are shaken up by grassroots activity like Keli Carender's. Her story, and others like it, show that individuals can make a difference, not just in political parties but also in the broader political arena. The key is to "just get it done."

CHAPTER GOALS

- ★ **Define political parties and their functions in politics (pp. 337–40)**
- ★ **Explain the roles that parties play in elections (pp. 340–44)**
- ★ **Describe how the major American parties are structured at the national, state, and local levels (pp. 344–48)**
- ★ **Explain how parties organize legislative business and influence policy (pp. 348–52)**
- ★ **Identify the reasons for and sources of party identification (pp. 352–60)**
- ★ **Describe how the party system in the United States has changed over time and its main features today (pp. 360–71)**

What Are Political Parties?

Define political parties and their functions in politics

Political parties, like interest groups (see Chapter 11), are organizations that seek influence over government. They can generally be distinguished from interest groups on the basis of their mission. A party seeks to control the government by nominating candidates and electing its members to office. As we will see in Chapter 11, interest groups do not control the operation of government and its personnel but rather try to influence government policies, often through lobbying elected officials and contributing to campaigns.

political parties organized groups that attempt to influence the government by electing their members to important government offices

Although the Founders did not envision the rise of political parties, they quickly became a core feature of the American political system. Parties and **partisanship** organize the political world and simplify complex policy debates for citizens and elected officials. Parties also play central roles in mobilizing citizens to vote, informing the public of government policy, and ensuring that the public voice is heard in policy debates.

partisanship identification with or support of a particular party or cause

Political parties have been the chief points of contact between government, on the one side, and individual citizens and interest groups, on the other. Through organized political parties, citizens and groups can influence government policies. As political scientist Walter Dean Burnham wrote, political parties "generate... collective power on behalf of the many [who are] individually powerless against the relatively few who are individually or organizationally powerful."[2] It may be difficult for ordinary citizens to have any real influence on government acting as individuals, but they can have an impact on what government does when they act collectively. Political parties also seek to organize and influence important groups in society to win elections and gain political power. They are instruments through which citizens and government attempt to influence each other.

In a landmark book written over a half-century ago, political scientist E. E. Schattschneider advocated for a political system run by party politics instead of interest groups.[3] To be an equal democracy where all groups are represented, there must be competitive and responsible political parties that provide real choices to the electorate so that the public can participate in the government's decision-making process. Parties, he believed, are able to mobilize more people than interest groups because they can expand the "scope of conflict" or the policy debate to include most or all of the electorate. While interest groups (see Chapter 11) benefit from focusing on specific policy issues, political parties broaden political conflict to the public arena and focus on a range of policy issues, from the economy to foreign policy, in order to win elections.

It is not enough, however, to simply have political parties: parties must be "competitive" and "responsible." When political parties compete with one another to win elections, Schattschneider contended, they have incentives to continually expand public debates to include nonvoting members of the electorate in order to gain a majority of voters and win the election. This strategy has been evident in the extremely competitive presidential elections since 2000, with widespread voter-mobilization campaigns on the part of the Democratic and Republican parties. Voter turnout in 2008, 2012, and 2016 was at the highest levels since 1960, largely because of the get-out-the-vote campaign drives organized by the political parties.

Political parties must also act "responsibly" by continually informing the people of current political issues that are in their best interests. And once in power, political parties must enact laws that represent their members' interests. In this idealized view, competitive and responsible parties can help increase voter turnout, creating more equal representation for those in lower socioeconomic classes.

Some political scientists argue that Schattschneider's vision is far from reality. Today, we have large, powerful, and active political parties, but party candidates are often subsidized by big businesses and the wealthy. Political scientist Larry Bartels found that on economic issues both the Democratic and Republican parties are more responsive to the preferences of the upper and middle classes and ignore the policy wishes of the lower class. Bartels calls this "unequal democracy."[4] Stagnating wages for the middle class and rising income inequality help explain why many voters have grown increasingly frustrated by the Democratic and Republican parties; in the 2016 presidential election, many supported populist candidates, such as Republican Donald Trump and Independent Bernie Sanders, who sought to reform the political system.

Another criticism of parties stems from the idea that they are in fact controlled more by interest groups and wealthy campaign donors than by politicians and the public. This influence causes parties to be less likely to respond to voter preferences, and parties may even take advantage of the public's lack of attention to politics to promote their own agenda.[5]

Some observers believe that the problem in the United States today is that the two parties and political elites in Congress are too polarized along liberal and conservative lines, whereas the majority of Americans hold moderate opinions and values; thus, Congress and the parties do a poor job of representing the citizens.[6] Others argue that the rules governing our election system need reform so that there are more than two major political parties to better represent citizens' views.[7] Both of these topics are covered in more detail near the end of this chapter.

As long as political parties have existed, they have been criticized for introducing selfish, "partisan" concerns into public debates and national policy. Yet political parties are extremely important to the functioning of a democracy. Most Americans affiliate or lean toward one of the two major parties, Democrats or Republicans. As we will see, parties can increase participation in politics, provide a central cue for citizens to cast informed votes, and organize the business of legislatures and governing.

While both major parties often claim to be looking out for lower-income individuals (as did the Bernie Sanders and Trump campaigns in 2016), studies have shown that both Democrats and Republicans in Congress respond more to the interests of the affluent and middle-class Americans.

HOW DO POLITICAL PARTIES FORM AND CHANGE?

Historically, parties form in one of two ways. The first, which could be called *internal mobilization*, occurs when political conflicts prompt officials and competing factions within government to mobilize popular support. This is precisely what happened during the early years of the American Republic. Competition in Congress between northeastern merchants and southern farmers led each group to attempt to organize their supporters. The result was the foundation of America's first national parties: the Federalists, whose strength was greatest in the New England states and the Jeffersonians or Antifederalists, whose primary base was in the South.

The second way that parties form is called *external mobilization*, which takes place when a group of politicians outside of government organizes popular support to win governmental power. For example, during the 1850s a group of state politicians who opposed slavery, especially the expansion of slavery in U.S. territorial possessions, built what became the Republican Party by constructing party organizations and mobilizing popular support in the Northeast and West.

America's two major parties now are the Democrats and the Republicans. Both trace their roots back over 150 years, and both have evolved over time. Since they were formed, the two major parties have undergone significant changes in their policy positions and their membership. These changes have been prompted both by issues and events (economic change, the civil rights movement, immigration, etc.) and by demographic and social change in the United States. Today growing differences in the demographic profiles of Republicans and Democrats suggest more change in the party system is under way. Younger voters and racial and ethnic minorities increasingly affiliate with the Democratic Party, while white, older people are more likely to vote Republican. In the 2016 presidential campaign, a lack of trust in and frustration with the federal government mobilized many to support "outsider" populist candidates on both the ideological right and left. The success of outsider candidates may signal that change to the political parties is under way (see discussion in this chapter on the history of party systems and party realignments).

THE UNITED STATES' TWO-PARTY SYSTEM

Over the past 200 years, Americans' conception of political parties has changed considerably. In the early years of the Republic, parties were seen as threats to the social order and were referred to as "factions." In the *Federalist Papers*, both Alexander Hamilton and James Madison condemned factions that pursued narrow self-interest over the broader well-being of the nation as a whole.[8] In his 1796 Farewell Address, President George Washington warned his countrymen to shun partisan politics. Nonetheless, a **two-party system** emerged early in the new Republic. Beginning with the Federalists and the Jeffersonian Republicans in the late 1780s, two major parties have dominated national politics, although which two parties has changed with the times and issues. (See "Party Systems," which follows.)

two-party system a political system in which only two parties have a realistic opportunity to compete effectively for control

Most other countries in the world use a proportional representation system, in which seats in government (national legislature or parliament) are allocated to political parties based on their share of the total vote cast in the election. In contrast, the United States uses geographic single-member districts combined with winner-take-all elections. It doesn't matter, for example, if the contest for a U.S. House seat is won with 40 percent or 80 percent of the total vote; the candidate with the largest number of votes (a plurality) in that district wins the seat in Congress or a state legislature. That is why the system is "winner take all" or a plurality electoral system: unlike in proportional systems, runners-up do not gain seats in government (see Chapter 10 as well). The U.S. system is also called "first past the post" because the candidate with the most votes wins the election, even if she did not win a majority of the popular vote. In the United States, proportional voting rules are uncommon, especially above the local level, and are absent at the national level.

Election rules largely determine how many political parties there are in a country. Plurality voting rules in the United States create its two party–dominant system, and third parties have generally not won seats in Congress, state legislatures, or the presidency. Under U.S. election rules, voters have an incentive not to vote for small- or third-party candidates for fear of "wasting" their vote when only one party (usually one of the two largest parties) can win the election. Concern about wasting one's vote on third parties is called the spoiler effect or strategic voting. Proportional representation systems used in many other countries tend to result in multiple parties in government. If U.S. rules were to change, the number of political parties would likely change as well.

FOR CRITICAL ANALYSIS

What rules governing the American electoral process promote a two-party system? How might different rules impact the party system?

WHAT POLITICAL PARTIES DO

Without political parties, democracy as we know it would be difficult to achieve. In the United States, citizens take for granted that leaders will run for public office, that there will be competition among candidates, that they will have the opportunity to learn about candidates and policy issues from campaigns and cast their ballots in fair elections, and that once in office, political leaders will work together to make policy and govern. Each of these tasks is complex, however, and would be all the more so if political parties did not exist. Parties mobilize citizens in the electorate to vote, offer choices to voters in elections, and provide officeholders with organization for running government. As political scientist John Aldrich argues in *Why Parties*, parties solve three fundamental problems of democracy: how to regulate the number of people seeking public office, how to mobilize voters, and how to achieve and maintain the majorities needed to pass legislation once in office.[9]

Parties, Voter Mobilization, and Elections

Explain the roles that parties play in elections

Parties have always been central to the electoral process, and in recent years they have taken on a renewed role in recruiting candidates, coordinating campaigns, mobilizing voters, and raising money.[10] Just as companies seek to brand their products in the commercial marketplace using ad campaigns, branding and marketing now regularly happen in candidate campaigns. As campaigns become more candidate-centered, branding has become central. Barack Obama, for example, was especially effective in branding his campaign with the words "hope" and "change." In 2016, Donald Trump branded his campaign with the ubiquitous "Make American Great Again" red baseball caps. Parties succeed when they win elections; thus, we begin with parties and elections.

AMERICA SIDE by SIDE

Two-Party and Multi-Party Systems

The American political system is dominated by two political parties, the Republican Party and the Democratic Party, but many other countries have more than two parties. The number varies depending on the electoral rules in place. Countries such as the United States, which use a first-past-the-post system (in which the candidate with the most votes wins the seat), tend to have two major parties that dominate the system. In contrast, the Netherlands uses a proportional representation system and has 13 parties in their current legislature, with 4 of the parties working together to form a coalition government.

In proportional representation systems like the Netherlands, voters select parties to represent them nationally rather than candidates to represent their region, and parties receive roughly the same percentage of votes in parliament as they received in the election. Thus, the legislature tends to more accurately resemble how the national electorate voted. The party representation in the 2017 Dutch parliament is almost identical to the 2017 national vote, whereas in the United States, the largest parties tend to be overrepresented while smaller parties lose out.

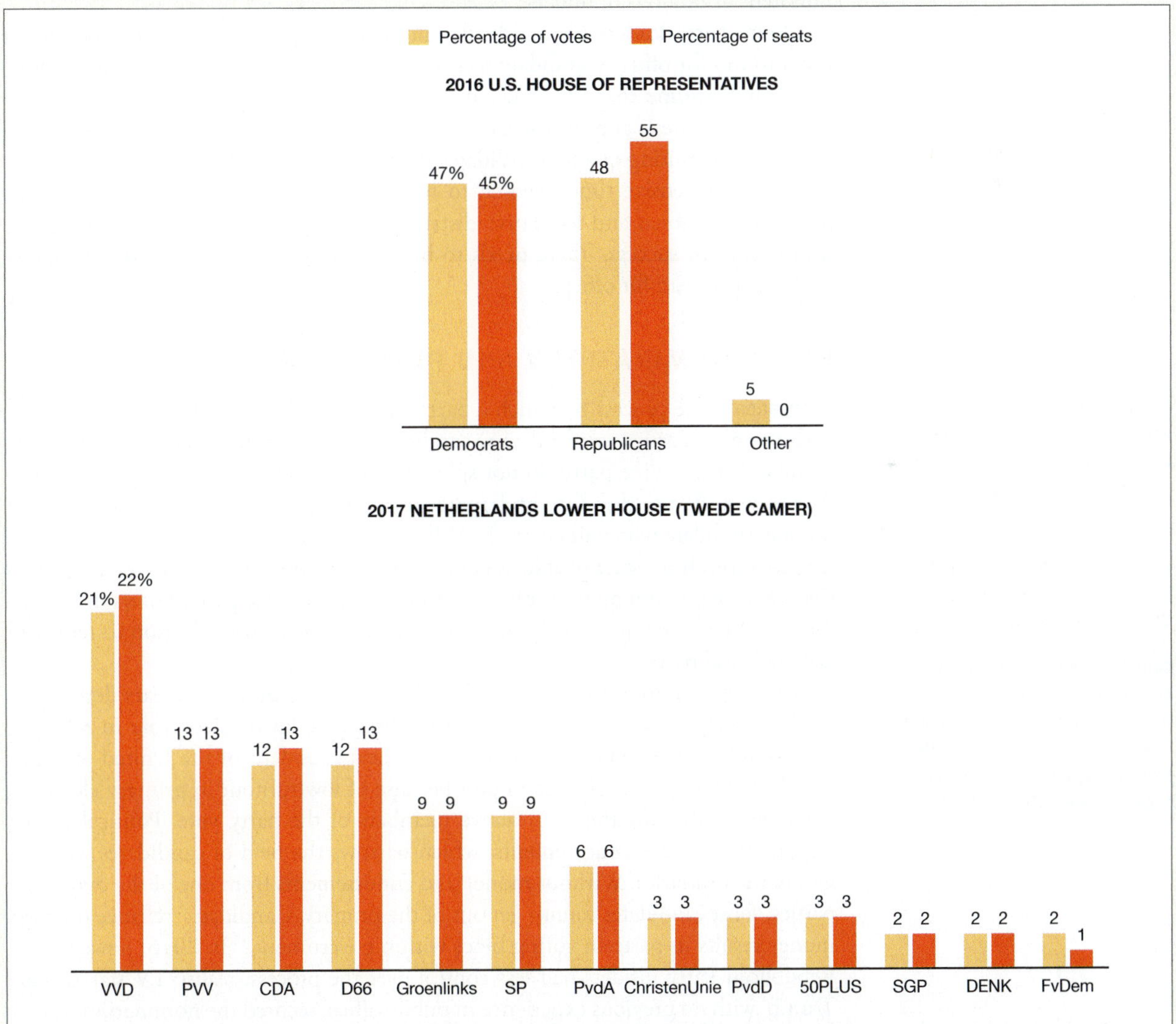

SOURCE: The U.S. Federal Election Commission, transition.fec.gov and the Kiesraad (Dutch Electoral Commission), www.kiesraad.nl (accessed 4/12/18).

RECRUITING CANDIDATES

One of the most important but least noticed party activities is the recruitment of candidates to run for office. As Schattschneider argued, "responsible parties" recruit candidates who are loyal to the party's philosophy and policy agenda, with the goal of controlling government and adopting laws that are consistent with the party's platform. Each election year, candidates run for thousands of state and local offices as well as congressional seats. When they do not have an incumbent running for re-election, party leaders attempt to identify strong candidates and encourage them to run for office in open-seat elections.

An ideal candidate will have a strong leadership record and the capacity to raise enough money to mount a serious campaign, especially if that candidate must challenge an incumbent or will face a well-funded opponent from the other party in the general election. Party leaders are usually not willing to provide financial backing to candidates who are unable to raise substantial funds on their own. For a U.S. House seat, this can mean several hundred thousand dollars; for a Senate seat, a serious candidate must be able to raise several million dollars. Presidential candidates raise hundreds of millions of dollars.

Often, party leaders have difficulty finding strong candidates and persuading them to run for office. Candidate recruitment is problematic in an era when politicians must assume that their personal lives will be intensely scrutinized on social media, in the press, and in negative campaign ads run by their opponents.[11] Other barriers to recruiting quality candidates include the extremely high cost of political campaigns, extensive time devoted to fundraising, and the numerous gerrymandered congressional and legislative districts (see Chapter 10), giving challengers a slim chance of success. There needs to be a decent chance of winning for quality challengers to run for office.

PARTY NOMINATIONS AND PRIMARIES

nomination the process by which political parties select their candidates for election to public office

primary elections elections held to select a party's candidate for the general election

caucus (political) a normally closed political party business meeting of citizens or lawmakers to select candidates, elect officers, plan strategy, or make decisions regarding legislative matters

Nomination is the process by which a party selects a single candidate to run for each elective office. Parties want only one candidate on the general-election ballot so that members of the same party do not split the vote, allowing the other party's candidate to win. Parties therefore undertake an internal process of nomination to settle on one candidate who will be on the ballot in the general election. The nomination process varies from state to state and office to office, but it usually involves a **primary election** or **caucus** among multiple candidates from the same party. Voters in the primary election select just one candidate to go on to the general election to represent each political party.

Scholars have found that although the nomination process appears democratic in that average citizens have a say, party elites play an outsized role in selecting the candidates who will compete to be the next president of the United States or member of Congress.[12] This is in part because of low turnout in primary elections, where generally only the most active members of the party vote. Political parties provide money and endorsements, which narrows the field of candidates who can win in the primaries. Without money and endorsements from one of the two major parties, most candidates cannot get out of the primary. Candidates' reliance on party money results in partisan voting blocs within government.[13] In 2016, however, the Republican Party insiders had less control over the process; reality-TV star Donald Trump, with no previous experience in public office, secured the nomination despite

With no incumbent running for New Hampshire's 1st Congressional District seat, Republican candidates debated one another in the primaries. Eddie Edwards, left, defeated four other Republican candidates to secure the party's nomination in the general election.

the fact that many members of the party emphatically spoke out against him. Only a handful of Republican members of Congress endorsed Trump for president.

GENERAL ELECTION AND MOBILIZING VOTERS

The general election begins after the nominations conclude. Throughout American history, the general election competition is a time of intense partisanship, when popular support for the parties is high. All the paraphernalia of party committees—from signs, bumper stickers, and buttons to social media slogans, hashtags, and YouTube ads—are on display, and party members are activated into local party workforces. One of the earliest activities of party workers is voter registration. Parties and candidate campaigns, along with nonprofit organizations, mail notices, call and email voters, organize voter-registration drives on college campuses, and knock on doors to ensure that citizens are registered. Confirming that citizens are registered to vote or helping them register, however, is only the first step.

The next step is turning out the vote. Convincing voters to actually show up to cast a ballot on Election Day is one of the hardest tasks that the parties face; it involves getting individuals to go to the polls, stand in line, and vote for the party's candidates on the ballot. If they are voting by mail—absentee ballots or mail voting is how one in three Americans now vote—each voter must fill out the ballot and return it. Some states, like Oregon and Washington, have all-mail elections, and all ballots are mailed to home addresses (see Chapter 8).

Voter mobilization, once an art, has now become a science. Campaigns now organize wide-scale voter-mobilization drives involving field offices with hundreds of thousands of volunteers and party workers contacting millions of voters. In recent years, the two major parties have developed an extensive database of over 240 million potential adult voters, combining state voter registration files, demographic data from the U.S. Census, and commercial behavior data, which allows the parties to more accurately seek out votes for their party candidates, contributions, and campaign volunteers. Using these vast computerized databases, modern

Research by political scientists and campaign organizations has shown that face-to-face, in-person contacts are much more effective than mailings, robocalls, or TV advertising in mobilizing voters.

micro-targeting when political campaigns tailor messages to individuals in small homogenous groups based on their group interests to support a candidate or policy issue

political campaigns can predict who you will vote for, and they are extremely effective at turning out the voters who are most likely to vote for their candidates. One way campaigns use these data is through **micro-targeting**, which involves tailoring campaign messages to individuals in small, homogeneous groups (e.g., suburban stay-at-home mothers or fans of NASCAR) and emphasizing specific, often heated issues, rather than a one-size-fits-all campaign message. This technique enables political parties to identify small groups based on specific characteristics—including geographic location—and to target candidates' strategies and messages to these groups.

Big data and targeted campaign messages have revolutionized how parties and candidates conduct voter-mobilization drives. It doesn't matter, after all, which party has more support if that party's voters stay home on Election Day. In 2008 the Obama campaign learned that face-to-face and in-person contacts are much more effective than mailings or robocalls at getting out the vote.[14] The lessons of 2008 were improved on in 2012 and 2016 as both parties built more accurate databases to use when developing their messages and turning out the vote. Facebook was especially important in turning out Republican voters for Trump in 2016.

Parties as Organizations

party organization the formal structure of a political party, including its leadership, election committees, active members, and paid staff

Describe how the major American parties are structured at the national, state, and local levels

In the United States **party organizations** exist at virtually every level of government (see Figure 9.1). These organizations are usually committees made up of a number of active party members. State law and party rules dictate how such committees are created. Usually, committee members are elected at local party business meetings, called caucuses, or as part of the regular primary election. The best-known examples of these

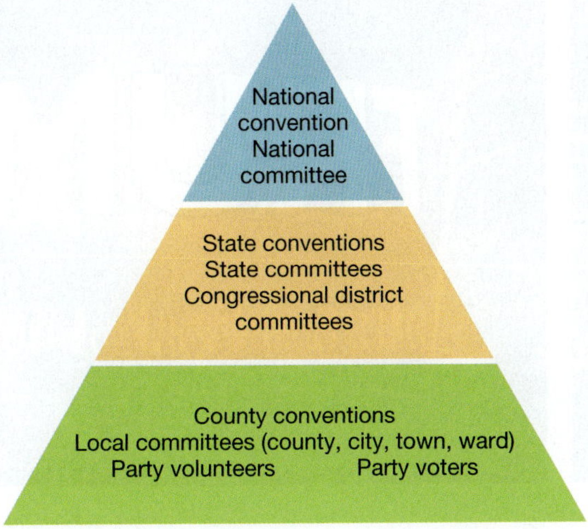

FIGURE 9.1

How American Parties Are Organized

committees are at the national level: the Democratic National Committee and the Republican National Committee.

NATIONAL CONVENTION

At the national level, the party's most important institution is the **national convention**. The convention, held every four years, is attended by delegates from each of the 50 states. The convention has three formal tasks, the most important of which is to nominate the party's presidential and vice-presidential candidates. Before World War II, presidential nominations occupied most of the time at the national convention, requiring days of negotiation and compromise. In recent years, however, presidential candidates have been chosen by winning enough delegates in state primary elections and caucuses to win the official nomination on the first ballot. Today, the convention serves as a media event to promote the party's candidates, not as a forum to decide which presidential candidate will represent the party.

national convention convened by the Republican National Committee or the Democratic National Committee to nominate official candidates for president and vice president in the upcoming election, establish party rules, and adopt the party's platform

The convention's other two formal tasks, determining the party's rules and its **platform**, are also important. Party rules can determine the influence of competing groups within the party, which may improve the party's chances for electoral success. In 1972, for example, the Democratic National Convention adopted a new set of rules favored by the party's liberal wing. State delegations to the Democratic Convention were required to include women and members of minority groups in rough proportion to those groups' representation among the party's membership in that state. The change also called for the use of the proportional voting rules. In the case of the Democratic Party, proportional representation increased the likelihood of women and minority delegates being elected, while in the Republican Party, which used proportional representation voting for the first time in 2012, it worked to increase representation of social conservatives and Tea Party members.

platform a party document, written at a national convention, that contains party philosophy, principles, and positions on issues

The convention also approves the party platform. Platforms are often dismissed as documents filled with promises that voters seldom read. To some extent this criticism is well founded: not one voter in a thousand so much as glances at the party platform, and even the news media pay little attention to the documents.

Today, the parties use their national conventions to provide more entertainment than substantive policy in order to attract media attention and promote their candidate.

Furthermore, the parties' presidential candidates make little use of the platforms in their campaigns and usually develop their own themes. Nonetheless, the platform is understood as a contract in which the various party groups attending the convention state their terms for supporting the ticket. Party platforms should be seen more as internal party documents than as public pledges.

NATIONAL COMMITTEES

Between conventions, each national political party is technically headed by its national committee. For the Democrats and Republicans, these are called the Democratic National Committee (DNC) and the Republican National Committee (RNC). Much of what these committees do is raise money for party candidates. The national committees also try to minimize disputes within the party and work to enhance the party's media image. The work of each national committee is overseen by its chairperson.

soft money money contributed directly to political parties and other organizations for political activities, such as voter mobilization drives, that is not regulated by federal campaign spending laws

The DNC and RNC each used to raise tens of millions of dollars of so-called **soft money** every election cycle, which could be used to support party candidates throughout the nation. The 2002 Bipartisan Campaign Reform Act outlawed this practice. To circumvent the law and raise the large amounts of money needed for political campaigns, however, each party and most candidates establish Super PACs as sources of outside money. These Super PACs promote and publicize political issues, including airing negative campaign ads. As nonprofit political advocacy groups, Super PACs can claim tax-exempt status under Section 527 of the Internal Revenue Code (see Chapter 10); therefore the committees that comprise each Super PAC are called 527 committees. Super PACs can raise and spend unlimited amounts of money as long as their activities are not *coordinated* with those of the formal party organizations or the candidates, and if their aim is to inform the public and increase voter turnout. Many Super PACs are directed by former Republican and Democratic party officials and run shadow campaigns on behalf of the parties.[15] Super PACs can have outsized influence in elections because they run expensive television and media ads for and against candidates. Because wealthy funders, corporations, and even foreign donors can mask their identity by forming Super PACs, they have become synonymous with political corruption in some circles.

CONGRESSIONAL, STATE, AND LOCAL CAMPAIGN COMMITTEES

Each party also forms House and Senate campaign committees, whose efforts may or may not be coordinated with the activities of the national committees (that is, the DNC and RNC). The congressional campaign committee is made up of members of each chamber that are expected to raise a certain sum of money, and doing so allows them to move up in the power structure. Congressional committees direct funds to the handful of very competitive House and Senate races each election. Presidential and congressional fundraising committees compete for dollars from the biggest donors, who are often corporations and billionaires. In recent years, both parties have attempted to better coordinate the fund-raising activities of all of their committees.

The Democrats and the Republicans also have a central committee in each state. The parties traditionally also have county committees and, in some instances, state Senate district committees, judicial district committees, and, in the case of larger cities, citywide party committees and local assembly district "ward" committees.

During the nineteenth and early twentieth centuries, many cities, counties, and occasionally even a few states had such well-organized parties that they were called **party machines**, whose leaders were called "bosses." The famous old machines of New York, Chicago, and Boston relied on "precinct captains" and a fairly tight group of party members around them. Precinct captains were usually leaders in neighborhood party clubhouses, which were important social centers and places for distributing favors (or bribes) to constituents.[16] Traditional party machines depended heavily on **patronage**, their power to control government jobs. With thousands of jobs to dispense, party bosses were able to recruit armies of political workers to turn out the vote. Voting for the party could mean the guarantee of a government job, such as a police officer, firefighter, or garbage collector. The party machines even distributed free turkeys on Thanksgiving, in exchange for support on Election Day.

Some of the major reform movements in American history, such as the Progressive movement in the early 1900s, were motivated by the excessive power, corruption, and abuses of these party machines and their bosses. Progressive reformers changed the rules of politics to reduce the power of parties and to give voters more voice in deciding who was elected to public office. A few of the many reforms to weaken the party machines included the direct election of U.S. senators; the secret ballot and long ballot, where the names of candidates running for both parties were listed; primary elections where voters, not parties, picked candidates; and voter registration, which reduced turnout and prevented party officials from casting false ballots for their candidate.

Few political machines are left today. With civil service and the merit system, party leaders no longer control many government jobs, which was a primary way the party rewarded loyal supporters. Nevertheless, state and local party organizations are very active in recruiting candidates and conducting voter-registration drives. In addition, under current federal law, state and local party organizations can spend unlimited amounts of money on "party-building" activities such as voter-registration and get-out-the-vote drives. National party organizations, which have enormous

party machines strong party organizations in late nineteenth- and early twentieth-century American cities; these machines were led by often corrupt "bosses" who controlled party nominations and patronage

patronage the resources available to higher officials, usually opportunities to make partisan appointments to offices and to confer grants, licenses, or special favors to supporters

Political parties used to be ruled by powerful local "bosses," who handed out jobs and favors in exchange for loyalty on Election Day. The cartoon shows "fat cat" New York boss Richard Croker controlling the Democratic Party organization (the donkey) with his pit bulls.

fund-raising abilities, transfer millions of dollars to the state and local party organizations. State and local parties, in turn, spend this soft money to promote national, state, and local political activities. Through the transfer of party campaign money, local organizations became linked financially to the national parties and American political parties became more integrated. State and local party organizations play an important role in elections despite the collapse of the old party machines.[17]

Parties in Government

Explain how parties organize legislative business and influence policy

When the bumps, bruises, and dust of the campaign and election have settled, does it matter which party has won? It does. Especially when the parties are sharply divided ideologically, as they have been in recent years, the party that controls government can make significant changes to law and policy.

PARTIES AND POLICY

For decades, one of the most familiar complaints about American politics was that the two major parties try to be all things to all people and are therefore indistinguishable from each other. But since the 1980s fundamental differences have emerged between the positions of Democratic and Republican party leaders on a number of key issues. For example, the national leadership of the Republican Party supports limiting immigration to the United States, maintaining high levels of military spending, cuts in social programs including health care, tax relief for corporations and upper-income voters, protecting rights for gun owners, and a social agenda backed by members of conservative religious denominations, including opposition to abortion. The Republican Party opposes government regulation on businesses, including environmental laws. The Democratic Party, on the other hand, supports expanded funding for public education, social services and national health care, public spending for infrastructure such as roads, cuts in military spending, increased regulation of business to address climate change, raising taxes on the wealthy and corporations to combat growing income inequality, restrictions on gun ownership, and a variety of consumer protection programs. Democrats favor more lenient immigration policies and have been strong supporters of so-called DREAMers—undocumented immigrants brought to the United States as children.

Partisan conflict has intensified in recent years. More Americans believe there are stronger conflicts between Democrats and Republicans in U.S. society today than between blacks and whites, the rich and the poor, and other social groups (see Figure 9.2). In 2018, 86 percent of Americans said conflicts between Democrats and Republicans are either strong or very strong.[18]

Beginning in the 1980s the Republican Party, led by Ronald Reagan, sought to expand its base by focusing on social issues that mattered to conservative religious voters. Ted Cruz (R-Tex.) announced his 2016 presidential campaign at Liberty University.

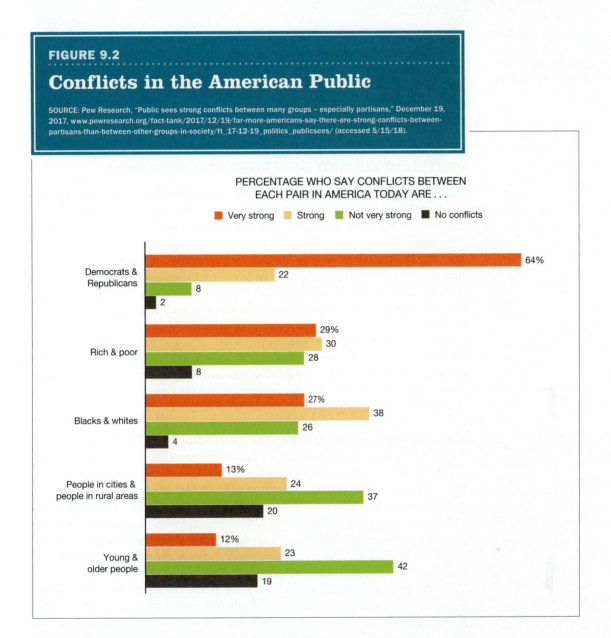

FIGURE 9.2

Conflicts in the American Public

SOURCE: Pew Research, "Public sees strong conflicts between many groups – especially partisans," December 19, 2017, www.pewresearch.org/fact-tank/2017/12/19/far-more-americans-say-there-are-strong-conflicts-between-partisans-than-between-other-groups-in-society/ft_17-12-19_politics_publicsees/ (accessed 5/15/18).

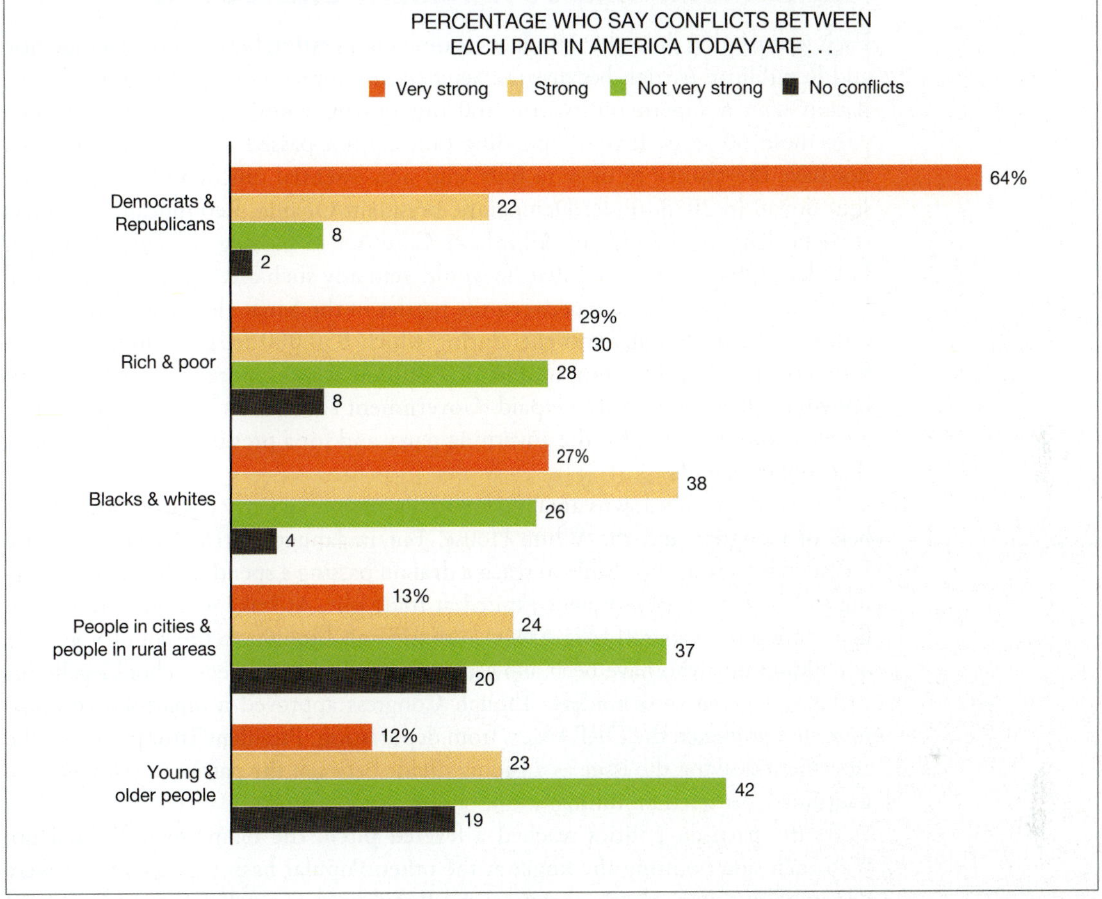

Party leaders often seek to develop issues they hope will add new groups to their party's constituent base. During the 1980s, for example, under the leadership of Ronald Reagan, the Republicans used social issues, including support for school prayer, opposition to abortion, and opposition to affirmative action, to gain the support of white southerners. This effort was successful at increasing Republican strength in the once solidly Democratic South. In 2008, Barack Obama campaigned on creating national health insurance for all Americans and ending the Iraq War; the effect was to build a coalition of working class and middle class voters. In the 2016 presidential election, Donald Trump proposed to build a wall between the southern U.S. border and Mexico to prevent illegal immigration, building a coalition of traditional conservatives and white working-class citizens who have faced economic hardship.

policy entrepreneur an individual who identifies a problem as a political issue and brings a policy proposal into the political agenda

As these examples suggest, party leaders can play the role of **policy entrepreneurs**, developing ideas and programs that will expand their party's base of support while eroding that of the opposition. Like their counterparts in the business world, party leaders seek to identify and develop programs and policies that will appeal to the public. The public, of course, has the ultimate voice. With its votes it decides whether or not to "buy" new policy offerings.

PARTISANSHIP AND GOVERNMENT SHUTDOWNS

Each year passing the federal budget requires cooperation between the Democratic and Republican parties, because the Senate must approve the spending bill for the nation with a supermajority vote (60 out of 100 votes)—and rarely does one party hold 60 seats. If these spending bills are not passed, the government does not have the money to operate fully, and non-essential offices and programs are shut down. In 2013, under Democratic president Obama, Republican lawmakers tried to delay or defund the Affordable Care Act in passing the federal budget. President Obama promised that he would veto any such attempt to end national health care. This stalemate between the parties in the Senate led to a 17-day shutdown of the federal government, during which 850,000 federal employees were furloughed (not paid), and another 1.3 million were required to work without knowing when they would be paid. Government shutdowns are costly, but there are also political costs, for the governing party and for a president unable to adopt their policy agenda.

Government shutdowns are rare, especially when one party controls both chambers of Congress and the White House. But in January 2018, Republicans and Democrats were again unable to reach a deal on passing a spending bill before funding for the federal government expired at midnight. At stake was protection from deportation for 700,000 DREAMers—immigrants brought to the country illegally as children but who have been allowed to live, work, and attend school legally for decades as green card holders. Though Congress approved a bipartisan compromise that protected the DREAMers from deportation, President Trump rejected the agreement, leaving the issue as a gaping divide between the parties as the stalemate continued, centered on immigration.

As the partisan politics reached a fevered pitch, the blame game heated up, with each side pointing the finger at the other. Popular hash tags on Twitter were #TrumpShutdown, clearly targeting the Republican-controlled government, and #SchumerShutdown, blaming the Senate leader of the Democratic Party who provided most of the votes for the shutdown. To end the stalemate a group of bipartisan moderate senators proposed a short-term stopgap spending bill to keep the government operating until early February. After five short-term spending bills, a final omnibus spending bill was passed in March 2018, but the fate of the DREAMers remains unclear.

FACTIONS WITHIN THE PARTIES

While party polarization, or the depth of divisions between Republicans and Democrats, is at an all-time high, the divisions *within* each political party may be nearly as important. Parties are broad coalitions of people and groups who agree on a common approach to address current challenges facing the nation, including foreign threats to security, economic growth, and social inequality. But political parties are also diverse and represent many people with competing interests for power and influence. For leaders in Congress and state legislatures, keeping these different groups working toward shared goals can be difficult. When cooperation among factions is not successful, a party's internal divisions can weaken the party itself.

The Republican Party today, for example, is divided in four ways. Pro-business conservatives, epitomized by Nebraska senator Benjamin Sasse, are traditional Republican conservatives, generally a relatively affluent group that favors small government and lower corporate taxes but also favors global free trade. Far-right or alt-right conservatives, such as President Trump, tend to be social conservatives, often with lower levels of education, and are opposed to immigration and U.S. involvement in the global economy and institutions like the United Nations. They favor tariffs on imports to the United States to protect American-made products. Social and religious conservatives, such as Texas senator Ted Cruz, are primarily driven by their socially conservative values, such as opposition to abortion and gay marriage. Finally, libertarians, such as Kentucky senator Rand Paul, believe in small government and reduced government regulations, and emphasize individual freedom. Libertarians are closer to traditional conservatives than to alt-right conservatives. These cleavages have presented severe challenges for governing. For example, far-right conservatives like Donald Trump favor very strict immigration policies in order to protect American workers, while pro-business conservatives see that immigration is important to maintain a healthy economy. These differences make it difficult to find common ground. Trump's electoral success in the 2016 Republican presidential primaries was due in part to a crowded field of candidates; no one candidate could secure a majority.

During his presidency, Donald Trump has waged a war, particularly through his use of Twitter, against many Republican leaders within his party, including Senate Majority Leader Mitch McConnell, former attorney general Jeff Sessions, former FBI director James Comey, the late Arizona senator John McCain, and Special Counsel Robert Mueller, among others.[19] Nonetheless, Republican lawmakers in Congress have generally rallied around the president even if they have personally been subject to his wrath on Twitter. Despite serious divisions within parties, when a job needs to get done, the parties often unify behind a shared goal.

The 2016 presidential election also revealed serious divides within the Democratic Party between its liberal wing (whose members favored Bernie Sanders) and traditional Democrats, who favored Hillary Clinton and who tend to be older and hold a mix of moderate and liberal values. Such divisions within the party may have contributed to the Democrats losing the White House and Congress in 2016, as many Sanders supporters refused to vote for Clinton in the general election. Today, however, the Democratic Party has renewed strength and has largely remained united in staunch opposition to President Trump. Within the Democratic Party, the coalitions all strongly favor social safety nets (national health care, etc.) but are divided in terms of government regulation of business.

PARTIES IN CONGRESS

Congress depends more on the party system than is generally recognized, as the parties form the basic organization for running Congress. The Speaker of the House is a party office. All the members of the House take part in the election of the Speaker, but the actual selection is made by the **majority party**—the party that holds a majority of seats in the House. (The other party is known as the **minority party**.)

majority party the party that holds the majority of legislative seats in either the House or the Senate

minority party the party that holds the minority of legislative seats in either the House or the Senate

When the majority party caucus presents a nominee for Speaker to the entire House, its choice is usually ratified in a straight vote along party lines. The committee system of both houses of Congress is also a product of the two-party system; the party with the most seats chairs the congressional committees, setting the policy agenda. Each party is also assigned a quota of members for each committee, depending on the percentage of total seats held by the party. As we shall see in Chapter 12, the assignment of individual members to committees is a party decision. Granting a member of Congress permission to transfer to another committee is also a party decision, as is advancement up the committee ladder toward serving as committee chair.

FOR CRITICAL ANALYSIS

How do parties attract the popular support they need to win elections?

Party Identification

Identify the reasons for and sources of party identification

One reason why parties are so important is that individual's tend to develop party identification with one of the major political parties. **Party identification** has been compared with wearing blue- or red-tinted glasses: they color voters' understanding of politics in general and are the most important cue in how to vote in elections. Party identification can create information bubbles and filters where citizens follow news media and candidates on social media that are of the same partisan leaning. Most Republicans vote for Republican party candidates, and most Democrats vote for Democrats. Slightly less than one-third of Americans are Republicans, while Democrats and Independents each make up slightly more than one-third of the population. However, most independents lean toward one of the major parties, and political scientists often consider independents who lean as identifying with that party. The number of people identifying as Democrats has outnumbered Republican identifiers for a long time (see Figure 9.3).

party identification an individual voter's psychological ties to one party or another

Although it is an emotional tie, party identification also has a rational component. Voters generally form attachments to the party that reflects their views and interests. Once those attachments are formed, usually in youth, they are likely to persist and even be handed down to children, unless some very strong factors convince individuals that their party is no longer serving their interests.

On any general-election ballot, there are a number of candidates about whom the average voter has little information. Without knowledge of local or judicial races, most voters fall back on their Republican or Democratic party identification or leaning. Some states allow a straight-ticket voting option, where individuals may check one box to cast a ballot for all the Republican or Democratic party candidates up and down the ballot, from local to national offices.

Party identification gives citizens a stake in election outcomes that goes beyond the particular race at hand. This is why strong party identifiers are more likely to go to the polls, to be contacted by political campaigns, and to support the party with which they identify. **Party activists** are drawn from rank and file members, but tend to be more ideologically extreme than the average person identifying with the party. Activists are those who not only vote but also contribute their time, money, and effort to party affairs, organization, and elections, thus giving them an outsize role in the party. No party could succeed without the thousands of

party activists partisans who contribute time, energy, and effort to support their party and its candidates

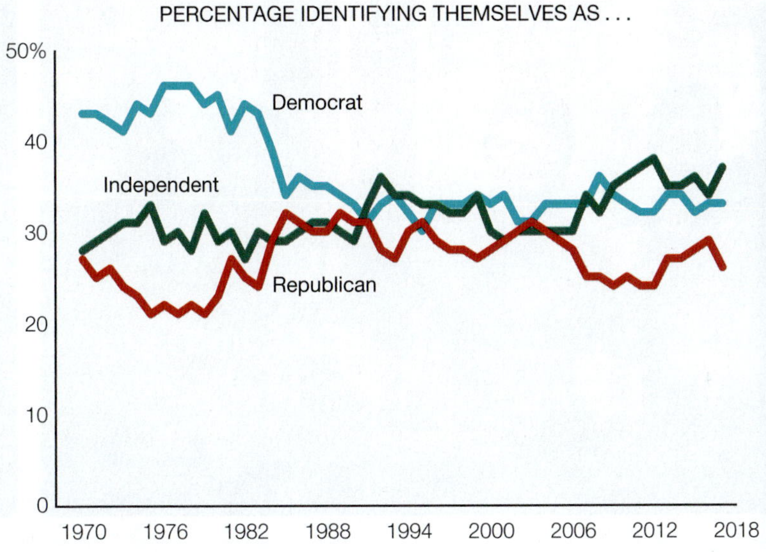

FIGURE 9.3

Trends in Party Identification, 1970–2017

Over time, the Democrats have lost strength as more Americans identified themselves as Republicans and independents. Since 2004, however, the number of Democrats has held steady and the number of Republicans has declined, while the number of Americans identifying as independent of either party has increased to an all-time high. Why do you think this is?

SOURCE: Pew Research Center, "Party Identification," March 20, 2018, www.people-press.org/2018/03/20/party-identification-trends-1992-2017/ (accessed 5/15/18).

volunteers who undertake the tasks needed to keep the organization going. Many party activists devote their time to politics because they have strong beliefs on particular policy issues.

WHO ARE REPUBLICANS AND DEMOCRATS?

The Democratic and Republican parties are currently the only truly national parties in the United States. They are the only political organizations that draw support from every region of the country and from Americans of every racial, economic, religious, and ethnic group. The two parties do not draw equal support from members of every social and demographic stratum, however. In the United States today, several group characteristics are associated with each party. These include race and ethnicity, gender, religion, class (income and education), ideology, region, and age.

The parties have different philosophies and seek to appeal to different core constituencies. The Democratic Party at the national level seeks to unite organized labor, the poor and working class, college-educated middle-class professionals, members of racial and ethnic groups, the young, and government workers. The Republicans, by contrast, appeal to business, white non-Hispanics, white working-class voters, upper-class and affluent voters, military families, religious conservatives, and libertarian-leaning conservatives who want less government interference in all aspects of society and the economy. Rural and suburban areas provide more votes for the Republicans, while urban areas are dominated by Democrats.

Race and Ethnicity The United States' growing racial and ethnic diversity is reflected in changing partisanship and growing divisions among the Republican and Democratic parties. Since the 1930s and Franklin Delano Roosevelt's New Deal,

For many voters, race and ethnicity play a major role in party identification. Members of racial and ethnic minority groups tend to favor Democratic candidates. In 2016, Hillary Clinton gained strong support from African Americans, Asian Americans, and Latinos.

more African Americans have supported the Democratic Party than the Republican Party. Today more than 90 percent of African Americans describe themselves as Democrats and support Democratic candidates in national, state, and local elections. In 2016, 92 percent of African Americans voted for Democrat Hillary Clinton for president.[20]

Latino voters are less monolithic. Cuban Americans, for example, have generally leaned Republican whereas Mexican Americans have favored the Democrats. As a group, however, Latinos increasingly support the Democratic Party. A strong shift toward the Democratic Party occurred in 2008, when the exit polls showed that 67 percent of Latinos supported Obama. This trend has continued, with 65 percent voting for Hillary Clinton in 2016. Latino party affiliation is particularly important because it has the potential to alter the electoral map and change traditionally "red" states (states that reliably vote for the Republican presidential candidate) to "blue" states (states that reliably vote for the Democratic presidential candidate).[21]

Asian Americans have been divided in past elections but now solidly favor Democratic candidates. In 2016, 65 percent of Asian Americans voted for Hillary Clinton, and 29 percent voted for Donald Trump, according to exit polls. Asian Americans, like Latinos, are extremely diverse (see Chapter 8), reflecting cultural differences from their home countries, ranging from India, China, Korea, the Philippines, and more.

The affiliation of African Americans and Latinos with the Democratic Party can be traced to the party's historical policy positions. The Democrats were the party of the civil rights movement, desegregation, and affirmative action policies that solidified African American support. Similarly, Democrats tend to be more supportive than Republicans of policies that favor an easier path to citizenship for immigrants. Support for immigration is often critically important for Latino and Asian voters, especially in states like California, where 28 percent of the population are legal immigrants.

While to overgeneralize these groups is a disservice to the unique characteristics that make up these peoples, we also seek broad patterns to understand how Latinos, Asians, and African Americans are forming coalitions that may create the foundations for the Democratic Party.

Gender Women are somewhat more likely to support Democrats than Republicans, and men are somewhat more likely to support Republicans. This reflects the fact that women tend to prioritize health, education, and social services, issues favored by the Democratic Party, while men tend to prioritize fiscal and economic issues and national security, issues favored by the Republican Party. This difference is known as the **gender gap**. The gender gap has hovered at 10 percent since 1992.

gender gap a distinctive pattern of voting behavior reflecting the differences in views between women and men

The widest gender gap was in 2016, with the first female major-party presidential candidate. There was a 24 percentage-point gap between women and men in the 2016 election. The 2018 midterm elections, dubbed another year of the women, resulted in at least 125 women in Congress. Women voted for Democrats 59 to 40 percent; men split 47 to 51 percent. That 23-point gender gap is the biggest in a midterm election dating back to 1982. In 2016, 54 percent of women supported Democrat Hillary Clinton, compared to 41 percent of men.[22] Still, this is not much more than the Democratic advantage among women in 2012 and 2008. The advantage for Trump among men, however, was significantly larger than the 7-point advantage Romney had among men in 2012 and the one-point advantage Obama had over McCain in 2008. In 2016, 53 percent of men supported Trump compared to 41 percent for Clinton.[23]

Religion Just as racial and ethnic diversity continues to grow, so does religious diversity in the United States. Jews are among the Democratic Party's most loyal constituent groups and have been since the New Deal. Nearly 90 percent of Jewish Americans describe themselves as Democrats. Catholics were also once a strongly pro-Democratic group but have been shifting toward the Republican Party since the 1970s, when

Republicans began focusing on abortion and other social issues important to Catholics. White Protestants are more likely to identify with the Republican Party. Evangelical Protestants, in particular, have been drawn to the Republicans' conservative stands on social issues, such as marriage and abortion. Those who are unaffiliated with a religion—a growing segment of the population at roughly 25 percent—strongly favor the Democratic Party.[24] Today 56 percent of American adults believe it is not necessary to believe in God to be moral and have good values.[25]

The importance of religious conservatives to the Republican Party became more evident after 2000, when George W. Bush awarded federal grants and contracts to religious groups. By using so-called faith-based groups as federal contractors, Bush sought to ensure that these groups and churches would have a continuing stake in Republican success. Religious conservatives, particularly white born-again Christians, overwhelmingly supported Bush in 2004, accounting for one-third of his votes. In 2012 and 2016 white evangelical Protestants continued to vote overwhelmingly Republican.[26]

Class Rising income inequality is an important trend that has recently led to economic populism. The patterns of class voting that emerged from the New Deal of the 1930s were simple: upper-income Americans were considerably more likely to be Republican whereas lower-income Americans were far more likely to identify with the Democrats. This divide is reflected in the differences between the two parties on economic issues. In general, Republicans support cutting taxes, decreased regulation of business, and lower social spending—positions that reflect the interests of the wealthy. The Democrats, however, favor increasing social spending and in some cases raising taxes on the wealthy—a position consistent with the interests of less affluent Americans. But beginning in the 1970s, many white working-class voters turned to the Republican Party. When class is measured by education, white workers without a college degree have favored Republicans in recent elections. While both the Democratic and Republican parties appeal to working-class voters, working-class whites with low levels of education tend to vote Republican, while working-class minorities tend to vote Democratic.[27] This trend accelerated in the 2016 election, contributing to Republicans' electoral success. A wide gap in presidential preferences emerged between those with and without a college degree. College graduates backed Clinton by a 9-point margin (52 percent to 43 percent), while those without a college degree backed Trump (52 percent to 44 percent) in what is the widest gap in support among college graduates and non-college graduates in exit polls dating back to 1980.

Ideology Ideology and party identification are very closely linked. Most individuals who describe themselves as conservatives identify with the Republican Party, whereas most who call themselves liberals support the Democrats. This division has increased in recent years as the two parties have taken very different positions on social and economic issues.

The Pew Research Center's political typology finds that 36 percent of Americans are "ideological" and identify strongly with one of the two major parties. For most Americans, however, party and ideological identification are not so clear-cut: 54 percent of Americans are less partisan and less predictable as to which candidates they will support. These voters are only sporadically interested in politics, such as during an election cycle. Finally, the remaining 10 percent of Americans are completely on the sidelines of politics—this group tends to be young and diverse.[28] This varied political typography of our nation suggests that the categories of liberal and conservative may not capture the full picture.

Region After the 2000 election, red and blue maps appeared showing the regional distribution of the vote. Democrats, represented as "blue America," tend to be clustered on the coasts, the upper Midwest, across the northern states, and in most urban areas. Republicans, represented as "red America," tend to be concentrated in the Mountain West and the South, and in suburbs and rural areas.

The explanations for these regional variations are complex. Between the Civil War and the 1960s, the Democrats controlled the South. Today, the South is where Republicans gain strength, but this is changing in some states and urban areas. Southern Republicanism has come about because conservative white southerners associate the Democratic Party with liberal positions and policies that benefit urban and minority voters. Republican strength in the South is also related to the weakness of organized labor in this region and a dependence on military programs supported by the Republicans. Democratic strength in the Northeast and Midwest is a function of the continuing influence of organized labor in the large cities of these regions and of the regions' large populations of minority voters. The coastal West, especially California and the Pacific Northwest, shifted toward the Democrats in the 1990s, in part because of growing young/millennial populations, the importance of the Latino vote, concerns with the environment, and a growing population of the religiously unaffiliated.[29]

Many states that used to be solidly red or blue are now turning "purple" where Republicans and Democrats battle to win elections. These states include Texas, North Carolina, Virginia, Arizona and other states where Republicans used to dominate. For example, Democrat Hillary Clinton lost Texas by just 9 percent of the vote in 2016. On the other hand, Midwest states that used to be solidly Democratic favored Republicans in 2016, including Wisconsin, Michigan, Iowa, Ohio, and Pennsylvania. Demographic change and modern electoral campaigns that mobilize high turnout are blurring the lines between red and blue states (Figure 9.4).

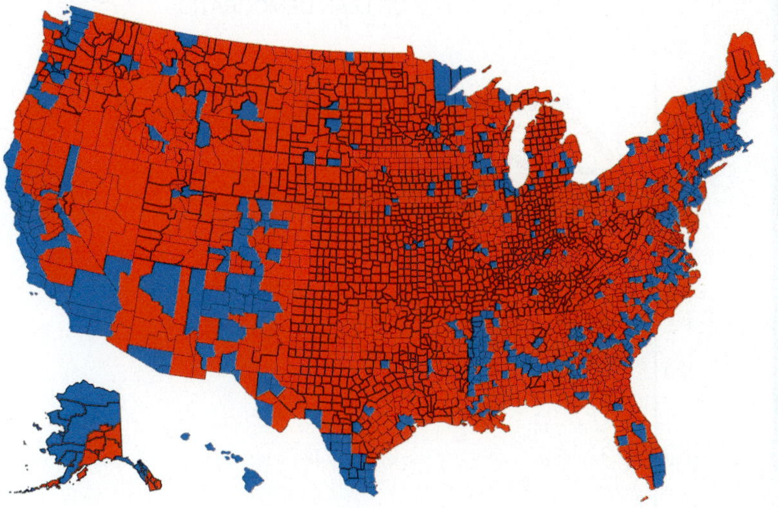

FIGURE 9.4

Presidential Vote by County, 2016

In 2016 the Republicans dominated in most counties in the center of the country. Though the map shows more "red" counties than "blue" covering a greater geographic area, Hillary Clinton and the Democrats won many of the most populous counties and several of the states with the most votes in the electoral college (see Chapter 10).

SOURCES: "Presidential Election Results: Donald Trump Wins," *New York Times*, www.nytimes.com/elections/results/president; Mark Newman, Maps of the 2016 U.S. presidential election results, www-personal.umich.edu/~mejn/election/2016/ (accessed 5/15/18).

Age Age is also associated with partisanship. Today young people are much more likely to be Democrats, while the oldest voters affiliate with the Republican Party. Why does age matter for partisanship? Individuals from the same age cohort are likely to have experienced a similar set of events during the period when their party loyalties were formed. Millennials, for example, who came of age during Bush's presidency and the Iraq War, also have a strong identification with the Democratic Party. The election of Barack Obama in 2008 saw a particularly striking shift among young voters toward the Democratic Party. In recent years, however, there has been a striking uptick in the percentage of young people who identify as independent, which may be a reflection of increasing frustration with government. Nonetheless, in 2016, 55 percent of people ages 18–29 voted for Hillary Clinton, compared to just 37 percent for Donald Trump.[30] As a group, young people have distinct policy preferences that overlap with those of the Democratic Party, including strong support for LGBTQ rights, legalization of marijuana, environmental protection, and greater economic equality.

FOR CRITICAL ANALYSIS

What are the major components of each party's political coalition? What factors tie these groups to their respective parties?

RECENT TRENDS IN PARTY AFFILIATION

After the 1960s many analysts began to express concern that American parties had become too weak to play their vital role in converting popular political participation into effective government. These scholars noted a decline in partisan attachment within the electorate, the growth in the numbers of voters identifying as independent, and a rise in so-called split-ticket voting. This overall trend, sometimes termed **dealignment**, was seen as a product of growing social diversity and educational attainment, which made voters less reliant on parties to guide their political decision-making (see Figure 9.5). The growth of the mass media, particularly television, also seemed to reduce the role of parties in elections as television tends to focus on the personalities of individual candidates rather than the "institution" of the party.

dealignment a movement away from the major political parties; a decline in partisan attachment

FIGURE 9.5

Education and Party Affiliation

Recently, people with higher levels of education have affiliated with the Democratic Party more and more. Do you think this trend will continue? How will this affect party platforms, long term?

SOURCE: Pew Research Center, "Gender, Education, Age, Divides in Party Affiliation," March 20, 2018, www.people-press.org/2018/03/20/wide-gender-gap-growing-educational-divide-in-voters-party-identification/1_2-19/ (accessed 10/16/18).

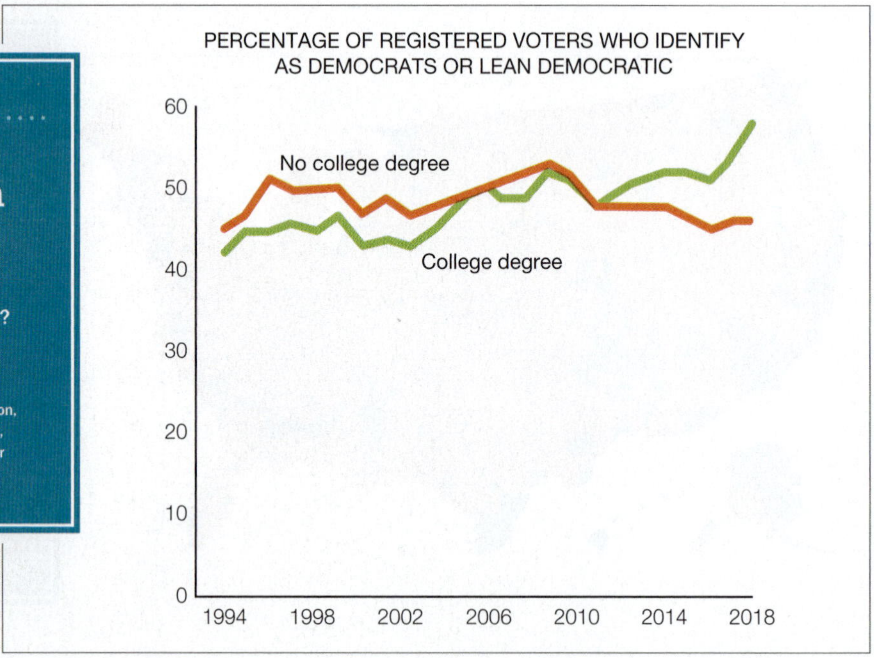

Who Identifies with Which Party?

Gender	Men	31%	40%	28%
	Women	27%	34%	39%
Age	18–29	24%	41%	35%
	30–49	25%	41%	34%
	50–64	32%	34%	34%
	65+	29%	37%	34%
Race	White	35%	37%	28%
	Black	4%	23%	73%
	Hispanic	16%	39%	46%
	Asian	27%	39%	34%
Education	Postgraduate	24%	33%	44%
	College graduate	35%	34%	31%
	Some college	30%	39%	31%
	High school diploma or less	26%	39%	35%
Income	< $20K	20%	40%	40%
	$20–$40K	23%	39%	38%
	$40K–$75K	31%	37%	32%
	>$75K	34%	35%	32%

NOTES: Percentages do not add to 100 because the category "Other/don't know" is omitted. ANES does not include rural/urban/suburban data.

SOURCE: American National Election Study 2016 time series, www.electionstudies.org (accessed 11/4/17).

Party identification varies by income, race, and gender. For example, as these statistics from 2016 show, Americans with higher incomes are more supportive of the Republican Party than are Americans with lower incomes. Women are significantly more likely than men to identify with the Democratic Party, whereas more men identify as independents.

Republican Party

Democratic Party

Independent

FOR CRITICAL ANALYSIS

1. How do younger Americans differ from older Americans in their party identification? What is the best predictor of party identification?
2. Do you think of yourself as a Democrat, Republican, or independent? Are other Americans of your gender, age, race, and income level likely to share your references?

While they often lean toward one of the two parties and vote for the Republicans or Democrats in national elections, independents have unique views and are more supportive of third parties and election reform efforts that create opportunities for groups outside of government to have a voice in government.[31] With congressional approval ratings at an all-time low, the number of Americans identifying as independents has grown to roughly 40 percent.[32] In nine states, independent voters outnumber the two major political parties, including Alaska, which has 55 percent registered independents; Connecticut, with 41 percent; Colorado, 38 percent; and Iowa, 36 percent.[33]

Today, party loyalties in America are in a state of flux. On the one hand, the percentage of voters who declare no party loyalty remains at an all-time high.[34] On the other hand, party identification among a large number of the most active voters has grown stronger.[35] The "Who Are Americans?" feature indicates the relationship between party identification and a number of social criteria. Race and ethnicity, age, education, religion, region, and income seem to have the greatest influence on Americans' party affiliations.

Party Systems

Describe how the party system in the United States has changed over time and its main features today

Historians often refer to the set of parties that are important at any given time as a nation's party system. The United States has usually had a two-party system, meaning that only two parties have a serious chance to win national elections. But the nation has not always had the same two parties and, as we shall see, minor parties often put forward candidates.

The term *party system*, however, refers to more than just the number of parties competing for power. It also includes the organization of the parties, the dominant form of campaigning, the main issue divisions between the parties, the balance of power between and within party coalitions, the parties' social and institutional bases, and the policies around which party competition is organized. Seen from this broader perspective, the character of a nation's party system can change even if the number of parties remains the same and even when the same two parties seem to be competing for power. Today's American party system is very different from the country's party system of 100 years ago, but the Democrats and Republicans continue to be the major competing forces. Over the course of American history, changes in political forces and alignments have produced six distinctive party systems.

THE FIRST PARTY SYSTEM: FEDERALISTS AND JEFFERSONIAN REPUBLICANS

The first party system emerged in the 1790s and pitted the Federalists, who favored a strong national government and president, against the Jeffersonian Republicans, or Antifederalists, who favored a weaker national government with the states retaining power protections for individuals from government interference. The Federalists were the establishment party at the time, and the Antifederalists were the outsiders. The Federalists represented mainly New England merchants and supported a program of protective tariffs to encourage manufacturing, forgiving states' Revolutionary

War debts, the creation of a national bank, and commercial ties with Britain. The Jeffersonians, led by southern agricultural interests, opposed these policies and instead favored free trade, the promotion of agricultural interests, and friendship with France. The Federalists sought, unsuccessfully, to use the force of law against the Jeffersonians by enacting the Alien and Sedition Acts to outlaw criticism of the government. These acts, however, proved virtually impossible to enforce, and the Jeffersonians gradually expanded their base from the South into the Middle Atlantic states. In the election of 1800, Thomas Jefferson defeated the incumbent Federalist president, John Adams, and led his party to power. Over the following years, the Federalists gradually weakened. The party disappeared after the pro-British sympathies of some Federalist leaders during the War of 1812 led to charges of treason against the party.

From the collapse of the Federalists until the 1830s, America had only one political party, the Jeffersonian Republicans, who gradually came to be known as the Democrats. This period of one-party politics was defined by an absence of party competition. Throughout this period, however, there was intense conflict within the Democratic Party, particularly between the supporters and opponents of General Andrew Jackson, America's great military hero of the War of 1812. Jackson was the first populist president with a wide base of mass support; he sought to give rank-and-file members more say in party politics. Jackson's opponents united to deny him the presidency in 1824, but Jackson won elections in 1828 and 1832. Jackson's support was in the South and West, and he generally espoused a program of free trade and policies that appealed to those regions.

In the 1830s the Whig Party emerged as the Democrats' main rival. This drawing depicts a Whig rally and parade during the 1840 election.

THE SECOND PARTY SYSTEM: DEMOCRATS AND WHIGS

During the 1830s, groups opposing Jackson united to form a new political force, the Whig Party, giving rise to the second American party system. Both the Democrats and the Whigs built party organizations throughout the nation and sought to enlarge their bases of support by expanding the right to vote. They increased the number of eligible voters—still only white males—through the elimination of the requirement of property ownership in order to be able to vote. Support for the new Whig Party was stronger in the Northeast than in the South and West and among merchants than among small farmers. Hence, in some measure, the Whigs were the successors of the Federalists. Yet conflict between the two parties revolved more around personalities than policies. The Whigs were a diverse group united more by opposition to the Democrats than by agreement on programs. In 1840 the Whigs won their first presidential election under the leadership of General William Henry Harrison. The Whig campaign carefully avoided issues—since the party could agree on almost none—and emphasized the personal qualities and heroism of the candidate. They also invested heavily in campaign rallies and entertainment to win the hearts, if not exactly the minds, of the voters.

During the late 1840s and early 1850s, conflicts over slavery produced sharp divisions within both the Whig and the Democratic parties. By 1856 the Whig Party had all but disintegrated under the strain, and many Whig politicians and voters, along with antislavery Democrats, joined the new Republican Party, which pledged to ban slavery from the western territories. In 1860 the new Republican Party nominated Abraham Lincoln for the presidency. Lincoln's victory in a four-way candidate race for president strengthened southern calls for secession from the Union and, soon thereafter, for all-out civil war.

THE CIVIL WAR AND POST–CIVIL WAR PARTY SYSTEM

During the course of the war, President Lincoln depended heavily on Republican governors and state legislatures to raise troops, provide funding, and maintain popular support for a long and bloody military conflict. The secession of the South had stripped the Democratic Party of many supporters, but the Democrats remained politically competitive throughout the war and nearly won the 1864 presidential election because of war weariness on the part of the northern public. With the defeat of the Confederacy in 1865, some Republicans sought to use Reconstruction to grant the right to vote to newly freed slaves, thus creating a large pro-Republican voting bloc. This Reconstruction program failed, in part because of violent resistance by southern whites via the Ku Klux Klan. With the end of Reconstruction, the former Confederate states regained full control of their internal affairs and party politics. Throughout the South, African Americans were deprived of political rights, including the right to vote, despite post–Civil War constitutional guarantees to the contrary. From the end of the Civil War to the 1890s, the Republican Party remained the party of the North, with strong business and middle-class support, while the Democrats were the party of the South, with support also from working-class and immigrant groups.

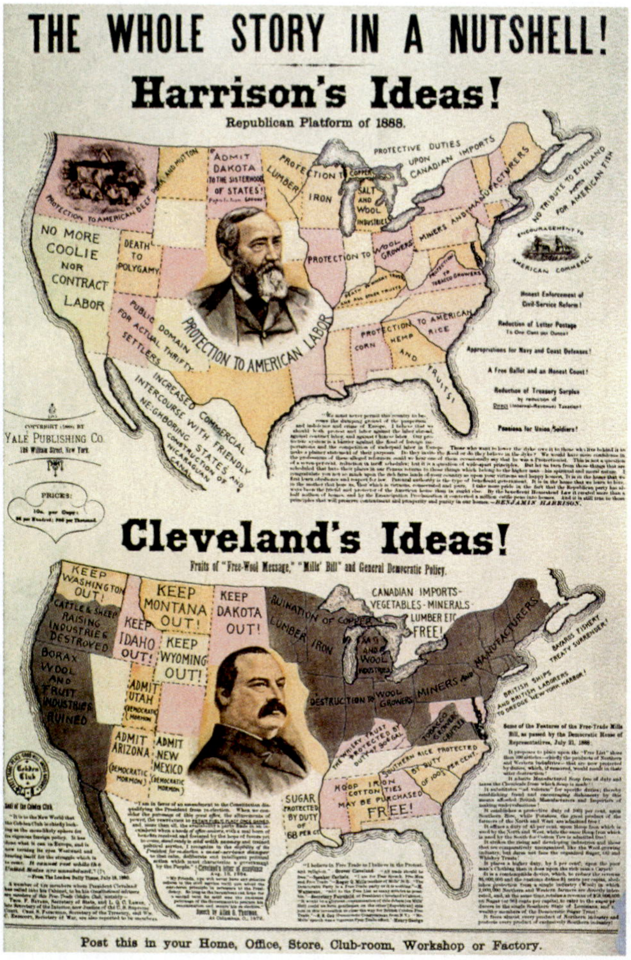

Following the Civil War, the Republican Party remained dominant in the North. This poster supporting Republican Benjamin Harrison in the 1888 election promises protective tariffs and other policies that appealed to the industrial states in the North.

THE SYSTEM OF 1896: POPULISM AND REPUBLICAN RESPONSES

During the 1890s, profound and rapid social and economic changes led to the emergence of a variety of protest parties, including the Populist Party, which won the support of hundreds of thousands of voters in the South and West. The Populists appealed mainly to small farmers but also attracted western mining interests and urban workers. In the 1892 presidential election, the Populist Party carried four states and elected governors in eight. In 1896 the Populist Party effectively merged with the Democrats, who nominated William Jennings Bryan, a Democratic senator with pronounced Populist sympathies, for the presidency. The Republicans nominated the conservative senator William McKinley. In the ensuing campaign, northern and midwestern businesses made an all-out effort to defeat what they saw as a radical threat from the Populist–Democratic alliance. When the dust settled, the Republicans had won a resounding victory. The GOP ("Grand Old Party"), or Republican Party, had carried the more heavily populated northern and midwestern states and confined the Democrats to their smaller bases of support in the South and far West. For the next 36 years, the Republicans were the nation's majority party, carrying seven of nine presidential elections and controlling both houses of Congress in 15 of 18 contests. The Republican Party was pro-business, advocating low taxes, high tariffs on imports, and a minimum of government regulation.

THE NEW DEAL PARTY SYSTEM: GOVERNMENT HELPS THE WORKING CLASS

Soon after the Republican presidential candidate Herbert Hoover won the 1928 presidential election, the nation's economy collapsed. The Great Depression, which produced unprecedented economic hardship, stemmed from a variety of causes; but from the perspective of millions of Americans, the Republican Party did not do enough to promote economic recovery when millions of Americans were starving and without jobs. In 1932, Americans elected Franklin Delano Roosevelt and a solidly Democratic Congress. Roosevelt developed a program for economic recovery that he dubbed the "New Deal." Under the auspices of the New Deal, the size of America's national government increased substantially. The federal government took responsibility for economic management and social welfare to an extent that was unprecedented in American history. For the first time, government took an active role in the individual lives of Americans, providing unemployment benefits, jobs, food, and more.

Roosevelt expanded the political base of the Democratic Party. He rebuilt and revitalized the party around unionized workers, upper-middle-class intellectuals and professionals, southern farmers, Jews, Catholics, and African Americans—the so-called New Deal coalition that made the Democrats the nation's majority party for the next 36 years. Groping for a response to the New Deal, Republicans often wound up supporting popular New Deal programs such as Social Security in what was sometimes derided as "me too" Republicanism. Even the relatively conservative administration of Dwight D. Eisenhower in the 1950s left the principal New Deal programs intact.

The New Deal coalition was severely strained during the 1960s by conflicts over civil rights and the Vietnam War. The struggle over civil rights initially divided northern Democrats, who supported the civil rights cause, from white southern Democrats, who defended the system of racial segregation. As the civil rights movement launched a northern campaign aimed at securing access to jobs and education and an end to racial discrimination in such realms as housing, northern Democrats also split, often along income lines. The struggle over the Vietnam War further divided the Democrats, with upper-income liberal Democrats strongly opposing the Johnson administration's decision to greatly expand the numbers of U.S. troops fighting in Southeast Asia. These divisions within the Democratic Party provided an opportunity for the GOP, which returned to power in 1968 under the leadership of Richard Nixon.

THE CONTEMPORARY AMERICAN PARTY SYSTEM

The Republican Party widened its appeal in the second half of the twentieth century. In 1964, for example, the Republican presidential candidate Barry Goldwater argued in favor of substantially reduced levels of taxation and spending, less government regulation of the economy, and the elimination of many federal social programs. Though Goldwater was defeated by Lyndon Johnson, his ideas continued to be major themes for the Republican Party. Richard Nixon's "southern strategy" gave GOP the votes it needed to end Democratic control of national politics. Nixon appealed to disaffected white southerners, and he sparked the shift that gave the party a strong position in all the states of the former Confederacy. The movement of white southerners to the Republican Party was spurred by opposition to desegregation of the South and to the civil rights movement supported by Democratic leaders, including President Kennedy. During the 1980s, under the leadership of President Ronald Reagan, Republicans added two additional important groups to their coalition. The first were religious conservatives, who were opposed to abortion and marriage equality and felt the Democrats were not protecting traditional family and religious values. The second were working-class whites, who were drawn to Reagan's tough approach to foreign policy and opposition to affirmative action. Many Republicans consider Reagan's tenure in office as a "golden era" that saw deregulation of many industries, reduced government intervention in the economy, and exhibited robust economic growth.

While Republicans built a political base around economic and social conservatives and white southerners, the Democratic Party maintained its support among a majority of unionized workers and upper-middle-class professionals. Democrats also appealed to racial and ethnic minorities. The 1965 Voting Rights Act had greatly increased black voter participation in the South and helped the Democratic Party retain some House and Senate seats in southern states. And whereas the Republicans appealed to social conservatives, the Democrats appealed to Americans concerned with economic fairness and inequality, women's rights, the environment and protections of public land, and other progressive social causes.

Republicans fared poorly at state and local levels until the 1990s, when conservative religious groups made a concerted effort to expand their influence within the Republican Party. This effort led to conflict between members of the "religious right" and more traditional fiscal Republicans, whose major concerns were economic matters such as taxes and federal regulation of business. In 2000, George W. Bush united the party behind a program of tax cuts, education reform, military strength, and family values.

However, Republicans fared poorly again in the 2008 elections, campaigning during the worst financial crisis since the 1930s. Democrat Barack Obama, the nation's first African American president, was elected in 2008 and reelected for a second term in 2012. He united racial and ethnic minorities, youth, and other liberals with older white moderates in a powerful national coalition, winning large popular majorities in the 2008 and 2012 elections. Obama helped the nation recover from global economic recession; reformed national health care, the financial sector, and immigration; and promoted clean energy and environmental protections, labor policy, and LGBTQ rights. He was championed globally as a progressive leader with strong alliances in Europe. However, he

Richard Nixon's "southern strategy" helped broaden the Republican Party's base in the late 1960s and the 1970s by appealing to white southerners. Here, Nixon meets supporters in Georgia in 1973.

became deeply unpopular with Republicans who objected to what they saw as overreach by the federal government. Republicans captured both houses of Congress in 2014, and in 2016, they retained both chambers and won the presidency in a tight race, signaling that sharp partisan differences and intense party conflict would continue to characterize American politics.

Transitions in the party systems over time are sometimes called **electoral realignments.** During these periods, the coalitions that support the parties and the balance of power between the parties change and are redefined. In historical terms, realignments occur when new issues, combined with economic or political crises, mobilize new voters and persuade large numbers of them to reexamine their traditional partisan loyalties and permanently shift their support from one party to another. Figure 9.6 charts the sequence of party systems and realignments in American history.

electoral realignment the point in history when a new party supplants the governing party, becoming in turn the dominant political force

Although scholars dispute the timing of realignments, there is some agreement that five have occurred since the Founding. The first took place around 1790–1800, when the Jeffersonian Republicans defeated the Federalists and became the dominant force in American politics. The second realignment occurred in 1828, when the Jacksonian Democrats seized control of the White House and the Congress. In the third period of realignment, centered on the 1860 election, the newly founded Republican Party, led by Abraham Lincoln, won power, in the process destroying the Whig Party, which had been one of the nation's two major parties since the 1830s. Many northern voters who had supported the Whigs or the Democrats on the basis of their economic policies shifted their support to the Republicans as slavery replaced tariffs and economic concerns as the central issue on the nation's agenda. Many southern Whigs shifted their support to the Democrats. The new regional alignment of forces that emerged was solidified by the trauma of the Civil War and persisted almost to the end of the nineteenth century. In the fourth alignment, the election of 1896 saw Republican candidate William McKinley, emphasizing business, industry, and urban interests, defeat Democrat William Jennings Bryan, who spoke for populist economic interests, farmers, and miners. Republican dominance lasted until the fifth realignment, during the period 1932–36, when the Democrats, led by Franklin Delano Roosevelt, took control of the White House and Congress during the economic crisis of the Great Depression. Despite sporadic interruptions, the Democrats maintained control of both through the 1960s. Since that time, American party politics has been characterized by **divided government**, wherein the presidency is controlled by one party while the other party controls one or both houses of Congress.

divided government the condition in American government wherein the presidency is controlled by one party while the opposing party controls one or both houses of Congress

Major party realignments are rare in America, occurring on average about once every 30 years. There are frequent false alarms, when pundits describe elections as realignments and they turn out not to be. In the 2016 presidential election, significant factions of the Republican Party were in disagreement over Donald Trump's candidacy, leading some observers to question whether the election was the beginning of a new party realignment. Many high-profile Republican politicians refused to support Trump, and some withdrew their support during the course of the campaign. However, during the first two years of the Trump administration, Republicans in Congress have generally supported the President's policy agenda.

PARTY POLARIZATION

party polarization the division between the two major parties on most policy issues, with members of each party unified around their party's positions with little crossover

A distinguishing feature of the contemporary party system is **party polarization.** The vast and growing gap between Democrats and Republicans has become a defining feature of American politics today, with more Democrats holding liberal positions

FIGURE 9.6

How the Party System Evolved

During the nineteenth century, the Democrats and Republicans emerged as the two dominant parties in American politics. As the American party system evolved, many third parties emerged; but few of them remained in existence for very long.

*Or, in some cases, fourth parties; most of these parties lasted through only one term.
**The Anti-Masonics had the distinction of being not only the first third party but also the first party to hold a national nominating convention and the first to announce a party platform.

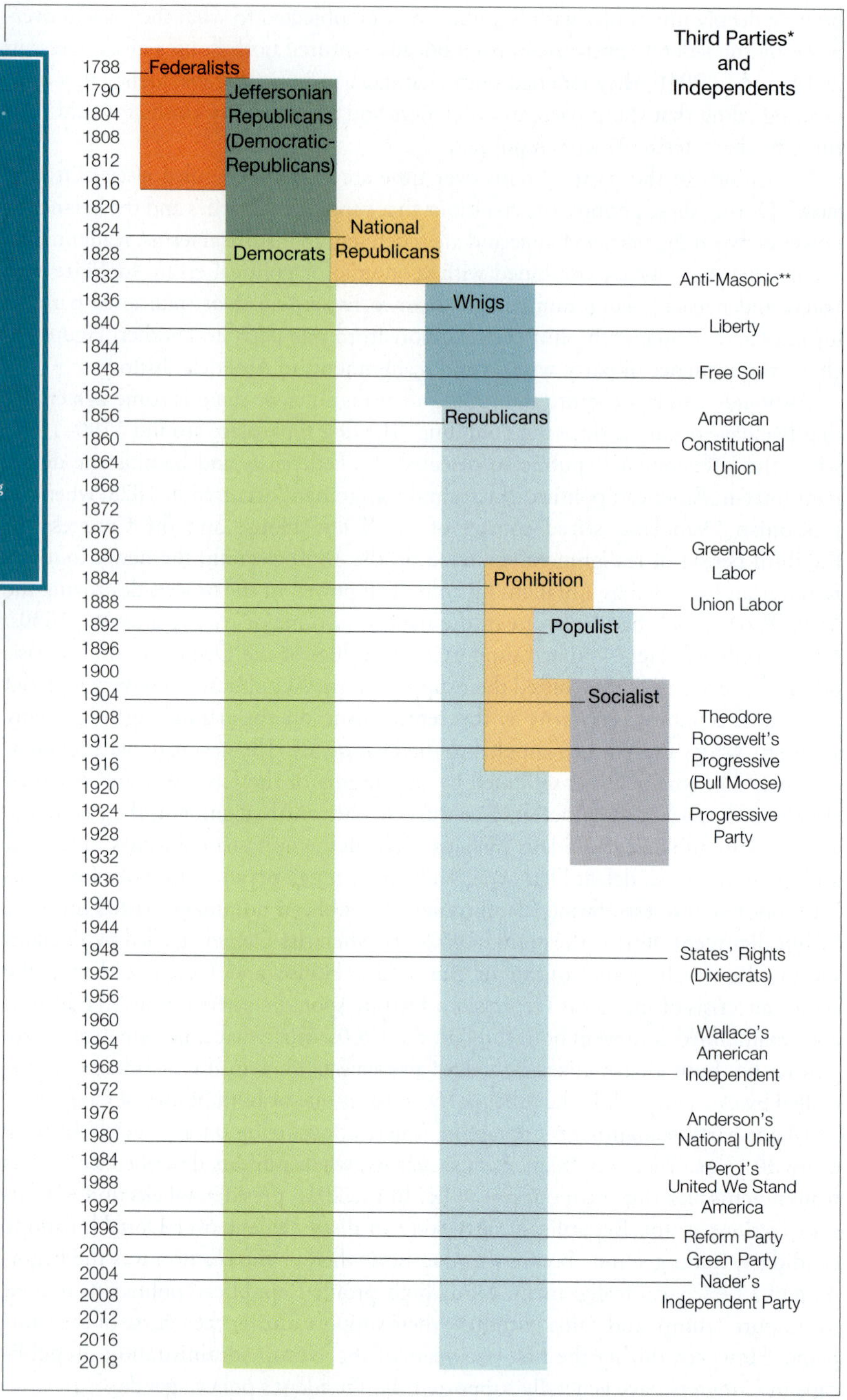

and more Republicans holding conservative views (see Figure 9.7). In Congress, polarization is measured by party unity in roll-call votes. Over 90 percent of the time, members of Congress vote in agreement with the majority of their party.[36] With this kind of party-line voting, legislation is often enacted by slim vote margins in Congress.

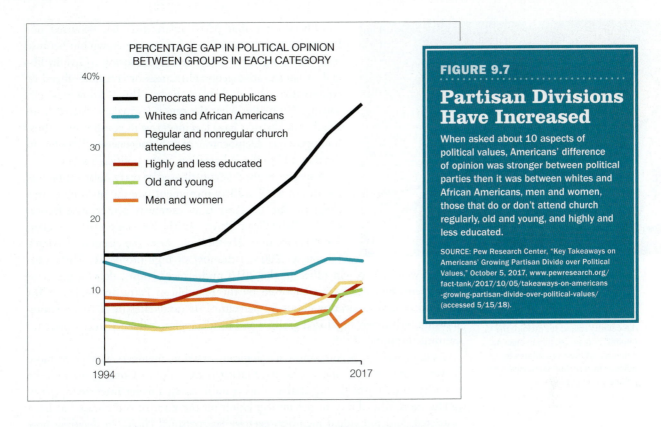

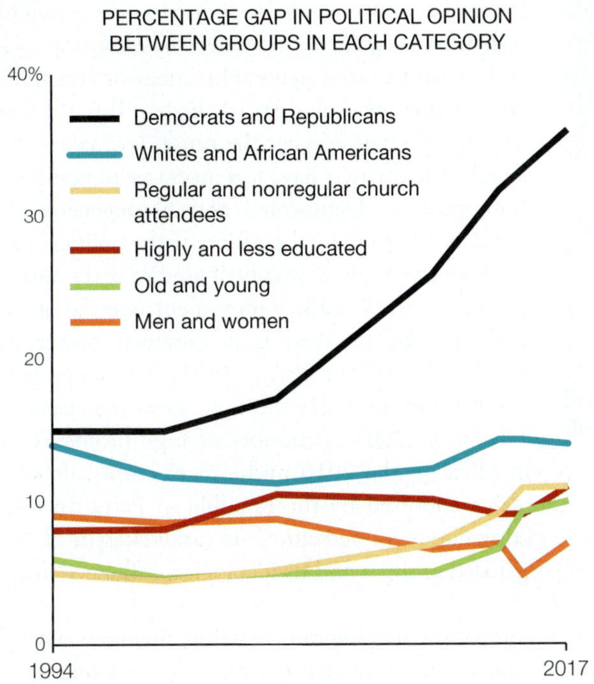

FIGURE 9.7

Partisan Divisions Have Increased

When asked about 10 aspects of political values, Americans' difference of opinion was stronger between political parties then it was between whites and African Americans, men and women, those that do or don't attend church regularly, old and young, and highly and less educated.

SOURCE: Pew Research Center, "Key Takeaways on Americans' Growing Partisan Divide over Political Values," October 5, 2017, www.pewresearch.org/fact-tank/2017/10/05/takeaways-on-americans-growing-partisan-divide-over-political-values/ (accessed 5/15/18).

The extent of party polarization in Congress was exemplified by party-line voting in 2017 for the most significant overhaul of the U.S. tax code in three decades.[37] The bill reduced taxes temporarily to varying degrees for some Americans but, provided the most benefits to affluent citizens. The bill also provided a massive tax cut to corporations, lowering the rate from 35 to 21 percent. Through concessions, threats, and extended negotiations, Republican leaders secured votes of support from every Republican member of the House but 12 and every Senate Republican but one. Democrats in the House and Senate were in unanimous opposition to the tax bill.

While lawmakers in Congress are generally strong conservatives or strong liberals, Congress does not match the ideology of the American public; most Americans are moderates in terms of their opinions on major issues.[38] Party polarization in Congress may be the result of how congressional representatives are elected. Every 10 years, congressional district geographic boundaries are redrawn so that each district has roughly the same population. These districts are increasingly drawn to be "safe" for one political party or another so that the district has a clear majority of either Republicans or Democrats. Most lawmakers are elected from safe, homogeneous districts, where a majority of voters identify with their party, which means they have little chance of losing in the next election. Incumbents, on average, win 70 percent of the popular vote compared with challengers' 30 percent.[39] Uncompetitive elections in Congress and safe seats are associated with growing party polarization. Without facing competition from the other party during general elections, those elected to Congress are strong partisans. Today lawmakers face the greatest threats during their own party's primary elections, which can have the effect of moving candidates more to the ideological extremes of their party in order to win in the primary.

FOR CRITICAL ANALYSIS

What are the principal issues dividing the two major parties today? What are the chief areas of agreement between the two parties?

The Tea Party emerged after the election of Barack Obama in 2008. During the 2010 midterm elections, Tea Party activists around the country rallied to "reclaim the Capitol" and succeeded in electing a number of their candidates to office, which further increased party polarization in Congress.

Others argue that party polarization has occurred not because of how congressional districts are drawn but because individuals segregate themselves by choosing to live in liberal or conservative geographic areas or consume liberal or conservative news and social media. This is known as self-sorting. No matter what the cause, lawmakers elected from solidly safe districts have less incentive to compromise; thus, homogeneous Democratic and homogeneous Republican districts add to the polarization of the political parties.

A specific event that contributed to party polarization was the rise of the Tea Party movement (see the opening of this chapter). The Tea Party is an extremely conservative faction of the Republican Party, which has supported President Trump since the 2016 election. After the election of Barack Obama in 2008, a number of high-profile Tea Party candidates went on to win office in the 2010 midterm elections, defeating several incumbents and candidates endorsed by the Republican Party. In total, the Tea Party succeeded in electing about 32 percent of its candidates in 2010—a strong showing for a newly organized group—and its ideological influence in elections has continued through 2018.

As Congress has become more ideologically extreme, members have given more power to their party leaders, who have changed the rules in Congress so that the majority can control the legislative process more easily, further intensifying party polarization. The ability to debate legislation on the floor of the House has been restricted, and individual members exercise less personal choice in deciding how to vote. Even strong party leaders are not immune to the pressure from their most ideologically extreme members. In 2015, House Speaker John Boehner resigned in the middle of his term. The historic event occurred because of deep divisions within the Republican Party, especially the opposition of 40 of the most conservative House members—Tea Party activists—who wanted him to take a harder line against Obama and the Democrats.

THIRD PARTIES

third parties parties that organize to compete against the two major American political parties

Although the United States has a two party–dominant system, it has always had more than two parties. Typically, **third parties** in the United States have represented social and economic interests that for one reason or another were not given voice by the two major parties.[40] Such parties often influence elections. The Populists, a party centered in the rural areas of the West and Midwest, and the Progressives, spokespersons for the urban middle class in the late nineteenth and early twentieth centuries, are the most important examples in the previous century. The most successful recent third party candidate, H. Ross Perot, who ran in 1992 as an independent and in 1996 as the Reform Party's nominee, won the votes of almost one in five Americans in 1992.

Because third parties almost always lose at the national level, such parties exist mainly as a protest movement against the two parties or to promote specific issues. Third parties often are sources of new ideas and party realignment, and they can profoundly affect elections, taking votes from one of the major parties and enabling the other to win. In the extremely close 2000 presidential election, for example, third-party candidate Ralph Nader won just 3 percent of the popular vote, but that

Third-party candidates rarely win elections, but they can influence campaigns. In 2016, Jill Stein (left) and Gary Johnson and his vice-presidential running mate William Weld (right) ran as alternatives to the Democratic and Republican candidates. Enough votes went to Johnson and Stein that they denied Clinton and Trump from winning a majority.

split the Democratic vote enough to swing the election in favor of Republican George W. Bush. Leaders in both major political parties fear third-party challenges in presidential elections. In the controversial 2016 election, Republican Donald Trump won 46 percent of the popular vote compared to 48 percent for Democrat Hillary Clinton. Neither candidate won a majority because votes for third parties stole votes from the two major party candidates.

Table 9.1 lists the top candidates in the presidential election of 2016, including the top third-party and independent candidates who ran. Third-party candidates fared better in 2016 than in the last three presidential elections, leading some observers to suggest that third parties were one reason Clinton lost key battleground states and thus the election. Third-party and independent candidacies also arise at the state and local levels. The Libertarian and Green parties in particular run candidates in many state and local elections. In 2012 independent candidates won Senate races in Maine and Vermont and were re-elected in 2018.

Obstacles Facing Third Parties Americans usually assume that only candidates nominated by one of the two major parties have any chance of winning an election. As noted above, voters who would prefer a third-party candidate may feel compelled to vote for the major-party candidate whom they regard as the "lesser of two evils," to avoid wasting their votes in a futile gesture. This is called *strategic voting*.

Under federal election law, only parties that receive more than 5 percent of the national presidential vote are entitled to federal funds. The Reform Party qualified by winning 8.2 percent in 1996, but since then third parties have not won federal matching money. As discussed earlier, third-party candidates are also hampered by single-member district system for allocating seats. In many other nations, several individuals can be elected to represent each legislative district—a system of multiple-member districts, more favorable to third-party candidates. Some American states do have multiple-member districts for state legislature, but the vast majority do not. The plurality system of voting discussed earlier in this chapter also discourages many minor parties in the United States.[41] In the proportional system used in other countries, parties can earn seats in government with 15–20 percent of the popular vote.

The Influence of Third Parties Although the Republican Party was the only American third party to make itself permanent (by replacing the Whigs), other third parties have enjoyed an influence far beyond their electoral size. This is because

TABLE 9.1

Parties and Candidates in 2016

CANDIDATE	PARTY	VOTE TOTAL	PERCENTAGE OF VOTES	ELECTORAL COLLEGE VOTES*
Hillary Clinton	Democratic	65,147,421	48%	227
Donald Trump	Republican	62,634,907	46%	304
Gary Johnson	Libertarian	4,454,855	3%	0
Jill Stein	Green	1,426,922	1%	0
Other candidates		1,047,140	0.8%	0

*As was their right, seven members of the electoral college voted for other candidates despite Trump or Clinton carrying the state.

SOURCE: U.S. Election Atlas, "2016 Presidential General Election Results," www.uselectionatlas.org/RESULTS/national.php?year=2016&minper=0&f=0&off=0&elect=0 (accessed 12/1/16).

large parts of their programs were adopted by one or both of the major parties, which sought to appeal to the voters mobilized by the new party and thus expand their own electoral strength. The Democratic Party, for example, became a great deal more liberal when it adopted most of the Progressive Party reforms in the early twentieth century. Many socialists felt that President Franklin Roosevelt's New Deal had adopted most of their party's platform including unemployment compensation and laws guaranteeing workers the right to organize into unions. This kind of influence explains the short lives of third parties. Their causes are usually eliminated when the major parties adopt their policies and draw their supporters into the mainstream.

Election Reform and Third Parties In part because third parties have become increasingly common in American politics despite election rules favoring a two-party system, one-third of all winning presidential candidates since the Civil War have been elected with a plurality (simply more votes than any other candidate) but not a majority (more than 50 percent of all votes) of the national popular vote.[42] If the party that wins the presidency in one out of three elections is not favored by a majority of voters, that calls into question the legitimacy of our election system. Some scholars suggest that the failure to secure majorities may continue in the future with the rise of independent candidates and dissatisfaction with the two major political parties.[43]

Some proponents of election reform argue that two major parties are not sufficient to represent the varied interests of America's 320 million people and that more political parties would improve representation. Forms of proportional representation, multiple-member districts, or instant runoff voting would increase the probability of third-party representation in American politics. State ballot access laws are another major impediment for third parties. Third parties often fail to meet criteria to get on the ballot, such as registration fees or petition requirements in which a certain number of voters must sign a petition in order for the third-party or independent candidate to gain ballot access. Those who favor a stronger role for third parties argue that states should make it easier to get on the ballot. Supporters of the current system, on the other hand, contend that America's two-party system creates stability in governing and prevents the need for a coalition government, where multiple small parties work together to form a majority to govern.

Ranked Choice Voting An example of an election reform that may reduce party polarization and increase opportunities for third parties is ranked choice voting. Ranked choice voting is a form of instant runoff voting in that it guarantees that the winner of an election has support from a majority of those voting in the election, rather than a plurality. Ranked choice voting (or preference voting) is a ballot form used in countries around the world, notably Australia, that is growing in popularity in numerous American cities and some states. Rather than casting a single vote for one's most preferred choice, a voter ranks candidates from the most preferred to the least preferred (usually the top three) on the ballot. If a candidate wins a majority of first-place votes (50 percent plus one), the candidate is declared the winner and second- or third-place votes are not counted. But if the top candidate does not receive a majority of the votes cast, the candidate with the fewest first-choice votes is eliminated, and those voters' ballots are redistributed to their second-choice candidates. The ballots are recounted; if the leading candidate has a majority of votes cast, a winner is declared. The process is repeated until a majority winner is declared. This system eliminates the "spoiler" effect that occurs when votes for a third-party candidate are discarded.

Research suggests that ranked choice voting leads to more civility in political campaigns, fewer negative campaigns, and cooperation among candidates who seek to be a voter's second choice if they cannot be a first choice.[44] It is also associated with more grassroots mobilization of voters. Though ranked choice voting is used in many countries around the world, in the United States only the state of Maine uses it, as well as a handful of U.S. cities. Successful local experiments in election reform may open the doors to use of this process at the state or even national level.

Political Parties
WHAT DO WE WANT?

Parties provide an important opportunity for citizen participation in American politics. They make it easier for ordinary citizens to understand politics, evaluate candidates, participate in elections, and have a voice in government policy. They are also important to the health of the democracy. The presence of an opposition party is an important check on those in power. And competition among the political parties gives citizens an incentive to vote and politicians an incentive to get them to vote.[45] Voter mobilization is one of political parties' most important tasks, as voter turnout in the United States remains relatively low, especially in primaries and caucuses (see the **"Who Participates?"** feature on p. 373).

Parties in the United States are considered to be ground-up organizations, meaning that they get their power from the members of the mass public who support them at the local level. A century ago, political party bosses controlled the party platform, the party message, and often, through early money to candidates, who held elected office and who won the nomination for president. But changes to politics ranging from the advent of primary elections to the digital revolution more recently have altered many aspects of party politics. As Keli Carender's mobilizing efforts that helped kick off the Tea Party movement show, the internet has decentralized party power, opening up the possibilities for citizen influence. The four resources that political parties use to contest and win elections (time, money, expertise, and organization) no longer belong solely to party organizations. Now citizens can volunteer and give money to the party without ever being contacted by a party official. Online fund-raising allows millions of donors to give small contributions to parties, and social media allow the party to spread its message far and wide online. These changes are beneficial for parties because more people are involved, but at the same time there are more divergent opinions that must be recognized and appeased. No longer can party leaders craft their own message and relay it to the field; they must also listen to what their supporters want.

Questions remain, however, over what influence new groups and parties will have on politics given current U.S. election rules. Will party leaders pay more attention to the preferences of the mass public and party members? Is the two-party system ideal for American politics, or would electoral reforms encourage more parties to form and, hence, provide more choice for voters?

Who Votes in Primaries and Caucuses?

Turnout in 2016 Primaries

Percentage of voting-eligible population

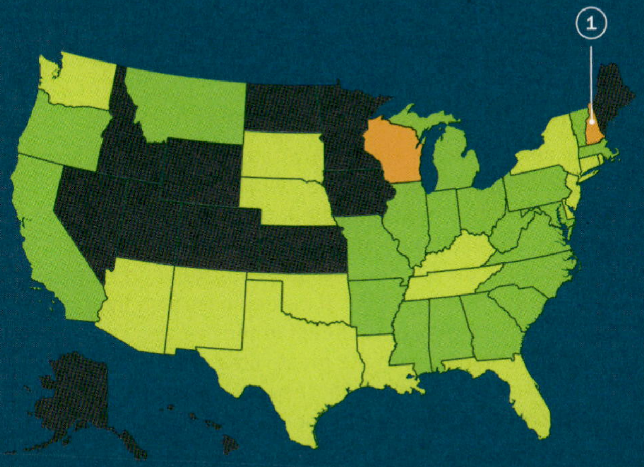

Turnout in 2016 Caucuses

Percentage of voting-eligible population

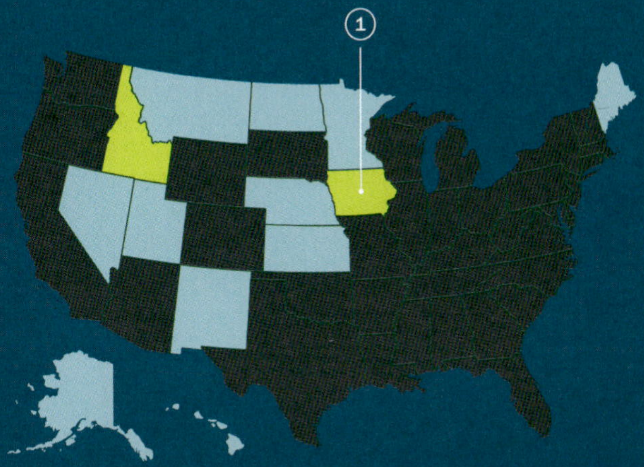

● 1–14% ● 15–29% ● 30–44% ● 45–60% (1) Earliest primary/caucus

SOURCE: Michael P. McDonald, "2016 Presidential Nomination Contest Turnout Rates," United States Election Project, September 21, 2016, www.electproject.org/ (accessed 11/27/17).
NOTES:
Montana: Caucus data are for credentialed Republicans (only party leaders are allowed to vote). Both parties participated in the primary.
South Carolina: Data are for the Democratic primary only. No data are available for Republican primary.
Nevada: Data are for Republican caucus only. No data are available for Democratic caucus.
Alaska, Hawaii, Maine, North Dakota: Data are for Democratic caucuses only. No data are available for Republican caucuses.
Kentucky: Data are for the Democratic primary only. No data are available for the Republican caucus.
Nebraska, Washington: Data are for the Republican primary only. No data are available for the Democratic caucus.
Idaho: Data are for the Democratic caucus only. No data are available for the Republican primary.
Wyoming: Republican caucus was canceled. No data are available.
Colorado: No data are available.

WHAT YOU CAN DO

Get Involved with Your Preferred Party

- ✔ Participate in the next primary or caucus in your state. When you register to vote (see p. 329), you may be asked to indicate your party affiliation.
- ✔ If you're unsure which party best represents your views, visit **www.politicalcompass.org/tests/** to take a test to find out.
- ✔ Volunteer to help your preferred party with a political campaign by making phone calls, knocking on doors, distributing literature, and otherwise working to get out the vote. You can sign up with the Republican Party at **www.gop.com/get-involved** and with the Democratic Party at **www.democrats.org/volunteer**, and with other parties through their websites.

STUDY GUIDE

What Are Political Parties?

Define political parties and their functions in politics (pp. 337–40)

A political party is an organization that seeks influence over government by electing its members to office. Although some people are critical of political parties, they are extremely important to the functioning of a democracy because they increase participation in politics, provide a central cue for citizens to cast informed votes, and organize the business of Congress and governing. While the particular parties have changed over time, the United States has had a two-party system since the 1780s. Today, America's two major parties are the Democrats and the Republicans.

Key Terms

political parties (p. 337)
partisanship (p. 337)
two-party system (p. 339)

Practice Quiz

1. A political party is different from an interest group in that a political party
   a) seeks to control the government by nominating candidates and electing its members to office.
   b) is constitutionally exempt from taxation.
   c) is entirely nonprofit.
   d) has a much larger membership.
   e) has a much smaller membership.
2. The congressional election system in the United States is called "first past the post" because
   a) candidates must win both a primary election and a general election before taking office.
   b) seats in the House of Representatives and Senate are allocated to political parties based on their share of the total vote cast in the election.
   c) the candidate with the most votes wins even if she did not win a majority of the popular vote.
   d) a candidate can win an election only if he wins a majority of the popular vote.
   e) more Americans now vote by mail than at their local polling places.

Parties, Voter Mobilization, and Elections

Explain the roles that parties play in elections (pp. 340–44)

Because parties succeed when they win elections, parties have a large role in recruiting candidates, coordinating campaigns, mobilizing voters, and raising money.

Key Terms

nomination (p. 342)
primary election (p. 342)
caucus (political) (p. 342)
micro-targeting (p. 344)

3. The practice of tailoring campaign messages to individuals in small, homogeneous groups is referred to as
   a) indexing.
   b) micro-targeting.
   c) winnowing.
   d) external mobilization.
   e) internal mobilization.

Parties as Organizations

Describe how the major American parties are structured at the national, state, and local levels (pp. 344–48)

Party organizations exist at virtually every level of government in the United States, and they play an important role in structuring electoral competition. At the national level, for example, party organizations assemble conventions every four years that nominate the party's presidential and vice-presidential candidates, draft the party's campaign platform for the presidential race, and approve changes in the rules governing party procedures. Similarly, at the state and local levels, party organizations are active in recruiting candidates to run for office and in conducting voter registration and get-out-the-vote drives.

Key Terms

party organization (p. 344)
national convention (p. 345)
platform (p. 345)
soft money (p. 346)
party machines (p. 347)
patronage (p. 347)

Practice Quiz

4. Which of the following is *not* determined at a party's national convention?
   a) the party's candidate for president
   b) the party's candidate for vice president
   c) the party's campaign platform for the presidential race
   d) the congressional committees party representatives will be assigned to
   e) the rules and regulations governing party procedures
5. Super PACs
   a) were outlawed by the 2002 Bipartisan Campaign Reform Act.
   b) are ineligible for tax-exempt status under Section 527 of the Internal Revenue Code.
   c) are campaign fund-raising organizations legally affiliated with the Democratic National Committee.
   d) are prohibited from running advertisements during election campaigns.
   e) can raise and spend unlimited amounts of money as long as their activities are not coordinated with those of the formal party organizations or the candidates.
6. The strength of traditional party machines depended most heavily on
   a) patronage.
   b) primaries.
   c) hard money.
   d) soft money.
   e) dark money.

Parties in Government

Explain how parties organize legislative business and influence policy (pp. 348–52)

Political parties exert a great deal of influence over public policy, the structure of Congress, and the behavior of presidents. The sharp ideological divisions between Democrats and Republicans in recent years mean that election outcomes matter greatly for the kinds of laws that government enacts. The fact that political parties are broad coalitions of diverse interests means that party leaders must always work to overcome divisions between the different factions within their parties. Many of the most important organizational features of Congress, such as the role of the House Speaker, the committee system, and seniority, also depend on the party system.

Key Terms

policy entrepreneur (p. 350)
majority party (p. 351)
minority party (p. 351)

Practice Quiz

7. By identifying problems and proposing policies that will expand their party's base of support, party leaders can act as
   a) whips.
   b) convention delegates.
   c) patrons.
   d) policy entrepreneurs.
   e) party activists.
8. Which of the following features of the House of Representatives is determined by a vote of the whole membership rather than by decisions within each party?
   a) the assignments of individual members to particular committees.
   b) advancement up the committee ladder.
   c) the ability of individual members to transfer from one committee to another.
   d) the use of the seniority system for determining committee chairs.
   e) selection of the Speaker of the House.

Party Identification

Identify the reasons for and sources of party identification (pp. 352–60)

Party identification refers to the psychological and emotional attachments people have to one of the political parties. In contemporary American politics, a wide variety of group characteristics, including race, ethnicity, gender, religion, class, ideology, region, and age, are associated with an individual's party identification. Party loyalties in the United States are currently in a state of flux, and more than one-third of Americans identify themselves as independents rather than as Democrats or Republicans.

Key Terms

party identification (p. 352)
party activists (p. 352)
gender gap (p. 355)
dealignment (p. 358)

Practice Quiz

9. The decline in partisan attachment in the electorate, the growth in the number of voters identifying as independent, and the rise in so-called split-ticket voting was referred to as
   a) partisan polarization.
   b) independentification.
   c) unalignment.
   d) realignment.
   e) dealignment.

Party Systems

Describe how the party system in the United States has changed over time and its main features today (pp. 360–71)

A nation's party system refers to the organization of the parties within the country, the dominant form of campaigning, the main divisions between the parties, the balance of power between and within party coalitions, the parties' social and institutional bases, and the issues and policies around which party competition is organized. Over the course of American history, changes in political forces and alignments have produced six distinctive party systems. Although third parties have occasionally influenced election outcomes and placed new ideas on the political agenda, numerous factors limit their long-term success and they have rarely been able to win elections at the national level.

Key Terms

electoral realignment (p. 365)
divided government (p. 365)
party polarization (p. 365)
third parties (p. 368)

Practice Quiz

10. Which party was formed in the 1830s in opposition to Andrew Jackson's presidency?
    a) American Independent
    b) Federalist
    c) Jeffersonian Republican
    d) Democratic
    e) Whig

11. The so-called New Deal coalition was severely strained
    a) during the 1860s by conflicts over slavery and southern secession.
    b) during the 1890s by conflicts over the gold standard.
    c) during the 1930s by conflicts over the Great Depression and America's involvement in World War II.
    d) during the 1960s by conflicts over civil rights and the Vietnam War.
    e) during the 1990s by conflicts over abortion and affirmative action.

12. The periodic episodes in American history in which an "old" dominant political party is replaced by a "new" dominant political party are called
    a) constitutional revolutions.
    b) divided governments.
    c) unified governments.
    d) dealignments.
    e) electoral realignments.

13. Voters who prefer a third-party candidate but vote for the major-party candidate whom they regard as the "lesser of two evils" are engaging in
    a) strategic voting.
    b) split-ticket voting.
    c) straight-ticket voting.
    d) ranked choice voting.
    e) rational abstention.

For Further Reading

Aldrich, John H. *Why Parties? A Second Look*. Chicago: University of Chicago Press, 2011.

Bartels, Larry. *Presidential Primaries and the Dynamics of Public Choice*. Princeton, NJ: Princeton University Press, 1988.

Burnham, Walter Dean. *Critical Elections and the Mainsprings of American Politics*. New York: W. W. Norton, 1970.

Cohen, Marty, David Karol, Hans Noel, and John Zaller. *The Party Decides: Presidential Nominations before and after Reform*. Chicago: University of Chicago Press, 2008.

Donovan, Todd, and Shaun Bowler. *Reforming the Republic: Democratic Institutions for the New America*. Englewood Cliffs, NJ: Prentice Hall, 2003.

Green, Donald, Bradley Palmquist, and Eric Schickler. *Partisan Hearts and Minds: Political Parties and the Social Identities of Voters*. New Haven, CT: Yale University Press, 2002.

Maisel, L. Sandy. *Political Parties and Elections: A Very Short Introduction*. New York: Oxford University Press, 2007.

McCarty, Nolan, Keith Poole, and Howard Rosenthal. *Polarized America: The Dance of Ideology and Unequal Riches*. Cambridge, MA: MIT Press, 2006.

Polsby, Nelson W. *The Consequences of Party Reform*. New York: Oxford University Press, 1983.

Redlawsk, David P., Caroline J. Tolbert, and Todd Donovan. *Why Iowa? How Caucuses and Sequential Elections Improve the Presidential Nominating Process*. Chicago: University of Chicago Press, 2011.

Schattschneider, E. E. *The Semisovereign People: A Realist's View of Democracy in America*. New York: Holt, Rinehart and Winston, 1960.

Shefter, Martin. *Political Parties and the State: The American Historical Experience*. Princeton, NJ: Princeton University Press, 1994.

Recommended Websites

D.C.'s Political Report
www.dcpoliticalreport.com

Here you can find almost every organization that identifies itself as a political party, including such obscure groups as the American Beer Drinker's Party and the Scorched Earth Party.

Democratic Party
www.democrats.org

Republican Party
www.GOP.com, www.rnc.org

These are the official websites for the Democrats and Republicans. Compare the platforms of the two main U.S. parties and see whether there's "not a dime's worth of difference" between them.

Green Party
www.gp.org

Libertarian Party
www.lp.org

The Green Party and Libertarian Party are two of the largest and most successful third parties in recent years. Find out what these parties are trying to accomplish.

National Annenberg Election Survey
http://annenbergpublicpolicycenter.org

Individual voters tend to develop psychological ties to one party or another. The National Annenberg Election Survey uses survey data to track party identification by state every two years. Find out if your state has more Democratic or Republican identifiers.

Pew Research Center, Political Polarization
www.pewresearch.org/packages/political-polarization

This Pew Research Center series presents interactive graphics illustrating dramatic shifts in party polarization over time as it explores the current political landscape and the implications of party polarization for the American public.

★ chapter ★

10

Campaigns and Elections

WHAT GOVERNMENT DOES AND WHY IT MATTERS Elections are the core of any democracy. In a democratic system like the United States, citizens self-govern by choosing among candidates and electing leaders to represent them in government. The rules for elections affect who runs, how they run, who votes, and who wins.

The presidential election of 2016 was historic in several regards. It was a race between Democrat Hillary Clinton, who was the nation's first female major-party nominee, and Republican Donald Trump, who became the first person to win the presidency who had not previously served in elective office or in the military. Although their share of the electorate varies from one election to another, young people as always played an important role. Brian Bodine of the Texas Young Republican Federation explained his support for candidate Trump: "As the months went by, his vision resonated with me more and more. . . . [His win sent] a powerful message to established politicians, struggling businesses, disenchanted blue-collar workers and tens of millions of people throughout the country. If he can accomplish even half of what he pledged to do during his

Even though many issues affect them deeply, young people do not vote in elections at the same rate as older Americans. However, countless young people have strong impact on campaigns, as epitomized by Brian Bodine (far left) and the members of the Texas Young Republican Federation.

campaign, it will be huge for the country and he will go down in history as a great President."[1] Jessica Valdes, a college student in Florida and naturalized citizen originally from Cuba, supported Clinton, who she viewed as wanting "to give (immigrants) the opportunity to achieve the American dream" and to make college more affordable.[2] Yet another student, Ethan Aliste, who attends community college in California, expressed frustration with some of his friends who were "apathetic about the political stakes or claimed registering to vote was too difficult."[3] Turnout among young voters remained lower than that of older age groups. Just over 46 percent of 18- to 29-year-olds voted in 2016, compared to 58.7 percent of 30- to 44-year-olds, 66.6 percent of 45- to 64-year-olds, and 70.9 percent of those aged 65 and older.[4] Clearly young people do not find the electoral arena as enticing as do their older counterparts, affecting whose voice gets heard in politics and government.

As a result of their low voter turnout, many young people miss out on one of the most remarkable features of democratic government: every few years, citizens are provided the means with which to change the government and select new leaders. In the United States, tens of thousands of political offices at the local, state, and national levels hold popular elections. Although most Americans do not often vote directly on specific policies and laws, they exert tremendous influence over political outcomes through the regular selection of their leaders. By allowing citizens to hold their elected representatives accountable for their actions, elections, like freedom of speech and a free press, are at the very heart of democracy. Without them, democratic self-government could not survive.

In this chapter, we will learn about how elections work in the United States and how electoral rules and other considerations influence campaign strategy. We will see how election laws, the candidates' campaigns, and voters' choices determined the outcome of the 2016 presidential and congressional elections, and thus determined who represents the American people in government.

CHAPTER GOALS

- ★ **Describe the major rules and procedures of elections in the United States (pp. 381–93)**
- ★ **Explain how campaigns are typically conducted (pp. 393–400)**
- ★ **Describe how candidates raise the money they need to run (pp. 400–405)**
- ★ **Identify the major factors that influence voters' decisions (pp. 406–8)**
- ★ **Analyze the strategies, issues, and outcomes of the 2016 and 2018 elections (pp. 409–21)**

Elections in America

Describe the major rules and procedures of elections in the United States

In the United States, elections are highly routinized events that occur on fixed dates and are subject to specific rules. National presidential elections take place every four years, on the first Tuesday after the first Monday in November. Congressional elections are held every two years, also on the first Tuesday after the first Monday in November. Congressional elections that do not coincide with a presidential election are often called **midterm elections**. Localities and states can choose when to hold their elections. Most Americans have the opportunity to vote in several elections each year. Voting in elections is the most common form of participation in American politics.

midterm elections congressional elections that do not coincide with a presidential election; also called *off-year elections*

THE BASIC RULES OF THE GAME FOR U.S. ELECTIONS

primary elections elections held to select a party's candidate for the general election

In the American federal system, the responsibility for running elections is decentralized, resting largely with state and local governments. Elections are administered by state, county, and city election boards that are responsible for establishing and staffing polling places, processing mail-in ballots, and verifying the eligibility of voters. State laws influence who may vote, how they vote, and where they vote. For example, states must choose whether to require photo identification to vote and whether or not to allow their residents to cast a ballot by mail, to vote early at an official polling place, and to register to vote and vote on the same day.

Election season begins with **primary elections**, which are held to select each party's candidates for the general election. Primary elections are used in races for offices at the national, state, and often local levels. They are used to select the best candidate to represent the political party in the general election. Thus, primary elections are races where Democrats compete against Democrats and Republicans against Republicans (except in states that have "top two primaries," in which candidates from

Elections are the most important way that Americans participate in politics. Some of the rules of elections have changed over time. (Left) African Americans vote for the first time in Wilcox County, Alabama, after the passage of the Voting Right Act in 1965. (Right) An 18-year-old woman registers to vote in Illinois after the Twenty-Sixth Amendment in 1971 lowered the nationwide voting age from 21 to 18.

all parties run against one another and the top two face each other in the general election; California and Washington State use this method). The winners of primary elections face one another as their parties' nominees in the **general election**, the decisive electoral contest. The winner of the general election is elected to office for a specified term.

general election a regularly scheduled election involving most districts in the nation or state, in which voters select officeholders; in the United States, general elections for national office and most state and local offices are held on the first Tuesday after the first Monday in November in even-numbered years (every four years for presidential elections)

The United States is one of the few nations in the world to hold primary elections. In most countries, nominations of candidates are controlled completely by party officials, as they once were in the United States. Primary elections were introduced at the turn of the twentieth century by reformers who hoped to weaken the power of party leaders; the introduction of primary elections for the first time enabled voters, rather than party elites, to pick the candidates to compete in the general election (see Chapter 9). In states with **closed primaries**, only registered members of a political party may vote in a primary election to select that party's candidates. States with **open primaries** allow all registered voters, including independents, to choose which party's primary they will participate in.

closed primary a primary election in which voters can participate in the nomination of candidates but only of the party in which they are enrolled for a period of time prior to primary day

open primary a primary election in which the voter can wait until the day of the primary to choose which party to enroll in to select candidates for the general election

WHAT IT TAKES TO WIN—WINNER TAKE ALL

On the surface, the basic idea of how an election works may seem simple: voters select their preferred candidate on the ballot, votes are counted, and the candidate with the most votes wins the election. But there are actually many possible variations in how people vote and how the votes are counted.

While we take this system for granted in the United States, there are three different ways that ballots are counted and aggregated in countries using democratic elections. In some countries, a candidate must receive an absolute majority (50 percent plus 1) of all the votes cast in the relevant district in order to win the election. This type of electoral system is called a **majority system**. Majority systems usually include a provision for a **runoff election** between the two top candidates because if the initial race draws several candidates, there is little chance that any one will receive a majority.

majority system a type of electoral system in which, to win a seat in the parliament or other representative body, a candidate must receive a majority of all the votes cast in the relevant district

runoff election a "second-round" election in which voters choose between the top two candidates from the first round

In some other countries, including the United States, candidates for office need not win an absolute majority of the votes cast to win an election. Instead, victory is awarded to the candidate who receives the most votes, regardless of the actual percentage this represents. A candidate receiving 50 percent or even 30 percent of the popular vote can win if no other candidate receives more votes. This type of electoral system is called a **plurality system** and is used in most elections in the United States. The winning candidate needs to win a plurality (the most but not necessarily a majority) of the votes cast in the election. These voting rules are commonly referred to as "winner take all." In the 2016 Republican primaries, for example, Donald Trump was frequently referred to by the media as the winner, but in most states he only won around 35 percent of the vote because there were three or more candidates in the race. Trump also did not win a majority of the popular vote in the general election.

plurality system a type of electoral system in which, to win a seat in the parliament or other representative body, a candidate need only receive the most votes in the election, not necessarily a majority of the votes cast

Most advanced democracies use a third type of electoral system, called **proportional representation**. Under proportional rules, competing political parties are awarded legislative seats in rough proportion to the percentage of popular votes that each party wins. A party that wins 30 percent of the popular vote will receive roughly 30 percent of the seats in the parliament or other representative body. Proportional representation benefits smaller groups and third parties, such as the Green Party, Libertarian Party, or even far-right populist parties, because it usually allows a party

proportional representation a multiple-member district system that allows each political party representation in proportion to its percentage of the total vote to win legislative seats with fewer votes than would be required under a majority or plurality system. A party that wins 10 percent of the national vote might win 10 percent of the parliamentary seats. In the United States, by contrast, a party that wins 10 percent of the vote would probably win no seats in Congress. Because they give small parties little chance of success, plurality and majority systems tend to reduce the number of political parties that can hold power. This is one of the reasons that the United States has only two significant political parties (see Chapter 9 for more on the two-party system in the United States).

THE BALLOT

Before the 1890s voters cast ballots according to political parties. Each party printed its own election ballots, listed only its own candidates for each office, and employed party workers to distribute the ballots at the polls. Because voters had to choose which party's ballot to use, it was very difficult for a voter to cast anything other than a **straight-ticket vote**, selecting candidates from the same political party for all offices on the ballot. The advent of a new, neutral ballot at the turn of the twentieth century brought a significant change to electoral procedure. The new ballot—called the Australian ballot or long-form ballot—was prepared and administered by the government rather than the political parties. Each ballot was identical and included the names of all candidates running for public office. This ballot reform made it possible for voters to make their choices on the merits of the individual candidates, rather than the overall party and to have their choice of candidates be private.

straight-ticket voting selecting candidates from the same political party for all offices on the ballot

Because all candidates for the same office now appeared on the same ballot, voters were no longer forced to choose straight-ticket voting. This practice gave rise to the phenomenon of split-ticket voting, where voters may, for example, vote for a Democrat for Senate and a Republican for governor. If a voter supports candidates from more than one party in the same election, he is said to be casting a split-ticket vote. Split-ticket voting for national elections is far less common today than it was in the 1970s and 80s; today most people cast straight-ticket ballots or vote for candidates of the same political party for Congress and the president.[5]

In the United States, it is the states and county governments, not the federal government, that run elections and print the voting ballots. Some counties employ

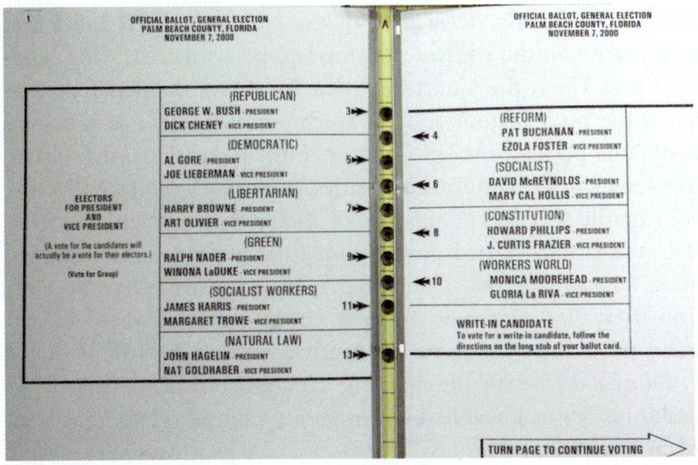

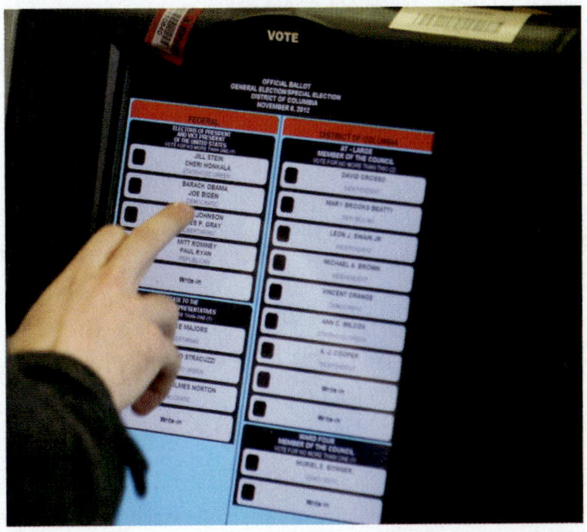

Ballots have changed dramatically over the years. In 2000 the configuration of the "butterfly" ballot (left) caused confusion in a key county in the swing state of Florida. This contested election led to the passage of the Help Americans Vote Act, which required states to upgrade their voting procedures. Many increased their use of computerized voting machines (right).

paper ballots, while most now use electronic or computerized voting systems. The controversial presidential election of 2000 led to a closer look at different ballot forms and voting systems used across the 3,000 counties in the United States. In 2000 the margin of victory for Republican George W. Bush over Democrat Al Gore in Florida was so small that the state ordered a recount. Careful examination of the results revealed that the punch card voting machines and butterfly ballot used in Florida had led to many voting and counting errors. The controversy made its way to the Supreme Court, which effectively reversed Florida's recount order, awarding the presidency to Bush. In the wake of the controversial election, Congress adopted the Help Americans Vote Act (HAVA) in 2003, requiring the states to use computerized voter registration databases. Critics of HAVA feared that such systems might be vulnerable to unauthorized use or hacking. In 2016, 21 states experienced intrusion by Russian hackers in their computerized state election systems, although to date there is no evidence that ballots were changed. In Illinois, for example, hackers viewed 300,000 active Illinois voter registration records (names, addresses, birthdates, voting history, etc.) but were unable to modify the data.[6] In the past, computerized voting machines have generally worked well and have significantly updated America's election system, but all computerized systems have vulnerabilities. Protecting state and county election systems from hackers is a new priority for reform.

LEGISLATIVE ELECTIONS AND ELECTORAL DISTRICTS

The boundaries for some elected offices are straightforward: all eligible U.S. citizens 18 years or older may vote for president; all eligible residents of each such state may vote for that state's governor and two U.S. Senators. Other political offices, such as members of the U.S. House of Representatives and state lawmakers, are elected from geographic legislative districts whose boundaries are drawn by state governments—either state legislatures or independent commissions or the courts. The boundaries for congressional and state legislative districts are redrawn every 10 years to reflect population changes, as determined by the U.S. Census. The process of redrawing district boundaries is called **redistricting**. The geographic shape of legislative district boundaries is influenced by several factors, including population size and existing government boundaries such as counties.

redistricting the process of redrawing election districts and redistributing legislative representatives; this happens every 10 years, to reflect shifts in population or in response to legal challenges in existing districts

Federal court decisions have played a major role in how legislative districts are drawn. In the 1962 landmark case *Baker v. Carr*, the Supreme Court ruled that federal courts can intervene on the issue of drawing legislative districts. In a series of decisions in 1963 and 1964, the Court held that legislative districts for Congress and state legislatures must include roughly equal populations so as to accord with the principle of "one person, one vote."[7] Prior to these decisions, many state legislative districts were simply county boundaries, with each county electing one representative, regardless of the population of the county. Drawing districts with roughly equal populations shifted power from rural areas to urban centers, where the population was higher. Today, average U.S. House districts have roughly 700,000 people (up from 30,000 people in 1800). State legislative districts vary from a few thousand people in some states to nearly a million (931,000) in the California Senate. During the 1980s the Supreme Court also declared that legislative districts should, insofar as possible, be contiguous, compact, and consistent with existing political subdivisions.[8]

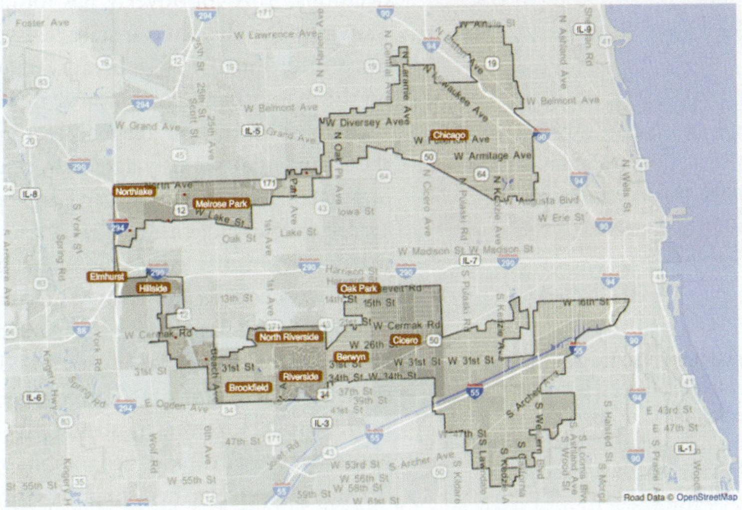

The original gerrymander was a districting plan attributed to the Massachusetts governor Elbridge Gerry (1744–1814) that had the shape of a salamander. This practice continues today across the country, as seen here in the odd shape of Illinois's 4th Congressional District, which was drawn to create a majority Latino district.

Despite these legal requirements, state lawmakers who are responsible for drawing the district boundaries for Congress and state legislatures regularly seek to influence electoral outcomes to favor one political party over another (or incumbents over challengers). This strategy of drawing legislative districts to favor a political party is called **gerrymandering**. Gerrymandering is named for a nineteenth-century Massachusetts governor, Elbridge Gerry, who was alleged to have designed an odd-shaped district in the shape of a salamander to promote his party's interests.[9]

The principle behind gerrymandering is simple: different populations of voters residing in geographically defined districts can produce different electoral results. For example, by dispersing the members of a political party across two or more districts, state lawmakers can dilute that group's voting power and prevent it from electing a representative in any district. This technique is known as "cracking." Alternatively, by concentrating the members of a party in as few districts as possible, state lawmakers can try to ensure that their opponents will elect as few representatives as possible, a technique called "packing." The controversial but widespread practice of gerrymandering has created many "safe" districts in Congress, and state legislatures where incumbents rarely face a serious challenger. This contributes to the frequency with which members of Congress are re-elected in landslide elections. In 2018, 86 percent of Senators and 93 percent of House members won re-election, but a historic 56 members did not even run for re-election.[10] When candidates do not face serious challengers in elections there is concern that public officials will not represent the interests of the people but will instead make laws that benefit special interests. To address this problem, some states use nonpartisan redistricting boards or commissions where boundaries are drawn not to advantage one party over the other and the partisanship of voters in the district is not a consideration in drawing geographic boundaries.

gerrymandering the apportionment of voters in districts in such a way as to give unfair advantage to one racial or ethnic group or political party

Partisan gerrymandering—that is, drawing districts to advantage one party over another—has recently become highly controversial. Critics of this practice claim that these techniques go against the principle of "one person, one vote." Others believe that the process of legislative districting is by nature political, and parties strategically drawing districts to gain an advantage is part of the electoral game. They also contend there is no agreed-upon standard for too much partisan tilt in these

partisan gerrymandering occurs when politicians from one party intentionally manipulate the boundaries for legislative election districts to disadvantage their political opponents' chance of winning an election and advantage their own political party

FOR CRITICAL ANALYSIS

How do district boundaries affect elections for the U.S. House and state legislatures? Should districts be drawn based on partisan considerations or other criteria?

decisions. This controversy has found its way into the courts. Legislative districts drawn by the Republican state legislature in Pennsylvania, for example, were ruled unconstitutional in 2018 because of gerrymandering. The U.S. Supreme Court took up the matter in *Gill v. Whitford*, in which Democratic voters of a Wisconsin district sued to overturn the allegedly gerrymandered state district map.[11] In June 2018 the Court unanimously agreed to send the case back to the district court, delaying Supreme Court action on partisan gerrymandering for at least another term.

majority-minority district an electoral district, such as a congressional district, in which the majority of the constituents belong to racial or ethnic minorities

The federal government has often supported congressional districts made up primarily of minority group members, a practice intended to increase the number of African Americans and Latinos elected to public office in accordance with the 1965 Voting Rights Act. Beginning with the 1993 case of *Shaw v. Reno*, however, the Supreme Court has generally opposed efforts to force the creation of **majority-minority districts**.[12] The Court has asserted that districting based exclusively on race/ethnicity is unlawful. However, most majority-minority districts in the United States occur naturally in states and geographic areas with large minority populations. Most African Americans in Congress, for example, are elected from districts with a majority of African American voters.

PRESIDENTIAL ELECTIONS

Presidential elections have special rules because they are the only public office in the U.S. elected by all American citizens (though the president is technically elected by the electoral college, not by direct popular vote of the citizens). Moreover, presidential candidates from the two major parties are officially nominated at the parties' national conventions, following a series of state-by-state primary elections and caucuses to select delegates to the conventions. While primary elections are also used to select candidates in congressional and other types of elections, the national convention delegate system for nominating candidates is unique to presidential elections.

Nominating Presidential Candidates: Primaries and Caucuses How do we pick presidential candidates in the United States? Before the presidential election every four years, the parties must select candidates to represent them in the general election. The process starts with primary elections and caucuses that are held by the major political parties to choose a candidate who will face the nominee from the other major party during the general election. Most states hold primary elections, but about one-third use caucuses instead.

Caucuses are essentially party business meetings. At the lowest level, precinct caucuses are meetings of registered voters within a local geographic area who are members of the same political party. There are hundreds of precinct caucuses in each state. The purpose of precinct caucuses is to elect delegates to county assemblies. The same process is repeated for county caucuses, which elect members to represent their preferences at the district caucuses, and finally for the state assembly. If members of a local precinct caucus prefer Bernie Sanders for president, for example, the delegates representing that precinct at the county, district, and state caucuses would continue to cast votes for Sanders. Thus citizens attending local caucuses end up electing delegates to statewide conventions, which is where delegates to the national party conventions are chosen. Compared to primary elections, caucuses give party leaders and activists a larger role in selecting candidates for public office.

Candidate strategies to win states holding primaries are very different than for states using caucuses. This is because voter turnout in caucuses tends to be much lower than in primary elections. Television and mass media campaigns typically are used to campaign in primary states, while face-to-face and retail politics are more common in caucus states.

The Iowa caucuses are especially famous, as the first state to select presidential candidates in the calendar year, as is the New Hampshire primary, as the second election in the presidential nomination process. Both the Iowa caucus and New Hampshire primary are characterized by **retail politics**, where presidential candidates spend a great deal of time in the state to meet with voters face to face. Like the general elections, early primaries and caucuses tend to be highly contested, with high levels of mass media coverage and intensive voter mobilization drives.

retail politics a style of campaigning where candidates connect to voters at intimate gatherings and local events

The primaries and caucuses traditionally begin in January of a presidential election year and end in June, with state elections roughly every two weeks. Iowa and New Hampshire's disproportionate role in picking presidential candidates is due to their being the first states to cast votes in the caucuses and primaries. These early voting states are important because they can help candidates gain momentum by securing national media attention, money in the form of campaign contributions, and higher ratings in public-opinion polls. Candidates that perform well in the Iowa caucuses and New Hampshire primary send signals to voters in states holding later primaries and caucuses that a candidate is viable (can win the nomination) and electable (can win the general election). A candidate who performs better than expected in Iowa and New Hampshire will usually be able to win public support and media coverage for subsequent races. A candidate who fares poorly in these two states may be written off as a loser and drop out of the race. In 2016, Donald Trump and Bernie Sanders beat expectations by both placing second in the Iowa caucuses and first in the New Hampshire primary. These early wins helped solidify Trump's nomination for the Republican party ticket, and indicated that Sanders would be a viable rival of Clinton throughout the Democratic party nomination. Today, the presidential nomination has become "front-loaded," with states vying to increase their political influence by holding their nominating processes earlier in the calendar year in order to receive more attention from candidates and the media.

Campaigning for early primaries and caucuses typically involves grassroots politics, with candidates attempting to connect directly with citizens. Here, 2016 presidential candidate Ted Cruz speaks to potential voters at a local diner in Keene, New Hampshire.

One study found that the change in mass media coverage that candidates receive before and after the Iowa caucuses predicts how well they will do in the New Hampshire primary and in presidential primaries nationwide measured by vote share.[13] This study suggests that it is not winning the Iowa caucuses that matters but doing better than expected by the national media. For example, if Barack Obama had not won the Iowa caucus in 2008, unexpectedly beating presumed Democratic front-runner Hillary Clinton, most commentators believe he would not have gone on to capture the Democratic nomination. Similarly, Republican candidate Donald Trump fared much better than expected by political elites and the mass media by placing second in the Iowa caucuses and first in the New Hampshire primary. In an era of viral digital social media, media coverage of early nominating events is even greater than before and may further increase the importance of states holding early primaries and caucuses.[14]

FOR CRITICAL ANALYSIS

Is it fair that two relatively small states (in terms of population) such as Iowa and New Hampshire should have such outsize influence in picking presidents?

delegate a representative who votes according to the preferences of his or her constituency

The result of the presidential primary or caucus determines how each state's **delegates** will vote at their party's national convention. As noted in Chapter 9, the Democratic Party requires that state presidential primaries allocate delegates on the basis of proportional representation; Democratic candidates win delegates in rough proportion to their percentage of the primary vote. The Republican Party does not require proportional representation, but many states now use the system. A few states use the winner-take-all system, by which the candidate with the most votes wins all the party's delegates in that state. When the primaries and caucuses are concluded, it is usually clear which candidates have won their parties' nominations.

Nominating Presidential Candidates: Party Conventions For more than 50 years after America's Founding, presidential nominations were controlled by each party's congressional caucus—all the party's members in the House and the Senate. Critics referred to this process as the "King Caucus" and charged that it did not fairly represent the views of party members throughout the nation. Thus, the King Caucus process was replaced by the system of national party conventions. As it developed over the next century, the convention became the decisive institution in the presidential nominating processes of the two major parties. Composed of delegates from each state who pledge loyalty to different presidential candidates, the convention was a deliberative body in which party elites argued, negotiated, and eventually chose a single candidate to support. The size of a state's delegation depended on the state's population, and each delegate was allowed one vote for the purpose of nominating the party's presidential and vice-presidential candidates. Between the 1830s and World War II, delegates to the national party conventions were selected by a state's party leaders. These individuals were public officials, political activists, and party notables from all regions of the state, representing most major party factions. Over time, reformers viewed the convention as a symbol of rule by party elites and the affluent. Around the turn of the twentieth century, many states adopted direct primary elections to choose presidential candidates, enabling average citizens to have a voice in picking their president. As we saw earlier in this chapter, today the nomination is determined in a series of primary elections and caucuses held in all 50 states during the months prior to the party's national convention. These elections determine how each state's convention delegates will vote. Candidates usually arrive at the convention knowing who has enough delegate support in hand to assure a victory in the first round of balloting. If one candidate does not win a majority of delegates, a second ballot is issued, and delegates can choose to vote for a different candidate.

Superdelegates are party elites who are not bound to the voting results in their state primaries and can vote as they wish. At the 2016 Democratic National Convention, most superdelegates backed Hillary Clinton, giving her a significant advantage over her opponent Bernie Sanders, despite Sanders's strong support among voters. The Republican Party does not use superdelegates, and the practice of reserving delegates for the party elite is increasingly controversial in the Democratic Party.

Even though the party convention no longer controls presidential nominations, it still has a number of important tasks. The convention makes the rules concerning delegate selection and future presidential primary elections. In 1972, for example, the Democratic Party adopted rules requiring convention delegates to be broadly representative of the party's membership in terms of race and gender. Another important task for the convention is the drafting of a **party platform**, a statement of principles and pledges around which the delegates can unite.

Although the party's nominees for the president and vice president are officially announced at the party conventions, they are actually selected much earlier through caucuses and primary elections. In 2016, Hillary Clinton and Tim Kaine formally accepted the Democratic nomination at the national convention.

Most importantly, the convention is an opportunity for the party to showcase its candidate in anticipation of the upcoming general election. On a national stage with the television cameras rolling, the presidential and vice-presidential nominees deliver acceptance speeches. These speeches are opportunities for the nominees to begin their formal general-election campaigns and make a positive impression on the media. In her speech at the 2016 Democratic National Convention, for example, Hillary Clinton repeated three times the theme of her general-election campaign, "stronger together," insisting that the phrase was not just a slogan for the campaign, but "a guiding principle for the country we've always been and the future we're going to build."

Picking Presidents: The Electoral College After they are officially nominated at the party convention, presidential candidates compete in the general election. As noted earlier, the presidential election differs from other elections in an important way: the voters do *not* directly elect the president. In the early history of popular voting, nations often made use of indirect elections. In these elections, voters would choose the members of an intermediate body. These members would, in turn, select public officials. The last vestige of this procedure in the United States is the **electoral college**, the group of electors who formally select the president and vice president of the United States.

party platform a party document, written at a national convention, that contains party philosophy, principles, and policy positions

electoral college the presidential electors from each state who meet after the general election to cast ballots for president and vice president

When Americans go to the polls on Election Day, they are technically not voting directly for presidential candidates, even though they mark ballots as such; they are instead choosing among slates of electors selected by each party in the state and pledged, if elected, to support that party's presidential candidate. Electors are allocated to each state based on the size of the state's congressional delegation (Senators plus House members). Larger-population states thus have more votes in the electoral college. North Dakota, for example, has 3 votes in the electoral college (based on its 2 senators plus 1 representative), while California has 55 (2 senators plus 53 representatives).

The president of the United States is the winner of the electoral college—the candidate who wins at least 270 of the college's 538 votes—not necessarily the candidate with the most votes from the people. This is in part because the electoral college and most elections in the United States are governed by plurality, winner-take-all rules. With only two exceptions, each state awards *all* of its electors to the candidate who receives the most votes in the state.[15] Thus, in 2016, Trump received all 29 of Florida's electoral votes, though he won only 49 percent of the votes in the state.

Since electoral votes are won on a state-by-state basis, it is mathematically possible for a candidate who receives the most popular votes nationwide to fail to carry states whose electoral votes would add up to a majority. Four times in the nation's history has the winner of the electoral college not won the popular vote (the most votes from the people). In 1876, Rutherford B. Hayes was the winner in the electoral college despite receiving fewer popular votes than his rival, Samuel Tilden. In 1888, Grover Cleveland received more popular votes than Benjamin Harrison but fewer electoral votes. The third instance was the election of 2000, discussed earlier, when the lengthy legal battle over recounting votes in Florida ultimately ended with the Supreme Court's decision in *Bush v. Gore* that handed George W. Bush the presidency, even though he had not won the popular vote.[16] Bush won a majority in the electoral college, but Democratic candidate Al Gore won 500,000 more votes from the people nationwide. And the fourth instance was in 2016 when Hillary Clinton won almost 3 million more votes than Donald Trump, but Trump won the majority in the electoral college. Because of these contentious cases where the popular vote winner has lost the election, calls for eliminating the electoral college and using a national popular vote for president are widespread. Public-opinion polls continue to show that most Americans prefer a direct election for the president.[17]

Replacing the electoral college with another system would require a constitutional amendment that most agree would be extremely difficult to pass. However, reform is still possible since the Constitution allows states to choose the method of selecting presidential electors. One example of a recent attempt to reform the electoral college is the National Popular Vote plan, which has been introduced and adopted in a number of state legislatures. Under the proposed rule change, a state's electoral college votes would go to the candidate who won the national popular vote, not the candidate with a plurality of votes in that specific state. States would enter a compact with other states making the same change, which would go into effect when a number of states representing a majority in the electoral college (270 electoral votes) approved it. The reform would effectively bypass the electoral college without the need for an amendment to the U.S. Constitution. As of 2018, 10 states plus Washington, D.C., for a total of 165 electoral college votes, have enacted the bill into law. The bill will take effect when enacted by states possessing an additional 105 electoral votes pass the law.

Another limitation of the electoral college system is that some presidents do not have widespread support. Few democracies in the world elect a president who does not win a majority of the popular vote. Since the Civil War, roughly one-third of American presidents have been elected with only a plurality (less than 50 percent) rather than a majority vote.[18] Notably, Abraham Lincoln won just 40 percent of the popular vote in a four-way election, Bill Clinton was elected with just 43 percent of the popular vote in 1992 and Trump with 46 percent in 2016.[19] This often happens when a third-party candidate receives a significant percentage of votes. If the third-party candidate is more closely aligned ideologically with the losing

FIGURE 10.1

Electing the President: Steps in the Process

Formation of an Exploratory Committee
Formed 18 to 24 months before the election, this committee begins fundraising and bringing the candidate's name to the attention of the media and influential groups.

↓

Fundraising
Presidential candidates must develop fundraising strategies, hire expert fundraisers, and quickly build a substantial "war chest" early on to show they are serious contenders.

↓

Campaigning
Months before the primaries, candidates begin meetings with local leaders, public appearances, ad campaigns, and other strategies.

↓

Primaries and Caucuses
Candidates need to do well in early contests such as Iowa and New Hampshire in order to build momentum and win their party's nomination. Party debates give candidates an opportunity to impress large television audiences.

↓

The Convention
The Democratic and Republican parties hold national conventions in September prior to the November general election. The parties' nominees for president and vice president are officially announced.

↓

The General Election Campaign
In the months leading up to the November election, candidates focus on battleground or swing states as they aim to win at least 270 votes in the electoral college. They run television ads and use new media to reach voters. They must continue to raise money throughout this process.

↓

The Debates
In October, the major-party candidates engage in several televised debates along with one vice-presidential debate.

↓

The General Election
On the Tuesday following the first Monday in November, voters in each state cast ballots. In most states, the candidate who wins the most votes in the state wins all of the state's votes in the electoral college.

↓

The Electoral College
The electors meet in their state capitals in December, and their votes are officially counted in January.

↓

The Inauguration
The president is officially inaugurated on January 20.

major-party candidate, then a majority of voters may not support the winning presidential candidate.

DIRECT-DEMOCRACY ELECTIONS

ballot initiative a proposed law or policy change that is placed on the ballot by citizens or interest groups for a popular vote

referendum the practice of referring a proposed law passed by a legislature to the vote of the electorate for approval or rejection

Beyond presidential and congressional elections, 24 states also provide for the initiative process. **Ballot initiatives** allow citizens to circulate petitions to place policy change or proposed laws directly on the ballot for a popular vote. If a ballot initiative receives majority support, it becomes law (in Florida, a super majority is required to adopt constitutional initiatives). Controversial issues frequently appear on the ballots of states with the initiative process. In recent years, voters in several states have raised taxes, lowered taxes, prohibited social services for undocumented immigrants, provided universal health care, created nonpartisan redistricting, protected the environment, legalized marijuana, and much more. At the turn of the twentieth century, ballot initiatives were used to grant women the right to vote, prevent child labor, limit the workday to eight hours, and allow voters to elect U.S. senators directly (rather than having them chosen by state legislatures). All 50 states have the legislative **referendum**, in which the state legislature refers certain laws to the voters for a popular vote. Referendum votes are required for changes to state constitutions.

The initiative and the referendum, both referred to as *ballot measures,* are examples of direct democracy. They allow voters to govern directly and make laws without intervention by government officials or the political parties. Ballot measure campaigns often involve high spending by proponents and opponents, and mass media campaigns that can rival those of congressional and presidential candidates within a state. The validity of ballot measure results, however, is subject to judicial action. If a court finds that an initiative violates the state or national constitution, it can overturn the result. This happened in 2012 when the federal courts overturned California's Proposition 8, which banned same-sex marriage.[20]

Ballot initiatives not only change policy but also appear to affect political behavior. One study found that states with initiatives on the ballot have higher voter turnout over time. Citizens living in direct-democracy states report more interest in politics and are more likely to discuss politics. Why is this so? Ballot propositions offer voters the opportunity to directly make public policy and change government laws, which may have an "educative" effect on the people.[21] When they have more opportunities to act politically, citizens may learn to participate more and come to believe their participation has meaning.

Elections with policy choices on the ballot provide information to voters in the form of political campaigns and attention in the mass media. Ballot measures concerning controversial policy issues generate their own campaigns with television, newspaper, and digital media, and rely on volunteers for mobilization drives that contact potential voters.[22] Hundreds of initiatives and referenda appear on state election ballots every two years. In 2018 ballot measures included anti–sanctuary city initiatives in Missouri, Oklahoma, and Nevada, raising the minimum wage in Michigan, and paid family and medical leave in Massachusetts. An initiative in Maine in 2016 created a new system of voting called "ranked choice voting," discussed earlier, in which voters choose three candidates to rank in order of preference, rather than choosing only one. The new voting system applies to gubernatorial, congressional, and state legislative elections. Ballot initiatives are increasingly common: more initiatives and referenda have appeared on state ballots over the last 30 years than at any other time in American history, outside of the Progressive era at the turn of the twentieth century. In 2018, 157 ballot measures were certified for the ballot in 37 states.[23]

In addition, ballot measures can help shape both the national agenda and evaluations of candidates.[24] In 2006 coordinated ballot measures raising the minimum wage in multiple states may have influenced voters to focus on the economy, priming voters to cast ballots for Democrats in Congress and for Democratic governors. Placing issues on the ballot as part of an effort to influence candidate elections is an important strategy for political campaigns attempting to shape the political agenda.

Eighteen states also have legal provisions for **recall** elections, which allow voters to remove governors and other state officials from office prior to the expiration of their terms. In California, for example, if 12 percent of those who voted in the last general election sign petitions demanding a special recall election, one must be scheduled by the state board of elections. In 2003 many California voters blamed Governor Gray Davis for the state's $38-billion budget deficit; Davis became only the second governor in American history to be recalled by his state's electorate; the actor Arnold Schwarzenegger was elected in his place. In 2012, Wisconsin governor Scott Walker won a highly visible recall election, keeping his position. Federal officials, such as the president and members of Congress, are not subject to recall.

recall a procedure to allow voters to remove state officials from office before their terms expire by circulating petitions to call a vote

Election Campaigns

Explain how campaigns are typically conducted

A **campaign** is an effort by political candidates (and their political party) to win the backing of donors, elected officials, and voters in their quest for elected office. Campaigns precede every primary and general election. Because of the complexity of the campaign process and the amount of money that candidates must raise, presidential campaigns often begin almost two years before the November election; and congressional campaigns, 12 months in advance of the election. The campaign for any office consists of a number of steps. Candidates often form an exploratory committee consisting of supporters who will help them raise funds and bring their names to the attention of the media, potential donors, and voters. Money from corporations and affluent citizens is an important component of U.S. elections since public funding is limited. **Incumbents**, who already hold elected office, have an advantage over the candidates challenging them. Incumbents usually are already well known and have little difficulty attracting supporters and campaign contributors—unless, of course, they have been subject to damaging publicity while in office.

campaign an effort by political candidates and their supporters to win the backing of donors, political activists, and voters in their quest for political office

incumbent a candidate running for re-election to a position that he or she already holds

CAMPAIGN CONSULTANTS

A formal organization and professional campaign managers are critical for campaign success. For a local campaign, candidates generally need hundreds of volunteers and some paid professionals. State-level campaigns call for thousands of volunteers, and presidential campaigns require tens of thousands of volunteers and paid staff nationwide. Virtually all serious contenders for national and statewide office retain the services of professional campaign consultants. Most candidates need a professional campaign manager, media consultants, pollsters and a data analytics

Candidates for national office rely on campaign advisers to guide their campaigns and direct volunteers. Here, Hillary Clinton collaborates with Huma Abedin, her longtime aide and her campaign's vice chairwoman; Brian Fallon (left), her national press secretary; and Nick Merrill (right), her traveling press secretary.

team, financial advisers, a press spokesperson, and staff directors to coordinate the activities of volunteer and paid workers. Consultants offer candidates the expertise necessary to craft appealing campaign messages, conduct accurate opinion polls, produce television and social media ads, organize direct-mail campaigns, open field offices, and leverage valuable information about their constituents from massive digital voter files or from surveys. Most consultants who direct campaigns specialize in politics, corporate advertising and strategic communication, public relations, communications, and computing. They may work with commercial clients in addition to politicians.

FUNDRAISING

Modern national political campaigns are fueled by enormous amounts of money, with more money necessary for highly competitive elections and federal offices. Candidates generally begin raising funds long before they face an election, and many politicians spend more time soliciting donations than engaging in any other campaign activity. Members of Congress spend a significant portion of their time fundraising; the Democratic leadership recommends that 40 to 50 percent of their time be spent on fundraising.[25] Serious fundraising efforts involve appealing to both small and large donors. To have a reasonable chance of winning a seat in the House of Representatives, a candidate may need to raise more than $1 million; in 2014 candidates in the most competitive House races spent $10 million or more. In the 2018 Senate races, candidates in the most competitive elections spent $31–94 million.[26]

Once elected to office, members of Congress find it much easier to raise campaign funds and are thus able to outspend their challengers (see Figure 10.2).[27] Incumbents can out-raise their opponent by significant amounts because most businesses and corporations, interest group contributions, and PAC money donations go to incumbents. These groups seek a voice in government from their investment in

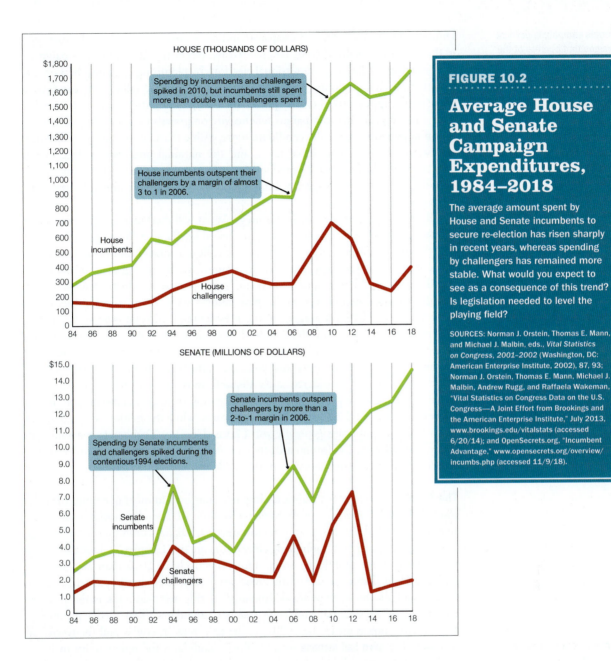

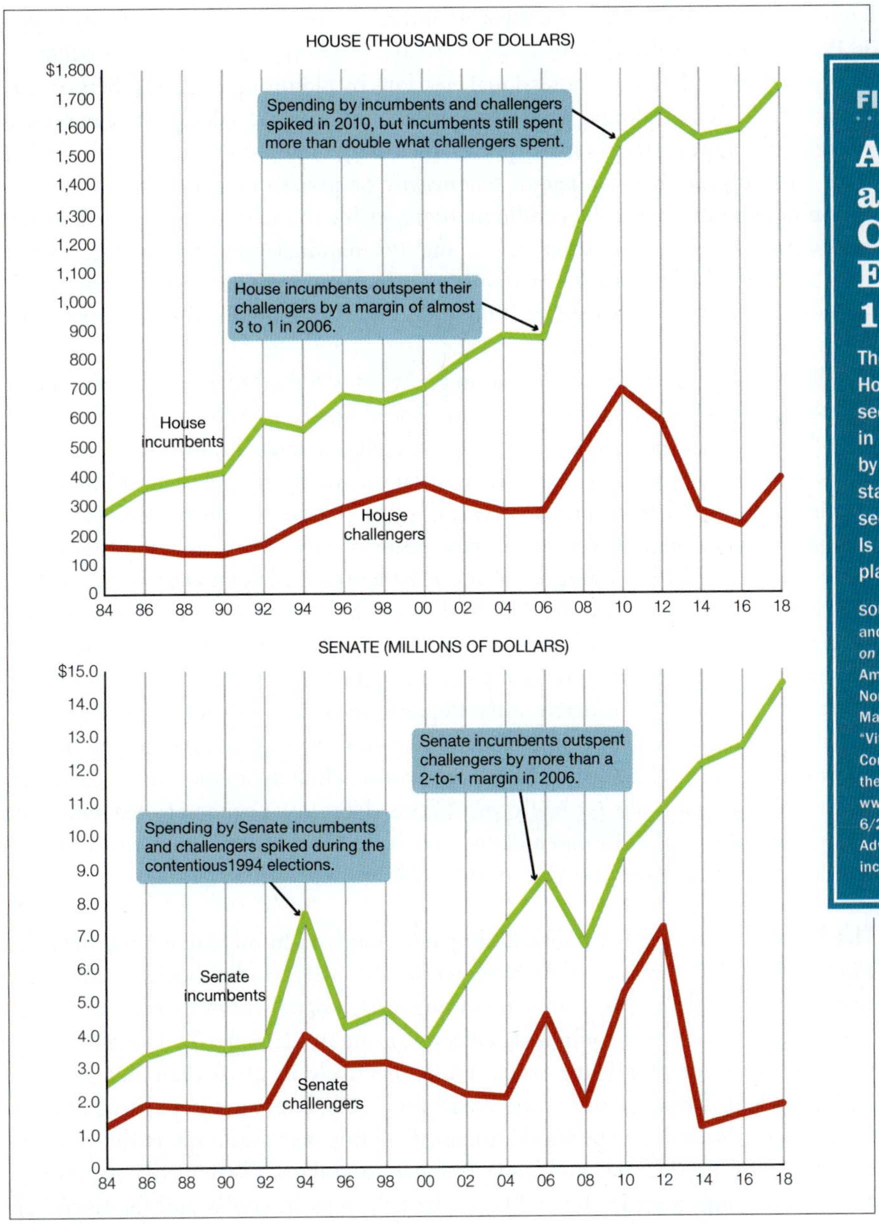
HOUSE (THOUSANDS OF DOLLARS)
Spending by incumbents and challengers spiked in 2010, but incumbents still spent more than double what challengers spent.
House incumbents outspent their challengers by a margin of almost 3 to 1 in 2006.
House incumbents
House challengers
SENATE (MILLIONS OF DOLLARS)
Senate incumbents outspent challengers by more than a 2-to-1 margin in 2006.
Spending by Senate incumbents and challengers spiked during the contentious1994 elections.
Senate incumbents
Senate challengers

FIGURE 10.2

Average House and Senate Campaign Expenditures, 1984–2018

The average amount spent by House and Senate incumbents to secure re-election has risen sharply in recent years, whereas spending by challengers has remained more stable. What would you expect to see as a consequence of this trend? Is legislation needed to level the playing field?

SOURCES: Norman J. Orstein, Thomas E. Mann, and Michael J. Malbin, eds., *Vital Statistics on Congress, 2001–2002* (Washington, DC: American Enterprise Institute, 2002), 87, 93; Norman J. Orstein, Thomas E. Mann, Michael J. Malbin, Andrew Rugg, and Raffaela Wakeman, "Vital Statistics on Congress Data on the U.S. Congress—A Joint Effort from Brookings and the American Enterprise Institute," July 2013, www.brookings.edu/vitalstats (accessed 6/20/14); and OpenSecrets.org, "Incumbent Advantage," www.opensecrets.org/overview/incumbs.php (accessed 11/9/18).

campaign contributions; thus, these organizations—businesses, labor unions, public interest groups, and others—want to invest in the candidate most likely to win, and incumbents win a large percentage of the time. Members of the majority party in the House and Senate are particularly attractive to donors who want access to those in power.[28] In the "Money and Politics" section later in this chapter, we will discuss further the critical role that money plays in the electoral process.

CAMPAIGN STRATEGY

For those candidates who win the nomination process, the last hurdle is the general election. There are essentially two types of general election campaigns in the

grassroots campaigns political campaigns that operate at the local level, often using face-to-face communication to generate interest and momentum by citizens

United States today: **grassroots campaigns** and mass media campaigns. The first type is the organizationally driven, labor-intensive election. Candidates campaign in local elections and many congressional elections by recruiting large numbers of volunteers to knock on doors, hand out leaflets, and organize rallies. The candidates make public appearances in many places, including university campuses. Generally, local and congressional campaigns rely heavily on grassroots outreach and mobilization designed to make the candidate more visible than her opponent. Statewide campaigns, some congressional races, and the national presidential election fall into the second category: the media-driven, money-intensive electoral campaign. President Obama's campaigns in 2008 and 2012 were notable in combining both types of campaigns.

All campaigns must decide on a strategy: What will their main message be? How will they allocate their resources (television, social media, face-to-face mobilization)? Which voters will they target? The electoral college is one election rule that influences the campaign strategy of presidential candidates by forcing them to campaign heavily in a dozen battleground, or swing, states—those in which Democrats and Republicans are roughly even in the population—while often ignoring the rest of the country. In 2016, 94 percent of the presidential campaign events occurred in 12 battleground states, with the bulk in the populous swing states of Florida, Ohio, Pennsylvania, and Virginia.[29] Presidential candidates in the general election focus not on winning the most individual votes but rather on winning the electoral votes of states that are not considered safely Republican or safely Democratic. Residents of battleground states get smothered with attention from the candidates and media as presidential candidates vie for that state's votes, while the millions of residents of states where Republicans generally win (Texas, Utah) or Democrats generally win (New York, Illinois, California) are often ignored. Without electoral competition in safe states, the needs and concerns of the residents may well be ignored.

The Media Contemporary political campaigns rely on a number of communication tools to reach the voters they want to target for support, including social media, massive computerized databases, and micro-targeting. Digital communication strategy is especially important in mobilizing citizens to vote (see Chapter 7). Donald Trump used Facebook for mobilizing voters more effectively in 2016 than any previous U.S. president. Extensive use of the broadcast media, television in particular, is the hallmark of the modern political campaign. Airing television ads is the primary cost faced by presidential and congressional candidates. Two media techniques that became important in the 1990s are the talk show interview and the town hall meeting. The **town hall meeting** format allows candidates the opportunity to interact with ordinary citizens, thus showing the candidates' concern with the views and needs of the voters. Both talk show appearances and town hall meetings (when televised) allow candidates to deliver their messages to millions of Americans without the input of journalists or commentators who might criticize or question the candidates' assertions.

town hall meeting an informal public meeting in which candidates meet with ordinary citizens; allows candidates to deliver messages without the presence of journalists or commentators

Candidates spend millions of dollars for *paid media* time in the form of television and radio ads, as discussed in the previous section. Many of these ads consist of 15-, 30-, or 60-second spots (advertisements) that deliver a candidate's message to a target audience. One notable example was Lyndon Johnson's 1964 "daisy" ad, which suggested that Johnson's opponent, Barry Goldwater, would lead the United States into nuclear war. Television ads are used to establish candidate name recognition, create a favorable image of the candidate and a negative image of the opponent, link the candidate with desirable groups in the community, and communicate the candidate's stands on selected issues.

Often in the later stages of a campaign, candidates and the political advocacy groups that support them will "go negative," airing ads that criticize their opponents' policy positions, qualifications, or character. Though voters consistently say they reject so-called negative campaigning, political scientist John Geer found that negative campaign ads can benefit voters more than positive ads in some cases.[30] Negative ads are more likely to address important policy differences and provide supporting evidence, while positive ads tend to focus on candidates' personal characteristics. And even when negative ads are misleading or patently false, they are effective in that voters remember more from negative ads than from positive ads, possibly because negative ads are designed to elicit emotional responses, such as fear, anxiety, or anger.

In addition to ads sponsored by the candidates, a growing percentage of campaign ads are sponsored by the political parties and by political advocacy groups seeking to influence the outcome of the election. The 2010 *Citizens United* decision (discussed later in this chapter) allowed corporations, unions, and interest groups to spend unlimited amounts of their own money to advocate for political candidates. Corporations, unions, and interest groups can form Super PACs and run unlimited campaign ads for or against candidates, as long as the organizations are "independent" of the candidate's campaign. When viewers see attack ads against a candidate, it can be difficult to determine who sponsored the ad because a Super PAC with a generic name—Citizens for America, for example—paid for the ad. The effect of unlimited spending on television advertising remains unclear.

Candidates also benefit from *free media*, where the cost of airtime is borne by the media themselves when the media cover the candidates' statements and activities as news. In the 2016 presidential primaries, Donald Trump, largely due to his many controversial statements and tweets, benefited from free media coverage.[31] Critics claimed that the networks' tendency to focus on Trump, rather than provide balanced political coverage of all candidates, occurred because he drew the biggest audience.

Online media is free and has become a major weapon in modern political campaigns as more Americans turn to the internet and social media for news.

While voters often complain about the prevalence of negative advertising in campaigns, research shows that negative ads are more memorable, and sometimes contain more information about candidates' policy differences than positive ads.

Today, every presidential campaign and most campaigns for Congress and major state offices develop a social media strategy for fundraising, generating interest in the candidate, mobilizing supporters, and getting out the vote. (See Chapters 7 and 8 for a fuller discussion of political candidates' digital strategy.) One reason digital media are so effective at organizing presidential campaigns is cost: the internet enables inexpensive organization of volunteers and offers more opportunities for free advertising, such as on Twitter and YouTube. Online political videos may be more effective than television ads because viewers make a conscious choice to watch them, instead of having their television program interrupted by an unwanted ad.

Debates Public debates were a critical part of the democratic process of ancient Greece, where they were both a vital form of public entertainment and the principal means of what today would be called "voter education." Many successful American politicians, such as Abraham Lincoln and Barack Obama, came to prominence largely because of their skill as debaters. Today, both presidential and vice-presidential candidates hold debates, as do candidates for statewide and even local offices. Debates give voters the opportunity to see how the candidates fare in direct, face-to-face exchanges outside the "campaign bubble" of stage-managed public appearances and carefully scripted speeches. Candidates who can think on their feet may be seen as demonstrating the kind of on-the-spot decision-making that is more like actual governing than anything else they do in a campaign.

Televised presidential debates began with the famous 1960 Kennedy–Nixon clash. Kennedy's strong performance in the debate and the perception of many voters that the youthfully vigorous Kennedy "looked presidential" were major factors in bringing about his victory over the much better-known Richard Nixon. Indeed, candidates can make or break their campaigns with the strength of their debate performances, including high-profile gaffes during the debates and even unconscious gestures and the nuances of their facial expressions. Presidential debates usually involve civilized disagreement about substantive policy issues. The Republican primary debates in 2016, however, uncharacteristically included fierce arguments, harsh character attacks, and personal insults, many of which stemmed from the bombastic style of Donald Trump and his opponents' occasional attempts to match it. When Trump faced off against Democrat Hillary Clinton in the general election, the antagonistic tone continued, and their first televised debate broke viewership records as the most watched in U.S. history.[32]

Micro-Targeting and Polling The media and televised debates allow candidates to communicate their policy goals and promises to voters. While this method is efficient for campaigns, it is also blunt; different voters care about different issues, after all. As we saw in Chapter 9, the idea behind micro-targeting is to send different campaign ads or messages to different demographic groups of voters and potential voters. Suburban "soccer moms," for instance, would be targeted with ads different from those targeting rural "cowboy dads." Republican president George W. Bush is credited with successfully using micro-targeting in the 2000 and 2004 presidential elections. His campaign focused on wedge issues—issues where a voter's preferences diverge from those of his political party. By targeting such voters with messages focusing on Bush's position on the wedge issue, the campaign hoped to convince these voters to cast a ballot for Bush rather than for his opponent.[33]

Micro-targeting became more sophisticated during the 2008 presidential campaign as Democrats built an extensive organization to contact and turn out voters. The Obama campaign made use of an unprecedented volume of survey data, conducting thousands of short- and long-form random sample interviews each week to gauge voters' preferences. Statistical algorithms looked for patterns in these opinions and the many other data points the campaign had assembled for every voter based on massive state voter-registration files, consumer data warehouses, commercial data, and past campaign contacts. The campaign used this mountain of information to generate different, carefully targeted messages for different demographic, regional, and ideological groups to persuade them to turn out and vote for Obama.[34] It was the first time big data had been used to win a presidential election. Because of micro-targeting, millions of Americans heard from other Americans about issues that mattered the most to them. Virtually all campaigns for national and statewide offices make extensive use of random sample opinion polling (see Chapter 6). To be competitive, a candidate must use random sample public-opinion polls to gauge public support. Polls of likely voters are conducted throughout most political campaigns. These polls provide the basic information that candidates and their staff use to craft campaign messages and strategies—that is, to select issues, assess the candidates' strengths and weaknesses and those of the opposition, and measure voter responses to the campaign.

Once campaigns have identified specific groups of voters, they reach out via face-to-face contacts, phone calls, mailings, and social media to their target audiences for fundraising and voter mobilization. Personal contact has been found to be the most effective at mobilizing voters to turn out but requires field offices and volunteers. Staffs of paid or volunteer telephone callers, using computer-assisted dialing systems and prepared scripts, also place calls to deliver their candidate's message. The targeted groups are often those identified by polls as either uncommitted or weakly committed, but strong supporters of the candidate are also contacted and encouraged to vote and donate money to the campaign. Since 2008 the presidential campaigns of both parties have also placed millions of automated "robocalls" urging voters to support their candidates.

Since John Kennedy and Richard Nixon debated on live television in 1960 (left), presidential debates have been one of the most closely watched events in election campaigns. The intense, bitter debates in 2016 between Donald Trump and Hillary Clinton (right) drew the largest audience for presidential debates in American history.

Contemporary presidential campaigns gather large amounts of data on potential voters in order to effectively tailor campaign messages to specific demographics. Armed with these data, volunteers for both the Trump and Clinton campaigns made thousands and thousands of phone calls to urge individuals to support their candidate on Election Day in 2016.

Direct mail is another vehicle for communicating with voters. After obtaining the appropriate mailing lists, candidates usually send pamphlets, letters, and brochures describing themselves and their views to voters believed to be sympathetic. Often, the letters sent to voters are personalized: the recipient is addressed by name in the text, and the letter appears actually to have been signed by the candidate. In addition to its use as a political advertising medium, direct mail is an important source of campaign funds. Computerized mailing lists permit campaign strategists to pinpoint individuals whose interests, background, and activities suggest that they may be potential donors to the campaign.

"People power" remains critical in modern political campaigns. Research suggests that direct mail and robocalls are less effective than in-person and phone contacts.[35] Candidates continue to use the political services of tens of thousands of volunteers, especially for grassroots get-out-the-vote drives. Still, even the recruitment of campaign volunteers has become a job for electronic technology. Employing a technique called "instant organization," paid staff use phone banks to contact not only potential voters but also potential campaign workers in areas targeted by a computer. Volunteer workers are recruited from among those called.

Money and Politics

Describe how candidates raise the money they need to run

Although online fundraising has made raising money for campaigns more convenient, modern campaigns require a great deal of money. A 60-second spot on prime-time network television costs hundreds of thousands of dollars each time it is aired. Polling, social media campaigns, and data analytics can easily reach or exceed the six-figure mark. Campaign consultants can charge substantial fees.

FOR CRITICAL ANALYSIS

Do American political campaigns help voters make a decision? Or do they produce more confusion than enlightenment?

In the nineteenth century, labor-intensive campaigns allowed parties whose chief support came from groups nearer the bottom of the socioeconomic scale to use their numerical superiority as a partial counterweight to the institutional and economic resources more readily available to the opposition. As many as 2.5 million individuals worked on political campaigns during the 1880s.[36] The money-intensive campaign of the modern era, by contrast, has given a major boost to the political fortunes of candidates whose supporters are able to furnish the large sums now needed to compete effectively.[37]

Candidates with the most campaign dollars often win. In 2008 and 2012, Barack Obama raised more than his Republican opponents. In 2016, though Hillary Clinton spent more than her opponent, Donald Trump, she did not win. Nonetheless, the 2016 election shattered previous records. Combined spending by candidates, parties, and interest groups on the congressional and presidential races was $6.5 billion in 2016 compared with $6.2 billion in 2012 and $5.3 billion in 2008. Of the $6.5 billion, $4.3 billion was spent on congressional races and $2.6 billion on the presidential race.[38]

THE COURTS AND CAMPAIGN SPENDING

The United States is rare among democracies in allowing candidates to raise unlimited sums of money to spend on their campaigns with no time restrictions of when the money can be spent. In most democratic countries, publicly financed campaigns are the norm; in such a system, candidates or parties are provided with a set amount of money to spend by the government. In the United States, candidates may raise ever-increasing amounts of money from private individuals, corporations, and interest groups. Reformers have long been concerned about the potential for corruption that exists when candidates are actively soliciting private interests for funding campaigns. In an attempt to limit the influence of money in politics, the federal government has adopted a number of laws to limit and regulate contributions to political campaigns. But two Supreme Court decisions adopted over a 40-year period have dismantled most of these restrictions on money in politics.

The first, *Buckley v. Valeo* (1976), was a landmark Supreme Court case that struck down several provisions of the Federal Election Campaign Act of 1974, including limits on candidate spending, use of personal funds, and independent expenditures. (Independent expenditures are sums of money spent to influence a campaign, but the donating organization is not allowed to coordinate with a candidate's official campaign.) The decision introduced the idea that money (in this case, campaign contributions) counts as "speech" under the First Amendment and that candidates could spend unlimited amounts of their own money on their own campaign. However, the Court left intact the provision of the law that sets limits on individuals' campaign contributions.[39]

In 2010 the U.S. Supreme Court ruled in *Citizens United v. Federal Election Commission* that the government could not restrict independent expenditures by corporations or unions in support of candidates.[40] The Court said restrictions on independent expenditures violated the First Amendment. With this decision, the United States entered a new era of campaign finance in which corporations and unions can spend unlimited sums. Following the *Citizens United* decision, *SpeechNow v. FEC* allowed wealthy individuals and organizations to form

Recently courts have ruled that campaign contributions are a form of speech and, for the most part, cannot be restricted. However, many people worry that these decisions reinforce the influence of the very affluent in American politics at the expense of everyone else.

committees, called Super PACs, which can raise unlimited amounts of money to run advertising for and against candidates so long as their efforts are not coordinated with those of the candidates.[41] These groups can spend unlimited amounts for or against candidates, but they cannot contribute directly to their campaign. This resulted in a significant increase in campaign spending in the 2010 midterm election and unprecedented spending in the 2012 and 2016 presidential elections.

FOR CRITICAL ANALYSIS

What purpose do limits on monetary contributions to political campaigns serve? Should there be limits? How do monetary contributions affect the outcomes of elections?

As the Court struggles to balance free speech with preventing political corruption, the sum of these three court decisions tips the scale in favor of speech. Opponents raise concerns that unlimited spending by wealthy donors, corporations, and other organizations could worsen existing corruption in American politics. This concern is bolstered by a number of new studies finding that members of Congress make decisions that represent the interests of wealthy campaign donors, not average voters.[42]

SOURCES OF CAMPAIGN FUNDS

Although restrictions remain on how money is raised and spent on elections, there is today a great deal of latitude on where money comes from and what it is used for. Campaigns have at least six potential sources of funds.

Individual Donors Politicians spend a great deal of time asking people for money. Money is solicited via direct mail, through the internet, over the phone, and in numerous face-to-face meetings. Under federal law, individuals may donate as much as $2,700 per candidate per election, $5,000 per federal PAC per calendar year,

AMERICA SIDE by SIDE

Campaign Laws in Comparison

Electoral campaigns are more expensive in the United States than in any other country, with only India approaching the same amount of spending.[a] Both the United States and India are large federal countries, so spending is high partly because these countries have multiple levels of government to elect. India's population, however, is approximately four times the U.S. population, so the United States still spends significantly more per voter. Critics have argued that the amount of money in these campaigns creates an unfair advantage for certain candidates, increases the importance and influence of large campaign donors, and potentially undermines the quality of democracy.

Some countries have rules that limit campaign contributions or campaign spending. The United States has extensive rules regarding campaign contributions for candidates, but has few spending limits. The United Kingdom, in contrast, does not limit contributions but has strict rules on campaign spending. Some countries also allow qualified parties and/or candidates free or subsidized access to media, which reduces the need to raise huge sums.

However, a considerable amount of campaign spending is determined by the nature of the election. Norway bans political advertising on television and the radio and campaigns run for two weeks. Even though Norway sets no restrictions on campaign spending or fundraising, roughly 74.4 percent comes from public funds.[b]

	UNITED STATES	INDIA	UNITED KINGDOM	NORWAY
Campaign spending in a recent election (in U.S. dollars)	$6.5 billion (2016)	Roughly $5 billion (2014)	$55.7 million (2017)	Roughly $6.5 million (2013)
Length of national election	Unlimited	2+ weeks*	One month	2 weeks
Are public funds available?	Only for presidential candidates (federal funds)	No	Yes	Yes
Is media access free or subsidized?	No	Yes (for parties, not candidates)	Yes (for parties, not candidates)	No
Bans on television advertising?	No	No	No	Yes
Approximate spending per voter (in U.S. dollars)	$25.97	$6.35	$1.09	$1.76

*While the Electoral Commission of India lists the official campaign as only two weeks, (http://eci.nic.in/eci_main1/the_function.aspx#campaign) with all campaigning required to end the day before the election, polling took 5 weeks in 2014, as different regions of the country were scheduled to go to the polls on different days.

SOURCES: Campaign Laws from The International Institute for Democracy and Electoral Assistance Political Finance Database, www.idea.int (accessed 4/15/18); Christopher Ingraham, "Somebody Just Put a Price Tag on the 2016 Election. It's a Doozy," *Washington Post*, April 14, 2017, www.washingtonpost.com (accessed 4/15/18); The UK Electoral Commission, "Political Party Spending at Previous Elections," 2018, www.electoralcommission.org.uk (accessed 4/15/18); and "International Campaign Finance," CNN World, reporting of the 2013 election campaign contributions from Statistics Norway, www.ssb.no (accessed 4/30/16).

[a] Sruthi Gottipati and Rajesh Kumar Singh. "India Set to Challenge U.S. for Election-Spending Record," Reuters, March 9, 2014, www.reuters.com/article/2014/03/09/us-india-election-spending-idUSBREA280AR20140309#XxEPYA752ikcQRB5.97 (accessed 4/15/18).

[b] Office for Democratic Institutions and Human Rights, "Election Expert Team Report: Norway Parliamentary Elections 11 September 2017," p. 7, December 4, 2017. www.osce.org/odihr/elections/norway/360336?download=true (accessed 4/15/18).

$33,400 per national party committee per calendar year, and $10,000 to state and local committees per calendar year. (There is no limit to the number of candidates or PACs that an individual can give to, however—a result of the Supreme Court's decision in *McCutcheon et al. v. Federal Election Commission*.[43]) Bernie Sanders's 2016 presidential campaign raised an unprecedented $231 million in individual contributions, 58 percent of which was made up of small contributions under $200.[44] The "Who Participates?" feature at the end of this chapter looks at the characteristics of donors to political campaigns.

political action committee (PAC) a private group that raises and distributes funds for use in election campaigns

Political Action Committees **Political Action Committees (PACs)** are organizations established by corporations, labor unions, or interest or advocacy groups to channel the contributions of their members and employees into political campaigns. Under the terms of the 1971 Federal Election Campaign Act, which governs campaign finance in the United States, PACs are permitted to make larger contributions to any given candidate than individuals are allowed to make. Moreover, allied or related PACs often coordinate their campaign contributions, greatly increasing the amount of money a candidate actually receives from the same interest group. More than 4,600 PACs are registered with the Federal Election Commission, which oversees campaign finance practices in the United States. Nearly two-thirds of all PACs represent corporations, trade associations, and other business and professional groups. Many congressional and party leaders have established PACs, known as "leadership PACs," to provide funding for their political allies.

Soft Money Before 2002 most campaign dollars took the form of "soft money," unregulated contributions to the national parties nominally to assist in party building, voter registration efforts, and voter mobilization rather than for particular campaigns. Federal campaign finance legislation crafted by Senators John McCain and Russell Feingold and enacted in 2002 sought to ban soft money by prohibiting the national parties from receiving contributions from corporations, unions, or individuals and preventing them from directing such funds to their affiliated state parties. However, it did not reduce the overall importance of money in politics. Under federal rules, a national political party committee may make unlimited "independent expenditures" advocating support for its own presidential candidate or defeating an opposing party's candidate as long as these expenditures are not coordinated with the candidate's own campaign.

527 committee (Super PAC) a nonprofit independent political action committee that may raise unlimited sums of money from corporations, unions, and individuals but is not permitted to contribute to or coordinate directly with parties or candidates

501(c)(4) committees (dark money) politically active nonprofits; under federal law, these nonprofits can spend unlimited amounts on political campaigns and not disclose their donors as long as their activities are not coordinated with the candidate campaigns and political activities are not their primary purpose

Outside Spending: Super PACs and Dark Money **527 committees (Super PACs)** and **501(c)(4) committees (dark money)** are independent groups that are currently not covered by the campaign spending restrictions imposed in 2002 by the Bipartisan Campaign Reform Act, but now raise much of the money used for political campaigns. These groups, named for the sections of the tax code under which they are organized, can raise and spend unlimited amounts as long as their efforts are not coordinated with those of any candidate's campaign. As a result, each presidential campaign raises millions from sympathetic outside groups. A 527 is a group established specifically for the purpose of political advocacy and is required to report to the IRS. A 501(c)(4) is a nonprofit group that also engages in campaign advocacy but may not spend more than half its revenue for political purposes. Unlike a 527, a 501(c)(4) is not required to disclose where it gets its funds or exactly what it does with them—as a result, its funding has earned the name "dark money" and has raised growing concern that the lack of transparency in campaign funding threatens fair elections. Indeed, it has become a common practice for wealthy and corporate donors, as well as foreigners, to route campaign contributions through 501(c)(4)s to avoid the legal limits on contributions through other channels.

Outside spending via Super PACs and dark money (527s and 501(c)(4)s) played an unprecedented role in the 2012 and 2016 presidential races and 2018 midterm elections as outside groups ran extensive television and online ads. Super PACs on both sides relied on very large contributions. A growing concern is that elections in the United States can be bought with big money from corporations and wealthy donors, who will then hold significant influence when that candidate is elected. Political corruption and undue influence from Wall Street were recurring themes among the 2016 presidential candidates. But 2016 was characterized by lopsided campaign spending: Clinton raised and spent double that of the Trump campaign. By October 2016, Clinton had raised nearly $500 million, with an additional $189 million from outside money (Super PACs) compared to just $247 million raised by Trump, with another $59 million from outside money.

Public Funding The Federal Election Campaign Act also provides for public funding of presidential campaigns, as discussed earlier. Candidates running as a major party in the presidential primaries are eligible for public funds by raising at least $5,000 in individual contributions of $250 or less in each of 20 states. Candidates who reach this threshold may apply for federal funds to match, on a dollar-for-dollar basis, all contributions of $250 or less. But by accepting matching funds they agree to spend no more than $48.07 million in their presidential primary campaigns, including limits on using their personal funds and funds from private donors.

Under current law, no candidate is required to accept public funding for either the nominating races or the general presidential election. Candidates who do not accept public funding are not affected by any expenditure limits. In 2008, John McCain accepted public funding for the general election campaign, receiving $84 million, but Barack Obama declined, choosing to rely on his own fundraising prowess. Obama was ultimately able to outspend McCain by a wide margin. Neither major-party candidate accepted public financing in 2012 or 2016. As a result, many observers believed that the 2008 race was the last time that a major-party candidate would forgo personal fundraising in favor of public funding. The United States is unique from most other democratic countries, which rely on public funding for political campaigns to prevent corruption.

Unlimited Spending by Candidates of Their Own Money On the basis of the Supreme Court's 1976 decision in *Buckley v. Valeo*, the right of individuals to spend their *own* money to campaign for office is a constitutionally protected matter of free speech and is not subject to limitation.[45] Thus, extremely wealthy candidates often contribute millions of dollars to their own campaigns; Donald Trump, for example, spent millions of his own money on his 2016 campaign, as did Ross Perot in 1992 and 1996.

How Voters Decide

Identify the major factors that influence voters' decisions

Even if well-funded groups and powerful individuals influence the electoral process, it is the millions of individual decisions on Election Day that ultimately determine electoral outcomes. Sooner or later the choices of voters weigh more heavily than the schemes of campaign advisers or the leverage of interest groups. Three factors influence voters' decisions at the polls: partisan loyalty, issues and policy preferences, and candidate characteristics.

PARTISAN LOYALTY

Most voters feel a certain sense of identification or kinship with the Democratic Party or the Republican Party. This sense of identification is often handed down from parents to children and reinforced by social and cultural ties (see Chapter 9). Partisan identification predisposes voters to favor their party's candidates and oppose those of the other party (see Figure 10.3). At the level of the presidential contest, issues and candidate personalities may become very important. But partisanship is more likely to assert itself in the less visible races, where issues and the candidates are not as well known. State legislative races, for example, are often decided by voters' partisanship.

Once formed, voters' partisan loyalties seldom change. Individuals tend to keep their party affiliations unless some crisis causes them to reexamine the bases of their loyalties and to conclude that they have not given their support to the appropriate party. During these relatively infrequent periods of electoral change, millions of voters can change their party ties. For example, at the beginning of the New Deal era, between 1932 and 1936, millions of former Republicans transferred their allegiance to Franklin Roosevelt and the Democrats.

FIGURE 10.3

The Effect of Party Identification on the Vote, 2016

In 2016 around 90 percent of Democrats and Republicans supported their party's presidential candidate. Should candidates devote their resources to converting voters who identify with the opposition or to winning more support among independents? What factors might make it difficult for candidates to simultaneously pursue both courses of action?

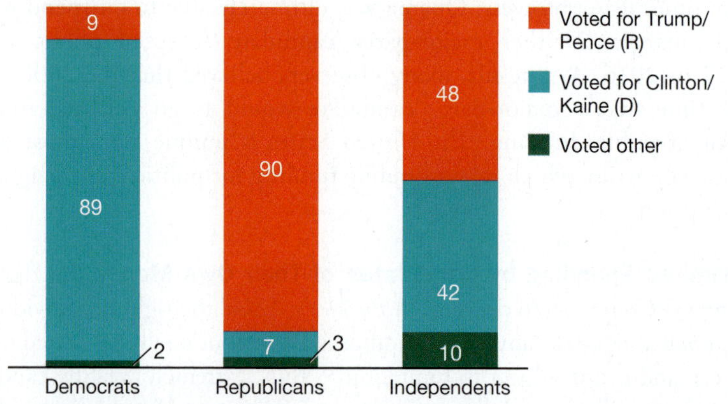

ISSUES AND POLICY PREFERENCES

Policy preferences are a second factor influencing voters' choices at the polls. Voters may cast their ballots for the candidate whose position on economic issues they believe to be closest to their own or the candidate who has what they believe to be the best record on foreign policy or immigration. Though candidates for the presidency or Congress are often held accountable for the economy, other policy issues vary in importance depending on the election. In 2008, for example, Obama made ending the war in Iraq and providing national health care for all Americans his core issues. In 2016, Donald Trump made curbing immigration and building a wall along the U.S.–Mexico border a key issue in his campaign for the presidency. If candidates articulate and publicize very different positions on important policy issues, voters are more likely to be able to identify and act on whatever policy preferences they may have. The ability of voters to make choices on the basis of policy preferences is diminished, however, if voters are uninformed or misinformed about the issues and candidates. Voters' issue choices usually involve a mix of their judgments about the past behavior of competing parties and candidates and their hopes and fears about candidates' future behavior. Political scientists call choices that focus on future behavior **prospective voting**, whereas those based on past performance are called **retrospective voting**. Retrospective economic voting, in which voters evaluate candidates on the strength of the economy, has been found to be more important than prospective voting.

prospective voting voting based on the imagined future performance of a candidate or political party

retrospective voting voting based on the past performance of a candidate or political party

To some extent, whether prospective or retrospective evaluation is more important in a particular election depends on the strategies of competing candidates. Candidates always endeavor to define the issues of an election in terms that will serve their interests. Incumbents running during a period of prosperity will seek to take credit for the economy's strength and will define the election as revolving around their record of success. This strategy encourages voters to make retrospective judgments. By contrast, an insurgent running during a period of economic uncertainty will tell voters it is time for a change and ask them to make prospective judgments. Donald Trump focused on change in 2016 and "making America great again" and, through well-crafted media campaigns, was able to define voters' agenda of choices.

The Economy As we identify the strategies and tactics employed by opposing political candidates and parties, we should keep in mind that the best-laid plans of politicians often go awry. Election outcomes are affected by a variety of forces that candidates for office cannot fully control. Among the most important of these forces is the condition of the economy. If voters are satisfied with their economic conditions, they tend to support the party in power, while concern about the economy tends to favor the opposition. Thus, the 2008 financial crisis gave Barack Obama and the Democrats a significant advantage. Over the past quarter-century, the Consumer Confidence Index, calculated by the Conference Board, a business research group, has been a fairly accurate predictor of presidential outcomes. The index is based on surveys asking voters how optimistic they are about the future of the economy. It would appear that a generally rosy view, indicated by a score over 100, bodes well for the party in power. An index score under 100, indicating that voters are pessimistic about the economy's trend, suggests that incumbents should worry about their own job prospects (see Figure 10.4). In recent presidential elections personal economic conditions were an important factor in explaining voter decisions in the election.

FIGURE 10.4

Consumer Confidence and Presidential Elections

Since 1968 the Consumer Confidence Index has been a fairly reliable predictor of incumbents' political fortunes. Was the result of the 2016 election consistent with this trend? What issues other than the economy influenced the 2016 election?

*Survey was bimonthly prior to 1977 so figures for 1968, 1972, and 1976 are for October and they are for September from 1983 on.
**Gore and Clinton won the popular vote, but Bush and Trump were elected by the electoral college.

NOTE: A score above 100 means most people are optimistic about the economy. A score below 100 means most people are pessimistic about the economy. The candidate who won the election appears in bold.

SOURCE: The Conference Board, www.conference-board.org/data/consumerdata.cfm (accessed 10/25/16).

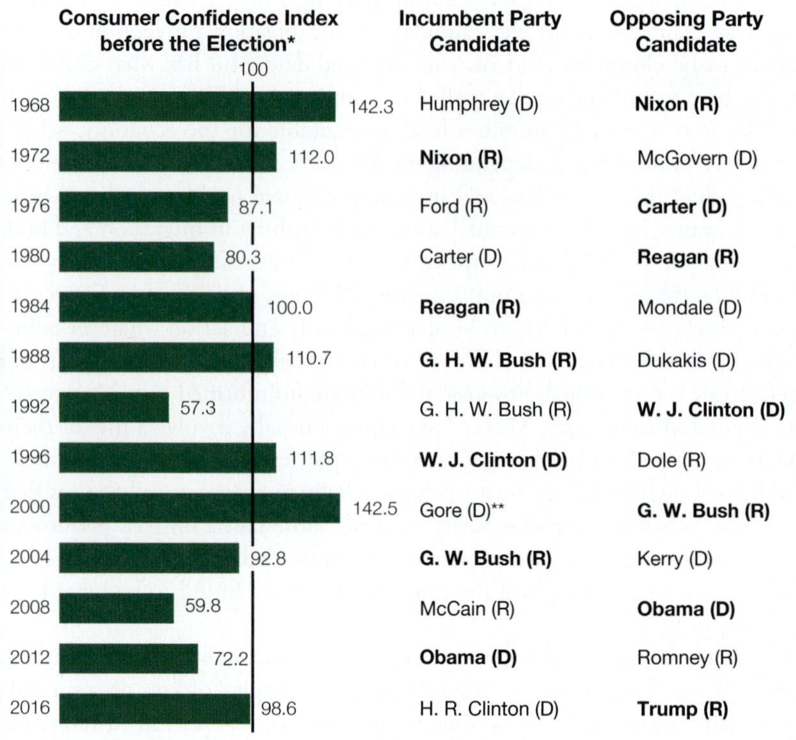

CANDIDATE CHARACTERISTICS

Candidates' personal attributes can influence voters' decisions. The more important candidate characteristics that affect voters' choices are race, ethnicity, religion, gender, geography, and socio-economic background. In general, voters may be proud to see someone of their gender or of their ethnic, religious, or geographic background in a position of leadership. They may presume that such candidates are likely to have views and perspectives close to their own. This is why politicians often seek to "balance the ticket," by making certain that their party's ticket included members of as many important groups as possible.

Just as candidates' personal characteristics may attract some voters, they may repel others. Some voters are prejudiced against candidates from certain ethnic, racial, or religious groups. And for many years, voters were reluctant to support the candidacies of women, although this is slowly changing. Indeed, the fact that the 2008 Democratic candidate was an African American man and the 2016 Democratic candidate a woman indicates the increasing diversity of candidates for public office.

FOR CRITICAL ANALYSIS

What factors influence voters' choices? What factors matter most to you when you decide how to cast your ballot?

Voters also pay attention to candidates' personality characteristics, such as "decisiveness," "honesty," and "vigor." In recent years, integrity has become a key election issue. In the 2016 presidential election many Americans questioned the trustworthiness of both Hillary Clinton and Donald Trump. Nonetheless, Trump supporters saw their candidate as unafraid to speak his mind. Clinton supporters, on the other hand, admired her ambition, toughness, and discipline.

The 2016 and 2018 Elections

Analyze the strategies, issues, and outcomes of the 2016 and 2018 elections

In 2016, Democrat Hillary Clinton faced Republican Donald Trump in a dramatic and bitterly fought presidential race. Despite media predictions of Democratic success, Trump won a surprise victory with a majority of votes in the electoral college, though Clinton won the popular vote, receiving 2.9 million more votes than Trump. The GOP also retained control of both houses of Congress. In the 2018 midterm elections, Democrats won control of the House of Representatives for the first time since 2010. Republicans, however, were able to expand their majority in the U.S. Senate.

In this section, we analyze how the 2016 and 2018 races unfolded and the major factors that contributed to the results. We conclude by considering what these elections might mean for the future of American government and politics.

THE 2016 PRESIDENTIAL NOMINATION

As we saw in Chapter 9, over the past 50 years America's two major political parties have experienced an ideological realignment that has made both parties more ideologically homogeneous. Today, the Republican Party is the party of conservatives, while the Democratic Party is the political home of those who view themselves as politically liberal. Within each party, though, there are some differences of political perspective. The Democratic camp includes different varieties of liberal opinion ranging from traditional social welfare liberalism, which traces its roots to the New Deal, to left-liberal progressivism, which envisions a substantially expanded role for the federal government. The Republican camp includes many shades of conservative opinion, ranging from business conservatives who support reducing government regulation and taxes, to social conservatives who oppose abortion and same-sex marriage. In 2016 each party's nomination was sharply contested by candidates representing different factions within the two parties as well as by "outsider" populist candidates.

The Democratic Primaries On the Democratic side, Hillary Clinton faced a serious challenge from Vermont senator Bernie Sanders, a left-liberal progressive and self-described Democratic Socialist. Though Clinton's experience, control of the party machinery, support in minority communities, and fund-raising prowess seemed to make her nomination a foregone conclusion, Sanders mounted an aggressive candidacy that gained momentum in large part through mobilizing young voters. Sanders's populist platform—which, to some, contained bold new ideas such as free college education—called for a political revolution to counter political corruption, corporate influence, and inequality. Though outmatched in money and organization, Sanders proved a tenacious competitor. He was widely seen as more trustworthy and "authentic" than Clinton, especially by young Americans. Ultimately, Sanders won 43 percent of the Democratic primary vote and carried 23 states and territories compared to Clinton's 34.

The 2016 Democratic National Convention exposed conflicts within the Democratic Party. While Hillary Clinton was ultimately nominated, Senator Bernie Sanders attracted many supporters.

The Republican Primaries On the Republican side, the 2016 presidential nomination battle also revealed deep divisions within the party. Seventeen candidates competed in the Republican primaries, including "establishment" candidates such as Jeb Bush and Marco Rubio, libertarian Rand Paul, and social conservatives like Ted Cruz. Real estate mogul and reality-TV star Donald Trump was an "outsider" populist candidate, claiming to represent the interests of ordinary Americans rather than elites. His platform included the enactment of harsher immigration laws, the repeal of Obamacare, the appointment of more conservative judges to the federal courts, an end to environmental and other regulations that increased manufacturing costs in the United States, and changes to international economic agreements to better serve American interests. With slogans like "Make America Great Again" and "America First," Trump's stances more closely mirrored those of European nationalist and radical right populist candidates than the views of mainstream conservatives in the United States.

In the early weeks of the Republican race, Donald Trump was not taken seriously as a presidential candidate by most pundits and party leaders. During the Republican primaries, however, Trump campaigned cleverly, making use of huge noisy rallies, social media (especially Twitter and Facebook), and the propensity of the broadcast media to focus on sound bites and sensationalism. At the first televised Republican presidential primary debate in August 2015, Trump sought to drive the agenda by insulting his rivals and making bold, outlandish, and even false political claims that served to make his opponents' carefully developed talking points seem pale and boring. Throughout the course of his campaign, Trump continued to command headlines with controversial and incendiary comments, including his assertions that he would build a wall along the U.S.–Mexico border and place a temporary ban on Muslim immigration to the United States. As Trump's provocative statements dominated the news media for much of the primary season, other Republican candidates dropped from the race.

THE GENERAL ELECTION

With their parties' nominations in hand, Clinton and Trump faced one another in the general election. Clinton seemed to possess several advantages, especially her experience in public office and the Democrats' seeming advantage in the electoral college. Based on voting patterns in recent elections, states with a total of roughly 217 electoral votes were considered "blue states," either safely Democratic or favorable to the Democrats. States with another 32 electoral votes leaned toward the Democrats, potentially putting the Democratic candidate within 21 of the 270 votes needed to win. The Republicans, by contrast, could generally only count on around 191 electoral votes from reliably "red" states.

Democratic candidates, moreover, usually receive support from the most rapidly growing segments of the electorate—namely, minority voters—along with women and young people. Republicans, on the other hand, rely primarily on the votes of white Americans, especially men, who represent a declining fraction of the electorate. As recently as 1976, 89 percent of the electorate was white, while in 2016 only about 69 percent was white non-Hispanic.[46] Clinton also entered

Donald Trump's provocative campaign rhetoric, including a promise to build a wall at the U.S.–Mexico border, helped energize supporters and generate media coverage.

the race with an enormous fund-raising edge over Trump. This ultimately allowed the former secretary of state to spend more than twice as much as her rival.

The Trump campaign was confident it could overcome the Democrats' advantages. Trump believed his appeal to blue-collar white voters, especially men, would make him competitive in Democratic strongholds in Midwestern states. He also calculated that he would increase Republican support among white voters sufficiently to offset the Democratic edge among nonwhite voters. Moreover, Trump hoped that his provocative style would continue to encourage extensive free media coverage, offsetting Clinton's fund-raising advantage and ability to spend freely on paid campaign ads.

Early in the general-election race, several trends emerged. First, Clinton and Trump were the two most disliked presidential nominees in modern American history. Both candidates had far lower favorability ratings than past presidential candidates, and as scandals raged on throughout the general-election campaign, many Americans reported that the election left them feeling "disgusted."[47]

Second, gender played a significant, though ultimately not decisive, role in 2016. Not only did this election see the first female presidential candidate representing a major party, but gender issues were also headline news throughout much of the election. Donald Trump made comments about women that many people deemed offensive and similar past comments of his were unearthed (discussed below). The Trump campaign countered that Clinton's husband had also treated women inappropriately. Nonetheless, by November, exit polls showed a gender gap of 13 percentage points, with 54 percent of women supporting Clinton compared with 41 percent of men.

Third, the media played an outsized role in 2016. Many observers, including President Obama, criticized the media for focusing excessively on Trump, with the goal of making headlines and viral news. In the general election, Trump received more than double Clinton's free media attention.[48] He excelled on the campaign trail, tweeting his daily campaign messages and effectively writing his own headline news. At the same time, some people, including Trump himself, believed that the news media's political bias favored Clinton. Trump began declaring that the mainstream media published and broadcast "fake news" and should be ignored.

And fourth, money mattered—and it didn't. Clinton raised and spent twice as much as the Trump campaign and had superior organization, with more field offices than Trump in almost every state. However, Trump's enormous free media coverage (estimated to be worth as much as $2 billion) more than offset Clinton's financial edge. Almost every morning, a new and ever more outrageous Trump tweet or Facebook post would dominate the news, leaving little space for Clinton to set the media agenda.

Personal Attacks, Scandal, and Campaign Strategy From the earliest years of the Republic, personal attacks have been an important weapon in the arsenals of competing political forces, but the 2016 campaign seemed to many observers to represent a new phase in aggressive mudslinging.

Leading up to the presidential election, Republicans in 2015 launched a congressional investigation of Hillary Clinton's role in the deaths of U.S. embassy officials in Benghazi, Libya, and another investigation of Clinton's use of a private email server to handle official State Department correspondence during her tenure as secretary of state. Democrats charged that the primary purpose of these investigations was to damage Clinton's reputation as the presumptive 2016 Democratic presidential nominee. While the investigations did not lead to formal charges against Clinton, they served to convince many Americans that the former secretary of state was dishonest and untrustworthy. During the course of the race, WikiLeaks made available a large quantity of Democratic National Committee emails and stolen emails from Clinton's campaign director, John Podesta. The emails revealed Clinton said different things in public and private, which, to some, showed she was disconnected from ordinary Americans. Democrats disputed the content of the leaks and suggested that WikiLeaks had been given its information by the Russian government, which had launched hacks as part of an effort to influence the American election—a claim later proved to be true.

For their part, Democratic opposition researchers had begun to develop a dossier on Trump as soon as he emerged as a potential GOP candidate. Democrats focused on his many controversial remarks—such as his comments about women and statements blaming undocumented immigrants for drugs, rape, and other crime—labeling them as offensive and Trump as xenophobic, racist, and sexist. On October 7, 2016, with one month before the November election, the *Washington Post* released a video from 2005 that contained audio of Trump making lewd comments about women and boasting about how his celebrity status gave him license to touch women inappropriately—comments that many people felt condoned sexual assault. The release of the tape was followed by allegations from more than a dozen women who reported having experienced unwanted sexual advances by Trump or who accused the candidate of sexual assault. Most of these accounts concerned events that had taken place some years in the past, and Trump contested their veracity. However, an increasingly unflattering image of Trump emerged. The recording, which Trump could not dispute, created explosive negative media coverage and a sharp drop in his polling numbers. Following these revelations, by mid-October most polls showed Clinton with a strong lead over Trump.

In October 2016 the *Washington Post* released a 2005 video in which Donald Trump was heard bragging that his fame gave him license to touch women inappropriately. After the video was released, multiple women—including Karena Virginia (right)—came forward to accuse Trump of sexual assault or unwanted sexual contact.

Two groups that were crucial to Trump's success were men and white working-class voters. White working-class voters in particular were unhappy with the economy and turned to Trump to bring factory jobs back to the United States. Here, Trump supporters celebrate his victory on election night.

Eleven days before the election, however, scandal and personal attacks turned back on Clinton. FBI director James Comey sent a letter to Congress saying his agency was investigating 650,000 newly discovered emails that could be pertinent to their earlier investigation of Clinton's use of a private email server during her time as secretary of state. The letter effectively reopened the investigation of Clinton's mishandling of email communications and the possibility of a national security breach, and the Trump campaign capitalized on the announcement as further proof of Clinton's alleged corruption. Two days before the election, Comey announced that the emails in fact did not support new charges; and as Americans went to the polls, most analysts gave Clinton a 70 to 80 percent chance of winning.

UNDERSTANDING THE 2016 RESULTS

In the end, the 2016 presidential election was a historic upset in which the national media and the polling forecasts were mistaken. On election night, the forecasts swung wildly, from the earlier predictions of a safe Clinton victory to reports indicating a Trump victory by wide margins. Many Americans who had been following the opinion polls and media analyses before the election were stunned by Trump's surprise win and by the Republicans' success in retaining control of both houses of Congress.

Trump swept every southern state and nearly all of the Midwest. He won most of the 15 battleground states that were considered competitive in the 2016 election, including the battleground states of Florida and Ohio. Trump's unexpected success in the northern industrial states of Michigan, Wisconsin, and Pennsylvania—all of which had gone to Obama in 2012—ultimately tipped the balance, leading to his victory in the electoral college (see Figure 10.5 and the "Who Are Americans?" feature). For only the fourth time in U.S. history the candidate who won a majority in the electoral college did not win the popular vote. Republicans also retained control of both houses of Congress as well as a majority of the state legislatures.

FOR CRITICAL ANALYSIS

In 2016 more Americans chose Hillary Clinton for president, but Donald Trump won the electoral college and thus the presidency. Should the electoral college system be replaced?

FIGURE 10.5

Distribution of Electoral Votes in the 2016 Election

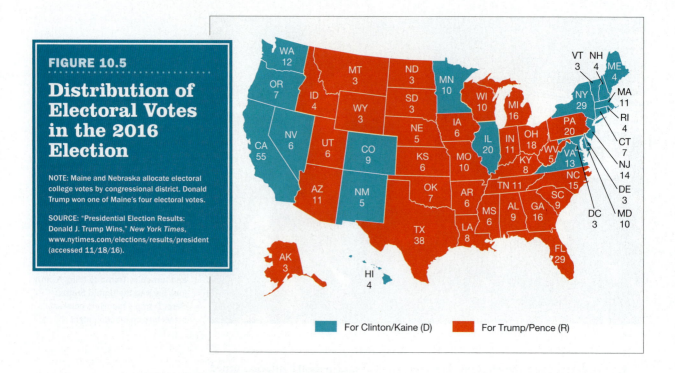

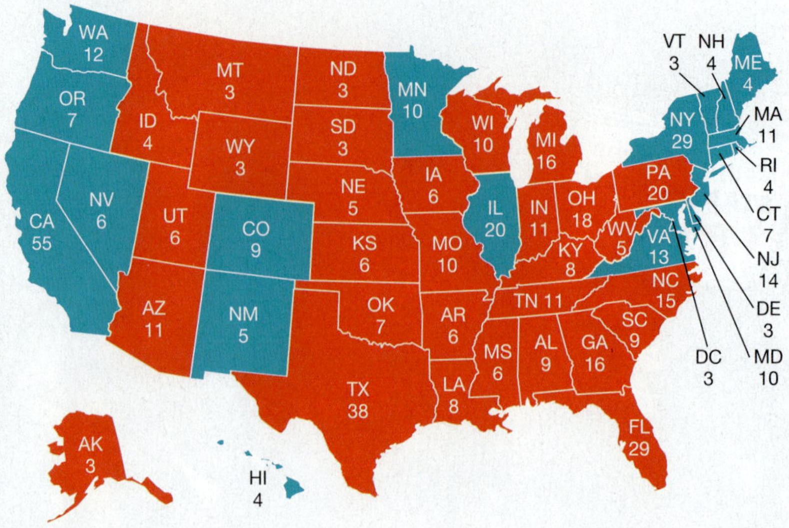

NOTE: Maine and Nebraska allocate electoral college votes by congressional district. Donald Trump won one of Maine's four electoral votes.

SOURCE: "Presidential Election Results: Donald J. Trump Wins," *New York Times*, www.nytimes.com/elections/results/president (accessed 11/18/16).

Voters' Choices Trump's popularity among working-class white Americans, especially white men, was crucial to his winning coalition. This demographic group had the most negative views of the economy and was generally opposed to the trade policies favored by the Democrats and mainstream conservatives. They looked to Trump to bring back factory jobs that had moved overseas and saw Clinton as representing Wall Street, government, and—as one Trump ad put it—"more of the same." According to exit polls, Trump won 67 percent of the votes among whites without a college degree compared to just 28 percent for Clinton—a 14 percentage point gain for Trump compared with the Republican vote from this group in 2012. This support enabled Trump to build a winning coalition that also included traditional Republican partisans. He won 90 percent of the votes among registered Republicans, 81 percent of the vote among ideological conservatives, and 81 percent among white born-again or evangelical Christians. The exit polls revealed that Trump also earned more of the votes among men, white voters in general, and voters over age 45. Among respondents who felt the country was "seriously off track," Trump won almost 70 percent of their votes.[49]

Among those who felt the country was generally going in the right direction, Hillary Clinton won 90 percent support. Clinton also received a majority of votes from women, African Americans, Latinos, Asian Americans, and college-educated voters, although blacks and Latinos voted at slightly lower rates for Clinton than they had for Obama four years earlier. She won 71 percent of the votes of minority college graduates and 75 percent among minorities without a college degree. Young voters favored Clinton (55 percent compared to only 37 percent for Trump), but high youth support for third-party candidates (10 percent, up from 3 percent in 2012) meant lower support for the Democratic candidate. In the swing states of

Who Supported Trump in 2016?

Donald Trump won enough votes in the electoral college to defeat Hillary Clinton in the 2016 presidential election, though he lost the popular vote. The map in Figure 10.5, to the left, shows who won each state; there, red clearly dominates. If we adjust the map to show each state in proportion to its population (below), red states still dominate, but there is more blue on the map, reflecting the fairly tight race.

Election Results by State's Population

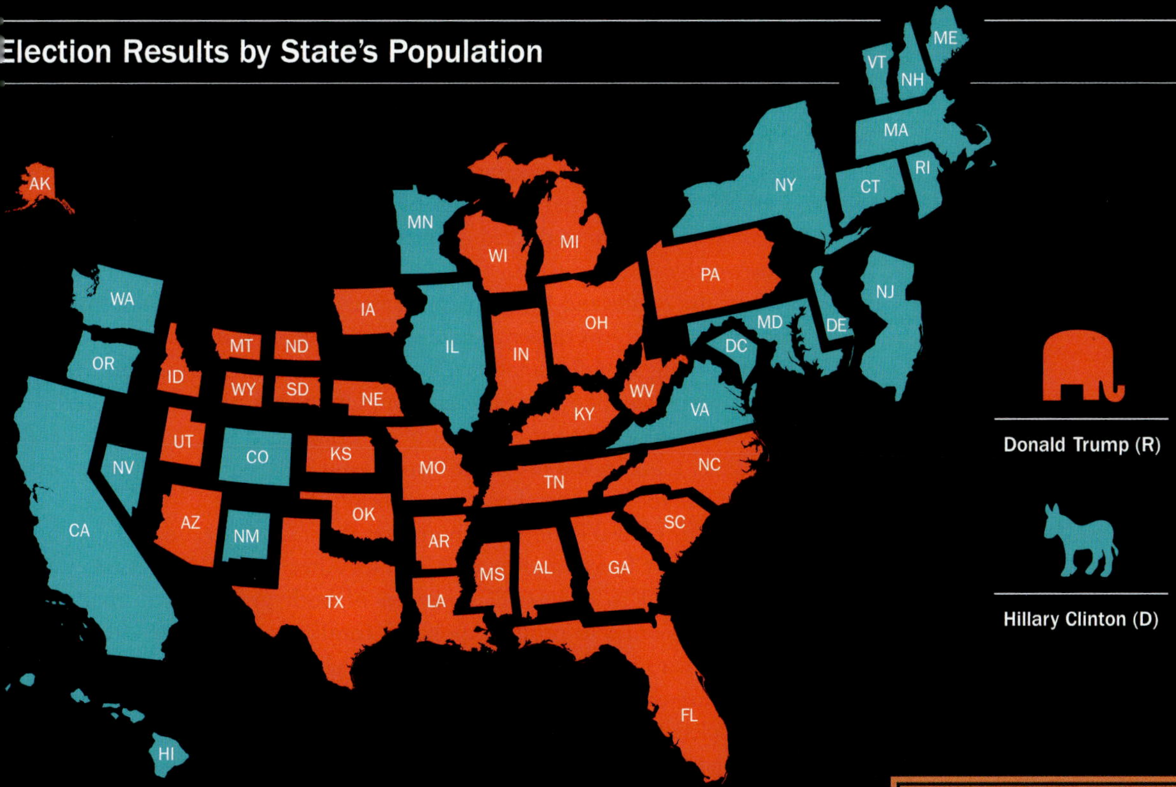

Votes in Electoral College

55	California	10	Maryland	06	Utah
38	Texas	10	Minnesota	05	New Mexico
29	Florida	10	Wisconsin	05	Nebraska
29	New York	10	Missouri	05	West Virginia
20	Illinois	09	Colorado	04	Hawaii
20	Pennsylvania	09	Alabama	03 / 01	Maine
18	Ohio	09	South Carolina	04	New Hampshire
16	Michigan	08	Louisiana	04	Rhode Island
16	Georgia	08	Kentucky	04	Idaho
15	North Carolina	07	Connecticut	03	Delaware
14	New Jersey	07	Oregon	03	District Of Columbia
13	Virginia	07	Oklahoma	03	Vermont
12	Washington	06	Iowa	03	Alaska
11	Massachusetts	06	Nevada	03	Montana
11	Indiana	06	Arkansas	03	North Dakota
11	Arizona	06	Kansas	03	South Dakota
11	Tennessee	06	Mississippi	03	Wyoming

FOR CRITICAL ANALYSIS

1. Clinton won three of the five states with the largest populations: California, New York, and Illinois. How are these states different from states with smaller populations? What do these differences tell us about the political differences between more densely populated areas (urban areas) and those with lower populations (rural areas)?
2. What do you think causes the differences between urban and rural America? Do you think these differences will continue long into the future?

Michigan, Pennsylvania, and Wisconsin, votes for third-party candidates may have cost Clinton those very close races. To many Americans Trump seemed authentic—a candidate with a bold vision he was not afraid to assert. He seemed to represent Americans who felt disenfranchised and left behind by the social and economic changes buffeting the nation.

Russian Interference Soon after the conclusion of the campaign, Democrats charged that Trump had been helped by Russian hacking of the Democratic National Committee and Clinton emails and "trolls" mounting a social media campaign aimed at defeating Clinton. Multiple reports from the national intelligence agencies confirmed the Russian government did seek to intervene in the 2016 election. For example, in October 2018, Twitter released millions of tweets from some 3,400 accounts linked to a Russian "troll farm" known as the Internet Research Agency run by the Kremlin.[50] At this agency, approximately 1,000 Russian agents, working 24 hours a day, spent more than a million dollars a week creating thousands of social media accounts impersonating Americans. These agents also purchased thousands of political ads promoting their posts on Facebook and other platforms. Russian groups also organized campaign rallies in the United States on behalf of Donald Trump and sought to discredit Hillary Clinton, portraying her as a criminal and untrustworthy.

Analysis of the tweets and Facebook posts emanating from Russian sources suggests that the Russian government's main goal was to sow discord in the United States by promoting an inflammatory discourse on such matters as race, religion, gun control, and police shootings of black men. Often troll farm agents would tweet on both sides of the issue to stir up trouble. Beginning in 2015 when it became clear that Hillary Clinton was the likely Democratic presidential candidate, Russian tweets and social media pages became uniformly hostile to Clinton. And once Trump became the official Republican nominee, Russia's propaganda campaign uniformly condemned Clinton and backed Trump. After the 2016 election, Russian interference returned to the familiar pattern of both praising and condemning Trump's actions in order to promote political conflict in the United States and to undermine popular confidence in the American electoral process. These activities continued during the 2018 election despite efforts by social media platforms to identify and delete fictitious Russian accounts as well as accounts traced to Iran and other foreign governments.

Both Republicans and Democrats recognized the gravity of foreign government interference with American elections. Former House Speaker Paul Ryan (R-Wisc.) said, "The Russians engaged in a sinister and systematic attack on our political system. It was a conspiracy to subvert the process, and take aim at democracy itself," while Senate Democratic Leader Chuck Schumer (D-N.Y.) said investigations had provided "proof that [Russian president] Vladimir Putin directed a campaign to interfere with our elections, with the goal of tipping the outcome."[51]

The fact that the Russians meddled in the 2016 election raised questions about whether the Trump campaign had knowledge of Russian efforts or in any way worked with the Russians. To answer these questions, a probe led by Special Counsel and former FBI director Robert Mueller was launched in May 2017. As a result of the Mueller probe, a half dozen Trump campaign officials have been indicted for various federal crimes and violations of campaign laws. President Trump has vehemently denied allegations of impropriety and denounced the Mueller probe as a "witch hunt" organized by his political foes. At the time of this writing the relationship between the Trump campaign and the Russian government remains unclear.

Immediately after the 2018 national elections, President Trump requested and received the resignation of Attorney General Jeff Sessions and named Sessions's chief of staff, Matthew Whitaker, acting attorney general. Whitaker had frequently criticized the Mueller probe and had suggested restricting its authority by cutting its budget to stop the investigation of the president. If Whitaker follows through on these ideas, the stage will be set for a tumultuous battle between the Trump administration and congressional Democrats.

THE 2018 ELECTION: A BLUE WAVE MEETS A RED WALL

Generally speaking, American national elections follow a pattern, sometimes called the cycle of surge and decline. In a presidential year like 2016, the party that captures the White House also gains seats in the House and Senate as many voters, drawn to the polls by the presidential contest, will also cast their ballots for other members of the president's party. In the ensuing off-year election, however, some of these "extra" seats are almost sure to be lost.

This normal cycle might already have given Democrats reason for confidence as they considered their tactics for 2018. But Democrats had even more reason to be optimistic. In office, President Trump continued his practice of making bombastic, misleading, and divisive statements that seemed inconsistent with the gravitas that Americans expect of a president. This behavior helped undermine Trump's public approval which, throughout his presidency, hovered near historically low levels. Trump, moreover, engaged in a number of bitter struggles with his opponents on such issues as immigration, environmental policy, and judicial appointments as he sought to implement programs based upon the promises presented in his campaign. These struggles helped energize Democrats to redouble their determination to take control of Congress and deal a setback to Trump's agenda.

Unique factors help decide the elections in each state and congressional district, but the 2018 election, more than most midterm contests, revolved around the president. Trump's outsized personality and frequent inflammatory rhetoric inspired anger on the part of some voters and fierce loyalty on the part of others. Between 2016 and 2018, across the nation, hundreds of thousands of Democrats who had never previously been much involved in politics, especially women and young people, entered the political arena to oppose Donald Trump. These Democrats engaged in political activity by signing petitions, attending rallies and protests, and contacting public officials. Republicans were also active, but according to a Kaiser Family Foundation survey, Democrats were almost twice as likely to be politically engaged as Republicans during this period.[52] In March 2018, for example, nearly 800,000 protestors in Washington, D.C., and a million more around the nation demonstrated in favor of gun control measures and against the president's failure to take action on the matter.[53] In addition, an unusually large number of women launched campaigns for national and state office, usually as Democrats. Some were veterans of the Bernie Sanders campaign, but many others were newcomers, drawn to politics as a result of the #MeToo movement. These women saw the GOP, and President Trump in particular, as insufficiently attentive to issues of sexual harassment. This view was underscored by Republican support for Brett Kavanaugh's nomination to the Supreme Court despite allegations of sexual assault made against him.

After Donald Trump's surprising win in 2016, Democrats across the country increased their efforts to organize and press for progress on key issues. In light of recent gun violence and what they saw as Trump administration inaction, in 2018 over 800,000 protestors in Washington, D.C., joined other protests around the country to push for stricter gun control regulation.

This grassroots enthusiasm gave Democratic candidates a sizable financial edge over the Republicans. Of course, major donors contributed hundreds of millions of dollars to both sides, but, in another sign of Democratic grass-roots enthusiasm, a record-shattering 5 million ordinary individuals contributed money to Democratic candidates through ActBlue and other Democratic fund-raising organizations. Sixty percent of these donors were first-time contributors and more than half were women.[54] All these developments led Democrats to hope that a "blue wave" would sweep the GOP from power in both Houses of Congress and even from many state governments as an expression of anger at Donald Trump and his fellow Republicans.

While Democrats mobilized their blue wave, the Republicans also planned their campaigns. The same issues that energized Democrats also invigorated Republicans. In particular, the battle over the Kavanaugh appointment convinced Republicans that they needed to fight hard to retain control of Congress. While Democrats had generally believed the charges against Kavanaugh, Republicans saw them as false and politically motivated. President Trump made the Kavanaugh fight along with such other hot-button issues as Trump's determination to stop a caravan of Central American immigrants from crossing the U.S. border major themes as he crisscrossed the country speaking to large and usually raucous Republican rallies in states and congressional districts that he had carried in 2016 and where incumbents were now threatened. At his rallies and in his tweets, Trump also pointed with pride to the strong economy, the renegotiation of U.S. trade deals, talks with North Korea, and to other achievements that pleased his political base. In 2016 many Republicans had been leery of too close an association with Trump. Now, most embraced him. In 2016, Trump had promised to build a wall on America's southern border to hold back immigrants. That wall was never built, but now President Trump was attempting to build a red wall around GOP strongholds to hold back the Democrats' blue wave.

The Outcome On November 6, 2018, the blue wave crashed against Trump's red wall with mixed results. Democrats won control of the U.S. House of Representatives for the first time since 2010, while Republicans expanded their majority in the Senate. Democrats won seven governor's races gained control of handful of state legislatures, and also won four new state attorney general offices.[55] The voter turnout in 2018 was 49 percent—the highest level since 1966 and a strong increase over recent midterm elections. Youth voter turnout, which is historically very hard to increase, soared by 10 percentage points to 31 percent of voters aged 18–29.

In House races, Democrats gained at least 38 seats for a 233-to-200 majority. (At the time of publication, two races were still undecided.) A number of close races were still to be decided in the days following the election with some recounts possible. Many of these "flipped" seats were in competitive states like Pennsylvania, Michigan, Wisconsin, and Iowa that had been carried by Trump in 2016. Women were critical to Democratic victories. Women made up more than half the 2018 electorate and supported Democratic candidates by margins of as much as 20 percentage points. The new 116th Congress will include over 100 women in the

House and more than 20 in the Senate, an all-time record. Two of the newly elected women, Democrats Rashida Tlaib of Michigan and Ilhan Omar of Minnesota, became the first Muslim women ever elected to the Congress. At the same time, Democrats Sharice Davids of Kansas and Debra Haaland of New Mexico were the first Native American women to win congressional elections.

In Senate races, Democrats began with a disadvantage. Of the 31 seats at stake in 2018, 23 were held by Democrats and only 8 by Republicans. This meant that the GOP had fewer seats to defend. Of the 23 Democratic seats, moreover, several were in "red" states where Republicans had the advantage. By the end of the night, Republicans had defeated Democratic incumbents in three red states—Indiana, Missouri, and North Dakota—while staving off a surprisingly strong Democratic challenge to Senator Ted Cruz in Texas. Two Senate seats previously held by Republicans went to the Democrats in Nevada and Arizona. These outcomes guaranteed GOP control of the Senate with at least 52 seats.

Democrats were generally successful in gubernatorial contests, taking seven seats, including Illinois, Kansas, Michigan, and Wisconsin, from the Republicans. Results in three other states, however, were disappointing to the Democratic Party. In the battleground state of Ohio, Republican Mike DeWine defeated Richard Cordray, former head of the Federal Consumer Financial Protection Bureau. Democrats had also hoped to elect African American governors in Florida and Georgia for the first time with Andrew Gillum and Stacey Abrams. Both had raised large sums of money and drawn tremendous media attention. In closely fought races, however, Gillum and Abrams were defeated. The margins were so close that recounts and court challenges seemed likely, though both candidates eventually conceded. Democrats did achieve a first in a gubernatorial race when Jared Polis won in Colorado to become the nation's first openly gay governor.

Democratic gubernatorial victories in Kansas, Michigan, and Wisconsin were especially important because in these states both houses of the legislature remained in Republican hands. Generally speaking, when one party controls both houses of

After the 2018 elections there will be a record number of female members of Congress, most of them Democrats. Here, Sharice Davids (left) celebrates after ousting Republican Kevin Yoder. With this victory, Davids became Kansas's first openly gay member of Congress and the first Native American woman elected to Congress. (She shares the latter distinction with New Mexico's Deb Haaland, another Native American Democrat elected to Congress in 2018.)

In 2018, Republicans increased their advantage in the Senate, winning critical races against vulnerable Democratic incumbents. Here, Republican Josh Hawley of Missouri celebrates his win over incumbent Democratic senator Claire McCaskill. This race was one of the most watched, and expensive, campaigns nationwide.

the state legislature and the governor's mansion it is likely to engage in partisan gerrymandering, drawing state legislative and congressional district boundaries that favor its own side. When control of a state government is divided, the two parties are often compelled to reach an agreement that protects incumbents on both sides of the aisle. New Democratic governors in Kansas, Michigan, and Wisconsin would likely prevent gerrymandering favorable to the Republicans after the 2020 census. At the same time, the Democrats won full control over state governments in Illinois, Maine, Nevada, and New Mexico and expected to be able to control post-census redistricting in all four states, to their own party's advantage. Overall, Republicans would have solid control of the governments in 21 states, Democrats in 14 states, and in 13 states control would be divided between the two parties.

Ballot Measures In a number of states, voters were also asked to decide ballot measures. Gerrymandering itself was on the ballot in some states. Voters in Colorado, Michigan, and Missouri overwhelmingly supported ballot initiatives creating independent commissions to draw district boundaries. Such commissions were established in Arizona in 2000 and California in 2010 and have long been practiced in Iowa. Supporters of the commission idea oppose gerrymandering—whether partisan or bipartisan—and favor a level electoral playing field.

Voters in Michigan and Missouri approved legalization of medical marijuana; voters in Arkansas and Missouri approved increases in the minimum wage; restrictions on abortion carried in Alabama and West Virginia. In Massachusetts, voters rejected a measure that would have repealed a 2016 law prohibiting discrimination in public places based on gender identity. In North Carolina and Arkansas, citizens approved state constitutional amendments requiring voters to present official photo IDs when casting ballots. A Florida referendum restored voting rights for most ex-felons.

Interestingly, voters in some solidly red states approved progressive ballot initiatives while voters in some solidly blue states approved initiatives generally associated with conservative forces. Voters in deeply red Idaho, Nebraska, and Utah approved referenda expanding Medicaid coverage, while voters in solidly blue Washington turned back a ballot measure imposing a fee on industries responsible for greenhouse gas emissions.[56] These results may appear peculiar, but ballot initiatives carry no party label. Stripped of party as a cue, voters often stray from their expected behavior. Whether, as a result, they become more or less rational is an open question.

FOR CRITICAL ANALYSIS

Given the factors that went into the 2018 elections, and the results, do you think Democrats or Republicans are more likely to control Congress going forward? Why?

THE 2018 ELECTION AND AMERICA'S FUTURE

The mixed results of the 2018 election were something of a disappointment to Democrats who thought they would hand President Trump a more crushing defeat. As Democrats had hoped, however, voter turnout increased sharply in 2018. Some 114 million Americans or 49 percent of the nation's eligible voters participated. In the last midterm election, 2014, voter turnout was only 36 percent. A majority of the nation's voters, according to exit polls, saw the election as a referendum on President Trump's performance in office. Given Trump's low levels of public approval, this should have helped the Democrats and, indeed, many more voters said they cast their votes to oppose Trump than voted to support him. On a national basis, Democrats received a clear majority of the votes cast in congressional elections, approximately 5 million more than were cast for Republicans.

The challenge, though, is that American elections are not national. They are a set of individual state by state and district by district contests. For the most part, the Democrats' blue wave meant that opposition to Trump increased sharply in states and urban and suburban districts where the president was already unpopular, without having much impact upon states and districts in America's small towns and rural areas, where the president drew his strongest support. Trump had spent the weeks before the election bolstering GOP enthusiasm in those areas, building a red wall to hold back the Democrats' blue wave.

Despite losses in the Senate, taking control of the House of Representatives was an important achievement. With control of the House, Democrats are in a position to block Trump's legislative efforts and to conduct investigations into the president's conduct as well as the activities of Trump appointees in the executive branch. Conceivably, House Democrats might work with the president in some areas, but the chance of any significant cooperation seems low. Democrats are unlikely to see any reason to help the president achieve anything for which he might claim credit in 2020. The president will almost certainly feel compelled to rely ever more heavily on executive orders and other forms of executive action that bypass the Congress. With the Senate firmly in Republican hands, Trump will continue to use his appointment powers to reshape the bureaucracy and the courts. The stage seems set for two more years of the partisan struggle that characterizes American democratic politics.

The 2018 elections also made clear that if the Republican Party is to remain competitive nationally it must develop a message that appeals to voters outside its current base of older white men in America's small towns and rural areas. The Democrats have built a coalition that includes women, minorities, and young people. It is no accident that the first Muslim and Native American women elected to Congress along with the first openly gay governor are all Democrats. The Democratic electorate is growing while the GOP's base represents a shrinking percentage of the national electorate and even of the electorate in rapidly growing red states like Texas where as formidable a Republican politician as Senator Ted Cruz had to scramble to avoid defeat. If the Republican Party cannot find a way to expand its constituency, 2018 may be the last time the red wall can hold back the blue wave.

Campaigns and Elections
WHAT DO WE WANT?

As politicians ponder the questions just discussed, individual Americans must think about what the 2016 and 2018 elections might mean for them. Will Republican economic policies create more jobs or leave Americans with less secure economic futures? What will Republican plans to eliminate Obamacare mean for Americans' access to medical services? Will Republican national security policies make us more or less safe? How will America's diverse communities be affected by potential GOP efforts to crack down on illegal immigration? Should we be more critical consumers of opinion polls and the political information circulated on social media?

Another question about elections concerns campaign finance and whose interests will be represented in government. Donald Trump was a unique candidate who was able to generate unprecedented free media coverage, but his campaign still raised and spent hundreds of millions of dollars, much of it collected as small donations from individuals. In a nation as large and diverse as the United States, to be sure, campaign contributors represent many different groups and, often, clashing interests. The fact remains, however, that those with more money will be able to give more and that, once in office, elected officials can be expected to represent the interests of those who supported them. The **"Who Participates?"** feature on the facing page shows who donated to the 2016 presidential campaign.

Two trends in campaign finance may play a role in how elections are funded in the future and, thus, who is elected to office and what policies are enacted. On the one hand, recent decisions by the Supreme Court have overturned federal laws that sought to set some limits on who could give and how much they could give. The laws existed in hopes of limiting the influence of affluent interests over the electoral process and government. But the Court has held that giving money is (in some circumstances) a form of political speech that is essential to the country's democratic process. Will moneyed interests continue to play a large role in the election process? What new laws may be needed to make the rules of the game fair? Will campaign spending increase to the point that the citizens of tomorrow enact reform for public financing or free media for all qualified candidates?

Who Donates to Political Campaigns?

Percentage of Adults Who Donated, 2016*

*To a political campaign, candidate, or organization

Income

11% | <$20k **15%** | $20–$40k **21%** | $40–$80k **30%** | $80k+

Age

17% | 18–25 **15%** | 26–44 **22%** | 45–64 **30%** | 65+

Education**

**Highest level attained

12% | High school or less **23%** | Some college **26%** | College diploma **37%** | Postgraduate degree

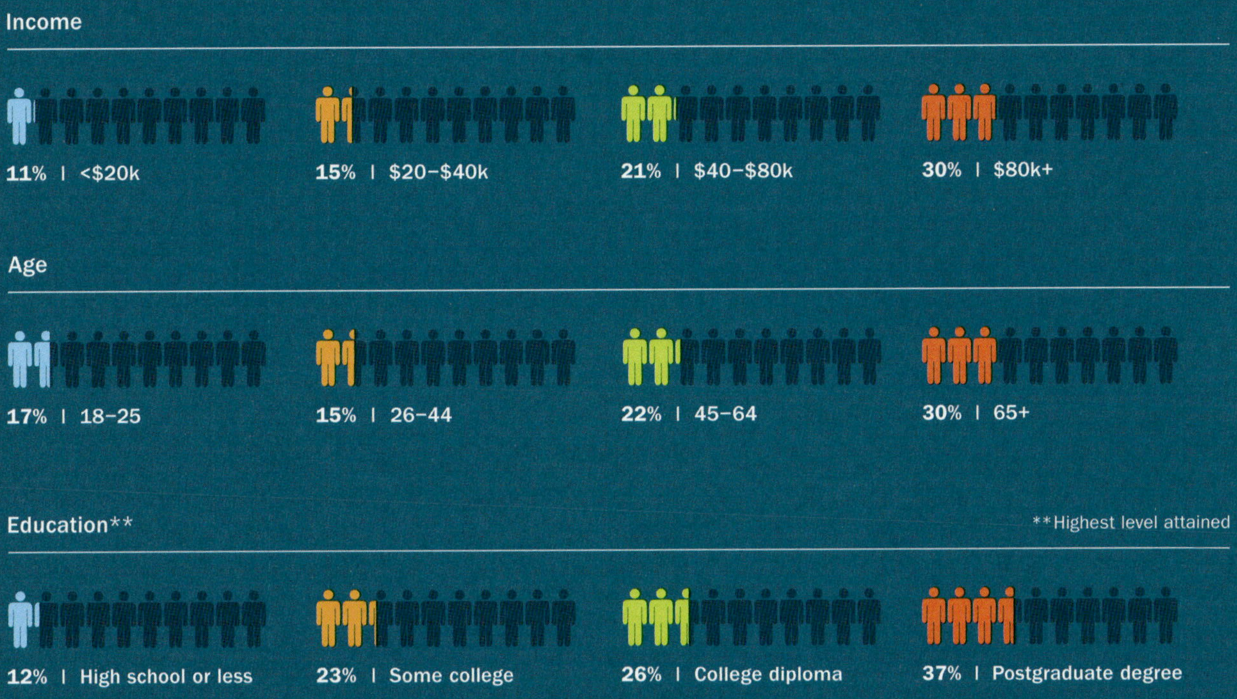

SOURCE: Cooperative Congressional Election Study (CCES) 2016, www.electproject.org/2016P (accessed 11/20/17).

★ WHAT YOU CAN DO ★

Your Views on Money in Politics

 Track campaign contributions at the federal level at **www.opensecrets.org** and at the state level at **www.followthemoney.org**.

 If you're concerned about the role of money in politics, voice your opinion on social media platforms such as Facebook and Twitter.

 You can also contact groups working to raise awareness of the role of money in politics, such as Common Cause (**www.commoncause.org**), Move to Amend (**www.movetoamend.org**), or Democracy Is for People (**www.democracyisforpeople.org**).

STUDY GUIDE

Elections in America

Describe the major rules and procedures of elections in the United States (pp. 381–93)

American elections are subject to many specific rules. The responsibility for administering elections rests mainly with states and counties, and most elections in the United States today use the Australian ballot and operate under a plurality, rather than a majority or proportional representation, system. The United States is also one of the few nations in the world to hold primary elections in addition to a general election. Unlike members of the House of Representatives, who are elected through a direct vote from districts that are redrawn every 10 years, presidents are elected indirectly by the electoral college.

Key Terms

midterm elections (p. 381)
primary elections (p. 381)
general election (p. 382)
closed primary (p. 382)
open primary (p. 382)
majority system (p. 382)
runoff election (p. 382)
plurality system (p. 382)
proportional representation (p. 382)
straight-ticket voting (p. 383)
redistricting (p. 384)
gerrymandering (p. 385)
partisan gerrymandering (p. 385)
majority-minority district (p. 386)
retail politics (p. 387)
delegate (p. 388)
party platform (p. 389)
electoral college (p. 389)
ballot initiative (p. 392)
referendum (p. 392)
recall (p. 393)

Practice Quiz

1. An open primary is a primary election in which
   a) one's vote is made public.
   b) only registered members of the party may vote.
   c) all registered voters, including independents, are able to choose which party primary they will participate in.
   d) only two candidates are allowed to run.
   e) voting is conducted by mail.
2. To win under the plurality system used in most American elections a candidate must receive
   a) more than 50 percent of the popular vote.
   b) more than 50 percent in the runoff election.
   c) more than two-thirds of the popular vote.
   d) more than 75 percent of the popular vote.
   e) more votes than his or her opponents, regardless of the percentage.
3. If a voter supports candidates from more than one party in the same election, she is said to be engaging in
   a) retrospective voting.
   b) two-way voting.
   c) prospective voting.
   d) straight-ticket voting.
   e) split-ticket voting.
4. If a state has 10 members in the U.S. House of Representatives, how many votes in the electoral college does that state have?
   a) 2
   b) 10
   c) 12
   d) 20
   e) The number of votes cannot be determined from this information.

Election Campaigns

Explain how campaigns are typically conducted (pp. 393–400)

In order to successfully run for national or statewide office, candidates must create formal campaign organizations that employ a campaign manager, a media consultant, a pollster, a financial adviser, a press spokesperson, and a staff director. Modern national political campaigns are expensive to run, and candidates must start raising money well before the election. Campaigns must decide on a message and a strategy for communicating that message to the voters they want to target.

Key Terms

campaign (p. 393)
incumbent (p. 393)
grassroots campaigns (p. 396)
town hall meeting (p. 396)

Practice Quiz

5. An incumbent is a candidate who
   a) does not currently hold office.
   b) has the support of both major parties.
   c) already holds the office he or she is running for.
   d) has won his or her party's primary election.
   e) has been nominated at the party convention.
6. In nearly every election since 1980, the average amount of money spent by House incumbents to secure re-election has
   a) been about the same as the average amount of money spent by challengers.
   b) been greater than the average amount of money spent by challengers.
   c) been less than the average amount of money spent by challengers.
   d) been $0 due to federal laws that provide campaign funds for incumbents.
   e) been $1 million due to federal laws that provide campaign funds for incumbents.

Money and Politics

Describe how candidates raise the money they need to run (pp. 400–405)

Modern political campaigns in the United States are enormously expensive, and candidates with the most money often win. Supreme Court cases since the mid-1970s have removed many restrictions on campaign finance. Candidates finance their campaigns with money from individual donors, political action committees, political parties, and the candidates' own bank accounts. Election spending by Super PACs, 527s, 501(c)(4)s, and nonprofit groups must be independent of candidates' campaigns. The Federal Elections Campaign Act also provides for public funding of presidential campaigns.

Key Terms

political action committee (PAC) (p. 404)
527 committee (Super PAC) (p. 404)
501(c)(4) committees (dark money) (p. 404)

Practice Quiz

7. In *Buckley v. Valeo*, the Supreme Court ruled that
   a) PAC donations to campaigns are constitutionally protected.
   b) candidates cannot spend any of their own money to run for office.
   c) the right of individuals to spend their own money to campaign is constitutionally protected.
   d) there is no limit to the number of candidates to whom an individual can contribute.
   e) the Bipartisan Campaign Reform Act is unconstitutional.
8. The main difference between a 527 committee and a 501(c)(4) committee is that
   a) a 527 is not legally required to disclose where it gets its money while a 501(c)(4) is legally required to do so.
   b) a 501(c)(4) is not legally required to disclose where it gets its money while a 527 is legally required to do so.
   c) a 527 can only contribute to one campaign while a 501(c)(4) can contribute to many.
   d) a 501(c)(4) can only contribute to one campaign while a 527 can contribute to many.
   e) a 527 can legally coordinate its spending with a candidate's campaign while a 501(c)(4) cannot.
9. Public funding of presidential campaigns was
   a) outlawed by the Federal Election Campaign Act.
   b) declared unconstitutional by the Supreme Court in *McCutcheon et al. v. Federal Election Commission*.
   c) accepted by both major-party presidential candidates in 2016.
   d) rejected by all four major-party presidential candidates in 2012 and 2016.
   e) limited to only $25 million in 2008, 2012, and 2016.

How Voters Decide

Identify the major factors that influence voters' decisions (pp. 406–8)

Three factors influence the decisions that voters make at the polls: partisan loyalty, issues and policy preferences, and candidate characteristics. Partisan attachments do not change frequently and are an important influence on which candidates a voter chooses to support. Voters may also consider the past and future behavior of competing parties and candidates. A candidate's race, ethnicity, religion, gender, and social background are also weighed by voters on Election Day.

Key Terms

prospective voting (p. 407)

retrospective voting (p. 407)

Practice Quiz

10. When a voter decides which candidate to vote for based on imagined future performance, the voter is engaged in
- a) prospective voting.
- b) retrospective voting.
- c) introspective voting.
- d) straight-ticket voting.
- e) split-ticket voting.

11. The Consumer Confidence Index
- a) measures how business leaders rate the federal government's regulation of the economy during election years.
- b) was a federal government program designed to increase economic growth during the Reagan administration.
- c) has been an inaccurate predictor of presidential outcomes.
- d) has been a fairly accurate predictor of presidential outcomes.
- e) is based on government reports of objective economic indicators.

The 2016 and 2018 Elections

Analyze the strategies, issues, and outcomes of the 2016 and 2018 elections (pp. 409–21)

In a stunning upset, Donald Trump was elected president in 2016 over Hillary Clinton. After the elections, the Democrats regrouped and organized effectively to energize voters and win back the House of Representatives in 2018, though the Republicans retained control of the Senate. Voter turnout was the highest in decades, and the incoming Congress will have more women members than ever.

Practice Quiz

12. In the 2016 general election, voters who said they felt the country and the economy were headed in the wrong direction were most likely to vote for
- a) Hillary Clinton
- b) Donald Trump
- c) Jill Stein
- d) Gary Johnson
- e) Jeb Bush

13. In 2016, Trump and the Republicans received a majority of votes from
- a) whites and Asian Americans
- b) whites, Latinos, and women
- c) whites and men
- d) African Americans and more affluent voters
- e) Latinos and young voters

14. Which of the following states flipped from Democratic to Republican in the 2016 election?
- a) Florida, Ohio, and Pennsylvania
- b) California, New York, and Massachusetts
- c) Texas, Alabama, and Kentucky
- d) West Virginia, Missouri, and Kansas
- e) Oregon, Washington, and Delaware

15. Which of the following statements is true about the 2018 elections?
- a) Youth turnout increased significantly.
- b) Democrats won control of the Senate.
- c) Overall turnout was down from the 2014 midterm elections.
- d) After 2018 most incoming female members of Congress were Republicans.
- e) Republicans raised more money than Democrats in the 2018 election cycle.

16. In 2018 the Republicans won Senate seats in which of the following states:
- a) Arizona and Nevada
- b) Indiana, Missouri, and North Dakota
- c) Ohio and Pennsylvania
- d) California and New York
- e) New Mexico, Virginia, and West Virginia

For Further Reading

Abramson, Paul, John Aldrich, and David Rohde. *Change and Continuity in the 2008 Elections*. Washington, DC: CQ Press, 2009.

Ackerman, Bruce, and Ian Avres. *Voting with Dollars*. New Haven, CT: Yale University Press, 2004.

Browning, Graeme. *Electronic Democracy*. New York: Cyberage, 2002.

Ginsberg, Benjamin, and Martin Shefter. *Politics by Other Means: Institutional Conflict and the Declining Significance of Elections in America*. New York: W. W. Norton, 1999.

Heilemann, John, and Mark Halperin. *Game Change: Obama and the Clintons, McCain and Palin, and the Race of a Lifetime*. New York: Harper, 2010.

Maass, Matthias. *The World Views of the 2008 U.S. Presidential Election*. New York: Palgrave, 2009.

Nelson, Michael, ed. *The Elections of 2008*. Washington, DC: CQ Press, 2009.

Polsby, Nelson, Aaron Wildavsky, and David Hopkins. *Presidential Elections*. 12th ed. New York: Rowman and Littlefield, 2007.

Raymond, Allen, and Ian Spiegelman. *How to Rig an Election*. New York: Simon & Schuster, 2008.

Schier, Steven. *You Call This an Election?* Washington, DC: Georgetown University Press, 2003.

Wayne, Stephen. *Is This Any Way to Run a Democratic Election?* 3rd ed. Washington, DC: CQ Press, 2007.

Recommended Websites

Dark Money
www.opensecrets.org/dark-money/
Dark money refers to politically active organizations whose finances do not need to be disclosed. Learn more about how dark money spending works and its growing influence on election campaigns.

ElectionMail.com
www.electionmail.com
Are you thinking about running for office? Whether you aspire to be student government president or president of the United States, here you can find links to affordable political printing, including political brochures, campaign literature, and campaign signs.

FairVote
www.fairvote.org
FairVote is dedicated to open access to voting, equal representation, and a voice for all Americans. Read about some of their electoral reform proposals such as runoff elections, proportional representation, and alternatives to the electoral college.

Federal Election Commission
www.fec.gov
The Federal Election Commission (FEC) is an independent government agency that was created in 1975 to administer and enforce the Federal Election Campaign Act. At the official FEC website you can read about the rules and regulations that govern the financing of federal elections and other topics of interest.

JibJab.com
www.jibjab.com
This website became famous for its political video clips during the 2004 presidential campaign. For a good laugh check out some of the political jokes or rummage through the video archives to find one of the original Bush or Kerry clips.

National Archives and Records Administration
www.archives.gov/federal-register/electoral-college/index.html
The National Archives and Records Administration's U.S. Electoral College page is a great resource on presidential elections. Find answers to frequently asked questions about our electoral system, read about how electors vote, or try predicting who will win the next presidential election with the electoral college calculator.

OpenSecrets.org
www.opensecrets.org
Campaign funds come from a variety of sources, including individual donors, political action committees, self-contributions, independent spending, parties, and public funding. At this site you can research funding for all federal officials, including your own members of Congress.

Pew Research Center, Election 2016
www.pewresearch.org/topics/2016-election/
Pew Research Center's resource for the 2016 presidential election includes survey data, facts, figures, and public opinion.

Project Vote Smart
www.votesmart.org
Project Vote Smart is a nonpartisan site dedicated to providing citizens with information on political candidates and elected officials. Here you can easily view a candidate's biographical information, position on issues, and voting record so that you can make an informed choice on Election Day.

Voter Information Services
www.vis.org
Voter Information Services is a nonpartisan, nonprofit organization dedicated to helping interested citizens learn about their elected members of Congress. Here you can obtain a congressional report card for your members of Congress and find out where they stand on the issues.

★ chapter ★

11

Groups and Interests

WHAT GOVERNMENT DOES AND WHY IT MATTERS After graduating from college with a degree in physics, 25-year-old Ben Brown was working in New York City in the energy business when he read a newspaper article quoting former senator Alan Simpson, Republican of Wyoming. Simpson asserted that young people would lack political power until a young person "could walk into his office and say, 'I'm from the American Association of Young People. We have 30 million members, and we're watching you, Simpson.'"[1] He was referencing the political clout of AARP, formerly known as the American Association of Retired Persons, the largest membership organization in the country. AARP is known for its formidable defense of Social Security, Medicare, and other issues of interest to older Americans.

In contrast, young Americans have not had a broad-based membership group representing their interests, and in 2016 Brown decided to found one. Individuals can join the Association of Young Americans (AYA) for $20 per year and enjoy discounts on transportation and movies, much as AARP members have long enjoyed travel and insurance services. While those benefits are intended to entice members, the real purpose of AYA is to lobby on issues such as preserving net neutrality, stopping

Interest groups have a strong influence in American political life, but whose interests do these groups serve? Young people have struggled to have a strong voice in politics, but Ben Brown founded the Association for Young Americans to change that.

unpaid internships, and protecting student debt repayment programs. The organization has a weekly newsletter and provides a "Contact Our Reps" tool to "make it easy for anyone to connect with their elected officials" and make their preferences known. "We work to insert the voices of the 80 million Americans ages 18 to 35 into everyday politics," the group's website says.[2] Since 2016, AYA has grown to include 8,000 members. AYA demonstrates interest groups in action.

Tens of thousands of organized groups have formed in the United States, ranging from civic associations to huge nationwide organizations such as the National Rifle Association (NRA), whose chief cause is opposition to restrictions on gun ownership, and Common Cause, a public interest group that advocates for such issues as limits on campaign spending. Indeed, Alexis de Tocqueville, a famous nineteenth-century French writer, once wrote that America was "a nation of joiners."[3] This defining characteristic of American political life has not changed since Tocqueville made his observation. Americans are much more likely to join political and social organizations than people in other countries, and America has more organized interest groups than other nations.

Many believe this unique trend has a positive impact on democracy. But others worry that the power and money wielded by these groups can dominate Congress, the president, and the political process—such as elections—at the expense of average citizens and the public welfare. Another concern is that despite the array of interest groups in American politics, not all interests—like those of young people—are represented equally, and the results of competition among various interests are not always consistent with the common good. In this chapter we will examine the nature and consequences of interest group politics in the United States.

Despite the array of interest groups in American politics, however, not all interests—like those of young people—are represented equally, and the results of competition among various interests are not always consistent with the common good. In this chapter we will examine the nature and consequences of interest group politics in the United States.

CHAPTER GOAL

- ★ **Describe the major types of interest groups and whom they represent (pp. 431–39)**
- ★ **Describe how interest groups and social groups organize (pp. 439–45)**
- ★ **Analyze why the number of interest and advocacy groups has grown in recent decades (pp. 446–47)**
- ★ **Explain how interest groups try to influence government and policy (pp. 447–59)**

Defining Interest Groups

Describe the major types of interest groups and whom they represent

The framers of the U.S. Constitution feared the power that could be wielded by organized interests. Yet they believed that interest groups thrived because of liberty—the freedom that all Americans have to organize and to express their views. In the eighteenth and nineteenth centuries, organized groups were called "associations." The Federalists and the anti-Federalists themselves were organized groups of political elites that had different views about how to create America's new democracy. Both the Federalists and anti-Federalists agreed that if the government were given the power to regulate or in any way to forbid efforts by organized interests to participate in the political process, it would in effect have the power to suppress individual liberty. The solution to this dilemma was presented by James Madison in the *Federalist Papers* no. 10:

> Take in a greater variety of parties and interests [and] you make it less probable that a majority of the whole will have a common motive to invade the rights of other citizens. . . . [Hence the advantage] enjoyed by a large over a small republic.[4]

According to Madison, a good government encourages multitudes of interests so that no single interest, which he called a "faction," can ever consistently dominate the others. The basic assumption is that all the competing interests will regulate one another, producing balance.[5]

Today, this Madisonian principle is called **pluralism**. Pluralism is a theory of democracy based on the balancing of interests in society via groups that compete for policy outcomes from government. While an interest group may lose on one issue, it may win on the next; and overall the vast majority of society will be represented in government. According to pluralist theory, all interests are and should be free to compete for influence in government and politics. Moreover, according to the theory of pluralism, the outcome of this competition is compromise and moderation since no group is likely to be able to achieve any of its goals without accommodating itself to some of the views of its many competitors.[6]

pluralism the theory that all interests are and should be free to compete for influence in the government; the outcome of this competition is compromise and moderation

Pluralism was long the dominant view of the U.S. political system, but critics point out that not all interests are equally represented in the competition for political influence. Some interests speak with loud voices (i.e., affluent corporations), while others can barely make themselves heard (i.e., Midwest farmers). Pluralism does not guarantee political equality. Indeed, important research indicates that, through group politics, economic elites have considerably more influence than mass-based forces in the American political process.[7] This version of pluralism is called elite pluralism and more accurately describes American politics.

An **interest group** is an organized group of people that lobbies government to change public policy. This definition includes membership organizations (citizen groups) as well as businesses, corporations, universities, labor unions, and other institutions that restrict membership to particular occupational groups or other categories of persons. Individuals form groups to increase the chance that their views will be heard and their interests treated favorably by the government. Interest groups are sometimes negatively referred to as "lobbies," "special interests," or "pressure groups," or positively discussed as advocacy organizations or citizen groups. They are

interest group individuals who organize to influence the government's programs and policies

Although public school teachers are a minority of the total population, they are an influential interest group in many states because they are highly informed and act as a group in support of issues related to their profession, including teachers' salaries.

also sometimes confused with political action committees (PACs), which are groups that raise and distribute money for use in election campaigns (see Chapter 10). Many interest groups create PACs in their name to be the money-giving arm of the interest group. For example, the NRA Political Victory Fund donates money to political candidates and officeholders on behalf of the NRA, which represents the interests of gun owners.

One final distinction is that interest groups are also different from political parties: interest groups tend to focus on the *policies* of government, while parties tend to concern themselves with the *personnel* of government. Parties organize to win elected office and interest groups do not, although interest groups are increasingly engaged in political campaigns and seek to help candidates favorable to their policy goals win elections.

The number of interest groups in the United States is enormous, and millions of Americans are members of one or more groups, at least to the extent of paying dues, attending an occasional meeting, following a group on social media, reading news from the group, or being on an email list. By representing the interests of such large numbers of people and encouraging political participation, organized groups can and do enhance American democracy. Organized groups educate their members on policy issues and mobilize their members for elections and grassroots lobbying efforts using sophisticated social media campaigns, email listservs, letters and news reports, media campaigns, and more. Groups lobby members of Congress and the executive, engage in litigation, and generally represent their members' interests in the political arena. Interest groups also monitor government programs to make certain that these programs do not adversely affect their members. In all these ways, organized interest groups help promote democratic politics.

Because not all interests are represented equally in society, interest group politics works to the advantage of some and the disadvantage of others. Homeless people are generally not organized, for example, while the National Realtors Association spends more than most organized lobbyists in Washington, D.C. Furthermore, not all organized interests are successful. Organized interest groups in the United States are predominantly economic groups. Groups working on behalf of businesses and industry far outweigh citizen groups in terms of their number of registered lobbyists in Washington, D.C., and in state capitals, and of their financial resources to influence government and elections. The ability of economic groups to mobilize resources for elections often results in legislative victories when lawmakers win office and support policies that benefit their industry. Examples of such groups include the oil and gas industries (who supported recent legislation that opened up drilling in Alaska), telecommunication firms (who supported repealing of "net neutrality" regulations), and pharmaceutical companies (who seek fewer government regulations of drugs).

COMMON TYPES OF INTEREST GROUPS

Economic and Corporate Groups Interest groups come in as many shapes and sizes as the interests they represent. The most obvious are groups with a direct economic interest in governmental policy. Businesses and corporations make up over a third of the groups with lobbying offices in Washington, with trade associations comprising another 23 percent and labor unions just 2 percent of groups registered to lobby.[8] Trade associations are generally supported by groups of producers or manufacturers in a particular economic sector, such as the National Association of Manufacturers or the American Fuel and Petrochemical Manufacturers. Trade associations care about broad industrywide issues, and they lobby and make financial contributions to gain access to elected officials. In addition to these broadly representative groups, specific companies may be active in Washington on certain issues that are of particular concern to them. Combined, over 6 in 10 groups lobbying in Washington represent businesses, corporations, or trade associations.

Trade associations spent more than $716 million to lobby the federal government and Congress in 2017.[9] Some of the biggest spenders included the U.S. Chamber of Commerce, Blue Cross Blue Shield, the American Medical Association, Boeing, and The National Association of Realtors.

Which industry spends the most money on lobbying activities? Table 11.1 lists the top spenders from 1998–18. At the top of the list are financial groups, insurance, the real estate industry, and the pharmaceutical industry, which has spent more than $4 billion lobbying lawmakers in an effort to maintain high drug prices and patent protection for their products.[10]

Wealthy corporate interest groups usually find it easier to gain attention from elected officials than do other types of groups. Here, Maine governor Paul LePage speaks at a news conference to discuss a report from the Pharmaceutical Research and Manufacturers of America (PhRMA), an interest group representing biopharmaceutical companies and researchers.

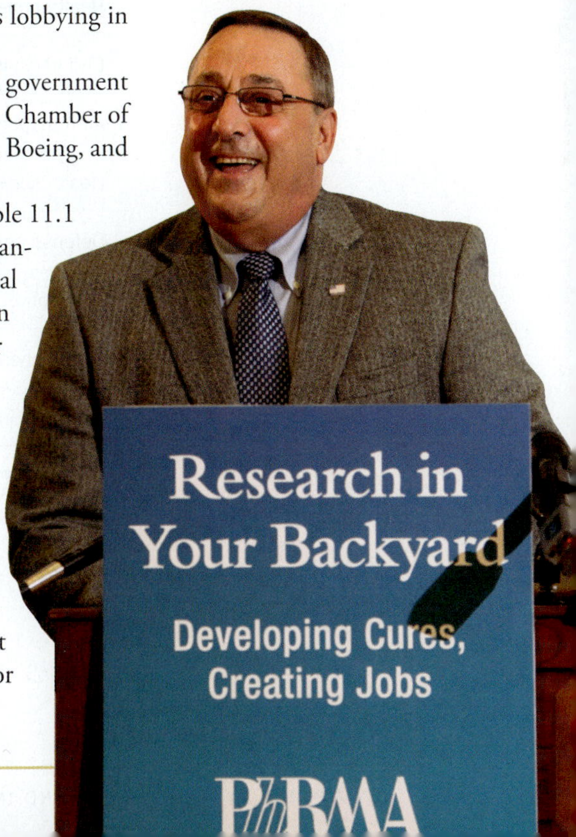

Labor Groups Labor organizations are also active in lobbying government. The AFL-CIO, the United Mine Workers, and the Teamsters all lobby on behalf of organized labor. American Federation of State, County and Municipal Employees (AFSCME), represents 1.4 million members who work in public service and health care. AFSCME represents its members on thousands of issues, from improving unemployment benefits to raising the minimum wage. Labor unions represent all sectors of the American workforce, but according to one study, labor

TABLE 11.1

Top Spending on Lobbying by Industry, 1998–2018

INDUSTRY	TOTAL
Pharmaceuticals and health products	$4,001,631,064
Insurance	$2,751,743,572
Electric utilities	$2,384,646,037
Electronics manufacturing and equipment	$2,265,674,175
Business associations	$2,254,317,913
Oil and gas	$2,130,959,766
Miscellaneous manufacturing and distributing	$1,711,453,232
Education	$1,651,855,249
Hospitals and nursing homes	$1,628,529,677
Securities and investment	$1,571,585,579
Real estate	$1,560,196,283
Telecom services	$1,559,003,678
Health professionals	$1,473,898,726
Civil servants and public officials	$1,455,196,910
Air transport	$1,415,833,437
Health services and HMOs	$1,116,511,600
Defense aerospace	$1,114,819,742
Automotive	$1,109,408,742
Miscellaneous issues	$1,069,275,817
Television, movies, and music	$1,049,917,835

SOURCE: Center for Responsive Politics, "Top Spenders," www.opensecrets.org/lobby/top.php?indexType=i&showYear=a (accessed 11/8/18).

unions represent just 2 percent of the total number of interest groups registered to lobby in Washington.[11]

Despite being out-lobbied, labor unions continue to exercise influence in Washington. Union members vote, and organized labor can have a significant impact upon elections. Few members of Congress can ignore labor's power at the polls.

Professional Associations Professional lobbies such as the American Bar Association and the American Medical Association have been particularly successful at furthering their members' interests in state and federal legislatures. Trial lawyers are represented by the American Association for Justice. Accountants, real estate agents, dentists, teachers and even college faculty have professional associations. Professional associations comprise just over 10 percent of the total number of groups lobbying in Washington. Financial institutions, represented by organizations such as the American Bankers Association and the National Savings and Loan League, although often less visible than other lobbies, also play an important role in shaping legislative policy.

Public Interest Groups Recent years have witnessed the growth of a powerful "public interest" lobby, purporting to represent the general good rather than its own economic interests. **Public interest groups,** or citizen groups, have been most visible in the consumer protection and environmental policy areas, although public interest groups cover a broad range of issues. Citizen groups comprise only 20 percent of the groups with lobbying offices in Washington. However, a survey of 315 lobbyists and government officials, about 98 randomly selected policy issues, found that citizen groups were more likely to be mentioned as being influential in the debate than any other type of group.[12]

public interest groups groups that claim they serve the general good rather than only their own particular interests

The Natural Resources Defense Council, the Sierra Club, the National Civic League, and Common Cause are all examples of public interest groups. Claims to represent *only* the public interest should be viewed with caution, however. It is not uncommon to find decidedly private interests seeking to hide behind the term *public interest.* For example, the benign-sounding Partnership to Protect Consumer Credit is a coalition of credit card companies fighting for less federal regulation of credit abuses, and Project Protect is a coalition of logging interests promoting increased timber cutting.[13] Economic interests often mask their financial interests by organizing public interest groups.

Ideological Groups and Advocacy Groups Closely related to and overlapping with public interest groups are ideological groups, organized in support of a particular political or philosophical perspective. The National Right to Life and the Christian Coalition, for example, promote conservative values and social goals, such as opposing abortion. The National Taxpayers Union and the Center for American Progress campaign to reduce the size of the federal government and cut taxes. Liberal-leaning groups, including EMILY's List and MoveOn.org, support causes such as protecting national parks and public lands, climate action, free college, and increasing the minimum wage.

Public-Sector Groups The perceived need for representation on Capitol Hill has generated a public-sector lobby in the past several years, including the National League of Cities, the National Conference of State Legislatures, and the "research" lobby. The latter group comprises think tanks and universities that have an interest in obtaining government funds for research and support, and it includes such institutions as Harvard University, the Brookings Institution, and the American

AMERICA SIDE by SIDE

Civil Society around the World

Political scientists who study democracy around the world emphasize the important role society may play in shaping democracy. Interest groups are part of what is known more broadly as civil society: organizations outside the state that help people define and promote their interests. These groups play an important role in maintaining the overall health of democracy. Countries with an active civil society may be more likely to transition to democracy. South Africa's strong civil society played a major role in protesting for democracy against a repressive Apartheid regime. In contrast, civil society membership was heavily co-opted by authoritarian regimes in Germany and Japan; rebuilding the independence and engagement of these groups remains a major democratic challenge to this day. So, while de Tocqueville may have been writing about the United States as a "nation of joiners," many other democracies have also joined this club.

PERCENTAGE OF POPULATION THAT REPORTS AS ACTIVE MEMBERS OF INTEREST GROUPS

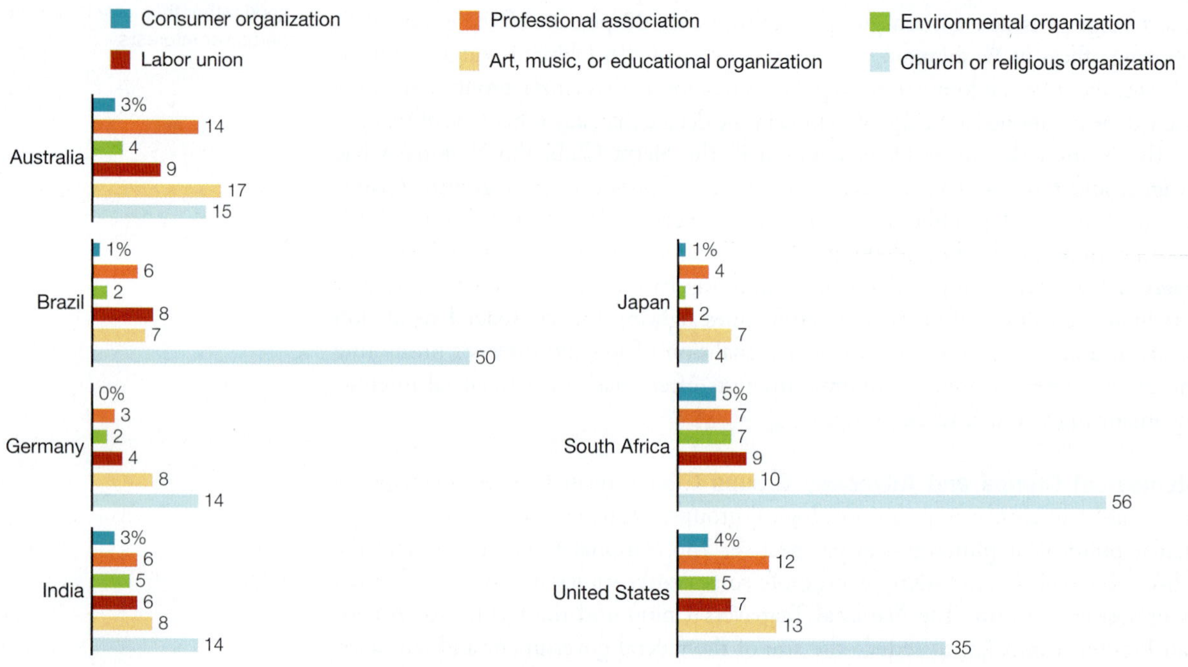

SOURCE: R. Inglehart et al., eds., "World Values Survey: Round Six—Country-Pooled Datafile Version," 2014, www.worldvaluessurvey.org (accessed 5/28/18).

Enterprise Institute. These groups represent roughly 10 percent of the total number of groups lobbying in Washington.

WHAT INTERESTS ARE NOT REPRESENTED?

It is difficult to categorize unrepresented interests precisely because they are not organized and are not able to demonstrate to government their identity and their demands. The political scientist David Truman referred to these interests as "potential interest groups."[14] He is undoubtedly correct that at any time, as long as there is freedom, it is possible that any interest shared by a lot of people can develop through "voluntary association" into a genuine interest group that can demand, usually successfully. But the fact remains that many widely shared interests are not represented by organized groups. Two such "potential" groups are the homeless and the poor. Both groups have shared interests in policy outcomes, such as job programs and affordable housing. But the groups lack organization through which to push for government policy to address these concerns.[15]

Unequal Representation and the Upper-Class Bias of Group Membership

Despite the benefits of interest groups in terms of mobilizing and educating the public and the arguments in favor of pluralism, there are concerns about the influence of special interests in the United States. One long-standing critic is E. E. Schattschneider, who argued in a famous quote, "The flaw in the pluralist heaven is that the heavenly chorus sings with a strong upper-class accent."[16] Critics contend that pressure politics, or interest group politics, is heavily skewed in favor of corporate, business, and upper-class groups, leaving those with lower socioeconomic status less able to participate in and influence politics.

Economic and upper class groups were strongly in favor of reducing corporate taxes and funded the election campaigns of Republican lawmakers who shared their interest in major tax reform. In December 2017 President Trump signed the Tax Cuts and Jobs Act that reduced corporate tax rates from 35 to 21 percent and reduced the top individual tax rate from nearly 40 to 37 percent, a sweeping tax cut

In a demonstration of the upper-class bias of interest group politics, Congress worked swiftly to relieve flight delays caused by budget cuts in 2013, prioritizing the issue over concerns about funding for public health and education affecting lower-income Americans.

Though interest groups are prevalent in America, certain people do not have a strong voice in government. These include the homeless, the unemployed, and students. Often these groups have little financial backing to help them organize.

for the wealthiest Americans and corporations. The total cost to taxpayers of the tax bill is $448 billion in lost revenue that will result in cuts to programs that benefit primarily lower and middle-class Americans.[17]

People with higher incomes, more education, and management or professional occupations are much more likely to become members of groups than are those who occupy the lower rungs on the socioeconomic ladder.[18] Well-educated, upper-income business and professional people are more likely to have the time, money, and skills needed to play a role in a group or association or contribute financially to an organized interest. Moreover, for business and professional people, group membership may provide personal contacts, access to information that can help advance their careers, travel perks, discounted insurance, and many other financial benefits. At the same time, of course, corporate entities—businesses and the like—usually have ample resources to form or participate in groups that seek to advance their interests.

The result is that interest group politics in the United States tends to have a pronounced upper-class bias. Certainly, many interest groups and political associations have a working- or lower-class membership—labor organizations or welfare rights organizations, for example—but the vast majority of interest groups and their members are drawn from the middle and upper-middle classes. Even when interest groups take opposing positions on issues and policies, the conflicting positions they take on policy issues usually reflect divisions among upper-income strata rather than conflicts between the upper and lower classes. Many policy issues critical to working and middle class people—quality public education, efficient transportation, affordable housing, safe neighborhoods—are often ignored by government. Thus, when the political system is run by interest groups, democracy will be unequal and many issues important to average Americans will be ignored.

Schattschneider believed that in order to have equal representation in government America needs strong competitive, responsible political parties willing and able to mobilize the lower classes and nonvoters. Interest groups are not enough. That is, citizens from the bottom rungs of the socioeconomic ladder must be organized on the massive scale associated with political parties. Competitive political parties provide alternative choices so that the public can participate in the

government's decision-making process. Interest groups benefit from a limited scope, When political parties compete with one another to win elections, they have incentives to continually expand political discussion to nonvoting members of the electorate to gain a majority of voters. Finally, political parties must also act "responsibly" by informing the public of salient issues in the public interest, not narrow economic interests.

By representing broad public interests, competitive parties could create more equal representation in American politics. Thus, the relative importance of political parties and interest groups in politics has far-ranging implications for the distribution of political power in the United States and for how well the interests of the lower and middle classes are represented. (It should be noted that some public interest and political advocacy groups discussed later seek to educate and inform the public and bring in new members, much like political parties.)

How Groups Organize

Describe how interest groups and social groups organize

Although interest groups are many and varied, most share certain key organizational components. These include leadership, money, an agency or office, and members.

Leadership and decision-making structure are critical for group organization. For some groups, this structure is very simple. For others, it can be quite elaborate and involve hundreds of local chapters that are melded into a national apparatus. Political entrepreneurs initially organize interest groups with a strong commitment to a particular set of goals. Such entrepreneurs see the formation of a group as a means both for achieving those goals and for enhancing their own influence in the political process. And just as is true in the business world, successful groups often become bureaucratized; a paid professional staff replaces the initial entrepreneurial leadership.

For example, MoveOn.org initially formed in 1998 as an email group by software entrepreneurs Joan Blades and Wes Boyd to push for the censure, but not

MoveOn.org is one of America's most influential liberal interest groups. They have claimed to have millions of members and have 250 local chapters across the country. Here, MoveOn holds a rally encouraging Congress to reject President Trump's nomination of Mike Pompeo for Secretary of State.

impeachment, of President Bill Clinton so the country could "move on" to important national issues. Beginning as a ragtag band of liberal activists, MoveOn.org in the past two decades has raised millions of dollars for candidates and progressive policy issues such as legislation protecting consumers, the environment, immigrants, and the working class. Today MoveOn.org has millions of members and 250 local chapters in every state. It is a significant player in the network of progressive organized interest groups in the United States.

Today every group needs a social media strategy. Both progressive and conservative online advocacy groups often have a streamlined staff structure with little bureaucracy. As computer scientist Clay Shirky explains in *Here Comes Everybody*, the internet has given rise to a proliferation of online organizations without formal organizing structures.[19] An example is Wikipedia, whose content is provided by volunteers from around the world. But the real impact of the digital media revolution is the advent of new forms of organization. Leadership remains a priority for online organizations. Entrepreneurship and leadership are important for all interest groups but especially so for those with little staff and formal organization as the leader holds the organization together.

The second key organizational component of interest groups is a financial structure capable of sustaining the organization and funding the group's activities. Because the cost of maintaining groups with a significant online presence is lower than for traditional lobbying groups, more and varied types of organized interests have been able to form and succeed. These groups often raise money via targeted email campaigns for voluntary contributions rather than regular annual membership dues. Many groups also sell some ancillary services to members, such as insurance and vacation tours. In addition, many groups establish an agency that actually carries out the group's tasks, which may be a research organization, a public relations office, or a lobbying office in Washington or a state capital.

membership association an organized group in which members play a substantial role, sitting on committees and engaging in group projects

Finally, almost all interest groups must attract and keep members, whether membership is defined formally or informally. Groups must persuade individuals to invest the money, time, energy, or effort required to take part in the group's activities. Members play a larger role in some groups than in others. In **membership associations**, group members actually serve on committees and engage in projects. In the case of labor unions, members pay significant dues and attend rallies or march in picket lines. In the case of political or ideological groups, members may participate in demonstrations and protests. In another set of groups, **staff organizations**, a professional staff conducts most of the group's activities while members are called on only to make contributions. Among the well-known public interest groups, some, such as the National Organization for Women, are membership groups; others, such as the Children's Defense Fund, are staff organizations. Many online organized interests do not require membership beyond signing up for an online newsletter or signing an online petition.

staff organization a type of membership group in which a professional staff conducts most of the group's activities

THE "FREE-RIDER" PROBLEM

Whether they need individuals to volunteer or merely to write checks, groups need to recruit and retain members. Yet many groups find this task difficult, even when it comes to recruiting members who agree strongly with the group's goals. Why? As the economist Mancur Olson explains, the benefits of a group's success are often broadly available and cannot be denied to nonmembers.[20] Such benefits are called **collective goods.** This term is usually associated with certain government benefits, but it can also be applied to beneficial outcomes of interest group activity.

collective goods benefits sought by groups that are broadly available and cannot be denied to nonmembers

Olson offers this example: suppose a number of private property owners live near a mosquito-infested swamp. Each owner wants this swamp cleared. But if one or a few of the owners were to clear the swamp alone, their actions would benefit all the other owners as well, without any effort on the part of those other owners. Each of the inactive owners would be a **free rider** on the efforts of the ones who cleared the swamp. Thus, there is a disincentive for any of the owners to undertake the job alone. Since the number of concerned owners is small in this particular case, they might eventually be able to organize themselves to share the costs as well as to enjoy the benefits of clearing the swamp.

free riders those who enjoy the benefits of collective goods but did not participate in acquiring or providing them

But suppose the number of interested people is increased. Suppose the common concern is not the neighborhood swamp but polluted air or groundwater involving thousands or even millions of residents. National defense is the most obvious collective good whose benefits are shared by all residents, regardless of the taxes they pay or the support they provide. As the number of involved persons increases or as the size of the group increases, the free-rider phenomenon becomes more of a problem. The group would no doubt be more influential if all concerned individuals were active members—if there were no free riders. This collective action problem is one of the major reasons why many groups do not form.

WHY JOIN GROUPS?

Individuals do not have much incentive to become active members of a group that is already working more or less on their behalf. To overcome this free-rider problem, groups offer members "selective benefits" available only to group members. These benefits can be informational, material, solidary, purposive, or a combination of benefits. A community association, for example, can offer its members a sense of belonging (solidary benefit), involvement in community decision-making (purposive benefit), and reduced rates on homeowners' insurance (material benefit) or a community swimming pool (material benefit). Table 11.2 gives some examples of the range of benefits in each of these categories.

TABLE 11.2

Selective Benefits of Interest Group Membership

CATEGORY	BENEFITS
Informational benefits	Conferences Professional contacts Publications Coordination among organizations Research Legal help Professional codes Collective bargaining
Material benefits	Travel packages Insurance Discounts on consumer goods
Solidary benefits	Friendship Networking opportunities
Purposive benefits	Advocacy Representation before government Participation in public affairs

SOURCE: Adapted from Jack Walker, Jr., *Mobilizing Interest Groups in America: Patrons, Professions, and Social Movements* (Ann Arbor: University of Michigan Press, 1991), 86.

informational benefits special newsletters, periodicals, training programs, conferences, and other information provided to members of groups to entice others to join

material benefits special goods, services, or money provided to members of groups to entice others to join

solidary benefits selective benefits of group membership that emphasize friendship, networking, and consciousness-raising

purposive benefits selective benefits of group membership that emphasize the purpose and accomplishments of the group

Informational benefits are the most widespread and important category of selective benefits offered to group members. Information is provided through online communication such as email, conferences, training programs, and newsletters and other periodicals sent automatically to those who have paid membership dues. **Material benefits** include anything that can be measured monetarily, such as gifts, discount purchasing, shared advertising, and, perhaps most valuable of all, health and retirement insurance. **Solidary benefits** include the friendship and networking opportunities that membership provides. Extremely important to many of the newer citizen groups is "consciousness-raising," including the satisfaction of working toward a common goal with like-minded individuals. One example of this can be seen in the claims of many women's organizations that active participation conveys to each member an enhanced sense of her own value and a stronger ability to advance individual as well as collective rights. Members of associations based on ethnicity, race, or religion also derive solidary benefits from interacting with individuals they perceive as sharing their own backgrounds, values, and perspectives.

A fourth type of benefit involves the appeal of the purpose of an interest group. An example of these **purposive benefits** is businesses joining trade associations to further their economic interests. Similarly, individuals join consumer, environmental, or other civic groups to pursue goals important to them. Many of the most successful interest groups of the past 20 years have been citizen groups or public interest groups organized largely around shared ideological goals, including government reform, civil rights, economic equality, "family values," and even opposition to government itself.

DIGITAL COMMUNICATION AND INTEREST GROUPS

Digital communication is changing how interest groups encourage participation in politics and sustained collective action by citizens. Political scientist and former vice president of the Sierra Club David Karpf has argued that digital media and social media have created a new kind of interest group politics in America that has revolutionized political advocacy. For example, liberal-leaning MoveOn.org and conservative-leaning Americans for Prosperity have arisen over the past two decades to play an increasingly important role in citizen participation in politics. These grassroots online activist organizations have redefined membership and fund-raising practices via innovative methods for communicating with their members, measuring the opinions of their members, and moving their members into action—in terms of influencing public opinion, contributing money to campaigns, and working on behalf of the organization.[21]

Traditional interest groups are expensive to organize (one reason why group membership has an upper-class bias), and they rely on professional advocates and direct mail. They are also slow to change. By contrast, many of today's advocacy groups are relatively inexpensive to organize and quick to adapt to an ever-changing world of politics. Rather than requiring an annual membership fee to join, membership is free and defined by receiving communication from the group or working on behalf of the group. Targeted fund-raising drives—over local, state, or federal government legislation; over a salient event, such as raising money for victims of Hurricane Maria in Puerto Rico; or over an election—is how the organization raises funds to maintain itself. While most traditional interest groups are focused on a single issue—for instance, the Sierra Club seeks protection of the environment while AARP advocates on behalf of older Americans—online advocacy groups are often issue generalists that have a wide umbrella of issues for which they lobby.

Advocacy groups with a significant online structure are less expensive to organize because they have a streamlined staff structure with fewer staff who often work from virtual offices. In contrast, traditional interest groups must maintain offices in Washington, D.C., and other regional locations. The modified staff structure engages in different work routines that prioritize communication with members through email, Twitter, and other digital platforms rather than mailing expensive glossy newsletters or engaging in direct lobbying of members of Congress.

Today's advocacy groups employ grassroots strategies to pressure elected officials. These strategies may include the use of social media to organize rallies, generate news headlines, and promote fund-raising events, letter-writing campaigns, boycotts, and protests. Online advocacy groups may improve representation for citizens, counteracting the disproportionate influence of business and corporate interests in Washington. Liberal and conservative groups, as well as economic interest groups, have been better able to organize and affect government policy in the past decade with the help of the internet and social media.

APPROACHES TO INTEREST GROUP MEMBERSHIP: TWO CASE STUDIES

Online advocacy organizations may also differ from traditional groups in the types of benefits they offer members, as the cases of MoveOn and AARP illustrate.

MoveOn Rather than offering members material selective incentives to join the group, online activist groups like MoveOn offer informational selective benefits to members via daily or weekly news updates and solidary benefits of volunteering or donating money on behalf of the organization. Unlike mainstream news organizations, online advocacy groups are decidedly partisan in the information they provide members. In addition, the group offers their members purposive benefits—the knowledge that one is contributing to a dearly held cause. Purposive benefits may be the most important of all in maintaining the new online citizen advocacy groups.

AARP One group that has been extremely successful in recruiting members and mobilizing them for political action is AARP. The organization was founded as the American Association of Retired Persons in 1958 as a result of the efforts of a retired California high school principal, Ethel Percy Andrus, to find affordable health insurance for herself and the thousands of members of the National Retired Teachers Association. For the insurer, it provided an expanded market; for Andrus, it was a way to serve the ever-growing elderly population, whose problems and needs were expanding along with their numbers and their life

MoveOn.org pioneered a new model of interest group membership and operations. Founded in 1998 and claiming 2 million members, MoveOn seeks to leverage technology to lower the barriers to political participation. In 2018, MoveOn, along with pro-choice groups like NARAL, helped organize online to protest the confirmation of Supreme Court nominee Brett Kavanaugh.

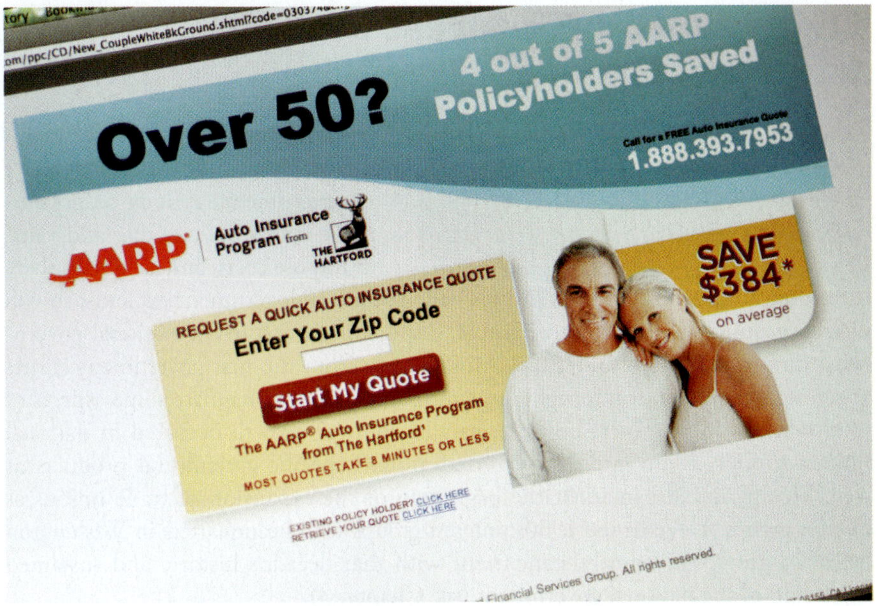

AARP is one of the largest interest groups in the country. One way that AARP attracts members is through selective benefits, such as hotel discounts, credit and identity theft prevention, free health tests, and all types of affordable insurance coverage.

expectancy. Today, AARP is a large and powerful organization with 38 million members and an annual income of $900 million.[22]

How did this large organization overcome the free-rider problem and recruit 38 million older people as members? First, no other organization has ever more successfully provided the selective benefits necessary to overcome the free-rider problem. It helps that AARP began as an organization to provide affordable health insurance for aging members rather than as an organization to influence public policy. But that fact only strengthens the argument that members need short-term individual benefits if they are to invest effort in a longer-term and less concrete set of benefits. As AARP evolved into a political interest group, its leadership added more selective benefits for individual members. It provided guidance against consumer fraud, offered low-interest credit cards, evaluated and endorsed products that were deemed valuable to members, and provided auto insurance and a discounted mail-order pharmacy.

The resources of AARP are so extensive that its leadership has been able to mobilize itself on issues of importance to the group. One of its most successful methods of mobilization for political action is a "telephone tree," with which AARP leaders can quickly mobilize thousands of members for and against proposals that affect Social Security, Medicare, and other questions of security for the aging. A "telephone tree" in each state enables the state AARP chair to phone all of the AARP district directors, who then can phone the presidents of the dozens of local chapters, who can call their local officers and individual members. Within 24 hours, thousands of individual AARP members can be contacting local, state, and national officials to express their opposition to proposed legislation. Other organizations have borrowed strategy from AARP, creating digital versions of the telephone tree using social media and email to allow members to contact their elective representatives over important policy issues.

The Growth of Interest and Advocacy Groups

Analyze why the number of interest and advocacy groups has grown in recent decades

Interest groups and concerns about them are not new. As long as there is government, as long as government makes policies that add value or impose costs, and as long as there is freedom to organize, interest groups will abound. If government expands, so will interest groups. There was, for example, a spurt of growth in the national government during the 1880s and '90s, arising largely from the first government efforts at economic intervention to fight large monopolies and to regulate some aspects of interstate commerce. In response, a parallel spurt of growth occurred in national interest groups. Many groups organized around specific agricultural products as well. This period also marked the beginning of the expansion of trade unions as interest groups. Later, in the 1930s, interest groups with headquarters in Washington began to grow significantly, concurrent with that decade's historic and sustained expansion of the national government (see Chapter 3).

Over the past half-century there has been an even greater increase both in the number of interest groups seeking to play a role in the American political process and in their ability to influence that process. Interest and advocacy groups have become much more numerous, more active, and more influential in American politics, with lobby groups and Super PACs playing major roles in Congress and in electoral politics. This explosion of interest group activity has two basic origins: first, the expansion of the role of government during this period and, second, the coming-of-age of a new and dynamic set of political forces in the United States—forces that have relied heavily on "public interest" groups to advance their causes.

THE EXPANSION OF GOVERNMENT

Modern governments' extensive economic and social programs have powerful politicizing effects, often sparking the organization of new groups and interests. Interest group activity is often a consequence of government. Government involvement in any area can be a powerful stimulus for political organization and action by those whose interests are affected.

For example, during the 1970s expanded federal regulation of the automobile, oil, gas, education, and health care industries compelled each of these industries to increase substantially its efforts to influence the government's laws and regulations. These efforts, in turn, spurred the organization of other groups to counter the activities of the first.[23] Similarly, federal social programs have sparked political organization. For example, federal programs and court decisions in such areas as abortion and school prayer were one factor leading to the rise of fundamentalist religious groups. Thus, the expansion of government in recent decades has also stimulated increased group activity and organization.

Like the federal government, the states too have expanded their scope of government and have likewise witnessed a growth in the number and diversity of interest groups. But interest group activity isn't uniform across the states. One study, for example, found that large-population, affluent states with higher per capita income and higher government expenditures have more trade associations than other states. These large-population, affluent states legislate on more policy areas, and thus activate the business community to lobby to protect their economic interests. Economists call this "rent seeking."[24]

GROWTH OF PUBLIC INTEREST GROUPS IN THE 1960S AND '70S

Public interest groups often advocate for interests that are not addressed by traditional lobbies. For example, in addition to many other activities, the Public Interest Research Group (PIRG) publishes an annual toy safety report to help protect consumers and to encourage policy makers to address problems in this area.

The second factor accounting for the explosion of interest group activity was the emergence of a new set of forces in American politics that can collectively be called the "New Politics movement," which began in the 1960s and '70s. For this cohort of upper-middle-class professionals, the civil rights and antiwar movements were formative political experiences. They formed groups to crusade against racial discrimination and the Vietnam War, and this experience taught them the political efficacy of organized group activity to affect politics. In more recent years, these citizens have focused attention on issues such as environmental protection, social and economic inequality, women's rights, and rights for the LGBTQ community. Members of this movement founded or strengthened public interest groups such as Common Cause, the Sierra Club, the Environmental Defense Fund, and NOW. Such groups were able to influence the media, Congress, and even the judiciary, and enjoyed a remarkable degree of success during the late 1960s and early '70s in securing the enactment of environmental, consumer, and occupational health and safety legislation.

A host of advocacy organizations also exist for the ideological right and have been equally successful. Founded in 1964, the American Conservative Union was one of the first public interest groups to form to advocate for conservative issues. Their primary concerns are liberty, personal responsibility rather than government welfare programs, traditional values, and national defense. Other examples include the American Family Association, one of the leading national Christian advocacy organizations concerned with the moral foundations of American culture, which lobbies for policies that strengthen traditional families; and Citizens United, which uses a combination of education, advocacy, and grassroots organization to seek to restore traditional American values of limited government, free markets, strong families, and national security. These organizations are also active in electoral campaigns, running ads to advantage Republican candidates and against Democratic candidates for public office.

Interest Group Strategies

Explain how interest groups try to influence government and policy

Interest groups work to improve the likelihood that their policy interests will be heard and treated favorably by the government. The quest for political influence or power takes many forms. Insider strategies include access to key decision makers, lobbying, and litigating cases in courts. Outsider strategies include going public and using electoral politics. These strategies do not exhaust all the possibilities, but they paint a broad picture of ways that groups use their resources in the fierce competition for power (see Figure 11.1).

Many groups employ a mix of insider and outsider strategies. For example, environmental groups such as the Sierra Club lobby members of Congress and key congressional staff members, participate in bureaucratic rule making by offering comments and suggestions to agencies on new environmental rules, and bring lawsuits under various environmental acts such as the Endangered Species Act, which authorizes groups and citizens to come to court if they believe the act is being violated. At the same time, the Sierra Club attempts to influence public opinion through media campaigns and to influence electoral politics by supporting candidates who it believes share its environmental views and by opposing candidates it views as foes of environmentalism. While most groups win sometimes and lose sometimes when advocating for their policy goals, in general groups that are well organized and have resources, including citizen groups, are more effective.

FIGURE 11.1

How Interest Groups Influence Congress

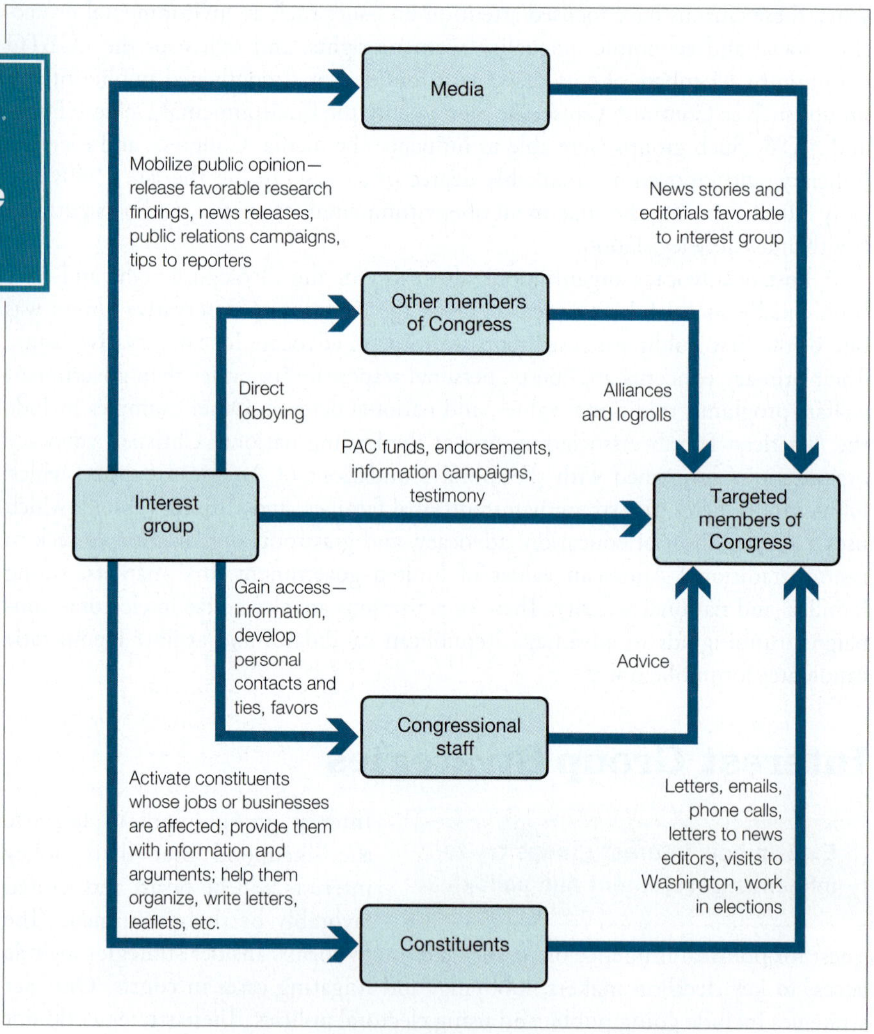

DIRECT LOBBYING

Lobbying is an attempt by a group to influence the policy process through persuasion of government officials. Most Americans tend to believe that interest groups exert their influence through direct contact with members of Congress, but lobbying encompasses a broad range of activities that groups engage in with all sorts of government officials and the public as a whole.

lobbying a strategy by which organized interests seek to influence the passage of legislation by exerting direct pressure on government officials

The 1946 Federal Regulation of Lobbying Act defines a lobbyist as "any person who shall engage himself for pay or any consideration for the purpose of attempting to influence the passage or defeat of any legislation of the Congress of the United States." The 1995 Lobbying Disclosure Act requires all organizations employing lobbyists to register with Congress and to disclose whom they represent, whom they lobby, what they are looking for, and how much they are paid. Approximately 9,443 lobbyists are currently registered, down from a height of over 14,000 in 2007.[25]

Lobbying involves a great deal of activity on the part of someone speaking for an interest, and lobbyists attempt to influence the policy process in a variety of ways.[26] Lobbyists first and foremost provide information to lawmakers, administrators, and committee staff about their interests and the legislation at hand. They often testify on behalf of their clients at congressional committee and agency hearings. Lobbyists talk to reporters, place ads in newspapers, and organize letter-writing, phone call, and email campaigns. Many lobbying efforts occur in private meetings with lawmakers and campaign leaders, and behind closed doors. They also play an important role in fund-raising, helping to direct clients' contributions to certain members of Congress and presidential candidates.

Lobbying Congress Traditionally, the term *lobbyist* referred mainly to individuals who sought to influence the passage of legislation in Congress. The First Amendment to the Constitution provides for the right to "petition the Government for a redress of grievances." But as early as the 1870s, *lobbying* became the common term for petitioning. And since petitioning cannot take place on the floor of the House or Senate, petitioners must confront members of Congress in the lobbies of the legislative chamber—hence the term *lobbying*.

Sophisticated lobbyists win influence by providing information about policies to busy members of Congress. Although interest groups do not necessarily buy votes, they do buy time, expertise, and influence. Studies have found that those interest groups providing the most money to representatives are more likely to be consulted by that representative and asked to provide information and expertise in discussing a bill pertaining to that group's area of interest. This, in essence, gives interest groups a voice in shaping how legislation is written; and while it cannot ensure votes for laws preferred by the group, by participating in the policy process, organized interests are influencing policy.

The influence of lobbyists, in many instances, is based on personal relationships and the behind-the-scenes services they are able to perform for lawmakers. Many of Washington's top lobbyists have close ties to important members of Congress or were themselves important political figures, thus virtually guaranteeing that their clients will have direct access to congressional leaders. Some important lobbyists have more than a business relationship to lawmakers: quite a few, in fact, are married to prominent political figures.

Through their lobbyists, interest groups also have substantial influence in setting the legislative agenda. They help to craft specific language in legislation and build coalitions and comprehensive campaigns around particular policy issues.[27]

Like many of their colleagues, John Boehner (R-Ohio, left) and Mary Landrieu (D-La., right) worked as lobbyists after leaving Congress. Members of Congress have knowledge and contacts that make them particularly attractive to lobbying firms.

These coalitions do not rise from the grassroots but instead are put together by Washington lobbyists who launch comprehensive campaigns that combine simulated grassroots activity with information and campaign funding for members of Congress.

What happens to interests that do not engage in extensive lobbying? They often find themselves "Microsofted"; that is, marginalized in the political process. In 1998 the software giant was facing antitrust action from the Justice Department and had few friends in Congress. One member of the House, Representative Billy Tauzin (R-La.), told Microsoft's chair, Bill Gates, that without an extensive investment in lobbying, the corporation would continue to be "demonized." Gates responded by quadrupling Microsoft's lobbying expenditures and hiring lobbyists with strong ties to Congress. The result was congressional pressure on the Justice Department that led to a settlement of the Microsoft suit on terms favorable to the company.[28] Today massive companies like Amazon and Facebook may be in a situation similar to Microsoft's in the '90s in that they need to increase lobbying efforts. President Trump and other leaders publically criticized Amazon for becoming too large in terms of market share and Facebook for not protecting the privacy of its members' information.

Lobbying the President So many individuals and groups clamor for the president's time and attention that only the most skilled and best-connected members of the lobbying community can hope to influence presidential decisions. Typically, a president's key political advisers and fund-raisers will include individuals with ties to the lobbying industry who can help their friends gain access to the White House.

Lobbying the president took an odd twist in 2018 when Donald Trump's personal lawyer, Michael Cohen, was widely criticized for accepting millions of dollars from corporations including AT&T and international drug companies for "insights" on the president's decision making, although Cohen is not registered as a lobbyist. Cohen is under investigation by the federal prosecutor for bank fraud, wire fraud, and campaign finance violations; crimes to which he plead guilty in August 2018.

Lobbying the Executive Branch Even when an interest group is successful at getting its bill passed by Congress and signed by the president, the prospect of full and faithful implementation of that law is not guaranteed. Often a group and its allies do not pack up and go home as soon as the president turns the new law they

Business leaders are often able to gain special access to elected officials. Here, Maximo Alvarez, president of Sunshine Gasoline Distributors (left), and Irina Vilarino, owner of Las Vegas Cuban Cuisine (right), meet with President Trump to discuss tax cuts for small businesses.

lobbied for over to the appropriate agency. In some respects, interest group access to the executive branch is facilitated by federal law. The Administrative Procedure Act, first enacted in 1946 and frequently amended in subsequent years, requires most federal agencies to provide notice and an opportunity for comment before implementing proposed new rules and regulations. This "notice and comment rule making" is designed to allow interests an opportunity to make their views known and to participate in the implementation of federal legislation that affects them. Congress enacted the Negotiated Rulemaking Act in 1990 to encourage administrative agencies to engage in direct and open negotiations with affected interests when developing new regulations. These two pieces of legislation have played an important role in opening the bureaucratic process to interest group influence. Today, few federal agencies would consider attempting to implement a new rule without consulting affected interests, known in Washington as "stakeholders."[29]

How Interest Groups Make Policy; Iron Triangles and Issue Networks The development of government policy is the product of the so-called **iron triangle**, which has one angle in an executive branch program (bureaucratic agency), another angle in a Senate or House committee or subcommittee, and a third angle in some highly stable and well-organized interest group. In policy areas such as farming and agriculture policy or energy policy, interest groups, government agencies, and congressional committees routinely work together for mutual benefit. The interest group provides campaign contributions for members of Congress, lobbies for larger budgets for the agency, and provides policy expertise to lawmakers. The agency, in turn, provides government contracts for the interest group and constituency services for friendly members of Congress. The congressional committee or subcommittee, meanwhile, supports the agency's budgetary requests and the programs the interest group favors. Together the three actors that make up the angles in the triangle create a mutually supportive relationship that can last over a long period of time, especially if a committee member has considerable seniority in Congress. An interest cannot feel

iron triangle the stable, cooperative relationship that often develops among a congressional committee, an administrative agency, and one or more supportive interest groups; not all of these relationships are triangular, but the iron triangle is the most typical

FIGURE 11.2

The Iron Triangle in the Defense Sector

Defense contractors are powerful actors in shaping defense policy; they act in concert with defense committees and subcommittees in Congress and executive agencies concerned with defense.

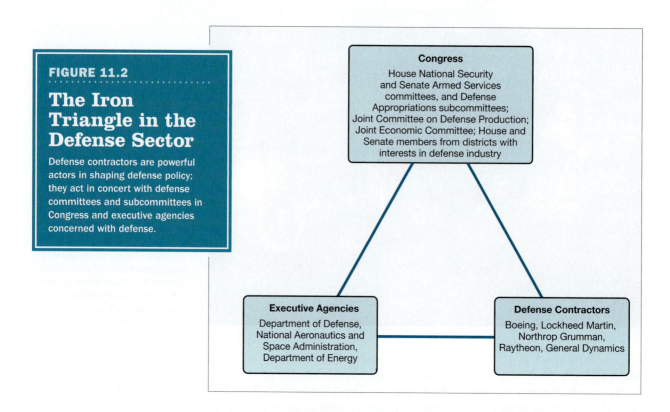

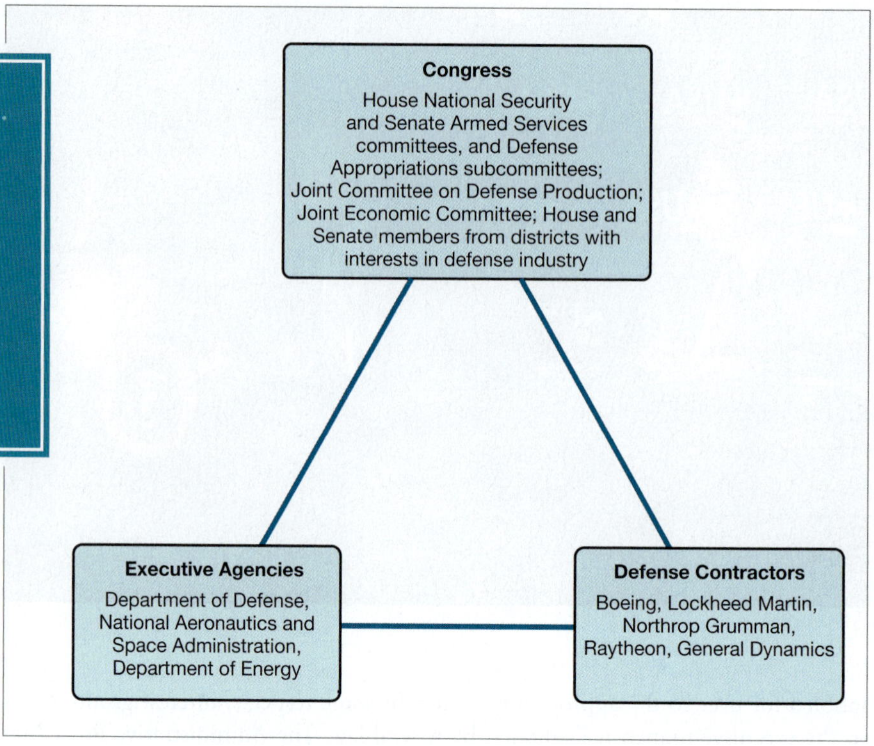

comfortable about its access to Congress until it has one or more of its "own" people with 10 or more years of continuous service on the relevant committee or subcommittee. Figure 11.2 illustrates an important iron triangle in recent American political history: that of the defense industry.

issue network a loose network of elected leaders, public officials, activists, and interest groups drawn together by a specific policy issue

A number of important policy domains, such as the environment, tax policy, and immigration policy, are controlled not by highly structured and unified iron triangles but by broader **issue networks.** These networks consist of like-minded politicians, consultants, public officials, activists, and interest groups that care about the issue in question. Activists and interest groups recognized as being involved in the issue (the stakeholders) are customarily invited to testify before congressional committees or give their views to government agencies considering action in their domain. Issue networks and iron triangles may be overlapping and may coexist.

REGULATING LOBBYING

Sometimes the actions of lobbyists are outside of the law. In 2005 a prominent Washington lobbyist, Jack Abramoff, was indicted on numerous charges of fraud and violations of federal lobbying laws. During the investigation of his activities, it was revealed that Abramoff, along with his associate Michael Scanlon, had collected tens of millions of dollars from several American Indian tribes that operated lucrative gambling casinos. (Indian gambling is currently a $30 billion industry in the United States.) What Abramoff provided in exchange was access to key Republican members of Congress, who helped his clients shut down rival casino operators. Abramoff was closely associated with several House members, including the former House majority leader Tom DeLay. Millions of tribal dollars found their way into the campaign war chests of Abramoff's friends in Congress. Thus, through a well-connected lobbyist, money had effectively purchased access and influence. Abramoff and several of his associates subsequently pleaded guilty to federal bribery and fraud charges, and Abramoff was sentenced to more than five years in prison.

Because lobbyists are so influential in Washington, D.C., Congress has tried to limit their role by adopting stricter guidelines. However, the effectiveness of the new rules is unclear. For example, businesses may no longer deduct lobbying costs as a business expense. Trade associations must report to members the proportion of their dues that goes toward lobbying, and that proportion of the dues may not be reported as a business expense. The most important new regulation was the 1995 Lobbying Disclosure Act, which expanded the definition of the organization and individuals that must register to lobby.

In 1996, Congress passed legislation limiting the size of gifts to its own members and banned the practice of honoraria for giving speeches, which special interests had used to supplement congressional salaries. In 2007 new rules prohibited lobbyists from paying for most meals, trips, parties, and gifts for members of Congress. Lobbyists were also required to disclose the amounts and sources of small campaign contributions they collected from clients and "bundled" into large contributions. And interest groups were required to disclose the funds they used to rally voters to support or oppose legislative proposals. According to the *Washington Post*, however, within a few weeks, lobbyists had learned how to circumvent many of the new rules, and lobbying firms were as busy as ever.[30]

USING THE COURTS

Interest groups sometimes turn to litigation when they lack access or when they feel they have insufficient influence to change a policy. Interest groups can use the courts to affect public policy in at least three ways: (1) by bringing suit directly on behalf of the group itself, (2) by financing suits brought by individuals, or (3) by filing a companion brief as an *amicus curiae* (literally "friend of the court") to an existing court case (see Chapter 15 for a discussion of amicus briefs).

Among the best-known illustrations of using the courts for political influence is found in the history of the National Association for the Advancement of Colored People (NAACP). In *Brown v. Board of Education of Topeka, Kansas*, the U.S. Supreme Court held that legal segregation of the schools was unconstitutional.[31] Later, extensive litigation accompanied the women's rights movement in the 1960s and the movement for rights for gays and lesbians in the 1990s. In 2015 the case of *Obergefell v. Hodges* illustrated the success of this litigation strategy as the Supreme Court declared that the Fourteenth Amendment prohibited states from refusing to issue marriage licenses to same-sex couples.[32]

The 1973 Supreme Court case of *Roe v. Wade*, which took away a state's power to ban abortions, sparked a controversy that organized conservatives nationwide.[33] Since 1973, conservative groups have made extensive use of the courts to whittle away at the scope of the privacy doctrine initially defined by the Supreme Court in *Roe v. Wade*. They obtained rulings, for example, that prohibit the use of federal funds to pay for voluntary abortions. And in 1989 right-to-life groups were able to use the case of *Webster v. Reproductive Health Services* to restore the right of states to place restrictions on abortion, thus undermining the

When the Food and Drug Administration (FDA) required cigarette packages to carry new warning labels such as the one below, a coalition of tobacco companies sued the government, claiming the labels violated First Amendment rights. The companies won their suit. In response, anticigarette groups such as the Campaign for Tobacco-Free kids are urging the FDA to develop new warnings.

Roe v. Wade decision (see Chapter 4).[34] The *Webster* case brought more than 300 interest groups on both sides of the abortion issue to the Supreme Court's door. On the other side of the political spectrum, the American Civil Liberties Union (ACLU) regularly uses litigation to challenge state and federal laws that restrict the rights of individuals and groups. This includes recent successful challenges to laws ending affirmative action in the states.

Litigation involving large businesses is voluminous in such areas as taxation, antitrust, interstate transportation, patents, and product quality and standardization. Often a business is brought to litigation against its will by virtue of initiatives taken against it by other businesses or by government agencies. But many individual businesses bring suit themselves to influence government policy, and business groups also frequently use the courts because of the number of government programs applied to them. Major corporations and their trade associations pay tremendous amounts of money each year in fees to the most prestigious Washington law firms. Much of this money is used to keep the best and most experienced lawyers prepared to represent the corporations in court or before administrative agencies when necessary.

institutional advertising
advertising designed to create a positive image of an organization

MOBILIZING PUBLIC OPINION

Going public is a strategy to mobilize the widest and most favorable public opinion for an issue or societal problem, and a favored strategy of citizen groups, membership groups, and online advocacy groups. Many groups consider it imperative to maintain this climate at all times. As early as the 1930s, political analysts were distinguishing between the "old lobby" of direct group representation before Congress and the "new lobby" of public-relations professionals addressing the public at large as a way to ultimately reach Congress.[35]

One of the best-known ways of going public is the use of **institutional advertising**. A casual scanning of websites, newspapers, and television ads will provide numerous examples of expensive and well-designed ads by the major oil and gas companies, automobile and steel companies, other large corporations, and trade associations. The ads attempt to show how much these organizations are doing for the country. Their purpose is to create and maintain a positive association between an organization

Throughout American history, groups have staged mass protests to bring greater attention to their causes. These have included (from left) the Selma to Montgomery march for civil rights, organized by Martin Luther King, Jr., and others in 1965; Tea Party rallies for lower taxes and smaller government, which erupted in 2009; the Occupy Wall Street movement of 2011, which protested income inequality; and the Black Lives Matter movement, which began in 2013 in response to the killing of Trayvon Martin by George Zimmerman.

and the community at large in the hope of drawing on these favorable feelings as needed for specific political campaigns later on.

As discussed earlier, citizen groups and advocacy groups rely heavily on mobilizing the public opinion of their members via social media, such as Twitter campaigns and targeted email messages. On any given day a new viral media story may become headline news, and in most cases an interest group is behind the story. Such groups span the ideological spectrum from liberal to conservative and can wield significant pressure on elected officials to act.

Protests and Demonstrations Many groups resort to going public because they lack the resources, the contacts, or the experience to use other political strategies. The sponsorship of boycotts, sit-ins, mass rallies, and marches by Martin Luther King, Jr.'s, Southern Christian Leadership Conference and related organizations during the 1950s and '60s is one of the most significant and successful cases of going public to create a more favorable climate of opinion by calling attention to abuses. The success of these events inspired similar efforts by women's groups.

The 2010 Republican takeover of the House of Representatives began with the spontaneous self-organization of the Tea Party movement in 2009 as an angry response to the Obama administration's health care initiatives. In 2011 the Occupy Wall Street movement sparked demonstrations across America and around the world, giving voice to those who are outraged by economic inequality. In 2013 the Black Lives Matter movement took off after the shooting of an unarmed black teenager by a member of the local neighborhood watch and quickly spread across the nation. Shootings of black people by police and vigilantes across the country have led to major demonstrations protesting institutionalized racism, and calling in particular for the elimination of racial inequality in the criminal justice system.

Grassroots Mobilization Another form of going public is **grassroots mobilization**, in which a lobby group mobilizes its members and their families throughout the country to call or email their elected representatives in support of the group's position. Among the most effective users of the grassroots effort in contemporary American politics is the religious right. Networks of evangelical churches have the capacity to generate hundreds of thousands of letters, phone calls, and emails to Congress and

grassroots mobilization a lobbying campaign in which a group mobilizes its membership to contact government officials in support of the group's position

the White House. Similarly, the NRA maintains a powerful grassroots lobbying effort, spending more on mobilization of its members than on professional lobbyists. The NRA's 5 million dues-paying members can be mobilized to flood congressional offices with letters and phone calls, and few members of Congress are eager to pick a fight with the group.[36] The interests of the NRA were seriously challenged in 2018 when, in the aftermath of a mass shooting at a high school in Parkland, Florida, in February 2018, students there used social media to mobilize Americans across the nation in support of stronger gun laws. Under the label "March for Our Lives," these students successfully coordinated a mass rally in Washington, D.C., as well as rallies around the country. Largely as a result of their efforts, and those of supporters they attracted, several states enacted tougher gun laws. Grassroots campaigns have been so effective in recent years that a number of Washington consulting firms have begun to specialize in this area.[37]

Sometimes, what initially appears to be an upswelling of grassroots mobilization is not in fact a genuine grassroots campaign but instead represents "Astroturf lobbying" (a play on the name of the artificial grass used on many sports fields). Such campaigns, often using email, have increased in frequency in recent years, yet members of Congress often continue to respond more to lobbyists than to public demonstrations of support for specific policy issues.

USING ELECTORAL POLITICS

In addition to attempting to influence members of Congress and other government officials, interest groups seek to use the electoral process to elect the right legislators in the first place and to ensure that those who are elected will owe them a debt of gratitude for their support. If we view matters in perspective, groups invest more resources in lobbying than in electoral politics. Nevertheless, financial support and campaign activism can be important tools for organized interests. The NRA, for example, dramatically increased its spending in the 2016 election, spending $30 million to support Trump.[38]

Political Action Committees and Super PACs By far the most common electoral strategy employed by interest groups is that of giving financial support to political parties or specific candidates running for office. But such support can easily cross the threshold into outright bribery. Therefore, Congress has occasionally attempted to regulate this strategy, but with limited success. The Federal Election Campaign Act of 1971 (amended in 1974) requires that each candidate or campaign committee itemize the full name and address, occupation, and principal business of each person who contributes more than $100. These provisions create an open record of which organizations and individuals fund the campaigns of candidates for public office.

The 1972 Watergate scandal was triggered by the illegal entry of a group of clandestine agents employed by the president's re-election committee into the office of the Democratic National Committee in the Watergate apartment and hotel complex. An investigation quickly revealed numerous violations of campaign finance laws, involving millions of dollars in unregistered cash from corporate executives to President Nixon's re-election committee. Reaction to Watergate produced further legislation on campaign finance in 1974 and 1976, but the effect was to restrict individuals rather than interest group campaign activity. In the 2017–18 election cycle, individuals could contribute no more than $2,700 to any candidate for federal office in any

Who Is Represented by PACs?

In the 2016 election cycle, political action committees (PACs) spent a grand total of $1.7 billion to elect and defeat political candidates. PACs representing the financial sector spent the most, followed closely by agribusiness. For many sectors, the amount donated to Republican candidates exceeded that donated to Democratic candidates.

PAC Contributions to Federal Candidates, 2016

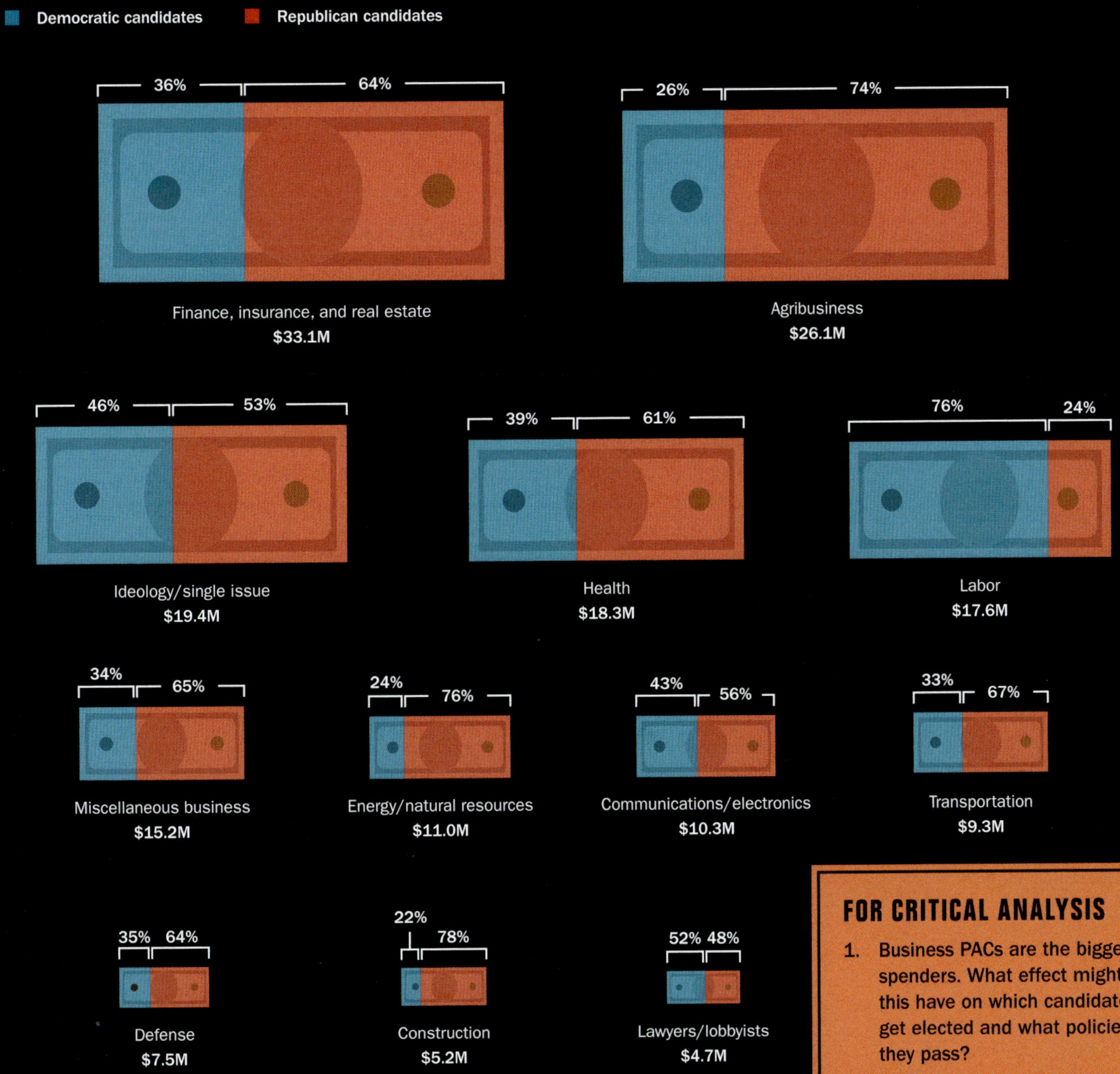

■ Democratic candidates ■ Republican candidates

36% 64%
Finance, insurance, and real estate
$33.1M

26% 74%
Agribusiness
$26.1M

46% 53%
Ideology/single issue
$19.4M

39% 61%
Health
$18.3M

76% 24%
Labor
$17.6M

34% 65%
Miscellaneous business
$15.2M

24% 76%
Energy/natural resources
$11.0M

43% 56%
Communications/electronics
$10.3M

33% 67%
Transportation
$9.3M

35% 64%
Defense
$7.5M

22% 78%
Construction
$5.2M

52% 48%
Lawyers/lobbyists
$4.7M

FOR CRITICAL ANALYSIS

1. Business PACs are the biggest spenders. What effect might this have on which candidates get elected and what policies they pass?

2. Why do you think PACs are more likely to donate to Republican candidates than to Democratic candidates?

political action committee (PAC) a private group that raises and distributes funds for use in election campaigns

primary or general election. A **political action committee (PAC)**, however, can contribute $5,000, provided it contributes to at least five different federal candidates each year. (Campaign finance regulations are discussed in more detail in Chapter 10.) The laws permit corporations, unions, and other interest groups to form PACs. PACs represent interest groups in electoral politics. The option to form a PAC was made available by law in the early 1970s. Before then it was difficult, if not downright illegal, for corporations, including unions, to get directly involved in elections by supporting parties and candidates.

The flurry of reform legislation in the 1970s attempted to reduce the influence that interest groups have over elections, but the effect has been almost the exact opposite. Electoral spending by interest groups has been increasing dramatically.

Given the enormous costs of running political campaigns, most politicians are eager to receive contributions and at least willing to give a friendly hearing to the needs and interests of contributors. While most politicians do not "sell out" to the interests that fund their campaigns, there is evidence that interest groups' campaign contributions do influence the overall pattern of political behavior in Congress and in the state legislatures, and that lawmakers represent affluent individuals and groups more than the middle class.[39] (See the "Who Are Americans?" feature for one depiction of who is represented by PACs.)

Concern about PACs grew through the 1980s and '90s, creating a constant drumbeat for reform of federal election laws. Proposals to abolish PACs were introduced in Congress on many occasions, with perhaps the most celebrated being the "McCain-Feingold bill" (the Bipartisan Campaign Reform Act of 2002). When originally proposed in 1996, McCain-Feingold was aimed at reducing or eliminating PACs. But in a stunning about-face, when the act was adopted in 2002, it did not restrict PACs in any significant way.

527 committee (Super PAC) a nonprofit independent political action committee that may raise unlimited sums of money from corporations, unions, and individuals but is not permitted to contribute to or coordinate directly with parties or candidates

One consequence of this reform, was the creation of new organizations, to fund candidates: **Super PACs** and **527 committees.** As we saw above, a PAC has a maximum contribution limit of $5,000 per candidate in each election cycle. Super PACs, on the other hand, cannot donate to candidates or parties directly, but they can spend unlimited sums of money on campaigns to influence an election in favor of candidates or parties as long as their activity (for example, campaign ads or mobilization efforts) is not coordinated with the candidates or parties. Because there are no limits on the amount of money Super PACs may raise from corporations, unions, and interest groups, they have become more important than PACs and have had the effect of strengthening interest groups. As long as a group's campaign expenditures are not coordinated with those of a candidate's campaign, the group is free to spend as much money as it wishes. Such expenditures are viewed as "issue advocacy" and are protected by the First Amendment. The Supreme Court's landmark decision *Citizens United v. Federal Election Commission* (2010) dramatically increased the flow of money from interest groups, 527s, and Super PACs into politics and electoral campaigns. *Citizens United* removed restrictions on corporate and union political spending.[40]

In the 2016 presidential election, independent expenditures (commonly referred to as outside spending) totaled about $1.3 billion, of which $594 million came from Super PACs. Candidates Hillary Clinton and Donald Trump raised $1.5 billion total, and the Super PACs supporting them raised $618 million, according to the Center for Responsive Government.[41] Super PAC financing of U.S. elections represents a significant amount of all dollars spent on electoral campaigns. In 2016, Super PACs spent more than $1.1 billion on House and Senate races.[42] In the 2018 election there were 2,224 Super PACs, which together spent $815 million.[43]

The amount of money spent by organized interests on elections has increased dramatically in the last decade. This cartoon raises the concern that influence in government is for sale and only the extremely wealthy can buy it.

Campaign Activism Financial support is not the only way that organized groups seek influence through electoral politics. Sometimes activism can be even more important than campaign contributions. Campaign activism on the part of conservative groups played a very important role in bringing about the Republican capture of both houses of Congress in 1994. For example, Christian Coalition activists played a role in many races, including those in which Republican candidates were not strongly identified with the religious right. One postelection study suggested that more than 60 percent of the more than 600 candidates supported by the Christian right were successful in state, local, and congressional races in 1994, especially in the South.[44] In many congressional districts, Christian Coalition efforts were augmented by grassroots campaigns launched by the NRA, which had been outraged by Democratic support for gun control legislation. Both groups are well organized at the local level and were able to mobilize their members across the country to participate in congressional races. In the 2012 presidential elections, prochoice groups mobilized their supporters to turn out and vote for Democratic candidate Obama via telephone get-out-the-vote drives.

Ballot Initiatives Another political tactic that interest groups use is sponsorship of ballot initiatives at the state level. The initiative, available in half the states allows proposed laws to be placed on the general election ballot and submitted directly to the voters, bypassing the state legislature and the governor. The initiative was originally promoted by late-nineteenth-century Populists and Progressives as a mechanism that would allow the people to govern directly—an antidote to interest group influence in the legislative process.

Some studies have suggested that, ironically, many initiative campaigns today are actually sponsored by interest groups seeking to circumvent legislative opposition to their goals. In recent years, for example, initiative campaigns have been sponsored by the insurance industry, the automobile industry, trial lawyers' associations, and tobacco companies.[45] The success of business groups promoting successful tax limitation ballot measures in the 1970s and 1980s has led liberal activists to develop their own issue campaigns. Liberal activists established the Ballot Initiative Strategy Center to provide national coordination for these efforts, which led to successful statewide ballot measures to raise the minimum wage, protect the environment in Colorado, and increase taxes for corporations and high-income wage earners in Oregon and California. Both corporate and grassroots groups have had success with ballot initiatives over the past two decades.

But while businesses may sponsor ballot initiatives, such measures are much more likely to be rejected by voters on Election Day than initiatives sponsored by citizen groups. In an important study, political scientist Elisabeth Gerber finds that citizen groups and unions are the most effective at sponsoring ballot measures, whereas businesses, trade associations, and professional associations are more effective at lobbying state legislatures. The implication is that mechanisms of direct democracy, like the initiative process, favor citizen interests while lobbying favors economic interests.[46]

Interest Groups
WHAT DO WE WANT?

We would like to think that government policies are products of legislators representing the public interest. The truth of the matter is that few programs and policies ever reach the public agenda without the vigorous efforts of important national interest groups. In the realm of economic policy, social policy, and international trade policy, the activity of interest groups is of critical importance.

James Madison wrote that "liberty is to faction as air is to fire."[47] By this he meant that the organization and proliferation of interests are inevitable in a free society. As long as competition among different interests was free, open, and vigorous—that is, as long as pluralism thrived—there would be some balance of power among them, and no one interest would be able to dominate the political or governmental process.

Indeed, there is considerable competition among organized groups in the United States. Prochoice and antiabortion forces, for example, continue to be locked in a bitter struggle, as are the NRA and gun control groups. Nevertheless, interest group politics is not as balanced as Madison's theory and pluralism might suggest. Although the weak and poor do occasionally become organized to assert their interests, interest group politics is generally a form of political competition best suited to the wealthy and powerful.

Moreover, although groups sometimes organize to promote broad public concerns, they more often represent relatively narrow, selfish interests. Small groups seeking narrow interests can be organized much more easily than large and diffuse collectives. The members of relatively small groups—say, bankers or hunting enthusiasts—are usually able to recognize their shared interests and the need to pursue them in the political arena. Members of large and diffuse groups—say, consumers or the unemployed—often find it difficult to recognize their shared interests or the need to engage in collective action to achieve them.[48] Whether Ben Brown's new Association of Young Americans can grow and achieve legislative success remains to be seen, as younger Americans' activism may be undercut by the diverse array of interests they have and by the many immediate concerns that dominate their time (school, work, and family, among others).

Organized interest groups sometimes seem to have a greater impact than voters on the government's policies and programs, especially through lobbying and financial contributions to political candidates. (The "**Who Participates?**" feature on the facing page shows how much major groups spend on lobbying activities). Yet, before we decide that we should do away with interest groups, we should think carefully: If there were no organized interests, would the government pay more attention to ordinary voters? Would young people be better or worse off if there were no interest groups in the United States? Or would the government simply pay less attention to everyone? In his work *Democracy in America*, Alexis de Tocqueville argued that the proliferation of groups promoted democracy by encouraging governmental responsiveness. Does group politics foster democracy or impede democracy? It does both.

WHO PARTICIPATES?

How Much Do Major Groups Spend?

Lobbying Expenditures, 2016 (top spenders)

[money stack icon] = $1,000,000

- **$103,950,000** U.S. Chamber of Commerce
- **$64,821,111** National Association of Realtors
- **$25,006,109** Blue Cross/Blue Shield
- **$22,006,109** American Hospital Association
- **$19,730,000** Pharmaceutical Research & Manufacturers of America
- **$19,410,000** American Medical Association
- **$17,020,000** Boeing Co.
- **$16,438.000** National Association of Broadcasters
- **$16,370,000** AT&T Inc.
- **$15,700,000** Business Roundtable
- **$15,430,000** Alphabet Inc.
- **$14,330,000** Comcast Corp.
- **$13,900,000** Southern Co.
- **$13,635,982** Dow Chemical
- **$13,615,811** Lockheed Martin
- **$13,420,000** The Internet & Television Association (NCTA)
- **$12,541,000** FedEx Corp.
- **12,050,000** Northrop Grumman
- **$11,840,000** ExxonMobil
- **$11,354,000** Amazon.com

SOURCE: Center for Responsive Politics, www.opensecrets.org/lobby (accessed 11/21/17).

★ WHAT YOU CAN DO ★

Get Involved with Interest Groups and Lobbying

- ☑ Find an interest group that appeals to you at **votesmart.org/interest-groups**, then follow that group on Facebook or Twitter.
- ☑ Find out which groups give the most money to your representatives in Congress by clicking "Congress" at **www.opensecrets.org/politicians**. You can look up your representatives by zip code.
- ☑ Contact your Center for Campus Life to find out if groups you're interested in have chapters on your campus. Many groups will gladly help students start campus chapters.

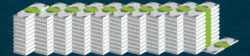

STUDY GUIDE

Defining Interest Groups

Describe the major types of interest groups and whom they represent (pp. 431–39)

An interest group is an organized group of people that makes policy-related appeals to government. Common types of interest groups include economic and corporate groups, labor groups, and citizen (or public interest) groups. Well-educated, upper-income, professional people are more likely to have the time, money, and skills to participate in interest groups. As a result, interest groups tend to skew in favor of corporate, business, and upper-class interests, leaving those with lower socioeconomic status less able to participate in and influence politics.

Key Terms

pluralism (p. 431)
interest group (p. 431)
public interest groups (p. 435)

Practice Quiz

1. The theory that competition among organized interests will produce balance and compromise, with all the interests regulating one another, is
   a) pluralism.
   b) elite power politics.
   c) democracy.
   d) socialism.
   e) libertarianism.

2. The Natural Resources Defense Council, the Sierra Club, the National Civic League, and Common Cause are all examples of
   a) membership associations.
   b) public interest groups.
   c) professional associations.
   d) ideological groups.
   e) public-sector groups.

How Groups Organize

Describe how interest groups and social groups organize (pp. 439–45)

Almost all interest groups share a similar set of organizational components, including leadership, money, an office, and members. In order to overcome the free-rider problem, interest groups attempt to provide their potential members with informational, material, solidary, and purposive benefits. Online advocacy groups have established new approaches to organization and membership.

Key Terms

membership association (p. 440)
staff organization (p. 441)
collective goods (p. 441)
free riders (p. 441)
informational benefits (p. 442)
material benefits (p. 442)
solidary benefits (p. 442)
purposive benefits (p. 442)

Practice Quiz

3. Benefits sought by groups that are broadly available and cannot be denied to nonmembers are called
   a) purposive benefits.
   b) informational benefits.
   c) solidary benefits.
   d) material benefits.
   e) collective goods.

4. Friendship and networking are examples of
   a) purposive benefits.
   b) informational benefits.
   c) solidary benefits.
   d) material benefits.
   e) collective goods.

5. Discount purchasing and health insurance are examples of
   a) purposive benefits.
   b) informational benefits.
   c) solidary benefits.
   d) material benefits.
   e) collective goods.

The Growth of Interest and Advocacy Groups

Analyze why the number of interest and advocacy groups has grown in recent decades (pp. 446–47)

In recent decades there has been a significant growth in the number of interest groups seeking to influence the American political process. One reason for this change has been the dramatic expansion of the role of American government over the last four decades. Another reason for this change has been the emergence of a new set of political forces in the United States called the "New Politics" movement.

Practice Quiz

6. Which of the following is an important reason for the enormous increase in the number of groups seeking to influence the American political system?
   a) the decrease in the size and activity of government during the last few decades
   b) the increase in the size and activity of government during the last few decades
   c) the increase in the amount of soft money in election campaigns in recent decades
   d) the increase in legal protection provided to interest groups as a result of the Supreme Court's evolving interpretation of the First Amendment
   e) the increase in the number of people identifying themselves as independent in recent decades

Interest Group Strategies

Explain how interest groups try to influence government and policy (pp. 447–59)

Interest groups take action to improve the probability that their policy interests will be treated favorably by all branches and all levels of government. These actions often take many different forms. Insider strategies include direct lobbying, cultivating access to decision makers, and using the court system. Outsider strategies include mobilizing public opinion and using electoral politics.

Key Terms

lobbying (p. 449)
iron triangle (p. 451)
issue network (p. 452)
institutional advertising (p. 454)
grassroots mobilization (p. 455)
political action committee (PAC) (p. 458)
527 committee (Super PAC) (p. 458)

Practice Quiz

7. Which of the following best describes the federal government's laws regarding lobbying?
   a) Federal law allows lobbying but only on issues related to taxation.
   b) Federal law allows lobbying but only if the lobbyists receive no monetary compensation for their lobbying.
   c) Federal law strictly prohibits any form of lobbying.
   d) Federal law requires all organizations employing lobbyists to register with Congress and to disclose whom they represent, whom they lobby, what they are looking for, and how much they are paid.
   e) There are no laws regulating lobbying because the federal government has never passed any legislation on the legality of the activity.
8. A loose network of elected leaders, public officials, activists, and interest groups drawn together by a public policy issue is referred to as
   a) an issue network.
   b) a public interest group.
   c) a political action committee.
   d) pluralism.
   e) an iron triangle.
9. Which of the following is a way that interest groups use the courts to influence public policy?
   a) supplying judges with solidary benefits
   b) joining an issue network
   c) creating an iron triangle
   d) forming a political action committee
   e) filing amicus curiae briefs

10. Which of the following are examples of the "going public" strategy?
    a) free riding, pluralism, and issue networking
    b) donating money to political parties, endorsing candidates, and sponsoring ballot initiatives
    c) institutional advertising, grassroots advertising, and protests and demonstrations
    d) providing informational benefits, providing solidary benefits, and providing material benefits
    e) filing an amicus brief, bringing a lawsuit, and financing those who are filing a lawsuit

11. Which of the following is *not* an activity in which interest groups frequently engage?
    a) starting their own political party
    b) litigation
    c) sponsoring ballot initiatives at the state level
    d) lobbying
    e) contributing to campaigns

12. One of the major differences between PACs and Super PACs is that
    a) a PAC has a maximum contribution limit of $500 per candidate in each election cycle while a Super PAC has a maximum contribution limit of $1,000.
    b) a PAC has a maximum contribution limit of $1,000 per candidate in each election cycle while a Super PAC has a maximum contribution limit of $5,000.
    c) a PAC has a maximum contribution limit of $5,000 per candidate in each election cycle while a Super PAC has a maximum contribution limit of $10,000.
    d) a PAC has a maximum contribution limit of $5,000 per candidate in each election cycle while a Super PAC cannot donate to candidates directly.
    e) a Super PAC has a maximum contribution limit of $5,000 per candidate in each election cycle while a PAC cannot donate to candidates directly.

For Further Reading

Alexander, Robert, ed. *The Classics of Interest Group Behavior.* New York: Wadsworth, 2005.

Baumgartner, Frank, Jeffrey M. Berry, Beth L. Leech, David C. Kimball, and Marie Hojnacki. *Lobbying and Policy Change: Who Wins, Who Loses, and Why.* Chicago: University of Chicago Press, 2009.

Berry, Jeffrey. *Interest Group Society.* 5th ed. New York: Longman, 2008.

Cigler, Allan J., and Burdett A. Loomis, eds. *Interest Group Politics.* 9th ed. Washington, DC: CQ Press, 2015.

Drutman, Lee. *The Business of America Is Lobbying: How Corporations Became Politicized and Politics Became More Corporate.* New York: Oxford University Press, 2015.

Goldstein, Kenneth. *Interest Groups, Lobbying, and Participation in America.* New York: Cambridge University Press, 2008.

Herrnson, Paul, and Christopher Deering. *Interest Groups Unleashed.* Washington, DC: CQ Press, 2012.

Holyoke, Thomas. *Interest Groups and Lobbying: Pursuing Political Interests in America.* Boulder, CO: Westview, 2014.

Kaiser, Robert. *So Damn Much Money: The Triumph of Lobbying and the Corrosion of American Government.* New York: Vintage, 2010.

Karpf, David. *The MoveOn Effect: The Unexpected Transformation of American Political Advocacy.* New York: Oxford University Press, 2012.

Lessig, Lawrence. *Republic, Lost: How Money Corrupts Congress—and a Plan to Stop It.* New York: Twelve/Hachette Book Group, 2011.

Lowi, Theodore J. *The End of Liberalism: The Second Republic of the United States.* 2nd ed. New York: W. W. Norton, 1979.

Moe, Terry M. *The Organization of Interests: Incentives and the Internal Dynamics of Political Interest Groups.* Chicago: University of Chicago Press, 1980.

Nownes, Anthony. *Total Lobbying: What Lobbyists Want and How They Try to Get It.* New York: Cambridge University Press, 2006.

Olson, Mancur, Jr. *The Logic of Collective Action: Public Goods and the Theory of Groups.* Cambridge, MA: Harvard University Press, 1965.

Shirky, Clay. *Here Comes Everybody: The Power of Organizing without Organizations.* New York: Penguin Press, 2008.

Strolovitch, Dara. *Affirmative Advocacy: Race, Class, and Gender in Interest Group Politics.* Chicago: University of Chicago Press, 2007.

Recommended Websites

AARP
www.aarp.org
AARP (formerly the American Association of Retired Persons) is one of the largest and most significant interest groups in the United States. Read about the history of this organization, its group benefits, and how it is affecting political issues and elections.

AFL-CIO Legislative Alerts
www.aflcio.org/Legislation-and-Politics/Legislative-Alerts
Created in 1955, the AFL-CIO represents more than 10 million working men and women. See how this influential labor group is active and involved in political issues.

American Civil Liberties Union
www.aclu.org

American Conservative Union
www.conservative.org
The American Civil Liberties Union and the American Conservative Union are two of the nation's largest and most influential ideological interest groups. See what these opposing groups have to say about our government and current political issues.

American Israel Public Affairs Committee
www.aipac.org
Due to globalization, interest groups cannot limit their activities to one country. Decisions made in Washington, D.C., can affect countries around the world. The American Israel Public Affairs Committee works with Republicans and Democrats to maintain a strong relationship between the United States and Israel.

MoveOn
www.moveon.org
This progressive interest group is dedicated to bringing ordinary citizens back into the political process and electing liberal members of government. See how this group uses electoral politics, via political action committees and campaign activism, to achieve its agenda.

National Rifle Association
www.nra.org

Coalition to Stop Gun Violence
www.csgv.org

Brady Campaign to Prevent Gun Violence
www.bradycampaign.org
Lobbying is an attempt by a group to influence the policy process by persuading government officials. These three groups employ a variety of lobbying techniques on the issue of gun control.

U.S. Public Interest Research Group
www.uspirg.org
This public interest group stands up for ordinary citizens. Its special emphasis is on consumer rights and the environment. U.S. Public Interest Research Group (U.S. PIRG) mobilizes public opinion via institutional advertising, social movements, and grassroots efforts. U.S. PIRG chapters can be found in most states and at many colleges and universities.

World Wildlife Fund
www.wwf.org
The World Wildlife Fund is dedicated to protecting nature. It provides information to policy makers about conservation and advocates for policies to help preserve the natural environment.

issue, it is important for the American people to learn about what Congress is doing. As the example of the near government shutdown indicates, actions taken—or not taken—in Congress affect the everyday experiences we take for granted. With its power to spend and tax, Congress also affects the choices that people face and the opportunities they can expect in life. With so much information about Congress available on the internet, it is not hard to get beyond the heated rhetoric and simplistic headlines and ask your own questions about a proposed law. How will it affect my life and the lives of people I care about? What is the impact on my country? Making laws is a complex and often messy process. Even so, it is vital for citizens to monitor what Congress does because the laws it passes are so central to their lives.

CHAPTER GOALS

- ★ **Describe who serves in Congress and how they represent their constituents (pp. 469–82)**
- ★ **Explain how party leadership, the committee system, the staff system, and caucuses help structure congressional business (pp. 482–89)**
- ★ **Outline the steps in the process of passing a law (pp. 489–94)**
- ★ **Analyze the factors that influence which laws Congress passes (pp. 494–502)**
- ★ **Describe Congress's influence over other branches of government (pp. 502–5)**

Congress: Representing the American People

Describe who serves in Congress and how they represent their constituents

Congress is the most important representative institution in American government. Each member's primary responsibility in theory is to the district, to his or her **constituency**, not to the congressional leadership, a party, or even Congress itself. Yet the task of representation is not a simple one. Views about what constitutes fair and effective representation differ, and constituents may have very different expectations of their representatives. Members of Congress must consider these diverse views and expectations as they represent their districts.

constituency the residents in the area from which an official is elected

HOUSE AND SENATE: DIFFERENCES IN REPRESENTATION

The framers of the Constitution provided for a **bicameral** legislature—that is, a legislative body consisting of two chambers. As we saw in Chapter 2, the framers intended each of these chambers, the House of Representatives and the Senate, to serve a different constituency. Members of the Senate, appointed by state legislatures for six-year terms, were to represent society's elite. Today, members of both the House and the Senate are elected directly by the people. The 435 members of the House are elected from districts apportioned according to population; the 100 members of the Senate are elected in a statewide vote, with two senators from each state. Senators continue to have much longer terms in office and usually represent much larger and more diverse constituencies than do their counterparts in the House (see Table 12.1).

bicameral having a legislative assembly composed of two chambers or houses, distinguished from *unicameral*

The House and Senate play different roles in the legislative process. In essence, the Senate is the more deliberative of the two bodies—the forum in which any and all ideas that senators raise can receive a thorough public airing. The House is the

TABLE 12.1

Differences between the House and the Senate

	HOUSE	SENATE
Minimum age of member	25 years	30 years
U.S. citizenship	At least 7 years	At least 9 years
Length of term	2 years	6 years
Number representing each state	1-53 per state (depends on population)	2 per state
Constituency	Local	Statewide

For its first 128 years, Congress was a decidedly masculine world. In 1917, Jeanette Rankin (R-Mont.; pictured back row, far right) became the first woman to serve in the House or Senate. As of 2016, a total of 297 women had served as U.S. representatives or senators, while 11,804 men have served.

more centralized and organized of the two bodies—better equipped to play a routine role in the governmental process. In part, this difference stems from the different rules governing the two bodies. These rules give House leaders more control over the legislative process and allow House members to specialize in certain legislative areas. The rules of the much smaller Senate give its leadership relatively little power and discourage specialization.

Both formal and informal factors contribute to differences between the two chambers of Congress. Differences in the length of terms and requirements for holding office, specified by the Constitution, generate differences in how members of each body develop their constituencies and exercise their powers of office. For the House, the small size and relative homogeneity of their constituencies and the frequency with which they must seek re-election—every two years—make members more attuned to the legislative needs of local interest groups. The result is that members of the House most effectively and frequently serve as the agents of well-organized local interests with specific legislative agendas—for instance, used-car dealers seeking relief from regulation, labor unions seeking more favorable legislation, or farmers looking for higher subsidies. Because House members seek re-election every two years, they are interested in doing what their constituents want right *now*.

Senators, on the other hand, serve larger and more heterogeneous constituencies. As a result, they are somewhat better able than members of the House to act as the agents for groups and interests organized on a statewide or national basis. Moreover, with longer terms in office (six years), senators have more time to consider "new ideas" or to bring together new coalitions of interests rather than simply serving existing ones.

TRUSTEE VERSUS DELEGATE REPRESENTATION

delegate a representative who votes according to the preferences of his or her constituency

trustee a representative who votes based on what he or she thinks is best for his or her constituency

For the Founders, Congress was the national institution that best embodied the ideals of representative democracy. But what is the role of a representative? A member of Congress can interpret her job as representative in two different ways: as a **delegate**, acting on the express preferences of her constituents, or as a **trustee**, more loosely tied to constituents and empowered to make the decisions she thinks best. The delegate role appears to be the more democratic because it forces representatives to heed the desires of their constituents. But this requires the representative to be in constant touch with constituents; it also requires constituents to follow each policy issue very closely. The problem with this form of representation is that most people do not follow every issue so carefully; instead, they focus only on the issue or issues of particular interest to them. Many people are too busy to get the information necessary to make informed judgments even on issues they care about. Thus, adhering to the delegate form of representation runs the risk that the voices of only a few active and informed constituents get heard. Although it seems more democratic at first glance, the delegate form of representation may actually open Congress up to even more influence by special interests.

When congressional members act as trustees, on the other hand, they may not pay sufficient attention to the wishes of their constituents. In this scenario, the only way the public can exercise influence is by voting every two years for representatives and every six years for senators. In fact, most members of Congress take this electoral check very seriously. They try to anticipate the wishes of their constituents even when they don't know exactly what those wishes are because they know that unpopular decisions can be used against them in the coming election.

SOCIOLOGICAL VERSUS AGENCY REPRESENTATION

We have become so accustomed to the idea of representative government that we tend to forget what a peculiar concept representation really is. A representative claims to act or speak for some other person or group. But how can one person be trusted to speak for another? How do we know that those who call themselves our representatives are actually speaking on our behalf, rather than simply pursuing their own interests?

There are two circumstances under which one person reasonably might be trusted to speak for another. The first occurs if the two individuals are so similar in background, character, interests, and perspectives that anything said by one would very likely reflect the views of the other as well. This principle is at the heart of what is sometimes called **sociological representation**—the sort of representation that takes place when representatives have the same racial, gender, ethnic, religious, or educational backgrounds as their constituents. The assumption is that sociological similarity helps to promote good representation; thus, the composition of a properly constituted representative assembly should mirror the composition of society.

sociological representation a type of representation in which representatives have the same racial, gender, ethnic, religious, or educational backgrounds as their constituents; it is based on the principle that if two individuals are similar in background, character, interests, and perspectives, then one can correctly represent the other's views

The second circumstance under which one person might be trusted to speak for another occurs if the two are formally bound together so that the representative is in some way accountable to those he is supposed to represent. If representatives can somehow be punished for failing to speak properly for their constituents, then we know they have an incentive to provide good representation even if their own personal backgrounds, views, and interests differ from the backgrounds of those they represent. This principle is called **agency representation**—the sort of representation that takes place when constituents have the power to hire and fire their representatives.

agency representation a type of representation in which a representative is held accountable to a constituency if he or she fails to represent that constituency properly; this is incentive for the representative to provide good representation when his or her personal backgrounds, views, and interests differ from those of his or her constituency

Both sociological and agency representation play a role in the relationship between members of Congress and their constituencies, but in many ways, members of Congress do not reflect the American population (see the "Who Are Americans?" feature on p. 473).

The Social Composition of the U.S. Congress The extent to which the U.S. Congress is representative of the American people in a sociological sense can be seen by examining social characteristics of the House and Senate today. For example, the religious affiliations of members of both the House and Senate are overwhelmingly Protestant—the distribution is very close to the proportion in the population at large. Catholics are the second-largest category of religious affiliation and Jews a much smaller, third category.[4] Religious affiliations directly affect congressional debate on a limited range of issues where different moral views are at stake, such as abortion.

FOR CRITICAL ANALYSIS

Why is sociological representation important? If congressional representatives have racial, religious, or educational backgrounds similar to those of their constituents, are they better representatives? Why or why not?

African Americans, women, Latinos, and Asian Americans have increased their congressional representation in the past two decades (see Figure 12.1), but the representation of minorities in Congress is still not comparable to their proportions in the general population. After the 2018 elections, Congress was 9 percent African American, 7 percent Latino, and 3 percent Asian American. By contrast, the American population was far more diverse, with 13.3 percent African Americans, 17.6 percent Latinos, and 5.6 percent Asian Americans.[5] As the United States has

FIGURE 12.1

Number of Women, African Americans, and Latinos in the U.S. Congress, 1971–2019

Congress has become much more socially diverse since the 1970s. After a gradual increase from 1971 to 1990, the number of female and African American members grew quickly during the first half of the 1990s. Do you think these numbers will rise in the future? Why or why not?

SOURCES: Harold W. Stanley and Richard G. Niemi, eds., *Vital Statistics on American Politics 2003-2004* (Washington, DC: CQ Press, 2003), 207, Table 5-2; Jennifer E. Manning, *Membership of the 113th Congress: A Profile*, Congressional Research Service 7-5700, January 13, 2014, www.fas.org/sgp/crs/misc/R42964.pdf (accessed 2/24/14); Jennifer E. Manning, *Membership of the 114th Congress: A Profile*, Congressional Research Service, 7-5700 September 17, 2015, www.fas.org/sgp/crs/misc/R43869.pdf (accessed 9/28/15); R. Eric Petersen, *Representatives and Senators: Trends in Member Characteristics since 1945*, Congressional Research Service 7-5700, February 17, 2012, www.fas.org/sgp/crs/misc/R42365.pdf (accessed 9/28/15); 2019 data were calculated by the authors.

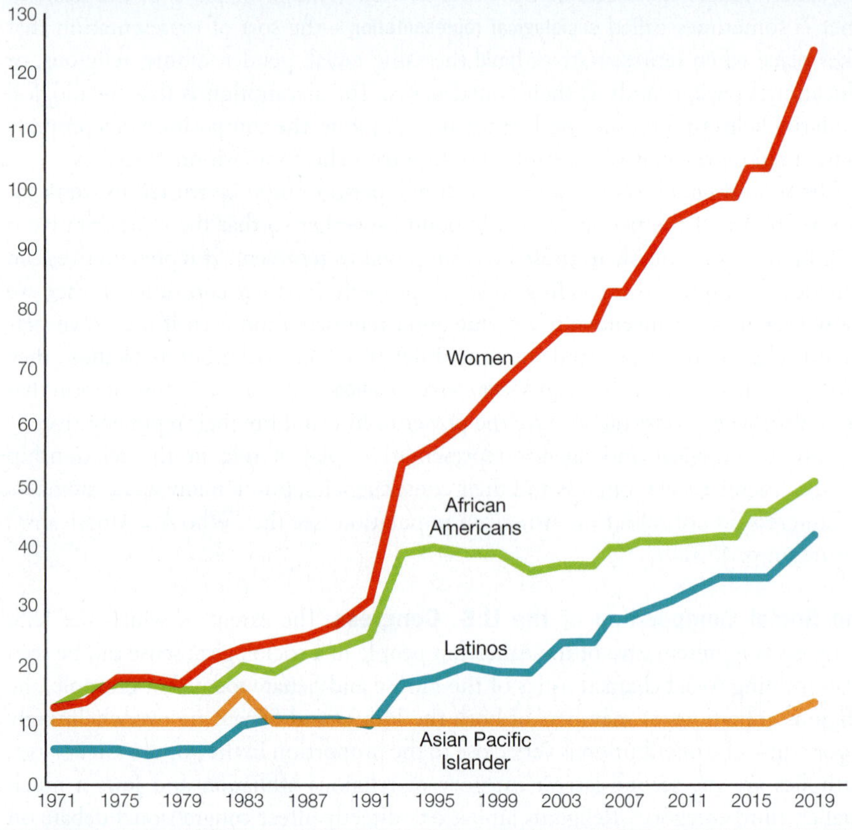

become more diverse, Congress has lagged behind in sociological representation. Similarly, the number of women in Congress continues to trail far behind their proportion of the population. In 2006, Nancy Pelosi (D-Calif.) became the first female Speaker of the House. Following the 2018 elections, the 116th Congress (2019–21) included at least 102 women in the House and 23 women in the Senate, an all-time high. Since many important contemporary issues cut along racial and

Who Are the Members of Congress?

Gender

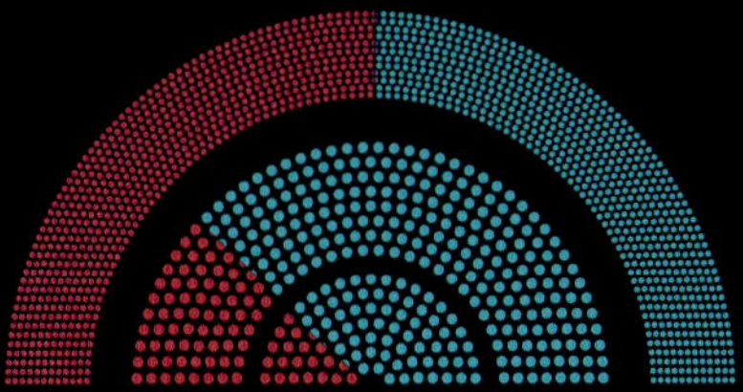

	Senate	House	U.S. pop.
Female	24%	23%	51%
Male	76%	77%	49%

Party

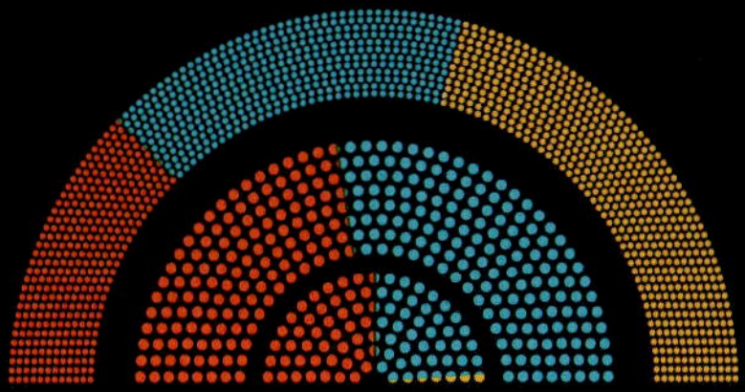

	Senate	House	U.S. pop.*
Republican	51%	45%	25%
Democratic	46%	52%	33%
Independent	2%	0%	36%

Key

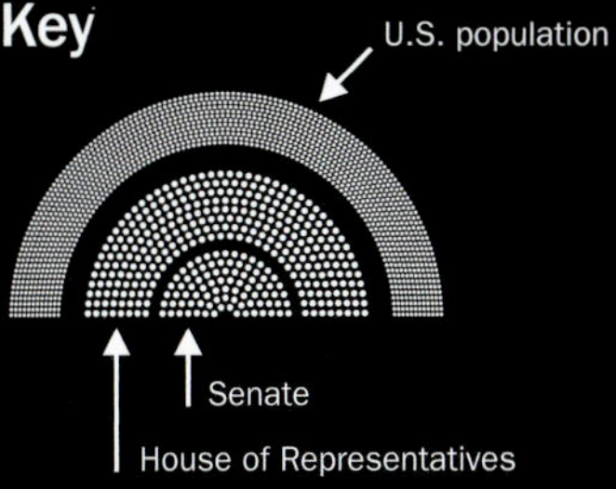

Although the number of women, African Americans, and Latinos in Congress has increased in recent decades, Congress is still much less diverse than the American population. Members of Congress are predominantly male, white, Protestant, and a large percentage hold a law degree. These data compare the 116th Congress, which took office in 2019, with the U.S. population as a whole.

Race

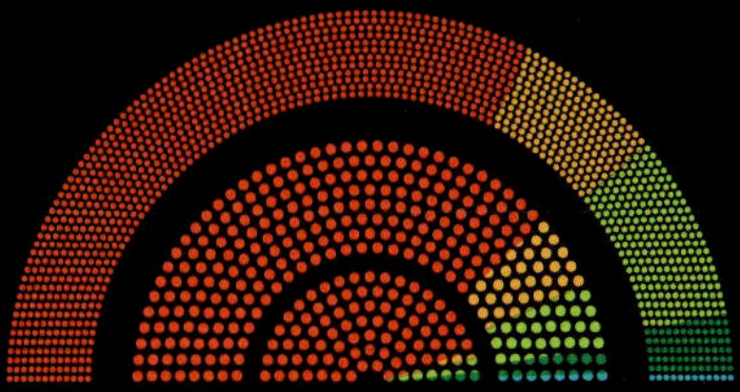

	Senate*	House	U.S. pop.*
White	90%	77%	64%
Black	3%	11%	13%
Hispanic	4%	9%	16%
Asian	3%	3%	5%
Native American	0%	1%	1%

Religion

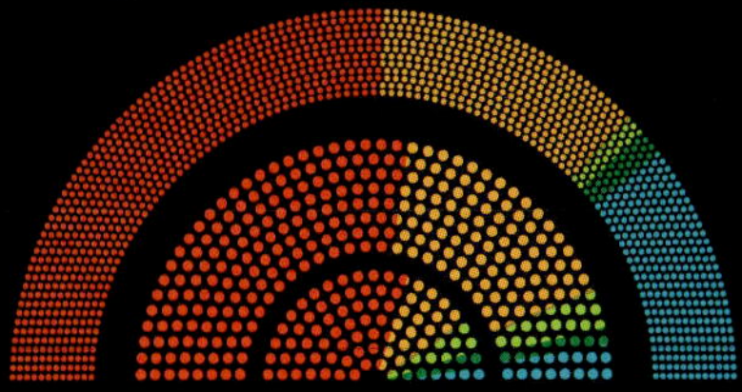

	Senate	House	U.S. pop.
Protestant	60%	55%	51%
Catholic	22%	33%	24%
Jewish	9%	5%	2%
Mormon	5%	2%	2%
All others	4%	5%	21%

Foreign birth

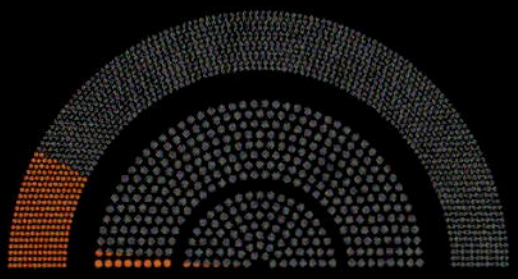

Senate	1%
House	3%
U.S. population	13%

Military service

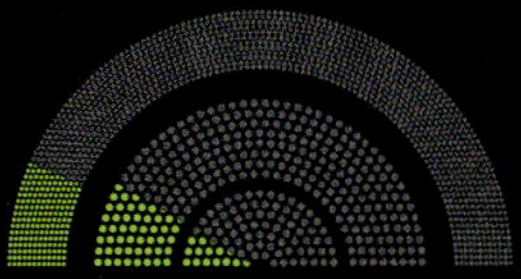

Senate	16%
House	17%
U.S. population	13%

Holds a law degree

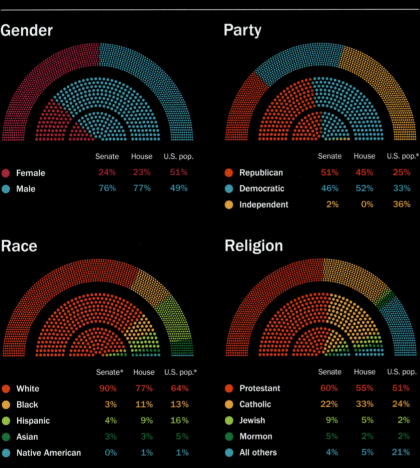

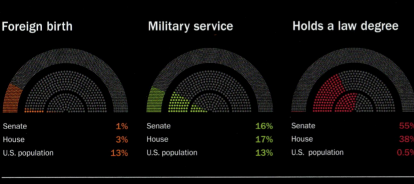

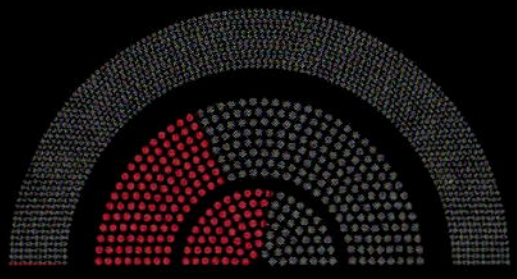

Senate	55%
House	38%
U.S. population	0.5%

Average age

Senate 61 House 57 U.S. population 37

NOTES: As of November 13, 2018, 10 House races and 2 Senate races remain undecided.
Data for religion are from the 115th Congress.
*Percentages do not sum to 100 because some Americans identify with other categories.
SOURCES: Jennifer E. Manning, "Membership of the 115th Congress: A Profile," Congressional Research Service, www.fas.org/sgp/crs/misc/R43869.pdf (accessed 11/12/18); U.S. Census Bureau, www.census.gov/population/age/-data/2012comp.html (accessed 3/19/14); and author's updates.

FOR CRITICAL ANALYSIS

1. Does it matter if the backgrounds of members of Congress reflect the population as a whole? Can members still represent their constituents effectively if they do not come from similar backgrounds?
2. Visit www.house.gov and www.senate.gov to identify your representatives in Congress and visit their web pages. How similar are their backgrounds to yours? How closely do their policy positions, as expressed on their web pages, match your own?

To more effectively promote a legislative agenda addressing issues that disproportionately affect racial and ethnic minority groups, members of Congress from those groups have formed caucuses. Here, Rep. Michelle Lujan Grisham (D-N. Mex.), former chair of the Congressional Hispanic Caucus, speaks out about Donald Trump's proposed changes to immigration policies.

gender lines, pressure for reform in the representative process is likely to continue until all groups are fully represented.

The occupational backgrounds of members of Congress have always been a matter of interest because many issues split along economic lines that are relevant to occupations and industries. The legal profession is the dominant career of most members of Congress prior to their election, and public service or politics is also a significant background. In addition, many members of Congress have important ties to business and industry.[6] Moreover, members of Congress are much more highly educated than most Americans. More than 9 in 10 members hold university degrees, and more than one-third of them have law degrees.[7] This is not a portrait of the U.S. population; Congress is not a sociological microcosm of American society.

Can Congress still legislate fairly or take account of a diversity of views and interests if it is not a sociologically representative assembly? There is reason to believe it can. Representatives, as we shall see shortly, can serve as the agents of their constituents even if they do not precisely mirror their sociological attributes. Yet sociological representation is a matter of some importance. At the least, the social composition of a representative assembly is important for symbolic purposes: to demonstrate to groups in the population that the government takes them seriously. If Congress is not representative symbolically, then its own authority, and indeed that of the entire government, is reduced.[8]

Representatives as Agents A good deal of evidence indicates that whether or not members of Congress share their constituents' sociological characteristics, they *do* work very hard to speak for their constituents' views and to serve their constituents' interests. The idea of representative as agent is similar to the relationship of lawyer and client. True, the relationship between the House member and an average of 710,767 "clients" in the district, or the senator and millions of "clients" in the state, is very different from that of the lawyer and client. But the criteria of performance are comparable. One expects at the very least that each representative will constantly seek to discover the interests of the constituency and take those interests into account as she governs. Whether members of Congress always represent the interests of their constituents is another matter, as we will see later in this chapter.[9]

There is constant communication between constituents and congressional offices, and the volume of email from constituents and advocacy groups has grown so large so quickly that congressional offices have struggled to find effective ways to respond in a timely manner.[10] At the same time, members of Congress have found new ways to communicate with constituents. They have created websites describing their achievements, established a presence on social networking sites, and issued e-newsletters that alert constituents to current issues. Many also have set up blogs and Twitter accounts to establish a more informal style of communication with constituents.

The seriousness with which members of the House attempt to behave as representatives can be seen in the amount of time they spend on behalf of their constituents. One way to measure the amount of time members of Congress devote to constituency service (called "casework") is to look at the percentage of personal House and Senate staff (personal staff being non-committee member staff) assigned to district and state offices. In 1972, 22.5 percent of House members' personal staff were located in district offices; by 2016 the number had grown to 47.3 percent. For the Senate, the staff in state offices grew from 12.5 percent in 1972 to 43.2 percent in 2016.[11] The service that these offices provide is not merely a matter of handling correspondence. It includes talking to constituents; providing them with minor services; presenting special bills for them; attempting to influence decisions by regulatory commissions on their behalf; helping them apply for federal benefits such as Social Security and Small Business Administration loans; and assisting them with immigration cases. For example, during his fight for re-election in 2014, Senate Minority Leader Mitch McConnell (R-Ky.) ran a campaign ad featuring Noelle Hunter, a Kentucky resident whose ex-husband abducted their daughter and took her to Africa. According to Hunter, McConnell "took up my cause personally" and worked with the State Department to bring her daughter back home. Senator Pat Roberts (R-Kans.) struck a similar tone when touting his success in helping Kate Forristall, a Kansan whose daughter was taken hostage while teaching English in Ethiopia. Roberts says in the ad, "We got the call. Top priority. We went to work."[12]

In many districts, there are two or three issues that are top priorities for constituents and, therefore, for the representatives. For example, representatives from districts that grow wheat, cotton, or tobacco will likely give legislation on these subjects great attention. In oil-rich states such as Oklahoma and Texas, senators and members of the House are likely to be leading advocates of oil interests. For one thing, representatives are probably fearful of voting against their district interests; for another, the districts are unlikely to have elected representatives who would *want* to vote against them. On the other hand, on many issues, constituents do not have very strong views, and representatives are free to act as they think best. Foreign policy issues often fall into this category.

The influence of constituencies is so pervasive that both parties generally agree that nothing should be done to endanger the re-election chances of any member. Party leaders obey this rule fairly consistently by not asking any member to vote in a way that might conflict with a district interest.

THE ELECTORAL CONNECTION

The sociological composition of Congress and the activities of representatives once they are in office are very much influenced by electoral considerations. Three factors related to the U.S. electoral system affect who gets elected and what they do once in office. The first factor concerns who decides to run for office and which candidates have an edge over others. The second issue is that of incumbency advantage. Finally, the way congressional district lines are drawn can greatly affect the outcome of an election. Let us examine more closely the impact that these considerations have on representation.

Who Runs for Congress Voters' choices are restricted from the start by who decides to run for office. In the past, decisions about who would run for a particular elected office were made by local party officials. A person who had a record of service to the party, who was owed a favor, or whose "turn" had come up might be nominated by party leaders. Today, few party organizations have the power to slate candidates in this way. Instead, parties try to ensure that well-qualified candidates run for Congress. During the 1990s the Republican Party developed "farm teams" of local officials who were groomed to run for Congress. Their success led Democrats to attempt a similar strategy. Even so, the decision to run for Congress is a personal one, and one of the most important factors determining who runs for office is an individual candidate's ambition.[13] A potential candidate may also assess whether he can attract enough money to mount a credible campaign. The ability to raise money depends on connections with other politicians, interest groups, and national party organizations.

Features distinctive to each congressional district also affect the field of candidates. For example, the way the congressional district overlaps with state legislative boundaries may affect a candidate's decision to run. A state-level legislator who is considering running for the U.S. Congress is more likely to assess her prospects favorably if her state district coincides with the congressional district (because the voters will already know her).

incumbency holding the political office for which one is running

Incumbency **Incumbency** plays a very important role in the American electoral system and in the kind of representation citizens get in Washington. Once in office, members of Congress gain access to an array of tools they can use to stack the deck in favor of their re-election. Their success in winning re-election is evident in the high rates of re-election for congressional incumbents: as high as 98 percent for House members and 90 percent for members of the Senate in recent years (see Figure 12.2). It is also evident in what is called "sophomore surge"—the tendency for candidates to win a higher percentage of the vote when seeking subsequent terms in office. In 2018 approximately 93 percent of incumbents in the House and 86 percent in the Senate were re-elected.[14] Furthermore, incumbents often win by large margins: in 2018 only 76 of the 435 House races were decided by a margin of less than 10 percent.[15]

Incumbency can help a candidate by scaring off potential challengers. In many races, potential candidates may decide not to run because they fear that the incumbent simply has too much money or is too well liked or too well known or that a district's partisan leanings are too unfavorable. The efforts of incumbents to raise funds to ward off potential challengers start early. In addition to incumbents' own efforts, each political party makes a special effort to reelect incumbents viewed as especially vulnerable. The Democratic Congressional Campaign Committee (DCCC) places vulnerable incumbents in its "Frontline" program to receive extra funding, choice committee assignments, and high-profile speaking engagements. For the 2018 midterm elections, the DCCC placed 19 incumbents on its Frontline list, many of whom had won in 2016 in districts carried by Trump. For its part, the Republican Congressional Campaign Committee (RCCC) named 10 members to its own incumbent protection program.[16]

The advantage of incumbency thus tends to preserve the status quo in Congress. This fact has implications for the social composition of Congress. For example,

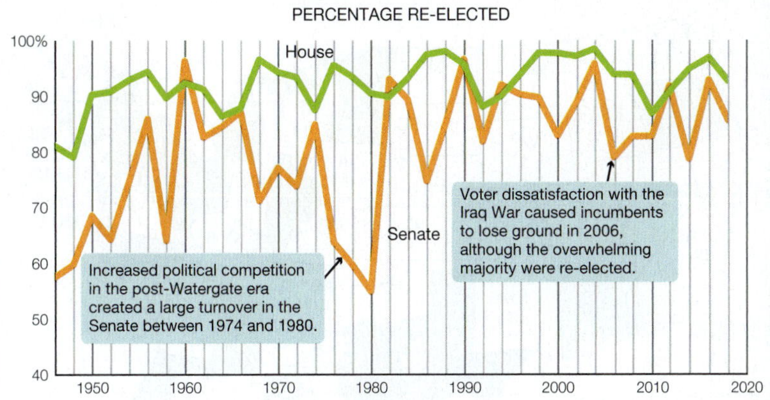
PERCENTAGE RE-ELECTED
100%
90
80
70
60
50
40
1950
1960
1970
1980
1990
2000
2010
2020
House
Senate
Increased political competition in the post-Watergate era created a large turnover in the Senate between 1974 and 1980.
Voter dissatisfaction with the Iraq War caused incumbents to lose ground in 2006, although the overwhelming majority were re-elected.

FIGURE 12.2

The Power of Incumbency

Members of Congress who run for re-election have a very good chance of winning. Has the incumbency advantage generally been greater in the House or in the Senate? What are the consequences of the incumbency advantage for who serves in Congress?

SOURCES: Norman J. Ornstein et al., eds., *Vital Statistics on Congress, 1999-2000* (Washington, DC: AEI Press, 2000), 57-8; "Reelection Rates over the Years," opensecrets.org; and authors' update.

incumbency advantage makes it harder for women to increase their numbers in Congress because most incumbents are men. Women who run for open seats—that is, seats for which there are no incumbents—are just as likely to win as male candidates.[17] Supporters of **term limits** argue that such limits are the only way to get new faces into Congress. They believe that incumbency advantage and the tendency of many legislators to view politics as a career mean that very little turnover will occur in Congress unless limits are imposed on the number of terms a legislator may serve.

term limits legally prescribed limits on the number of terms an elected official can serve

Yet the percentage of incumbents who are returned to Congress after each election also depends on how many members decide to run again. Because each year some members decide to retire, turnover in Congress is greater than the re-election rates of incumbents suggest. On average, 10 percent of the House and Senate decide to retire each election.

The precarious economy and the backlash against the party in power made 2008 and 2010 difficult election years for some incumbents, particularly Democrats, given that their party controlled the presidency and both houses of Congress in a year when economic woes contributed to strong anti-incumbent sentiment.[18] Incumbents have fared better in recent elections. In 2016, Trump's surprise victory in the presidential race benefited Republican incumbents, who appeared to be in danger of losing their seats. In 2018, 5 incumbents in the Senate and over 20 incumbents in the House lost their seats.

Apportionment and Redistricting The final factor affecting who wins a seat in the House is the way congressional districts are drawn. Every 10 years, state legislatures must redraw congressional districts to reflect population changes. Because the number of congressional seats has been fixed at 435 since 1929, redistricting is a zero-sum process: in order for one state to gain a seat, another must lose one. The process of allocating congressional seats among the 50 states is called **apportionment**. States with population growth gain additional seats; states with a population decline or with less population growth lose seats. Over the past several decades, the shift of the American population to the South and the West has greatly increased the size of the congressional delegations from those regions. This trend continued after the 2010 census and

apportionment the process, occurring after every decennial census, that allocates congressional seats among the 50 states

FIGURE 12.3

Projected Congressional Reapportionment, 2020

States in the South and the West will likely be the big winners in the reapportionment of House seats following the 2020 census. The old manufacturing states in the Midwest and Mid-Atlantic regions will be the biggest losers. Is this shift likely to favor Democrats or Republicans?

SOURCE: Rebecca Tippett, "2020 Congressional Reapportionment: An Update," December 21, 2017, Carolina Population Center, University of North Carolina, demography.cpc.unc.edu (accessed 6/8/18).

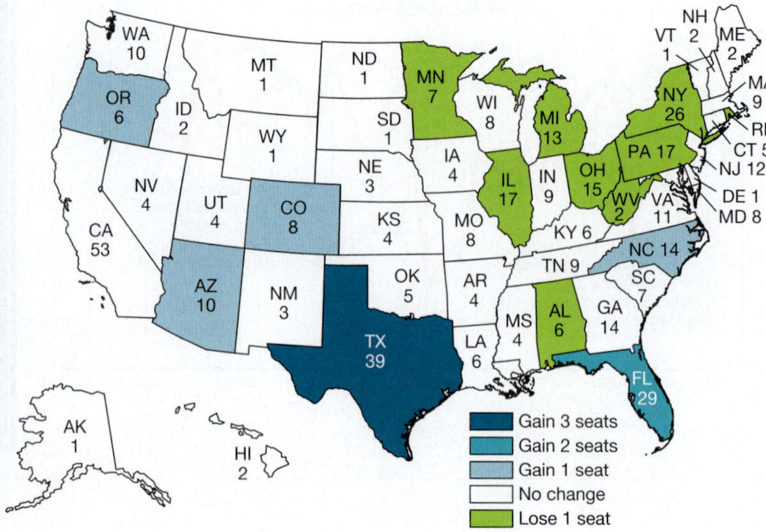

will likely continue after 2020 (see Figure 12.3). Texas is likely to gain three seats (after gaining four after 2010), and Florida will likely gain two. States in the Northeast and "rust belt" are likely to lose seats. Latino voters are nearly three times as prevalent in states that gained seats than in states that lost seats, suggesting that the growth of the Latino population is a major factor in the American political landscape.[19]

redistricting the process of redrawing election districts and redistributing legislative representatives; this happens every 10 years to reflect shifts in population or in response to legal challenges to existing districts

gerrymandering the apportionment of voters in districts in such a way as to give unfair advantage to one racial or ethnic group or political party

States that gain or lose seats must then redraw their congressional district borders. Not surprisingly, **redistricting** is a highly political process: districts are shaped to create an advantage for the party with a majority in the state legislature, which controls the redistricting process in most states. In this complex process, those charged with drawing districts use sophisticated computer technologies to come up with the most favorable district boundaries. Redistricting can create open seats and may pit incumbents of the same party against one another, ensuring that one of them will lose. Redistricting can also give an advantage to one party by clustering voters with some ideological or sociological characteristics in a single district or by separating those voters into two or more districts. The manipulation of electoral districts to serve the interests of a particular group is known as **gerrymandering** (see Chapter 10).

Some analysts claim that Republicans have benefited from partisan gerrymandering since the 2010 redistricting cycle because they controlled the majority of state legislatures at the time. To support this argument, they point to the 2012 congressional election, in which the Republican Party maintained its majority in the House despite winning 1.4 million fewer votes than Democratic House candidates.[20] But others question whether districting that favors Republicans is a product of deliberate gerrymandering. They argue that these districts may reflect the natural clustering of Democrats in urban areas, not deliberate bias.[21] Even so, concern about partisan gerrymandering has led some states to take redistricting power away from state legislatures and give it to independent commissions. In the 2010 redistricting cycle,

Redrawing legislative districts is a difficult task because it has implications for who will be elected. Here, the attorney for Arizona's Independent Redistricting Commission discusses a possible layout with a city council member from Casa Grande. Arizona gained one congressional seat following the 2010 census.

six states—California, Arizona, Idaho, New Jersey, Washington, and Montana—required district lines to be drawn by commissions.[22] In 2015 a challenge to the use of commissions failed when the Supreme Court upheld the legality of relying on commissions to draw congressional district lines.[23] In 2018 the Supreme Court declined to rule on cases arising from charges of partisan gerrymandering in Wisconsin and Maryland. In the Wisconsin case, challengers had asked the Court to rule that the legislative districting of the state as a whole was designed to give Republicans a lopsided majority of congressional seats. The case was sent back to lower courts for further review.[24] The Supreme Court is, however, expected to rule on a North Carolina case where the Republican state official who led the state's recent redistricting efforts announced that the congressional map was drawn to give the GOP a large majority of the state's congressional seats.

FOR CRITICAL ANALYSIS

How does redistricting alter the balance of power in Congress? Why do political parties care so much about the redistricting process?

As we saw in Chapter 10, since the passage of the 1982 amendments to the Voting Rights Act of 1965, race has become a major, and controversial, consideration in drawing voting districts. These amendments, which encouraged the creation of districts in which members of racial minorities have decisive majorities, have greatly increased the number of minority representatives in Congress. After the 1990 redistricting cycle, the number of predominantly minority districts doubled, rising from 26 to 52. Among the most fervent supporters of the new minority districts were white Republicans, who used the opportunity to create more districts dominated by white Republican voters. These developments raise thorny questions about representation. Some analysts argue that the system may grant minorities greater sociological representation but has made it more difficult for minorities to win substantive policy goals, while others dispute this argument.[25]

In the case of *Miller v. Johnson* (1995), the Supreme Court limited racial redistricting by ruling that race could not be the predominant factor in creating electoral districts.[26] The distinction between race being the "predominant" factor and its being one factor among many is hazy. As a result, concerns about redistricting and representation have not disappeared.[27] Questions about minority representation emerged in 2011 in Texas, which gained four new seats as a result of reapportionment. The Republican legislature drew a map that advantaged Republicans in three of those districts. But the plan drew a legal challenge on the grounds that it underrepresented Hispanic voters, who accounted for most of the state's population growth. Although federal judges drew a map more favorable to minorities (and Democrats), the Supreme Court ruled that the state did not have to use the map drawn by judges. The state ultimately agreed to a map that added two Latino-dominated districts. However, federal courts ruled that this map also weakened Latino and African American political power by creating too few minority districts.

The future of race in redistricting became more uncertain after the 2013 Supreme Court decision in *Shelby County v. Holder*. That decision invalidated a section of the Voting Rights Act requiring that the Justice Department approve the redistricting plans of jurisdictions with a history of racial discrimination.[28] Many Democrats expressed disappointment with the decision, fearing that the previously covered states, several of which are controlled by Republican majorities, might try to redraw district lines to partisan ends and further bias districts toward Republicans.[29] In 2015, Alabama's black legislators challenged that state's redistricting under the Voting Rights Act. They charged that the Republican legislature had diluted the vote of African Americans by packing black voters into districts that already had strong minority representation, thus enhancing the chances of white Republican candidates in the remaining districts. The legislature claimed, on the contrary, that it was acting in accordance with the Voting Rights Act by concentrating black voters. Although the Supreme Court did not declare the districting unconstitutional, it ruled that the lower court had erred in approving the districts.[30] The ruling signaled that state legislatures would not be able to use the Voting Rights Act to justify packing minority voters into districts. Because the drawing of district boundaries affects incumbents as well as the field of candidates who decide to run for office, it continues to be a key battleground on which political parties fight about the meaning of representation.

DIRECT PATRONAGE

As agents of their constituents, members of Congress have numerous opportunities to provide direct benefits, or **patronage**, for their districts. The most important such opportunity for direct patronage is in so-called **pork-barrel** legislation, which specifies a project to be funded within a particular district. Many observers of Congress argue that pork-barrel bills are the only ones that some members are serious about moving toward actual passage because they are seen as so important to members' re-election bids.

patronage the resources available to higher officials, usually opportunities to make partisan appointments to offices and to confer grants, licenses, or special favors to supporters

pork barrel (or pork) appropriations made by legislative bodies for local projects that are often not needed but that are created so that local representatives can win re-election in their home districts

A common form of pork-barreling is the "earmark," by which members of Congress insert into bills language that provides special benefits for their own constituents. When the Democrats took over Congress in 2007, they vowed to limit the use of earmarks, which had grown from 1,439 per year in 1995 to 15,268 in 2006. More troubling, earmarks were connected to congressional scandals. For example, the Republican House member Randy "Duke" Cunningham (R-Calif.) was sent to jail in 2005 for accepting bribes by companies hoping to receive earmarks in return.[31] The House passed a new rule requiring that those representatives supporting each earmark identify themselves and guarantee that they have no personal financial stake in the requested project. A new ethics law applied similar provisions to the Senate. Though the new requirements appear to have had some impact, nonetheless, in the midst of the sharp economic downturn in 2009, Congress passed an economic stimulus bill that contained more than 8,000 earmarks. In his 2010 State of the Union address, President Obama called for Congress to publish a list of all earmark requests on a single website. Congress not only failed to enact such legislation but in 2010 set a new record by passing 11,320 earmarks worth $32 billion. Still, in 2011 the House and the Senate agreed to a two-year moratorium on earmarks in spending bills and renewed the ban for the 113th, 114th, and 115th Congresses.[32] In 2018, President Trump suggested to Congress that it should consider restoring earmarks as a way of enhancing congressional power vis à vis the bureaucracy and to help "grease" the legislative wheels by giving members an incentive to support legislative programs. Trump's comments were greeted favorably by many congressional leaders.[33]

FOR CRITICAL ANALYSIS

Would Congress work more effectively if it brought back earmarks? Why are earmarks so difficult to eliminate?

Some analysts claim that the lack of earmarks contributes to congressional gridlock. They argue that earmarks provide congressional leaders with incentives to promote compromise among members. Supporters of this position contend that earmarks are not inherently an abuse of power and note that they often support legitimate district projects, such as transportation and parks.[34]

There are a few other types of direct patronage (see Figure 12.4). One important form of constituency service is intervention with federal administrative agencies on behalf of constituents. Members of the House and Senate and their staff spend a great deal of time on the telephone and in administrative offices seeking to secure favorable treatment for constituents and supporters. For example, members of Congress can assist senior citizens who are having Social Security or Medicare benefit eligibility problems. Most members of Congress have a "constituent services" section on their websites, providing information about what they can and cannot do to assist their constituents.

A different form of patronage is the **private bill**. Unlike a public bill, which is supposed to deal with general rules and categories of behavior, people, and institutions, a private bill proposes to grant some kind of relief, special privilege, or exemption to the person named in the bill. As many as 75 percent of all private bills introduced (and one-third of those that pass) are concerned with obtaining citizenship for

private bill a proposal in Congress to provide a specific person with some kind of relief, such as a special exemption from immigration quotas

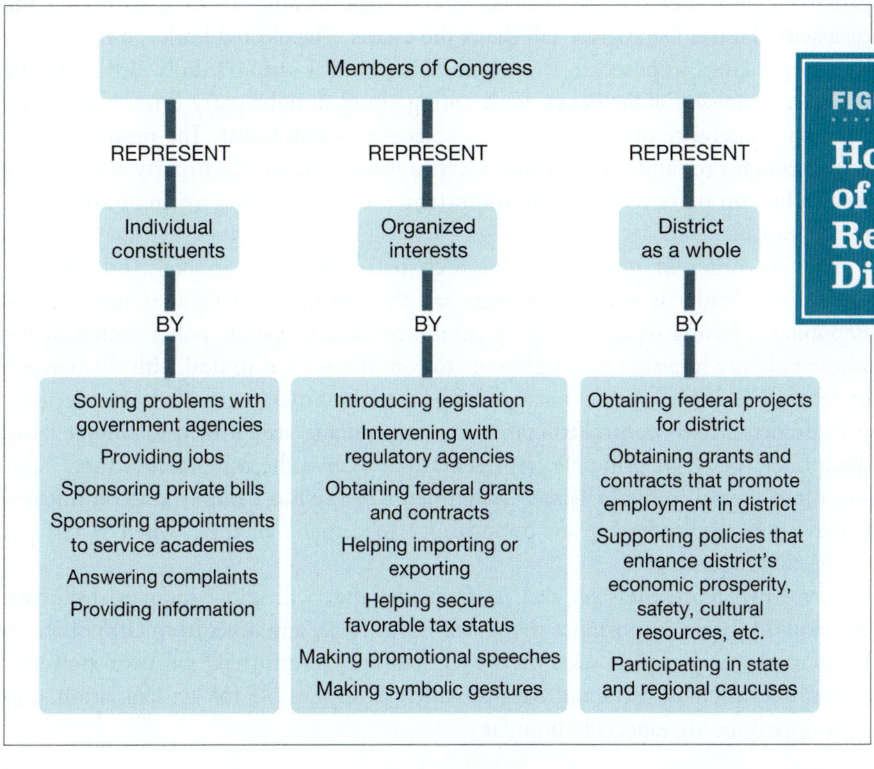

FIGURE 12.4

How Members of Congress Represent Their Districts

foreign nationals who do not have resident status in the United States. Other private bills address a diverse set of issues involving a claim against the federal government, such as problems with veterans' benefits or taxation. Private legislation is a congressional privilege that can be abused, but it is impossible to imagine members of Congress completely giving up one of the easiest, cheapest, and most effective forms of patronage available to them. It can be defended as an indispensable part of the process by which members of Congress seek to fulfill their role as representatives. And obviously they like the privilege because it helps them win re-election.

The Organization of Congress

Explain how party leadership, the committee system, the staff system, and caucuses help structure congressional business

The U.S. Congress is not only a representative assembly but also a legislative body. To exercise its power to make laws, Congress must first bring about something close to an organizational miracle. The building blocks of congressional organization include the political parties, the committee system, congressional staff, the caucuses, and the parliamentary rules of the House and Senate. Each of these factors plays a key role in the organization of Congress and in the process through which Congress formulates and enacts laws.

conference a gathering of House Republicans every two years to elect their House leaders; Democrats call their gathering the "caucus"

caucus (political) a normally closed political party business meeting of citizens or lawmakers to select candidates, elect officers, plan strategy, or make decisions regarding legislative matters

Speaker of the House the chief presiding officer of the House of Representatives; the Speaker is the most important party and House leader and can influence the legislative agenda, the fate of individual pieces of legislation, and members' positions within the House

majority leader the elected leader of the majority party in the House of Representatives or in the Senate; in the House, the majority leader is subordinate in the party hierarchy to the Speaker of the House

minority leader the elected leader of the minority party in the House or Senate

whip a party member in the House or Senate responsible for coordinating the party's legislative strategy, building support for key issues, and counting votes

PARTY LEADERSHIP IN THE HOUSE

Every two years, at the beginning of a new Congress, the members of each party gather to elect their House leaders. House Republicans call their gathering the **conference**. House Democrats call theirs the **caucus**. The elected leader of the majority party is later proposed to the whole House and is automatically elected to the position of **Speaker of the House**, with voting along straight party lines. The House majority conference or caucus then also elects a **majority leader**. The minority party goes through the same process and selects a **minority leader**. Each party also elects a **whip** to line up party members on important votes and to relay voting information to the leaders.

Next in order of importance for each party after the Speaker and majority or minority leader is what Democrats call the Steering and Policy Committee—Republicans have a separate steering committee and a separate policy committee—whose tasks are to assign new legislators to committees and to deal with the requests of incumbent members for transfers from one committee to another. At one time, party leaders strictly controlled committee assignments, using them to enforce party discipline. Today, in principle, representatives receive the assignments they want. But often several individuals seek assignments to the most important committees, which gives the leadership an opportunity to cement alliances when it resolves conflicting requests.

Generally, representatives seek assignments that will allow them to influence decisions of special importance to their districts. Representatives from farm districts, for example, may request seats on the Agriculture Committee.[35] Seats on powerful committees such as Ways and Means, which is responsible for tax legislation, and Appropriations are especially popular.

PARTY LEADERSHIP IN THE SENATE

Within the Senate, the majority party usually designates a member with the greatest seniority to serve as president pro tempore, a position of primarily ceremonial leadership. Real power is in the hands of the majority leader and minority leader, each elected by party conference. Together they control the Senate's calendar, or agenda for legislation. Each party also elects a policy committee, which advises the leadership on legislative priorities. The structure of majority party leadership in the House and the Senate is shown in Figures 12.5 and 12.6.

THE COMMITTEE SYSTEM

The committee system is central to the operation of Congress. At each stage of the legislative process, Congress relies on committees and subcommittees to do the hard work of sorting through alternatives and writing legislation. There are several different kinds of congressional committees: standing committees, select committees, joint committees, and conference committees.

Standing Committees The most important arenas of congressional policy making are **standing committees.** These committees remain in existence from one session of Congress to the next; they have the power to propose and write legislation. The jurisdiction of each standing committee covers a particular subject matter, which in most cases parallels a major department or agency in the executive branch (see Table 12.2). Among the most important standing committees are those in charge of finances. The House Ways and Means Committee and the Senate Finance Committee are powerful because of their jurisdiction over taxes, trade, and expensive entitlement programs such as Social Security and Medicare. The Senate and House Appropriations committees also play important ongoing roles because they decide how much funding various programs will actually receive; they also determine exactly how the money will be spent. A seat on an appropriations committee allows a member the opportunity to direct funds to a favored program—perhaps one in his home district.

standing committee a permanent committee with the power to propose and write legislation that covers a particular subject, such as finance or agriculture

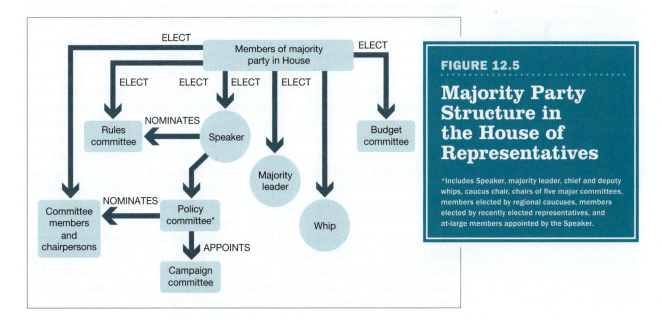

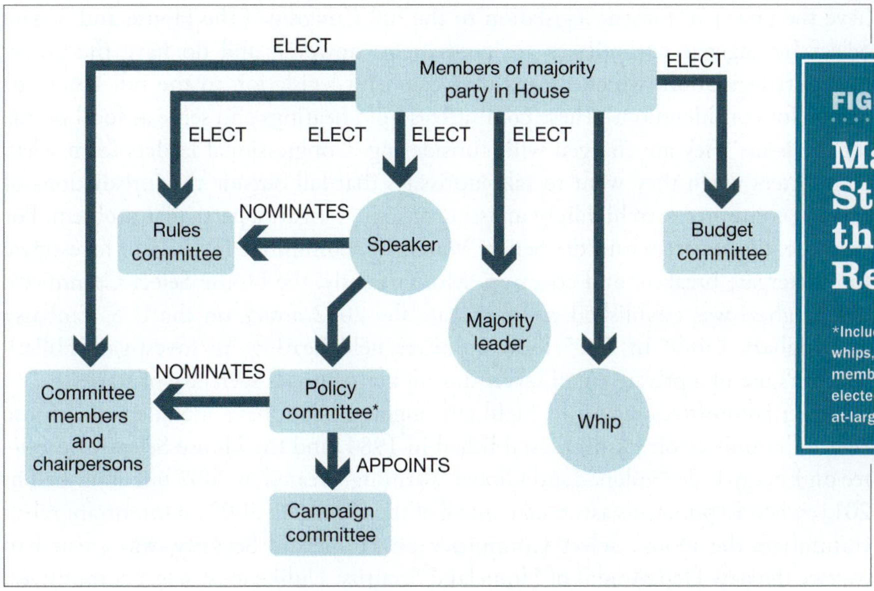

FIGURE 12.5

Majority Party Structure in the House of Representatives

*Includes Speaker, majority leader, chief and deputy whips, caucus chair, chairs of five major committees, members elected by regional caucuses, members elected by recently elected representatives, and at-large members appointed by the Speaker.

FIGURE 12.6

Majority Party Structure in the Senate

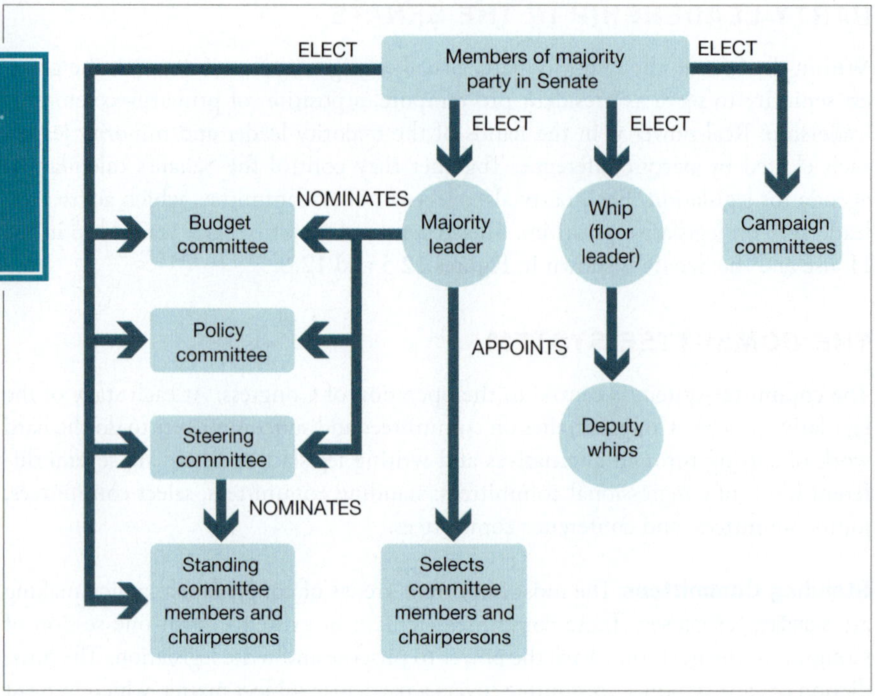

Except for the House Rules Committee, all standing committees receive proposals for legislation and process them into official bills. The House Rules Committee decides the order in which bills come up for a vote on the House floor and determines the specific rules that govern the length of debate and opportunity for amendments. The Senate, which has less formal organization and fewer rules, does not have a rules committee.

select committees (usually) temporary legislative committees set up to highlight or investigate a particular issue or address an issue not within the jurisdiction of existing committees

Select Committees **Select committees** are usually not permanent and usually do not have the power to present legislation to the full Congress. (The House and Senate Select Intelligence committees are permanent, however, and do have the power to report legislation, which means they can send legislation to the full House or Senate for consideration.) These committees hold hearings and serve as focal points for the issues they are charged with considering. Congressional leaders form select committees when they want to take up issues that fall outside the jurisdictions of existing committees, to highlight an issue, or to investigate a particular problem. For example, the Senate set up the Senate Watergate Committee in 1973 to investigate the Watergate break-in and cover-up. More recently, the House Select Committee on Benghazi was established to investigate the 2012 attack on the U.S. Embassy in Benghazi, Libya. In 2015 the committee held hearings to investigate Hillary Clinton's use of a private email server during her tenure as secretary of state.

Select committees set up to highlight ongoing issues have included the House Select Committee on Hunger, established in 1984, and the House Select Committee on Energy Independence and Global Warming, created in 2007 but abolished in 2011, when Republicans assumed control of the House. In 2003 an important select committee, the House Select Committee on Homeland Security, was created to oversee the new Department of Homeland Security. Unlike most select committees,

TABLE 12.2

Permanent Committees of Congress

HOUSE COMMITTEES		
Agriculture	Financial Services	Oversight and Government Reform
Appropriations	Foreign Affairs	Rules
Armed Services	Homeland Security	Science, Space, and Technology
Budget	House Administration	Small Business
Education and the Workforce	Intelligence	Transportation and Infrastructure
Energy and Commerce	Judiciary	Veterans' Affairs
Ethics	Natural Resources	Ways and Means
SENATE COMMITTEES		
Agriculture, Nutrition, and Forestry	Energy and Natural Resources	Intelligence
Appropriations	Environment and Public Works	Judiciary
Armed Services	Finance	Rules and Administration
Banking, Housing, and Urban Affairs	Foreign Relations	Small Business and Entrepreneurship
Budget	Health, Education, Labor, and Pensions	Veterans' Affairs
Commerce, Science, and Transportation	Homeland Security and Governmental Affairs	

this one had the ability to present legislation. Initially the committee had only temporary status. It was made a regular permanent committee in 2005.

Joint Committees **joint committees** involve members from both the Senate and the House. There are four such committees: economic, taxation, library, and printing. These joint committees are permanent, but they do not have the power to present legislation. The Joint Economic Committee and the Joint Taxation Committee have often played important roles in collecting information and holding hearings on economic and financial issues.

joint committees legislative committees formed of members of both the House and Senate

Conference Committees Finally, **conference committees** are temporary committees whose members are appointed by the Speaker of the House and the presiding officer of the Senate. These committees are charged with reaching a compromise on legislation once it has been passed by the House and the Senate. Conference committees play an extremely important role in determining the laws that are actually passed

conference committees joint committees created to work out a compromise on House and Senate versions of a piece of legislation

Committees hold hearings to gather information for legislation or investigate the activities of government agencies. Here, President Trump's first attorney general, Jeff Sessions, testifies in front of the House Judiciary Committee.

because they must reconcile any differences in the legislation passed by the House and Senate.

When control of Congress is divided between two parties, each is guaranteed significant representation in conference committees. When a single party controls both houses, the majority party is not obligated to offer such representation to the minority party. In 2003, Democrats complained that Republicans took this power to the extreme by excluding them and adding new provisions to legislation at the conference committee stage. Democrats even prevented several conference committees from convening to protest their near exclusion from conference committees on major energy, health care, and transportation laws. After they returned to power in 2007, the Democrats also largely bypassed the conference committees; when their early efforts to reach compromises in committee were derailed by partisan differences, the Democrats began making closed-door agreements between top leaders in the House and the Senate. Although the process facilitated compromises across the two chambers, it meant that important changes to bills were made in private, without the transparency that would have been part of the conference committee process. After 2010, Congress continued to avoid conference committees. Instead, the Republican House and Democratic Senate exchanged amendments as they sought to reach agreement on the final version of a bill, a practice known informally as "ping-pong."[36]

seniority the ranking given to an individual on the basis of length of continuous service on a committee in Congress

Politics and the Organization of Committees Within each committee, hierarchy has usually been based on **seniority**, determined by years of continuous service on that particular committee. In general, each committee is chaired by the most senior member of the majority party. But the principle of seniority is not absolute. When the Republicans took over the House in 1995, they violated the principle of seniority in the selection of key committee chairs. House Speaker Newt Gingrich defended the new practice, saying, "You've got to carry the moral responsibility of fielding the team that can win or you cheat the whole conference."[37] Since then, Republicans have continued to depart from the seniority principle, often choosing committee chairs on the basis of loyalty or fund-raising abilities rather than seniority. In 2007, Democrats returned to the seniority principle for choosing committee chairs but altered traditional practices in other ways by offering freshmen Democrats choice committee assignments to increase their chances of re-election.[38]

Over the years, Congress has reformed its organizational structure and operating procedures. Most changes have been made to improve efficiency, but some reforms have also been a response to political considerations. For example, the Republican leadership of the 104th Congress (1995–97), seeking to concentrate more authority in the party leadership, reduced the number of subcommittees and limited the time committee chairs could serve to three terms. They made good on this in 2001, when they replaced 13 committee chairs.

As a consequence of these changes, committees no longer have the central role they once held in policy making. Furthermore, sharp partisan divisions have made it difficult for committees to deliberate and bring bipartisan expertise to bear on policy making as in the past. With committees less able to engage in effective decision making, they typically do not deliberate for very long or call witnesses, and it has become more common in recent years for party-driven legislation to go directly to the floor, bypassing committees altogether.[39] Nonetheless, committees continue to play a role in the legislative process, especially on issues that are not sharply partisan.[40]

THE STAFF SYSTEM: STAFFERS AND AGENCIES

The congressional institution second in importance only to the committee system is the staff system. Every member of Congress employs many staff members whose tasks include handling constituent requests and, to a large extent, dealing with legislative details and the activities of administrative agencies. Staffers often bear the primary responsibility for formulating and drafting proposals, organizing hearings, dealing with administrative agencies, and negotiating with lobbyists. Indeed, legislators typically deal with one another through staff, rather than through direct personal contact. Staffers even develop policy ideas, draft legislation, and, in some instances, have a good deal of influence over the legislative process. Representatives and senators together employ roughly 11,500 staffers in their Washington and home offices. In addition, Congress employs more than 2,000 committee staffers.[41] These individuals make up the permanent staff that stays attached to every House and Senate committee regardless of turnover in Congress and that is responsible for organizing and administering the committee's work, including doing research, scheduling, organizing hearings, and drafting legislation. Committee staffers can play key roles in the legislative process.

staff agencies legislative support agencies responsible for policy analysis

Not only does Congress employ personal and committee staff, but it has also established **staff agencies** designed to provide the legislative branch with resources and expertise independent of the executive branch. These agencies enhance Congress's capacity to oversee administrative agencies and to evaluate presidential programs and proposals. They include the Congressional Research Service, which performs research for legislators who wish to know the facts and competing arguments relevant to policy proposals or other legislative business; the Government Accountability Office, through which Congress can investigate the financial and administrative affairs of any government agency or program; and the Congressional Budget Office, which assesses the economic implications and likely costs of proposed federal programs.

Members of Congress rely heavily on their personal staffs and on committee staffs, who often play an important role in the legislative process.

Women's Parliamentary Representation Worldwide

In April 2018 a special election in Arizona propelled Republican Debbie Lesko into the House, raising the number of women in Congress to 107.[a] This marked the first time in U.S. history that women comprised 20 percent of Congress, with 19.3 percent of the House and 23 percent of the Senate being women. While this may seem an impressive achievement, when we look around the world we find that the United States lags behind many countries in gender representation in government. As of 2018, the Inter-Parliamentary Union ranked the United States as 102 (out of 188) in women's parliamentary representation. Examining the lower house of parliament only (since not all countries have an upper house) reveals that the United States ranks between Saudi Arabia (19.9 percent) and Kyrgyzstan (19.2 percent).

Past research on women's global representation offers a few suggestions for why the U.S. percentage is so low, with the main explanations focusing on election rules and party systems.[b] Women candidates benefit from gender quotas and may be at a disadvantage in "winner-take-all" elections like those in the United States. In Rwanda, women comprise 61 percent of parliament, and there is both a gender quota (30 percent of the legislature is required to be women) and proportional representation (election rules where parties receive seats based on the percentage of the vote they received). Party recruitment also plays a major role, as cross-country research has found that "new left" parties (parties that favor environmental and social justice issues) also more actively recruit women into running for public office.

PARLIAMENTARY REPRESENTATION OF WOMEN

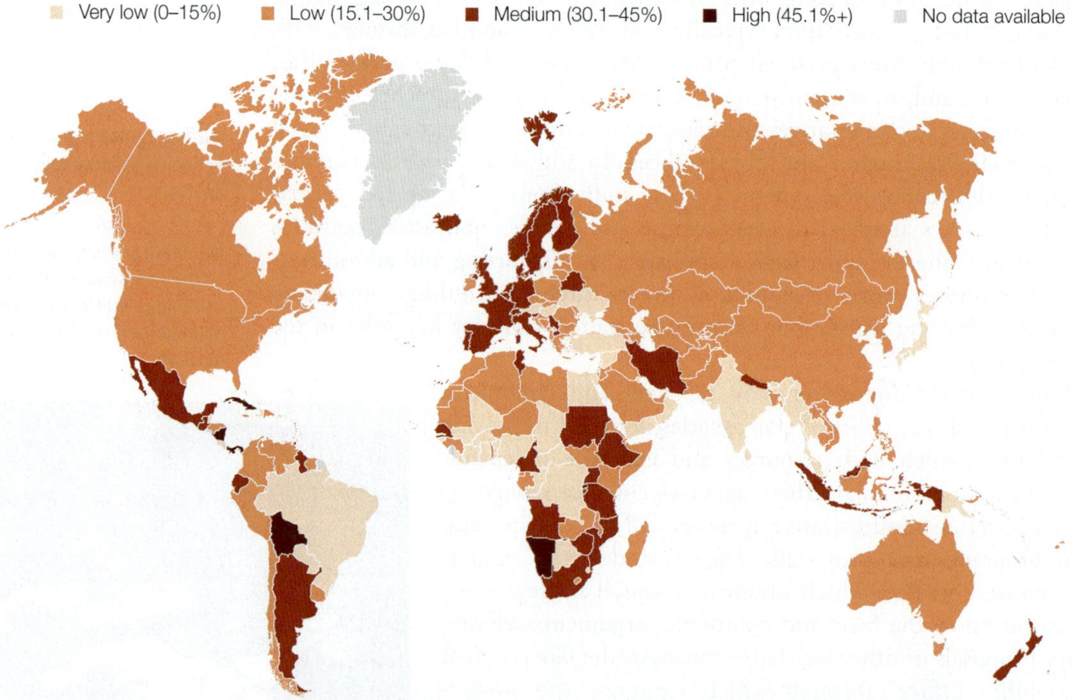

SOURCE: The Inter-Parliamentary Union (IPU), "Women in National Parliaments," April 1, 2018, archive.ipu.org (accessed 5/18/18).

[a] The Center for American Women and Politics (CAWP), "With Election of Debbie Lesko (AZ-08), Record Number of Women in Congress," April 24, 2018, cawp.rutgers.edu/sites/default/files/resources/18.4.24_pr_lesko_az08.pdf (accessed 5/18/18).

[b] Lena Wängnerud, "Women in Parliaments: Descriptive and Substantive Representation," *Annual Review of Political Science*, 12 (2009): 51–69.

INFORMAL ORGANIZATION: THE CAUCUSES

In addition to the official organization of Congress, an unofficial organizational structure also exists: the caucuses. **Caucuses** are groups of senators or representatives who share certain opinions, interests, or social characteristics. A large number of caucuses are composed of legislators representing particular economic or policy interests, such as the Travel and Tourism Caucus, the Steel Caucus, and Concerned Senators for the Arts. Legislators who share common backgrounds have organized caucuses such as the Congressional Black Caucus, the Congressional Caucus for Women's Issues, and the Congressional Hispanic Caucus. All these caucuses seek to advance the interests of the groups they represent by promoting legislation, encouraging Congress to hold hearings, and pressing administrative agencies for favorable treatment. In recent years, some caucuses have evolved into powerful lobbying organizations, well funded by interest groups. For example, the Sportsmen's Caucus receives funds from a nonprofit foundation that itself benefits from donations from the National Rifle Association, sports equipment manufacturers, and firearms manufacturers. In 2010 conservative Republicans in the House and Senate formed the Tea Party Caucus (now called the Freedom Caucus) to advance antispending policies.

caucuses (congressional) associations of members of Congress based on party, interest, or social group, such as gender or race

Rules of Lawmaking: How a Bill Becomes a Law

Outline the steps in the process of passing a law

The institutional structure of Congress is a key factor in shaping the legislative process. A second and equally important set of factors is the rules of congressional procedure. These rules govern everything from the introduction of a **bill** through its submission to the president for signing (see Figure 12.7). Not only do these regulations influence the fate of every bill, but they also help determine the distribution of power in the Congress.

bill a proposed law that has been sponsored by a member of Congress and submitted to the clerk of the House or Senate

COMMITTEE DELIBERATION

The first step in getting a law passed is drafting legislation. Members of Congress, the White House, and federal agencies all take roles in developing and drafting initial legislation. Bills can originate in the House or the Senate, but only the House can introduce "money bills," those that spend or raise revenues. The framers inserted this provision in the Constitution because they believed that the chamber closest to the people should exercise greater authority over taxing and spending. The bill is then officially submitted by a senator or representative to the clerk of the House or Senate and referred to the appropriate committee for deliberation. During the course of its deliberations, the committee typically refers the bill to one of its subcommittees, which may hold hearings, listen to expert testimony, and amend the proposed legislation before referring it to the full committee for consideration. The full committee may then accept the recommendation of the subcommittee or hold its own hearings and prepare its own amendments.

The next steps in the process are the **committee markup** sessions, in which committees rewrite bills to reflect changes discussed during the hearings. In the

committee markup the session in which a congressional committee rewrites legislation to incorporate changes discussed during hearings on a bill

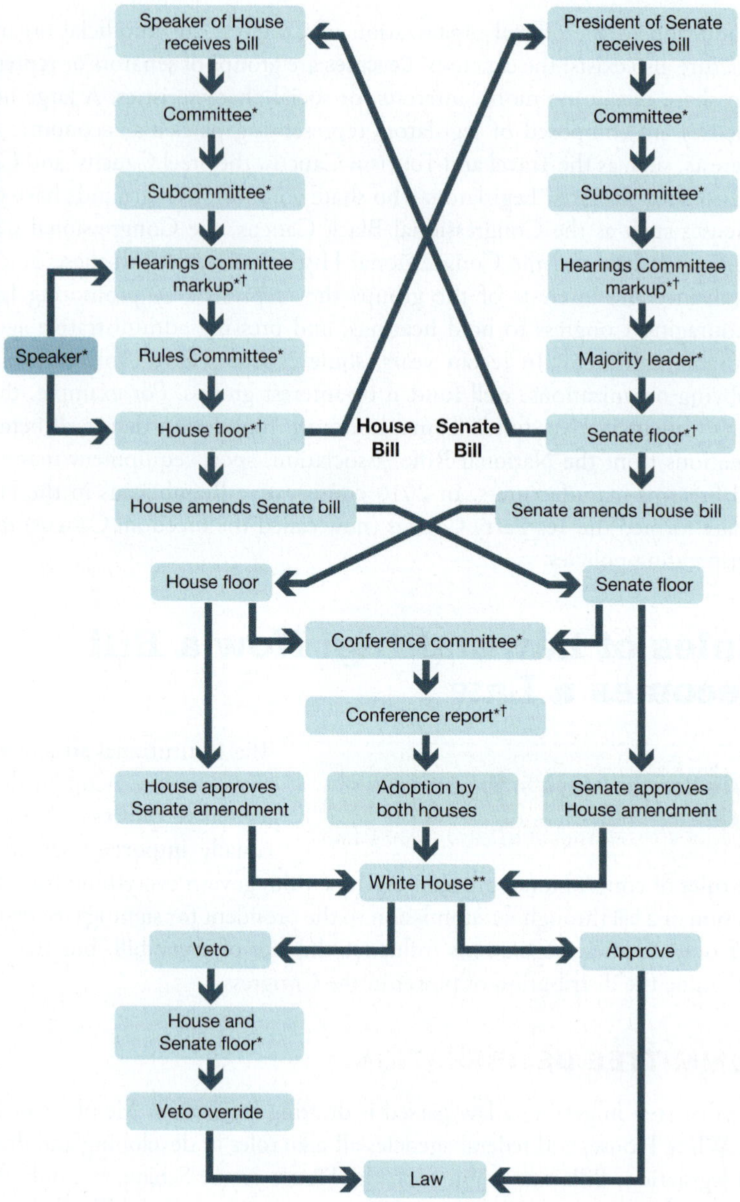

FIGURE 12.7

How a Bill Becomes a Law

*Points at which a bill can be amended.
**If the president neither signs nor vetoes a bill within 10 days, it automatically becomes law.
†Points at which a bill can die by vote.

partisan fighting that has characterized Congress in recent years, the minority party has charged that its members are often not given enough time to study proposed legislation before markup. In 2003 conflict over this issue drew the Capitol police to the House and almost resulted in a fistfight among representatives when Democrats protested their treatment by the House Ways and Means Committee. Charging that they had been given a complex pension bill only 10 hours before markup, House Democrats walked out. The ensuing commotion, with Republicans calling the police and a Democratic congressperson threatening a Republican, presented a sorry spectacle for the evening news. Though the committee chair apologized,

Democrats lost a resolution to censure the committee for its actions. At every stage of the legislative process, members protest that they are not given enough time to read proposals. In March 2018, members were handed a 2,200-page omnibus appropriations bill which would come to a vote in just 52 hours. Not allowing much time for readings of committee markups or bills themselves is usually a leadership tactic designed to push legislation forward before members can find items with which to disagree.

Frequently, the committee and subcommittee do little or nothing with a bill that has been submitted to them. Many bills are simply allowed to "die in committee" without serious consideration. Often, members of Congress introduce legislation that they neither expect nor even desire to see enacted into law but present mainly to please a constituency group by taking a stand. Many such bills are of narrow interest or stand little chance of passing given the political climate. For example, Representative Barbara Lee (D-Calif.) introduced the Department of Peacebuilding Act of 2015 to establish a "Department of Peacebuilding" in the executive branch, dedicated to promoting peace in international affairs.

As with most bills that are not reported out of committee, Lee's bill attracted little serious interest and only 26 cosponsors.[42] These bills die a quick and painless death. Other pieces of legislation have ardent supporters and die in committee only after a long battle. But in either case, most bills are never reported out of the committees to which they are assigned. In a typical congressional session, 80 to 90 percent of the more than 10,000 bills introduced die in committee.[43]

In the House, the relative handful of bills that are presented out of committee must pass one last hurdle within the committee system—the Rules Committee, which determines the rules that will govern action on the bill on the House floor. In particular, the Rules Committee allots the time for debate and decides to what extent amendments to the bill can be proposed from the floor. A bill's supporters generally prefer a **closed rule**, which puts severe limits on floor debate and amendments. Opponents of a bill usually prefer an **open rule**, which permits potentially damaging floor debate and makes it easier to add amendments that may cripple the bill or weaken its chances for passage. Thus, the outcome of the Rules Committee's deliberations can be extremely important, and the committee's hearings can be an occasion for sharp conflict. In recent years, the Rules Committee has become less powerful because the House leadership exercises so much influence over its decisions.

closed rule a provision by the House Rules Committee limiting or prohibiting the introduction of amendments during debate

open rule a provision by the House Rules Committee that permits floor debate and the addition of new amendments to a bill

DEBATE

The next step in getting a law passed is debate on the floor of the House and Senate. Party control of the agenda is reinforced by the rule giving the Speaker of the House and the president of the Senate the power of recognition during debate on a bill. Usually the chair knows the purpose for which a member intends to speak well in advance of the occasion. Spontaneous efforts to gain recognition are often foiled. For example, the Speaker may ask, "For what purpose does the member rise?" before deciding whether to grant recognition.

In the House, virtually all the time allotted by the Rules Committee for debate on a given bill is controlled by the bill's sponsor and by its leading opponent. In almost every case, these two people are the committee chair and the ranking minority member of the committee that processed the bill—or those they designate. These two participants are, by rule and tradition, granted the power to allocate most of the debate time in small amounts to members who are seeking to speak for or against

Once a senator is granted the floor, Senate rules permit him to speak for as long as he wishes. Although "talking filibusters" are rare today, in May 2015 Senator Rand Paul (R-Ky.) spoke continuously for 10½ hours, challenging the legality of government surveillance in his opposition to renew the Patriot Act.

filibuster a tactic used by members of the Senate to prevent action on legislation they oppose by continuously holding the floor and speaking until the majority backs down; once given the floor, senators have unlimited time to speak, and it requires a vote of three-fifths of the Senate to end a filibuster

cloture a rule or process in a legislative body aimed at ending debate on a given bill; in the U.S. Senate, 60 senators (three-fifths) must agree in order to impose a time limit and end debate

the measure. Preference in the allocation of time goes to the members of the committee whose jurisdiction covers the bill.

Filibuster In the Senate, the leadership has much less control over floor debate. Indeed, the Senate is unique among the world's legislative bodies for its commitment to unlimited debate. Once given the floor, a senator may speak as long as she wishes. On a number of memorable occasions, senators have used this opportunity to prevent action on legislation that they opposed. Through this tactic, called the **filibuster**, small minorities or even one individual in the Senate can force the majority to give in. Filibusters can be ended by a Senate vote to cut off debate, called **cloture**. From 1917 to 1975, it took two-thirds of the Senate or 67 votes to end a filibuster. In 1975 the Senate changed the rules to three-fifths of the Senate or 60 votes needed for cloture. The threat of a filibuster ensures that, in crafting legislation and proposing judicial appointments, the majority takes into account the viewpoint of the political minority.

For much of American history, senators only rarely used the filibuster, though during the 1950s and '60s, opponents of civil rights legislation often used filibusters to block its passage. In the last 20 years, the filibuster has become so common that observers routinely note that it takes 60 votes to get anything passed in the Senate. The 113th Congress (2013–15) broke the record with 218 cloture votes.[44] The 115th Congress held 192 cloture votes as of November 1, 2018.

In 2013 the Democratic Senate leader Harry Reid (Nev.) mobilized his party to alter the filibuster rules for the first time in many decades. Frustrated by the repeated failure of the Senate to vote on many of the president's nominees to fill positions in the executive branch, as well as judgeships to important federal courts, Reid invoked what senators had come to call "the nuclear option," a change to the filibuster rules. Under the new rules, nominees for positions in the executive branch and the federal courts—except the Supreme Court—could not be filibustered. This means that they can be approved by a simple majority vote. Not surprisingly, the two parties had different views on the decision. Reid defended it as necessary, due to what he called "unbelievable, unprecedented obstruction." Republicans denounced the new rule, stating, in the words of Pat Roberts (R-Kans.), "We have weakened this body permanently."[45] After winning control of both houses of Congress and the White House in 2016, however, Republicans expanded Reid's rule to include Supreme Court justices and so were able to secure the appointment of Justice Neil Gorsuch, who would undoubtedly have been blocked by Senate Democrats under the old rules. Legislation is still subject to filibuster, though some Republicans, along with President Trump, have declared that it is time to bring an end to the filibuster altogether.

Amendments and Holds The filibuster is not the only technique used to block Senate debate. Under Senate rules, members have virtually unlimited ability to propose amendments to a pending bill. Each amendment must be voted on before the bill can come to a final vote. The introduction of new amendments can be stopped only by unanimous consent. This, in effect, can permit a determined minority to filibuster by amendment, indefinitely delaying the passage of a bill. Senators can also place "holds," or stalling devices, on bills to delay debate. Senators place holds on bills when they fear that openly opposing them will be unpopular. Because holds are kept secret, the senators placing the holds do not have to take public responsibility for their actions. There have been several efforts to eliminate holds. In 2007 reformers succeeded in passing the Honest Leadership and Open Government

Act. Although the new law did not eliminate holds, it contained provisions requiring senators who imposed a hold to identify themselves in the *Congressional Record* after six days and state the reasons for the hold.[46] Even with this provision, senators continued to impose holds on legislation and especially on presidential appointees. Senator Lindsey Graham (R-S.C.) aroused the ire of the White House in 2013 for threatening to use holds on all of President Obama's nominees unless the administration made survivors of the 2012 terrorist attack on the U.S. mission in Benghazi, Libya, available to Congress for questioning.[47]

FOR CRITICAL ANALYSIS

Two of Congress's chief responsibilities are representation and lawmaking. How do these responsibilities support and reinforce each other? How might they also conflict with each other?

Voting Once a bill is debated on the floor of the House and the Senate, the leaders schedule it for a vote on the floor of each chamber. Leaders do not bring legislation to the floor unless they are fairly certain it is going to pass. On rare occasions, the last moments of the floor vote can be very dramatic as each party's leadership puts its whip organization into action to make sure that wavering members vote with the party. In 2015 the House of Representatives failed to pass a spending bill to fund the Department of Homeland Security hours before the agency was to run out of money and begin to shut down. Despite having a majority in the chamber and an early vote that suggested that the bill would pass easily, House Republican Party leaders failed to prevent the most conservative members of the party from suddenly abandoning the bill over objections that it left out provisions to block President Obama's executive actions on immigration. As midnight approached, the House agreed on a one-week extension to keep the department open.[48] Leaders later secured sufficient support to enact longer-term funding for Homeland Security. The importance of being able to attract wavering members with "pork" for their districts is one reason President Trump urged Congress in 2018 to restore earmarks, which have been banned since 2011.

CONFERENCE COMMITTEE: RECONCILING HOUSE AND SENATE VERSIONS OF LEGISLATION

Getting a bill out of committee and through both houses of Congress is no guarantee that the bill will be enacted into law; it must be considered by a conference committee. Frequently, bills that begin with similar provisions in both chambers emerge with little resemblance to each other. Alternatively, a bill may be passed by one chamber but undergo substantial revision in the other chamber. In such cases, a conference committee composed of the senior members of the committees or subcommittees that initiated the bill may be required to iron out differences between the two now dissimilar pieces of legislation. Sometimes members or leaders will let objectionable provisions pass on the floor, knowing that they will get the chance to make changes in conference. Usually, conference committees meet behind closed doors. Agreement requires a majority of each of the two delegations. Legislation that emerges successfully from a conference committee is more often a compromise than a clear victory for one side. In recent years, as we have seen, polarization in Congress has led to much less reliance on conference committees. Instead, leaders exchange amendments in the hope of reaching agreement.

When a bill comes out of conference, it faces one more hurdle. Before it can be sent to the president for signing, the House-Senate conference committee's version of the bill must be approved on the floor of each chamber. Usually such approval is given quickly. Occasionally, however, a bill's opponents use this round of approval as one last opportunity to defeat a piece of legislation.

PRESIDENTIAL ACTION

veto the president's constitutional power to turn down acts of Congress; a presidential veto may be overridden by a two-thirds vote of each house of Congress

pocket veto a presidential veto that is automatically triggered if the president does not act on a given piece of legislation passed during the final 10 days of a legislative session

The final step in passing a law is presidential approval. Once adopted by the House and Senate, a bill goes to the president, who may choose to sign the bill into law or veto it. If the president does not sign the bill or veto it within 10 days and Congress is in session, the bill automatically becomes law. The **veto** is the president's constitutional power to reject a piece of legislation. To veto a bill, the president returns it unsigned within 10 days to the house of Congress in which it originated. If Congress adjourns during the 10-day period and the president has taken no action, the bill is also considered to be vetoed. This latter method is known as the **pocket veto.** The possibility of a presidential veto affects how willing members of Congress are to push for different pieces of legislation at different times. If they think a proposal is likely to be vetoed, they might shelve it until a later time.

A presidential veto may be overridden by a two-thirds vote in both the House and Senate. A veto override says much about the support that a president can expect from Congress, and it can deliver a stinging blow to the executive branch. Presidents will often back down from a veto threat if they believe that Congress will override the veto.

How Congress Decides

Analyze the factors that influence which laws Congress passes

What determines the kinds of legislation that Congress ultimately produces? According to the simplest theories of representation, members of Congress respond to the views of their constituents. In fact, the process of creating a legislative agenda, drawing up a list of possible measures, and deciding among them is a very complex one, in which a variety of influences from inside and outside government play important roles. External influences include a legislator's constituency and various interest groups. Influences from inside government include party leadership, congressional colleagues, and the president. Let us examine each of these influences individually and then consider how they interact to produce congressional policy decisions.

Representatives spend a lot of time meeting with constituents in their districts to explain how they have helped their district and learn what issues their constituents care about. Such meetings are often informal events at local restaurants or fairs, or town halls where constituents can ask questions. Here, Senator Chuck Grassley (R-Iowa) meets with constituents.

CONSTITUENCY

Because members of Congress, for the most part, want to be re-elected, we would expect the views of their constituents to be a primary influence on the decisions that they make. Yet constituency influence is not so straightforward. In fact, most constituents pay little attention to politics and often do not even know what policies their representatives support. Nonetheless, members of Congress spend a lot of time worrying about what their constituents think because they realize that the choices they make may be scrutinized in a future election and used as ammunition by an opposing candidate. Because of this possibility, members of Congress do try to anticipate their constituents' policy views, especially if they think that voters will take them into account during elections.[49] In this way, constituents may affect congressional policy choices even when there is little direct evidence of their influence. In October 1998, for example, 31

House Democrats broke party ranks and voted in favor of an impeachment inquiry against President Clinton because they believed a "no" vote could cost them re-election that November. In 2017, despite a personal effort by President Trump to persuade dissident Republicans, the House GOP leadership could not muster enough Republican votes to pass a measure that would have repealed Obamacare. Some Republicans from swing districts feared upsetting constituents who favored Obamacare, while more conservative Republicans thought the bill did not go far enough in dismantling government-sponsored health insurance. Then-White House press secretary Sean Spicer said, "This isn't a dictatorship and we've got to expect members to ultimately vote how they will according to what they think."[50]

INTEREST GROUPS

Interest groups are another important external influence on congressional policies. Members of Congress pay close attention to interest groups for a number of reasons: interest groups can mobilize constituents, serve as watchdogs on congressional action, and supply candidates with money. When members of Congress are making voting decisions, those interest groups that have some connection to constituents in particular districts are most likely to be influential, and those groups with the ability to mobilize followers in many congressional districts may be especially influential. In recent years, Washington-based interest groups with little grassroots strength have recognized the importance of locally generated activity. Accordingly, they have sought to simulate grassroots pressure with so-called Astroturf lobbying (see Chapter 11). Such campaigns encourage constituents to sign form letters, postcards, or emails, which are then sent to congressional representatives. Lobbying campaigns set up toll-free telephone numbers for a system in which simply reporting your name and address to the listening computer will generate a letter to your congressional representative. One Senate office estimated that such organized campaigns to demonstrate "grassroots" support account for two-thirds of the mail the office received. As such campaigns increase, however, they become less influential because members of Congress are aware of how rare real constituent interest actually is.[51]

Many interest groups also use legislative "scorecards" that rate how members of Congress vote on issues of importance to that group. A high or low rating by an important interest group may provide a potent weapon in the next election. Interest groups can increase their influence over a particular piece of legislation by signaling their intention to include it in their scoring. Among the most influential groups that use scorecards, often posting them on their websites for members and the public to see, are the National Federation of Independent Business, the American Federation of Labor-Congress of Industrial Organizations (AFL-CIO), National Right to Life, the League of Conservation Voters, and the National Rifle Association.

Interest groups also have substantial influence in setting the legislative agenda and in helping to craft specific language in legislation. Today, sophisticated lobbyists win influence by providing information about policies, as well as campaign contributions, to busy members of Congress. The $1.1 trillion end-of-year spending bill passed at the end of 2014 included an amendment exempting many financial transactions from federal regulation under the Dodd-Frank Act. The amendment language was taken from a bill originally written by Citigroup lobbyists, with 70 of 85 lines of the bill directly copying Citigroup's language.[52] After further lobbying by the banking industry, legislation enacted in 2018 loosened a number of Dodd-Frank rules and exempted regional banks from a number of remaining rules. In recent years, interest groups have also begun to build broader coalitions and comprehensive campaigns around particular policy issues. These coalitions do not rise from the grass roots but instead are put together by Washington lobbyists, who launch comprehensive lobbying campaigns that combine simulated grassroots activity with information and campaign funding for members of Congress.

Close financial ties between members of Congress and interest group lobbyists often raise eyebrows because they suggest that interest groups get special treatment in exchange for political donations. Concerns about the influence of lobbyists in Congress mounted in the early 2000s when Republicans launched the K Street Project, named after the street in Washington where many high-powered lobbyists have offices. The K Street Project placed former Republican staffers in key lobbying positions and ensured a large and steady flow of corporate cash into Republican coffers. Congressional relationships to lobbyists came under close scrutiny when the lobbyist Jack Abramoff, a self-proclaimed big supporter of the K Street Project, pleaded guilty in early 2006 to charges of conspiracy, mail fraud, and tax evasion.

Concern over such corruption led Congress to enact new ethics legislation in 2007. Now lobbyists are required to disclose the names of the individual contributors to these political donations. Although the new law provides additional transparency, revealing more about the relationship between lobbyists and members of Congress, it is widely viewed as lacking sufficient authority to go after those who are suspected of ethics violations. Moreover, the large sums of cash raised by "Super PACs" (political action committees)—discussed in Chapter 10—have introduced a whole new set of questions about the role of special interests in politics, especially because donors to Super PACs can remain anonymous. Although they cannot openly coordinate with candidates, Super PACs can endorse candidates by name and are often run by people close to the candidates they support. In 2016, Super PACs poured unprecedented sums of money into the race for president, but they also targeted key congressional contests in an effort to affect the balance of power between the parties in Congress. In 2018, 10 individuals—5 Democrats and 5 Republicans—collectively contributed several hundred million dollars to Super PACs supporting congressional candidates all across the country as the two parties fought for control of Congress.[53]

FOR CRITICAL ANALYSIS

How does congressional ethics legislation address concerns about corruption? Why is it important that lawmakers identify the earmarks they add to legislation?

PARTY

In both the House and Senate, party leaders have a good deal of influence over the behavior of their party members. This influence, sometimes called "party discipline," was once so powerful that it dominated the lawmaking process. In the late 1800s, party leaders could often command the allegiance of more than 90 percent of their members. A vote in which half or more of the members of one party take one position while at least half of the members of the other party take the opposing position is called a **party unity vote**. At the beginning of the twentieth century, nearly half of all **roll-call votes** in the House of Representatives were party votes. For much of the twentieth century, the number of party votes declined as bipartisan legislation became more common. The 1990s witnessed a return to strong party discipline as partisan polarization drew sharper lines between Democrats and Republicans, and congressional party leaders aggressively used their powers to promote party discipline. By 2015 party discipline has been at an all-time high.

party unity vote a roll-call vote in the House or Senate in which at least 50 percent of the members of one party take a particular position and are opposed by at least 50 percent of the members of the other party

roll-call vote a vote in which each legislator's yes or no vote is recorded as the clerk calls the names of the members alphabetically

Typically, party unity is greater in the House than in the Senate. House rules grant greater procedural control of business to the majority party leaders, which gives them more influence over House members. In the Senate, however, the leadership has few sanctions over its members. The former Senate minority leader Tom Daschle once observed that a Senate leader seeking to influence other senators has as incentives "a bushel full of carrots and a few twigs."[54]

Though it has not reached nineteenth-century levels, party unity has been on the rise in recent years because the divisions between the parties have deepened on many high-profile issues such as abortion, health care, and financial reform (see Figure 12.8). Party unity scores rise when congressional leaders try to put a partisan stamp on legislation. For example, in 1995 then-Speaker Newt Gingrich sought to enact a Republican "Contract with America" that few Democrats supported. The result was more party unity in the House than in any year since 1954. Since then, the polarization of political parties has resulted in very high party unity scores. In 2016, House Democrats voted with the majority 96 percent of the time, marking an all-time high, at least in modern times. That year Senate Democrats voted with their caucus 92 percent of the time, seven points below the record set in 2014. Republicans were also very united. In 2016, House Republicans voted with their party 96 percent of the time, an all-time record high; Senate Republicans voted with their party 86 percent of the time, only five points below the record set in 2015.[55]

To some extent, party unity is based on ideology and background. Republican members of the House are more likely than Democrats to have been elected by rural or suburban districts. Democrats are likely to be more liberal on economic and social questions than their Republican colleagues in both houses. These differences certainly help to explain roll-call divisions between the two parties. Ideology and background, however, are only part of the explanation for party unity. The other part has to do with party organization and leadership. Among the resources that

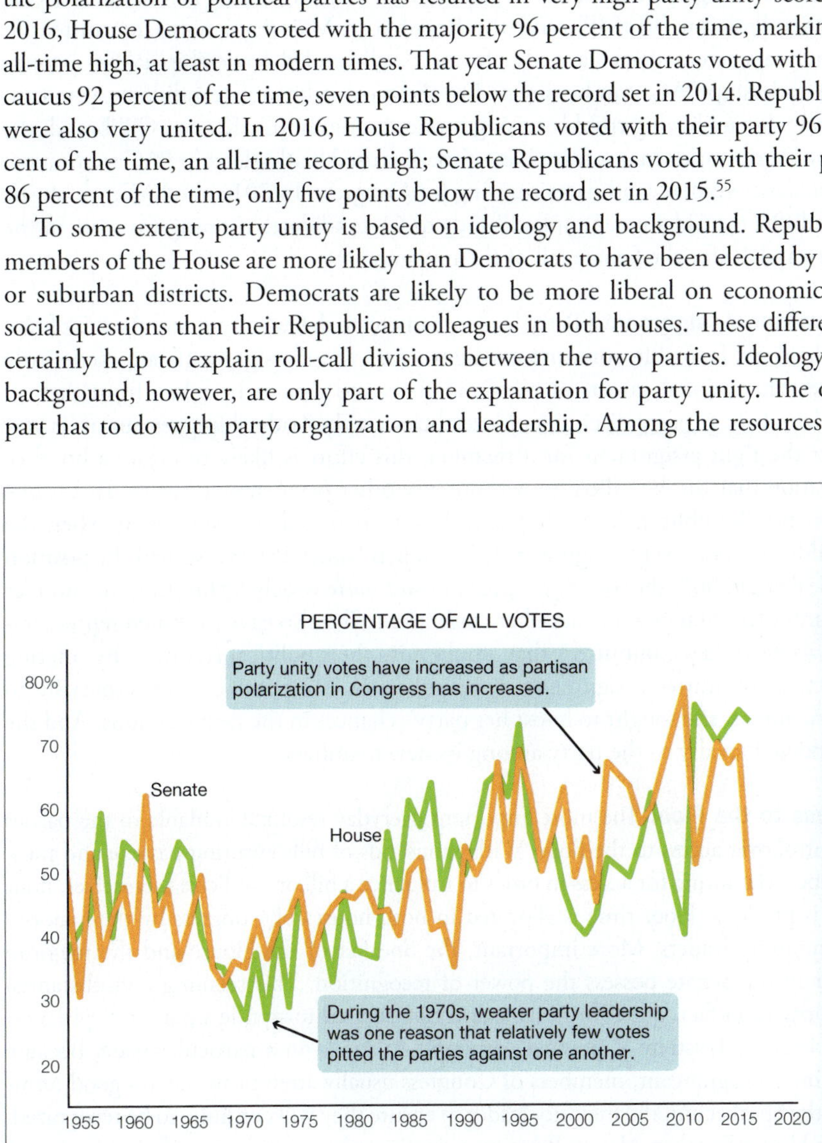
PERCENTAGE OF ALL VOTES
Party unity votes have increased as partisan polarization in Congress has increased.
80%
70
60
50
40
30
20
Senate
House
During the 1970s, weaker party leadership was one reason that relatively few votes pitted the parties against one another.
1955 1960 1965 1970 1975 1980 1985 1990 1995 2000 2005 2010 2015 2020

FIGURE 12.8

Party Unity Votes by Chamber

Party unity votes are roll-call votes in which a majority of one party lines up against a majority of the other party. Party unity votes increase when the parties are polarized and when the party leadership can enforce discipline. Why did the percentage of party unity votes decline in the 1970s? Why has it risen in recent years?

SOURCES: CQ Roll Call's Vote Studies, http://media.cq.com/votestudies (accessed 6/9/14); Eliza Newlin Carney, "Standing Together against Any Action," *CQ Weekly* (March 16, 2015); and "2015 Vote Studies: Party Unity Remained Strong," *CQ Weekly* (February 8, 2016); Vital Statistics, "Table 8-3 Party Unity Votes in Congress, 1953–2016," Brookings, May 21, 2018, www.brookings.edu/multi-chapter-report/vital-statistics-on-congress/ (accessed 11/9/18).

party leaders have at their disposal to reward loyal members who vote with the party are (1) leadership PACs, (2) committee assignments, (3) access to the floor, (4) the whip system, (5) logrolling, and (6) the presidency.

Leadership PACs Leaders have increased their influence over members in recent years with aggressive use of leadership PACs. Leadership PACs are organizations that members of Congress use to raise funds that they then distribute to other members of their party running for election. Republican congressional leaders pioneered the aggressive use of leadership PACs to win their congressional majority in 1995, and the practice has spread widely since that time. The former House majority leader Tom DeLay was especially aggressive in raising funds, creating several important PACs, including Americans for a Republican Majority (ARMPAC), Retain Our Majority Program (ROMP), and the Republican Majority Issues Committee. In recent years, Democrats have also formed well-funded leadership PACs. Money from leadership PACs can be directed to the most vulnerable candidates or to candidates who are having trouble raising money. For example, Kirsten Gillibrand, the junior Democratic senator from New York, has used her leadership PAC to promote Democratic women candidates running for Congress. In 2016 the PAC, which she named Off the Sidelines, supplied funds to 61 candidates running for seats in the House and 10 for the Senate, all of them women.[56]

Committee Assignments Party leaders can create debts among members by helping them get favorable committee assignments. These assignments are made early in the congressional careers of most members and cannot be taken from them if they later balk at party discipline. Nevertheless, if the leadership goes out of its way to get the right assignment for a member, this effort is likely to create a bond of obligation that can be called on without any other payments or favors. This is one reason the Republican leadership gave freshmen favorable assignments when the Republicans took over Congress in 1995. When Nancy Pelosi assumed the position of Speaker in 2007, she sought to spread power more widely by limiting the number of committees that any one member could chair. She also gave freshmen representatives access to key committees that would raise their political stature.[57] By offering attractive committee assignments to members in competitive races, especially to new members, she sought to boost her party's chances in the next elections. And she engendered loyalty to the party among its new members.

Access to the Floor The most important everyday resource available to the parties is control over access to the floor. With thousands of bills awaiting passage and most members clamoring for access in order to influence a bill or publicize themselves, floor time is precious. Floor time is allocated in both houses of Congress by the majority and minority leaders. More important, the Speaker of the House and the majority leader in the Senate possess the power of recognition. This seemingly insubstantial authority is, in fact, quite formidable and can be used to stymie a piece of legislation completely or frustrate a member's attempts to speak on a particular issue. Because the power is significant, members of Congress usually attempt to stay on good terms with the Speaker and the majority leader to ensure they will continue to be recognized.

As House Speaker, Nancy Pelosi was particularly generous in offering freshmen Democrats and other especially vulnerable Democrats an opportunity to speak on the floor. When Republicans assumed control of the House in 2010, they likewise ensured that the voices of freshmen Republicans were heard on the House floor.[58] As we saw above, each party makes an effort to protect potentially vulnerable members, and freshmen are often high on that list.

The Whip System Some influence accrues to party leaders through the whip system, which is primarily a communications network for conveying the leaders' wishes and plans to the members. Between 12 and 20 assistant and regional whips are selected to operate at the direction of the majority or minority leader and the whip. They poll all the members to learn their intentions on specific bills, enabling the leaders to know if they have enough support to allow a vote as well as whether the vote is so close that they will need to put pressure on undecided members. In those instances, the Speaker or a lieutenant will go to a few party members who have indicated they will switch if their vote is essential—an expedient that the leaders try to limit to a few times per session.

The whip system helps maintain party unity in both houses of Congress, but it is particularly critical in the House of Representatives because of the large number of legislators whose positions and votes must be accounted for. The majority and minority whips and their assistants must be adept at inducing compromise among legislators who hold widely differing viewpoints. In 2015 a group of conservative Republicans, organized into the House Freedom Caucus, regularly disputed the positions of the party leadership. Frustrated with the lack of discipline, House majority whip Steve Scalise (R-La.) expelled several members from his whip team for failing to support party positions.[59] Indeed, conflict with these same rebellious Republicans prompted Speaker John Boehner to make the stunning announcement in September 2015 of his retirement from the speakership and from the House.

logrolling a legislative practice whereby agreements are made between legislators in voting for or against a bill; vote trading

Logrolling An agreement between two or more members of Congress who have nothing in common except the need for support is called **logrolling**. The agreement states, in effect, "You support me on bill X, and I'll support you on another bill of your choice." Since party leaders are the center of the communications networks in the two chambers, they can help members create large logrolling coalitions. Hundreds of logrolling deals are made each year, and although there are no official record-keeping books, it would be a poor party leader whose whips did not know who owed what to whom. In some instances, logrolling produces strange alliances. A most unlikely alliance emerged in Congress in October 1991, an alliance that one commentator dubbed "the corn for porn plot."[60] The alliance joined Senate supporters of the National Endowment for the Arts (NEA) with senators seeking limits on the cost of grazing rights on federal lands. The NEA, which provides federal funding to the arts, had been under fire from the conservative senator Jesse Helms (R-N.C.) for funding some controversial artists whose work Helms believed to be indecent. In an effort to block federal support for such works, Helms attached a provision to the NEA's funding that would have prohibited the agency from awarding grants to any work that in a "patently offensive way" depicted "sexual or excretory activities or organs." Supporters of the NEA condemned such restrictions as a violation of free speech and pointed out that many famous works of art could not have been funded under such restrictions. When it appeared that the amendment would pass, NEA supporters offered western senators a deal. In exchange for voting down the Helms amendment, they would eliminate a planned increase in grazing fees. Republican senators from 16 western states switched their votes and defeated the Helms amendment. Although Helms called his defeat

When John Boehner became Speaker of the House in 2010, he was overwhelmingly backed by House Republicans. By 2015, the most conservative factions of the party, frustrated that Boehner hadn't been more effective against the Obama administration, pressured him to resign.

After Democrats took control of the House of Representatives in November 2018, former House minority leader Nancy Pelosi (D-Calif.) was poised to take over the role of Speaker of the House from retiring Speaker Paul Ryan (R-Wisc.). She had previously served in the same position from 2007–11.

the product of "back-room deals and parliamentary flimflam," his amendment was simply the victim of the time-honored congressional practice of logrolling.[61]

The Presidency Of all the influences that maintain the clarity of party lines in Congress, the influence of the presidency is probably the most important. Indeed, the office is a touchstone of party discipline in Congress. Since the late 1940s, under President Harry Truman, presidents each year have identified a number of bills that they want to be considered part of their administration's program. By the mid-1950s both parties in Congress began to look to the president for these proposals, which became the most significant part of Congress's agenda. The president's support is a criterion for party loyalty, and party leaders are able to use it to rally some members. Though President Trump was personally unpopular with many members of Congress, legislators still looked to him to set the agenda and most of the major legislative initiatives of 2017 and 2018, including border security, immigration, the repeal of Obamacare, and tax reform originated in the White House.

WHEN CONGRESS CAN'T DECIDE

We've considered the major factors that influence congressional decisions, but what happens if Congress as a whole can't decide and fails to act? Some recent congresses have been notable for their inability to pass laws. The 114th Congress (2015–17), 113th Congress (2013–15), and the 112th Congress (2011–13) were the three least productive Congresses in modern history.[62]

As the end of its second session neared, the 115th Congress seemed likely to become the least productive Congress in modern history in terms of number of new laws enacted. A number of those new laws, however, were important. These included a sanctions law targeting Russia, Iran, and North Korea; the enactment of a major revision of the tax code; a budget bill that averted a government shutdown; and bills overturning a number of Obama-era regulations.[63] The Republican-controlled Senate also approved the appointment of two conservatives, Neil Gorsuch and Brett Kavanaugh, to the Supreme Court. These appointments are likely to affect Supreme Court decisions for years to come.

In 2018, President Trump and congressional leaders agreed on a spending bill that provided for increased defense and domestic social spending. Though the bill was opposed by Republican "deficit hawks," and by some Democrats who demanded legislation to protect undocumented immigrants, a majority of Republicans and more than 73 House Democrats supported the legislation. In the Senate, Rand Paul (R-Ky.) briefly filibustered the bill, but it was ultimately passed by a large majority and signed into law. By increasing overall spending levels, Trump and congressional leaders provided funding for programs that each party supported. The GOP got more money for the military, and the Democrats won more money for domestic programs.[64] It was the sort of classic logroll hated by ideological purists but necessary in a democratic legislature.

FOR CRITICAL ANALYSIS

Why has it become so difficult for members of Congress to compromise? How is American democracy harmed when Congress is unable to agree on major pieces of legislation?

Congressional Polarization Congress's frequent inability to decide reflects the deep ideological differences that separate the two parties. Efforts to measure the ideological distance between the two parties show that since the mid-1970s

Republicans and Democrats have been diverging sharply and are now more polarized than at any time in the last century. Democrats have become more liberal and Republicans have become more conservative on issues related to the economy and the role of government.[65] But as Figure 12.9 shows, the Republican Party has experienced the greatest ideological shift, becoming sharply more conservative. Moreover, because congressional districts are increasingly homogeneous in their ideology—in part due to gerrymandering but mainly because of natural clustering of the population—most members of Congress are in safe seats. Their constituents will not punish them for failing to compromise. Moreover, active mobilization by organizations on the right, such as the Club for Growth, means that Republican members of Congress who support compromises might be punished. These outside organizations have financed alternative candidates to challenge members who vote against

FIGURE 12.9

Polarization in Congress

In recent decades Democrats and Republicans in Congress are increasingly polarized as Democrats have become more liberal and Republicans more conservative. One way of measuring polarization is to estimate the ideology of members of Congress based on their roll-call votes and then graph the ideologies of each party's members. As the graph shows, polarization was lower in the 1940s and 1950s, with some Democrats and some Republicans even overlapping in their ideologies.

SOURCE: Voteview, http://voteview.com/dwnl.htm (accessed 10/15/18).

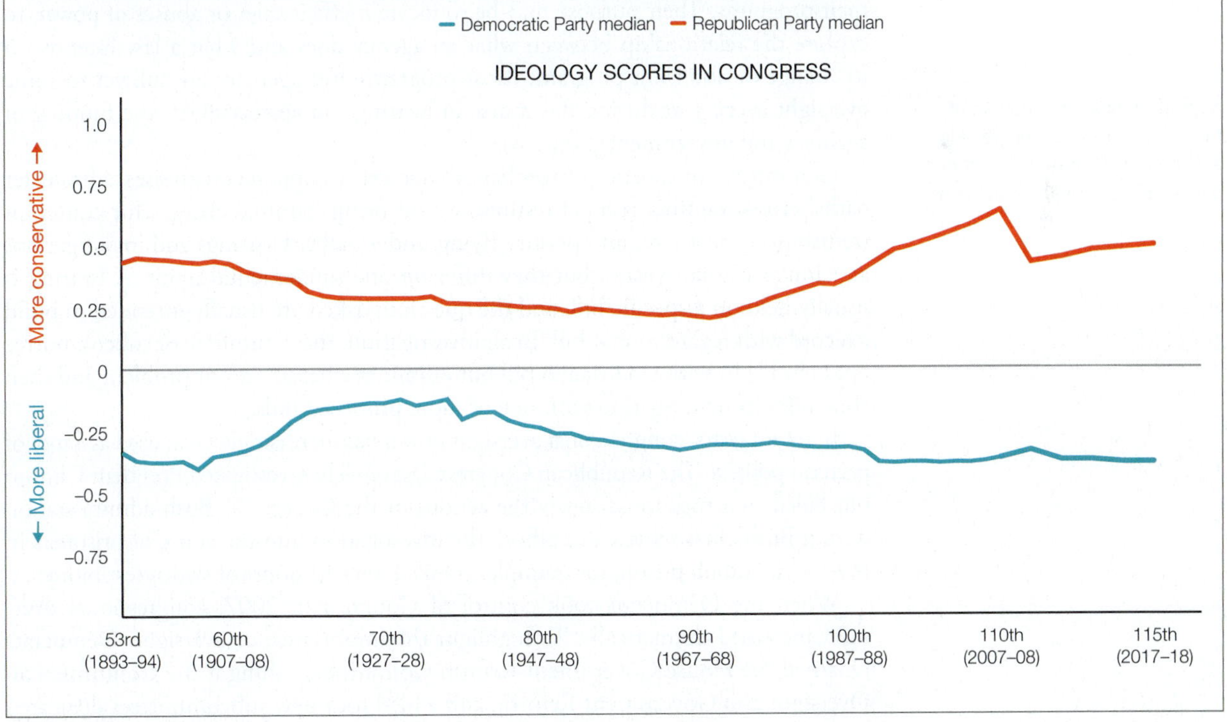

FOR CRITICAL ANALYSIS

How does polarization contribute to congressional gridlock? How has the use of congressional procedures made it more difficult to enact legislation in recent years?

the organizations' positions. Despite rebukes by Republican congressional leadership, groups such as the Club for Growth actively worked to recruit and support candidates in the 2016 election.[66]

However, congressional polarization is here to stay so long as voters elect representatives with sharply different views about what government should and shouldn't do. Until there is more agreement about the role of government and the best way to manage the budgetary challenges that face the country, congressional stand-offs on major legislation will remain a regular feature of American politics.

Beyond Legislation: Other Congressional Powers

Describe Congress's influence over other branches of government

In addition to the power to make the law, Congress has at its disposal an array of other instruments through which to influence the process of government. The Constitution gives the Senate the power to approve treaties and appointments. And Congress has a number of other powers through which it can share with the other branches the capacity to administer the laws.

OVERSIGHT

oversight the effort by Congress, through hearings, investigations, and other techniques, to exercise control over the activities of executive agencies

appropriations the amounts of money approved by Congress in statutes (bills) that each unit or agency of government can spend

Oversight, as applied to Congress, refers to the effort to oversee or to supervise how the executive branch carries out legislation. Oversight is carried out by committees or subcommittees of the Senate or the House, which conduct hearings and investigations to analyze and evaluate bureaucratic agencies and the effectiveness of their programs. Their purpose may be to locate inefficiencies or abuses of power, to explore the relationship between what an agency does and what a law intends, or to change or abolish a program. Most programs and agencies are subject to some oversight every year during the course of hearings on **appropriations**, the funding of agencies and government programs.

Committees or subcommittees have the power to subpoena witnesses, administer oaths, cross-examine, compel testimony, and bring criminal charges for contempt (refusing to cooperate) and perjury (lying under oath). Hearings and investigations are similar in many ways, but they differ on one fundamental point. A hearing is usually held on a specific bill, and the questions asked are usually intended to build a record with regard to that bill. In an investigation, the committee or subcommittee does not begin with a particular bill but examines a broad area or problem and then concludes its investigation with one or more proposed bills.

In recent years, congressional oversight power has increasingly been used as a tool of partisan politics. The Republican Congress aggressively investigated President Clinton but failed to scrutinize seriously the actions of the George W. Bush administration during Bush's first six years in office. The investigation into the abuse of prisoners in Iraq's Abu Ghraib prison, for example, entailed only 12 hours of sworn testimony.

When the Democrats took control of Congress in 2007, congressional oversight increased dramatically. To highlight the importance of oversight, Democrats renamed the House Government Reform Committee, calling it the Committee on Oversight and Government Reform, and added four new subcommittees dedicated to oversight. They also hired more than 200 new investigative staffers.[67] Armed with these resources, the Democratic Congress held 942 oversight hearings during its first six months in power, compared with 579 for the same period when Republicans controlled Congress in 2005.[68] Congressional leaders are quite aware of oversight hearings as political tools. After 2010 the Republican House used the oversight power to highlight the politically weak points in President Obama's record, holding extensive hearings on the Affordable Care Act and on the militant attack of the American consulate in Benghazi, Libya, that resulted in American deaths.[69] First convened in 2014, the Select Committee on Benghazi became enmeshed in partisan contention after Hillary Clinton, secretary of state during the attacks, announced that she would run for president. In 2015, as revelations emerged that Clinton had used a private email server during her tenure as secretary of state, the committee began to investigate whether appropriate procedures had been followed and whether national security was compromised.[70] When the FBI undertook an investigation into the matter in 2016, FBI director James Comey recommended no criminal charges against Clinton but also questioned her judgment and called her actions "extremely careless."

Almost as soon as Donald Trump took office in 2017, Democrats called for investigations into allegations the Trump administration had colluded with Russian operatives to help Trump win the 2016 election. House and Senate committees, chaired by Republicans, failed to find evidence of presidential wrongdoing. Democrats, however, demanded the appointment of a special counsel after President Trump's firing of FBI director James Comey. Over the course of the investigation, the special counsel indicted several close Trump aides for improper contacts with Russian officials. As of October 2018, four former Trump aides—George Papadopoulos, Paul Manafort, Rick Gates, and Michael Flynn—had pleaded guilty to a variety of crimes related to the investigation.

ADVICE AND CONSENT: SPECIAL SENATE POWERS

The Constitution has given the Senate another special power, one that is not based on lawmaking. The president has the power to make treaties and to appoint top executive officers, ambassadors, and federal judges—but only "with the Advice and Consent of the Senate" (Article II, Section 2). For treaties, two-thirds of those present must concur; for appointments, a simple majority is required.

The power to approve or reject presidential requests includes the power to set conditions. In fact, the Senate only occasionally exercises its power to reject treaties and appointments, and despite recent debate surrounding judicial nominees, only a small number of judicial nominees have been rejected by the Senate or withdrawn by the president to avoid rejection during the past century, whereas hundreds have been approved. However, the recent increase in use of the filibuster to block judicial nominees led the Democratic Senate to bar the filibuster in deliberations about judicial and executive branch appointments.

Most presidents make every effort to take potential Senate opposition into account in treaty negotiations with foreign powers. Instead of treaties, presidents frequently resort to **executive agreements** that do not need Senate approval. The Supreme Court has held that such agreements are equivalent to treaties.[71] In the past, presidents sometimes concluded secret agreements without informing Congress of the agreements' contents or even their existence. For example, American involvement in the Vietnam War grew in part out of a series of secret arrangements made between American presidents and the South Vietnamese during the 1950s and '60s. Congress did not even learn of the existence of these agreements until 1969. In 1972,

executive agreement an agreement, made between the president and another country, that has the force of a treaty but does not require the Senate's "advice and consent"

The Constitution provides the Senate with the power to confirm executive branch appointments such as Supreme Court nominee Neil Gorsuch (left). Congress also has the power to approve or reject treaties made by the President. Secretary of State John Kerry (bottom right) and other members of President Obama's cabinet testified before the Senate Foreign Relations Committee on behalf of a nuclear weapons agreement with Iran.

Congress passed the Case Act, which requires that the president inform Congress of any executive agreement within 60 days of its having been reached. This provides Congress with the opportunity to cancel agreements it opposes. In addition, Congress can limit the president's ability to conduct foreign policy through executive agreement by refusing to appropriate the funds needed to implement an agreement. In this way, for example, Congress can modify or even cancel executive agreements to provide American economic or military assistance to foreign governments.

IMPEACHMENT

impeachment the formal charge by the House of Representatives that a government official has committed "Treason, Bribery, or other high Crimes and Misdemeanors"

The Constitution also grants Congress the power of impeachment over the president, vice president, and other executive officials. **Impeachment** means to charge a government official (president or otherwise) with "Treason, Bribery, or other high Crimes and Misdemeanors" and bring him before Congress to determine guilt. Impeachment is thus like a criminal indictment in which the House of Representatives acts like a grand jury, voting (by simple majority) on whether the accused ought to be impeached. If a majority of the House votes to impeach, the impeachment trial moves to the Senate, which acts like a trial jury by voting whether to convict and forcibly remove the person from office (which requires a two-thirds majority of the Senate). The impeachment power is a considerable one; its very existence in the hands of Congress is a highly effective safeguard against the executive tyranny so greatly feared by the framers of the Constitution. The House has initiated impeachment proceedings more than 60 times in U.S. history. Fewer than 20 officials were ultimately impeached, and only eight—all federal judges—were convicted by the Senate and removed from office.[72]

Controversy over Congress's impeachment power has arisen over the grounds for impeachment, especially the meaning of "high Crimes and Misdemeanors." A strict reading of the Constitution suggests that the only impeachable offense is an actual crime. But a more common working definition is that "an impeachable offense is whatever the majority of the House of Representatives considers it to be at a given moment in history."[73] In other words, impeachment, especially impeachment of a president, is a political decision.

FOR CRITICAL ANALYSIS

Under what circumstances should Congress exercise its power of impeachment? Why has impeachment been used so rarely in U.S. history?

The political nature of impeachment was very clear in the two instances of presidential impeachment that have occurred in American history. In the first, in 1867, President Andrew Johnson, a southern Democrat who had battled a congressional Republican majority over Reconstruction, was impeached by the House but saved

The Senate possesses the power to impeach federal officials. In American history, 16 federal officials have been impeached, including two presidents. Andrew Johnson was impeached in 1868 for improperly removing the Secretary of War. In 1998 the House impeached President Bill Clinton for lying under oath about his affair with White House intern Monica Lewinsky.

from conviction by one vote in the Senate. In 1998 the House impeached President Bill Clinton on two counts, for lying under oath and obstructing justice during the investigation into his sexual affair with the White House intern Monica Lewinsky. The vote was highly partisan, with only five Democrats voting for impeachment on each charge. In the Senate, where a two-thirds majority was needed to convict the president, only 45 senators voted to convict on the first count of lying and 50 voted to convict on the second charge of obstructing justice. As in the House, the vote for impeachment was highly partisan, with all Democrats and only five Republicans supporting the president's ultimate acquittal.

Congress
WHAT DO WE WANT?

Much of this chapter has described the major institutional components of Congress and has shown how they work as Congress makes policy. But what do these institutional features mean for how Congress represents the American public? As we saw with Guy Berkebile and Hazel Hoffman at the beginning of the chapter, congressional actions—and inaction—have profound effects on Americans' lives. Does the organization of Congress promote the equal representation of all Americans? Or are there institutional features of Congress that allow some interests more access and influence than others? What can we learn from a tax cut that passes congress and a CHIP reauthorization that almost fails?

As we noted at the beginning of this chapter, Congress instituted a number of reforms in the 1970s to make itself more accessible and to distribute power more widely within the institution. These reforms sought to respond to public views that

Congress had become a stodgy institution ruled by a powerful elite that made decisions in private. We have seen that these reforms increased the number of subcommittees, prohibited most secret hearings, and increased the staff support for Congress. These reforms spread power more evenly throughout the institution and opened new avenues for the public to contact and influence Congress.

But the opening of Congress ultimately did not benefit the broad American public as reformers had envisioned. In fact, the congressional reforms enacted during the 1970s actually made Congress less effective and, ironically, more permeable to special interests. Open committee meetings made it possible for sophisticated interest groups to monitor and influence every aspect of developing legislation. The unanticipated, negative consequences of these reforms highlighted the trade-off between representation and effectiveness in Congress.[74] Efforts to improve representation by opening Congress up made it difficult for Congress to be effective.

When Congress is ineffective, American democracy suffers. As we have seen in this chapter, prolonged stalemates in Congress have led to a reduction in America's credit rating and a costly government shutdown. Moreover, Americans have lost confidence in Congress as it has lurched from crisis to crisis. Is it time for some major changes to make Congress work better? Disillusionment with congressional gridlock has led some to say that the United States should become a parliamentary system, where the winning party can enact the legislation it promised in its party platform. Such a system is more accountable to voters and less prone to stalemate. But Americans would have to jettison the presidency and become a unicameral body to operate as a true parliamentary system, like that of Britain.

Changes in the way Congress conducts its business could also promote more bipartisan decision making. For example, former House Speaker John Boehner decided that he would only bring legislation to the floor if a majority of Republicans supported it. Speaker Paul Ryan also followed the same practice. The "Hastert rule," as this practice is called, could easily be abandoned, allowing bipartisan majorities to enact legislation. Another significant change—eliminating the filibuster in the Senate—would heighten partisan differences but ease gridlock. As we have seen, the Senate voted to eliminate the filibuster for executive branch appointments and judicial candidates in 2013 and for the Supreme Court in 2017. Abandoning the filibuster altogether would allow legislation to move more smoothly through the Senate. Will any of these changes—or other measures—be adopted? Each carries risks to political parties and to politicians. Yet, gridlock also carries political risks, as the public grows frustrated with congressional inaction on important policy areas. What areas of public policy might suffer if Congress continues its inability to decide? How politicians weigh these different choices will shape how—and whether—Congress fills its central position in American democracy.

Gridlock and bitter disagreements in Congress turn some Americans off to politics. However, as the core representative institution of government, Congress is supposed to represent all Americans. As the "**Who Participates?**" feature on the facing page shows, the electorate that turns out to vote for Congress is on average older, whiter, and more affluent than the average American.

Who Elects Congress?

2018 Voters as Compared with U.S. Population

← U.S. population

↑ Electorate

*Numbers may not add up to 100 percent due to rounding.

SOURCES: CNN House Exit Polls, www.cnn.com/election/2018/exit-polls (accessed 11/12/18); U.S. Census Bureau, 2014 American Community Survey, www.census.gov/programs-surveys/acs/data.html (accessed 10/22/15).

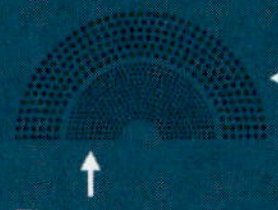

Gender	U.S. pop.	Electorate
● Women	51%	52%
● Men	49%	48%

Age	U.S. pop.	Electorate
● 18–29	22%	13%
● 30–44	25%	22%
● 45–64	34%	39%
● 65+	19%	26%

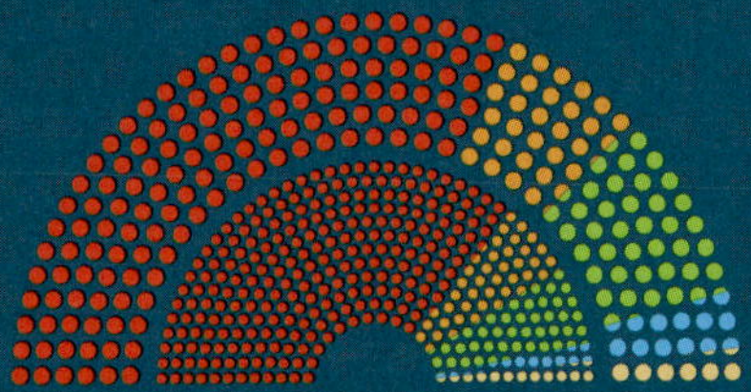

Race	U.S. pop.	Electorate
● White	62%	72%
● Black	13%	11%
● Latino	17%	11%
● Asian	5%	3%
● Other	3%	3%

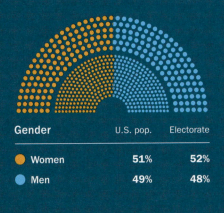

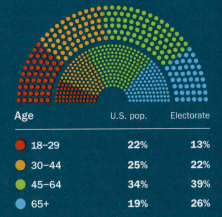

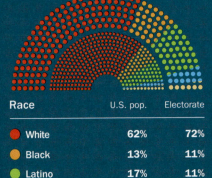

Income	U.S. pop.	Electorate*
● Under $30k	52%	17%
● $30–$50k	20%	21%
● $50–$100k	20%	29%
● $100–$200k	6%	25%
● Over $200k	2%	9%

★ WHAT YOU CAN DO ★

Know Your Members of Congress

 Vote in the next congressional election. If you haven't registered, see page 329 for instructions on how to do so.

 Discover what bills are currently under consideration in Congress by visiting **www.congress.gov**.

 Contact your member of Congress to state your opinion. Go to **www.house.gov** and enter your ZIP code to find your representative. Go to **www.senate.gov** and find your state in the drop-down menu to find your two U.S. senators.

STUDY GUIDE

Congress: Representing the American People

Describe who serves in Congress and how they represent their constituents (pp. 469–82)

A member of Congress's primary responsibility is to his or her constituency. While the number of African Americans, women, Latinos, and Asian Americans in Congress has increased over the last two decades, these groups are still significantly underrepresented relative to their proportions in the general population. Regardless of whether members of Congress share their constituents' sociological characteristics, however, representatives do work hard to speak for their constituents' views and to serve their constituents' interests. Generally speaking, there are three factors related to the U.S. electoral system that affect who gets elected and what they do once in office: who decides to run for Congress, the incumbency advantage, and the way congressional districts are drawn.

Key Terms

constituency (p. 469)
bicameral (p. 469)
delegate (p. 470)
trustee (p.470)
sociological representation (p. 471)
agency representation (p. 471)
incumbency (p. 476)
term limits (p. 477)
apportionment (p. 477)
redistricting (p. 478)
gerrymandering (p. 478)
patronage (p. 480)
pork-barrel (or pork) (p. 480)
private bill (p. 481)

Practice Quiz

1. Which of the following is a way in which the House and the Senate are different?
   a) The House is a more deliberative legislative body than the Senate.
   b) The House is more centralized and organized than the Senate.
   c) Senators serve smaller and more homogeneous constituencies than members of the House.
   d) Senators are often more attuned to the legislative needs of local interest groups than members of the House.
   e) There are no important differences between the House and the Senate.

2. What type of representation is described when constituents have the power to hire and fire their representative?
   a) agency representation
   b) sociological representation
   c) philosophical representation
   d) ideological representation
   e) economic representation

3. Which of the following statements best describes the social composition of the U.S. Congress?
   a) The majority of representatives do not have university degrees.
   b) Men and women are equally represented in Congress.
   c) Most members of Congress do not affiliate with any specific religion.
   d) The legal profession is the dominant career of most members of Congress prior to their election.
   e) The number of African American, Latino, and Asian American representatives has decreased over the last 20 years.

4. The Supreme Court has ruled that
   a) only the House of Representatives has the constitutional authority to redraw congressional district lines.
   b) race can be the predominant factor in drawing congressional districts.
   c) race cannot be the predominant factor in drawing congressional districts.
   d) states cannot use unelected, nonpartisan committees to draw congressional districts.
   e) only the Senate has the constitutional authority to redraw congressional district lines.

5. An *earmark* is
   a) a rule in the House of Representatives that limits who can be heard during legislative debates.
   b) a congressional district drawn to advantage candidates from a certain racial or ethnic group.
   c) a law that grants some special privilege or exemption to a single individual.
   d) language inserted into a bill by a member of Congress that provides special benefits for the member of Congress's constituents.
   e) a weekly, informal meeting between members of Congress and their constituents.

The Organization of Congress

Explain how party leadership, the committee system, the staff system, and caucuses help structure congressional business (pp. 482–89)

Congress is not only a representative body but also a lawmaking institution. The political parties, the committee system, congressional staff, the caucuses, and the parliamentary rules of the House and Senate play key roles in the process by which Congress formulates and enacts law. The committee system is particularly important because Congress relies on committees and subcommittees to do the difficult work of sorting through alternatives and writing bills.

Key Terms

conference (p. 482)
caucus (political) (p. 482)
Speaker of the House (p. 482)
majority leader (p. 482)
minority leader (p. 482)
whip (p. 482)
standing committee (p. 483)
select committees (p. 484)
joint committees (p. 485)
conference committees (p. 485)
seniority (p. 486)
staff agencies (p. 487)
caucuses (congressional) (p. 489)

Practice Quiz

6. Which of the following types of committees include members of both the House and the Senate?
   a) standing committee
   b) select committee
   c) conference committee
   d) rules committee
   e) No committees include both House members and senators.
7. A series of reforms instituted by Congress in the 1970s, including an increase in the number of subcommittees and greater autonomy for subcommittee chairs, had the effect of
   a) reducing the power of committee chairs.
   b) increasing the power of committee chairs.
   c) eliminating the incumbency advantage in congressional elections.
   d) ending the filibuster.
   e) expanding the number of joint committees in Congress.

Rules of Lawmaking: How a Bill Becomes a Law

Outline the steps in the process of passing a law (pp. 489–94)

The rules of congressional procedure influence the fate of every bill and determine the distribution of power in Congress. Debate over bills is much less restricted in the Senate than in the House, and the filibuster gives tremendous power to individual senators. The president's veto power also exerts an important influence on Congress's lawmaking because the possibility of a presidential veto affects how willing members of Congress are to push for different pieces of legislation.

Key Terms

bill (p. 489)
committee markup (p. 489)
closed rule (p. 491)
open rule (p. 491)
filibuster (p. 492)
cloture (p. 492)
veto (p. 494)
pocket veto (p. 494)

Practice Quiz

8. What is the difference between a closed rule and an open rule in the House?
   a) A closed rule puts severe limits on floor debate and amendments, whereas an open rule permits floor debate and makes amendments easier.
   b) An open rule puts severe limits on floor debate and amendments, whereas a closed rule permits floor debate and makes amendments easier.
   c) A closed rule allows journalists and members of the public to listen to debates about a bill, whereas an open rule prevents journalists and members of the public from listening to debates about the bill.
   d) An open rule allows journalists and members of the public to listen to debates about a bill, whereas a closed rule prevents journalists and members of the public from listening to debates about the bill.
   e) A closed rule prevents the federal judiciary from declaring a bill unconstitutional once passed, whereas an open rule allows the federal judiciary to declare a bill unconstitutional.

9. Which of the following statements about the filibuster is most accurate?
   a) The filibuster was first used in 1975.
   b) The votes of 67 senators are currently required to end a filibuster.
   c) The filibuster was used far more frequently in the 1930s and 1940s than it has been in the last two decades.
   d) Nominees for positions in the executive branch and the federal courts cannot currently be filibustered.
   e) Filibusters were declared unconstitutional by the Supreme Court in 2013.

How Congress Decides

Analyze the factors that influence which laws Congress passes (pp. 494–502)

A variety of influences from inside and outside government play a role in congressional decision making. External influences include the policy preferences of the legislator's constituency and the lobbying of various interest groups. Party leaders within Congress use many methods, including leadership PACs, logrolling, and the president's support, to influence how representatives behave. The growing polarization of Democrats and Republicans has significantly hindered the legislative productivity of Congress in recent years.

Key Terms

party unity vote (p. 496)

roll-call vote (p. 496)

logrolling (p. 499)

Practice Quiz

10. Members of Congress take their constituents' views into account because
    a) the Supreme Court can invalidate laws passed without majority support in the public.
    b) interest groups are forbidden from lobbying during legislative votes.
    c) most constituents pay close attention to what's going on in Congress at all times.
    d) they worry that their voting record will be scrutinized at election time.
    e) they can be impeached if they go against their constituents' policy preferences.
11. Which of the following is *not* a resource that party leaders in Congress use to create party discipline?
    a) leadership PACs
    b) committee assignments
    c) access to the floor
    d) the whip system
    e) party unity votes
12. An agreement between members of Congress to trade support for each other's bills is known as
    a) oversight.
    b) filibuster.
    c) logrolling.
    d) patronage.
    e) cloture.

Beyond Legislation: Other Congressional Powers

Describe Congress's influence over other branches of government (pp. 502–5)

Congress has many other powers than simply lawmaking. Using hearings, investigations, and other techniques, Congress exercises control over the agencies of the executive branch. Under the Constitution, the president can only make treaties and appoint top executive officers, ambassadors, and federal judges "with the Advice and Consent of the Senate." The Constitution also grants Congress the power of impeachment over the president, vice president, and other executive officials.

Key Terms

oversight (p. 502)

appropriations (p. 502)

executive agreement (p. 503)

impeachment (p. 504)

Practice Quiz

13. When Congress conducts an investigation to explore the relationship between what a law intended and what an executive agency has done, it is engaged in
    a) oversight.
    b) advice and consent.
    c) appropriations.

d) executive agreement.
e) direct patronage.

14. Which of the following statements about impeachment is *not* true?
    a) The president is the only official who can be impeached by Congress.
    b) Impeachment means to charge a government official with "Treason, Bribery, or other high Crimes and Misdemeanors."
    c) The House of Representatives decides by simple majority vote whether the accused ought to be impeached.
    d) The Senate decides whether to convict and remove the person from office.
    e) There have only been two instances of presidential impeachment in American history.

For Further Reading

Adler, E. Scott, and John D. Wilkerson. *Congress and the Politics of Problem Solving*. New York: Cambridge University Press. 2013.

Chafetz, Josh. *Congress's Constitution: Legislative Authority and the Separation of Powers*. New Haven, CT: Yale University Press, 2017.

Connelly, William F., John J. Pitney, and Gary Schmitt, eds. *Is Congress Broken? The Virtues and Defects of Partisanship and Gridlock*. Washington, DC: Brookings Institution Press, 2017.

Dodd, Lawrence C., and Bruce I. Oppenheimer, eds. *Congress Reconsidered*. 10th ed. Washington, DC: CQ Press, 2012.

Dodson, Debra L. *The Impact of Women in Congress*. New York: Oxford University Press, 2006.

Fenno, Richard F. *Homestyle: House Members in Their Districts*. Boston: Little, Brown, 1978.

Fiorina, Morris. *Congress: Keystone of the Washington Establishment*. 2nd ed. New Haven, CT: Yale University Press, 1989.

Koger, Gregory. *Filibustering: A Political History of Obstruction in the House and Senate*. Chicago: University of Chicago Press, 2010.

Lee, Frances E. *Beyond Ideology: Politics, Principles, and Partisanship in the U.S. Senate*. Chicago: University of Chicago Press, 2009.

Mann, Thomas E., and Norman J. Ornstein. *It's Even Worse Than It Looks: How the American Constitutional System Collided with the New Politics of Extremism*. New York: Basic Books, 2012.

Mayhew, David R. *Congress: The Electoral Connection*. New Haven, CT: Yale University Press, 1974.

Palmer, Barbara, and Denise Simon. *Breaking the Political Glass Ceiling: Women and Congressional Elections*. 2nd ed. New York: Routledge, 2008.

Schickler, Eric, and Frances E. Lee. *The Oxford Handbook of the American Congress*. New York: Oxford University Press, 2011.

Tate, Katherine. *Concordance: Black Lawmaking in the U.S. Congress from Carter to Obama*. Ann Arbor: University of Michigan Press, 2014.

Wawro, Gregory J., and Eric Schickler. *Filibuster: Obstruction and Lawmaking in the U.S. Senate*. Princeton, NJ: Princeton University Press, 2006.

Recommended Websites

Cook Political Report
www.cookpolitical.com
The Cook Political Report, by Charlie Cook, is a nonpartisan analysis of electoral politics. Check out current House and Senate races for an in-depth analysis of past elections and previews of future congressional elections.

Roll Call
www.rollcall.com
Roll Call, the newspaper of Capitol Hill, provides daily coverage on the members, legislation, and events taking place in and around the U.S. legislature.

The Sunlight Foundation and Taxpayers for Common Sense Open Congress
www.opencongress.org
Informative and very user-friendly means to explore legislation passed and proposed, compare legislators, and keep up with recent action on bills.

U.S. House of Representatives
www.house.gov

U.S. Senate
www.senate.gov
These are the official websites for the U.S. House of Representatives and the U.S. Senate. Here you can find information on your members of Congress, key congressional leaders, bills currently under consideration, and legislative committees.

★ chapter ★

13

The Presidency

WHAT GOVERNMENT DOES AND WHY IT MATTERS Kevin Hartley of Tennessee was 21 years old in April 2017 when he collapsed and died from cardiac arrest after using methylene chloride to strip paint from a bathtub during a renovation job. Although the chemical was associated with dozens of deaths dating back to the 1940s, the Environmental Protection Agency, established in 1970, had lacked the regulatory teeth to remove such widely available products from the market. Wendy Cleland-Hamnett, the EPA's top official overseeing pesticides and toxic chemicals, lamented, "How is it possible that you can go to a home improvement store and buy a paint remover that can kill you?"[1]

In summer 2016, Congress passed and President Obama signed a reform of the Toxic Substances Control Act of 1976, giving the EPA more power to regulate toxic chemicals. Passed with bipartisan support, the new law required the EPA to evaluate both new and existing chemicals, including the 10 most toxic chemicals in wide use. In the last days of the Obama administration in January 2017, after 10 years of research, the EPA proposed banning certain uses of methylene chloride,

While presidents inherit policies and regulations implemented during previous administrations, they are empowered to reverse or alter them according to their beliefs. As a former businessman, President Trump rejected the regulations put in place by the Obama administration that could put restraints on some businesses.

especially by ordinary consumers and non-industrial businesses.

But as presidential administrations switched from Obama to Trump, these new rules remained mere proposals. As a candidate Donald Trump said that he wanted to eliminate two regulations for every one that his agencies enacted. And when the Trump Administration took office in January 2017, it froze rules and proposed regulations across government, including those at the EPA. Kevin Hartley died three months later.

The Trump EPA did release new rules about toxic chemicals in summer 2017. They were written by Nancy Beck, a toxicologist who, between stints at the EPA under Presidents George W. Bush and Trump, had worked for the American Chemistry Council, contesting EPA regulations over what she called "phantom risks." The new rules reflected changes that had been requested by the chemical industry and did not include a ban on methylene chloride. The new leadership at the EPA also overturned Cleland-Hamnett's recommendation to ban the use of the pesticide chlorpyrifos, associated with development disabilities in children, and undermined tracking of the health effects of a chemical once used in nonstick pans associated with birth defects and kidney cancer. Recognizing that the agency's leadership was going in a different direction, Cleland-Hamnett, who had worked for the EPA since 1979, under presidents of both parties, announced her retirement. "It's time for me to go." In the face of continued public concern over toxic paint strippers, then-EPA head Scott Pruitt indicated in May 2018 that the agency would implement the methylene chloride ban. But months of inaction passed, and in October 2018 a coalition of consumer groups threatened to sue the EPA for delaying the ban after four more people died.

In this chapter, we examine the foundations of the American presidency and assess the origins and character of presidential power. Presidents are empowered by democratic political processes and, increasingly, by their ability to control and expand the institutional resources of the office. They sit atop the executive branch, a large bureaucracy of departments and agencies such as the EPA. They influence policy with their appointments to the Cabinet, the White House staff, and to the Executive Office of the President, choosing officials who are sympathetic to their policy goals and using regulatory review as with the EPA and executive orders to make policy. They set the tone for government as well, as the sole elected official representing the entire country. But, as we will see, presidential power is not without limit, nor should it be. The U.S. Constitution emphasizes checks and balances among the branches of government, not unlimited power. The framers thought a powerful and energetic president would make the U.S. government more effective but knew that presidential power needed to be subject to constraints to prevent it from becoming a threat to citizens' liberties.

CHAPTER GOALS

- ★ **Understand the expressed, implied, delegated, and inherent powers of the presidency (pp. 515–29)**
- ★ **Identify the institutional resources presidents have to help them exercise their powers (pp. 529–33)**
- ★ **Explain how modern presidents have become even more powerful (pp. 533–43)**

The Constitutional Powers of the Presidency

Understand the expressed, implied, delegated, and inherent powers of the presidency

The presidency was established by Article II of the Constitution, which begins by asserting that "The executive power shall be vested in a President of the United States of America." This language is known as the Constitution's "vesting clause." The president's executive power is underscored in Section 3 of Article II, the "take care clause," which confers upon the president the duty to "take care that the laws be faithfully executed. The president's oath of office at the end of Section 1, moreover, obligates—and thus empowers—the chief executive to "preserve, protect and defend the Constitution of the United States." This language seems to require the president to take action, without specifying any limits to that action, if constitutional government is threatened. President Abraham Lincoln cited his oath of office as justification for suspending the writ of habeas corpus in 1861. He declared that his oath would be broken if the government was overthrown. Suspension of the writ, he said, was necessary to prevent that calamity from taking place. By vesting the executive power in the president, Article II also implies that the president serves as America's head of state and is, therefore, entitled to special deference and respect. In Europe, the chief executives and heads of state were monarchs. While presidents are not monarchs, as the holders of executive power, they might appear to be entitled to the kingly respect due a head of state. On the basis of Article II, presidents make use of three types of powers. These are called the expressed powers of the office, implied powers, and delegated powers. A fourth type of power claimed by presidents does not appear in Article II. This is called the inherent power of the office.

Abraham Lincoln, like many other presidents, cited the presidential oath of office as providing the president the authority to take all the necessary actions to protect the nation.

EXPRESSED POWERS

expressed powers specific powers granted by the Constitution to Congress (Article I, Section 8) and to the president (Article II)

The **expressed powers** of the presidency are those specifically established by the language of the Constitution. These fall into several categories:

1. *Military.* Article II, Section 2, provides for the power as "Commander in Chief of the Army and Navy of the United States, and of the Militia of the several States, when called in to the actual Service of the United States."
2. *Judicial.* Article II, Section 2, also provides the power to "grant Reprieves and Pardons for Offences against the United States, except in Cases of Impeachment."
3. *Diplomatic.* Article II, Section 2, further provides the power "by and with the Advice and Consent of the Senate to make Treaties." Article II, Section 3, provides the power to "receive Ambassadors and other public Ministers."
4. *Executive.* Article II, Section 3, also authorizes the president to see to it that all the laws are faithfully executed; Section 2 gives the chief executive power to appoint, remove, and supervise all executive officers and to appoint all federal judges.
5. *Legislative.* Article I, Section 7, and Article II, Section 3, give the president the power to participate authoritatively in the legislative process.

commander in chief the role of the president as commander of the national military and the state National Guard units (when called into service)

Military Power The president's military powers are among the most important exercised by the chief executive. The position of **commander in chief** makes the president the highest military authority in the United States, with control of the entire defense establishment. The president is also head of the nation's intelligence network, which includes not only the Central Intelligence Agency (CIA) but also the National Security Council (NSC), the National Security Agency (NSA), the Federal Bureau of Investigation (FBI), and a host of less well-known but very powerful international and domestic security agencies.

Military Sources of Domestic Power The president's military powers extend into the domestic sphere. Article IV, Section 4, provides that the "United States shall [protect] every State . . . against . . . Invasion . . . and . . . domestic Violence." Congress has made this an explicit presidential power through statutes directing the president as commander in chief to discharge these obligations.[2] The Constitution restrains the president's use of domestic force by providing that a state legislature (or governor when the legislature is not in session) must request federal troops before the president can send them into the state to provide public order. Yet this proviso is not absolute. First, presidents are not obligated to deploy national troops merely because the state legislature or governor makes such a request. More important, the president may deploy troops in a state or city without a specific request from the state legislature or governor if the president considers it necessary to maintain an essential national service during an emergency, enforce a federal judicial order, or protect federally guaranteed civil rights.[3]

One historic example of the unilateral use of presidential emergency power, even when the states don't request it, is the decision by President Dwight D. Eisenhower in 1957 to send troops into Little Rock, Arkansas, against the wishes of the state of Arkansas, to enforce court orders to integrate Little Rock's Central High School. The governor of Arkansas, Orval Faubus, had posted the Arkansas National Guard at the entrance to Central High School to prevent the court-ordered admission

One of the president's responsibilities is the maintenance of public order in times of crisis. In 1951, President Eisenhower used this to justify sending the troops to Little Rock to enforce racial integration of public schools (left). President Trump sent troops to Puerto Rico to assist in the aftermath of Hurricane Maria in 2017.

of nine black students. After an effort to negotiate with Governor Faubus failed, President Eisenhower reluctantly sent 1,000 paratroopers from the U.S. Army's 101st Airborne Division to Little Rock; they stood watch while the black students took their places in the all-white classrooms.

In most instances of domestic disorder, whether from human or from natural causes, presidents tend to exercise unilateral power by declaring a "state of emergency," as President Trump did in response to the three hurricanes striking America in 2017, thereby making available federal grants, insurance, and direct aid.

Judicial Power The presidential power to grant reprieves, pardons, and amnesty involves power over all individuals who may be a threat to the security of the United States. Presidents may use this power on behalf of a particular individual, as did Gerald Ford when he pardoned Richard Nixon in 1974 "for all offenses against the United States which he...has committed or may have committed." Or they may use it on a large scale, as did President Andrew Johnson in 1868, when he gave full amnesty to all southerners who had participated in the "Late Rebellion." Presidents' use of the pardon power can be very controversial. President Trump was criticized for pardoning former Arizona sheriff Joe Arpaio after Arpaio was found guilty of criminal contempt for ignoring a court order that directed his office to halt illegal racial profiling practices. The pardon was criticized because Trump did not first consult with the Justice Department's office of pardons and it was issued before Arpaio had been sentenced.

Diplomatic Power The president is America's "head of state," its chief representative in dealings with other nations, having the power to make treaties for the United States (with the advice and consent of the Senate) as well as the power to "recognize" other countries. Diplomatic recognition means that the United States acknowledges a government's legitimacy and territorial claims. In 2015, President Obama restored American diplomatic ties with Cuba, which had been severed by President Eisenhower in 1961 after the United States' relations with the Castro regime deteriorated. In 2017, after several staffers at the U.S. embassy in Cuba demonstrated neurological symptoms after being exposed to strange sounds, some blamed these "sonic attacks" on the Cuban government, which prompted President Trump to revisit newly restored American ties with Cuba. In 2018, President Trump met with North

As the head of state, the president is America's chief representative in dealings with other countries. Here, President Trump meets with North Korea's Supreme Leader Kim Jong-un in 2018 to discuss nuclear disarmament on the Korean Peninsula.

Korean leader, Kim Jong-un in an effort to defuse tensions on the Korean Peninsula. Earlier in the year, North Korea and America had exchanged threats in the wake of North Korean nuclear missile tests.

executive agreement an agreement, made between the president and another country, that has the force of a treaty but does not require the Senate's "advice and consent"

In recent years, presidents have expanded the practice of using executive agreements instead of treaties to establish relations with other countries.[4] An **executive agreement** is exactly like a treaty because it is a contract between two countries, but it does not require Senate approval. There are actually two types of executive agreements. One is the *executive–congressional agreement*. For this type of agreement, the president will submit the proposed arrangement to Congress for a simple majority vote in both houses, usually easier for presidents to win than the two-thirds approval of the Senate that is required for a treaty. The United States' 2015 accord with Iran is a recent example of an executive–congressional agreement. The other type of executive agreement is the *sole executive agreement*, which is simply an understanding between the president and a foreign state and is not submitted to Congress for approval. In the past, sole executive agreements were used to flesh out commitments already made in treaties or to arrange for matters well below the level of policy. Since the 1930s, however, presidents have entered into sole executive agreements on important issues when they were uncertain about their prospects for securing congressional approval. For example, the General Agreement on Tariffs and Trade (GATT), one of the cornerstones of U.S. international economic policy in the post–World War II era, was based on an executive agreement. The courts have held that executive agreements have the force of law, as though they were formal treaties.

Executive Power The Constitution focuses executive power and legal responsibility on the president. The most important basis of the president's power as chief executive is found in Article II, Section 3, of the Constitution, which stipulates that the president must see that all the laws are faithfully executed, and Section 2, which provides that the president will appoint and supervise all executive officers and appoint all federal judges (with Senate approval; after some early controversy, presidents' sole power to remove executive branch officials was accepted). The power to appoint the principal executive officers and to require each of them to report to the president on subjects relating to the duties of their departments makes the president the true chief executive officer (CEO) of the nation. The president is subject to some limitations because the appointment of all such officers, including ambassadors, ministers, and federal judges, is subject to a majority approval by the Senate. But these appointments are at the discretion of the president, and the loyalty and the responsibility of each appointee are presumed to be directed toward the president.

The Supreme Court's decision in *United States v. Nixon* is often seen as a blow to presidential power because Nixon was required to turn over secret tapes related to the Watergate scandal, despite his claims of executive privilege. Here, Nixon points to transcripts of the tapes that he is turning over to House impeachment investigators.

Another component of the president's power as chief executive is **executive privilege**, the claim that confidential communications between a president and close advisers should not be revealed without presidential consent. Presidents have made this claim ever since George Washington refused a request from the House of Representatives to deliver documents concerning negotiations of an important treaty. Washington refused (successfully) on the grounds that, first, the House was not constitutionally part of the treaty-making process and, second, diplomatic negotiations required secrecy.

Although many presidents have claimed executive privilege, the concept was not tested in the courts until the 1971 "Watergate" affair, when President Richard Nixon refused congressional demands that he turn over secret White House tapes that congressional investigators suspected would establish his complicity in illegal activities. In *United States v. Nixon* (1974), the Supreme Court ordered Nixon to turn over the tapes.[5] The president complied with the order and was forced to resign from office. The *United States v. Nixon* case is often seen as a blow to presidential power, but in actuality, the Court's ruling recognized for the first time the legal validity of executive privilege, though holding that it did not apply in this particular instance. Subsequent presidents have cited *United States v. Nixon* in support of their claims of executive privilege. The Obama administration invoked executive privilege once, in response to congressional demands for records from Attorney General Eric Holder relating to Operation Fast and Furious, an arms-trafficking sting operation that went awry, with federal agents losing track of hundreds of guns they sold to suspected gun smugglers.

executive privilege the claim that confidential communications between a president and close advisers should not be revealed without the consent of the president

Legislative Power The president plays a role not only in the administration of government but also in the legislative process. Two constitutional provisions are the primary sources of the president's power in the legislative arena. The first of these is the portion of Article II, Section 3, providing that the president "shall from time to time give to the Congress Information of the State of the Union, and recommend to their Consideration such Measures as he shall judge necessary and expedient." Delivering a "State of the Union" address may at first appear to be little more than the president's obligation to make recommendations for Congress's consideration. But as political and social conditions began to favor an increasingly prominent presidential role, each president, especially since FDR, began to rely on this provision in order to become the primary initiator of proposals for legislative action in Congress and the most important single participant in legislative decision making, as well as the principal source for public awareness of national issues.[6]

The second of the president's legislative powers is the veto power assigned by Article I, Section 7.[7] The **veto** is the president's constitutional power to reject acts of Congress (see Figure 13.1), making the president the most important single legislative leader.[8] No bill vetoed by the president can become law unless both the

veto the president's constitutional power to turn down acts of Congress; a presidential veto may be overridden by a two-thirds vote of each house of Congress

FIGURE 13.1

The Veto Process

*PL = public law; 107 = number of Congress (107th was 2001–02); 999 = number of the law.

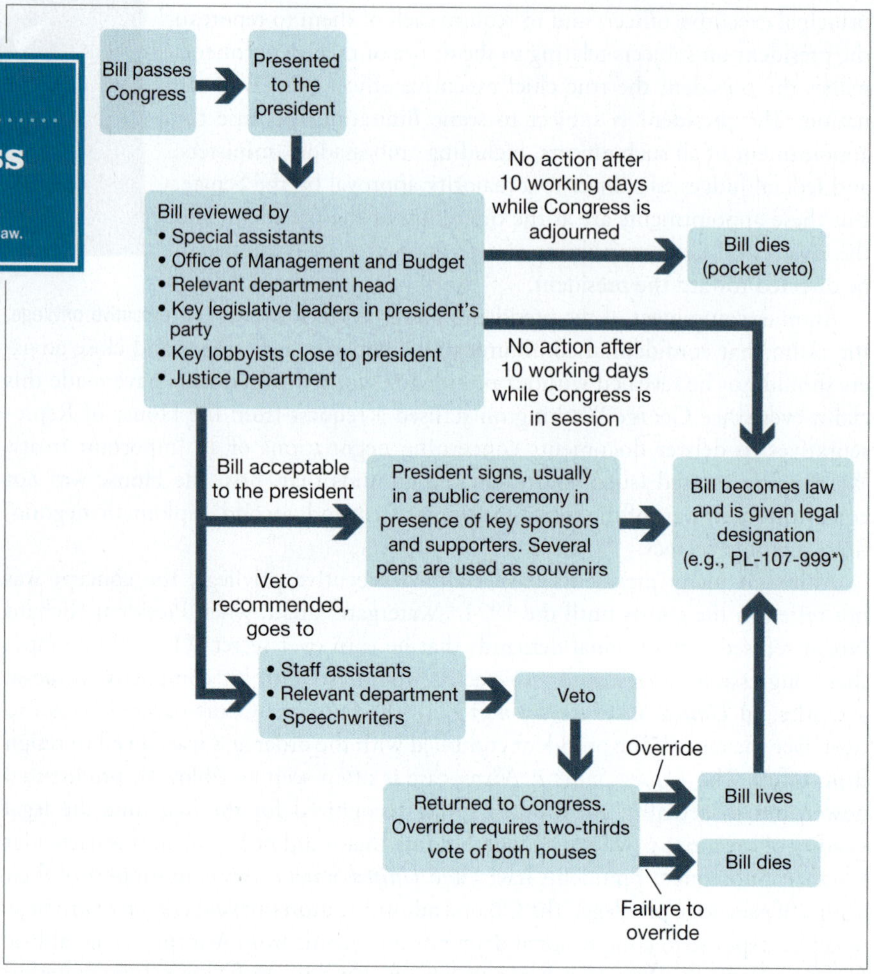
Bill passes Congress
Presented to the president
Bill reviewed by
• Special assistants
• Office of Management and Budget
• Relevant department head
• Key legislative leaders in president's party
• Key lobbyists close to president
• Justice Department
No action after 10 working days while Congress is adjourned
Bill dies (pocket veto)
No action after 10 working days while Congress is in session
Bill acceptable to the president
President signs, usually in a public ceremony in presence of key sponsors and supporters. Several pens are used as souvenirs
Bill becomes law and is given legal designation (e.g., PL-107-999*)
Veto recommended, goes to
• Staff assistants
• Relevant department
• Speechwriters
Veto
Override
Returned to Congress. Override requires two-thirds vote of both houses
Bill lives
Bill dies
Failure to override

pocket veto a presidential veto that is automatically triggered if the president does not act on a given piece of legislation passed during the final 10 days of a legislative session

House and Senate override the veto by a two-thirds vote. In the case of a **pocket veto**, Congress does not have the option of overriding the veto but must reintroduce the bill in the next session. Usually, if a president is presented with a bill and does not sign it within 10 days, it automatically becomes law. But this is true only while Congress is in session. If a president chooses not to sign a bill presented within the last 10 days of a legislative session and Congress is out of session when the 10-day limit expires, instead of becoming law, the bill is vetoed.

Use of the veto varies according to the political situation each president confronts. During his last two years in office, when Democrats had control of both houses of Congress, Republican president George W. Bush vetoed 10 bills, including legislation designed to prohibit the use of harsh interrogation tactics, saying it "would take away one of the most valuable tools in the war on terror."[9] Similarly, 10 of President Obama's 12 vetoes occurred during his last two years in office, when Republicans held the majority in both Houses. Among Obama's most significant vetoes was his 2015 decision to veto a bill authorizing construction of the Keystone XL oil pipeline that would have carried oil from Canada to U.S. refineries. The bill had been opposed by environmentalists and other interests. An attempt to override

FOR CRITICAL ANALYSIS

How might the anticipation of a veto affect the behavior of Congress? And how might the anticipation of a congressional override affect the president's behavior?

In his 2018 State of the Union address, President Trump emphasized the need to tighten immigration laws and highlighted the importance of recently passed tax-overhaul legislation.

the president's veto failed to obtain the necessary two-thirds majority of both houses of Congress. Since the time of George Washington, presidents have used their veto power over 3,000 times, and on only 111 occasions has Congress overridden them. As of November 2018, despite several threats to use his veto power, President Trump had not vetoed a single bill.

Though not explicitly, the Constitution provides the president with the power of **legislative initiative**—the implied power to bring a legislative agenda before Congress. The framers of the Constitution clearly saw legislative initiative as one of the keys to executive power. *Initiative* implies the ability to formulate proposals for important policies, and the president, as an individual with a great deal of staff assistance, is able to initiate decisive action more frequently than Congress, with its large assemblies that have to deliberate and debate before taking action. With some important exceptions, Congress depends on the president to set the agenda of public policy. For example, under the terms of the 1921 Budget and Accounting Act, the president is required to submit a budget to the Congress. In the case of the budget and other matters, initiative confers the power of being able to set the terms of discourse in the making of public policy.

legislative initiative the president's inherent power to bring a legislative agenda before Congress

For example, during the weeks immediately following September 11, George W. Bush took many presidential initiatives to Congress, and each was given almost unanimous support. President Obama made health care his chief domestic priority and engaged in sharp battles with congressional Republicans to bring about the enactment of the Affordable Care Act, informally known as "Obamacare." President Trump sought to lead Congress in the elimination of Obamacare and in a massive tax reform effort but found it difficult to unite the fractious Republicans behind his agenda. Congress was unable to muster a majority for the repeal of Obamacare but did enact a sweeping reform of the tax system and a major new budget that substantially lifted spending on military and domestic programs.

FOR CRITICAL ANALYSIS

Although Congress passes laws, the president has influence too. What is the president's role in the legislative process?

IMPLIED POWERS

implied powers powers derived from the necessary and proper clause of Article I, Section 8, of the Constitution; such powers are not specifically expressed but are implied through the expansive interpretation of delegated powers

The list of expressed presidential powers is brief, but each expressed power has become the foundation of a second set of presidential powers, the so-called **implied powers** of the office. An implied power is one that can be said to be necessary to allow presidents to exercise their expressed power. For example, the Constitution expressly gives the president the power to appoint "all other officers of the United States . . . which shall be established by law." Article II does not, however, expressly grant the president the power to remove such officials from office. There is no reason to assume *a priori* that the power to appoint necessarily indicates the power to remove an official. The president of France appoints the prime minister but only the national legislature can remove that official from office. From the earliest years of the Republic, though, presidents claimed that the removal power was implied by the appointment power. This claim was generally accepted until 1867 when, during its struggles with President Andrew Johnson, Congress enacted the *Tenure of Office Act* (repealed in 1887) requiring the president to obtain senatorial approval to remove officials whose appointments had required Senate confirmation. Johnson's refusal to comply with this Act led to the president's 1868 impeachment and trial. Johnson escaped his own removal from office by a one-vote margin. Fifty years later, the U.S. Supreme Court held in the case of *Myers* v. *United States* that the removal power was, indeed, implied by the appointment power.[10]

Presidents have also made much of the very first sentence of Article II, which declares, "The executive power shall be vested in a President of the United States of America." This grant of power, along with the subsequent admonition to presidents to see to it that the laws are faithfully executed, as well as the president's oath of office, have been cited by successive White Houses as justifications for actions not expressly sanctioned by the Constitution. In recent years, the vesting clause has been said by presidents and their advisers to support what has come to be known as the "theory of the unitary executive."[11]

Unitary executive theory holds that all executive power inheres in the president except as explicitly limited by the Constitution.[12] Thus, according to this view, the president is a sovereign subject to some restraints, such as Congress's control of revenues, its impeachment power, and its power to override presidential vetoes. Some proponents of unitary executive theory also maintain that presidents have their own power to interpret the Constitution as it applies to the executive branch and need not necessarily defer to the judiciary. This claim was advanced by President George W. Bush when he signed a Defense Appropriation Bill that included language on the treatment of terrorist suspects—the so-called anti-torture provision introduced by Senator John McCain—that the president had opposed. In his signing statement, Bush declared that he would construe the portion of the act relating to the treatment of detainees, "in a manner consistent with the constitutional authority of the President to supervise the unitary executive branch and as Commander in Chief and consistent with the constitutional limitations on the judicial power."[13] The president was claiming, in other words, that particularly in the military realm, he possessed the authority to execute acts of Congress according to his own understanding of the law and the nation's interests. He also seemed to be claiming that the authority of the courts to interfere with his actions was limited.

Unitary executive theory particularly holds that the president controls all policy making by the executive branch with Congress wielding only limited, if any, direct power over executive agencies. Only presidents, say unitary executive theorists, may exercise discretionary authority over the actions of these agencies. This idea has been the basis for such presidential programs as "regulatory review," to be discussed below, which has been used by every president since Ronald Reagan to guide rule making by the various federal agencies, sometimes using this process to write authoritative rules when they could not persuade Congress to enact laws they sought.[14]

The president is, of course, a unitary chief executive. But the principle of constitutional checks and balances would appear to provide Congress with powers over the many important agencies of the executive branch through what has come to be called "congressional oversight" of the executive. Article I of the Constitution gives Congress a number of powers, including the power to appropriate funds, to raise and support armies and navies, to regulate interstate commerce, and to impeach officials of the executive branch. Article I also gives Congress the authority "to make all laws which shall be necessary and proper for carrying into execution the foregoing powers." Congressional oversight, which includes legislative hearings, investigations, studies, and reports, is arguably implied by this language. If Congress is to carry out its constitutional responsibilities, it must possess the ability to obtain information regarding the activities of executive branch agencies and officials. Thus, the stage is set for conflict between the implied powers of Congress and those of the president.

DELEGATED POWERS

Many of the powers exercised by the president and the executive branch are not found in the Constitution but are **delegated powers**, the products of congressional statutes and resolutions. Over the past century, Congress has voluntarily delegated a great deal of its own legislative authority to the executive branch. To some extent, this delegation of power has been an almost inescapable consequence of the expansion of government activity in the United States since the New Deal. Given the vast range of the federal government's responsibilities, Congress cannot execute and administer all of the programs it creates and the laws it enacts. Inevitably, Congress must turn to the hundreds of departments and agencies in the executive branch or, when necessary, create new agencies to implement its goals. Thus, for example, in 2002, when Congress sought to protect America from terrorist attacks, it established the Department of Homeland Security, with broad powers in the realms of law enforcement, public health, and immigration.

delegated powers constitutional powers that are assigned to one governmental agency but that are exercised by another agency with the express permission of the first

As they implement congressional legislation, federal agencies collectively develop thousands of rules and regulations and issue thousands of orders and findings every year. Agencies interpret Congress's intent, promulgate rules aimed at implementing that intent, and issue orders to individuals, firms, and organizations to impel them to conform to the law. When it establishes an agency, Congress sometimes grants it only limited discretionary authority, providing very specific guidelines and standards that must be followed by the administrators charged with the program's implementation. Take the Internal Revenue Service (IRS), for example. Most Americans view the IRS as a powerful agency whose dictates can have an immediate and sometimes unpleasant impact on their lives. In fact, congressional tax legislation is very specific and detailed, leaving little to the discretion of IRS administrators.[15] The agency certainly develops numerous rules and procedures to enhance tax collection. It is Congress, however, that establishes the structure of the tax liabilities, tax exemptions, and tax deductions that determine each taxpayer's burdens and responsibilities.

AMERICA SIDE by SIDE

Executive Branches in Comparison

All democracies have an executive branch, but the specific form it takes varies. In presidential systems, such as the United States, the position of the head of state (the symbolic leader of a country) and the head of government (the leader in charge of the day-to-day running of the government) is combined into one position—the president. In parliamentary systems, these roles are often held by different people, with the head of government being the more powerful position. For example, in Germany, the head of government is the prime minister (called the chancellor), while the head of state is the president, who plays a largely ceremonial role similar to the United Kingdom's queen.

Most democracies use parliamentary executive systems, though presidential systems are common in the Americas, in part due to the historical influence of the United States. Political scientists have long debated which system is "best," contrasting parliamentary and presidential systems on their effectiveness, stability, and representativeness. In presidential systems, for example, the separation of powers may protect against the "tyranny of the majority," in which a majority pursues its interests without regard to those of minority groups (see Chapter 2), but it can also lead to deadlock, policy inefficiencies, and polarization.

A small but growing group of countries uses a hybrid "semipresidential" system. France, for instance, divides the executive between a powerful head of state (the president) and the head of government (the prime minister) who have different but (theoretically) equal powers. While this arrangement is intended to combine the best of both systems, conflict can emerge in semi-presidential systems between the prime minister and president over differences in legislation or constitutional authority. In most semi-presidential systems, the president holds the majority of the power, including the power to appoint and dismiss the prime minister. Occasionally, presidents in these systems can use their power advantage to undermine the legislature and threaten democracy.

	PRESIDENTIAL	PARLIAMENTARY
Examples	United States, Mexico, Brazil, Chile, Ghana, South Korea	United Kingdom, India, Germany, Japan, Canada, Austria, Norway
Executive title	President	Prime Minister, Chancellor, etc.
Is the executive the . . .		
Head of state?	Yes	No
Head of government?	Yes	Yes
Executive elected by . . .	Voters*	Parliament
Term in office	Fixed by law	Subject to support of the parliament
Separation of powers	Yes	No; the Prime Minister is a member of the parliament
Executive role in legislating	Veto power	Initiates most bills

*In the United States, the president is elected by the Electoral College, not by the voters directly. Other presidential systems have the voters directly elect the president.

In most instances, though, congressional legislation is not very detailed. Often, Congress defines a broad goal or objective and delegates enormous discretionary power to administrators to determine how that goal is to be achieved. Agency administrators have the power to draft rules and regulations that have the effect of law. Indeed, the courts treat these administrative rules like congressional statutes. For all intents and purposes, when Congress creates an agency such as the Department of Homeland Security, giving it a broad mandate to achieve some desirable outcome, it transfers its own legislative power to the executive branch.

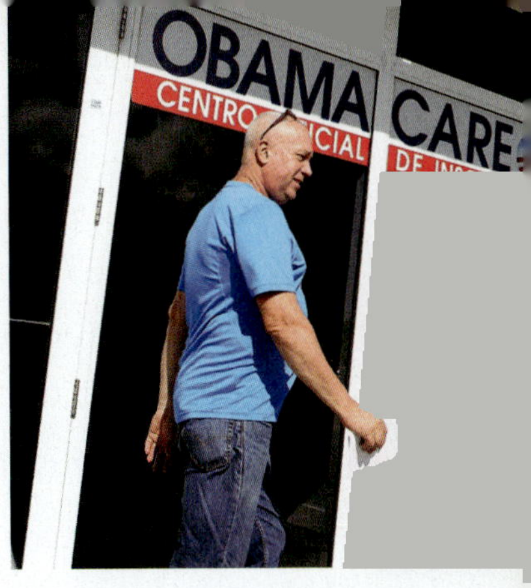

The influence of the president and the executive branch is widespread as the executive is responsible for the implementation of many laws that Congress passes. For example, after Congress passed the Affordable Care Act, it was up to the executive branch to orchestrate the health insurance enrollment process for millions of Americans.

At least since the New Deal, Congress has tended to give executive agencies broad mandates and to draft legislation that offers few clear standards or guidelines for implementation by the executive. For example, the 1933 National Industrial Recovery Act gave the president the authority to set rules to bring about fair competition in key sectors of the economy without ever defining what the term meant or how it was to be achieved.[16] This pattern of broad delegation became typical in the ensuing decades. The 1972 Consumer Product Safety Act, for example, authorizes the Consumer Product Safety Commission to reduce unreasonable risk of injury from household products but offers no suggestions to guide the commission's determination of what constitutes reasonable and unreasonable risks or how these are to be reduced.[17] This means the executive branch, under the president's direction, has wide discretion to make rules that impact American citizens and businesses. A recent example of the executive branch's role is the 2010 Affordable Care Act. After the law passed, several members of Congress admitted that they did not fully understand how the act would work and were depending upon the Department of Health and Human Services, the agency with primary administrative responsibility for the act, to explain it to them. The case of the Affordable Care Act is fairly typical. As administrative scholar Jerry L. Nashaw has observed, "Most public law is legislative in origin but administrative in content."[18]

In the nineteenth century there were relatively well-defined congressional guidelines for administrators. During much of the nineteenth century, the federal government had relatively few domestic responsibilities, and Congress could pay close attention to details. Today, the operation of an enormous executive establishment and literally thousands of programs under varied and changing circumstances requires that administrators be allowed some considerable measure of discretion to carry out their jobs. Nevertheless, the end result is to shift power from Congress to the executive branch.

INHERENT POWERS

Presidents have also claimed a fourth source of power. These are powers not specified in the Constitution but said to stem from "the rights, duties and obligations of the presidency." These are referred to as **inherent powers** and are most often asserted by presidents in time of war or national emergency. President Lincoln relied upon a claim of inherent power to raise an army after the fall of Fort Sumter. Similarly, Presidents Roosevelt (World War II), Truman (Korean War), and both Presidents Bush (Persian Gulf and Middle East wars) claimed inherent powers to defend the nation. Since the Korean War, presidents have used their claim of inherent powers along with their constitutional power as Commander in Chief to bypass the constitutional provision giving Congress the power to declare war. Congress declared war after the Japanese attack on Pearl Harbor on December 7, 1941. Since that time, American forces have been sent to fight foreign wars on more than one hundred occasions but not once was Congress asked for a Declaration of War. In 1973, Congress passed the War

inherent powers powers claimed by a president that are not expressed in the Constitution but are inferred from it

Powers Resolution designed to restore its role in military policy. Presidents, however, have regarded the resolution as an improper limitation on the inherent powers of the presidency and have studiously ignored the provisions of the War Powers Resolution.

The difference between inherent and implied powers is often subtle and the two are frequently jointly claimed in support of presidential action. Implied powers can be traced to the powers expressed in the actual language of the Constitution.[19] Inherent powers, on the other hand, derive from national sovereignty. Under international law and custom, sovereign states possess a number of inherent rights and powers. The most important of these are the right to engage in relations with other nations, the right of self-defense against attacks from other states, and the right to curb internal violence and unrest. Who is actually to act to give effect to the nation's various rights and powers? The executive power is vested by the Constitution in the president, who is acknowledged to have the power to "make" if not "declare" war, to negotiate treaties with other nations and to see to it that the laws are faithfully executed. Thus, it might be said to be constitutionally implied that it is the president who possesses the inherent power to act to defend the nation, to conduct its foreign relations, and to safeguard law and order.

Most presidents believe that they and only they are constitutionally authorized to manage the nation's relations with foreign states. If challenged, presidents and their aides will cite the words of John Marshall's 1800 speech to the House of Representatives where the future Chief Justice called the president, "the sole organ of the nation in its external relations, and its sole representative with foreign nations."[20] According to constitutional scholar Louis Fisher, Marshall meant that the president was the sole organ in implementing, not making, foreign policy.[21] Yet, the Supreme Court took the more expansive view in its famous *Curtiss-Wright* decision, which cites Marshall in support of the idea that the president possesses broad inherent power in the making of foreign policy.[22]

A number of presidents have claimed that the presidency also possessed inherent powers in military affairs and in dealing with domestic emergencies—powers that were not necessarily spelled out in the Constitution or sanctioned by law.[23] In 1861, Abraham Lincoln suspended the writ of habeas corpus, ordered martial law in a number of areas, called out the state militias, withdrew funds from the Treasury, and ordered a naval blockade of Southern ports, all without congressional authorization.

No president has acted so frequently on the basis of inherent powers as President George W. Bush. He claimed that the inherent powers of the presidency gave him the authority to create military commissions, designate U.S. citizens as enemy combatants, engage in "extraordinary renditions" of captured suspects who would be moved to unknown facilities in unnamed countries for interrogation, and authorize the National Security Agency (NSA) to monitor phone conversations between the United States and other nations.[24] When challenged, some but not all of these actions were overturned by the courts. We will examine these decisions in some detail in Chapter 15. It is worth noting, however, that the decisions hardly put to rest the idea of inherent power. Indeed, Bush's successor, President Barack Obama, continued to rely on the concept of inherent power in ordering drone strikes against suspected terrorists and ordering American air strikes in Libya. Testifying before Congress in 2014, Attorney General Eric Holder defended the president's unilateral actions, saying, "Given what the president's responsibility is in running the executive branch, I think there is an inherent power there for him to act in the way that he has."[25] In 2017, President Trump's order banning travelers from several Muslim

WHO ARE AMERICANS?

Who Are America's Presidents?

American presidents have all been men. Until the election of Barack Obama in 2008, they had all been white. As the data show, a majority of presidents have come from the eastern United States, with Virginia producing the most American presidents, especially in the nation's first decades.

Gender

Race

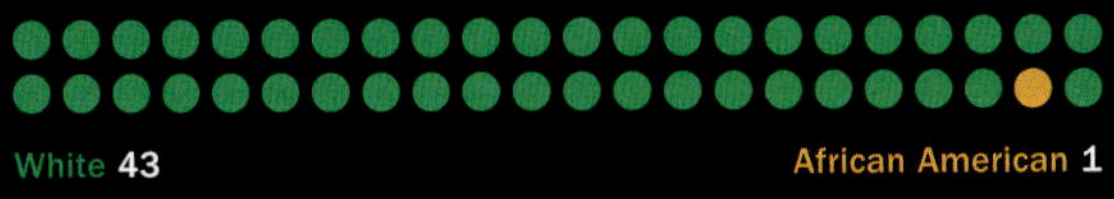

Age

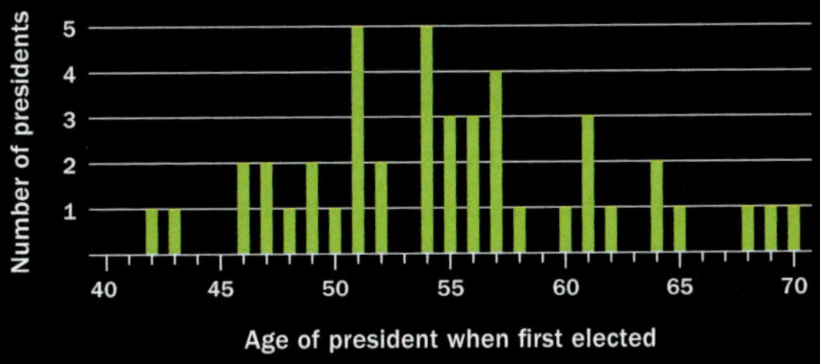

Party*

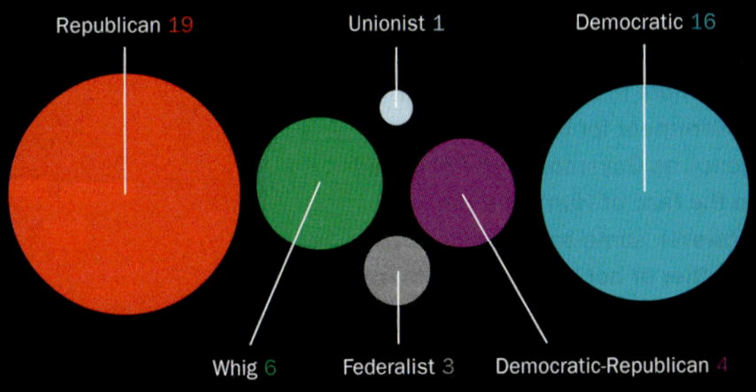

Top Occupations**

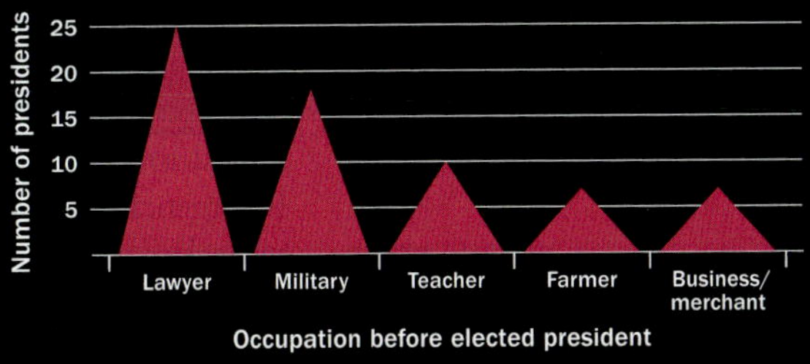

Region†

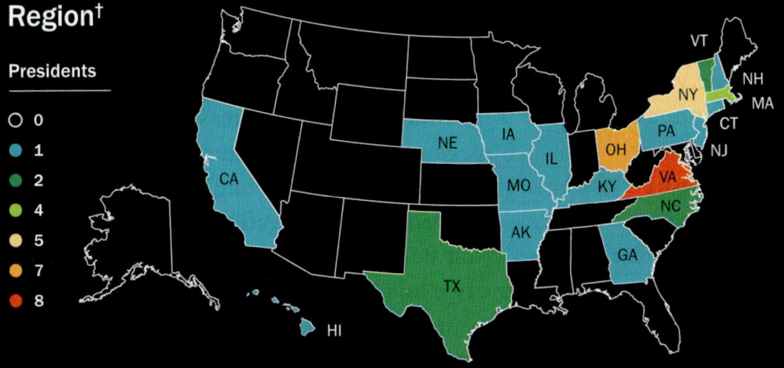

NOTE: Grover Cleveland served as America's 22nd and 24th presidents. He is counted only once in the demographic data here, thus the total number of people who have served as U.S. president is 44.

*Some presidents switched parties during their political careers, thus the numbers sum to more than 44.

**This chart reflects the top nonpolitical careers of U.S. presidents. (All presidents except George Washington and Donald Trump had previous political and/or public service experience.) Presidents may have had more than one occupation, and some occupations do not appear on this list, thus the numbers do not sum to 44.

† Andrew Jackson was born in the Waxhaw area, on the North Carolina–South Carolina border.

SOURCES: Roper Center, www.ropercenter.uconn.edu/elections/common/pop_vote.html; David Leip, http://uselectionatlas.org/RESULTS/; the American Presidency Project, www.presidency.ucsb.edu/showelection.php?year=1840; Miller Center, University of Virginia, http://millercenter.org/president (accessed 3/17/14).

FOR CRITICAL ANALYSIS

1. Why do you think all presidents have been men and all but one have been white? Do you think this is likely to change in coming years?
2. Why do you think so many presidents have come from the South and the East? What electoral or historical factors may have produced this trend?

THE CABINET

Cabinet the secretaries, or chief administrators, of the major departments of the federal government; Cabinet secretaries are appointed by the president with the consent of the Senate

In the American system of government, the **Cabinet** is the traditional but informal designation for the heads of all the major federal government departments. The Cabinet has no constitutional status. Unlike in Great Britain and many other parliamentary countries, where the cabinet *is* the government, the American Cabinet is not a collective body. It meets but makes no decisions as a group. Each appointment must be approved by the Senate, but Cabinet members are not responsible to the Senate or to Congress at large. However, cabinet secretaries and their deputies frequently testify before congressional committees to justify budgets and policy objectives, or explain policies or recent major events or issues.

All U.S. Cabinet departments, and about half the other agencies, were created by acts of Congress. The remaining agencies were created by executive order, the orders of department secretaries, or through the reorganization of existing agencies.[29] Major agencies created by executive order include the Environmental Protection Agency (EPA), the Federal Emergency Management Agency (FEMA), and the Drug Enforcement Administration (DEA). Presidents have claimed the power to create agencies and Congress has acquiesced by providing funding.

Each of the 15 government departments is led by a secretary who is a member of the president's Cabinet. Reporting to the secretary is a deputy secretary, while individual offices and activities are led by undersecretaries and assistant secretaries. The major independent agencies, such as the Social Security Administration, are usually headed by a senior official whose title might be commissioner, administrator, or director and who is in turn supported by deputies and assistant deputies. Government departments range in size from the tiny Department of Education, which employs only about 4,200 individuals, to the massive Department of Defense (DoD), which oversees some 700,000 civilian employees and 1.3 million military personnel. The DoD is also responsible for maintaining the military readiness of 1.1 million reserve and National Guard troops.

The independent agencies also vary in size. The Social Security Administration employs about 60,000 individuals, while some of the smaller agencies are staffed by only a few dozen individuals.

THE WHITE HOUSE STAFF

White House staff analysts and advisers to the president, each of whom is often given the title "special assistant"

The White House staff is composed mainly of analysts and advisers.[30] Although many of the top **White House staff** members hold such titles as "adviser to the president," "assistant to the president," "deputy assistant," and "special assistant" for a particular task or sector, the judgments and advice they are supposed to provide are a good deal broader and more generally political than those coming from the Executive Office of the President or from the Cabinet departments. The members of the White House staff also tend to be more closely associated with the president than are other presidentially appointed officials. This is especially true in the Trump White House, where the president's daughter Ivanka is an assistant to the president, and her husband, Jared Kushner, is a senior adviser to the president.

THE EXECUTIVE OFFICE OF THE PRESIDENT

Executive Office of the President (EOP) the permanent agencies that perform defined management tasks for the president; created in 1939, the EOP includes the OMB, the CEA, the NSC, and other agencies

Created in 1939, the **Executive Office of the President (EOP)** is a major part of the institutional presidency. Somewhere between 1,500 and 2,000 highly specialized people work for EOP agencies.[31] The importance of each agency in the EOP varies according to the personal orientation of each president. The most important and the largest EOP agency is the Office of Management and Budget (OMB). Its roles in preparing the national budget, designing the president's program, reporting on agency activities, and overseeing regulatory proposals connect the OMB to every conceivable presidential responsibility. The status and power of the OMB have grown in importance with each successive president, and the director of the OMB is now one of the most powerful officials in Washington. At one time the process of budgeting was a "bottom-up" procedure, with expenditure and program requests passing from the lowest bureaus through the departments to "clearance" in the OMB and thence to Congress, where each agency could be called in to explain what its "original request" was before the OMB revised it. Now the budgeting process is "top-down": the OMB sets the terms of discourse for agencies as well as for Congress.

The staff of the Council of Economic Advisers (CEA) constantly analyzes the economy and economic trends in order to help the president anticipate events rather than waiting and reacting to them. The Council on Environmental Quality was designed to do for environmental issues what the CEA does for economic issues. The **National Security Council (NSC)** is composed of designated Cabinet officials who meet regularly with the president to give advice on the large national security picture. The staff of the NSC assimilates and analyzes data from all intelligence-gathering agencies (CIA, etc.). In some administrations, the head of the NSC, the president's national security adviser, has held the president's confidence and been a more important figure in the making of American foreign and military policy than the cabinet secretaries in these domains. Henry Kissinger, President Nixon's national security adviser, was such an individual. Other national security advisers have been disappointments to the presidents who appointed them. For example, General Michael Flynn, President Trump's first national security adviser, was forced to resign amid charges of improper relations with Russian officials.

National Security Council (NSC) a presidential foreign policy advisory council composed of the president, the vice president, the secretary of state, the secretary of defense, and other officials invited by the president

THE VICE PRESIDENCY

The vice presidency is a constitutional anomaly, even though the office was created along with the presidency by the Constitution. The vice president exists for two purposes only: to succeed the president in case of death, resignation, or incapacity, and to preside over the Senate, casting a tie-breaking vote when necessary.[32]

The main value of the vice president as a political resource for the president is electoral. Traditionally, presidential candidates choose running mates who can win the support of at least one state (preferably a large one) that may not otherwise support the ticket. It is very doubtful that John Kennedy would have won in 1960 without his vice-presidential candidate, Lyndon Johnson, and the contribution Johnson made to winning in Texas. Another traditional guideline holds that the vice-presidential nominee should provide some regional balance and, wherever possible, ideological or ethnic balance as well. In 2016, Donald Trump chose Governor Mike Pence of Indiana as his running mate for a number of reasons. First, Pence, a former host of conservative radio and television talk shows, was well known among conservatives. Second, Pence served in Congress for 12 years. He worked to reassure skeptical party leaders that Trump was a qualified candidate. Third and most important, Pence is a devout Christian who is very well regarded by social conservatives. As vice president, Pence is often the person Trump relies on to smooth relations with Republican members of Congress.

The vice president is also important because, in the event of the death or incapacity of the president, he or she will succeed to the nation's highest office. During

Mike Pence, who served as a member of Congress and then governor of Indiana, is devoutly Christian and socially conservative. He helped improve Donald Trump's electoral appeal among social conservatives and establishment Republicans.

the course of American history, eight vice presidents have had to replace presidents who died in office. One vice president, Gerald Ford, found himself at the head of the nation when President Richard Nixon was forced to resign as a result of the Watergate scandal.

Until the ratification of the Twenty-Fifth Amendment in 1965, the succession of the vice president to the presidency was a tradition, launched by John Tyler when he assumed the presidency after William Henry Harrison's death, rather than a constitutional or statutory requirement. The Twenty-Fifth Amendment codified this tradition by providing that the vice president would assume the presidency in the event of the chief executive's death or incapacity and setting forth the procedures that would be followed. The Twenty-Fifth Amendment also provides that if the vice presidency becomes vacant, the president will nominate an individual who must be confirmed by a majority vote of both houses of Congress. Thus, in 1973 when Vice President Spiro Agnew was forced to resign, President Nixon nominated Gerald Ford, who was confirmed. Later, when Nixon was forced to resign, Ford became president. In the event that both the president and vice president are killed, the Presidential Succession Act of 1947 establishes an order of succession, beginning with the Speaker of the House and continuing with the president pro tempore of the Senate and the Cabinet secretaries. This piece of legislation, adopted during the Cold War and prompted by fear of a nuclear attack, has taken on new importance in an age of global terrorism.

THE FIRST SPOUSE

The president serves as both chief executive and chief of state—the equivalent of Great Britain's prime minister and monarch rolled into one, simultaneously leading the government and representing the nation at official ceremonies and functions.

Because they are generally associated exclusively with the head-of-state aspect of America's presidency, presidential spouses are usually not subject to the same sort of media scrutiny or partisan attack as that aimed at the president. Traditionally,

First Lady Melania Trump is an immigrant from Slovenia and a former model. During the 2016 presidential campaign, Mrs. Trump campaigned for her husband, speaking at the Republican National Convention and occasionally at rallies.

most first ladies have limited their activities to the ceremonial portion of the presidency: greeting foreign dignitaries, visiting other countries, and attending important national ceremonies.

Some first spouses, however, have had considerable influence over policy. Franklin Roosevelt's wife, Eleanor, was widely popular but also widely criticized for her active role in many elements of her husband's presidency. During the 1992 campaign, Bill Clinton often implied that his wife would be active in the administration; he joked that voters would get "two for the price of one." And indeed, after the election, Hillary Clinton took a leading role in many policy areas, most notably heading the administration's health care reform effort. She also became the first first lady to seek public office on her own, winning a seat in the U.S. Senate in 2000 and then running for president in 2008 and 2016, having served in between as President Obama's secretary of state.

Melania Trump is the first foreign-born first lady in almost 200 years. With no political or public affairs experience, Mrs. Trump said that she would be a traditional first lady. Given the current expectation that the first spouse should assume some public responsibility, however, Mrs. Trump may become a visible advocate for an important social cause. Thus far, she has spoken out against online bullying.

The Contemporary Bases of Presidential Power

Explain how modern presidents have become even more powerful

During the nineteenth century, Congress was America's dominant institution of government, and members of Congress sometimes treated the president with disdain. Today, however, no one would assert that the presidency is unimportant. Presidents seek to dominate the policy-making process and claim the power to lead the nation in time of war. The expansion of presidential power over the course of the past century has come about not by accident but as the result of an ongoing effort by successive presidents to enlarge the powers of the office.

Generally, presidents can expand their power in two primary ways: through popular mobilization and through the administration. First, presidents may use popular appeals to create a mass base of support that will allow them to dominate their political foes, a tactic called "going public."[33] Second, presidents may seek to bolster their control of established executive agencies or to create new administrative institutions and procedures that will reduce their dependence on Congress and give them a more independent governing and policy-making capability. Perhaps the most obvious example of this is the use of executive orders to achieve policy goals in lieu of seeking to persuade Congress to enact legislation.

Presidents do have a third, less reliable tool: their political party. Most presidents have relied on their own party to implement their legislative agenda. For example, in 2009–10, President Obama relied on congressional Democrats to pass the Affordable Care Act ("Obamacare") in the face of virtually unanimous Republican opposition. However, the president does not control his party; party members have considerable autonomy. President Trump was unable to rally enough Republican legislators to repeal Obamacare, although he was able to bring about the enactment of tax reform. Consequently, although the party is valuable to chief executives, it has not been a fully reliable presidential tool.

Moreover, in America's system of separated powers, the president's party may be in the minority in Congress and unable to do much for the chief executive's programs. As a result, contemporary presidents are more likely to use the two other methods, popular mobilization and executive administration, to achieve their political goals.

GOING PUBLIC

In the nineteenth century, it was considered inappropriate for presidents to engage in personal campaigning on their own behalf or in support of programs and policies. When Andrew Johnson broke this unwritten rule and made a series of speeches vehemently seeking public support for his Reconstruction program, even some of his supporters were shocked at what they saw as his lack of decorum and dignity. The president's opponents cited his "inflammatory" speeches in one of the articles of impeachment drafted by the Congress.[34]

In the twentieth century, though, popular mobilization became a favored weapon in the political arsenals of most presidents. The first to make systematic use of appeals to the public were Theodore Roosevelt and Woodrow Wilson, but the president who used public appeals most effectively was Franklin Delano Roosevelt. FDR was "firmly persuaded of the need to form a direct link between the executive office and the public."[35] He developed a number of tactics for forging such a link. He often embarked on speaking trips around the nation to promote his programs. On one such tour, he told a crowd, "I regain strength just by meeting the American people."[36] In addition, FDR made effective use of a new electronic medium, the radio, to reach millions of Americans. In his famous "fireside chats," the president's voice could be heard in every living room in the country, discussing programs and policies and generally assuring Americans that Franklin Delano Roosevelt was aware of their difficulties and working diligently toward solutions.

Roosevelt was also an innovator in the realm of what now might be called press relations. When he entered the White House, FDR faced a mainly hostile press, typically controlled by conservative members of the business establishment.[37] To circumvent the editors and publishers who were generally unsympathetic to his goals, the president worked to cultivate the reporters who covered the White House. FDR made himself available for biweekly press conferences, where he offered candid answers to reporters' questions and made certain to make important policy announcements that would provide the reporters with significant stories for their papers.[38] Franklin Roosevelt's press secretary, Stephen Early, was charged with organizing press conferences and making certain that reporters observed the informal rules distinguishing those presidential comments that could be attributed directly to the president from those that were off the record.

Over the last century, presidents and candidates have made more and more used of direct appeals to the American people. President Franklin Roosevelt made effective use of radio to build public support for his programs (top). Donald Trump (bottom) has likewise used Twitter to promote his message, both as a candidate and as president.

Every president since FDR has sought to craft a public-relations strategy that would emphasize the incumbent's strengths and maximize his popular appeal. For John F. Kennedy, who was handsome and quick-witted, the televised press conference was an excellent public-relations vehicle. Both Bill Clinton and Barack Obama held televised town meetings—carefully staged events that gave these presidents opportunities to appear to consult with rank-and-file citizens about their goals and policies without having to face the sorts of pointed questions preferred by reporters.

Bill Clinton introduced an innovation that continued to be used by Bush, Obama, and Trump. This was to make the White House Communications Office an important institution within the EOP. The Communications Office became responsible not only for responding to reporters' queries but also for developing and implementing a coordinated communications strategy—promoting the president's policy goals, developing responses to adverse news stories, and making certain that a favorable image of the president would, insofar as possible, dominate the news.

Going Public Online President Obama was the first chief executive to make full use of another new communication medium—the internet. Drawing on the interactive tools of the web, Obama's 2008 and 2012 campaigns changed the way politicians organize supporters, advertise to voters, defend against attacks, and communicate with their constituents.[39] In the 2016 presidential campaign, candidates Hillary Clinton and especially Donald Trump made particular use of Twitter to communicate with millions of voters, bypassing traditional media. Trump usually tweeted many times a day, often making outrageous claims that guaranteed that he would dominate media coverage as reporters rushed to analyze and criticize Trump's assertions. Trump did not care if the media criticized him or refuted his claims—his goal was to dominate coverage. During the course of the campaign, Trump received a quantity of free coverage that would have cost several billion dollars if he had purchased advertising time. The Clinton campaign spent much more money than Trump, but Trump's clever use of Twitter and his manipulation of the media gave him an enormous air-time advantage.

The internet has changed not only the way modern presidents campaign but also how they govern. The Whitehouse.gov website keeps the president's constituents abreast of his policy agenda with a weekly streaming video address by the president, press briefings, speeches and remarks, a daily blog, photos of the president, the White House schedule, and other information. Virtually everything the president does is recorded online. YouTube aired Obama's press conferences and public appearances on a daily basis. Every presidential address is now streamed live online. Obama also created a website that allowed citizens to submit petitions to the White House. Any petition receiving 100,000 signatures was slated for review by the administration and a response issued. For example, in 2015 the president issued extensive comments on the death of Michael Brown, a black man shot by a white police officer in Ferguson, Missouri, in response to citizen petitions demanding a federal investigation of the incident.

FOR CRITICAL ANALYSIS

What are the advantages and disadvantages of presidents governing via digital media? How do these pros and cons compare with "going public" in the age of television?

Circumventing television and other traditional media, the internet allows the president to broadcast his policy ideas directly to the citizens. Every Trump legislative initiative and policy direction is preceded by a flurry of tweets repeated by the broadcast and print media. And, Trump's language seems tailored to the twitter age. Calling North Korean leader Kim Jong-un "Little Rocket Man" in his tweets allowed Trump to boil down his sense of contempt and harsh posture toward North Korea into a tweet-sized threat to use force.

The Limits of Going Public Some presidents have been able to make effective use of popular appeals to overcome congressional opposition. Popular support, though, has not been a firm foundation for presidential power: President George W. Bush maintained an approval rating of over 70 percent for more than a year following the September 11 terrorist attacks. By the end of 2005, however, Bush's approval rating had dropped to 39 percent as a result of the growing unpopularity of the Iraq War, the administration's inept handling of hurricane relief, and a number of White House scandals, including the conviction of Vice President Cheney's chief of staff on charges of lying to a federal grand jury. Between the time President Obama took office in January 2009 and May 2016, his public approval ranged from a high of 76 percent in January 2009 to a low of 36 percent in the fall of 2014.[40] Such declines in popular approval during a president's term in office are nearly inevitable and follow a predictable pattern.[41] Both before and after they are elected, presidents generate popular support by promising to undertake important programs that will contribute directly to the well-being of large numbers of Americans. Almost without exception, presidential performance falls short of promises and popular expectations, leading to a decline in public support and the ensuing weakening of presidential influence.[42] It is a rare American president, such as Bill Clinton, who exits the White House more popular than when he went in. Donald Trump's approval rating had risen to 45 percent by June 2018, after hitting a low of 35 percent in 2017.[43]

THE ADMINISTRATIVE STRATEGY

Contemporary presidents have increased the administrative capabilities of their office in three ways. First, they have enhanced the reach and power of the EOP. Second, they have sought to increase White House control over the federal bureaucracy. Third, they have expanded the role of executive orders and other instruments of direct presidential governance. Taken together, these three components of what might be called the White House "administrative strategy" have given presidents a capacity to achieve their programmatic and policy goals even when they are unable to secure congressional approval. Indeed, some recent presidents have been able to accomplish a great deal with remarkably little congressional, partisan, or even public support.

The Growth of the EOP The EOP has grown from six administrative assistants in 1939 to several hundred employees working directly for the president in the White House office, along with some 2,500 individuals staffing the several divisions of the

Executive Office. The creation and growth of the White House staff have given the president an enormously enhanced capacity to gather information, plan programs and strategies, communicate with constituencies, and exercise supervision over the executive branch. The staff multiplies the president's eyes, ears, and arms, becoming a critical instrument of presidential power.[44]

In particular, the OMB, an agency within the EOP, serves as a potential instrument of presidential control over federal spending and hence a mechanism through which the White House has greatly expanded its power. The OMB has the capacity to analyze and approve all legislative proposals, not only budgetary requests, emanating from all federal agencies before being submitted to Congress. This procedure, now a matter of routine, greatly enhances the president's control over the entire executive branch. All legislation originating in the White House as well as all executive orders also go through the OMB.[45] Thus, through one White House agency, the president has the means to exert major influence over the flow of money and the shape and content of national legislation.

Regulatory Review A second instrument that presidents have used to increase their power and reach is an agency within OMB called the Office of Information and Regulatory Affairs (OIRA), which supervises the process of regulatory review through which presidents have sought to seize control of rule-making by the agencies of the executive branch. Whenever Congress enacts a statute, its actual implementation requires the promulgation of hundreds of rules by the agency charged with administering the law and giving effect to the will of Congress. For example, if Congress wishes to improve air quality, it must delegate to an agency—say the Environmental Protection Agency (EPA)—the power to establish numerous rules and regulations that will govern the actions of the government agencies, firms, and individuals whose conduct may have an impact upon the atmosphere. The agency rule-making process is, itself, governed by a number of statutory requirements concerning public notice (most importantly publication in the *Federal Register*), hearings, and appeals, but once completed and published in the massive *Code of Federal Regulations*, administrative rules have the effect of law and will be enforced by the federal courts.

The discretion Congress delegates to administrative agencies has provided recent presidents with an important avenue for expanding their own power. Beginning with little fanfare during the Nixon administration, presidents—through regulatory review—gradually have endeavored to take control of the rule-making process and to use it as a quasi-legislative mechanism through which they can engage in lawmaking without the interference of the legislature.

For example, during the course of his presidency, Clinton issued 107 directives to administrators, ordering them to propose specific rules and regulations and, pursuant to the requirements of the Administrative Procedures Act, to publish them in the *Federal Register* for public commentary. Clinton's presidential rulemaking directives covered a wide variety of topics. For example, Clinton ordered the Food and Drug Administration (FDA) to develop rules designed to restrict the marketing of tobacco products to children.[46] President George W. Bush continued the Clinton-era practice of issuing presidential directives to agencies to spur them to issue new rules and regulations. The Obama administration not only issued a number of major regulatory directives to federal agencies but also launched a "look back" program. Under this program, the administration sought to eliminate several hundred existing rules it deemed obsolete.[47] In 2015, Obama sought new regulations governing power plant emissions, overtime pay for workers, the educational practices of career (for-profit) colleges, and a host of other matters. President Trump moved aggressively to reverse these and other directives by issuing new rules or repealing existing ones to roll back environmental regulations, reduce banking regulations, eliminate workplace safety regulations, and remove protections for transgender workers, among others. Most notably, in the first year of his presidency, Trump eliminated nearly 70 environmental regulations.[48]

Governing by Decree: Executive Orders and Memoranda A third mechanism through which contemporary presidents have sought to enhance their power to govern unilaterally is through the use of executive orders and other forms of presidential decrees, including executive agreements, national security findings and directives, proclamations, reorganization plans, and memoranda.

executive order a rule or regulation issued by the president that has the effect and formal status of legislation

An **executive order** is a direct presidential directive to the bureaucracy to undertake some action, bypassing Congress and the legislative process. Executive orders have a long history in the United States and have been the instruments for a number of important policies, including the purchase of Louisiana, the annexation of Texas, the emancipation of the slaves, the wartime internment of Japanese Americans, the desegregation of the military, the initiation of affirmative action, and the creation of a number of federal agencies including the Environmental Protection Agency, the Food and Drug Administration, and the Peace Corps.[49]

Historically, executive orders were most often used during times of war or national emergency. President Lincoln relied heavily on executive orders in the early months of the Civil War to mobilize troops, purchase warships, and obtain funds from the U.S. Treasury.[50] During World War II, President Roosevelt issued 286 executive orders, establishing wartime agencies and authorizing the government to take control of factories and property for wartime needs.[51] In recent years, though, executive orders have become routine instruments of presidential governance rather than emergency wartime measures (Figure 13.3).

President George W. Bush issued more than 300 executive orders, many relating to the war on terrorism but others pertaining to domestic policy matters, such as his ban on the use of federal funds to support international family planning groups and his prohibition of the use of embryonic stem cells in federally funded research projects. President Obama issued an executive action halting the deportation of undocumented immigrants who had come to the United States as children, prohibiting federal agencies and contractors from discriminating against transgender employees, and declaring more than 700,000 square miles of the central Pacific Ocean off-limits to fishing. President Trump rescinded most of Obama's orders on immigration and opened the way for the deportation of those who had been protected by the previous president's orders. Trump also issued a number of orders, including a controversial "travel ban" decree seeking to prevent travelers from several majority-Muslim countries from entering the United States. Trump's orders led to a number of lawsuits, but the Supreme Court ultimately upheld the ban.

Presidential use of executive orders is constrained by law. When presidents issue executive orders, in principle they do so pursuant to the powers granted to them by the Constitution or delegated to them by Congress. When presidents issue orders they generally must state the constitutional or statutory basis for their actions. For example, when President Johnson ordered U.S. government contractors to initiate programs of affirmative action in hiring, he said the order was designed to implement the 1964 Civil Rights Act, which prohibited employment discrimination.

FIGURE 13.3

Presidential Executive Orders*

Executive orders are a tool presidents have for influencing policy. Their use has varied considerably over time. Each bar in the graph shows the average number of executive orders each president issued per year in office. Which presidents issued the most executive orders? What events in U.S. history were occurring when those presidents were in office?

*Does not include memoranda or other forms of executive action
**As of October 2018.

SOURCE: Gerhard Peters, www.presidency.ucsb.edu/data/orders.php (accessed 10/1/18).

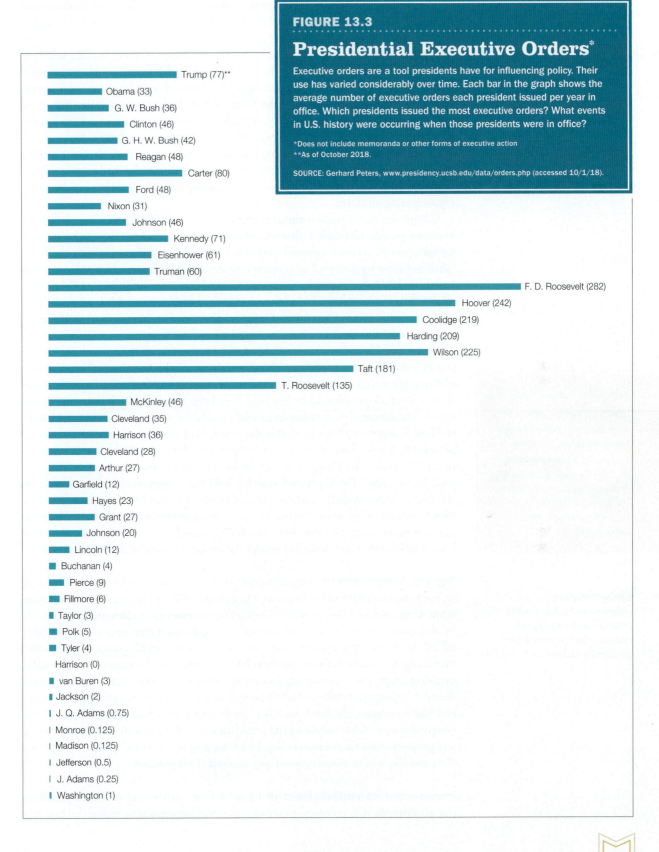

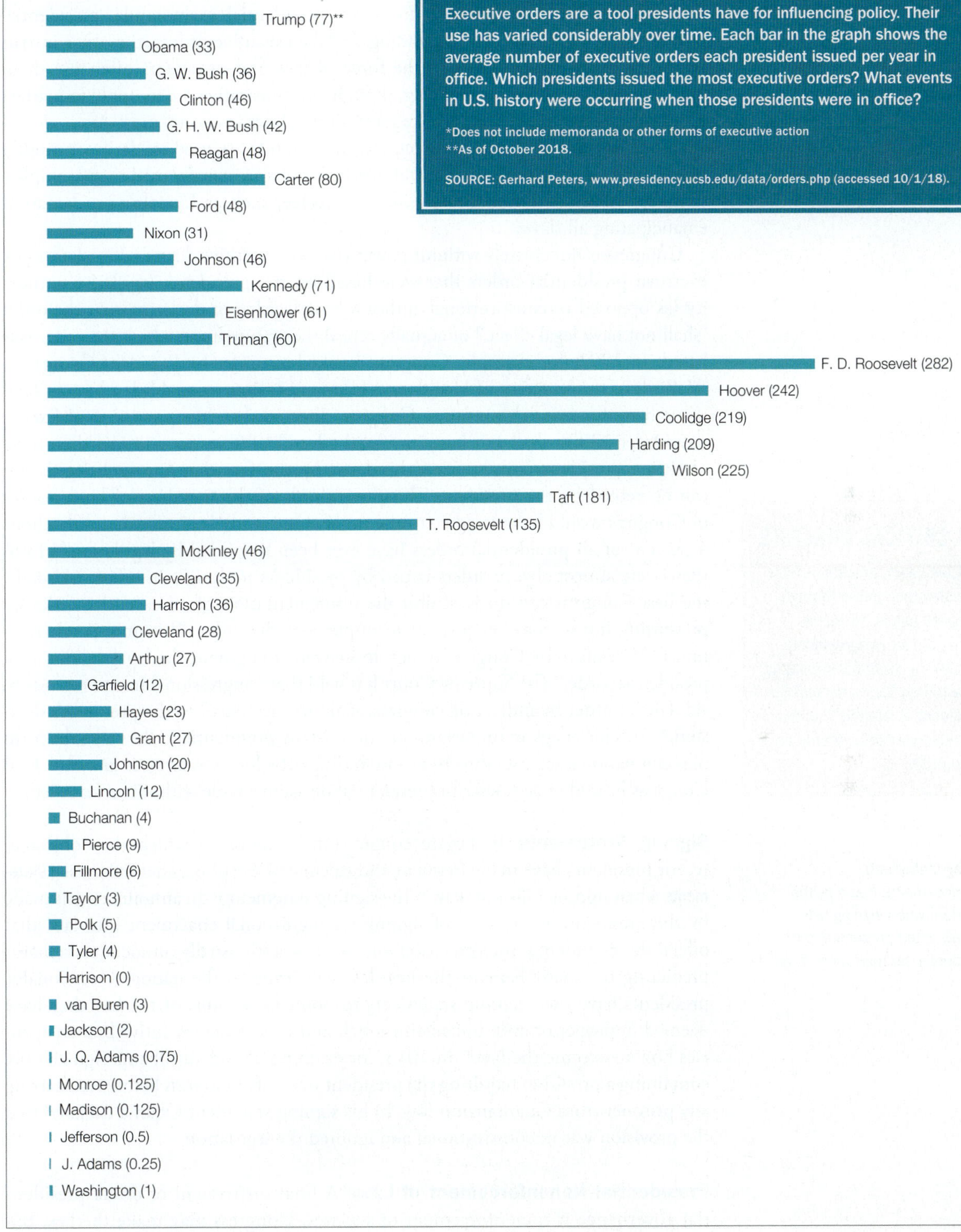

Where the courts have found no constitutional or statutory basis for a presidential order they have invalidated it. Such cases, however, are rare. Generally, the judiciary has accepted executive orders as the law of the land.

Executive orders are one form of presidential decree. Others include administrative orders, national security directives, presidential memoranda, presidential proclamations, and presidential findings.[52] Like executive orders, the other instruments establish policy and have the force of law, and presidents often use them interchangeably. Generally speaking, though, administrative orders apply to matters of administrative procedure and organization; directives seem most often associated with national or homeland security; memoranda are used to clarify or modify presidential positions and orders; and proclamations are usually used to give emphasis to an especially important presidential decree, such as Lincoln's proclamation emancipating all slaves.

Congress is not entirely without power vis-à-vis executive decrees. Legislators can overturn presidential orders that were based on the president's legislative authority (as opposed to constitutional authority) via legislation declaring that the order "shall not have legal effect," or actually repeal the statute upon which the order was based. In 1993, for example, Congress revoked an order by President George H. W. Bush to the secretary of Health and Human Services to establish a human fetal tissue bank for research purposes. Congress directed that "the provisions of Executive Order 12806 shall not have any legal effect."[53] Efforts to overturn the orders of sitting presidents are, however, hindered by the fact that any such legislation can be vetoed by the president. Thus, two-thirds of the members of both houses of Congress would have to agree to the move. One study indicates that only about 4 percent of all presidential orders have ever been rescinded by legislation.[54] Even these were almost always orders issued by presidents no longer in office.[55] Usually, the best Congress can do is inhibit the implementation of an executive order by preventing funds from being spent to implement the order. This, too, is relatively unusual.[56] Failure by Congress to act, moreover, strengthens the legal validity of a presidential order. The Supreme Court has held that congressional inaction tends to validate an order by indicating congressional "acquiescence" to the president's decision.[57] This idea begs an important question. Many presidential orders take the form of secret national security directives and findings of which Congress is unaware. Can Congress be said to acquiesce in presidential decisions made without its knowledge?

FOR CRITICAL ANALYSIS

In recent years, presidents have expanded their power through increased use of executive orders, executive agreements, and other unilateral instruments. Is the United States becoming a "presidential republic"? Is this a development to be feared or welcomed?

Signing Statements To negate congressional actions to which they objected, recent presidents have made frequent and calculated use of presidential **signing statements** when signing bills into law.[58] The signing statement is an announcement made by the president, at the time of signing a congressional enactment into law, that offers the president's interpretation of the law and usually innocuous remarks predicting the many benefits the new law will bring to the nation. Occasionally, presidents have used signing statements to point to sections of the law they have deemed improper or even unconstitutional, and to instruct executive branch agencies how to execute the law.[59] In 2013, for example, President Obama signed a bill containing a provision requiring the president to notify Congress before transferring any prisoner from Guantánamo Bay. In his signing statement Obama declared that the provision was unconstitutional and ignored the legislation.

signing statements
announcements made by the president when signing bills into law, often presenting the president's interpretation of the law

Presidential Nonenforcement of Laws A final instrument of direct presidential governance is nonenforcement of statutes. Congress may make the law, but

In 2017, President Trump signed an Executive Order on health care. The administration claimed this order would provide patients expanded options for health insurance, though many felt it would undermine the stability of Obamacare.

presidents implement and enforce it. If the president decides that a particular law is not to his liking and refuses to enforce it, Congress may find that its intent is stymied. President Obama, for example, suspended enforcement of portions of the Affordable Care Act when the rollout of "Obamacare" produced public confusion and inefficient implementation. President Trump, in an effort to undercut the ACA, has effectively ordered the IRS to not enforce a provision of the Affordable Care Act requiring taxpayers to indicate on their tax returns that they had health insurance—a major blow to the law's mandate. Since the president is the nation's chief law enforcer, refusal to enforce a law can become a unilateral negation of its effects.

The Advantages of the Administrative Strategy Through the course of American history, party leadership and popular appeals have played important roles in presidential efforts to overcome political opposition, and both continue to be instruments of presidential power. Yet, as we have seen, in the modern era presidents have not always been able to rely upon support from their own parties, and the effects of popular appeals have often proven evanescent. The limitations of the alternatives have increasingly impelled presidents to try to expand the administrative capabilities of the office and their own capacity for unilateral action as means of achieving their policy goals. In recent decades, the expansion of the Executive Office, the development of regulatory review, and the use of executive orders and signing statements have given presidents a substantial capacity to achieve significant policy results despite congressional opposition to their legislative agendas.

In principle, perhaps, Congress could respond more vigorously to unilateral policy making by the president than it has. Certainly, a Congress willing to impeach a president should have the mettle to overturn the chief executive's administrative directives. But the president has significant advantages in such struggles with Congress. In battles over presidential directives and orders, Congress is on the defensive, reacting to presidential initiatives. The framers of the Constitution saw "energy," or the ability to take the initiative, as a key feature of executive power.[60] When the president takes action by issuing an order or an administrative directive, Congress must respond through the cumbersome and time-consuming lawmaking process, overcome internal divisions, and enact legislation that the president may ultimately veto. Moreover, as the political scientist Terry Moe has argued, in such battles Congress faces a significant collective action problem: members are likely to be more sensitive to the substance of a president's actions and its short-term effects on their constituents than to the more general long-term implications of presidential power for the vitality of their institution.[61]

THE LIMITS OF PRESIDENTIAL POWER: CHECKS AND BALANCES

From the Constitution, presidents derive expressed, implied, and delegated powers. Claims of inherent powers are derived from the basic principles of national sovereignty coupled with the constitutional grant of executive power. But while the framers sought an energetic executive, they were also concerned that executive power could be abused and might stifle citizens' liberties. To guard against this possibility, the framers contrived a number of checks on executive power. The president's term is limited to four years, though with the possibility of reappointment. The Congress is empowered to impeach and remove the president, to reject presidential appointments and refuse to ratify treaties, to refuse to enact laws requested by the president, to deny funding for the president's programs, and to override presidential vetoes of congressional enactments.

The framers viewed the threat of impeachment as an important check upon executive power. The Constitution provides that a president may be impeached for "high crimes and misdemeanors." Such offenses are to be charged by the House and tried in the Senate, with the Chief Justice presiding and a two-thirds vote needed for conviction. During the course of American history, only two presidents, Andrew Johnson and Bill Clinton, have been impeached though neither was convicted. Johnson's impeachment was, as noted earlier, triggered by his veto of the Tenure in Office Act; and Clinton's by charges of sexual improprieties and lying under oath about them. A third president, Richard Nixon, would almost certainly have been impeached for his misdeeds in the Watergate affair, but Nixon chose to resign to avoid the impeachment process.

The requirement that the Senate concur in treaties and presidential appointments was seen by the framers as another important check on executive power. However in recent years severe partisan disagreements often have led presidents to resort to "recess appointments." These are authorized by Article II, Section 2, which states, "The President shall have power to fill up all Vacancies that may happen during the Recess of the Senate, by granting Commissions which shall expire at the End of their next Session." Until recent years, recess appointments were made only between Senate sessions or when the Senate was adjourned for lengthy periods. However, recess appointments have become more frequent and the Senate has resorted to a strategy similar to the one employed to prevent pocket vetoes. One senator is assigned the task of calling the chamber to order for a few moments every day for a pro forma session during periods of recess so that the president cannot claim the Senate was closed for business. Presidents have viewed this procedure as nothing more than a subterfuge since the Senate is incapable of actually conducting business during these periods.

And, of course, under the Constitution, only the Congress would have the power to enact legislation or to levy taxes or to appropriate funds. Indeed, so many were the constitutional checks on executive power that some delegates to the Constitutional Convention feared that the executive would be too weak and the potential energy of executive power lost. As we can see, however, from the many actions of presidents in recent years, presidential power has grown significantly beyond the framers' vision.

Presidential Power
WHAT DO WE WANT?

The framers of the Constitution created a system of government in which the Congress and the executive branch were to share power. At least since the New Deal, however, the powers of Congress have waned, whereas those of the presidency have expanded dramatically. There is no doubt that Congress continues to be able to confront presidents and even, on occasion, hand the White House a sharp rebuff.

In the larger view, however, presidents' occasional defeats, however dramatic, have to be seen as temporary setbacks in a gradual but decisive shift toward increased presidential power. Louis Fisher, a leading authority on the separation of powers, recently observed that in what are arguably the two most important policy arenas, national defense and the federal budget, the powers of Congress have been in decline for at least the past 50 years.[62]

What might the growth of executive power mean to students reading this book today? It might mean, on the one hand, that policies they favor can more easily become the law of the land. Congress works slowly while the president can work quickly, making law by the stroke of a pen or an instruction to the federal bureaucracy. Presidential strength works both ways, however: for those who oppose a particular policy or have qualms about some aspect of it, the stroke of the presidential pen might seem hasty and autocratic. The consequences can even be deadly, as we saw in the chapter opener, when a ban on a toxic chemical is at stake.

Today's students should also consider one of the chief concerns about presidential power expressed by the framers of the Constitution. The framers feared that executives were often too ready to go to war. Legislatures, they thought, were more likely to consider the costs and sacrifices entailed by war. Accordingly, the war power was given to Congress to "leash the dogs of war."[63] The framers possessed a good deal of practical experience, and their views merit consideration. Does presidential unilateralism or congressional deliberation offer better protection from the dogs of war so feared by the framers? In an era of significant international tension and trouble spots, including Iran, North Korea, Iraq, Syria, Libya, and Ukraine, the ease with which the country's leaders enter armed conflict may be a real concern.

A powerful presidency, a weak Congress, and a partially apathetic electorate make for a dangerous mix. Who we vote into the office of the president matters, as the example of EPA policy on toxic chemicals demonstrates. (The "**Who Participates?**" feature on the facing page shows who voted for Donald Trump in 2016.)

Presidents have increasingly asserted the right to govern unilaterally. Presidential power, to be sure, can be a force for good. To cite one example from the not-so-distant past, it was President Lyndon Johnson, more than Congress or the judiciary, who faced up to the task of smashing America's racial apartheid system. Yet, as the framers knew, unchecked power—whether executive or legislative—is always dangerous. The framers of the Constitution believed that liberty required checks and balances. However useful presidential power may seem, we should always be mindful of the framers' concern.

Who Voted for Donald Trump in 2016?

Age

Age	Trump	Clinton
18–29	37%	55%
30–44	42%	50%
45–64	53%	44%
65+	53%	45%

Race

Race	Trump	Clinton
White	58%	37%
African American	8%	88%
Hispanic	29%	65%
Asian American	29%	65%
Other	37%	56%

Income

Income	Trump	Clinton
<$50,000	41%	52%
$50,000–$99,999	50%	46%
$100,000+	48%	47%

Legend: ● Trump ● Clinton ● Other candidates

Sex

Sex	Trump	Clinton
Men	53%	41%
Women	42%	54%

SOURCE: "2016 Election Exit Polls," *Washington Post*, November 10, 2016, www.washingtonpost.com/graphics/politics/2016-election/exit-polls/ (accessed 11/10/16).

★ WHAT YOU CAN DO ★

Contact the White House

☑ After he or she is elected, the president is expected to represent all Americans. Ask a question or share your view on a policy with the president and White House staff via **www.whitehouse.gov/contact**.

☑ Create a petition at **http://petitions.whitehouse.gov** regarding an issue you care about, and try to get as many signatures as possible.

☑ Watch a few recent presidential speeches, including this year's State of the Union address, on YouTube. Share your views with your fellow students, friends, and family.

STUDY GUIDE

The Constitutional Powers of the Presidency

Understand the expressed, implied, delegated, and inherent powers of the presidency (pp. 515–29)

Presidents have four kinds of powers: expressed, implied, delegated, and inherent. The president's expressed powers, as defined by Article II of the Constitution, include military, judicial, diplomatic, executive, and legislative powers. The expressed powers also entail a set of implied powers, which can be considered necessary in order to carry out the expressed powers. The president's delegated powers are not found in the Constitution but are, instead, the product of congressional statutes and resolutions. The president's inherent powers grow from "the rights, duties and obligations of the presidency" that presidents often assert during times of war and national crisis.

Key Terms

expressed powers (p. 516)
commander in chief (p. 516)
executive agreement (p. 518)
executive privilege (p. 519)
veto (p. 519)
pocket veto (p. 520)
legislative initiative (p. 521)
implied powers (p. 522)
delegated powers (p. 523)
inherent powers (p. 525)

Practice Quiz

1. Which of the following does *not* require the Senate's approval?
   a) a sole executive agreement
   b) a treaty
   c) an appointment of an ambassador
   d) a Supreme Court nomination
   e) an appointment of an executive officer
2. What did the Supreme Court rule in *United States v. Nixon*?
   a) Nixon had to turn his secret White House tapes over to congressional investigators because presidents do not have the power of executive privilege.
   b) Nixon did not have to turn his secret White House tapes over to congressional investigators because, in general, presidents have the power of executive privilege.
   c) Nixon had to turn his secret White House tapes over to congressional investigators but, in general, presidents have the power of executive privilege.
   d) Nixon did not have to turn his secret White House tapes over to congressional investigators but, in general, presidents do not have the power of executive privilege.
   e) All presidents are immune from criminal investigations and cannot, therefore, be tried in any court of law.
3. What are the requirements for overriding a presidential veto?
   a) 50 percent plus one vote in both houses of Congress
   b) two-thirds vote in both houses of Congress
   c) two-thirds vote in the Senate only
   d) three-fourths vote in both houses of Congress
   e) A presidential veto cannot be overridden by Congress.
4. The Supreme Court has ruled that
   a) the power to remove executive appointees belongs exclusively to the Senate.
   b) the power to remove executive appointees belongs exclusively to the House of Representatives.
   c) the power to remove executive appointees belongs exclusively to the president.
   d) the power to remove executive appointees belongs exclusively to the federal judiciary.
   e) executive appointees can only be removed from office through formal impeachment hearings in both houses of Congress.
5. The "theory of the unitary executive" argues that
   a) Congress should control all policy making by the executive branch and the president should wield only limited power over executive agencies.
   b) the president should control all policy making by the executive branch and Congress should wield only limited power over executive agencies.
   c) all executive agencies should be independent from the influence of both the president and Congress.
   d) presidents should be limited to serving only a single term in office.
   e) the presidency should be replaced by a three-person executive council.
6. A system in which the positions of head of state and head of government are held by a single individual is referred to as
   a) a presidential system.
   b) a parliamentary system.
   c) a semi-parliamentary system.
   d) a semi-presidential system.
   e) a plural executive system.

7. President Harry S. Truman justified his attempt to seize the nation's steel mills during the Korean War on the basis of
   a) the president's expressed powers to deal with national emergencies.
   b) the president's inherent powers to deal with national emergencies.
   c) the president's delegated powers to deal with national emergencies.
   d) the president's implied powers to deal with national emergencies.
   e) the president's imperial powers to deal with national emergencies.
8. Which of the following statements about presidential declarations of national emergency is *not* accurate?
   a) Presidents can only declare a state of national emergency in response to foreign threats with the approval of Congress.
   b) Once the president has declared a state of national emergency, constitutional rights, including the right of habeas corpus, may be temporarily suspended.
   c) A declaration of national emergency in response to foreign threats allows the president to embargo trade, seize foreign assets, and prohibit transactions with whatever foreign nations are involved.
   d) Declarations of national emergency remain in force for only one year unless they are renewed by the president.
   e) Congress may, by a joint resolution of the two houses, terminate a declaration of national emergency.

The Presidency as an Institution

Identify the institutional resources presidents have to help them exercise their powers (pp. 529–33)

The institutionalized presidency is made up of the cabinet, the White House staff, the Executive Office of the President, the vice presidency, and the first spouse. Through their advice and assistance, these thousands of individuals give the president a capacity for action that he could never have by himself. When coupled with the president's formal powers, the institutionalized presidency makes the chief executive an important player in the country's policy-making process.

Key Terms

Cabinet (p. 530)
White House staff (p. 530)
Executive Office of the President (EOP) (p. 530)
National Security Council (NSC) (p. 531)

Practice Quiz

9. The EOP agency responsible for preparing the national budget, designing the president's program, and overseeing regulatory proposals is called
   a) the Office of Management and Budget.
   b) the National Security Council.
   c) the Council of Economic Advisers.
   d) the Congressional Budget Office.
   e) the Bureau of Economic Analysis.
10. Approximately how many people work for agencies within the Executive Office of the President?
   a) 25 to 50
   b) 700 to 1,000
   c) 1,500 to 2,000
   d) 4,500 to 5,000
   e) 25,000 to 30,000
11. Which of the following statements about vice presidents is *not* true?
   a) The vice president succeeds the president in case of death, resignation, or incapacitation.
   b) The vice president casts the tie-breaking vote in the Senate when necessary.
   c) The vice president serves as an honorary member of the Supreme Court.
   d) Eight vice presidents have had to replace American presidents who died in office.
   e) Presidential candidates often select a vice-presidential candidate who is likely to bring the support of a state that would not otherwise support the ticket.

The Contemporary Bases of Presidential Power

Explain how modern presidents have become even more powerful (pp. 533–43)

Although Congress was the dominant institution in the American political system throughout the nineteenth century, modern presidents have expanded the policy-making power of their office in a number of ways. While some presidents have relied primarily on the support of party members to advance their legislative goals, contemporary presidents more commonly turn to popular mobilization and executive administration in pursuing policy change.

Key Terms

executive order (p. 538)
signing statements (p. 540)

Practice Quiz

12. What are two primary ways that presidents can expand their power?
- a) avoiding popular appeals and loosening their control of executive agencies
- b) using popular appeals and bolstering their control of executive agencies
- c) using popular appeals and loosening their control of executive agencies
- d) avoiding popular appeals and bolstering their control of executive agencies
- e) weakening national partisan institutions and bolstering their control of executive agencies

13. The Environmental Protection Agency and the Food and Drug Administration were created through the use of
- a) a pocket veto.
- b) an executive-congressional agreement.
- c) a sole executive agreement.
- d) an executive order.
- e) executive privilege.

14. When the president makes an announcement about his interpretation of a congressional enactment that he is signing into law, it is called
- a) a signing statement.
- b) a line-item veto.
- c) an executive order.
- d) legislative initiative.
- e) regulatory review.

For Further Reading

Edwards, George. *Why the Electoral College Is Bad for America*. New Haven, CT: Yale University Press, 2004.

Fisher, Louis. *Constitutional Conflicts between President and Congress*, 6th ed. Lawrence: University Press of Kansas, 2014.

Gellman, Barton. *Angler: The Cheney Vice Presidency.* New York: Penguin, 2008.

Gerhardt, Michael J. *The Forgotten Presidents: Their Untold Constitutional Legacy.* New York: Oxford University Press, 2013.

Ginsberg, Benjamin. *Presidential Government*. New Haven, CT: Yale University Press, 2016.

Griffin, Stephen. *Long Wars and the Constitution*. Cambridge, MA: Harvard University Press, 2013.

Hendrickson, Ryan. *Obama at War.* Lexington: University Press of Kentucky, 2015.

Kumar, Martha J. *Managing the President's Message: The White House Communications Operation*. Baltimore: Johns Hopkins University Press, 2010.

Milkis, Sidney. *The American Presidency: Origins and Development.* Washington, DC: CQ Press, 2011.

Nelson, Michael. *The Presidency and the Political System*. Washington, DC: CQ Press, 2013.

Neustadt, Richard E. *Presidential Power: The Politics of Leadership from Roosevelt to Reagan*. Rev. ed. New York: Free Press, 1990.

Ragsdale, Lyn. *Vital Statistics on the Presidency*. Washington, DC: CQ Press, 2014.

Schlesinger, Arthur. *The Imperial Presidency.* Reprint, New York: Mariner, 2004.

Skowronek, Stephen. *The Politics Presidents Make: Leadership from John Adams to Bill Clinton*. Cambridge, MA: Belknap Press of Harvard University Press, 1997.

Suri, Jeremy. *The Impossible Presidency.* New York: Basic Books, 2017.

Tulis, Jeffrey K. *The Rhetorical Presidency.* Princeton, NJ: Princeton University Press, 2017.

John Yoo. *The Powers of War and Peace: The Constitution and Foreign Affairs after 9/11*. Chicago: University of Chicago Press, 2006.

Recommended Websites

The American Presidency Project
www.americanpresidency.org

Directed by Gerhard Peters and John T. Woolley at the University of California Santa Barbara, this site contains over 88,000 documents related to the study of the presidency, including party platforms, candidates' remarks, statements of administration policy, documents released by the Office of the Press Secretary, and election debates. This site is also an excellent resource for data related to the study of the presidency.

Dave Leip's Atlas of U.S. Presidential Elections
www.uselectionatlas.org

For information on upcoming and past presidential elections, refer to this website. Experiment with the electoral college calculator to see how your state could affect the electoral outcome.

The National Archives: Executive Branch
www.archives.gov/executive

Research official executive branch documents at the Executive Branch website, provided by the U.S. National Archives and Records Administration.

The White House
www.whitehouse.gov

This is the official website of the White House. Here you can read about current presidential news, the president's Cabinet, executive orders, and presidential appointments.

White House Historical Association
www.whitehousehistory.org

The White House Historical Association is dedicated to the understanding, appreciation, and preservation of the White House. At its website you can find historical facts and take a detailed online tour of the numerous rooms and the property.

The White House: Past First Ladies
www.whitehouse.gov/history/firstladies/

The first lady is an important resource for the president in his role as head of state. Read about the current and past first ladies on this website.

★ chapter ★

14

Bureaucracy in a Democracy

WHAT GOVERNMENT DOES AND WHY IT MATTERS Lee Ann Walters couldn't figure out what was wrong with her 4-year-old twins. They had just moved to a new house in Flint, Michigan, and had rashes all over their bodies. One doctor thought it was contact dermatitis, another eczema. The prescribed creams had no effect. Yet another doctor suspected scabies, but tests were negative. Then Walters had an epiphany: every time her sons swam in the kiddie pool in the yard, or took a bath, the rash flared up. She told her family to stop drinking the tap water, which was orange-brown even after running through a filter she had installed.

That was December 2014. Eight months earlier, the cash-strapped city of Flint, under a state-appointed emergency manager, had switched its water supply to save money. Rather than draw water from the Detroit system, the city switched to the Flint River, which had been an industrial dumping ground for years. Soon, the local General Motors engine plant stopped using the river water, which was corroding the auto parts. Walters had the city test her tap water: the lead count was 104 parts per billion (ppb); the legal limit is 15. A follow-up test a week later: 397 parts per billion. Flint's utility administrator told her not to use the water. A researcher from Virginia Tech began testing water around the city: one-third of the samples had elevated lead levels, one as high as 13,200 ppb. A local pediatrician announced a spike

Government bureaucracies affect ordinary Americans in countless ways. The Flint water crisis, exposed by Lee Ann Walters, demonstrates how the failures of bureaucracy on every level of government can affect citizens' lives directly.

in lead levels among young children. Lead exposure can cause developmental delays and disability in children. The damage is permanent.

Walters tracked down an EPA drinking water expert who discovered that in switching to the Flint River, city officials had failed to add anti-corrosive chemicals to the water (despite a federal regulation requiring corrosion control). Running through old pipes, the untreated river water was leaching lead into the drinking supply. An official from Michigan's Department of Environmental Quality assured the EPA that there was corrosion control in place. Meanwhile, the city had been testing for lead but telling residents to flush their water before collecting their samples and retesting in houses where the initial lead levels were low, not high.[1]

Finally, in January 2016, in the face of growing outcry from city residents, researchers, and advocates such as the ACLU, the EPA declared a state of emergency in Flint and took over lead testing in the city. In March 2016 the Flint Water Advisory Task Force, appointed by Michigan governor Rick Snyder to examine the crisis, issued its final report. The report cited a "series of government failures" at all levels: the local water department rushed to switch the water supply without corrosion control; the state Departments of Environmental Quality and Health and Human Services ignored mounting evidence of unsafe water; the federal EPA delayed enforcement of the Safe Water Drinking Act and Lead and Copper Rule; and the governor's office failed to reverse the poor decisions of the emergency manager and state agencies despite the urgings of senior staff members.[2]

The Flint water crisis is a dramatic example of bureaucratic failure. Americans depend on public bureaucracies for providing services they use every day and in emergencies. On a typical day, a college student might check the weather forecast, drive on an interstate highway, mail the rent check, drink from a public water fountain, check the calories on the side of a yogurt container, attend a class, go online, and meet a relative at the airport. Each of these activities is possible because of the work of a government bureaucracy: the U.S. Weather Service, the U.S. Department of Transportation, the U.S. Postal Service, the Environmental Protection Agency, the Food and Drug Administration, the student loan programs of the U.S. Department of Education, the Advanced Research Projects Agency (which developed the internet in the 1960s), and the Federal Aviation Administration. Without the ongoing work of these agencies, many of these common activities would be impossible, unreliable, or more expensive. When bureaucracies work well, we barely notice.

But when they fail, the results can be truly alarming, like the Flint crisis, or the September 11 terror attacks, widely viewed as a failure of the national security bureaucracy.[3] Such failures play into Americans' ambivalence about the role of government. Some disasters prompt politicians to promise that they will slash the bureaucracy, especially at the federal level. Yet others result in an increase in the bureaucracy, like the creation of the federal Department of Homeland Security after September 11. Each instance raises a number of questions: should the bureaucracy be smaller or larger? How can it become more efficient and effective? How can the bureaucracy be made more responsive to the needs of the American people?

CHAPTER GOALS

- ★ **Define bureaucracy, and describe the basic features of the executive branch (pp. 553–62)**
- ★ **Describe the major goals we expect federal agencies to promote (pp. 563–73)**
- ★ **Evaluate some of the ways politicians have tried to make the bureaucracy more efficient (pp. 573–79)**
- ★ **Explain why it is often difficult to control the bureaucracy (pp. 579–83)**

Bureaucracy and Bureaucrats

Define bureaucracy, and describe the basic features of the executive branch

Although Congress, the president, and the courts may garner more attention in the American system as they make policy, the **bureaucracy** plays a crucial role in administering public policy on the ground. Bureaucrats carry out the normal work of government, implementing the policies that Congress and the president have passed and that the court system may have adjudicated. The teachers you had in elementary school, the Social Security officer who approved your grandmother's retirement pension, the air traffic controller who guided the plane on your last vacation, the engineers who designed the roads that carried you to class, and the inspector who approved the meat in this morning's breakfast sausage are all bureaucrats.

bureaucracy the complex structure of offices, tasks, rules, and principles of organization that is employed by all large-scale institutions to coordinate the work of their personnel

At its best, bureaucracy ensures fair, accountable administration performed by expert professionals. To provide services, government bureaucracies employ specialists such as meteorologists, doctors, and scientists. To do their jobs effectively, these specialists require resources and tools (ranging from paper to complex computer software). They must coordinate their work with others (for example, traffic engineers must communicate with construction engineers). And they must effectively reach out to the public (for example, doctors must be made aware of health warnings). Bureaucracy is a means of coordinating the many different parts that must work together for the government to provide useful services.

When bureaucracy runs well, it can be virtually invisible. When it fails, the results can be spectacularly public, as when Hurricane Katrina breached levies built by the Army Corps of Engineers and the Federal Emergency Management Agency reacted ineffectually, or when the Department of Veterans Affairs was criticized in 2014 for long waiting lists for veterans seeking medical care and even blamed for veteran deaths in Phoenix.[4] How bureaucrats carry out their responsibilities shapes individuals' experiences of government in profound ways.

WHAT BUREAUCRATS DO

Bureaucrats execute and implement laws, determining who is eligible for Medicare, studying whether a new medicine is safe and effective. They deliver mail, tell national park campers that they can build a fire *here* but not *there*, calculate how long it would take a spacecraft to reach the edge of the solar system. They gather data and conduct research. Some, like customs officials, are "street-level bureaucrats" who regularly interact with the public. Yet others, like researchers at the National Institutes of Health, work in specialized facilities with other experts. As they carry out their responsibilities, implementing and enforcing laws, making rules, and innovating, they exercise discretion and help define how public policy gets expressed.

Bureaucrats Implement Laws Congress is responsible for making the laws, but in most cases legislation only sets the broad parameters for government action. Bureaucracies are responsible for filling in the blanks by determining how the laws should be implemented. This requires bureaucracies to draw up detailed rules that guide the process of **implementation** and to play a key role in enforcing the laws. Congress needs the bureaucracy to engage in rule making and implementation for several

implementation the efforts of departments and agencies to translate laws into specific bureaucratic rules and actions reasons. One is that bureaucracies employ people who have much more specialized expertise in specific policy areas than do members of Congress. Decisions about how to achieve many policy goals—from managing the national parks to regulating air quality to ensuring a sound economy—rest on the judgment of specialized experts. A second reason that Congress needs bureaucracy is that because updating legislation can take many years, bureaucratic flexibility can ensure that laws are administered in ways that take new conditions into account. Finally, members of Congress often prefer to delegate politically difficult decision-making to bureaucrats.

Bureaucrats Make Rules One of the most important activities that government agencies do is issue rules that provide more detailed and specific indications of what a given congressional policy will actually mean. For example, the Clean Air Act empowers the Environmental Protection Agency (EPA) to assess whether current or projected levels of air pollutants pose a threat to public health, determine whether motor vehicle emissions are contributing to such pollution, and create rules designed to regulate these emissions. After the Supreme Court ruled in 2007 that the EPA had the authority to regulate auto emissions, the agency in the Obama administration imposed new emission standards for automobiles, which would raise the average fuel economy for new vehicles to 35.5 miles per gallon starting in 2016, a standard later boosted to 54.4 miles per gallon by 2025.[5] In 2014 the EPA extended its reach to regulate factories and power plants that emit greenhouse gases. Especially controversial was the Clean Power Plan, requiring power plants to reduce greenhouse gas emissions by 32 percent by 2030. The plan never went into effect due to lawsuits filed by a number of states, and in 2017 the head of the EPA in the Trump administration repealed the plan.[6]

The rule-making process is thus a highly political one. Once a new law is passed, the relevant agency studies the legislation and proposes a set of rules to guide implementation. These proposed rules are then open to comment by anyone who wishes to weigh in. Representatives for the regulated industries and advocates of all sorts commonly submit comments. But anyone who wishes to can go to the website www.regulations.gov to read proposed rules, enter comments, and view the comments of others. Once rules are approved, they are published in the *Federal Register* and have the force of law. That said, the Trump administration's repeal of the Obama EPA's Clean Power Plan demonstrates the fragility of government by bureaucratic rule-making, compared to government by congressional legislation.[7] If Congress passes a new law, changing it usually requires another congressional action, while rules made by the bureaucracy in one administration can be easily reversed by the next.

During the 1970s and '80s, the length of time required to develop an administrative rule from a proposal to actual publication in the *Federal Register* (when it takes on full legal status) grew from an average of 15 months to an average of 35 to 40 months. Inefficiency? No. Most of the increased time is attributable to new procedures requiring more public notice, more public hearings in Washington and elsewhere, more cost-benefit analysis, and stronger legal obligations to prepare "environmental impact statements" demonstrating that the proposed rule or agency action will not have an unacceptably large negative impact on the human or physical environment.[8] Thus, a great deal of what is popularly decried as the lower efficiency of public agencies can be attributed to the political, judicial, legal, and public-opinion restraints and extraordinarily high expectations imposed on public bureaucrats. If a private company such as Apple were required to open up all its decision processes and management practices to full view by the media, its

An example of bureaucratic rules that affect Americans both positively and negatively are the regulations set forth by the Environmental Protection Agency (EPA). When President Obama extended the EPA's authority to regulate greenhouse gas emissions in 2014, many people applauded the benefits to the environment, but at the same time, thousands lost jobs because of the new rules.

competitors, and all interested citizens, Apple—despite its profit motive and the pressure of competition—would likely appear far less efficient, perhaps no more efficient than public bureaucracies.

Bureaucrats Enforce Laws In addition to rule making, bureaucracies play an essential role in enforcing the laws, thus exercising considerable power over private actors. In 2015 the EPA charged Volkswagen with cheating on emissions tests of its diesel vehicles. For over seven years, the company had installed software that showed emissions at legal levels during testing conditions, but once the cars were on the road emissions were actually 10 to 40 percent higher. After the EPA threatened to bar the company from selling some of its 2016 cars in the United States, Volkswagen admitted that it had cheated. The financial repercussions for the company will be long-lasting. In 2016 the company agreed to a $15.8-billion settlement that required it to buy back the faulty vehicles and compensate owners. As part of the settlement, Volkswagen also agreed to fund several clean air programs. Even with these payments, Volkswagen faced additional lawsuits from states and investors.[9]

Bureaucrats Innovate A good case study of the important role agencies can play is the story of how ordinary federal bureaucrats created the internet. Yes, it's true: what became the internet was developed largely by the U.S. Department of Defense, and defense considerations still shape the basic structure of the internet. In 1957, immediately following the profound American embarrassment over the Soviet Union's launching of *Sputnik*, the first satellite to orbit the Earth, Congress authorized the establishment of the Advanced Research Projects Agency (ARPA) to develop, among other things, a means of maintaining communications in the event of a strategic attack on the existing telecommunications network (the telephone system). Since the telephone network was highly centralized and therefore could have been completely disabled by a single attack, ARPA developed a decentralized, highly redundant network with an improved probability of functioning after an attack. The full design, called *ARPANET*, took almost a decade to create. By 1971 around

20 universities were connected to the ARPANET. The forerunner to the internet was born.[10]

WHO ARE BUREAUCRATS?

Bureaucrats are considered members of the "civil service" and work under the **merit system** created by the Civil Service Act of 1883. With this act, the federal government attempted to imitate business by requiring appointees to public office be qualified for the job to which they were appointed. The goal was to end political appointments under the "spoils system," which awarded jobs based on political connections, and to create a system of competitive examinations through which the very best candidates were to be hired for every job. As a further safeguard against political interference, merit-system employees were given legal protection against being fired without a show of cause. Reasonable people may disagree about the value of such job security and how far it should extend in the civil service, but the justifiable objective of this job protection, cleansing bureaucracy of political interference while upgrading performance, cannot be disputed. At the higher levels of government agencies, including such posts as cabinet secretaries and assistant secretaries, many jobs are filled with political appointees and are not part of the merit system.

merit system a product of civil service reform, in which appointees to positions in public bureaucracies must objectively be deemed qualified for those positions

The State Department's foreign service officer corps represents U.S. interests abroad. To become a foreign service officer, you must take both a written and an oral exam. Approximately 75 percent of the 20,000 or so applicants who take the exam each year do not pass.

8 STEPS TO BECOMING A FOREIGN SERVICE OFFICER
······· FSO SELECTION PROCESS ·······

STEP 1: CHOOSE A CAREER TRACK ?

While all U.S. diplomats are expected to communicate U.S. foreign policy and interact effectively with host country governments to help advance U.S. interests worldwide, each career track has a specific focus. Selecting a career track is an important decision, as you may not change career tracks once you choose a track during the registration for the Foreign Service Officer Test (FSOT).

Learn more about each career track

CONSULAR ★
ECONOMIC ★
MANAGEMENT ★
POLITICAL ★
PUBLIC DIPLOMACY ★

STEP 2: REGISTER FOR THE FSOT ?

You may register for the test up until the deadlines or until capacity is reached. Pearson VUE, the test administrator, will send you a confirmation email on the first business day following submission of your registration.

Register for the FSOT

FSOT

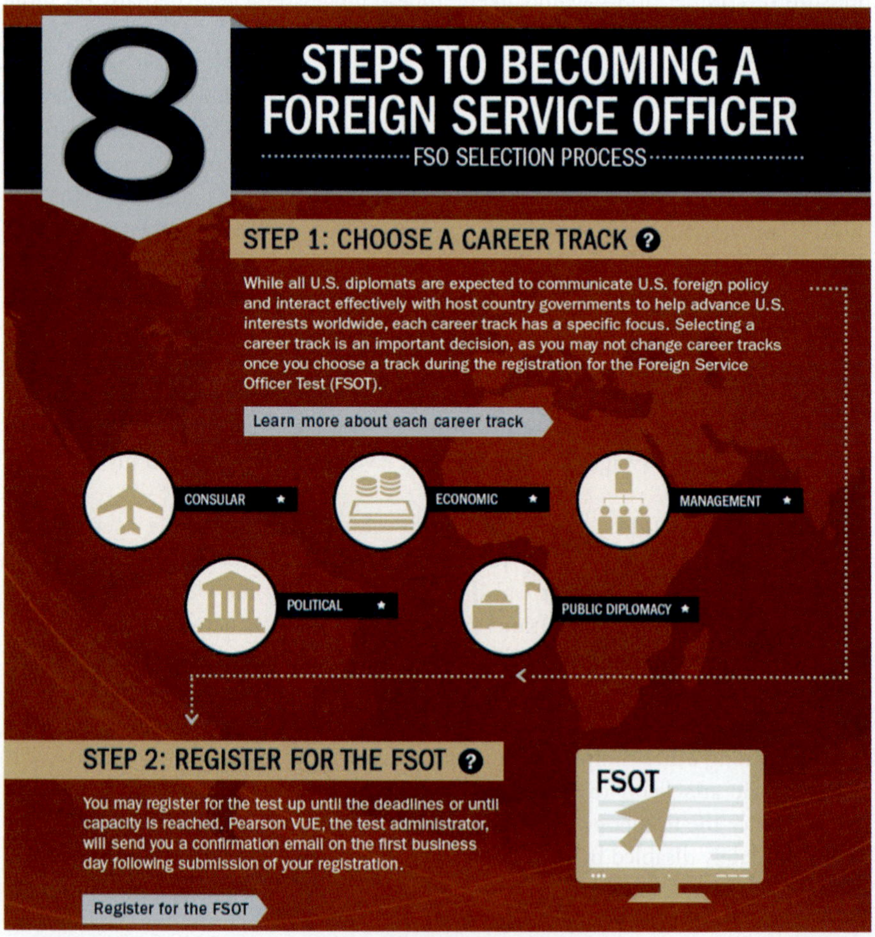

Who Are "Bureaucrats"?

Bureaucrats are often stereotyped as being more concerned with procedure and forms than with helping people. But the reality is that the millions of executive branch employees that work in agencies in D.C. and around the country are essential to keeping America running smoothly. Bureaucrats manage everything from national security and veterans services to providing help for needy families and ensuring that Americans have clean and safe drinking water. But who are bureaucrats? How is the bureaucracy similar to the American population? How is it different?

Executive Branch Employees, 2017

Sex

Female Male

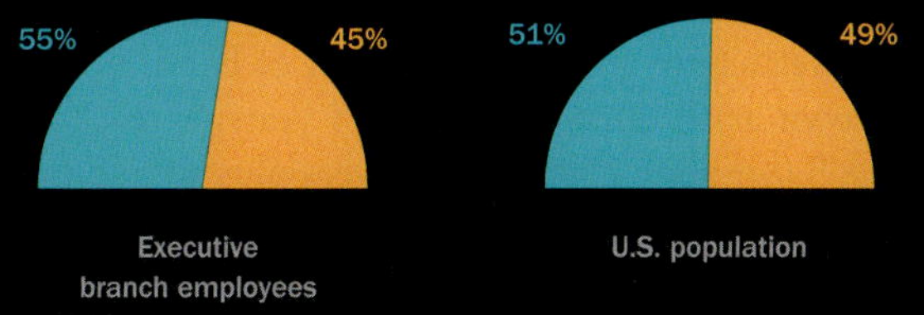

Race / ethnicity

White Black Latino Asian

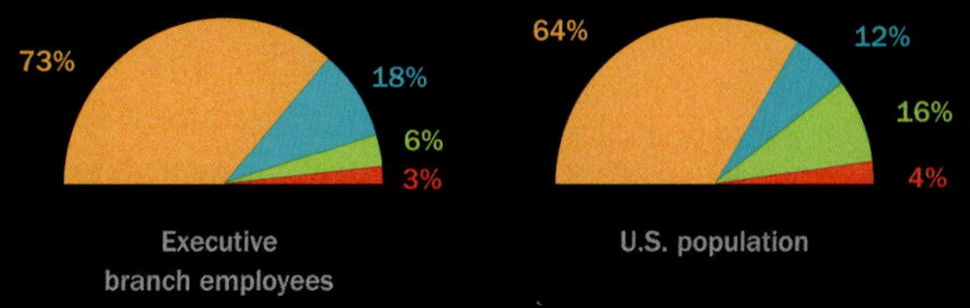

Education

Less than high school High school degree Some college College degree Postgraduate degree

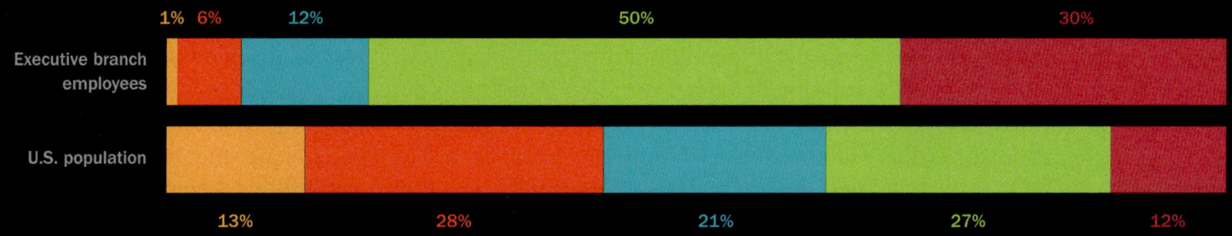

Military service

Yes No

Location, 2017

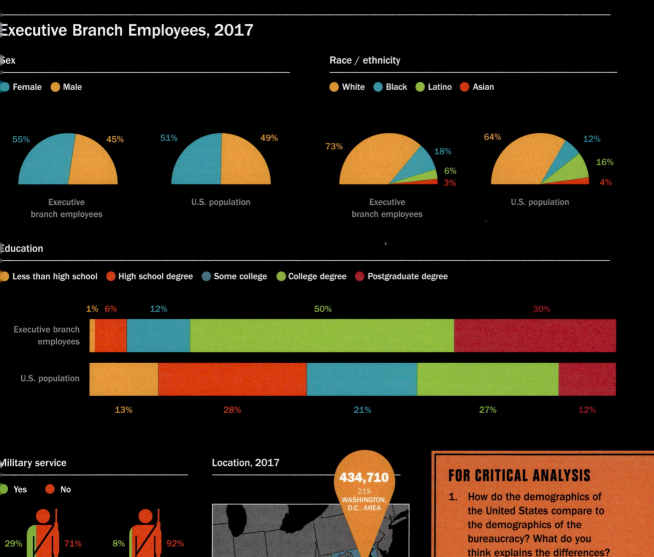

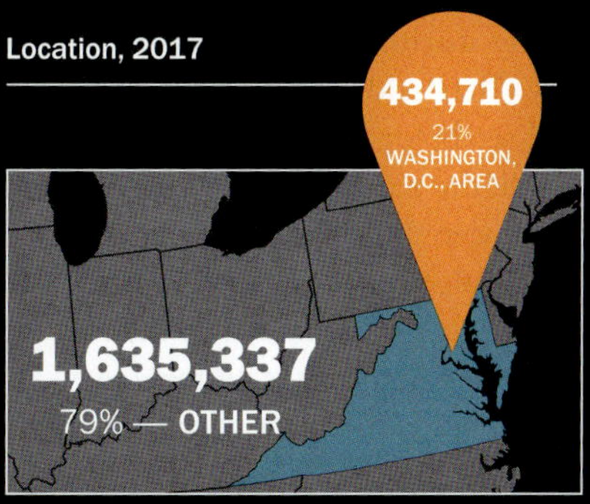

FOR CRITICAL ANALYSIS

1. How do the demographics of the United States compare to the demographics of the bureaucracy? What do you think explains the differences?
2. With 2 million people working for the executive branch, mostly outside of the Washington, D.C., area, how can Congress and the president be sure that they are serving the public's interests?

NOTE: Numbers may not add up to 100 percent due to rounding. The category of "other" has been omitted.
SOURCES: American Community Survey 5-year Estimates, www.factfinder.census.gov (accessed 3/9/18); Gallup, news.gallup.com (accessed 3/9/18).

Today's federal bureaucrats are distributed around the country—nearly 4 out of 5 federal employees work outside of Washington, D.C. For example, California has over 141,000 federal workers, and Texas has more than 114,000.[11] Compared to private sector workers, members of the full-time civilian federal workforce are more educated—more hold college and advanced degrees—and are more likely to hold professional occupations in science, engineering, diplomacy, and other advanced fields.[12] Federal workers are more diverse than the private workforce: as of 2017, 36.7 percent were minority group members, 18.2 percent black, 8.8 percent Hispanic, 6 percent Asian, 2.2 percent Native Hawaiian/Pacific Islander/American Indian/Alaska Native, and 1.5 percent non-Hispanic multiracial. Federal workers are more likely to be male than private sector workers (57 percent compared to 54 percent in the private sector),[13] and nearly one-third of federal workers are veterans.[14]

The size of the federal service has been a subject of political contention for decades. Particularly in the post–Watergate era of low trust in government, politicians from both parties, from Reagan to Clinton, have asserted that the federal government is too big. President Barack Obama struck a different note in his first inaugural address, saying, "The question we ask today is not whether our government is too big or too small, but whether it works."[15] President Trump's first budget proposed major decreases in federal departments outside of Defense and Homeland Security. Despite fears of bureaucratic growth getting out of hand, however, the federal service has hardly grown at all during the past 35 years; it reached its peak postwar level in 1968, with 3.0 million civilian employees plus an additional 3.6 million military personnel (a figure swollen by the war in Vietnam). The number of civilian federal employees has since fallen to fewer than 2.7 million in 2017; the number of military personnel totals 1.29 million.[16]

FOR CRITICAL ANALYSIS

How has the size of the federal service changed over the past six decades? How are calls for smaller government related to the size of the federal service?

The growth of the federal service over the past 50 years is even less imposing when placed in the context of the total workforce and when compared with the size of state and local public employment. Figure 14.1 indicates that since 1950 the ratio of federal employment to the total workforce has in fact *declined* slightly in the past 60 years. Figure 14.2 shows that although the dollar increase in federal spending shown by the bars is impressive, the trend line indicating the relation of federal spending to the gross domestic product remained close to what it had been in 1960 (that is, the size of the federal government as a proportion of the total economy has been flat). Meanwhile, state and local employment has grown: in 1950 there were 4.3 million state and local civil service employees (about 6.5 percent of the country's workforce). In 2015 there were roughly 19.3 million state and local employees (nearly 14 percent of the nation's employed workforce).[17] Federal employment, in contrast, exceeded 6 percent of the workforce only during World War II, and almost all of that temporary growth was military. That said, the number of federal contractors has grown considerably, as we shall see below.

In sum, the national government is indeed "very large," but it has not been growing any faster than the economy or society. Bureaucracy keeps pace with society, despite people's seeming dislike of it, because the airport control towers, the prisons, the Social Security system, and other essential elements of modern-day society cannot be operated without bureaucracy. Indeed, the recent growth of government spending does not reflect a growth in the federal bureaucracy or even growth in federal contractors but rather an increase in payments to individuals for valued social programs such as Social Security and Medicare (which provides health care for people over age 65).

FIGURE 14.1

Employees in the Federal Service as a Percentage of the National Workforce, 1950–2018

Since 1950, the ratio of federal employment to the total workforce has gradually declined. Today, federal employees make up less than 2 percent of the total workforce in the United States. Even at its height, federal employees made up less than 6 percent. What do these numbers suggest about the size of the federal government today?

NOTE: Employment numbers are for December of each year; 2018 numbers are from September.

SOURCE: Bureau of Labor Statistics, Current Employment Statistics, "Employment, Hours, and Earnings from the Current Employment Statistics Survey (National)," https://data.bls.gov/timeseries/CES9091000001 (accessed 10/13/18).

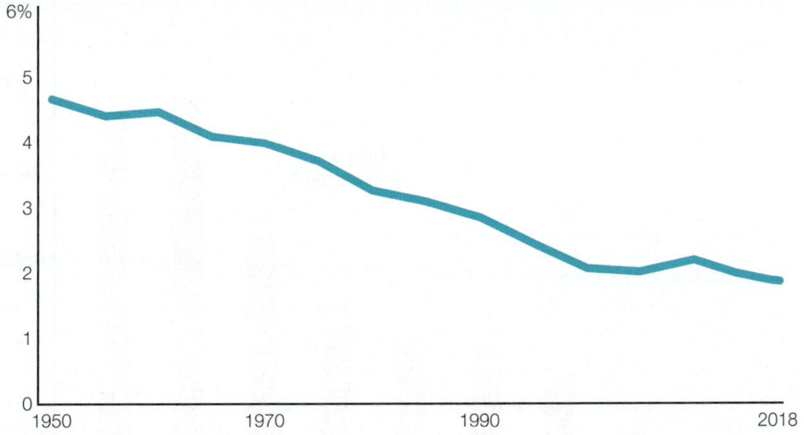

THE ORGANIZATION OF THE EXECUTIVE BRANCH

Cabinet **departments**, agencies, and bureaus are the operating parts of the bureaucratic whole. At the top is the head of the department, who in the United States is called the "secretary" of the department.[18] Below the secretary and the deputy secretary is a second tier of "undersecretaries," who have management responsibilities for one or more operating agencies. Those operating agencies are the third tier of the department, yet they are the highest level of responsibility for the actual programs around which the entire department is organized. This third tier is generally called the "bureau level." Each bureau-level agency usually operates under a statute, enacted by Congress, that set up the agency and gave it its authority and jurisdiction. The names of these bureau-level agencies are often quite well known to the public—the Forest Service and the Food Safety and Inspection Service, for example. These are the so-called line agencies, those that deal directly with the public. Sometimes these agencies are officially called "bureaus," such as the Federal Bureau of Investigation (FBI), which is part of the third tier of the Department of Justice. But *bureau* is also the conventional

department the largest subunit of the executive branch; the secretaries of the 15 departments form the Cabinet

FIGURE 14.2

Annual Federal Outlays, 1950–2018*

As the bars in the figure indicate, when measured in dollars, federal government spending has gone up over time, from $423 billion in 1950 to over $3 trillion in 2017. (The amounts here are measured in constant 2009 dollars, which means the numbers have been adjusted for inflation.) But as the red line shows, federal spending as a percentage of gross domestic product (GDP) has moved up and down just slightly over time. Thus, while government spending has grown, it has basically kept pace with the growing size of the U.S. economy.

*Data for 2017–18 are estimated.

SOURCE: Office of Management and Budget, "Table 1.3—Summary of Receipts, Outlays, and Surpluses or Deficits in Current Dollars, Constant (FY 2009) Dollars, and as Percentages of GDP: 1940–2023," www.whitehouse.gov/omb/budget/historicals (accessed 10/13/18).

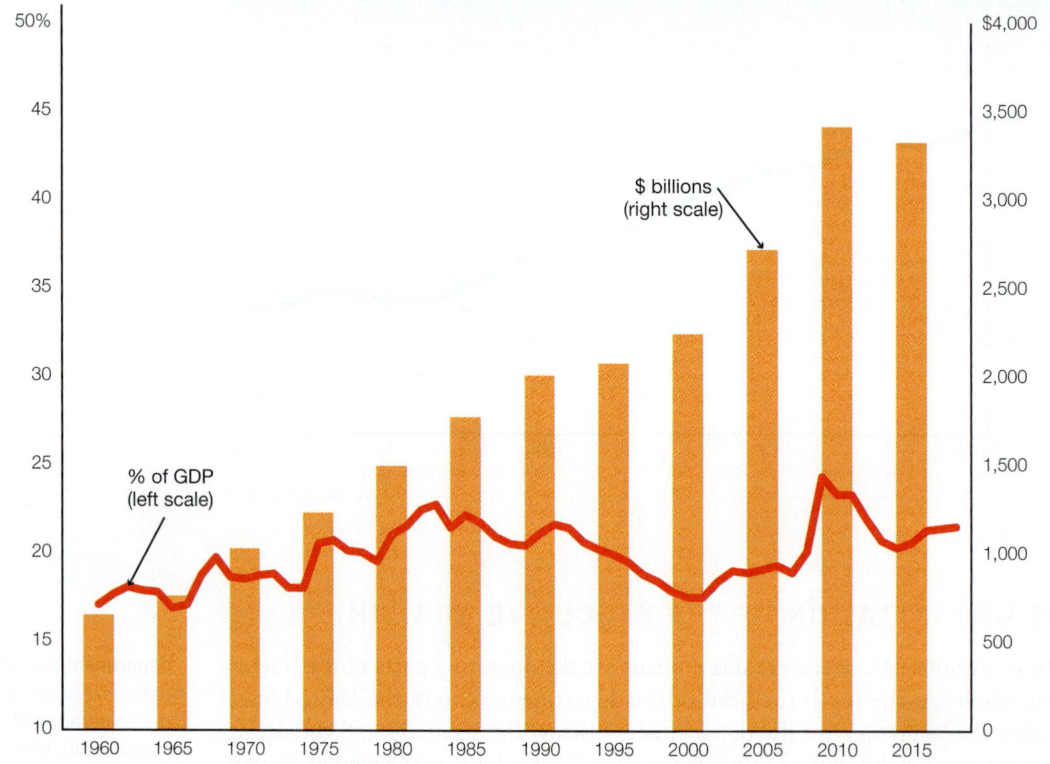

term for this level of administrative agency, even though many agencies or their supporters have preferred over the years to adopt a more politically palatable designation, such as "service" or "administration." Each bureau is, of course, even further subdivided into divisions, offices, or units—all are parts of the bureaucratic hierarchy.

independent agency agency that is not part of a Cabinet department

Not all government agencies are part of Cabinet departments. Some **independent agencies** are set up by Congress outside the departmental structure altogether, even

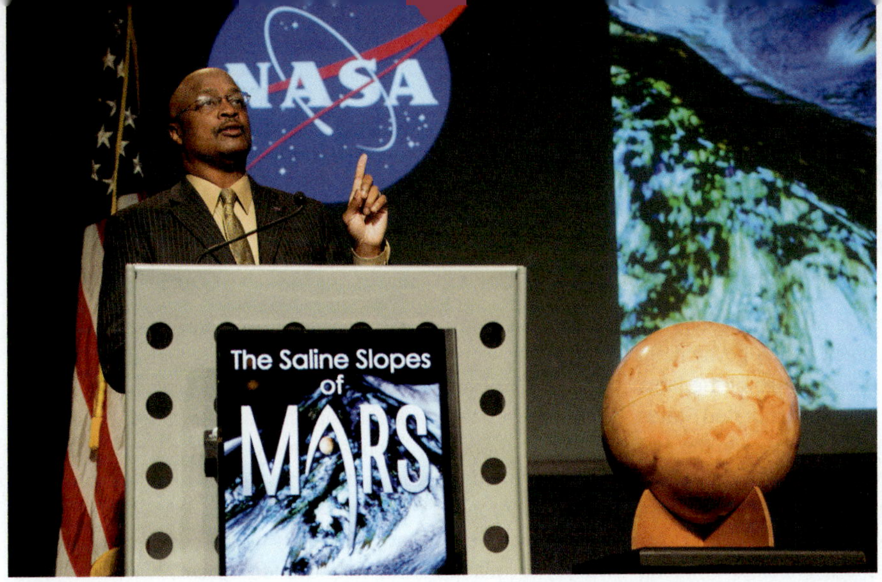

The National Aeronautics and Space Administration (NASA), an independent agency of the federal government, was established by President Eisenhower in 1958. Its mission is "To reach for new heights and reveal the unknown so that what we do and learn will benefit all humankind." Here, NASA public affairs officer Dwayne Brown announces the presence of water on Mars.

though the president appoints and directs the heads of these agencies. Independent agencies usually have broad powers to provide public services that are either too expensive or too important to be left to private initiatives. Some examples of independent agencies are the National Aeronautics and Space Administration (NASA), the Central Intelligence Agency (CIA), and the EPA. **Government corporations** are a third type of government agency but are more like private businesses in performing and charging for a market service, such as transporting railroad passengers (Amtrak).

government corporation
government agency that performs a market-oriented public service and raises revenues to fund its activities

Yet a fourth type of agency is the independent regulatory commission, given broad discretion to make rules. The first regulatory agencies established by Congress, beginning with the Interstate Commerce Commission in 1887, were set up as independent regulatory commissions because Congress recognized that regulatory agencies are "mini-legislatures," whose rules are exactly the same as legislation but require the kind of expertise and full-time attention that is beyond the capacity of Congress. Until the 1960s most of the regulatory agencies set up by Congress, such as the Federal Trade Commission (1914) and the Federal Communications Commission (1934), were independent regulatory commissions. But beginning in the late 1960s and the early 1970s, all new regulatory programs, with two or three exceptions (such as the Federal Election Commission), were placed within existing departments and made directly responsible to the president. After the financial crisis that began in 2008, Congress passed legislation to improve regulation of banks and other nonbank financial institutions. The legislation also created an important new regulatory agency, the Consumer Financial Protection Bureau. The bureau enforces consumer protection laws, for example, regulating bank practices that affect credit cards and mortgages. The agency aims to eliminate deceptive practices and act as the voice of consumers. Its website (www.consumerfinance.gov) also takes complaints from consumers and provides easy-to-understand information on many topics, including student debt repayment.

Bureaucracy in Comparison

As one of the world's largest and most populous countries, the United States has a vast bureaucracy to run government programs and services. However, as a percentage of the labor force, the number of government employees in the United States is not especially high. As the first graph below shows, the size of government bureaucracies, relative to each country's work force, varies widely. For example, the Norwegian government employs nearly 30 percent of the labor force, whereas only around 8 percent of Japanese workers work for the government.

We can also see differences in whether most government employees work at the national level or the subnational level in each country. In the United States, most government employees work at the state or local level, rather than the national level. In other countries, such as Turkey, most bureaucrats work for the national government. What do you think accounts for these differences? How does federalism influence American bureaucracy, and what differences do we see in countries like Turkey or Ireland that do not have federalism?

TOTAL GOVERNMENT EMPLOYMENT AS A PERCENTAGE OF THE LABOR FORCE MARKET

Country	Percentage
Norway	30%
Canada	18
Greece	18
South Africa*	17
Czech Republic	16
Spain	16
United States	16
Ireland	15
Turkey*	12
Brazil*	12
Mexico*	12
Japan	8

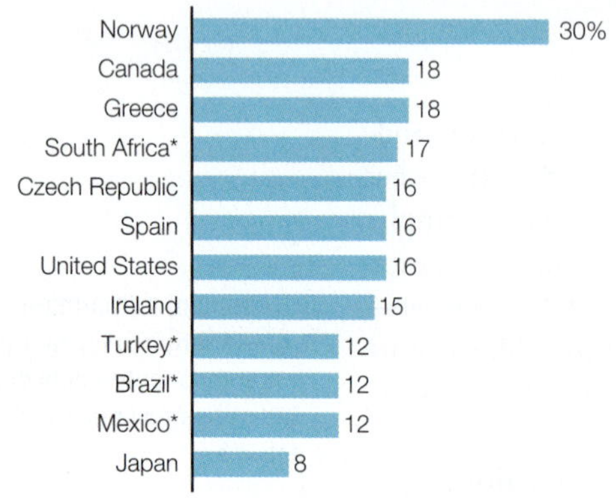

NOTE: Includes national and sub-national government employees.
*Brazil, Mexico, South Africa, and Turkey data are from 2014.

GOVERNMENT EMPLOYMENT BY LEVEL OF GOVERNMENT

■ National ■ Subnational

Country	National	Subnational
Turkey	91%	8%
Ireland	90	10
Greece	77	20
Czech Republic	45	54
Norway	37	63
South Africa*	30	70
Mexico*	30	70
Spain	20	80
United States	19	81
Japan	14	86
Brazil*	12	88
Canada	12	88

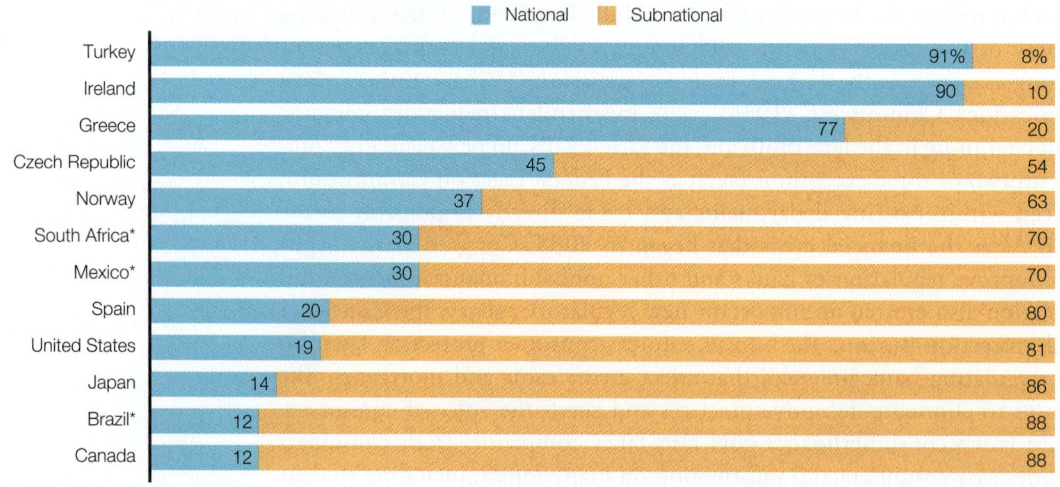

*Brazil, Mexico, and South Africa data are from 2013.

SOURCE: OECD, "Public employment and Pay," Government at a Glance, 2017, www.stats.oecd.org (accessed 4/16/18).

Goals of the Federal Bureaucracy

Describe the major goals we expect federal agencies to promote

The different agencies of the executive branch can be classified into three main groups by the services they provide to the American public. The first category of agencies provides services and products that seek to promote the public welfare. The second group of agencies works to promote national security. The third group provides services that help maintain a strong economy. Let us look more closely at what each set of agencies offers to the American public.

regulatory agency department, bureau, or independent agency whose primary mission is to impose limits, restrictions, or other obligations on the conduct of individuals or companies in the private sector

PROMOTING PUBLIC WELL-BEING

One of the most important activities of the federal bureaucracy is to promote the public good by providing services, building infrastructure, and enforcing regulations that serve citizen needs. Departments that have important responsibilities for promoting public well-being include the Departments of Housing and Urban Development, Health and Human Services, Veterans Affairs, the Interior, Education, and Labor. Ensuring the public welfare is also the main activity of agencies in other departments, such as the Department of Agriculture's Food and Nutrition Service, which administers the federal school lunch program and the Supplemental Nutrition Assistance Program (SNAP, formerly known as food stamps). In addition, multiple independent regulatory agencies enforce regulations that aim to safeguard the public health and welfare.

The Department of Health and Human Services (HHS) administers the cash assistance program Temporary Assistance for Needy Families (TANF). Yet this program is one of the smallest activities of the department. HHS also oversees the National Institutes of Health (NIH), which is responsible for cutting-edge biomedical research, and the two major health programs of the federal government: Medicaid, which provides health care for low-income families and for many elderly and disabled people; and Medicare, which is the health insurance available to most elderly people in the United States.

A different notion of public well-being, but one highly valued by most Americans, is provided by the National Park Service, under the Department of the Interior. First created in 1916, the National Park Service is responsible for the care and upkeep of national parks. Since the nineteenth century, Americans have seen protection of the natural environment as an important public goal and have looked to federal agencies to implement laws and administer programs that preserve natural areas and keep them open to the public.

The federal bureaucracy also promotes the public good through the watchdog activities of many **regulatory agencies.** These include the Food and Drug Administration (FDA), within the HHS; the Occupational Safety and Health Administration (OSHA), in the Department of Labor; as well as numerous independent regulatory commissions, such as the Consumer Product Safety Commission, the Federal Communications Commission, and the EPA.

The National Institutes of Health (NIH) is an example of a federal bureaucracy that promotes the public welfare by conducting cutting-edge biomedical research. NIH research has helped doctors to treat diabetes and cardiovascular disease, among many other illnesses. This scientist is studying pancreatic beta cells, which play a role in diabetes.

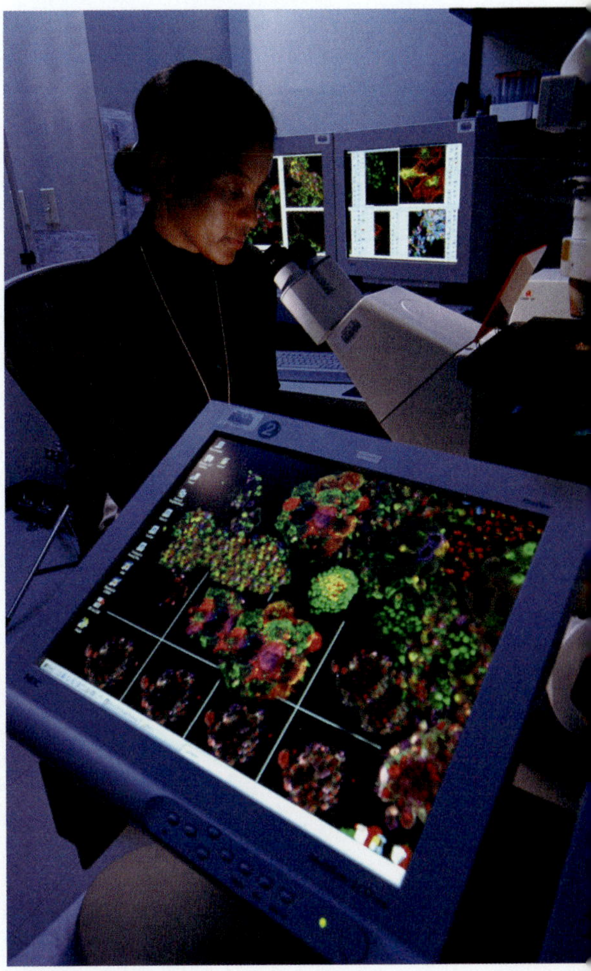

An agency or commission is regulatory if Congress delegates to it relatively broad powers over a sector of the economy or a type of commercial activity and authorizes it to make rules within that jurisdiction. Rules made by regulatory agencies have the force and effect of law.

Bureaucracies, Clienteles, and the Public Some of the public agencies that provide services are tied to a specific group or segment of American society that is often thought of as the main clientele of that agency. For example, the Department of Agriculture was established in 1862 to promote the interests of farmers. Likewise, the Department of Veterans Affairs has strong links to veterans' organizations such as the American Legion and the Veterans of Foreign Wars. The Department of Education relies on teachers' organizations for support. Figure 14.3 is a representation of this type of politics. This configuration is known as an iron triangle, a pattern of stable relationships among an agency in the executive branch, a congressional committee or subcommittee, and one or more organized groups of agency clientele. (Iron triangles are discussed in detail in Chapter 11.)

These relationships with particular clienteles are often important in preserving agencies from political attack. During his 1980 campaign, Ronald Reagan promised to dismantle the Department of Education as part of his commitment to get government "off people's backs." After his election, Reagan even appointed a secretary of

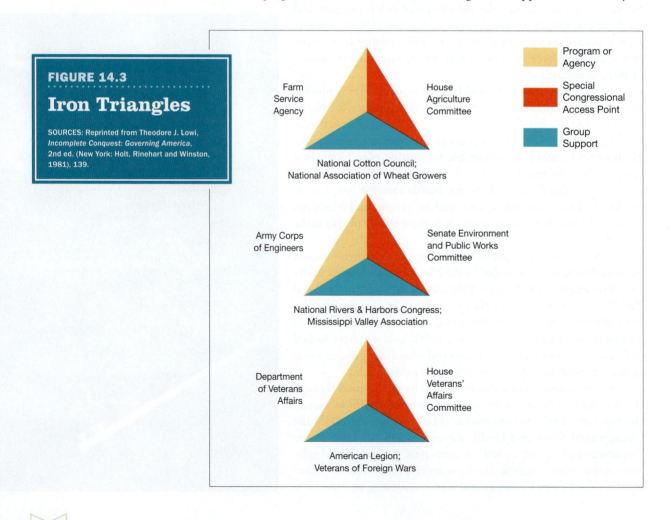

FIGURE 14.3

Iron Triangles

SOURCES: Reprinted from Theodore J. Lowi, *Incomplete Conquest: Governing America*, 2nd ed. (New York: Holt, Rinehart and Winston, 1981), 139.

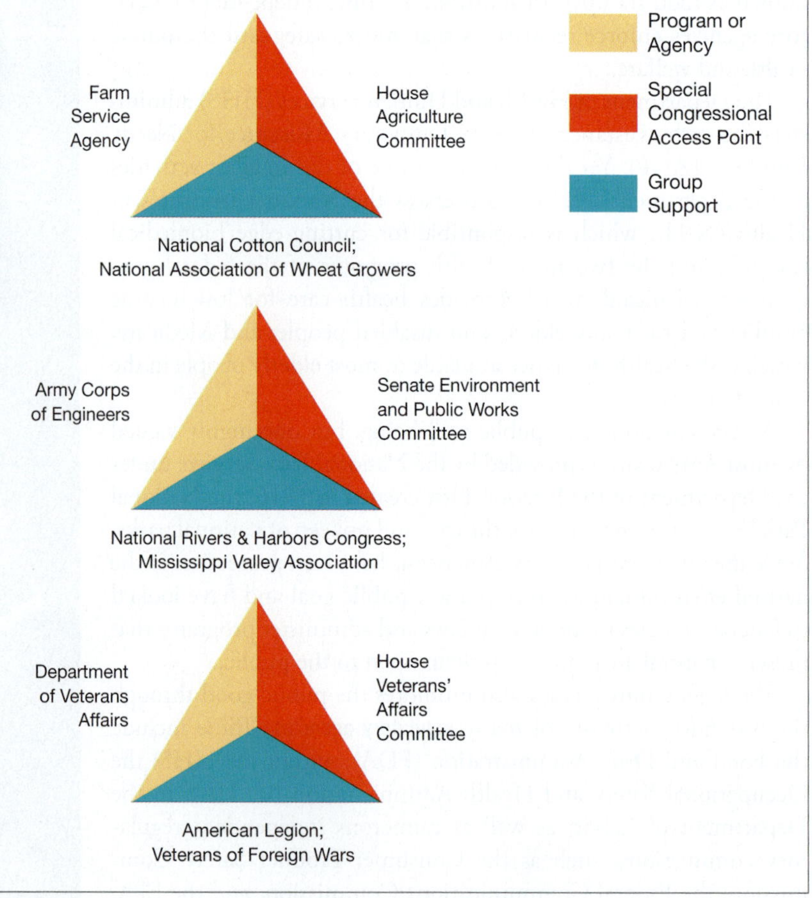

the department who was publicly committed to eliminating it. Yet by the end of his administration, the Department of Education was still standing and barely touched. In 1995 the Republican Congress vowed to eliminate the Department of Education, along with two other departments; but it, too, failed. The educational constituency of the department (its clientele) mobilized to save it each time. Teachers' unions and educational administrators formed a powerful alliance to defend the department. Trump administration Education Secretary Betsy DeVos has not proposed eliminating the department but has clashed with teacher unions over her promotion of charter schools and private school choice initiatives.[19]

Indeed, the ability of clientele groups to get their way is not automatic, as agencies have to balance limited resources, competing interests, and political pressures. For example, the Department of Veterans Affairs long resisted the efforts of Vietnam veterans to be compensated for exposure to Agent Orange, a chemical defoliant used extensively during the Vietnam War. Veterans charged that exposure to Agent Orange had left them with a variety of diseases ranging from cancer to severe birth defects in their children. Only after decades of lobbying, lawsuits, and federally sponsored studies did the Department of Veterans Affairs provide assistance to affected veterans.

FOR CRITICAL ANALYSIS

What is the impact of iron triangles on government services in the United States? Do the ties among agencies, congressional committees, and organized groups promote the efficient provision of government services?

PROVIDING NATIONAL SECURITY

One of the remarkable features of American federalism is that the most vital agencies for providing security for the American people (namely, the police) are located in state and local governments. But some agencies vital to maintaining national security are located in the national government, and they can be grouped into two categories: agencies to confront threats to internal national security and agencies to defend American security from external threats. The departments of greatest influence in these areas are Homeland Security, Justice, Defense, and State.

Agencies for Internal Security The task of maintaining domestic security changed dramatically after the terrorist attacks of September 11, 2001. The creation of the

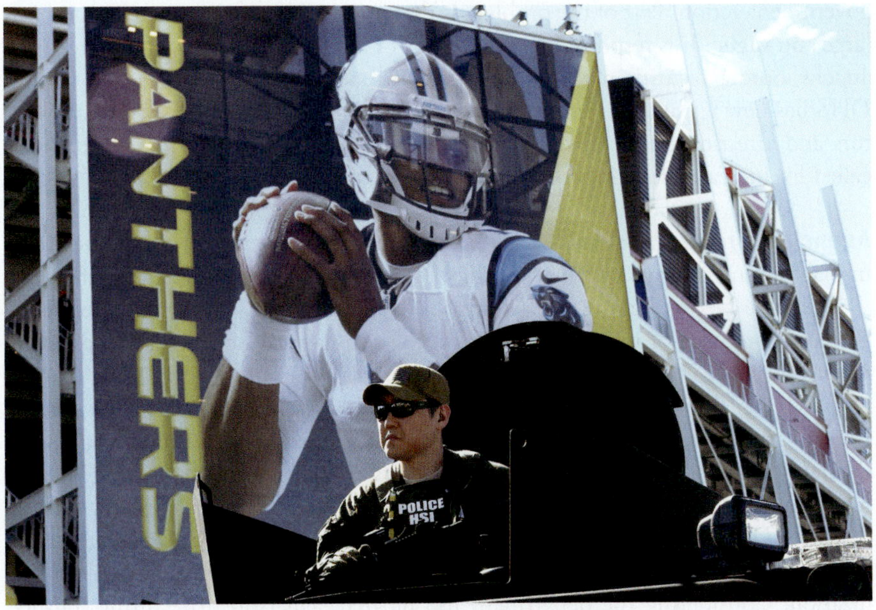

The Department of Homeland Security (DHS) is tasked with the broad goal of keeping America safe. Its 240,000 employees work in jobs as diverse as aviation security, emergency response, and chemical facility inspection. The DHS also provides security for the Super Bowl.

Department of Homeland Security in late 2002 signaled the high priority that domestic security would now have. The orientation of domestic agencies also shifted as agencies geared up to prevent terrorism, a very different task from their former charge of investigating crime. With this shift in responsibility came broad new powers, many of them controversial, including the power to detain terrorist suspects and to engage in extensive domestic intelligence gathering about possible terrorists.

Before September 11, most of the effort put into maintaining internal national security took the form of legal work related to prosecuting federal crimes. The largest and most important unit of the Justice Department is the Criminal Division. Lawyers in the Criminal Division represent the U.S. government when it is the plaintiff enforcing federal criminal laws, except for those cases (about 25 percent) specifically assigned to other divisions or agencies. Criminal litigation is handled by U.S. attorneys, who are appointed by the president. There is one U.S. attorney in each of the 94 federal judicial districts; he or she supervises the work of a number of assistant U.S. attorneys.

The Civil Division of the Justice Department deals with litigation in which the United States is the defendant being sued for injury and damages allegedly inflicted by a government official or agency. The missions of the other divisions of the Justice Department—Antitrust, Civil Rights, Environment and Natural Resources, and Tax—are described by their names.

In 2002 the new Department of Homeland Security joined the Justice Department as the major bureaucracy charged with domestic security. The department took over some of the security-oriented agencies previously controlled by other departments. (See Table 14.1 for a look inside the Department of Homeland Security.) Growing pains were evident in Homeland Security's first years. Different bureaucratic cultures, now part of a single operation, quickly became embroiled in turf battles with one another and with the FBI (which remained in the Justice Department) as the two departments attempted to sort out their respective responsibilities. These early problems signaled deeper challenges that the Department of Homeland Security has continued to face throughout its existence. DHS has been unable to establish itself as a strong institutionally coherent presence capable of coordinating government action. Part of the problem is that its portfolio of responsibilities is both large and vague. It is responsible for all kinds of internal security including terrorist attacks, border security, natural disasters, and food safety. Under President Trump DHS has new visibility in implementing the president's travel bans on certain visitors and arresting undocumented immigrants, and his first two budget proposals called for increased funding for the department.[20]

FOR CRITICAL ANALYSIS

Why was the Department of Homeland Security created? What problems has the new department faced?

Agencies for External National Security Two departments occupy center stage in maintaining external national security: the Departments of State and Defense.

The State Department's primary mission is diplomacy. As the most visible public representative of American diplomacy, the secretary of state works to promote American perspectives and interests in the world. For example, President Trump's first Secretary of State Rex Tillerson traveled to Moscow in 2017 in a bid to weaken Russia's support for Syrian President Bashar al-Assad amid concerns about his use of chemical weapons.[21]Although diplomacy is the primary task of the State Department, diplomatic missions are only one of its organizational dimensions. As of 2016 the State Department comprised several dozen bureau-level units, each under the direction of an undersecretary, although Tillerson proposed a departmental reorganization. Considering the department too bloated, Tillerson froze hiring, pushed

TABLE 14.1

Department of Homeland Security

SELECTED OFFICES	FUNCTION	2018 BUDGET, IN BILLION $	ESTIMATED NUMBER OF EMPLOYEES
U.S. Customs and Border Protection	Responsible for securing America's borders to protect the United States against terrorist threats and prevent the illegal entry of inadmissible persons and contraband, while facilitating lawful travel, trade, and immigration	14	59,753
U.S. Immigration and Customs Enforcement	The principal investigative arm of the Department of Homeland Security	7.1	21,289
Transportation Security Administration	Provides security for the nation's transportation system	7.9	52,956
Coast Guard	Safeguards our nation's maritime interests and natural resources on our rivers, in U.S. ports, on the high seas, and in the maritime domain around the world	12.1	14,117
U.S. Secret Service	Protects national leaders and safeguards the nation's financial infrastructure and payment systems	1.99	
National Protection and Programs Directorate	Combats cyber-attacks and foreign espionage by enhancing infrastructure and preventing hacking	1.9	
Federal Emergency Management Agency	Manages and coordinates the federal response to and recovery from major domestic disasters and emergencies of all types	7.9	

SOURCE: U.S. House Appropriations Committee, "FY 2018 Omnibus: Homeland Security," March 21, 2018, https://appropriations.house.gov (accessed 3/29/18); House Appropriations Committee, "Fiscal Year 2018 Homeland Security Bill," March 21, 2018, https://appropriations.house.gov (accessed 3/29/18).

out top career officials, and limited promotions, steps that earned criticism from some in Congress.[22] Secretary of State Mike Pompeo lifted Tillerson's hiring freeze, although many positions remain unfilled.

These bureaus support the responsibilities of the elite foreign-service officers, who staff U.S. embassies around the world and who hold almost all of the most powerful positions in the department below the rank of ambassador.[23] The ambassadorial positions, especially the plum positions in the major capitals of the world, are filled by presidential appointees, many of whom get their posts by having been important donors to victorious political campaigns.

Despite the importance of the State Department in foreign affairs, fewer than 20 percent of all U.S. government employees working abroad are directly under its authority. By far the largest number of career government professionals working abroad are under the authority of the Defense Department.

The Defense Department is charged with providing the military forces needed to deter war and protect the nation. Headquartered in the Pentagon, across the Potomac River from Washington, D.C., the Department of Defense (DoD) is one of the largest bureaucracies in the world, composed of 2 million people across five sets of institutions.[24] The president, as commander-in-chief, appoints the Secretary

The Departments of Defense and State are the most important parts of the federal bureaucracy focused on national security. Secretary of Defense James Mattis (left) is the civilian head of the military (reporting to the president as commander in chief). Secretary of State Mike Pompeo (center right) is the United States' chief diplomat. He is pictured meeting with Qatari foreign minister Sheikh Mohammed bin Abdulrahman Al Thani in 2018. The State Department runs embassies around the world. U.S. embassy to Grenada principal officer Stephen Frahm (right) speaks with U.S. citizens in Grenada about how to access government services in case of emergency.

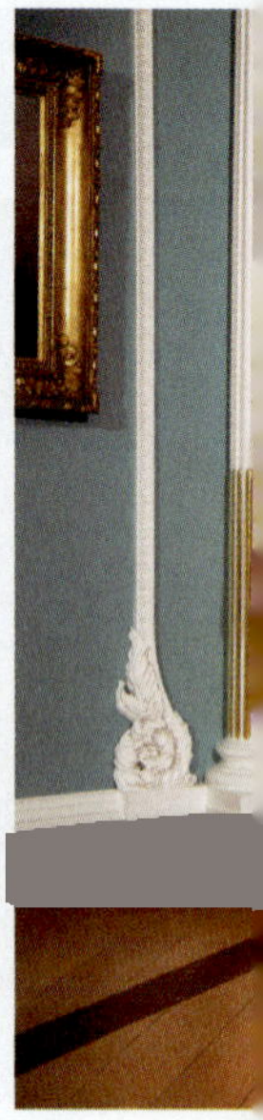

of Defense, whose Office of the Secretary of Defense (OSD) plans and carries out the nation's security policies as directed by the secretary and president. The OSD provides civilian oversight of the military. The second institution is the Joint Chiefs of Staff, consisting of the Chairman of the Joint Chiefs of Staff, who is the president's principal military adviser, and the five military service chiefs (Army, Navy, Air Force, Marine Corps, and National Guard; the Coast Guard is in the Department of Homeland Security except in wartime). Third, there are three military departments, each with its own civilian secretary and military secretary (Army, Navy, Air Force; the Marine Corps is part of the Department of the Navy). The military departments train and equip military forces. Fourth, the Unified Combatant Commands (COCOMs) are the entities that execute military operations. There are six regional COCOMs (Africa Command; European Command; Central Command; Northern Command; Southern Command; and Pacific Command) and three functional COCOMS (Strategic Command; Special Operations Command; and Transportation Command). Finally there are the defense agencies that perform supply or service activities that are common to more than one military department. There are currently 20 such defense agencies.[25]

The Department of Defense is an enormously complex organization, and has been reformed several times to increase efficiency and effectiveness. The contemporary DoD was created in 1947, after concerns arose during World War II that the Departments of War and Navy, then separate entities, were insufficiently integrated to fight effectively. Another major reorganization came in 1986, when the Goldwater-Nichols Defense Reform Act made the Chairman of the Joint Chiefs of Staff the president's main military adviser, rather than the service chiefs. Also, operational control was moved from the service chiefs to the unified commands, permitting those commanders to use all military assets available on an integrated basis. More recently, the Budget Control Act of 2011 (see "sequestration," discussed later in this chapter) reduced annual defense appropriations (outside of current military operations) by 5 percent from 2013 on, prompting further efforts to prioritize DoD's many tasks.[26] However, the 2018 federal spending bill signed by President Trump in

March 2017 raised the sequestration caps and increased both defense and domestic spending.

National Security and Democracy Of all the agencies in the federal bureaucracy, those charged with providing national security most often come into conflict with the norms and expectations of American democracy. Two issues in particular arise as these agencies work to ensure national security: (1) the trade-offs between respecting the personal rights of individuals versus protecting the general public, and (2) the need for secrecy in matters of national security versus the public's right to know what the government is doing. Needless to say, Americans often disagree about what activities the government should be able to pursue to defend U.S. national security.

When national security is at stake, federal agencies have taken actions that are normally considered incompatible with individual rights. For example, during World War II President Franklin Roosevelt ordered thousands of American citizens of Japanese descent to be relocated to internment camps due to national security concerns. Although the Supreme Court approved this action, the federal government has since acknowledged that it constituted unjustified discrimination and has offered reparations to those who were interned.

Protecting national security often requires the government to conduct its activities in secret. Yet, as Americans have come to expect a more open government, many believe that federal agencies charged with national security keep too many secrets from the American public. The effort to make information related to national security more available began in 1966 with the passage of the Freedom of Information Act (FOIA). Strengthened in 1974 after Watergate, the act allows any person to request classified information from any federal agency. The information obtained often reveals unflattering or unsuccessful aspects of national security activities. One private organization, the National Security Archive, makes extensive use of FOIA requests to obtain information about the activities of national security agencies; it has published many of these documents on its website and maintains an archive in Washington, D.C., that is open to the public. The website's "The Torture Archive,"

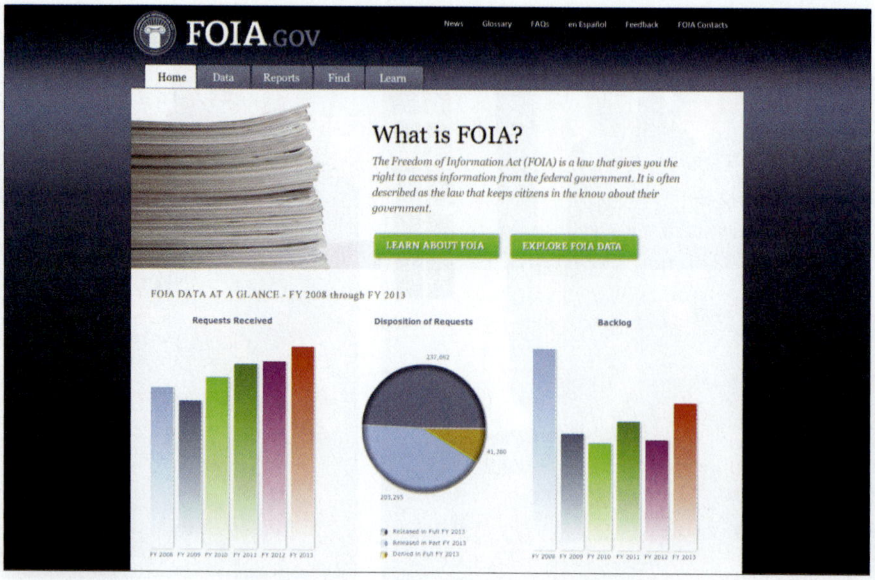

The U.S. media have used Freedom of Information Act requests to obtain important information, such as federal drug safety reports and conditions at local jails. Americans are likely to always debate just how much secrecy their government is entitled to.

for example, is a searchable database of documents related to the authorized use of torture by the American government.

With the advent of the war on terrorism, the government gained unprecedented powers to detain foreign suspects, carry out wiretaps and searches, conduct secret military tribunals, and build an integrated law-enforcement and intelligence system. Congress hastily enacted many of these sweeping provisions of the USA PATRIOT Act several weeks after the terrorist attacks, with little debate.

The threat of terrorism also dramatically sharpened the tension between secrecy and democracy. After the September 11 attacks, access under the FOIA was curtailed, and the range of information deemed sensitive greatly expanded. Some analysts worried that secrecy would prevent Congress from carrying out its basic oversight responsibilities. They also claimed that much of the secrecy had nothing to do with national security. President Obama ordered federal agencies to administer the FOIA law more liberally and signed an executive order to speed declassification of secret documents. However, Obama's campaign to make government more transparent was challenged by national security contract worker Edward Snowden's leak of sensitive national security documents in 2013. The Snowden documents exposed the extent, and potential illegality, of the National Security Agency's (NSA) global surveillance operations. Following the revelation that the NSA was collecting private data on millions of Americans and foreign nationals—tracking not only phone calls but also email messages, web browser histories, and personal contacts—concern mounted among the American public, government watchdog groups, and representatives in Congress, while foreign allies threatened to suspend cooperation on global antiterrorism efforts.[27] A panel of intelligence experts appointed by President Obama to assess the NSA's activities concluded that its massive data collection "made only a modest contribution to the nation's security." They recommended, among dozens of other reforms, that the government stop the collection program and relinquish the files to a third party.[28] Congress barred the bulk collection of telephone data and instituted other limits on government surveillance in the 2015 USA Freedom Act. The restrictions in the new legislation sought to ensure security without jeopardizing privacy, although critics remain concerned about the scope of government surveillance.[29]

MAINTAINING A STRONG ECONOMY

In our capitalist economic system, the government does not directly run the economy. Yet many federal government activities are critical to maintaining a strong economy. Foremost among these are the agencies responsible for fiscal and monetary policy. Other agencies, such as the Internal Revenue Service (IRS), collect private resources into use for public purposes. Tax policy may also strengthen the economy through decisions about whom to tax, how much, and when. Finally, the federal government, through such agencies as the Department of Transportation, the Commerce Department, and the Energy Department, may directly provide services or goods that bolster the economy.

Fiscal and Monetary Agencies **Fiscal policy** can refer to any government policy having to do with public finance. However, Americans often reserve *fiscal* for taxing and spending policies and use *monetary* for policies having to do with banks, credit, and currency.

fiscal policy the government's use of taxing, monetary, and spending powers to manipulate the economy

While the responsibility for making fiscal policy lies with Congress, the administration of fiscal policy occurs primarily in the Treasury Department. In addition to collecting income, corporate, and other taxes, the Treasury manages the national debt: $21 trillion in 2018.[30] The Treasury Department is also responsible for printing U.S. currency, but currency is only a tiny proportion of the entire money economy. Most of the trillions of dollars used in the transactions of the private and public sectors of the U.S. economy exist virtually—in computerized accounts rather than as actual currency. The Treasury Department also performs tax and economic policy analysis, as does the Council of Economic Advisors, located within the Executive Office of the President.

A key monetary agency is the **Federal Reserve System** (called simply the Fed), which is headed by the Federal Reserve Board. The Fed has authority over the interest rates and lending activities of the nation's most important banks. Congress established the Fed in 1913 as a clearinghouse responsible for adjusting the supply of money and credit to the needs of commerce and industry in different regions of the country. The Fed is also responsible for ensuring that banks do not overextend themselves, a policy that guards against bank failures during a sudden economic scare, such as occurred in 1929. The Treasury and the Federal Reserve took center stage when a string of bank failures threatened economic catastrophe in 2008. These agencies designed a $700-billion bailout package and convinced Congress that a rapid response was needed to avert a worldwide depression. Although the Treasury and the Federal Reserve sprang into action when economic calamity loomed, critics charged that the crisis could have been prevented if these agencies had exercised more regulatory oversight over the financial sector during the previous decade. In 2010, Congress and the president created the Financial Stability Oversight Council to identify systemwide risks to the financial sector. As part of its duties, the council devised a rule to identify "systemically important" nonbank financial companies that would pose a grave threat to U.S. financial stability in the event that they failed and to prompt stiffer regulatory oversight of those companies.[31]

Federal Reserve System a system of 12 Federal Reserve banks that facilitates exchanges of cash, checks, and credit; regulates member banks; and uses monetary policies to fight inflation and deflation

Revenue Agencies One of the first actions Congress took under President George Washington was to create the Department of the Treasury, and probably its oldest function is the collection of taxes on imports, called tariffs. Now part of the Department of Homeland Security, federal customs agents are located at every U.S. seaport

Several government agencies are focused on maintaining a strong economy. These include the Federal Reserve, headed by Jerome Powell (left), which regulates interest rates and lending activity. The Treasury Department (which oversees the IRS and thus collects taxes) is headed by Secretary Steven Mnuchin (center). The federal government also provides small business loans and other incentives for economic development in large and small sectors of the economy. In 2015 the Obama administration announced more money for research to protect bee habitats (right).

revenue agency an agency responsible for collecting taxes. Examples include the Internal Revenue Service for income taxes; the U.S. Customs Service for tariffs and other taxes on imported goods; and the Bureau of Alcohol, Tobacco, Firearms and Explosives for collection of taxes on the sale of those particular products

and international airport to oversee the collection of tariffs. But far and away the most important of the **revenue agencies** is the Internal Revenue Service, a bureau within the Treasury Department.

The IRS is the government agency that Americans love to hate. As one expert put it, "probably no organization in the country, public or private, creates as much clientele *dis*favor as the Internal Revenue Service. The very nature of its work brings it into an adversarial relationship with vast numbers of Americans every year [emphasis added]."[32] Taxpayers complain about the IRS's needless complexity, its lack of sensitivity and responsiveness to individual taxpayers, and its overall lack of efficiency. Such complaints led Congress to pass the IRS Restructuring and Reform Act of 1998, which instituted a number of new protections for taxpayers. Yet Congress continued to cut the IRS budget—$900 million over eight years through 2018—despite Treasury Secretary Steven Mnuchin's request for a larger budget and more staff to allow the agency to enhance enforcement, bring in more tax revenue, fend off hackers, and restore customer service.[33]

Economic Development Agencies Federal agencies also conduct programs designed to strengthen particular segments of the economy or to provide specific services aimed at strengthening the entire economy. Created in 1889, the Department of Agriculture is the fourth-oldest Cabinet department. Its initial mission, to strengthen American agriculture by providing information about effective farming practices, reflected the enormous importance of farming in the American economy. Through its Agricultural Extension Service, the Department of Agriculture established a significant presence in rural areas throughout the country. It also built strong support for its activities among the nation's farmers and at the many land-grant colleges, where agricultural research has been conducted for over 100 years.

At first glance, the Department of Transportation, which oversees the nation's highway and air traffic systems, may seem to have little to do with economic development. But effective transportation is the backbone of a strong economy. The interstate highway system, for example, is widely acknowledged as a key factor in

promoting economic growth in the decades after World War II. The Small Business Administration, in the Department of Commerce, provides loans and technical assistance to small businesses across the country.

Can the Bureaucracy Be Reformed?

Evaluate some of the ways politicians have tried to make the bureaucracy more efficient

When citizens complain that government is too bureaucratic, what they often mean is that government bureaucracies seem inefficient, waste money, and perform poorly. The botched roll-out of healthcare.gov, the federal government's online health insurance marketplace, handicapped the implementation of the Affordable Care Act when it opened and subsequently crashed in October 2013. A report by the Inspector General of the Department of Health and Human Services concluded afterward that the Centers for Medicare and Medicaid Services, tasked with overseeing the website, lacked the necessary managerial and technical capacity and ignored warnings that the enormous software project was headed for trouble.[34] In the waiting list scandal that rocked the Veterans Health Administration in 2014, some VHA hospitals that had not met the target of getting appointments for veterans within 14 days had created unofficial lists to make their waiting times look better. A VA audit and FBI investigation found that over 120,000 veterans were left waiting or never got appointments. Congress passed and President Obama signed new legislation in late 2014 that added funding, allowed some veterans to get private health care at government expense, and gave the VA Secretary increased authority to fire poorly performing managers.[35] When citizens have negative personal experience with the federal government—mountains of forms to fill out, lengthy waits, and unsympathetic service—they wonder why government can't do better.

The government has often sought to find ways to make the federal bureaucracy more efficient. In 1993, President Bill Clinton launched the National Performance Review—part of his promise to "reinvent government"—to make the federal bureaucracy more efficient, accountable, and effective. The National Performance Review sought to prompt federal agencies to adopt flexible, goal-driven practices. Clinton promised that the result would be a government that would "work better and cost less." Virtually all observers agreed that the review made substantial progress. Its original goal was to save more than $100 billion over five years, in large part by cutting the federal workforce by 12 percent (more than 270,000 jobs) by the end of 1999. In fact, by 2000, $136 billion in savings were already assured through legislative or administrative action, and the federal workforce had been cut by 426,200.[36]

In 2015, President Obama created a Social and Behavioral Sciences team to help departments incorporate insights from behavioral science—how people make decisions and act on them—to make government processes more efficient. The team launched a number of experiments to improve services, such as an effort to boost military service members' enrollment in the government retirement savings plan, which was lower than that of other federal employees. By requiring service members to make a choice as part of their orientation upon arrival at a new military base, the experiment increased enrollment by over 8 percent.[37]

Beyond these efforts seeking greater efficiency and effectiveness, government reorganization is a recurrent theme. Presidents Nixon, Carter, Clinton, and Obama each ordered a reorganization of the executive branch. Nixon, for example, sought to retain the Departments of State, Defense, Treasury, and Justice but streamline other departments by function (Natural Resources, Human Resources, Community Development, and Economic Development). However, Congress objected, as executive branch structures reflect committee and subcommittee jurisdictions in Congress, which are important to lawmakers who wish to address constituent concerns and who therefore resist consolidation.[38] At the beginning of his term, President Trump too issued an executive order asking each department to file reorganization plans, but after his administration's first year, only a few departments had done so.[39]

In recent decades there have been several attempts to "reinvent government." In 1993, President Bill Clinton and Vice President Al Gore established the National Performance Review for this purpose. Gore promoted this on David Letterman's show, where he railed against the government's procurement requirements, which even specified the number of pieces into which a government ashtray may shatter.

Although streamlining efforts like Clinton's did help make government work more effectively, it did not institute the more sweeping approach to reform demanded by some political leaders. Reform has instead been pursued through efforts to terminate, devolve, or contract out government functions. In general, Democratic administrations have aimed to make the existing bureaucracy work more effectively, whereas Republican administrations have sought to sideline the bureaucracy, especially by contracting out government work to private companies.

ELIMINATING PROGRAMS AND AGENCIES

The only certain way to reduce the size of the bureaucracy is to eliminate programs through termination, a rare occurrence. Even in the 12 years of the Reagan and George H. W. Bush administrations, both of which proclaimed a strong commitment to the reduction of the national government, not a single national government agency or program was terminated. In the 1990s, Republicans did succeed in eliminating two small agencies. The 2018 spending bill, passed by a Republican-led Congress, not only increased federal spending but also prohibited agencies from eliminating programs or offices without congressional authorization.[40]

The overall difficulty in terminating bureaucracy is a reflection of Americans' love–hate relationship with the national government. As antagonistic as Americans may be toward bureaucracy in general, they benefit from the services being rendered and the protections being offered by particular bureaucratic agencies. They fiercely defend their favorite agencies while perceiving no inconsistency in their hostility toward the bureaucracy in general. A good case in point is the agonizing problem of closing military bases in the wake of the end of the Cold War with the former Soviet Union, when the United States no longer needed so many bases. Since every base was in some congressional member's district, it proved impossible for Congress to decide to close any of them. Consequently, beginning in 1988, Congress established the Defense Base Closure and Realignment Commission (BRAC) to decide on base closings, allowing Congress only an up or down vote on the commission's proposals.[41] Five different BRAC reports, the most recent in 2005, formed the basis for closing bases and modifying the operations in the remaining bases. When the Pentagon proposed another round of base closings in 2014, it met with resistance from members of Congress, few of whom wanted to run the risk that a base in their district could close.[42]

Elected leaders have come to rely on a more incremental approach to downsizing the bureaucracy. Much has been done by budgetary means. In 2011, due to concerns among House Republicans about the size of the national debt, Congress failed to raise the nation's debt ceiling—the amount of national debt that can be issued by the Treasury—usually an uncontroversial step to keep government in operation. The Treasury Department came within days of being unable to pay bondholders and other creditors. The resolution to the crisis was the Budget Control Act of 2011, which required Congress to pass a deficit-cutting budget in exchange for raising the debt ceiling or else trigger sequestration, across-the-board cuts to both domestic and defense spending. Congress failed to pass a budget, triggering cuts.[43] As a result, a number of agencies made personnel reductions at that time. President Trump imposed a federal hiring freeze upon taking office, but did not issue a formal

Americans may desire smaller government in the abstract, but they defend the agencies that affect them. Closing military bases in the United States has proved particularly controversial. Citizens mobilized across the country to urge the Base Closure and Realignment Commission not to close military bases in their areas.

plan. Some agencies operated as if under a freeze, and some, like the Social Security Administration, made early buyout offers to their workforce in summer 2017, but the size of the federal workforce remained largely unchanged.[44]

DEVOLUTION

devolution a policy to remove a program from one level of government by delegating it or passing it down to a lower level of government, such as from the national government to the state and local governments

The next most effective approach to reducing the size of the federal bureaucracy is **devolution**, downsizing the federal bureaucracy by delegating the implementation of programs to state and local governments (also see Chapter 3, Federalism). Devolution often alters the pattern of who benefits most from government programs. Opponents of devolution in social policy, for example, charge that it reduces the ability of the government to remedy inequality. They argue that state governments, which cannot run deficits as the federal government does and which have more limited taxing capabilities, will inevitably cut spending on programs that serve low-income residents. They point to the State Children's Health Insurance Program (SCHIP), which was created in 1997 to extend health insurance to low-income children. When the economy was booming, states added children to the rolls and some states even extended benefits to the children's parents. But during the recession of the early 2000s, as states faced significant budget crises, many cut back on SCHIP. And during the Great Recession that began in 2008, Arizona closed SCHIP to new enrollments altogether and did not reopen the program until late 2016, long after the recession was over.[45] States, with their tight fiscal circumstances, can have difficulty keeping pace with economic need.

Often the central aim of devolution is to provide more efficient and flexible government services. Yet, by its very nature, devolution entails variation across the states. In some states, government services may improve as a consequence of devolution. In other states, services may deteriorate as the states use devolution as an opportunity to cut spending and reduce services. This has been the pattern in the implementation of the welfare reform passed in 1996, the most significant devolution of federal government social programs in many decades. Some states, such as Oregon, have used the flexibility of the reform to design innovative programs that respond to clients' needs; other states, such as Idaho, have virtually dismantled their welfare programs. The recession that began in 2008 provided the first real evidence about what increased state flexibility meant for low-income Americans. Studies showed that the number of people on public assistance rose by 14 percent even as the unemployment rate increased by 88 percent between 2007 and 2010.[46] Moreover, states varied widely in how they responded: for example, although the unemployment rate rose by 146 percent in Arizona—increasing from 4 percent at the end of 2007 to almost 10 percent in 2010—public-assistance rolls actually fell by 48 percent. In Oregon, by contrast, public-assistance cases rose by 70 percent, although unemployment grew by only 41 percent. The overall lack of growth and state variation in welfare contrast sharply with the rise in food stamp recipients during 2008–09, a program run by the federal government. Recipients of food stamps (now called the Supplemental Nutrition Assistance Program) grew by 45 percent between 2009 and 2010 and pulled an estimated 8 percent of Americans out of poverty in 2009.[47] Critics argued that devolution gave the states too much flexibility in designing their own welfare programs and that the result has been a program unable to assist the poor when they need it most.

FOR CRITICAL ANALYSIS

Dissatisfied citizens have supported a range of bureaucratic reforms, including termination of agencies, devolution of responsibility to lower levels of government, and privatization. Are such reforms likely to make the bureaucracy more responsive to public wishes?

This is the dilemma that devolution poses. Up to a point, variation can be considered one of the virtues of federalism. But in a democracy, it is inherently dangerous to have large variations in the provisions of services and benefits.

PRIVATIZATION AND CONTRACTING OUT

Most of what is called "privatization" is the provision of government goods and services by private contractors under direct government supervision. Except for top-secret strategic materials, virtually all military hardware, from boats to bullets, is produced on a privatized basis by private contractors. Research services worth billions of dollars are bought under contract by governments from universities and from ordinary industrial corporations and private "think tanks." **Privatization** simply means that a formerly public activity is picked up under contract by a private company or companies. But such programs are still very much government programs—paid for by government and supervised by government. Privatization downsizes the government only in that the workers providing the service are no longer counted as part of the government bureaucracy. Privatization may not mean less government but rather a different role for government, as managerial expertise is needed to write contracts and oversee private companies carrying out government work.[48]

privatization a formerly public service that is now provided by a private company but paid for by the government

The central aim of privatization is to reduce the cost of government. When private contractors can perform a task as well as government can but for less money, taxpayers win. President George W. Bush made privatization a central component of his effort to reform the federal bureaucracy. He introduced new procedures that would subject more than 800,000 federal jobs, nearly half the federal civilian workforce, to competitive outsourcing. If it were determined that a company could do the job more efficiently, the work would be contracted out. Under Bush, government outsourcing grew dramatically as the government sought to staff the new Department

One strategy to carry out the tasks of government is privatization. The U.S. military and Department of Defense contract many services to companies such as Booz Allen Hamilton, which provides systems for personnel management, program support, and assessment, among other services.

FIGURE 14.4

Outsourcing the Government

The number of contractors employed by the federal government has increased, especially after September 11, 2001. Does contracting out government jobs save money, or does it create problems of oversight and accountability? Or both?

NOTE: Includes both new contracts and payments against existing contracts.

SOURCES: Paul Light, "The True Size of Government," *The Volcker Alliance*, October 2017, www.volckeralliance.org (accessed 4/4/18).

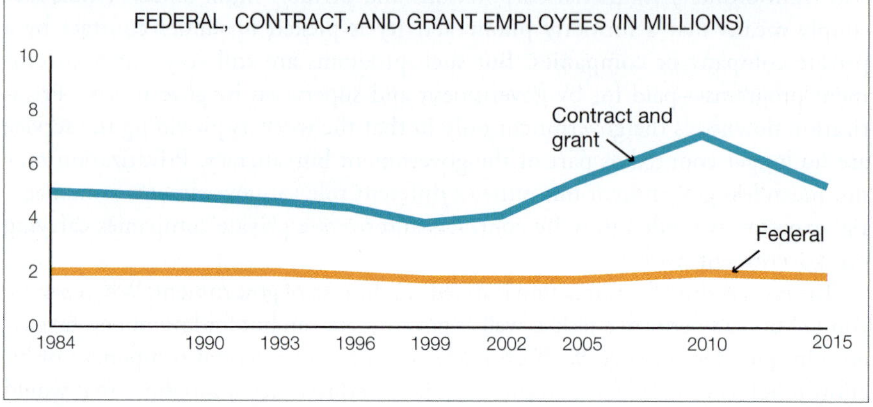

of Homeland Security and pursue wars in Afghanistan and Iraq without increasing the numbers of federal employees. Payments for federal contracts grew from $209 billion in 2000 to $537 billion in 2011.[49] Although military contracts account for much of the growth, contracting is common throughout the federal bureaucracy. In fact, contracting has become so widespread that it has been called a "virtual fourth branch of government"[50] (Figure 14.4).

Depending on how it is conducted, competitive outsourcing may not lead to extensive privatization; instead, competition may improve government performance by forcing federal agencies to reexamine how they can do their work more efficiently. But when public bureaucracies are *not* granted a fair chance to bid in the contracting competition and, too, if there is little competition among private firms, private firms have a monopoly on service provision and often end up being less efficient and more costly than government. In 2015 close to 60 percent of all contracts were awarded competitively. But that year was an exception: from 2000 to 2011, less than half of existing contracts were subject to open competition. In fact, there is no good evidence that privatization saves the government money.

In most aspects of government activity, contract employees work side by side with government employees in what has been called a "blended workforce."[51] Many agencies that rely on technical expertise, such as the National Oceanographic and Atmospheric Administration, routinely rely on contractors. Although federal regulations forbid the outsourcing of "inherently governmental work," no clear line separates governmental and nongovernmental work.[52]

Concerns about adequate government oversight, accountability, and performance of private contractors escalated when the scale of contracting dramatically increased. In 2008, Congress responded to the concerns about contractors by creating a "Commission on Wartime Contracting." Its final report sharply criticized the use of private contractors, estimating that the practice had wasted between $31 and $60 billion during the wars in Afghanistan and Iraq. It made numerous recommendations for reform but noted that successful reforms would require congressional action and funding for new oversight capabilities.[53] Congress created databases to record contractor performance and to keep track of legal or contractual violations.[54] However, both the Government Accountability Office (GAO) and government transparency groups found the databases poorly documented and of little use in agency decision-making or congressional oversight.[55]

FOR CRITICAL ANALYSIS

Private firms play a significant role in providing government services, including both internal and external security. What are the advantages and disadvantages of relying on private firms to provide essential services? Can government provide adequate oversight of these private companies?

Some members of Congress have sought far-reaching regulations on contractors, including forbidding contractors from performing sensitive functions in war settings such as interrogations, security, and intelligence activities. Proposals for such major reforms, however, are difficult to enact given the political connections of many federal contractors.

The Obama administration sought to address the concerns about contracting in several ways. In July 2009 the White House Office of Management and Budget (OMB) took steps to reduce the government's reliance on outside contractors. Departments and agencies were told to cut contract spending by 7 percent over the next two years.[56] By 2011 the administration announced that for the first time in 13 years, spending on outside contractors had declined.[57] In 2016 the Obama Department of Justice decided to end the use of private prisons for federal inmates after an audit found more safety and security problems than in government-run facilities.[58]

In 2013 the national security leaks by Edward Snowden and a mass shooting at the Washington Navy Yard, a U.S. military base—both by government contractors—raised fresh concerns about the outsourcing of government and prompted Congress to pass legislation calling for a review of contractors' security clearances.[59] The White House also drafted an executive order requiring government contractors to disclose their political donations, though Congress blocked those efforts by passing a federal spending bill in 2014 that prohibits any funding to require contractors to disclose campaign donations.[60] In addition, in 2015 Obama set new requirements for federal contractors in a very different area, compelling contractors to pay a $10.10 minimum wage and to provide paid sick leave for their employees (even if he had failed to win congressional approval for measures to assist workers in general).[61] In March 2017, President Trump signed legislation rolling back several Obama regulations, including a rule barring companies from receiving a federal contract if they had violated labor, wage, or workplace safety rules.[62]

Managing the Bureaucracy

Explain why it is often difficult to control the bureaucracy

By their very nature, bureaucracies pose challenges to democratic governance. Although bureaucracies provide the expertise needed to implement the public will, they can also become entrenched organizations that serve their own interests. The public's task is neither to retreat from bureaucracy nor to attack it but to take advantage of its strengths while making it more accountable to the demands of democratic politics and representative government.

THE PRESIDENT AS CHIEF EXECUTIVE

In 1937, President Franklin Roosevelt's Committee on Administrative Management officially addressed a plea that had been growing increasingly urgent: "The president needs help." The national government had grown rapidly during the preceding 25 years, but the structures and procedures necessary to manage the burgeoning executive branch had not yet been established. The response to the call for "help" for the president initially took the form of three management policies: (1) all communications and decisions that related to executive policy decisions must pass through the Executive Office of the President (EOP); (2) in order to cope with such a flow, the EOP must have an adequate staff of specialists in research, analysis, legislative and legal writing, and public affairs; and (3) the EOP must have additional staff to ensure that presidential decisions are made, communicated to Congress, and carried out by the appropriate agency.

Making the Managerial Presidency The story of the modern presidency can be told largely as a series of responses to the plea for managerial help as the scope of the federal government—and presidential power—has grown.[63]

The president heads the federal government, which is the largest employer in the country and the largest purchaser of goods and services in the world.[64] As the CEO of this enormous organization, the president may have goals associated with management (striving for efficiency) and control (shaping policy outcomes). Presidents have several tools at their disposal. They have appointment power over the top layer of the executive branch, the political appointees who sit on top of the career civil service. They can issue executive orders, making policy and shaping the executive branch unilaterally. They can also alter an agency's budget or organizational scheme. Indeed, the presidency has been marked by waves of executive branch reorganization by presidents seeking to exert administrative and political control.[65]

After Roosevelt's reforms, perhaps the most important were those under President Jimmy Carter, whose reorganization of the civil service will long be recognized as one of the most significant contributions of his presidency. The Civil Service Reform Act of 1978 was the first major revamping of the federal civil service since its creation in 1883. The 1978 act created the Merit Systems Protection Board to defend competitive merit recruitment and promotion from political encroachment. The separate Federal Labor Relations Authority was set up to administer collective bargaining and to address individual personnel grievances. The third new agency, the Office of Personnel Management, was created to manage recruiting, testing, training, and the retirement system. The Senior Executive Service, a top management rank for civil servants, was also created to recognize and foster "public management" as a profession and to facilitate the movement of "super-grade" career officials across agencies and departments.[66]

President Bill Clinton was often criticized for the way he managed his administration—his loose approach to administration included all-night "bull sessions," complete with pizza—yet, as we have seen, he inaugurated one of the most systematic efforts "to change the way government does business" in his National Performance Review. Heavily influenced by the theories of management consultants who prized decentralization, customer responsiveness, and employee initiative, Clinton sought to infuse these new practices into government.[67]

Subsequent presidents have made their own mark. George W. Bush was the first president with a degree in business. He followed the standard business school dictum to select skilled subordinates and then delegate responsibility to them. Critics contended, however, that his administration's distrust of the bureaucracy led it to exercise inappropriate political control over agency experts. Obama's approach to the managerial presidency featured a deep belief in the importance of scientific expertise, which was reflected in his appointments to key regulatory agencies such as the FDA, OSHA, and the EPA. But he had his own critics, who complained about micromanagement and centralization.[68]

President Trump called for deep budget cuts and reorganization in a number of executive branch departments and agencies. His presidency has also raised the specter of a "deep state" of bureaucrats who exert power independent of political control. Political scientist Michael Glennon has used the term "the double state" to describe a phenomenon in which, for example, Bush-era national security policies such as covert drone strikes and use of the Guantánamo Bay prison continued under President Obama, even though Obama as a candidate had criticized them. Glennon raises the possibility of a "double government" of bureaucrats that continues to pursue policies of its preference outside of political or democratic control.[69] Episodes such as EPA employees informing the media about a report on climate change they feared would be suppressed seemed to confirm Trump supporters' fears of the limits of presidential control over the bureaucracy.[70] There is little evidence of the truly rogue bureaucracy that figures in the most extreme versions of conspiracy theories, but questions of who controls the bureaucracy and how much autonomy bureaucrats should have have occupied political scientists and government leaders for decades.

CONGRESSIONAL OVERSIGHT

Another lever of control over the bureaucracy is Congress. Congress passes legislation, which the bureaucracy must then implement. Such delegation derives from the constitutionally mandated roles for each branch of government; the president must "faithfully execute" the laws Congress passes. But because Congress cannot possibly stipulate every detail of every law, the bureaucracy must interpret legislative intent.[71] The delegation of implementation introduces the principal-agent problem: does the bureaucracy (the agent) implement laws in the manner Congress (the principal) intended?

One way Congress can hold the bureaucracy accountable is **oversight**. Congressional committees and subcommittees have jurisdictions roughly parallel to one or more departments and agencies in the executive branch, and members of Congress who sit on these committees can develop expertise equal to that of the bureaucrats. The most visible indication of Congress's oversight efforts is the use of public hearings, before which bureaucrats and other witnesses are summoned to discuss and defend agency budgets and past decisions.

oversight the effort by Congress, through hearings, investigations, and other techniques, to exercise control over the activities of executive agencies

Studies show that congressional committee and subcommittee hearings and meetings grew quite dramatically in the late 1960s and 1970s, as Congress tried to keep pace with the expansion of the executive branch; this growth was especially pronounced in the House, which conducts more total days of oversight hearings than the Senate.[72] However, concern has grown in recent years about failures of oversight.[73] There appears to be less **"police patrol" oversight**—regular or even preemptive

"police patrol" oversight regular or even preemptive congressional hearings on bureaucratic agency operations

"fire alarm" oversight episodic, as-needed congressional hearings on bureaucratic agency operations, usually prompted by media attention or advocacy group complaints

FOR CRITICAL ANALYSIS

What are some of the important topics on which Congress has held oversight hearings? What did Congress try to achieve by holding oversight hearings?

hearings on agency operations—and more **"fire alarm" oversight** prompted by media attention or advocacy group complaints. For example, consumer outrage prompted the House Oversight and Government Reform Committee's 2016 inquiry into a 500-percent price hike on EpiPens used to treat severe allergic reactions.[74] There are also more oversight hearings under divided government, when the executive branch and at least one chamber of Congress are controlled by different parties.[75] For example, the House select committee on Benghazi, the eighth committee in the Republican-led Congress to investigate the attack on the American mission in Benghazi, Libya, called former secretary of state Hillary Clinton to appear for a second time in 2015. Republican members of the committee questioned the former secretary for more than eight hours, while Democrats charged that the hearing was designed to harm Clinton's presidential campaign.[76] Some observers worry that the extreme partisan polarization of recent years has politicized oversight, with the hearings that do occur dismissed as partisan while other issues are ignored.[77]

Individual members of Congress can also carry out oversight inquiries. Such standard congressional "casework" can address significant questions of public

The most visible aspect of congressional oversight is the use of public hearings. Following the 2012 attack on the U.S. embassy in Benghazi, Libya, Congress held multiple highly publicized—and highly politicized—hearings to investigate the matter, focusing on the activities of former secretary of state Hillary Clinton.

responsibility even when they are motivated only by the demands of an individual constituent. Oversight also encompasses the communications between congressional staff and agency staff. In addition, Congress has created for itself three large agencies whose obligations are to engage in constant research on matters related to the executive branch. These are the General Accounting Office (GAO), the Congressional Research Service, and the Congressional Budget Office, each designed to give Congress information independent of the information it can get directly from the executive branch through hearings and other communications.[78] Another source of information for oversight is directly from citizens through the FOIA, which, as we have seen, gives ordinary citizens the right to gain access to agency files and agency data. Nevertheless, the information citizens gain through the FOIA can be made effective only through the institutionalized channels of congressional committees and, though rarely, through public interest litigation in the federal courts.

FOR CRITICAL ANALYSIS

Through elected officials (the president and Congress), the public can achieve some control over the bureaucracy. What are the relative advantages and disadvantages of presidential and congressional control of the bureaucracy?

Bureaucracy
WHAT DO WE WANT?

Americans' views about the federal government bureaucracy present something of a paradox. On the one hand, the public expresses dislike for "big government," exemplified by bureaucracy. From this perspective, the federal government is too large, inherently wasteful, and at odds with individual freedom. On the other hand, Americans support many government programs and have high expectations for government. Indeed, high expectations lead many Americans to blame bureaucrats when the country faces problems, such as the prolonged economic downturn of recent years. One consequence of these divergent views is that public discussion about bureaucracy is often high on emotion and short on facts. Another consequence can be that bureaucracies try to maximize one value but undermine others. As we saw in the chapter opener, the decision to switch the Flint water supply was made to save money, but it endangered the health of Flint residents.

Arguments contending that the federal government is too large ignore the fact that the number of government employees has not grown disproportionately large when compared with the size of the American workforce. Charges that government wastes the taxpayers' money must also be put into perspective. As we have seen in this chapter, outsourcing government activities to private contractors does not offer a remedy for wasteful spending. In fact, private firms may be more wasteful than the public sector unless there is strong government oversight of private activities. Finally, it is true that bureaucratic rules often limit the freedom of individuals and corporations. But the laws that bureaucracies implement were enacted by our elected representatives in Congress. They are, in fact, the product of our democratic political system. As these considerations suggest, building a bureaucracy that reflects American values is not a simple task. Adequate congressional oversight is one important part of the solution because a bureaucracy that is shielded from the public eye may wind up pursuing its own interests rather than those of the public. Even so, an administration whose every move is subject to intense public scrutiny may be hamstrung in its efforts to carry out the public interest. (The "**Who Participates?**" feature on the facing page shows the bureaucracy's response to public concerns about health care accessibility for veterans.) Finding the right balance between bureaucratic autonomy and public scrutiny is a central task of creating an effective government; it requires both presidential and congressional vigilance to build an effective and responsive bureaucracy.

The emergence of "big data" is likely to change the way bureaucracies operate in the future. The term *big data* refers to very large data sets that compile information on a wide range of topics including climate, traffic, and health, and the NSA's huge database of phone calls and use of social media. Big data have the potential to improve government performance by linking sources of information that were previously unconnected. They also will allow the government to analyze information that was stored as text or went uncollected. Advances in government's ability to implement programs in public health, food safety, and transportation are only the beginning of what big data promise. At the same time, however, big data pose a threat to individual privacy, as the revelations about the NSA's data suggest. As bureaucracies tap into the promise of big data to create more effective programs, a close public eye on the implications for the right to privacy will be needed. How might big data improve the government's delivery of services in the future? What additional safeguards might be needed to protect individuals' privacy?

Waiting for a Veterans Affairs Health Care Appointment

After media reports about excessive waits endured by veterans seeking health care appointments, and widespread fraud in reporting those wait times, Congress passed the 2014 Veterans Choice Act, which allows veterans to go to private doctors if they would otherwise have to wait more than 30 days to see a Veterans Affairs provider. This act was supplemented in 2017 by the website, Access to Care (accesstocare.va.gov), which reports wait times at veterans clinics around the country. The vast majority of veterans seeking health care appointments are now able to schedule one at their local VA within 30 days.

93%
195,604,902 total

Total appointments requested in 2017:
208,065,313

4%
7,306,571 total

1.4%
2,835,626 total

0.3%
545,582 total

Scheduled Within 30 days

Scheduled Within 31–60 days

Scheduled Within 61–90 days

Scheduled Within 90+ days

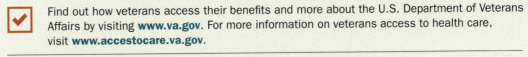

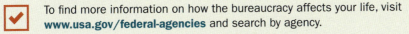

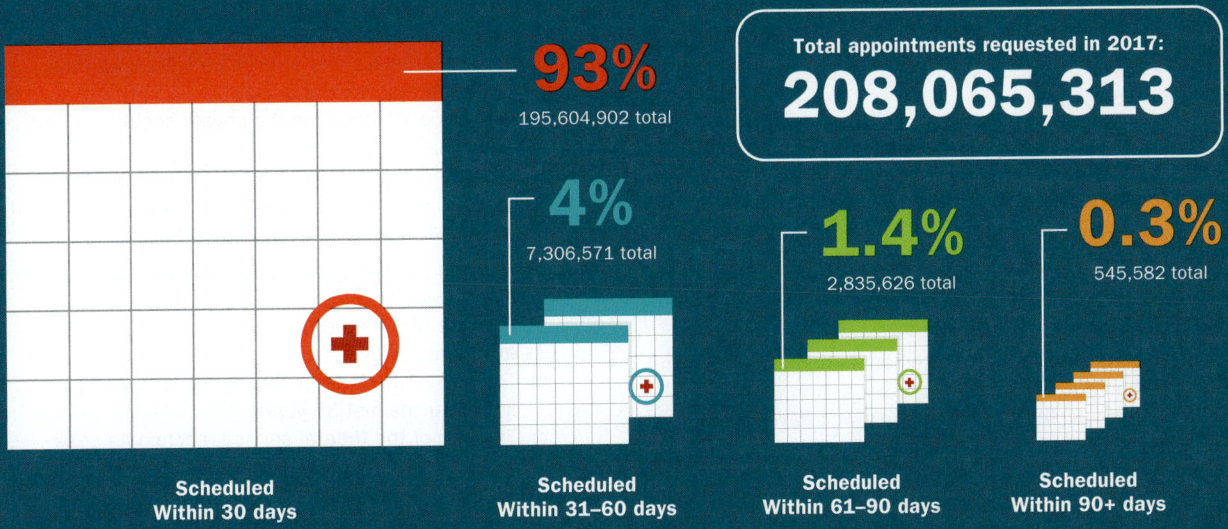

Note: Numbers may not add up to 100 percent due to rounding.

SOURCES: "Attempted Fix for VA Health Delays Creates New Bureaucracy," npr.org; Patient Access Data, www.va.gov (accessed 3/9/18).

★ WHAT YOU CAN DO ★

Ask Questions about Federal Agencies

- ☑ Find out how veterans access their benefits and more about the U.S. Department of Veterans Affairs by visiting **www.va.gov**. For more information on veterans access to health care, visit **www.accestocare.va.gov**.

- ☑ To find more information on how the bureaucracy affects your life, visit **www.usa.gov/federal-agencies** and search by agency.

- ☑ Ask a question about how federal agencies can help you. Most agencies have FAQ and contact pages on their websites.

STUDY GUIDE

Bureaucracy and Bureaucrats

Define bureaucracy, and describe the basic features of the executive branch (pp. 553–62)

Bureaucracy is defined as the complex structure of offices, tasks, and rules that private and public organizations use to coordinate the work of their personnel. The federal executive branch is composed of cabinet departments, independent agencies, government corporations, and independent regulatory commissions. Through their implementation, innovation, rule making, and enforcement decisions, the federal service touches on many important aspects of daily life.

Key Terms

bureaucracy (p. 553)
implementation (p. 553)
merit system (p. 556)
department (p. 559)
independent agency (p. 560)
government corporation (p. 561)

Practice Quiz

1. Which of the following statements about Congress and the bureaucracy is *not* true?
   a) Bureaucracies employ people who have much more specialized expertise in specific policy areas than do members of Congress.
   b) Members of Congress often prefer to delegate politically difficult decision-making to bureaucrats.
   c) While Congress is responsible for making laws, the bureaucracy is responsible for filling in the blanks by determining how the laws should be implemented.
   d) Congress banned rule making by the federal bureaucracy in 1995.
   e) Congress relies heavily on bureaucratic flexibility in implementing laws because updating legislation can take many years and bureaucrats can ensure that laws are administered in ways that take new conditions into account.

2. The Civil Service Act of 1883 required that appointees to positions within the federal bureaucracy
   a) pledge an oath of loyalty to the United States.
   b) register as independents rather than as members of an organized political party.
   c) be qualified for the job to which they were appointed.
   d) serve for no more than 10 years.
   e) serve for no fewer than 10 years.

3. Federal bureaucrats
   a) all work in Washington, D.C.
   b) are more likely to be female than private sector workers.
   c) are more racially and ethnically diverse than the private sector workforce.
   d) are less educated than the private sector workforce.
   e) are less likely to hold professional occupations in science, engineering, diplomacy, and other advanced fields than the private sector workforce.

4. Which of the following best describes the size of the federal service?
   a) The size of the federal service has grown exponentially over the last 35 years.
   b) The size of the federal service has changed very little over the last 35 years.
   c) The size of the federal service reached its peak in 1955 and has been dramatically declining ever since.
   d) The federal service has employed at least 15 percent of the American workforce every year since 1950.
   e) The federal service was eliminated during the 1990s in order to hire more state government employees.

5. Which of the following is an example of a government corporation?
   a) National Aeronautics and Space Administration
   b) Amtrak
   c) Federal Bureau of Investigation
   d) Environmental Protection Agency
   e) Department of Justice

Goals of the Federal Bureaucracy

Describe the major goals we expect federal agencies to promote (pp. 563–73)

The federal bureaucracy promotes public well-being through a diverse set of services, products, and regulations. Some federal agencies, such as the Department of Defense, the Department of Justice, and the Department of Homeland Security, protect the country against internal and external security threats. Other federal agencies, such as the Federal Reserve System and the Internal Revenue Service, promote the public's welfare by helping maintain a strong economy.

Key Terms

regulatory agency (p. 563)
fiscal policy (p. 571)
Federal Reserve System (p. 571)
revenue agency (p. 572)

Practice Quiz

6. A stable relationship between a bureaucratic agency, a clientele group, and a legislative committee is called
   a) a standing committee.
   b) a conference committee.
   c) a cabinet.
   d) an issue network.
   e) an iron triangle.

7. Americans refer to government policy about banks, credit, and currency as
   a) interstate commerce policy.
   b) deficit policy.
   c) fiscal policy.
   d) monetary policy.
   e) regulatory policy.

Can the Bureaucracy Be Reformed?

Evaluate some of the ways politicians have tried to make the bureaucracy more efficient (pp. 573–79)

Many Americans express frustration with the performance of the federal bureaucracy. As a result, politicians have frequently explored various methods of making the federal bureaucracy more efficient. In general, politicians have attempted to promote bureaucratic reform through reorganization, termination of programs, devolution, and privatization.

Key Terms

devolution (p. 576)
privatization (p. 577)

Practice Quiz

8. Which president instituted the bureaucratic reform of the National Performance Review?
   a) Richard Nixon
   b) Lyndon Johnson
   c) Jimmy Carter
   d) Bill Clinton
   e) George W. Bush

9. *Devolution* refers to
   a) the gradual decline in efficiency that always comes when government begins to implement a new program.
   b) moving all or part of a program from the public sector to the private sector.
   c) a policy of reducing or eliminating regulatory restraints on the conduct of individuals or private institutions.
   d) a policy to remove a program from one level of government by passing it down to a lower level of government.
   e) reducing the overall number of regulatory agencies in the federal bureaucracy.

10. Which of the following statements best describes termination of government programs?
    a) In the 12 years of the Reagan and George H. W. Bush administrations over 50 national government programs were terminated.
    b) In the 12 years of the Reagan and George H. W. Bush administrations over 100 national government programs were terminated.
    c) In the 12 years of the Reagan and George H. W. Bush administrations over 1,000 national government programs were terminated.
    d) The Supreme Court has ruled that government programs can only be terminated through a constitutional amendment.
    e) Terminating government programs is a difficult process that rarely occurs at the federal level.

11. Which of the following has been referred to as the "virtual fourth branch of government"?
    a) independent regulatory commissions
    b) government contracting
    c) the Government Accountability Office
    d) the Defense Base Closure and Realignment Commission
    e) the White House Office of Management and Budget

Managing the Bureaucracy

Explain why it is often difficult to control the bureaucracy (pp. 579–83)

The federal bureaucracy provides the expertise that is needed to implement the law. However, parts of the bureaucracy can also become entrenched organizations that serve their own interests rather than the public will. Presidents have several powerful tools at their disposal to exert administrative and political control over the federal bureaucracy, including high-level appointments and executive orders. Congress can also exert influence over bureaucratic behavior by enacting specific legislation and engaging in vigorous oversight.

Key Term

oversight (p. 581)

"police patrol" oversight (p. 581)

"fire alarm" oversight (p. 582)

Practice Quiz

12. The concept of *oversight* refers to the effort made by
    a) Congress to make executive agencies accountable for their actions.
    b) the president to make executive agencies accountable for their actions.
    c) the president to make Congress accountable for its actions.
    d) the courts to make executive agencies responsible for their actions.
    e) the states to make the executive branch accountable for its actions.

13. "Police patrol" oversight refers to
    a) hearings conducted by the FBI to investigate lawbreaking by members of Congress.
    b) any congressional hearings related to state or local law enforcement agencies.
    c) episodic, as-needed congressional hearings on bureaucratic agency operations, usually prompted by media attention or advocacy group complaints.
    d) regular or even preemptive congressional hearings on bureaucratic agency operations.
    e) any congressional hearings related to federal law enforcement agencies.

14. Which of the following agencies were created to give Congress independent information about matters related to the executive branch?
    a) Government Accountability Office, Congressional Research Service, Congressional Budget Office
    b) Department of Justice, Department of the Interior, Department of the Treasury
    c) Congressional Oversight Organization, Bureau of Government Performance, National Performance Review Association
    d) Office of Management and Budget, Council of Economic Advisers, Oversight and Government Reform
    e) Government Accountability Office, National Performance Review, Troubled Asset Relief Program

For Further Reading

Aberbach, Joel D., and Mark A. Peterson, eds. *Institutions of American Democracy: The Executive Branch*. Institutions of American Democracy Series. New York: Oxford University Press, 2006.

Arnold, Peri E. *Making the Managerial Presidency: Comprehensive Organization Planning.* Princeton, NJ: Princeton University Press, 1986.

DiIulio, John J., Jr. *Bring Back the Bureaucrats: Why More Federal Workers Will Lead to Better (and Smaller!) Government.* West Conshohocken, PA: Templeton Press, 2014.

Glennon, Michael J. *National Security and Double Government.* New York: Oxford University Press, 2015.

Gormley, William, and Stephen Balla. *Bureaucracy and Democracy: Accountability and Performance.* 3rd ed. Washington, DC: CQ Press, 2012.

Kettl, Donald F. *System under Stress: The Challenge to 21st Century Government.* 3rd ed. Los Angeles: Sage/CQ Press, 2014.

Kettl, Donald F., and James W. Fesler. *The Politics of the Administrative Process.* 4th ed. Washington, DC: CQ Press, 2008.

Light, Paul C. *A Government Ill Executed: The Decline of the Federal Service and How to Reverse It.* Cambridge, MA: Harvard University Press, 2008.

Moffitt, Susan. *Making Public Policy: Participatory Bureaucracy in American Democracy.* New York: Cambridge University Press, 2014.

Wilson, James Q. *Bureaucracy: What Government Agencies Do and Why They Do It.* New York: Basic Books, 1989.

Zegart, Amy B. *Spying Blind: The CIA, The FBI, and the Origins of 9/11.* Princeton, NJ: Princeton University Press, 2009.

Recommended Websites

Central Intelligence Agency
www.cia.gov
The Central Intelligence Agency (CIA) is one of several bureaucracies responsible for providing national security. A major problem facing this clandestine agency is how to provide security and meet the public's right to know what the government is doing. At the official website for the CIA, see what questions are often asked.

Department of Homeland Security
www.dhs.gov
The Department of Homeland Security was created after September 11 to promote bureaucratic communication and domestic security. See what the department is doing to protect America from foreign threats.

Federal Emergency Management Agency
www.fema.gov
In the aftermath of Hurricane Katrina, the Federal Emergency Management Agency (FEMA) became infamous for its role in the disaster relief efforts. View the disaster history of your state, and see what FEMA is currently doing to prevent disasters and assist Americans in need.

Office of Personnel Management
www.opm.gov/
OPM manages the federal government's civil service, listing federal jobs, conducting background and security checks, upholding the merit system, managing health and retirement benefits, and providing training and development programs for federal employees.

Official U.S. Executive Branch Websites
www.loc.gov/rr/news/fedgov.html
This resource page at the Library of Congress website provides links to every federal department, independent agency, and regulatory commission in the federal bureaucracy.

Project on Government Oversight
www.pogo.org
The Project on Government Oversight is an independent, nonprofit organization that seeks to make government more accountable by investigating corruption and misconduct. Originally set up to focus on the military, this organization now examines all types of government bureaucracies.

Reason Foundation
reason.org
The Reason Foundation is dedicated to promoting libertarian principles and limited government. Its website includes studies and opinion pieces on a range of policy issues, including many related to the size and effectiveness of the federal bureaucracy.

USAFacts
www.usafacts.org/
A project of former Microsoft CEO Steve Ballmer and Seattle design studio Artefact, USAFacts assembles and presents data from a variety of U.S. government jurisdictions in an accessible interface.

U.S. Agency for International Development
www.usaid.gov
In 1961 Congress created the U.S. Agency for International Development (USAID) to provide economic and social development assistance to foreign countries. Often criticized for promoting American values and foreign policy objectives, USAID is currently involved in numerous global issues.

★ chapter ★

15

The Federal Courts

WHAT GOVERNMENT DOES AND WHY IT MATTERS Mark Janus works for the Illinois Department of Healthcare and Family Services as a child support specialist. He is not a member of the union representing many public sector workers in the state, the American Federation of State, County, and Municipal Employees (AFSCME). Nonetheless, he is required to pay a "fair-share" fee to the union on the grounds that nonmembers benefit from the union's bargaining activities over issues such as pay and benefits. Nonmembers do not have to contribute to the union's political activities, such as endorsements of political candidates.[1]

Janus argues, however, that *all* activity that public sector unions engage in is inherently political. In particular, he disagrees with the union's bargaining for increased benefits when Illinois was facing a budget crisis due in part to mismanagement of the state pension program. "The union's fight is not my fight," he says. "For years it supported politicians who put the state into its current budget and pension crises. . . . That's not public service." He believes that being forced to pay a fee that supports the union's activities violates his First Amendment rights.

His case went to the Supreme Court, which heard oral arguments in February 2018. Janus's

Although the Supreme Court is often viewed as the least political of the three branches, its rulings touch on major political issues that affect Americans in many ways. Here, Mark Janus (left) celebrates with supporters after winning his Supreme Court case, which could have a profound effect on how unions operate.

lawsuit challenged a 1977 case, *Abood v. Detroit Board of Education*, in which the Court allowed state and local governments to require public employees to pay union fees, a practice in 22 states. The Court almost overturned *Abood* in 2015 in a case in which a California teacher sued the local teachers' union over such fees. But after Justice Antonin Scalia died in February 2016, the Court split 4–4 in the California case.[2]

After taking office in 2017, Trump nominated conservative appeals court judge Neil Gorsuch to the vacant seat. With the Gorsuch appointment, conservatives once again enjoyed a 5–4 Supreme Court majority. Perhaps not surprisingly, the Gorsuch appointment resulted in a conservative decision in *Janus v. AFSCME*, and Janus's First Amendment rights would be upheld. But union supporters say the decision will have devastating effects on public-sector unions' ability to protect workers, including female, African American, and Hispanic employees, who face a smaller gap in pay in union jobs compared to nonunion jobs, according to the Economic Policy Institute and the National Women's Law Center.[3]

For both Democrats and Republicans, the importance of the Supreme Court's 5–4 decision underscored the significance of President Trump's Supreme

Court appointments. Had Obama nominee Merrick Garland, rather than Trump nominee Neil Gorsuch, been seated on the High Court, the mandatory-dues requirement would likely have been upheld. With the *Janus* decision in mind, Democrats and Republicans prepared to redouble their efforts to win subsequent battles over judicial appointments, as President Trump announced the nomination of Brett Kavanaugh, another conservative judge, to take the place of Justice Anthony Kennedy, who announced his retirement in July 2018. After a divisive political battle, Kavanaugh was confirmed by the Senate and joined the Court in October.

Every year, nearly 25 million cases are tried in American courts. Cases can arise from disputes between citizens, from efforts by government agencies to punish wrongdoing, from citizens' efforts to prove that their rights have been infringed on as a result of government action—or inaction—and from efforts by interest groups to promote their agendas. Many critics of the U.S. legal system assert that Americans have become too litigious (ready to use the courts for all purposes). But the heavy use that Americans make of the courts is also an indication of the extent of conflict in American society. And given the existence of social conflict, it is far better that Americans seek to settle their differences through the courts than resort to violence or otherwise take matters into their own hands. The framers of the Constitution called the Supreme Court the "least dangerous branch" of American government. Today, though, it is not unusual to hear the Court described as an all-powerful "imperial judiciary." But before we can understand this transformation and its consequences, we must look in some detail at America's judicial process.

CHAPTER GOALS

- ★ **Identify the general types of cases and types of courts in our legal system (pp. 593–97)**
- ★ **Describe the different levels of federal courts and their functions (pp. 598–603)**
- ★ **Explain how the Supreme Court exercises the power of judicial review (pp. 604–10)**
- ★ **Describe the process the Supreme Court follows in the exercise of its power of judicial review (pp. 610–18)**
- ★ **Consider the personal and political influences on judges and the courts (pp. 618–24)**

The Legal System

Identify the general types of cases and types of courts in our legal system

Originally, a "court" was the place where a sovereign ruled—where the king or queen governed. Settling disputes between citizens was part of governing. In modern democracies, courts and judges have taken over the power to settle conflicts by hearing the facts on both sides and deciding which side possesses the greater merit. But since judges are not kings and queens, they must have a basis for their authority. That basis in the United States is the Constitution and the law. Courts decide cases by hearing the facts on both sides of a quarrel and applying the relevant law or principle to the facts. This can be a sensitive matter because courts have been given the authority to settle disputes not only between citizens but also between citizens and the government itself, where the courts are obliged to maintain the same neutrality and impartiality as they do in disputes involving two citizens. This is the essence of the "rule of law": that "the state" and its officials must be judged by the same laws as the citizenry.

CASES AND THE LAW

Court cases in the United States proceed under two broad categories of law: criminal law and civil law, each with myriad subdivisions.

Cases of **criminal law** are those in which the government charges an individual with violating a statute that has been enacted to protect public health, safety, morals, or welfare. In criminal cases, the government is always the **plaintiff** (the party that brings charges) and alleges that a criminal violation has been committed by a named **defendant**. Most criminal cases arise in state and municipal courts and involve matters ranging from traffic offenses to robbery and murder. Although the great bulk of criminal law is still a state matter, a large and growing body of federal criminal law deals with matters ranging from tax evasion and mail fraud to acts of terrorism and

criminal law the branch of law that regulates the conduct of individuals, defines crimes, and specifies punishment for proscribed conduct

plaintiff the individual or organization that brings a complaint in court

defendant the one against whom a complaint is brought in a criminal or civil case

In criminal cases, the government charges an individual with violating a statute protecting health, safety, morals, or welfare. Most such cases arise in state and municipal courts. Here, an Illinois county court hears testimony in a murder case.

the sale of narcotics. Defendants found guilty of criminal violations may be fined or sent to jail or prison.

civil law the branch of law that deals with disputes that do not involve criminal penalties

Cases of **civil law** involve disputes among individuals, groups, corporations, and other private entities or between such litigants and the government, in which no criminal violation is charged. Unlike in criminal cases, the losers in civil cases cannot be fined or incarcerated, although they may be required to pay monetary damages for their actions. The two most common types of civil cases involve contracts and torts. In a typical contract case, an individual or corporation charges that it has suffered because of another's violation of a specific agreement between the two. For example, the Smith Manufacturing Corporation may charge that Jones Distributors failed to honor an agreement to deliver raw materials at a specified time, causing Smith to lose business. Smith asks the court to order Jones to compensate it for the damage it allegedly suffered. In a typical tort case, one individual charges that he has been injured by another's negligence or malfeasance. Medical malpractice suits are one example of tort cases. Another important area of civil law is administrative law, which involves disputes over the jurisdiction, procedures, or authority of administrative agencies. A plaintiff may assert, for example, that an agency did not follow proper procedures when issuing new rules and regulations. A court will then examine the agency's conduct in light of the Administrative Procedure Act, the legislation that governs agency rule making.

precedent prior case whose principles are used by judges as the basis for their decision in a present case

In deciding cases, courts apply statutes (laws) and legal **precedents** (prior decisions). State and federal statutes, for example, often govern the conditions under which contracts are and are not legally binding. Jones Distributors might argue that it was not obliged to fulfill its contract with the Smith Manufacturing Corporation because actions by Smith, such as the failure to make promised payments, constituted fraud under state law. Precedents established in previous cases also guide courts' decisions in new cases. Attorneys for a physician being sued for malpractice might search for prior instances in which courts ruled that actions similar to those of their client did not constitute negligence. Such precedents are applied under the doctrine of **stare decisis**, a Latin phrase meaning "let the decision stand."

stare decisis literally, "let the decision stand"; the doctrine that a previous decision by a court applies as a precedent in similar cases until that decision is overruled

If a case involves the actions of the federal government or a state government, a court may also be asked to examine whether the government's conduct was consistent with the Constitution. In a criminal case, for example, defendants might assert that their constitutional rights were violated when the police searched their property. Similarly, in a civil case involving federal or state restrictions on land development, plaintiffs might assert that government actions violated the Fifth Amendment's prohibition against taking private property without just compensation. Thus, both civil and criminal cases may raise questions of constitutional law.

TYPES OF COURTS

In the United States, systems of courts have been established both by the federal government and by the governments of the individual states. Both systems have several levels, as shown in Figure 15.1. More than 97 percent of all court cases in the United States are heard in state courts. The overwhelming majority of criminal cases, for example, involve violations of state laws prohibiting such actions as murder, robbery, fraud, theft, and assault. If such a case is brought to trial, it will be heard at a state **trial court**, in front of a judge and sometimes a jury, who will determine whether the defendant violated state law. If the defendant is convicted, she may appeal the conviction to a higher court, such as a state **court of appeals**, and from there to a court

trial court the first court to hear a criminal or civil case

court of appeals a court that hears appeals of trial court decisions

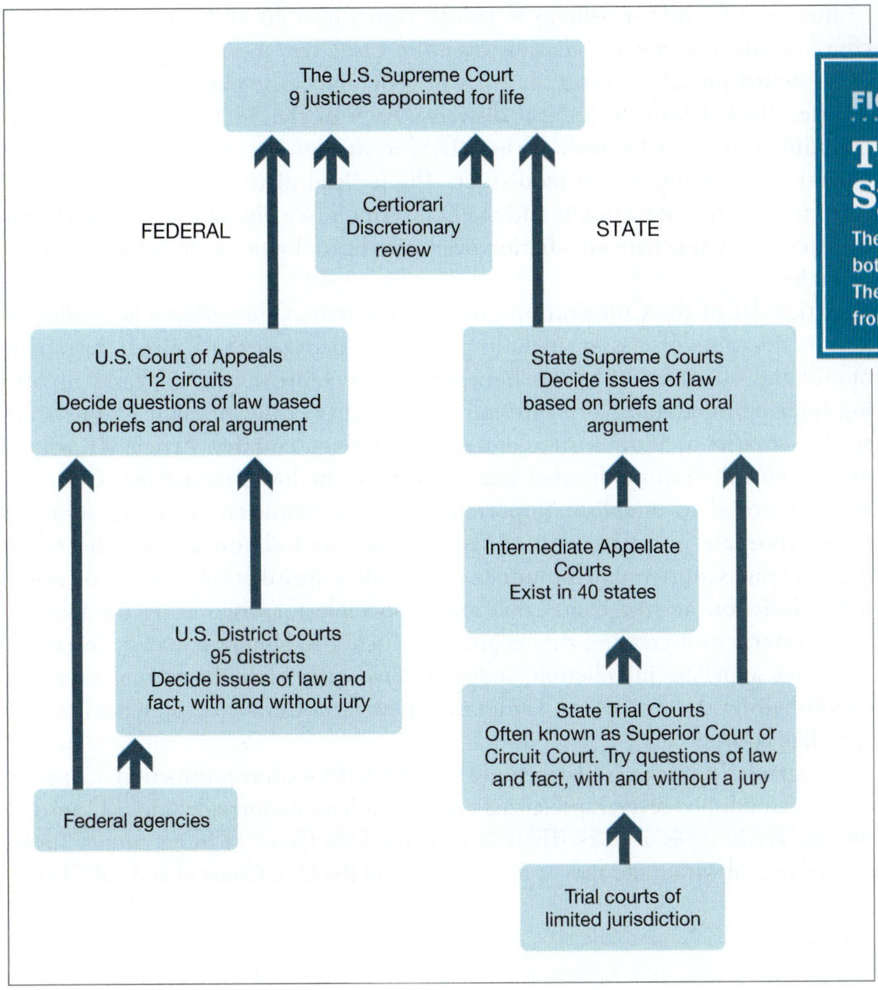

The U.S. Supreme Court
9 justices appointed for life
FEDERAL
Certiorari
Discretionary
review
STATE
U.S. Court of Appeals
12 circuits
Decide questions of law based on briefs and oral argument
State Supreme Courts
Decide issues of law based on briefs and oral argument
Intermediate Appellate Courts
Exist in 40 states
U.S. District Courts
95 districts
Decide issues of law and fact, with and without jury
State Trial Courts
Often known as Superior Court or Circuit Court. Try questions of law and fact, with and without a jury
Federal agencies
Trial courts of limited jurisdiction

FIGURE 15.1

The U.S. Court System

The state and federal court systems both include several types of courts. The Supreme Court hears appeals from both systems.

of last resort, usually called the state's **supreme court**. The government is not entitled to appeal if the defendant is found not guilty in a criminal case.

The party filing an appeal, known as an *appellant*, usually must show that the trial court made a legal error in deciding the case. Appeals courts do not hear witnesses or examine additional evidence and will consider new facts only under unusual circumstances. Thus, for example, a physician who loses a malpractice case might appeal on the basis that the trial court misapplied the relevant law or incorrectly instructed the jury. It should be noted that in both criminal and civil matters most cases are settled before trial through negotiated agreements between the parties. In criminal cases these agreements are called **plea bargains.**

Cases are heard in the federal courts if they involve federal laws, treaties with other nations, or the U.S. Constitution; these areas are the official **jurisdiction** of the federal courts. In addition, any case in which the U.S. government is a party is heard in the federal courts. If, for example, an individual is charged with violating a federal criminal statute, such as evading the payment of income taxes, charges are brought before a federal judge by a federal prosecutor. Civil cases involving the citizens of more than one state and in which more than $75,000 is at stake may be heard in either the federal or the state courts, usually depending on the preference of the plaintiff.

supreme court the highest court in a particular state or in the United States; this court primarily serves an appellate function

plea bargain a negotiated agreement in a criminal case in which a defendant agrees to plead guilty in return for the state's agreement to reduce the severity of the criminal charge or prison sentence the defendant is facing

jurisdiction the sphere of a court's power and authority

But even if a matter belongs in federal court, how do we know which federal court should exercise jurisdiction over the case? For the most part, Congress has assigned jurisdictions on the basis of geography. The nation is currently, by statute, divided into 94 judicial districts. Each of the 94 U.S. district courts, including one court for each of three U.S. territories, exercises jurisdiction over federal cases arising within its district. The judicial districts are, in turn, organized into 11 regional circuits and the D.C. circuit (see Figure 15.2). Each circuit court exercises appellate jurisdiction over cases heard by the district courts within its region.

original jurisdiction the authority to initially consider a case; distinguished from appellate jurisdiction, which is the authority to hear appeals from a lower court's decision

Article III of the Constitution gives the Supreme Court **original jurisdiction** in a limited variety of classes, including (1) cases between the United States and one of the 50 states, (2) cases between two or more states, (3) cases involving foreign ambassadors or other ministers, and (4) cases brought by one state against citizens of another state or against a foreign country. Article III assigns original jurisdiction in all other federal cases to the lower courts that Congress was authorized to establish. Importantly, the Constitution gives the Supreme Court appellate jurisdiction in all federal cases, and almost all cases heard by the Supreme Court today are under its appellate jurisdiction. Courts of original jurisdiction are the courts that are responsible for discovering the facts in a controversy and creating the record on which a judgment is based. In courts that have appellate jurisdiction, judges receive cases after the factual record is established by the trial court. Ordinarily, new facts cannot be presented before appellate courts.

Geography, however, is not the only basis for federal court jurisdiction. Congress has also established several specialized courts that have nationwide original jurisdiction in certain types of cases. These include the U.S. Court of International Trade, created to deal with trade and customs issues; and the U.S. Court of Federal Claims,

FIGURE 15.2

Federal Appellate Court Circuits

The 94 federal district courts are organized into 12 regional circuits: the 11 shown here, plus the District of Columbia, which has its own circuit. Each circuit court hears appeals from lower federal courts within the circuit. A thirteenth federal circuit court, the U.S. Court of Appeals for the Federal Circuit, hears appeals from a number of specialized courts such as the U.S. Court of Federal Claims.

SOURCE: www.uscourts.gov/court_locator.aspx (accessed 7/27/10).

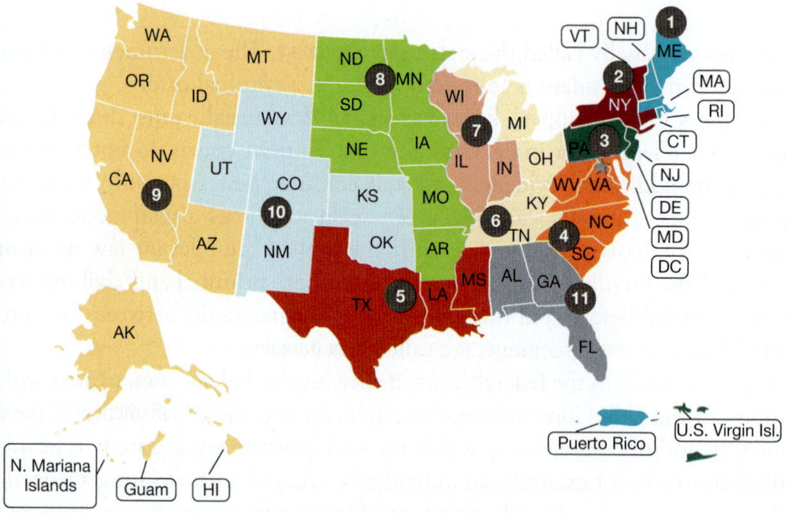

which handles damage suits against the United States. Congress has also established a court with nationwide appellate jurisdiction, the U.S. Court of Appeals for the Federal Circuit, which hears appeals involving patent law and those arising from the decisions of the trade and claims courts. Other federal courts assigned specialized jurisdictions by Congress include the U.S. Court of Appeals for Veterans Claims, which exercises exclusive jurisdiction over cases involving veterans' claims, and the U.S. Court of Military Appeals, which deals with questions of law arising from trials by court-martial.

With the exception of the claims court and the Court of Appeals for the Federal Circuit, these specialized courts were created by Congress on the basis of the powers the legislature exercises under Article I, rather than Article III, of the Constitution. Article III is designed to protect judges from political pressure by granting them life tenure and prohibiting reduction of their salaries while they serve. The judges of Article I courts, by contrast, are appointed by the president for fixed terms of 15 years and are not protected by the Constitution from salary reduction. As a result, these "legislative courts" are generally viewed as less independent than the courts established under Article III of the Constitution. The three territorial courts (for Guam, the U.S. Virgin Islands, and the Northern Mariana Islands) were also established under the provisions in Article I, and their judges are appointed for 10-year terms.

The appellate jurisdiction of the federal courts extends to cases originating in the state courts. In both civil and criminal cases, a decision of the highest state court can be appealed to the U.S. Supreme Court by raising a federal issue. A defendant who appeals a lower-court decision in federal court might assert, for example, that he or she was denied the right to counsel or was otherwise deprived of the **due process of law** guaranteed by the federal Constitution or that important issues of federal law were at stake in the case. The U.S. Supreme Court is not obligated to accept such appeals and will do so only if it believes that the matter has considerable national significance. In addition, in criminal cases, defendants who have been convicted in a state court may request a **writ of habeas corpus** from a federal district court. Sometimes known as the "Great Writ," habeas corpus is a court order to the authorities to show cause for a prisoner's incarceration. The court will then evaluate the sufficiency of the cause and may order the release of a prisoner deemed to be held in violation of her legal rights. In 1867 its distrust of southern courts led Congress to authorize federal district judges to issue such writs to prisoners who they believed had been deprived of constitutional rights in state court. Generally speaking, state defendants seeking a federal writ of habeas corpus must show that they have exhausted all available state remedies and must raise issues not previously raised in their state appeals. Federal courts of appeals and, ultimately, the U.S. Supreme Court have appellate jurisdiction for federal district court habeas decisions.

due process of law the right of every individual against arbitrary action by national or state governments

writ of habeas corpus a court order that the individual in custody be brought into court and shown the cause for detention; habeas corpus is guaranteed by the Constitution and can be suspended only in cases of rebellion or invasion

Although the federal courts hear only a small fraction of all the civil and criminal cases decided each year in the United States, their decisions are extremely important. It is in the federal courts that the Constitution and federal laws that govern all Americans are interpreted and their meaning and significance established. Moreover, it is in the federal courts that the powers and limitations of the increasingly powerful national government are tested. Finally, through their power to review the decisions of the state courts, it is ultimately the federal courts that dominate the American judicial system.

Federal Courts

Describe the different levels of federal courts and their functions

During the year ending in March 2017, federal district courts (the lowest federal level) received 362,628 cases. Though large, this number is less than 1 percent of the number of cases heard by state courts (see Figure 15.3). The federal courts of appeal listened to 58,951 cases during the same period. Generally, about 15 percent of the verdicts rendered by the lower courts are appealed to the U.S. Supreme Court. Most of the 9,000 or so cases filed with the Supreme Court each year are dismissed without a ruling on their merits. The Court has broad latitude to decide what cases it will hear and generally listens to

FIGURE 15.3

Caseloads of American Courts

This figure shows the total incoming caseloads of U.S. courts in 2016 (the most recent year for which complete state court data are available is 2010). More than 97 percent of the cases heard in American courts every year are heard in state courts. At both the federal and the state levels, lower-court decisions can be appealed to the appropriate court of appeals. Why do you think a larger percentage of federal district court decisions are appealed compared with state trial court decisions?

SOURCES: Court Statistics Project, National Center for State Courts, www.courtstatistics.org/; Supreme Court, 2017 Year-End Report on the Federal Judiciary, www.supremecourt.gov/publicinfo/year-end/2017year-endreport.pdf White House Office of Management and Budget, Historical Tables, Table 3.1, https://www.whitehouse.gov/omb/historical-tables/ (accessed 7/20/18).

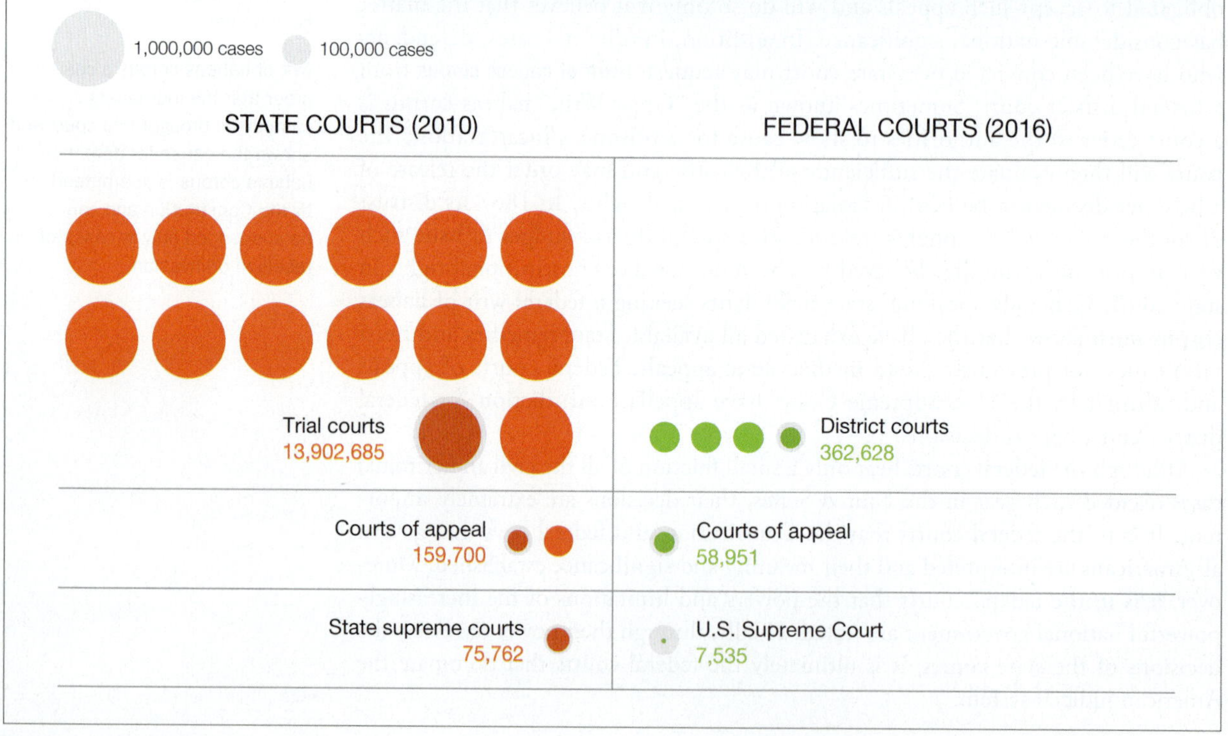

only those cases it deems raise the most important issues. In recent years, fewer than 80 cases per year have received full-dress Supreme Court reviews.[4]

FEDERAL TRIAL COURTS

Most of the cases of original federal jurisdiction are handled by the federal district courts. Although the Constitution gives the Supreme Court original jurisdiction in several types of cases, such as those affecting ambassadors and those in which a state is one of the parties, most original jurisdiction goes to the lowest courts—the trial courts.

Congress has authorized the appointment of 678 federal district judges to staff the 94 federal district courts. At any given time, some of these positions may be vacant and awaiting the appointment of new judges. District judges are assigned to district courts according to the workload; the busiest of these courts may have as many as 28 judges. Only one judge is assigned to each case, except where statutes provide for three-judge courts to deal with special issues. The routines and procedures of the federal district courts are essentially the same as those of the state trial courts except that federal procedural requirements tend to be stricter. States, for example, do not have to provide a grand jury, a 12-member trial jury, or a unanimous jury verdict. Federal courts must follow all these procedures.

FEDERAL APPELLATE COURTS

Roughly 20 percent of all lower-court cases, along with appeals from some federal agency decisions, are subsequently reviewed by federal appeals courts. As noted earlier, the country is divided geographically into 11 regional circuits and the D.C. circuit, each of which has a U.S. Court of Appeals. A thirteenth appellate court, the U.S. Court of Appeals for the Federal Circuit, has a subject matter, rather than a geographical, jurisdiction. Congress has authorized the appointment of 179 court of appeals judges, though, as in the case of the district courts, some spots may be vacant at any given point in time.

Except for cases selected for review by the Supreme Court, decisions made by the appeals courts are final. Because of this finality, certain safeguards have been built into the system. The most important is the provision of more than one judge for every appeals case. Each court of appeals has from 6 to 28 permanent judgeships, depending on the workload of the circuit. Although normally three judges hear appealed cases, in some instances a larger number of judges sit together en banc.

Another safeguard is provided by the assignment of a Supreme Court justice as the circuit justice for each of the 12 circuits. The circuit justice deals with requests for special action by the Supreme Court. The most frequent and best-known action of circuit justices is that of reviewing requests for stays of execution when the full Court is unable to do so—primarily during the summer, when the Court is in recess.

THE SUPREME COURT

The Supreme Court is America's highest court. Article III of the Constitution vests "the judicial power of the United States" in the Supreme Court, and this court is supreme in fact as well as form. The Supreme Court is the only federal court established by the Constitution. The lower federal courts are created by statute and can be restructured or, presumably, even abolished by the Congress. The Supreme Court

chief justice justice on the Supreme Court who presides over the Court's public sessions and whose official title is "chief justice of the United States"

is made up of the chief justice of the United States and eight associate justices. The **chief justice** presides over the Court's public sessions and conferences and is always the first to speak and vote when the justices deliberate; voting then proceeds in order of seniority. In the Court's actual deliberations and decisions, the chief justice has no more authority than his colleagues. Each justice casts one vote. In addition, if the chief justice has voted with the majority, she decides which of the justices will write the formal opinion for the Court. The character of the opinion can be an important means of influencing the evolution of the law beyond the mere affirmation or denial of the appeal on hand. To some extent, the influence of the chief justice is a function of her own leadership ability. Some chief justices, such as the late Earl Warren, have been able to lead the Court in a new direction. In other instances, forceful associate justices, such as the late Felix Frankfurter or William Brennan, are the dominant figures on the Court.

The Constitution does not specify the number of justices who should sit on the Supreme Court; Congress has the authority to change the Court's size. In the early nineteenth century, there were six Supreme Court justices; later there were seven. Congress set the number of justices at nine in 1869, and the Court has remained that size ever since.

HOW JUDGES ARE APPOINTED

Federal judges are nominated by the president and confirmed by the Senate. They are generally selected from among the more prominent or politically active members of the legal profession. Many federal judges previously served as state court judges or state or local prosecutors.

There are no formal qualifications for service as a federal judge. In general, presidents endeavor to appoint judges who possess legal experience and good character and whose partisan and ideological views are similar to their own. Once the president has formally nominated an individual, the nominee must be considered by the Senate Judiciary Committee and confirmed by a majority vote in the full Senate. In recent years, a good deal of partisan conflict has surrounded judicial appointments. Senate Democrats have sought to prevent Republican presidents from appointing conservative judges, while Senate Republicans have worked to prevent Democratic presidents from appointing liberal judges. During the early months of the Obama administration, Republicans were able to slow the judicial appointment process through filibusters and other procedural maneuvers so that only 3 of the president's 23 nominations for federal judgeships were confirmed by the Senate.[5] Some of Obama's allies urged the president to take a more aggressive stance or risk allowing Republicans to block what had been considered a key Democratic priority. In November 2013 the Senate voted 52 to 48 to end the use of the filibuster against all executive branch and judicial nominees except those to the Supreme Court, allowing President Obama to quickly secure the appointment of more than 300 new district court judges and 55 new appeals court judges.

In 2017, as we saw earlier, Republicans turned the tables and extended these rule changes to include Supreme Court nominees, thus blocking Democratic efforts to prevent President Trump from appointing Neil Gorsuch to the High Court. In July 2018, Justice Anthony Kennedy, who had been a swing vote on the Court, announced his resignation. President Trump nominated Judge Brett Kavanaugh to replace Kennedy. Kavanaugh was generally seen as a conservative in the Gorsuch mold. Liberal groups promised an all-out fight to block the nomination but, with Republican control of the Senate and the elimination of filibusters on judicial appointments, there was little chance Democrats could derail the Kavanaugh appointment.

Senate Republicans' strategy to not take up Obama's nomination of Merrick Garland, and to eliminate filibusters on Supreme Court nominations, paid off when President Trump nominated Neil Gorsuch in 2017. Gorsuch was confirmed in a 54-to-45 vote, with several Senate Democrats voting for the Republican nominee.

Supreme Court Appointments While political factors play an important role in the selection of district and appellate court judges, they are decisive when it comes to Supreme Court appointments. Because the high court has so much influence over American law and politics, virtually all presidents have made an effort to select justices who share their political philosophies.

Five of the nine current justices, as of October 2018, were appointed by Republican presidents (Table 15.1). With the exception of the months between the passing of Antonin Scalia in February 2016 and the confirmation of Neil Gorsuch in April 2017, the Court has had a conservative majority for 46 years, most recently consisting of Chief Justice Roberts and justices Alito, Thomas, Gorsuch, and Kavanaugh. As we saw in earlier chapters, this majority propelled the Court in a more conservative direction in a variety of areas, including civil rights (Chapter 5) and election law (Chapter 10).

In recent decades, Supreme Court nominations have come to involve intense partisan struggle. Typically, after the president has named a nominee, interest

TABLE 15.1

Supreme Court Justices, 2019* (in Order of Seniority)

NAME	YEAR OF BIRTH	LAW SCHOOL ATTENDED	PRIOR EXPERIENCE	APPOINTED BY	YEAR OF APPOINTMENT
Clarence Thomas	1948	Yale	Federal judge	G. H. W. Bush	1991
Ruth Bader Ginsburg	1933	Columbia	Federal judge	Clinton	1993
Stephen Breyer	1938	Harvard	Federal judge	Clinton	1994
John Roberts, Jr. *(Chief Justice)*	1955	Harvard	Federal judge	G. W. Bush	2005
Samuel Alito	1950	Yale	Federal judge	G. W. Bush	2006
Sonia Sotomayor	1954	Yale	Federal judge	Obama	2009
Elena Kagan	1960	Harvard	Solicitor general	Obama	2010
Neil Gorsuch	1967	Harvard	Federal judge	Trump	2017
Brett Kavanaugh	1965	Yale	Federal judge	Trump	2018

*As of October 2018

After Justice Anthony Kennedy announced his retirement in 2018, Trump nominated Brett Kavanaugh to the Supreme Court. After a contentious confirmation process, Kavanaugh took his seat on the Court. Many feel that Kavanaugh will shift the Court in a more conservative direction.

groups opposed to the nomination mobilize opposition in the media, among the public, and in the Senate. One bitter struggle occurred in 1987 when President Ronald Reagan nominated Robert Bork to the Supreme Court. Bork had been a Yale law professor, a federal judge, and Solicitor General of the United States. Despite this distinguished record, liberal political forces were very concerned about Bork's conservative views and angrily recalled that it was Bork who, as Solicitor General, had done Richard Nixon's bidding and fired the Watergate special prosecutor in what went down in history as the "Saturday Night Massacre." Senate Democrats subjected Bork to a relentless grilling, using excerpts from his speeches, writings, and judicial opinions to paint him as a right-wing extremist. The Bork nomination was defeated, and this type of attack came to be known as "borking" a nominee.

The next year, when President George H. W. Bush proposed the conservative judge Clarence Thomas for the Court, liberal groups launched a campaign to discredit Thomas, promising to bork him as well. After extensive research into his background, opponents of the nomination were able to produce evidence suggesting that Thomas had sexually harassed a former subordinate, Anita Hill. Thomas denied the charge. After contentious Senate Judiciary Committee hearings, highlighted by testimony from both Thomas and Hill, Thomas narrowly won confirmation.

Republicans severely criticized Obama's nomination of Sonia Sotomayor in 2009 and Elena Kagan in 2010, though both were ultimately confirmed by the Senate. In 2016, however, the death of conservative justice Antonin Scalia gave President Obama an opportunity to replace Scalia with a more liberal jurist, and Obama named Judge Merrick Garland. Republicans held a majority in the Senate and, as we saw earlier, refused to act on Garland. In 2017 newly elected President Trump secured the appointment of a conservative jurist, Neil Gorsuch.

Senate Democrats vowed to filibuster the Gorsuch appointment. Republicans, however, used their Senate majority to change the rules and prevent such a filibuster. In so doing, the GOP followed and extended a playbook that had been developed by the Democrats when they held a Senate majority. In 2018, President Trump nominated Judge Brett Kavanaugh to replace retiring Justice Anthony Kennedy. Kavanaugh promised to push the Court a bit further to the political right.

The Kavanaugh nomination touched off one of the most intense political struggles in recent American history. Days before the Senate was to vote, Christine Blasey Ford, who had known Kavanaugh in high school, came forward to assert that the judge had attempted to sexually assault her 36 years ago when he was 17 and she was 15. Kavanaugh vehemently denied the accusation as well as accusations of sexual impropriety by two other women who had known him in college. Televised testimony before the Senate Judiciary Committee by Kavanaugh and Ford divided the Senate and the nation, primarily along partisan lines. Democrats argued that Kavanaugh was unfit to serve on the Court while Republicans asserted that the charges against Kavanaugh had been invented for political reasons. An FBI investigation failed to shed light on the allegations, and Kavanaugh was confirmed, receiving the votes of all but one Republican and only one Democrat.[6]

Vho Are Federal Judges?

e factor among many that presidents may take into account when selecting judicial nominees is diversity. The number Supreme Court justices is relatively small, so it is easy to count the number of African Americans who have served as preme Court justices (2), female justices (4), and Hispanic justices (1). How diverse is the rest of the federal judiciary? e first section below shows the racial, ethnic, and gender composition of the lower federal courts.

ederal Judges in 2018,* by Race and Gender

*As of March 2018

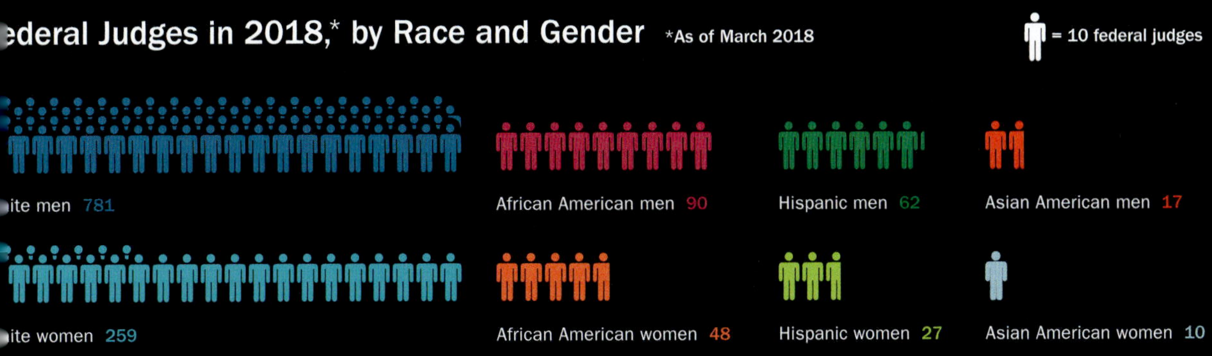

ppointments to Federal Courts, by Administration

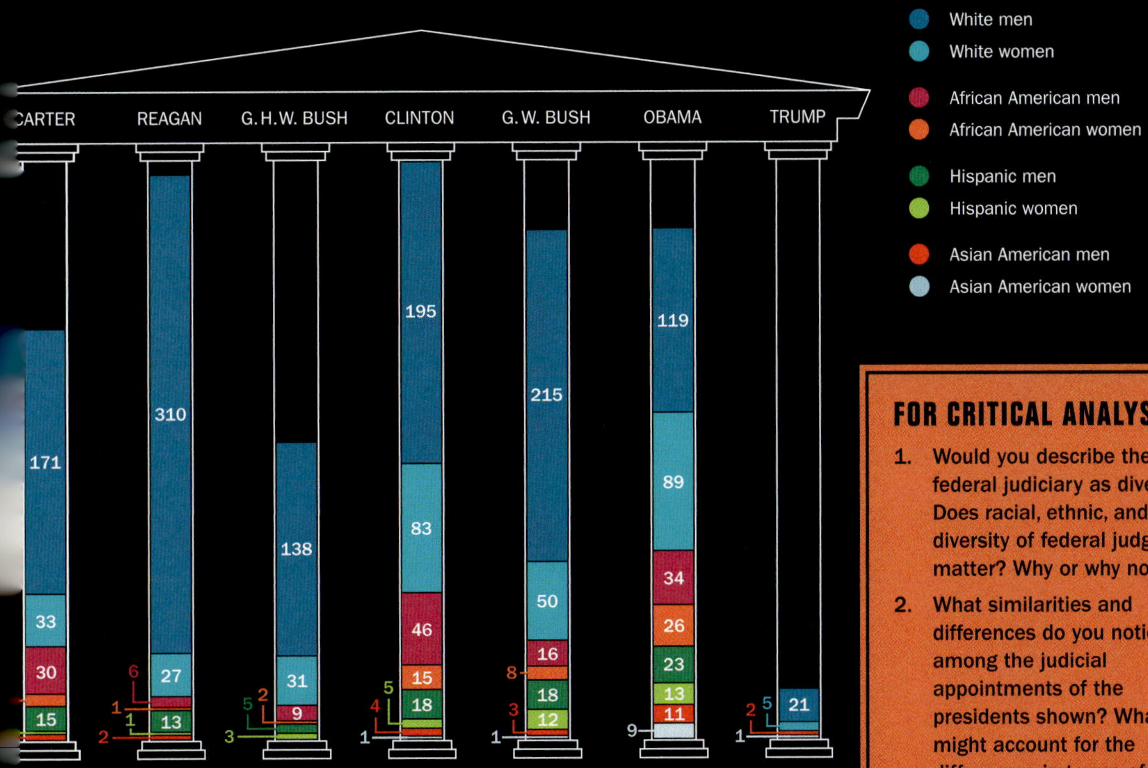

JRCE: Federal Judicial Center, www.fjc.gov/, (accessed 3/6/18).

FOR CRITICAL ANALYSIS

1. Would you describe the federal judiciary as diverse? Does racial, ethnic, and gender diversity of federal judges matter? Why or why not?
2. What similarities and differences do you notice among the judicial appointments of the presidents shown? What might account for the differences in terms of the diversity of their appointees?

The Power of the Supreme Court: Judicial Review

judicial review the power of the courts to review and, if necessary, declare actions of the legislative and executive branches invalid or unconstitutional; the Supreme Court asserted this power in *Marbury v. Madison* (1803)

Explain how the Supreme Court exercises the power of judicial review

The term **judicial review** refers to the power of the judiciary to examine and, if necessary, invalidate actions undertaken by the legislative and executive branches if it finds them unconstitutional. The term is sometimes also used to describe the scrutiny that appellate courts give to the actions of trial courts, but, strictly speaking, this is an improper use. A higher court's examination of a lower court's decisions might be called "appellate review," but it is not judicial review.

JUDICIAL REVIEW OF ACTS OF CONGRESS

Because the Constitution does not give the Supreme Court the power of judicial review over congressional enactments, the Court's exercise of it seems like something of a usurpation. Judicial review was discussed at the Constitutional Convention. Some delegates expected the courts to exercise this power, while many others were "departmentalists," believing that each branch of the new government would interpret the Constitution as it applied to its own actions, with the judiciary mainly ensuring that individuals did not suffer injustices.

Ambiguity over the framers' intentions was settled in 1803 in the case of *Marbury v. Madison*.[7] This case arose after Thomas Jefferson replaced John Adams in the White House. Jefferson's secretary of state, James Madison, refused to deliver an official commission to William Marbury, who had been appointed to a minor office by Adams and approved by the Senate just before Adams left the presidency. Marbury petitioned the Supreme Court to order Madison to deliver the commission. Jefferson and his followers did not believe that the Court had the power to undertake such an action and might have resisted the order. Chief Justice John Marshall was determined to assert the power of the judiciary but knew he must avoid a direct confrontation with the president. Accordingly, Marshall turned down Marbury's petition but gave as his reason the unconstitutionality of the legislation upon which Marbury had based his claim. Thus, Marshall asserted the power of judicial review but did so in a way that would not provoke a battle with Jefferson. The Supreme Court's decision in this case established the power of judicial review:

> It is emphatically the province and duty of the Judicial Department [the judicial branch] to say what the law is. Those who apply the rule to particular cases must, of necessity, expound and interpret that rule. If two laws conflict with each other, the Courts must decide on the operation of each.... So, if a law [e.g., a statute or treaty] be in opposition to the Constitution, if both the law and the Constitution apply to a particular case, so that the Court must either decide that case conformably to the law, disregarding the Constitution, or conformably to the Constitution, disregarding the law, the Court must determine which of these conflicting rules governs the case. This is of the very essence of judicial duty.

The Court's legal power to review acts of Congress has not been seriously questioned since 1803. One reason for that is that the Supreme Court makes a self-conscious effort to give acts of Congress an interpretation that will make them constitutional.

For example, in its 2012 decision upholding the constitutionality of the Affordable Care Act, the Court agreed with the many legal scholars who had argued that the Congress had no power under the Constitution's commerce clause to order Americans to purchase health insurance. But, rather than invalidate the act, the Court declared that the law's requirement that all Americans purchase insurance was actually a tax and, thus, represented a constitutionally acceptable use of Congress's power to levy taxes.[8]

In more than two centuries, the Court has concluded that fewer than 160 acts of Congress directly violated the Constitution.[9] These cases are often highly controversial. For example, in 2007 and 2014, the high court struck down key portions of the Bipartisan Campaign Reform Act, through which Congress had sought to regulate spending in political campaigns.[10] The Court found that provisions of the act limiting political advertising violated the First Amendment. And as we saw in Chapter 4 with the 2017 case of *Matal v. Tam*, the Court also cited free speech concerns in striking down a federal law that prohibited trademarks that disparaged people or groups. The decision was cheered by fans of the Washington Redskins football team. These cases are important but unusual in that the Court rarely overturns acts of Congress.

JUDICIAL REVIEW OF STATE ACTIONS

The power of the Supreme Court to review state legislation or other state action and to determine its constitutionality is neither granted by the Constitution nor inherent in the federal system. But the logic of the **supremacy clause** of Article VI of the Constitution, which declares the Constitution itself and laws made under its authority to be the supreme law of the land, is very strong. Furthermore, in the Judiciary Act of 1789, Congress conferred on the Supreme Court the power to reverse state constitutions and laws whenever they are clearly in conflict with the U.S. Constitution, federal laws, or treaties.[11] This power gives the Supreme Court appellate jurisdiction over all the millions of cases that American courts handle each year.

supremacy clause Article VI of the Constitution, which states that laws passed by the national government and all treaties are the supreme law of the land and superior to all laws adopted by any state or any subdivision

The supremacy clause of the Constitution not only established the federal Constitution, statutes, and treaties as the "supreme Law of the Land" but also provided that "the Judges in every State shall be bound thereby, any Thing in the Constitution or Laws of the State to the Contrary notwithstanding." Under this authority, the Supreme Court has frequently overturned state constitutional provisions or statutes, state court decisions, and local ordinances it deems to contravene rights or privileges guaranteed under the federal Constitution or federal statutes.

The civil rights arena abounds with examples of state laws that the Supreme Court has overturned because the statutes violated guarantees of due process and equal protection contained in the Fourteenth Amendment to the Constitution. For example, in the 1954 case of *Brown v. Board of Education*, the Court overturned statutes from Kansas, South Carolina, Virginia, and Delaware that either required or permitted segregated public schools, ruling that such statutes denied black schoolchildren equal protection under the law.[12] In 2003 the Court ruled that Texas's law criminalizing sodomy violated the right to liberty protected by the due process clause.[13] In the 2017 case of *Pavan v. Smith*, the Court overturned an Arkansas law that denied same-sex couples the right to include a spouse's name on a birth certificate—a right granted to other couples. The Court said the statute denied same-sex couples equal protection of the law.[14]

AMERICA SIDE by SIDE

Term Limits for High Court Justices

Once appointed, Supreme Court justices "shall hold their Offices during good Behaviour,"[a] which has effectively meant they serve for life. Only once (in 1804) has the Senate started impeachment proceedings against a Supreme Court justice, and this judge was ultimately acquitted.[b]

While the founding fathers may have created life terms with the intention of preserving judicial independence and isolating justices from partisan pressures, the life term limits may have created other political problems. Scholars point out that the extreme partisan nature and tensions that emerge during Supreme Court appointment hearings (as described in this chapter) may be due to the life term rule.[c] After all, appointing a justice favorable to your partisan position is considered a major political coup given that the average Supreme Court justice serves over 25 years.

Constitutional courts (courts with the power of judicial review) aim to preserve judicial independence as they play an important role in guaranteeing democracy by checking executive overreach. Other countries, however, have sought to balance this with the need of also having a more dynamic and changing court. Canada, for instance, sets a mandatory retirement age of 75 for their Supreme Court justices. Other countries have set term limits so that justices serve one long, non-renewable term. This system insulates justices from political pressures yet still promotes judicial turnover. If the United States used the same rules as Germany (see below), only 3 of the 9 current justices—Sotomayor, Kagan, and the recently appointed Gorsuch—would still be on the court.

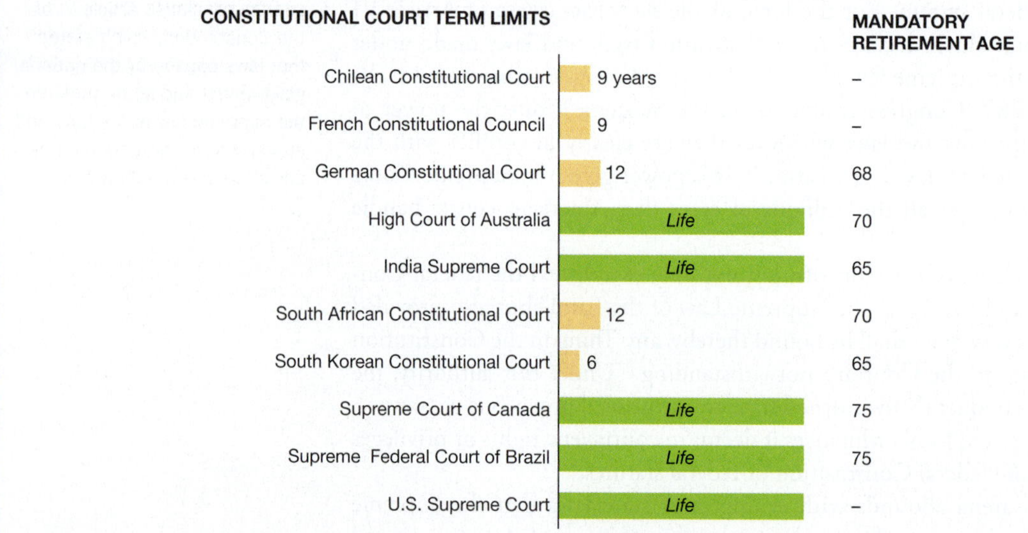

SOURCE: Central Intelligence Agency, "Judicial Branch," The World Factbook, https://www.cia.gov/index.html (accessed 4/15/18).

[a] U.S. Constitution, Article III, Section 1.

[b] U.S. Senate, "Senate Prepares for Impeachment Trial," www.senate.gov/artandhistory/history/minute/Senate_Tries_Justice.htm (accessed 4/15/18).

[c] Steven G. Calabresi and James Lindgren, "Term Limits for the Supreme Court: Life Tenure Reconsidered," *Harvard Journal of Law & Public Policy*, 29, no. 3 (2005): 769–878.

State statutes in other areas of law are equally subject to challenge. Many of the Supreme Court's recent decisions overturning state law have come in cases concerning election law. In 2015, for example, the Court ruled against an Alabama legislative districting plan that opponents charged was designed to reduce the influence of black voters.[15] During the same year the Court ruled against an effort by the Arizona legislature to invalidate a districting plan drawn up by an independent commission created by a voter referendum.[16] In the 2017 case of *Cooper v. Harris*, the Court invalidated a North Carolina legislative districting plan that moved tens of thousands of black voters into congressional districts that already had large black majorities.[17] This tactic is known as "packing," and is designed to reduce the number of seats that might be affected by some group of voters by packing them all into as few districts as possible.

The Supreme Court has the power to review state action. In *Pavan v. Smith*, the Supreme Court overturned Arkansas's law that disallowed same-sex parents to have both of their names listed on their children's birth certificates. Here, Marisa Pavan, the plaintiff in the case, holds her daughter and her birth certificate showing both parents' names.

One realm in which the Court constantly monitors state conduct is that of law enforcement. As we saw in Chapter 4, over the years, the Supreme Court has developed a number of principles regulating police conduct to ensure that the police do not violate constitutional liberties. These principles, however, must often be updated to keep pace with changes in technology. In a 2012 decision, the Supreme Court found that police use of a GPS tracker—a device invented more than two centuries after the adoption of the Bill of Rights—constituted a "search" as defined by the Fourth Amendment.[18] And in the 2014 case of *Riley v. California*, the Court held that the police could not undertake a warrantless search of the digital contents of a cell phone—another device hardly imagined by the framers.[19]

JUDICIAL REVIEW OF FEDERAL AGENCY ACTIONS

Although Congress makes the law, as we saw in Chapters 12 and 14, it can hardly administer the thousands of programs it has enacted and must therefore delegate power to the president and to a huge bureaucracy to achieve its purposes. For example, if Congress wishes to improve air quality, it cannot possibly anticipate all the conditions and circumstances that may arise with respect to that general goal. Inevitably, Congress must delegate to the executive substantial discretionary power to make judgments about the best ways to bring about improved air quality in the face of changing circumstances. Thus, over the years, almost any congressional program will result in thousands upon thousands of pages of administrative regulations developed by executive agencies nominally seeking to implement the will of the Congress.

Delegation of power to the executive poses a number of problems for Congress and the federal courts. If Congress delegates broad authority to the president, it risks seeing its goals subordinated to and subverted by those of the executive branch.[20] If Congress attempts to limit executive discretion by enacting precise rules and standards to govern the conduct of the president and the executive branch, it risks writing laws that do not conform to real-world conditions and that are too rigid to be adapted to changing circumstances.[21]

Over the past two centuries, the issue of delegation of power has led to a number of court decisions regarding the scope of the delegation. Courts have also been called on to decide whether the regulations adopted by federal agencies are consistent with Congress's express or implied intent.

As presidential power expanded during the New Deal era, one indication of increased congressional subordination to the executive was the enactment of laws that contained few, if any, principles limiting executive discretion. Congress enacted legislation, often at the president's behest, that gave the executive virtually unfettered authority to address a particular concern. For example, the Emergency Price Control Act of 1942 authorized the executive to set "fair and equitable" prices without spelling out what those terms might mean.[22] Although the Court initially challenged these delegations of power to the president during the New Deal, it retreated from its position when faced with a confrontation with President Franklin Delano Roosevelt. Perhaps as a result, no congressional delegation of power to the president since then has been struck down as impermissibly broad. Particularly in recent years, the Supreme Court has found that so long as federal agencies developed rules and regulations "based upon a permissible construction" or "reasonable interpretation" of Congress's statute, the judiciary would accept the views of the executive branch. Generally, the courts also give considerable deference to administrative agencies as long as those agencies engage in a formal rule-making process as prescribed by the various statutes governing agency rule making.

JUDICIAL REVIEW AND PRESIDENTIAL POWER

The federal courts are also called on to review the actions of the president. On many occasions, members of Congress as well as individuals and groups have challenged presidential orders and actions in the federal courts. In recent years, the federal bench has, more often than not, upheld assertions of presidential power in such realms as foreign policy, war and emergency powers, legislative power, and administrative authority. In June 2004, however, the Supreme Court ruled on three cases involving President George W. Bush's antiterrorism initiatives and claims of executive power and in two of the three cases appeared to place some limits on presidential authority.

One important case was *Hamdi v. Rumsfeld*.[23] Yaser Esam Hamdi, apparently a Taliban soldier, was captured by American forces in Afghanistan and brought to the United States, where he was incarcerated at the Norfolk Naval Station. Hamdi was classified as an enemy combatant and denied civil rights, including the right to counsel, despite the fact that he had been born in Louisiana and held American citizenship. In June 2004 the Supreme Court ruled that Hamdi was entitled to a lawyer and "a fair opportunity to rebut the government's factual assertions." Thus the Supreme Court did assert that presidential actions were subject to judicial scrutiny and that the Court could place some constraints on the president's power. But at the same time the Court affirmed the president's single most important claim: the unilateral power to declare individuals, including U.S. citizens, "enemy combatants," who could be detained by federal authorities under adverse legal circumstances. Several of the justices intimated that once designated an enemy combatant, a U.S. citizen might be tried before a military tribunal, without the normal presumption of innocence.

In the 2006 case of *Hamdan v. Rumsfeld*,[24] Salim Hamdan, a Taliban fighter, was captured in Afghanistan and held at the Guantánamo Bay naval base. The Bush administration planned to try Hamdan before a military commission authorized by a 2002 presidential order. The Supreme Court ruled that the commissions created by the president planned to use procedures that would violate federal law and U.S. treaty obligations. President Bush responded by demanding that Congress rewrite the law. Congress quickly obliged and enacted the Military Commissions

The courts may be called on to review the actions of the president. After President Trump's "travel ban" was implemented in early 2017, many court cases challenged this decision, and eventually one case was tried before the Supreme Court. In a 5–4 decision, the Court upheld the travel ban, sparking outrage from Democratic lawmakers.

Act, which gave the president statutory authority for his actions. In Section 7 of the act, Congress declared that Guantánamo prisoners could not bring habeas corpus petitions to federal courts to seek their release. In the 2008 case of *Boumediene v. Bush*, however, the Supreme Court struck down Section 7 and declared habeas corpus to be a fundamental right.[25] Judicial review of presidential actions is not limited to presidential war powers and the realm of terrorism. In 2013 the Fourth U.S. Circuit Court of Appeals ruled that President Obama violated the Constitution when he made so-called recess appointments to the National Labor Relations Board in order to avoid the need to secure Senate confirmation. Recess appointments are customarily used only when the Senate adjourns at the end of the year, but the president made the appointments in question when the Senate was on a short break. In June 2014 the Supreme Court ruled that a Senate recess of less than 10 days was "presumptively too short" to justify a recess appointment. In this case, the Senate had recessed for only 3 days.[26]

In its 2018 decision in the case of *Trump v. Hawaii,* however, the Court upheld the use of presidential power.[27] Through an executive order, President Trump had prohibited travel into the United States by people from several Muslim-majority countries. In a 5–4 decision, the Court held that the president had broad authority, given by statute, to determine that certain travelers might impose a risk to the security of the United States.

FOR CRITICAL ANALYSIS

During his 2005 confirmation hearings, senators asked Chief Justice Roberts why the Supreme Court was more willing to declare acts of Congress unconstitutional than it was to confront the president on the constitutionality of his actions. What reasons might you identify?

JUDICIAL REVIEW AND LAWMAKING

Much of the work of the courts involves the application of statutes to the particular case at hand. Over the centuries, judges have also developed a body of rules and principles of interpretation that are not grounded in specific statutes. This body of judge-made law is called **common law**. For example, **tort case**, which determines whether one person is liable for causing harm to another, is based more upon cases and precedents than statute.

common law law made through court precedent rather than legislative enactments

tort case a lawsuit by one individual (the plaintiff) demanding compensation for harm allegedly caused by the actions of another (the defendant)

The appellate courts, however, are in another realm. Their rulings can be considered laws, but they govern the behavior only of the judiciary. The written opinion of an appellate court is about halfway between common law and statutory law. As in common law, the opinion is judge-made and draws heavily on the precedents of previous cases. But, as in statutory law, it tries to articulate the rule of law controlling the case in question and future cases like it. It differs from a statute in that a statute addresses itself to the future conduct of citizens, whereas a written opinion addresses itself mainly to the future willingness or ability of courts to take cases and render favorable opinions. Decisions by appellate courts affect citizens by opening or closing access to the courts.

The Supreme Court in Action

Describe the process the Supreme Court follows in the exercise of its power of judicial review

Given the millions of disputes that arise every year, the job of the Supreme Court would be impossible if it were not able to control the flow of cases and its own caseload. Over the years, the courts have developed specific rules that govern which cases within their jurisdiction they will and will not hear. In order to be heard by the courts, cases must meet certain criteria that are initially applied by the trial court but may be reconsidered by appellate courts. These rules of access can be broken down into three major categories: case or controversy, standing, and mootness.

Article III of the Constitution and Supreme Court decisions define judicial power as extending only to "cases and controversies." This means that the case before a court must be an actual controversy, not a hypothetical one, with two truly adversarial parties. The courts have interpreted this language to mean that they do not have the power to render advisory opinions to legislatures or agencies about the constitutionality of proposed laws or regulations. Furthermore, even after a law is enacted, the courts will generally refuse to consider its constitutionality until it is actually applied.

standing the right of an individual or organization to initiate a court case, on the basis of having a substantial stake in the outcome

Parties to a case must also have **standing**—that is, they must show that they have a substantial stake in the outcome of the case. The traditional requirement for standing has been to show injury to oneself; that injury can be personal, economic, or even aesthetic, such as a neighbor's building a high fence that blocks one's view of the ocean. In order for a group or class of people to have standing (as in class-action suits), each member must show specific injury. This means that a general interest in the environment, for instance, does not provide a group with sufficient basis for standing.

mootness a criterion used by courts to screen cases that no longer require resolution

The Supreme Court also uses a third criterion in determining whether it will hear a case: that of **mootness**. In theory, this requirement disqualifies cases that are brought too late—after the relevant facts have changed or the problem has been resolved by other means. The criterion of mootness, however, is subject to the discretion of the courts, which have begun to relax the rules of mootness, particularly in cases where a situation that has been resolved is likely to come up again. In the abortion case *Roe v. Wade*, for example, the Supreme Court rejected the lower court's argument that because the pregnancy in question had already come to term, the case was moot. The Court agreed to hear the case because no pregnancy was likely to outlast the lengthy appeals process.[28] Related to mootness but less frequently cited is the idea of *ripeness*, which means the readiness of a case for litigation. The courts try to avoid becoming entangled in issues that remain hypothetical or events that may never occur.

Putting aside the formal criteria, the Supreme Court is most likely to accept cases that involve conflicting decisions by the federal circuit courts, cases that present important questions of civil rights or civil liberties, and cases in which the federal government is the appellant. Ultimately, however, the question of which cases to accept can come down to the preferences and priorities of the justices. If a group of justices believes that the Court should intervene in a particular area of policy or politics, they are likely to look for a case or cases that will serve as vehicles for judicial intervention. For many years, the Court was not interested in considering challenges to affirmative action or other programs designed to provide particular benefits to minorities. In recent years, however, several of the Court's more conservative justices have been eager to push back the limits of affirmative action and racial preference and have therefore accepted a number of cases that would allow them to do so. In the 2014 case *Schuette v. Coalition to Defend Affirmative Action*, for example, the Court ruled that a Michigan ballot initiative that resulted in a ban on racial preferences in college admissions was constitutional.[29] The decision paved the way for other states to prohibit the use of race as a factor in college admissions. In the 2016 case of *Fisher v. University of Texas*, however, the Court ruled that race could be one of the factors taken into account in college admissions if the school so desired.[30]

Writs Most cases reach the Supreme Court through a **writ of certiorari**. Certiorari is an order to a lower court to deliver the records of a particular case to be reviewed for legal errors. The term *certiorari* is sometimes shortened to *cert*, and cases deemed to merit certiorari are referred to as "certworthy." An individual who loses in a lower federal court or state court and wants the Supreme Court to review the decision has 90 days to file a petition for a writ of certiorari with the clerk of the U.S. Supreme Court. Petitions for thousands of cases are filed with the Court every year (see Figure 15.4).

writ of certiorari a decision of at least four of the nine Supreme Court justices to review a decision of a lower court; *certiorari* is Latin, meaning "to make more certain"

Since 1972 most of the justices have participated in a "certiorari pool" in which their law clerks work together to evaluate the petitions. Each petition is reviewed by one clerk, who writes a memo for all the justices participating in the pool, summarizing the facts and issues and making a recommendation. Clerks for the other justices add their comments to the memo. After the justices have reviewed the memos, any one of them may place any case on the "discuss list," which is circulated by the chief justice. If a case is not placed on the discuss list, it is automatically denied certiorari. Cases placed on the discuss list are considered and voted on during the justices' closed-door conference.

For certiorari to be granted, four justices must be convinced that the case satisfies rule 10 of the Rules of the Supreme Court of the United States. Rule 10 states that certiorari is not a matter of right but is to be granted only when there are special and compelling reasons. These include conflicting decisions by two or more circuit courts, conflicts between circuit courts and state courts of last resort, conflicting decisions by two or more state courts of last resort, decisions by circuit courts on matters of federal law that should be settled by the Supreme Court, and a circuit court decision on an important question that conflicts with Supreme Court decisions. It should be clear from this list that the Court will usually take action under only the most compelling circumstances—when there are conflicts among the lower courts about what the law should be, when an important legal question has been raised in the lower courts but not definitively answered, or when a lower court

FIGURE 15.4

Cases Filed in the U.S. Supreme Court, 1938–2017 Terms*

*Number of cases filed in term starting in year indicated.

SOURCES: Years 1938–69, 1970–83, 1984–99: reprinted with permission from *The United States Law Week* (Washington, DC: Bureau of National Affairs), vol. 56, no. 3102; vol. 59, no. 3064; vol. 61, no. 3098; vol. 63, no. 3134; vol. 65, no. 3100; vol. 67, no. 3167; vol. 69, no. 3134 (copyright © Bureau of National Affairs Inc.); 2000–05 U.S. Bureau of the Census, *Statistical Abstract of the United States*; 2006–07: Office of the Clerk, Supreme Court of the United States; and Supreme Court of the United States, Cases on Docket, www.uscourts.gov/statistics-reports/caseload-statistics-data-tables; Supreme Court, 2017 Year-End Report on the Federal Judiciary, www.supremecourt.gov/publicinfo/year-end/2017year-endreport.pdf (accessed 4/5/18).

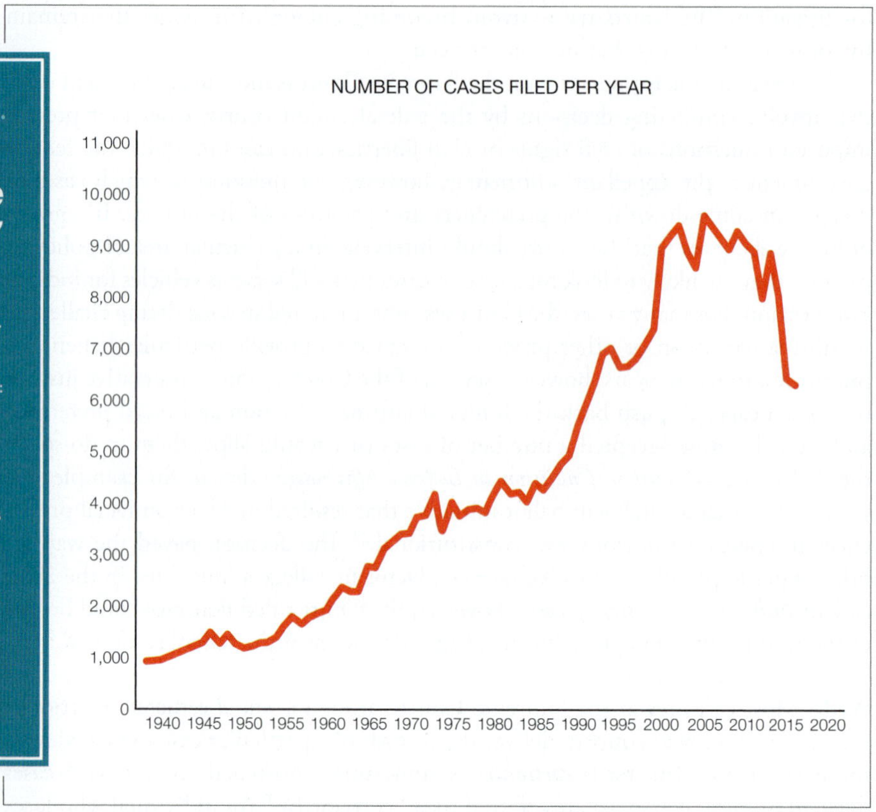

solicitor general the top government lawyer in all cases before the Supreme Court where the government is a party

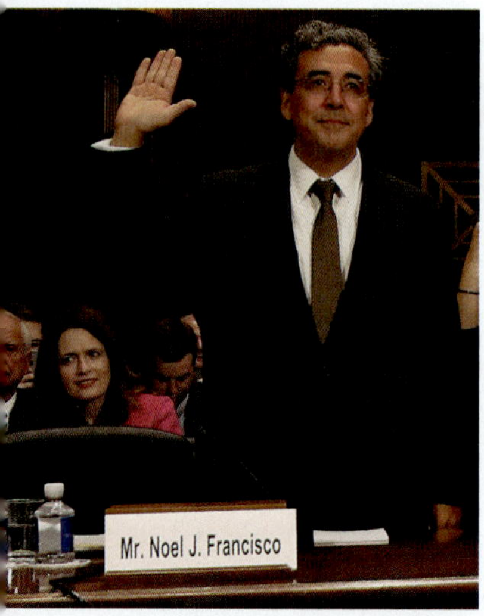

Before becoming solicitor general in the Trump administration, Noel Francisco has had experience in the Justice Department and in private practice, where he argued several cases in front of the Supreme Court.

deviates from the principles and precedents established by the high court. Few cases are able to gain the support of four justices needed for certiorari. In recent sessions, although thousands of petitions were filed, the Court has granted certiorari to barely more than 80 petitioners each year—about 1 percent of those seeking a Supreme Court review.

A handful of cases reach the Supreme Court through avenues other than certiorari. One of these is the writ of certification, which can be used when a U.S. court of appeals asks the Supreme Court for instructions on a point of law that has never been decided. A second alternative avenue is the writ of appeal, which is used to appeal the decision of a three-judge district court.

CONTROLLING THE FLOW OF CASES

In addition to the judges, other actors play important roles in shaping the flow of cases through the federal courts: the solicitor general and federal law clerks.

The Solicitor General If any single person has greater influence than individual judges over the federal courts, it is the **solicitor general** of the United States. The solicitor general is the third-ranking official in the Justice Department (below the attorney general and the deputy attorney general) but the top government lawyer in virtually all cases before the Supreme Court in which the government is a party. The solicitor general has the greatest control over the flow of cases; his or her actions are not reviewed by any higher authority in the executive branch. More than half the Supreme Court's total workload consists of cases under the direct charge of the solicitor general.

The solicitor general exercises especially strong influence by screening cases before any agency of the federal government can appeal them to the Supreme Court.[31] Agency heads may lobby the president or otherwise try to circumvent the solicitor general, and a few of the independent agencies have a statutory right to make direct appeals; but without the solicitor general's support, these requests are seldom reviewed by the Court. Congress has given only a few agencies, including the Federal Communications Commission, the Federal Maritime Commission, and in some cases the Department of Agriculture (even though it is not an independent agency), the right to appeal directly to the Supreme Court without going through the solicitor general.

The solicitor general can enter a case even when the federal government is not a direct litigant by writing an **amicus curiae** ("friend of the court") brief. A friend of the court is not a direct party to a case but has a vital interest in its outcome. Thus, when the government has such an interest, the solicitor general can file an amicus brief or a federal court can invite such a brief because it wants an opinion in writing. Other interested parties may file briefs as well.

amicus curiae literally, "friend of the court"; individuals or groups who are not parties to a lawsuit but who seek to assist the Supreme Court in reaching a decision by presenting additional briefs

In addition to exercising substantial control over the flow of cases, the solicitor general can shape the arguments used before the federal courts. Indeed, the Supreme Court tends to give special attention to the way the solicitor general characterizes the issues. The solicitor general is the person who appears most frequently before the Court and, theoretically at least, is the most disinterested. The credibility of the solicitor general is not hurt when several times each year he comes to the Court to withdraw a case with the admission that the government has made an error.

Law Clerks Every federal judge employs law clerks to research legal issues and assist with the preparation of opinions. Each Supreme Court justice is assigned four clerks, almost always honors graduates of the nation's most prestigious law schools. A clerkship with a Supreme Court justice is a great honor and generally indicates

Federal judges, including Supreme Court justices, rely on their clerks for research and help in preparing opinions. Serving as a law clerk to a Supreme Court justice is a prestigious position. Four current justices—Roberts (pictured here), Breyer, Kagan, and Gorsuch—clerked for a Supreme Court justice early in their careers.

that the fortunate individual is likely to reach the very top of the legal profession. The work of the Supreme Court clerks is a closely guarded secret, but it is likely that some justices rely heavily on their clerks for advice in writing opinions and in deciding whether the Court should hear specific cases. In a recent book, a former law clerk to the late justice Harry Blackmun charged that Supreme Court justices yielded "excessive power to immature, ideologically driven clerks, who in turn use that power to manipulate their bosses."[32]

LOBBYING FOR ACCESS: INTERESTS AND THE COURT

At the same time that the Court exercises discretion over which cases it will review, groups and forces in society often seek to persuade the justices to listen to their problems. Lawyers representing interest groups try to choose the proper client and the proper case so that the issues in question are most dramatically and appropriately portrayed. When possible, they also pick a district or jurisdiction with a sympathetic judge in which to bring the case. Sometimes they even have to wait for an appropriate political climate. They must also attempt to develop a proper record at the trial court level, one that includes some constitutional arguments and even, when possible, errors on the part of the trial court.

One of the most effective strategies that litigants use in getting cases accepted for review by the appellate courts is to bring the same type of suit in more than one circuit (that is, to develop a "pattern of cases") in the hope that inconsistent treatment by two different courts will improve the chance of a Supreme Court review. The two most notable users of the pattern-of-cases strategy in recent years have been the National Association for the Advancement of Colored People (NAACP) and the American Civil Liberties Union (ACLU). For many years, the NAACP (and its Defense Fund—now a separate group) has worked through local chapters and with many individuals to encourage litigation on issues of racial discrimination and segregation. Sometimes it distributes petitions to be signed by parents and filed with local school boards and courts, deliberately sowing the seeds of future litigation. The NAACP and the ACLU often encourage private parties to bring suit and then join the suit as amici curiae.

In many states, it is considered unethical and illegal for attorneys to engage in "fomenting and soliciting legal business in which they are not parties and have no pecuniary right or liability." The NAACP was sued by the state of Virginia in the late 1950s in an attempt to restrict or eliminate its efforts to influence the pattern of cases. The Supreme Court reviewed the case in 1963, recognized that the strategy was being used, and held that the NAACP strategy was protected by the First and Fourteenth amendments, just as other forms of speech and petition are protected.[33]

Thus, many pathbreaking cases are eventually granted certiorari because repeated refusal to review one or more of them would amount to a rule of law just as much as if the courts had handed down a written opinion. In this sense, the flow of cases, especially the pattern of significant cases, influences the behavior of the appellate judiciary.

THE SUPREME COURT'S PROCEDURES

The Supreme Court's decision to accept a case is the beginning of what can be a lengthy and complex process (see Figure 15.5). After a petition is filed and certiorari is granted, the Court considers the reasoning on both sides as presented in

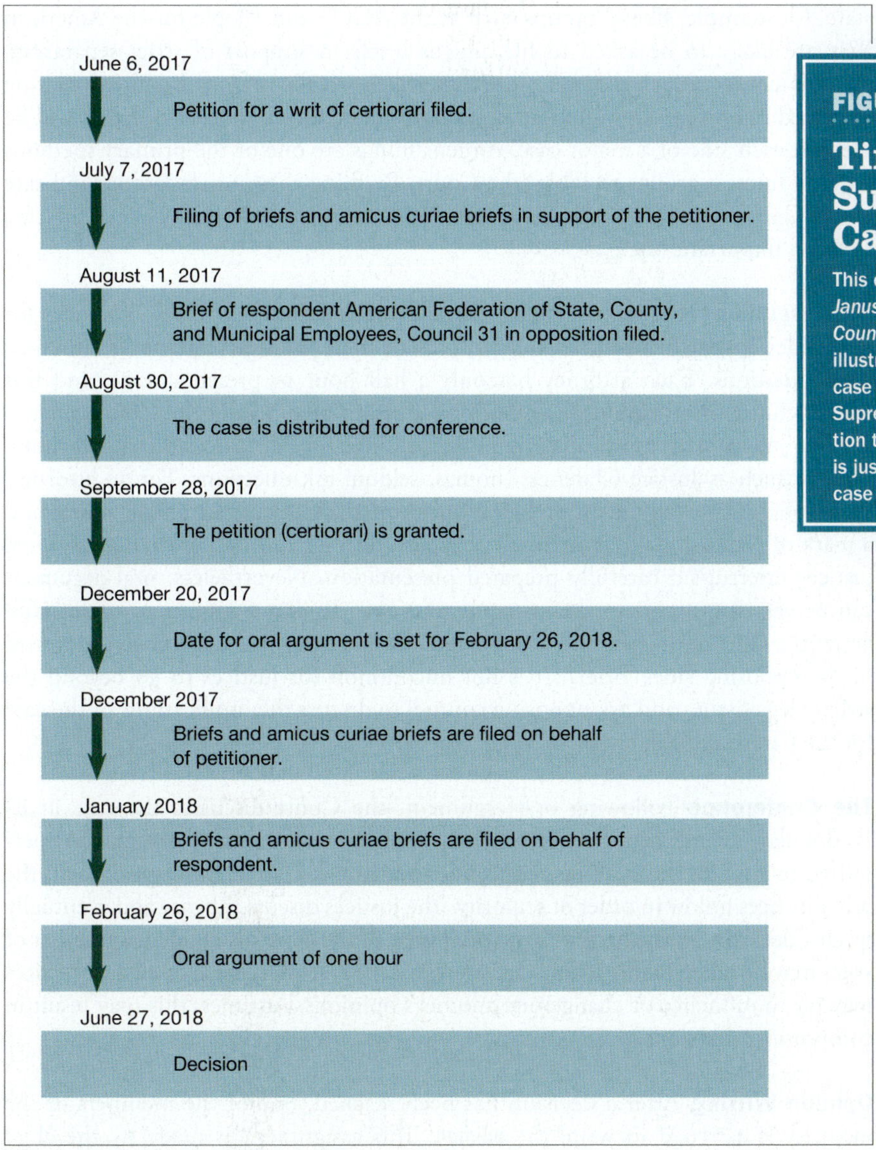
June 6, 2017
Petition for a writ of certiorari filed.
July 7, 2017
Filing of briefs and amicus curiae briefs in support of the petitioner.
August 11, 2017
Brief of respondent American Federation of State, County, and Municipal Employees, Council 31 in opposition filed.
August 30, 2017
The case is distributed for conference.
September 28, 2017
The petition (certiorari) is granted.
December 20, 2017
Date for oral argument is set for February 26, 2018.
December 2017
Briefs and amicus curiae briefs are filed on behalf of petitioner.
January 2018
Briefs and amicus curiae briefs are filed on behalf of respondent.
February 26, 2018
Oral argument of one hour
June 27, 2018
Decision

FIGURE 15.5

Time Line of a Supreme Court Case

This calendar of events in the case of *Janus v. American Federation of State, County, and Municipal Employees* illustrates the steps of the process a case goes through as it moves through the Supreme Court. The total time from petition to the Supreme Court to the decision is just over one year, although the initial case was filed years ago in a lower court.

briefs and oral argument, the justices discuss the case in conference, and opinions are carefully drafted.

Briefs First, the attorneys on both sides must prepare **briefs**, written documents in which the attorneys explain why the Court should rule in favor of their client. Briefs are filled with referrals to precedents specifically chosen to show that other courts have frequently ruled in the same way the attorneys are requesting that the Supreme Court rule. The attorneys for both sides muster the most compelling precedents they can in support of their arguments.

briefs written documents in which attorneys explain, using case precedents, why the court should find in favor of their client

As the attorneys prepare their briefs, they often ask sympathetic interest groups for their help. These groups are asked to file amicus curiae briefs that support the claims of one or the other litigant. In a case involving separation of church and state, for example, liberal groups such as the ACLU and People for the American Way are likely to be asked to file amicus briefs in support of strict separation, whereas conservative religious groups are likely to file amicus briefs advocating increased public accommodation of religious ideas. Often, dozens of briefs will be filed on each side of a major case. Amicus filings are one of the primary methods used by interest groups to lobby the Court. By filing these briefs, groups indicate to the Court where they stand and signal to the justices that they believe the case to be an important one.

oral argument the stage in the Supreme Court procedure in which attorneys for both sides appear before the Court to present their positions and answer questions posed by justices

Oral Argument The next stage of a case is **oral argument**, in which attorneys for both sides appear before the Court to present their positions and answer the justices' questions. Each attorney has only a half hour to present a case, and this time includes interruptions for questions. Certain members of the Court, such as the late Justice Antonin Scalia, are known to interrupt attorneys dozens of times. Others, such as Justice Clarence Thomas, seldom ask questions. For an attorney, the opportunity to argue a case before the Supreme Court is a singular honor and a mark of professional distinction. It can also be a harrowing experience, as when justices interrupt a carefully prepared presentation. Nevertheless, oral argument can be very important to the outcome of a case. It allows justices to understand better the heart of the case and to raise questions that might not have been addressed in the opposing sides' briefs. It is not uncommon for justices to go beyond the strictly legal issues and ask opposing counsel to discuss the implications of the case for the Court and the nation at large.

The Conference Following oral argument, the Court discusses the case in its Wednesday or Friday conference, a strictly private meeting that no outsiders are permitted to attend. The chief justice presides over the conference and speaks first; the other justices follow in order of seniority. The justices discuss the case and eventually reach a decision on the basis of a majority vote. If the Court is divided, a number of votes may be taken before a final decision is reached. As the case is discussed, justices may try to influence or change one another's opinions. At times, this may result in compromise decisions.

opinion the written explanation of the Supreme Court's decision in a particular case

Opinion Writing After a decision has been reached, one of the members of the majority is assigned to write the **opinion**. This assignment is made by the chief justice or by the most senior justice in the majority if the chief justice is on the losing side. The assignment of the opinion can make a significant difference to the interpretation of a decision. Every opinion of the Supreme Court sets a major precedent for future cases throughout the judicial system. Lawyers and judges in the lower courts will examine the opinion carefully to ascertain the Supreme Court's intent. Differences in wording and emphasis can have important implications for future litigation. Thus, in assigning an opinion, the justices must give serious thought to the impression the case will make on lawyers and on the public and to the probability that one justice's opinion will be more widely accepted than another's.

One of the more dramatic instances of this tactical consideration occurred in 1944, when Chief Justice Harlan F. Stone chose Justice Felix Frankfurter to write the opinion in the "white primary" case *Smith v. Allwright*.[34] The chief justice believed that this sensitive case, which overturned the southern practice of prohibiting black participation in nominating primaries, required the efforts of the most brilliant and

The Supreme Court allocates just one hour to hear oral arguments, even in difficult and contentious cases. Attorneys for both sides must make their arguments succinctly and respond to questions from the nine justices, which are often very pointed.

scholarly jurist on the Court. But the day after Stone made the assignment, Justice Robert H. Jackson wrote a letter to Stone urging a change of assignment and arguing that Frankfurter, a foreign-born Jew from New England, would not win the South with his opinion, regardless of its brilliance. Stone accepted the advice and substituted Justice Stanley Reed, an American-born Protestant from Kentucky and a southern Democrat in good standing.

Once the majority opinion is drafted, it is circulated to the other justices. Some members of the majority may agree with both the outcome and the rationale but wish to emphasize or highlight a particular point. For that purpose, they draft a concurring opinion, called a *regular concurrence*. In other instances, one or more justices may agree with the majority decision but disagree with the rationale presented in the majority opinion. These justices may draft *special concurrences*, explaining their own rationale for the decision and how it differs from the majority's rationale.

Dissent Justices who disagree with the majority decision of the Court may choose to publicize the character of their disagreement in the form of a **dissenting opinion**. The dissenting opinion is generally assigned by the senior justice among the dissenters. Dissents can be used to express irritation with an outcome or to signal to defeated political forces in the nation that their position is supported by at least some members of the Court. Ironically, the most dependable way an individual justice can exercise a direct and clear influence on the Court is to write a dissent. Because there is no need to please a majority, dissenting opinions can be more eloquent and less guarded than majority opinions. The current Supreme Court often produces 5–4 decisions, with dissenters writing long and detailed opinions that, they hope, will help them persuade a swing justice to join their side on the next round of cases dealing with a similar topic. During the Court's 2006–07 term, Justice Ruth Bader Ginsburg was so unhappy about the majority's decisions in a number of cases that she began to read forceful dissents from the bench, a practice she has continued

dissenting opinion a decision written by a justice in the minority in a particular case in which the justice wishes to express his or her reasoning in the case to underscore her disagreements with several recent decisions and point the way toward other possibilities.

Dissent plays a special role in the work and impact of the Court because it amounts to an appeal to lawyers all over the country to keep bringing similar cases. Therefore, an effective dissent influences the flow of cases through the Court and the arguments that lawyers will use in later cases. Even more important, dissent points out that although the Court speaks with a single opinion, it is the opinion only of the majority—and one day the majority might go the other way.

Often, the division between the majority and the dissenting justices in major cases reflects deep divisions in American society. Take the 2015 same-sex marriage case of *Obergefell v. Hodges* in which the majority opinion, written by Justice Anthony Kennedy, asserted that state same-sex marriage bans violated the Fourteenth Amendment by arbitrarily intruding upon personal choices, "central to individual dignity and autonomy," and thus denying such persons due process and equal protection of the laws.[35] The dissenters, Chief Justice Roberts and Justices Alito, Scalia, and Thomas, declared that the Fourteenth Amendment had never been intended or interpreted as providing a right to same-sex marriage, and they criticized the majority opinion as little more than an effort by jurists to write their own views into the Constitution. In its split decision, the Court mirrored a division in American society between those who see gay rights as a natural extension of civil rights and those offended, often for religious reasons, by open expressions of same-sex partnership. The dissenting justices hope to encourage further litigation in this realm, but generally speaking, once a right is granted it is seldom subject to revocation.

Supreme Court justices can use a dissenting opinion to express their opposing viewpoint with the hope of influencing future cases on similar questions. Justice Ruth Bader Ginsburg is known for her forceful dissents such as in the 2014 Hobby Lobby case, which allowed a corporation to claim religious grounds for refusing to provide contraceptive coverage in its health insurance program.

Explaining Supreme Court Decisions

Consider the personal and political influences on judges and the courts

The Supreme Court makes its mark on American politics and society through the decisions it hands down. But judicial decision-making does not take place in a vacuum, of course. Like other actors in government, justices are influenced by institutional concerns, prior experience, and personal philosophy. In addition, the Court as a whole is affected by the overarching political system in which it plays a role. Over time, that role has shifted as a result of political developments both inside and outside the Court.

INFLUENCES ON SUPREME COURT DECISION-MAKING

The Supreme Court explains its decisions in terms of law and precedent. But it is the Court itself that decides what the laws actually mean and what importance the precedent will actually have. Throughout its history, the Court has shaped and reshaped the law. In the late nineteenth and early twentieth centuries, for example, the Supreme Court held that the Constitution, law, and precedent permitted racial segregation in the United States. Beginning in the 1950s, however, the Court found that the Constitution prohibited segregation on the basis of race and indicated that the use of racial categories in legislation was always suspect. By the 1970s and '80s the Court once again held that the Constitution permitted the use of racial categories—when such categories were needed to help members of minority groups achieve full participation in American society. Since the 1990s the Court has retreated from this position, too, indicating that governmental efforts to provide extra help to racial minorities could represent an unconstitutional infringement on the rights of the majority.

Institutional Interests The Supreme Court's justices are acutely aware of the Court's place in history, and they care about protecting the Court's power and reputation. This desire to protect the institutional integrity of the Court can sometimes influence judicial thinking. During the 1930s, for example, the Supreme Court became embroiled in a political struggle with President Franklin Roosevelt over his "New Deal" programs. During the 1935–36 term, the Court struck down several of the president's initiatives in a series of 5–4 votes. Furious, the president responded by proposing a Court-reform plan that would have increased the size of the Court to as many as 15 justices. Roosevelt hoped to pack the Court with his own appointees and, thus, win future cases over New Deal programs. Justice Owen Roberts, who had been one of the five justices voting against the president's initiatives, made a sudden reversal, voting in favor of an important New Deal policy he had been expected to oppose. The media dubbed Roberts's shift "The switch in time that saved nine."

Such institutional concerns are not isolated incidents, however. More recently, Chief Justice John Roberts seemed to have institutional concerns in mind when he surprised fellow conservatives by casting the deciding vote in favor of the constitutionality of the Affordable Care Act in 2012. The Court's conservative majority had come under increasing political fire for its positions on such matters as campaign finance and affirmative action. Roberts, according to one commentator, saw himself as "uniquely entrusted with the custodianship of the Court's legitimacy, reputation, and stature" and was determined to show that the Court stood above mere political ideology.[36] As we saw above, Roberts repeated his support of the Affordable Care Act in 2015 in the case of *King v. Burwell.*

Activism and Restraint Judicial philosophy also plays a role in the decisions of all judges, including those on the Supreme Court. One element of judicial philosophy is the issue of activism versus restraint. Over the years, some justices have believed that courts should interpret the Constitution according to the stated intentions of its framers and defer to the views of Congress when interpreting federal statutes. Justice Felix Frankfurter, for example, advocated judicial deference to legislative bodies and avoidance of the "political thicket" in which the Court would entangle itself by deciding questions that were essentially political rather than legal in character. Some, but not all, advocates of **judicial restraint** are also called "strict constructionists" because they look strictly to the words of the Constitution in interpreting its meaning. The late Justice Scalia, along with Justice Thomas, Justice Gorsuch, and Justice Kavanaugh advocate originalism in interpreting the Constitution and textualism in interpreting statutes.

The alternative to restraint is **judicial activism.** Activist judges such as Chief Justice Earl Warren believed that the Court should go beyond the words of the Constitution or a statute to consider the broader societal implications of its decisions. Activist judges sometimes strike out in new directions, promulgating new interpretations or inventing new legal and constitutional concepts when they

judicial restraint judicial philosophy whose adherents refuse to go beyond the clear words of the Constitution in interpreting the document's meaning

judicial activism judicial philosophy that posits that the Court should go beyond the words of the Constitution or a statute to consider the broader societal implications of its decisions believe these to be socially desirable. For example, Justice Harry Blackmun's opinion in *Roe v. Wade* was based on a constitutional right to privacy that is not found in the words of the Constitution but was, rather, from the Court's prior decision in *Griswold v. Connecticut*.[37] Blackmun and the other members of the majority in the *Roe* case argued that the right to privacy was implied by other constitutional provisions. In this instance of judicial activism, the Court knew the result it wanted to achieve and was not afraid to make the law conform to the desired outcome.

Activism and restraint can overlap with but are not always the same as liberalism and conservatism. For example, conservative politicians often castigate "liberal activist" judges and call for the appointment of conservative jurists who will refrain from reinterpreting the law. But the Rehnquist Court, dominated by conservatives, was among the most activist courts in American history, particularly in such areas as federalism and election law. The Roberts Court is continuing along the same route. For example, in the 2014 case of *McCutcheon v. Federal Election Commission*, the Court struck down one of the major remaining elements of Congress's efforts to regulate campaign finance. The Court's five more conservative justices said that limits on how much individuals could contribute in any given election were a restraint on free speech.[38] This decision could be described as "activist" because it broadens the interpretation of "speech" and overturns congressional legislation that has significant public support. As the examples of these conservative courts illustrate, a judge may be philosophically conservative and believe in strict construction of the Constitution but also be jurisprudentially activist and believe that the courts must play an active and energetic role in policy making, if necessary striking down acts of Congress to ensure that the intent of the framers is fulfilled.

FOR CRITICAL ANALYSIS

In its 2010 decision in *McDonald v. Chicago*, the Supreme Court applied the doctrine of selective incorporation and ruled that the Second Amendment right to bear arms applies to the states as well as to the federal government. What is "selective incorporation"? What is its significance in American constitutional history?

Political Ideology and Partisanship The philosophy of activism versus restraint is sometimes a smokescreen for political ideology, and indeed, the liberal or conservative attitudes or partisan leanings of justices play an important role in their decisions.[39] In the past, liberal judges have often been activists, willing to use the law to achieve social and political change, whereas conservatives have been associated with judicial restraint. Interestingly, however, in recent years some conservative justices who have long called for restraint have actually become activists in seeking to undo some of the work of liberal jurists.

From the 1950s to the 1980s the Supreme Court took an activist role in such areas as civil rights, civil liberties, abortion, voting rights, and police procedures. For example, the Supreme Court was more responsible than any other governmental institution for breaking down America's system of racial segregation. In the following decades, however, the conservative justices appointed by presidents Ronald Reagan, George H. W. Bush, and George W. Bush became the dominant bloc on the Court and, as we saw earlier, moved the Court to the right on a number of issues, including affirmative action and abortion.

The political struggles of recent years amply illustrate the importance of judicial ideology. Is abortion a fundamental right or a criminal activity? How much separation must there be between church and state? Does application of the Voting Rights Act to increase minority representation constitute a violation of the rights of whites? The answers to these and many other questions cannot be found in the words of the Constitution. They must be located, instead, in the hearts and minds of the judges who interpret that text.

Judicial philosophy, ideology, and institutional interest all influence the thinking of justices. In the end, however, the Supreme Court is a court of law and must pay heed to statutes and legal precedent. A decision that cannot be justified by law and precedent cannot be issued. To ignore the law would be to undermine the rule of law and to destroy the constitutional structure in which the Supreme Court occupies such a prominent place.

JUDICIAL POWER AND POLITICS

One of the most important institutional changes to occur in the United States during the past half-century has been the striking transformation of the role and power of the federal courts, and of the Supreme Court in particular. Understanding how this transformation came about is the key to understanding the contemporary role of the courts in America.

Traditional Limitations on the Federal Courts For much of American history, the power of the federal courts was subject to a number of limitations.[40] First, unlike other governmental institutions, courts cannot exercise power on their own initiative. Judges must wait until a case is brought to them before they can make authoritative decisions. Traditionally, moreover, courts were constrained by judicial rules of standing that limited access to the bench. Claimants who simply disagreed with governmental action or inaction could not obtain access to the courts, which was limited to individuals who could show that they were specifically affected by the government's behavior in some area. This limitation on access diminished the judiciary's capacity to forge links with important political and social forces.

Second, courts were traditionally limited in the character of the relief they could provide. In general, courts acted only to offer relief or assistance to individuals and not to broad social classes, again inhibiting the formation of alliances between the courts and important social forces.

Third, courts lacked enforcement powers of their own and were compelled to rely on executive or state agencies to ensure compliance with their edicts. If the executive or state agencies were unwilling to assist the courts, judicial enactments could go unheeded, as when President Andrew Jackson declined to enforce Chief Justice John Marshall's 1832 order to the state of Georgia to release two missionaries it had arrested on Cherokee lands. Marshall asserted that the state had no right to enter the lands without the Cherokees' assent.[41] Jackson is reputed to have said, "John Marshall has made his decision, now let him enforce it."

Fourth, federal judges are, of course, appointed by the president (with the consent of the Senate). As a result, the president and Congress can shape the composition of the federal courts and ultimately, perhaps, the character of judicial decisions. Finally, Congress has the power to change both the size and jurisdiction of the Supreme Court and other federal courts. In many areas, federal courts obtain their jurisdiction not from the Constitution but from congressional statutes. On a number of occasions, Congress has threatened to take matters out of the courts' hands when it was unhappy with the courts' policies.[42] For example, in 1996, Congress enacted several pieces of legislation designed to curb the jurisdiction of the federal courts. One of these laws was the Prison Litigation Reform Act, which limits the ability of federal judges to issue "consent decrees," under which the judges could take control of state prison systems. As to the size of the Court, on one memorable occasion that

FOR CRITICAL ANALYSIS

Are the federal courts "imperial," or are they subordinate to the elected branches of government? In what respect does the federal judiciary still play a "checks and balances" role?

we mentioned earlier, presidential and congressional threats to expand the size of the Supreme Court—Franklin Delano Roosevelt's "Court packing" plan—encouraged the justices to drop their opposition to New Deal programs.

As a result of these limitations on judicial power, through much of their history the chief function of the federal courts was to provide judicial support for executive agencies and to legitimize acts of Congress by declaring them to be consistent with constitutional principles. Only on rare occasions have the federal courts dared to challenge Congress or the executive branch.[43]

Two Judicial Revolutions Since the Second World War, however, the role of the federal judiciary has been strengthened and expanded. There have been two judicial revolutions in the United States since then. The first and more visible of these was the substantive revolution in judicial policy. As we saw earlier in this chapter and in Chapters 4 and 5, in many policy areas, including school desegregation, legislative apportionment, and criminal procedure, and in obscenity, abortion, and voting rights, the Supreme Court was at the forefront of a series of sweeping changes in the role of the U.S. government and, ultimately, the character of American society.[44]

At the same time that the courts were introducing important policy innovations, they were also bringing about a second, less visible revolution. During the 1960s and '70s the Supreme Court and other federal courts instituted a series of changes in judicial procedures that fundamentally expanded the power of the courts in the United States.

First, the federal courts liberalized the concept of standing to permit almost any group that seeks to challenge the actions of an administrative agency to bring its case before the federal bench. In 1971, for example, the Supreme Court ruled that public interest groups could use the National Environmental Policy Act to challenge the actions of federal agencies by claiming that the agencies' activities might have adverse environmental consequences.[45]

Congress helped to make it even easier for groups dissatisfied with government policies to bring their cases to the courts by adopting Section 1983 of the U.S. Code, which permits the practice of "fee shifting"—that is, allowing citizens who successfully bring a suit against a public official for violating their constitutional rights to collect their attorneys' fees and costs from the government. Thus, Section 1983 encourages individuals and groups to bring their problems to the courts rather than to Congress or the executive branch. These changes have given the courts a far greater role in the administrative process than ever before. Many federal judges are concerned that federal legislation in areas such as health care reform will create new rights and entitlements that give rise to a deluge of court cases. "Any time you create a new right, you create a host of disputes and claims," warned Barbara Rothstein, chief judge of the federal district court in Seattle, Washington.[46]

Second, the federal courts broadened the scope of relief to permit themselves to act on behalf of broad categories or classes of persons in "class-action" cases, rather than just on behalf of individuals.[47] A **class-action suit** is a procedural device that permits large numbers of persons with common interests to join together under a representative party to bring or defend a lawsuit. One example of a class-action suit is the case of *In re Agent Orange Product Liability Litigation*, in which a federal judge in New York certified Vietnam War veterans as a class with standing to sue

class-action suit a legal action by which a group or class of individuals with common interests can file a suit on behalf of everyone who shares that interest a manufacturer of herbicides for damages allegedly incurred from exposure to the defendant's product while in Vietnam.[48] The class potentially numbered in the tens of thousands.

Third, the federal courts began to employ so-called structural remedies, in effect retaining jurisdiction of cases until the court's mandate had actually been implemented to its satisfaction.[49] The best known of these instances was the effort of federal judge W. Arthur Garrity, Jr., to operate the Boston school system from his bench in order to ensure its desegregation. Between 1974 and 1985, Judge Garrity issued 14 decisions relating to different aspects of the Boston school desegregation plan that had been developed under his authority and put into effect under his supervision.[50] In 1985, as a result of a suit brought by the NAACP five years earlier, federal judge Leonard B. Sand imposed fines that would have forced the city of Yonkers, New York, into bankruptcy if it had refused to accept his plan to build public housing in white neighborhoods. Twenty-two years and $1.6 million in fines later, the city finally gave in to the judge's ruling in 2007.

Through these three judicial mechanisms, the federal courts paved the way for an unprecedented expansion of national judicial power. In essence, liberalization of the rules of standing and expansion of the scope of judicial relief drew the federal courts into linkages with important social interests and classes, while the introduction of structural remedies enhanced the courts' ability to serve these constituencies. Thus, during the 1960s and '70s, the power of the federal courts expanded in the same way the power of the executive expanded during the 1930s: through links with

Today, the Supreme Court is frequently at the center of major political issues. In a historic decision in 2015, the Court declared same-sex marriage a fundamental right protected by the due process and equal protection clauses of the Fourteenth Amendment to the Constitution.

constituencies, such as civil rights, consumer, environmental, and feminist groups, that staunchly defended the Supreme Court in its battles with Congress, the executive, and other interest groups.

FOR CRITICAL ANALYSIS

In what ways are courts, judges, and justices shielded from politics and political pressure? In what ways are they vulnerable to political pressure? Are the courts an appropriate place for politics?

The Federal Judiciary
WHAT DO WE WANT?

In the original conception of the framers, the judiciary was to be the institution that would protect individual liberty from the government. As we saw in Chapter 2, the framers believed that in a democracy the great danger was what they termed "tyranny of the majority"—the possibility that a popular majority, "united or actuated by some common impulse or passion," would "trample on the rules of justice."[51] The framers hoped that the courts would protect liberty from the potential excesses of democracy. And for most of American history, the federal courts' most important decisions were those that protected the freedoms—to speak, worship, publish, vote, and attend school—of groups and individuals whose political views, religious beliefs, or racial or ethnic backgrounds made them unpopular.

Today, Americans of all political persuasions seem to view the courts as useful instruments through which to pursue their goals rather than as protectors of individual rights. Conservatives want to ban abortion and help business maintain its profitability, whereas liberals want to promote school integration and help enhance the power of workers in the workplace. (The "**Who Participates?**" feature on the facing page looks at efforts to influence the Supreme Court through amicus briefs.) These may all be noble goals, but they present a basic dilemma for students of American government. If the courts are simply one more set of policy-making institutions, who is left to protect the liberty of individuals?

The decisions made by the Supreme Court today will have important consequences for our lives and futures. The Court's campaign-finance decisions will have consequences for who will govern the nation you inherit. The Court's decisions on health care will influence the type of care you receive and its cost. The Court's decisions in the realm of immigration will affect who will and will not be able to call themselves Americans. The Court's decision in Mark Janus's case against public-sector unions could influence your future job and taxes. The Supreme Court is not an abstract entity in far-off Washington. It reaches directly into your life.

Influencing the Supreme Court?

Average Amicus Briefs per Case

1 — 1960s
2 — 1970s
4 — 1980s
5 — 1990s
8 — 2000s
11 — 2010s (through 2017)

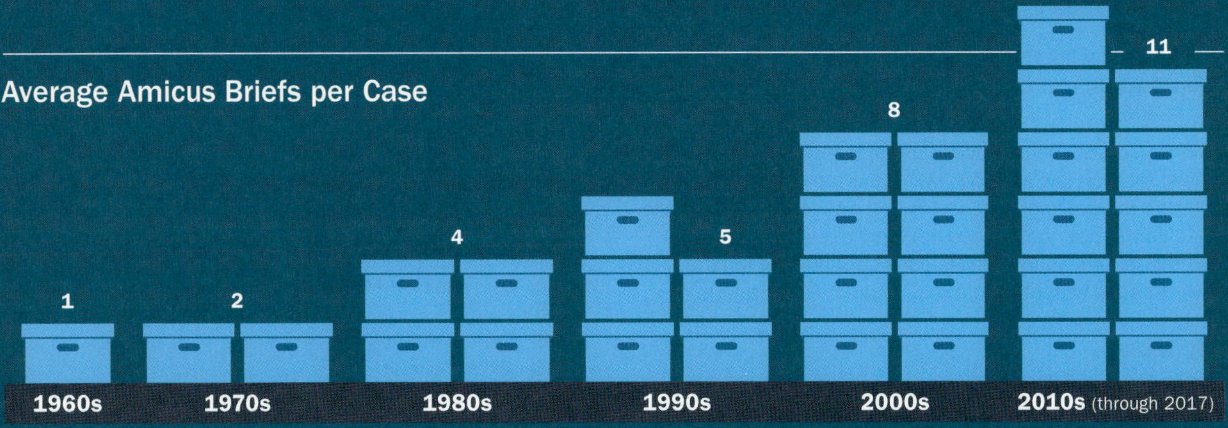

Amicus Briefs for Selected Landmark Cases

6 — *Brown v. Board of Education, 1954* (racial segregation)

107 — *Grutter v. Bollinger, 2003* (affirmative action admissions policy)

136 — *National Federation of Independent Business v. Sebelius, 2012* (Affordable Care Act, individual mandate)

147 — *Obergefell v. Hodges, 2015* (marriage equality)

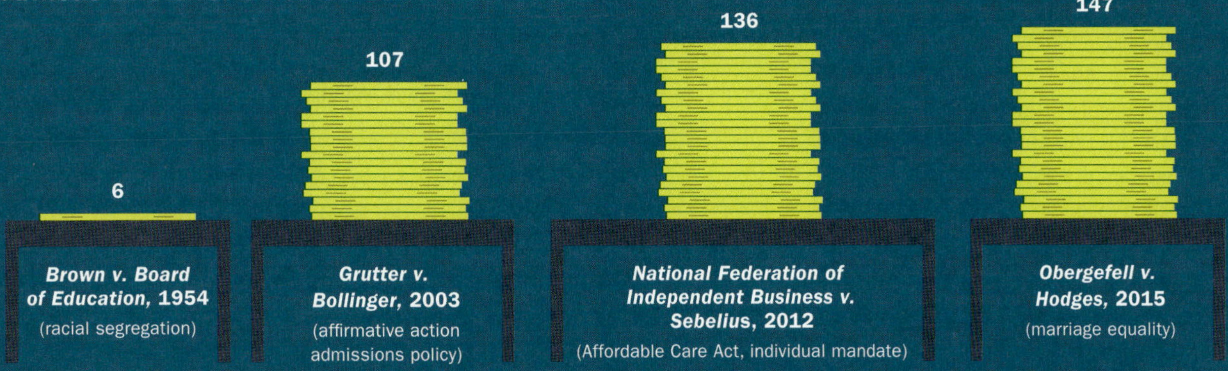

SOURCES: Anthony J. Franze and R. Reeves Anderson, "Record Breaking Term for Amicus Curiae in Supreme Court Reflects New Norm," *The National Law Journal*, August 19, 2015, www.nationallawjournal.com/supremecourtbrief/id=1202735095655/Record-Breaking-Term-for-Amicus-Curiae-in-Supreme-Court-Reflects-New-Norm (accessed 12/8/15); Thomas G. Hansford and Kristen Johnson, "The Supply of Amicus Curiae Briefs in the Market for Information at the U.S. Supreme Court," *Justice System Journal*, 35, no. 4 (2014): 362–82; and Anthony J. Franze and R. Reeves Anderson, "In Quiet Term, Drop in Amicus Curiae at the Supreme Court," *Supreme Court Brief*, September 6, 2017, www.law.com (accessed 12/23/17).

★ WHAT YOU CAN DO ★

Look inside the Federal Courts

☑ Find which groups filed amicus briefs for U.S. Supreme Court cases at **www.scotusblog.com**, and read a few of the briefs.

☑ Click on the "Court Locator" tab at **www.uscourts.gov** to find which federal courts are near you and to view their calendar of oral arguments. Court dockets and some case files are available at **www.pacer.gov**.

☑ Watch videos of cases from the Cameras in Courts pilot project at **www.uscourts.gov/about-federal-courts/cameras-courts**.

STUDY GUIDE

The Legal System

Identify the general types of cases and types of courts in our legal system (pp. 593–97)

American court cases proceed under two broad categories of law: criminal law and civil law. There are court systems at both the federal and state levels in the United States. While state courts hear only cases involving questions of state law, the federal courts decide cases addressing federal laws, treaties with other nations, and the Constitution.

Key Terms

criminal law (p. 593)
plaintiff (p. 593)
defendant (p. 593)
civil law (p. 594)
precedent (p. 594)
stare decisis (p. 594)
trial court (p. 594)
court of appeals (p. 594)
supreme court (p. 595)
plea bargain (p. 595)
jurisdiction (p. 595)
original jurisdiction (p. 596)
due process of law (p. 597)
writ of habeas corpus (p. 597)

Practice Quiz

1. What is the name for the body of law that involves disputes between private entities such as individuals, groups, and corporations?
   a) civil law
   b) privacy law
   c) criminal law
   d) household law
   e) common law

2. The doctrine that previous court decisions should apply as precedents in similar cases is known as
   a) habeas corpus.
   b) a writ of certiorari.
   c) stare decisis.
   d) rule of four.
   e) senatorial courtesy.

3. Where do most trials in America take place?
   a) U.S. Court of Federal
   b) claims
   c) federal district courts
   d) federal circuit courts
   e) the Supreme Court of the United States

4. Which of the following is not included in the original jurisdiction of the Supreme Court?
   a) cases between the United States and one of the 50 states
   b) cases brought by one state against citizens of another state or against a foreign country
   c) cases involving challenges to the constitutionality of state laws
   d) cases between two or more states
   e) cases involving foreign ambassadors or other ministers

5. The term *writ of habeas corpus* refers to
   a) a short, unsigned decision by an appellate court, usually rejecting a petition to review the decision of a lower court.
   b) a criterion used by courts to screen cases that no longer require resolution.
   c) a decision of at least four of the nine Supreme Court justices to review a decision of a lower court.
   d) a court order that an individual in custody be brought into court and shown the cause for his or her detention.
   e) a brief filed by the solicitor general when the federal government is not a direct litigant in a Supreme Court case.

Federal Courts

Describe the different levels of federal courts and their functions (pp. 598–603)

The federal judiciary is composed of 94 district courts, 12 circuit courts, several specialized courts that have nationwide original jurisdiction in certain types of cases, and the U.S. Supreme Court. The federal courts hear a very small percentage of the cases decided in the United States each year. Presidents typically nominate judges for the federal judiciary who are prominent members of the legal profession and who share their partisan and ideological views. The importance of appointments to the federal judiciary has made the confirmation process in the Senate increasingly contentious in recent years.

Key Term

chief justice (p. 600)

Practice Quiz

6. The size of the Supreme Court is determined by
   a) the president.
   b) the chief justice.
   c) the Department of Justice.
   d) Congress.
   e) the Constitution.

7. The formal requirements for service as a federal judge include
   a) experience as a state-level judge.
   b) a minimum age of 30.
   c) a minimum of 10 years' legal experience.
   d) a neutral political background.
   e) There are no formal requirements for service as a federal judge.

The Power of the Supreme Court: Judicial Review

Explain how the Supreme Court exercises the power of judicial review (pp. 604–10)

The U.S. Supreme Court has the power to review the constitutionality of acts of Congress and the federal executive branch, as well as state actions. Although this power is not explicitly provided for in the Constitution, the Supreme Court asserted the power of judicial review in its 1803 *Marbury v. Madison* decision; and this power has generally been accepted since then.

Key Terms

judicial review (p. 604)
supremacy clause (p. 605)
common law (p. 609)
tort case (p. 609)

Practice Quiz

8. The Supreme Court's decision in *Marbury v. Madison* was important because
   a) it invalidated state laws prohibiting interracial marriage.
   b) it ruled that the recitation of prayers in public schools is unconstitutional under the establishment clause of the First Amendment.
   c) it established that arrested people have the right to remain silent, the right to be informed that anything they say can be held against them, and the right to counsel before and during police interrogation.
   d) it provided an expansive definition of *commerce* under the interstate commerce clause.
   e) it established the power of judicial review.

9. The U.S. Supreme Court's power to review state actions comes from
   a) tort law.
   b) *Hamdi v. Rumsfeld* and *Hamdan v. Rumsfeld.*
   c) the supremacy clause of the Constitution and the Judiciary Act of 1789.
   d) certiorari and amicus curiae.
   e) The Supreme Court does not have the power to review state actions.

The Supreme Court in Action

Describe the process the Supreme Court follows in the exercise of its power of judicial review (pp. 610–18)

Most cases reach the Supreme Court by a writ of certiorari. The Supreme Court is most likely to grant a writ of certiorari to cases that involve conflicting decisions by the federal circuit courts, cases that present important questions of civil rights or civil liberties, and cases in which the federal government is the appellant. Much of the Supreme Court's power in the American political system comes from its power to invalidate actions taken by the legislative and executive branches of government if these actions violate the Constitution.

Key Terms

standing (p. 610)
mootness (p. 610)
writ of certiorari (p. 611)
solicitor general (p. 612)
amicus curiae (p. 613)
briefs (p. 615)
oral argument (p. 616)
opinion (p. 616)
dissenting opinion (p. 617)

Practice Quiz

10. Which of the following is *not* included as a "special and compelling" reason to hear a case under Rule 10 of the Rules of the Supreme Court of the United States?
   a) the president of the United States authors an amicus curiae brief on the issue in question
   b) a circuit court decision on the issue in question conflicts with previous Supreme Court decisions
   c) there are conflicting decisions by two or more state courts of last resort on the issue in question
   d) there are conflicting decisions between circuit courts and state courts of last resort on the issue in question
   e) there are conflicting decisions by two or more circuit courts on the issue in question

11. Which of the following play an important role in shaping the flow of cases heard by the Supreme Court?
   a) the attorney general and the secretary of state
   b) the solicitor general and federal law clerks
   c) the president and Congress
   d) state legislatures
   e) the federal district and circuit courts

12. Which of the following is a brief submitted to the Supreme Court by someone other than one of the parties in the case?
   a) amicus curiae brief
   b) writ of habeas corpus
   c) writ of certiorari
   d) dissenting opinion
   e) de jure brief

Explaining Supreme Court Decisions

Consider the personal and political influences on judges and the courts (pp. 618–24)

Through most of American history, the federal courts avoided confrontations with the other branches of government and worked primarily to provide support for executive actions and congressional laws by declaring them to be consistent with constitutional principles. During the 1960s and '70s the federal courts liberalized the concept of standing, broadened the scope of relief courts could provide, and began to employ structural remedies. As a result of these changes, the power of the federal court system expanded dramatically.

Key Terms

judicial restraint (p. 619)
judicial activism (p. 619)
class-action suit (p. 622)

Practice Quiz

13. If a justice refuses to go beyond the clear words of the Constitution in interpreting the document's meaning, he or she would be considered an advocate of which judicial philosophy?
   a) judicial restraint
   b) judicial activism
   c) stare decisis
   d) judicial liberalism
   e) judicial conservatism

14. Which of the following procedures adopted by the federal courts after 1960 fundamentally expanded the power of the judiciary in the United States?
   a) banning the practice of "fee shifting"
   b) prohibiting the courts from acting on behalf of broad categories of persons in "class-action" cases
   c) expanding the concept of standing to permit almost any group that seeks to challenge the actions of an administrative agency to bring its case before the federal bench
   d) creating a "Department of Judicial Enforcement" to independently implement the federal judiciary's decisions
   e) granting federal courts the ability to exercise power on their own initiative through the issuance of "mootness" rulings

For Further Reading

Baum, Lawrence. *Ideology in the Supreme Court*. Princeton, NJ: Princeton University Press, 2017.

Baum, Lawrence. *The Supreme Court*. 12th ed. Washington, DC: CQ Press, 2015.

Block, Frederick. *Disrobed: An Inside Look at the Life and Work of a Federal Trial Judge*. New York: Westlaw, 2012.

Breyer, Stephen. *The Court and the World: American Law and the New Global Realities*. New York: Knopf, 2015.

Chermerinsky, Erwin. *Closing the Courthouse Door: How Your Constitutional Rights Became Unenforceable*. New Haven, CT: Yale University Press, 2017.

Cross, Frank. *Decision Making in the U.S. Courts of Appeals*. Stanford, CA: Stanford University Press, 2007.

Greenhouse, Linda. *The U.S. Supreme Court: A Very Short Introduction*. New York: Oxford University Press, 2012.

Hirshman, Linda. *Sisters in Law: How Sandra Day O'Connor and Ruth Bader Ginsburg Went to the Supreme Court and Changed the World*. New York: Harper, 2015.

Peppers, Todd, and Artemus Ward. *In Chambers: Stories of Supreme Court Law Clerks and Their Justices*. Charlottesville: University of Virginia Press, 2012.

Posner, Richard. *Reflections on Judging*. Cambridge, MA: Harvard University Press, 2013.

Posner, Richard A. *The Federal Judiciary: Strengths and Weaknesses*. Cambridge, MA: Harvard University Press, 2017.

Raskin, Jamin B. *We the Students: Supreme Court Decisions for and about Students*. Washington, DC: CQ Press, 2003.

Rosenberg, Gerald. *The Hollow Hope: Can Courts Bring about Social Change?* 2nd ed. Chicago: University of Chicago Press, 2008.

Rossum, Ralph. *Antonin Scalia's Jurisprudence*. Lawrence: University Press of Kansas, 2006.

Stevens, John Paul. *Five Chiefs: A Supreme Court Memoir*. Boston: Little, Brown, 2011.

Sunstein, Cass. *Are Judges Political?* Washington, DC: Brookings Institution Press, 2006.

Toobin, Jeffrey. *The Nine: Inside the Secret World of the Supreme Court*. New York: Anchor Books, 2008.

Toobin, Jeffrey. *The Oath: The Obama White House and the Supreme Court*. New York: Anchor Books, 2013.

Trachtman, Michael. *The Supreme Court's Greatest Hits: The 44 Supreme Court Cases That Most Directly Affect Your Life*. 3rd ed. New York: Sterling, 2016.

Tribe, Lawrence. *Uncertain Justice: The Roberts Court and the Constitution*. New York: Picador, 2015.

Urofsky, Melvin. *Dissent and the Supreme Court: Its Role in the Court's History and the Nation's Constitutional Dialogue*. New York: Pantheon, 2015.

Whittington, Keith. *Political Foundations of Judicial Supremacy: The President, the Supreme Court, and Constitutional Leadership in U.S. History*. Princeton, NJ: Princeton University Press, 2008.

Recommended Websites

Concourts
www.concourts.net
The U.S. Supreme Court has the responsibility for examining and interpreting the Constitution. The Concourts website assumes a comparative perspective and looks at systems of constitutional review in over 150 countries.

FindLaw
www.findlaw.com
FindLaw's website provides answers to most legal questions and helps individuals find legal counsel.

Justice Talking
www.justicetalking.org
Justice Talking is a public radio program that examines current legal issues and important court cases.

Legal Information Institute
www.law.cornell.edu
The Legal Information Institute at Cornell University is a wonderful website for conducting legal research.

Office of the Solicitor General
www.usdoj.gov/osg
The solicitor general conducts litigation on behalf of the U.S. Supreme Court and has a tremendous amount of control over the cases that it hears. See what cases are currently being considered by this powerful official of the Justice Department.

U.S. Courts
www.uscourts.gov
The U.S. court system consists of trial, appellate, and supreme courts. The U.S. Courts website provides a look at the different types of courts in the federal judiciary.

U.S. Supreme Court
www.supremecourtus.gov
The website for the U.S. Supreme Court provides information on recent decisions. Take a moment to read some oral arguments, briefs, or court opinions.

U.S. Supreme Court Media
www.oyez.org
The website for U.S. Supreme Court Media has a great search engine for finding information on such landmark cases as *Marbury v. Madison*, *Miranda v. Arizona*, and *Roe v. Wade*.

Appendix

The Declaration of Independence

In Congress, July 4, 1776

The unanimous Declaration of the thirteen united States of America,

When in the Course of human events, it becomes necessary for one people to dissolve the political bands which have connected them with another, and to assume among the powers of the earth, the separate and equal station to which the Laws of Nature and of Nature's God entitle them, a decent respect to the opinions of mankind requires that they should declare the causes which impel them to the separation.

We hold these truths to be self-evident, that all men are created equal, that they are endowed by their Creator with certain unalienable Rights, that among these are Life, Liberty and the pursuit of Happiness.—That to secure these rights, Governments are instituted among Men, deriving their just powers from the consent of the governed.—That whenever any Form of Government becomes destructive of these ends, it is the Right of the People to alter or to abolish it, and to institute new Government, laying its foundation on such principles and organizing its powers in such form, as to them shall seem most likely to effect their Safety and Happiness. Prudence, indeed, will dictate that Governments long established should not be changed for light and transient causes; and accordingly all experience hath shewn, that mankind are more disposed to suffer, while evils are sufferable, than to right themselves by abolishing the forms to which they are accustomed. But when a long train of abuses and usurpations, pursuing invariably the same Object evinces a design to reduce them under absolute Despotism, it is their right, it is their duty, to throw off such Government, and to provide new Guards for their future security.—Such has been the patient sufferance of these Colonies; and such is now the necessity which constrains them to alter their former Systems of Government. The history of the present King of Great Britain is a history of repeated injuries and usurpations, all having in direct object the establishment of an absolute Tyranny over these States. To prove this, let Facts be submitted to a candid world.

He has refused his Assent to Laws, the most wholesome and necessary for the public good.

He has forbidden his Governors to pass Laws of immediate and pressing importance, unless suspended in their operation till his Assent should be obtained; and when so suspended, he has utterly neglected to attend to them.

He has refused to pass other Laws for the accommodation of large districts of people, unless those people would relinquish the right of Representation in the Legislature, a right inestimable to them and formidable to tyrants only.

He has called together legislative bodies at places unusual, uncomfortable, and distant from the depository of their public Records, for the sole purpose of fatiguing them into compliance with his measures.

He has dissolved Representative Houses repeatedly, for opposing with manly firmness his invasions on the rights of the people.

He has refused for a long time, after such dissolutions, to cause others to be elected; whereby the Legislative powers, incapable of Annihilation, have returned to the People at large for their exercise; the State remaining in the mean time exposed to all the dangers of invasion from without, and convulsions within.

He has endeavoured to prevent the population of these States; for that purpose obstructing the Laws for Naturalization of Foreigners; refusing to pass others to encourage their migrations hither, and raising the conditions of new Appropriations of Lands.

He has obstructed the Administration of Justice, by refusing his Assent to Laws for establishing Judiciary powers.

He has made Judges dependent on his Will alone, for the tenure of their offices, and the amount and payment of their salaries.

He has erected a multitude of New Offices, and sent hither swarms of Officers to harrass our people, and eat out their substance.

He has kept among us, in times of peace, Standing Armies without the Consent of our legislatures.

He has affected to render the Military independent of and superior to the Civil power.

He has combined with others to subject us to a jurisdiction foreign to our constitution, and unacknowledged by our laws; giving his Assent to their Acts of pretended Legislation:

For Quartering large bodies of armed troops among us:

For protecting them, by a mock Trial, from punishment for any Murders which they should commit on the Inhabitants of these States:

For cutting off our Trade with all parts of the world:

For imposing Taxes on us without our Consent:

For depriving us in many cases, of the benefits of Trial by Jury:

For transporting us beyond Seas to be tried for pretended offences:

For abolishing the free System of English Laws in a neighboring Province, establishing therein an Arbitrary government, and enlarging its Boundaries so as to render it at once an example and fit instrument for introducing the same absolute rule into these Colonies:

For taking away our Charters, abolishing our most valuable Laws, and altering fundamentally the Forms of our Governments:

For suspending our own Legislatures, and declaring themselves invested with power to legislate for us in all cases whatsoever.

He has abdicated Government here, by declaring us out of his Protection and waging War against us.

He has plundered our seas, ravaged our Coasts, burnt our towns, and destroyed the lives of our people.

He is at this time transporting large Armies of foreign Mercenaries to compleat the works of death, desolation and tyranny, already begun with circumstances of Cruelty & perfidy scarcely paralleled in the most barbarous ages, and totally unworthy the Head of a civilized nation.

He has constrained our fellow Citizens taken Captive on the high Seas to bear Arms against their Country, to become the executioners of their friends and Brethren, or to fall themselves by their Hands.

He has excited domestic insurrections amongst us, and has endeavoured to bring on the inhabitants of our frontiers, the merciless Indian Savages, whose known rule of warfare, is an undistinguished destruction of all ages, sexes and conditions.

In every stage of these Oppressions We have Petitioned for Redress in the most humble terms: Our repeated Petitions have been answered only by repeated injury. A Prince whose character is thus marked by every act which may define a Tyrant, is unfit to be the ruler of a free people.

Nor have We been wanting in attentions to our Brittish brethren. We have warned them from time to time of attempts by their legislature to extend an unwarrantable jurisdiction over us. We have reminded them of the circumstances of our emigration and settlement here. We have appealed to their native justice and magnanimity, and we have conjured them by the ties of our common kindred to disavow these usurpations, which, would inevitably interrupt our connections and correspondence. They too have been deaf to the voice of justice and of consanguinity. We must, therefore, acquiesce in the necessity, which denounces our Separation, and hold them, as we hold the rest of mankind, Enemies in War, in Peace Friends.

We, Therefore, the Representatives of the United States of America, in General Congress, Assembled, appealing to the Supreme Judge of the world for the rectitude of our intentions, do, in the Name, and by Authority of the good People of these Colonies, solemnly publish and declare, That these United Colonies are, and of Right ought to be Free and Independent States; that they are Absolved from all Allegiance to the British Crown, and that all political connection between them and the State of Great Britain, is and ought to be totally dissolved; and that as Free and Independent States, they have full Power to levy War, conclude Peace, contract Alliances, establish Commerce, and to do all other Acts and Things which Independent States may of right do. And for the support of this Declaration, with a firm reliance on the protection of divine Providence, we mutually pledge to each other our Lives, our Fortunes and our sacred Honor.

The foregoing Declaration was, by order of Congress, engrossed, and signed by the following members:

John Hancock

NEW HAMPSHIRE
Josiah Bartlett
William Whipple
Matthew Thornton

MASSACHUSETTS BAY
Samuel Adams
John Adams
Robert Treat Paine
Elbridge Gerry

RHODE ISLAND
Stephen Hopkins
William Ellery

CONNECTICUT
Roger Sherman
Samuel Huntington
William Williams
Oliver Wolcott

NEW YORK
William Floyd
Philip Livingston
Francis Lewis
Lewis Morris

NEW JERSEY
Richard Stockton
John Witherspoon
Francis Hopkinson
John Hart
Abraham Clark

PENNSYLVANIA
Robert Morris
Benjamin Rush
Benjamin Franklin
John Morton
George Clymer
James Smith
George Taylor
James Wilson
George Ross

DELAWARE
Caesar Rodney
George Read
Thomas M'Kean

MARYLAND
Samuel Chase
William Paca
Thomas Stone
Charles Carroll,
of Carrollton

VIRGINIA
George Wythe
Richard Henry Lee
Thomas Jefferson
Benjamin Harrison
Thomas Nelson, Jr.
Francis Lightfoot Lee
Carter Braxton

NORTH CAROLINA
William Hooper
Joseph Hewes
John Penn

SOUTH CAROLINA
Edward Rutledge
Thomas Heyward, Jr.
Thomas Lynch, Jr.
Arthur Middleton

GEORGIA
Button Gwinnett
Lyman Hall
George Walton

Resolved, That copies of the Declaration be sent to the several assemblies, conventions, and committees, or councils of safety, and to the several commanding officers of the continental troops; that it be proclaimed in each of the United States, at the head of the army.

The Articles of Confederation

Agreed to by Congress November 15, 1777;
ratified and in force March 1, 1781

To all whom these Presents shall come, we the undersigned Delegates of the States affixed to our Names, send greeting. Whereas the Delegates of the United States of America, in Congress assembled, did, on the fifteenth day of November, in the Year of Our Lord One thousand Seven Hundred and Seventy seven, and in the Second Year of the Independence of America, agree to certain articles of Confederation and perpetual Union between the States of Newhampshire, Massachusetts-bay, Rhodeisland and Providence Plantations, Connecticut, New-York, New-Jersey, Pennsylvania, Delaware, Maryland, Virginia, North-Carolina, South-Carolina and Georgia in the words following, viz. "Articles of Confederation and perpetual Union between the states of Newhampshire, Massachusettsbay, Rhodeisland and Providence Plantations, Connecticut, New-York, New-Jersey, Pennsylvania, Delaware, Maryland, Virginia, North-Carolina, South-Carolina and Georgia.

Art. I. The Stile of this confederacy shall be "The United States of America."

Art. II. Each state retains its sovereignty, freedom and independence, and every Power, Jurisdiction and right, which is not by this confederation expressly delegated to the United States, in Congress assembled.

Art. III. The said states hereby severally enter into a firm league of friendship with each other, for their common defence, the security of their Liberties, and their mutual and general welfare, binding themselves to assist each other, against all force offered to, or attacks made upon them, or any of them, on account of religion, sovereignty, trade, or any other pretence whatever.

Art. IV. The better to secure and perpetuate mutual friendship and intercourse among the people of the different states in this union, the free inhabitants of each of these states, paupers, vagabonds and fugitives from Justice excepted, shall be entitled to all privileges and immunities of free citizens in the several states; and the people of each state shall have free ingress and regress to and from any other state, and shall enjoy therein all the privileges of trade and commerce, subject to the same duties, impositions and restrictions as the inhabitants thereof respectively, provided that such restriction shall not extend so far as to prevent the removal of property imported into any state, to any other state, of which the Owner is an inhabitant; provided also that no imposition, duties or restriction shall be laid by any state, on the property of the united states, or either of them.

If any Person guilty of, or charged with treason, felony, or other high misdemeanor in any state, shall flee from Justice, and be found in any of the united states, he shall, upon demand of the Governor or executive power, of the state from which he fled, be delivered up and removed to the state having jurisdiction of his offence.

Full faith and credit shall be given in each of these states to the records, acts and judicial proceedings of the courts and magistrates of every other state.

Art. V. For the more convenient management of the general interests of the united states, delegates shall be annually appointed in such manner as the legislature of each state shall direct, to meet in Congress on the first Monday in November, in every year, with a power reserved to each state, to recall its delegates, or any of them, at any time within the year, and to send others in their stead, for the remainder of the Year.

No state shall be represented in Congress by less than two, nor by more than seven Members; and no person shall be capable of being a delegate for more than three years in any term of six years; nor shall any person, being a delegate, be capable of holding any office under the united states, for which he, or another for his benefit receives any salary, fees or emolument of any kind.

Each state shall maintain its own delegates in a meeting of the states, and while they act as members of the committee of the states.

In determining questions in the united states, in Congress assembled, each state shall have one vote.

Freedom of speech and debate in Congress shall not be impeached or questioned in any Court, or place out of Congress, and the members of congress shall be protected in their persons from arrests and imprisonments, during the time of their going to and from, and attendance on congress, except for treason, felony, or breach of the peace.

Art. VI. No state without the Consent of the united states in congress assembled, shall send any embassy to, or receive any embassy from, or enter into any conference, agreement, or alliance or treaty with any King, prince or state; nor shall any person holding any office or profit or trust under the united states, or any of them, accept of any present, emolument, office or title of any kind whatever from any king, prince or foreign state; nor shall the united states in congress assembled, or any of them, grant any title of nobility.

No two or more states shall enter into any treaty, confederation or alliance whatever between them, without the consent of the united states in congress assembled, specifying accurately the purposes for which the same is to be entered into, and how long it shall continue.

No state shall lay any imposts or duties, which may interfere with any stipulations in treaties, entered into by the united states in congress assembled, with any king, prince or state, in pursuance of any treaties already proposed by congress, to the courts of France and Spain.

No vessels of war shall be kept up in time of peace by any state, except such number only, as shall be deemed necessary by the united states in congress assembled, for the defence of such state, or its trade; nor shall any body of forces be kept up by any state, in time of peace, except such number only, as in the judgment of the united states, in congress assembled, shall be deemed requisite to garrison the forts necessary for the defence of such state; but every state shall always keep up a well regulated and disciplined militia, sufficiently armed and accoutred, and shall provide and constantly have ready for use, in public stores, a due number of field pieces and tents, and a proper quantity of arms, ammunition and camp equipage.

No state shall engage in any war without the consent of the united states in congress assembled, unless such state be actually invaded by enemies, or shall have received certain advice of a resolution being formed by some nation of Indians to invade such state, and the danger is so imminent as not to admit of a delay, till the united states in congress asssembled can be consulted; nor shall any state grant commissions to any ships or vessels of war, nor letters of marque or reprisal, except it be after a declaration of war by the united states in congress assembled, and then only against the kingdom or state and the subjects thereof, against which war has been so declared, and under such regulations as shall be established by the united states in congress assembled, unless such state be infested by pirates; in which case vessels of war may be fitted out for that occasion, and kept so long as the danger shall continue, or until the united states in congress assembled shall determine otherwise.

Art. VII. When land-forces are raised by any state for the common defence, all officers of or under the rank of colonel, shall be appointed by the legislature of each state respectively, by whom such forces shall be raised, or in such manner as such state shall direct, and all vacancies shall be filled up by the state which first made the appointment.

Art. VIII. All charges of war, and all other expences that shall be incurred for the common defence or general welfare, and allowed by the united states in congress assembled, shall be defrayed out of a common treasury, which shall be supplied by the several states in proportion to the value of all land within each state, granted to or surveyed for any Person, as such land and the buildings and improvements thereon shall be estimated according to such mode as the united states in congress assembled, shall from time to time direct and appoint.

The taxes for paying that proportion shall be laid and levied by the authority and direction of the legislatures of the several states within the time agreed upon by the united states in congress assembled.

Art. IX. The united states in congress assembled, shall have the sole and exclusive right and power of determining on peace and war, except in the cases mentioned in the sixth article—of sending and receiving ambassadors—entering into treaties and alliances, provided that no treaty of commerce shall be made whereby the legislative power of the respective states shall be restrained from imposing such imposts and duties on foreigners, as their own people are subjected to, or from prohibiting the exportation of any species of goods or commodities whatsoever—of establishing rules for deciding in all cases, what captures on land or water shall be legal, and in what manner prizes taken by land or naval forces in the service of the united states shall be divided or appropriated—of granting letters of marque and reprisal in times of peace—appointing courts for the trial of piracies and felonies committed on the high seas and establishing courts for receiving and determining finally appeals in all cases of captures, provided that no member of congress shall be appointed a judge of any of the said courts.

The united states in congress assembled shall also be the last resort on appeal in all disputes and differences now subsisting or that hereafter may arise between two or more states concerning boundary, jurisdiction or any other cause whatever; which authority shall always be exercised in the manner following. Whenever the legislative or executive authority or lawful agent of any state in controversy with another shall present a petition to congress stating the matter in question and praying for a hearing, notice thereof shall be given by order of congress to the legislative or executive authority of the other state in controversy, and a day assigned for the appearance of the parties by their lawful agents, who shall then be directed to appoint by joint consent, commissioners or judges to constitute a court for hearing and determining the matter in question: but if they cannot agree, congress shall name three persons out of each of the united states, and from the list of such persons each party shall alternately strike out one, the petitioners beginning, until the number shall be reduced to thirteen; and from that number not less than seven, nor more than nine names as congress shall direct, shall in the presence of congress be drawn out by lot, and the persons whose names shall be so drawn or any five of them, shall be commissioners or judges, to hear and finally determine the controversy, so always as a major part of the judges who shall hear the cause shall agree in the determination: and if either party shall neglect to attend at the day appointed, without shewing reasons, which congress shall judge sufficient, or being present shall refuse to strike, the congress shall proceed to nominate three persons out of each state, and the secretary of congress shall strike in behalf of such party absent or refusing; and the judgment and sentence of the court to be appointed, in the manner before prescribed, shall be final and conclusive; and if any of the parties shall refuse to submit to the authority of such court, or to appear to defend their claim or cause, the court shall nevertheless proceed to pronounce sentence, or judgment, which shall in like manner be final and decisive, the judgment or sentence and other proceedings being in either case transmitted to congress, and lodged among the acts of congress for the security of the parties concerned: provided that every commissioner, before he sits in judgment, shall take an oath to be administered by one of the judges of the supreme or superior court of the state, where the cause shall be tried, "well and truly to hear and determine the matter in question, according to the best of his judgment, without favour, affection or hope of reward:" provided also, that no state shall be deprived of territory for the benefit of the united states.

All controversies concerning the private right of soil claimed under different grants of two or more states, whose jurisdictions as they may respect such lands, and the states which passed such grants are adjusted, the said grants or either of them being at the same time claimed to have originated antecedent to such settlement of jurisdiction, shall on the petition of either party to the congress of the united states, be finally determined as near as may be in the same manner as is before prescribed for deciding disputes respecting territorial jurisdiction between different states.

The united states in congress assembled shall also have the sole and exclusive right and power of regulating the alloy and value of coin struck by their own authority, or by that of the respective states—fixing the standard of weights and measures throughout the united states—regulating the trade and managing all affairs with the Indians, not members of any of the states, provided that the legislative right of any state within its own limits be not infringed or violated—establishing and regulating post-offices from one state to another, throughout all the united states, and exacting such postage on the papers passing thro' the same as may be requisite to defray the expences of the said office—appointing all officers of the land forces, in the service of the united states, excepting regimental officers—appointing all the officers of the naval forces, and commissioning all officers whatever in the service of the united states—making rules for the government and regulation of the said land and naval forces, and directing their operations.

The united states in congress assembled shall have authority to appoint a committee, to sit in the recess of congress, to be denominated "A Committee of the States," and to consist of one delegate from each state; and to appoint such other committees and civil officers as may be necessary for managing the general affairs of the united states under their direction—to appoint one of their number to preside, provided that no person be allowed to serve in the office of president more than one year in any term of three years; to ascertain the necessary sums of Money to be raised for the service of the united states, and to appropriate and apply the same for defraying the public expenses—to borrow money, or emit bills on the credit of the united states, transmitting every half year to the respective states an account of the sums of money so borrowed or emitted,—to build and equip a navy—to agree upon the number of land forces, and to make requisitions from each state for its quota, in proportion to the number of white inhabitants in such state; which requisition shall be binding, and thereupon the legislature of each state shall appoint the regimental officers, raise the men and cloath, arm and equip them in a soldier like manner, at the expense of the united states; and the officers and men so cloathed, armed and equipped shall march to the place appointed, and within the time agreed on by the united states in congress assembled: But if the united states in congress assembled shall, on consideration of circumstances judge proper that any state should not raise men, or should raise a smaller number than its quota, and that any other state should raise a greater number of men than the quota thereof, such extra number shall be raised, officered, cloathed, armed and equipped in the same manner as the quota of such state, unless the legislature of such state shall judge that such extra number cannot be safely spared out of the same, in which case they shall raise officer, cloath, arm and equip as many of such extra number as they judge can be safely spared. And the officers and men so cloathed, armed and equipped, shall march to the place appointed, and within the time agreed on by the united states in congress assembled.

The united states in congress assembled shall never engage in a war, nor grant letters of marque and reprisal in time of peace, nor enter into any treaties or alliances, nor coin money, nor regulate the value thereof, nor ascertain the sums and expenses necessary for the defence and welfare of the united states, or any of them, nor emit bills, nor borrow money on the credit of the united states, nor appropriate money, nor agree upon the number of vessels of war, to be built or purchased, or the number of land or sea forces to be raised, nor appoint a commander in chief of the army or navy, unless nine states assent to the same: nor shall a question on any other point, except for adjourning from day to day be determined, unless by the votes of a majority of the united states in congress assembled.

The congress of the united states shall have power to adjourn to any time within the year, and to any place within the united states, so that no period of adjournment be for a longer duration than the space of six Months, and shall publish the Journal of their proceedings monthly, except such parts thereof relating to treaties, alliances or military operations, as in their judgment require secrecy; and the yeas and nays of the delegates of each state on any question shall be entered on the Journal, when it is desired by any delegate; and the delegates of a state, or any of them, at his or their request shall be furnished with a transcript of the said Journal, except such parts as are above excepted, to lay before the legislatures of the several states.

Art. X. The committee of the states, or any nine of them, shall be authorised to execute, in the recess of congress, such of the powers of congress as the united states in congress assembled, by the consent of nine states, shall from time to time think expedient to vest them with; provided that no power be delegated to the said committee, for the exercise of which, by the articles of confederation, the voice of nine states in the congress of the united states assembled is requisite.

Art. XI. Canada acceding to this confederation, and joining in the measures of the united states, shall be admitted into, and entitled to all the advantages of this union: but no other colony shall be admitted into the same, unless such admission be agreed to by nine states.

Art. XII. All bills of credit emitted, monies borrowed and debts contracted by, or under the authority of congress, before the assembling of the united states, in pursuance of the present confederation, shall be deemed and considered as a charge against the united states, for payment and satisfaction whereof the said united states and the public faith are hereby solemnly pledged.

Art. XIII. Every state shall abide by the determinations of the united states in congress assembled, on all questions which by this confederation are submitted to them. And the Articles of this confederation shall be inviolably observed by every state, and the union shall be perpetual; nor shall any alteration at any time hereafter be made in any of them; unless such alteration be agreed to in a congress of the united states, and be afterwards confirmed by the legislatures of every state.

And Whereas it hath pleased the Great Governor of the World to incline the hearts of the legislatures we respectively represent in congress, to approve of, and to authorize us to ratify the said articles of confederation and perpetual union. Know Ye that we the undersigned delegates, by virtue of the power and authority to us given for that purpose, do by these presents, in the name and in behalf of our respective constituents, fully and entirely ratify and confirm each and every of the said articles of confederation and perpetual union, and all and singular the matters and things therein contained: And we do further solemnly plight and engage the faith of our respective constituents, that they shall abide by the determinations of the united states in congress assembled, on all questions, which by the said confederation are submitted to them. And that the articles thereof shall be inviolably observed by the states we respectively represent, and that the union shall be perpetual. In Witness whereof we have hereunto set our hands in Congress. Done at Philadelphia in the state of Pennsylvania the ninth day of July, in the Year of our Lord one Thousand seven Hundred and Seventy-eight, and in the third year of the independence of America.

The Constitution of the United States of America

[PREAMBLE]

We the People of the United States, in Order to form a more perfect Union, establish Justice, insure domestic Tranquility, provide for the common defence, promote the general Welfare, and secure the Blessings of Liberty to ourselves and our Posterity, do ordain and establish this Constitution for the United States of America.

ARTICLE I

SECTION 1

[LEGISLATIVE POWERS]

All legislative Powers herein granted shall be vested in a Congress of the United States, which shall consist of a Senate and House of Representatives.

SECTION 2

[HOUSE OF REPRESENTATIVES, HOW CONSTITUTED, POWER OF IMPEACHMENT]

The House of Representatives shall be composed of Members chosen every second Year by the People of the several States, and the Electors in each State shall have the Qualifications requisite for Electors of the most numerous Branch of the State Legislature.

No Person shall be a Representative who shall not have attained to the Age of twenty five Years, and been seven Years a Citizen of the United States, and who shall not, when elected, be an Inhabitant of that State in which he shall be chosen.

Representatives and *direct Taxes*[1] shall be apportioned among the several States which may be included within this Union, according to their respective Numbers, *which shall be determined by adding to the whole Number of free Persons, including those bound to Service for a Term of Years, and excluding Indians not taxed, three fifths of all other Persons.*[2] The actual Enumeration shall be made within three Years after the first Meeting of the Congress of the United States, and within every subsequent Term of ten Years, in such Manner as they shall by Law direct. The Number of Representatives shall not exceed one for every thirty Thousand, but each State shall have at Least one Representative; *and until such enumeration shall be made, the State of New Hampshire shall be entitled to chuse three, Massachusetts eight, Rhode-Island and Providence Plantations one, Connecticut five, New-York six, New Jersey four, Pennsylvania eight, Delaware one, Maryland six, Virginia ten, North Carolina five, South Carolina five, and Georgia three.*[3]

When vacancies happen in the Representation from any State, the Executive Authority thereof shall issue Writs of Election to fill such Vacancies.

The House of Representatives shall chuse their Speaker and other Officers; and shall have the sole Power of Impeachment.

SECTION 3

[THE SENATE, HOW CONSTITUTED, IMPEACHMENT TRIALS]

The Senate of the United States shall be composed of two Senators from each State, *chosen by the Legislature thereof,*[4] for six Years; and each Senator shall have one Vote.

Immediately after they shall be assembled in Consequence of the first Election, they shall be divided as equally as may be into three Classes. The Seats of the Senators of the first Class shall be vacated at the Expiration of the second Year, of the second Class at the Expiration of the fourth Year, and of the third Class at the Expiration of the sixth Year, so that one third may be chosen every second Year; *and if Vacancies happen by Resignation, or otherwise, during the Recess of the Legislature of any State, the Executive thereof may make temporary Appointments until the next Meeting of the Legislature, which shall then fill such Vacancies.*[5]

No Person shall be a Senator who shall not have attained to the Age of thirty Years, and been nine Years a Citizen of the United States, and who shall not, when elected, be an Inhabitant of that State for which he shall be chosen.

The Vice President of the United States shall be President of the Senate, but shall have no Vote, unless they be equally divided.

The Senate shall chuse their other Officers, and also a President pro tempore, in the Absence of the Vice President, or when he shall exercise the Office of President of the United States.

[1]Modified by Sixteenth Amendment.

[2]Modified by Fourteenth Amendment.

[3]Temporary provision.

[4]Modified by Seventeenth Amendment.

[5]Modified by Seventeenth Amendment.

The Senate shall have the sole Power to try all Impeachments. When sitting for that Purpose, they shall be on Oath or Affirmation. When the President of the United States is tried, the Chief Justice shall preside: And no Person shall be convicted without the Concurrence of two thirds of the Members present.

Judgment in Cases of Impeachment shall not extend further than to removal from Office, and disqualification to hold and enjoy any Office of honor, Trust or Profit under the United States: but the Party convicted shall nevertheless be liable and subject to Indictment, Trial, Judgment and Punishment, according to Law.

SECTION 4

[ELECTION OF SENATORS AND REPRESENTATIVES]

The Times, Places and Manner of holding Elections for Senators and Representatives, shall be prescribed in each State by the Legislature thereof; but the Congress may at any time by Law make or alter such Regulations, except as to the Places of chusing Senators.

The Congress shall assemble at least once in every Year, and such Meeting shall be on the first Monday in December, unless they shall by Law appoint a different Day.[6]

SECTION 5

[QUORUM, JOURNALS, MEETINGS, ADJOURNMENTS]

Each House shall be the Judge of the Elections, Returns and Qualifications of its own Members, and a Majority of each shall constitute a Quorum to do Business; but a smaller Number may adjourn from day to day, and may be authorized to compel the Attendance of absent Members, in such Manner, and under such Penalties as each House may provide.

Each House may determine the Rules of its Proceedings, punish its Members for disorderly Behaviour, and, with the Concurrence of two thirds, expel a Member.

Each House shall keep a Journal of its Proceedings, and from time to time publish the same, excepting such Parts as may in their Judgment require Secrecy; and the Yeas and Nays of the Members of either House on any questions shall, at the Desire of one fifth of those Present, be entered on the Journal.

Neither House, during the Session of Congress, shall, without the Consent of the other, adjourn for more than three days, nor to any other Place than that in which the two Houses shall be sitting.

SECTION 6

[COMPENSATION, PRIVILEGES, DISABILITIES]

The Senators and Representatives shall receive a Compensation for their Services, to be ascertained by Law, and paid out of the Treasury of the United States. They shall in all Cases, except Treason, Felony and Breach of the Peace, be privileged from Arrest during their Attendance at the Session of their respective Houses, and in going to and returning from the same; and for any Speech or Debate in either House, they shall not be questioned in any other Place.

No Senator or Representative shall, during the Time for which he was elected, be appointed to any civil Office under the Authority of the United States, which shall have been created, or the Emoluments whereof shall have been encreased during such time; and no Person holding any Office under the United States, shall be a Member of either House during his Continuance in Office.

SECTION 7

[PROCEDURE IN PASSING BILLS AND RESOLUTIONS]

All Bills for raising Revenue shall originate in the House of Representatives; but the Senate may propose or concur with Amendments as on other Bills.

Every Bill which shall have passed the House of Representatives and the Senate, shall, before it become a Law, be presented to the President of the United States: If he approve he shall sign it, but if not he shall return it, with his Objections to that House in which it shall have originated, who shall enter the Objections at large on their Journal, and proceed to reconsider it. If after such Reconsideration two thirds of that House shall agree to pass the Bill, it shall be sent, together with the Objections, to the other House, by which it shall likewise be reconsidered, and if approved by two thirds of that House, it shall become a Law. But in all such Cases the Votes of both Houses shall be determined by yeas and Nays, and the Names of the Persons voting for and against the Bill shall be entered on the Journal of each House respectively. If any Bill shall not be returned by the President within ten Days (Sundays excepted) after it shall have been presented to him, the Same shall be a Law, in like Manner as if he had signed it, unless the Congress by their Adjournment prevent its Return, in which Case it shall not be a Law.

Every Order, Resolution, or Vote to which the Concurrence of the Senate and House of Representatives may be necessary (except on a question of Adjournment) shall be presented to the President of the United States; and before the Same shall take Effect, shall be approved by him, or being disapproved by him, shall be repassed by two thirds of the Senate and House of Representatives, according to the Rules and Limitations prescribed in the Case of a Bill.

SECTION 8

[POWERS OF CONGRESS]

The Congress shall have Power

To lay and collect Taxes, Duties, Imposts and Excises, to pay the Debts and provide for the common Defence and general Welfare of the United States; but all Duties, Imposts and Excises shall be uniform throughout the United States;

To borrow Money on the credit of the United States;

[6]Modified by Twentieth Amendment.

To regulate Commerce with foreign Nations, and among the several States, and with the Indian Tribes;

To establish an uniform Rule of Naturalization, and uniform Laws on the subject of Bankruptcies throughout the United States;

To coin Money, regulate the Value thereof, and of foreign Coin, and fix the Standard of Weights and Measures;

To provide for the Punishment of counterfeiting the Securities and current Coin of the United States;

To establish Post Offices and post Roads;

To promote the Progress of Science and useful Arts, by securing for limited Times to Authors and Inventors the exclusive Right to their respective Writings and Discoveries;

To constitute Tribunals inferior to the supreme Court;

To define and punish Piracies and Felonies committed on the high Seas, and Offences against the Law of Nations;

To declare War, grant Letters of Marque and Reprisal, and make Rules concerning Captures on Land and Water;

To raise and support Armies, but no Appropriation of Money to that Use shall be for a longer Term than two Years;

To provide and maintain a Navy;

To make Rules for the Government and Regulation of the land and naval Forces;

To provide for calling forth the Militia to execute the Laws of the Union, suppress Insurrections and repel Invasions;

To provide for organizing, arming, and disciplining, the Militia, and for governing such Part of them as may be employed in the Service of the United States, reserving to the States respectively, the Appointment of the Officers, and the Authority of training the Militia according to the discipline prescribed by Congress;

To exercise exclusive Legislation in all Cases whatsoever, over such District (not exceeding ten Miles square) as may, by Cession of particular States, and the Acceptance of Congress, become the Seat of the Government of the United States, and to exercise like Authority over all Places purchased by the Consent of the Legislature of the State in which the Same shall be, for the Erection of Forts, Magazines, Arsenals, dock-Yards, and other needful Buildings;—And

To make all Laws which shall be necessary and proper for carrying into Execution the foregoing Powers, and all other Powers vested by this Constitution in the Government of the United States, or in any Department or Officer thereof.

SECTION 9

[SOME RESTRICTIONS ON FEDERAL POWER]

The Migration or Importation of such Persons as any of the States now existing shall think proper to admit, shall not be prohibited by the Congress prior to the Year one thousand eight hundred and eight, but a Tax or duty may be imposed on such Importation, not exceeding ten dollars for each Person.[7]

The Privilege of the Writ of Habeas Corpus shall not be suspended, unless when in Cases of Rebellion or Invasion the public Safety may require it.

No Bill of Attainder or ex post facto Law shall be passed.

No Capitation, or other direct, Tax shall be laid, unless in Proportion to the Census or Enumeration herein before directed to be taken.[8]

No Tax or Duty shall be laid on Articles exported from any State.

No Preference shall be given by any Regulation of Commerce or Revenue to the Ports of one State over those of another; nor shall Vessels bound to, or from, one State, be obliged to enter, clear, or pay Duties in another.

No Money shall be drawn from the Treasury, but in Consequence of Appropriations made by Law; and a regular Statement and Account of the Receipts and Expenditures of all public Money shall be published from time to time.

No Title of Nobility shall be granted by the United States: And no Person holding any Office of Profit or Trust under them, shall, without the Consent of the Congress, accept of any present, Emolument, Office, or Title, of any kind whatever, from any King, Prince, or foreign State.

SECTION 10

[RESTRICTIONS UPON POWERS OF STATES]

No State shall enter into any Treaty, Alliance, or Confederation; grant Letters of Marque and Reprisal; coin Money; emit Bills of Credit; make any Thing but gold and silver Coin a Tender in Payment of Debts; pass any Bill of Attainder, ex post facto Law, or Law impairing the Obligation of Contracts, or grant any Title of Nobility.

No State shall, without the Consent of the Congress, lay any Imposts or Duties on Imports or Exports, except what may be absolutely necessary for executing its inspection Laws: and the net Produce of all Duties and Imposts, laid by any State on Imports or Exports, shall be for the Use of the Treasury of the United States; and all such Laws shall be subject to the Revision and Control of the Congress.

No State shall, without the Consent of Congress, lay any Duty of Tonnage, keep Troops, or Ships of War in time of Peace, enter into any Agreement or Compact with another State, or with a foreign Power, or engage in War, unless actually invaded, or in such imminent Danger as will not admit of delay.

ARTICLE II

SECTION 1

[EXECUTIVE POWER, ELECTION, QUALIFICATIONS OF THE PRESIDENT]

The executive Power shall be vested in a President of the United States of America. *He shall hold his Office during the Term of*

[7]Temporary provision.

[8]Modified by Sixteenth Amendment.

four Years, and, together with the Vice President, chosen for the same Term, be elected, as follows[9]

Each State shall appoint, in such Manner as the Legislature thereof may direct, a Number of Electors, equal to the whole Number of Senators and Representatives to which the State may be entitled in the Congress: but no Senator or Representative, or Person holding an Office of Trust or Profit under the United States, shall be appointed an Elector.

The electors shall meet in their respective States, and vote by ballot for two Persons, of whom one at least shall not be an Inhabitant of the same State with themselves. And they shall make a List of all the Persons voted for, and of the Number of Votes for each; which List they shall sign and certify, and transmit sealed to the Seat of the Government of the United States, directed to the President of the Senate. The President of the Senate shall, in the Presence of the Senate and House of Representatives, open all the Certificates, and the Votes shall then be counted. The Person having the greatest Number of Votes shall be the President, if such Number be a Majority of the whole Number of Electors appointed; and if there be more than one who have such Majority, and have an equal Number of Votes, then the House of Representatives shall immediately chuse by Ballot one of them for President; and if no Person have a Majority, then from the five highest on the List the said House shall in like Manner chuse the President. But in chusing the President, the Votes shall be taken by States, the Representation from each State having one Vote; A quorum for this Purpose shall consist of a Member or Members from two thirds of the States, and a Majority of all the States shall be necessary to a Choice. In every Case, after the Choice of the President, the person having the greatest Number of Votes of the Electors shall be the Vice President. But if there should remain two or more who have equal Votes, the Senate shall chuse from them by Ballot the Vice President.[10]

The Congress may determine the Time of chusing the Electors, and the Day on which they shall give their Votes; which Day shall be the same throughout the United States.

No Person except a natural born Citizen, or a Citizen of the United States, at the time of the Adoption of this Constitution, shall be eligible to the Office of President; neither shall any Person be eligible to that Office who shall not have attained to the Age of thirty five Years, and been fourteen Years a Resident within the United States.

In Case of the Removal of the President from Office, or his Death, Resignation, or Inability to discharge the Powers and Duties of the said Office, the Same shall devolve on the Vice President, and the Congress may by Law provide for the Case of Removal, Death, Resignation or Inability, both of the President and Vice President, declaring what Officer shall then act as President, and such Officer shall act accordingly, until the Disability be removed, or a President shall be elected.

[9]Number of terms limited to two by Twenty-Second Amendment.

[10]Modified by Twelfth and Twentieth Amendments.

The President shall, at stated Times, receive for his Services, a Compensation, which shall neither be increased nor diminished during the Period for which he shall have been elected, and he shall not receive within that Period any other Emolument from the United States, or any of them.

Before he enter on the Execution of his Office, he shall take the following Oath or Affirmation:—"I do solemnly swear (or affirm) that I will faithfully execute the Office of President of the United States, and will to the best of my Ability, preserve, protect and defend the Constitution of the United States."

SECTION 2

[POWERS OF THE PRESIDENT]

The President shall be Commander in Chief of the Army and Navy of the United States, and of the Militia of the several States, when called into the actual Service of the United States; he may require the Opinion, in writing, of the principal Officer in each of the executive Departments, upon any Subject relating to the Duties of their respective Offices, and he shall have Power to grant Reprieves and Pardons for Offences against the United States, except in Cases of Impeachment.

He shall have Power, by and with the Advice and Consent of the Senate, to make Treaties, provided two thirds of the Senators present concur; and he shall nominate, and by and with the Advice and Consent of the Senate, shall appoint Ambassadors, other public Ministers and Consuls, Judges of the supreme Court, and all other Officers of the United States, whose Appointments are not herein otherwise provided for, and which shall be established by Law: but the Congress may by Law vest the Appointment of such inferior Officers, as they think proper, in the President alone, in the Courts of Law, or in the Heads of Departments.

The President shall have Power to fill up all Vacancies that may happen during the Recess of the Senate, by granting Commissions which shall expire at the End of their next Session.

SECTION 3

[POWERS AND DUTIES OF THE PRESIDENT]

He shall from time to time give to the Congress Information of the State of the Union, and recommend to their Consideration such Measures as he shall judge necessary and expedient; he may, on extraordinary Occasions, convene both Houses, or either of them, and in Case of Disagreement between them, with Respect to the Time of Adjournment, he may adjourn them to such Time as he shall think proper; he shall receive Ambassadors and other public Ministers; he shall take Care that the Laws be faithfully executed, and shall Commission all the Officers of the United States.

SECTION 4

[IMPEACHMENT]

The President, Vice President and all civil Officers of the United States, shall be removed from Office on Impeachment for, and Conviction of, Treason, Bribery, or other high Crimes and Misdemeanors.

ARTICLE III

SECTION 1

[JUDICIAL POWER, TENURE OF OFFICE]

The judicial Power of the United States, shall be vested in one supreme Court, and in such inferior Courts as the Congress may from time to time ordain and establish. The Judges, both of the supreme and inferior Courts, shall hold their Offices during good Behaviour, and shall, at stated Times, receive for their Services, a Compensation, which shall not be diminished during their Continuance in Office.

SECTION 2

[JURISDICTION]

The judicial Power shall extend to all Cases, in Law and Equity, arising under this Constitution, the Laws of the United States, and Treaties made, or which shall be made, under their Authority;—to all Cases affecting Ambassadors, other public Ministers and Consuls;—to all Cases of admiralty and maritime Jurisdiction;—to Controversies to which the United States shall be a Party;—to Controversies between two or more States;—*between a State and Citizens of another State;*—between Citizens of different States,—between Citizens of the same State claiming Lands under Grants of different States, *and between a State,* or the Citizens thereof, *and foreign States, Citizens or Subjects.*[11]

In all Cases affecting Ambassadors, other public Ministers and Consuls, and those in which a State shall be Party, the supreme Court shall have original Jurisdiction. In all the other Cases before mentioned, the supreme Court shall have appellate Jurisdiction, both as to Law and Fact, with such Exceptions, and under such Regulations as the Congress shall make.

The Trial of all Crimes, except in Cases of Impeachment, shall be by Jury; and such Trial shall be held in the State where the said Crimes shall have been committed; but when not committed within any State, the Trial shall be at such Place or Places as the Congress may by Law have directed.

SECTION 3

[TREASON, PROOF, AND PUNISHMENT]

Treason against the United States, shall consist only in levying War against them, or in adhering to their Enemies, giving them Aid and Comfort. No Person shall be convicted of Treason unless on the Testimony of two Witnesses to the same overt Act, or on Confession in open Court.

The Congress shall have Power to declare the Punishment of Treason, but no Attainder of Treason shall work Corruption of Blood, or Forfeiture except during the Life of the Person attainted.

[11]Modified by Eleventh Amendment.

ARTICLE IV

SECTION 1

[FAITH AND CREDIT AMONG STATES]

Full Faith and Credit shall be given in each State to the public Acts, Records, and judicial Proceedings of every other State. And the Congress may by general Laws prescribe the Manner in which such Acts, Records and Proceedings shall be proved, and the Effect thereof.

SECTION 2

[PRIVILEGES AND IMMUNITIES, FUGITIVES]

The Citizens of each State shall be entitled to all Privileges and Immunities of Citizens in the several States.

A Person charged in any State with Treason, Felony or other Crime, who shall flee from Justice, and be found in another State, shall on Demand of the executive Authority of the State from which he fled, be delivered up, to be removed to the State having Jurisdiction of the Crime.

No person held to Service or Labour in one State, under the Laws thereof, escaping into another, shall, in Consequence of any Law or Regulation therein, be discharged from such Service or Labour, but shall be delivered up on Claim of the Party to whom such Service or Labour may be due.[12]

SECTION 3

[ADMISSION OF NEW STATES]

New States may be admitted by the Congress into this Union; but no new State shall be formed or erected within the Jurisdiction of any other State; nor any State be formed by the Junction of two or more States, or Parts of States, without the Consent of the Legislatures of the States concerned as well as of the Congress.

The Congress shall have Power to dispose of and make all needful Rules and Regulations respecting the Territory or other Property belonging to the United States; and nothing in this Constitution shall be so construed as to Prejudice any Claims of the United States, or of any particular State.

SECTION 4

[GUARANTEE OF REPUBLICAN GOVERNMENT]

The United States shall guarantee to every State in this Union a Republican Form of Government, and shall protect each of them against Invasion; and on Application of the Legislature, or of the Executive (when the Legislature cannot be convened), against domestic Violence.

ARTICLE V

[AMENDMENT OF THE CONSTITUTION]

The Congress, whenever two thirds of both Houses shall deem it necessary, shall propose Amendments to this Constitution, or, on the Application of the Legislatures of two thirds of the

[12]Repealed by the Thirteenth Amendment.

several States, shall call a Convention for proposing Amendments, which, in either Case, shall be valid to all Intents and Purposes, as Part of this Constitution, when ratified by the Legislatures of three fourths of the several States, or by Conventions in three fourths thereof, as the one or the other Mode of Ratification may be proposed by the Congress; *Provided that no Amendment which may be made prior to the Year One thousand eight hundred and eight shall in any Manner affect the first and fourth Clauses in the Ninth Section of the first Article;*[13] and that no State, without its Consent, shall be deprived of its equal Suffrage in the Senate.

ARTICLE VI

[DEBTS, SUPREMACY, OATH]

All Debts contracted and Engagements entered into, before the Adoption of this Constitution, shall be as valid against the United States under this Constitution, as under the Confederation.

This Constitution, and the Laws of the United States which shall be made in Pursuance thereof; and all Treaties made, or which shall be made, under the Authority of the United States, shall be the supreme Law of the Land; and the Judges in every State shall be bound thereby, any Thing in the Constitution or Laws of any State to the Contrary notwithstanding.

The Senators and Representatives before mentioned, and the Members of the several State Legislatures, and all executive and judicial Officers, both of the United States and of the several States, shall be bound by Oath or Affirmation, to support this Constitution; but no religious Test shall be required as a Qualification to any Office or public Trust under the United States.

ARTICLE VII

[RATIFICATION AND ESTABLISHMENT]

The Ratification of the Conventions of nine States, shall be sufficient for the Establishment of this Constitution between the States so ratifying the Same.[14]

Done in Convention by the Unanimous Consent of the States present the Seventeenth Day of September in the Year of our Lord one thousand seven hundred and Eighty seven and of the Independence of the United States of America the Twelfth. *In Witness* whereof We have hereunto subscribed our Names,

[13]Temporary provision.

[14]The Constitution was submitted on September 17, 1787, by the Constitutional Convention, was ratified by the conventions of several states at various dates up to May 29, 1790, and became effective on March 4, 1789.

G:° WASHINGTON—
Presidt. and deputy from Virginia

NEW HAMPSHIRE
John Langdon
Nicholas Gilman

MASSACHUSETTS
Nathaniel Gorham
Rufus King

CONNECTICUT
Wm. Saml. Johnson
Roger Sherman

NEW YORK
Alexander Hamilton

NEW JERSEY
Wil: Livingston
David Brearley
Wm. Paterson
Jona: Dayton

PENNSYLVANIA
B Franklin
Thomas Mifflin
Robt. Morris
Geo. Clymer
Thos. FitzSimons
Jared Ingersoll
James Wilson
Gouv Morris

DELAWARE
Geo: Read
Gunning Bedford jun
John Dickinson
Richard Bassett
Jaco: Broom

MARYLAND
James McHenry
Dan of St Thos. Jenifer
Danl. Carroll

VIRGINIA
John Blair—
James Madison Jr.

NORTH CAROLINA
Wm. Blount
Richd. Dobbs Spaight
Hu Williamson

SOUTH CAROLINA
J. Rutledge
Charles Cotesworth Pinckney
Charles Pinckney
Pierce Butler

GEORGIA
William Few
Abr Baldwin

Amendments to the Constitution

Proposed by Congress and Ratified by the Legislatures of the Several States, Pursuant to Article V of the Original Constitution.

Amendments I–X, known as the Bill of Rights, were proposed by Congress on September 25, 1789, and ratified on December 15, 1791.

AMENDMENT I

[FREEDOM OF RELIGION, OF SPEECH, AND OF THE PRESS]

Congress shall make no law respecting an establishment of religion, or prohibiting the free exercise thereof; or abridging the freedom of speech, or of the press; or the right of the people peaceably to assemble, and to petition the Government for a redress of grievances.

AMENDMENT II

[RIGHT TO KEEP AND BEAR ARMS]

A well regulated Militia, being necessary to the security of a free State, the right of the people to keep and bear Arms, shall not be infringed.

AMENDMENT III

[QUARTERING OF SOLDIERS]

No Soldier shall, in time of peace be quartered in any house, without the consent of the Owner, nor in time of war, but in a manner to be prescribed by law.

AMENDMENT IV

[SECURITY FROM UNWARRANTABLE SEARCH AND SEIZURE]

The right of the people to be secure in their persons, houses, papers, and effects, against unreasonable searches and seizures, shall not be violated, and no Warrants shall issue, but upon probable cause, supported by Oath or affirmation, and particularly describing the place to be searched, and the persons or things to be seized.

AMENDMENT V

[RIGHTS OF ACCUSED PERSONS IN CRIMINAL PROCEEDINGS]

No person shall be held to answer for a capital, or otherwise infamous crime, unless on a presentment or indictment of a Grand Jury, except in cases arising in the land or naval forces, or in the Militia, when in actual service in time of War or in public danger; nor shall any person be subject for the same offence to be twice put in jeopardy of life or limb; nor shall be compelled in any criminal case to be a witness against himself, nor be deprived of life, liberty, or property, without due process of law; nor shall private property be taken for public use, without just compensation.

AMENDMENT VI

[RIGHT TO SPEEDY TRIAL, WITNESSES, ETC.]

In all criminal prosecutions, the accused shall enjoy the right to a speedy and public trial, by an impartial jury of the State and district wherein the crime shall have been committed, which district shall have been previously ascertained by law, and to be informed of the nature and cause of the accusation; to be confronted with the witnesses against him; to have compulsory process for obtaining witnesses in his favor, and to have the Assistance of Counsel for his defence.

AMENDMENT VII

[TRIAL BY JURY IN CIVIL CASES]

In suits at common law, where the value in controversy shall exceed twenty dollars, the right of trial by jury shall be preserved, and no fact tried by a jury, shall be otherwise reexamined in any Court of the United States, than according to the rules of the common law.

AMENDMENT VIII

[BAILS, FINES, PUNISHMENTS]

Excessive bail shall not be required, nor excessive fines imposed, nor cruel and unusual punishments inflicted.

AMENDMENT IX

[RESERVATION OF RIGHTS OF PEOPLE]

The enumeration in the Constitution, of certain rights, shall not be construed to deny or disparage others retained by the people.

AMENDMENT X

[POWERS RESERVED TO STATES OR PEOPLE]

The powers not delegated to the United States by the Constitution, nor prohibited by it to the States, are reserved to the States respectively, or to the people.

AMENDMENT XI

[Proposed by Congress on March 4, 1794; declared ratified on January 8, 1798.]

[RESTRICTION OF JUDICIAL POWER]

The Judicial power of the United States shall not be construed to extend to any suit in law or equity, commenced or prosecuted against one of the United States by Citizens of another State, or by Citizens or Subjects of any Foreign State.

AMENDMENT XII

[Proposed by Congress on December 9, 1803; declared ratified on September 25, 1804.]

[ELECTION OF PRESIDENT AND VICE PRESIDENT]

The Electors shall meet in their respective states and vote by ballot for President and Vice-President, one of whom, at least, shall not be an inhabitant of the same state with themselves; they shall name in their ballots the person voted for as President, and in distinct ballots the person voted for as Vice-President, and they shall make distinct lists of all persons voted for as President, and of all persons voted for as Vice-President, and of the number of votes for each, which lists they shall sign and certify, and transmit sealed to the seat of the government of the United States, directed to the President of the Senate;—the President of the Senate shall, in presence of the Senate and House of Representatives, open all the certificates and the votes shall then be counted;—The person having the greatest number of votes for President, shall be the President, if such number be a majority of the whole number of Electors appointed; and if no person have such majority, then from the persons having the highest numbers not exceeding three on the list of those voted for as President, the House of Representatives shall choose immediately, by ballot, the President. But in choosing the President, the votes shall be taken by states, the representation from each state having one vote; a quorum for this purpose shall consist of a member or members from two-thirds of the states, and a majority of all the states shall be necessary to a choice. And if the House of Representatives shall not choose a President whenever the right of choice shall devolve upon them, before the fourth day of March next following, then the Vice-President shall act as President, as in the case of the death or other constitutional disability of the President.—The person having the greatest number of votes as Vice-President, shall be the Vice-President, if such number be a majority of the whole number of Electors appointed, and if no person have a majority, then from the two highest numbers on the list, the Senate shall choose the Vice-President; a quorum for the purpose shall consist of two-thirds of the whole number of Senators, and a majority of the whole number shall be necessary to a choice. But no person constitutionally ineligible to the office of President shall be eligible to that of Vice-President of the United States.

AMENDMENT XIII

[Proposed by Congress on January 31, 1865; declared ratified on December 18, 1865.]

SECTION 1

[ABOLITION OF SLAVERY]

Neither slavery nor involuntary servitude, except as a punishment for crime whereof the party shall have been duly convicted, shall exist within the United States, or any place subject to their jurisdiction.

SECTION 2

[POWER TO ENFORCE THIS ARTICLE]

Congress shall have power to enforce this article by appropriate legislation.

AMENDMENT XIV

[Proposed by Congress on June 13, 1866; declared ratified on July 28, 1868.]

SECTION 1

[CITIZENSHIP RIGHTS NOT TO BE ABRIDGED BY STATES]

All persons born or naturalized in the United States, and subject to the jurisdiction thereof, are citizens of the United States and of the State wherein they reside. No State shall make or enforce any law which shall abridge the privileges or immunities of citizens of the United States; nor shall any State deprive any person of life, liberty, or property, without due process of law; nor deny to any person within its jurisdiction the equal protection of the laws.

SECTION 2

[APPORTIONMENT OF REPRESENTATIVES IN CONGRESS]

Representatives shall be apportioned among the several States according to their respective numbers, counting the whole number of persons in each State, excluding Indians not taxed. But when the right to vote at any election for the choice of electors for President and Vice-President of the United States, Representatives in Congress, the Executive and Judicial officers of a State, or the members of the Legislature thereof, is denied to any of the male inhabitants of such State, being twenty-one years of age, and citizens of the United States, or in any way abridged, except for participation in rebellion, or other crime, the basis of representation therein shall be reduced in the proportion which the number of such male citizens shall bear to the whole number of male citizens twenty-one years of age in such State.

SECTION 3

[PERSONS DISQUALIFIED FROM HOLDING OFFICE]

No person shall be a Senator or Representative in Congress, or elector of President and Vice-President, or hold any office, civil or military, under the United States, or under any State, who, having previously taken an oath, as a member of Congress, or as an officer of the United States, or as a member of any State legislature, or as an executive or judicial officer of any State, to support the Constitution of the United States, shall have engaged in insurrection or rebellion against the same, or given aid or comfort to the enemies thereof. But Congress may by a vote of two-thirds of each House, remove such disability.

SECTION 4

[WHAT PUBLIC DEBTS ARE VALID]

The validity of the public debt of the United States, authorized by law, including debts incurred for payment of pensions and bounties for services in suppressing insurrection or rebellion, shall not be questioned. But neither the United States nor any State shall assume or pay any debt or obligation incurred in aid of insurrection or rebellion against the United States, or any claim for the loss or emancipation of any slave; but all such debts, obligations and claims shall be held illegal and void.

SECTION 5

[POWER TO ENFORCE THIS ARTICLE]

The Congress shall have power to enforce, by appropriate legislation, the provisions of this article.

AMENDMENT XV

[Proposed by Congress on February 26, 1869; declared ratified on March 30, 1870.]

SECTION 1

[NEGRO SUFFRAGE]

The right of citizens of the United States to vote shall not be denied or abridged by the United States or by any State on account of race, color, or previous condition of servitude.

SECTION 2

[POWER TO ENFORCE THIS ARTICLE]

The Congress shall have power to enforce this article by appropriate legislation.

AMENDMENT XVI

[Proposed by Congress on July 2, 1909; declared ratified on February 25, 1913.]

[AUTHORIZING INCOME TAXES]

The Congress shall have power to lay and collect taxes on incomes, from whatever source derived, without apportionment among the several States, and without regard to any census or enumeration.

AMENDMENT XVII

[Proposed by Congress on May 13, 1912; declared ratified on May 31, 1913.]

[POPULAR ELECTION OF SENATORS]

The Senate of the United States shall be composed of two Senators from each State, elected by the people thereof, for six years; and each Senator shall have one vote. The electors in each State shall have the qualifications requisite for electors of the most numerous branch of the State legislatures.

When vacancies happen in the representation of any State in the Senate, the executive authority of such State shall issue writs of election to fill such vacancies: *Provided,* That the legislature of any State may empower the executive thereof to make temporary appointments until the people fill the vacancies by election as the legislature may direct.

This amendment shall not be so construed as to affect the election or term of any Senator chosen before it becomes valid as part of the Constitution.

AMENDMENT XVIII

[Proposed by Congress December 18, 1917; declared ratified on January 29, 1919.]

SECTION 1

[NATIONAL LIQUOR PROHIBITION]

After one year from the ratification of this article the manufacture, sale, or transportation of intoxicating liquors within, the importation thereof into, or the exportation thereof from the United States and all territory subject to the jurisdiction thereof for beverage purposes is hereby prohibited.

SECTION 2

[POWER TO ENFORCE THIS ARTICLE]

The Congress and the several States shall have concurrent power to enforce this article by appropriate legislation.

SECTION 3

[RATIFICATION WITHIN SEVEN YEARS]

This article shall be inoperative unless it shall have been ratified as an amendment to the Constitution by the legislatures of the several States, as provided in the Constitution, within seven years from the date of the submission hereof to the States by the Congress.[1]

AMENDMENT XIX

[Proposed by Congress on June 4, 1919; declared ratified on August 26, 1920.]

[WOMAN SUFFRAGE]

The right of citizens of the United States to vote shall not be denied or abridged by the United States or by any State on account of sex.

Congress shall have power to enforce this article by appropriate legislation.

[1]Repealed by the Twenty-First Amendment.

AMENDMENT XX

[Proposed by Congress on March 2, 1932; declared ratified on February 6, 1933.]

SECTION 1

[TERMS OF OFFICE]

The terms of the President and Vice President shall end at noon on the 20th day of January, and the terms of Senators and Representatives at noon on the 3d day of January, of the years in which such terms would have ended if this article had not been ratified; and the terms of their successors shall then begin.

SECTION 2

[TIME OF CONVENING CONGRESS]

The Congress shall assemble at least once in every year, and such meeting shall begin at noon on the 3d day of January, unless they shall by law appoint a different day.

SECTION 3

[DEATH OF PRESIDENT-ELECT]

If, at the time fixed for the beginning of the term of the President, the President elect shall have died, the Vice President elect shall become President. If a President shall not have been chosen before the time fixed for the beginning of his term, or if the President elect shall have failed to qualify, then the Vice President elect shall act as President until a President shall have qualified; and the Congress may by law provide for the case wherein neither a President elect nor a Vice President elect shall have qualified, declaring who shall then act as President, or the manner in which one who is to act shall be selected, and such person shall act accordingly until a President or Vice President shall have qualified.

SECTION 4

[ELECTION OF THE PRESIDENT]

The Congress may by law provide for the case of the death of any of the persons from whom the House of Representatives may choose a President whenever the right of choice shall have devolved upon them, and for the case of the death of any of the persons from whom the Senate may choose a Vice President whenever the right of choice shall have devolved upon them.

SECTION 5

[AMENDMENT TAKES EFFECT]

Sections 1 and 2 shall take effect on the 15th day of October following the ratification of this article.

SECTION 6

[RATIFICATION WITHIN SEVEN YEARS]

This article shall be inoperative unless it shall have been ratified as an amendment to the Constitution by the legislatures of three-fourths of the several States within seven years from the date of its submission.

AMENDMENT XXI

[Proposed by Congress on February 20, 1933; declared ratified on December 5, 1933.]

SECTION 1

[NATIONAL LIQUOR PROHIBITION REPEALED]

The eighteenth article of amendment to the Constitution of the United States is hereby repealed.

SECTION 2

[TRANSPORTATION OF LIQUOR INTO "DRY" STATES]

The transportation or importation into any State, Territory, or Possession of the United States for delivery or use therein of intoxicating liquors, in violation of the laws thereof, is hereby prohibited.

SECTION 3

[RATIFICATION WITHIN SEVEN YEARS]

This article shall be inoperative unless it shall have been ratified as an amendment to the Constitution by conventions in the several States, as provided in the Constitution, within seven years from the date of the submission hereof to the States by the Congress.

AMENDMENT XXII

[Proposed by Congress on March 21, 1947; declared ratified on February 27, 1951.]

SECTION 1

[TENURE OF PRESIDENT LIMITED]

No person shall be elected to the office of President more than twice, and no person who has held the office of President or acted as President, for more than two years of a term to which some other person was elected President shall be elected to the office of the President more than once. But this Article shall not apply to any person holding the office of President when this Article was proposed by the Congress, and shall not prevent any person who may be holding the office of President, or acting as President, during the term within which this Article becomes operative from holding the office of President or acting as President during the remainder of such term.

SECTION 2

[RATIFICATION WITHIN SEVEN YEARS]

This article shall be inoperative unless it shall have been ratified as an amendment to the Constitution by the legislatures of three-fourths of the several States within seven years from the date of its submission to the States by the Congress.

AMENDMENT XXIII

[Proposed by Congress on June 16, 1960; declared ratified on March 29, 1961.]

SECTION 1

[ELECTORAL COLLEGE VOTES FOR THE DISTRICT OF COLUMBIA]

The District constituting the seat of Government of the United States shall appoint in such manner as the Congress may direct:

A number of electors of President and Vice President equal to the whole number of Senators and Representatives in Congress to which the District would be entitled if it were a State, but in no event more than the least populous State; they shall be in addition to those appointed by the States, but they shall be considered, for the purposes of the election of President and Vice President, to be electors appointed by a State; and they shall meet in the District and perform such duties as provided by the twelfth article of amendment.

SECTION 2

[POWER TO ENFORCE THIS ARTICLE]

The Congress shall have power to enforce this article by appropriate legislation.

AMENDMENT XXIV

[Proposed by Congress on August 27, 1962; declared ratified on January 23, 1964.]

SECTION 1

[ANTI-POLL TAX]

The right of citizens of the United States to vote in any primary or other election for President or Vice President, for electors for President or Vice President, or for Senator or Representative of Congress, shall not be denied or abridged by the United States or any State by reason of failure to pay any poll tax or other tax.

SECTION 2

[POWER TO ENFORCE THIS ARTICLE]

The Congress shall have power to enforce this article by appropriate legislation.

AMENDMENT XXV

[Proposed by Congress on July 6, 1965; declared ratified on February 10, 1967.]

SECTION 1

[VICE PRESIDENT TO BECOME PRESIDENT]

In case of the removal of the President from office or his death or resignation, the Vice President shall become President.

SECTION 2

[CHOICE OF A NEW VICE PRESIDENT]

Whenever there is a vacancy in the office of the Vice President, the President shall nominate a Vice President who shall take the office upon confirmation by a majority vote of both houses of Congress.

SECTION 3

[PRESIDENT MAY DECLARE OWN DISABILITY]

Whenever the President transmits to the President pro tempore of the Senate and the Speaker of the House of Representatives his written declaration that he is unable to discharge the powers and duties of his office, and until he transmits to them a written declaration to the contrary, such powers and duties shall be discharged by the Vice President as Acting President.

SECTION 4

[ALTERNATE PROCEDURES TO DECLARE AND TO END PRESIDENTIAL DISABILITY]

Whenever the Vice President and a majority of either the principal officers of the executive departments, or of such other body as Congress may by law provide, transmit to the President pro tempore of the Senate and the Speaker of the House of Representatives their written declaration that the President is unable to discharge the powers and duties of his office, the Vice President shall immediately assume the powers and duties of the office as Acting President.

Thereafter, when the President transmits to the President pro tempore of the Senate and the Speaker of the House of Representatives his written declaration that no inability exists, he shall resume the powers and duties of his office unless the Vice President and a majority of either the principal officers of the executive department, or of such other body as Congress may by law provide, transmit within four days to the President pro tempore of the Senate and the Speaker of the House of Representatives their written declaration that the President is unable to discharge the powers and duties of his office. Thereupon Congress shall decide the issue, assembling within forty eight hours for that purpose if not in session. If the Congress, within twenty one days after receipt of the latter written declaration, or, if Congress is not in session, within twenty one days after Congress is required to assemble, determines by two-thirds vote of both Houses that the President is unable to discharge the powers and duties of his office, the Vice President shall continue to discharge the same as Acting President; otherwise, the President shall resume the powers and duties of his office.

AMENDMENT XXVI

[Proposed by Congress on March 23, 1971; declared ratified on July 1, 1971.]

SECTION 1

[EIGHTEEN-YEAR-OLD VOTE]

The right of citizens of the United States, who are eighteen years of age or older, to vote shall not be denied or abridged by the United States or by any State on account of age.

SECTION 2

[POWER TO ENFORCE THIS ARTICLE]

The Congress shall have power to enforce this article by appropriate legislation.

AMENDMENT XXVII

[Proposed by Congress on September 25, 1789; declared ratified on May 8, 1992.]

[CONGRESS CANNOT RAISE ITS OWN PAY]

No law varying the compensation for the services of the Senators and Representatives, shall take effect, until an election of representatives shall have intervened.

The Federalist Papers

NO. 10: MADISON

Among the numerous advantages promised by a well constructed Union, none deserves to be more accurately developed than its tendency to break and control the violence of faction. The friend of popular governments never finds himself so much alarmed for their character and fate, as when he contemplates their propensity to this dangerous vice. He will not fail therefore to set a due value on any plan which, without violating the principles to which he is attached, provides a proper cure for it. The instability, injustice, and confusion introduced into the public councils have, in truth, been the mortal diseases under which popular governments have everywhere perished, as they continue to be the favorite and fruitful topics from which the adversaries to liberty derive their most specious declamations. The valuable improvements made by the American constitutions on the popular models, both ancient and modern, cannot certainly be too much admired; but it would be an unwarrantable partiality to contend that they have as effectually obviated the danger on this side, as was wished and expected. Complaints are everywhere heard from our most considerate and virtuous citizens, equally the friends of public and private faith and of public and personal liberty, that our governments are too unstable, that the public good is disregarded in the conflicts of rival parties, and that measures are too often decided, not according to the rules of justice and the rights of the minor party, but by the superior force of an interested and overbearing majority. However anxiously we may wish that these complaints had no foundation, the evidence of known facts will not permit us to deny that they are in some degree true. It will be found, indeed, on a candid review of our situation, that some of the distresses under which we labor have been erroneously charged on the operation of our governments; but it will be found, at the same time, that other causes will not alone account for many of our heaviest misfortunes; and, particularly, for that prevailing and increasing distrust of public engagements and alarm for private rights which are echoed from one end of the continent to the other. These must be chiefly, if not wholly, effects of the unsteadiness and injustice with which a factious spirit has tainted our public administration.

By a faction I understand a number of citizens, whether amounting to a majority or minority of the whole, who are united and actuated by some common impulse of passion, or of interest, adverse to the rights of other citizens, or to the permanent and aggregate interests of the community.

There are two methods of curing the mischiefs of faction: the one, by removing its causes; the other, by controlling its effects.

There are again two methods of removing the causes of faction: the one, by destroying the liberty which is essential to its existence; the other, by giving to every citizen the same opinions, the same passions, and the same interests.

It could never be more truly said than of the first remedy, that it is worse than the disease. Liberty is to faction what air is to fire, an aliment without which it instantly expires. But it could not be a less folly to abolish liberty, which is essential to political life, because it nourishes faction, than it would be to wish the annihilation of air, which is essential to animal life, because it imparts to fire its destructive agency.

The second expedient is as impracticable, as the first would be unwise. As long as the reason of man continues fallible, and he is at liberty to exercise it, different opinions will be formed. As long as the connection subsists between his reason and his self-love, his opinions and his passions will have a reciprocal influence on each other; and the former will be objects to which the latter will attach themselves. The diversity in the faculties of men, from which the rights of property originate, is not less an insuperable obstacle to a uniformity of interests. The protection of these faculties is the first object of Government. From the protection of different and unequal faculties of acquiring property, the possession of different degrees and kinds of property immediately results; and from the influence of these on the sentiments and views of the respective proprietors, ensues a division of the society into different interests and parties.

The latent causes of faction are thus sown in the nature of man; and we see them everywhere brought into different degrees of activity, according to the different circumstances of civil society. A zeal for different opinions concerning religion, concerning Government, and many other points, as well of speculation as of practice; an attachment to different leaders ambitiously contending for pre-eminence and power; or to persons of other descriptions whose fortunes have been interesting to the human passions, have in turn divided mankind into parties, inflamed them with mutual animosity, and rendered them much more disposed to vex and oppress each other, than to co-operate for their common good. So strong is this propensity of mankind to fall into mutual animosities, that where no substantial occasion presents itself, the most frivolous and fanciful distinctions have been sufficient to kindle their unfriendly passions, and excite their most violent conflicts. But the most common and durable source of factions has been the various and unequal distribution of property. Those who hold and those who are without property have ever formed distinct interests in society. Those who are creditors, and those who are debtors, fall under a like discrimination. A landed interest, a manufacturing interest, a mercantile interest, a moneyed interest, with many lesser interests, grow up of necessity in civilized nations, and divide them into different classes, actuated by different sentiments and views. The regulation of these various and interfering interests forms the principal task of modern Legislation, and involves the spirit of party and faction in the necessary and ordinary operations of Government.

No man is allowed to be judge in his own cause, because his interest would certainly bias his judgment and, not improbably, corrupt his integrity. With equal, nay with greater reason, a body of men are unfit to be both judges and parties at the same time; yet what are many of the most important acts of legislation but so many judicial determinations, not indeed concerning the rights of single persons, but concerning the rights of large bodies of citizens; and what are the different classes of legislators but advocates and parties to the causes which they determine? Is a law proposed concerning private debts? It is a question to which the creditors are parties on one side and the debtors on the other. Justice ought to hold the balance between them. Yet the parties are, and must be, themselves the judges; and the most numerous party, or in other words, the most powerful faction must be expected to prevail. Shall domestic manufacturers be encouraged, and in what degree, by restrictions on foreign manufacturers? are questions which would be differently decided by the landed and the manufacturing classes, and probably by neither with a sole regard to justice and the public good. The apportionment of taxes on the various descriptions of property is an act which seems to require the most exact impartiality; yet there is, perhaps, no legislative act in which greater opportunity and temptation are given to a predominant party to trample on the rules of justice. Every shilling with which they overburden the inferior number is a shilling saved to their own pockets.

It is in vain to say that enlightened statesmen will be able to adjust these clashing interests and render them all subservient to the public good. Enlightened statesmen will not always be at the helm. Nor, in many cases, can such an adjustment be made at all without taking into view indirect and remote considerations, which will rarely prevail over the immediate interest which one party may find in disregarding the rights of another or the good of the whole.

The inference to which we are brought is that the *causes* of faction cannot be removed and that relief is only to be sought in the means of controlling its *effects*.

If a faction consists of less than a majority, relief is supplied by the republican principle, which enables the majority to defeat its sinister views by regular vote. It may clog the administration, it may convulse the society; but it will be unable to execute and mask its violence under the forms of the Constitution. When a majority is included in a faction, the form of popular government, on the other hand, enables it to sacrifice to its ruling passion or interest both the public good and the rights of other citizens. To secure the public good and private rights against the danger of such a faction, and at the same time to preserve the spirit and the form of popular government, is then the great object to which our enquiries are directed. Let me add that it is the great desideratum by which alone this form of government can be rescued from the opprobrium under which it has so long labored and be recommended to the esteem and adoption of mankind.

By what means is this object attainable? Evidently by one of two only. Either the existence of the same passion or interest in a majority at the same time must be prevented, or the majority, having such co-existent passion or interest, must be rendered, by their number and local situation, unable to concert and carry into effect schemes of oppression. If the impulse and the opportunity be suffered to coincide, we well know that neither moral nor religious motives can be relied on as an adequate control. They are not found to be such on the injustice and violence of individuals, and lose their efficacy in proportion to the number combined together, that is, in proportion as their efficacy becomes needful.

From this view of the subject it may be concluded that a pure Democracy, by which I mean a Society consisting of a small number of citizens, who assemble and administer the Government in person, can admit of no cure for the mischiefs of faction. A common passion or interest will, in almost every case, be felt by a majority of the whole; a communication and concert results from the form of Government itself; and there is nothing to check the inducements to sacrifice the weaker party or an obnoxious individual. Hence it is that such Democracies have ever been spectacles of turbulence and contention; have ever been found incompatible with personal security or the rights of property; and have in general been as short in their lives as they have been violent in their deaths. Theoretic politicians, who have patronized this species of Government, have erroneously supposed that by reducing mankind to a perfect equality in their political rights, they would at the same time be perfectly equalized and assimilated in their possessions, their opinions, and their passions.

A Republic, by which I mean a Government in which the scheme of representation takes place, opens a different prospect and promises the cure for which we are seeking. Let us examine the points in which it varies from pure Democracy, and we shall comprehend both the nature of the cure and the efficacy which it must derive from the Union.

The two great points of difference between a Democracy and a Republic are: first, the delegation of the Government, in the latter, to a small number of citizens elected by the rest; secondly, the greater number of citizens and greater sphere of country over which the latter may be extended.

The effect of the first difference is, on the one hand, to refine and enlarge the public views by passing them through the medium of a chosen body of citizens, whose wisdom may best discern the true interest of their country and whose patriotism and love of justice will be least likely to sacrifice it to temporary or partial considerations. Under such a regulation it may well happen that the public voice, pronounced by the representatives of the people, will be more consonant to the public good than if pronounced by the people themselves, convened for the purpose. On the other hand, the effect may be inverted. Men of factious tempers, of local prejudices, or of sinister designs, may, by intrigue, by corruption, or by other means, first obtain the suffrages, and then betray the interests of the people. The question resulting is, whether small or extensive Republics are most favorable to the election of proper guardians of the public weal; and it is clearly decided in favor of the latter by two obvious considerations.

In the first place it is to be remarked that however small the Republic may be, the Representatives must be raised to a certain number in order to guard against the cabals of a few; and that however large it may be they must be limited to a certain number in order to guard against the confusion of a multitude. Hence, the number of Representatives in the two cases not being in proportion to that of the Constituents, and being proportionally greatest in the small Republic, it follows that if the proportion of fit characters be not less in the large than in the small Republic, the former will present a greater option, and consequently a greater probability of a fit choice.

In the next place, as each Representative will be chosen by a greater number of citizens in the large than in the small Republic, it will be more difficult for unworthy candidates to practise with success the vicious arts by which elections are too often carried; and the suffrages of the people being more free, will be more likely to centre on men who possess the most attractive merit and the most diffusive and established characters.

It must be confessed that in this, as in most other cases, there is a mean, on both sides of which inconveniencies will be found to lie. By enlarging too much the number of electors, you render the representative too little acquainted with all their local circumstances and lesser interests; as by reducing it too much, you render him unduly attached to these, and too little fit to comprehend and pursue great and national objects. The Federal Constitution forms a happy combination in this respect; the great and aggregate interests being referred to the national, the local and particular to the State legislatures.

The other point of difference is the greater number of citizens and extent of territory which may be brought within the compass of Republican than of Democratic Government; and it is this circumstance principally which renders factious combinations less to be dreaded in the former than in the latter. The smaller the society, the fewer probably will be the distinct parties and interests composing it; the fewer the distinct parties and interests, the more frequently will a majority be found of the same party; and the smaller the number of individuals composing a majority, and the smaller the compass within which they are placed, the more easily will they concert and execute their plans of oppression. Extend the sphere and you take in a greater variety of parties and interests; you make it less probable that a majority of the whole will have a common motive to invade the rights of other citizens; or if such a common motive exists, it will be more difficult for all who feel it to discover their own strength and to act in unison with each other. Besides other impediments, it may be remarked, that where there is a consciousness of unjust or dishonorable purposes, communication is always checked by distrust in proportion to the number whose concurrence is necessary.

Hence, it clearly appears that the same advantage which a Republic has over a Democracy in controlling the effects of faction is enjoyed by a large over a small republic—is enjoyed by the Union over the States composing it. Does this advantage consist in the substitution of representatives whose enlightened views and virtuous sentiments render them superior to local prejudices and to schemes of injustice? It will not be denied that the representation of the Union will be most likely to possess these requisite endowments. Does it consist in the greater security afforded by a greater variety of parties, against the event of any one party being able to outnumber and oppress the rest? In an equal degree does the increased variety of parties comprised within the Union increase this security? Does it, in fine, consist in the greater obstacles opposed to the concert and accomplishment of the secret wishes of an unjust and interested majority? Here again the extent of the Union gives it the most palpable advantage.

The influence of factious leaders may kindle a flame within their particular States but will be unable to spread a general conflagration through the other States: a religious sect may degenerate into a political faction in a part of the Confederacy; but the variety of sects dispersed over the entire face of it must secure the national Councils against any danger from that source: a rage for paper money, for an abolition of debts, for an equal division of property, or for any other improper or wicked project, will be less apt to pervade the whole body of the Union than a particular member of it; in the same proportion as such a malady is more likely to taint a particular county or district than an entire State.

In the extent and proper structure of the Union, therefore, we behold a republican remedy for the diseases most incident to Republican Government. And according to the degree of pleasure and pride we feel in being republicans ought to be our zeal in cherishing the spirit and supporting the character of federalist.

PUBLIUS
November 22, 1787

NO. 51: MADISON

To what expedient, then, shall we finally resort, for maintaining in practice the necessary partition of power among the several departments as laid down in the constitution? The only answer that can be given is that as all these exterior provisions are found to be inadequate the defect must be supplied, by so contriving the interior structure of the government as that its several constituent parts may, by their mutual relations, be the means of keeping each other in their proper places. Without presuming to undertake a full development of this important idea I will hazard a few general observations which may perhaps place it in a clearer light, and enable us to form a more correct judgment of the principles and structure of the government planned by the convention.

In order to lay a due foundation for that separate and distinct exercise of the different powers of government, which to a certain extent is admitted on all hands to be essential to the preservation of liberty, it is evident that each department should have a will of its own; and consequently should be so constituted that the members of each should have as little agency as possible in the appointment of the members of the others. Were this principle rigorously adhered to, it would require that all the appointments for the supreme executive, legislative, and judiciary magistracies should be drawn from the same fountain of authority, the people, through channels having no communication whatever with one another. Perhaps such a plan of constructing the several departments would be less difficult in practice than it may in contemplation appear. Some difficulties, however, and some additional expense would attend the execution of it. Some deviations, therefore, from the principle must be admitted. In the constitution of the judiciary department in particular, it might be inexpedient to insist rigorously on the principle: first, because peculiar qualifications being essential in the members, the primary consideration ought to be to select that mode of choice which best secures these qualifications; second, because the permanent tenure by which the appointments are held in that department must soon destroy all sense of dependence on the authority conferring them.

It is equally evident that the members of each department should be as little dependent as possible on those of the others for the emoluments annexed to their offices. Were the executive magistrate, or the judges, not independent of the legislature in this particular, their independence in every other would be merely nominal.

But the great security against a gradual concentration of the several powers in the same department consists in giving to those who administer each department the necessary constitutional means and personal motives to resist encroachments of the others. The provision for defence must in this, as in all other cases, be made commensurate to the danger of attack. Ambition must be made to counteract ambition. The interest of the man must be connected with the constitutional rights of the place. It may be a reflection on human nature that such devices should be necessary to control the abuses of government. But what is government itself but the greatest of all reflections on human nature? If men were angels, no government would be necessary. If angels were to govern men, neither external nor internal controls on government would be necessary. In framing a government which is to be administered by men over men, the great difficulty lies in this: You must first enable the government to control the governed; and in the next place oblige it to control itself. A dependence on the people is, no doubt, the primary control on the government; but experience has taught mankind the necessity of auxiliary precautions.

This policy of supplying, by opposite and rival interests, the defect of better motives, might be traced through the whole system of human affairs, private as well as public. We see it particularly displayed in all the subordinate distributions of power, where the constant aim is to divide and arrange the several offices in such a manner as that each may be a check on the other; that the private interest of every individual may be a sentinel over the public rights. These inventions of prudence cannot be less requisite in the distribution of the supreme powers of the State.

But it is not possible to give to each department an equal power of self-defense. In republican government, the legislative authority necessarily predominates. The remedy for this inconveniency is to divide the legislature into different branches; and to render them, by different modes of election and different principles of action, as little connected with each other as the nature of their common functions and their common dependence on the society will admit. It may even be necessary to guard against dangerous encroachments by still further precautions. As the weight of the legislative authority requires that it should be thus divided, the weakness of the executive may require, on the other hand, that it should be fortified. An absolute negative on the legislature appears, at first view, to be the natural defense with which the executive magistrate should be armed. But perhaps it would be neither altogether safe nor alone sufficient. On ordinary occasions it might not be exerted with the requisite firmness, and on extraordinary occasions it might be perfidiously abused. May not this defect of an absolute negative be supplied by some qualified connection between this weaker branch of the stronger department, by which the latter may be led to support the constitutional rights of the former, without being too much detached from the rights of its own department?

If the principles on which these observations are founded be just, as I persuade myself they are, and they be applied as a criterion to the several State constitutions, and to the federal Constitution, it will be found that if the latter does not perfectly correspond with them, the former are infinitely less able to bear such a test.

There are, moreover, two considerations particularly applicable to the federal system of America, which place that system in a very interesting point of view.

First. In a single republic, all the power surrendered by the people is submitted to the administration of a single government; and usurpations are guarded against by a division of the government into distinct and separate departments. In the compound republic of America, the power surrendered by the people is first divided between two distinct governments, and then the portion allotted to each subdivided among distinct and separate departments. Hence a double security arises to the rights of the people. The different governments will control each other, at the same time that each will be controlled by itself.

Second. It is of great importance in a republic not only to guard the society against the oppression of its rulers, but to guard one part of the society against the injustice of the other part. Different interests necessarily exist in different classes of citizens. If a majority be united by a common interest, the rights of the minority will be insecure. There are but two methods of providing against this evil: The one by creating a will in the community independent of the majority—that is, of the society itself; the other, by comprehending in the society so many separate descriptions of citizens as will render an unjust combination of a majority of the whole very improbable, if not impracticable. The first method prevails in all governments possessing an hereditary or self-appointed authority. This, at best, is but a precarious security; because a power independent of the society may as well espouse the unjust views of the major as the rightful interests of the minor party, and may possibly be turned against both parties. The second method will be exemplified in the federal republic of the United States. Whilst all authority in it will be derived from and dependent on the society, the society itself will be broken into so many parts, interests and classes of citizens, that the rights of individuals, or of the minority, will be in little danger from interested combinations of the majority. In a free government the security for civil rights must be the same as that for religious rights. It consists in the one case in the multiplicity of interests, and in the other in the multiplicity of sects. The degree of security in both cases will depend on the number of interests and sects; and this may be presumed to depend on the extent of country and number of people comprehended under the same government. This view of the subject must particularly recommend a proper federal system to all the sincere and considerate friends of republican government: Since it shows that in exact proportion as the territory of the Union may be formed into more circumscribed Confederacies, or States, oppressive combinations of a majority will be facilitated; the best security, under the republican form, for the rights of every class of citizens, will be diminished; and consequently the stability and independence of some member of the government, the only other security, must be proportionally increased. Justice is the end of government. It is the end of civil society. It ever has been and ever will be pursued until it be obtained, or until liberty be lost in the pursuit. In a society under the forms of which the stronger faction can readily unite and oppress the weaker, anarchy may as truly be said to reign as in a state of nature, where the weaker individual is not secured against the violence of the stronger: And as, in the latter state, even the stronger individuals are prompted, by the uncertainty of their condition, to submit to a government which may protect the weak as well as themselves: So, in the former state, will the more powerful factions or parties be gradually induced, by a like motive, to wish for a government which will protect all parties, the weaker as well as the more powerful. It can be little doubted that if the State of Rhode Island was separated from the Confederacy and left to itself, the insecurity of rights under the popular form of government within such narrow limits would be displayed by such reiterated oppressions of factious majorities that some power altogether independent of the people would soon be called for by the voice of the very factions whose misrule had proved the necessity of it. In the extended republic of the United States, and among the great variety of interests, parties, and sects which it embraces, a coalition of a majority of the whole society could seldom take place on any other principles than those of justice and the general good; and there being thus less danger to a minor from the will of the major party, there must be less pretext, also, to provide for the security of the former, by introducing into the government a will not dependent on the latter, or, in other words, a will independent of the society itself. It is no less certain than it is important, notwithstanding the contrary opinions which have been entertained, that the larger the society, provided it lie within a practicable sphere, the more duly capable it will be of self-government. And happily for the *republican cause*, the practicable sphere may be carried to a very great extent by a judicious modification and mixture of the *federal principle.*

PUBLIUS
February 6, 1788

The Anti-Federalist Papers

Essay by Brutus in the *New York Journal*

When the public is called to investigate and decide upon a question in which not only the present members of the community are deeply interested, but upon which the happiness and misery of generations yet unborn is in great measure suspended, the benevolent mind cannot help feeling itself peculiarly interested in the result.

In this situation, I trust the feeble efforts of an individual, to lead the minds of the people to a wise and prudent determination, cannot fail of being acceptable to the candid and dispassionate part of the community. Encouraged by this consideration, I have been induced to offer my thoughts upon the present important crisis of our public affairs.

Perhaps this country never saw so critical a period in their political concerns. We have felt the feebleness of the ties by which these United-States are held together, and the want of sufficient energy in our present confederation, to manage, in some instances, our general concerns. Various expedients have been proposed to remedy these evils, but none have succeeded. At length a Convention of the states has been assembled, they have formed a constitution which will now, probably, be submitted to the people to ratify or reject, who are the fountain of all power, to whom alone it of right belongs to make or unmake constitutions, or forms of government, at their pleasure. The most important question that was ever proposed to your decision, or to the decision of any people under heaven, is before you, and you are to decide upon it by men of your own election, chosen specially for this purpose. If the constitution, offered to your acceptance, be a wise one, calculated to preserve the invaluable blessings of liberty, to secure the inestimable rights of mankind, and promote human happiness, then, if you accept it, you will lay a lasting foundation of happiness for millions yet unborn; generations to come will rise up and call you blessed. You may rejoice in the prospects of this vast extended continent becoming filled with freemen, who will assert the dignity of human nature. You may solace yourselves with the idea, that society, in this favoured land, will fast advance to the highest point of perfection; the human mind will expand in knowledge and virtue, and the golden age be, in some measure, realised. But if, on the other hand, this form of government contains principles that will lead to the subversion of liberty—if it tends to establish a despotism, or, what is worse, a tyrannic aristocracy; then, if you adopt it, this only remaining assylum for liberty will be shut up, and posterity will execrate your memory.

Momentous then is the question you have to determine, and you are called upon by every motive which should influence a noble and virtuous mind, to examine it well, and to make up a wise judgment. It is insisted, indeed, that this constitution must be received, be it ever so imperfect. If it has its defects, it is said, they can be best amended when they are experienced. But remember, when the people once part with power, they can seldom or never resume it again but by force. Many instances can be produced in which the people have voluntarily increased the powers of their rulers; but few, if any, in which rulers have willingly abridged their authority. This is a sufficient reason to induce you to be careful, in the first instance, how you deposit the powers of government.

With these few introductory remarks, I shall proceed to a consideration of this constitution:

The first question that presents itself on the subject is, whether a confederated government be the best for the United States or not? Or in other words, whether the thirteen United States should be reduced to one great republic, governed by one legislature, and under the direction of one executive and judicial; or whether they should continue thirteen confederated republics, under the direction and controul of a supreme federal head for certain defined national purposes only?

This enquiry is important, because, although the government reported by the convention does not go to a perfect and entire consolidation, yet it approaches so near to it, that it must, if executed, certainly and infallibly terminate in it.

This government is to possess absolute and uncontroulable power, legislative, executive and judicial, with respect to every object to which it extends, for by the last clause of section 8th, article 1st, it is declared "that the Congress shall have power to make all laws which shall be necessary and proper for carrying into execution the foregoing powers, and all other powers vested by this constitution, in the government of the United States; or in any department or office thereof." And by the 6th article, it is declared "that this constitution, and the laws of the United States, which shall be made in pursuance thereof, and the treaties made, or which shall be made, under the authority of the United States, shall be the supreme law of the land; and the judges in every state shall be bound thereby, any thing in the constitution, or law of any state to the contrary notwithstanding." It appears from these articles that there is no need of any intervention of the state governments, between the Congress and the people, to execute any one power vested in the general government, and that the constitution and laws of every state are nullified and declared void, so far as they are or shall be inconsistent with this constitution, or the laws made in pursuance of it, or with treaties made under the authority of the United States.—The government then, so far as it extends, is a complete one, and not a confederation. It is as much one complete government as that of New York or Massachusetts, has as absolute and perfect powers to make and execute all laws, to appoint officers, institute courts, declare offences, and annex penalties, with respect to every object to which it extends, as any other in the world. So far therefore as its powers reach, all ideas of confederation are given up and lost. It is true this government is limited to certain objects, or to speak more properly, some small degree of power is still left to the states, but a little attention to the powers vested in the general government, will convince every candid man, that if it is capable of being executed, all that is reserved for the individual states must very soon be annihilated, except so far as they are barely necessary to the organization of the general government. The powers of the general legislature extend to every case that is of the least importance—there is nothing valuable to human nature, nothing dear to freemen, but what is within its power. It has authority to make laws which will affect the lives, the liberty, and property of every man in the United States; nor can the constitution or laws of any state, in any way prevent or impede the full and complete execution of every power given. The legislative power is competent to lay taxes, duties, imposts, and excises;—there is no limitation to this power, unless it be said that the clause which directs the use to which those taxes, and duties shall be applied, may be said to be a limitation: but this is no restriction of the power at all, for by this clause they are to be applied to pay the debts and provide for the common defence and general welfare of the United States; but the legislature have authority to contract debts at their discretion; they are the sole judges of what is necessary to provide for the common defence, and they only are to determine what is for the general welfare; this power therefore is neither more nor less, than a power to lay and collect taxes, imposts, and excises, at their pleasure; not only [is] the power to lay taxes unlimited, as to the amount they may require, but it is perfect and absolute to raise them in any mode they please. No state legislature, or any power in the state governments, have any more to do in carrying this into effect, than the authority of one state has to do with that of another. In the business therefore of laying and collecting taxes, the idea of confederation is totally lost, and that of one entire republic is embraced. It is proper here to remark, that the authority to lay and collect taxes is the most important of any power that can be granted; it connects with it almost all other powers, or at least will in process of time draw all other after it; it is the great mean of protection, security, and defence, in a good government, and the great engine of oppression and tyranny in a bad one. This cannot fail of being the case, if we consider the contracted limits which are set by this constitution, to the late [state?] governments, on this article of raising money. No state can emit paper money—lay any duties, or imposts, on imports, or exports, but by consent of the Congress; and then the net produce shall be for the benefit of the United States: the only mean therefore left, for any state to support its government and discharge its debts, is by direct taxation; and the United States have also power to lay and collect taxes, in any way they please. Every one who has thought on the subject, must be convinced that but small sums of money can be collected in any country, by direct taxe[s], when the foederal government begins to exercise the right of taxation in all its parts, the legislatures of the several states will find it impossible to raise monies to support their governments. Without money they cannot be supported, and they must dwindle away, and, as before observed, their powers absorbed in that of the general government.

It might be here shewn, that the power in the federal legislative, to raise and support armies at pleasure, as well in peace as in war, and their controul over the militia, tend, not only to a consolidation of the government, but the destruction of liberty.—I shall not, however, dwell upon these, as a few observations upon the judicial power of this government, in addition to the preceding, will fully evince the truth of the position.

The judicial power of the United States is to be vested in a supreme court, and in such inferior courts as Congress may from time to time ordain and establish. The powers of these courts are very extensive; their jurisdiction comprehends all civil causes, except such as arise between citizens of the same state; and it extends to all cases in law and equity arising under the constitution. One inferior court must be established, I presume, in each state, at least, with the necessary executive officers appendant thereto. It is easy to see, that in the common course of things, these courts will eclipse the dignity, and take away from the respectability, of the state courts. These courts will be, in themselves, totally independent of the states, deriving their authority from the United States, and receiving from them fixed salaries; and in the course of human events it is to be expected, that they will swallow up all the powers of the courts in the respective states.

How far the clause in the 8th section of the 1st article may operate to do away all idea of confederated states, and to effect an entire consolidation of the whole into one general government, it is impossible to say. The powers given by this article are very general and comprehensive, and it may receive a construction to justify the passing almost any law. A power to make all laws, which shall be *necessary and proper*, for carrying into execution, all powers vested by the constitution in the government of the United States, or any department or officer thereof, is a power very comprehensive and definite [indefinite?], and may, for ought I know, be exercised in a such manner as entirely to abolish the state legislatures. Suppose the legislature of a state should pass a law to raise money to support their government and pay the state debt, may the Congress repeal this law, because it may prevent the collection of a tax which they may think proper and necessary to lay, to provide for the general welfare of the United States? For all laws made, in pursuance of this constitution, are the supreme law of the land, and the judges in every state shall be bound thereby, any thing in the constitution or laws of the different states to the contrary notwithstanding.—By such a law, the government of a particular state might be overturned at one stroke, and thereby be deprived of every means of its support.

It is not meant, by stating this case, to insinuate that the constitution would warrant a law of this kind; or unnecessarily to alarm the fears of the people, by suggesting, that the federal legislature would be more likely to pass the limits assigned them by the constitution, than that of an individual state, further than they are less responsible to the people. But what is meant is, that the legislature of the United States are vested with the great and uncontroulable powers, of laying and collecting taxes, duties, imposts, and excises; of regulating trade, raising and supporting armies, organizing, arming, and disciplining the militia, instituting courts, and other general powers. And are by this clause invested with the power of making all laws, *proper and necessary*, for carrying all these into execution; and they may so exercise this power as entirely to annihilate all the state governments, and reduce this country to one single government. And if they may do it, it is pretty certain they will; for it will be found that the power retained by individual states, small as it is, will be a clog upon the wheels of the government of the United States; the latter therefore will be naturally inclined to remove it out of the way. Besides, it is a truth confirmed by the unerring experience of ages, that every man, and every body of men, invested with power, are ever disposed to increase it, and to acquire a superiority over every thing that stands in their way. This disposition, which is implanted in human nature, will operate in the federal legislature to lessen and ultimately to subvert the state authority, and having such advantages, will most certainly succeed, if the federal government succeeds at all. It must be very evident then, that what this constitution wants of being a complete consolidation of the several parts of the union into one complete government, possessed of perfect legislative, judicial, and executive powers, to all intents and purposes, it will necessarily acquire in its exercise and operation.

Let us now proceed to enquire, as I at first proposed, whether it be best the thirteen United States should be reduced to one great republic, or not? It is here taken for granted, that all agree in this, that whatever government we adopt, it ought to be a free one; that it should be so framed as to secure the liberty of the citizens of America, and such an one as to admit of a full, fair, and equal representation of the people. The question then will be, whether a government thus constituted, and founded on such principles, is practicable, and can be exercised over the whole United States, reduced into one state?

If respect is to be paid to the opinion of the greatest and wisest men who have ever thought or wrote on the science of government, we shall be constrained to conclude, that a free republic cannot succeed over a country of such immense extent, containing such a number of inhabitants, and these encreasing in such rapid progression as that of the whole United States. Among the many illustrious authorities which might be produced to this point, I shall content myself with quoting only two. The one is the baron de Montesquieu, spirit of laws, chap. xvi. vol. I [book VIII]. "It is natural to a republic to have only a small territory, otherwise it cannot long subsist. In a large republic there are men of large fortunes, and consequently of less moderation; there are trusts too great to be placed in any single subject; he has interest of his own; he soon begins to think that he may be happy, great and glorious, by oppressing his fellow citizens; and that he may raise himself to grandeur on the ruins of his country. In a large republic, the public good is sacrificed to a thousand views; it is subordinate to exceptions, and depends on accidents. In a small one, the interest of the public is easier perceived, better understood, and more within the reach of every citizen; abuses are of less extent, and of course are less protected." Of the same opinion is the marquis Beccarari.

History furnishes no example of a free republic, any thing like the extent of the United States. The Grecian republics were of small extent; so also was that of the Romans. Both of these, it is true, in process of time, extended their conquests over large territories of country; and the consequence was, that their governments were changed from that of free governments to those of the most tyrannical that ever existed in the world.

Not only the opinion of the greatest men, and the experience of mankind, are against the idea of an extensive republic, but a variety of reasons may be drawn from the reason and nature of things, against it. In every government, the will of the sovereign is the law. In despotic governments, the supreme authority being lodged in one, his will is law, and can be as easily expressed to a large extensive territory as to a small one. In a pure democracy the people are the sovereign, and their will is declared by themselves; for this purpose they must all come together to deliberate, and decide. This kind of government cannot be exercised, therefore, over a country of any considerable extent; it must be confined to a single city, or at least limited to such bounds as that the people can conveniently assemble, be able to debate, understand the subject submitted to them, and declare their opinion concerning it.

In a free republic, although all laws are derived from the consent of the people, yet the people do not declare their consent by themselves in person, but by representatives, chosen by them, who are supposed to know the minds of their constituents, and to be possessed of integrity to declare this mind.

In every free government, the people must give their assent to the laws by which they are governed. This is the true criterion between a free government and an arbitrary one. The former are ruled by the will of the whole, expressed in any manner they may agree upon; the latter by the will of one, or a few. If the people are to give their assent to the laws, by persons chosen and appointed by them, the manner of the choice and the number chosen, must be such, as to possess, be disposed, and consequently qualified to declare the sentiments of the people; for if they do not know, or are not disposed to speak the sentiments of the people, the people do not govern, but the sovereignty is in a few. Now, in a large extended country, it is impossible to have a representation, possessing the sentiments, and of integrity, to declare the minds of the people, without having it so numerous and unwieldly, as to be subject in great measure to the inconveniency of a democratic government.

The territory of the United States is of vast extent; it now contains near three millions of souls, and is capable of containing much more than ten times that number. Is it practicable for a country, so large and so numerous as they will soon become, to elect a representation, that will speak their sentiments, without their becoming so numerous as to be incapable of transacting public business? It certainly is not.

In a republic, the manners, sentiments, and interests of the people should be similar. If this be not the case, there will be a constant clashing of opinions; and the representatives of one part will be continually striving against those of the other. This will retard the operations of government, and prevent such conclusions as will promote the public good. If we apply this remark to the condition of the United States, we shall be convinced that it forbids that we should be one government. The United States includes a variety of climates. The productions of the different parts of the union are very variant, and their interests, of consequence, diverse. Their manners and habits differ as much as their climates and productions; and their sentiments are by no means coincident. The laws and customs of the several states are, in many respects, very diverse, and in some opposite; each would be in favor of its own interests and customs, and, of consequence, a legislature, formed of representatives from the respective parts, would not only be too numerous to act with any care or decision, but would be composed of such heterogenous and discordant principles, as would constantly be contending with each other.

The laws cannot be executed in a republic, of an extent equal to that of the United States, with promptitude.

The magistrates in every government must be supported in the execution of the laws, either by an armed force, maintained at the public expence for that purpose; or by the people turning out to aid the magistrate upon his command, in case of resistance.

In despotic governments, as well as in all the monarchies of Europe, standing armies are kept up to execute the commands of the prince or the magistrate, and are employed for this purpose when occasion requires: But they have always proved the destruction of liberty, and [are] abhorrent to the spirit of a free republic. In England, where they depend upon the parliament for their annual support, they have always been complained of as oppressive and unconstitutional, and are seldom employed in executing of the laws; never except on extraordinary occasions, and then under the direction of a civil magistrate.

A free republic will never keep a standing army to execute its laws. It must depend upon the support of its citizens. But when a government is to receive its support from the aid of the citizens, it must be so constructed as to have the confidence, respect, and affection of the people. Men who, upon the call of the magistrate, offer themselves to execute the laws, are influenced to do it either by affection to the government, or from fear; where a standing army is at hand to punish offenders, every man is actuated by the latter principle, and therefore, when the magistrate calls, will obey: but, where this is not the case, the government must rest for its support upon the confidence and respect which the people have for their government and laws. The body of the people being attached, the government will always be sufficient to support and execute its laws, and to operate upon the fears of any faction which may be opposed to it, not only to prevent an opposition to the execution of the laws themselves, but also to compel the most of them to aid the magistrate; but the people will not be likely to have such confidence in their rulers, in a republic so extensive as the United States, as necessary for these purposes. The confidence which the people have in their rulers, in a free republic, arises from their knowing them, from their being responsible to them for their conduct, and from the power they have of displacing them when they misbehave: but in a republic of the extent of this continent, the people in general would be acquainted with very few of their rulers: the people at large would know little of their proceedings, and it would be extremely difficult to change them. The people in Georgia and New-Hampshire would not know one another's mind, and therefore could not act in concert to enable them to effect a general change of representatives. The different parts of so extensive a country could not possibly be made acquainted with the conduct of their representatives, nor be informed of the reasons upon which measures were founded. The consequence will be, they will have no confidence in their legislature, suspect them of ambitious views, be jealous of every measure they adopt, and will not support the laws they pass. Hence the government will be nerveless and inefficient, and no way will be left to render it otherwise, but by establishing an armed force to execute the laws at the point of the bayonet—a government of all others the most to be dreaded.

In a republic of such vast extent as the United-States, the legislature cannot attend to the various concerns and wants of its different parts. It cannot be sufficiently numerous to be acquainted with the local condition and wants of the different districts, and if it could, it is impossible it should have sufficient time to attend to and provide for all the variety of cases of this nature, that would be continually arising.

In so extensive a republic, the great officers of government would soon become above the controul of the people, and abuse their power to the purpose of aggrandizing themselves, and oppressing them. The trust committed to the executive offices, in a country of the extent of the United-States, must be various and of magnitude. The command of all the troops and navy of the republic, the appointment of officers, the power of pardoning offences, the collecting of all the public revenues, and the power of expending them, with a number of other powers, must be lodged and exercised in every state, in the hands of a few. When these are attended with great honor and emolument, as they always will be in large states, so as greatly to interest men to pursue them, and to be proper objects for ambitious and designing men, such men will be ever restless in their pursuit after them. They will use the power, when they have acquired it, to the purposes of gratifying their own interest and ambition, and it is scarcely possible, in a very large republic, to call them to account for their misconduct, or to prevent their abuse of power.

These are some of the reasons by which it appears, that a free republic cannot long subsist over a country of the great extent of these states. If then this new constitution is calculated to consolidate the thirteen states into one, as it evidently is, it ought not to be adopted.

Though I am of opinion, that it is a sufficient objection to this government, to reject it, that it creates the whole union into one government, under the form of a republic, yet if this objection was obviated, there are exceptions to it, which are so material and fundamental, that they ought to determine every man, who is a friend to the liberty and happiness of mankind, not to adopt it. I beg the candid and dispassionate attention of my countrymen while I state these objections—they are such as have obtruded themselves upon my mind upon a careful attention to the matter, and such as I sincerely believe are well founded. There are many objections, of small moment, of which I shall take no notice—perfection is not to be expected in any thing that is the production of man—and if I did not in my conscience believe that this scheme was defective in the fundamental principles—in the foundation upon which a free and equal government must rest—I would hold my peace.

BRUTUS
October 18, 1787

Presidents and Vice Presidents

	PRESIDENT	VICE PRESIDENT		PRESIDENT	VICE PRESIDENT
1	George Washington *(Federalist 1789)*	John Adams *(Federalist 1789)*	12	Zachary Taylor *(Whig 1849)*	Millard Fillmore *(Whig 1849)*
2	John Adams *(Federalist 1797)*	Thomas Jefferson *(Dem.-Rep. 1797)*	13	Millard Fillmore *(Whig 1850)*	
3	Thomas Jefferson *(Dem.-Rep. 1801)*	Aaron Burr *(Dem.-Rep. 1801)* George Clinton *(Dem.-Rep. 1805)*	14	Franklin Pierce *(Democratic 1853)*	William R. D. King *(Democratic 1853)*
			15	James Buchanan *(Democratic 1857)*	John C. Breckinridge *(Democratic 1857)*
4	James Madison *(Dem.-Rep. 1809)*	George Clinton *(Dem.-Rep. 1809)* Elbridge Gerry *(Dem.-Rep. 1813)*	16	Abraham Lincoln *(Republican 1861)*	Hannibal Hamlin *(Republican 1861)* Andrew Johnson *(Unionist 1865)*
5	James Monroe *(Dem.-Rep. 1817)*	Daniel D. Tompkins *(Dem.-Rep. 1817)*	17	Andrew Johnson *(Unionist 1865)*	
6	John Quincy Adams *(Dem.-Rep. 1825)*	John C. Calhoun *(Dem.-Rep. 1825)*	18	Ulysses S. Grant *(Republican 1869)*	Schuyler Colfax *(Republican 1869)* Henry Wilson *(Republican 1873)*
7	Andrew Jackson *(Democratic 1829)*	John C. Calhoun *(Democratic 1829)* Martin Van Buren *(Democratic 1833)*	19	Rutherford B. Hayes *(Republican 1877)*	William A. Wheeler *(Republican 1877)*
8	Martin Van Buren *(Democratic 1837)*	Richard M. Johnson *(Democratic 1837)*	20	James A. Garfield *(Republican 1881)*	Chester A. Arthur *(Republican 1881)*
9	William H. Harrison *(Whig 1841)*	John Tyler *(Whig 1841)*	21	Chester A. Arthur *(Republican 1881)*	
10	John Tyler *(Whig and Democratic 1841)*		22	Grover Cleveland *(Democratic 1885)*	Thomas A. Hendricks *(Democratic 1885)*
11	James K. Polk *(Democratic 1845)*	George M. Dallas *(Democratic 1845)*	23	Benjamin Harrison *(Republican 1889)*	Levi P. Morton *(Republican 1889)*

	PRESIDENT	VICE PRESIDENT
24	Grover Cleveland *(Democratic 1893)*	Adlai E. Stevenson *(Democratic 1893)*
25	William McKinley *(Republican 1897)*	Garret A. Hobart *(Republican 1897)*
		Theodore Roosevelt *(Republican 1901)*
26	Theodore Roosevelt *(Republican 1901)*	Charles W. Fairbanks *(Republican 1905)*
27	William H. Taft *(Republican 1909)*	James S. Sherman *(Republican 1909)*
28	Woodrow Wilson *(Democratic 1913)*	Thomas R. Marshall *(Democratic 1913)*
29	Warren G. Harding *(Republican 1921)*	Calvin Coolidge *(Republican 1921)*
30	Calvin Coolidge *(Republican 1923)*	Charles G. Dawes *(Republican 1925)*
31	Herbert Hoover *(Republican 1929)*	Charles Curtis *(Republican 1929)*
32	Franklin D. Roosevelt *(Democratic 1933)*	John Nance Garner *(Democratic 1933)*
		Henry A. Wallace *(Democratic 1941)*
		Harry S. Truman *(Democratic 1945)*
33	Harry S. Truman *(Democratic 1945)*	Alben W. Barkley *(Democratic 1949)*
34	Dwight D. Eisenhower *(Republican 1953)*	Richard M. Nixon *(Republican 1953)*
35	John F. Kennedy *(Democratic 1961)*	Lyndon B. Johnson *(Democratic 1961)*
36	Lyndon B. Johnson *(Democratic 1963)*	Hubert H. Humphrey *(Democratic 1965)*
37	Richard M. Nixon *(Republican 1969)*	Spiro T. Agnew *(Republican 1969)*
		Gerald R. Ford *(Republican 1973)*
38	Gerald R. Ford *(Republican 1974)*	Nelson Rockefeller *(Republican 1974)*
39	James E. Carter *(Democratic 1977)*	Walter Mondale *(Democratic 1977)*
40	Ronald Reagan *(Republican 1981)*	George H. W. Bush *(Republican 1981)*
41	George H. W. Bush *(Republican 1989)*	J. Danforth Quayle *(Republican 1989)*
42	William J. Clinton *(Democratic 1993)*	Albert Gore, Jr. *(Democratic 1993)*
43	George W. Bush *(Republican 2001)*	Richard Cheney *(Republican 2001)*
44	Barack H. Obama *(Democratic 2009)*	Joseph R. Biden, Jr. *(Democratic 2009)*
45	Donald J. Trump *(Republican 2017)*	Michael R. Pence *(Republican 2017)*

Endnotes

CHAPTER 1

1. Lindsey Bever, "Meet Saira Blair, 18, Soon to Be the Nation's Youngest Lawmaker," *Washington Post,* November 7, 2014, www.washingtonpost.com/news/morning-mix/wp/2014/11/07/meet-saira-blair-18-soon-to-be-the-nations-youngest-lawmaker/?utm_term=.708303648d03 (accessed 1/16/18); Lucy McCalmont, "Conservative, Lawmaker, Student," *Politico,* November 5, 2014, www.politico.com/story/2014/11/saira-blair-west-virginia-112602 (accessed 11/16/18); Jae Jones, "This Texas City Just Elected the Youngest City Council Member in the State," *The Nation,* June 1, 2017, www.thenation.com/article/texas-city-just-elected-youngest-person-hold-office-state/ (accessed 1/16/18); City of Prairie View, TX, "Kendric Jones—Position #3," www.prairieviewtexas.gov/departments/kendric_jones_-_pos_3.php (accessed 1/16/18).
2. Arch Puddington and Tyler Roylance, Freedom in the World, 2016, freedomhouse.org/sites/default/files/FH_FITW_Report_2016.pdf (accessed 4/10/16).
3. Eugen Weber, *Peasants into Frenchmen: The Modernization of Rural France, 1870–1914* (Stanford, CA: Stanford University Press, 1976), chap. 5.
4. V. O. Key, *Politics, Parties, and Pressure Groups* (New York: Crowell, 1964), 201.
5. Harold Lasswell, *Politics: Who Gets What, When, How* (New York: Meridian Books, 1958).
6. Abby Goodnough, "Maine Voters Approve Medicaid Expansion, a Rebuke of Gov. LePage," *New York Times,* November 7, 2017, www.nytimes.com/2017/11/07/us/maine-medicaid-healthcare.html (accessed 12/27/17); "2018 Ballot Measures," Ballotpedia, https://ballotpedia.org/2018_ballot_measures (accessed 10/10/18).
7. This definition is taken from Norman H. Nie, Jane Junn, and Kenneth Stehlik-Barry, *Education and Democratic Citizenship in America* (Chicago: University of Chicago Press, 1996).
8. Kyle Dropp and Brendan Nyhan, "One-Third Don't Know Obamacare and Affordable Care Act Are The Same," *New York Times,* The Upshot, February 7, 2017, www.nytimes.com/2017/02/07/upshot/one-third-dont-know-obamacare-and-affordable-care-act-are-the-same.html?_r=0 (accessed 12/28/17).
9. John B. Horrigon and Lee Rainie, "Americans' Views on Open Government Data," Pew Research Center, April 21, 2015, www.pewinternet.org/2015/04/21/open-government-data/ (accessed 7/22/15).
10. Pew Research Center, "Beyond Distrust," November 23, 2015, http://assets.pewresearch.org/wp-content/uploads/sites/5/2015/11/11-23-2015-Governance-release.pdf (accessed 4/15/18).
11. Pew Research Center, "Beyond Distrust."
12. U.S. Census Bureau, Population Clock, April 15, 2018, www.census.gov/popclock/ (accessed 4/15/18).
13. Susan B. Carter, Scott Sigmund Gartner, Michael R. Haines, Alan L. Olmstead, Richard Sutch, and Gavin Wright, eds., *Historical Statistics of the United States: Millennial Edition Online* (New York: Cambridge University Press, 2006), Table Aa145-184, Population, by Sex and Race: 1790–1990, 23. Data from 2016 available at U.S. Census Bureau, "2016 American Community Survey 1-Year Estimates: Selected Characteristics of the Native and Foreign-Born Populations," https://factfinder.census.gov/faces/tableservices/jsf/pages/productview.xhtml?pid=ACS_16_1YR_S0501&prodType=table (accessed 12/26/17).
14. Carter et al., *Historical Statistics of the United States,* Table Aa145-184, Population, by Sex and Race: 1790–1990, 23.
15. Carter et al., *Historical Statistics of the United States,* Table Aa145-184, Population, by Sex and Race: 1790–1990, 23; Table Aa2189-2215, Hispanic Population Estimates.
16. Campbell J. Gibson and Emily Lennon, "Historical Census Statistics on the Foreign-Born Population of the United States: 1850–1990," February 1999, www.census.gov/population/www/documentation/twps0029/twps0029.html (accessed 4/10/16).
17. Carter et al., *Historical Statistics of the United States,* Table Aa22-35, Selected Population Characteristics.

18. Michael B. Katz and Mark J. Stern, *One Nation Divisible: What America Was and What It Is Becoming* (New York: Russell Sage Foundation, 2006), 16.
19. Carter et al., *Historical Statistics of the United States*, Table Aa145-184, Population, by Sex and Race: 1790–1990, 23. Karen R. Humes, Nicholas A. Jones, and Roberto R. Ramirez, "Overview of Race and Hispanic Origin: 2010. *2010 Census Briefs*," no. C2010BR-02 (Washington, DC: U.S. Census Bureau, March 2011), 4, www.census.gov/prod/cen2010/briefs/c2010br-02.pdf (accessed 10/14/2011).
20. U.S. Census Bureau, "2016 American Community Survey 1-Year Estimates: Selected Characteristics of the Native and Foreign-Born Populations."
21. U.S. Census Bureau, "2016 American Community Survey 1-Year Estimates: Selected Characteristics of the Native and Foreign-Born Populations."
22. U.S. Census Bureau, "2016 American Community Survey 1-Year Estimates: Selected Characteristics of the Foreign-Born Population by Region of Birth: Latin America," https://factfinder.census.gov/faces/tableservices/jsf/pages/productview.xhtml?pid=ACS_16_1YR_S0506&prodType=table (accessed 12/26/17).
23. U.S. Census Bureau, "2016 American Community Survey 1-Year Estimates: Selected Characteristics of the Foreign-Born Population by Region of Birth: Asia," https://factfinder.census.gov/faces/tableservices/jsf/pages/productview.xhtml?pid=ACS_16_1YR_S0505&prodType=table (accessed 12/2/17).
24. U.S. Census Bureau, "2016 American Community Survey 1-Year Estimates: Selected Characteristics of the Foreign-Born Population by Region of Birth: Europe," https://factfinder.census.gov/faces/tableservices/jsf/pages/productview.xhtml?pid=ACS_16_1YR_S0503&prodType=table (accessed 12/26/17).
25. Bryan Baker and Nancy Rytina, "Estimates of the Unauthorized Immigrant Population Residing in the United States: January 2012," *Population Estimates*, Office of Immigration Statistics, Department of Homeland Security, March 2013, www.dhs.gov/sites/default/files/publications/Unauthorized%20Immigrant%20Population%20Estimates%20in%20the%20US%20January%202012_0.pdf (accessed 12/26/17).
26. Anthony Faiola, "States' Immigrant Policies Diverge," *Washington Post*, October 15, 2007, A1.
27. *Plyler v. Doe*, 457 U.S. 202 (1982).
28. Robert P. Jones and Daniel Cox, "America's Changing Religious Identity, 2016," Public Religion Research Institute, September 6, 2017, www.prri.org/wp-content/uploads/2017/09/PRRI-Religion-Report.pdf (accessed 11/4/17).
29. Jones and Cox, "America's Changing Religious Identity."
30. U.S. Census Bureau, "Demographic Trends in the 20th Century, Table 5: Population by Age and Sex for the United States: 1900 to 2000," www.census.gov/prod/2002pubs/censr-4.pdf (accessed 4/11/16); U.S. Census Bureau, "Population Estimates, Age and Sex," www.census.gov/quickfacts/fact/table/US/PST045217 (accessed 12/26/17).
31. World Bank, "Population Ages 65 and Above (% of Total)," March 1, 2018, http://data.worldbank.org/indicator/SP.POP.65UP.TO.ZS (accessed 4/15/18).
32. U.S. Census Bureau, "2010 Census Urban Area Facts," www.census.gov/geo/reference/ua/uafacts.html (accessed 4/11/16); Central Intelligence Agency, "World Factbook: Urbanization," 2017, www.cia.gov/library/publications/the-world-factbook/fields/2212.html (accessed 4/15/18).
33. Thomas Piketty and Emmanuel Saez, "Income Inequality in the United States, 1913–1998," *Quarterly Journal of Economics* 118, no. 1 (2003) (Tables and Figures Updated to 2015), http://eml.berkeley.edu/~saez/TabFig2015prel.xls (accessed 12/26/17).
34. U.S. Census Bureau, "Income: Historical Income Data. Tables F-2, F-3, and F-6." www.census.gov/hhes/www/income/data/historical/index.html (accessed 4/12/16).
35. U.S. Census Bureau, "Historical Poverty Tables, Table 2: Poverty Status of People by Family Relationship, Race, and Hispanic origin: 1959 to 2016," www.census.gov/data/tables/time-series/demo/income-poverty/historical-poverty-people.html (accessed 4/15/18).
36. U.S. Census Bureau, "Historical Poverty Tables, Table 2: Poverty Status of People by Family Relationship, Race, and Hispanic Origin: 1959 to 2014," www.census.gov/hhes/www/poverty/data/historical/hstpov2.xls (accessed 4/11/16).
37. Jesse Sussell and James A. Thomson, "Are Changing Constituencies Driving Rising Polarization in the U.S. House of Representatives?" RAND Corporation Research Report RR-396-RC, 2015, www.rand.org/pubs/research_reports/RR896.html (accessed 1/15/18).
38. See Judith N. Shklar, *American Citizenship: The Quest for Inclusion* (Cambridge, MA: Harvard University Press, 1991).
39. Herbert McClosky and John Zaller, *The American Ethos: Public Attitudes toward Capitalism and Democracy* (Cambridge, MA: Harvard University Press, 1984), 19.
40. *Burwell v. Hobby Lobby Stores, Inc.*, 573 U.S. __ (2014).
41. Kevin McCoy and Kevin Johnson, "U.S. Demands Apple Unlock Phone in Drug Case," April 10, 2016, www.usatoday.com/story/news/2016/04/08/justice-moving-forward-separate-apple-case/82788824 (accessed 4/10/16).
42. J. R. Pole, *The Pursuit of Equality in American History* (Berkeley: University of California Press, 1978), 3.
43. *Plessy v. Ferguson*, 163 U.S. 537 (1896).
44. *Brown v. Board of Education*, 347 U.S. 483 (1954).
45. See Rogers M. Smith, *Liberalism and American Constitutional Law* (Cambridge, MA: Harvard University Press, 1985), chap. 6.
46. The case was *San Antonio Independent School District v. Rodriguez*, 411 U.S. 1 (1973). See the discussion in Smith, *Liberalism and American Constitutional Law*, 163–4;

see also Alana Semuels, "Good School, Rich School; Bad School, Poor School," *The Atlantic*, August 25, 2016, www.theatlantic.com/business/archive/2016/08/property-taxes-and-unequal-schools/497333/ (accessed 12/26/17).

47. Janell Fetterolf, "Many Around the World Say Women's Equality Is Very Important," Pew Research Center, January 19, 2017, www.pewresearch.org/fact-tank/2017/01/19/many-around-the-world-say-womens-equality-is-very-important/ (accessed 2/16/18); John Gramlich, "10 Things We Learned about Gender Issues in the U.S. in 2017," Pew Research Center, December 28, 2017, www.pewresearch.org/fact-tank/2017/12/28/10-things-we-learned-about-gender-issues-in-the-u-s-in-2017/ (accessed 2/16/18); "The Partisan Divide on Political Values Grows Even Wider," Pew Research Center, October 5, 2017, www.people-press.org/2017/10/05/1-partisan-divides-over-political-values-widen/ (accessed 2/16/18); Pew Research Center, "Support for Same-Sex Marriage Grows, Even among Groups That Had Been Skeptical," June 26, 2017, www.people-press.org/2017/06/26/support-for-same-sex-marriage-grows-even-among-groups-that-had-been-skeptical/ (accessed 2/16/18); Pew Research Center, "Trends in American Values, 1987–2012," June 4, 2012; Pew Research Center for the People and the Press and for the Public, "For the Public, It's Not about Class Warfare, but Fairness," March 2, 2012, www.peoplepress.org/2012/03/02/for-the-public-its-not-about-class-warfare-but-fairness (accessed 2/16/18).
48. See the discussion in Eileen McDonagh, "Gender Political Change," in *New Perspectives on American Politics*, ed. Lawrence C. Dodd and Calvin C. Jillson (Washington, DC: CQ Press, 1994), 58–73. The argument for moving women's issues into the public sphere is made by Jean Bethke Elshtain, *Public Man, Private Woman* (Princeton, NJ: Princeton University Press, 1981).
49. Roger Lowenstein, "The Way We Live Now: The Inequality Conundrum," *New York Times Magazine*, June 10, 2007, 11.
50. New York Times/CBS News Poll, "Americans' Views on Income Inequality and Workers' Rights," www.nytimes.com/interactive/2015/06/03/business/income-inequality-workers-rights-international-trade-poll.html (accessed 12/27/17); Frank Newport, "Majority Say Wealthy Americans, Corporations Taxed Too Little," April 18, 2017, news.gallup.com/poll/208685/majority-say-wealthy-americans-corporations-taxed-little.aspx (accessed 12/27/17).
51. Kevin Phillips, *Arrogant Capital: Washington, Wall Street, and the Frustration of American Politics* (Boston: Little, Brown, 1994); Richard L. Hasen, *Plutocrats United: Campaign Money, the Supreme Court, and the Distortion of American Elections* (New Haven, CT: Yale University Press, 2016).
52. FairVote, "Voter Turnout," www.fairvote.org/voter_turnout#voter_turnout_101 (accessed 4/10/16).
53. Center for the Study of the American Electorate, "2008 Turnout Report: African-Americans, Anger, Fear and Youth Propel Turnout to Highest Level since 1960," December 17, 2008, www.american.edu/research/news/loader.cfm?csModule5security/getfile&pageid523907 (accessed 2/19/16).
54. Lydia Saad, "Conservatives Lead in U.S. Ideology Down to Single Digits," Gallup News, January 11, 2018, http://news.gallup.com/poll/225074/conservative-lead-ideology-down-single-digits.aspx?g_source=IDEOLOGY&g_medium=topic&g_campaign=tiles (accessed 1/15/18).
55. Art Swift, "Majority in U.S. Say Federal Government Has Too Much Power," Gallup News, October 5, 2017, news.gallup.com/poll/220199/majority-say-federal-government-power.aspx (accessed 1/15/18); Pew Research Center, "Summer 2017 Political Landscape Survey," Final Toplines, October 24, 2017, http://assets.pewresearch.org/wp-content/uploads/sites/5/2017/10/04163936/10-05-2017-Political-landscape-toplines-for-release.pdf (accessed 4/3/18).
56. Pew Research Center, "How Republicans and Democrats View Federal Spending," April 24, 2017, www.people-press.org/2017/04/24/how-republicans-and-democrats-view-federal-spending/ (accessed 1/15/18).
57. Benjamin I. Page and Lawrence R. Jacobs, *Class War? What Americans Really Think about Economic Inequality* (Chicago: University of Chicago Press, 2009).
58. Pew Research Center, "Public Trust in Government, 1958–2017," www.people-press.org/2017/05/03/public-trust-in-government-1958-2017/ (accessed 12/27/17).
59. Pew Research Center, "Public Trust in Government, 1958–2017."
60. Joseph S. Nye, Jr., "Introduction: The Decline of Confidence in Government," in *Why People Don't Trust Government*, ed. Joseph S. Nye, Jr., Philip D. Zelikow, and David C. King (Cambridge, MA: Harvard University Press, 1997), 4.

CHAPTER 2

1. "Jim Obergefell," *Biography*, www.biography.com/people/jim-obergefell (accessed 3/4/18).
2. Jim Obergefell, "Gay Activist Jim Obergefell: Love, Loss and Steadfast Commitment Lead a Nation Forward," *Variety*, June 29, 2015, http://variety.com/2015/biz/news/gay-activist-jim-obergefell-love-loss-commitment-lead-nation-forward-1201529672/ (accessed 3/4/18).
3. *Obergefell v. Hodges,* 576 U.S. __ (2015).
4. Obergefell, "Love, Loss and Steadfast Commitment."
5. Richard E. Neustadt, *Presidential Power and the Modern Presidents: The Politics of Leadership from Roosevelt to Reagan* (New York: Simon & Schuster, 1991), 29.
6. The social makeup of colonial America and some of the social conflicts that divided colonial society are discussed in Jackson Turner Main, *The Social Structure of*

Revolutionary America (Princeton, NJ: Princeton University Press, 1965).

7. George B. Tindall and David E. Shi, *America: A Narrative History*, 8th ed. (New York: W. W. Norton, 2010), 202.
8. For a discussion of events leading up to the Revolution, see Charles M. Andrews, *The Colonial Background of the American Revolution* (New Haven, CT: Yale University Press, 1924).
9. See Carl Becker, *The Declaration of Independence* (New York: Knopf, 1942).
10. An excellent and readable account of the development from the Articles of Confederation to the Constitution will be found in Alfred H. Kelly, Winfred A. Harbison, and Herman Belz, *The American Constitution: Its Origins and Development*, 7th ed., vol. 1 (New York: W. W. Norton, 1991), chap. 5.
11. Reported in Samuel E. Morrison, Henry Steele Commager, and William Leuchtenburg, *The Growth of the American Republic*, vol. 1 (New York: Oxford University Press, 1969), 244.
12. Quoted in Morrison, Commager, and Leuchtenburg, *Growth of the American Republic*, 242.
13. Charles A. Beard, *An Economic Interpretation of the Constitution of the United States* (New York: Macmillan, 1913).
14. Max Farrand, ed., *The Records of the Federal Convention of 1787*, vol. 1 (New Haven, CT: Yale University Press, 1966).
15. Madison's notes, along with the somewhat less complete records kept by several other participants in the convention, are available in a four-volume set. See Max Farrand, ed., *The Records of the Federal Convention of 1787*, 4 vols., rev. ed. (New Haven, CT: Yale University Press, 1966).
16. Farrand, *Records of the Federal Convention of 1787*, 476.
17. Alexander Hamilton, James Madison, and John Jay, *The Federalist Papers*, ed. Clinton L. Rossiter (New York: New American Library, 1961), no. 71.
18. *Federalist Papers*, no. 70.
19. Max Farrand, *The Framing of the Constitution of the United States* (New Haven, CT: Yale University Press, 1962), 49.
20. Melancton Smith, quoted in Herbert J. Storing, *What the Anti-Federalists Were For* (Chicago: University of Chicago Press, 1981), 17.
21. "Essays of Brutus," no. 1, in *The Complete Anti-Federalist*, ed. Herbert Storing (Chicago: University of Chicago Press, 1981).
22. *Federalist Papers*, no. 57.
23. "Essays of Brutus," no. 15, in Storing, *Complete Anti-Federalist*.
24. *Federalist Papers*, no. 10.
25. "Essays of Brutus," no. 7, in Storing, *Complete Anti-Federalist*.
26. "Essays of Brutus," no. 6, in Storing, *Complete Anti-Federalist*.
27. Storing, *What the Anti-Federalists Were For*, 28.
28. *Federalist Papers*, no. 51.
29. Quoted in Storing, *What the Anti-Federalists Were For*, 30.
30. *Federalist Papers*, no. 10.

CHAPTER 3

1. Steph Sherer, "Medical Marijuana Users Caught in State-Federal Conflict," CNN.com, November 10, 2014, www.cnn.com/2014/09/05/opinion/sherer-medical-marijuana-prosecutions/index.html (accessed 7/31/17).
2. "33 Legal Medical Marijuana States and DC," November 7, 2018, https://medicalmarijuana.procon.org/view.resource.php?resourceID=000881 (accessed 11/7/18).
3. Sherer, "Medical Marijuana Users."
4. Brady Dennis, "Obama Administration Will Not Block State Marijuana Laws, If Distribution Is Regulated," *Washington Post*, August 29, 2013, http://articles.washingtonpost.com/2013-08-29/national/41566270_1_marijuana-legalization-attorney-general-bob-ferguson-obama-administration (accessed 11/17/13).
5. John Hudak, "The Disorienting Effect of Marijuana on the Trump Administration," Brookings Institution, April 20, 2017, www.brookings.edu/blog/fixgov/2017/04/20/disorienting-effects-of-marijuana-on-the-trump-administration/ (accessed 7/31/17).
6. The public policy exception stems from developments in case law tracing back to the 1930s. In Section 283 of the Restatement (Second) of Conflict of Laws (1971) a group of judges and academics codified existing case law related to marriage: "A marriage which satisfies the requirements of the state where the marriage was contracted will everywhere be recognized as valid unless it violates the strong public policy of another state which had the most significant relationship to the spouses and the marriage at the time of the marriage." However, in *Baker v. General Motors Corp*, 522 U.S. 222 (1998), the Supreme Court explicitly stated that its decision "creates no general exception to the full faith and credit command."
7. Adam Liptak, "Bans on Interracial Unions Offer Perspective on Gay Ones," *New York Times*, March 17, 2004, A22.
8. *Loving v. Virginia*, 388 U.S. 1 (1967). The Lovings were charged with violating Virginia's miscegenation laws and were sentenced to one year in jail, which would be suspended if they left the state for 25 years. Five years later, with the assistance of the American Civil Liberties Union, the Lovings filed a motion to vacate their conviction. The Supreme Court heard the case and overturned the Lovings' conviction, finding Virginia's miscegenation law unconstitutional under the due process clause and equal protection clause of the Fourteenth Amendment.
9. Ken I. Kersch, "Full Faith and Credit for Same-Sex Marriages?" *Political Science Quarterly* 112 (Spring 1997):

117–36; Joan Biskupic, "Once Unthinkable, Now under Debate," *Washington Post*, September 3, 1996, A1.

10. *United States v. Windsor*, 570 U.S. __ (2013).
11. *Obergefell v. Hodges*, 576 U.S. __ (2015).
12. Elliot C. McLaughlin, "Most States to Abide by Supreme Court's Same-Sex Marriage Ruling, but . . . ," CNN, June 30, 2015, www.cnn.com/2015/06/29/us/same-sex-marriage-state-by-state/ (accessed 8/16/15).
13. *Hicklin v. Orbeck*, 437 U.S. 518 (1978).
14. *Sweeny v. Woodall*, 344 U.S. 86 (1952).
15. Council of State Governments, "Interstate Compacts Toolkit—Backgrounder," www.csg.org/knowledgecenter/docs/ToolKit05InterstateCompacts.pdf (accessed 6/5/18).
16. A good discussion of the constitutional position of local governments is in Richard Briffault, "Our Localism: Part I, the Structure of Local Government Law," *Columbia Law Review* 90, no. 1 (January 1990): 1–115. For more on the structure and theory of federalism, see Larry N. Gerston, *American Federalism: A Concise Introduction* (Armonk, NY: M. E. Sharpe, 2007), and Martha Derthick, "Up-to-Date in Kansas City: Reflections on American Federalism" (1992 John Gaus Lecture), *PS: Political Science and Politics* 25 (December 1992): 671–75.
17. *McCulloch v. Maryland*, 4 Wheaton 316 (1819).
18. *Gibbons v. Ogden*, 9 Wheaton 1 (1824).
19. The Sherman Antitrust Act, adopted in 1890, for example, was enacted not to restrict commerce but rather to protect it from monopolies, or trusts, in order to prevent unfair trade practices and to enable the market again to become self-regulating. Moreover, the Supreme Court sought to uphold liberty of contract to protect businesses. For example, in *Lochner v. New York*, 198 U.S. 45 (1905), the Court invalidated a New York law regulating the sanitary conditions and hours of labor of bakers on the grounds that the law interfered with liberty of contract.
20. The key case in this process of expanding the power of the national government is generally considered to be *NLRB v. Jones & Laughlin Steel Corporation*, 301 U.S. 1 (1937), in which the Supreme Court approved federal regulation of the workplace and thereby virtually eliminated interstate commerce as a limit on the national government's power.
21. Kenneth T. Palmer, "The Evolution of Grant Policies," in *The Changing Politics of Federal Grants*, ed. Lawrence D. Brown, James W. Fossett, and Kenneth T. Palmer (Washington, DC: Brookings Institution Press, 1984), 15.
22. Palmer, "Evolution of Grant Policies," 6.
23. Morton Grodzins, *The American System*, ed. Daniel J. Elazar (Chicago: Rand McNally, 1966).
24. See Terry Sanford, *Storm over the States* (New York: McGraw-Hill, 1967).
25. James L. Sundquist, *Making Federalism Work*, with David W. Davis (Washington, DC: Brookings Institution Press, 1969), 271. George Wallace was mistrusted by the architects of the War on Poverty because he was a strong proponent of racial segregation and "states' rights."
26. See Donald F. Kettl, *The Regulation of American Federalism* (Baton Rouge: Louisiana State University Press, 1983).
27. Cindy Skrzycki, "Trial Lawyers on the Offensive in Fight against Preemptive Rules," *Washington Post*, September 11, 2007, D2.
28. *Gonazales v. Oregon*, 546 U.S. 243 (2006).
29. *Wyeth v. Levine*, 555 U.S. 555 (2009).
30. Philip Rucker, "Obama Curtails Bush's Policy of 'Preemption,'" *Washington Post*, May 22, 2009, A3.
31. Evan Halper, "Trump and California Are Set to Collide Head-On over Fuel Standards," *Los Angeles Times*, April 27, 2018, www.latimes.com/politics/la-na-pol-mileage-20180427-story.html (accessed 5/1/18).
32. The phrase "laboratories of democracy" was coined by Supreme Court Justice Louis Brandeis in his dissenting opinion in *New State Ice Co. v. Liebmann*, 285 U.S. 262 (1932).
33. *United States v. Darby Lumber Co.*, 312 U.S. 100 (1941).
34. W. John Moore, "Pleading the 10th," *National Journal*, July 29, 1996.
35. *United States v. Lopez*, 14 U.S. 549 (1995).
36. *Printz v. United States*, 521 U.S. 98 (1997).
37. Timothy Conlan, *New Federalism: Intergovernmental Reform from Nixon to Reagan* (Washington, DC: Brookings Institution Press, 1988); U.S. Advisory Commission on Intergovernmental Relations, *Federal Regulation of State and Local Governments*.
38. For an assessment of the achievements of the 104th and 105th Congresses, see Timothy Conlan, *From New Federalism to Devolution: Twenty-Five Years of Intergovernmental Reform* (Washington, DC: Brookings Institution Press, 1998).
39. Robert Frank, "Proposed Block Grants Seen Unlikely to Cure Management Problems," *Wall Street Journal*, May 1, 1995, 1.
40. Sarah Kershaw, "U.S. Rule Limits Emergency Care for Immigrants," *New York Times*, September 22, 2007, A1.
41. Education Commission of the States, "50-State Comparison: Charter School Policies," January 2018, www.ecs.org/charter-school-policies/ (accessed 6/5/18).
42. Zach Winn, "A List of States That Allow Concealed Guns on Campus," *Campus Safety Magazine*, August 30, 2017, www.campussafetymagazine.com/university/list-of-states-that-allow-concealed-carry-guns-on-campus/ (accessed 10/12/18).
43. National Council of State Legislatures, "NCSL Fiscal Brief: State Balanced Budget Requirements," October 2010, www.ncsl.org/documents/fiscal/StateBalancedBudgetProvisions2010.pdf (accessed 7/26/17).
44. Robert Jay Dilger and Richard S. Beth, "Unfunded Mandates Reform Act: History, Impact, and Issues" (Washington, DC: Congressional Research Service, April 19, 2011), 40, http://digital.library.unt.edu/ark:/67531/metadc40084/m1/1/high_res_d/R40957_2011Apr19.pdf (accessed 11/16/13).

45. See U.S. Advisory Commission on Intergovernmental Relations, *Federal Regulation of State and Local Governments: The Mixed Record of the 1980s* (Washington, DC: Advisory Commission on Intergovernmental Relations, July 1993).
46. Congressional Budget Office, "A Review of CBO's Activities in 2014 under the Unfunded Mandates Reform Act," March 31, 2015, www.cbo.gov/sites/default/files/114th-congress-2015-2016/reports/50051-UMRA2_0.pdf (see Appendix B, p. 39) (accessed 8/16/15).
47. Adam Liptak, "Justices to Hear Health Care Case as Race Heats Up," *New York Times*, November 15, 2011, A1.
48. Kaiser Family Foundation, "Status of State Medicaid Expansion Decisions," May 31, 2018, www.kff.org/health-reform/slide/current-status-of-the-medicaid-expansion-decision/ (accessed 6/5/18); Ballotopedia, "2018 Ballot Measure Election Results," https://ballotpedia.org/2018_ballot_measure_election_results (accessed 11/7/18).
49. U.S. Committee on Federalism and National Purpose, *To Form a More Perfect Union* (Washington, DC: National Conference on Social Welfare, 1985). See also the discussion in Paul E. Peterson, *The Price of Federalism* (Washington, DC: Brookings Institution Press, 1995), esp. chap. 8.
50. Malcolm Gladwell, "Remaking Welfare: In States' Experiments, a Cutting Contest," *Washington Post*, March 10, 1995, 6.
51. Ashley Burnside and Ife Floyd, "TANF Benefits Remain Low Despite Recent Increases in Some States," Center on Budget and Policy Priorities, October 12, 2018, www.cbpp.org/sites/default/files/atoms/files/10-30-14tanf.pdf (accessed 10/12/18).
52. Cohen, Elissa, Sarah Minton, Megan Thompson, Elizabeth Crowe, and Linda Giannarelli, "Welfare Rules Databook: State TANF Policies as of July 2015," OPRE Report 2016-67 (Washington, DC: Office of Planning, Research and Evaluation, Administration for Children and Families, U.S. Department of Health and Human Services, 2016), http://wrd.urban.org/wrd/data/databooks/2015%20Welfare%20Rules%20Databook%20(Final%2009%2026%2016).pdf (accessed 7/30/17); and Mary Jo Pitzi, "Arizona Limits Poverty Aid to 1 Year; Strictest in U.S." azcentral.com, July 1, 2016, www.azcentral.com/story/news/politics/arizona/2016/07/01/arizona-limits-poverty-aid-1-year-strictest-us/86499262/ (accessed 7/30/17).
53. Andrea Louise Campbell, *Trapped in America's Safety Net: One Family's Struggle* (Chicago: University of Chicago Press, 2014), 82.
54. Frank J. Thompson, *Medicaid Politics: Federalism, Policy Durability, and Health Reform* (Washington, DC: Georgetown University Press, 2012).
55. Insurance Institute for Highway Safety, "Motor Vehicle Fatalities in 1996 Were 12 Percent Higher on Interstates, Freeways in 12 States That Raised Speed Limits," press release, October 10, 1997.
56. *Gonzales v. Raich*, 545 U.S. 1 (2005). For more, see William Yardley, "New Federal Crackdown Confounds States That Allow Medical Marijuana," *New York Times*, May 8, 2011, A13.
57. *Gonzales v. Oregon*, 546 U.S. 243 (2006).
58. Josh Sanburn, "Colorado Approves a 'Right to Die' for Terminally Ill Patients," *Time*, November 9, 2016, time.com/4563632/colorado-right-to-die-approved/ (accessed 11/10/16).
59. National Conference of State Legislatures, "Collecting E-Commerce Taxes," www.ncsl.org/research/fiscal-policy/collecting-ecommerce-taxes-an-interactive-map.aspx (accessed 11/17/13).
60. Richard Rubin, "States Set Up Fight over Web Sales Tax," *Wall Street Journal*, February 23, 2016, www.wsj.com/articles/states-seek-new-ways-to-tax-online-sales-1456262265 (accessed 4/11/16).
61. *United States v. Texas*, 579 U.S. __ (2016).
62. Alexander Bolton, "GOP Looks for Plan B after Failure of Immigration Measures," The Hill, February 16, 2018, thehill.com/homenews/senate/374143-gop-looks-for-plan-b-after-failure-of-immigration-measures (accessed 2/18/18).
63. Kate Linthicum, "Obama Ends Secure Communities Program as Part of Immigration Action," *Los Angeles Times*, November 21, 2014, www.latimes.com/local/california/la-me-1121-immigration-justice-20141121-story.html (accessed 8/16/15).
64. "Enhancing Public Safety in the Interior of the United States," Executive Order 13768, January 25, 2017, www.federalregister.gov/documents/2017/01/30/2017-02102/enhancing-public-safety-in-the-interior-of-the-united-states (accessed 7/27/17).
65. Camila Domonoske, "Judge Blocks Trump Administration from Punishing 'Sanctuary Cities,'" NPR, November 21, 2017, www.npr.org/sections/thetwo-way/2017/11/21/565678707/enter-title (accessed 2/18/18).
66. Nicole Rodriguez, "Trump Administration Wants to Arrest Mayors of 'Sanctuary Cities,'" *Newsweek*, January 16, 2018, www.newsweek.com/trump-administration-wants-arrest-mayors-sanctuary-cities-783010 (accessed 2/18/18).
67. *NFIB v. Sebelius*, 567 U.S. 519 (2012).
68. Adam Liptak, "In Health Law, Asking Where U.S. Power Stops," *New York Times*, November 14, 2011, A1.
69. Robert Barnes, "Affordable Care Act Survives Supreme Court Challenge," *Washington Post*, June 25, 2015, www.washingtonpost.com/politics/courts_law/obamacare-survives-supreme-court-challenge/2015/06/25/af87608e-188a-11e5-93b7-5eddc056ad8a_story.html (accessed 8/16/15).
70. National League of Cities, "City Rights in an Era of Preemption: A State-by-State Analysis," 2017, http://nlc.org/preemption (accessed 7/27/17).
71. Emma G. Ellis, "Guess How Much That Anti-LGBTQ Law Is Costing North Carolina," *Wired*, Sepember 18, 2016, www.wired.com/2016/09/guess-much-anti-lgbtq-law-costing-north-carolina/ (accessed 7/27/17).

72. Celeste Bott, "St. Louis $10 Minimum Wage to Revert Back to $7.70 in August, Greitens Announces," *St. Louis Post-Dispatch,* July 1, 2017, www.stltoday.com/news/local/govt-and-politics/st-louis-minimum-wage-will-revert-back-to-in-august/article_0428b488-d4e2-5778-895b-f44ad92cc65a.html (accessed 7/27/17); Celeste Bott, "More Than 100 St. Louis Businesses Opt to Keep $10 Minimum Wage, Despite New State Law," *St. Louis Post-Dispatch,* August 7, 2017, www.stltoday.com/news/local/metro/more-than-st-louis-businesses-opt-to-keep-minimum-wage/article_920788cd-47b2-5a39-b494-8ee7e6c0f676.html (accessed 2/18/18); CBS St. Louis, "McDonalds 'Save the Raise' Protest Happening Today," August 17, 2017, stlouis.cbslocal.com/2017/08/17/mcdonalds-save-the-raise-protest-happening-today/ (accessed 2/18/18).
73. Melia Robinson, "Here's Where You Can Legally Smoke Weed in 2018," *Business Insider,* January 23, 2018, www.businessinsider.com/where-can-you-can-legally-smoke-weed-2018-1/#alaska-1 (accessed 2/13/18); "33 Legal Medical Marijuana States and DC," November 7, 2018, https://medicalmarijuana.procon.org/view.resource.php?resourceID=000881 (accessed 11/7/18).

CHAPTER 4

1. This account taken from April Baer, "The Slants: Trading in Stereotypes," NPR, June 11, 2008, www.npr.org/templates/story/story.php?storyId=90278746; Katy Steinmetz, "'The Slants' Suit: Asian-American Band Goes to Court over Name," *Time,* October 23, 2013, http://entertainment.time.com/2013/10/23/the-slants-suit-asian-american-band-goes-to-court-over-name/; Kat Chow, "The Slants: Fighting for the Right to Rock a Racial Slur," NPR, January 19, 2017, www.npr.org/sections/codeswitch/2017/01/19/510467679/the-slants-fighting-for-the-right-to-rock-a-racial-slur; *Matal v. Tam,* 582 U.S. __ (2017); Ian Shapira and Ann E. Marimow, "Washington Redskins Win Trademark Fight over the Team's Name," *Washington Post,* June 29, 2017, www.washingtonpost.com/local/public-safety/2017/06/29/a26f52f0-5cf6-11e7-9fc6-c7ef4bc58d13_story.html?utm_term=.22ed3bf39917 (accessed 2/4/18).
2. Alexander Hamilton, James Madison, and John Jay, *The Federalist Papers*, ed. Clinton Rossiter (New York: New American Library, 1961), no. 84, 513.
3. *Federalist Papers*, no. 84, 513.
4. Clinton Rossiter, *1787: The Grand Convention* (New York: W. W. Norton, 1987), 302.
5. Rossiter, *1787,* 303. Rossiter also reports that "in 1941 the States of Connecticut, Massachusetts, and Georgia celebrated the sesquicentennial of the Bill of Rights by giving their hitherto withheld and unneeded assent."
6. *Barron v. Baltimore*, 7 Peters 243, 246 (1833).
7. The Fourteenth Amendment also seems designed to introduce civil rights. The final clause of the all-important Section 1 provides that no state can "deny to any person within its jurisdiction the equal protection of the laws." It is not unreasonable to conclude that the purpose of this provision was to obligate the state governments as well as the national government to take positive actions to protect citizens from arbitrary and discriminatory actions, at least those based on race. Civil rights will be explored in Chapter 5.
8. For example, *The Slaughterhouse Cases*, 16 Wallace 36 (1883).
9. *Chicago, Burlington and Quincy Railroad Company v. Chicago*, 166 U.S. 226 (1897).
10. *Gitlow v. New York*, 268 U.S. 652 (1925).
11. *Near v. Minnesota*, 283 U.S. 697 (1931); *Hague v. C.I.O.*, 307 U.S. 496 (1939).
12. *Palko v. Connecticut*, 302 U.S. 319 (1937).
13. All of these were implicitly included in the *Palko* case as "not incorporated" into the Fourteenth Amendment as limitations on the powers of the states.
14. There is one interesting exception, which involves the Sixth Amendment right to public trial. In the 1948 case *In re Oliver*, 33 U.S. 257, the right to a public trial was, in effect, incorporated as part of the Fourteenth Amendment. However, the issue in that case was put more generally as "due process," and public trial itself was not actually mentioned in so many words. Later opinions, such as *Duncan v. Louisiana*, 391 U.S. 145 (1968), cited the *Oliver* case as the precedent for more explicit incorporation of public trials as part of the Fourteenth Amendment.
15. *Abington School District v. Schempp*, 374 U.S. 203 (1963).
16. *Engel v. Vitale*, 370 U.S. 421 (1962).
17. *Wallace v. Jaffree*, 472 U.S. 38 (1985).
18. *Lemon v. Kurtzman*, 403 U.S. 602 (1971). The *Lemon* test is still good law, but as recently as the 1994 Court term, four justices have urged that the test be abandoned. Here is a settled area of law that may soon become unsettled.
19. *Rosenberger v. Rector and Visitors of the University of Virginia*, 515 U.S. 819 (1995).
20. *Elk Grove United School District v. Newdow,* 542 U.S. 1 (2004).
21. *Van Orden v. Perry*, 545 U.S. 677 (2005).
22. *McCreary County v. American Civil Liberties Union of Kentucky*, 545 U.S. 844 (2005).
23. *West Virginia State Board of Education v. Barnette*, 319 U.S. 624 (1943). The case it reversed was *Minersville School District v. Gobitus*, 310 U.S. 586 (1940).
24. *Cantwell v. Connecticut*, 310 U.S. 296 (1940).
25. *Holt v. Hobbs*, 574 U.S. __ (2015).
26. *Equal Employment Opportunity Commission v. Abercrombie & Fitch Stores, Inc.*, 575 U.S. __ (2015).
27. *Burwell v. Hobby Lobby Stores,* 573 U.S. __ (2014).
28. *Abrams v. United States*, 250 U.S. 616 (1919).
29. *United States v. Carolene Products Company*, 304 U.S. 144 (1938), n4. This footnote is one of the Court's most important doctrines. See Alfred H. Kelly, Winfred A. Harbison, and Herman Belz, *The American Constitution: Its Origins and Development*, 7th ed. (New York: W. W. Norton, 1991), 2:519–23.

30. *Schenck v. United States*, 249 U.S. 47 (1919).
31. *Brandenburg v. Ohio*, 395 U.S. 444 (1969).
32. *Buckley v. Valeo*, 424 U.S. 1 (1976).
33. *McConnell v. Federal Election Commission*, 540 U.S. 93 (2003).
34. *Federal Election Commission v. Wisconsin Right to Life*, 551 U.S. 449 (2007).
35. *Citizens United v. Federal Election Commission*, 558 U.S. 310 (2010).
36. *McCutcheon v. Federal Election Commission*, 572 U.S. __ (2014).
37. Arthur Delaney, "Supreme Court Rolls Back Campaign Finance Restrictions," Huffington Post, March 23, 2010, updated May 25, 2011, www.huffingtonpost.com/2010/01/21/supreme-court-rolls-back_n_431227.html (accessed 7/9/12).
38. *Chaplinsky v. State of New Hampshire*, 315 U.S. 568 (1942).
39. *Dennis v. United States*, 341 U.S. 494 (1951), which upheld the infamous Smith Act of 1940 that provided criminal penalties for those who "willfully and knowingly conspire to teach and advocate the forceful and violent overthrow and destruction of the government."
40. Laura Kipness, *Unwanted Advances* (New York: Harper, 2017).
41. *Capitol Broadcasting Company v. Acting Attorney General*, 405 U.S. 1000 (1972).
42. *R.A.V. v. City of St. Paul*, 505 U.S. 377 (1992).
43. *United States v. Schwimmer*, 279 U.S. 644 (1929).
44. *Bethel School District No. 403 v. Fraser*, 478 U.S. 675 (1986).
45. *Hazelwood School District v. Kuhlmeier*, 484 U.S. 260 (1988).
46. *Morse v. Frederick*, 551 U.S. 393 (2007).
47. *City Council v. Taxpayers for Vincent*, 466 U.S. 789 (1984).
48. Louis Fisher, *American Constitutional Law* (New York: McGraw-Hill, 1990), 546.
49. *Bigelow v. Virginia*, 421 U.S. 809 (1975).
50. *Virginia State Board of Pharmacy v. Virginia Citizens Consumer Council*, 425 U.S. 748 (1976). Later cases restored the rights of lawyers to advertise their services.
51. *Lorillard Tobacco v. Reilly*, 533 U.S. 525 (2001).
52. *Hague v. Committee for Industrial Organization*, 307 U.S. 496 (1939).
53. *Texas v. Johnson*, 491 U.S. 397 (1989).
54. Charles Babington, "Senate Rejects Flag Desecration Amendment," *Washington Post*, June 28, 2006, www.washingtonpost.com/wp-dyn/content/article/2006/06/27/AR2006062701056.html (accessed 11/13/13).
55. *Snyder v. Phelps*, 562 U.S. __ (2011).
56. For a good general discussion of speech plus, see Fisher, *American Constitutional Law*, 544–46. The case upholding the buffer zone against the abortion protesters is *Madsen v. Women's Health Center*, 512 U.S. 753 (1994).
57. *Near v. Minnesota*, 283 U.S. 697 (1931).
58. *New York Times Co. v. United States*, 403 U.S. 713 (1971).
59. *Branzburg v. Hayes*, 408 U.S. 665 (1972).
60. *New York Times Co. v. Sullivan*, 376 U.S. 254 (1964).
61. Shannon Hutzler, "Protecting Informed Public Participation," *Valparaiso University Law Review* 41, no. 3 (Spring 2007): 1235–84.
62. See *Zeran v. America Online*, 129 F3d 327 (4th Cir. 1997).
63. *Roth v. United States*, 354 U.S. 476 (1957).
64. Concurring opinion in *Jacobellis v. Ohio*, 378 U.S. 184 (1964).
65. *Miller v. California*, 413 U.S. 15 (1973).
66. *Reno v. American Civil Liberties Union*, 521 U.S. 844 (1997).
67. *United States v. Williams*, 553 U.S. 285 (2008).
68. *United States v. Playboy Entertainment Group*, 529 U.S. 803 (2000).
69. *Brown v. Entertainment Merchants Association*, 564 U.S. __ (2011).
70. *District of Columbia v. Heller*, 554 U.S. 570 (2008).
71. *McDonald v. Chicago*, 561 U.S. 742 (2010).
72. *In re Winship*, 397 U.S. 358 (1970). An outstanding treatment of due process in issues involving the Fourth through Seventh amendments will be found in Fisher, *American Constitutional Law*, chap. 13.
73. *Horton v. California*, 496 U.S. 128 (1990).
74. *Mapp v. Ohio*, 367 U.S. 643 (1961). Although Mapp went free in this case, she was later convicted in New York on narcotics trafficking charges and served 9 years of a 20-year sentence.
75. For a good discussion of the issue, see Fisher, *American Constitutional Law*, pp. 884–9.
76. *United States v. Grubbs*, 547 U.S. 90 (2006).
77. *National Treasury Employees Union v. Von Raab*, 489 U.S. 656 (1989).
78. *Skinner v. Railway Labor Executives' Association*, 489 U.S. 602 (1989).
79. *Vernonia School District 47J v. Acton*, 515 U.S. 646 (1995).
80. *Chandler v. Miller*, 520 U.S. 305 (1997).
81. *Florida v. Jardines*, 569 U.S. __ (2013).
82. *United States v. Jones*, 132 S. 565 U.S. __ (2012).
83. *Maryland v. King*. 569 U.S. __ (2013).
84. *Riley v. California*, 573 U.S. __ (2014).
85. *Terry v. Ohio*, 392 U.S. 1 (1968).
86. Marjorie Cohn, "NSA Metadata Collection: Fourth Amendment Violation," JURIST, January 15, 2014, http://jurist.org/forum/2014/01/marjorie-cohn-nsa-metadata.php (accessed 4/19/16).
87. Edwin S. Corwin and J. W. Peltason, *Understanding the Constitution* (New York: Holt, 1967), 286.
88. *Benton v. Maryland*, 395 U.S. 784 (1969).
89. *Miranda v. Arizona*, 348 U.S. 436 (1966).
90. *Berman v. Parker*, 348 U.S. 26 (1954). For a thorough analysis of the case, see Benjamin Ginsberg, "*Berman v. Parker*: Congress, the Court, and the Public Purpose," *Polity* 4 (1971): 48–75. For a later application of the case that suggests that "just compensation"—defined as something approximating market value—is about all a

property owner can hope for protection against a public taking of property, see Theodore Lowi et al., *Poliscide: Big Government, Big Science, Lilliputian Politics*, 2nd ed. (Lanham, MD: University Press of America, 1990), 267–70.

91. *Kelo v. City of New London*, 545 U.S. 469 (2005).
92. *Gideon v. Wainwright*, 372 U.S. 335 (1963).
93. *Wiggins v. Smith*, 539 U.S. 510 (2003).
94. For further discussion of these issues, see Corwin and Peltason, *Understanding the Constitution*, 319–23.
95. *Furman v. Georgia*, 408 U.S. 238 (1972).
96. *Gregg v. Georgia*, 428 U.S. 153 (1976).
97. Death Penalty Information Center, "Facts about the Death Penalty," October 11, 2018, https://deathpenaltyinfo.org/documents/FactSheet.pdf (accessed 10/12/18).
98. *Kennedy v. Louisiana*, 554 U.S. 407 (2008).
99. *Snyder v. Louisiana*, 552 U.S. 472 (2008).
100. *Glossip v. Gross*, 576 U.S. __ (2015).
101. *Hudson v. McMillan*, 503 U.S. 1 (1992).
102. *Miller v. Alabama*, 567 U.S. __ (2012).
103. *Olmstead v. United States*, 277 U.S. 438 (1928). See also David M. O'Brien, *Constitutional Law and Politics*, vol. 1, 6th ed. (New York: W. W. Norton, 2005), 76–84.
104. *West Virginia State Board of Education v. Barnette* 319 U.S. 624 (1943).
105. *NAACP v. Alabama ex rel. Patterson*, 357 U.S. 449 (1958).
106. *Griswold v. Connecticut*, 381 U.S. 479 (1965).
107. *Griswold*, concurring opinion. In 1972 the Court extended the privacy right to unmarried women: *Eisenstadt v. Baird*, 405 U.S. 438 (1972).
108. *Roe v. Wade*, 410 U.S. 113 (1973).
109. *Webster v. Reproductive Health Services*, 492 U.S. 490 (1989), which upheld a Missouri law that restricted the use of public medical facilities for abortion. The decision opened the way for other states to limit the availability of abortion.
110. *Planned Parenthood of Southeastern Pennsylvania v. Casey*, 505 U.S. 833 (1992).
111. *Ayotte v. Planned Parenthood*, 546 U.S. 320 (2006).
112. *Gonzales v. Carhart*, 550 U.S. 124 (2007).
113. *Bowers v. Hardwick*, 478 U.S. 186 (1986).
114. *Lawrence v. Texas*, 539 U.S. 558 (2003).
115. *Lawrence* (2003).
116. It is worth recalling here the provision of the Ninth Amendment: "The enumeration in the Constitution, of certain rights, shall not be construed to deny or disparage others retained by the people."
117. *Obergefell v. Hodges*, 576 U.S. __ (2015).
118. Arthur L. Caplan, ed., *The Case of Terri Schiavo: Ethics at the End of Life* (Amherst, NY: Prometheus Books, 2016).
119. *Gonzales v. Oregon*, 546 U.S. 243 (2006).
120. Daniel J. Solove, *Nothing to Hide: The False Tradeoff between Privacy and Security* (New Haven, CT: Yale University Press, 2011).

CHAPTER 5

1. Maia Silber, "A Trailblazing Transgender Midshipman Navigates an Uncertain Path in the Wake of Trump's Tweet." *Washington Post*, July 29, 2017, www.washingtonpost.com/lifestyle/style/a-trailblazing-transgender-midshipman-navigates-an-uncertain-path-in-the-wake-of-trumps-tweet/2017/07/29/bf92a6c6-73c5-11e7-9eac-d56bd5568db8_story.html?utm_term=.34e163b1fd55 (accessed 2/3/18).
2. Silber, "Trailblazing Transgender Midshipman." See also "A Transgender Midshipman Fights Trump's Ban," CNN, November 21, 2017, www.cnn.com/2017/11/21/politics/trump-transgender-military-ban-second-order/index.html (accessed 2/3/18).
3. Mark Joseph Stern, "Trump Administration Relents, for Now: Trans Americans May Enlist in the Military Starting Monday," Slate, December 30, 2017, slate.com/news-and-politics/2017/12/trump-administration-wont-appeal-trans-troops-ban-to-the-supreme-court.html (accessed 2/3/18).
4. Paula Baker, "The Domestication of Politics: Women and American Political Society, 1780–1920," *American Historical Review* 89 (June 1984): 620–47.
5. *Dred Scott v. Sandford*, 60 U.S. 393 (1857).
6. August Meier and Elliott Rudwick, *From Plantation to Ghetto* (New York: Hill and Wang, 1976), 184–88.
7. Jill Dupont, "Susan B. Anthony," New York Notes (Albany: New York State Commission on the Bicentennial of the U.S. Constitution, 1988), 3.
8. *Plessy v. Ferguson*, 163 U.S. 537 (1896).
9. Dupont, "Susan B. Anthony," 4.
10. The prospect of a "fair employment practices" law tied to the commerce power produced the Dixiecrat break with the Democratic Party in 1948. The Democratic Party organization of the States of the Old Confederacy seceded from the national party and nominated its own candidate, the then-Democratic governor of South Carolina, Strom Thurmond, who later became a Republican senator. This almost cost President Truman the election.
11. This was based on the provision in Article VI of the Constitution that "all treaties made...under the Authority of the United States" shall be the "supreme Law of the Land." The commission recognized that if the U.S. Senate ratified what became the Universal Declaration of Human Rights (a treaty), then that power could be used as the constitutional umbrella for effective civil rights legislation. The Supreme Court had recognized in *Missouri v. Holland*, 252 U.S. 416 (1920), that a treaty could enlarge federal power at the expense of the states.
12. *Missouri ex rel. Gaines v. Canada*, 305 U.S. 337 (1938).
13. *Sweatt v. Painter*, 339 U.S. 629 (1950).
14. *Shelley v. Kraemer*, 334 U.S. 1 (1948).
15. The District of Columbia case came up, too; but since the District of Columbia is not a state, this case did not

directly involve the Fourteenth Amendment and its equal protection clause. The plaintiffs confronted the Court on the same grounds, however—that segregation is inherently unequal. Their victory in effect was "incorporation in reverse," with equal protection moving from the Fourteenth Amendment to become part of the Bill of Rights. See *Bolling v. Sharpe*, 347 U.S. 497 (1954).

16. *Brown v. Board of Education of Topeka, Kansas*, 347 U.S. 483 (1954).
17. The Supreme Court first declared that race was a suspect classification requiring strict scrutiny in the decision *Korematsu v. United States*, 323 U.S. 214 (1944). In this case, the Court upheld President Roosevelt's executive order of 1941 allowing the military to exclude persons of Japanese ancestry from the West Coast and to place them in internment camps. It is one of the few cases in which classification based on race survived strict scrutiny.
18. The two most important cases were *Cooper v. Aaron*, 358 U.S. 1 (1958), which required Little Rock, Arkansas, to desegregate, and *Griffin v. Prince Edward County School Board*, 377 U.S. 218 (1964), which forced all the schools of that Virginia county to reopen after five years of closing to avoid desegregation.
19. In *Cooper v. Aaron*, the Supreme Court ordered immediate compliance with the lower court's desegregation order and went beyond that with a stern warning that it is "emphatically the province and duty of the judicial department to say what the law is."
20. *Shuttlesworth v. Birmingham Board of Education of Jefferson City* 358 U.S. 101 (1958) upheld a "pupil placement" plan purporting to assign pupils on various bases, with no mention of race. This case interpreted *Brown* to mean that school districts had to stop explicit racial discrimination but were under no obligation to take positive steps to desegregate. For a while black parents were doomed to a case-by-case approach.
21. For good treatments of this long stretch of the struggle of the federal courts to integrate the schools, see Paul Brest and Sanford Levinson, *Processes of Constitutional Decision-Making: Cases and Materials*, 2nd ed. (Boston: Little, Brown, 1983), 471–80; and Alfred H. Kelly, Winfred A. Harbison, and Herman Belz, *The American Constitution: Its Origins and Development*, 6th ed. (New York: W. W. Norton, 1983), 610–16.
22. Aimee Green, "Elmer's Restaurant Says It Made Black Man Prepay Because He Sat in a Bar, Ordered Alcohol," *Oregon Live*, October 29, 2015, www.oregonlive.com/clark-county/index.ssf/2015/10/elmers_told_state_investigator.html (accessed 8/2/18).
23. See Hamil Harris, "For Blacks, Cabs Can Be Hard to Get," *Washington Post*, July 21, 1994, J1.
24. For a thorough analysis of the Office for Civil Rights, see Jeremy Rabkin, "Office for Civil Rights," in *The Politics of Regulation*, ed. James Q. Wilson (New York: Basic Books, 1980).
25. This was an accepted way of using quotas or ratios to determine statistically that blacks or other minorities were being excluded from schools or jobs and then, on the basis of that statistical evidence, to authorize the Justice Department to bring suits in individual cases and class-action suits. In most segregated situations outside the South, it is virtually impossible to identify and document an intent to discriminate.
26. *Swann v. Charlotte-Mecklenberg Board of Education*, 402 U.S. 1 (1971).
27. *Milliken v. Bradley*, 418 U.S. 717 (1974).
28. For a good evaluation of the Boston effort, see Gary Orfield, *Must We Bus? Segregated Schools and National Policy* (Washington, DC: Brookings Institution, 1978), 144–6. See also Bob Woodward and Scott Armstrong, *The Brethren: Inside the Supreme Court* (New York: Simon and Schuster, 1979), 426–27; and J. Anthony Lukas, *Common Ground* (New York: Random House, 1986).
29. *Board of Education v. Dowell*, 498 U.S. 237 (1991).
30. *Parents Involved in Community Schools v. Seattle School District No. 1*, 551 U.S. 701 (2007).
31. *Griggs v. Duke Power Company*, 401 U.S. 424 (1971). See also Allan Sindler, *Bakke, DeFunis, and Minority Admissions* (New York: Longman, 1978), 180–89.
32. For a good treatment of these issues, see Charles O. Gregory and Harold A. Katz, *Labor and the Law* (New York: W. W. Norton, 1979), chap. 17.
33. In 1970 this act was amended to outlaw for five years literacy tests as a condition for voting in all states.
34. Joint Center for Political Studies, *Black Elected Officials: A National Roster—1988* (Washington, DC: Joint Center for Political Studies Press, 1988), 9–10. For a comprehensive analysis and evaluation of the Voting Rights Act, see Bernard Grofman and Chandler Davidson, eds., *Controversies in Minority Voting: The Voting Rights Act in Perspective* (Washington, DC: Brookings Institution, Press, 1992).
35. Ford Fessenden, "Ballots Cast by Blacks and Older Voters Were Tossed in Far Greater Numbers," *New York Times*, November 12, 2001, A17.
36. Aaron Blake, "Texas Redistricting Case: Five Things You Need to Know," *Washington Post*, December 13, 2011, www.washingtonpost.com/blogs/the-fix/post/texas-redistricting-case-five-things-you-need-to-know/2011/12/13/gIQAdowHsO_blog.html; Manny Fernandez, "Federal Judges Approve Final Texas Redistricting Maps," *New York Times*, February 28, 2012, www.nytimes.com/2012/02/29/us/final-texas-redistricting-maps-approved.html (accessed 6/22/12).
37. *Shelby County v. Holder*, 570 U.S. __ (2013).
38. *Crawford v. Marion County Election Board*, 553 U.S. 181 (2008). See also David Stout, "Supreme Court Upholds Voter Identification Law in Indiana," *New York Times*, April 29, 2008, www.nytimes.com/2008/04/29/washington/28cnd-scotus.html (accessed 1/13/14).
39. See Douglas S. Massey and Nancy A. Denton, *American Apartheid: Segregation and the Making of the Underclass* (Cambridge, MA: Harvard University Press, 1993), chap. 7.

40. Michael Powell, "Bank Accused of Pushing Mortgage Deals on Blacks," *New York Times*, June 6, 2009, www.nytimes.com/2009/06/07/us/07baltimore.html; Charlie Savage, "Countrywide Will Settle a Bias Suit," *New York Times*, December 22, 2011, B1.
41. *Loving v. Virginia*, 388 U.S. 1 (1967).
42. *Windsor v. United States*, 699 F.3d 169 2nd Cir. (2012).
43. *Adarand Constructors Inc. v. Pena*, 515 U.S. 200 (1995).
44. *Fisher v. University of Texas*, 570 U.S. __ (2013).
45. *Fisher v. University of Texas*, 579 U. S. __ (2016).
46. See Jane J. Mansbridge, *Why We Lost the ERA* (Chicago: University of Chicago Press, 1986); and Gilbert Steiner, *Constitutional Inequality* (Washington, DC: Brookings Institution Press, 1985).
47. See *Frontiero v. Richardson*, 411 U.S. 677 (1973).
48. See *Craig v. Boren*, 429 U.S. 190 (1976).
49. Claire Zillman, "Barnes & Noble Is Latest Retailer to Face Transgender Discrimination Lawsuit," *Fortune*, May 7, 2015, http://fortune.com/2015/05/07/barnes-noble-transgender-lawsuit/ (accessed 12/23/15).
50. *Franklin v. Gwinnett County Public Schools*, 503 U.S. 60 (1992).
51. Jennifer Halperin, "Women Step Up to Bat," *Illinois Issues* 21 (September 1995): 11–14.
52. Joan Biskupic and David Nakamura, "Court Won't Review Sports Equity Ruling," *Washington Post*, April 22, 1997, A1.
53. Debra DeMeis and Rosanna Hertz, "Sex, Sports, and Title IX on Campus: The Triumphs and Travails," Daily Beast, June 22, 2012, www.dailybeast.com/articles/2012/06/22/sex-sports-and-title-ix-on-campus-the-triumphs-and-travails.html (accessed 6/22/12).
54. *United States v. Virginia*, 518 U.S. 515 (1996).
55. Judith Havemann, "Two Women Quit Citadel over Alleged Harassment," *Washington Post*, January 13, 1997, A1.
56. Petula Dvorak, "The Citadel Didn't Want to Admit Women. but Once This Woman Got In, She Was Unstoppable," *Washington Post*, October 27, 2016, www.citadel.edu/root/the-citadel-didnt-want-to-admit-women-but-once-this-woman-got-in-she-was-unstoppable (accessed 10/9/18).
57. *Meritor Savings Bank v. Vinson*, 477 U.S. 57 (1986). See also Gwendolyn Mink, *Hostile Environment: The Political Betrayal of Sexually Harassed Women* (Ithaca, NY: Cornell University Press, 2000), 28–32.
58. *Harris v. Forklift Systems, Inc.*, 510 U.S. 17 (1993).
59. *Burlington Industries v. Ellerth*, 524 U.S. 742 (1998); *Faragher v. City of Boca Raton*, 524 U.S. 775 (1998).
60. Laura Kipness, *Unwanted Advances: Sexual Paranoia Comes to Campus* (New York: Harper, 2017).
61. *Ledbetter v. Goodyear Tire and Rubber Co.*, 550 U.S. 618 (2007).
62. Sarah Kliff, "A Stunning Chart Shows the True Cause of the Gender Wage Gap," Vox, February 19, 2018, www.vox.com/2018/2/19/17018380/gender-wage-gap-childcare-penalty (accessed 10/9/18).
63. New Mexico had a different history because not many Anglos settled there initially. (*Anglo* is the term for a non-Hispanic white, generally of European background.) Mexican Americans had considerable power in territorial legislatures between 1865 and 1912. See Lawrence H. Fuchs, *The American Kaleidoscope* (Hanover, NH: University Press of New England, 1990), 239–40.
64. *Salvatierra v. Del Rio Independent School District*, 33 S.W.2d 790 (Tex. Civ. App. 1930).
65. *Mendez v. Westminster*, 64 F. Supp. 544 (S.D. Cal. 1946), aff'd, 161 F.2d 774 (9th Cir. 1947) (en banc).
66. On the United Farm Workers and César Chávez, see Marshall Ganz, *Why David Sometimes Wins: Leadership, Organization, and Strategy in the California Farm Worker Movement* (New York: Oxford University Press, 2009); Miriam Pawel, *The Union of Their Dreams: Power, Hope and Struggle in Cesar Chavez's Farm Worker Movement* (New York: Bloomsbury Press, 2010); and Jacques E. Levy, *Cesar Chavez: Autobiography of La Causa* (Minneapolis: University of Minnesota Press, 2007).
67. *United States v. Texas*, 579 U.S. __ (2016).
68. Dick Kirschten, "Not Black and White," *National Journal*, March 2, 1991, 497.
69. *Arizona v. United States*, 567 U.S. __ (2012); Robert Barnes, "Supreme Court Rejects Much of Arizona Immigration Law," *Washington Post*, June 25, 2012, www.washingtonpost.com/politics/supreme-court-rules-on-arizona-immigration-law/2012/06/25/gJQA0Nrm1V_story.html?hpid5zl (accessed 6/25/12).
70. *United States v. Wong Kim Ark*, 169 U.S. 649 (1898).
71. *Korematsu v. United States*, 323 U.S. 214 (1944).
72. Children of the Camps, "Historical Documents: Civil Liberties Act of 1988," http://pbs.org/childofcamp/history/civilact.html (accessed 2/17/08).
73. *Lau v. Nichols*, 414 U.S. 563 (1974).
74. Not all Native American tribes agreed with this, including the Navajos. See Ronald Takaki, *A Different Mirror: A History of Multicultural America* (Boston: Little, Brown, 1993), 238–45.
75. On the resurgence of Native American political activity, see Stephen Cornell, *The Return of the Native: American Indian Political Resurgence* (New York: Oxford University Press, 1990); and Dee Brown, *Bury My Heart at Wounded Knee* (New York: Holt, Rinehart, 1971).
76. See the discussion in Robert A. Katzmann, *Institutional Disability: The Saga of Transportation Policy for the Disabled* (Washington, DC: Brookings Institution Press, 1986).
77. For example, after pressure from the Justice Department, one of the nation's largest rental-car companies agreed to make special hand controls available to any customer requesting them. See "Avis Agrees to Equip Cars for Disabled," *Los Angeles Times*, September 2, 1994, D1.
78. For more, see Dale Carpenter, *Flagrant Conduct: The Story of* Lawrence v. Texas (New York: W. W. Norton, 2013).
79. *Bowers v. Hardwick*, 478 U.S. 186 (1986).
80. *Romer v. Evans*, 517 U.S. 620 (1996).

81. *Lawrence v. Texas*, 539 U.S. 558 (2003).
82. *Obergefell v. Hodges*, 576 U.S. __ (2015).
83. Pew Research Center, "Changing Attitudes on Gay Marriage," June 26, 2017, www.pewforum.org/fact-sheet/changing-attitudes-on-gay-marriage/ (accessed 10/9/18).
84. The Department of Health, Education, and Welfare (HEW) was the cabinet department charged with administering most federal social programs. In 1980, when education programs were transferred to the newly created Department of Education, HEW was renamed the Department of Health and Human Services.
85. *Regents of the University of California v. Bakke*, 438 U.S. 265 (1978).
86. See, for example, *United Steelworkers v. Weber*, 443 U.S. 193 (1979); and *Fullilove v. Klutznick*, 448 U.S. 448 (1980).
87. *Adarand Constructors Inc. v. Peña*.
88. *Gratz v. Bollinger*, 539 U.S. 244 (2003).
89. *Grutter v. Bollinger*, 539 U.S. 306 (2003).
90. *Fisher v. University of Texas*.
91. There are still many genuine racists in America, but with the exception of a lunatic fringe, made up of neo-Nazis and members of the Ku Klux Klan, most racists are too ashamed or embarrassed to take part in normal political discourse. They are not included in either category here.
92. *Slaughterhouse Cases*, 83 U.S. 36 (1873).

CHAPTER 6

1. Suzanna Hupp, "In Their Own Words: The Gun Rights Advocate," *Texas Monthly,* March 23, 2016, www.texasmonthly.com/list/in-their-own-words/the-gun-rights-advocate/ (accessed 3/3/18).
2. Brianna Sacks, "After Florida School Shooting, Several Survivors and Victims' Parents Pan Trump's Idea to Arm Teachers," BuzzFeed News, February 24, 2018, www.buzzfeed.com/briannasacks/students-and-parents-react-to-armed-teacher-proposal?utm_term=.rtNPqM580#.xrVbnry1A (accessed 3/3/8).
3. Jeffrey M. Jones, "U.S. Preference for Stricter Gun Laws Highest since 1993," Gallup Social & Policy Issues, March 14, 2018, http://news.gallup.com/poll/229562/preference-stricter-gun-laws-highest-1993.aspx (accessed 5/30/18).
4. Alvin Chang, "Gun Sales Usually Skyrocket after Mass Shootings. But Not This Time," Vox, March 7, 2018, www.vox.com/2018/3/7/17066352/gun-sales-mass-shooting-data (accessed 5/30/18).
5. Samantha Smith, "Young People Less Likely to View Iraqi, Syrian Refugees as Major Threat to U.S.," Pew Research Center, February 3, 2017, www.pewresearch.org/fact-tank/2017/02/03/young-people-less-likely-to-view-iraqi-syrian-refugees-as-major-threat-to-u-s/ (accessed 4/3/18).
6. Milton Lodge and Charles Taber, "Three Steps toward a Theory of Motivated Political Reasoning," in *Elements of Reason: Cognition, Choice, and the Bounds of Rationality*, ed. Arthur Lupia, Mathew D. McCubbins, and Samuel L. Popkin (London: Cambridge University Press, 2000); David Redlawsk, "Hot Cognition or Cool Consideration? Testing the Effects of Motivated Reasoning on Political Decision Making," *Journal of Politics* 64 (2002): 1021–44; David Redlawsk, Andrew Civettini, and Karen Emmerson, "The Affective Tipping Point: Do Motivated Reasoners Ever 'Get It'?" *Political Psychology* 31, no. 4 (2010): 563–93.
7. Caroline J. Tolbert, David P. Redlawsk,, and Kellen J. Gracey, "Racial Attitudes and Emotional Responses to the 2016 Republican Candidates," *Journal of Elections, Public Opinion and Parties* 28, no. 2 (2018): 245–62.
8. George E. Marcus, W. Russell Neuman, and Michael MacKuen, *Affective Intelligence and Political Judgment* (Chicago: University of Chicago Press, 2000).
9. Juliana Menasce Horowitz, "In 2017, Americans Narrowly Opposed Allowing Teachers and School Officials to Carry Guns," Pew Research Center, Fact Tank, February 23, 2018, www.pewresearch.org/fact-tank/2018/02/23/in-2017-americans-narrowly-opposed-allowing-teachers-and-school-officials-to-carry-guns/ (accessed 3/17/18).
10. Pew Research Center, "Beyond Red vs. Blue: The Political Typology. Section 6: Foreign Affairs, Terrorism and Privacy," June 26, 2014, www.people-press.org/2014/06/26/section-6-foreign-affairs-terrorism-and-privacy/ (accessed 3/11/16).
11. Richard Wike and Katie Simmons, "Global Support for Principle of Free Expression, but Opposition to Some Forms of Speech: Americans Especially Likely to Embrace Individual Liberties," Pew Research Center, November 18, 2015, www.pewglobal.org/2015/11/18/global-support-for-principle-of-free-expression-but-opposition-to-some-forms-of-speech/ (accessed 11/18/15).
12. Anthony Cilluffo, "5 Facts about Student Loans," Pew Research Center, Fact Tank, August 24, 2017, www.pewresearch.org/fact-tank/2017/08/24/5-facts-about-student-loans/ (accessed 3/17/18).
13. Paul R. Abramson, *Political Attitudes in America* (San Francisco: Freeman, 1983).
14. Pew Research Center, "Large Majorities See Checks and Balances, Right to Protest as Essential for Democracy," March 2, 2017, www.people-press.org/2017/03/02/large-majorities-see-checks-and-balances-right-to-protest-as-essential-for-democracy/ (accessed 3/2/18).
15. Jocelyn Kiley, "U.S. Public Sees Russian Role in Campaign Hacking, But Is Divided Over New Sanctions." Pew Research Center, January 10, 2017, www.pewresearch.org/fact-tank/2017/01/10/u-s-public-says-russia-hacked-campaign/ (accessed 3/17/18).
16. Rob Suls, "Share of Democrats Calling Russia 'Greatest Danger' to U.S. Is at Its Highest since End of Cold War."

Pew Research Center, April 20, 2017, www.pewresearch.org/fact-tank/2017/04/20/share-of-democrats-calling-russia-greatest-danger-to-u-s-at-its-highest-since-end-of-cold-war/ (accessed 4/3/18).

17. See Paul M. Sniderman and Edward G. Carmines, *Reaching beyond Race* (Cambridge, MA: Harvard University Press, 1997).
18. Lydia Saad, "Conservative Lead in U.S. Ideology Is Down to Single Digits," Gallup, January 11, 2018, http://news.gallup.com/poll/225074/conservative-lead-ideology-down-single-digits.aspx (accessed 3/17/18).
19. Douglas R. Oxley et al., "Political Attitudes Vary with Physiological Traits," *Science* 321, no. 5896 (September 19, 2008): 1667–70. See also Jeffrey Mondak, *Personality and the Foundation of Political Behavior* (Cambridge: Cambridge University Press, 2010).
20. John Alford, Carolyn Funk, and John Hibbing, "Are Political Orientations Genetically Transmitted?" *American Political Science Review* 99, no. 2 (2005): 153–67; Rich Morin, "Study on Twins Suggests Our Political Beliefs May Be Hard-Wired," Pew Research Center, Fact Tank, December 9, 2013, www.pewresearch.org/fact-tank/2013/12/09/study-on-twins-suggests-our-political-beliefs-may-be-hard-wired/ (accessed 1/20/14).
21. See Angus Campbell et al., *The American Voter* (New York: Wiley, 1960), 147.
22. Betsy Sinclair, *The Social Citizen: Peer Networks and Political Behavior* (Chicago: University of Chicago Press, 2012).
23. Pew Research Center, "Support for Same-Sex Marriage Grows, Even among Groups That Had Been Skeptical," June 26, 2017, www.people-press.org/2017/06/26/support-for-same-sex-marriage-grows-even-among-groups-that-had-been-skeptical/ (accessed 5/21/18).
24. Jennifer A. Heerwig and Brian J. McCabe, "Education and Social Desirability Bias: The Case of a Black Presidential Candidate," *Social Science Quarterly* 90, no. 3 (2009): 674–86.
25. Raymond E. Wolfinger and Steven J. Rosenstone, *Who Votes?* (New Haven, CT: Yale University Press, 1980). See also Steven J. Rosenstone and John Mark Hansen, *Mobilization, Participation, and Democracy in America* (New York: Macmillan, 1993).
26. Frey, William. "The U.S. Will Become Minority White in 2045, Census Predicts: Youthful Minorities Are Engines Future Growth." Brookings Institution, March 14, 2018, www.brookings.edu/blog/the-avenue/2018/03/14/the-us-will-become-minority-white-in-2045-census projects/?utm_campaign=Brookings%20Brief&utm_source=hs_email&utm_medium=email&utm_content=61375295 (accessed 3/17/18).
27. Katherine Tate, *Black Faces in the Mirror* (Princeton, NJ: Princeton University Press, 1993).
28. Pew Research Center. "On Views of Race and Inequality, Blacks and Whites Are Worlds Apart: About Four-in-Ten Blacks Are Doubtful That the U.S. Will Ever Achieve Racial Equality," June 27, 2016, www.pewsocialtrends.org/2016/06/27/on-views-of-race-and-inequality-blacks-and-whites-are-worlds-apart/ (accessed 4/3/18).
29. Tate, *Black Faces*.
30. Brakkton Booker, "How Equal Is American Opportunity? Survey Shows Attitudes Vary by Race," National Public Radio, September 21, 2015, www.npr.org/sections/thetwo-way/2015/09/21/442068004/how-equal-is-american-opportunity-survey-shows-attitudes-vary-by-race (accessed 3/11/16).
31. Pew Research Center, "Across Racial Lines, More Say Nation Needs to Make Changes to Achieve Racial Equality," August 5, 2015, www.people-press.org/2015/08/05/across-racial-lines-more-say-nation-needs-to-make-changes-to-achieve-racial-equality/8-4-2015_02a/ (accessed 2/24/16).
32. Jens Manuel Krogstad, "Key Facts about the Latino Vote in 2016," October 14, 2016; and Flores, Antonio, "Facts on U.S. Latinos, 2015. Statistical Portrait of Hispanics in the United States," September 18, 2017, Pew Research Center, www.pewresearch.org/fact-tank/2016/10/14/key-facts-about-the-latino-vote-in-2016/ and www.pewhispanic.org/2016/04/19/statistical-portrait-of-hispanics-in-the-united-states-key-charts/ (accessed 3/17/18).
33. Anna Brown and Renee Stepler, "Statistical Portrait of the Foreign-Born Population in the United States, 1960–2013," Pew Research Center, September 28, 2015, www.pewhispanic.org/2015/09/28/statistical-portrait-of-the-foreign-born-population-in-the-united-states-1960-2013-key-charts/#2013-fb-origin (accessed 12/22/15).
34. Author analysis of 2014 Cooperative Election Study, Harvard University, released February 2015, http://projects.iq.harvard.edu/cces/home (accessed 3/4/16); Pew Research Center, "Broad Public Support for Legal Status for Undocumented Immigrants, Other Attitudes About Immigration More Mixed, June 4, 2015," www.people-press.org/2015/06/04/broad-public-support-for-legal-status-for-undocumented-immigrants/ (accessed 3/17/18).
35. Pew Research Center, "Latinos and the New Trump Administration," February 23, 2017, www.pewhispanic.org/2017/02/23/latinos-and-the-new-trump-administration/ (accessed 4/3/17).
36. Matt Barreto and Gary M. Segura, *Latino America: How America's Most Dynamic Population Is Poised to Transform the Politics of the Nation* (New York: Public Affairs, 2014).
37. "Trump Gets Negative Ratings for Many Personal Traits, but Most Say He Stands Up for His Beliefs," Pew Research Center, October 1, 2018, www.people-press.org/2018/10/01/trump-gets-negative-ratings-for-many-personal-traits-but-most-say-he-stands-up-for-his-beliefs/ (accessed 10/10/18).

38. Michael Lipka, "Religious 'Nones' Are Not Only Growing, They're Becoming More Secular," Pew Research Center, Fact Tank, November 11, 2015, www.pewresearch.org/fact-tank/2015/11/11/religious-nones-are-not-only-growing-theyre-becoming-more-secular/ (accessed 11/11/15).
39. 2014 Cooperative Comparative Election Study.
40. See Richard Lau and David Redlawsk, *How Voters Decide: Information Processing during an Election Campaign* (New York: Cambridge University Press, 2006).
41. Brian Schaffner and Stephen Ansolabehere, "CCES Common Content, 2014," Harvard Dataverse, V2, http://dx.doi.org/10.7910/DVN/XFXJVY (accessed 5/4/16).
42. Morris Fiorina, Samuel Abrams, and Jeremy Pope, *Culture War? The Myth of a Polarized America* (New York: Longman, 2004).
43. Nathan J. Kelly and Peter K. Enns, "Inequality and the Dynamics of Public Opinion: The Self-Reinforcing Link between Economic Inequality and Mass Preferences," *American Journal of Political Science* 54, no. 4 (2010): 855–70; Jacob S. Hacker and Paul Pierson, *Winner-Take-All Politics: How Washington Made the Rich Richer—and Turned Its Back on the Middle Class* (New York: Simon and Schuster, 2010).
44. Larry M. Bartels, "Homer Gets a Tax Cut: Inequality and Public Policy in the American Mind," *Perspectives on Politics* 3, no. 1 (2005): 15–31; Larry Bartels, *Unequal Democracy: The Political Economy of the New Gilded Age* (Princeton, NJ: Princeton University Press, 2008).
45. Thomas E. Mann and Norman J. Ornstein, *It's Even Worse Than It Looks: How the American Constitutional System Collided with the New Politics of Extremism* (New York: Basic Books, 2012).
46. Shaun Bowler, Gary Segura, and Stephen Nicholson, "Earthquakes and Aftershocks: Race, Direct Democracy, and Partisan Change," *American Journal of Political Science* 50 (2006): 146–59. For a more general discussion of the spillover effects of ballot measures on public opinion, see Stephen Nicholson, *Voting the Agenda: Candidates, Elections, and Ballot Propositions* (Princeton, NJ: Princeton University Press, 2005).
47. John R. Zaller, *The Nature and Origins of Mass Opinion* (New York: Cambridge University Press, 1992).
48. Milton Lodge, Kathleen McGraw, and Patrick Stroh, "An Impression-Driven Model of Candidate Evaluation," *American Political Science Review* 83, no. 2 (1989): 399–419.
49. Benjamin I. Page and Robert Y. Shapiro, *The Rational Public: Fifty Years of Trends in Americans' Policy Preferences* (Chicago: University of Chicago Press, 1995); Eugene Wittkopf, *Faces of Internationalism: Public Opinion and Foreign Policy* (Durham, NC: Duke University Press, 1990).
50. Pew Research Center, "In Gay Marriage Debate, Both Supporters and Opponents See Legal Recognition as 'Inevitable,'" June 6, 2013, www.people-press.org/2013/06/06/in-gay-marriage-debate-both-supporters-and-opponents-see-legal-recognition-as-inevitable (accessed 3/19/14).
51. *Varnum v. Brien*, 763 N.W.2d 862 (Iowa 2009).
52. Rebecca J. Kreitzer, Allison J. Hamilton, and Caroline J. Tolbert, "Does Policy Adoption Change Opinions on Minority Rights? The Effects of Legalizing Same-Sex Marriage," *Political Research Quarterly* 67, no. 4 (July 10, 2014): 795–808.
53. *Obergefell v. Hodges*, 576 U.S. __ (2015).
54. Monica Anderson, "For Earth Day, Here's How Americans View Environmental Issues," Pew Research Center, April 20, 2017, www.pewresearch.org/fact-tank/2017/04/20/for-earth-day-heres-how-americans-view-environmental-issues/ (accessed 3/17/18); Brian Kennedy, "Two-Thirds of Americans Give Priority to Developing Alternative Energy over Fossil Fuels," Pew Research Center, January 23, 2017, www.pewresearch.org/fact-tank/2017/01/23/two-thirds-of-americans-give-priority-to-developing-alternative-energy-over-fossil-fuels/ (accessed 3/17/18); Michael Shea, "Trump Will Withdraw U.S. from Paris Climate Agreement," *New York Times*, June 1, 2017, www.nytimes.com/2017/06/01/climate/trump-paris-climate-agreement.html (accessed 3/17/18).
55. Zaller, *Nature and Origins*.
56. Carroll Glynn et al., *Public Opinion*, 2nd ed. (Boulder, CO: Westview, 2004), 293. See also Michael X. Delli Carpini and Scott Keeter, *What Americans Know about Politics and Why It Matters* (New Haven, CT: Yale University Press, 1996).
57. Delli Carpini and Keeter, *What Americans Know*.
58. Adam J. Berinsky, "Assuming the Costs of War: Events, Elites and American Support for Military Conflict," *Journal of Politics* 69, no. 4 (2007): 975–97; Zaller, *Nature and Origins*.
59. Richard R. Lau and David P. Redlawsk, "Advantages and Disadvantages of Cognitive Heuristics in Political Decision Making," *American Journal of Political Science* 45 (October 2001): 951–71; Lau and Redlawsk, *How Voters Decide*.
60. For a discussion of the role of information in politics, see Arthur Lupia and Matthew D. McCubbins, *The Democratic Dilemma: Can Citizens Learn What They Need to Know?* (New York: Cambridge University Press, 1998). See also Shaun Bowler and Todd Donovan, *Demanding Choices: Opinion and Voting in Direct Democracy* (Ann Arbor: University of Michigan Press, 1998). See also Samuel Popkin, *The Reasoning Voter: Communication and Persuasion in Presidential Campaigns* (Chicago: University of Chicago Press, 1991); Arthur Lupia, "Shortcuts versus Encyclopedias: Information and Voting Behavior in California Insurance Reform Elections," *American Political Science Review* 88 (1994): 63–76; and Wendy Rahn, "The Role of Partisan Stereotypes in Information Processing about Political Candidates," *American Journal of Political Science* 37 (1993): 472–96.

61. James Druckman, Erik Petersen, and Rune Slothuus, "How Elite Partisan Polarization Affects Public Opinion Formation," *American Political Science Review* 107, no. 1 (February 2013): 57–79.
62. Lee Rainie et al., "Social Media and Political Engagement," Pew Research Center, October 19, 2012, www.pewinternet.org/2012/10/19/social-media-and-political-engagement (accessed 8/14/14).
63. Tony Dokoupil, "Is the Internet Making Us Crazy? What the New Research Says," *Newsweek*, July 9, 2012, http://mag.newsweek.com/2012/07/08/is-the-internet-making-us-crazy-what-the-new-research-says.html (accessed 3/19/14); Nicholas Carr, *The Shallows: What the Internet Is Doing to Our Brains* (New York: W. W. Norton, 2011).
64. Benjamin Ginsberg, *The American Lie: Government by the People and Other Political Fables* (Boulder, CO: Paradigm, 2007).
65. Gerald F. Seib and Michael K. Frisby, "Selling Sacrifice," *Wall Street Journal*, February 5, 1993, 1.
66. Peter Marks, "Adept in Politics and Advertising, 4 Women Shape a Campaign," *New York Times*, November 11, 2001, B6.
67. Donald J. Trump (@realDonaldTrump), "I am being investigated for firing the FBI director by the man who told me to fire the FBI director! Witch Hunt" Twitter, June 16, 2017, 6:07 a.m., https://twitter.com/realdonaldtrump/status/875701471999864833?lang=en (accessed 4/3/18).
68. Donald J. Trump (@realDonaldTrump), "You are witnessing the single greatest WITCH HUNT in American political history - led by some very bad and conflicted people! #MAGA" Twitter, June 15, 2017, 4:57 a.m., https://twitter.com/realdonaldtrump/status/875321478849363968?lang=en (accessed 4/3/18).
69. Jason Gainous and Kevin Wagner, *Tweeting to Power: The Social Media Revolution in American Politics* (New York: Oxford University Press, 2013).
70. *Roe v. Wade*, 410 U.S. 113 (1973).
71. See Gillian Peele, *Revival and Reaction* (Oxford: Clarendon, 1985). See also Connie Paige, *The Right-to-Lifers* (New York: Summit, 1983).
72. See Shanto Iyengar, *Is Anyone Responsible? How Television Frames Political Issues* (Chicago: University of Chicago Press, 1991); and Shanto Iyengar, *Do the Media Govern?* (Thousand Oaks, CA: Sage, 1997).
73. David W. Moore, "Support for Invasion of Iraq Remains Contingent on U.N. Approval," Gallup, November 12, 2002, www.gallup.com/poll/7195/support-invasion-iraq-remains-contigent-un-approval.aspx (accessed 3/2/18); Pew Research Center, "Public Attitudes toward the War in Iraq: 2003–2008," March 19, 2008, www.pewresearch.org/2008/03/19/public-attitudes-toward-the-war-in-iraq-20032008 (accessed 2/19/14).
74. Campbell et al., *The American Voter*.
75. Benjamin I. Page and Robert Y. Shapiro, "The Rational Public: Fifty Years of Trends in Americans' Policy Preferences," (Chicago: University of Chicago Press, 1992).
76. Gerald C. Wright, Rober S. Erikson, and John P. McIver, "Public Opinion and Policy Liberalism in the American States," *American Journal of Political Science* 31, no. 4 (November 1987): 980–1001.
77. Pew Research Center, "Mixed Views of Economic Policies and Health Care Reform Persist: Support for Health Care Principles, Opposition to Package," October 8, 2009, www.people-press.org/2009/10/08/mixed-views-of-economic-policies-and-health-care-reform-persist/ (accessed 2/15/14).
78. Christopher Wlezien, "The Public as Thermostat: Dynamics of Preferences for Spending," *American Journal of Political Science* 39, no. 4 (1995): 981–1000.
79. See Julianna Pacheco, "Attitudinal Policy Feedback and Public Opinion: The Impact of Smoking Bans on Attitudes toward Smokers, Secondhand Smoke, and Anti-Smoking Policies," *Political Research Quarterly* 77, no. 3 (2013): 714–34; Barbara Norrander, "The Multi-Layered Impact of Public Opinion on Capital Punishment Implementation in the American States," *Political Research Quarterly* 53, no. 4 (2000): 771–93; Suzanne Mettler and Joe Soss, "The Consequences of Public Policy for Democratic Citizenship: Bridging Policy Studies and Mass Politics," *Perspectives on Politics* 2, no. 1 (2004): 55–73; Andrea Hetling and Monika L. McDermott, "Judging a Book by Its Cover: Did Perceptions of the 1996 U.S. Welfare Reforms Affect Public Support for Spending on the Poor?" *Journal of Social Policy* 37, no. 3 (2008): 471–87; Joe Soss, "Lessons of Welfare: Policy Design, Political Learning, and Political Action," *American Political Science Review* 93, no. 2 (1999): 363–80; Joe Soss and Sanford F. Schram, "A Public Transformed? Welfare Reform as Policy Feedback," *American Political Science Review* 101, no. 1 (2007): 111.
80. Malcolm E. Jewell, *Representation in State Legislatures* (Lexington: University Press of Kentucky, 1982).
81. Lawrence R. Jacobs and Robert Y. Shapiro, *Politicians Don't Pander: Political Manipulation and the Loss of Democratic Responsiveness* (Chicago: University of Chicago Press, 2000).
82. John Griffin and Brian Newman, "Are Voters Better Represented?" *Journal of Politics* 67 (2005): 1206–27.
83. Bartels, *Unequal Democracy*.
84. Other authors have endorsed Bartels's view that government policy exacerbates income inequality. See, for example, Hacker and Pierson, *Winner-Take-All Politics*.
85. Martin Gilens, "Inequality and Democratic Responsiveness," *Public Opinion Quarterly* 69, no. 5 (2005): 778–96; and Martin Gilens, "Preference Gaps and Inequality in Representation," *PS: Political Science and Politics* 42, no. 2 (2009): 335–41.
86. Robert Dahl, *A Preface to Democratic Theory* (Chicago: University of Chicago Press, 1956).
87. Herbert Asher, *Polling and the Public* (Washington, DC: CQ Press, 2001), 64.

88. Drew DeSilver and Scott Keeter, "The Challenges of Polling When Fewer People Are Available to be Polled," July 21, 2015, www.pewresearch.org/fact-tank/2015/07/21/the-challenges-of-polling-when-fewer-people-are-available-to-be-polled/ (accessed 3/1/16).
89. Michael Kagay and Janet Elder, "Numbers Are No Problem for Pollsters, Words Are," *New York Times*, August 9, 1992, E6.
90. Adam J. Berinsky, "The Two Faces of Public Opinion," *American Journal of Political Science* 43, no. 4 (1999): 1209–30.
91. Lynn Vavreck and Douglas Rivers, "The 2006 Cooperative Congressional Election Study," *Journal of Elections, Public Opinion and Parties* 18, no. 4 (2008): 355–66. See also Simon Jackman and Lynn Vavreck, "Primary Politics: Race, Gender, and Age in the 2008 Democratic Primary," *Journal of Elections, Public Opinion and Parties* 20, no. 2 (2010): 153–86.
92. Nate Silver, "FiveThirtyEight's Pollster Ratings," August 5, 2016, *FiveThirtyEight* (blog), http://projects.fivethirtyeight.com/pollster-ratings/ (accessed 10/16/16).
93. Berinsky, "Two Faces of Public Opinion." See also Adam Berinsky, "Political Context and the Survey Response: The Dynamics of Racial Policy Opinion," *Journal of Politics* 64, no. 2 (2002): 567–84.
94. Pew Research Center. "Are Telephone Polls Understating Support for Trump?" March 31, 2017, www.pewresearch.org/2017/03/31/are-telephone-polls-understating-support-for-trump/ (accessed 3/17/18)
95. Nate Silver, "Which Polls Fared Best (and Worst) in the 2012 Presidential Race," *FiveThirtyEight* (blog), November 10, 2012, http://fivethirtyeight.blogs.nytimes.com/2012/11/10/which-polls-fared-best-and-worst-in-the-2012-presidential-race/ (accessed 2/24/16).
96. Redlawsk, Tolbert, and Donovan, *Why Iowa?*
97. Sasha Issenberg, *The Victory Lab: The Secret Science of Winning Campaigns* (New York: Broadway Books, 2012); Sasha Issenberg, "A More Perfect Union: How President Obama's Campaign Used Big Data to Rally Individual Voters," *MIT Technology Review*, December 19, 2012, www.technologyreview.com/featuredstory/509026/how-obamas-team-used-big-data-to-rally-voters/ (accessed 11/25/15).
98. Nanette Byrnes, "Twitter May Have Predicted the Election," *Technology Review*, December 2, 2016, www.technologyreview.com/s/603010/twitter-may-have-predicted-the-election/ (accessed 8/2/18).
99. Katerina Eva Matsa, Amy Mitchell, and Galen Stocking, "Searching for News: The Flint Water Crisis," April 27, 2017, www.journalism.org/essay/searching-for-news/ (accessed 3/17/18).
100. Chris Taylor, "Triumph of the Nerds: Nate Silver Wins in 50 States," November 7, 2012, http://mashable.com/2012/11/07/nate-silver-wins/#6aWvyWVGcaqq (accessed 2/24/16).
101. "How Popular/Unpopular Is Donald Trump? An Updating Calculation of the President's Approval Rating, Accounting for Each Poll's Quality, Recency, Sample Size and Partisan Lean" *FiveThirtyEight* (blog), June 23, 2017, www.fivethirtyeight.com/features/how-were-tracking-donald-trumps-approval-ratings/ (accessed 3/17/18).
102. Christopher Wlezien and Stuart Soroka, "The Relationship between Public Opinion and Policy," in *Oxford Handbook of Political Behavior*, ed. Russell Dalton and Hans-Dieter Klingemann (New York: Oxford University Press, 2009), 799–817.
103. Gilens, "Inequality and Democratic Responsiveness"; Bartels, *Unequal Democracy*.
104. Ryan Claassen and Benjamin Highton, "Does Policy Debate Reduce Information Effects in Public Opinion? Analyzing the Evolution of Public Opinion on Health Care," *Journal of Politics* 68, no. 2 (2006): 410–20.

CHAPTER 7

1. Patrick Anderson, "Net Neutrality Protest Reaches Sioux Falls, Lincoln Student Takes on the FCC," *Argus Leader*, December 7, 2017, www.argusleader.com/story/news/business-journal/2017/12/07/net-neutrality-protest-sioux-falls-fcc/930819001/ (accessed 3/26/18).
2. Meg McIntyre, "Local High School Students Protest Proposed Rollback of Net Neutrality Rules," *Keene Sentinel*, December 8, 2017, www.sentinelsource.com/news/local/local-high-school-students-protest-proposed-rollback-of-net-neutrality/article_204cec19-3104-58f4-930a-404c65d84e65.html (accessed 3/26/18).
3. Cecilia Kang, "In Protests of Net Neutrality Repeal, Teenage Voices Stood Out," *New York Times*, December 20, 2017, www.nytimes.com/2017/12/20/technology/net-neutrality-repeal-teens.html (accessed 3/26/18).
4. Julian P. Boyd et al., eds., *The Papers of Thomas Jefferson* (Princeton, NJ: Princeton University Press), http://press-pubs.uchicago.edu/founders/documents/amendI_speechs8.html (accessed 5/30/14).
5. Shanto Iyengar, *Media Politics* (New York: W.W. Norton & Company, 2015).
6. Quoted in Rodney Tiffen, "Journalism in the Trump Era," Inside Story, February 24, 2017, http://insidestory.org.au/journalism-in-the-trump-era (accessed 4/4/18).
7. David Folkenflik, "AT&T Deal for Time Warner Casts Renewed Attention on CNN," *NPR*, October 25, 2016, www.npr.org/2016/10/25/499299869/at-t-deal-for-time-warner-casts-renewed-attention-on-cnn (accessed 5/21/18).
8. Columbia Journalism Review, "Resources," https://archives.cjr.org/resources/index.php (accessed 8/2/18).
9. For a criticism of the increasing consolidation of the media, see the essays in Patricia Aufderheide et al., *Conglomerates and the Media* (New York: New Press, 1997).
10. Pew Research Center, "2017 Pew Research Center's American Trends Panel," March 27, 2017,

http://assets.pewresearch.org/wp-content/uploads/sites/13/2017/05/09125944/PJ_2017.05.10_Media-Attitudes_TOPLINE.pdf (accessed 1/22/18).

11. Pew Research Center, "Amid Criticism, Support for Media's 'Watchdog' Role Stands Out," August 8, 2013, www.people-press.org/2013/08/08/amid-criticism-support-for-medias-watchdog-role-stands-out (accessed 4/27/14).
12. Pew Research Center, "Digital News Fact Sheet" August 7, 2017, www.journalism.org/fact-sheet/digital-news/ (accessed 1/22/18).
13. Clay Shirky, *Here Comes Everybody: The Power of Organizing without Organizations* (New York: Penguin Books, 2008).
14. Amy Mitchell, Jesse Holcomb, and Rachel Weisel, "State of the News Media 2016," Pew Research Center, June 15, 2016, www.journalism.org/2016/06/15/state-of-the-news-media-2016/?utm_content=buffer6871f&utm_medium=social&utm_source=twitter.com&utm_campaign=buffer (accessed 3/19/18).
15. Shirky, *Here Comes Everybody*; Mitchell, Holcomb, and Weisel, "State of the News Media 2016."
16. Robert McChesney and John Nichols, *The Death and Life of American Journalism: The Media Revolution That Will Begin the World Again* (New York: Nation Books, 2010).
17. "Newspapers Fact Sheet," Pew Research Center, June 13, 2018, www.journalism.org/fact-sheet/newspapers/ (accessed 10/10/18).
18. Darrell West, *The Next Wave: Using Digital Technology to Further Social and Political Innovation* (Washington, DC: Brookings Institution Press, 2011).
19. Laura Wamsley, "Big Newspapers Are Booming: 'Washington Post' to Add 60 Newsroom Jobs," NPR, December 27, 2016, www.npr.org/sections/thetwo-way/2016/12/27/507140760/big-newspapers-are-booming-washington-post-to-add-sixty-newsroom-jobs (accessed 1/22/18).
20. Michael Barthel, "Circulation and Revenue Fall for Industry Overall," Pew Research Center, June 1, 2017, www.pewresearch.org/fact-tank/2017/06/01/circulation-and-revenue-fall-for-newspaper-industry/(accessed 1/22/18).
21. Eugene Kim, "Jeff Bezos Reinvented the *Washington Post*," *Business Insider*, May, 15 2016, www.businessinsider.com/how-the-washington-post-changed-after-jeff-bezos-acquisition-2016-5/#because-of-its-affiliation-with-bezos-the-post-says-its-now-finding-it-a-lot-easier-to-recruit-engineers-bezos-has-also-instilled-a-much-stronger-culture-of-customer-obsession-post-execs-often-receive-reader-complaint-emails-forwarded-by-bezos-12 (accessed 1/22/18).
22. Mitchell, Holcomb, and Weisel, "State of the News Media 2016."
23. Robert O'Harrow, Jr., "Trump's Bad Bet: How Too Much Debt Drove His Biggest Casino Aground," *Washington Post*, January 18, 2016, www.washingtonpost.com/investigations/trumps-bad-bet-how-too-much-debt-drove-his-biggest-casino-aground/2016/01/18/f67cedc2-9ac8-11e5-8917-653b65c809eb_story.html (accessed 3/9/16); Robert O'Harrow, Jr., "Trump Swam in Mob-Infested Waters in Early Years as an NYC Developer," *Washington Post*, October 16, 2015, www.washingtonpost.com/investigations/trump-swam-in-mob-infested-waters-in-early-years-as-an-nyc-developer/2015/10/16/3c75b918-60a3-11e5-b38e-06883aacba64_story.html (accessed 3/9/16).
24. Tim Hains, "Donald Trump Jr.'s Emails Are Not A 'Smoking Gun' of Anything," RealClear Politics, July 14, 2017, www.realclearpolitics.com/video/2017/07/14/greenwald_donald_trump_jrs_emails_are_not_a_smoking_gun_for_anything_not_evidence_of_any_crime.html (accessed 1/22/18).
25. Mitchell, Holcomb, and Weisel, "State of the News Media 2016."
26. Pew Research Center, "Audio and Podcasting Fact Sheet," July 12, 2018, www.journalism.org/fact-sheet/audio-and-podcasting/ (accessed 9/22/18).
27. Mitchell, Holcomb, and Weisel, "State of the News Media 2016."
28. Pew Research Center, "The Internet's Broader Role in Campaign 2008," January 11, 2008, www.people-press.org/2008/01/11/internets-broader-role-in-campaign-2008/; and "Journalism, Satire or Just Laughs? '*The Daily Show* with Jon Stewart' Examined," May 8, 2008, www.journalism.org/2008/05/08/journalism-satire-or-just-laughs-the-daily-show-with-jon-stewart-examined/ (accessed 9/7/12).
29. West, *The Next Wave*; Edward Glaeser, *Triumph of the City: How Our Greatest Invention Makes Us Richer, Smarter, Greener, Healthier, and Happier* (New York: Penguin Press, 2011).
30. Kristin Lu, "Growth in Mobile News Use Driven by Older Adults." Pew Research Center, June 12, 2017, www.pewresearch.org/fact-tank/2017/06/12/growth-in-mobile-news-use-driven-by-older-adults/ (accessed 3/20/18).
31. Jeffrey Gottfriend and Elisa Shearer, "Americans' Online News Use Is Closing in on TV News Use," Pew Research Center, September 7, 2017, www.pewresearch.org/fact-tank/2017/09/07/americans-online-news-use-vs-tv-news-use/ (accessed 3/20/18); Kristin Bialik and Katerina Eva Matsa, "Key Trends in Social and Digital Media Use," Pew Research Center, October 4, 2017, www.pewresearch.org/fact-tank/2017/10/04/key-trends-in-social-and-digital-news-media/ (accessed 3/20/18).
32. Aaron Smith and Maeve Duggan, "Online Political Videos and Campaign 2012," Pew Research Center, November 2, 2012, www.pewinternet.org/2012/11/02/online-political-videos-and-campaign-2012 (accessed 4/29/14).
33. Pew Research Center, "State of the News Media: Digital News Fact Sheet," August 7, 2017, www.journalism.org/fact-sheet/digital-news/ (accessed 5/21/18).
34. Aaron Smith and Monica Anderson, "Social Media Use in 2018," Pew Research Center, March 1, 2018, www.pewinternet.org/2018/03/01/social-media-use-in-2018/ (accessed 3/19/18).

35. Antony Wilhelm, *Digital Nation: Toward an Inclusive Information Society* (Cambridge, MA: MIT Press, 2006); Paul DiMaggio et al., "Social Implications of the Internet," *Annual Review of Sociology* 27, no. 1 (2001): 307–36.
36. Karen Mossberger, Caroline J. Tolbert, and Mary Stansbury, *Virtual Inequality: Beyond the Digital Divide* (Washington, DC: Georgetown University Press, 2003); Pippa Norris, *Digital Divide: Civic Engagement, Information Poverty, and the Internet Worldwide* (New York: Cambridge University Press, 2001).
37. Karen Mossberger, Caroline Tolbert and Ramona McNeal, "Digital Citizenship," MIT Press, Internet Broadband Fact Sheet, 2008; Pew Research Center, February 5, 2018, www.pewinternet.org/fact-sheet/internet-broadband/ (accessed 3/19/18).
38. U.S. Census Bureau, "Nearly 8 in 10 Americans Have Access to High-Speed Internet," American Community Survey, November 13, 2014, www.census.gov/newsroom/press-releases/2014/cb14-202.html (accessed 3/2/16).
39. Mossberger, Tolbert, and Stansbury, *Virtual Inequality*.
40. Karen Mossberger, Caroline J. Tolbert, and William W. Franko, *Digital Cities: The Internet and the Geography of Opportunity* (New York: Oxford University Press, 2013).
41. Elisa Shearer and Jeffrey Gottfried, "News Use across Social Media Platforms 2017," Pew Research Center, September 7, 2017, www.journalism.org/2017/09/07/news-use-across-social-media-platforms-2017/ (accessed 8/1/18).
42. Thom File, "Voting in America: A Look at the 2016 Presidential Election," *Census Blogs*, May 20, 2017, www.census.gov/newsroom/blogs/random-samplings/2017/05/voting_in_america.html (accessed 3/19/18).
43. Amy Mitchell, Jeffrey Gottfried, and Katerina Eva Matsa, "Political Interest and Awareness Lower among Millennials," Pew Research Center, June 1, 2015, www.journalism.org/2015/06/01/political-interest-and-awareness-lower-among-millennials/ (accessed 12/7/15).
44. Smith and Anderson, "Social Media Use 2018."
45. Elisa Shearer and Jeffrey Gottfried, "News Use across Social Media Platforms 2017," Pew Research Center, September 7, 2017, www.journalism.org/2017/09/07/NEWS-USE-ACROSS-SOCIAL-MEDIA-PLATFORMS-2017/ (accessed 5/21/18).
46. Michael Barthel et al., "The Evolving Role of News on Twitter and Facebook."
47. Jason Gainous and Kevin Wagner, *Tweeting to Power: The Social Media Revolution in American Politics* (New York: Oxford University Press, 2013).
48. Gainous and Wagner, *Tweeting to Power*, 1.
49. Politifact, "Donald Trump's File," www.politifact.com/personalities/donald-trump/ (accessed 1/22/18).
50. Greg Sargent, "This Brutal New Poll Shows That Trump's Safe Space Is Shrinking," *Washington Post*, August 8, 2017, www.washingtonpost.com/blogs/plum-line/wp/2017/08/08/this-brutal-new-poll-shows-that-trumps-safe-space-is-shrinking/?utm_term=.744ad3651728 (accessed 3/8/18).
51. Erin McCann, "United's Apologies: A Timeline," *New York Times*, April 14, 2017, www.nytimes.com/2017/04/14/business/united-airlines-passenger-doctor.html (accessed 5/21/18).
52. Richard Davis, "Interplay: Political Blogging and Journalism," in *iPolitics: Citizens, Elections, and Governing in the New Media Era*, ed. Richard L. Fox and Jennifer M. Ramos (Cambridge: Cambridge University Press, 2012), 76–99.
53. Pew Research Center Publications, "State of the News Media 2010," March 15, 2010, http://pewresearch.org/pubs/1523/state-of-the-news-media-2010 (accessed 9/11/12); West, *The Next Wave*.
54. Karen Mossberger and Caroline J. Tolbert, "Digital Democracy: How Politics Online Is Changing Electoral Participation," in *Oxford Handbook of American Elections and Political Behavior*, ed. Jan E. Leighley (New York: Oxford University Press, 2010), 200–18.
55. Caroline Tolbert and Ramona McNeal, "Unraveling the Effects of the Internet on Political Participation," *Political Research Quarterly* 56, no. 2 (2003): 175–85.
56. Karen Mossberger, Caroline Tolbert, and Ramona McNeal, *Digital Citizenship: The Internet, Society, and Participation* (Cambridge, MA: MIT Press, 2008). See Richard L. Fox and Jennifer M. Ramos, eds., *iPolitics: Citizens, Elections, and Governing in the New Media Era* (Cambridge: Cambridge University Press, 2011).
57. W. R. Neuman, M. R. Just, and A. N. Crigler, *Common Knowledge: News and the Construction of Political Meaning* (Chicago: University of Chicago Press, 1992).
58. A. Healy and D. McNamara, "Verbal Learning and Memory: Does the Modal Model Still Work?" in *Annual Review of Psychology*, vol. 47, ed. J. Spense, J. Darley, and D. Foss (Palo Alto, CA: Annual Reviews, 1996), 143–72.
59. Cass Sunstein, *Republic.com* (Princeton, NJ: Princeton University Press, 2001). See also Mossberger and Tolbert, "Digital Democracy."
60. Michael Margolis and David Resnick, *Politics as Usual: The Cyberspace "Revolution"* (Thousand Oaks, CA: Sage, 2000).
61. West, *The Next Wave*; McChesney and Nichols, *Death and Life of American Journalism*.
62. Hannah Roberts, "This Is What Fake News Actually Looks Like—We Ranked 11 Election Stories That Went Viral on Facebook," *Business Insider*, November 17, 2016, www.businessinsider.com/fake-presidential-election-news-viral-facebook-trump-clinton-2016-11 (accessed 5/21/18).
63. Krysten Crawford, "Stanford Study Examines Fake News and the 2016 Presidential Election," *Stanford News*, January 18, 2017, www.news.stanford.edu/2017/01/18/stanford-study-examines-fake-news-2016-presidential-election/ (accessed 5/21/18).
64. Matthew A. Baum, "Preaching to the Choir or Converting the Flock: Presidential Communication Strategies in

the Age of Three Medias," in *iPolitics: Citizens, Elections, and Governing in the New Media Era*, ed. Richard L. Fox and Jennifer M. Ramos (Cambridge: Cambridge University Press, 2012), 183–205.

65. Eli Pariser, *The Filter Bubble: What the Internet Is Hiding from You* (New York: Penguin Press, 2011).
66. Markus Prior, "News vs. Entertainment: How Increasing Media Choice Widens Gaps in Political Knowledge and Turnout," *American Journal of Political Science* 49, no. 3 (2005): 577–92.
67. Delli Carpini and Keeter, *What Americans Know about Politics*; Sunstein, *Republic.com*.
68. Mossberger, Tolbert, and Stansbury, *Virtual Inequality*.
69. Jonathan M. Ladd, *Why Americans Hate the Media and How It Matters* (Princeton, NJ: Princeton University Press, 2012).
70. Pew Research Center, "Trust in the News Media," May 9, 2017, www.journalism.org/2017/05/10/americans-attitudes-about-the-news-media-deeply-divided-along-partisan-lines/pj_2017-05-10_media-attitudes_a-05/[0] (accessed 3/20/18).
71 Amy Wong, "'That's How Dictators Get Started': McCain Criticizes Trump for Calling Media 'the Enemy,'" *Washington Post*, February 8, 2017, www.washingtonpost.com/news/the-fix/wp/2017/02/18/thats-how-dictators-get-started-mccain-criticizes-trump-for-calling-media-the-enemy/?noredirect=on&utm_term=.90e929b9948d (accessed 5/21/18).
72. David J. Garrow, *Protest at Selma: Martin Luther King, Jr., and the Voting Rights Act of 1965* (New Haven, CT: Yale University Press, 2001).
73. See Todd Gitlin, *The Whole World Is Watching* (Berkeley: University of California Press, 1980).
74. Tim Groseclose, *Left Turn: How Liberal Media Bias Distorts the American Mind* (New York: St. Martin's Press, 2011).
75. Pew Research Center, "How Journalists See Journalists in 2004: Views on Profits, Performance and Politics," May 2004, http://people-press.org/files/legacy-pdf/214.pdf (accessed 9/7/12).
76. "Fake News," Lies and Propaganda: How to Sort Fact from Fiction," University of Michigan Library Research Guides, 2018, http://guides.lib.umich.edu/c.php?g=637508&p=4462444 (accessed 3/20/18).
77. Doris Graber, ed., *Media Power in American Politics*, 5th ed. (Washington, DC: CQ Press, 2006).
78. Amber E. Boydstun, Stefaan Walgrave, and Anne Hardy, "Two Faces of Media Attention: Media Storms vs. General Coverage," *Political Communication* 31, no. 4 (2014): 509–31.
79. Larry M. Bartels, *Presidential Primaries and the Dynamics of Public Choice* (Princeton, NJ: Princeton University Press, 1988).
80. David P. Redlawsk, Caroline J. Tolbert, and Todd Donovan, *Why Iowa? How Caucuses and Sequential Elections Improve the Presidential Nominating Process* (Chicago: University of Chicago Press, 2011).
81. Larry Bartels, *Unequal Democracy: The Political Economy of the New Gilded Age* (Princeton, NJ: Princeton University Press, 2008).
82. Pew Research Center, "Public Has Mixed Expectations for New Tax Law," January 24, 2018, www.people-press.org/2018/01/24/public-has-mixed-expectations-for-new-tax-law/ (accessed 5/21/18).
83. Robert Entman, "Framing: Toward Clarification of a Fractured Paradigm," *Journal of Communication* 43, no. 4 (1993): 51–58.
84. Shanto Iyengar and Donald R. Kinder, *News That Matters: Television and American Opinion* (Chicago: University of Chicago Press, 1987), 63.
85. *New York Times v. United States*, 403 U.S. 713 (1971).
86. United Nations General Assembly, "Report of the Special Rapporteur on the Promotion and Protection of the Right to Freedom of Opinion and Expression," 2011, www.ohchr.org/EN/Issues/FreedomOpinion/Pages/OpinionIndex.aspx (accessed 3/14/16).
87. Andrew Chadwick, *Internet Politics: States, Citizens, and New Communication Technologies* (Oxford: Oxford University Press, 2006).
88. See Martin Linsky, *Impact: How the Press Affects Federal Policymaking* (New York: W. W. Norton, 1986).

CHAPTER 8

1. Richard Fry, "Millennials and Gen-Xers Outvoted Boomers and Older Generations in 2016 election," July 31, 2017, www.pewresearch.org/fact-tank/2017/07/31/millennials-and-gen-xers-outvoted-boomers-and-older-generations-in-2016-election/ (accessed 1/31/18).
2. Gregory S. Schneider, "Historic Turnout of Young Voters in Virginia Election Poses Problem for Republicans," *Washington Post,* November 24, 2017, www.washingtonpost.com/local/virginia-politics/historic-turnout-of-young-voters-in-virginia-election-hints-at-national-problem-for-republicans/2017/11/24/8e90d978-cf03-11e7-9d3a-bcbe2af58c3a_story.html?utm_term=.4e20eb4f3eeb (accessed 1/31/18).
3. Gregory S. Schneider, Laura Vozzella, and Fenit Nirappil, "In the Final Spring to Election Day, a Historical Push to Turn Out Voters in Va.," *Washington Post,* November 4, 2017, www.washingtonpost.com/local/virginia-politics/in-the-final-sprint-to-election-day-an-historic-push-to-turn-out-voters-in-va/2017/11/04/ea833a58-bff6-11e7-97d9-bdab5a0ab381_story.html?utm_term=.3c809dcb4021 (accessed 1/31/18).
4. U.S. Census Bureau, "Voter Turnout Increases by 5 Million in 2008 Presidential Election, U.S. Census Bureau Reports," Newsroom Archive, www.census.gov/newsroom/releases/archives/voting/cb09-110.html (accessed 2/29/16).
5. Michael McDonald, "2016 November General Election Turnout Rates," United States Elections Project, www.electproject.org/2016g (accessed 11/11/16).

6. U.S. Census Bureau, "Table 10. Reasons for Not Voting, by Selected Characteristics: November 2012," Voting and Registration, www.census.gov/hhes/www/socdemo/voting/publications/p20/2012/tables.html.
7. National Conference of State Legislatures, "Same Day Voter Registration," March 27, 2018, www.ncsl.org/research/elections-and-campaigns/same-day-registration.aspx (accessed 6/12/18).
8. Catherine E. Shoichet, "Is Racism on the Rise? More in U.S. Say It's a 'Big Problem,' CNN/KFF Poll Finds," CNN, Race & Reality in America, November 25, 2015, www.cnn.com/2015/11/24/us/racism-problem-cnn-kff-poll/ (accessed 2/29/16).
9. Sidney Verba, Kay Lehman Schlozman, and Henry E. Brady, *Voice and Equality: Civic Voluntarism in American Politics* (Cambridge, MA: Harvard University Press, 2005), chap. 3, for kinds of participation; 66–67 for prevalence of local activity.
10. Michael P. McDonald, "American Voter Turnout in Historical Perspective," in *The Oxford Handbook of American Elections and Political Behavior*, ed. Jan Leighley (New York: Oxford University Press, 2010), 125–43.
11. Todd Donovan and Shaun Bowler, *Reforming the Republic: Democratic Institutions for the New America* (Upper Saddle River, NJ: Pearson Education, 2004).
12. For a discussion of the decline in voter turnout over time, see Ruy A. Teixeira, *The Disappearing American Voter* (Washington, DC: Brookings Institution Press, 1992). See also Michael McDonald and Samuel Popkin, "The Myth of the Vanishing Voter," *American Political Science Review*, 95 (2001): 963–74; and Michael McDonald, "2012 November General Election Turnout Rates," *United States Election Project*, www.electproject.org/2012g (accessed 9/14/12).
13. McDonald, "2016 November General Election Turnout Rates."
14. Elisa Shearer and Jeffrey Gottfried, "News Use across Social Media Platforms 2017," Pew Research Center, www.journalism.org/2017/09/07/news-use-across-social-media-platforms-2017/ (accessed 3/29/18).
15. Meredith Rolfe, *Voter Turnout: A Social Theory of Political Participation* (New York: Cambridge University Press, 2012).
16. Lee Rainie, et al., "Social Media and Political Engagement," Pew Research Center, Internet, Science & Tech, www.pewinternet.org/2012/10/19/social-media-and-political-engagement/ (accessed 6/24/14).
17. Helen Margetts, Peter John, Scott Hale, and Taha Yasseri, *Political Turbulence: How Social Media Shape Collective Action* (New York: Oxford University Press, 2017).
18. Philip Bump, "60 Minutes' profiles the genius who won Trump's campaign: Facebook," *Washington Post*, October 9, 2017, www.washingtonpost.com/news/politics/wp/2017/10/09/60-minutes-profiles-the-genius-who-won-trumps-campaign-facebook/?utm_term=.ad2bd8d8194a (accessed 3/29/18).
19. Caroline J. Tolbert and Ramona S. McNeal, "Unraveling the Effects of the Internet on Political Participation," *Political Research Quarterly* 56, no. 2 (2003): 175–85; see also Bruce Bimber, "Information and Political Engagement in America: The Search for Effects of Information Technology at the Individual Level," *Political Research Quarterly* 54 (2001): 53–67; Bimber, *Information and American Democracy: Technology and the Evolution of Political Power* (Cambridge: Cambridge University Press, 2009); J. Thomas and G. Streib, "The New Face of Government: Citizen-Initiated Contacts in the Era of E-Government," *Journal of Public Administration Theory and Research* 13, no. 1 (2003): 83–102; D. V. Shah et al., "Information and Expression in a Digital Age: Modeling Internet Effects on Civic Participation," *Communication Research* 32, no. 5 (2005): 531–65; K. Kenski and N. J. Stroud, "Connections between Internet Use and Political Efficacy, Knowledge, and Participation," *Journal of Broadcasting and Electronic Media* 50, no. 2 (2006): 173–92.
20. Sasha Issenberg, *The Victory Lab: The Secret Science of Winning Campaigns* (New York: Broadway Books, 2013); Andrew Chadwick, *The Hybrid Media System: Politics and Power* (New York: Oxford University Press, 2017).
21. Open Secrets, "Hillary Clinton (D)," www.opensecrets.org/pres16/candidate?id=N00000019 (accessed 6/20/18).
22. Open Secrets, "Donald Trump (R)," www.opensecrets.org/pres16/candidate?id=N00023864 (accessed 6/20/18).
23. Jason Gainous and Kevin Wagner, *Tweeting to Power: The Social Media Revolution in American Politics* (New York: Oxford University Press, 2013).
24. Gainous and Wagner, *Tweeting to Power.*
25. Karen Mossberger and Caroline J. Tolbert, "Digital Democracy: How Politics Online Is Changing Electoral Participation," in *Oxford Handbook of American Elections and Political Behavior*, ed. Jan E. Leighley (New York: Oxford University Press, 2010), 200–218.
26. Philip Bump, "'60 Minutes' Profiles the Genius Who Won Trump's Campaign: Facebook," *Washington Post*, October 9, 2017, www.washingtonpost.com/news/politics/wp/2017/10/09/60-minutes-profiles-the-genius-who-won-trumps-campaign-facebook/?utm_term=.ad2bd8d8194a (accessed 3/29/18).
27. W. R. Neuman, M. R. Just, and A. N. Crigler, *Common Knowledge: News and the Construction of Political Meaning* (Chicago: University of Chicago Press, 1992).
28. David P. Redlawsk, "Hot Cognition or Cool Consideration: Testing the Effects of Motivated Reasoning," *Journal of Politics* 64 (2002): 1021–44.
29. Caroline J. Tolbert, David P. Redlawsk, and Kellen J. Gracey, "Racial Attitudes and Emotional Responses to the 2016 Republican Candidates," *Journal of Election, Public Opinion and Parties* 28, no. 2 (2018): 245–62.
30. Manuel Castells, *The Rise of the Network Society: The Information Age: Economy, Society, and Culture* (Oxford: Blackwell, 1997).

31. Bruce Bimber and Richard Davis, *Campaigning Online: The Internet in U.S. Elections* (Cambridge: Cambridge University Press, 2003).
32. Robert Putnam, *Bowling Alone: The Collapse and Revival of American Community* (New York: Simon and Schuster, 2000).
33. Karen Mossberger, Caroline J. Tolbert, and Allison Hamilton, "Measuring Digital Citizenship: Mobile Access and Broadband," *International Journal of Communication* 6 (2012): 2492–528; Pippa Norris, *Digital Divide: Civic Engagement, Information Poverty, and the Internet Worldwide* (New York: Cambridge University Press, 2001); Benjamin Barber, "The New Telecommunications Technology: Endless Frontier or the End of Democracy?" *Constellations* 4, no. 2 (2011): 208–28; Tolbert and McNeal, "Unraveling the Effects of the Internet."
34. Russell Dalton, *The Good Citizen: How a Younger Generation Is Reshaping American Politics* (Washington, DC: CQ Press, 2008).
35. "Same-Sex Marriage Tweets Takeover the Internet," *USA Today*, June 27, 2015, www.usatoday.com/story/news/nation-now/2015/06/27/same-sex-marriage-scotus-gay-marriage-twitter-love-wins-trending/29389167/ (accessed 1/7/16).
36. Russell Dalton, "Citizenship Norms and the Expansion of Political Participation," *Public Choice* 56 (2008): 76–98.
37. Anamitra Deb, Stacy Donohue, and Tom Glaisyer, "Is Social Media a Threat to Democracy?" The Omidyar Group, October 1 2017, www.omidyargroup.com/wp-content/uploads/2017/10/Social-Media-and-Democracy-October-5-2017.pdf (accessed 3/29/18).
38. David S. Cloud, "Facebook Tells Congress 126 million Americans May Have Seen Russia-Linked Ads," *LA Times*, October 31, 2017, www.latimes.com/nation/la-na-russia-tech-20171031-story.html (accessed 3/29/18).
39. Josh Constine, "120K Instagrams by Russian Election Attackers Hit 20M Americans," Tech Crunch, November 1, 2017, techcrunch.com/2017/11/01/instagram-election-interference (accessed 3/29/18).
40. Julian Borger, Lauren Gambino, and Sabrina Siddiqui, "Tech Groups Face Congress as Showdown over Russian Election Meddling Looms," *The Guardian*, October 27, 2017, www.theguardian.com/technology/2017/oct/22/facebook-google-twitter-congress-hearing-trump-russia-election (accessed 3/29/18); Deb, Donohue, and Glaisyer, "Is Social Media a Threat to Democracy?"
41. Anthony Downs, *An Economic Theory of Democracy* (New York: Harper and Row, 1957); William H. Riker and Peter C. Ordeshook, "A Theory of the Calculus of Voting," *American Political Science Review* 62, no. 1 (1968): 25–42.
42. Julianna Pacheco and Jason Fletcher, "Incorporating Health into Studies of Political Behavior: Evidence for Turnout and Partisanship," *Political Research Quarterly* 68, no. 1 (2014): 104–16; Gustova López and Antonio Flores, "Dislike of Candidates or Campaign Issues Was Most Common Reason for Not Voting in 2016," Pew Research Center, June 1, 2017, www.pewresearch.org/fact-tank/2017/06/01/dislike-of-candidates-or-campaign-issues-was-most-common-reason-for-not-voting-in-2016/ (accessed 4/17/18).
43. Angus Campbell et al., *The American Voter* (New York: Wiley, 1960); Steven Rosenstone and John Mark Hansen, *Mobilization, Participation, and Democracy in America* (New York: Macmillan, 1993); Kay Lehman Scholzman, Sidney Verba, and Henry E. Brady, *The Unheavenly Chorus: Unequal Political Voice and the Broken Promise of American Democracy* (Princeton, NJ: Princeton University Press, 2012).
44. U.S. Census Bureau, "Table 7. Reported Voting and Registration of Family Members, by Age and Family Income: November 2016," Voting and Registration, www.census.gov/data/tables/time-series/demo/voting-and-registration/p20-580.html (accessed 3/29/18).
45. Sidney Verba and Norman H. Nie, *Participation in America: Political Democracy and Social Equality* (New York: Harper and Row, 1972); and www.census.gov/data/tables/time-series/demo/voting-and-registration/p20-580.html (accessed 3/15/18).
46. U.S. Census Bureau, "Voting and Registration in the Election of November 2016," May 2017, www.census.gov/data/tables/time-series/demo/voting-and-registration/p20-580.html (accessed 3/29/18).
47. Adam Hughs, "5 Facts about U.S. Political Donations," Pew Research Center, May 17, 2017, www.pewresearch.org/fact-tank/2017/05/17/5-facts-about-u-s-political-donations/ (accessed 3/29/18).
48. Julia Glum, "Youth Turnout for 2014 Midterm Election Lowest in 40 Years: Report," *International Business Times*, July 22, 2015, www.ibtimes.com/youth-voter-turnout-2014-midterm-election-lowest-40-years-report-2019813 (accessed 11/14/16); U.S. Census Bureau, "Voting and Registration in the Election of November 2016"; "Young People Dramatically Increase Their Turnout to 31%, Shape 2018 Midterm Elections," The Center for Information and Research on Civic Learning and Engagement, November 7, 2018 https://civicyouth.org/young-people-dramatically-increase-their-turnout-31-percent-shape-2018-midterm-elections/ (accessed 11/9/18).
49. Shiva Maniam and Samantha Smith, "A Wider Partisan and Ideological Gap between Younger, Older Generations," Pew Research Center, March 20, 2017, www.pewresearch.org/fact-tank/2017/03/20/a-wider-partisan-and-ideological-gap-between-younger-older-generations (accessed 3/29/18); Richard Frey, "Millennials and Gen Xers Outvoted Boomers and Older Generations in 2016 Election," Pew Research Center, July 31, 2017, www.pewresearch.org/fact-tank/2017/07/31/millennials-and-gen-xers-outvoted-boomers-and-older-generations-in-2016-election/ (accessed 3/29/18); Gary Langer, Christine Filer, Sofi Sinozich, and Allison De Jong, "Key Exit Poll Takeaways: Voters Negative on Trump, Most Interested

in Health Care, Immigration," ABC News, November 7, 2018, https://abcnews.go.com/Politics/negative-trump-divided-issues-voters-reshuffle-cards-washington/story?id=59025819 (accessed 11/9/18).

50. Julianna Pacheco, "Political Socialization in Context: The Effect of Political Competition on Youth Voter Turnout," *Political Behavior* 30, no. 4 (2008): 415–36.
51. Tyler Kingkade, "Youth Vote 2012 Turnout: Exit Polls Show Greater Share of Electorate than in 2008," Huffington Post, www.huffingtonpost.com/2012/11/07/youth-vote-2012-turnout-exit-polls_n_2086092.html (accessed 5/24/14).
52. Jennifer Lawless and Richard Fox, *Running from Office: Why Young Americans Are Turned Off to Politics* (New York: Oxford University Press, 2015).
53. Emily Hoban Kirby, Karlo Barrios Marcelo, and Kei Kawashima-Ginsberg, "Volunteering and the College Experience," Center for Information and Research on Civic Learning and Engagement, August 2009, www.civicyouth.org (accessed 11/25/09).
54. Rene Rocha et al., "Race and Turnout: Does Descriptive Representation in State Legislatures Increase Minority Voting?" *Political Research Quarterly* 63, no. 3 (2010): 890–907.
55. Susan Banducci, Todd Donovan, and Jeffrey Karp, "Minority Representation, Empowerment and Participation," *Journal of Politics* 66, no. 2 (2004): 534–56.
56. Mark Hugo Lopez and Paul Taylor, "Dissecting the 2008 Electorate: Most Diverse in U.S. History," Pew Research Center, Hispanic Trends, April 30, 2009, www.pewhispanic.org/2009/04/30/dissecting-the-2008-electorate-most-diverse-in-us-history/ (accessed 9/14/12).
57. Thom File, "The Diversifying Electorate—Voting Rates by Race and Hispanic Origin in 2012 (and Other Recent Elections)," U.S. Census Bureau, Current Population Survey, May 2013, www.census.gov/prod/2013pubs/p20-568.pdf (accessed 4/11/16).
58. Jens Manuel Krogstad and Mark Hugo Lopez, "Black Voter Turnout Fell in 2016, Even as a Record Number of Americans Cast Ballots," Pew Research Center, May 12, 2017, www.pewresearch.org/fact-tank/2017/05/12/black-voter-turnout-fell-in-2016-even-as-a-record-number-of-americans-cast-ballots/ (accessed 3/29/18).
59. See William Julius Wilson, *The Truly Disadvantaged: The Inner City, the Underclass, and Public Policy* (Chicago: University of Chicago Press, 1987); and Douglas Massey and Nancy Denton, *American Apartheid: Segregation and the Making of the American Underclass* (Cambridge, MA: Harvard University Press, 1993).
60. Jan E. Leighley and Jonathan Nagler, "Individual and Systemic Influences on Turnout: Who Votes? 1984," *Journal of Politics* 54 no. 3 (1992): 718–40.
61. Michael Dawson, *Black Visions: The Roots of Contemporary African-American Political Ideologies* (Chicago: University of Chicago Press, 2003).
62. File, "The Diversifying Electorate."
63. Matt Barreto and Gary Segura, *Latino America: How America's Most Dynamic Population Is Poised to Transform the Politics of the Nation* (New York: Public Affairs, 2014).
64. Matt Barreto, Gary Segura, and Nathan Woods, "The Mobilizing Effect of Majority–Minority Districts on Latino Turnout," *American Political Science Review* 98 (2004): 65–75, and authors' update.
65. Barreto and Segura, *Latino America*; Langer, Filer, Sinozich, and De Jong, "Key Exit Poll Takeaways: Voters Negative on Trump, Most Interested in Health Care, Immigration."
66. John Griffin and Brian Newman, *Minority Report: Evaluating Political Equality in America* (New York: Cambridge University Press, 2008); Rodney R. Hero, *Latinos and the U.S. Political System: Two-Tiered Pluralism* (Philadelphia: Temple University Press, 1992); Daniel Bowen and Christopher Clark, "Revisiting Descriptive Representation in Congress: Assessing the Effect of Race on the Constituent–Legislator Relationship," *Political Research Quarterly* 67, no. 3 (2014): 695–707.
67. Adrian Pantoja and Gary Segura, "Does Ethnicity Matter? Descriptive Representation in the Statehouse and Political Alienation Among Latinos," *Social Science Quarterly* 84 (2003): 441–60.
68. File, "The Diversifying Electorate."
69. Thom File, "Voting in America: A Look at the 2016 Presidential Election," *Census Blogs*, May 10, 2017, www.census.gov/newsroom/blogs/random-samplings/2017/05/voting_in_america.html (accessed 3/29/18).
70. "Election 2016: Exit Polls," *New York Times*, November 8, 2016, www.nytimes.com/interactive/2016/11/08/us/politics/election-exit-polls.html (accessed 11/11/16).
71. "Election 2016: Exit Polls."
72. Kira Sanbonmatsu, "Political Parties and the Recruitment of Women to State Legislatures," *Journal of Politics* 64, no. 3 (August 2002): 791–809; Jennifer L. Lawless and Richard L. Fox, *Why Are Women Still Not Running for Public Office?* (Washington, DC: Brookings Institution Press, 2008).
73. Center for American Women and Politics, *The Impact of Women in Public Office: Findings at a Glance* (New Brunswick, NJ: Rutgers University Press, 1991); Lawless and Fox, *Why Are Women Still Not Running for Public Office?*
74. See Richard A. Brody, "The Puzzle of Political Participation in America," in *The New American Political System*, ed. Anthony King (Washington, DC: American Enterprise Institute, 1978), chap. 8.
75. Rosenstone and Hansen, *Mobilization, Participation, and Democracy*, 59.
76. Alan S. Gerber and Donald P. Green, "The Effects of Canvassing, Telephone Calls, and Direct Mail on Voter Turnout: A Field Experiment," *American Political Science Review* 94, no. 3 (September 2000): 660.
77. Rolfe, *Voter Turnout.*
78. Robert M. Bond et al., "A 61-Million-Person Experiment in Social Influence and Political Mobilization," *Nature* 489 (2012): 295–98.

79. Bond et al., "A 61-Million-Person Experiment."
80. Katerina Eva Matsa and Kristine Lu, "10 Facts about the Changing Digital News Landscape," Pew Research Center, September 14, 2016, www.pewresearch.org/fact-tank/2016/09/14/facts-about-the-changing-digital-news-landscape/ (accessed 10/16/16).
81. Eitan D. Hersh, *Hacking the Electorate: How Campaigns Perceive Voters* (New York: Cambridge University Press, 2015); Sasha Issenberg, *The Victory Lab: The Secret Science of Winning Campaigns* (New York: Crown Publishers, 2012).
82. Theda Skocpol, *The Tea Party and the Remaking of Republican Conservatism* (New York: Oxford University Press, 2013).
83. Michael P. McDonald and John Samples, eds., *The Marketplace of Democracy: Electoral Competition and American Politics* (Washington, DC: Brookings Institution Press, 2006).
84. Mark N. Franklin, "Electoral Participation," in *Comparing Democracies: Elections and Voting in Global Perspective*, ed. Lawrence LeDuc, Richard G. Niemi, and Pippa Norris (Thousand Oaks, CA: Sage, 1996), 216–35; G. Bingham Powell, "American Voter Turnout in Comparative Perspective," *American Political Science Review* 80, no. 1 (1986): 17–43.
85. Todd Donovan, "A Goal for Reform: Make Elections Worth Stealing," *PS: Political Science and Politics* 40, no. 4 (2007): 681–6.
86. Donovan, "A Goal for Reform"; Gary W. Cox and Michael C. Munger, "Closeness, Expenditures, and Turnout in the 1982 U.S. House Elections," *American Political Science Review* 83, no. 1 (1989): 217–31; James G. Gimpel, Karen M. Kaufmann, and Shanna Pearson-Merkowitz, "Battleground States versus Blackout States: The Behavioral Implications of Modern Presidential Campaigns," *Journal of Politics* 69, no. 3 (2007): 786–97.
87. Gimpel, Kaufmann, and Pearson-Merkowitz, "Battleground States versus Blackout States"; Julianna Sandell Pacheco, "Political Socialization in Context: The Effect of Political Competition on Youth Voter Turnout," *Political Behavior* 30, no. 4 (2008): 415–36; Keena Lipsitz, "The Consequences of Battleground and 'Spectator' State Residency for Political Participation," *Political Behavior* 31, no. 2 (2009): 187–209.
88. David P. Redlawsk, Caroline J. Tolbert, and Todd Donovan, *Why Iowa? How Caucuses and Sequential Elections Improve the Presidential Nominating Process* (Chicago: University of Chicago Press, 2011).
89. Caroline J. Tolbert, Daniel C. Bowen, and Todd Donovan, "Initiative Campaigns: Direct Democracy and Voter Mobilization," *American Politics Research* 37, no. 1 (2009): 155–92.
90. Caroline J. Tolbert, John A. Grummel, and Daniel A. Smith, "The Effects of Ballot Initiatives on Voter Turnout in the American States," *American Politics Research* 29, no. 6 (2001): 625–48; Mark A. Smith, "The Contingent Effects of Ballot Initiatives and Candidate Races on Turnout," *American Journal of Political Science* 45, no. 3 (2001): 700–706; Caroline J. Tolbert and Daniel A. Smith, "The Educative Effects of Ballot Initiatives on Voter Turnout," *American Politics Research* 33, no. 2 (2005): 283–309; Frederick Boehmke and Daniel Bowen, "Direct Democracy and Individual Interest Group Membership," *Journal of Politics* 72, no. 3 (2010): 659–71.
91. Stephen Nicholson, *Voting the Agenda: Candidates, Elections, and Ballot Propositions* (Princeton, NJ: Princeton University Press, 2005).
92. John Myers, "That Blockbuster California Ballot Will Be a $452-Million Battle," *Los Angeles Times*, February 18, 2016, www.latimes.com/local/california/la-pol-sac-november-ballot-500-million-20160215-story.html (accessed 10/18/16).
93. Daniel A. Smith and Caroline J. Tolbert, *Educated by Initiative: The Effects of Direct Democracy on Citizens and Political Organizations in the American States* (Ann Arbor: University of Michigan Press, 2004).
94. Bruce E. Cain, Todd Donovan, and Caroline J. Tolbert, *Democracy in the States: Experiments in Election Reform* (Washington, DC: Brookings Institution Press, 2008).
95. U.S. Census Bureau, "Table 10. Reasons for Not Voting, by Selected Characteristics: November 2012," Voting and Registration, www.census.gov/hhes/www/socdemo/voting/publications/p20/2012/tables.html.
96. National Conference of State Legislatures, "Same Day Voter Registration."
97. Domenico Montanaro, "Would Automatic Voter Registration Increase Turnout?" NPR, March 18, 2015, www.npr.org/sections/itsallpolitics/2015/03/18/393645667/would-automatic-voter-registration-increase-turnout (accessed 11/14/16).
98. National Conference of State Legislatures, "Voter Identification Requirements," www.ncsl.org/research/elections-and-campaigns/voter-id.aspx (accessed 10/12/18).
99. Michael D. Regan, "What Does Voter Turnout Tell Us about the 2016 Election?" November 20, 2016, PBS News Hour, www.pbs.org/newshour/politics/voter-turnout-2016-elections (accessed 4/17/18); and "Oppose Voter ID Legislation—Fact Sheet," ACLU, www.aclu.org/other/oppose-voter-id-legislation-fact-sheet (accessed 4/17/18).
100. Michael Wines, "Wisconsin Strict ID Law Discouraged Voters, Study Finds," *New York Times*, September 25, 2017, www.nytimes.com/2017/09/25/us/wisconsin-voters.html (accessed 3/29/18).
101. National Conference of State Legislatures, "Voter Identification Requirements."
102. E. Ann Carson, "Prisoners in 2013," U.S. Department of Justice, Bureau of Justice Statistics, September 30, 2014, www.bjs.gov/content/pub/pdf/p13.pdf (accessed 4/11/16); National Conference of State Legislatures, "Felon Voting Rights," April 30, 2017 www.ncsl.org/research/elections-and-campaigns/felon-voting-rights.aspx (accessed 10/12/18).

103. Justin Wolfers, David Leonhardt and Kevin Quealy, "1.5 Million Missing Black Men," The Upshot, *New York Times*, April 20, 2015, www.nytimes.com/interactive/2015/04/20/upshot/missing-black-men.html?_r50&abt50002&abg51 (accessed 1/6/16).
104. Jean Chung, *Felon Disenfranchisement: A Primer* (Washington, DC: The Sentencing Project, 2016), www.sentencingproject.org/wp-content/uploads/2015/08/Felony-Disenfranchisement-Primer.pdf (accessed 10/12/16).
105. National Conference of State Legislatures, "Same Day Voter Registration."
106. Robert A. Jackson, Robert D. Brown, and Gerald C. Wright, "Registration, Turnout and the Electoral Representativeness of U.S. State Electorates," *American Politics Quarterly* 26, no. 3 (July 1998): 259–87. See also Benjamin Highton, "Easy Registration and Voter Turnout," *Journal of Politics* 59, no. 2 (April 1997): 565–87.
107. Stephen Knack and James White, "Election-Day Registration and Turnout Inequality," *Political Behavior* 22, no. 1 (2000): 29–44; Craig Leonard Brians and Bernard Grofman, "When Registration Barriers Fall, Who Votes? An Empirical Test of a Rational Choice Model," *Public Choice* 99 (1999): 161–76; Michael J. Hanmer, *Discount Voting: Voter Registration Reforms and Their Effects* (New York: Cambridge University Press, 2009); Mary Fitzgerald, "Greater Convenience but Not Greater Turnout: The Impact of Alternative Voting Methods on Electoral Participation in the United States," *American Politics Research* 33, no. 6 (2005): 842–67.
108. National Conference of State Legislatures, "Absentee and Early Voting," September 20, 2018, www.ncsl.org/research/elections-and-campaigns/absentee-and-early-voting.aspx (accessed 10/10/18).
109. Paul Gronke, Eva Galanes-Rosenbaum, and Peter Miller, "Early Voting and Turnout," *PS: Political Science and Politics* 40, no. 4 (October 2007): 639–45; Fitzgerald, "Greater Convenience but Not Greater Turnout"; Adam J. Berinsky, "The Perverse Consequences of Electoral Reform in the United States," *American Politics Research* 33, no. 4 (2005): 471–91.
110. Jeffrey Karp and Susan Banducci, "Going Postal: How All-Mail Elections Influence Turnout," *Political Behavior* 22, no. 3 (2000): 223–39.
111. Michael J. Hamner, *Discount Voting: Voter Registration Reforms and Their Effects* (New York: Cambridge University Press, 2009).
112. John Griffin and Michael Keane, "Are Voters Better Represented?" *Journal of Politics* 67, no. 4 (2005): 1206–27.
113. Larry Bartels, *Unequal Democracy: The Political Economy of the New Gilded Age* (Princeton, NJ: Princeton University Press, 2008).

CHAPTER 9

1. Taxdayteaparty.com, "Meet Keli Carender, Tea Party Organizer in Seattle, Washington," March 15, 2009, http://taxdayteaparty.com/2009/03/meet-keli-carender-tea-party-organizer-in-seattle-washington/ (accessed 1/26/18).
2. Walter Dean Burnham, *Critical Elections and the Mainsprings of American Politics* (New York: W. W. Norton, 1970).
3. E. E. Schattschneider, *The Semisovereign People: A Realist's View of Democracy in America* (New York: Holt, Rinehart & Winston, 1960).
4. Larry Bartels, *Unequal Democracy: The Political Economy of the New Gilded Age* (Princeton, NJ: Princeton University Press, 2008).
5. Kathleen Bawn et al., "A Theory of Political Parties: Groups, Policy Demands and Nominations in American Politics." *Perspectives on Politics* 10, no. 3 (2012): 571–97.
6. Morris Fiorina, Samuel Abrams, and Jeremy Pope, *Culture War? The Myth of a Polarized America* (New York: Pearson Longman, 2004).
7. Todd Donovan and Shaun Bowler, *Reforming the Republic: Democratic Institutions for the New America* (Upper Saddle River, NJ: Prentice Hall, 2003).
8. James Madison, *The Federalist Papers*, no. 10, http://thomas.loc.gov/home/histdox/fed_10.html (accessed 11/11/12).
9. John H. Aldrich, *Why Parties? A Second Look* (Chicago: University of Chicago Press, 2011).
10. Raymond J. La Raja, "Political Parties in the Era of Soft Money," in *The Parties Respond: Changes in American Parties and Campaigns*, 4th ed., ed. Sandy L. Maisel (Boulder, CO: Westview Press, 2002), 163–88.
11. For an excellent analysis of the parties' role in recruitment, see Paul Herrnson, *Congressional Elections: Campaigning at Home and in Washington* (Washington, DC: CQ Press, 1995).
12. Marty Cohen et al., *The Party Decides: Presidential Nominations before and after Reform* (Chicago: University of Chicago Press, 2008).
13. Seth E. Masket, *No Middle Ground: How Informal Party Organizations Control Nominations and Polarize Legislatures* (Ann Arbor: University of Michigan Press, 2011).
14. Sasha Issenberg, *Victory Lab: The Secret Science of Winning Campaigns* (New York: Crown, 2012).
15. Glen Justice, "F.E.C. Declines to Curb Independent Fund Raisers," *New York Times*, May 14, 2004, A16.
16. See Harold Gosnell, *Machine Politics: Chicago Model*, rev. ed. (Chicago: University of Chicago Press, 1968).
17. For a useful discussion, see John Bibby and Thomas Holbrook, "Parties and Elections," in *Politics in the American States*, ed. Virginia Gray and Herbert Jacob (Washington, DC: CQ Press, 1996), 78–121.
18. John Gramlich, "Far More Americans Say There Are Strong Conflicts between Partisans Than between Other Groups in Society," Pew Research Center, December 19, 2017, www.pewresearch.org/fact-tank/2017/12/19/far-more-americans-say-there-are-strong-conflicts-between-partisans-than-between-other-groups-in-society/ (accessed 5/12/18).

19. Tara Golshan, "'Reckless, Outrageous, and Undignified Behavior': Sen. Flake Quits the Senate Over Trump," Vox, October 24, 2017, www.vox.com/2017/10/24/16536756/flake-retitrement-over-trump-announcement (accessed 5/12/18).
20. "Election 2016: Exit Polls," *New York Times*, November 8, 2016, www.nytimes.com/interactive/2016/11/08/us/politics/election-exit-polls.html (accessed 11/11/16).
21. Alex Leary, "Hispanics Voting in Record Numbers in Florida, Other States, Boosting Hillary Clinton," *Miami Herald*, November 6, 2016, www.miamiherald.com/news/politics-government/election/article112958953.html (accessed 11/11/16).
22. "Election 2016: Exit Polls."
23. "Behind Trump's Victory: Divisions by Race, Gender and Education," November 9, 2016, Pew Research Center," www.pewresearch.org/fact-tank/2016/11/09/behind-trumps-victory-divisions-by-race-gender-education/ (accessed 5/12/18); Gary Langer, Christine Filer, Sofi Sinozich, and Allison De Jong, "Key Exit Poll Takeaways: Voters Negative on Trump, Most Interested in Health Care, Immigration," ABC News, November 7, 2018, https://abcnews.go.com/Politics/negative-trump-divided-issues-voters-reshuffle-cards-washington/story?id=59025819 (accessed 11/9/18).
24. Pew Research Center, Religious Landscape Study, www.pewforum.org/religious-landscape-study/ (accessed 12/16/15).
25. Gregory Smith, "A Growing Share of Americans Say It's Not Necessary to Believe in God to Be Moral," Pew Research Center, October 16, 2017, www.pewresearch.org/fact-tank/2017/10/16/a-growing-share-of-americans-say-its-not-necessary-to-believe-in-god-to-be-moral/ (accessed 5/12/18).
26. "Election 2016: Exit Polls."
27. Christopher Shea, "Who Are You Calling Working Class?" *Boston Globe*, February 12, 2006, www.boston.com/news/globe/ideas/articles/2006/02/12/who_are_you_calling_working_class/ (accessed 2/24/08).
28. Pew Research Center, "Beyond Red vs. Blue: The Political Typology," U.S. Politics & Policy, June 26, 2014, www.people-press.org/2014/06/26/the-political-typology-beyond-red-vs-blue (accessed 2/28/16).
29. Shaun Bowler, Gary Segura, and Stephen Nicholson, "Earthquakes and Aftershocks: Race, Direct Democracy, and Partisan Change," *American Journal of Political Science* 50 (January 2006): 146–59.
30. "Election 2016: Exit Polls."
31. Jeffrey A. Karp and Caroline J. Tolbert, "Support for Nationalizing Presidential Elections," *Presidential Studies Quarterly* 40, no. 4 (2010): 771–93.
32. Jeffrey M. Jones, "Democratic, Republican Identification Near Historical Lows," Gallup, January 11, 2016, www.gallup.com/poll/188096/democratic-republican-identification-near-historical-lows.aspx (accessed 8/3/16).
33. Alexa Mikalaski, "9 States Where Registered Independents Outnumber Both Major Political Parties," Independent Voter Network, August 8, 2018, https://ivn.us/2018/08/08/9-states-registered-independents-outnumber-major-political-parties/ (accessed 11/9/18).
34. See Morris Fiorina, "Parties and Partisanship: A Forty Year Retrospective," *Political Behavior* 24, no. 2 (2002): 93–115.
35. On the limited polarization among ordinary voters, see Fiorina, Abrams, and Pope, *Culture War?*; on growing partisan attachment among a subset of voters, see Alan Abramowitz and Kyle Saunders, "Why Can't We Just Get Along? The Reality of a Polarized America," *The Forum* 3, no. 2 (2005): 1–22.
36. "CQ Roll Call's Vote Studies—2013 in Review," February 3, 2014, http://media.cq.com/votestudies/ (accessed 7/25/16).
37. David Hawkings, "Ahead, the First Pure Party-Line Modern Tax Cut?" Roll Call, October 31, 2017, www.rollcall.com/news/hawkings/party-line-tax-cut (accessed 8/15/18).
38. Benjamin Page and Martin Gilens, *Democracy in America: What Has Gone Wrong and What We Can Do about It* (Chicago: University of Chicago Press, 2017).
39. Donovan and Bowler, *Reforming the Republican*. See also Marty Gilen, *Affluence and Influence: Economic Inequality and Political Power in America* (Princeton, NJ: Princeton University Press, 2014).
40. For a discussion of third parties in the United States, see Daniel Mazmanian, *Third Parties in Presidential Elections* (Washington, DC: Brookings Institution Press, 1974).
41. See Maurice Duverger, *Political Parties* (New York: Wiley, 1954).
42. Donovan and Bowler, *Reforming the Republic*.
43. Andri Blais, *To Keep or to Change First Past the Post? The Politics of Election Reform* (New York: Oxford University Press, 2008).
44. Todd Donovan, Caroline J. Tolbert, Kellen Gracey, "Campaign Civility under Preferential and Plurality Voting," *Electoral Studies* 42 (2016): 157–163.
45. Stanley Kelley, Jr., Richard E. Ayres, and William Bowen, "Registration and Voting: Putting First Things First," *American Political Science Review* 61 (June 1967): 359–70.

CHAPTER 10

1. BBC Newsbeat, "'I'm One of the Young Voters Who Backed Donald Trump,'" November 12, 2016, www.bbc.co.uk/newsbeat/article/37961355/im-one-of-the-young-voters-who-backed-donald-trump (accessed 1/26/18).
2. Emily Richmond, Mikhail Zinshteyn, and Natalie Gross, "Dissecting the Youth Vote," *The Atlantic,* November 11, 2016, www.theatlantic.com/education/archive/2016/11/dissecting-the-youth-vote/507416/ (accessed 1/26/17).
3. Richmond et al., "Dissecting the Youth Vote."
4. Thom File, "Voting in America: A Look at the 2016 Presidential Election," *Census Blogs*, May 10, 2017, www.census.gov/newsroom/blogs/random-samplings/2017/05/voting_in_america.html (accessed 1/26/18).

5. Amber Phillips, "Is Split-Ticket Voting Officially Dead?" *Washington Post*, November 17, 2016, www.washingtonpost.com/news/the-fix/wp/2016/11/17/is-split-ticket-voting-officially-dead/?utm_term=.ace9dff09c60 (accessed 5/14/18).
6. Sarah Zimmerman, "Illinois Protecting against Russian Election Tampering," February 28, 2018, *U.S. News and World Reports*, www.usnews.com/news/best-states/illinois/articles/2018-02-28/illinois-protecting-against-russian-election-tampering (accessed 5/14/18).
7. *Baker v. Carr* 369 U.S. 186 (1962); *Gray v. Sanders*, 372 U.S. 368 (1963); *Wesberry v. Sanders*, 376 U.S. 1 (1964); *Reynolds v. Sims*, 377 U.S. 533 (1964).
8. *Thornburg v. Gingles*, 478 U.S. 613 (1986).
9. Christopher Ingraham "This Is the Best Explanation of Gerrymandering You Will Ever See. How to Steal an Election: A Visual Guide," *Washington Post*, March 1, 2015, www.washingtonpost.com/news/wonk/wp/2015/03/01/this-is-the-best-explanation-of-gerrymandering-you-will-ever-see/?utm_term=.97e9bcf9a627 (accessed 7/25/18).
10. "Reelection Rates over the Years," Center for Responsive Politics, www.opensecrets.org/overview/reelect.php (accessed 11/9/18).
11. Christopher Ingraham, "'Sprawling,' Rorsarchian,' 'Corrosive' to Democracy: Pennsylvania's Top Court Condemns State Gerrymandered District," *Washington Post*, February 8, 2018, www.washingtonpost.com/news/wonk/wp/2018/02/08/sprawling-rorschachian-corrosive-to-democracy-pas-top-court-condemns-states-gerrymandered-districts/?noredirect=on&utm_term=.a009cd0645f9 (accessed 7/25/18).
12. *Shaw v. Reno*, 509 U.S. 630 (1993).
13. David Redlawsk, Caroline J. Tolbert, and Todd Donovan, *Why Iowa? How Caucuses and Sequential Elections Improve the Presidential Nomination Process* (Chicago: University of Chicago Press, 2011).
14. Redlawsk, Tolbert, and Donovan, *Why Iowa*?
15. State legislatures determine the system by which electors are selected. Almost all states use this "winner-take-all" system. Maine and Nebraska, however, provide that one electoral vote goes to the winner in each congressional district and two electoral votes go to the winner statewide.
16. *Bush v. Gore*, 531 U.S. 98 (2000).
17. Jeffrey Karp and Caroline J. Tolbert, "Polls and Elections: Support for Nationalizing Presidential Elections." *Presidential Studies Quarterly*, 40, no. 4 (2010): 771–93.
18. Todd Donovan and Shaun Bowler, *Reforming the Republic: Democratic Institutions for the New America* (Upper Saddle River, NJ: Pearson Press, 2003).
19. André Blais, *To Keep or to Change First Past the Post? The Politics of Electoral Reform* (Oxford: Oxford University Press, 2008).
20. Adam Nagourney, "Court Strikes Down Ban on Gay Marriage in California," *New York Times*, February 7, 2012, www.nytimes.com/2012/02/08/us/marriage-ban-violates-constitution-court-rules.html (accessed 8/21/12).
21. Daniel Smith and Caroline J. Tolbert, *Educated by Initiative: The Effects of Direct Democracy on Citizens and Political Organizations in the American States* (Ann Arbor: University of Michigan Press, 2004).
22. Shaun Bowler, Todd Donovan, and Caroline J. Tolbert, *Citizens as Legislators: Direct Democracy in the United States* (Columbus: Ohio State University Press, 1998).
23. BallotPedia, "2018 Ballot Measures," www.ballotpedia.org/2018_ballot_measures (accessed 11/8/18).
24. Stephen Nicholson, *Voting the Agenda: Candidates, Elections, and Ballot Propositions* (Princeton, NJ: Princeton University Press, 2005).
25. Ryan Grim and Sabrina Siddiqui, "Call Time for Congress Shows Dominates Bleak Work Life," Huffington Post, January 9, 2013, www.huffingtonpost.com/2013/01/08/call-time-congressional-fundraising_n_2427291.html (accessed 8/8/16).
26. "Most Expensive Races," Center for Responsive Politics, November 9, 2018, www.opensecrets.org/overview/topraces.php (accessed 11/9/18).
27. Stephen Ansolabehere and James Snyder, "Campaign War Chests and Congressional Elections," *Business and Politics* 2 (2000): 9–34.
28. Gary W. Cox and Eric Magar, "How Much Is Majority Status in the U.S. Congress Worth?" *American Political Science Review* 93 (1999): 299–309.
29. "Two-Thirds of Presidential Campaign Is in Just 6 States," Nationalpopularvote.com, www.nationalpopularvote.com/campaign-events-2016 (accessed 5/14/18); Daron Shaw, *The Race to 270: The Electoral College and the Campaign Strategies of 2000 and 2004* (Chicago: University of Chicago Press, 2006).
30. John Geer, *In Defense of Negativity: Attack Ads in Presidential Campaigns* (Chicago: University of Chicago Press, 2006).
31. Nicholas Confessore, Karen Yourish, "$2 Billion of Free Media for Donald Trump," *New York Times*, March 16, 2016, www.nytimes.com/2016/03/16/upshot/measuring-donald-trumps-mammoth-advantage-in-free-media.html (accessed 7/25/18).
32. Brian Stelter, "Debate Breaks Record as Most-Watched in U.S. History," CNN Money, September 27, 2016, www.money.cnn.com/2016/09/27/media/debate-ratings-record-viewership/ (accessed 10/17/16).
33. D. Sunshine Hillygus and Todd G. Shields, *The Persuadable Voter: Wedge Issues in Political Campaigns* (Princeton, NJ: Princeton University Press, 2009).
34. Sasha Issenberg, *The Victory Lab: The Secret Science of Winning Campaigns* (New York: Crown, 2012).
35. Alan S. Gerber and Donald P. Green, "The Effects of Canvassing, Telephone Calls, and Direct Mail on Voter Turnout: A Field Experiment," *American Political Science Review* 94, no. 3 (2000): 660.
36. M. Ostrogorski, *Democracy and the Organization of Political Parties* (New York: Macmillan, 1902).

37. For discussions of the consequences of this, see Thomas Edsall, *The New Politics of Inequality* (New York: W. W. Norton, 1984). See also Thomas Edsall, "Both Parties Get the Company's Money—but the Boss Backs the GOP," *Washington Post*, National Weekly Edition, September 16, 1986, 14; and Benjamin Ginsberg, "Money and Power: The New Political Economy of American Elections," in *The Political Economy*, ed. Thomas Ferguson and Joel Rogers (Armonk, NY: M. E. Sharpe, 1984).
38. Center for Responsive Politics, "Cost of Election," www.opensecrets.org/overview/cost.php (accessed 11/9/16); and Christopher Ingraham, "Somebody Just Put a Price Tag on the 2016 Election. It's a Doozy," *Washington Post*, April 14, 2017, www.washingtonpost.com/news/wonk/wp/2017/04/14/somebody-just-put-a-price-tag-on-the-2016-election-its-a-doozy/?utm_term=.6ecccc4dc35f (accessed 6/5/18).
39. *Buckley v. Valeo*, 424 U.S. 1 (1976).
40. *Citizens United v. Federal Election Commission*, 558 U.S. 50 (2010).
41. *Citizens United.*
42. Martin Gilens, *Affluence and Influence: Economic Inequality and Political Power in America* (Princeton, NJ: Princeton University Press; New York: Russell Sage, 2012).
43. *McCutcheon et al. v. Federal Election Commission*, 572 U.S. __ (2014).
44. OpenSecrets.org, Sen. Bernie Sanders, www.opensecrets.org/politicians/summary.php?cid=N00000528 (accessed 6/23/16).
45. *Buckley v. Valeo.*
46. Steve Phillips, "What about White Voters?" *Center for American Progress*, February 5, 2016, www.americanprogress.org/issues/race/news/2016/02/05/130647/what-about-white-voters/ (accessed 11/14/16).
47. Jonathan Martin, Dalia Sussman, and Megan Thee-Brenan, "Voters Express Disgust over U.S. Politics in New Times/CBS Poll," *New York Times*, November 3, 2016, www.nytimes.com/2016/11/04/us/politics/hillary-clinton-donald-trump-poll.html (accessed 11/11/18).
48. GDELT Project, "Presidential Campaign 2016: Candidate Television Tracker," television.gdeltproject.org/cgi-bin/iatv_campaign2016/iatv_campaign2016 (accessed 11/11/16).
49. "Election 2016: Exit Polls," *New York Times*, November 8, 2016, www.nytimes.com/interactive/2016/11/08/us/politics/election-exit-polls.html (accessed 11/11/16).
50. Nancy Scola, "Massive Twitter Data Release Sheds Light on Russia Trump Strategy," *Politico*, October 17, 2018, www.politico.com/story/2018/10/17/twitter-foreign-influence-operations-910005 (accessed 11/11/8).
51. Devlin Barrett, Sari Horwitz and Rosalind S. Helderman, "Russian Troll Farm, 13 Suspects Indicted in 2016 Election Interference," *Washington Post*, February 16, 2018, www.washingtonpost.com/world/national-security/russian-troll-farm-13-suspects-indicted-for-interference-in-us-election/2018/02/16/2504de5e-1342-11e8-9570-29c9830535e5_story.html?noredirect=on&utm_term=.1d49970b3df7 (accessed 11/9/18).
52. "One in Five Adults Have Attended a Political Protest, Rally, or Speech," *Washington Post*–Kaiser Family Foundation Survey (Jan. 24–Feb. 22, 2018), April 21, 2018, www.washingtonpost.com/page/2010-2019/WashingtonPost/2018/04/06/National-Politics/Polling/release_516.xml (accessed 11/9/18).
53. Ryan Sit, "More Than 2 Million in 90 Percent of Voting Districts Joined March for Our Lives Protests," *Newsweek*, March 26, 2018, www.newsweek.com/march-our-lives-how-many-2-million-90-voting-district-860841 (accessed 11/9/18).
54. Michelle Ye Hee Lee and Anu Narayanswamy, "Democratic Candidates for Congress Have Raised a Record-Shattering $1 Billion This Election," *Washington Post*, October 17, 2018, www.washingtonpost.com/politics/democratic-candidates-for-congress-have-raised-a-record-shattering-1-billion-this-election/2018/10/17/afedfe66-d231-11e8-8c22-fa2ef74bd6d6_story.html?utm_term=.350602226c5b (accessed 11/9/18).
55. Tim Craig, "Democrats' Gains in State Capitols Mark a Significant Turnaround for Party," *Washington Post*, November 8, 2018, A27.
56. Brady Dennis and David Weigel, "Progressive Ballot Measures Win over Even Red-State Voters," *Washington Post*, November 8, 2018, A33.

CHAPTER 11

1. Matt Miller, "Young Americans Get the Shaft," *Washington Post*, June 13, 2012, www.washingtonpost.com/opinions/young-americans-get-the-shaft/2012/06/13/gJQAeHp4ZV_story.html?utm_term=.4a68ebb3076f 9 (accessed 1/26/18).
2. This account drawn from Araz Hachadourian, "Who's Lobbying for Millennial Interests? Meet the 'AARP for Young People,'" *Yes! Magazine*, May 19, 2016, www.yesmagazine.org/people-power/millennials-have-the-numbers-to-move-our-politics-and-theyre-about-to-get-their-own-lobbyists-20160519 (accessed 1/26/18); and Association of Young Americans, joinaya.com/ (accessed 1/26/18).
3. Alexis de Tocqueville, *Democracy in America*, ed. J. P. Mayer and trans. George Lawrence (New York: Harper Collins, [1835–40] 1988), 513.
4. Alexander Hamilton, James Madison, and John Jay, *The Federalist Papers*, ed. Clinton L. Rossiter (New York: New American Library, 1961), no. 10, 83.
5. *The Federalist Papers*, no. 10.
6. The best statement of the pluralist view is in David Truman, *The Governmental Process* (New York: Knopf, 1951), chap. 2.
7. Martin Gilens and Benjamin I. Page, "Testing Theories of American Politics: Elites, Interest Groups, and Average Citizens," *Perspectives on Politics* 12, no. 3 (Sept. 2014):

564–81; Martin Gilens, *Affluence & Influence: Economic Inequality and Political Power in America* (Princeton, NJ: Princeton University Press, 2012); Benjamin I. Page and Martin Gilens, *Democracy in America? What Has Gone Wrong and What We Can Do about It* (Chicago: University of Chicago Press, 2017).

8. Beth L. Leech, National Survey of Governmental Relations, 2012; Center for Responsive Politics, "Political Action Committees," www.opensecrets.org/pacs/.
9. Megan R. Wilson, "Lobbying's Top 50: Who's Spending Big," The Hill, February 7, 2017, www.thehill.com/business-a-lobbying/business-a-lobbying/318177-lobbyings-top-50-whos-spending-big (accessed 4/5/18).
10. Center for Responsive Politics, "Interest Groups," www.opensecrets.org/industries/ (accessed 11/11/18).
11. Frank Baumgartner et al., *Lobbying and Policy Change: Who Wins, Who Loses, and Why* (Chicago: University of Chicago Press, 2009).
12. Baumgartner et al., *Lobbying and Policy Change.*
13. Erika Falk, Erin Grizard, and Gordon McDonald, "Legislative Issue Advertising in the 108th Congress: Pluralism or Peril?" *Harvard International Journal of Press/Politics* 11, no. 4 (Fall 2006): 148–64.
14. Truman, *Governmental Process.*
15. For an exploration of lower-class interest groups and social movements, see Frances Piven and Richard Cloward, *Poor People's Movements* (New York: Vintage, 1978).
16. E. E. Schattschneider, *The Semisovereign People: A Realist's View of Democracy in America* (New York: Holt, Rinehart and Winston, 1960).
17. The Tax Cuts and Jobs Act: Preliminary Economic Analysis, December 18, 2017, www.taxfoundation.org/tax-cuts-and-jobs-act-preliminary-analysis/ (accessed 4/5/18).
18. Kay Lehman Schlozman and John T. Tierney, *Organized Interests and American Democracy* (New York: Harper and Row, 1986), 60.
19. Clay Shirky, *Here Comes Everybody: The Power of Organizing without Organizations* (New York: Penguin Press, 2008).
20. Mancur Olson, *The Logic of Collective Action* (Cambridge, MA: Harvard University Press, 1965).
21. David Karpf, *The MoveOn Effect: The Unexpected Transformation of American Political Advocacy* (New York: Oxford University Press, 2012).
22. Christine Day, *AARP: America's Largest Interest Group and Its Impact* (Westport, CT: Praeger, 2017).
23. John Herbers, "Special Interests Gaining Power as Voter Disillusionment Grows," *New York Times*, November 14, 1978.
24. Jack Walker, "The Diffusion of Innovations among the American States," *American Political Science Association* 63, no. 3 (1969): 880–99; Thomas Dye, *Understanding Public Policy*, 15th ed. (Boston: Pearson, 2017).
25. Center for Responsive Politics, "Lobbying Database," www.opensecrets.org/lobby/ (accessed 5/15/18).
26. For discussions of lobbying, see Allan J. Cigler and Burdett A. Loomis, eds., *Interest Group Politics* (Washington, DC: CQ Press, 1983). See also Jeffrey M. Berry, *Lobbying for the People* (Princeton, NJ: Princeton University Press, 1977).
27. Marie Jojnacki, "Interest Groups' Decisions to Join Alliances or Work Alone," *American Journal of Political Science* 41 (1997): 61–87; Kevin W. Hula, *Lobbying Together: Interest Groups Coalitions in Legislative Politics* (Washington, DC: Georgetown University Press, 1999).
28. Andrew Chin, "A Case of Insecure Browsing," Newsobserver.com, September 30, 2004, www.unclaw.com/chin/scholarship/nando.pdf (accessed 3/30/16).
29. For an excellent discussion of the political origins of the Administrative Procedure Act, see Martin Shapiro, "APA: Past, Present, Future," *Virginia Law Review* 72, no. 477 (March 1986): 447–92.
30. David Kirkpatrick, "Congress Finds Ways of Avoiding Lobbyist Limits," *Washington Post*, February 11, 2007, 1.
31. *Brown v. Board of Education of Topeka, Kansas*, 347 U.S. 483 (1954).
32. *Obergefell v. Hodges*, 576 U.S. __ (2015).
33. *Roe v. Wade*, 410 U.S. 113 (1973).
34. *Webster v. Reproductive Health Services*, 492 U.S. 490 (1989).
35. E. Pendleton Herring, *Group Representation before Congress* (New York: McGraw-Hill, 1936).
36. National Rifle Association, www.home.nra.org (accessed 5/15/18).
37. Robert Maguire, "Audit Shows NRA Spending Surged $100 Million amidst Pro-Trump Push in 2016," Center for Responsive Politics, November 15, 2017, www.opensecrets.org/news/2017/11/audit-shows-nra-spending-surged-100-million-amidst-pro-trump-push-in-2016/ (accessed 7/27/18).
38. Martin Gilens, *Economic Inequality and Political Power in America* (New York: Oxford University Press, 2012).
39. *Citizens United v. Federal Election Commission*, 558 U.S. __ (2010).
40. Center for Responsive Politics, "Behind the Candidates: Campaign Committees and Outside Groups," www.opensecrets.org/pres16/raised-summ (accessed 4/6/18).
41. Center for Responsive Politics, "2016 Outside Spending, by Super PAC," www.opensecrets.org/outsidespending/summ.php?chrt=V&type=S (accessed 11/10/16).
42. Center for Responsive Politics, "2016 Outside Spending, by Super PAC," www.opensecrets.org/outsidespending/summ.php?chrt=V&type=S (accessed 1/15/18).
43. Center for Responsive Politics, "2018 Outside Spending, by Super PAC," November 8, 2018, www.opensecrets.org/outsidespending/summ.php?chrt=V&type=S (accessed 11/8/18).
44. Elisabeth R. Gerber, *The Populist Paradox* (Princeton, NJ: Princeton University Press, 1999).
45. Gerber, *Populist Paradox.*
46. *The Federalist Papers*, no. 10.
47. Olson, *Logic of Collective Action.*

CHAPTER 12

1. "Small Business Owners Praise GOP Tax Bill," Fox Business, December 20, 2017, www.foxbusiness.com/politics/2017/12/20/small-business-owners-praise-gop-tax-bill.html (accessed 2/3/18).
2. Erin Dooley and Meridith McGraw, "Program That Provides Low-Cost Health Care to 9M Children Set to Expire," ABC News, September 29, 2017, abcnews.go.com/US/program-low-cost-health-care-9m-children-set/story?id=50188069 (accessed 2/4/18).
3. Juliette Cubanski and Tricia Neuman, "The Facts of Medicare Spending and Financing," Kaiser Family Foundation Issue Brief, July 18, 2017, www.kff.org/medicare/issue-brief/the-facts-on-medicare-spending-and-financing/ (accessed 2/4/18).
4. Jennifer E. Manning, *Membership of the 113th Congress: A Profile* (Washington, DC: Congressional Research Service, October 31, 2013), www.senate.gov/CRSReports/crs-publish.cfm?pid=%260BL%2BR%5CC%3F%0A (accessed 12/1/13).
5. "Growing Racial and Ethnic Diversity in Congress," Pew Research Center, January 24, 2017, www.pewresearch.org/fact-tank/2017/01/24/115th-congress-sets-new-high-for-racial-ethnic-diversity/ft_17-01-23_congressdiversity/ (accessed 3/22/18).
6. Manning, *Membership of the 113th Congress.*
7. Jennifer E. Manning, *Membership of the 114th Congress: A Profile* (Washington, DC: Congressional Research Service, June 11, 2015), www.fas.org/sgp/crs/misc/R43869.pdf (accessed 9/14/15).
8. Manning, *Membership of the 113th Congress.*
9. For a discussion, see Benjamin Ginsberg, *The Consequences of Consent* (New York: Random House, 1982), chap. 1.
10. See Kristen D. Burnett, *Congressional Apportionment,* U.S. Census Bureau, November 2011, www.census.gov/prod/cen2010/briefs/c2010br-08.pdf (accessed 1/23/12). For some interesting empirical evidence, see Angus Campbell et al., *Elections and the Political Order* (New York: Wiley, 1966), chap. 11; for more recent considerations about the relationship between members of Congress and their constituents, see Lawrence Jacobs and Robert Y. Shapiro, *Politicians Don't Pander: Political Manipulation and the Loss of Democratic Responsiveness* (Chicago: University of Chicago Press, 2000); and Larry M. Bartels, *Unequal Democracy: The Political Economy of the New Gilded Age* (Princeton, NJ: Princeton University Press, 2008).
11. Norman J. Ornstein et al., *Vital Statistics on Congress* (Washington, DC: Brookings Institution Press, 2017), Tables 5–3 and 5–4, www.brookings.edu/,/media/Research/Files/Reports/2013/07/vital-statistics-congress-mann-ornstein/Vital-Statistics-Full-Data-Set.pdf?la5en (accessed 3/22/18); Norman J. Ornstein, Thomas E. Mann, and Michael J. Malbin, *Vital Statistics on Congress 2008* (Washington, DC: Brookings Institution Press, 2009), 111–12.
12. Ashley Parker, "Spotlighting Constituents to Buoy Congressional Candidates," *New York Times* (October 8, 2014), www.nytimes.com/2014/10/09/us/politics/out-of-the-mouths-of-constituents-candidates-find-a-message.html (accessed 9/14/15); Juana Summers, "Constituent Services Give Voters Something to Remember," National Public Radio, www.npr.org/2014/10/28/359615965/constituent-services-give-voters-something-to-remember (accessed 9/14/15).
13. Linda Fowler and Robert McClure, *Political Ambition: Who Decides to Run for Congress* (New Haven, CT: Yale University Press, 1989); and Alan Ehrenhalt, *The United States of Ambition: Politicians, Power, and the Pursuit of Office* (New York: Three Rivers Press, 1992).
14. Center for Responsive Politics, "Reelection Rates over the Years," www.opensecrets.org/bigpicture/reelect.php (accessed 11/9/18).
15. Author's calculations from Ballotpedia.org
16. Michael Leahy, "House Rules," *Washington Post,* June 10, 2007, W12. Simone Pathé, "Democrats Identify Vulnerable Incumbent Members for 2018," Roll Call, March 6, 2017, www.rollcall.com/politics/democrats-identify-vulnerable-members-2018 (accessed 3/22/18).
17. Barbara C. Burrell, *A Woman's Place Is in the House: Campaigning for Congress in the Feminist Era* (Ann Arbor: University of Michigan Press, 1994); and David Broder, "Key to Women's Political Parity: Running," *Washington Post,* September 8, 1994, A17.
18. Dan Balz, "Dodd, Dorgan, and Ritter to Retire as Democrats Face a Difficult Mid-Term Year," *Washington Post,* January 7, 2010.
19. Mark Hugo Lopez and Paul Taylor, "The 2010 Congressional Reapportionment and Latinos," Pew Research Center, www.pewhispanic.org/2011/01/05/the-2010-congressional-reapportionment-and-latinos/ (accessed 2/24/14).
20. Greg Giroux, "Republicans Win Congress as Democrats Get Most Votes," Bloomberg, March 18, 2013, www.bloomberg.com/news/2013-03-19/republicans-win-congress-as-democrats-get-most-votes.html (accessed 12/2/13).
21. Eric McGhee, "Are the Democrats Still at a Disadvantage in Redistricting?" *The Monkey Cage* (blog), July 9, 2013, themonkeycage.org/2013/07/09/are-the-democrats-still-at-a-disadvantage-in-redistricting/ (accessed 12/2/13).
22. Royce Crocker, *Congressional Redistricting: An Overview* (Washington, DC: Congressional Research Service, November 21, 2012), www.fas.org/sgp/crs/misc/R42831.pdf (accessed 12/2/13).
23. Adam Liptak, "Supreme Court Rebuffs Lawmakers over Independent Redistricting Plan," *New York Times,* June 29, 2015, www.nytimes.com/2015/06/30/us/supreme-court-upholds-creation-of-arizona-redistricting-commission.html?_r50 (accessed 9/14/15).

24. *Gill v. Whitford*, 585 U.S. __ (2018).
25. R. E. Cohen, "Did Redistricting Sink the Democrats?" *National Journal*, December 17, 1994, 2984.
26. *Miller v. Johnson*, 515 U.S. 900 (1995).
27. Bernie Becker, "Reapportionment Roundup," *New York Times*, December 24, 2009, http://thecaucus.blogs.nytimes.com/2009/12/24/reapportionment-roundup/ (accessed 1/31/10).
28. *Shelby County v. Holder*, 570 U.S. __ (2013); L. Paige Whitaker, *Congressional Redistricting and the Voting Rights Act: A Legal Overview* (Washington, DC: Congressional Research Service, August 30, 2013), www.fas.org/sgp/crs/misc/R42482.pdf (accessed 12/2/13).
29. Chris Cillizza, "What the Supreme Court's Voting Rights Act Decision Means for Politics," *Washington Post*, June 25, 2013, www.washingtonpost.com/blogs/the-fix/wp/2013/06/25/what-the-voting-rights-act-decision-means-for-politics/ (accessed 12/2/13).
30. Tarini Parti, "High Court Reasserts Voting Rights Act in Alabama Decision," *Politico*, March 25, 2015, www.politico.com/story/2015/03/supreme-court-alabama-redistricting-ruling-116384 (accessed 9/14/15).
31. Tom Hamburger and Richard Simon, "Everybody Will Know if It's Pork," *Los Angeles Times*, January 6, 2007, A1.
32. Don Seymour, "House Republicans Renew Earmark Ban for 113th Congress," website of the Speaker of the House, November 16, 2012, www.speaker.gov/general/house-republicans-renew-earmark-ban-113th-congress (accessed 12/1/13).
33. Aaron Blake, "Trump Wants to Bring Earmarks Back," *Washington Post*, January 10, 2018, www.washingtonpost.com/news/the-fix/wp/2018/01/10/trump-wants-to-bring-earmarks-back-heres-why-its-not-so-crazy/?utm_term=.5748db2288a1 (accessed 3/22/18).
34. Martin Frost and Tom Davis, "How to Fix What Ails Congress: Bring Back Earmarks," *Los Angeles Times*, February 8, 2015, www.latimes.com/opinion/op-ed/la-oe-frost-earmark-spending-20150209-story.html (accessed 9/14/15).
35. Richard Fenno, Jr., *Home Style: House Members in Their Districts* (Boston: Little, Brown, 1978).
36. Edward Epstein, "Dusting Off Deliberation," *CQ Weekly*, June 14, 2010, 1436–42. Sarah Binder, "Where Have All the Conference Committees Gone?" *The Monkey Cage* (blog), December 21, 2011, themonkeycage.org/blog/2011/12/21/where-have-all-the-conference-committees-gone/ (accessed 2/7/12).
37. Derek Willis, "Republicans Mix It Up When Assigning House Chairmen for the 108th," *Congressional Quarterly Weekly*, January 11, 2003, 89.
38. Rebecca Kimitch, "CQ Guide to the Committees: Democrats Opt to Spread the Power," *Congressional Quarterly Weekly*, April 16, 2007, 1080.
39. Richard E. Cohen, "Crackup of the Committees," *National Journal*, July 31, 1999, 2210–16.
40. See, for example, the announcement of an agreement on the Agricultural Act of 2014, House Committee on Agriculture, "House–Senate Negotiators Announce Bipartisan Agreement on Final Farm Bill," press release, http://agriculture.house.gov/news/documentsingle.aspx?DocumentID51220 (accessed 9/21/15).
41. Norman J. Ornstein, et al., *Vital Statistics on Congress* (Washington, DC: Brookings Institution and American Enterprise Institute, July 2013), chap. 5, www.brookings.edu/research/reports/2013/07/vital-statistics-congress-mann-ornstein (accessed 6/13/16).
42. H.R. 1111: Department of Peacebuilding Act of 2015, govtrack.us, www.govtrack.us/congress/bills/114/hr1111 (accessed 9/21/15).
43. "Statistics and Historical Comparisons: Bills by Final Status," govtrack.us, www.govtrack.us/congress/bills/statistics (accessed 9/21/15).
44. U.S. Senate, "Senate Actions on Cloture Motions," www.senate.gov/pagelayout/reference/cloture_motions/clotureCounts.htm (accessed 11/29/13).
45. Jeremy W. Peters, "Senate Vote Curbs Filibuster Power to Stall Nominees," *New York Times*, November 22, 2013, A1.
46. Jonathan Weisman, "House Votes 411–18 to Pass Ethics Overhaul," *Washington Post*, August 1, 2007, A1.
47. Leigh Munsil, "Graham Won't Lift Nominee-Hold Threat over Benghazi," Politico, November 11, 2013, www.politico.com/blogs/politico-live/2013/11/graham-wont-lift-nomineehold-threat-over-benghazi-177154.html (accessed 11/30/13).
48. Sean Sullivan and Mike DeBonis, "Congress Averts Homeland Security Shutdown with One-Week Extension," *Washington Post*, February 28, 2015, www.washingtonpost.com/politics/house-gop-hopes-to-pass-stopgap-dhs-funding-before-midnight-shutdown/2015/02/27/22021530-be88-11e4-b274-e5209a3bc9a9_story.html (accessed 9/21/15).
49. John W. Kingdon, *Congressmen's Voting Decisions* (New York: Harper and Row, 1973), chap. 3; and R. Douglas Arnold, *The Logic of Congressional Action* (New Haven, CT: Yale University Press, 1990).
50. Ben Jacobs and David Smith, "Donald Trump Blames Democrats for Stunning Failure to Repeal Obamacare," *Guardian*, March 25, 2017, www.theguardian.com/us-news/2017/mar/24/republican-healthcare-plan-bill-vote-pulled-obamacare-trump (accessed 3/22/18).
51. Jane Fritsch, "The Grass Roots, Just a Free Phone Call Away," *New York Times*, June 23, 1995, A1.
52. Eric Lipton and Ben Protess, "Banks' Lobbyists Help in Drafting Financial Bills," *New York Times*, May 23, 2013, dealbook.nytimes.com/2013/05/23/banks-lobbyists-help-in-drafting-financial-bills/ (accessed 9/21/15); Michael Corkery, "Citigroup Becomes the Fall Guy in the Spending Bill Battle" *New York Times*, December 12, 2014, dealbook.nytimes.com/2014/12/12/citigroup-becomes-the-fall-guy-in-the-spending-bill-battle/ (accessed 9/21/15).

53. Eliza Newlin Carney, "For Ethics Hawks, Congress Could Be Next," *National Journal Online*, February 17, 2009, http://freerepublic.com/focus/f-new/2187821/posts (accessed 2/5/10); Center for Responsive Politics, "Top Individual Contributors: All Federal Contributions (2018)," OpenSecrets, www.opensecrets.org/overview/topindivs.php (accessed 10/12/18).
54. Holly Idelson, "Signs Point to Greater Loyalty on Both Sides of the Aisle," *Congressional Quarterly Weekly Report*, December 19, 1992, 3849.
55. Norman J. Ornstein and Thomas E. Mann, *Vital Statistics on Congress* (Washington DC: Brookings Institution, 2018), www.brookings.edu/multi-chapter-report/vital-statistics-on-congress/ (accessed 7/25/18).
56. Center for Responsive Politics, "Contributions to Federal Candidates, 2016," www.opensecrets.org/pacs/pacgot.php?cmte=C00525600&cycle=2016 (accessed 10/13/16).
57. Kimitch, "CQ Guide to the Committees," 1080.
58. Leahy, "House Rules," W12; Marin Cogan, "Freshmen Jump Line for Floor Speeches," *Politico*, January 18, 2011, www.politico.com/news/stories/0111/47791.html (accessed 2/9/12).
59. Daniel Newhauser, "Three Booted from GOP Whip Team as Leaders Crack Down," *National Journal*, June 16, 2015, www.nationaljournal.com/congress/2015/06/16/Three-Booted-From-GOP-Whip-Team-Leaders-Crack-Down (accessed 9/21/15).
60. James J. Kilpatrick, "Don't Overlook Corn for Porn Plot," *Chicago Sun-Times*, January 3, 1992, 23.
61. Dennis McDougal, "Cattle Are Bargaining Chip of the NEA," *Los Angeles Times*, November 2, 1991, F1.
62. Mann and Ornstein, "Vital Statistics," 2017, Table 6-4.
63. "115th Congress (2017–2018)," www.congress.gov (accessed 11/9/18).
64. Thomas Kaplan, "Congress Approves $1.3 Trillion Spending Bill, Averting a Shutdown," *New York Times*, March 22, 2018, www.nytimes.com/2018/03/22/us/politics/house-passes-spending-bill.html?login=email&auth=login-email (accessed 7/30/18).
65. Geoffrey C. Layman, Thomas M. Carsey, and Juliana Menasce Horowitz, "Party Polarization in American Politics: Characteristics, Causes, and Consequences," *Annual Review of Political Science*, no. 9 (2006): 83–110.
66. For example, Fredreka Schouten, "Club for Growth Plans New Push in House Races," *USA Today*, August 17, 2015, http://onpolitics.usatoday.com/2015/08/17/club-for-growth-plans-new-push-in-house-races/ (accessed 9/21/15).
67. Elizabeth Williamson, "Revival of Oversight Role Sought; Congress Hires More Investigators, Plans Subpoenas," *Washington Post*, April 25, 2007, A1.
68. Susan Milligan, "Congress Reduces Its Oversight Role; Since Clinton, a Change in Focus," *Boston Globe*, November 20, 2005, A1; Bill Shaikin, "Clemens Is Star Attraction at Hearing," *Los Angeles Times*, February 12, 2008, D1.
69. Eric Lipton and Sheryl Gay Stolberg, "Health Law Rollout Provides Rich Target for Oversight Chief," *New York Times*, November 12, 2013, www.nytimes.com/2013/11/13/us/politics/health-law-rollout-provides-rich-target-for-oversight-chief.html?_r50 (accessed 12/12/13).
70. Michael S. Schmidt and Maggie Haberman, "Aides for Hillary Clinton and Benghazi Committee Dispute Testimony Plan," *New York Times*, July 25, 2015, www.nytimes.com/2015/07/26/us/clinton-to-testify-publicly-before-house-committee-investigating-benghazi-attacks.html (accessed 9/21/15).
71. Gregory Krieg, "FBI Boss Comey's 7 Most Damning Lines on Clinton," CNN, July 5, 2016, www.cnn.com/2016/07/05/politics/fbi-clinton-email-server-comey-damning-lines/ (accessed 9/21/16).
72. *United States v. Pink*, 315 U.S. 203 (1942). For a good discussion of the problem, see James W. Davis, *The American Presidency* (New York: Harper and Row, 1987), chap. 8.
73. U.S. House, "Impeachment," http://history.house.gov/Institution/Origins-Development/Impeachment/ (accessed 4/18/14).
74. Carroll J. Doherty, "Impeachment: How It Would Work," *Congressional Quarterly Weekly Report*, January 31, 1998, 222.

CHAPTER 13

1. This account is drawn from Amy Nixon, "Community Raises Funds to Support Hartley Family after Son Dies in Work Accident," *Tennessean*, May 4, 2017, www.tennessean.com/story/news/local/cheatham/2017/05/04/community-raises-funds-support-hartley-family-after-son-dies-work-accident/101283588/ (accessed 3/2/18); Eric Lipton, "Why Has the E.P.A. Shifted on Toxic Chemicals? An Industry Insider Helps Call the Shots," *New York Times*, October 21, 2017, www.nytimes.com/2017/10/21/us/trump-epa-chemicals-regulations.html (accessed 3/2/18); and Jamie Smith Hopkins, "EPA Wants to Restrict Sometimes-Deadly Paint Stripped Chemical," The Center for Public Integrity, January 12, 2017, www.publicintegrity.org/2017/01/12/20589/epa-wants-restrict-sometimes-deadly-paint-stripper-chemical (accessed 3/2/18).
2. These statutes are contained mainly in Title 10 of the U.S. Code, Sections 331, 332, and 333.
3. The best study covering all aspects of the domestic use of the military is that of Adam Yarmolinsky, *The Military Establishment* (New York: Harper and Row, 1971). Probably the most famous instance of a president's unilateral use of the power to protect a state "against domestic violence" was President Grover Cleveland's dealing with the Pullman strike of 1894. The famous Supreme Court case that ensued was *In re Debs*, 158 U.S. 564 (1895).
4. In *United States v. Pink*, 315 U.S. 203 (1942), the Supreme Court confirmed that an executive agreement is the legal equivalent of a treaty, despite the absence of Senate

approval. This case approved the executive agreement that was used to establish diplomatic relations with the Soviet Union in 1933. An executive agreement, not a treaty, was used in 1940 to exchange "fifty over-age destroyers" for 99-year leases on some important military bases.

5. *United States v. Nixon*, 418 U.S. 683 (1974).
6. For a different perspective, see William F. Grover, *The President as Prisoner: A Structural Critique of the Carter and Reagan Years* (Albany: State University of New York Press, 1988).
7. A third source of presidential power is implied from the provision for "faithful execution of the laws." This is the president's power to impound funds—that is, to refuse to spend money Congress has appropriated for certain purposes. One author referred to this as a "retroactive veto power" (Robert E. Goostree, "The Power of the President to Impound Appropriated Funds," *American University Law Review* 11 [January 1962]: 32–47). This impoundment power has been used freely and to considerable effect by many modern presidents, and Congress has occasionally delegated such power to the president by statute. But in reaction to the Watergate scandal, Congress adopted the Congressional Budget and Impoundment Control Act of 1974, which was designed to circumscribe the president's ability to impound funds by requiring that the president must spend all appropriated funds unless both houses of Congress consented to an impoundment within 45 days of a presidential request. Therefore, since 1974, the use of impoundment has declined significantly. Presidents have had either to bite their tongues and accept unwanted appropriations or to revert to the older and more dependable but politically limited method of vetoing the entire bill.
8. For more on the veto, see Robert J. Spitzer, *The Presidential Veto: Touchstone of the American Presidency* (Albany: State University of New York Press, 1989).
9. Dan Eggen, "Bush Announces Veto of Waterboarding Ban," *Washington Post*, March 8, 2008, www.washingtonpost.com/wp-dyn/content/article/2008/03/08AR2008030800304.html (accessed 6/10/10).
10. *Myers v. United States*, 272 U.S. 52 (1926). In the later case of *Humphrey's Executor v. United States*, 295 U.S. 602 (1935), the Court ruled that the executives of independent commissions could only be removed for cause.
11. John Yoo, *The Powers of War and Peace* (Chicago: University of Chicago Press, 2003). See also Dana D. Nelson, "The 'Unitary Executive' Question," *Los Angeles Times*, October 11, 2008, www.latimes.com/opinion/la-oe-nelson11-2008oct11-story.html (accessed 4/20/18).
12. See Eric Posner and Adrian Vermeule, *The Executive Unbound: After the Madisonian Republic* (Chicago: University of Chicago Press, 2011).
13. "Unchecked Abuse," *Washington Post*, January 11, 2006, www.washingtonpost.com/wp-dyn/content/article/2006/01/10/AR2006011001536.html (accessed 3/25/18).
14. Elena Kagan, "Presidential Administration," *Harvard Law Review* 114 (June 2001): 2262.
15. Kenneth F. Warren, *Administrative Law*, 3rd ed. (Upper Saddle River, NJ: Prentice-Hall, 1996), 250.
16. National Industrial Recovery Act, 48 Stat. 200 (1933).
17. Theodore J. Lowi, *The End of Liberalism*, 2nd ed. (New York: W. W. Norton, 1979), 117.
18. Jerry L. Nashaw, *Greed, Chaos, and Governance: Using Public Choice to Improve Public Law* (New Haven, CT: Yale University Press, 1997), 106.
19. Louis Fisher, "The Unitary Executive and Inherent Executive Power," *Journal of Constitutional Law*, 12, no. 1 (February 2010): 586.
20. 10 Annals of Cong. 613 (1800).
21. Louis Fisher, "Presidential Inherent Power: The 'Sole Organ' Doctrine," *Presidential Studies Quarterly* 37, no.1 (March 2007): 139.
22. *United States v. Curtiss-Wright Corp.*, 299 U.S. 304 (1936).
23. Clement Fatovic, *Outside the Law: Emergency and Executive Power* (Baltimore: Johns Hopkins University Press, 2009).
24. Louis Fisher, "Invoking Inherent Powers."
25. John Gramlich, "Holder Sees Constitutional Basis for Obama's Executive Actions," *Roll Call*, January 29, 2014, www.rollcall.com/news/holder_sees_constitutional_basis_for_obamas_executive_actions-230528-1.html?pg=1 (accessed 4/20/18).
26. Harold C. Relyea, "National Emergency Powers," Congressional Research Service, 2007, http://fas.org/sgp/crs/natsec/98-505.pdf (accessed 3/27/18).
27. Matthew Crenson and Benjamin Ginsberg, *Presidential Power: Unchecked and Unbalanced*, New York: W. W. Norton, 2007, pp. 341–342.
28. Andrew Reeves, "Political Disaster: Unilateral Powers, Electoral Incentives, and Presidential Disaster Declarations," *Journal of Politics* 73, no. 4 (October 2011): 1142–51.
29. William G. Howell and David E. Lewis, "Agencies by Presidential Design," *Journal of Politics* 64, no. 4 (November 2002): 1095–114.
30. A substantial portion of this section is taken from Theodore J. Lowi, *The Personal President* (Ithaca, NY: Cornell University Press, 1985), 141–50.
31. The actual number is difficult to estimate because, as with White House staff, some EOP personnel, especially in national security work, are detailed to the EOP from outside agencies.
32. Article I, Section 3, provides that "The Vice-President . . . shall be President of the Senate, but shall have no Vote, unless they be equally divided." This is the only vote the vice president is allowed.
33. Samuel Kernell, *Going Public: New Strategies of Presidential Leadership*, 3rd ed. (Washington, DC: CQ Press, 1997); also Jeffrey K. Tulis, *The Rhetorical Presidency* (Princeton, NJ: Princeton University Press, 1987).
34. Tulis, *Rhetorical Presidency*, 91.

35. Sidney M. Milkis, *The President and the Parties* (New York: Oxford University Press, 1993), 97.
36. James MacGregor Burns, *Roosevelt: The Lion and the Fox* (New York: Harcourt, Brace, 1956), 317.
37. Burns, *Roosevelt*, 317.
38. Kernell, *Going Public*, 79.
39. Claire Cain Miller, "How Obama's Internet Campaign Changed Politics," *New York Times*, November 7, 2008, bits.blogs.nytimes.com/2008/11/07/how-obamas-internet-campaign-changed-politics/?_php5true&_type5blogs&_r5o (accessed 4/7/14); David Plouffe, *The Audacity to Win: The Inside Story and Lessons of Barack Obama's Historic Victory* (New York: Viking, 2009).
40. "Presidential Job Approval Center," Gallup, www.gallup.com/poll/124922/presidential-approval-center.aspx (accessed 3/14/14).
41. Lowi, *Personal President*.
42. Lowi, *Personal President*, 11.
43. Gallup, "Trump Job Approval (Weekly)," July 22, 2018, https://news.gallup.com/poll/203207/trump-job-approval-weekly.aspx (accessed 7/27/18).
44. Milkis, *President and the Parties*, 128.
45. Milkis, *President and the Parties*, 160.
46. Kagan, "Presidential Administration," 2265.
47. John M. Broder, "Powerful Shaper of U.S. Rules Quits, with Critics in Wake," *New York Times*, August 4, 2012, A1.
48. Nadja Popovich, "67 Environmental Rules on the Way Out under Trump," *New York Times*, January 31, 2018, www.nytimes.com/interactive/2017/10/05/climate/trump-environment-rules-reversed.html (accessed 2/20/18).
49. Terry M. Moe and William G. Howell, "The Presidential Power of Unilateral Action," *Journal of Law, Economics and Organization* 15, no. 1 (January 1999): 133–34.
50. Todd F. Gaziano, "The Uses and Abuses of Executive Orders and Other Presidential Directives," *Texas Review of Law and Politics* 5 (Spring 2001): 267–315.
51. Kenneth R. Mayer, *With the Stroke of a Pen: Executive Orders and Presidential Power* (Princeton, NJ: Princeton University Press, 2001), 71–73.
52. Harold C. Relyea, "Presidential Directives: Background and Overview," Congressional Research Service, November 26, 2008, http://fas.org/sgp/crs/misc/98-611.pdf (accessed 3/25/18).
53. Vivian S. Chu and Ted Garvey, "Executive Orders: Issuance, Modification, and Revocation," Congressional Research Service, April 16, 2014, http://fas.org/sgp/crs/misc/RS20846.pdf (accessed 3/25/18).
54. Adam L. Warber, *Executive Orders and the Modern Presidency* (Boulder, CO: Lynne Rienner Publishers, 2006), 118–120.
55. Chu and Garvey, "Executive Orders."
56. Chu and Garvey, "Executive Orders," 10.
57. *Dames & Moore v. Regan*, 453 U.S. 654 (1981).
58. Philip Cooper, *By Order of the President* (Lawrence: University Press of Kansas, 2002), 201.
59. Edward S. Corwin, *The President: Office and Powers*, 5th ed. (New York: NYU Press, 1984), 283.
60. Alexander Hamilton, James Madison, and John Jay, *The Federalist Papers*, ed. Clinton Rossiter (New York: New American Library, 1961), no. 70, 423–30.
61. Terry Moe, "The Presidency and the Bureaucracy: The Presidential Advantage," in *The Presidency and the Political System*, ed. Michael Nelson (Washington, DC: CQ Press, 2002), 416–20.
62. Louis Fisher, *Congressional Abdication on War and Spending* (College Station: Texas A&M Press, 2000).
63. Letter from Thomas Jefferson to James Madison (September 6, 1789), in *The Papers of Thomas Jefferson*, ed. Julian P. Boyd (Princeton, NJ: Princeton University Press, 1958), 392, 397.

CHAPTER 14

1. This account draws from Abby Goodnough, Monica Davey, and Mitch Smith, "When the Water Turned Brown," *New York Times*, January 23, 2016; Amy Davidson, "The Contempt That Poisoned Flint's Water," *The New Yorker*, January 22, 2016; and Lindsey Smith, "This Mom Helped Uncover What Was Really Going on With Flint's Water," Michigan Public Radio, December 4, 2015, michiganradio.org/post/mom-helped-uncover-what-was-really-going-flint-s-water (accessed 8/11/17).
2. Flint Water Advisory Task Force, Final Report, March 2016, www.michigan.gov/documents/snyder/FWATF_FINAL_REPORT_21March2016_517805_7.pdf (accessed 8/11/17).
3. Amy B. Zegart, *Spying Blind: The CIA, The FBI, and the Origins of 9/11* (Princeton, NJ: Princeton University Press, 2009).
4. Paul C. Light, "A Cascade of Failures: Why Government Fails, and How to Stop It," Brookings Institution, July 14, 2014, www.brookings.edu/research/a-cascade-of-failures-why-government-fails-and-how-to-stop-it/ (accessed 8/5/17).
5. Environmental Protection Agency, "Regulations and Standards: Light Duty," www3.epa.gov/otaq/climate/regs-light-duty.htm#new1 (accessed 7/9/16).
6. Lisa Friedman and Brad Plumer, "E.P.A. Announces Repeal of Major Obama-Era Carbon Emissions Rule," *New York Times*, October 9, 2017, www.nytimes.com/2017/10/09/climate/clean-power-plan.html (accessed 10/24/17).
7. Thanks to Andy Rudalevige for this formulation.
8. Juliet Eilperin, "EPA Needed More Data before Ruling on Greenhouse Gas Emissions, Report Says," *Washington Post*, September 28, 2011, www.washingtonpost.com/national/health-science/epa-needed-more-data-before-ruling-on-greenhouse-gas-emissions-report-says/2011/09/28/gIQABs2X5K_story.html (accessed 1/2/12).

9. Margaret Cronin Fisk, Kartikay Mehrotra, Alan Katz, and Jeff Plungis, "Volkswagen Agrees to $15 Billion Diesel-Cheating Settlement," Bloomberg News, June 28, 2016, www.bloomberg.com/news/articles/2016-06-28/volkswagen-to-pay-14-7-billion-to-settle-u-s-emissions-claims (accessed 7/8/16).
10. Gary Bryner, *Bureaucratic Discretion* (New York: Pergamon Press, 1987).
11. "Federal Employees by State," *Governing,* www.governing.com/gov-data/federal-employees-workforce-numbers-by-state.html (accessed 8/10/17).
12. Congressional Budget Office, "Comparing the Compensation of Federal and Private-Sector Employees, 2011–2015," April 2017, www.cbo.gov/system/files/115th-congress-2017-2018/reports/52637-federalprivatepay.pdf (accessed 12/20/17).
13. U.S. Office of Personnel Management, "Women in Federal Service," www.fedview.opm.gov/2014files/2014_Womens_Report.pdf (accessed 8/10/17); Office of Personnel Management, "Profile of Federal Civilian Non-Postal Employees," September 30, 2017, www.opm.gov/policy-data-oversight/data-analysis-documentation/federal-employment-reports/reports-publications/profile-of-federal-civilian-non-postal-employees/ (accessed 10/13/18).
14. The President's Budget FY18, Analytical Perspectives, www.whitehouse.gov/omb/budget (accessed 8/10/17).
15. President Barack Obama, First Inaugural Address, January 21, 2009, https://obamawhitehouse.archives.gov/blog/2009/01/21/president-barack-obamas-inaugural-address (accessed 8/5/17).
16. Office of Personnel Management, "Federal Civilian Employment," September 2017, www.opm.gov/policy-data-oversight/data-analysis-documentation/federal-employment-reports/reports-publications/federal-civilian-employment/ (accessed 10/13/18); George M. Reynolds and Amanda Shendruk, "Demographics of the U.S. Military," Council on Foreign Relations, April 24, 2018, www.cfr.org/article/demographics-us-military (accessed 10/13/18).
17. Bureau of Labor Statistics, Current Employment Statistics, "Table B-1. Employees on Nonfarm Payrolls by Industry Sector and Selected Industry Detail," www.bls.gov/webapps/legacy/cesbtab1.htm (accessed 7/15/16).
18. There are historical reasons that American Cabinet-level administrators are called "secretaries." During the Second Continental Congress and the subsequent confederal government, standing committees were formed to deal with executive functions related to foreign affairs, military and maritime issues, and public financing. The heads of those committees were called "secretaries" because their primary task was to handle all correspondence and documentation related to their areas of responsibility.
19. Lauren Camera, "DeVos Outlines Vision for 'American Education,'" *U.S. News and World Report,* October 11, 2017, www.usnews.com/news/education-news/articles/2017-10-11/betsy-devos-outlines-vision-for-american-education (accessed 12/20/17).
20. Morgan Chalfant, "Homeland Security Sees Power Grow under Trump," The Hill, October 19, 2017, http://thehill.com/policy/national-security/356131-homeland-security-sees-power-grow-under-trump (accessed 11/10/17); Department of Homeland Security, "Budget Will Advance DHS Priorities," February 12, 2018, www.dhs.gov/news/2018/02/12/department-homeland-security-statement-president-s-fiscal-year-2019-budget (accessed 10/13/18).
21. Laura Koran, Elise Labott, and Nicole Gaouette, "Tillerson Visits Russia as Tensions over Syria Flare," CNN.com, April 11, 2017, www.cnn.com/2017/04/11/politics/rex-tillerson-putin-russia-g7/index.html (accessed 8/11/17).
22. U.S. Department of State, "Department Organization Chart: November 2016," www.state.gov/r/pa/ei/rls/dos/99484.htm (accessed 8/5/17); Robbie Gramer, "Lawmakers Slam Tillerson's Bungled State Department Reforms," *Foreign Policy,* November 15, 2017, http://foreignpolicy.com/2017/11/15/lawmakers-slam-tillersons-bungled-state-department-reforms-diplomacy-foreign-service-trump-administration-redesign-congress-corker-cardin/ (accessed 1/5/18).
23. For more details, consult John E. Harr, *The Professional Diplomat* (Princeton, NJ: Princeton University Press, 1972), 11; and Nicholas Horrock, "The CIA Has Neighbors in the 'Intelligence Community,'" *New York Times,* June 29, 1975, sec. 4, 2. See also Morton H. Halperin and Priscilla Clapp, *Bureaucratic Politics and Foreign Policy,* 2nd ed., with Arnold Kanter (Washington, DC: Brookings Institution Press, 2007).
24. In 2017 the Department of Defense had over 1.3 million active duty personnel and nearly 750,000 civilian employees. U.S. Department of Defense, "About the Department of Defense," www.defense.gov/About/ (accessed 12/20/17).
25. Congressional Research Service, "Defense Primer: The Department of Defense," December 13, 2016, https://fas.org/sgp/crs/natsec/IF10543.pdf (accessed 8/10/17).
26. The 5 percent reduction is compared to a 2012 baseline. Congressional Budget Office, "The U.S. Military's Force Structure: A Primer," July 29, 2016, www.cbo.gov/publication/51535 (accessed 8/10/17).
27. Louise Osborne, "Europeans Outraged over NSA Spying, Threaten Action," *USA Today,* October 29, 2013, www.usatoday.com/story/news/world/2013/10/28/report-nsa-spain/3284609/ (accessed 1/24/14).
28. Warren Strobel and Mark Hosenball, "White House Review Panel Proposes Curbs on Some NSA Programs," Reuters, December 18, 2013, www.reuters.com/article/2013/12/18/us-usa-surveillance-obama-idUSBRE9BG1AQ20131218 (accessed 1/24/14).
29. David Cole, "Here's What's Wrong with the USA Freedom Act," *The Nation,* May 6, 2015, www.thenation

.com/article/heres-whats-wrong-usa-freedom-act/ (accessed11/10/17).

30. U.S. Department of the Treasury, "The Debt to the Penny and Who Holds It," www.treasurydirect.gov/NP/debt/current (accessed 3/27/18).
31. Financial Stability Oversight Council, "Designations," www.treasury.gov/initiatives/fsoc/designations/Pages/default.aspx (accessed 1/23/14).
32. Lisa Rein, "IRS Conference in Anaheim Featured Gifts, Other Excesses Approved by Top Officials, Report Says," *Washington Post*, June, 6, 2013, www.washingtonpost.com/blogs/federal-eye/wp/2013/06/04/irs-conference-in-anaheim-featured-gifts-other-excesses-approved-by-top-officials-report-says/ (accessed 1/31/14).
33. Alan Rappeport, "Under Trump, An Already Depleted I.R.S. Could Face Deep Cuts," *New York Times* March 2, 2017, www.nytimes.com/2017/03/02/us/politics/trump-mnuchin-irs.html (accessed 8/5/17); Joe Davidson, "IRS Chief Says Trump's Budget Would Sharply Cut Taxpayer Service," *Washington Post*, June 1, 2018, www.washingtonpost.com/news/powerpost/wp/2018/06/01/irs-chief-says-trumps-budget-would-sharply-cut-taxpayer-service/?utm_term=.5c64e7ca25e9 (accessed 10/13/18).
34. U.S. Department of Health and Human Services, Office of the Inspector General, "CMS Management of the Federal Marketplace: A Case Study," February 2016, https://oig.hhs.gov/oei/reports/oei-06-14-00350.pdf (accessed 8/6/17).
35. U.S. Department of Veterans Affairs, "Veterans Access, Choice, and Accountability Act of 2014 Fact Sheet," www.va.gov/opa/choiceact/documents/choice-act-summary.pdf (accessed 8/6/17).
36. Vice President Gore's National Partnership for Reinventing Government, "Appendix F, History of the National Partnership for Reinventing Government: Accomplishments, 1993–2000, A Summary," http://govinfo.library.unt.edu/npr/whoweare/appendixf.html (accessed 3/28/08).
37. Social and Behavioral Sciences Team 2016 Annual Report, September 2016, https://sbst.gov/download/2016%20SBST%20Annual%20Report.pdf (accessed 8/6/17).
38. Andy Rudalevige, "Trump Wants to Reorganize the Executive Branch. Good Luck with That." *The Monkey Cage* (blog), March 16, 2017, www.washingtonpost.com/news/monkey-cage/wp/2017/03/16/trump-wants-to-reorganize-the-executive-branch-good-luck-to-him/?utm_term=.8b1417c138a2 (accessed 8/6/17).
39. Mick Mulvaney, Office of Management and Budget, "Comprehensive Plan for Reforming the Federal Government and Reducing the Federal Civilian Workforce" memorandum, April 12, 2017, www.whitehouse.gov/sites/whitehouse.gov/files/omb/memoranda/2017/M-17-22.pdf (accessed 8/6/17); Eric Katz, "Transferring Responsibility and Consolidating Offices Highlight Trump Reorganization Plan," Government Executive, February 12, 2018, www.govexec.com/management/2018/02/transferring-responsibilities-and-consolidating-offices-highlight-trump-reorganization-plan/145936/ (accessed 3/27/18).
40. Nicole Ogrysko, "Omnibus Spending Bill Complicates Administration's Reorg Plans," Federal News Radio, March 22, 2018, https://federalnewsradio.com/budget/2018/03/omnibus-complicates-administrations-reorganization-plans-as-congress-begins-votes/ (accessed 3/27/18).
41. Public Law 101-510, Title XXIX, Sections 2,901 and 2,902 of Part A (Defense Base Closure and Realignment Commission); see the 2005 commission's website, Defense Base Closure and Realignment Commission, www.brac.gov (accessed 1/3/12).
42. Walter Pincus, "For Pentagon, It's Always a Tough Battle to Get Congress to Close Military Bases, Facilities," *Washington Post*, March 17, 2014, www.washingtonpost.com/world/national-security/for-pentagon-its-always-a-tough-battle-to-get-congress-to-close-military-bases-facilities/2014/03/17/a7eda064-a887-11e3-8599-ce7295b6851c_story.html (accessed 9/30/15).
43. Dylan Mathews, "Everything You Could Possibly Need to Know," *Washington Post,* February 20, 2013, www.washingtonpost.com/news/wonk/wp/2013/02/20/the-sequester-absolutely-everything-you-could-possibly-need-to-know-in-one-faq/?utm_term=.6785d26f55af (accessed 8/6/17).
44. Eric Katz, "Social Security Offers Nearly Its Entire Workforce Early Retirement," *Government Executive,* August 4, 2017, http://m.govexec.com/pay-benefits/2017/08/social-security-has-sent-early-out-offers-nearly-its-entire-workforce/140008/?oref=govexec_today_pm_nl (accessed 8/11/17); Louis Jacobson, "Taking the Measure of the Federal Workforce under Donald Trump," Politifact, January 22, 2018, www.politifact.com/truth-o-meter/article/2018/jan/22/taking-measure-federal-workforce/ (accessed 3/27/18).
45. Lenny Bernstein, "Arizona Becomes Last State to Provide Health Insurance to Low-Income Children," *Washington Post,* July 25, 2016, www.washingtonpost.com/news/to-your-health/wp/2016/07/25/arizona-becomes-the-last-state-to-provide-health-insurance-to-low-income-children/?utm_term=.8c9293c169f2 (accessed 8/5/17).
46. Sheila R. Zedlewski, Pamela J. Loprest, and Erika Huber, "What Role Is Welfare Playing in This Period of High Unemployment?" Urban Institute, Fact Sheet 3, August 17, 2011, www.urban.org/UploadedPDF/412378-Role-of-Welfare-in-this-Period-of-High-Unemployment.pdf (accessed 7/4/12).
47. Sabrina Tavernise, "Food Stamps Helped Reduce Poverty Rate, Study Says," *New York Times*, April 10, 2012, A16.
48. John J. DiIulio, Jr., *Bring Back the Bureaucrats: Why More Federal Workers Will Lead to Better (and Smaller!) Government* (West Conshohocken, PA: Templeton Press, 2014); Kimberly J. Morgan and Andrea Louise Campbell, *The Delegated Welfare State* (New York: Oxford University Press, 2011).

49. Paul C. Light, "The New True Size of Government," Organizational Performance Initiative, Research Brief no. 2, Wagner School of Public Service, New York University, 8, https://wagner.nyu.edu/files/performance/True%20Size%20Research%20Brief.pdf (accessed 3/11/08); OMB Watch, "Total Spending by Year," FedSpending.org, www.fedspending.org/fpds/chart_total.php (accessed 1/2/12).
50. Scott Shane and Ron Nixon, "In Washington, Contractors Take On Biggest Role Ever," *New York Times*, February 4, 2007, A1.
51. Daniel Patrick Moynihan, "The Culture of Secrecy," *Public Interest* (Summer 1997): 55–71.
52. Thomas E. Mann and Norman J. Ornstein, *The Broken Branch: How Congress Is Failing America and How to Get It Back on Track* (New York: Oxford University Press, 2006), 155.
53. For the estimates on waste, see Commission on Wartime Contracting in Iraq and Afghanistan, *Transforming Wartime Contracting: Controlling Costs, Reducing Risks: Final Report to Congress*, 18, August 2011, www.wartimecontracting.gov (accessed 1/4/12).
54. Neil Gordon, "Move over FCMD, Make Way for FAPIIS," *POGO* (blog), September 11, 2009, http://pogoblog.typepad.com/pogo/2009/09/move-over-fcmd-make-way-for-fapiis.html (accessed 2/26/10).
55. Government Accountability Office, *Federal Contractors: Better Performance Information Needed to Support Agency Contract Award Decisions*, April 2009, GAO-09-374, www.gao.gov/new.items/d09374.pdf (accessed 2/26/10); Tom Lee, "FAPIIS May Be the Worst Government Website We've Ever Seen," Sunlight Foundation, April 19, 2011, sunlightfoundation.com/blog/2011/04/19/fapiis-may-be-the-worst-government-website-weve-ever-seen/ (accessed 1/23/14).
56. Joe Davidson, "OMB Moves to Cut Outside Contractors," Federal Diary, *Washington Post*, July 29, 2009, www.washingtonpost.com/wp-dyn/content/article/2009/07/28/AR2009072802812.html (accessed 2/18/10).
57. Joe Davidson, "Deficit-Cutters Must Also Weigh the Cost of Contractors," Federal Diary, *Washington Post*, February 4, 2011, www.washingtonpost.com/wp-dyn/content/article/2011/02/03/AR2011020306809.html?nav5emailpage (accessed 1/2/12).
58. Charlie Savage, "U.S. to Phase Out Use of Private Prisons for Federal Inmates," *New York Times*, August 18, 2016, www.nytimes.com/2016/08/19/us/us-to-phase-out-use-of-private-prisons-for-federal-inmates.html?_r=0 (accessed 11/8/17).
59. Marjorie Censer, "Five Provisions in the New Defense Policy Legislation for Contractors to Watch," *Washington Post*, January 5, 2014, www.washingtonpost.com/business/capitalbusiness/five-provisions-in-the-new-defense-policy-legislation-for-contractors-to-watch/2014/01/0/f6d-d00ec-6c10-11e3-a523-fe73f0ff6b8d_story.html (accessed 1/24/14).
60. Dan Egan, "Democrats Proposing New Limits on Corporate Campaign Donations," *Boston Globe*, February 12, 2010, www.boston.com/news/nation/washington/articles/2010/02/12/democrats_proposing_new_limits_on_corporate_campaign_donations/ (accessed 2/27/10).
61. Peter Baker, "Obama Orders Federal Contractors to Provide Workers Paid Sick Leave," *New York Times*, September 7, 2015, www.nytimes.com/2015/09/08/us/politics/obama-to-require-federal-contractors-to-provide-paid-sick-leave.html?_r50 (accessed 9/30/15).
62. Gregory Korte, "Trump Signs Four Bills to Roll Back Obama-Era Regulations," *USA Today*, March 27, 2017, www.usatoday.com/story/news/politics/2017/03/27/trump-signs-four-bills-roll-back-obama-era-regulations/99690456/ (accessed 11/8/17).
63. The title of this section was inspired by Peri Arnold, *Making the Managerial Presidency* (Princeton, NJ: Princeton University Press, 1986).
64. Daniel P. Gitterman, *Calling the Shots: The President, Executive Orders, and Public Policy* (Washington, DC: Brookings Institution Press, 2017).
65. Paul C. Light, *A Government Ill Executed: The Decline of the Federal Service and How To Revive It* (Cambridge, MA: Harvard University Press, 2008).
66. For more details and evaluations, see David Rosenbloom, *Public Administration* (New York: Random House, 1986), 186–221; Charles H. Levine, *The Quiet Crisis of the Civil Service: The Federal Personnel System at the Crossroads*, with the assistance of Rosslyn S. Kleeman (Washington, DC: National Academy of Public Administration, 1986).
67. John Micklethwait, "Managing to Look Attractive," *New Statesman* 125, November 8, 1996, 24.
68. Robert M. Gates, *Duty: Memoirs of a Secretary at War* (New York: Alfred A. Knopf, 2014); Leon Panetta, *Worthy Fights: A Memoir of Leadership in War and Peace* (New York: Penguin, 2014).
69. Michael J. Glennon, *National Security and Double Government* (New York: Oxford University Press, 2015).
70. Michael Crowley, "The Deep State Is Real. But It Might Not Be What You Think," *Politico Magazine*, September/October 2017, www.politico.com/magazine/story/2017/09/05/deep-state-real-cia-fbi-intelligence-215537 (accessed 11/10/17).
71. David Epstein and Sharyn O'Halloran, *Delegating Powers: A Transaction Cost Politics Approach to Policymaking under Separate Powers* (Cambridge: Cambridge University Press, 1999).
72. Robert J. McGrath, "Congressional Oversight Hearings and Policy Control," *Legislative Studies Quarterly* 38, no. 3 (2013): 349–76.
73. Mann and Ornstein, *The Broken Branch*.
74. Linette Lopez and Lydia Ramsey, "'You Asked for It'—Congress Railed on the Maker of EpiPen," *Business Insider*, September 21, 2016, www.businessinsider.com/mylan

-ceo-heather-bresch-house-oversight-committee-hearing-epipen-2016-9 (accessed 11/9/17); see Mathew D. McCubbins and Thomas Schwartz, "Congressional Oversight Overlooked: Police Patrols versus Fire Alarms," *American Journal of Political Science* 28, no. 1 (1984): 165–79.

75. Douglas Kriner and Liam Schwartz, "Divided Government and Congressional Investigations," *Legislative Studies Quarterly* 33, no. 2 (2008): 295–321.
76. Michael D. Shear and Michael S. Schmidt, "Benghazi Panel Engages Clinton in Tense Session," *New York Times*, October 22, 2015, www.nytimes.com/2015/10/23/us/politics/hillary-clinton-benghazi-committee.html?_r50 (accessed 10/29/15).
77. Thomas E. Mann and Norman J. Ornstein, *It's Even Worse Than It Looks: How the American Constitutional System Collided with the New Politics of Extremism* (New York: Basic Books, 2012); Francine Kiefer, "Comey Hearing: Why Congressional Oversight Has Broken Down," *Christian Science Monitor*, July 7, 2016, www.csmonitor.com/USA/Politics/2016/0707/Comey-hearing-Why-congressional-oversight-has-broken-down (accessed 11/9/17).
78. The Office of Technology Assessment was a fourth research agency serving Congress until 1995. It was one of the first agencies scheduled for elimination by the 104th Congress. Until 1983, Congress had still another tool of legislative oversight: the legislative veto. Each agency operating under such provisions was obliged to submit to Congress every proposed decision or rule, which would then lie before both chambers for 30 to 60 days. If Congress took no action by one-house or two-house resolution explicitly to veto the proposed measure during the prescribed period, the measure became law. The legislative veto was declared unconstitutional by the Supreme Court in 1983 on the grounds that it violated the separation of powers—the resolutions Congress passed to exercise its veto were not subject to presidential veto, as required by the Constitution. See *Immigration and Naturalization Service v. Chadha*, 462 U.S. 919 (1983).

CHAPTER 15

1. This account draws from Austin Berg, "Meet the Man Who Could End Forced Union Fees for Government Workers," Illinois Policy, 2018, www.illinoispolicy.org/story/meet-the-man-who-could-end-forced-union-fees-for-government-workers/ (accessed 3/3/18); and P. R. Lockhart, "What the Latest Union Case Before the Supreme Court Could Mean for Workers of Color," Vox, February 26, 2018, www.vox.com/policy-and-politics/2018/2/26/17053328/janus-afscme-supreme-court-unions-minorities (accessed 3/3/18).
2. *Abood v. Detroit Board of Education*, 431 U.S. 209 (1977).
3. Celine McNicholas and Janelle Jones, "Black Women Will Be Most Affected by *Janus*," Economic Policy Institute, Economic Snapshot, February 13, 2018, www.epi.org/publication/black-women-will-be-most-affected-by-janus/ (accessed 3/3/18); and Kayla Patrick, "Public Sector Unions Promote Economic Security and Equality for Women," National Women's Law Center Fact Sheet, January 2018, https://nwlc.org/resources/public-sector-unions-promote-economic-security-and-equality-for-women/ (accessed 3/3/18).
4. U.S. Courts Statistical Tables, www.uscourts.gov/statistics-reports/analysis-reports/statistical-tables-federal-judiciary (accessed 9/19/2015).
5. Michael A. Fletcher, "Obama Criticized as Too Cautious, Slow on Judicial Posts," *Washington Post*, October 16, 2009, www.washingtonpost.com/wp-dyn/content/article/2009/10/15/AR2009101504083.html (accessed 3/1/10).
6. John Bowden, "Timeline: Brett Kavanaugh's Nomination to the Supreme Court," The Hill, October 6, 2018, https://thehill.com/homenews/senate/410217-timeline-brett-kavanaughs-nomination-to-the-supreme-court (accessed 10/16/18).
7. *Marbury v. Madison*, 5 U.S. 137 (1803).
8. *National Federation of Independent Business v. Sebelius*, 567 U.S. __ (2012).
9. Acts of Congress held unconstitutional in whole or in part by the Supreme Court of the United States, General Printing Office, www.gpo.gov/fdsys/pkg/GPO-CONAN-2013/pdf/GPO-CONAN-2013-11.pdf (accessed 4/20/14).
10. *Federal Election Commission v. Wisconsin Right to Life*, 551 U.S. 449 (2007); *McCutcheon v. Federal Election Commission*, 572 U.S. __ (2014).
11. This review power was affirmed by the Supreme Court in *Martin v. Hunter's Lessee*, 14 U.S. 304 (1816).
12. *Brown v. Board of Education*, 347 U.S. 483 (1954).
13. *Lawrence v. Texas*, 539 U.S. 558 (2003).
14. *Paven v. Smith*, 582 U.S. __ (2017).
15. *Alabama Legislative Black Caucus v. Alabama*, 575 U.S. __ (2015).
16. *Arizona State Legislature v. Arizona Independent Redistricting Commission*, 576 U.S. __ (2015).
17. *Cooper v. Harris*, 581 U.S. __ (2017).
18. *United States v. Jones*, 565 U.S. __ (2012).
19. *Riley v. California*, 573 U.S. __ (2014).
20. Theodore J. Lowi, *The End of Liberalism*, 2nd ed. (New York: W. W. Norton, 1979); also David Schoenbrod, *Power without Responsibility: How Congress Abuses the People through Delegation* (New Haven, CT: Yale University Press, 1993).
21. Kenneth Culp Davis, *Discretionary Justice* (Baton Rouge: Louisiana State University Press, 1969), 15–21.
22. Emergency Price Control Act, 56 Stat. 23 (1942).

23. *Hamdi v. Rumsfeld*, 542 U.S. 507 (2004).
24. *Hamdan v. Rumsfeld*, 548 U.S. 557 (2006).
25. *Boumediene v. Bush*, 553 U.S. 723 (2008).
26. *National Labor Relations Board v. Noel Canning*, 573 U.S. — (2014).
27. *Trump v. Hawaii*, 585 U.S. __ (2018).
28. *Roe v. Wade*, 410 U.S. 113 (1973).
29. *Schuette v. Coalition to Defend Affirmative Action*, 572 U.S. __ (2014).
30. *Fisher v. University of Texas*, 579 U.S. __ (2016).
31. Robert Scigliano, *The Supreme Court and the Presidency* (New York: Free Press, 1971), 162. For an interesting critique of the solicitor general's role during the Reagan administration, see Lincoln Caplan, "Annals of the Law," *New Yorker*, August 17, 1987, 30–62.
32. Edward Lazarus, *Closed Chambers* (New York: Times Books, 1998), 6.
33. *NAACP v. Button*, 371 U.S. 415 (1963). The quotation is from the opinion in this case.
34. *Smith v. Allwright*, 321 U.S. 649 (1944).
35. *Obergefell v. Hodges*, 576 U.S. __ (2015).
36. Charles Krauthammer, "Why Roberts Did It," *Washington Post*, June 29, 2012, www.washingtonpost.com/opinions/charles-krauthammer-why-roberts-did-it/2012/06/28/gJQA4X0g9V_story.html (accessed 4/22/14).
37. *Griswold v. Connecticut*, 381 U.S. 479 (1965).
38. *McCutcheon v. Federal Election Commission*, 572 U.S. __ (2014).
39. R. W. Apple, Jr., "A Divided Government Remains, and with It the Prospect of Further Combat," *New York Times*, November 7, 1996, B6.
40. For limits on judicial power, see Alexander Bickel, *The Least Dangerous Branch* (Indianapolis, IN: Bobbs-Merrill, 1962).
41. *Worcester v. Georgia*, 31 U.S. 515 (1832).
42. Walter Murphy, *Congress and the Court* (Chicago: University of Chicago Press, 1962).
43. Robert Dahl, "The Supreme Court and National Policy Making," *Journal of Public Law* 6 (1958): 279.
44. Martin Shapiro, "The Supreme Court: From Warren to Burger," in *The New American Political System*, ed. Anthony King (Washington, DC: American Enterprise Institute, 1978).
45. *Citizens to Preserve Overton Park v. Volpe*, 401 U.S. 402 (1971).
46. Toni Locy, "Bracing for Health Care's Caseload," *Washington Post*, August 22, 1994, A15.
47. See "Developments in the Law—Class Actions," *Harvard Law Review* 89 (1976): 1318.
48. *In re Agent Orange Product Liability Litigation*, 100 F.R.D. 718 (E.D.N.Y. 1983).
49. Donald Horowitz, *The Courts and Social Policy* (Washington, DC: Brookings Institution Press, 1977).
50. *Morgan v. McDonough*, 540 F2d 527 (1 Cir., 1976; *cert. denied*, 429 U.S. 1042 [1977]).
51. Alexander Hamilton, James Madison, and John Jay, *The Federalist Papers*, ed. Clinton Rossiter (New York: New American Library, 1961), no. 10, 78.

Answer Key

Chapter 1
1. d
2. c
3. c
4. c
5. d
6. e
7. a
8. d
9. b
10. e
11. c
12. a
13. a
14. d
15. b

Chapter 2
1. b
2. a
3. b
4. c
5. e
6. c
7. c
8. d
9. b
10. e
11. e
12. b
13. d
14. a

Chapter 3
1. c
2. c
3. b
4. e
5. a
6. c
7. d
8. b
9. b
10. b
11. a
12. d
13. d
14. b

Chapter 4
1. a
2. e
3. b
4. e
5. b
6. e
7. b
8. b
9. d
10. a
11. e
12. c
13. a
14. d

Chapter 5
1. b
2. e
3. a
4. c
5. b
6. d
7. a
8. a
9. d
10. a
11. d
12. a
13. c
14. c

Chapter 6
1. c
2. c
3. a
4. d
5. e
6. d
7. e
8. a
9. c
10. b
11. a
12. b

Chapter 7
1. b
2. a
3. b
4. c
5. e
6. c
7. a
8. b
9. b
10. c
11. b
12. c
13. c

Chapter 8
1. e
2. a
3. d
4. e
5. e
6. c
7. d
8. d
9. c
10. d
11. d
12. c

Chapter 9
1. a
2. c
3. b
4. d
5. e
6. a
7. d
8. e
9. e
10. e
11. d
12. e
13. a

Chapter 10
1. c
2. e
3. e
4. c
5. c
6. b
7. c
8. b
9. d
10. a
11. d
12. c
13. c
14. a
15. a
16. b

Chapter 11
1. a
2. b
3. e
4. c
5. d
6. b
7. d
8. a
9. e
10. c
11. a
12. d

Chapter 12
1. b
2. a
3. d
4. c
5. d
6. c
7. a
8. a
9. d
10. d
11. e
12. c
13. a
14. a

Chapter 13
1. a
2. c

3. b
4. e
5. b
6. b
7. b
8. a
9. a
10. c
11. c
12. b
13. b
14. a

Chapter 14

1. d
2. c
3. c
4. b
5. b
6. e
7. c
8. d
9. d
10. e
11. b
12. a
13. d
14. a

Chapter 15

1. a
2. c
3. a
4. c
5. d
6. d
7. e
8. e
9. c
10. a
11. b
12. a
13. a
14. c

Credits

PHOTOGRAPHS

Frontmatter: Page vii: AP Photo/Cliff Owen; p. viii (top): Alex Wong/Getty Images; (bottom): Rob Hotakainen/MCT/Newscom; p. ix: Anthony Pidgeon/Redferns/Getty Images; p. x: US Navy/Erwin Jacob V. Miciano; p. xi (top): Jay Mallin/ZUMAPRESS.com/Alamy live news; (bottom): Lyndon French/The New York Times/Redux; p. xii: NextGen America; p. xiii: Rod Lamkey/Getty Images; p. xiv (top): Courtesy The Texas Young Republicans; (bottom): American Benefits Council; p. xv: Courtesy Guy Berkebile; p. xvi (top): Cheriss May/ZUMA Press/Newscom; (bottom): © G92, MJ3, F31/Zuma Press; p. xvii: AP Photo/Andrew Harnik.

Chapter 1: Page 2: Shutterstock; p. 3 (left): AP Photo/Cliff Owen; (right): Courtesy Kendric Jones; p. 8 (both): Bettmann/Corbis via Getty Images; p. 10: Erik McGregor/Pacific Press/Newscom; p. 11 (left): Erik McGregor/Pacific Press/Newscom; (right): Peter Casolino/Alamy Stock Photo; p. 14: Library of Congress; p. 16: Rue des Archives/Granger, NYC—All rights reserved; p. 18: Jim West/Alamy Stock Photo; p. 22: Keith Lane/McClatchy/TNS/Alamy Live News; p. 23: Bettmann/Corbis via Getty Images; p. 25 (left): Christian Hansen/The New York Times/Redux; (right): Scott Sommerdorf/The Salt Lake Tribune via AP; p. 26: Mike Nelson/EPA/Shutterstock; p. 29 (left): © Ira Lippke/ZUMA Press/Alamy Stock Photo; (right): Ethan Miller/Getty Images; p. 30: Screenshot 2016 U.S. Department of Education Office of Federal Student Aid; p. 31: Daniel Acker/Bloomberg via Getty Images.

Chapter 2: Page 40: Shutterstock; p. 41: Alex Wong/Getty Images; p. 43: Granger, NYC—All rights reserved; p. 45: Bettmann/Corbis via Getty Images; p. 46: Paul J. Richards/AFP/Getty Images; p. 48: Sarin Images/Granger, NYC—All rights reserved; p. 49: Howard Sun/Alamy Stock Photo; p. 52: Samuel Jennings (active 1789–1834). *Liberty Displaying the Arts and Sciences, or The Genius of America Encouraging the Emancipation of the Blacks*, 1792. Oil on canvas. 60 1/4" × 74" Library Company of Philadelphia. Gift of the artist, 1792; p. 57: Billion Photos/Shutterstock; p. 63: Library of Congress; p. 64: Paul J. Richards/AFP/Getty Images; p. 68: Rohn Engh/FPG/Getty Images; p. 69: Alex Wong/Getty Images.

Chapter 3: Page 76: Sergey Pykhonin/Alamy Stock Vector; p. 77: Rob Hotakainen/MCT/Newscom; p. 83: AP Photo/Adam Beam; p. 86: © Collection of the New-York Historical Society/Bridgeman Images; p. 88: Library of Congress; p. 89: Library of Congress; p. 95 (top): AP Photo/Sue Ogroki (bottom): Library of Congress; p. 99: Ilene MacDonald/Alamy Stock Photo; p. 101 (left): AP Photo; (right): AP Photo/Paul Vathis; p. 106: Ethan Miller/Getty Images; p. 107: AP Photo/Skip Foreman.

Chapter 4: Page 114: Shutterstock; p. 115: Anthony Pidgeon/Redferns/Getty Images; p. 124: ©The Star-Ledger/Aristide Economopoulos/The Image Works; p. 125 (left): Gary Tramontina/Getty Images; (right): Gary Tramontina/Getty Images; p. 126: Chip Somodevilla/Getty Images; p. 128: Everett Collection/Alamy Stock Photo; p. 131: © G92, MJ3, F31/Zuma Press; p. 132: Michael S. Williamson/The Washington Post via Getty Images; p. 133 (left): Saul Loeb/AFP/Getty Images; (right): Kyodo via AP Images; p. 138: Drew Angerer/

Getty Images; p. 140: AP Photo/Matt York; p. 141: Michael Matthews—Police Images/Alamy Stock Photo; p. 143: Bettmann/Getty Images; p. 145: Tracy A. Woodward/The Washington Post via Getty Images; p. 148: Win McNamee/Getty Images; p. 151: Gabriella Demczuk/The New York Times/Redux.

Chapter 5: Page 158: Shutterstock; p. 59: US Navy/ Erwin Jacob V. Miciano; p. 161 (left): Lanmas/Alamy Stock Photo; (right): MPI/Getty Images; p. 163: World History Archive/Alamy Stock Photo; p. 164: Library of Congress; p. 165 (left): Library of Congress; (right): Underwood Photo Archives/Superstock; p. 168: Bettmann/ Getty Images; p. 170 (left): Bettmann/Getty Images; (right): AP Photo/File; p. 171 (left): AP Photo; (right): Tony Savino/The Image Works; p. 173: www.Stanley Formanphotos.com Pulitzer Prize 1977; p. 178: Marilyn Humphries/Newscom; p. 179: Bettmann/Getty Images; p. 182 (left): Ben Solomon/NCAA Photos via Getty Images; (right): Dina Rudick/The Boston Globe via Getty Images; p. 183 (left): AP Photo/Ron Edmonds; (right): Scott Olson/Getty Images; p. 186 (left): Kent Sievers/ The World-Herald via AP; (right): AP Photo/Elliott Spagat, File; p. 187: Alex Milan Tracy/Sipa via AP Images; p. 189: Stephanie Strasburg/Pittsburgh Post-Gazette via AP; p. 193: Drew Angerer/CNP/AdMedia/Newscom.

Chapter 6: Page 204: Shutterstock; p. 205 (left): Jay Mallin/ZUMAPRESS.com/Alamy live news; (right): Tom Brenner/The New York Times/Redux; p. 208: AP Photo/Evan Vucci; p. 213: Chip Somodevilla/Getty Images; p. 214: Cheriss May/NurPhoto via Getty Images; p. 216: Shelly Rivoli/Alamy Stock Photo; p. 217: Gabriel Olsen/WireImage/Getty Images; p. 222 (left): Alex Wong/Getty Images; (right): Ed Lefkowicz Photography; p. 224: AP Photo/Carmen Taylor; p. 226 (left): Saul Loeb/AFP/Getty Images; (right): Twitter/@ realDonaldTrump; p. 229: AP Photo/Jose Luis Magana; p. 230: Jaap Arriens/NurPhoto via Getty Images; p. 233 (left): ©The Star-Ledger/Robert Sciarrino/The Image Works; (right): John Rudoff/Polaris/Newscom; p. 235: CALVIN AND HOBBES © 1994 Watterson. Reprinted with permission of Andrews McMeel Syndication. All rights reserved; p. 236: Bo Rader/The Wichita Eagle via AP, File; p. 243 (left): Bettmann/Getty Images; (right): Lionel Hahn/ABACAPRESS.com/Sipa via AP Images.

Chapter 7: Page 254: Shutterstock; p. 255: Lyndon French/The New York Times/Redux; p. 258: Richard B. Levine/Newscom; p. 259: AP Photo/Branden Camp; p. 262 (left): Mike Blake/REUTERS/Newscom; (right): Mandel Ngan/AFP/Getty Images; p. 263: Vario images GmbH & Co.KG/Alamy Stock Photo; p. 268: Drew Kelly/The New York Times/Redux; p. 269: Bryan Thomas/The New York Times/Redux; p. 272 (left): Albin Lohr-Jones/Pacific Press/Sipa via AP Images; (right): Tim Carroll/Redux; p. 274 (left): Bob Daemmrich/ Alamy Stock Photo; (right): Brendan Smialowski/Getty Images; p. 276 (left): Paul Marotta/Getty Images; (right): AP Photo/Richard Drew; p. 277: FactCheck.org, a project of the Annenberg Public Policy Center; p. 280: Melina Mara/The Washington Post via Getty Images; p. 281: Charles Moore/Getty Images; p. 283: Paul Davey/ Barcroft Images/Barcroft Media via Getty Images; p. 284: AP Photo/Nick Ut; p. 286: AP Photo/Mary Altaffer.

Chapter 8: Page 294: Shutterstock; p. 295: NextGen America; p. 298: Richard Ellis/Alamy Stock Photo; p. 299 (left): AP Photo/Stephen Brashear; (right): Samuel Corum/AnadoluAgency/GettyImages;p.301:Bettmann/ Getty Images; p. 306 (top): Xinhua/Eyevine/Redux; (bottom): The Photo Works/Alamy Stock Photo; p. 307: Inked Pixels/Shutterstock; p. 312: AP Photo/Matt Rourke, File; p. 313: Josh Brasted/Getty Images; p. 315 (left): Brooks Kraft/Getty Images; (right): AP Photo/ David Goldman; p. 318 (left): Jonathan Ernst/REUTERS/ Newscom; (right): Brooks Kraft/Getty Images; p. 320: Mario Tama/Getty Images; p. 323: Smith Collection/ Gado/Getty Images; p. 327: Scott Olson/Getty Images; p. 328: Irfan Khan/Los Angeles Times via Getty Images

Chapter 9: Page 334: Shutterstock; p. 335 (photo): Rod Lamkey/Getty Images; (vector): Shutterstock; p. 338 (left): Duane Prokop/Getty Images for MoveOn.org; (right): Tom Brenner/The New York Times/Redux; p. 343: AP Photo/Elise Amendola; p. 344: Melina Mara/The Washington Post via Getty Images; p. 346 (left): Michael Robinson Chavez/The Washington Post via Getty Images; (right): Samuel Corum/Anadolu Agency/Getty Images; p. 347: Bettmann/Getty Images; p. 348 (top): Bettmann/Getty Images; (bottom): Paul J. Richards/ AFP/Getty Images; p. 354: Darren Huack/Getty Images; p. 355 (left): Barbara Davidson/Los Angeles Times via Getty Images; (right): Brooks Kraft/Getty Images; p. 361: Granger, NYC—All rights reserved; p. 362: Granger, NYC—All rights reserved; p. 364: Nixon Presidential Library & Museum; p. 368: EPA European Press Photo Agency B.V./Alamy Stock Photo; p. 369 (left): Drew Angerer/Getty Images; (right): Jim Thompson/ The Albuquerque Journal via AP.

Chapter 10: Page 378: Shutterstock; p. 379: Courtesy The Texas Young Republicans; p. 381: Bettmann Archive/ Getty Images; p. 383 (left): Marc Serota/Reuters/Newscom; (right): Nicholas Kamm/AFP/Getty Images; p. 385 (left): Granger, NYC—All rights reserved; (right): OpenStreetMap contributors; p. 387: Port Gifford/Getty Images; p. 389: Chip Somodevilla/Getty Images; p. 394: Brendan Smialowski/AFP/Getty Images; p. 398 (left): Andrew Lichtenstein/Corbis via Getty Images; (right): Hillary for America, Campaign; p. 397 (left): Bettmann/Getty Images; (right): Yin Bogu Xinhua/eyevine/Redux; p. 400: Matthew Cavanaugh/Getty Images; p. 402 © G92, MJ3, F31/Zuma Press; p. 409: Robyn Beck/AFP/Getty Images; p. 410: Richard Ellis/Alamy Stock Photo; p. 412: AP Photo/Richard Drew; p. 413: Mike Segar/ Reuters/Newscom; p. 418: Visions of America/UIG via Getty Images; p. 419: Whitney Curtis/Getty Images; p. 420: Michael B. Thomas/Getty Images.

Chapter 11: Page 428: Shutterstock; p. 429: American Benefits Council; p. 432: AP Photo/Sue Ogrocki; p. 433: AP Photo/Robert F. Bukaty; p. 437: Brandon Sloter via AP; p. 438: Amanda Cowan/The Columbian via AP; p. 439 (left): Matthew Busch/Bloomberg via Getty Images; (right): AP Photo/Bloomington Herald-Times, Jeremy Hogan; p. 440: Tasos Katopodis/Getty Images for MoveOn.org; p. 444: Karl Sonnenberg/ Shutterstock; p. 445: Net Photos/Alamy Stock Photo; p. 447: Alex Wong/Getty Images; p. 450 (left): AP Photo/Alex Brandon, File; (right): AP Photo/Jacquelyn Martin; p. 451: Scott McIntyre/Bloomberg via Getty Images; p. 453: U.S. Food and Drug Administration; p. 454 (left): Steve Schapiro/Corbis via Getty Images; (right): © North County Times/ZUMAPRESS .com/Alamy Stock Photo; p. 455 (left): Tomas Abad/ Alamy Stock Photo; (right): Justin Sullivan/Getty Images; p. 459: Theresa McCracken/www.Cartoon Stock.com.

Chapter 12: Page 466: Shutterstock; p. 467 (left): Courtesy Guy Berkebile; (right): Scott Olson/Getty Images; p. 470: Bettmann/Getty Images; p. 474: Chip Somodevilla/ Getty Images; p. 479: AP Photo/Ross D. Franklin; p. 486: Brendan Smialowski/AFP/Getty Images; p. 487: Scott J. Ferrell/Getty Images; p. 492: Senate TV via AP; p. 494: Rachel Mummey for The Washington Post via Getty Images; p. 499: DPA Picture Alliance/ Alamy Stock Photo; p. 500: Tom Williams/CQ Roll Call/Getty Images; p. 504 (left): Olivier Douliery/Abaca/ Sipa via AP Images; (right): AP Photo/Andrew Harnik; p. 505 (left): Science History Images/Alamy Stock Photo; (right): William Philpott/Getty Images.

Chapter 13: Page 512: Shutterstock; p. 513: Cheriss May/ ZUMA Press/Newscom; p. 515: Bettmann/Getty Images; p. 517 (left): AP Photo/File; (right): U.S. Army photo by Capt. Tyson Friar; p. 518: Anthony Wallace/AFP/ Getty Images; p. 519: AP Photo/File; p. 521: The Asahi Shimbun via Getty Images; p. 525: Joe Raedle/Getty Images; p. 528: Jim Watson/AFP/Getty Images; p. 532: Bill Pugliano/Getty Images; p. 533: Chip Somodevilla/Getty Images; p. 535 (top): Bettmann/Getty Images; (bottom): Twitter/@realDonaldTrump; p. 541: T.J. Kirkpatrick/ Bloomberg via Getty Images.

Chapter 14: Page 550: Shutterstock; p. 551: © G92, MJ3, F31/Zuma Press; p. 555: Michael Williamson/The Washington Post via Getty Images; p. 556: U.S. Department of State; p. 561: NG Images/Alamy Stock Photo; p. 563: Richard T. Nowitz/Science Source; p. 565: Timothy A. Clary/AFP/Getty Images; p. 568: Yasin Ozturk/Anadolu Agency/Getty Images; p. 569 (left): Yasin Ozturk/Anadolu Agency/Getty Images; (right): Robert Nickelsberg/Getty Images; p. 570: Department of Justice/FOIA.gov; p. 572: Saul Loeb/AFP/Getty Images; p. 573 (left): Tom Williams/CQ Roll Call/ Getty Images; (right): Joe Raedle/Getty Images; p. 574: Alan Singer/CBS via Getty Images; p. 575: AP Photo/ Ben Chrisman; p. 577: Jeffrey MacMillan/For The Washington Post via Getty Images; p. 582: Andrew Harrer/ Bloomberg via Getty Images.

Chapter 15: Page 590: Shutterstock; p. 591: AP Photo/ Andrew Harnik; p. 593: AP Photo/Michael Tarm; p. 601: Cheriss May/NurPhoto via Getty Images; p. 602: The Asahi Shimbun via Getty Images; p. 607: Michael Hibblen/KUAR News; p. 609: Mark Wilson/Getty Images; p. 612: Mark Wilson/Getty Images; p. 613: Jonathan Ernst/REUTERS/Newscom; p. 617 Dana Verkouteren via AP Photo; p. 618: Bill O'Leary/The Washington Post via Getty Images; p. 623: Alex Wong/Getty Images.

TEXT

Figure 3.7: State Marijuana Laws in 2018 Map, originally published by Governing.com, March 30, 2018. Reprinted by permission of Governing.

Figure 6.1: Graph from "Large Majorities See Checks and Balances, Right to Protest as Essential for Democracy,"

Pew Research Center, Washington, DC (May 2017) http://www.people-press.org/2017/03/02/large-majorities-see-checks-and-balances-right-to-protest-as-essential-for-democracy/democracy_11/. Reprinted with permission.

Figure 9.7: Figure from "Key Takeaways on Americans' Growing Partisan Divide over Political Values," Pew Research Center, Washington, DC (October, 2017) http://www.pewresearch.org/fact-tank/2017/10/05/takeaways-on-americans-growing-partisan-divide-over-political-values/. Reprinted with permission.

Table 11.1: Table: "Top Spending on Lobbying Activities by Industry, 1998–2018" from OpenSecrets.org. Reprinted by permission of Center for Responsive Politics.

Figure 14.3: "Iron Triangles" republished with permission of Wadsworth, a division of Cengage Learning from *Incomplete Conquest: Governing America*, 2nd ed. by Theodore J. Lowi (New York: Holt, Rinehart and Winston, 1981), p. 139. © 1981 by CBS College.

Figure 14.4: "Number of Federal, Contract, and Grant Employees (in millions)," from *The True Size of Government: Tracking Washington's Blended Workforce, 1984–2015* (New York: The Volcker Alliance, 2017), p. 4. Reprinted by permission.

Glossary/Index

Page numbers in *italic* refer to figures or photos.

Communications Decency Act (CDA), 135, 285
community, online, 304–7
Community Reinvestment Act of 1977, 178
compacts, 83–84

concurrent powers, 82 authority possessed by *both* state and national governments, such as the power to levy taxes

confederation, 46 a system of government in which states retain sovereign authority except for the powers expressly delegated to the national government

conference, 482, 616 a gathering of House Republicans every two years to elect their House leaders; Democrats call their gathering the "caucus"

conference committees, 485–86, 493 joint committees created to work out a compromise on House and Senate versions of a piece of legislation

Congress, 466–507; *see also* House of Representatives; Senate
advice and consent by, 503–4
and Affordable Care Act, 106
caucuses, 489
committee system of, 352, 483–87, *485*
conference committees, 493
congressional oversight of executive branch, 523
Constitutional provision for, 55–56
decision making by, 494–502
and democracy, 505–6
differences between House and Senate, *469*, 469–70
direct patronage by, 480–82
election of, 475–80
emergency power limitations, 528
federal courts and, 621–22
and impeachment, 504–5
impeachment power of, 542
implied powers of, 79
influence of interest groups on, *448*, 449–52
iron triangles, 451–52
and limits of presidential power, 522, 541–43
lobbying, 449–52
majority party structure, *483–84*
member demographics, *473*
natural disaster response, 528
organization of, 482–89
oversight by, 502–3, 581–83
parties in, 351–52
party leadership in, 482–83, 496–500
party polarization in, 367–68, *501*
and population shift, 20, 22
powers delegated by, 523, 525
power under Articles of Confederation, 46, 48
presidential orders revoked by, 540
and presidential policy-making, 522, 533, 541–42
profile of, *473*
and regulatory review process, 537
representation by, *481*
rules of lawmaking in, 489–94, *490*
and separation of powers, 58, *59*
sociological vs. agency representation, 471–75, 474–75
staff system of, 487, *487*
and Supreme Court, 619–20
and Twenty-Seventh Amendment, 68
unfunded mandates of, 99
and voter demographics, *507*
waning powers of, 543
war power of, 525
congressional campaign committees, 347–48
Congressional Hispanic Caucus, *474*
congressional oversight, 523
Connecticut, 146, 360
Connecticut Compromise, 50; *see also* Great Compromise
conservatism, 30–31, 213, *214*, 366, 367, 619–20

constituency, 469, 474–75, *484*, *494*, 494–95 the residents in the area from which an official is elected

constituent services, 481
Constitution, U.S., 40–42, 53–59
amending, 58; *see also* amendments to the Constitution
Annapolis Convention, 48
Articles of Confederation vs., *54*
Bill of Rights, 59
executive branch, 56
on federal courts, 596
federalism in, 79–84
Founding and, 53–75
judicial branch, 56–57
legislative branch, 55–56
liberty in, 23
limits on power of national government, 30, 58, 59
local government and, 84
nationalistic interpretation of, 87–88
national unity and power provisions, 57–58
original rights in, *118*
powers of the presidency, 515–29
presidency established by, 515
president's interpretation of, 522
on racial discrimination, 171
ratification of, 58, 60–65, *63*
and weakness of Articles of Confederation, 47–48
Constitutional Convention of 1787, *49*, 49–53, 64–65, 604
constitutional democracy, 7–8

constitutional government, 7 a system of rule in which formal and effective limits are placed on the powers of the government

constitutional rights, in states of emergency, 528
consultants, campaign, 393–94, *394*
Consumer Confidence Index, 407, *408*
Consumer Financial Protection Bureau (CFPB), 561
Consumer Product Safety Act of 1972, 525
Controlled Substances Act, 105
convenience voting, *327*
Coons, Chris, 308
Cooperative Congressional Election Study, 241

cooperative federalism, *91*, 91–93, 97 a type of federalism existing since the New Deal era in which grants-in-aid have been used strategically to encourage states and localities (without commanding them) to pursue nationally defined goals; also known as *intergovernmental cooperation*

Cooper v. Harris, 607
Council of Economic Advisers (CEA), 531, 571
Council on Environmental Quality, 531
counsel, right to, 144
court cases, 593–94
Courtney, Joe, 476

court of appeals, 594 a court that hears appeals of trial court decisions

courts, 593; *see also* federal courts
cracking technique, 385
criminal cases, 593–97
criminal justice
rights of the criminally accused, *137*, 138–46
states' return of fugitives, 83

criminal law, 593 the branch of law that regulates the conduct of individuals, defines crimes, and specifies punishment for proscribed conduct

Croker, Richard, *347*
cross burning, 130
cruel and unusual punishment, 83, 144–45

digital citizen a daily internet user with broadband (high-speed) home internet access and the technology and literacy skills to go online for employment, news, politics, entertainment, commerce, and other activities; *see also* internet
defined, 11, 268
offline political participation of, 304–7

digital divide, 268, 309 the gap in access to the internet among demographic groups based on education, income, age, geographic location, and race/ethnicity

digital media, 267–71; *see also* internet

digital political participation, 303–10 activities designed to influence politics using the internet, including visiting a candidate's website, organizing events online, and signing an online petition

digital revolution, 261–63
digital subscription models, 264
diplomatic power (president), 517–18
diplomatic recognition, 517
direct-action politics, 10

direct democracy, 9, 392–93 a system of rule that permits citizens to vote directly on laws and policies

direct lobbying, 449–52
direct mail campaigns, 400
direct patronage, 480–82
Disability Rights Education and Defense Fund, 191–92
disabled Americans, civil rights for, 191–92

discrimination the use of any unreasonable and unjust criterion of exclusion; *see also* segregation
against African Americans, 95
against Asian Americans, 189–91
based on sexual orientation, 192–93
against citizens of other states, 83
defined, 161
against disabled Americans, 99, 191–92
employment, 171, 174–75, 195
gender, 180–85
in housing, 177–78
against Latinos/Hispanics, 184–89, *186*
in lending, 177–78
against Native Americans, 191–92
positive, 198
racial, 161–79
against white Americans, 198
against women, 171

Disney, 260

dissenting opinion, 617 a decision written by a justice in the minority in a particular case in which the justice wishes to express his or her reasoning in the case

district courts, federal, *596*, 596–97, 598, 599
district judges, appointment of, 599
District of Columbia, 82, 143, 167, 326, 327
District of Columbia v. Heller, 136–38
diversity, news media and, 273

divided government, 365 the condition in American government wherein the presidency is controlled by one party while the opposing party controls one or both houses of Congress

DNA testing, 140–41
DNC. *See* Democratic National Committee
Dodd–Frank Act, 495–96
Dole, Bob, 95
domestic military power, 516–17
domestic social spending, 500
donations (political campaigns). *See* fund-raising
Donovan, Todd, 245, 321
"Don't Ask, Don't Tell," 192
double government, 581

double jeopardy, 120, 142 the Fifth Amendment right providing that a person cannot be tried twice for the same crime

Douglas, William O., 146
Douglass, Frederick, 162
DREAM Act, 187, *229*
Dreamers. *See* DACA (Deferred Action for Childhood Arrivals)
Dred Scott v. Sandford, 162
Druckman, James, 229
Drudge Report, 264
Drug Enforcement Administration (DEA), 76, 530
drug testing, 140

dual federalism, 85–86, *91* the system of government that prevailed in the United States from 1789 to 1937 in which most fundamental governmental powers were shared between the federal and state governments

Du Bois, W.E.B., 165
due process clause, 120

due process of law, 138–46 the right of every individual against arbitrary action by national or state governments
cruel and unusual punishment, 144–45
defined, 597
double jeopardy, 142
eminent domain, 143
grand juries, 142
right to counsel, 144
and same-sex marriage ruling, 193
searches and seizures, 139–41
self-incrimination, 142–43

Duke Power Company, 175

E

Early, Stephen, 535

early voting, 327 the option in some states to cast a vote at a polling place or by mail before the election

earmarks, 480–81
East India Company, 44, 45, *45*
e-commerce, 105
economic class, public opinion and, 222–24
economic crisis of 2008. *See* financial crisis and recession of 2008
economic development agencies, 572–73
economic equality/inequality, 20, *21*, 25–26
economic freedom, 24–25
economic growth, environmental policy vs., 238
economic inequality. *See* income equality/inequality
Economic Opportunity Act, 91–92
economic populism, 356
economic power, political power and, 28
economy
bureaucracy for maintaining, 571–73
as campaign influence, 407
and federal control, 88
education
of Congress members, *473*, 474
and gender discrimination, 182–83
party affiliation and, *359*
and political participation, 310–11, *311*
and public opinion, 217
school segregation/desegregation, 25–26, 167–70, 623
state laws on, 86
Education, Department of, 530, 552, 564–65
Education Act of 1972, 182
EEOC. *See* Equal Employment Opportunity Commission
Eighth Amendment, 144–45
Eisenhower, Dwight D., 168–69, 363, 516–17, *517*

elastic clause, 56, 64 The concluding paragraph of Article I, Section 8, of the Constitution (also known as the "necessary and proper clause"), which provides Congress with the authority to make all

electoral college, 53, 299, 389–90, 392, 396 the presidential electors from each state who meet after the general election to cast ballots for president and vice president

electoral realignment, *366* the point in history when a new party supplants the governing party, becoming in turn the dominant political force

eminent domain, 143 the right of government to take private property for public use

equality of opportunity, 25–28, 209–10 a widely shared American ideal that all people should have the freedom to use whatever talents and wealth they have to reach their fullest potential

equal protection clause, 161, 179–80, 195 provision of the Fourteenth Amendment guaranteeing citizens "the equal protection of the laws." This clause has been the basis for the civil rights of African Americans, women, and other groups

equal time rule, 286 the requirement that broadcasters provide candidates for the same political office equal opportunities to communicate their messages to the public

establishment clause, 123–25 the First Amendment clause that says that "Congress shall make no law respecting an establishment of religion"; this law means that a "wall of separation" exists between church and state

exclusionary rule, 139 the ability of courts to exclude evidence obtained in violation of the Fourth Amendment

executive agreement, 503, 518 an agreement, made between the president and another country, that has the force of a treaty but does not require the Senate's "advice and consent"

Executive Office of the President (EOP), *529*, 530–31, 536–38 the permanent agencies that perform defined management

judicial activism, 619–21 judicial philosophy that posits that the Court should go beyond the words of the Constitution or a statute to consider the broader societal implications of its decisions

judicial restraint, 619–21 judicial philosophy whose adherents refuse to go beyond the clear words of the Constitution in interpreting the document's meaning

judicial review, 57, 69, 604–10 the power of the courts to review and, if necessary, declare actions of the legislative and executive branches invalid or unconstitutional; the Supreme Court asserted this power in *Marbury v. Madison* (1803)

jurisdiction, 595 the sphere of a court's power and authority

K

L

laissez-faire capitalism, 24 an economic system in which the means of production and distribution are privately owned and operated for profit with minimal or no government interference

legislative initiative, 521 the president's inherent power to bring a legislative agenda before Congress

***Lemon* test, 124** a rule articulated in *Lemon v. Kurtzman* that government action toward religion is permissible if it is secular in purpose, neither promotes nor inhibits the practice of religion, and does not lead to "excessive entanglement" with religion

and the addition of new amendments to a bill

Operation Fast and Furious, 519

opinion the written explanation of the Supreme Court's decision in a particular case; *see also* public opinion
defined, 207
dissenting, 617–18
forming of, 216–25
and political knowledge, 228–32
stability of, 225–32, *227*
of the Supreme Court, 616–17

OPM (Office of Personnel Management), 580
opportunity, equality of, 25–28, 209–10

oral argument, 616, *617* the stage in the Supreme Court procedure in which attorneys for both sides appear before the Court to present their positions and answer questions posed by justices

Oregon, 93, 105, 327, 576
Oregon Music News, 114
organized labor, 433
"originalist" judges, 602

original jurisdiction, 596–97 the authority to initially consider a case; distinguished from appellate jurisdiction, which is the authority to hear appeals from a lower court's decision

outsourcing, *578*, 583; *see also* privatization

oversight, 502–3, 581–83 the effort by Congress, through hearings, investigations, and other techniques, to exercise control over the activities of executive agencies

P

packing, 385, 607
PACs. *See* political action committee; Super PACs
Page, Benjamin, 235
Pai, Ajit, 254, 255
paid media time, 397
Palko, Frank, 120, 142
Palko v. Connecticut, 120, 122, 142
Parents Involved in Community Schools v. Seattle School District No. 1, 175
Paris Agreement, 227
Parks, Rosa, 169, *170*
parliaments, 8
participation, political. *See* political participation

partisan gerrymandering, 385–86 occurs when politicians from one party intentionally manipulate the boundaries for drawing legislative election districts to disadvantage their political opponents' chance of winning an election and advantage their own political party

partisan loyalty, 406
partisan media, 276
partisan politics, 339, 500–501; *see also* party polarization

partisanship, 207, 337 identification with or support of a particular party or cause

party activists, 352–53 partisans who contribute time, energy, and effort to support their party and its candidates

party affiliation, 221–22

party identification, 352–60, *353*, *359*, *406* an individual voter's psychological ties to one party or another

party leadership, in Congress, 482–83, 496–500
party-line voting, 366, 367

party machines, 320, 347, *347* strong party organizations in late nineteenth- and early twentieth-century American cities; these machines were led by often corrupt "bosses" who controlled party nominations and patronage

party organization, 344 the formal structure of a political party, including its leadership, election committees, active members, and paid staff

party platform a party document, written at a national convention, that contains party philosophy, principles, and policy positions

party polarization, 276–77, 339, *367*, 367–68, 500–501, *501* the division between the two major parties on most policy issues, with members of each party unified around their party's positions with little crossover

party systems, 360–61, *366*

party unity vote, 496, *497* a roll-call vote in the House or Senate in which at least percent of the members of one party take a particular position and are opposed by at least 50 percent of the members of the other party

Paterson, William, 50
Patient Protection and Affordable Care Act of 2010. *See* Affordable Care Act of 2010
Patriot Act. *See* USA PATRIOT Act
"patrol mode," 280, 281

patronage, 347, 480 the resources available to higher officials, usually opportunities to make partisan appointments to offices and to confer grants, licenses, or special favors to supporters

pattern-of-cases strategy, 614
Paul, Rand, 214, *492*
Pavan v. Smith, 605
Paxton, Ken, 83
pay, congressional, 68
PBS, 259
Pelosi, Nancy, 472, 498, *500*
Pence, Mike, 531, *532*
Pennsylvania, 47, 148, 322, 386

penny press, 267 cheap, tabloid-style newspaper produced in the nineteenth century, when mass production of inexpensive newspapers first became possible due to the steam-powered printing press; a penny press newspaper cost one cent compared with other papers, which cost more than five cents

Pentagon Papers, 133, 234, 283, 284

permanent absentee ballots, 327 the option in some states to have a ballot sent automatically to your home for each election, rather than having to request an absentee ballot each time

permanent committees. *See* standing committee
Perot, Ross, 368, 405
Persian Gulf War, 525
personal freedom, 23
petition, right of, 132, 133
petitions, 536
Pew Research Center, 226, 272
phone banks, 400
photo IDs, 324
physician-assisted suicide, 93, 105, 149–50
PIRG (Public Interest Research Group), *447*

plaintiff, 593 the individual or organization that brings a complaint in court

Planned Parenthood of Southeastern Pennsylvania v. Casey, 148–49

platform, 345, 389 a party document, written at a national convention, that contains party philosophy, principles, and positions on issues

plea bargain, 595 a negotiated agreement in a criminal case in which a defendant agrees to plead guilty in return for the state's agreement to reduce the severity of the criminal charge or prison sentence the defendant is facing

Pledge of Allegiance, 124–25, 146
Plessy v. Ferguson, 26, 164

pluralism, 9, 431 the theory that all interests are and should be free to compete for influence in the government; the outcome of this competition is compromise and moderation

plurality system, 382 a type of electoral system in which, to win a seat in the parliament or other representative body, a candidate need only receive the most votes in the election, not necessarily a majority of the votes cast

Plyler v. Doe, 18

pocket veto, 494, 520 a presidential veto that is automatically triggered if the president does not act on a given piece of legislation passed during the final 10 days of a legislative session

polarization. *See* party polarization
police brutality, 170

"police patrol" oversight, 581–82 regular or even preemptive congressional hearings on bureaucratic agency operations

police power, 82 power reserved to the state government to regulate the health, safety, and morals of its citizens

policy entrepreneur, 350 an individual who identifies a problem as a political issue and brings a policy proposal into the political agenda

policy feedback, 226
policy preferences, 407

political action committee (PAC), 404, 432, 456–58, *457*, 498 a private group that raises and distributes funds for use in election campaigns; *see also* Super PACs

political culture, 2–39 broadly shared values, beliefs, and attitudes about how the government should function; American political culture emphasizes the values of liberty, equality, and democracy
Americans' view of government, 29–33
and changes in American people, 13–22
citizenship, 10–13
defined, 23
and democracy, 28–29
and equality, 25–28
and ethnic diversity, 14–16, *15*
future of, 33–34
government, 5–10
and immigration, 13–22
and liberty, 24–25
and race, *15*, 16
thinking critically about, 22–29

political efficacy, 12 the ability to influence government and politics

political environment
ballot measures, 322–23
electoral competition, 321–22
mobilization, 319–21
and political participation, 319–23
and public opinion, 224–25
state electoral laws, 323–27, *325*

political equality, 25 the right to participate in politics equally, based on the principle of "one person, one vote"

political ideology, a cohesive set of beliefs that forms a general philosophy about the role of government

conservatism, 213, *214*
current American state of, 215, *215*
defined, 207
liberalism, 211, *213*
libertarianism, 214
and party identification, 356, *359*
and public opinion, 211–15
and Supreme Court decisions, 620–21

political knowledge, 11–13, *12* possessing information about the formal institutions of government, political actors, and political issues
costs to democracy, 230, 232
defined, 10
digital media's effect on, 230
necessity of, 11–13
and public opinion, 228–32
shortcuts and cues, 229–30

political participation, 297–328, *300*; *see also* turnout; voting
and access to government, 8–9
by African Americans, 313–14
age and, 311, *311*, 311–13
by Asian Americans, 316
and beliefs about political efficacy, 12–13
citizenship and, 10–13
democracy and, 28–29
digital, 303–10
forms of, 297–310
gender and, 316–17
influencing government through, 9–10
by Latinos, 314–15
online vs. offline, 304–7
and political environment, 319–23
political equality and, 25
religious identity and, 318–19
socioeconomic status and, 310–11
and state electoral laws, 323–27, *325*
through voting, 299–300, *311*; *see also* voting
traditional, 297–302

political parties, 334–73, *341*, *366* organized groups that attempt to influence the government by electing their members to important government offices; *see also specific parties*
and campaign funding, 404–5
congressional party unity, 496–98
defined, 337
in election of 2012, *370*
and elections, 340–44
electoral alignments and realignments, *366*
factions within, 350–51
formation of, 339
function of, 337–38
functions of, 339, 340
in government, 348–52
House steering committees of, 482
influence of money on, 29
influence of the wealthy on, *236*
interest groups vs., 334, 438–39
as organizations, 344–48
party identification, 352–60
party polarization, 339, 367–68
party systems, 360–61
and political socialization, 221–22
and presidential powers, 534
recent affiliation trends, 358–60, *359*
as source of power for the presidency, 534
third parties, 368–71
two-party system, 339

political power, economic power and, 28

political socialization, 216–17 the induction of individuals into the political culture; learning the underlying beliefs and values on which the political system is based

political speech, 127–29
political values, public opinion and, 209–11
Politico, 264

politics, 9–10 conflict over the leadership, structure, and policies of governments
defined, 5, 9
media's influence on, 278, 280–82
and money, 400–405
retail, 387

U

White House staff, 530, *529*, 537 analysts and advisers to the president, each of whom is often given the title "special assistant"

writ of certiorari, 611–12 a decision of at least four of the nine Supreme Court justices to review a decision of a lower court; *certiorari* is Latin, meaning "to make more certain"

writ of habeas corpus, 118, 597, 609 a court order that the individual in custody be brought into court and shown the cause for detention; habeas corpus is guaranteed by the Constitution and can be suspended only in cases of rebellion or invasion

Y

Z

Voter Registration Information

State	Registration Deadline before Election*	Early Voting Permitted?**	Identification Required to Vote?**	More Information
Alabama	14 days	No	Photo ID requested	alabamavotes.gov
Alaska	30 days	Yes	ID requested; photo not required	elections.alaska.gov
Arizona	29 days	Yes	ID required; photo not required	azsos.gov/election
Arkansas	30 days	Yes	Photo ID requested	sos.arkansas.gov
California	15 days; election-day registration permitted	Yes	No	sos.ca.gov
Colorado	8 days by mail or online; no in-person deadline	Yes (all voting by mail)	ID requested; photo not required	sos.state.co.us
Connecticut	14 days by mail; 7 days in person; election-day registration permitted	No	ID requested; photo not required	ct.gov/sots
Delaware	24 days	No	ID requested; photo not required	elections.delaware.gov
District of Columbia	30 days by mail or online; no in-person deadline	Yes	No	dcboee.org
Florida	29 days	Yes	Photo ID requested	dos.myflorida.com/elections
Georgia	28 days	Yes	Photo ID required	sos.ga.gov
Hawaii	30 days; no in-person deadline	Yes	Photo ID requested	hawaii.gov/elections
Idaho	25 days; election-day registration permitted	Yes	Photo ID requested	idahovotes.gov
Illinois	27 days; 16 days online	Yes	No	elections.il.gov
Indiana	29 days	Yes	Photo ID required	in.gov/sos/elections
Iowa	10 days; election-day registration permitted	Yes	Photo ID required	sos.iowa.gov
Kansas	21 days	Yes	Photo ID required	kssos.org
Kentucky	27 days	No	ID requested; photo not required	elect.ky.gov
Louisiana	30 days; 20 days online	Yes	Photo ID requested	sos.la.gov
Maine	21 days by mail; no in-person deadline	Yes	No	maine.gov/sos
Maryland	21 days	Yes	No	elections.state.md.us
Massachusetts	20 days	No	No	www.sec.state.ma.us
Michigan	30 days	No	Photo ID requested	michigan.gov/sos
Minnesota	21 days; election-day registration permitted	Yes	No	mnvotes.org
Mississippi	30 days	No	Photo ID required	sos.ms.gov
Missouri	Fourth Wednesday prior to election	No	ID requested; photo not required	sos.mo.gov
Montana	30 days by mail; no in-person deadline	Yes	ID requested; photo not required	sos.mt.gov

State	Registration Deadline before Election*	Early Voting Permitted?**	Identification Required to Vote?**	More Information
Nebraska	Third Friday prior to election by mail; second Friday prior to election in person	Yes	No	www.sos.ne.gov
Nevada	31 days by mail; 21 days in person	Yes	No	nvsos.gov
New Hampshire	10 days; election-day registration permitted	No	ID requested; photo not required	sos.nh.gov
New Jersey	21 days	Yes	No	njelections.org
New Mexico	28 days	Yes	No	sos.state.nm.us
New York	25 days	No	No	www.elections.ny.gov
North Carolina	25 days	Yes	No	ncsbe.gov
North Dakota	No voter registration required	Yes	ID required; photo not required	vote.nd.gov
Ohio	30 days	Yes	ID required; photo not required	sos.state.oh.us
Oklahoma	24 days	Yes	ID requested; photo not required	ok.gov/elections
Oregon	21 days	Yes (all voting by mail)	No	sos.oregon.gov
Pennsylvania	30 days	No	No	votespa.com
Rhode Island	30 days; election-day registration permitted	No	Photo ID requested	www.elections.state.ri.us
South Carolina	30 days	No	ID requested; photo not required	scvotes.org
South Dakota	15 days	Yes	Photo ID requested	sdsos.gov
Tennessee	30 days	Yes	Photo ID required	tn.gov/sos/election
Texas	30 days	Yes	Photo ID requested	votetexas.gov
Utah	30 days by mail; 7 days in person; election-day registration permitted	Yes	ID requested; photo not required	elections.utah.gov
Vermont	Wednesday before the election; no in-person deadline	Yes	No	www.sec.state.vt.us/elections
Virginia	22 days	Yes	Photo ID required	sbe.virginia.gov
Washington	30 days by mail and online; 8 days in person	Yes (all voting by mail)	ID requested; photo not required	sos.wa.gov/elections/
West Virginia	21 days	Yes	ID requested; photo not required	sos.wv.gov
Wisconsin	20 days by mail; election-day registration permitted	Yes	Photo ID required	www.sos.state.wi.us
Wyoming	14 days; election-day registration permitted	Yes	No	soswy.state.wy.us

* Information collected from Project Vote Smart, votesmart.org/elections/voter-registration (accessed 11/1/18).

** Information collected from National Conference of State Legislatures, www.ncsl.org (accessed 11/1/18). In states where an ID is "requested," voters who do not bring ID to the polls may be required to sign an affidavit of identity, vote on a provisional ballot, have a poll worker vouch for their identity, or take additional steps after Election Day to make sure their vote is counted.

Note: In November 2018, Arkansas and North Carolina passed ballot measures requiring a photo ID to vote. Michigan passed ballot measures to implement same-day and automatic voter registration.